To Mrs. Buck,
Love Sal Miragliotta

THE NORTON/GROVE
HANDBOOKS IN MUSIC

MUSIC PRINTING
AND
PUBLISHING

THE NORTON/GROVE
HANDBOOKS IN MUSIC

MUSIC PRINTING AND PUBLISHING

Edited by D. W. KRUMMEL and STANLEY SADIE

W. W. NORTON & COMPANY

NEW YORK   LONDON

Parts of this material first published in
The New Grove Dictionary of Music and Musicians®,
edited by Stanley Sadie, 1980

The New Grove and *The New Grove Dictionary of Music and Musicians*
are registered trademarks of Macmillan Publishers Limited, London

First published in the UK 1990 by
THE MACMILLAN PRESS LTD
Houndmills, Basingstoke, Hampshire RG21 2XS
and London
Companies and representatives throughout the world

British Library Cataloguing in Publication Data
Music printing and publishing. – (The New Grove
handbooks in musicology).
1. Western music. Publishing
I. Sadie, Stanley, *1930* – II. The new grove
dictionary of music and musicians
070.5'794

ISBN 0-333-47044-3

First American Edition, 1990

All Rights Reserved

ISBN 0-393-02809-7

W.W. Norton & Company, Inc.,
500 Fifth Avenue, New York, NY 10110

Typeset by Florencetype Ltd, Kewstoke, Avon
Printed in Hong Kong

1 2 3 4 5 6 7 8 9 0

Contents

Illustration Acknowledgments	vi
General Abbreviations	vii
Bibliographical Abbreviations	ix
Author Abbreviations	xi
Preface	xiii

PART ONE

Music Printing   *H. Edmund Poole*

I	Definition, Early Stages and Woodblock Printing	3
II	Printing Music from Type	11
III	Engraving	40
IV	Lithography and More Recent Processes	55
V	Music Printing by Computer *Richard Vendome*	66

Music Publishing   *D.W. Krummel*

VI	Definitions and Origins	79
VII	The Age of Letterpress 1501–1700	82
VIII	The Age of Engraving 1700–1860	98
IX	The Age of Offset Printing 1860–1975	117
X	Music Publishing Today	129

PART TWO

Dictionary of Music Printers and Publishers   135

PART THREE

Glossary   *Stanley Boorman*   489

PART FOUR

Bibliography   *D. W. Krummel*   553

Index   564

Illustration Acknowledgments

We are grateful to the following for permission to reproduce illustrative material. (Every effort has been made to contact copyright holders; we apologise to anyone who may have been omitted.): British Library, London: pp.2, 8, 90, 139, 144, 160, 245, 263, 341, 379, 385, 400, 459, 488 and 503; Museum Plantin-Moretus, Antwerp: pp.19, 545; Newberry Library, Chicago: p.22 (top); Bibliothèque Nationale, Paris: pp.22 (bottom), 25, and 42; Giraudon, Paris: p.24 (top); Edmund Poole: pp.29, 38, 45 and 248 (p.248 photo John R. Freeman & Co. Ltd, London); Österreichische Nationalbibliothek, Vienna: pp.41, 151, 333 and 446; Guildhall Library, City of London: p.44; G. Henle Verlag, Munich, and H. Stürtz AG, Würzburg: p.48; Bayerische Staatsbibliothek, Munich: pp.56, 108, 367, 440 and 464; photo St Bride Printing Library, London: pp.57 (fig.20 from C. Wagner, *Alois Senefelder, sein Leben und Wirken*, Leipzig, 1914) and 530; Fentone Music Ltd, Corby: p.63 (above); Boosey & Hawkes Ltd, London: p.63 (below); Music Print Corporation, Boulder, CO: p.64; Armando Dal Molin, Music Reprographics Ltd, Oyster Bay, NY: p.67; Xerox Corp., Palo Alto, CA: pp.70 and 71; Practical Computing (August 1985): p.72; © 1986 Oxford University Press: p.76 (bottom); Toppan Printing Co. (UK) Ltd: p.77; Bibliothèque royale Albert 1er, Brussels: pp.85 and 252–253; English Folk Dance and Song Society, London: p.93; Richard Macnutt, Withyham, Sussex: pp.96, 109, 112, 281, 300, 303, 312, 412 and 450; Bodleian Library, Oxford: p.121 (Harding Collection, Box 542) and p.240 (Harding Collection, Box 406) (p.121 also by permission of Chappell Music Ltd., London and Chappell & Co., Inc, Los Angeles); G. Schirmer, Inc., New York: p.123; Library of the Boston Athenaeum, Boston: p.154; Breitkopf & Härtel, Wiesbaden, and Dover Publications Inc., New York (facs.1966): p.185; Music Division, Library of Congress, Washington, DC: p.200; Archiv der Gesellschaft der Musikfreunde, Vienna: p.216; Editions Durand & Cie, Paris: p.223; A. L. van Gendt & Co. bv, Amsterdam: from H. D. L. Vervliet, *Sixteenth Century Printing Types of the Low Countries* (1968): p.370; Metropolitan Museum of Art (Harris Brisbane Dick Fund, 1953), New York: p.406; B. Schott's Söhne, Mainz: p.417; Civico Museo Bibliografico Musicale, Bologna: p.421; Brice Farwell, Morgan Hill, CA: p.471; Stanley Boorman: pp.523 and 524.

The drawing on p.529 is by Alan Forster, London and is based on the wooden press (probably dating from the first decade of the 19th century) in the St Bride Printing Library, London

General Abbreviations

ABC	American Broadcasting Company; Australian Broadcasting Commission	Feb	February
		fig.	figure [illustration]
		fl	floruit [he/she flourished]
Abt.	Abteilung [section]	Ger.	German
ACA	American Composers' Alliance	GmbH	Gesellschaft mit beschränkter Haftung [limited-liability company]
addn,	addition(s)		
addns		H	Hoboken catalogue [Haydn]; Helm catalogue [C. P. E. Bach]
arr.	arrangement, arranged by/for		
ASCAP	American Society of Composers, Authors and Publishers	HMS	His/Her Majesty's Ship
		Hnos.	Hermanos [brothers]
attrib.	attribution, attributed to	hpd	harpsichord
Aug	August	IAML	International Association of Music Libraries
b	born		
bap.	baptized	ibid	ibidem [in the same place]
bc	basso continuo	IMS	International Musicological Society
BMI	Broadcast Music Inc. (USA)		
bur.	buried	Inc.	Incorporated
BVM	Blessed Virgin Mary	inc.	incomplete
c	circa	incl.	includes, including
CA	California (USA)	inst, insts	instrument, instruments
CeBeDeM	Centre Belge de Documentation Musicale	Jan	January
		Jb	Jahrbuch [yearbook]
chap.	chapter	Jg.	Jahrgang [year of publication/ volume]
Cia	Compañía		
Cie	Compagnie	jr	junior
CNRS	Centre National de la Recherche Scientifique (F)	K	Kirkpatrick catalogue [D. Scarlatti]; Köchel catalogue [Mozart]
Co.	Company; County		
col., cols	column(s)	KY	Kentucky (USA)
comp.	compiler, compiled (by)	£	libra, librae [pound, pounds sterling]
CT	Connecticut (USA)		
d	died	LA	Louisiana (USA)
D	Deutsch catalogue [Schubert]; Dounias catalogue [Tartini]	Ltd	Limited
		M.	Monsieur
DC	District of Columbia (USA)	MA	Massachusetts (USA); Master of Arts
Dec	December		
diss.	dissertation	MI	Michigan (USA)
e.g.	exempli gratia [for example]	mm	millimetre(s)
ed., eds.	editor(s), edited (by)	Mme	Madame
edn., edns.	edition(s)	MN	Minnesota (USA)
Eng.	English	MS, MSS	manuscript(s)
esp.	especially	NBC	National Broadcasting Corporation
etc	et cetera [and so on]		
f, ff	following page, following pages	n.d.	no date of publication
		NJ	New Jersey (USA)
f., ff.	folio, folios	no., nos.	number, numbers
facs.	facsimile	Nor.	Norwegian
fasc., fascs.	fascicle, fascicles	Nov	November

General Abbreviations

n.p.	no place of publication	s.	solidus, solidi [shilling, shillings]
nr.	near		
n.s.	new series	SC	South Carolina (USA)
NY	New York State (USA)	Sept	September
Oct	October	ser.	series
OH	Ohio (USA)	sr	senior
op., opp.	opus, opera	suppl., suppls.	supplement(s), supplementary
org	organ		
OUP	Oxford University Press	trans.	translation, translated by
p.	pars	TX	Texas (USA)
p, pp	*piano, pianissimo*	U.	University
pl.	plate; plural	UNESCO	United Nations Educational, Scientific and Cultural Organization
pt.	part		
pubd	published		
pubn	publication	USA	United States of America
R	[in signature] editorial revision	USSR	Union of Soviet Socialist Republics
R	photographic reprint	v, vv	voice, voices
RCM	Royal College of Music, London	VEB	Volkseigener Betrieb [people's own industry]
repr.	reprinted	vol., vols.	volume, volumes
rev.	revision, revised (by/for)	v.p.	various publishers
RI	Rhode Island (USA)	W.	west, western
S	San, Santa, Santo, São [Saint]	WoO	Werke ohne Opuszahl [works without opus number]
S.	south, southern		
$	dollars		

Library Sigla

A-Wgm	Austria, Gesellschaft der Musikfreunde	*F-Pm*	France, Paris Bibliothèque Mazarine
A-Wn	Austria, Österreichische Nationalbibliothek, Musiksammlung	*GB-Och*	Great Britain, Oxford, Christ Church
		GB-Lbm	Great Britain, London, British Library, Reference Division (formerly British Museum) (= *LbI*)
B-Br	Belgium, Bibliothèque Royale Albert 1er/Koninklijke Bibliotheek Albert I		
D-Mbs	Germany, Bayerische Staatsbibliothek	*I-Bc*	Italy, Civico Museo Bibliografico Musicale

Bibliographical Abbreviations

AcM	*Acta musicologica*	*ES*	*Enciclopedia dello spettacolo*
AMP	Antiquitates musicae in Polonia; Associated Music Publishers		(Rome and Florence, 1954–62)
		FAM	*Fontes artis musicae*
AMw	*Archiv für Musikwissenschaft*	*FétisB*	F.-J. Fétis: *Biographie*
AMZ	*Allgemeine musikalische Zeitung*	*(FétisBs)*	*universelle des musiciens*
AMz	*Allgemeine Musik-Zeitung*		(Brussels, 2/1860–65) (and
AnMc	*Analecta musicologica*		suppl.)
AnnM	*Annales musicologiques*	*GerberL*	R. Gerber: *Historisch-*
Baker 5(–7)	*Baker's Biographical Dictionary of Musicians* (5/1958, 6/1978, 7/1984)		*biographisches Lexikon der Tonkünstler*
		GerberNL	R. Gerber: *Neues historisch-*
BJb	*Bach-Jahrbuch*		*biographisches Lexikon der*
BMw	*Beiträge zur Musikwissenschaft*		*Tonkünstler*
BNB	*Biographie nationale [belge]* (Brussels, 1866–)	*Grove1(–5)*	G. Grove, ed.: *A Dictionary of Music and Musicians*, 2nd–5th
BSIM	*Bulletin français de la S[ociété] I[nternationale de] M[usique]* [previously *Le Mercure musical*]		edns. as *Grove's Dictionary of Music and Musicians*
		Grove6	S. Sadie, ed.: *The New Grove Dictionary of Music and*
BurneyH	C. Burney: *A General History of Music from the Earliest Ages to the Present* (London, 1776–89)		*Musicians* (London, 1980)
		GroveAM	H. W. Hitchcock and S. Sadie, eds.: *The New Grove Dictionary of American Music* (London,
CaM	Catalogus musicus		1986)
CHM	*Collectanea historiae musicae* (in series Biblioteca historiae musicae cultores) (Florence, 1953–)	*HawkinsH*	J. Hawkins: *A General History of the Science and Practice of Music* (London, 1776)
CMc	*Current Musicology*	*HRo*	*Hudební rozhledy*
CMM	Corpus mensurabilis musicae (Rome, 1947–)	*HV*	*Hudební věda*
		IMi	Istituzioni e monumenti
ČSHS	*Československý hudební slovník*		dell'arte musicale italiana
DAB	Dictionary of American Biography (New York, 1928–36; 7 suppls., 1944–81)	*IMSCR*	*International Musicological Society Congress Report* [1930–]
		IMusSCR	*International Musical Society Congress Report* [1906–11]
DBI	*Dizionario biografico degli italiani* (Rome, 1960–)	ISAMm	Institute for Studies in American Music, monograph
DJbM	*Deutsches Jahrbuch der Musikwissenschaft*	*JAMS*	*Journal of the American Musicological Society*
DNB	*Dictionary of National Biography* (London, 1885–1901)	*JbMP*	*Jahrbuch der Musikbibliothek Peters*
DTO	Denkmäler der Tonkunst in Österreich	*JEFDSS*	*The Journal of the English Folk Dance and Song Society*
EDM	Das Erbe deutscher Musik (Berlin, 1935–)	*JMT*	*Journal of Music Theory*
		MA	*The Musical Antiquary*
EitnerQ	R. Eitner: *Biographisch-bibliographisches Quellen-Lexikon* (Leipzig, 1900–04)	MB	Musica britannica
		MD	*Musica disciplina*
		MEJ	*Music Educators Journal*

Bibliographical Abbreviations

Mf	*Die Musikforschung*	*RicordiE*	*Enciclopedia della musica*
MGG	*Die Musik in Gerschichte und*		(Milan: Ricordi, 1963–4)
	Gegenwart	*RIM*	*Rivista italiana di musicologia*
MJb	*Mozart-Jahrbuch des*	*RISM*	*Répertoire international des*
	Zentralinstituts für		*sources musicales*
	Mozartforschung	*RMARC*	*R[oyal] M[usical] A[ssociation]*
ML	*Music and Letters*		*Research Chronicle*
MMg	*Monatshefte für Musikgeschichte*	*RMI*	*Rivista musicale italiana*
MO	*Musical Opinion*	SCMA	Smith College Music Archives
MQ	*The Musical Quarterly*	*SIMG*	*Sammelbände der*
MR	*The Music Review*		*Internationalen Musik-*
MRM	Monuments of Renaissance		*Gesellschaft*
	Music	*SM*	*Studia musicologica Academiae*
MSD	Musicological Studies and		*scientiarum hungaricae*
	Documents, ed. A.	*SMN*	*Studia musicologica norvegica*
	Carapetyan (Rome, 1951–)	*SMP*	*Słownik muzyków polskich*
MT	*The Musical Times*	*SMw*	*Studien zur Musikwissenschaft*
MusAm	*Musical America*	*SMz*	*Schweizerische Musikzeitung/*
NA	*Note d'archivio per la storia*		*Revue musicale suisse*
	musicale	*STMf*	*Svensk tidskrift för*
NBJb	*Neues Beethoven-Jahrbuch*		*musikforskning*
NDB	*Neue deutsche Biographie*	*TVNM*	*Tijdschrift van de Vereniging*
	(Berlin, 1953–)		*voor Nederlandse*
NRMI	*Nuova rivista musicale italiana*		*muziekgeschiedenis*
NZM	*Neue Zeitschrift für Musik*	UVNM	Uitgaven der Vereniging voor
ÖMz	*Österreichische Musikzeitschrift*		Nederlandse
PAMS	*Papers of the American*		muziekgeschiedenis
	Musicological Society	*VMw*	*Vierteljahrsschrift für*
PGfM	Publikationen der		*Musikwissenschaft*
	Gesellschaft für	*VogelB*	E. Vogel: *Bibliothek der*
	Musikforschung		*gedruckten wettlichen Vocalmusik*
PMA	*Proceedings of the Musical*		*Italiens, aus den Jahren 1500 bis*
	Association		*1700* (Berlin, 1892); rev.,
PRMA	*Proceedings of the Royal Musical*		enlarged, by A. Einstein
	Association		(Hildesheim, 1962); further
PSB	*Polskich słownik*		addns in *AnMc*, nos. 4, 5, 9
	biograficzny (Kraków, 1935)		and 12; further rev. by
RBM	*Revue belge de musicologie*		F. Lesure and C. Sartori as
RdM	*Revue de musicologie*		*Bibliografia della musica italiana*
ReM	*La revue musicale* [1920–]		*vocale profana pubblicata dal*
RHCM	*Revue d'histoire et de critique*		*1500 al 1700* (?Geneva, 1978)
	musicales [1901]; *La revue*		
	musicale [1902–10]		

Author Abbreviations

Key to abbreviations used in the Dictionary section of this book.

A.C.(i)	Adriano Cavicchi	E.B.	Eric Blom
A.C.(ii)	Alexis Chitty	E.C.K.	Ernst C. Krohn
A.D.(i)	Anik Devriès	E.D.	Etienne Darbellay
A.D.(ii)	Albert Dunning	E.G.	Emily Good
A.D.S.	Anne Dhu Shapiro	E.K.	Emil Katzbichler
A.H.(i)	Anthony Hicks	E.M.	Einari Marvia
A.H.(ii)	Arthur Hutchings	F.B.	Frances Barulich
A.H.K.	Alec Hyatt King	F.D.(i)	Frank Daunton
A.L.	Adolf Layer	F.D.(ii)	Frank Dobbins
A.M.R.	Ann Marie Rigler	F.K.	Frank Kidson
A.P.(i)	Alan Page	F.L.	François Lesure
A.P.(ii)	Alan Pope	F.S.	Fritz Stein
A.P.B.	A. Peter Brown	F.S.M.	Franklin S. Miller
A.S.(i)	August Scharnagl	G.H.	Gunter Hempel
A.S.(ii)	Anne Schnoebelen	G.H.B.	Garrett H. Bowles
A.S.(iii)	Alexander Silbiger	G.H.S.	George H. Shorney
A.W.	Alexander Weinmann	G.N.	Geoffrey Norris
A.Z.L.	Agostina Zecca Laterza	G.O.	Geraldine Ostrove
B.B.	Brian Boydell	G.S.	Godelieve Spiessens
B.C.	Barton Cantrell	H.-C.M.	Hans-Christian Müller
B.F.	Bea Friedland	H.E.	Harry Eskew
B.M.	Beth Miller	H.E.J.	H. Earle Johnson
B.T.	Barbara Turchin	H.E.P.	H. Edmund Poole
C.A.H.	Cynthia Adams Hoover	H.G.	Harvey Grace
C.C.	Clifford Caesar	H.G.F.	Henry George Farmer
C.E.	Calvin Elliker	H.-M.P.	Hans-Martin Plesske
C.F.	Corey Field	H.R.	Hans Radke
C.H.P.	Charles H. Purday	H.S.	Hans Schmid
C.I.N.	Clare Iannotta Nielsen	H.V.	Henri Vanhulst
C.J.	Cari Johansson	I.M.	Ilona Mona
C. de P.L.	Carlos de Pontes Leça	I.G.	Inger Gustavsson
C.R.	Caroline Richmond	J.A.B.	Jane A. Bernstein
C.T.	Colin Timms	J.A.E.	John A. Emerson
D.A.L.	Douglas A. Lee	J.A.F.M.	J. A. Fuller Maitland
D.F.	Dan Fog	J.B.Y.	J. Bradford Young
D.H.(i)	Daniel Heartz	J.E.H.	John Edward Hasse
D.H.(ii)	David Hiley	J.H.	Jean Harden
D.H.(iii)	David Hunter	J.H.A.	J. Heywood Alexander
D.J.	David Johnson	J.H.B.	John H. Baron
D.J.B.	D. J. Blaikley	J.G.	Jean Geil
D.J.E	Dena J. Epstein	J.L.	Jan Ledeč
D.L.	Denise Launay	J.L.-C.	José López-Calo
D.L.R.	Deane L. Root	J.M.B.(i)	Jean M. Bonin
D.M.	Davitt Moroney	J.M.B.(ii)	James M. Burk
D.R.H.	D. Ross Harvey	J.M.V.	Juan Maria Veniard
D.T.(i)	Donald Thompson	J.R.B.	Joel R. Berendzen
D.T.(ii)	David Tunley	J.S.	Jürg Stenzl
D.W.K.	D. W. Krummel	J.S.W.	John S. Weissman

J.T.	John Tyrrell	R.L.	Rudolf Lück
J.W.W.	John W. Wagner	R.L.S.	Ronnie L. Smith
K.M.(i)	Kornel Michałowski	R.L.W.	Robert Lee Weaver
K.M.(ii)	Kari Michelsen	R.M.	Richard Macnutt
K.R.S.	Kenneth R. Snell	R.N.	Rosa Newmarch
K.S.	Kettil Skarby	R.S.(i)	Richard Schaal
K.V.	Karl Ventzke	R.S.(ii)	Robert Stevenson
L.A.T.	Leslie A. Troutman	R.S.(iii)	Robert Strizich
L.D.	Lasairíona Duignan	R.S.N.	Robert S. Nichols
L.G.	Laurent Guillo	R.T.W.	Ruth T. Watanabe
L.L.	Leanne Langley	R.W.	Roland Würtz
L.M.-S.	Luise Marretta-Schär	S.A.	Stefano Ajani
L.P.F.	Lloyd P. Farrar	S.B.(i)	Susan Bain
L.R.	Lennart Reimers	S.B.(ii)	Shirley Beary
M.C.	Maria Calderisi	S.B.(iii)	Stanley Boorman
M.D.	Mariangela Donà	S.C.-V.	Samuel Claro-Valdés
M.D.M.	Martha D. Minor	S.D.	Shelley Davis
M.D.-S.	Margaret Dean-Smith	S.F.P.	Samuel F. Pogue
M.D.T.	Mary D. Teal	S.G.C.	Suzanne G. Cusick
M.J.	Mark Jacobs	S.M.	Sylvette Milliot
M.K.	Marion Korda	S.M.W.	Steven Moore Whiting
M.K.D.	Mary Kay Duggan	S.S.B.	Samuel S. Brylawski
M.L.G.	Marie Louise Göllner	T.C.(i)	Tim Carter
M.M.	Miriam Miller	T.C.(ii)	Teresa Chylińska
M.S.L.	Mary S. Lewis	T.D.W.	Thomas D. Walker
M.W.	Marlene Wehrle	T.H.P.	Thomas H. Porter
N.E.T.	Nicholas E. Tawa	T.L.	Thomasin LaMay
N.F.	Nigel Fortune	T.-M.L.	T.-M. Langner
N.S.	Nigel Simeone	T.W.	Theodor Wohnhaas
O.E.	Owain Edwards	T.W.B.	Thomas W. Bridges
O.E.A.	Otto E. Albrecht	V.C.	Viorel Cosma
P.-A.G.	Paul-André Gaillard	V.D.	Vincent Duckles
P.C.E.	Paul C. Echols	V.H.	Veslemöy Heintz
P.G.	Peter Gradenwitz	V.H.M.	Victor H. Mattfeld
P.L.	Paul Landau	V.P.	Vivian Perlis
P.M.(i)	Paul Merrick	W.B.S.	William Barclay Squire
P.M.(ii)	Paula Morgan	W.C.S.	William C. Smith
P.W.J.	Peter Ward Jones	W.E.	Walter Emery
R.A.	Rudolph Angermüller	W.G.	Walter Gerstenberg
R.A.L.	R. Allen Lott	W.H.H.	William Henry Husk
R.B.(i)	Richard Baum	W.K.	Willi Kahl
R.B.(ii)	Rita Benton	W.P.	Wolfgang Plath
R.B.(iii)	Richard Burbank	W.R.(i)	Wolfgang Rehm
R.C.(i)	Raoul Camus	W.R.(ii)	Wilhelm Rohm
R.C.(ii)	Richard Crawford	W.R.C.	Wilma Reid Cipolla
R.D.W.	Richard D. Wetzel	W.S.(i)	Watkins Shaw
R.E.	Rudolf Elvers	W.S.(ii)	Wolfgang Spindler
R.E.E.	Robert E. Eliason	W.S.S.	Warren Storey Smith
R.G.	Richard Griscom	W.T.M.	W. Thomas Marrocco
R.H.M.	Rita H. Mead	W.Y.E.	William Y. Elias
R.J.	Richard Jackson	Z.C.	Zdeněk Culka
R.J.A.	Richard J. Agee		

Preface

This volume is one of a series of specialist handbooks arising out of *The New Grove Dictionary of Music and Musicians* (1980) and the perspectives implicit in that work. Designed to reflect and to meet the increasing interest over recent years in music collecting, music bibliography and music printing generally, it incorporates material on the printing and publishing of music that appeared in *The New Grove* and *The New Grove Dictionary of American Music* (1986), brought up to date and substantially supplemented. We hope that it will meet the interests of all enthusiasts for printed music, including collectors, bibliographers and librarians, who may find it useful in reference and cataloguing.

Part One is based on the *New Grove* article 'Printing and Publishing'. The text on Printing, as originally submitted by the late H. Edmund Poole, includes several substantial passages that (with his consent) were omitted from *The New Grove* as lying somewhat beyond the scope of a general music dictionary. These we have been happy to restore for the present more specialized work. The ending of the essay on Printing has been amended in the light of recent developments, and an extra chapter dealing in particular with computer printing techniques, by Richard Vendome, has been subjoined. The two earlier texts on Publishing have been merged, considerably expanded and reorganized in the light of recent events.

Part Two of this book consists of a dictionary of music publishers and printers. This is based on the roughly 500 entries on music publishers and printers in the 1980 and 1986 sets now supplemented by over 150 additional entries, to give the present work the substantially greater depth and wider geographical sweep appropriate to a more specialized work. All the entries originally written for *The New Grove* were sent to their original writers for any emendation; where the original writer was not available, it was sent to an alternative specialist in the field concerned. A few articles have been replaced in the light of recent work.

The changing structure of music publishing in recent years has raised a particular problem in the assemblage of the dictionary. Many major firms are now part of larger financial empires and holdings corporations and are frequently traded or taken over. We have mentioned at least the major names involved, in dictionary entries (and in the index). The choice of entry has generally been made with a view to the broader historical perspective, as we naturally prefer to choose those names through which the character of an imprint came to be established and its impact on the musical world came to be defined rather than that of a large and functionally anonymous financial organization.

Part Three, which is entirely new, is a glossary dealing with the terminology of music printing and publishing; it is hoped that this material, contributed by Stanley Boorman (New York University), will provide a useful new feature in the light of the lack hitherto of any terminological list concerned specifically with music printing in particular.

The bibliography to the book has been planned afresh and substantially extended compared with the one published in *The New Grove*. A new feature is the index, which should enhance the book's usefulness for specialists and non-specialists alike by permitting different types of access to the information in the volume.

*

We would like to acknowledge the help of a number of scholars who have generously offered their assistance towards the enhancement of the dictionary section in particular; many of them have supplied invaluable advice on the coverage of countries hitherto only scantily considered. These include several who did not specifically contribute, notably Herman Baron, Joseph Boonin, Peggy Daub, Mary Wallace Davidson, Malena Kuss, Anders Lönn, Maxey H. Mayo and Ercilia Morena Cha, as well as many who did contribute, among them Maria Calderisi, Mary K. Duggan, Harry Eskew, Robert Stevenson and George H. Shorney. We are especially grateful to Nigel Simeone not only for supplying new articles but for kindly looking over and bringing up to date some of those by contributors no longer living. Of those working on the dictionary section in Urbana we would particularly like to acknowledge the help of Richard Burbank, Julie Crawley, Calvin Elliker, David Hunter, Martha D. Minor, Thomas D. Walker and James Whittle. The basic work on the assembly of the book was done in London, particularly by Leanne Langley and Christina Bashford, with Sarah Roberts and Fiona Little.

Urbana, Illinois and London, 1989   D. W. KRUMMEL, STANLEY SADIE

PART ONE

Music Printing and Publishing

Page from the Roman Gradual, formerly known as the Constance Gradual (GB-Lbm IB 15154, f.lr), probably the first printed music (? southern Germany, c1473) [64% of actual size]

CHAPTER I

Definition, Early Stages and Woodblock Printing

Printing is a technique for producing many identical copies taken from raised, incised or plane surfaces: that is, from type or from wood or metal blocks cut in relief; from copper, pewter or other metals engraved and punched; from stone or metal plates bearing an image imperceptibly raised. These, generally called letterpress, intaglio and lithographic printing, have each been used for printing music, and each has enjoyed a period of pre-eminence. This waxing and waning was not in the lineal order of a successor taking the place of its antecedent: over long periods the processes were in use side by side, the unique qualities of each employed for some particular purpose. At the beginning of the 19th century, for example, Breitkopf & Härtel were printing music from type, from engraved plates and from lithographic stones concurrently. It is only since about the 1960s that music type has all but disappeared from the case rooms of printing offices and hand engraving has been supplanted by computerized production of visual text from which photographic plates are prepared.

Before the technique of printing was established and exploited widely, music was preserved and circulated in manuscript, or survived as a repertory carried in oral tradition among priests and professional lay musicians. During the latter part of the 15th century and the 16th printing became the accepted means by which works of literature, history, philosophy and scientific speculation were multiplied and disseminated in hundreds of copies – school primers by the thousand; but vocal and instrumental music was still circulated in handwritten form. Manuscripts were prepared for sale in this way at least until the beginning of the 19th century: the names of Foucault in Paris, Traeg in Vienna, Breitkopf in Leipzig and Ricordi in Milan recall the continuity and significance of this tradition. The dichotomy between the means chosen to perpetuate the 'word' on the one hand and the 'note' on the other arises no less from social and economic factors than from technological ones: and it raises questions about the spread of musical literacy, about the regulation of printing by state institutions, about the size and nature of the musical public and the scale of the market – national and international – at any given time. These issues have to be borne in mind, for each was one of the forces influencing, and reacting with, changes in technology.

The early stages of music printing show a diversity of technical solutions, for it cannot be claimed that music adapted itself immediately to the printed page. It first appeared, albeit in manuscript, in the Mainz psalter issued by Fust and Schoeffer in 1457. Sir Irvine Masson in his study of the surviving copies of this superb book found evidence that 'although no music was printed the compositors made the most careful provision for its being added by hand', and after citing examples suggested that 'no doubt the compositors of the psalter worked from manuscript which was musically complete'. If that is so, then those who subsequently wrote the music – using different styles of notation – were very careless. For example in the exceptionally fine copy in the library of the queen at Windsor a splendid red printed initial on folio 29*b* driven well into the vellum has been unskilfully erased to accommodate a melody notated in Gothic style: in the British Library copy the corresponding initial has been written over.

This pattern with its resulting infelicities was characteristic of many liturgical books printed during the 15th century and even into the 16th. Sometimes space for music was left blank on the page, sometimes the staff lines were printed (in red, only exceptionally in black). Presumably the music necessary to complete the text was added by professional scribes attached to the court, cathedral or monastery where the books were to be used, but however well written, the result favours the words over the music, which, while often beautifully written, elsewhere uses dull ink or is modestly drawn or omitted entirely. The space allotted to music, while usually adequate, was still determined by compositors whose standards and ideals were those of the literary text, and whose achievements in this speciality are typically very impressive, on occasion spectacular and noble.

The principal reason for the survival of this makeshift technique has often been assumed to be that liturgical usage in music, even in the words of the Offices, was not uniform throughout the Western Church in the 15th century. Dioceses and monastic establishments introduced variants of the accepted text of Rome and the musical expression of the different uses diverged even more. It was common sense for the printer, therefore, to omit from his books – expensive as they were to produce – those elements that would restrict his sale to one market. Even though many titles exist which suggest that only one diocese could use them, they were in fact often suitable for sale elsewhere, if the music were not printed. Martin Morin of Rouen signed a *Missale ad usum Sarum* 12 October 1492 in which a space was left for music and for the English in the marriage service to be added; in about 1500 he printed another *Missale ad usum Sarum* where blanks were left for the music but the responses in the marriage service were printed in English (both in The British Library, London).

The basic problems of music printing using wholly typographic means were solved in the 1470s, most notably and probably first in a South German gradual often associated with the Constance diocese and extant in a single copy (The British Library, London) with notes, staves, clefs (F and C), two vertical lines that abut on to the staves at each end, and text, all printed in black at two impressions (*see* illustration opposite chapter opening). Large initials for which the printer left space have been rubricated by hand and an additional red line has been drawn on the staves to indicate the position of F. Unfortunately the book does not bear a date, nor is the printer or the place of printing known, but the pages themselves are eloquent: they have been planned and achieved by a rational mind thinking in typographic terms. The relationship between the depth of the type area and the measure between the vertical lines that extend above and below the seven five-line systems is nicely judged; so is the interval between the individual staff lines in relation to the size of the Gothic notes and the size and the visual 'weight' of the text type, although it appears from the irregularity of the fount that the matrices were not well struck and justified.

A passage on leaf viia of Jean Charlier de Gerson's *Collectorium super Magnificat* (Esslingen: Conrad Fyner, 1473) where five identical black squares – often but incorrectly thought to have been printed from inverted type sorts – are shown descending in regular steps above the names of the principal notes of a scale qualifies only in a minimal way as music printing. Probably about contemporaneous with the South German gradual is a missal printed in Rome by Ulrich Han; in its colophon, dated 12 October 1476, he claimed to be the first to print music 'non calamo ereove stilo: sed novo artis ac solerti industrie genere Rome conflatum impressumque unacum cantu: quod numquam factum extitit' (not by the pen or copper stylus but by a new method ingeniously and carefully devised and printed in Rome, together with music, such as has never before been done). Han's work is outstanding in quality. The text of the Office is printed in red and black with a superb type in two columns. The notes in Roman notation are printed in black on red staff lines made up from pieces of rule the length of the column measure. Initials in red or blue, with touches of yellow in some capitals, are added by hand. As in the South German gradual, but here in a masterly way, the relationship of the parts is calculated to achieve a unity that satisfies, and one which is wholly efficient.

The missal was Han's only book containing music, but his methods were copied throughout Europe. Damiano da Moilli printed a *Graduale* in Parma in 1477; Richel printed a *Missale constantiensis* in Basle before 1481; Reyser printed a *Missale herbipolense* at Würzburg in 1481; Scotus printed two missals in Venice in 1482, and in the same year at Milan Valdarfer printed a *Missale ambrosianum*. In 1489 in Paris Higman and Hopyl printed a *Missale andegavense*; two years later the Compañeros Alemanes produced an *Antiphonarium Ord. S. Hieronymi* in Seville. It was not until 1500 that Han's technique reached England, but the *Missale Sarum* printed by Pynson in London in that year was a splendid book worthy to be set alongside the finest of its precursors.

Altogether, liturgical books with music – notes and staves – printed at two impressions were produced in at least 25 towns by 66 printers between 1476 and 1500. Most of the printers are represented by only one or two books, but others clearly were specialists: Ratdolt, the splendid printer of Venice and Augsburg, was responsible for 13;

Johann Emerich in Venice printed no fewer than 13 in seven years; Higman, a most refined craftsman, produced 12 in Paris; Johann Hamman printed 11 in Venice; Planck, Han's successor, printed eight; Sensenschmidt of Bamberg produced seven; and Wenssler of Basle produced five.

Those who needed printed books for the celebration of religious Offices were well served, as were the authors of works on the theory of music, though by different technical methods. For historical reasons, discussions of music theory during the Middle Ages and early Renaissance were built on an arithmetical basis: thus manuscripts contain diagrams of ratios and relationships as well as notes. When these treatises and polemical discourses were printed, the diagrams and sometimes simple arithmetic were reproduced by woodcuts. (The tradition of block cutting was already well established throughout Europe in the 15th century and many early printed books had been decorated with splendid woodcut initials and borders, and with representations of buildings, animals and people.) It was therefore easy to extend the practice to the music, though in some texts spaces were left in the printed page for the notes and staves to be written in. The technique offered great advantages. The musical material was not complicated and the examples were usually short; many models of the required notation were available. Unless musical types and the knowledge of how to use them were available locally it was natural that the printer should turn to a woodcutter, a craftsman more likely to be within call than a typesetter.

It is nevertheless difficult to account for the poor quality of much of early woodcut music. The technique was essentially simple. But it demanded judgment and manual dexterity and control from the operator to produce a block with the text and music reading from right to left, precise in every detail on a flat surface with everything else cut away. The graphic nature of music – a system of horizontal and vertical lines crossing at right angles with associated elements, notes, clefs and other signs, imposing shapes and angles of their own – presented difficulties. Unless the point of intersection of staff and note stem were cut very clean, and subsequently inked and printed with care, the ink tended to blob or spread at the junction. To avoid this some cutters left a small nick breaking the surface at the intersection, to reduce the density of the film of ink at this point. For the same reason it was not easy to cut open (white) notes with a staff line at its proper thickness running through.

Woodcut music from the 15th and 16th centuries varies enormously in extent and quality: this is to be expected, taking into consideration the large amount that was produced. By 1500, 12 works with woodcut music had been issued in Italy: nine theory books, two missals (one with 46 pages of music) and a four-part song. From 1500 to 1600, 326 separate works on the theory of music were issued in a total of 611 editions by 225 printers in 75 towns throughout Europe (see Davidsson, 1965). Some of the texts were remarkably popular, running through 30 editions in 49 years, or 40 editions in 63 years, repeated sometimes in the same form by the first printer, sometimes with new blocks for the music, sometimes with the originals, and sometimes by a different printer in the same town or elsewhere.

The following well-known early examples of music printed from blocks may be cited. The *Grammatica brevis* of Franciscus Niger, in its second edition printed in Basle (c1485) has a few pages with four lines of notes without staves (but with a clef) to illustrate the rhythms of five different poetic metres using verses from Virgil, Lucan, Ovid and Horace. This was followed by the *Musices opusculum* of Nicolaus Burtius, printed in Bologna by Ugo de Rugeriis for Benedictus Hectoris in 1487 (see fig.1*a*). Woodcuts were used to show the hymn *Ut quaeant laxis*, specimens of note forms and ligatures and, in the section on counterpoint, a short complete composition for three voices, all with staves. The cutting is thick and unskilful. In contrast to this hesitant performance the treatment of the music in *Flores musice omnis cantus Gregoriani* by Hugo Spechtshart of Reutlingen, printed in Strasbourg by Johann Prüss in 1488, is accomplished. As its title suggests, the practice of plainchant is treated in detail: the music, in Gothic notation on five lines with clef and directs, appears on 67 pages mostly occupying the whole panel. The second edition (c1490) is usually overlooked, but the cutting and printing of new blocks for the music in quite different notation is equally accomplished. The last two pages of *Historica beatica* (a play by Carolus Veradrus) printed by Eucharius Silber (Rome, 1493) are followed by a four-part song, which is the first printing of dramatic music, although the cutting of the block is not good. As King wrote, 'what is probably the earliest German secular song, found in *Von sant Ursulen schifflin* (Strasbourg, 1497) is also reproduced by an unusual use of this process – the notes (in Gothic form), the staves, and the text all being cut on wood'. Perhaps Andrea Antico was unaware of this when in *Liber quindecim missarum* (*RISM* 1516[1]) he said that he cut the notes in wood which nobody before him had done. This splendid folio of 161 pages is set off with fine initial letters and the work is a remarkable technical achievement, though the impression is rather flat and heavy (fig.1*b*). Antico had no imitators in printing large-scale collections of music from woodblocks, though woodcutting of the highest artistry may be seen in Luther's *Geistliche Lieder* printed by Valentin Bapst (Leipzig, 1545). Although these books are oustanding, there is much to admire in the decorative touches that enliven many more workaday theoretical treatises, for example, the illustration showing a priest playing an organ in the *Theorica musicae* of Gaffurius (Milan, 1492). In Gregor Reisch's *Margarita philosophica*, a full-page cut is printed as a part title before the main divisions. The section devoted to arithmetic, music, geometry and astronomy is prefaced with a woodcut showing among other features a group of musicians. The composition and cutting of the block in the first edition of 1503 (Freiburg: Johann Schott) is somewhat rudimentary but the corresponding block in the edition of 1504 (Strasbourg: J. Grüninger) is finer both in design and in execution.

It is normally stated of such works that the blocks were cut in wood. It might be more precise to say 'wood or perhaps metal'. It is very difficult to resolve which is used by inspecting a well-printed page. It is feasible

(a)

1. Two examples of music printed from woodblocks: (a) page showing note forms and ligatures from the 'Musices opusculum' of Nicolaus Burtius, printed by Ugo de Rugeriis for Benedictus Hectoris (Bologna, 1487); (b) beginning of the Kyrie from Pipelare's 'Missa L'homme armé', part of a page from the 'Liber quindecim missarum' printed by Andrea Antico (Rome, 1516), exemplifying woodcutting of the highest technical and artistic achievement [(a) 79%, (b) 46% of actual size]

(b)

that an ill-prepared woodblock, inadequately inked, might show grain, though no examples are known. Nor is evidence for the use of metal easier to come by. Comparison of numerous copies of a book in a single edition, or of copies in different editions, sometimes yields results. In the first edition of *Practica musicae* by Gaffurius, printed by Guillermus Le Signerre for Johannes Petrus de Lomatio (Milan, 1496), the examples of plainchant and mensural notation are well cut and printed without blemish. The editions of 1497 and 1508 (Brescia: Angelo Britannico) were printed using the same blocks, but small circles appear in association with music on two folios. This suggests that the music was cut on a plate nailed to a wooden mount, and that a careless beater inked the heads of the nails, which printed. In the edition of 1512 (Venice: Agostino Zani) some musical examples are slanting, which again suggests that the printing surface was mounted – and carelessly – because the forme could not have been locked up unless all the type, furniture and associated material were properly squared: this again suggests a metal plate rather than a woodblock. Such plates for illustrations in 16th-century books have survived with flanges pierced to take mounting nails.

However this may be, the use of wood or metal blocks to print music was more extensive than the complexities of musical notation might be thought to allow. The year 1472, for instance, is not only the conjectural date of the South German gradual mentioned above, but also the firm date of the earliest music printing in Japan. A recently discovered book of *shōmyō* (Buddhist hymns chanted in the services of the Shingon sect), printed by the priest Kaizen at Kōyasan on 21 June 1472 and now at the Research Archives for Japanese Music at Ueno Gakuen College in Tokyo, employed blocks that were re-used in an edition of 1478, and again in 1541 and 1561. Block printing was temporarily supplanted in the late 16th century by the Korean method known as 'old typography' and by the European-style typography used by Jesuit missionaries, but as early as 1601 secular music was again being printed from blocks; the process was used widely thereafter in the extensive production of *utaibon* (Noh texts with music). In the West, librettos and other small books continued into the 19th century to include music printed from blocks. The first music to be printed in the British colonies of North America, the ninth edition of the *Bay Psalm Book* (Boston: B. Green and J. Allen, 1698), was taken from woodblocks.

CHAPTER II

Printing Music from Type

In 1450 Johann Gutenberg established a system of taking copies from single types, accurate to shape and size, systematized into pages and printed on paper or vellum with a varnish-based ink with a press; the same process was adopted several decades later to make the first music types. Gutenberg's system of type making had three basic components. First, a letter or any other character, as written or drawn, was worked by means of gravers, punches, files and other tools on to the end of a piece of mild steel rod, somewhat larger in section than the intended character. It was finished so that the required outline was standing free in a horizontal plane across the section of the rod, with every stroke of the drawn model reproduced in steel. The spaces in and around the model were cut away from the metal, and when the rendering of the original was deemed satisfactory the steel was tempered hard. The finished tool was called a punch.

In the second stage of the process, the punch was driven with a hammer or pressed by means of a screw vice into a piece of copper of a chosen size – it had to be substantial enough to withstand its handling – to make a 'strike'. This, when smoothed, squared up to correct the bulging caused by the operation of the punch, and, adjusted so that the character was in a predetermined position on its plane side and sunk to a calculated depth, became a matrix, with the original character stamped in intaglio. A punch and a matrix were required for every character that was called for.

Finally, to make type, the matrix was placed into a casting mould. The matrix and the casting mould were always considered together, and indeed were made in relation one with another. If all the matrices were properly struck and justified, the types cast in them, if assembled into words, would rest so that the characters they carried would appear to have been lined up along a straight edge; types placed one above another would show a predetermined space above and below (or 'north and south'), and sufficient space around the individual characters to allow of a harmonious relationship between them when they were combined into words. These desiderata were realized by means of the variable casting mould: this delivered type of a fixed size, or body, north and south (made up of the visible character and invisible pieces of metal which gave the white spaces above and below), and allowed the casting of letters of any desired width.

The mould was made of iron in two complementary halves, each covered with wood on the outside. When the pieces were put together they gave an aperture to the limits required by the individual characters to be cast. The walls of the aperture were vertical and engineered to give true right angles at the four corners: they thus formed a shaft of standard height which opened into a plane walled funnel at the top and an aperture with an accurately machined section at the bottom. The matrix was put against the bottom of the shaft with the sunk character facing upwards and standing north and south to the fixed walls (this position was established by the structure of the mould) and supported underneath by a tie or spring. The halves of the mould were adjusted to the width of the character, allowing for the necessary space left and right, and stops were screwed down to prevent the mould closing further. The mould was turned so that the funnel was vertical, molten metal was poured in, and the mould was given a 'flick' to force the metal into every part of the matrix. The composition of the type metal used by the earliest printers is not precisely known, but an alloy of lead, tin and antimony in varying proportions has been reported for many samples of type used in the 16th century and subsequently. After casting, the mould was opened and the type (including the waste metal from the funnel) loosened with a hook and tossed out. The mould was reassembled with the matrix to cast again and again until sufficient types had been cast. The matrix was changed, the mould readjusted to the appropriate width for the new character, and casting continued.

The waste metal was broken from the casting, and each type was then rubbed down on abrasives, the face planed, and the whole finished by hand to ensure that the sides were smooth, the foot flat and all planes square one with another. Every character had to be cast and finished ('dressed') individually, and every type produced had to be uniform in size with all the others in the fount, as the collection of types – capitals and lower-case letters, roman and italic, figures, marks of punctuation and the like – cast in the same mould was called. In order for the characters to line up harmoniously, they had to appear in the same position on the shank; even italic (sloping) characters were cast on rectangular bodies. However, unless special provision was made for the letters y, f and j their bodies would be much wider than those required for such letters as i, b and c, and in a word like 'fairly' there would be unsightly gaps between f and a, l and y. To avoid this the mould was adjusted so that the character was cast on a body of average width, and part of the letter was made to hang over beyond the shank; this projection was called a 'kern'. Although kerning characters needed careful handling, they were quite safe in use because their over-hanging parts were supported on the shank of the preceding or following type.

The letters in a fount of type were supplied in numbers proportional to the frequency of their use – there were many more of e than of q, for example. Spaces of various widths, cast in the same mould as the type but only to the height of the shank without the character, were also included. These were necessary because although standard terms, such as 'pica' and 'petit canon' were used to describe founts, the type sizes themselves might well vary considerably according to their origin, and the printer who unwittingly mixed them would have great difficulty with alignment. In fact it was not until the 18th century that attempts were made to standardize type sizes against an agreed unit in such a way that a pica type cast by one founder could be used with a pica type cast elsewhere.

The printer distributed his type for use in a 'case'. This was a shallow tray divided into compartments of sizes appropriate to the frequency with which individual letters occurred in the fount: the boxes for e and i were larger than those used for v or z, for instance. The most frequently used letters were grouped in the middle boxes, little-used letters in boxes around the edge. When not in use the cases were stored on runners in racks; above these there were frames with a double slope, and it was on these that the cases were put when required by the compositor.

The compositor was given his copy – in manuscript for a new work, usually printed for a new edition of an existing work – and worked through it to estimate its extent in the light of instructions about the type to be used, the page size, type area and general style. He counted off the text word by word in order to determine where the page-breaks would fall when it was set. This process, called 'casting off' was especially important if the copy was extensive, because it was split between a number of compositors. Many examples of printer's copy have survived with such markings, enabling us to judge how accurate this planning could be.

With these essentials determined the compositor was ready for work. He sat or (from the mid-17th century onwards) stood with his cases of type and sheets of his copy in front of him; nearby was a 'galley', a shallow tray rather larger than his page with a raised edge on three sides. In his hand he held a composing stick, or setting stick. In the 16th century and perhaps earlier, this was a narrow piece of wood with a rabbet along one edge which was stopped at each end to accommodate a line of type of given 'measure' (length). By the 17th century it had developed into an iron tool which could be adjusted to produce columns of type to the required width. It consisted of a flat bed, or 'plate', about 200 mm long and 44 mm wide, with one long edge turned up to make a flange about 16 mm high, known as the 'back'. At one end it was joined precisely at right angles to a solid iron stop (or 'head') the same height as the back and as long as the plate was wide. The other long edge of the plate was left open. Resting on the plate was a slide in the form of a reversed L (⌐), with its longer arm the same length and depth as the head and exactly parallel to it. The shorter arm moved along the flange and could be fixed either by means of a screw, which passed into the slide through one of the series of holes drilled through the back, or by a clamping device, of which many kinds existed.

The compositor adjusted his stick to the length ('measure') of the lines of type he was to set and placed his setting rule, a thin slip of brass plate the same length as the intended line and of the same height as the type, against the back of the stick. He then started to compose. Holding the stick in his left hand with his thumb on the setting rule, he picked up the letters of the first word one by one with the thumb and first two fingers of his right hand and placed them in the correct order in the stick. When he came to the end of his first word he put in a space and then continued with the next word and so on, until he reached the end of his line. He then adjusted the spacing between the words so that the line exactly and comfortably fitted the chosen measure. He then moved his setting rule from the back of the stick to the front of the line he had just set and started his second line, letter by letter; his left hand and stick followed it over the case as his right hand moved from box to box taking up the letters and spaces one by one and placing each upon the setting rule, 'supporting and placing them together by the action of the left thumb, the other hand being instantly disengaged for picking up the next letter'. Thomas Curson Hansard, in his venerable *Typographia* (1825), describes these movements as 'performed with a degree of facility not easily conceived by a stranger to the art'. The compositor carried on setting, adjusting ('justifying') his lines to their proper length as he went along, keeping an eye on his type to check his accuracy – for he got no pay for correcting his errors later – until he could accommodate no more lines on the plate of his stick. Resting the stick on the lower of his two cases, he placed the setting rule in front of the last line set; then, holding the forefinger of each hand in front of the rule, he pressed his middle fingers against the ends of the lines and his thumb behind the first line, lifted the whole stickful and placed it on the waiting galley. He then resumed setting, filling and emptying his stick until he had set enough lines to make a page; he next set the page's running head and folio number, and the direction line at the bottom of the page, and then tied the whole round with page cord, removed it from the galley on a paper wrapper and stored it under his frame or in some other convenient safe place. He then recommenced his setting.

A printer had only a certain amount of type available to share between his compositors, and in order to maintain a comfortable supply of letters in the cases at any one time it was usually necessary to start printing a book long before it was completely set. Indeed a compositor was often called upon to set his copy out of its narrative order so that eight or 16 pages of type could be assembled for printing.

If a sheet of paper is folded at right angles midway along its long edge, two leaves, four pages, are formed. If these are numbered from the front consecutively from 1 to 4 and the fold is opened again, then pages 1 and 4 will appear on one side of the sheet and pages 2 and 3 on the other. Similarly, if a second fold is made across the first, four leaves, eight pages, are produced; if these are numbered consecutively from 1 to 8 then pages 1, 4, 5 and 8 will appear on one side of the opened sheet and pages 2, 3, 6 and 7 on the other; and so on, the number of pages multiplying as fold succeeds fold. This system of folding gave its name to formats, the arrangements of the type pages of a book that are necessary for the author's text to read continuously (they have nothing to do with size). The term 'folio' describes a book printed on sheets folded once, as in the first example above; 'quarto', a book made of sheets folded twice, as in the second example; and 'octavo', the format in which a third fold is made across the second to give eight leaves, 16 pages (for illustration *see* Format).

The format was decided by the printer before setting began and the markings made in casting off showed where the ends of pages in type would fall. If, therefore, it had been decided to work a manuscript as a quarto book and to set and print one side of a sheet before the setting of the pages of the other side was complete, then the compositor would know that he should set the copy for pages 1, 4, 5 and 8 first. That done, he would record the page numbers on the manuscript and indicate where on the sheet the matter was to be found. A manuscript for Christopher Simpson's *Principles of Practical Musick* (1665) is marked in this way (Bodleian Library, Oxford). If a second compositor was given copy for the other four pages required to complete the sheet, he would know that his front page was page 2 and that pages 3, 6 and 7 would follow.

When it was decided to print, the pages of type, tied round and resting on papers, were taken to the imposing stone, a flat level surface the height of the frame on which the cases of type were reared. Using the catchwords at the feet of pages as a guide to order, the compositor arranged his type on the stone in correct sequence according to the chosen format. He placed round the type a rectangular iron frame of square section with two iron cross-pieces, which divided it into four equal areas. This was the chase. Lengths of wood, called 'furniture', were put between the sides of the type pages and the intersecting cross-pieces and between the type pages and the outer frame of the chase. Along these sides long wedges were laid, and outside them short wedges ('quoins') were introduced, pressing the type upward and inward. The type was then untied, any irregularities in the surface were corrected by blows on a smooth piece of wood which was moved across the pages, and finally the quoins were driven tight. The type, furniture and chase together were called a forme, and if everything had been properly adjusted it could be handled as one integrated piece without fear of the type falling out. The pages to be printed on the other side of the sheet would then be assembled so that page 2 would fall exactly on the back of page 1, page 4 on the back of page 3 and so on. The forme in which the first and last pages appear is called the 'outer forme', the second one the 'inner forme'. Once the compositor was satisfied with his formes one of them would be taken to the press for proofing. A 'pull' was taken on one side of a sheet and this, together with the pieces of manuscript that had been set, was sent to the reader for correction. After any errors or other imperfections had been marked and the reader was satisfied with the sheet, the proof was sent back to the compositor, who would make such alterations to the type as were required. Any corrections and alterations made by the author were also incorporated. If the changes were many, a second proof – a 'revise' or 'review' – would be pulled and read. Once finally approved, the forme was ready for the press.

From the earliest days to about 1800 the printing press, or 'common press' as it was called, was made of wood (for a diagram *see* PRESS, fig.1). It consisted of two interlocking elements: a strong vertical frame, or body, which housed the impression system, and a pair of rails about 75 cm from the ground supported at both ends and running through the body at right angles to its width. This arrangement allowed passage to the paper and type system, made up of the carriage and its component fittings. The carriage itself consisted of a strong wooden plank upon which was mounted the coffin, a shallow box with strong raised iron corners. In this was bedded the press stone, a carefully smoothed piece of marble or Purbeck limestone about 62 cm long and 47 cm wide. At the end of the coffin furthest from the body of the press was hinged the outer tympan, a frame of wood and iron slightly smaller than the press stone. It was covered with parchment and contained a hole in each of its long sides in which a square bolt with a pointed end could be inserted. Within this frame was fitted another frame covered with parchment, the inner tympan, and between the two parchments cloth or paper was packed. The tympans were attached to a supporting frame (the 'gallows') which was fixed to the plank; hinged to the top of them was a thin iron frame covered with parchment or paper, the frisket.

In the body of the press was a spindle about 42 cm long. It was cut into a screw for a distance of 8.25 cm from the upper end, and was free to turn in a nut housed above it. Below the screw a short section of the spindle was squared and bolted to take the bar, a curved piece of iron rod with a wooden handle. Its lower end touched a depression in a plate fixed to the upper side of the impressing surface, or 'platen', a piece of hardwood scrupulously finished smooth and flat. This was 35.6 cm long, 22.9 cm wide and 5.1 cm thick and was fixed with its length across the body, parallel with the short edge of the press stone.

Before printing could start the press had to be made ready. The chosen forme was lifted on to the press stone and fixed by means of quoins between the chase and the corner pieces of the coffin so that the type would be correctly aligned for the paper. This was judged in relation to the points on the tympan, which controlled the position of the sheet; once the necessary adjustments had been made, a sheet of paper from the heap provided for the book was pasted in correct position on the tympan, and the parchment was treated with water to soften it. Two blankets were passed between the outer and inner tympan.

Two men, or 'companions' formed a press team and shared duties (for illustration *see* PRESS, fig.2). While the senior man was making ready, his partner worked up the ink on the mix block, a small table fixed to the side of the press, using a flexible knife and a kind of pestle. Once the ink – a mixture of varnish and colour, lampblack for black and ground vermillion for red – was of the correct consistency, the second press-man, or 'beater', took some of it up on his ink-balls, pelts stuffed with wool or horsehair which were nailed to wooden cups and handles. He took one in each hand, rolling them together to spread the mix well and evenly on the spherical surface of each. He then moved the balls over the type with a rocking motion, the handles revolving in his hands meanwhile. Once the type was correctly inked, the leading man, or 'puller', turned down the frisket on to the tympan and then turned down the two together on to the type. With his left hand he turned the 'rounce', which connected to a windlass slung under the frame, and thereby operated a system of belts to move the carriage bodily along the rails. The puller stopped the carriage when half of the forme was under the platen, caught hold of the bar with his right hand and drew it smoothly towards him through an angle of about 90°. The spindle turned, and the action of the screw sent the platen down about 15 mm, driving the tympan with considerable force on to the type. He released the bar and the tympan rose. Next he turned the rounce to the left, and the carriage moved so that the second half of the forme was under the platen; the bar was then pulled a second time and released. The rounce was turned clockwise and the carriage was drawn back to its original position. The tympan was raised and the frisket, its cover bearing an impression of the type, was removed. Using a sharp knife, the puller cut the printed rectangles out of the cover and replaced the frisket; this would now act as a mask, holding the paper against the tympan, permitting the type to reach the paper in the correct places and preventing the rest of the sheet from becoming soiled by the forme. The beater went over the type again with the ink-balls, and the puller took a sheet from the heap of paper already damped and laid it accurately on the sheet pasted on the tympan. He turned down the frisket, which simultaneously pressed the paper on to the tympan and forced the points through the sheet, holding it firmly against the tympan. He then folded the frisket and tympan together on to the type, and an impression was taken with two pulls as described above. The carriage was drawn back, the tympan and frisket raised and the printed sheet lifted off and laid down near the imprinted paper. The same sequence of events was repeated until the required number of copies had been taken off. The forme was then removed; the type was cleaned and taken up into a setting stick, and the individual types were dropped one by one into their appointed places in the case.

Meanwhile the second forme was made ready on the bed of the press to print the 'reiteration' on the back of the white paper. The heap of paper already printed on one side was turned over end to end, and printing restarted. The sheets were fed one by one on to the tympan so that the points passed through the holes already made in them, ensuring that the impressions of the type on both sides backed one on to the other.

The two pressmen exchanged roles after an agreed number of 'tokens' had been finished, each of 150 sheets printed on one side. As Moxon (1683–4) says, 'the *first* and *second* take their spell of *Pulling* and *Beating* an agreed number of *Tokens*: Sometimes they agree to change every three *Tokens*, which is three hours' work, and sometimes every six *Tokens*; that they may both *Pull and Beat* a like number of *Tokens* in one day'.

It was customary to turn the heap over and print the reiteration immediately after the printing of the white paper. Indeed, according to Gaskell (1972/R1974, 1975), 'the printer would be unwilling to leave the heap for long with only one side printed, for the paper would begin to dry and shrink – or would be liable to change shape differentially if it had to be redamped – so that it became impossible to fit the point holes over the points and make register'.

These considerations were particularly important when a sheet had to be printed with two colours on the same side or had to go through the press twice for any other reason. If red and black were required to be printed on the same side, a number of techniques were available. The most laborious was to set and impose the forme complete with both the black and red type in position and then to remove the red type and ink it separately, ink the rest of the type with black and replace the red type before locking up the forme and taking an impression. This method ensured good fitting of the red and black words when printed, but it was slow because the forme had to be unlocked after each impression.

Alternative procedures were much preferred. In one, the complete forme was proofed in black and the words that were to appear red were underlined. An impression of the forme was then taken in black on a frisket sheet, the frisket was removed, and the words that were to appear in red were carefully cut out. The corresponding type was removed from the forme and spacing material substituted, leaving blanks. An ordinary frisket was fitted to the tympan, the forme was inked in black, and the required number of copies were printed off. Next the spacing pieces were taken out, and thin pieces of card were cut exactly to fit the same areas and laid on the press stone. The red type was then placed in position on the card and this stood rather higher than the surrounding black type. The specially prepared 'colours frisket' was fitted, the red type was inked red, and the sheet was put through the press again, printing red only; for the colour frisket 'hinders any thing to print but what prints through the holes cut in it; which holes these underlined words fall exactly through' (Moxon).

This simplified account of the main procedures of typographic printing applies broadly to the 17th and 18th centuries, but as tradition is so strong in the craft the description may well hold in essentials for 16th-century practices too: certainly early woodcuts showing printers at work support this view. The press itself changed little until the 19th century. During the years 1800–03 Earl Stanhope built one with an iron frame and a full-size platen which gave good impressions at a single pull and which would accommodate a larger sheet than the wooden press. Other iron presses followed and were much used for book printing until about 1830, but gradually the hand press was replaced by the cylinder and later the rotary press, machines of different construction powered by steam and in time by electricity.

The same processes were used to print music from type (see fig.2). As in the making of text type, the number of copies cast of each pattern varied according to need (there were more minims than breves, for example); spaces of varying widths were also cast so that notes could be separated as required by the music. The copy manuscript from which the compositor worked was similarly marked to show line-ends and other details of layout. The actual printing of the prepared copy was not affected by the material to be printed – text, pictures or music – and the normal press was used. The techniques of printing plainchant were highly developed by 1500, but there was no corresponding evolution in the printing of mensural music from type during the same period:

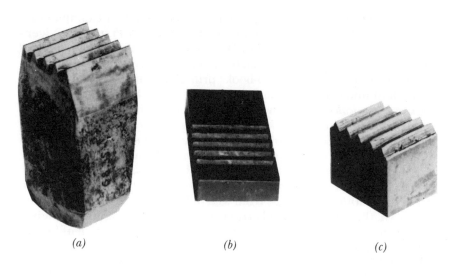

(a)   (b)   (c)

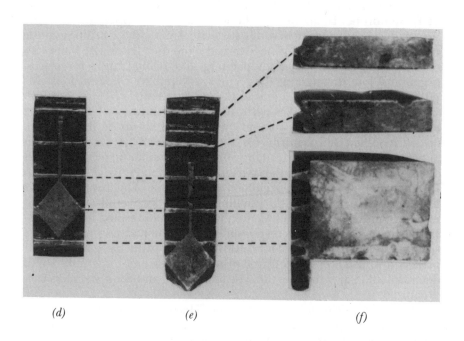

(d)   (e)   (f)

2. Steps in making music type illustrated by material from the 'grande musicque' cut by Hendrik van den Keere for Christopher Plantin (1577): (a) steel punch with a five-line staff system engraved in relief on its end; (b) matrix produced by striking the punch into a billet of copper (here c20 mm wide) to leave the staff lines recessed; (c) type cast from the matrix; (d) type cast with the matrix in 'normal' position in the mould; (e) note head from the same matrix projecting below the normal position of the lowest staff line; (f) type shown in (e) turned on its side to show that the projecting note head was cast with only three lines attached and completed by two additional types, each carrying a separately cast segment of staff line; (d), (e) and (f) illustrate the principle of 'kerning' or overhang

19

attempts were isolated and restricted in scope. The first example, four lines on a single page, appeared in the first edition of Franciscus Niger's *Grammaticus* (Venice: Theodor of Würzburg, 1480): only the notes and clef were printed, accurately aligned for anybody to rule the staves. Other examples appear in two books printed by Michel de Toulouse in Paris, both undated and assigned to about 1496. One was an edition of *Utilissime musicales regule* by Guillermus Guerson and the other an anonymous treatise *L'art et instruction de bien danser* (a unique copy is in the Library of the Royal College of Physicians, London). Music appears on 18 pages of the latter, mostly in chant notation, printed black on four red lines, but there are almost two pages of music in mensural notation. At first glance the achievement is not impressive but closer examination shows that, although the type from which the notes are printed has been badly cast, their typographical arrangement was workmanlike. A slightly later example is a mensural Credo printed by Johann Emerich of Speyer in his *Graduale* of 1499.

In Venice there were moves that transformed music printing and made polyphonic music generally available in greater quantity and over wider areas than ever before. The innovator was Ottaviano dei Petrucci of Fossombrone. In about 1490 he went to Venice apparently to study the technique of printing in order to devise a method for printing music from movable type. In 1498 he obtained from the Signoria of Venice an exclusive 20-year privilege for printing and selling music for voices, organ and lute throughout the Venetian Republic. His first book was published in 1501: *Harmonice musices odhecaton A* (*RISM* 1501), a collection of 96 pieces arranged as partsongs with the cantus and tenor on the left-hand page of an opening and the altus and bassus on the right – a layout modified satisfactorily for three-part items. A second edition appeared in 1502/3 and a third in 1503/4. All together he printed at least 43 musical titles in Venice, the latest in 1509. When Petrucci returned to Fossombrone in 1511, a typecutter named Jacomo Ungaro applied for his patent for printing music, claiming to have discovered how to print mensural music in the city of Venice, where he had resided for 40 years. It is likely that Ungaro was responsible for cutting and casting Petrucci's type in Venice, and probably several of the plainchant founts that preceded it. Petrucci's later music printing in Fossombrone (until 1520) deteriorated in appearance: the type looks worn and the system less well organized.

Petrucci's music printing was splendid. His note forms were abundant and with their equivalent rests varied enough to set the most elaborate works of the composers of his day. The characters were elegant, the punchcutting, justification of the matrices and typecasting were accomplished. The presswork was so meticulous that he was consistently able to achieve perfect register of notes, staves and text though (at least initially) three impressions were required: first for the notes, second for the staves, and third for the text, initial letters, signatures and page numbers. The whole achievement immediately conveys typographical conviction which on analysis is found to derive from a skilful choice of size for individual elements – notes, key signatures, the staff system, clefs etc – and from the manner in which they are related. For example, the length of a note stem is the depth of four spaces on the staff, a relationship that has persisted to our own day: the stem of the B♭ key signature is longer than the stem of a note and in this way maintains its role as a flag. The directs are very noticeable, serve their purpose and balance the large initials and other display material at the left of the staves. Only by the use of notes, letters and spaces, all casts in sizes that worked exactly together without bodging, could such results be achieved. (Petrucci had equal success with his system of tablature, the first to be printed from movable type; see fig.3.) It is not known who cut the punches for these founts and justified the matrices. Francesco Griffo of Bologna, a brilliant punchcutter, who was the first to cut 'littera cursiva' (italic) types, under commission from the printers Soncino and Aldus Manutius, worked with Petrucci in Fossombrone in 1511, but there is no evidence that they had collaborated earlier in Venice.

The shining example of Petrucci encouraged other printers into imitation. The first was Erhard Oeglin of Augsburg who issued *Melopoeiae sive Harmoniae* (1507: settings by Petrus Tritonius and others of Horace's odes) and a few later titles. The books do not achieve the elegance of Petrucci but Oeglin made good register with his two workings. His staff lines are assembled from short pieces of type. A book on the grand scale (folio: 44 × 28.5 cm) which approaches Petrucci's quality is the *Liber selectarum cantionum quas vulgo mutetas appellant, sex quinque et quatuor vocum* (Augsburg: Grimm and Wirsung, 1520[4]). The hand of a master is seen in *Rerum musicarum*, a treatise by Johannes Frosch (Strasbourg: Peter Schoeffer jr and Mathias Apiarius, 1535): the scale of the work is much along the lines of Petrucci's and the achievement, by two impressions, is comparable. The sole surviving part (triplex) of *XX Songes* printed 'at the sign of the Black Morens' in London in 1530 (*RISM* 1530[6]) is equally elegant and well printed (see fig.4).

In 1532 Jean de Channey printed at Avignon, at the composer's expense, the first of four volumes of sacred music by Carpentras. Although oval note heads had appeared in the woodcut music of J. F. Locher's *Historia de rege frantie* (Freiburg: F. Riederer, 1495; copy in the National Library of Scotland, Edinburgh), the Carpentras books are remarkable as the first to use type cast with a rounded, almost oval note form instead of the traditional lozenge and square. Cut by Etienne Briard of Bar-le-Duc, the open notes have stems with a strong downward stroke followed through with a splendid calligraphic swing, swelling and diminishing to reconnect with the stem. The black notes are rather lifeless by comparison. Briard not only abandoned the accepted note forms but cast aside the whole system of proportional notation and replaced complicated ligatures with single notes. The music was printed in two impressions (see fig.5).

By this time a great step forward had been taken elsewhere, marked by the survival of fragments of two anonymous pieces printed by John Rastell in London (perhaps in 1526, or earlier) each of which survives in a unique copy (The British Library, London). One, printed on part of a broadside, is an incomplete song for one voice; the other is a three-part

3. *Part of a page from Joan Ambrosio Dalza's 'Intabolatura de lauto' (f.3v) printed by Petrucci (Venice, 1508); the decorative initial and unbroken staff lines indicate that the sheet was passed through the press at least twice, as in the method devised by Petrucci for printing mensural music*

4. *Part of a page from 'XX Songes' (London, 1530), showing the beginning of Taverner's 'Love wyll I' [67% of actual size]*

5. *Part of a page from the 'Liber primus missarum' of Carpentras (signature A2), the first printed music with oval note heads (Avignon, 1532; cut by Etienne Briard, printed by Jean de Channey)*

song 'Tyme to pas with goodly sport' which is in Rastell's play *A New Interlude and a Mery of the Nature of the iiii Elements* (for illustration *see* RASTELL, JOHN). The fragments are remarkable because the music – notes and staves – the clefs, indications of key, and the words were all printed together at one impression. This was made possible by casting the note and a fragment of a complete set of staff lines on the same type body. Spacing-pieces of various widths bearing only fragments of staff lines were used to maintain continuous systems between notes. The type, not undistinguished in design, looks rather shaky on the page, and as far as is known was used only once more – in Coverdale's *Goostly Psalmes* (*c*1538); but if the date assigned to it by King is accepted – and his argument is closeknit and persuasive – Rastell 'can be credited with several achievements: the earliest mensural music printed in England; the earliest broadside with music printed from type anywhere in Europe; the earliest song printed in an English dramatic work. Rastell also made the first attempt at printing a score, by any process in any country'.

If this survival has no known progenitor and is without issue the latter cannot be said of the work of Pierre Attaingnant in Paris, who was often held to be the first to devise and use the technique of printing music from type at one impression. He issued his first book, *Chansons nouvelles en musique a quatre parties: naguere imprimees a Paris*, on 4 April 1527/8 (*RISM* 1528[3]) and until 1551 maintained a steady output of music from the collections of the finest composers of the late 15th century and of his own day. His typographical apparatus was accomplished in design and finish, and he used it with neat authority, demonstrating his powers as a publisher as well as a printer who gave to posterity a system that was to survive, little altered, for more than 200 years (see fig.6).

The techniques of Attaingnant were much imitated, and his repertory of music was raided. The high estimation in which both were held can be measured by the speed with which printers inside and outside France procured types for single-impression music. Jacques Moderne, in Lyons, produced his *Motetti del fiore* in 1532 (*RISM* 1532[10], 1532[11]), printed in elegant note forms based on those of Petrucci rather than upon the squatter types of Attaingnant (for illustration *see* MODERNE, JACQUES). The enterprising Christian Egenolff of Frankfurt am Main printed at one impression *Melodide in odas Horatij: et quaedam alia carminum genera*, by Petrus Tritonius, in 1532. In Nuremburg Hieronymus Formschneider ('Grapheus') issued Senfl's *Varia carminum genera* in 1534. Georg Rhau of Wittenberg printed more than 60 primers and works of musical theory with examples cut in woodblock, and also music at single impression from 1538. Joanne de Colonia, in Naples, is said to have been the first (in 1537) to print music at one impression in Italy, but it was Antonio Gardano and the Scotto family in Venice who established that city as the pre-eminent centre of Italian music printing. Though the printing of music at one impression was not practised in the Low Countries until 1540 (by Willem van Vissenaecken at Antwerp), the process flourished in the hands of Tylman Susato (for illustration *see*

6. *Two examples of music printed by one pass through the press: extract from Janequin's 'Fyes vous' (above), in the 'Tiers livre contenant XXI chansons musicales a quatre parties' (F-Pm MS 2, f.152v), printed and published by Pierre Attaingnant (Paris, 1536); part of the discantus of Byrd's 'Miserere mihi, Domine' (below), from 'Cantiones sacrae' (with Tallis; London, 1575), printed by Thomas Vautrollier with type imported from France; both demonstrate the simplicity and logic, but also the shortcomings, of the one-note-one-type system with note head and stem cast on a single type containing segments of a complete staff system: observe also Attaingnant's use of alternative, 'squatter' type to print notes one above the other [(above) 70%, (below) 66% of actual size]*

SUSATO, TYLMAN). Susato used a splendid character which aligned very well with the staves and may be seen to advantage in his *Premier livre des chansons a quatre parties* (*RISM* 1543[16]). He was soon joined by Pierre Phalèse at Louvain and Christopher Plantin who published important partbooks in the 1570s at Antwerp.

There were capable and energetic followers in France, of whom Robert Granjon and Philippe Danfrie were historically the most important. In 1549 Granjon, one of the great French punchcutters, obtained a privilege to print music, but it was not until ten years later that he took advantage of it to print, at Lyons, some compositions by Barthélemy Beaulaigue (see fig.7). He used a music type that follows generally the style of the notes used for Carpentras' music at Avignon, though scaled down: the open notes are freely cut and calligraphic, the black notes rounded. Granjon's refined and elegant types match very well his *civilité* letter ('lettre françoise d'art de main') in which he set the words of Beaulaigue's songs. In 1558 Philippe Danfrie, an accomplished engraver, copied Granjon's music fount and called his version 'musique en copie' or 'musique d'escriture'. His notes too are rounded, but lack authority.

In 1559 the elder Guillaume Le Bé started to cut a system with rounded notes, large and small, for a 'tablature d'espinette', but designed for double impression. They were used for two tablatures by Adrien Le Roy and Ballard, founders of a dynasty of French music printers. Towards the end of the 17th century Pierre Ballard had a character engraved in which the points at the corners of the lozenge and the open notes were rounded and the black notes were completely circular, with the stem central (for illustration *see* GANDO). With these exceptions the typographical music of France and the rest of Europe was published in the square and lozenge notation of Attaingnant, however distant in quality and style from its exemplar, and continued to be so for a century – in France until the last decade of the 18th century.

So far it has been assumed that (in general) the methods of setting and printing the type in music volumes were the same as those used for text, always bearing in mind that the nature of music might well call for modifications in detail. Books are set vertically because the reading eye is more efficient in dealing with short lines (10 to 12 cm according to the size of character) than with long ones. For aesthetic and practical reasons musicians have generally liked their music lines long, with the depth of the page less than its width. Because of these preferences, 'special layout patterns have been found desirable for musical notation. These in turn have called for peculiar formats requiring appropriate imposition schemes' (Krummel, 1971). This practice, adopted for music books in

7. *Granjon's types for words and music in Beaulaigue's 'Chansons nouvelles'* (*Lyons, 1558–9*) [98% of actual size]

the 16th and 17th centuries, prevailed for many years. In the first edition of *The Letter-Press Printer* (London, 1876), Joseph Gould showed among his schemes of imposition 'A sheet of Quarto the Broad Way commonly used in Works of Music'; in the second edition (1881) a sheet of octavo was shown arranged the broad way to meet the same need.

Evidence of the technical processes involved in printing music can often be discovered from examination of surviving copies. Some printed music shows the importance of the frisket. For example, on f.59v of the *Liber selectarum cantionum* (1520[4]), some short printed staves at the left of the page break off sharply, leaving a blank on the right. Inspection shows that the staves are continuous across the whole page but beyond the short pieces printed with notes they appear as blind impressions. Clearly the short pieces of the staff system needed for the few notes of music were inked just beyond the desired limit, and the frisket cover was cut to act as a mask, allowing the required staves to print through with a crisp vertical edge. The remaining length of the staff, uninked, and acting as bearers, supported the frisket and tympan and so prevented the paper from sagging into an otherwise empty space in the forme. Similar support may have been provided when the notes in the music forme were printed. In Oeglin's *Harmonie Petri Tritonii super odis Horatii Flacci* (1507; *GB-Lbm*) there is a blind impression of uninterrupted rows of notes, of a different character from any used in the book, which were no doubt acting in this way (for example f.105). Finally, on the title-page of *Processionarum ordinis praedicatorum* (Seville: Meinardus Ungut and Stanislaus Polonus, 1494) there is a blind stamped frame composed entirely of capital letters P, marking the type area of a normal page, and perhaps arranged to support the sheet in the printing of an otherwise empty red forme.

It is clear from the impression of spaces that have risen in the forme and been inked, as well as from the nature of the damage that type sustains, that normal spacing quads in various sizes were used and that notes were cast full on their body. Such traces often show how well the red and black formes were imposed to register accurately. This is clear, for example, in *L'art et instruction de bien danser* (B iv and B iir and elsewhere), a book that is often dismissed as rough, or interesting as a curio only. The very close approach and overlapping of characters in the same forme show how freely kerning was used: Ratdolt's *Graduale* (1494, University Library, Cambridge) provides splendid examples, as does *Rerum musicarum* by Johannes Frosch, printed in 1535 by Peter Schoeffer and Mathias Apiarius.

The introduction of single-impression music type was welcomed and imitated; but the advantage of being able to build up a musical phrase, notes and staff complete, by the gathering of single types in the order they appeared in the copy was purchased at a price. Compared with the complexity of some text letters there was nothing intrinsically difficult about cutting a punch for a note designed for double-impression printing. Such a note was economical, too: few note forms were required; they could be cast in quantity; and they were of universal application, appropriate to any degree of any scale. To cut a punch for a note designed for single-impression printing was much more difficult. The note had to be given a fixed place in relation to fractional parts of staff lines worked with it on the same punch. The staff lines had to appear at exactly the same intervals on every punch, so that when the matrices were struck and type was cast from them, the staves made continuous and parallel lines. Fournier, a virtuoso punchcutter of the 18th century, commented on the difficulty of achieving this and described how he made patterns for laying parallel, evenly spaced lines on the surface of the end of the punch before he started to work the metal. Matrices were struck and justified with extreme care and then cast to their full width so that the staff lines extended right across the character, special attention being paid to the cleaning and finishing of their ends. Not many types achieved the perfection that the system called for, and in use they quickly lost their pristine excellence: the edges of the traversing lines were often damaged and caused breaks in the printed image. Making every allowance for chance damage, it is clear that many founts were not skilfully cut. Some writers have suggested that the primitive appearance of some founts, for example Rastell's, may be due to the use of a technique in which matrices were struck twice, once for the note and once for the staves; an attempt to strike a matrix in this way may produce a much deformed character, and better results are obtained by casting in a matrix that has been engraved with a burin wholly without the use of punches.

Although it was difficult to make satisfactory punches, the number required was limited by the character of the music for which they were prepared. The range of pitches and of note values was still relatively small. The 'grande musicque' cut for Plantin by Hendrik van den Keere in 1557 had notes for values ranging from the breve to the quaver (*fusa*) and cast with fragments of a five-line staff, but the number of each form was limited (for illustration *see* TYPE SIZE). Assuming a G clef, there were three minims, three crotchets and three quavers cast as g', a' and b'. If they were turned top to bottom the same types would serve for d'', c'' and b'. But if d' or f'' were required, some method would have to be found to change the disposition of the staff lines. Fortunately information about how this was done has been preserved in a letter from the punchcutter to Plantin. He says how many punches would be required and how much material, and continues (in H. D. L. Vervliet's translation), 'I certainly should not be able to finish one punch every day, and we shall have much trouble in casting, and other expense beyond the usual, because I shall have to use at least 3 moulds. But I hope I could help myself out with four moulds by packing [the bodies and jets] as needs be . . . I can't see my way to justify, even if I take on more hands, more than the 5 or 6 matrices a day'.

In Van den Keere's 'moyenne musicque' (which survives at the Plantin Moretus Museum, Inventory 237) some of the punches show five staff lines, some six; and some of the punches for Granjon's 'moyenne music' (Inventory 241) show seven. The matrices struck by these punches could be placed in a number of alternative positions in the mould to cast a note in a chosen position on the staves. Thus relatively few punches and matrices could be manipulated to produce a wide variety of notes. This versatility must have saved the printer a great deal of money and time. On the other hand, the printed image was not wholly satisfactory: slightly imperfect casting or other faults left minute gaps between the individual types in the line which the ink could not fill, and as a result white space showed: this was even more noticeable as the types became worn. To prevent this as far as possible, a system of 'bonding' or fitting was developed, using longer pieces of single or double staff line above or below a note cast on fewer staff lines. This was widely used, for example, in *Kirchengesäng darinnen die Heubtartickel* (1566) and *Selectae cantiones quinque et sex vocum* by Jacob Meiland (Nuremberg: Dietrich Gerlach, 1572).

Apart from the examples of Channey, Granjon and Danfrie mentioned earlier, note heads were cut as lozenges or squares and stems were centred: this style persisted almost to the end of the 17th century, but by that time it was so at variance with the taste of the day that punches were cut in the pattern of written notes, with the heads oval or roundish with stems to the left or right. The innovator of this style was the London printer John Heptinstall, who first used the face in John Carr's *Vinculum societatis* (*RISM* 1687[6]). The notes were cast with fractions of staves, and so were tails (for illustration *see* HEPTINSTALL, JOHN). Fractions of beam cut at a suitable angle – sometimes with a fragment of stem attached, sometimes not – were also provided to join successive quavers and semiquavers moving upwards and downwards. This feature gave the character its name 'the new tied note'. The note heads are overlarge and the type ill-fitted, but it continued in use until at least 1699.

Alternative types soon became available: Peter de Walpergen in Oxford cut two splendid examples which were used only once or twice. In 1699 William Pearson published *Twelve New Songs* (*RISM* 1699[5]), a collection of pieces by various composers, issued chiefly to encourage his 'new London character'. Smaller in scale than Heptinstall's, the type was better fitted and better cast and was used extensively by Pearson, most notably perhaps in *Orpheus Britannicus* (2/1706), and by his successors into the mid-18th century (see fig.8).

By this time, however, the mainstream of music printing was served by the engraver and the offerings of the type printer were found in the backwaters of hymnbooks, small songbooks and the like: but not for very long. In 1749/50 Jacques-François Rosart cut a series of punches for a revolutionary method of music printing which he offered to Johannes Enschedé at Haarlem. He received no encouragement and it was J. G. I. Breitkopf, working to the same principles as Rosart, who took the credit for the innovation and brought the system to fruition. In 1754 Breitkopf started to have his punches cut and in February 1755 he published a *Sonnet* to demonstrate the quality of his system. In a preface to the *Sonnet* he commended his work to 'lovers of the musical art' and to printers. He continued:

the method used until now has fallen somewhat into disrepute, since it possesses neither the beauty demanded nowadays nor is it adequate to

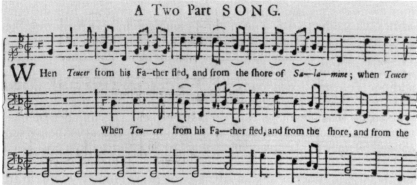

8. Two printed versions of a Purcell song in 'Orpheus Britannicus': (above) from the first edition (London, 1698), printed by John Heptinstall, and (below) from the second (London, 1706), printed by William Pearson; in both systems the stems of quavers occurring in groups of two or more are 'tied' with a beam, but there are great differences in the structure of the notes – in the Heptinstall character the quavers are cast in two parts, looking forward to the 'mosaic' music types of the 1750s [top 64%, bottom 71% of actual size]

meet the needs of the art of music which has been brought to a state of perfection. The printers themselves are not very satisfied with the old method, partly because its intricacy is burdensome, but mainly because the typesetting is not so regular that it can be achieved without a lot of ingenious devices and botching which the compositor first of all has to work out for himself.

Breitkopf did not explain the theoretical basis of his system, but P. -S. Fournier (Fournier *le jeune*), who enjoyed Breitkopf's confidence, described the essentials in his *Traité historique et critique sur l'origine et les progrès des caractères de fonte pour l'impression de la musique, avec des épreuves de nouveaux caractères de musique présentés aux imprimeurs de France* (1765). All the types were cast on the same-sized body, 'being the fifth part of the body of each line of music' (i.e. the size of only one staff line). All symbols used were formed to this dimension, so that the clefs, notes and other characters which were necessarily larger than the body were made up of several pieces 'set skilfully one above the other. A note, for

29

example, is made up of three and four pieces; a clef of two, the upper part formed by one punch, the lower part formed by another punch, and these parts joined together form the character of the complete clef'. Such founts are now called 'mosaic types' (see figs.9 and 10).

In 1756 Fournier published an *Essai d'un nouveau caractère de fonte pour l'impression de la musique, inventé et exécuté dans toutes les parties typographiques* as a specimen of a new character which aimed at rendering music from type as if it had been printed by copperplate engraving. It offered short dance movements, printed at two impressions to demonstrate the elegance and logic of the system. Fournier later developed this experimental character into a second music fount, this time for single-impression printing. It was based on a different system from that perfected by Breitkopf. While Breitkopf's type was designed on one body size and could be assembled into composite pieces as required, in Fournier's system the symbols were cut for casting on five different bodies, according to size. The minims, crotchets and simple quavers, key signatures, measures and other symbols of the same height were made in one piece (with segments of three or four staff lines incorporated), instead of in the three or four pieces that other systems required. In addition Fournier provided a wide range of characters which worked with the composite pieces. Fournier claimed that this arrangement made typesetting simpler, more reliable and quicker. The number of types required was reduced by half: as he wrote, his 'character being only about 160 matrices instead of at least 300 that other systems carry'. A third type for single impression was cut by J. M. Fleischman for Izaac Enschedé – founder of a great dynasty of printers in Haarlem, in the Netherlands – as a reply to Breitkopf's. It was a superlative achievement. By 1760 he had cut 226 punches and struck and justified 240 matrices so skilfully that the music printed from his type approached the clarity of engraved music (see fig.9*b*).

Three other systems of mosaic music are worthy of note. First W. Caslon & Son of London showed a music type in two sizes in a specimen book of 1763. It is not known who cut the punches, but the character offers a wide range of sorts and fits agreeably. The second appeared in a *Manifesto d'una nuova impressa di stampare la musica in caratteri gettati nel modo stesso come si scrive* published by Antonio de Castro (Venice, 1765). To show the capabilities of his type he printed a *Duetto* by Giuseppe Paolucci. The 'manifesto' type 'Inciso et Gettato dal M. Rev. Sig D. Giacomo Falconi' is ramshackle and loose but it holds together well enough to be read without confusion; it was used for extensive works – Paolucci's *Preces octo vocibus* (Venice, 1767), for example, and his *Arte pratica di contrappunto* (1765).

The third system of this group was offered by Henric Fougt, a native of Lapland working in Sweden in 1766; the next year he went to England and obtained a patent. Although his technique was basically the same as Breitkopf's, it was simpler and called for fewer punches; and it proved robustly effective. In his patent he described the analysis by which he arrived at his system and, as the only account of its kind, it is worth study (Poole, 1965–6).

The first major work in which Breitkopf used his type was *Il trionfo della fedeltà* by the Electress Maria Anna Walpurgis of Bavaria, issued in score in three volumes in 1756. In the same year he published a *Recueil d'airs à danser*, and thenceforth his output was extensive: according to Fournier, Breitkopf issued 51 musical works including operas, keyboard works and songs between 1755 and 1761. This output continued in bulk and variety well into the 19th century.

Fournier's small music is elegantly shown in the *Anthologie françoise* (1765; for illustration *see* FOURNIER, PIERRE-SIMON); Fleischman's types are best studied, for themselves and in relation to Breitkopf's, in the *Haerlemse zangen* that Izaac and Johannes Enschedé published in 1761. The poems were translations into Dutch of the texts that appeared in High German in the *Berlinische Oden und Lieder* (1756), and the settings were to the same music that Breitkopf had used (see figs.9*a* and *b*). A comparison between the work of Fleischman and the type used by Johann Jacob Lotter of Augsburg, one of Breitkopf's earliest imitators, is offered by editions of Leopold Mozart's violin method: Lotter's *Versuch einer gründlichen Violinschule* (1756) and Johannes Enschedé's *Grondig onderwys in het behandelen der viool* (1766).

Fougt printed extensively. His first work was an edition of *Six Sonatas for Two Violins and Bass* by Francesco Uttini, and he issued seven other important works principally of chamber music. He issued a large number of single sheets (82 have survived), mostly songs, before he left England to return to Sweden in 1770. His equipment is said to have been purchased by R. Falkener and used, with technical improvements, to produce songsheets.

The Caslon type, sturdy and economical, was used widely during the latter part of the 18th century, notably on songsheets, and is well represented on inserts in the *Lady's Magazine*, the *Hibernian Magazine* and elsewhere. Caslon's types were much used in America. Christopher Saur of Germanstown, Pennsylvania, was the first to print music from movable type in America with his *Geistreiche Lieder*, a collection of 40 tunes that he printed in 1752 from types he had cast himself. In October 1783 the *Boston Magazine*, printed and published by Norman & White, issued 'A New Song', *Throw an apple*, set to music by A. Hawkins. According to Isaiah Thomas, the famous Massachusetts printer, 'Norman cut the punches and made every tool to complete the ... types': he also cast them. Thomas himself had a complete series of the Caslon founts, including music, for in 1786 he issued *The Worcester Collection of Sacred Harmony*, 'printed typographically at Worcester, Massachusetts'. In addition to hymns and psalm tunes the collection includes the four-part vocal line of the 'Hallelujah' chorus from Handel's *Messiah* very competently set in score, eight lines to the oblong page.

Given a knowledge of music and the advice of an editor, the compositor setting types with note and staff incorporated would have few major difficulties, though the fitting of sorts cast on different bodies would have been time-consuming. The compositor setting mosaic music was faced with other and more searching problems. Some of them were

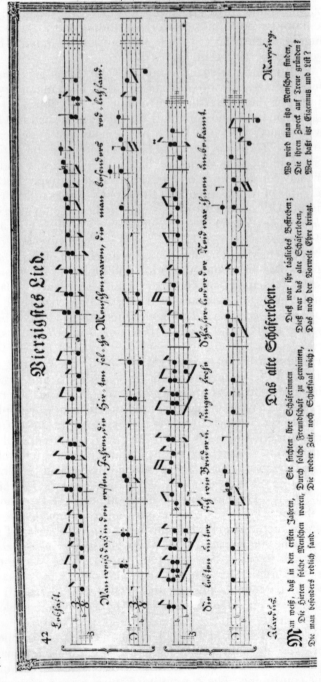

9. Two approaches to the same music: (a) German original published by Breitkopf (Leipzig, 1756), and (b) Dutch copy published by Enschedé (Haarlem, 1761) using Fleischman's types [both 63% of actual size]

examined by Christian Gottlob Täubel, a Leipzig printer, in his *Prak-tisches Handbuch der Buchdruckerkunst für Anfänger* (Leipzig, 1791). The setting of music, he warned, is much more difficult and needs more care than the setting of ordinary text; anybody proposing to become a music compositor must not have an irascible temperament or be in too much of a hurry; if he is too eager to get on he will overlook detail; music typesetting calls for the tedious and painstaking construction of involved pieces of music using only very small units; the compositor must be able to reproduce in type exactly what the author has drawn with his pen. Caution against hasty work runs through his advice about casting off copy, maintaining optical and musically even spacing, ensuring good underlay of words and arranging convenient turn-over breaks.

Whereas music type before Breitkopf was set line by line as ordinary text, mosaic music had to be set in blocks across the staff systems and the compositor needed cool judgment and an intimate knowledge of his cases, fitted as they were with hundreds of different characters, to build his musical jigsaw accurately. Täubel provided general advice and illustrative examples, but the beginner would have needed much practice under an experienced overseer before he could have carried on unsupervised.

Mosaic type was expensive and used large quantities of metal. Even with careful handling, the fine-cut pieces of note, stem and staff line – coming as they did to the edge of the type body – were easily damaged and the types seldom looked convincing and unbroken across even a narrow page. There was a great deal of experiment in the early 19th century to counter these difficulties. Many of these trials used notes with head and tail complete. In 1802 François Olivier obtained a patent for ten years to protect the development of a system which contained new features. The punches were cut in steel without fragments of staff lines, tempered, struck into copper matrices and justified. The staff lines were engraved in a chosen position in the matrices by means of a burin and were then cut to a predetermined depth by a special steel saw. The types were cast in the usual way, using one of seven moulds. The advantage of the method was that few punches were required – a quaver or a semibreve could be struck with the same punch into a number of matrices and defined as a particular note by the position in which the staves were engraved. In spite of all precautions the alignment of the staff lines was not smooth, and although Olivier and his partner Godefroi published albums and methods, success escaped them; Olivier died, a disappointed man, in 1812.

In 1820 Eugène Duverger of Paris obtained a 15-year patent for a system which among other desiderata would ensure that the staves were parallel and unbroken. In October 1834 an account of his process, including a specimen showing his characters in three sizes, appeared in the *Bulletin* of the Société d'Encouragement pour l'Industrie Nationale. His types did not incorporate fragments of the staves. Using a setting stick engraved with staff lines as a guide and with spaces similarly marked, he set his types, sometimes using notes with complete stems, sometimes with part only, in their correct positions vertically and horizontally. The other signs – words, key signature and the like – were also set. Long slurs were made of the very narrow strips of copper, bent and cut to the length required: bars tying the tails of successive quavers were made of pieces of pewter slipped into kerns made across the stems of the notes. The matter was proofed and corrected. The whole was then brushed over with oil and covered with a fine plaster which was allowed to set. When it was sufficiently firm the plaster was carefully removed from the type. A plane, fitted with a cutting iron bearing five sharp points at intervals corresponding with those engraved on the setting stick, was passed over the face of the plaster in accurately marked positions to make a trace of five lines, thus leaving the music with its staves complete. The plaster mould was baked in an oven, put into a casting box and type metal alloy poured in. When the metal was solid and cool enough to handle, the casting was removed from the box and separated from the plaster. Any defects were corrected by hand and the plate was squared up and planed over the back to a uniform thickness, mounted and imposed with other plates in a chase, ready for printing at one impression. The system, which received a 'Brevet d'addition et de perfectionnement' in October 1838, was widely used, and when skilfully manipulated produced very satisfactory results; but it was found costly and suitable only for editions in large numbers.

Many other systems were developed in France, some purely typographical, others combining type with plaster moulding. The typographical systems include those of Derriey – a tour de force of cutting and founding, but used only in a specimen sheet – and of T. Beaudoire, which was used in books and periodicals. Of the mixed methods those of Tantestein, Curmer and Reinhard of Strasbourg were the most successful.

In England, Edward Cowper, a prolific inventor of machinery and processes in printing technology, patented in 1827 a revolutionary method of music printing. The printing surface consisted mainly of the ends of pieces of copper wire passed through a three-ply block of wood and made to stand 1.6 mm above the surface of the block. The ends of the wire formed the black notes; the white notes were made up from two curved pieces, which were pushed into the surface of the wood to form the elliptical character. Other characters were created from curved shapes which had been drawn through holes in a steel plate in long pieces and then cut into units about 8 mm long. The edges of small pieces of brass printed the stems of notes, slurs, beams and the like and were tapped into the wooden block to stand at the same height as the notes. If the words of a song were to be printed they were set in type, moulded in plaster and cast into lines which were cut up and underlaid in grooves cut into the wood. The staves, with their clefs, were made on separate blocks (each system on its own narrow strip of wood) which were arranged in a chase to register accurately with the note blocks. The second part of the invention was centred on a revolving tympan. When taking impressions the note blocks were locked up in one chase and the staff blocks in another, and both were put in one forme, head to head, adjusted so that the staves would fall correctly on the notes if one chase had been folded over on to the other. Two sheets of paper were laid on the tympan and buttoned down by separate friskets. The forme was inked all over and an impression was taken. The tympan was lifted and as a result of a special mechanism the surface holding the paper and the friskets was turned through 180°. A second impression was taken, the notes and staves neatly overprinting to complete the music. This method was much used in the 1830s.

A second patent from which much was expected was taken out in 1856 by Gustav Scheurmann, a music seller and publisher of Newgate Street, London. It was designed to separate the staves from the notes and other necessary symbols and words into two formes, printed one after the other by a specially adapted press. The characters were cut and cast in the usual way but special attention was given to the casting of beams for joining the tails of successive quavers and the like. For this feature he devised a special mould that would cast bars at any angle on a body which mounted in steps from left to right and on which the kerned stems of the notes rested. From the short example given in *Grove 1* (iii, 248), the method produced excellent results, but the inventor was not satisfied until his music could be printed in one impression; and on this ultimate he foundered. It is a great pity that Scheurmann did not persist with his two-impression technique because, as he demonstrated, he could over-print his two formes accurately on lead and from this create an electrotype which, backed with metal, could be imposed as a plate for letterpress printing at one impression.

Although these various methods (and there were many more) had something to offer in technical ingenuity to improve various features of the earliest mosaic music types, it was the descendants of Breitkopf who won the day. It was remarkable how many different complete systems of type in different sizes were offered during the 19th century, in England, Germany and America, most of them demonstrating in the accuracy of their fit the superb quality of the punchcutting, matrix-striking and letter-founding of their day. These types, however, were not created merely to demonstrate technical brilliance: they were made to serve a market.

The relationship between the improvements in the processes of music printing and market demand may be illustrated by short quotations from sources published in 1834. In the preface to the first volume, 'Instrumental', of the *Musical Library*, it is stated:

> the Musical Library was commenced with a view to afford the same aid in the progress of the musical art that literature has so undeniably received from the cheap publications of the day ... before this work appeared, the exhorbitant sums demanded for engraved music amounted to a prohibition of its free circulation among the middle classes; at a time too when the most enlightened statesmen saw distinctly the policy of promoting the cultivation of the art in almost every class of society.

In an account of the 'various processes applied to printing music' on the first four pages of the first 'monthly supplement' to the *Musical Library* (April 1834) the writer said:

In each process [intaglio and lithography], the manual labour of printing off the copies involving considerable nicety and attention, is a source of constant recurring expense. In printing music from the *surface* of moveable types, or stereotype plates, either by the printing press or printing machine, the operation is rapid and certain; the market may be supplied at once to the extent of the demand; and the consumer may receive the full benefit of mechanical improvements, in the diminished cost of the article produced. Such a work as the 'Musical Library' could only be undertaken with the aid of musical typography.

The system that the publisher of the *Musical Library* had adopted was 'a secret process of music printing invented by M. Duverger of Paris'.

The wisdom of the commercial argument summarized above, brilliantly demonstrated in practice by Alfred Novello some years later, was well served by the typefounders. In 1820 William Clowes, printer of the *Harmonicon* and other music, imported from Germany punches and matrices for music type and developed the technique they offered to real excellence in his own foundry. In the 1830s Hugh Hughes of Dean Street, London, offered two sizes of music type and V. Figgins, the Patent Letter Foundry and Miller & Richard all had founts to offer the music publisher (see figs.10*a* and *b*), in such variety that by 1876 manuals of instruction could give no reliable general information about typesetting. There was so much music printed from type in London during the latter half of the 19th century that the compositors engaged exclusively in music typesetting were numerous enough to establish and maintain their own trade union, the London Society of Music Compositors (1872).

John Southward indicated something of the market in his handbook *Practical Printing* (1882):

In many of the large offices in London and the country, music composition is regularly done, but in the metropolis it has been made into an independent department of the printing business. There are offices which undertake hardly any other kind of work. If the manager of a periodical desires to give a page of music, he sends the copy to one of the music-printing establishments, and in due time receives back a stereo or electro plate which he can work with the rest of his pages ... the fact of the demand for music work being altogether beyond the means of supply, originally called this trade into existence.

He treated of the principles of music typesetting in general terms because although 'most of the letter-founders supply music types their systems, unfortunately, differ somewhat'. He used the type of the Patent Letter Foundry for his illustrations as this system was 'the most complete'.

The demand for typographical music was not a wholly British phenomenon. The publication of manuals of instruction, taking the beginner step by step through the rudiments of notation to the setting of scores and other intricacies, much more thoroughly than Täubel had done in 1791, provides some evidence of this. In Germany there were three such

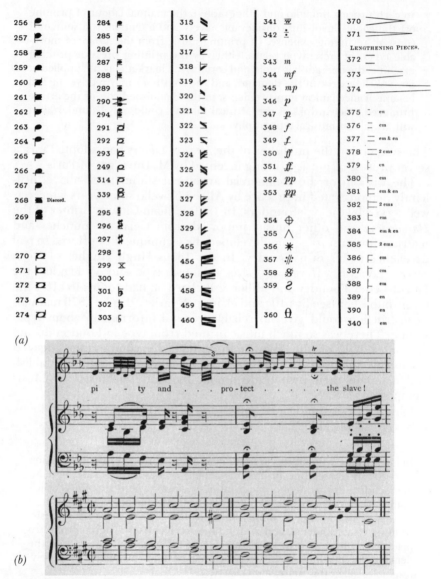

(a)

(b)

10. By the 19th century 'mosaic' music type systems had reached their maximum complexity: (a) part of the specimen sheet of Diamond Music, offered by V. & J. Figgins in London, containing 452 separate types in the fount which had to be supplemented by a large supply of specially cast spacing material; (b) Diamond no.3 music type offered by Stevens, Shanks & Sons, London [both 85% of actual size]

books, one in two editions, between 1844 and 1875. Typefounders provided founts of type, each being offered as better than the last, not only during the 19th century but well into the 20th.

In America Thomas Adams (*Typographia*, 1856) devoted a page to music, with examples set in the type of L. Johnson & Co., Philadelphia. Thomas MacKellar (*The American Printer*, 1873 and 1879) was much more thorough, using the types of MacKellar, Smiths & Jordan of Philadelphia, and as late as 1904 Theodore Low de Vinne devoted 18 pages of his treatise *Modern Methods of Book Composition* to music.

This account of the development of music printing from type has been concerned largely with method: even with the same techniques, standards achieved varied enormously. This was particularly true during the 16th and 17th centuries, when the punchcutter (who made the moulds, struck and justified the matrices) and the founder (who cast the types) had to be remarkably skilful to manipulate current engineering techniques if type of sufficient merit and versatility was to give acceptable printed results. For every outstanding printer using type of good quality with skill – Attaingnant, Moderne, Ballard (sometimes), Petrucci, Gardano, Scotto, Susato, Vautrollier and Day – there were others whose work left much to be desired, who used types that were badly fitted, indifferently cast and with only a limited range of characters. Some founts produced such broken staff-line systems that the page almost defied reading at the required speed of performance; others were so inadequate that the printer had to set a special warning between the staff lines to instruct the performer that a quaver with an asterisk above it should be read as a semiquaver.

CHAPTER III

Engraving

The polyphonic music of the 16th and 17th centuries was printed in partbooks, or in books showing all parts on facing pages, or in score. Attaingnant arranged moving parts together on the same set of staves in some of his keyboard volumes, the unknown German printer of an early collection of *Kirchengeseng* of the Bohemian Brethren (1566) used the same technique and William Godbid managed to print Thomas Tomkins's *Musica Deo sacra* (1668) in four parts on a two-staff system. The ingenuity shown by the printers of these pieces draws attention to the limitations of their type (carrying integrated notes and staff segments), and to its clumsy inability to show, confidently, more than one part on one set of staves. The inadequacy of the system to reproduce elaborate keyboard music with its rapid succession of short notes and dense chords, to render satisfactorily solo and concerted string and wind music extended in tonal range and scalar agility, or to notate florid song, became increasingly obvious. The hand equipped with the nimble and flexible pen was able to meet all these challenges in manuscript, and it was the hand-driven line engraved in copper that furnished the needs of the composer and the connoisseur from the latter part of the 16th century onwards.

The earliest date known on any intaglio engraving is 1446 although there is evidence that plates were being produced at least ten years earlier. It is not known how they were printed. The first mention of a copper-plate printing press is probably that in a document of 1540 in the Antwerp archives, cited by Goovaerts (1880); but the hand mangle had been developed commercially in the 14th century. The maps for editions of Claudius Ptolemy's *Geographia* issued in Bologna (1477), Rome (1478) and Florence (1482) were printed from copper plates and show place names splendidly cut in various sizes of Roman capital. It seems curious that music was not prepared for printing from incised copper plates, too: perhaps the techniques of copper-plate engraving and, particularly, printing were not widely known, for, after the editions of Ptolemy's *Geographia* and a map of central Europe printed in 1491, very few maps were produced from engraved plates until about 1540. The earliest known practical music to be produced by copper-plate engraving seems to be *Intabolatura da leuto del divino Francesco da Milano novamenta stampada* (fig.11), published without printer or date but attributed by A. J. Ness in his edition to some time before 1536, when Marcolini da Forlì issued *Intabolatura di liuto de diversi, con la bataglia, et altre cose bellissime, di M. Francesco da Milano, stampata nuovamente.* Ness

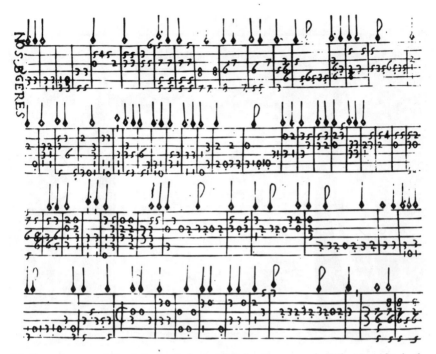

11. *Part of a page of 'Intabolatura da leuto del divino Francesco da Milano', said to be the first music printed from engraved plates (before 1536)*

suggested that Francesco Marcolini (the publisher of the latter volume) may have been responsible for the other title too, because in his preface he claimed that he had been experimenting with 'engraving on wood and metal' (perhaps copper) in seeking Petrucci's 'secrets' of printing lute tablature. After this, there was a gap of some decades before music was again engraved.

The table showing the finals and dominants of the 12 modes in Vincenzo Galilei's *Dialogo ... della musica antica e della moderna* (Florence: Giorgio Marescotti, 1581) is not fully mensural music. Otherwise, engraved music is next found in a number of devotional prints made after paintings or drawings by Marten de Vos and other Flemish artists. In some of the engravings a whole score is shown as an open book; in others the separate vocal parts – nine in one case –are disposed about the picture on scrolls or on tablets held by angels. The engravings contain complete works, some of them by known composers such as Andreas Pevernage, Cornelis Verdonck and Cornelis Schuyt, some by composers otherwise unknown, such as D. Raymundi. The earliest example, the Virgin and St Anne with Jesus, engraved in masterly style by Johan Sadelar after de Vos, appeared in Antwerp in 1584 (for illustration *see* SADELAR, JOHAN) and was reprinted in Rome (1586) and in Antwerp (1587). Others (all but one by the same engraver) were published in Mainz (1587) or Frankfurt (undated). The engravings are superb as pictorial compositions,

12. Devotional text showing a motet by Pevernage, supported by the figures of Harmonia, Musica and Mensura: engraving by A. and C. Collaert from 'Encomium musices' (Antwerp: Philip Galle, c1590)

and the notation of the music, though small, is clear and accurately reproduced. In the same vein is *Encomium musices*, a book made up of 18 plates, each illustrating a different scene from the Bible (Antwerp: Philip Galle, *c*1590). The designs by Jaen von de Straet provide a mass of information about musical instruments of the day which the brilliant engraving of Adriaen Collaert and others has preserved in the copper. The title-page shows three female figures, Harmonia, Musica and Mensura, framed by a fine show of musical instruments and supporting an open score of a motet for six voices by Pevernage (*see* fig.12).

By this time Simone Verovio, a calligrapher and engraver, had issued in Rome two collections of pieces printed from engraved copper plates. The first was *Diletto spirituale: canzonette a tre et a quattro voci composte da diversi ecc.mi musici, raccolte da Simone Verovio, intagliate et stampate dal medesimo: con l'intavolatura del cimbalo et liuto* (*RISM* 1586[3]), a folio of 23 leaves (for illustration *see* VEROVIO, SIMONE). The title describes the nature of the work. Each two-page opening shows the separate vocal parts with words, a version for keyboard in three or four parts and another for lute in Italian tablature, all elegantly engraved and skilfully printed. Verovio produced similar works until 1608, sometimes entirely on his own, sometimes with the assistance of a compatriot engraver Martin van Buyten. His methods were adopted by his successors in Rome, some anonymous (as was the printer of J. H. Kapsberger's *Libro primo di mottetti* of 1612), but one of whom, Nicolò Borboni, was as accomplished as Verovio himself. He is best known for his *Musicale concenti a une, et due voci . . . libro primo* (1618), which he composed and engraved, and for the editions of Frescobaldi's keyboard works, superbly engraved by Christofori Bianchi (from 1615), which he published.

Meanwhile, music printed from engraved copper plates had appeared in England (1612–13) and the Netherlands (1615), but it was not known for about another 40 years in France (*c*1660) and in Germany not until 1689 (though engraved music appeared in typeset books in France and Germany in the 1620s and 30s). The English work was *Parthenia or The Maydenhead of the First Musicke that Ever was Printed for the Virginalls: composed by Three Famous Masters: William Byrd, Dr John Bull and Orlando Gibbons* (*RISM* 1613[14]) engraved by William Hole for Dorothy Evans, and printed by G. Lowe. It is an accomplished piece of engraving showing a command equal to Verovio's, but with the parts so condensed that the music would have been extremely difficult to play. The first Dutch example was issued by Joannes Janssen in Amsterdam: *Paradisus musicus testudinis* by Nicolas Vallet, engraved by Joannes Berwinckel (*RISM* 1618[16]). The Ballard monopoly of typographic music printing in France did not extend to printing from copper plates, and composers who did not wish to entrust their music to Ballard published it on their own account or through a music seller. The first of these was Michel Lambert who, before 1660, published in Paris *Les airs de Monsieur Lambert* engraved by Richers. Eventually the technique spread across the Atlantic where it was used in 1721 for *An Introduction to the Singing of Psalm Tunes* by John Tufts, published by Samuel Gerrish in Boston, and for *The Grounds and Rules of Music Explained* by Thomas Walter (Boston: J. Franklin).

In England, Roger North described (*c*1695) how he bought a copper plate 'polish't and grounded' and etched some music on it. He used the acid too strong and the result was not satisfactory. Later (*c*1715–20) he related how 'etching, with a litle graving (and perhaps worse ways) have been used' to meet the demand for printed music. He refers to the work of 'Stephen Rogers in Holland' whose music was 'wonderfull fair'. In a well-known passage from his *History of the Science and Practice of Music*, Hawkins also referred to Roger and those Dutch artificers who found a means to soften copper so as 'to render it susceptible of an impression from the stroke of a hammer or a punch, the point whereof had the form of a musical note'. The inventive Dutch music printing activity in the 1680s and 90s was extensive, complicated and obscure (as with Coster and the prototypographers who may have preceded Gutenberg himself), and while much of it was typographic, the importance of engraving is suggested in the name of one Johannes Stichter, a printer and publisher who in 1686 announced that he sold various sorts of music 'printed in a newly invented way'. There is no ambiguity in the claims of

Thomas Cross (see fig.13) who in *Dear Sally, a New Song* (*c*1690) said of himself that he:

> arriv'd to such perfection in musick that Gent may have their works fairly engraved, as cheap as Puncht & Sooner; he having good hands to assist him, covenanted for a term of years; he can cut miniture, without having it writ with ungum'd ink, to take off upon the plate as they do for other people.

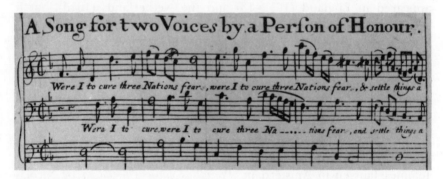

13. *Engraving by Thomas Cross of London of a song by Purcell (Z517); the small note heads and compressed writing of the underlay are characteristic of the songsheets which Cross and others produced to be sold cheaply and in quantity* [71% of actual size]

However elusive these flickers of information may be, they are given substance in the first account of the methods of music engraving to be written by a practitioner. It occurs in *L'encyclopédie*, where Mme Delusse provided a commentary on the second of two plates concerned with 'Gravure en lettres, en géographie et en musique' (fig.14). She said that when music was first engraved on copper the notes were drawn with a steel point – sometimes in their ordinary written form, sometimes as lozenges – and were then bitten in with acid. She cited collections of organ music, a large proportion of the operas of Lully and Mouret, the motets of Campra and Lalande and the cantatas of Bernier and Clérambault as examples of music engraved in this manner. The notes, she wrote, were not as regular in form as those later produced by punches. By correcting this irregularity and bringing the characteristics to conform as closely as possible with the written notes, the style of music engraving had come gradually to the state of perfection in which it existed at the time of her writing.

At the outset of her description of the current technique Mme Delusse stated that the aim of the engraver was to reproduce the manuscript copy exactly, on a copper or pewter plate, freehand; and she went on to summarize methods that have persisted, with slight modification, to the 20th century. The plate was first squared up and a rectangle drawn with a point and ruler close to the four edges of the metal. The area was then scaled against the copy to determine how the music was to be laid out. She described this important stage in the process inadequately. Fortunately, manuscripts that have been through the engraver's hands during the 18th century have survived, and much can be learnt from them. The number of notes seems to have been counted, to determine how much space a work would take. In scores, consideration was given to the relative movement of the parts and to the ranges which determined the number of leger lines required. The engraver knew the size of the punches and of the plates used for certain kinds of music – keyboard, vocal, orchestral and so on. With this information he could calculate how many lines the music would occupy, making necessary provision for clefs, key and time signatures, and the titles to the whole work and to the individual movements. He then decided how many lines could be accommodated on a plate, and worked through the piece marking the places for line breaks. This was not a simple mechanical count because the planning had to take account of the logic of the music, allowing space, as far as possible,

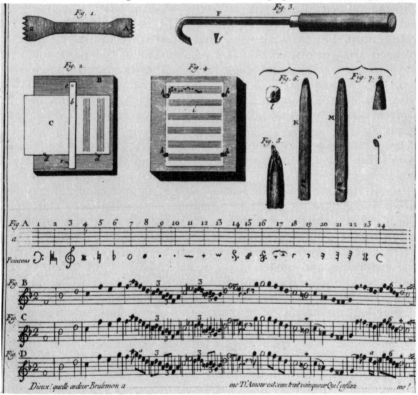

14. *18th-century music engravers' tools, reproduced from 'L'encyclopédie': 'Fig.1' shows the five-pointed tool for pricking the position of staff systems (in two sizes) on the metal engraving plates; in 'Fig.2' a squared-up plate rests flat on a stone under a straight edge (b), with two systems already cut by a scorer ('Fig.3'); 'Fig.4' shows the plate completely scored, with some characters (made by the punches indicated in 'Figs.6–7') already in position; 'Figs.A–D' show a variety of punches; the text in the last line was engraved with a burin*

in proportion to the value of the notes. This proved relatively simple in the quicker movements, but there are many indications in the manuscripts of second thoughts and recalculation in the slower movements. With his estimates made, the engraver was ready to work his plate. He set his compass to the calculated interval between the top lines of each staff system and scribed these positions on each long edge of the rectangle. He then used a five-pointed marker to make five equidistant scratches at each edge: these were used to align the staff lines, which were drawn with the sharp tooth of a scorer (a burin with a wide cutting edge). The single-tooth scorer was later superseded by a five-point scorer or raster which could engrave a system of staff lines in one operation; this was preferred by most engravers, though the single-tooth scorer was retained by some practitioners for cutting bar-lines.

When the ruling was finished, the burr raised by the cutting tools was removed with a scraper, working across the lines with a light hand. This done (Mme Delusse wrote), everything on the manuscript was lightly drawn on the plate with a steel point, working from right to left so that all would appear the correct way round when printed. If a song were being set, the words and music had to be indicated in their correct relationship. The marking would have to observe the same logic that dictated the cast-off, so that the relationship of the parts could be grasped as a whole at sight, and to achieve this the engraver might well have had to modify some of the detail written on the manuscript at the planning stage. The pitch and the value of each note were shown by conventional signs at the end of the mark indicating the position of their stems.

Once the plate was completely marked, the copy was laid aside. Apparently the favoured practice in France in the late 18th century was to engrave any words below the music first with a burin, and then to stamp the note heads, rests, clefs, sharps, flats, naturals, directs and so on, using punches driven by a hammer with a flat face. This done, the plate was transferred from the thick, smooth stone that supported it during the punching and laid on an anvil, where it was planished or flattened using a hammer with a slightly convex face, to remove the distortions and bulges in the metal caused by the action of the punches. The plate was then laid on a smooth surface to be finished. The note stems, bar-lines, slurs, tails to single quavers, the beams connecting the stems of groups of quavers, and subdivisions of quavers, were put in with a burin or with a scorer. To enable all cutting to be done from right to left the plate had to be turned around and about; indeed to cut slurs the engraver often held his graver still and turned the plate on to it. When the cutting was finished the scores were drawn through the staves again to open any lines that might have been closed up during punching. The plate was examined carefully, touched up as necessary, burrs scraped, and unrequired scratches and dots burnished away. A proof copy was pulled and any errors noticed by the composer and the printer's reader were marked for amendment. For correction, the plate was rested on the edge of the bench, between the arms of correcting callipers, each of which carried a point turned inwards at its end. The point of the arm over the face of the plate was placed on the character to be changed and pressed down; the point of the arm resting on the bench under the plate met it and located the position of the fault through the metal. The mark on the back was ringed, the plate was turned over face down on the stone and the area around the error was struck with a dot punch. The plate was turned over again, and the metal raised on the surface was burnished to obliterate the defective work. The back was also gently tapped with a hammer over the same area. Once the surface was smooth and flat, the corrections were made; care was taken not to disturb the original work around it. The plate was then ready for printing at the rolling press (see also fig.15).

The first comprehensive account of the printing of music from engraved plates is in *Nouvel manuel complet de l'imprimeur en taille douce* by Berthiaud, revised by P. Boitard (1837), in which a whole section is devoted to music. According to them, music was rarely engraved on copper with a burin but was usually worked on pewter with a hammer and punches. If music came to the printer on copper plates then it was printed as any other copper-plate engraving, but the printing of music from pewter plates required procedures different from those usual with copper. The preliminary cleaning was modified, the inking was carried out cold with specially formulated ink, the force of the press was reduced, and the top roller had to be of sufficient diameter to prevent the plate from bowing as it passed through the press and curving upwards to take the shape of the roller.

It is not always easy to discover the methods used by printers and publishers to impose music printed from engraved plates, because much of the evidence is bound up tightly in the spines of library volumes. But it is possible to notice trends from broken-down and incomplete pieces and from superlative copies specially retained in their original condition. It seems that Roger engraved his vertical folios on large plates (278 mm deep × 516 mm wide, for example) with two pages to view, to provide a fold down the middle; his oblong music is usually printed on a single plate to a page (for an example of his engraving *see* ROGER, ESTIENNE). Walsh followed no fixed practice, as W. C. Smith found: 'Any attempt to apply to Walsh's music the usual rules based on the foldings of the paper, direction of lines, or position of watermarks is out of the question, as it is clear that he used to cut his paper without regard to such, and as it suited his purpose at the time'; later 'It can be added that at times he used paper folded once, giving 4 pp. folio stitched through the folds . . . but this was not always the case and he appears to have used cut single sheets sewn together'.

Berthiaud and Boitard said that it was rare for music to be printed in single plates; more often two or four plates were printed on a sheet of paper which, when it was folded down the middle, showed the impressions paged in correctly numbered order. This was achieved by printing the first page, turning the paper over and then printing the

15. The basic processes used in engraving from the 18th century to the present (showing the German practice, with punches): (a) cutting the staff lines on the metal plate, (b) translating the music from manuscript on to a spaced plate (working from right to left), (c) striking punches (music or lettering) into the plate, (d) cutting a slur, (e) pulling a proof

third page, imposed as the first but in the other half of the sheet. After allowing the sheet to dry for 24 hours, the second and fourth pages were printed in the same way.

The printing quality of pewter plates depended on the alloy from which they were made. Generally the alloys were more brittle as the proportion of antimony was greater. This, taken with the reaction of the metal to the punch and working at the press, may explain the cracks that disfigure some music printed direct from plates, particularly during the 19th century. Some runs were considerable: on the evidence of R. J. S. Stevens (1778; MS, Pendlebury Library of Music, Cambridge) 4000 copies were taken by Thomas Straight from a pewter plate before it was worn out. Cracks rarely appear in copper plates; wear can be attributed to other causes: 'the abrasive action of the plate printers' wiping canvasses . . . could break down fine work on a copper plate within a hundred impressions, and during a long run the cost of rebiting and repairs could absorb almost as much as the expenditure on the original work' (Bain, quoting Pye). This experience related to book illustration where detail was much finer than in music printing, but the points are valid for copperplate printing generally.

These imperfections give rise to bibliographical distractions, because cracks, missing or damaged notes and faint copies suggest late impressions taken from worn metal or new editions taken from 'the original plates'. Instead, many faults arose from causes intrinsic in metals and processes, and might have declared themselves early as well as late or arisen too from human shortcomings. Cracks may be attributable to any one of several causes: they might have been in the blank plate before working, they might have been opened by a burin where the metal was weak, or they might have spread under machine pressure at any stage of the printing run. Discrepancies in engraving style that occur through the parts of an instrumental work might stir thoughts of cancelled and re-engraved plates, but, since other evidence is lacking, it is safe to attribute such differences to trade practices. It is not always safe to accept 'T. Cross *sculp.*' as proof that all, or even most, of the music in a work has been engraved by Thomas Cross: he had 'good hands' to assist him. William Forster shared between engravers the work of punching his edition of certain Haydn symphonies, as the surviving manuscripts show and as the printed copies betray.

In France the subdivisions of labour followed another pattern. Three first-class engravers were called on to present the *Pièces de clavecin composées par M. Couperin* (1713), though only one, Du Plessy, seems to have been responsible for the music. The title-page of *Pièces de clavecin avec voix ou violon . . . par Mr Mondonville oeuvre V* (c1745) shows the names of F. Baillieul (*scripsit*), Hué (*sculpsit*), Rigaud (*inventit*) and Aubert (*sculpsit*). The *fermier-général* composer Jean-Benjamin de La Borde was rich enough to be able to commission Mlle Vendôme (the most famous of a group of outstanding music engravers) and Mora to engrave his insipid *Choix de chansons* (1773; fig.16) and Moreau le Jeune, Le Bouteux, Le Barbier and Saint-Quentin, the leading illustrators of the day, to create one of the most superbly decorated books of the century.

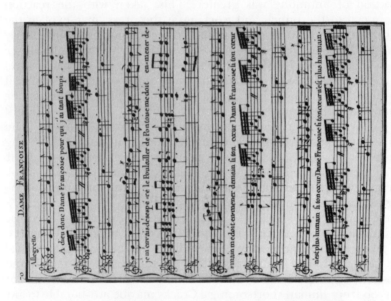

16. *Part of a song from La Borde's 'Choix de chansons' (Paris, 1773), the music engraved without punches, with the full-page engraving by Saint-Quentin that illustrates it [69% of actual size]*

This work's unique technical excellence shows only the best of a great deal of very good engraving which set the standard for the rest of Europe.

Once established in the 18th century, the music engraver's activities apparently changed very little. Tastes and standards of quality no doubt emerged, as with all crafts. What little is known of the work itself, however, must be inferred mostly from the vast number of surviving editions. Only rarely are particulars mentioned in secondary sources, since the techniques themselves, involving a coordination of the skilled hand with the trained eye, were well-guarded secrets passed on from master craftsmen through long years of apprenticeship. Effective control was maintained, it is assumed, through business opportunities and access to punches and other tools. Even today there are probably fewer than a dozen sets of tools extant in libraries, museums or other public institutions. Music engraving also remained remarkably decentralized, and it seems not unreasonable to speculate that at the high point of production, just after 1900, music engravers were active in several hundred cities throughout the world. To be sure, large firms often did the work for smaller firms and personal publishers, undertaking the engraving, running off copies and storing the plates for later press runs. Late 19th-century publishers as far away as London, St Petersburg and Latin America, for instance, were served by specialist engravers in Leipzig, of whom Röder, Brandstetter and Engelmann were the best known, and whose warehouses were largely destroyed in World War II. Other major engraving firms included Lowe and Brydone in London and the New York publisher G. Schirmer.

Predictably, music came in the 19th century to be increasingly standardized in its graphic character. Lines became finer in their execution, presumably because of the use of harder pewter with less lead in its alloy. The visual contrast between thin and thick lines could thus be emphasized, for instance between the endings and the middle of a tie or slur, or between the verticals and the diagonals on note heads or, most notably, in sharp signs. In subtle ways the standard appearance of musical signs changed over the years: the G-clef, for instance, rounded at the top around 1800, by 1850 was typically pointed. The musical page acquired a more dramatic appearance, but always short of interfering with the demands of performers. (These demands perhaps explain why music had no William Morris.) Standardization aside, engravers no doubt argued over the ideal layout and placement on the page for optimum legibility. Engraving house style thus emerged, enabling the workmanship of particular firms or even workmen to be identified, whether by contemporary persons in the trade (for instance as evidence of piracy in litigation) or by later scholars (as evidence of the date and source of particular exemplars). Priority and authenticity of editions can sometimes be inferred from such particulars, sometimes even by the evidence of the printing process itself. German music after 1850, for instance late Schumann or early Brahms, often exists in two forms, an earlier one printed directly from the plates and a later one printed by lithographic transfer, to be discussed below. After 1850 publishers

17(a) Terms used by Gamble and Ross for the sizes of punches and scorers

Gamble (1923) identifies eight punch sizes, with a number, name and examples of use for each. Ross (1971) gives a similar account of staff (scorer) sizes. Both agree that the numbers for staff sizes are consistently used for scorers, but that there is no unique correspondence with the numbers for punch sizes.

	Gamble: Punch Sizes			Ross: Staff Sizes	
no.	*name*	*measure of C clef mm*	*no.*	*name*	*measure of staff inches*
1	Stempel Zeug	7.9	1	Giant	5/16
2	Maho Zeug	7.4	2	English	19/64
3	Gewohnlich Zeug	6.8	3	Regular, Ordinary or Common	9/32
4	Peter Zeug	6.2	4	Peter	17/64
5	Grosse Mittel Zeug	5.9	5	Large Middle	15/64
6	Kleine Mittel Zeug	5.3	6	Small Middle	7/32
7	Cadenza Zeug	4.7	7	Cadenza	3/16
8	Pearl Zeug	3.2	8	Pearl	5/32

no.	*use*
1, 2	Tutors, orchestral music
3	Songs and pianoforte (sheet music)
4	Songs and pianoforte (albums)
5	Band parts, operatic music
6	Choral music
7	Pocket editions, violin lines in piano and violin pieces
8	Thematic advertisements, incidental purposes

Note: The Gamble figures identify the height of a C clef, which is intended to match the height of the staff. A treble clef or a rest will vary slightly from fount to fount within 'Maho' or 'Peter'; a crotchet will differ depending on the intended length of the stem (some engravers use only a note-hand punch and add stems with a graver). Punches slightly smaller than the corresponding staff sizes may be used to achieve a general feeling of precision of statement, conceivably at the expense of legibility from a distance. Considerably smaller punches are often used for grace notes or cues.

(b) Illustration of the staff line sizes from 'Music Engraving and Printing: Historical and technical Treatise', published in 1923 by William Gamble.

increasingly used wove paper that was coated and, unfortunately, high in acid content (Ricordi being among the notable exceptions).

The critics of engraving in England, France and elsewhere said that the process, although elegant, fluent and suited to music, was slow and expensive. Some offered a new typography as a means of capturing the charms of engraving without its disadvantages, but this proved a not very satisfactory alternative; others, later, adopted lithography to achieve the same ends.

CHAPTER IV

Lithography and More Recent Processes

Lithography is defined in the *Oxford English Dictionary* as 'the art or process of making a drawing, design or writing on a special kind of stone (called a "lithographic stone") so that impressions in ink can be taken from it'. The practice is based on the phenomenon that one greasy substance will receive another but any greasy substance will repel water. The man who used this principle to develop a quite novel method of printing was Alois Senefelder. He wanted to be a playwright but could not afford to publish at his own expense through the trade; he accordingly took up the study of printing techniques. He found the most promising was that of etching on a copper plate. He later substituted a piece of kellheim limestone and found that he could write with more command and more distinctly on the stone than on the copper plates. He used his own ink prepared with wax, soap and lampblack and decided to try the effect of biting the stone with 'aqua fortis' (nitric acid), wondering 'whether, perhaps, it might not be possible to apply printing ink to it, in the same way as wood engravings, and so to take impressions from it'. After pouring off the acid he found the writing 'elevated about a tenth part of a line', or about 2 mm, and that satisfactory impressions could be taken.

A page of poorly printed music in a prayer book that he saw at Ingolstadt persuaded him that his 'new method of printing would be particularly applicable to music printing' and he began with the work of a friend, Franz Gleissner. It is usually accepted that the first of Gleissner's compositions to be printed was the *Feldmarsch der Churpfalzbayer'schen Truppen* (1796; fig.18), but in the first part of his *Complete Course of Lithography* (1818; Eng. trans., 1819 – from which the above quotations are taken), Senefelder gave primacy to *12 neue Lieder für's Klavier* (1796). He copied the music on stone and, using a copper-plate printing press, with the assistance of one printer, took 120 copies. The composing of the songs, the writing, engraving and printing took less than two weeks.

These techniques of relief etching and printing from stone, refined and developed by Senefelder, were much used for music printing up to at least the first decade of the 19th century. In his study of Senefelder's life and work (1914), Carl Wagner showed a stone plate with music etched in high relief from the printing office of H. Gombart of Augsburg, dating from about 1800 (fig. 19). Music printed by this method can sometimes be identified by the impression left in the paper by the raised characters, for example in *Sonate à quatre mains pour le pianoforte ... Oeuvre II* by Franz Danzi (Munich: Falter, *c*1797).

Senefelder continued to experiment, observing the chemical and physical affinities between different substances. He noticed that gum-water prevented the chemical writing ink made of soap and wax from adhering to the stone; he drew lines with soap on a polished stone, moistened the whole surface with gum water and applied oil-based ink which adhered only to the soap lines. He described his experiments:

> In trying to write music on the stone, with a view to print it in this way, I found that the ink ran on the polished surface; this I obviated by washing the stone with soap water, or linseed-oil before I began to write; but in order to remove again this cover of grease which extended over the whole surface (so that the whole stone would have been black on the application of the colour [printing ink]) after I had written or drawn on the stone, it was necessary to apply aqua fortis, which took it entirely away, and left the characters or drawings untouched.

Out of these principles, rationalized in 1798, Senefelder developed the 'chemical printing' of true lithography, which allowed impressions to be taken from lines barely raised above the flat surface of a stone. He quickly extended the range of his procedures, or 'manners' as he called them. With the engraved manner the drawing was engraved in the surface of the stone with needles without being etched; this was used in the first work he produced after his discovery of chemical printing, *Eine*

18. *Part of Gleissner's Feldmarsch der Chrupfalzbayer'schen Truppen' (1796), traditionally accepted as the first piece of music successfully reproduced by Senefelder from etched stone [44% of actual size]*

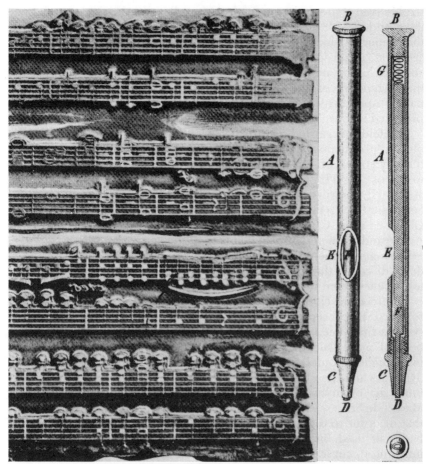

19. *Part of a stone plate etched with music in high relief, from the printing office of H. Gombart in Augsburg*

20. *Device for laying down identical note heads in succession (from G. Engelmann's 'Traité théorique et pratique de lithographie', Mulhouse, 1839–40), which consisted of a metal tube through which a rod (F) passed, enclosing at G a small spring: at the lower extremity of the rod a note head was engraved in relief, with lithographic ink being introduced round the rod through an aperture (E) in the outer case; a step cut in the rod blocked the flow of ink to the nozzle (C) until the end of the rod (D) was pressed against the stone, raising the road (F) and allowing the ink to be moved by capillary attraction down the nozzle on to the note head; when the pressure was released the spring (G) forced the rod down and cut off the ink supply, leaving enough in the nozzle to keep the note head covered for the next application*

Symphonie von vier obligaten Stimmen by Gleissner, where, to make the title-page as neat as possible, the engraved manner was used. It was possible to combine the engraved manner with the elevated (surface) manner. In his *Rapport sur la lithographie . . . adressé a la Societé d'encouragement de Paris* (20 October 1815, p. 3), G. Engelmann showed a piece of music in which the notes had been written in ink and the staff lines engraved; and Senefelder combined the methods in title-pages, 'where the finest hair strokes [were] drawn in first with the needle, and the thicker, or shade lines, added with the pen'. By 1800 Senefelder had demonstrated that the chemical printing process was not limited to stone; other substances 'as wood, metal, paper, even fat substances, as wax, shellac and rosin' could be used under certain circumstances. He did not cease to refine the techniques of his earlier discoveries such as 'transferring from paper, upon which drawing or writing is previously executed with prepared ink'.

Senefelder regarded his process as of universal application – apt for quick reproduction, in any quantity, of originals as various as orders of the day struck off on the battlefield, bill heads, advertising copy and works of art. The early development of lithography was very much associated, however, with the printing of music, largely because Senefelder's own interests and needs, and because of his association with Gleissner (and Gleissner's wife, a remarkable woman), Falter, J. A. André and Steiner at critical points in his career.

During his experiments Senefelder laid out his music complete and in detail direct on the stone, working from right to left with a sharp black-lead pencil; pen-work remained the basis of the technique in its commercial development. It may well be that the early lithographers followed the procedures of the pewter-plate engravers: ruled their staff systems first (line by line), established clefs, key signatures and indications of pulse, laid the note heads in position and, aided by drawing instruments, completed stems, beams, slurs, binds, indications of dynamics and the like as required. The note heads in early lithographic music are often circular, and it is known from a well-informed writer, Marcel de Serres, who visited Munich and Vienna to study lithography, that in order to draw round and uniform note heads a special former had to be used. Similarly, for the same purpose, a resinous tampon was introduced, cut at one end to the size and shape of a note head, which was inked and stamped where required on the stone. Engelmann, one of the most important innovators of the lithographic science, reported that as it was time-consuming to form the note heads with a pen and difficult to make them uniform, German lithographers had developed a tool which under the pressure of a plunger and spring delivered a measured amount of chemical ink down a tube of circular or oval section, and at the end of the tube in contact with the stone formed a note head (see fig. 20). With the aid of this pen it was possible to lay quickly a large number of identical note heads. Considerable skill was required to manage the pen where lines crossed: if both lines were wet the ink might 'blob' at the intersection.

The procedures required for writing direct on the stone, however, were arduous: it is not surprising that once the so-called transfer process was understood it was much used, particularly for ephemera. In this, the writing or drawing was copied from left to right with a flexible pen, a common goose-quill for want of a steel pen of comparable elasticity, using chemical ink on transfer paper, which had a specially prepared surface on one side. When the work was finished and the ink dry, the back of the paper was sponged with very weak nitric acid and the leaf put between sheets of dry blotting paper to absorb superfluous liquid and ensure that the paper was uniformly damp. While still moist the sheet was laid on the surface of a highly polished stone face down and, protected with backing sheets, was passed two or three times through the press. The stone was then removed from the press and bitten in, and pure water was poured over it until the paper was disengaged, leaving an exact image, reversed right to left in the correct sense for printing. The stone was then prepared for printing in the manner used for stones on which the writing had been applied direct.

Although Senefelder acquired a British patent in 1801, he was still writing in the future tense, urging its adoption for music printing, in his *Complete Course* in 1818. It is impossible to judge by looking at printed sheets to what extent, and when, the process of transfer to stone from originals written on prepared paper in chemical ink became an accepted practice for music. The process was increasingly used in commerce and law from the 1820s onwards, and certainly Wagner's writing of the full score of *Tannhäuser* in 1845 (see fig.21) shows that the technique had by this time become reliable even in the hands of amateurs. In the same year, he wrote, he had 25 copies made of the scores of *Der fliegende Holländer* and *Rienzi*, 'by means of the so-called autographic transfer process, although only from the writing of copyists'.

Traditionally, music was laid direct on the stone with pen, brush and, sometimes, graver, or at one remove via transfer paper. In his British patent Senefelder described how 'plates of copper, tin, pewter, and various metallic compounds already etched or engraved' could be charged with a specially prepared ink and passed through a rolling press to yield impressions which could be readily transferred to stone. It is not known who was the first to compound the qualities and defects of engraving and lithographic techniques by transferring a proof taken from a punched and engraved plate to a lithographic stone for printing; nor is it known when that was first done. But it was a crucial development, and it set a pattern which has persisted in some guise or other.

Dans le temple d'industrie, a song dedicated to Louis XVIII on the Exhibition of the products of French industry, 'drawn, written and printed on the lithographic plates of A. Senefelder & Co., rue Servandoni no.13' (Paris, *c*1820) shows a splendid portrait and some accomplished writing, but the music 'engraved by Madame Pannetier' was printed from intaglio plates in a rolling press. In France the 1830s and 40s produced some examples that seem to have been transferred from intaglio plates to stone for printing. In 1848 it was stated that D'Almaine & Co. had 'recently introduced a new and very superior mode of printing music at a charge infinitely lower than by the old processes, whilst the notation is rendered beautiful and agreeable to the eye'. This company had facilities for printing by letterpress, intaglio and lithography, and the new process might well have been derived from a combination of the intaglio and lithographic methods. *The Official and Descriptive Catalogue* of the Great Exhibition provides clear evidence that such a combination was being worked in London in 1851, for it is recorded in Class 30 that Jullien & Co. of 214 Regent Street exhibited

21. *Beginning of Act 1 of 'Tannhäuser', printed from the composer's autograph; Wagner wrote the score on lithographic transfer paper which was then laid down on to the stone*

'specimens of ornamental printed music: three of the titles are printed in oil colours, and three printed in colours from stone. The music was engraved on pewter, and afterwards transferred and printed from stone'. During the 19th century developments in the design of printing machinery led to experiments with metal plates treated to give the same results as lithographic stone. Although zinc, for example, offered satisfactory properties for lithography, its adoption for music printing was belated. Lowe & Brydone, one of the largest British music printers, used stone until 1895, when they started to print from zinc.

The paper size of the earliest lithographic music was not at all uniform; some works were printed with two or more pages on a stone, others with one page on each stone. In 1797 Senefelder was using stones of about 2500 square cm in surface area for his music, but as presses improved it was possible to use larger stones and by the latter part of the 19th century stones and zinc plates were giving 16 pages in full music size or 64 pages in octavo, imposed in accord with the same principles as those governing imposition in letterpress printing.

The next great step forward came with the introduction of the camera into the field of the reproductive graphic arts. As soon as photography had become a practical process in 1839 as a result of the work of the Niepces, Louis Daguerre and W. H. Fox Talbot, attempts were made to apply it to lithography; but it was not until 1852 that R. J. Lemercier and his colleagues succeeded in devising a process – difficult and hazardous in its operation – which they described in *Lithophotographie: ou, Impressions obtenues sur pierre à l'aide de la photographie*. Alphonse Poitevin's process, in which the lithographic stone was sensitized with bichromated albumen, was perfected in 1855 and won general acceptance; it still persists in certain applications. In 1857 Eduard I. Asser of Amsterdam succeeded in making transfers from photographic prints on to a non-sensitized stone and in 1859 Henry James was the first to make photographic transfers on to grained zinc. Instead of being written on stone or on transfer paper and then chemically 'fixed', music could now be derived from any original that could be photographed, the negative printed down on to stone or zinc and subsequently treated to yield a printing surface.

It is not surprising that this technology gave tremendous impetus to the development of new methods – or old methods in new guises – in the origination of music for printing. Instead of writing and drawing in reverse on stone or from left to right on special paper it was now possible to write from left to right on ordinary smooth paper, photograph the result and transfer it on to the stone or zinc plate for printing. Instead of punching and engraving metal plates it was possible to adapt traditional practices to paper, using, instead of gravers, pens and drawing instruments, and special punches carrying note heads, clefs, letters and even complete frequently used words (for example *piano, accel., ped.*). This process was worked either on lithographic transfer paper for direct transfer to stone or metal; or on ordinary papers for the camera and subsequent printing down for lithography; or for line engraving in relief. In the 1920s and 30s the process was much used in

France, where it was known as *similigravure*: its late developments are represented in the work of the Grafische Industrie, Haarlem, Netherlands, and Caligraving of Thetford, England.

The Halstan Process, a system unique to the company of that name in Amersham, England, is also graphical in essence. It was devised by Harold Smith, a master music engraver, and developed from 1919 onwards by him and his brother Stanley, a photographer and engraver. The basis of the process is a meticulously planned original, four times the finished size, marked out in light blue pencil which will not reproduce photographically. Care is taken at this stage to ensure that the layout of the whole manuscript takes account of the nature of the music, with suitable page turns and correct spacing of individual symbols; this requires a mixture of musical and engraving skills. The image is then created in dense black ink using a variety of specially devised rulers and stencils, standard drawing instruments and pens. Any text on the page is set by photo-composition and laid down in position. After internal proof-reading the original is reduced photographically to produce either a proof or final bromide or film. Emphasis on quality and flexibility has ensured a strong worldwide following for the process. All the music examples in *Grove 6* are set by Halstan, as are the Britten scores printed for Faber & Faber and the new Verdi Edition published by Ricordi and the University of Chicago Press.

These graphical processes all require particular tools for making note heads, clefs and other musical symbols, whereas the equipment for ruling staves, stems, beams, slurs and the like is common to them all. Traditional procedures, however, have been strongly challenged by a system based on the technique of dry transfer, in which punches, stencils and other similar hand tools are not required. Instead, multiple copies of individual music symbols are printed in a dense black substance (plastic 'ink') on one side of a thin transparent film. When the face of the sheet is turned down on to paper and the form of any character is rubbed from the back, the 'ink' leaves the sheet and adheres to the paper. In this way a succession of note heads, clefs, rests and a wide range of other units in any quantity – each individual character in every respect uniform with its fellow – can be rubbed down in any position. Letraset in Great Britain offer music sheets, but the most comprehensive system has been developed in the Netherlands as Notaset, and is much used (see fig.22); such systems are also extensively used by Bärenreiter. Basically simple, the technique demands care in practice. Each work starts as a detailed layout made on previously ruled paper by a musically trained planner and is then developed by operators using transfer sheets, rubbing down the necessary characters in place as they appear. The whole is finished with a pen as required, after which it is photographed and printed down on to a zinc plate.

All the processes described in this section are relatively slow, and call for the work of many hands: yet they and variants of them have survived and sometimes prospered, while the amount of work done by the engravers of pewter plates has declined catastrophically. The shift from punching and engraving has been much accelerated by the rapid

(a)

(b)

22. *(a) Specimen Notaset transfer sheet; (b) Characters being rubbed down on to pre-determined positions*

development of efficient music typewriters. Attempts were made in the 18th century to use the action of a piano to record on paper notes as they were struck, but it was not until 1833 that the first practical typewriter for music was described in a French patent (no.3748) awarded to Xavier Progin of Marseilles for what he called 'une machine ou plume typographique'. Other machines followed, by Berry (1837) and Guillemot (1859), but the first serious, commercially distributed machine was probably the Tachigrafo Musicale introduced by Angelo Tessaro in 1887 and marketed in Italy by Ricordi. During the next 60 years there were literally hundreds of patents granted throughout the world, particularly in America, for music typewriters. Most, for one reason or another, fell by the wayside; some were developed; a few succeeded, as for example the machine patented by Lily Salmon (later Pavey) which was manufactured for a time by the Imperial Typewriter Co. in England. Two or three types of machine have enjoyed wide and continuing use over a long period. One of these is the Keaton Music Typewriter, invented and developed by Robert H. Keaton of San Francisco, formerly a professional violinist. Intended for the individual musician and the small publisher, it has been highly successful throughout the USA: the makers have made no attempt to promote sales elsewhere, though one or two machines have found their way to Europe.

If Keaton's machine has served a domestic market only, the typewriters invented and developed by Armando Dal Molin and Cecil Effinger have each attained a wide influence in the commercial sphere. Dal Molin, Italian engineer and amateur musician, invented a music typewriter for his own use in 1945. The following year he patented it in Italy and went to the USA to develop it further, exhibiting it as the Music Writer at the New York World's Fair of Music. He started a business to manufacture the machine, and also set up a music typing studio. Refinements were added in 1955, and by the late 1950s the system was so successful that Dal Molin stopped making the machine for sale in order to develop his music origination business. It has been estimated that by 1972 the process had produced some 400,000 pages. Effinger, a

23. *Musicwriter (1973 model) designed by Cecil Effinger*

composer and professor of music at the University of Colorado (1956), conceived the idea of a music typewriter in Paris in 1945. He had made his first model the 'size of a large table – not functional' by November 1947. It was patented in March 1954 and the first production model was shown at Denver, Colorado, in July 1955, since when the machine has been in demand throughout the world. It is simple and robust in construction and engineered to fine limits (see fig.23). It is best used by professionals working with previously planned copy.

CHAPTER V

Music Printing by Computer

Interest in computerized music printing began to grow in the early 1960s, when the potential of computing began to be understood beyond the realms of theoretical science; the possibility had been considered as early as 1953 by Dal Molin. Musical notation, with its elements of language on the one hand and mathematics on the other, presented a fascinating challenge to computer-literate musicians who could foresee benefits both for academic research and commercial enterprise.

Post-war developments in electronics had given rise both to 'analogue' (controlled by variable voltage) and 'digital' (controlled by numbers) devices: electro-cardiographs and similar mechanical pen recorders are examples of the former, computers (at first valve-powered and cumbersome) of the latter. These elements came together in the 1950s with the development of the digital plotter, a line-drawing device which can move a pen in small increments in response to numbers sent to it by a computer; the pen is either down (drawing a trace on the paper) or up (not touching). It was later widely used as a tool for computerized music printing.

In the 1960s initial confidence gave way to a realization that the conventions of musical notation would not easily yield to automation. Layers of complexity which could be handled empirically by a skilled engraver or copyist seemed almost impenetrable in terms of mathematical logic, especially as many early projects were geared towards the cheap printing of contemporary music, with its irregular notational practices. Furthermore, computing was still impossibly slow and expensive for the intensive number processing needed even for the simplest music. Much important groundwork was done, however, especially in the development of music encoding languages, such as the Plaine and Easie code, developed by Barry S. Brook at Queen's College, New York, in the early 1960s, initially for bibliographical purposes, and DARMS ('Digital Alternate Representation of Musical Scores'), conceived by Stefan Bauer-Mengelberg in 1963. Both are still in use.

The first successful attempts at automated music printing date from this time. A project was set up at the University of Illinois, involving Lejaren Hiller and R. A. Baker of the Experimental Music Studio, Robert M. Oliver of the School of Engineering and Cecil Effinger, in which an electric typewriter was reconstructed with Effinger's Musicwriter typeface and equipped with a paper-punch unit (perforated tape was a normal storage medium for coded information in the 1960s). Music was typed in as if on a standard Musicwriter machine, producing coded paper tape. This was read by an ILLIAC digital computer which used mathematical procedures to perform such operations as alignment and right-hand margin justification; the computer then produced a new 'output tape' which was fed back into the paper-punch unit on the Musicwriter, and the correctly formatted page of music was typed out automatically. Dal Molin followed a similar line of research with his process, producing the first commercial results in 1970 from a system which created a negative image on film. From this he developed the Musicomp (1977), a computer with two keyboards (a special one for encoding pitch and a conventional computer keyboard for musical and alphanumeric symbols) and a facility to display the music on screen (see fig.24). The system is used by Dal Molin's company Music Reprographics, which provides origination for a number of publishers, among them Belwin-Mills.

24. (a) The Musicomp, designed by Armando Dal Molin (1977): the keys on the left set the pitch (7 notes, 4 octaves, with 2 more octaves available) and the keys on the right select, from a comprehensive range, the required musical and plain-language symbols, with the notes disposed according to their value by a space bar; the music is displayed on the screen by keyboard command through computer coding and stored in a microcassette (capable of storing 30 pages of music) before passing on to print-out in a complete form (b) A reproduction of part of a line of music originated on the Musicomp: the tempo, beams, slurs, crescendos and bar-lines, normally added by hand in other systems, are here all an integrated part of the whole

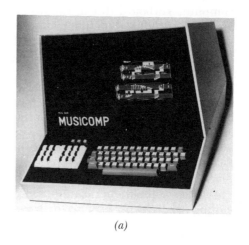

(a)

(b)

Academic institutions have been the source of most new computing techniques. In the 1970s a number of projects using university-based mainframe computers were started by individuals working on their own initiative: Mogens Kjaer at Aarhus, Denmark (Scan-Note), Thomas Hall at Princeton (the system used by A-R Editions), Leland Smith at Stanford (SCORE), Donald Byrd at Indiana (SMUT: 'System for Music Transcription') and Richard Vendome at Oxford (Oxford Music Processor). The first two have been taken over by printing houses; the others are being developed as software for desk-top publishing. The Scan-Note system, begun in 1970, was further developed by the Danish software house, Dataland, and produced its first results in 1976. It was taken over in 1984 by the Japanese printing house, Toppan, and has processed music for a number of publishers, including Bärenreiter. The music is input by skilled operators who enter a voice at a time, one hand on an electronic music keyboard (for pitch), the other at a special computer keyboard (for durations and musical symbols). The finished artwork is produced on film by laser-typesetter. The A-R process uses a simple alphanumeric code derived from FASTCODE (developed by Hall) and DARMS, entered at a standard computer terminal. Since 1977 it has mainly been used for scholarly projects by A-R Editions and other publishers. Output is by photo-typesetter.

The launching of the IBM PC (personal computer) in 1981 began a revolution in the world of computing. This machine, and its rival the Apple Macintosh, brought the power of computation to the office and even the home, opening up the exciting prospect of personal publishing; SCORE, SMUT and the Oxford Music Processor are being adapted and marketed to run on this inexpensive and rapidly developing hardware. Each uses alphanumeric input and provides the facility for screen editing (whereby the user can display music on the screen and make easy corrections). Output is by plotter or desk-top laser printer. Work on the SCORE program dates from 1971; it can now produce historic forms of notation, including neumes, mensural notation and lute tablature. SMUT is an offshoot of Jerome Wenker's MUSTRAN encoding language, based at Indiana University. The Oxford Music Processor first produced results in 1977 and has since been used by Oxford University Press.

An interesting system, used mainly for incipits, was developed by Norbert Böker-Heil at the Staatlichen Institut für Musikforschung in West Berlin; the music is entered in Plaine and Easie code and the system has been used for thematic catalogues in the *RISM* series. Another German project started in the 1970s, though in the commercial field, is the Amadeus system by Kurt Maas, which has been used by Schott. The MEG ('Music Editing and Graphics') system by Marco and Diego Minciacchi, run on the Apple II computer, has been used to prepare contemporary scores (by Stockhausen, for example) for publication by Universal Edition.

The pioneering work of the 1960s and 70s established a foundation of encoding systems and layout algorithms (formulated procedures) for music printing. The technology of the 1980s offered new opportunities to the musician, such as the means of playing music directly into the computer from a music keyboard by way of a MIDI (Musical Instrument Digital Interface), and the ability to move musical symbols about the screen with a 'mouse' (a hand-held device which can be moved over a flat surface to alter the position of a pointer on the screen). The most interesting developments of the 1980s are found in the IMS (Interactive Music System) conceived by Lippold Haken and Kurt Hebel as part of the CERL Music Project at the University of Illinois and the Mockingbird system developed by Severo Ornstein and John Maxwell at the Xerox Research Park, Palo Alto. IMS is an ambitious and comprehensive set of tools for music research, with applications for acoustics, analysis, composition, musicology and printing. Scores can be manipulated algorithmically and edited from a music keyboard or touch screen (a device operated by touching parts of the screen). This software is being adapted to run on all leading microcomputers, producing dot-matrix and laser printer output. The Mockingbird, described by its inventors as 'a composer's amanuensis', was written in 1980, using an experimental computer language, Mesa, and a Xerox 1132 computer, also experimental. The project, intended as a vehicle for technical research, was later abandoned, though some of the work has been incorporated in other programs. The purpose of the system, designed solely for two-staff piano music, was to capture a composer's playing on a keyboard and display it on a high-resolution screen in the form of a 'time plot' (note heads positioned on the staff according to the notes played and the time intervals between them); the resulting image resembled a piano roll. Next, stems, beams and other elements of notation were added by using a mouse to move a pointer to the relevant symbol displayed in a menu on the screen, then moving the symbol to its correct position. By this means the score could be built up, then automatically aligned and justified by the program. Mockingbird could play back the music and produce laser printer output (see fig.25).

Other valuable research has been done by Hélène Charnassé's team at the CNRS in Paris (projects include computer-printed editions of lute music), by John Dunn at North Staffordshire Polytechnic (music processing from DARMS input) and by a group at Nottingham University which includes Eric Foxley (a music-description language and preprocessor for use with the TROFF typesetting system) and John Morehen (a program to produce incipits of Renaissance madrigals from DARMS code).

Most present-day commercial music software is produced by the popular music world; much of it is designed by engineers or programmers whose background is technical rather than musical and who are influenced by powerful marketing considerations. The modern electronic music studio has equipment which enables a musician to compose without musical notation; the more powerful type of synthesizer combines the resources of a digital computer with an electronic keyboard, enabling music to be played in, and a microphone, enabling sounds to be 'sampled' (recorded digitally and stored as a computer file). A single note can be sung into a microphone, for

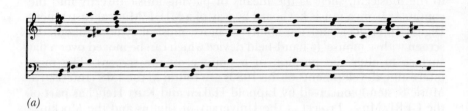

(a)

(b)

(c)

(d)

25. *Mockingbird – from keyboard input to finished score*
(a) 'piano-roll' input direct from the synthesizer keyboard (b) after alignment (c) with key and time signature and bar-lines added, after some redistribution of notes between staves (d) with some durations defined by the user

(e)

(f)

(g)

(h)

(25 continued)
(e) other durations automatically set (f) after correction by the user (g) after justification
(h) after adjustment by the user

example, and then played back at different pitches from the keyboard. Complex sounds can be created by FM (frequency modulation) or additive (harmonic) synthesis, and sampled sounds resynthesized. A musical composition can be assembled by using a 'sequencer', a computer program which enables a group of notes to be edited or modified (in pitch, sequence, tempo or timbre), or put into a 'loop' (repeated continuously). Leading synthesizer manufacturers of the 1980s include Kurzweil, Synclavier (USA), Fairlight (Australia) and Yamaha (Japan); all but the last of these produce expensive pieces of equipment intended primarily for studio use. Most synthesizers make use of a MIDI device and can be used in conjunction with some proprietary music-printing software. Since 1982 the Synclavier synthesizer has had its own high-quality printing facility: music can be played on the synthesizer or typed in alphanumerically at the computer keyboard, edited on-screen and output by a variety of printing devices.

A number of easy-to-use software packages are currently available and can produce music origination from a comparatively inexpensive combination of hardware: a microcomputer connected to a dot-matrix printer, plotter or desk-top laser printer. For the small publisher, the university or music college requiring its own facility, or any musical organization producing its own editions, such systems are an attractive economic proposition. However, at present only a few programs produce

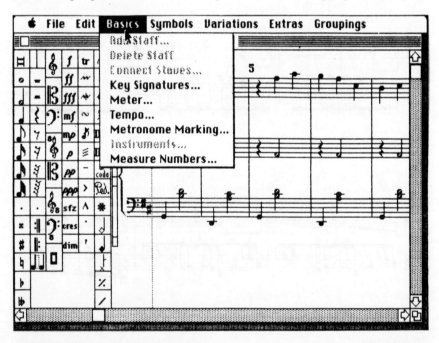

26. Professional Composer – screen display
The mouse-controlled cursor is seen pointing to the word 'Basics' at the top of the screen. The cursor is pointed to the required pitch on the staff and the mouse 'clicked' to select it. It is then pointed to a symbol on the palette at the left of the screen and clicked again. The symbol appears in the correct position on the staff.

results that approach the quality of traditional music engraving. Most programs were developed in connection with a specific musical repertory, and as a result no two 'music processors' have the same uniformity of operation and purpose (as opposed to word processors, most of which function in a similar way); this makes comparison between them difficult. Professional Composer, developed by Mark of the Unicorn for the Macintosh computer (1985), is proving successful. It takes full advantage of the Macintosh screen-graphics 'icon' system, which uses a mouse to move the required musical symbol from a 'palette' on the left of the screen into position on the staff (see fig.26). Notes are aligned automatically and facilities include beaming, transposition and playback. Macintosh graphics make it possible to add text in a number of styles and to 'cut-and-paste' portions of a score; output is by dot-matrix or laser printer. The system is used by Garland.

The mid-1980s saw a proliferation of music-printing software of varying quality, much of it based on similar principles to those described above. Among the better examples are MusPrint by Keith Hamel and the Deluxe Music Construction Set by Geoff Brown, both for the Macintosh, and The Music Factory by Stephen Dydo and La Ma de Guido by Llorenc Balsach, both for the IBM PC. The last of these comes from Spain, the others from the USA. Brown's program is of special interest because it uses the Adobe Systems' music fount (1986), a character set which gives excellent laser printer output.

The main techniques for entering musical data into a computer are alphanumeric code, music keyboard input and screen input. Alphanumeric codes were used in most of the earlier computer-printing systems. Music is entered at the computer keyboard in a code which represents musical notation as succinctly as possible but in as much detail as is required for the task in hand (a code which includes information about variant readings, for example, will be more complicated than one based on a single source). Ergonomic considerations, such as speed, ease and accuracy of use by a musician with no experience of computers, are important when using this technique. The Plaine and Easie and DARMS codes are alphanumeric (see fig.27); the latter exists in two syntactically distinct forms: User-DARMS for data input, where the music is entered a voice at a time ('linear decomposition mode') and Canonic DARMS for internal representation, consisting of a sequence of 'time slices' or synchronous events in the score. In some systems a music keyboard is used to input pitch, a computer keyboard being used to enter rhythm and other notational symbols. With the Scan-Note system the operator is able to use both simultaneously, 'playing' with the left hand and 'typing' with the right. This is an efficient method of data entry, but it requires skill on the part of the user. More recent systems use a MIDI device which enables both pitch and rhythm to be entered at a music keyboard, using a timing clock to calculate the latter. The MIDI standard (adopted by electronic instrument manufacturers in 1983) does not distinguish

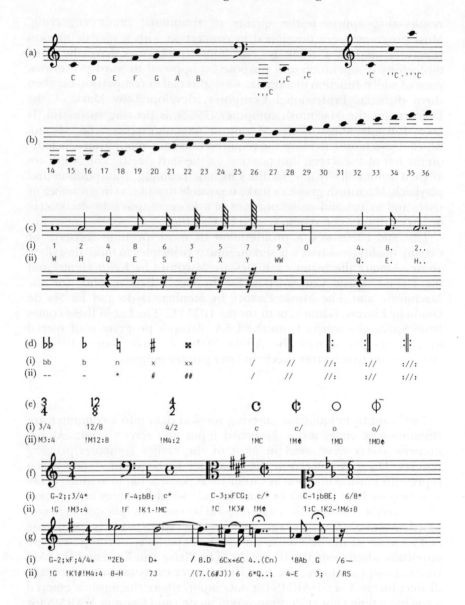

27. *Plaine and Easie and DARMS codes – basic structures compared*
(a) pitch: Plaine and Easie. The first pitch requires its octave to be specified; successive notes are assumed to be within the same octave until a new one is given. Similarly, a rhythmic value remains in force until changed. Rests are indicated by a hyphen '-' instead of a pitch character. (b) pitch: DARMS. 'Space codes', as they are called, define the vertical placing of notes, clefs and other symbols, within the range 00–49. Positions on the staff, 20–29, may be represented by 0–9 (single digit). The code may be omitted if it is the same as for the previous note. (c) rhythm: (i) P&E, (ii) DARMS (d) accidentals, bar-lines: (i) P&E (ii) DARMS (e) time signatures: (i) P&E (ii) DARMS (f) clefs, key and time signatures together: (i) P&E (ii) DARMS (g) example with various elements of notation (i) P&E (ii) DARMS

between enharmonic equivalences of pitch, such as F♯ and G♭. Errors of duration can arise if the music is rhythmically complex or if it is not played strictly in time. However, these difficulties can be overcome algorithmically (the computer predicting the intended notation) or by correction from the computer keyboard. Most programs which allow screen input are based on a proprietary computer-graphics facility (such as Macpaint, in the case of Macintosh software). Notation is placed and moved on the screen by use of a mouse (e.g. Professional Composer). Some programs have a limited 'intelligence', performing automatic alignment and spacing, for example, while others, such as MusPrint, can place symbols anywhere on the page without reference to notational legitimacy; this is particularly useful for contemporary music, but relies on the user to produce a satisfactory layout.

The first step in computing the layout of a score is the alignment of voices. The rhythmic values of all the voices are super-imposed to give a single 'composite' voice; see fig.28. Some elements of notation, such as clefs, key and time signatures, accidentals etc, require horizontal space to be inserted between notes independently of their rhythmic values; and where two notes of a chord are of adjacent pitch (i.e. a second apart) on the same staff, the lower must be displaced to the right if they have separate stems, and the upper if they use the same stem, regardless of its direction. Word underlay is another element which affects spacing; normally the notes are laid out first and the words fitted beneath, but if a word or syllable is too long for the available space the gaps between the

28. *J. S. Bach: Kyrie, Gott Vater in Ewigkeit (BWV669), bars 1–3*

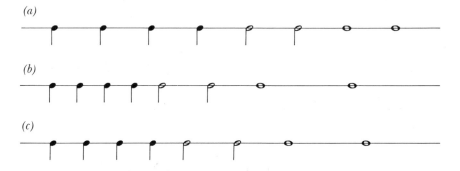

29. *Horizontal spacing*
(a) notes spaced equally, irrespective of duration (1:1) (b) notes spaced in direct proportion to duration (1:2) (c) notes spaced using the Golden Section ratio (1:1.618)

(a)

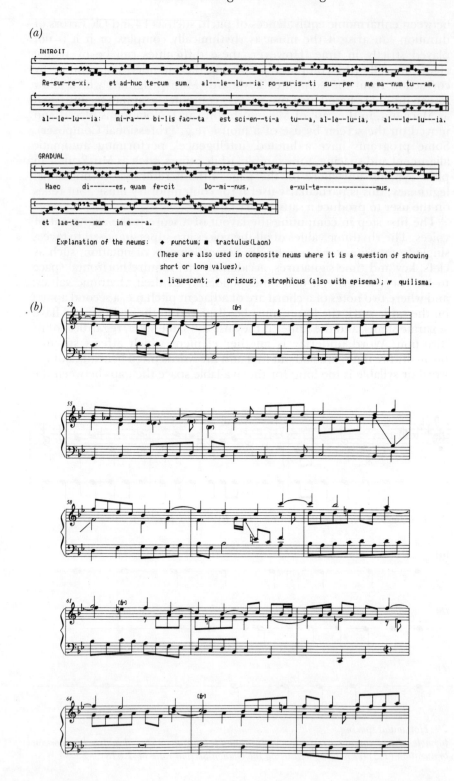

INTROIT

Re-sur-re-xi, et ad-huc te-cum sum, al---le--lu---ia: po--su-is--ti su---per me ma--num tu---am,

al--le--lu---ia: mi-ra---- bi-lis fac--ta est sci-en--ti-a tu---a, al-le--lu-ia, al--le--lu--ia.

GRADUAL

Haec di-------es, quam fe-cit Do--mi--nus, e-xul-te---------------mus,

et lae-te----mur in e----a.

Explanation of the neums: ◆ punctum; ■ tractulus(Laon)

(These are also used in composite neums where it is a question of showing short or long values).

■ liquescent; ♪ oriscus; ♪ strophicus (also with episema); ℣ quilisma.

(b)

(c)

30. (a) Dot-matrix output: Plainsong Program by Robert Sherlaw Johnson – Introit and part of the Gradual for Easter Sunday. The notation is intended to represent neume types used in the St Gall and Laon MSS. Note that in plainsong the spacing is determined by the words (produced on an Epson dot-matrix printer). (b) Graphics plotter output: Oxford Music Processor – Handel: Six Fugues or Voluntarys, ed. H. Diack Johnstone, no.3, bars 52–66 (OUP 1986) (produced on a Gould Colowriter 6320 plotter, resolution 0.025 mm, using a wet-ink pen at 12 cm per second). (c) Laser printer output: Toppan Scan-Note System – Mozart: Symphony no.40 (K550), first movement, bars 68–80 (sample, 1984).

notes are opened up. In traditional engraving practice there is a proportional relationship between rhythmic values and horizontal spacing within the same system of music. Notes of different value are not spaced equally, of course, but neither are they spaced directly in proportion to their duration. Analysis of the 'house style' of leading publishers has suggested a number of possible formulae. Visually pleasing results may be obtained by using the Golden Section ratio, 1:1.618 (i.e. if the distance between crotchets is 1 cm then the distance between minims will be 1.618 cm), though ratios as small as 1:1.15 are to be found in some printed music (see fig.29). Some researchers have proposed a 'fixed-variable' solution, combining a fixed proportion of a rhythmic value with its logarithm, for example. Certain musical textures need a particularly large or small ratio for easy legibility. Like most attempts to formulate rules to describe an empirical process, this is an area of conjecture.

Among other notational elements which can be computed are beams and slurs. In the case of a beamed group of notes the angle of the beam can be calculated by fitting a line through the notes (using a mathematical formula such as a 'least-squares-fit') and then off-setting it so that the shortest stem of the group is at least an octave in length. To avoid a visual clash with the staff lines, beams are placed vertically to start and end on a line, not in a space. Slur shapes are difficult to generate automatically, and are a weakness of many computerized processes; best results have been obtained by allowing the user to 'draw' the slur directly onto the screen using a mouse or light-pen. The shape can then be 'smoothed' by the computer.

After alignment, displacement and horizontal spacing have been calculated, the music is right-justified to fit the length of the staff. In some computer processes, system and page breaks are determined automatically, in others they can be set by the user. When the positions of all elements of notation have been calculated, the music can be printed out. Three types of device are used for this: dot-matrix printer, graphics plotter and laser printer (see fig.30). Some music-printing software includes facilities for automatic part-extraction and transposition. The user can enter a full score with all instruments untransposed, for example, and then extract a part or group of parts, transposed if necessary, with multiple rests concatenated and line breaks recalculated.

CHAPTER VI

Music Publishing:
Definition and Origins

The music publisher issues musical editions which consist primarily of musical notation, whether for performance or study; a publisher who issues books about music, certain kinds of instructional material, librettos and other primarily verbal texts but does not also issue musical editions, is not generally regarded as a music publisher. As with general publishers, the music publisher's activities involve obtaining a text and working with the composer or editor, financing the printing, promoting, advertising, storing and distributing the copies and, increasingly over the past century, negotiating and administering performing rights.

The present survey of music publishing, referring as it does to the major music publishers, establishes a general background for the entries in the dictionary (pp.135) as it also provides a cicerone for the study of music imprints. It describes the changing environment in which music publishers worked and inevitably comes close to being a summary of the cultural history of music in general, seen from the perspective of the student of musical documents. Music publishing is part of the history of society and commerce. It owes its existence to three phenomena that date back to the Renaissance: the invention of printing; the growth of modern mercantile practices which provided publishers with a framework for their economic and promotional activities; and the rise of the professional composer, who needed the services of the music publisher. Music printing is part of the history of technology, although printing and publishing are necessarily related and in fact many music publishers – before 1700 almost all, subsequently only a few – did their own printing.

Musical texts may be printed but not published. Luxurious editions were often prepared as keepsakes for private and limited circulation, as, for example, were the earliest copies of *Parthenia* (London, 1613/14); later impressions of this book, however, were intended for sale and should therefore be regarded as having been published. Other music was printed but not published in order to ensure control over performances. Ten partbooks make up John Barnard's *Selected Church Musick* (*RISM* 1641[5]), but there is no extant continuo part; apparently the vocal parts were printed so that the singers could learn the music, but no performance could take place without a continuo. In the 19th century full scores and instrumental parts for operas and some large symphonic works were often printed but not published, so that the owner could more effectively demand royalties or specify conditions of performance. Vocal scores, which were both printed and published, could be used to familiarize the public with a work and to train singers, but full-scale performances with orchestra could not be given until arrangements were made with the publisher, involving royalty payments in return for the rental of the instrumental parts and the conductor's score.

The opposite condition can also exist: music may be published but not printed. Through history there have been music copyists whose manuscripts were presumably intended to be equivalent to a printed copy. William Byrd and Thomas Tallis secured a patent in 1575 for music printing that also specified control over music paper; this implies that they had a special working relationship with copyists. Reports suggest that the money they made came mostly from the paper; and when Thomas Morley renegotiated the patent in 1599 he took pains to retain the coverage of music paper. In the early 18th century, Italian opera was rarely printed; yet, through manuscripts, it came to dominate European musical taste. Provincial newspaper announcements of the 18th and 19th centuries tell of men who made a living by copying music 'cheaper and more accurately' than printed editions. Today, through photography and lithography, any manuscript can be duplicated and hence can become the basis for a published edition. Various blueprint processes were also widely used, especially from 1920 to 1960, to copy and circulate contemporary music. The manuscript copy is an appropriate means of publishing a musical text of which few copies are likely to be needed.

Before Gutenberg's invention of printing, books were extensively distributed in manuscript; and the origins of book publishing are commonly seen as beginning well before that time. No evidence has been uncovered, however, of any copying shops that specialized in music. Music scribes were attached to courts and chapels, such as those at Mechlin or Ferrara; the music they copied was often widely circulated and much used, but their activity is distinct from the processes of publication.

During the period of incunabula, several dozen printers issued theoretical treatises, but few issued more than one such book. The printers of liturgical music, on the other hand, usually issued more than one book, perhaps because they had invested in music type. By 1480 liturgical books containing music in plainchant notation were being issued throughout Europe at the rate of several dozen a year.

Among the Italian printers who worked with music were Ulrich Han and Stephan Planck in Rome; Damiano and Bernardo Moilli in Parma; Christoph Valdarfer, Leonard Pachel and Antonio Zarotto in Milan; and, in Venice, a German lineage including Theodor Franck from Würzburg, Johann Hamman, active later in Speyer, and Johann Emerich from Speyer. Books for service use in Germany and central Europe were produced by Bernard Richel in Basle, Johann Sensenschmidt and later by Johann Pfeyl in Bamberg, Georg Reyser in Würzburg and Georg Stuchs in Nuremberg. For a few years just before 1490 about a dozen books a year came from the press of Michael

Wenssler in Basle. The most prolific German incunabula music printer was Erhard Ratdolt in Augsburg. Steffen Arndes, working between Italy and north Germany, also produced major liturgical music texts. In Paris in the 1480s several dozen missals were printed for various French bishoprics by Jean Du Pré, who left space for manuscript music; in the 1490s Jean Higman issued such books, using music type. These men were still essentially printers. There were two stimuli to the separation between printing and publishing; first, printers had to sub-contract the work to other printers; and second, financial support was sought outside the trade, in order to cover the costs of materials as well as labour, whether as manifestations of the desire to circulate a text (as with centralized distribution of diocesan service books or, later, congregational hymnals and psalters), to demonstrate patronage (as evidence of the munificence associated with the courtly chapels) or to invest capital (as in the case of reprinting, typically of anthologies). The first music publishers who were not also their own printers appeared after 1480, when the Venetian merchants Luc'Antonio Giunta and Ottaviano Scotto called on local printers, notably Johann Emerich and Johann Hamman, to print music books, mostly Roman missals. The Giunta family was to be the major Italian publisher of liturgical music books throughout the 16th century.

The history of Roman Catholic liturgical books in the 16th century has yet to be studied in detail, but it appears that the output in the Low Countries and Germany declined sharply about 1515; in France it flourished longer and did not disappear until after 1550. England produced liturgical books for a few years around 1500 and again during the reign of Mary Tudor. Elsewhere, Jan Haller in Kraków issued a splendid missal in 1503, and was succeeded by Hieronim Wietor, while Christophe van Remunde produced significant books in Antwerp at about the same time. Even so, more 16th-century liturgical music books probably came from the Giuntas than from all other publishers combined.

CHAPTER VII

The Age of Letterpress, 1501–1700

Petrucci has been called the Gutenberg of music printing. The comparison is not quite appropriate, since he was not the first to print music; but in matters of craftsmanship and artistry the comparison is apt. Besides being the first printer to use multiple-impression movable type, he deserves to be recognized as the first publisher of polyphony. Between 1501 and 1509 in Venice he issued the three *Canti* volumes of the *Odhecaton*, five books of *Motetti*, 16 mass books, 11 collections of popular frottolas and six lutebooks. Through them, the music of Josquin and his contemporaries became the earliest art-music repertory to appear in print. In 1511 Petrucci resumed printing in his native Fossombrone, with less exceptional results. His 61 known publications, the last dated 1520, provide an invaluable record of the musical works of Franco-Flemish polyphony and a testimony to their contemporary reputation.

Petrucci's success seems to have stimulated other printers to issue music. In Germany, Erhard Oeglin in Augsburg in the 1500s, and the itinerant Peter Schoeffer over the next two decades, used double-impression typography in direct imitation of Petrucci, as did Jean de Channey in Avignon in the 1530s. In Italy, on the other hand, Caneto, Sambonetto and particularly Dorico used woodblocks, as did Arnt von Aich in his noteworthy songbook from the 1510s, and Grimm & Wirsung in Augsburg in their sumptuous motet collection of 1520. Petrucci's most important successor, Andrea Antico, was, however, neither a printer nor a publisher but a woodcutter or engraver whose blocks were used by music printers in editions subsidized by others. The blocks can be identified in about a dozen books, most of them vocal canzonas, first issued when Antico was in Rome between 1510 and 1518. From 1520 to 1539 he worked in Venice, after 1532 in partnership with Ottaviano Scotto. About two dozen more music books were issued during this period, using his blocks. Blocks were also used in treatises and in instrumental anthologies such as Cavazzoni's tablature book of 1543, now thought to be the work of Bernardino Vitali.

The first really successful music publishing concern was established in Paris during the reign of François I, at the time of the so-called scholar printers by Pierre Attaingnant, who issued his first anthology in 1527/8. His typefaces are not without precedent but they contributed to the distinctive appearance of his editions and determined the speedy production of them, through which the chansons of Janequin, Costeley and their contemporaries were disseminated. Attaingnant flourished for a quarter of a century. His books follow formulae of many kinds – in their appearance, their content and even their titles for numbered series. Although he specialized in the early French chanson, which he issued in oblong partbooks, at first octavo and later quarto, he also issued several books of tablature and over a dozen folio mass collections, for which special music type was made.

Venetian music publishing after Petrucci and Antico is the story of two great names, Gardano and Scotto. Their output, devoted almost entirely to sacred and secular partbooks, was prodigious. Antoine Gardanoe (Antonio Gardano), originally from southern France, began printing in Venice in 1538, specializing in the music of Arcadelt and featuring series such as the *Motetti del frutto*. By 1545 he was issuing a dozen or more new titles every year; by 1600 the total had reached 30. His heirs continued to publish music up to 1685, sometimes retaining the name of Gardano, elsewhere using that of Magni, the founder's grandson-in-law. Over its long history the Gardano dynasty issued some 3000 musical editions. The firm founded by Girolamo Scotto produced perhaps half this total. It began in 1539 and for a time rivalled Gardano in the quantity and quality of its output. But before 1570 it had waned, and after 1590 its occasional publications were mostly reprints of Palestrina masses. Lesser Venetian publishers included Francesco Rampazetto (1561–8), who issued reprints in the 1560s; the composer Merulo ('Claudio da Correggio'), whose editions, from the same decade, were regarded as models of accuracy; and Alessandro Raverii, who printed over a dozen music books a year during his short career (1606–9).

The innovatory products of the 'nuove musiche' around 1600 were favoured by two younger Venetians, Ricciardo Amadino and Giacomo Vincenti, who were partners between 1583 and 1586 but worked separately thereafter. Amadino's firm disappeared during the economic decline of Venice and is last heard of in 1621; but the name of Vincenti persisted until 1667 and appeared on well over a thousand musical editions. The prolific Venetian trade in books, like Venetian commerce in general, enjoyed its greatest prosperity between 1540 and 1610: it was almost inevitable that the music publishers would also be important, although the quantity of their output is astonishing. The vast output of Venice – at its peak in the 1590s it was publishing more music than the whole of the rest of Europe – probably helped significantly in the spread of developments as different as polychoral and monodic styles.

The centre of early German music publishing was Nuremberg, thanks to two typecutters who also used their own type as printers: Hieronymus Formschneider ('Grapheus') and Johann Petreius. From 1532 Formschneider issued works by Hans Gerle, using woodcuts. He then cut a music face and used it in about a dozen music books that he printed between 1534 and 1539. (His name also appears in the imprint of Heinrich Isaac's *Choralus constantinus*, dated 1550–55.) He is also important because his music type was used by most of the Lutheran printers in north Germany later in the century. Petreius issued several dozen music books between 1536 and 1553; but he too is important as a designer of music type, which was used in south Germany, central Europe and as far away as Antwerp and Paris. His two music faces are particularly attractive and complex in their construction. The most prolific of the Nuremberg houses, however, was the partnership of Johann Berg ('Montanus') and Ulrich Neuber. They issued about a hundred editions, mostly partbooks and vernacular song collections, using Petreius type (1540–71), while their successors, Dietrich Gerlach (1567–93) and Paul Kauffmann (1594–1618), issued several hundred more.

Other music publishers became established in Paris after the death of Attaingnant. Of these, Nicolas Du Chemin issued about 200 music books (1549–76), including two series of chansons in the style of Attaingnant and about 30 folio mass books. Michel Fezandat issued several tablature books and Calvinist psalm books (1550–58). But it was the partners Adrian Le Roy and Robert Ballard who in 1551 obtained the exclusive royal privilege for music printing; this monopoly was to remain in force for over two centuries, determining the course of French music publishing up to the time of Lully and, indeed, as far as the French Revolution. Their earliest editions were mostly tablature books and psalters; in 1557–9, 22 folio choirbooks appeared. Thereafter secular partbook anthologies predominated in their catalogue. At first they used type from Petreius in Nuremberg, but shortly before 1560 they began to use founts, commissioned from the master punchcutter Guillaume Le Bé. These were to serve as a distinctive hallmark of the firm's music for the rest of its long existence. After the death of Le Roy in 1598, the Ballard name alone was used.

The fourth major music publishing centre in the mid-16th century was Antwerp. Though the first *Souterliedekens* was printed there by Symon Cock in 1539, the history begins effectively the following year with a privilege issued to Willem van Vissenaecken, who had music type specially cut for him but seems to have issued only one collection. His competitor and successor was Tylman Susato, who issued about 60 music books between 1543 and 1564; most were devoted to reprints of chansons and motets, but some were Flemish songbooks and psalm books. Jean de Laet and Hubert Waelrant produced about 20 attractive vocal collections (1554–65). The major music publisher in the Low Countries was Pierre Phalèse (i), who began his career in Louvain in 1545 and soon set up a partnership with Jean Bellère in Antwerp. After his death his son Pierre Phalèse (ii) moved to Antwerp, where the family continued to publish music up to 1691. The Phalèse imprint appears on nearly 200 chanson, motet and lute collections. It must be assumed that the Antwerp reprints reflected a considered judgment of market demands, thus providing us with a useful perspective on the popularity of different kinds of music. Music was also issued in Antwerp by Christopher Plantin, famed for the printing shop which survives today as a museum in Antwerp; his books are impressive and distinctive both visually and musically (see fig.31).

Like book publishing, music publishing favoured commercial centres in preference to university towns. Mostly before the ascendancy of the

31. Title-page of George de la Hèle's 'Octo missae', printed by Plantin (Antwerp, 1578)

four cities discussed above, Frankfurt, Lyons and Augsburg also housed music publishers. The Frankfurt printer Christian Egenolff worked for several decades from 1532, issuing collections of German folksongs and of settings of Horatian odes. Following sporadic activity in Lyons, including woodblock efforts by Antoine Du Ry in 1525 and Etienne Briard's double-impression round-note typography of 1532, Jacques Moderne began printing there with a folio missal and three motet collections, also in 1532. After five years of inactivity, he resumed with a series in the style of Attaingnant called *Le parangon des chansons*; 'Grand Jacques' (as Moderne called himself) also issued about a dozen other music books during his last years between 1541 and 1556, mostly reprints of Venice or Paris editions. His major successor was Godefroy Beringen, whose several extant music books, neat in appearance, are distinctly Calvinist in their repertory. In Augsburg anthologies were printed by Melchior Kriesstein (1540–49) and Philipp Ulhart (1537–79), devoted mostly to music taken from other publishers' books. Other printers around 1550 included Mathias Apiarius in Berne and the Zurich punchcutter turned lute-intabulator Rudolf Wyssenbach; the itinerant Jacob Baethen, whose music books were printed successively at Louvain, Maastricht and Düsseldorf; Johannese Honterus, the Romanian humanist scholar whose press at Braşov produced a songbook in 1548; and the Hungarian György Hoffgreff, who printed a songbook in 1552 at Kolozsvár (now Cluj-Napoca, Romania).

The commercial centres, in the mainstream of activity, could be expected to produce editions of a musical repertory that was stylish and distinguished but also essentially conservative. The character of the music produced in each centre was distinctive, but activity elsewhere varied much more widely in character and in quality, reflecting decisions that typically were either less informed or made in the light of local demands and circumstances. Because of religious conflict and the political decentralization of the country, German publishing was particularly diversified in appearance and scattered geographically. Nuremberg was the principal exception, producing attractive editions of the music of well-known composers and never completely losing its cosmopolitan outlook. But music was also issued by over a thousand different music printers in nearly 200 other German cities in the 16th and 17th centuries. Lutheran music books, at first using woodcuts, bear the imprints of more than a dozen different cities, most of them producing only a single title or two before 1540. Hans Hergot in Nuremberg was the first to print music to Luther's mass (1526), while his widow Kunegunde also printed pamphlets including music, as did her second husband, Georg Wachter. Wittenberg became the earliest important centre: Georg Rhau, who had printed some musical treatises as early as 1517, obtained a fount of music type from Formschneider in the 1530s and produced several dozen of the most important early Lutheran service books (1538–65). His successors included such men as Johann and Andreas Eichhorn in Frankfurt an der Oder (1556–1615), Andreas Hantzsch in Mühlhausen (1566–99), Johann Schwertel (1565–80) and Matthäus Welack in Wittenberg, Georg Baumann in Erfurt

(1557–97) and in Breslau (1590–1618), and Gimel Bergen in Dresden (1570–97, his heirs to 1687). In south Germany the major publishers included the shop of Adam Berg in Munich (1564–1629), whose many Lassus editions include the folio *Patrocinium musices* (1573–87), one of the most sumptuous musical editions ever produced; later collections of Lassus were issued by Nikolaus Henricus. In Frankfurt, Sigmund Feyerabend produced several major collections (1570–85), while to the east interesting editions were also produced, in Latin or the vernacular. These included sacred anthologies from Kraków from 1550 on, printed at first by Florian Ungler using woodcut music, later by Maciej Wirzbięta and the lineage of Szarfenberg, in whose editions movable type came to be intermixed; several elusive editions of the hymns of the Bohemian Brethren, in which the recurring music typefaces identify a fount that moved with the itinerant printers; and over a dozen collections issued by Jiří Černý (Nigrini) in Prague (1579–1604), either composed or at least encouraged by Jacob Handl.

In Germany around 1600 courtly patronage supported extensive music publishing activity by the Saxon printers Justus Hauck (1604–18) and Johann Forkel (1624–35, his successors to 1713) in Coburg, Johann Weidner in Jena (1605–29) and Nikolaus Stein in Frankfurt (1602–21, working mostly through the printer Wolfgang Richter); to the north by the Fürstliche Druckerei in Wolfenbüttel (1607–14) and by Philipp Van Ohr (1597–1609) and Heinrich Carstens (1609–25) in Hamburg; and to the south in Augsburg, Valentin Schönig (1591–1635) and Johannes Praetorius (1600–35). A great many 'occasional' works (*Gelegenheitskompositionen*), for events such as weddings, baptisms and funerals, appeared throughout the 17th century. The leading centre of such publishing in the 1620s was Leipzig, where Johann Lanckisch (1619–56) and Johann Gluck (1618–24) issued many of the works of Schein, among others. Jacob Reberlein in Hamburg (1632–60, his heirs to 1690) was the major printer of the 1630s. By far the most prolific centres for the publishing of occasional music, however, were those on the Baltic Sea, in Lübeck, Rostock, Greifswald, Stettin (Szczecin), Danzig (Gdańsk) and, above all, Königsberg (Kaliningrad), which included among its printers Georg Osterberger (1577–1612), Lorenz Segebade (1623–42), Pasche Mense (1643–51) and Johann and Friedrich Reusner (1639–93), who issued Heinrich Albert's song collections. Publishers of Lutheran hymnbooks included Georg Runge in Berlin (1616–39, his heirs to 1685), who issued many editions of Johannes Crüger's *Praxis pietatis melica*, Balthasar Wust in Frankfurt (1656–1702), and the Endter family in Nuremberg (1617–99). Major printers of the Catholic south included Georg Widmanstetter in Graz (1587–1614), Matthäus and later Tobias Nenninger in Passau (1602–19), succeeded by the shop of Georg Höller later in the century), Adam Meltzer in Dillingen (1603–10), Michael Wagner in Innsbruck (1639–68), Andreas Erfurt in Augsburg (1655–72), Rudolph Dreher in Kempten (1660–81), Johann Kaspar Bencard in Frankfurt and later Augsburg (1670–1723), and the Salzburg firm of Mayer, whose occasional output extends from the 1670s to past 1800. Frankfurt and Cologne were among the major centres producing Catholic service books. Among the earliest music distributors were Georg Willer and Caspar Flurschütz, both active in Augsburg early in the century, and responsible for particularly interesting early dealers' catalogues.

German music publishing declined during and after the Thirty Years War; but the disappearance of a number of large firms around 1600, particularly in Nuremberg, suggests that the war hastened rather than caused the decline. Decentralized as they were, German music publishers were also book publishers, to a greater extent than those of Italy or France: one also finds, particularly after 1630, imprints which name two men – a printer and a publisher – occasionally in different cities. From Germany, Lutheran music publishing spread to the east and north, to Prussia and Poland with Georg Rhetus in Danzig and Thorn (Torun; 1634–43, his heirs to 1664) and Andreas Hünefeld in Danzig (1608–47); to Copenhagen in 1537, where the major press was that of Henrick Waldkirch (1602–40); and to Stockholm in 1586 and Iceland in 1594. The Viennese firm of Cosmerovius (1636–1715) produced sumptuous librettos for court productions, often with engraved illustrations.

Calvinist psalm books were also printed in great quantities. Those before 1560 are modelled largely on Lutheran service books. In 1560, at Calvin's request, Antoine Vincent of Lyons arranged for various printers to issue 20,000 psalm books for service use. In recognition of the noteworthy tradition of punchcutting in France and Flanders at the time, a distinctive appearance came to identify both the psalm books themselves and a lineage of later books. Physically the latter are neat and well proportioned and printed from very small type. Examples include the lute books of Simon Gorlier and the partbooks of Godefroy Beringen, both in Lyons in the 1550s, along with the diminutive sets of Simon Du Bosc and Guillaume Guéroult in Geneva. Among the major punchcutters of the day whose music faces led to brief careers as music printers were Michel Du Boys, who issued several early books of Philibert Jambe de Fer; Jean Le Royer, whose work was issued under the name of the Lyons bookseller Charles Pesnot; Jean II de Laon, responsible for the 1582 edition of L'Estocart; Robert Granjon, famous for his typefaces even today, who issued music in various locations from Flanders to Rome; and Pierre Haultin in La Rochelle, whose aesthetic is reflected in the English madrigal partbook tradition begun by Thomas Vautrollier. Another printer whose repertory and printing style suggest a Calvinist character and who thus presumably enjoyed an exemption from the Ballard monopoly, was Jacques Mongeant, whose several anthologies date from the decades around 1600. The rich typographical resources of this tradition no doubt facilitated and inspired the Calvinist predilection for solfège music typefaces, manifest most notably in the 1560 psalm book of Pierre Davantes.

Editions of Calvinist psalms appeared in great profusion. Modest in scale and in time distinctly crabbed in appearance, they were at first largely modelled on Lutheran service books. Several hundred editions of the Marot and Bèze versions, many with music, were issued over the next two centuries, at first from Paris, Lyons (Jean de Tournes was the notable printer of them), Geneva and elsewhere, most frequently around 1650 in Charenton, near Paris. Geneva also produced a number of Italian psalm books for use by Piedmontese Calvinist congregations. Dutch psalm books, mostly in the Dathenius versions, were issued in the 17th century by Plantin in Antwerp and Gislain Manilius in Ghent, among others, usually in small format and with painfully tiny and ill-printed notation. The leading German printer of psalm books was Christoph Rab at Herborn in Nassau, who around 1600 brought out not only Lobwasser's German versions but also George Buchanan's Latin paraphrases and at least one Hungarian psalm book. In England, the psalms of Sternhold and Hopkins, which had first been printed in Geneva, went through many editions, based on Dutch models. While William Seres issued the forerunners of these in 1553, it was John Day – apparently exiled to Emden during the reign of Queen Mary but later returning to London – who in 1559 received a royal patent to print those psalm books that included music (see fig.32). He printed nearly 40 editions of Sternhold and Hopkins before his death in 1584; his son Richard inherited the patent and worked with several London printers in issuing nearly 50 more. In 1603 the Company of Stationers bought up the Day patent and used it to provide work for their printers. Between 1603 and 1650 several hundred more editions of the psalm book were printed with musical notation. John Playford later attempted to revitalize the music of the psalm book. In Scotland the publication of psalm books culminated in the edition printed by Andro Hart in Edinburgh in 1635.

Venice may have been the dominant centre of Italian music publishing before 1600, but it was not the only one. In Ferrara in the late 1530s a partnership of Johannes de Buglhat, Henrico Campis and Antonio Hucher issued several admirable sets of partbooks. In Rome the brothers Dorico used Antico's woodblock music as early as 1524 and later issued several dozen music books of their own (1533–72); the shops of Antonio Blado (1551–80) and Antonio Barré (1555–64) printed editions that were distinguished both musically and visually, while Alessandro Gardano (from the Venetian publishing family) issued several dozen editions in the 1580s. Some interesting madrigal partbooks came from Vincenzo Sabbio in Brescia (1579–88) and Vittorio Baldini in Ferrara (1582–1614), while Francesco Franceschi in Venice is named in the imprints of Zarlino's treatises (1562–99). Music printing in Bologna began with a 1584 partbook from the shop of Giovanni Rossi, whose heirs issued several collections by Banchieri in the 1610s.

In Florence the Marescotti family (1580–1611) produced epoch-making editions of Galilei, Caccini and Peri; their successors included Zanobi di Francesco Pignoni (1607–41) and Pietro Cecconcelli (1618–30). In Milan the Tradate family were succeeded by the prolific lineage begun by the heirs of Simone Tini, eventually managed by Filippo Lomazzo (1583–1628). Later Milanese publishers included Giorgio Rolla (1610–51) and the families Camagno (c1650–86) and Vigoni

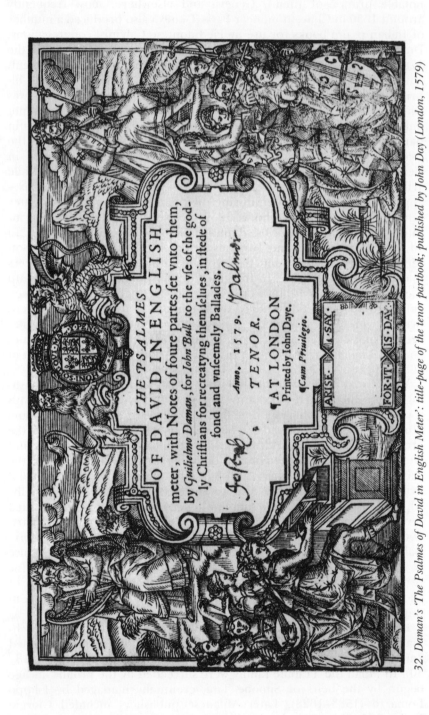

32. Daman's 'The Psalmes of David in English Meter': title-page of the tenor partbook; published by John Day (London, 1579)

(1680–*c*1750). This period also saw typographic adaptations of alphabetic notational systems, by Giovanni Ambrosio Colonna in Milan for guitar music and by Nicolò Tebaldini in Bologna. Music also appeared occasionally from Perugia, mostly from Pietroiacomo Petrucci (1577–1603); from Palermo, largely from the press of Giovanni Battista Maringo (1603–35); and from Naples, at first from Constantino Vitale (*fl* 1603–23) and Gargano & Nucci (1609–21), later from Giovanni Giacomo Carlino (1597–1616), whom Gesualdo engaged to print his own madrigal partbooks; and from Vicenza, where Angelo Salvadori issued several items in the 1620s. To sum up: around 1600 Venice was still the most prolific centre; Milan came second, albeit remotely; and printing took place in about a dozen other cities. As Venice waned, Rome became a centre for editions of the elaborate music of the Counter-Reformation; among the major publishers were Nicolo Mutii (1595–1602), Bartolomeo Zannetti (1602–21), Luca Antonio Soldi (1604–35), Giovanni Battista Robletti (1609–50), Andrea and Giacamo Fei (1615–85), Antonio Poggioli (1620–68), the Mascardi family (*c*1630–after 1719), Paolo Masotti (1621–37), Lodovico Grignani (*c*1630–50), Giovanni Battista Caifabri (1657–95), and Giovanni Angelo Mutii (1670–89). After 1650 Bologna slowly supplanted Rome as a printing centre (particularly for instrumental music), as Rome had supplanted Venice. The composer Maurizio Cazzati was particularly assiduous in seeing that his works were published; the printers of them included Vittorio Benacci (1659), Alessandro Pisarri (1660–62), the heirs of Evangelista Dozza (1663–4) and Gioseffo Micheletti (1687, also works by other composers in the surrounding decade). Giacomo Monti was active from 1636, and his successors issued large amounts of music between 1668 and 1709, often in partnership with the publisher Marino Silvani (1665–1727). Venice re-entered the scene with Giuseppe Sala (1676–1715), also mainly a publisher of instrumental music, and the Bortoli family, active mostly in the decade after 1700.

English secular music publishing began with Thomas Vautrollier, who in 1570 printed a Lassus anthology – apparently it was commercially unsuccessful. As we saw above, five years later Tallis and Byrd received a royal patent, covering music printing and music paper. Their own *Cantiones sacrae* (*RISM* 1575[3]), also printed by Vautrollier, sold badly too. A hiatus of 12 years followed; by 1585 Tallis was dead, and Vautrollier's music type had been acquired by the printer Thomas East. Between 1588 and 1596 East printed for Byrd well over a dozen important partbook collections, mostly of madrigals. Byrd's patent expired in 1596, and Peter Short then began printing music (as well as Thomas Morley's *Plaine and Easie Introduction to Practicall Musicke* in 1595); William Barley also sponsored music books. In 1598 Morley became the successor to Tallis and Byrd, by obtaining another royal patent (although psalm books were excluded). Barley became his associate, and East and Short were forbidden to print music. But in 1599 Morley failed in an attempt to take over part of Richard Day's psalm book patent, and he died in 1602. This allowed East and Short to resume their music printing, and in 1607 John Windet entered the field as a printer, as did the publisher

Thomas Adams as a claimant to the Barley patent. Their various successors were Humfrey Lownes (1604–13), Thomas Snodham (1609–24), William Stansby (1609–38) and Edward Allde (1610–15), all of whom printed madrigal partbooks. Folio books including lute tablature appeared alongside madrigal partbooks from 1597 but by 1610 the momentum to sustain an English music publishing industry was fading, and by 1620 new music was rarely published in England.

In northern and western Europe in the 17th century there arose a new kind of 'gentleman's musical edition', secular in its repertory, quiet, tasteful, often highly allusive in its texts in the manner of the emblem books of the day, and correspondingly neat and skilful in its printing. French *airs de cour*, issued by the Ballards in annual numbered series, were profitable enough to dominate the firm's production throughout the century; they also issued much French dramatic music, beginning with Cambert's *Pomone* (1671), continuing with more than a dozen tall folio scores of Lully operas (1679–88), and ending with another dozen by other composers (1688–94), mostly in large oblong quarto. In both of these genres one detects an aristocratic aura, in contrast to the mercantile character of their counterparts in other countries. German illustrated poetical-musical anthologies, for instance, challenge rather than flatter the reader to delight in them. Many of these song-books, involving the poet Johann Rist and his circle of friends in the Elbschwanenorden, were issued after 1650 by the Stern family of Lüneburg. Much the same nationalistic spirit informs Adriaen Valerius's famous Dutch folksong collection, the *Neder-landtsche gedenck-clanck*, published in Haarlem in 1626 (*RISM* 1626[14]), as well as the later anthologies of Hendrik Aertssens in Antwerp, and the Czech songs issued by Jiri Labaun in Prague at the end of the century. Distinctly Italianate gentlemanly tastes, on the other hand, are reflected in the music issued around 1600 by Phalèse in Antwerp and by Jan Bogard in Douai, in the 1640s by Paulus Matthysz in Amsterdam and in the 1650s by Jan van Geertsom in Rotterdam.

English music printing resumed with the elder John Playford (1650–84), who sensed the distinctive spirit of England's middle-class audience. He deserves to be recognized as the first great promoter among music publishers; and, judging from the quantity of his output and the extent to which many of the volumes seemed to be directed at a new musical market, he was one of the most successful. Printed at first by Thomas Harper and later by William Godbid, Playford's output ranged widely over song anthologies, psalm books, instrumental works and instruc-tional books (see fig.33). It served to establish England's musical identity in the period culminating in the music of Henry Purcell, and enhanced the country's musical literacy in the generation before the advent of the popular sheet-music edition just after 1700. Among Playford's imitators were John Carr and his son Richard in London, sometimes in partner-ship with Playford; John Forbes in Aberdeen (1662–1706), whose songbooks suggest an instructional market; and little-known Robert Thornton in Dublin (*fl* 1687–1701). On Playford's death his son Henry continued his work, but with notably less success. Whereas John

33. Title-page of 'The English Dancing Master', printed by Thomas Harper and published by John Playford in 1651

Playford's books had few competitors, Henry's shared the market with those of John Heptinstall (1686–1700) and William Pearson (1699–1735), both of whom used 'new round-note' music type in creating editions more legible and stylish than Playford's. Minor printers, mostly anonymous, issued broadside ballads with musical notation, many of them political in their messages, particularly during the days of the Popish Plots and conflicts over the succession during the final years of the century. The division of labour between printing and distribution is further reflected in the proliferation of music booksellers; John Hudgebut and in his later years Henry Playford were among the distributors, Edward Jones and Thomas Moore among the printers.

Music printing in the New World dates from the 1540s, when several plainchant books were issued in Mexico by Juan Pablos, followed by several other immigrant printers from Spain. In 1631 Juan Perez Bocanegra printed a ritual in Lima, in which polyphony appears in woodcuts on two pages, set to a vernacular text. The earliest surviving book printed in the English-speaking New World, the Bay Psalm Book, was issued in 1640 by Stephen Day at Cambridge in the Massachusetts Bay Colony. Containing no musical notation, it names the tunes to which the texts were to be sung, and the many editions that appeared during the next few decades showed a strong English influence in both content and method of production. Musical notation appeared for the first time only in the ninth edition ('printed by B. Green and J. Allen for Michael Perry' in Boston in 1698); crude woodcuts were used to produce the eight-page tune supplement and were re-used in several later editions.

Isolated single engravings notwithstanding (among them the superb picture motets executed by Johan Sadelar in the 1580s), the credit for being the first publisher to use engraving successfully belongs to Simone Verovio, who issued about 20 editions in Rome between 1586 and 1608. Although some were reprinted, he seems not to have recognized the powerful advantages of the process. Before the 18th century, music engraving was largely a luxury; it was useful because it conveyed better than letterpress printing the peculiarities of manuscript music notation, but it lacked the potential for the wide market of which merchants and earlier patrons assumed typeset music was capable. Music was printed from engraved plates before 1700 in several parts of Europe, almost all of it of considerable visual and musical distinction. Verovio's successor in Rome was Nicolò Borboni, who issued several lavish collections (1615–41). In Holland, the sumptuous Dutch *Bildmotetten* of c1580 were followed in the 1610s by several delightful books by Nicolas Vallet called *Le secret des muses*. The venerable *Parthenia* and parts of *Parthenia In-violata*, along with other collections, by Orlando Gibbons and Angelo Notari, were also engraved during this decade by William Hole in London. Occasional functional productions from around the mid-century (like William Slatyer's polyglot psalm book of 1652 and John Playford's edition of *Musick's Hand-Maide* of 1663) were followed by such sumptuous productions as the volumes of songs by Henry Bowman (1677) and Pietro Reggio (1680). In Germany, though broadside music engravings from the Augsburg shop of Lucas Kilian date from the early

17th century, extensive engraved editions, devoted mostly to instrumental music, do not appear to predate Sebastian Anton Scherer's *Tabulaturam* (Ulm, 1664). In France engraving seems to have been viewed at first as an alternative to the typography controlled by the Ballard patent. Most of the engraved music is instrumental; it includes collections by Lambert (1660–61), the Gaultiers (*c*1670), Chambonnières (1670), Corbetta (1671), Lebègue (?1678), Marais (1686–92), Raison (1688), D'Anglebert (1689), Nivers (1689) and Boyvin (1689–90). Hiérosme Bonneüil is named among the engravers. The hiatus during the 1690s reflects Ballard's successful injunction against the engraver Henri de Baussen and his publisher Henry Foucault. Resumption of engraving just before 1700, in editions that superseded the pretentious typeset Ballard editions of Lully operas of the previous decades, and in other works by Foucault and Pierre Ribou (1704–20) suggests that the commercial advantages of the process were now generally recognized.

In summary, the history of music publishing before 1700 is one of early brilliance and extended decline. The peak was reached before 1580, in Venice, Nuremberg, Paris and Antwerp. The decline was apparent by 1600 and is reflected in a diminished output, and in printing that was less spacious, less skilful and less original. Throughout the 17th century not only the same faces but, judging from the worn images, the same type was used, well past readability. The quality of the printing should be seen as a reflection of social conditions, which themselves reflect the changing interrelationships between composer, performer, patron and publisher as well as printer. Patronage was no doubt declining as a means of subsidizing music; thus, while lavish performances of new compositions continued to take place, publication of the scores was less frequently considered necessary (Lully's were the conspicuous exception).

The demise of music publishing over the course of the 17th century raises the question why printed scores might have been deemed necessary and desirable in the first place – especially in view of the apparently modest degree of musical literacy at the time. The belief that performers (chapel singers especially) were taught by rote, and the absence of signs of use on most extant copies (a counter-argument as much as a point in its own right) further support the speculation that early musical editions were printed less with the intention of circulating a composer's repertory, than as a demonstration of a patron's munificence and taste. Some works were clearly issued on the basis of guaranteed distribution of copies – hymnals, psalters and other service books for use by particular congregations, dioceses or churches, for instance, as well as *Gelegenheitskompositionen* – in order to obviate much of the need for formal publishing circumstances at all. Patronage, involving art music and made evident through a dedicatory text following the title-page, is presumably reflected in the great majority of other publications, although we still know little about the precise relationship between patron and musician (for instance as reflected in performance or other forms of subsistence rather than in subventions for publication)

ROLAND,
TRAGEDIE
MISE
EN MUSIQUE,

Par Monsieur de Lully, Escuyer, Conseiller
Secretaire du Roy, Maison, Couronne de
France & de ses Finances, & Sur-Intendant
de la Musique de Sa Majesté.

A PARIS,
Par CHRISTOPHE BALLARD, seul Imprimeur du Roy pour la Musique,
ruë Saint Jean de Beauvais, au Mont-Parnasse.
ET SE VEND
A la Porte de l'Academie Royale de Musique, ruë Saint Honoré.

M. DC. LXXXV.
AVEC PRIVILEGE DE SA MAJESTE'.

34. *Title-page of the tragédie lyrique 'Roland' (1685)*

or about the precise forms of intervention by the music publisher. Venture publishing, as generally understood today, may thus be indisputably evident only in reprints, presumably prepared at the publisher's own expense and thus issued on the basis of his calculated speculation that copies could be sold. It is noteworthy, moreover, that the production of reprints follows a curve that, if anything, reinforces the production curve of music publishing in general: few reprints at first, many just before 1600 (and most of these from the four commercial centres), a rapid decline in production soon after 1600, and very few for the rest of the century. Petrucci and his immediate followers had shown that music could be printed and published; it remained for the publishers of the 18th century to learn how this could be done most advantageously.

CHAPTER VIII

The Age of Engraving, 1700–1860

Music publishing during the next period – from the start of the careers of Bach and Handel to the height of the careers of Verdi, Wagner and Brahms – begins with the extensive commercial use of engraving and continues up to the first extensive use of offset lithography. It is a story of four cities: London from around 1700; Paris from between 1740 and 1760; Vienna from just before 1780; and Leipzig from around 1800. The activity in each city continued after the next rose to prominence; and the quantity of published music became cumulatively greater, as did the competition between publishers and the stimulation of general public interest in music.

In spite of the development of engraving, letterpress printing and manuscript copying continued to be used extensively throughout the 18th century. As late as the 1730s, Lelio Della Volpe in Bologna and Francesco Moücke in Florence were still issuing oblong anthologies of Italian cantatas badly printed from movable type. German publishers, chief among them J. J. Lotter in Augsburg, issued a variety of musical editions, notably treatises but also a few instrumental collections and songbooks, using crude but complicated movable type, most of which had been cut around 1680 for use in Nuremberg. In Vienna, Van Ghelen and, later, Trattner issued handsome typographic music books after 1750. Throughout the 18th century and into the 19th, in France, Spain and Italy, typeset liturgical books and treatises on plainchant were still printed from movable type, as were the many Dutch and Genevan psalm books and German and Scandinavian hymnbooks. In certain circumstances, letterpress printing remained the most desirable method: when the musical notation was simple (or, in some cases, complicated but not requiring speed in performance); when fixed and generally large press runs were involved; and when most of the volume consisted of text, as in treatises. After 1700 the publishing of typeset music thus came to be associated largely with pedagogic and amateur music and, to a degree, with the provincial more than with the cosmopolitan press. Conservative linear music type continued to be provided, notably by such firms as Gando in Paris and Caslon in London. Music typography was revived around 1750 through refinements introduced by men working in four countries; of these, however, Fournier in France and Enschedé (along with Rosart) in Holland produced little as publishers, while the English editions of Fougt and his successor, Robert Falkener, were mostly imitations of those of Leipzig engravers. The impact of Breitkopf throughout Germany and central Europe was much greater,

35. *Title-page and opening of the first violin part of Vanhal's 'Six Simphonies' op.7 no.2 (Berlin and Amsterdam, Hummel, c1770)*

since it was the only one of this group to survive into the next century and to involve a publishing programme built around the use of other graphic processes besides.

The competition between the various processes for disseminating musical documents involved not only letterpress and intaglio printing but also the manuscript-copying trade. One of the chief virtues of music 'publishing' in manuscript form, such as was used for 18th-century Italian opera, was that the use of manuscript offered the opera house or the composer a measure of control over the text unavailable when copies were printed and widely distributed. Before any forms of copyright were established, such a system of limited distribution seemed highly desirable. Furthermore, an opera house considering performance of a particular work that needed adjustments to suit local conditions could alter a neatly assembled typeset edition only with some difficulty; and because of the needs of singers and others involved in opera production, changes were always being called for. Instrumental music also came to appear often in manuscript rather than in typeset form, but for notational reasons. Type was harder to read than handwriting – short note values were particularly troublesome, since the beams were seldom continuous, and chords were impossible without breaking individual sorts of type. Such problems did not exist with manuscript or engraving. By 1700 most of the current musical repertory had moved outside the world of music publishing as it involved letterpress printing. Italian music, if it was printed at all, was printed abroad, usually in Amsterdam or London. J. S. Bach saw little of his music printed, almost all of it instrumental, with utilitarian titles such as 'Übung', while aspiring German publishers themselves, such as Johann Wilhelm Rönnagel, met with little success. In contrast, a study of the documents of the two dominant musical styles that were widespread throughout Europe in the 18th century – Neapolitan opera at the beginning and Viennese Classicism at the end – shows that manuscripts served the purposes of publication (in its widest functional sense) very effectively.

Extensive music publishing from engraved plates began in London and Amsterdam. Estienne Roger set up his shop in Amsterdam about 1690 and was soon engraving small oblong quarto piracies of Bolognese instrumental music. By 1700 his editions were large oblong folios, well executed with hand-drawn music on copper plates. His emphasis on Italian music suggests an international distribution of copies through northern and western Europe. After Roger's death in 1722, his widow and his son-in-law, Michel-Charles Le Cène, continued to publish until 1743. Dutch music publishing declined thereafter, although there were some important firms, among them Amédée Le Chevalier (1689–1702), Gerhard Fredrik Witvogel (1731–44), Joseph Schmitt (c1772–1791) and, especially, the family of Hummel (Amsterdam, 1754–1822; The Hague, 1755–c1801; also in Berlin after 1744; see fig.35). Nicolaas Barth (1775–1805) was succeeded by Lodewijk Plattner (1805–43) in Rotterdam, while the leading Belgian publisher from later in the century was Benoit Andrez in Liège.

London music publishers, inspired by the success of John Playford, experimented with new ways of printing and distributing music. While popular music was favoured by letterpress printers and their associates in London, engravers were attracted to Italianate instrumental music. Thomas Cross, who had engraved Purcell's *Sonnata's* in 1683, also prepared many single songsheets, undated but probably almost all from the last decade of the century; he later did the printing for the publisher Daniel Wright. He apparently used hard copper plates on which the signs were drawn by hand; in contrast the elder John Walsh, who began publishing in 1696, later in partnership with Joseph Hare, seems to have used soft plates of pewter or lead, on which the signs were impressed with punches. Although their catalogues consisted at first of songsheets (sometimes collected into periodical series) and works of other publishers which he sold at his shop, Walsh soon began to issue instrumental music, much of it taken from continental sources. His speciality, however, was the anthology of 'Favourite Songs' from the London stage; in time he became the principal publisher of Handel's music. By 1736, when the elder Walsh died, London music publishing was well established.

Few competitors challenged Walsh during his lifetime. John Young was active just after 1700, while John Cluer, mostly in the 1720s, issued some handsome scores of Handel operas, neatly engraved by hand rather than punched, and in small format; so did the younger Richard Meares and, somewhat later, Benjamin Cooke. English letterpress printers, such as John Watts, also issued early ballad-opera librettos and song anthologies that included crude woodcuts of the tunes. There also appeared a multitude of songsheets naming no printer or publisher, which must have been sold casually at music shops, much like the earlier broadside ballads. George Bickham, famed for his engraved drawings and writing book, also engraved music, drawn free-hand and decorated with delicate illustrations; his style served as a model for Benjamin Cole. The French engraver Fortier also did striking work on several books, perhaps most notably the superb 1738/9 edition of Domenico Scarlatti's *Essercizi*. Outside London, James Oswald, active in Edinburgh in the 1730s, later published Scottish music out of London, as William Thomson had done in the 1720s, while in Dublin John Neale was active in the 1730s, William Manwaring in the 1740s, and Samuel Lee from 1752.

Walsh's son John maintained the firm for another 30 years after his father's death. Other publishers came into prominence, notably John Simpson (1730s and 40s); John Johnson (c1740–1762, his widow to 1777); the Thompson family, including variously Ann, Peter, Charles, Samuel and Henry (c1750–1805); Robert Bremner (c1760–1789); Peter Welcker and his heirs (1762–85); William Forster, the violin-maker, with his son (c1762–1821); William Randall, the heir to Walsh (1766–83, in turn succeeded by Wright & Wilkinson, and Wright alone to 1801); William Napier (c1772–1791), Robert Wornum and his heirs (c1772–1900, also a piano maker); John Preston (c1774–1789), whose son Thomas ran the firm for the next 36 years; James Harrison (1779–1803); Joseph Dale and his heirs (1783–1837); John Longman (beginning *c*1767) with various partners, notably Francis Broderip (1776–98), important as the first music publisher to deposit his new publications at Stationers Hall for copyright purposes, and probably the most prolific of all London music publishers in the 1790s; Robert Birchall (1780–1819), whose catalogue is distinguished by music from the Continent, including early Beethoven editions of notable textual authenticity; and John Bland (*c*1776–1795), famous as one of the first publishers to announce his new editions through thematic catalogues. The editions of these publishers consisted of instrumental music in imitation of the editions which were appearing at this time from Paris and Amsterdam (including, for example, series of 'Periodical Ouvertures') and songs from English comic operas and from the pleasure gardens. Prominent music engravers whose names are occasionally inscribed in the editions include Henry Roberts (*c*1737–1765) and John Phillips (*c*1740–1775).

English music publishing continued to flourish during the 19th century as firms sprang up, dissolved, merged and separated, and sold their titles, plates and stocks. Thompson was succeeded by Robert Purday (with S. J. Button, 1806–8, thereafter as Button & Whitaker), Preston by Coventry & Hollier (1833–49). George Goulding (1786–98) merged with Thomas d'Almaine, who after further partnerships eventually managed the firm alone (1834–67), while Lewis Lavenu (1796–1844) shared several partners before his firm passed to Addison & Hodson. The flautist Tebaldo Monzani worked alone (1787–1800), then in partnership with Giambattista Cimador and Henry Hill, the latter eventually managed the firm alone (1829–45). Several workmen began firms early in the century that are still active, notably Samuel Chappell (1811–), Vincent Novello (1811–), Thomas Boosey (working in music after *c*1816) and Johann Baptist Cramer (alone after 1824). The last of these was one of several London firms established by a virtuoso pianist, the most important earlier one being that of Muzio Clementi; the Corri family and J. L. Dussek are among the other notable composer-publishers. Other firms included Metzler (1812–1931), and Keith, Prowse & Co. (1815–). By the 1840s special emphases were beginning to emerge: George Henry Davidson (1833–81) concentrated on cheap editions of popular music, as Novello did with serious music; Robert Cocks (1823–1904) maintained a large circulating library; Leader & Cock (1842–7) issued art songs of Sterndale Bennett; while Joseph Williams (1843–1961, based on his mother's firm, founded 1808) emphasized light opera. John Distin (1845–74) specialized in brass music, as did Boosey, which eventually acquired the firm. Christian Rudolph Wessel (in business with William Stodart in 1823, alone 1838–60, succeeded by Edwin Ashdown) specialized in foreign music and issued important Chopin editions, while Ewer (1823–67, merged to become Novello & Ewer to 1898) specialized in Mendelssohn. Augener (1853–), initially also an importer, at first issued only lithographed editions.

British music publishing was not confined to London. Samuel and later Philip Knapton worked in York (*c*1796–1829), while the elusive firm of Wheatstone was active around 1815 in Bath. Country psalmody printers flourished particularly in the 1740s, among them the itinerant Michael Beesly in the Berkshire-Oxfordshire area, and Michael Broome in Birmingham. Smollet Holden, specialist in military music, issued several collections in Dublin shortly after 1800. The Dublin haberdashery shop of Benjamin Rhames and his heirs (1756–1810) and later the family of Hime (before 1790–*c*1835), active in Liverpool, Dublin and Manchester, specialized in songsheets, many of them copied from London editions. William Power in Dublin, with his brother James in London, was responsible for two of the most famous editions of folk music, the *Irish Melodies* (1807–34) and *National Melodies* (1818–28) of Thomas Moore. Equally important were the editions of national songs by George Thomson in Edinburgh (1793–1845), to which Pleyel, Haydn, Beethoven, Weber and Hummel contributed. The Edinburgh firms of Bremner and Corri – branches of London firms bearing these names – often published their own music. Other Edinburgh publications bear the imprints of the cellist J. G. C. Schetky (mostly 1780s and 90s), Muir & Wood (1798–1818, in time succeeded by Penson, Robertson & Co., *c*1807–37) and Purdie (*c*1809–37). James Johnson (1772–1811) served as the engraver for most of these editions, although he also published several major works. The firm of Paterson (*c*1819–1964) eventually expanded from Edinburgh to several other Scottish towns as well as to London (where the name continues). Glasgow's music publishers began with James Aird, working around 1780, and culminated with J. Muir Wood (1848–99, earlier a branch of an Edinburgh shop begun in 1798 by John Muir and Andrew Wood). Irish music publishers included Dennis Connor, who issued harp music in the late 18th century, and Anthony Bunting, who was active around 1820.

British music publishing never forgot its origins in the popular songsheet. The annual output of several hundred such editions a year, a level established soon after 1700, appears to have persisted throughout the 18th century and into the 19th. Gradually the single sheet, printed on one side, was expanded into two sheets, printed on inside pages. A cover was often added; later, especially with the advent of lithography, a picture was often included. Most publishers were happy to include in their catalogues both songsheets and other popular forms, as well as more ambitious forms such as sonatas and symphonies. Through agreements for simultaneous publication between British publishers and continental publishers or composers, a kind of international copyright was effected. British music publishers remained largely committed to the process of engraving, and thus they tended to maintain their identity (apart from the publishers of religious service books and song anthologies issued in small format and in large press runs with movable type). Three 19th-century uses of movable music type by music publishers, however, deserve mention. Editions using solfège notation promoted by such firms as Curwen (founded 1863) were printed with type: they played a large part in the spread of the English choral tradition. William Clowes in London, later in Beccles, also used type for such popular publications as Charles Knight's *Musical Library* (1834–7). Novello used type for its 'cheap music' programme begun in 1847, through which major vocal works were widely circulated for many years.

In 18th-century France the Ballard family continued to hold its royal monopoly for music printing up to the Revolution. But the output of its press was neither particularly large nor central to Paris music, consisting mainly of popular songs and treatises. Music publishers were again established in Paris, based on a court decision that engravings fell outside the Ballard privilege, in effect thereby destroying its monopoly. Extensive activity did not flourish until the second third of the century, when some composers arranged for their music to be issued by Charles-Nicolas Le Clerc (1736–74), a violinist who served as publisher, and distributed by François Boivin (1721–53, whose wife was of the Ballard family). Typically,. these editions are small oblong folios, devoted to anthologies of dances, *airs* and cantatas and to current dramatic music.

The 'classical' period of Parisian music publishing, which began well before 1750, reached its peak in the 1770s and 80s. The main early operatic publisher was La Chevardière (1758–84); other publishers, such as Le Menu (1740s–1790), Marie-Anne Castagneri (1748–87), Jean-Baptiste Venier (1755–*c*1784), the Bureau d'Abonnement Musical (1765–*c*1783), Antoine Bailleux (1760s–1798) and Georges, and later Jacques-George, Cousineau (1760s–1822, the family later important as harp makers and harpists), specialized in instrumental music. François-Joseph Heina (1773–*c*1785) specialized in chamber music by his fellow Czechs. Whether issued serially, in annual cumulations, or as 'periodical' symphonies or overtures, editions from this period are mostly in large folio format, usually upright for operas but oblong for instrumental music. Many of the leading engravers of the period were women, among them Mme Leclair (wife of the composer) and Mlle Vendôme. This was the time when publishers' catalogues were commonly added to their editions – expandable lists engraved on separate plates which called attention to other available titles.

Parisian classical editions proved successful enough to be widely imitated in London and Amsterdam and eventually in Germany. In Lyons, Guéra (*c*1776–88) and Castaud were active; through Antoine Huberty, an engraver in Paris in the 1760s, French music publishing practices were transplanted to Vienna when he moved there about 1770. In Paris, the classical style persisted until the Revolution, after which three changes gradually took place: single songsheets began to be issued more frequently; the slender and well-spaced pre-Revolution opera score, with few instruments and on large staves, was replaced by a full score, thicker and with more parts exactly specified; and the method book, usually for specific instruments but also for singing and solfège, gained importance while the editions of chamber music parts slowly declined. Among the firms that particularly flourished in the decades after the Revolution were Jean-Georges Sieber (*c*1770–1822), Naderman (1770s–*c*1835), Lemoine (from 1772), Leduc (Pierre and, later, Auguste, 1775–1837), Imbault (*c*1782–1812), Pleyel (1795–1834) and the Gaveaux (1795–1829). This period also saw the establishment of two firms named Magasin de Musique, the first (1794–1825) resulting from government decree and later associated with the Conservatoire, the second (1802–11) based on a partnership between six composers.

Soon after 1750 the Breitkopf shop in Leipzig began to show an interest in music. His importance in music typography apart, Johann Gottlob Immanuel Breitkopf deserves mention for his music publishing strategy. His remarkable plan involved the three major methods of the day for committing music to paper: manuscript copying, engraving and letterpress printing. He chose to do battle with the engravers, now well established in London and Paris and beginning to appear in Amsterdam and various German cities, by using the other two graphic processes instead. His typeset music had the disadvantages and advantages of typeset books: the size of the edition needed to be determined in advance before copies were sold, and internal changes were difficult; but presswork was likely to be much cheaper once the type was set, and thus Breitkopf could print editions in large numbers and distribute them widely at a low price, creating his own market. His contribution to the rise of the sentimental German song of the *Sturm und Drang* period is probably considerable. He was also willing to sell his type to other printers and to print music for other publishers – among them Winter (1750–87) and Rellstab (1779–1812) in Berlin, Hartknoch (1763–1802) in Riga and Schwickert in Leipzig (1776–92) – thus increasing the use of his kind of musical edition. He developed his own copying programme, through which he provided on demand a very wide repertory of music that would not have justified large, typeset editions; his great thematic catalogues were issued for these manuscript copies. Breitkopf thus attempted, in effect, to head off the efforts of the music engravers: with his popular editions, set in type, he undersold them, and with his manuscript copies he circulated a larger repertory than they could afford. This strategy apparently succeeded for a time. Its effectiveness had declined by 1800, probably because the music engraving industry had become too extensive and thus was much closer than Breitkopf to the musicians themselves in Paris, England, the Netherlands and Italy. Even so, the firm was now well established as a music publisher, and much of the groundwork was laid for Leipzig to become the centre of European music publishing a few years later.

During the second half of the 18th century, music publishing spread from Paris and London to Amsterdam and various German cities. Several Nuremberg engravers from around the mid-century, including Balthasar Schmid (1725–c1786), Johann Ulrich Haffner (1740–70) and members of the Weigel family (active through most of the century) produced only a few editions, but with interesting music and distinctive appearance. The Dutch firm of Hummel, established in Amsterdam about 1754, competed strongly with Paris and London for many years, especially through its extensive chamber music catalogue. Particularly important about 1780, the firm declined around 1800, and Amsterdam ceased to be an important music centre. In several German cities music publishing was established before 1800, based on practices derived from Parisian engraving rather than from Breitkopf's typography. Among the important men who began to work at this time were Johann André in Offenbach (1774), Bernhard Schott in Mainz (1780), J. M. Götz, mostly in Mannheim (1780), H. P. Bossler, mostly in Speyer (1781), F. E. C. Leuckart in Breslau (from 1782, later in Leipzig), Macarius Falter in Munich (1787), Nicolaus Simrock in Bonn (c1790), J. A. Böhme in Hamburg (1794), J. P. Spehr in Brunswick (c1794) and G. Gombart in Augsburg (1795). Of these, André and Falter were additionally important in the first years of the 19th century as early users of the lithographic process.

Vienna became the earliest major centre of German music engraving, and the third important European centre, thanks mostly to the diversity of its musical market – manuscripts from Italy, engravings from Paris, typeset editions from Leipzig – but also because its music shops had been affiliated more closely with art dealers than with book sellers. Parisian-style engravings were first published in Vienna after about 1770, when the Parisian publisher Huberty settled there. No less important as an engraver was Christoph Torricella, and through the efforts of two other Italians, Carlo and Francesco Artaria, Viennese music publishing began to flourish in 1778. Artaria's editions were immediately successful, and this firm dominated Viennese music publishing until the end of the century. The composer Franz Anton Hoffmeister, who founded a firm in 1784, ranks alongside Artaria both for his important and ambitious editions and for his varied dealings with other publishers, notably his sale of selected titles to Artaria in the 1780s, his ties to Kühnel in Leipzig from 1800, and his eventual merger with Senefelder in 1807. Other early Viennese music publishers included Hieronymus Löschenkohl (1770–1806), a specialist in cheap engravings; Joseph Traeg (active as a dealer in manuscript material from 1781), later Breitkopf's agent as well as his own publisher; Laurenz Lausch (1782–?1801), also a copyist; the composer Leopold Kozeluch, trading as the Musikalisches Magazin (active 1784–1802); Joseph Eder, later in partnership with and eventually succeeded by his son-in-law, Jeremias Bermann (1789–c1840); the several partners who made up the Hoftheater-Musik-Verlag (1796–1822); Ignaz Sauer, later in partnership with Max Leidesdorf (1787–1840); and Carlo Mechetti, succeeded later by his nephew Pietro (1799–1855).

By 1798 Tranquillo Mollo had left Artaria and set up his own shop, and three years later Giovanni Cappi did likewise. In 1801 the Kunst und Industrie Comptoir (or Bureau d'Arts et d'Industrie) opened, managed by five men including Joseph Sonnleithner, the librettist of Beethoven's *Leonore* (1805). In 1803 the inventor of lithography, Alois Senefelder, moved to Vienna to establish his Chemische Druckerei, in competition with the various engravers of music, maps and other documents. Thus a period of diversification in Viennese music publishing began, as publishers experimented with new technical processes to challenge the established firms. Major aspirants from the next few years include Thaddäus Weigl (1803–31), Pietro Cappi (founded 1816), Ludwig Maisch (1810–16), Anton Paterno (founded 1820), modest in his ambitions, and Anton Pennauer (1825–34). Not until after 1820 did clear leaders begin to emerge. Anton Diabelli (founded 1817, jointly with Cappi in 1818) is also known for the famous piano waltz on which many composers, notably Beethoven, wrote variations. Sigmund Anton Steiner acquired Senefelder's shop in 1812 but soon returned to engraving for his editions, moving the lithographic production to the short-lived Lithographisches Institut. By the mid-century the two main publishers were S. A. Spina (partner of Diabelli 1824–51, alone to 1879) and Tobias Haslinger (1826–75 and successor to Steiner), whose catalogues were rich in earlier publishers' titles but also distinguished by ambitious and imaginative projects of their own. After 1857 the firm of Doblinger became important in the city's musical life. Viennese publishing owed much to the local community of composers, not only Mozart, Beethoven and Schubert, but also the many Kleinmeister whose efforts were devoted more to amateur instrumental music than to the songs so popular in Paris and London, and prepared the way for the lucrative properties of the Strauss waltz repertory. In appearance the early Viennese editions – clumsily punched with crudely designed signs, and printed from plates that were frequently cracked and were seldom wiped completely clean – recall the 18th century, in contrast with the handsome, well-executed London and Paris editions. As the centre of music publishing moved to Leipzig, Viennese editions improved in appearance, at a time when their repertory was moving in the direction of virtuoso keyboard music and Strauss waltzes.

About 1800 Leipzig began to emerge as a fourth centre of music publishing, and in due course the greatest. Breitkopf's firm, now Breitkopf & Härtel (and managed by G. C. Härtel), still experimented with different methods of printing, including lithography, but finally settled on engraving around 1811 (see fig.36). In 1801 the Viennese publisher Hoffmeister entered into a highly successful partnership with Ambrosius Kühnel as the Bureau de Musique: it was acquired by C. F. Peters in 1814. In 1807 Friedrich Hofmeister (not to be confused with Hoffmeister) began his activity as a publisher; he later acquired from Carl Friedrich Whistling the rights to the great bibliography of new German printed music now commonly known by his name. Other major Leipzig firms founded before 1860 include Heinrich Albert Probst (1823–36, thereafter in partnership with Carl Friedrich Kistner; in 1919 it merged with the firm of Siegel & Stoll, 1846–50, thereafter C. F. W. Siegel), Bartolf Senff (1844–1907), Merseburger (1849–, specializing in Lutheran church music), C. F. Kahnt (1851–) and Robert Forberg (1862–, important for its affiliation with the Moscow firm of Jürgenson). The firm of F. E. C. Leuckart moved from Breslau to Leipzig in 1870. Leipzig, drawing its support from the local book-publishing industry and from the Gewandhaus and the conservatory, inevitably became the centre of German music publishing at a time when German tastes prevailed in most of the Western world.

Established German firms outside Leipzig continued to flourish, among them André in Offenbach, Schott in Mainz (which in due course acquired the rights to Wagner) and Simrock (which moved from Bonn to Berlin in 1870, having established a close relationship with Brahms and, through him, Dvořák); so too did Spina, Mechetti and Haslinger in Vienna. Berlin challenged the primacy of Leipzig through Simrock as

36. *Haydn's 'The Seasons': title-page of the first edition with engraving by Amadeus Wenzel; published by Breitkopf & Härtel (Leipzig, 1802)*

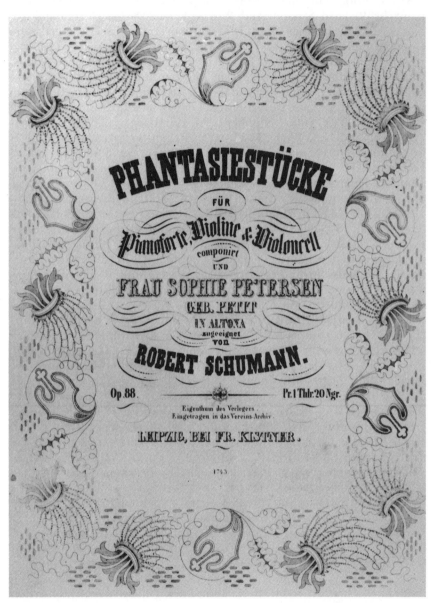

37. *Title-page of the first edition of Schumann's 'Phantasiestücke' op.88 (Leipzig: Kistner, 1850)*

well as important new firms such as A. M. Schlesinger (1810–64, succeeded by Robert Lienau), Traugott Trautwein (1820–1902), C. A. Challier (1835–1919, succeeded by Richard Birnbach), Bote & Bock (1838–), Adolf Fürstner (1868–, whose operatic properties included many by Richard Strauss) and Ries & Erler (1881–; Hermann Erler from 1872, Franz Ries from 1874). Important firms elsewhere were Gombart (1795–*c*1844) and Andreas Böhm (1803–) in Augsburg, Joseph Sidler (1818–28) and Josef Aibl (1825–1904) in Munich, August Cranz in Hamburg (1814–, later in Leipzig, and, through acquisition of the Spina firm, publisher for the Strauss family), Anton Benjamin in Altona (1818–, later in Hamburg, Leipzig and London), Tonger in Cologne (1822–), Julius Schuberth in Hamburg (1826–91, at times in Leipzig and New York), F. Pustet in Regensburg (1826–, specialists in Catholic church music, with offices in the USA and Rome), Karl Ferdinand Heckel in Mannheim (*c*1822–, who issued Hugo Wolf editions), Heinrichshofen in Magdeburg (active from 1797, but in music only from the mid-19th century), Henry Litolff in Brunswick (1828–1940), Adolf Nagel in Hanover (1835–1919) and the brothers Pazdírek (in Vienna, 1868–80, also in Moravia, and creators of the massive *Universal-Handbuch*, 1904–10, listing music in print). Music publishing involved both the music of famous composers like Schumann (see fig.37), Mendelssohn and Liszt as well as a vast output of salon orchestrations, arrangements of operatic favourites, sentimental songs (singly and in series) and instructional pieces.

Important new firms active in 19th-century Paris included Erard (1798–1840, an adjunct to the harp factory), Richault (1805–98), Carli (*c*1805–1919), Pacini (1806–46 and later), Janet & Cotelle (1810–91), Frey (1811–39), Maurice Schlesinger (*c*1821–1846, affiliated with the Berlin family firm), Troupenas (*c*1825–1850), Georges Schonenberger (1830–75), Heugel (1839–), Alphonse Leduc (1841–; not related to the earlier firm of Pierre and Auguste), Escudier (*c*1842–), Choudens (1854–), Brandus (1846–99), Flaxland (1847–69), Georges Hartmann (1866–91) and Costallat (founded in 1880 with the acquisition of the earlier firm of Enoch, 1867–, and known as Enoch Frères et Costallat). The musical repertory of Parisian publishing broadened considerably, although the three basic forms persisted. Songs, for instance, enjoyed a vogue after 1830 with the rise of lithography, although, as in England, works with rudimentary accompaniment and printed on a single sheet were replaced by songs with a florid vocal line and sentimental text, heavily accompanied by piano or often guitar, printed in an edition of several pages with a decorative cover. Thanks to current interest in music pedagogy, and stimulated by the Paris Conservatoire's acting as a publisher in its own right, the method book enjoyed great popularity. The published opera full score, on the other hand, did not prove feasible and declined during the first quarter of the century. About 1840 it was succeeded by the smaller vocal score in so-called Parisian format, which served to circulate the music of French and Italian Romantic grand opera.

Before 1810 there were very few music publishers in Italy, where the scene was dominated by copyists, and those who did attempt to publish, like Luigi Marescalchi (*c*1770–99) in Naples and Alessandri & Scattaglia (*c*1775–1803) and Antonio Zatta (1786–*c*1806) in Venice, encountered great difficulties. The control was not broken until 1808, when Giovanni Ricordi began issuing the operas of Rossini and his contemporaries. His firm's pre-eminence among Italian publishers was assured with the advent of his son Tito Ricordi, and their most successful composer, Giuseppe Verdi (see fig. 38); since then the name of Ricordi has been virtually synonymous with Italian opera, with rights to major works of the *verismo* period and onwards. Other firms included Luigi Bertuzzi (*c*1810–50), Ferdinando Artaria (1813–37), Luigi Scotti (1815–45), the Carulli family (1822–32), Lucca (1825–88), Giovanni Canti (1835–78) and Sonzogno (active in music after 1874) in Milan; Lorenzi (1812–19) and Guidi (1844–87) in Florence; Girard (1815–70) and his successor Teodoro Cottrau (1848–84), also Clausetti (*fl c*1850), in Naples; Ratti, Cencetti & Comp. (1821–37) in Rome; and Giudici & Strada (1859–1930) in Turin. Ricordi and Sonzogno in particular extended their activities beyond the work with scores into matters of production, reputedly involving the choice of singers and the inevitably convoluted politics of the opera house.

In Switzerland the firms of Hans Georg Nägeli in Zurich (1791–, renamed Gebrüder Hug in 1817) and Rieter-Biedermann in Winterthur (1849–84, later in Leipzig) followed the practices of their German and Viennese counterparts. Germans were also responsible for the important early work in countries to the east. The Kunst- und Industrie-Comptoir in Pesth (1805–22), for instance, began as a branch of the Vienna shop with the same name. Other Budapest shops included those of József Wagner (1839–58) and József Treichlinger (1845–77, successor to several earlier Budapest publishers), as well as Julius Rosenthaler (Gyula Rózsavölgyi, 1850–), who acquired most of the earlier firms and whose shop survives to today; Gusztáv Heckenast (1834–78); and Nándor Taborszky, who issued many Liszt editions. In Warsaw the leading early publishers were Franciszek Klukowski (1816–58), Antoni Brzezina (1822–31) and his successor, Gustaw Sennewald (1828–1905), and Rudolf Friedlein (1839–65) and his successors, Gebethner & Wolff (1857–1939); in Kraków, Stanisław Krzyżanowski (1870–1964) developed a catalogue strong in contemporary Polish music. Prague's earliest important publisher was Karel Vilém Enders (?1809–1832). Marco Berra (*c*1811–1853), who began work in Vienna before returning to Prague to become its major publisher, was succeeded by his son-in-law Jan Hoffmann and Hoffmann's heirs (*c*1841–?1918); also important in Prague were Emanuel Starý (1870–1949) and Urbánek (1872–1949). In Bucharest Anton Pann specialized in psalmody and native music publications around 1850; the firm of Gebauer also flourished there for nearly a century (1859–1945). In St Petersburg, J. D. Gerstenberg (1793–) acquired the stock of most of the smaller firms to become the leading publisher of his day. Among Swedish publishers, Olof Åhlström (1783–1835) was the earliest, while J. C. Hedbom (1827–52), Abraham Hirsch (1829–84) and Abraham

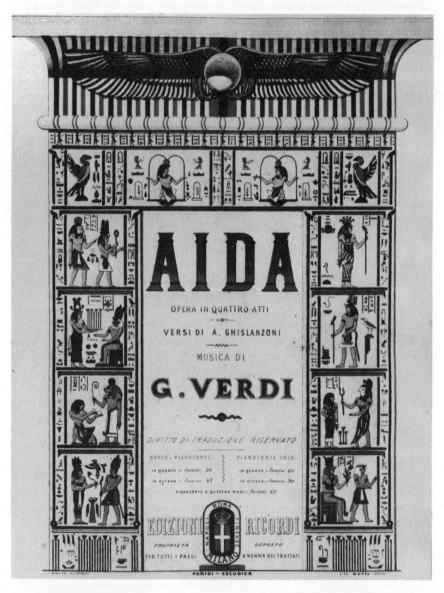

38. *Title-page of the first edition of the vocal score of Verdi's 'Aida', published by Ricordi in 1871*

Lundquist (1837–1915) were the most prolific; Carl Warmuth began publishing in Christiania (Oslo) in the 1840s. In Copenhagen, Søren Sønnichsen (1783–1826) was highly productive, as were the composer C. C. Lose (1802–79) and Horneman & Erslev (1846–79). Music publishing in the Hispanic world was slow to be established. The Lisbon firm of Sassetti began in 1848, while around 1900 the Bilbao firm of Ernesto Dotesio acquired many smaller Spanish firms and in 1914 became the Unión Musical Española.

Freehand music engraving was introduced into English colonies in New England as part of the reform movement of congregational singing, and in two celebrated instruction books published in Boston in 1721: John Tufts's *A Very Plain and Easy Introduction to the Singing of Psalm Tunes* (the first extant edition is the third, 1723, 'printed from copper-plates, neatly engraven . . . for Samuel Gerrish'), and Thomas Walter's *The Grounds and Rules of Musick*, printed by James Franklin, also for the bookseller Gerrish. Freehand engraving continued to be used in the early Yankee tunebooks, which bear the names of America's prominent copperplate engravers: Thomas Johnston, who engraved his own booklet of rules for singing (1755) as well as several editions of Walter's *The Grounds and Rules of Musick* around 1760; Henry Dawkins (James Lyon's *Urania*, 1761); Paul Revere (Josiah Flagg's *A Collection of the Best and Most Approved Tunes*, 1764, and *The New-England Psalm-singer* by William Billings, 1770); John Ward Gilman, who engraved several books around 1770, including American editions of works by the English psalmodist William Tans'ur; and Amos Doolittle, who prepared most of Daniel Read's compilations.

Movable type was introduced in the English colonies by Christopher Saur in Germantown, Pennsylvania; his sacred collection *Kern alter und neuer . . . geistreicher Lieder* (1752) was the first of several German religious books with music issued from his press in subsequent decades. Although Saur is thought to have cast the type himself, his matrices came from Europe, probably Frankfurt. The music typeface used in William Dawson's *The Youth's Entertaining Amusement* (Philadelphia, 1754) appears to be unique; Wolfe identifies the printer as Anton Armbrüster, who also issued the collection *Tunes in Three Parts* in 1763. The last of the early American music typefaces, acquired from the Dutch firm of Enschedé, is seen in two books printed for the Reformed Protestant Dutch Church in New York; Francis Hopkinson's translation of *The Psalms of David* (1767) and *A Collection of the Psalm and Hymn Tunes* (1774).

Moveable type began to be used more frequently in the 1780s, when the founts were first imported from the Caslon foundry in London. This also marks 'he rise of specialist publishing (exemplified by a broadside songsheet printed by William Norman in Boston in 1783) and of religious music publishing. In 1785 Isaiah Thomas in Boston and Worcester and William McCulloch in Philadelphia imported founts, and the adoption of this practice eventually led to the decline of freehand engraving, as well as to the establishment of a formal repertory of religious music and the tunebook as a distinct physical object. Set in movable type, such tunebooks were oblong in format and bound in heavy boards; a theoretical introduction generally preceded the music. Most of the several hundred different tunebooks that appeared around the turn of the century were printed in the Caslon typeface, in the special music type without staff lines developed by Andrew Law for his solfège system, or in a new and tidier face (which also had a special solfège version) introduced soon after 1800 by the Binney & Ronaldson foundry in Philadelphia. Centred at first in the cities of the East Coast, religious music publishing eventually spread to the west and south and resulted in the publication of collections of sacred music (especially hymns) by Lowell Mason and his contemporaries, as well as the shape-note tunebooks.

As early as 1768 John Mein and John Fleming prepared a broadside engraving of *The New and Favourite Liberty Song*, the plates for which were used in *Bickerstaff's Boston Almanack* for 1769. In 1786 Chauncey Langdon's *The Select Songster* was engraved in New Haven by Amos Doolittle, and during the course of the next few years a group of prominent Philadelphians – Alexander Reinagle the composer, John Aitken the engraver, Thomas Dobson the pressman, Henry Rice the bookseller, and Francis Hopkinson the composer and patron – assembled their talents to produce several major anthologies: vocal and instrumental collections by Reinagle (notably a set of keyboard variations thought to be America's first purely secular musical publication), Hopkinson's famous *Seven Songs* (1788), and a Roman Catholic service book. The introduction of music engraving punches in America can probably be traced to these books.

Sheet-music publishing was firmly established in America by the mid-1790s. In 1793 J. C. Moller and Henri Capron established a music shop in Philadelphia and published four issues of *Moller and Capron's Monthly Numbers*, a periodical collection of vocal and instrumental music, although their business was soon taken over by George Willig (1794–1845). Benjamin Carr settled in Philadelphia in 1793 and soon published music (1794–*c*1820); that year J. H. Smith and James Harrison founded short-lived companies in New York, as did the more successful James Hewitt (1793–1825) and George Gilfert (*c*1794–1814). In 1794 Carr's father Joseph moved from London and opened a shop in Baltimore and Frederick Rausch established another in New York. Peter Albrecht von Hagen started his own firm in Boston (*c*1798–1803). These firms, all located in urban centres, had close ties with the theatrical companies that were also being founded at the time. Many of the publishers themselves had been theatre musicians, and their catalogues consisted largely of theatre songs. At the turn of the century two more major publishers were established, Gottlieb Graupner in Boston (1796–1835) and George E. Blake in Philadelphia (1802–*c*18?). While Philadelphia maintained its leadership through the shops of Willig and Blake, New York grew in importance through the work of somewhat smaller firms, including those of Edward Riley (1806–51), John Paff (1811–17), Joseph Willson (1812–20), the Geib family (1814–58) and William Dubois (1813–54, successor to Paff). John Rowe Parker was important in the music trades in Boston (1817–24) as well as for many other musical activities, while Oliver Shaw in Providence (1817–48) was also a respected composer. Early publishers in Charleston included Charles Gilfert (1817–27) and John Siegling (1819–1970).

A significant development occurred in the late 1820s, when lithography, first used about 1822 by Henry Stone in Washington, was taken up more extensively in New York by Edward S. Mesier, Anthony Fleetwood and G. Melkham Bourne. Notable early examples of the process can be found in editions of *Jim Crow* and other works in the emerging repertory of blackface minstrelsy. These developments further reflect the rise of 'Jacksonian democracy', with its emphasis on the new values of the western frontier rather than the more traditional values cultivated in the eastern cities. Early music lithographs, with their imperfectly drawn musical text but better prospects for music illustration, interested a public different from the one that purchased engraved music editions, now largely devoted to the fashionable repertories of Italian opera and guitar songs. While the London repertory thus ceased to dominate music publishers' catalogues, the fashions of guitar accompaniments, sentimental texts and illustrated covers suggest that America's music publishers still generally retained their London models. Lithographic sheet music virtually disappeared in the 1830s, perhaps because the engraved editions looked so much less amateurish. The process re-emerged, however, in the 1840s with the development of chromolithography for cover illustrations; notable among the specialist shops using this technique, by which several colours could be printed, were John H. Bufford, W. S. and J. B. Pendleton, and B. W. Thayer in Boston; Peter S. Duval and Thomas Sinclair in Philadelphia; and Nathaniel Currier (famous through his later partnership with J. Merritt Ives), George Endicott, and Napoleon Sarony of Sarony, Major & Knapp in New York.

In the 1830s Baltimore publishers were particularly active, notably John Cole (1822–39, including the production of sacred music) and the younger George Willig (1829–1910). The 1840s saw the emergence in Boston of Henry Prentiss (1825–47), Charles Keith (1833–47), Elias Howe (1843–50, 1860–1931) and George D. Russell (variously with George P. Reed, Nathan Richardson and Henry Tolman, 1849–88); in Philadelphia James G. Osbourn (1831–48), Leopold Meignen (alone and in partnership with Augustus Fiot, 1834–55), Lee & Walker (1848–75) and, more famous but less extensive, the brothers Winner (Septimus and Joseph, 1845–1918); and in Baltimore Frederick Benteen (later Miller & Beacham, 1835–73). Also in the 1840s the family of William Cumming Peters (1810s–1892) became active in Pittsburgh, as well as in Baltimore, Cincinnati and Louisville. Music publishing in San Francisco flourished during the Gold Rush years, the firms of Atwill (1852–60), Matthias Gray (1858–92) and Sherman & Hyde (1870–) being particularly important. While several important new firms were active on the East Coast in the 1850s (among them S. T. Gordon, mostly in New York, 1846–1941, Henry McCaffrey in Baltimore, 1853–95, and Horace Waters in New York, 1845–1940s), more significant activity was taking place in the west, involving such major firms as Balmer & Weber in St Louis (1848–1907), Root & Cady in Chicago (1858–72) and Silas Brainard in Cleveland (1845–1931). Smaller firms in the west included William F. Colburn in Cincinnati (1849–59), Henry N. Hempsted in Milwaukee (1849–98), John Sage in Buffalo (1850–71), David P. Faulds (1854–1903) and Louis Tripp (c1857–1875) in Louisville, H. M. Higgins in Chicago (1855–67). Confederate firms included A. E. Blackmar (in Vicksburg, Mississippi; Augusta, Georgia; and New Orleans, 1858–88) and W. T. Mayo (1841–54), Philip P. Werlein (1853–) and Louis Grunewald (1858–1969) in New Orleans. Foremost among America's music publishers by the middle of the century were the various partnerships in New York of Firth, Hall & Pond (1815–75 and later; they issued much of the music of Stephen Foster) and Oliver Ditson in Boston (1835–1931, perhaps the most important of all American music publishers in the late 19th century).

CHAPTER IX

The Age of Offset Printing, 1860–1975

The third main era in the history of music publishing began with the introduction of offset lithography. In Leipzig, established as the centre of music publishing, the firm of C. G. Röder, specialists in music engraving and printing from 1846, successfully used a lithographic steam press as early as 1863, and by 1867 were engraving and printing music for Peters as well as other publishers in Leipzig and throughout Europe. The effect in time was a vast increase in the amount of printed music, the output of which reached a high point around 1910, gradually receding thereafter in response to the advent of sound recording and broadcasting. Throughout much of the world, music publishing prospered as never before in the late 19th and early 20th centuries, although particular firms have waxed and waned under the impact of commercial events and fashions in the musical repertory. Whether in Paris, London, Milan or New York, affluence is evident from the vast quantity of published music. Generally, the successful publishers were either those who were perceptive enough to identify emerging musical tastes or were able to fix the graphic appearance of their editions and devote their content mostly to salon music or other works that would sell – what is now frequently disparaged as musical trivia. The basic format became the single songsheet, supported by arrangements for salon orchestra or dance band. World War I stimulated the publication of patriotic songs, especially in the larger countries.

Qualitative considerations became interwoven with commercial considerations, however, as publishers promoted their titles beyond national boundaries. To the extent that quality is determinable through analysis, furthermore, the very function of the musical document may be seen to change. Before 1860 music was issued mostly for the use of performers, and thus was (as it still is) likely to be sold at stores that also sold violin strings, piano-tuning supplies, music stands, guitars, small instruments and the like, rather than at bookshops. Music designed for study purposes first appeared in the late 19th century, as a result of the rise of public concerts and, later, sound recordings, and the growth of the academic study of music and the rise of musicology. Public concerts and recordings have contributed to the popularity of the miniature score, while musicology has fostered historical and critical editions. Miniature scores, issued briefly in the mid-19th century by firms like Heckel in

Mannheim and Guidi in Florence, proliferated as the speciality of Albert Payne, who, working in his father's music shop in Leipzig, began his *Kleine Kammermusik Partiturausgabe* in 1886. Six years later he sold the series to Ernst Eulenburg (Leipzig, 1874–), whose editions have dominated the market ever since. Many of the small scores – variously designated as 'study', 'miniature', 'pocket' or 'reading' scores – are photographic reductions of conductor's scores; but in modern times some contain original material, such as analytical notes and scholarly corrections which are not found in print elsewhere. Other publishers slowly entered the market, including Ernst Donajowski in Leipzig (later Wiener Philharmonischer.Verlag) and Hawkes in London, publishing the standard classics; by the mid-20th century nearly every publisher issued 'study scores' of the most important of its copyright works.

The modern historical editions, intended for study rather than for use in performance, has many ancestors, such as Arnold's Handel edition (1787–97) and Breitkopf's 'Oeuvres complètes' of Mozart, Haydn and Clementi (*c*1800). Its modern beginnings derive from the mid-19th century and the collected editions by Breitkopf & Härtel of Beethoven, Mozart and other major composers. The same firm acted as publisher of the Bach Gesellschaft edition. Other auspicious series also appeared about this time, some of them not sponsored by either a commercial publisher or government patronage; Friedrich Chrysander's great Handel edition, produced largely in the editor's home, is an example. Informal assemblages of enthusiasts who published useful editions included the Musical Antiquarian Society in the 1840s, and the Plainsong and Mediaeval Music Society, beginning in 1888, both in London. The publication of scholarly editions was well established throughout Europe by the end of the 19th century.

The impact of scholarship may also be seen in the 'scholarly performing' edition, which reflects the publisher's scrupulous concern for accuracy of detail and respect for the composer's intentions. The firm of Steingräber (Hanover, later Leipzig, 1878–) was long respected in this field, particularly for its variorum edition of Bach's keyboard music prepared by Hans Bischoff. In the 1950s Bärenreiter in Kassel (1923–) became pre-eminent in the production of scholarly performing editions, a reputation shared in particular instances with the firm of Henle (Munich, Duisburg, 1948–) and the newer Wiener Urtext Edition (Vienna, 1972–), so as to offer performers, at least for the most celebrated works, a gratifying if bewildering choice between alternative conceptions of authenticity. The private press of L'Oiseau-Lyre (Paris, Oxford, Monaco, 1932–) is also noted for its sumptuous editions, imposing in their scholarship, of specialized repertories, while the American Institute of Musicology (Rome, Dallas, 1946–) has undertaken an ambitious publishing programme of scholarly editions of early music. Major publishers specializing in scholarly editions today include Arno Volk (Cologne, 1950–), A-R Editions (Madison, Wisconsin, 1962–) and Garland (New York, mid-1970s–).

The increasingly historical character of the music repertory during the early 20th century was fostered by, as it also influenced the outlook of, the major German publishers, particularly those, such as Breitkopf & Härtel, Peters, Schott and Simrock, who invested in editions of leading composers. The major addition to the group was Universal in Vienna (1901–) which began by acquiring several other major German firms, and after 1907, under the leadership of Emil Hertzka, entered into contracts with Mahler, Schoenberg, Bartók and many other major composers. Gustav Bosse in Regensburg (1912–) has been a major publisher of folk, school and church music. Max Brockhaus (Leipzig, 1893–) has promoted contemporary opera. Other firms came to be recognized for their particular niches in the rich and diversified world of central European music. Theodor Rättig in Vienna (c1877–1910) was an early champion of Bruckner; more diversified in its riches was the short-lived firm of Lauterbach & Kuhn (1902–8). Operettas were a speciality of Weinberger in Vienna (1885–1938) and the Drei Masken Verlag in Munich and Berlin (1910–), among others; Ars Viva (1950–53), founded by Hermann Scherchen to promote avant-garde composers, was acquired by Schott and contributed to that firm's strong presence in this field. Hänssler in Stuttgart (1919–) has emphasized Lutheran music, while Kallmeyer in Wolfenbüttel (1925–) has concentrated on scholarly works in general. Ugrino in Hamburg (1923–) catered originally to the Ugrino religious community. However much they are respected for art music, German publishers probably issue as high a proportion of popular tunes as does the rest of the world. Hans Sikorski in Hamburg (1928–) and Hans Gerig in Cologne (1946–) have served the pop and educational markets, while the Österreichischer Bundesverlag in Vienna (1771–) issues national folk and educational editions.

World War II devastated many German music publishers, many of whom moved to England or America, sometimes founding new firms but usually contributing to established ones. The bombing of German cities, Leipzig in particular, took a heavy toll of stocks and plates. In 1954 the Deutscher Verlag für Musik in Leipzig became the state music publishing house. Numerous firms had already moved to the West, for instance Benjamin and Fürstner to near London (the latter based on a pre-war office there), Breitkopf & Härtel to Wiesbaden, Brockhaus to Lörrach, Heinrichshofen to Wilhelmshaven, Kahnt to near Konstanz, Peters to Frankfurt (with separate firms as well in London, under the Hinrichsen name, and in New York) and Steingräber to Frankfurt; some of them had counterparts or rival offices in East Germany, and enjoyed only short-lived success. The arrival in England and the USA of experienced music publishers escaping the Holocaust – many of them from Universal, including Hans W. Heinsheimer, Edwin and Alfred Kalmus and Ernst Roth – helped serve the increasingly sophisticated tastes of performers and listeners during the 1950s.

The German musical hegemony prevailed throughout the 19th century, although German music publishers themselves were probably not notably more prolific than their counterparts elsewhere, who flourished mostly by providing songs in the vernacular languages, the distinctive dance music of the community and other material of regional interest. While the early nationalist composers typically began by publishing at home, later success usually found them happy to promote the cause of their country's distinctive music through German editions: Smetana may have published most of his music through Urbanek in Prague, for instance, but Dvořák worked to a great extent with Simrock; Grieg began publishing with his friend Horneman in Copenhagen but much of his later music was issued with the support of Peters; Sibelius was published mostly by Breitkopf & Härtel. In time Leipzig became the home of publishers from abroad, among them Bosworth (1889–), set up to protect English copyrights, and Arthur P. Schmidt from Boston (1889–1910).

Among significant new firms in Victorian England were Hutchings & Romer (1866–1916), Stanley Lucas, Weber & Co. (1873–1907) and Murdoch, Murdoch & Co. (c1880–1946). Popular music publishing became highly lucrative in the late 19th century through two promotional devices, the illustrated cover and the royalty system of publicity by star performers. Music-hall ballads and theatre tunes flourished alongside Gilbert and Sullivan. Chappell, thanks to the Dreyfus brothers – Louis in London and Max in New York – effectively controlled much of the music of the London and Broadway stages, sharing the market with Francis, Day & Hunter (1877–) and Ascherberg, Hopwood & Crew (1878–1970). Other firms were established by interests abroad, including Alfred Lengnick (1893–) by Simrock, Hinrichsen (1938–) as a branch of the Peters family and Galliard (1962–72) as a subsidiary of Galaxy in New York. Stainer & Bell (1907–) was originally established by a consortium of composers. Recent British publishers of art music have been sustained by their major composers, for instance Oxford University Press by Vaughan Williams and Walton, Boosey & Hawkes and later Faber Music (1966–) by Britten, Novello by Elgar, the London office of Schott by Tippett, and Joseph Williams (1819–1962), Chester (1874–) and Murdoch by others. Among firms outside London, Gwynn Williams in Llangollen (1937–) has developed a speciality of Welsh folk music.

Publishers in other countries have emphasized their national music, among them Alsbach in Rotterdam (1866–98) and Amsterdam (1898–). Wilhelm Hansen in Copenhagen (1853–, heir to Sønnichsen, Lose and Horneman) has been Scandinavia's major music publisher; alongside it in Denmark the Samfundet til Udgivelse af Dansk Musik (1871–) is more important for national historical editions, the Kgl. Hofmusikhandel (1880–1929) for theatre music, the scholarly antiquarian Dan Fog (1953–) for significant bibliographical works. In Norway, H. T. Winther (1823–78) and the Hals brothers (1847–1908), like many north European shops, worked both as publisher and rental library; their successor Carl Warmuth (1851–1908) was in turn succeeded by the Norsk Musikforlag (1909–). Sweden's major firm has been Gehrmans in Stockholm (1893–), while Finland's is Fazer in Helsinki (1897–).

As well as older-established firms such as Choudens, Costallat, Escudier, Heugel, Leduc and Lemoine, the array of major Paris

39. *Sheet-music cover of the first edition of the song 'Bess you is my woman' from Gershwin's 'Porgy and Bess' (1935)*

publishers includes more recently founded firms like Durand (1869–), the original publisher of most of Saint-Saëns, Debussy and Ravel; Hamelle (1877–), specializing in 19th-century French music, including most of early Fauré, Salabert (c1880s–), publisher for several of Les Six; Fromont (c1885–1922), the early publisher of Debussy; Célestin Joubert (1891–1970), known for operettas and other light works; Max Eschig (1907–), at first largely a French agency for foreign firms; and Jobert (1922–), successor to Fromont. Other publishers recognized as promoters of contemporary composers include Rouart-Lerolle (1905–41), Senart (1908–41) and Editions de la Sirène (1918–36). Foetisch in Lausanne (1865–) has been the major promoter of contemporary Swiss composers. The recent major Italian publishers of art music include Carisch in Milan (1887–), Curci in Naples (1912–), De Santis in Rome (1852–, latterly specializing in avant-garde music), Suvini Zerboni in Milan (1930–, specializing in contemporary music from Japan as well as Italy) and Zanibon at Padua (1908–). The major publisher in Portugal has been Valentim de Carvalho in Lisbon (1914–), in Spain Boileau Bernasconi in Barcelona (1906–), complementing the Instituto Español de Musicología in Madrid (1943–) set up by the Spanish government for scholarly works. Israeli Music Publications in Tel-Aviv (1949–) was set up to serve the needs of Israel's serious composers.

Russian composers, like those elsewhere, worked at first with nearby publishers, for example, Tchaikowsky in Moscow with Jürgenson (1861–1918), the 'Mighty Handful' in St Petersburg particularly with Bessel (1869–1907); Gutheil in Moscow (1859–1914) became as prominent as those two publishers, especially later on as the publisher of Rakhmaninov. As Russian music became increasingly popular abroad, M. P. Belyayev (1885–, originally from St Petersburg) set up a successful enterprise in Leipzig for distributing Russian music in the West and was able to secure copyright protection outside Russia. The last major firm to be established before the revolution was Editions Russes de Musique, founded by Sergey Koussevitzky (Moscow, 1909) to promote new Russian works, successor to Gutheil, and active later in Berlin and Paris as the major publisher of Stravinsky and other Russian émigré composers. Since the confiscation of Jürgenson in 1918, music in the USSR has been published exclusively by Muzïka.

Numerous firms established before the war in eastern Europe are today part of national enterprises. Polskie Wydawnictwo Muzyczne (1928–) is uncommon on three counts: it was established before World War II; it is a consortium of musicians and scholars; and it is located in Kraków rather than Warsaw. Among the earlier Polish firms was Michał Arct (1900–1949). The Czech firms of Urbánek and Starý were nationalized around 1949; today they are under the imprint of Supraphon, successor to Hudební Matice (1953–61). In Hungary, Editio Musica Budapest was created in 1950 through a merger of several firms, including Rózsavölgyi (1850–), Magyar Kórus (1931–, specialists in art music), and Rozsnyai (1889–, specialists in pedagogic materials). In Romania, the general firms of Doina in Bucharest (1916–47) and the Morawetz brothers in Timişoara (1930–33) and the pop firm of Stefan

40. Cover of an edition of two piano works by Edward MacDowell, published in the series
Schirmer's Library of Musical Classics; the distinctive cover design was adopted in 1939

Kiritescu in Bucharest (1941–8) have been succeeded by the state-managed Musikstaatsverlag.

The period between the Civil War and World War II in the United States saw an even greater expansion in publishing activity and an increase in specialization. A torrent of music for domestic use was published; indeed the label 'the age of parlor music' appropriately evokes the image of a piano stool in the home filled with sheet music. Oliver Ditson acquired many of the older small firms during the depressions of the late 19th century to become the country's major publisher. He was in a good position to become the prime mover behind the Board of Music Trade, founded in 1855 to address the common concerns of music publishers, though it was moribund by the end of the century. Ditson also set up subsidiaries, notably John Church & Co. in Cincinnati (1885–1930). Other firms were established, mostly by German immigrants, the largest and best known of these being G. Schirmer in New York (formally established in 1861 but active earlier); it was later known for its special series of the classics, and it extended its catalogue to contemporary music (see fig.40) under the wise guidance of Theodore Baker, Oscar Sonneck and, later, Carl Engel. Other firms established by German immigrants included Carl Fischer in New York (1872–), specializing at first in band music, then in choral and orchestral works; Arthur P. Schmidt in Boston (1876–1960), noted for its sponsorship of American composers; and the smaller firm of J. Fischer in Dayton, Ohio (1864–), specializing in Roman Catholic choral music. Theodore Presser, founded in Lynchburg, Virginia (1883), soon moved to Philadelphia and enhanced its catalogue by publishing what became the major music journal of the time, *The Etude*.

While the conspicuous thrust of America's major music publishers was towards the polite, German repertory – as earnest, classical, cosmopolitan and transcendental as the market would bear – in truth the vast bulk of the output, from these and countless minor firms, was of entertaining, commonplace, provincial and pedestrian repertory, which the market indeed would bear. The measure of music publishing after 1850 must involve not only the easily recognizable large firms but also the smaller regional and specialist firms, less easily describable as a reflection of the totality. Perhaps most conspicuous among the specialist firms were those that cultivated sacred music; they produced tunebooks, hymnals and school collections, usually set in type in quarto format, at first oblong, later upright. The major early publisher of these was Mason Bros. (1853–85), established by the family of Lowell Mason. From its model derive two music publishing traditions. One was devoted to evangelical song and included Biglow & Main in New York (1867–1922), James D. Vaughan (Lawrenceburg, Tennessee, 1890–), Homer Rodeheaver, mostly in Winona Lake, Indiana (1910–), Charles Henry Pace in Chicago (1910–, focusing on black gospel music) and J. R. Baxter in Dallas (1926–). The other tradition was devoted to public school and other educational music and included, among the firms originating in the 19th century, Silver Burdett in Boston (1885–) and the Boston Music Co. (1885–1977, originally a subsidiary of

G. Schirmer). The manifest trend, however, was towards an emphasis on popular song, such as would be reflected in the sentimental ballads that made up the monthly issues of *The Folio* of the White-Smith Co. (Boston, 1868–1976) as well as the catalogues of Benjamin Hitchcock of New York (1869–1941). It should also be noted that, much as music publishers served also as retailers, a number of firms best known as retailers were also occasional publishers, among them Lyon & Healy in Chicago (1864–, noted as a harp manufacturer as well).

American music publishing was by no means centralized in New York. Chicago enjoyed a bustling activity, its practitioners including the composer Will Rossiter (1891–1954) and Sol Bloom (1896–1910), who was later prominent in the US House of Representatives. Detroit publishers, beginning with Adam Couse (1844–59) and Stein & Buchheister (1854–65), came later to be known for musical comedy, firms including Clark J. Whitney (1857–95), Joseph Henry Whittemore (1858–93), Roe Stephens (1868–93) and Jerome H. Remick (1898–1930, also in New York); Sam Fox (1906–) originally worked in Cleveland before moving to Tin Pan Alley. Sedalia, Missouri, could claim John Stillwell Stark (1882–1922), who issued the early rags of Scott Joplin, while Memphis housed W. C. Handy's commercialized blues publishing, under the imprint of Pace & Handy (1908–20, later in New York). As Hollywood became the home of the film industry, Los Angeles developed a music publishing community of its own. In later years, however, it degenerated into the centre of 'song shark' practices, whereby dealers with questionable reputations extracted exorbitant fees from the gullible novices in return for printing and copyrighting songs and ostensibly 'plugging' them, with the help of famous performers and other influential parties, into lucrative hits.

American popular music publishing emerged as a specialism after the Civil War as publishers began to look for hit tunes. Its centre was an area of mid-town Manhattan, moving upwards from East 14th to West 28th and eventually West 50th Street, known as Tin Pan Alley. Among the major firms were Belwin, Inc. (1918–), founded by Max Winkler, which in 1949 merged with Mills Music, 1919–); Famous Music Co. (1928–66), with strong ties to several Hollywood studios; Leo Feist (1895–, which merged with Miller and Robbins to form the Big 3 Music Corporation: see below); Charles Foley; T. B. Harms (1881–1969), which enjoyed its greatest success when its manager, Louis Dreyfus, enlisted Jerome Kern and, later, Richard Rodgers among its composers; Miller Music (*c*1930–1973), an offshoot of Harms; J. J. Robbins (1927–39), active in the 'big band' movement; Shapiro, Bernstein & Co. (1895–); Joseph W. Stern (1894–1920), whose partner, Edward B. Marks, later acquired it; and M. Witmark & Sons (1885–1941), active among the founders of ASCAP. Composers also established their own firms, among them Harry Von Tilzer (1902–), George M. Cohan and Irving Berlin. The proximity of these firms, and later ones like Frank Music Corp. (1949–), to the Broadway musical stage, with its favourite performers and composers attuned to the rising mass audience, greatly enhanced their access to current tastes, while the commercial environment ensured that they were among the first participating publishers in the performing rights movement. Corporate flexibility was as important as musical insight in this world, as directors moved from firm to firm and mergers and acquisitions flourished. Many firms were absorbed into larger units, such as Warner Bros. Music of Los Angeles (1929–, through its Music Publishers Holding Corporation), the Big 3 Music Corporation (1939–, a subsidiary of MGM, later of United Artists), and MCA Music in New York (1965–); and they were unified through trade organizations such as the Music Publishers' Association of the United States (MPA, founded 1895, at first made up of publishers mostly of serious music), or the National Music Publishers' Association (NMPA, founded 1917 as the Music Publishers' Protective Association, made up of popular music publishers), or the Church Music Publishers' Association (CMPA). Recently many publishers have chosen to centralize their marketing, distribution or other activities through specialist firms such as Charles Hansen (1949–) and Hal Leonard (1949–). The spiritual home of America's pop music is probably neither New York nor Hollywood but rather Nashville, although in fact publishers, like record companies, are today scattered across the country.

Educational specialists also emerged to issue books for school use, band parts, music for large choirs, collections of favourite songs for amateurs, charts and other supplies for pedagogic purposes, and juvenile instructional music. In the United States the Lowell Mason tradition culminated in the 'basic series' (i.e. sets of graded materials for use at the elementary school level), which have sustained publishers such as the American Book Company, Allyn & Bacon, Follett, Ginn, Summy-Birchard (1888–) and Neil A. Kjos. Band music continued to be issued nationally by Carl Fischer and another general music firm, John Church, as well as by specialist publishers like E. F. Ellis in Washington, J. W. Pepper in Philadelphia, Vandersloot in Williamsport, Pennsylvania, and C. L. Barnhouse in Oskaloosa, Iowa. Choral music was a speciality of E. C. Schirmer (1921–) in Boston and H. W. Gray (1906–71) in New York, as well as Shawnee Press (1939–), which was devoted at first to Fred Waring choral arrangements. Major denominational firms of special prominence include James D. Vaughan (1890–), originally serving southern rural hymnody and now affiliated with the Church of God; Augsburg (1841–) in Minneapolis, serving various Lutheran churches, along with Concordia (1890–) in St Louis, active in promoting early music for service use; Lillenas (1925–) in Kansas City, with the Nazarene Church, and Broadman (1934–) in Nashville, with Southern Baptists. The gospel song was largely a speciality of Homer Rodeheaver of Winona Lake, Indiana, whose catalogue was acquired in 1969 by Word, Inc. (1951–) of Waco, Texas. Other major religious music publishers include the Hope Publishing Co. (1892–), originally in Chicago; E. S. Lorenz (1890–) of Dayton, Ohio; and the Zondervan Music Group of Nashville, specialists in evangelical song. Songbooks are also issued by or for innumerable political, ethnic, social, fraternal and occupational groups. Fred J. Rullman, associated with the Metropolitan Opera, long dominated the market for opera librettos, while Oak

Publications in New York (1950s–) has focused on folk music, and Hargail, also in New York (1941–), on recorder music. The possibilities of camera-copy music printing have also nourished the 'cottage industry' publishers, whose catalogues contain only a few titles, directed to highly specialized audiences, announced on a highly strategic basis and available only from the publishers directly. The range of specialist activity embraces a vast array of smaller American publishers: the *Musician's Guide* of 1980, for instance, listed 25,000 different firms.

American art music, meanwhile, found its early champions in Arthur P. Schmidt in Boston (who was apprenticed in Germany and, through P. L. Jung, acquired rights to the music of MacDowell), and in the Wa-Wan Press in Newton Centre, Massachusetts (1901–12), set up by the composer Arthur Farwell to encourage a distinctive national style based on American Indian music (for illustration *see* WA-WAN PRESS). The Society for the Publication of American Music (1919–69) prepared and promoted important new works, as did Henry Cowell's New Music series (1927–58), substantially underwritten by Charles Ives and prepared for publication by Herman Langinger. Serious music was also issued by academic presses, the activity around 1950 in the Smith College area of Northampton, Massachusetts, being noteworthy. The Cos Cob Press (1929–48, succeeded by Arrow Music Press, to 1956), Peer-Southern (1928–), Galaxy (1931–), Broude Bros. (1930s–), Alexander Broude (1954–82) and Boelke-Bomart (1948–) have also issued the music of American composers. Among the large general music firms, Schirmer over the decades 1920–50 specialized in American art songs, while since the 1960s C. F. Peters has been strong in avant-garde works. Belmont in Los Angeles (1960s–) concentrates on the music of Arnold Schoenberg. Distribution of music for a limited audience has been addressed by organizations like the American Composers Alliance (1938–) and the American Music Center (1940–), as well as by music rental services.

The problems in distributing European editions in the USA often led to special American offices, beginning with agencies in New York of Novello in the 1850s and later of Ricordi and, through P. L. Jung (1891–8), of Breitkopf & Härtel. Later cooperative agencies included Associated Music Publishers (1927–64), Peer (1940–, for several Latin American firms), Elkan-Vogel (1929–70, working mainly with French publishers), Am-Rus Music Corp. (directed by Eugene Weintraub, 1940–) and Leeds (*c*1940–1964) – the latter two handling music from the USSR – and European American Music Distributors (1977–). The situation after World War II in particular, when German music was generally unavailable in England and America and when the technology of offset lithography was well developed, gave rise to extensive reprinting, mostly of standard editions. From the 1960s, small editions of important out-of-print texts have been prepared for libraries and scholars; these have often been of monumental historical editions in reduced format. Among the major specialists in this activity are Edwin F. Kalmus (1926–), International Music Co. (1941–) and, more recently, Dover (1941–), all in New York.

Music was printed in Canada as early as 1800, with many different models reflecting various purposes. Prior to the Confederation in 1867, the major firm was A. & S. Nordheimer (1844–c1927) in Toronto, whose output reflects American sheet-music practices. Overseas ties are reflected in the Anglo-Canadian Music Publishers' Association (Toronto, 1885–1920), set up to protect English copyrights, as well as in the catalogue of Frederick Harris (1910–), originally an English agency but now specializing in conservatory editions. Among other specialist firms have been Whaley, Royce & Co. (1888–1930s) in Toronto, issuing salon music; Gordon Thompson (1909–) in Toronto, educational music; the Waterloo Music Co. (1922–), wind instruction and band music; and Berandol (Toronto, 1969–), whose serious music catalogue has grown out of earlier BMI commitments. Protestant hymnals, Sunday School books and similar texts also appeared in other parts of the British Empire in the 18th century and the 19th (e.g. *The Oriental Masonic Muse*, Calcutta, 1791, and a song, 'Jesus de Ware Zoondaars Vriend' by F. Logier, in a Cape Town newspaper of 1840, provisionally recognized as the first music publications of India and South Africa, respectively), but there was no continuing tradition of production in these areas. Australian music publishing began in Melbourne in 1850 with Joseph Wilkie, predecessor of the more important firm of Allan, and in Sydney a few years later with William Henry Paling and around 1890 with Jacques Albert. While Allan and Paling came to be noted for their support of Australian composers, Albert worked extensively with English and American firms, as did the branch of Chappell (1904).

Music publishing was also introduced in Latin America by European immigrants, who worked mainly as music teachers and retailers, and often impresarios. In addition to selling imported editions (sometimes presumably with subsidy from the European publishers) the imaginative shopkeepers identified and promoted music of a distinctively local character, issued separately or as supplements to literary journals devoted to music, cultural topics, general or current affairs. As early as 1824 sheet music was being issued in Rio de Janeiro, whose later imprints name J. B. Klier (1834–47), Pierre Laforge (1837–51), Filippone (1846–1911) or Bevilacqua e Napoleão (c1869–1968). Music was even published in the Amazon River settlements around 1900 during the rubber boom, also in São Paulo, where Vicente Vitale was particularly active after 1923. Europeans who kept music shops in Spanish communities included Engelmann (from Strasbourg) in Havana, Niemeyer (from Hamburg) in Valparaiso, Chile, Wagner in Mexico City and Breyer in Buenos Aires (both also from Germany), as well as Giusti (from Corsica) in San Juan, Puerto Rico. Local opera house repertories are also reflected in their catalogues, notably in Buenos Aires, where Ricordi was active as early as 1885 and after 1924 a powerful force in local music publishing. Among the major recent composers to benefit from a close working relationship with one particular publisher was Alberto Ginastera, with the Buenos Aires firm of Barry.

CHAPTER X

Music Publishing Today

The changing circumstances of today's music publishers, in historical perspective, reflect several larger trends. The first is based on measurement of production: more music is available than ever before, although the quantity seems actually to be decreasing slightly from the high point reached early in the century. The evidence is very incomplete, although the overall historical trend is obvious. Up to 1700, the annual world-wide production of musical editions probably never exceeded a hundred titles. Based on data suggested above, it seems fair to fix the total at no more than five titles a year before about 1525 (i.e. from the beginnings to the age of Petrucci); 30 titles a year from 1525 to 1550 (during Attaingnant's major activity); 80 titles a year from 1550 to 1600 (when the four major centres were particularly active); and 60 titles a year during the 17th century. The vast increase during the 18th century reflects the rise of engraved music and the proliferation of songsheets. While any estimates are frustrated by the practice of not dating music, the first half-century, with London as the main centre, probably produced about 150 titles a year; the next three decades probably saw around 300 new titles each year, as Parisian publishers entered the picture; while the last two decades saw a further proliferation, with the growth of Viennese and German publishers, so that the total swelled to about a thousand a year by 1800. The trend continued, stimulated by commercial pressures during the 19th century, with annual outputs reaching perhaps 2000 by 1835, 10,000 by 1850, 20,000 by 1870, and 50,000 by 1910, probably the apogee, just before the extensive distribution of commercial sound recordings. The totals are guesswork, which at best may give rise to questions of what exactly to count, although the slow decline over the intervening decades, when viewed in gross quantitative terms, is hard to regard as a cause for alarm. Underlying factors that contribute to the changes, however, deserve closer attention.

A quantitative decline is possible, in today's intensely active musical society, partly because music itself is more widely available than ever before. Concomitantly, local music retailing has declined disturbingly, as outlets have closed or been forced to provide a more limited range of services to their customers. The attrition, generally an international phenomenon, is partly compensated for by the rise of national and cooperative retailing activities and of public and academic music libraries, along with better bibliographies and repertory lists and (to music publishers themselves a dubious blessing) modern photocopying technology. Along with the benefit of a greater availability of musical documents probably also comes the loss of respect for those documents. The very abundance no doubt can contribute to a 'musical information overload' of sorts. At the same time, better access has clearly helped scholars to discover, and performers to promote, the little-known and forgotten repertories that enjoy wide favour today.

The resulting diffusion of musical taste may be less specific, but is readily appreciated by inspecting music shop inventories, catalogues, advertisements and collections. There is no longer such an institution as a general music publisher: specialities are called for. With a few notable exceptions, general music journals have also perished, to be replaced by the plethora of specialist periodicals that now overflow the library's current periodical shelves. Generally higher in quality than their departed brethren by being better focused, they nevertheless further contribute to the fragmentation of our musical communities. Similarly, over the course of the past century, music publishers have discovered the necessity (not to mention the pleasures) of becoming part of specific musical communities through the character of their catalogues, as favouring band or orchestra music, or choral music or songs; in offering conservative or adventurous repertories; in promoting particular composers, schools and trends; and whether catering for amateur or professional audiences.

The trends, once in motion, proliferate, as for each audience a different music publisher or group of publishers seems necessary. It is no longer a matter of the classical performer having trouble talking to the pop performer, so that 80 years ago this maxim could have been proposed: serious music publishers needed support, which popular music publishers earned. Wealth is no doubt still to be amassed in music publishing, particularly where commercial pop music is concerned and when a publisher can develop a successful relationship with recognized composers and styles. The recent experiences of many music publishers with the giant financial conglomerates suggest that the giants usually discover the successful innovators well after their vital and lucrative periods of activity. Yet in the 1960s many of the stable giants of music publishing found themselves, for better or worse, absorbed into the great financial conglomerates. While the music publisher's financial circumstances are probably no less mysterious today than they ever were, a high proportion of today's firms, both classical and popular, would appear to be in the business more as an outgrowth of a commitment to a particular musical community and repertory than in search of lucrative profits.

The music publishing industry has also been profoundly affected by the rise of the modern commercial sound recording, along with the all-pervading sound of music in modern society. The musical mass media, whatever the quality of their offerings, inevitably inspire cases in point of Gresham's law: listeners drive out performers, as bad music drives out good. The possibilities of coordinating a music publishing programme with the related activities of a recording company, a sound-equipment manufacturer, a film producer or the entertainment industry, has further attracted the more imaginative among music publishers, from smaller firms (particularly in areas without a rich music publishing tradition) to the giant conglomerates (notably those lured by potential marketing advantages), albeit so far with mixed results.

Declining concern for the physical objects of music publishing goes hand in hand with the increasing emphasis on music as intellectual and artistic property, which publishers share with or manage for the creator. Many major publishers still flourish by selling copies on paper, although one publisher enjoys recalling how in the 1920s, as sound recording and radio became more pervasive, his firm sold its entire stock – 70 tons of paper – for pulp, for $210. Still other music publishers, for the most part those commercially in the ascendant, find themselves drawn increasingly into the world of copyright law – involving both 'performance rights' over public presentation, broadcast and diffusion and 'mechanical rights' controlling sound recordings – and further away from the world of printing, promotion and distribution.

The distribution of performing parts in the form of manuscript copies during the 18th century no doubt provided a kind of protection, thanks to the restricted access to the musical texts themselves, but the proliferation of printed copies in the 19th century, while it provided for wider distribution, also limited the income of the creator. Thus in Great Britain the 'Bulwer-Lytton Act' of 1833, providing protection for performance of dramatic works, was in 1842 extended to cover music as well. Enforcement was not widespread until the 1870s, however, through the infamous Harry Wall and the Authors', Composers', and Artists' Copyright and Performing Right Protective Society. Revision of the British copyright act in 1911 led to the founding in 1914 of the Performing Right Society Ltd, which covers performance rights; the Mechanical-Copyright Protection Society Ltd (MCPS) was formed in 1924 through the amalgamation of several bodies which had been set up as early as 1910 for the purposes of covering mechanical rights. Previously the Société des Auteurs, Compositeurs et Éditeurs de Musique (SACEM) had been founded in 1851 in France, as well as the Anstalt für musikalische Aufführungsrechte (AFMA), established by the Genossenschaft deutscher Tonsetzer (Association of German Composers) in Germany in 1903, today succeeded in West Germany by the Gesellschaft für musikalischer Aufführungs- und mechanische Vervielfältigungsrechte (GEMA). The earliest such organization in the United States was the American Society of Composers, Authors and Publishers (ASCAP), founded in 1914, which in 1940 engaged in the pitched battle with the major radio networks that led to the incorporation of its major competitor, Broadcast Music, Inc. (BMI). SESAC (formerly the Society of European Stage Authors and Composers) is another group important in the United States and through bureaux in several other countries, many of which, however, also have their own national organizations. International coordination of these groups involves the Confédération Internationale de Sociétés d'Auteurs et Compositeurs (CISAC) for performance rights, and the Bureau International de l'Edition Mécanique (BIEM) for mechanical rights over sound carriers such as regular and compact disc recordings and tapes.

The rise of rapid photocopying machinery has no doubt further diminished the sale of copies for music publishers, calling for price increases, threatening publishers' historically close working relationship with performers and forcing them to look all the more to performance rights for their income. Such circumstances, influenced variously by the different kinds of repertory, documentation and audience, have no doubt served to diminish even further the features shared by music publishers. The general belief today is that, after a quarter-century of continued happy expansion, from about 1945 to 1970, the music publishing industry has been experiencing an unsettling period of economic uncertainty and volatility. At the same time, the overriding generalization to be drawn from the history summarized here suggests that published music can always be expected to fluctuate in its accessibility as well as in its significance, as a reflection of publishers' sensitivity to the changing musical, social, technological and commercial contexts of their activity, and of their ability to identify, prepare, distribute and promote the repertories that reflect those contexts.

PART TWO

Dictionary

A

Adams, Thomas (*d* London, 1620). English bookseller and publisher. He was established in London from 1591 and financed several significant musical publications, including John Dowland's *The Third and Last Booke of Songes or Aires*, printed by Peter Short in 1603, and Robert Dowland's *A Musicall Banquet*, printed by Thomas Snodham in 1610. He also had the right to reprint several other titles, but this was disputed by William Barley. Between 1611 and 1620 he traded at 'the Bell in St. Paul's churchyard'. He is thought to have published Orlando Gibbons's *Fantazies of III Parts* in 1620, which bears the imprint 'London. At the Bell in St. Paul's churchyard'.

Humphries and Smith (1954, 2/1970)

M.M.

Aertssens [Aertsen], **Hendrik** (*b* Antwerp, bap. 22 May 1586; *d* Antwerp, bur.14 April 1658). Flemish printer, active in Antwerp. He issued his first publication in 1613 and in 1640 his son Hendrik Aertssens (ii) (*b* Antwerp, bap. 17 April 1622; *d* Brussels, 30 Sept 1663) joined the firm. The Aertssens were well known for their publications of sacred vernacular songs, particularly *Het paradys der gheestelycke en kerckelycke lofsanghen* which was reprinted five times. Hendrik Aertssens (iii) (*b* Antwerp, bap. 27 Dec 1661; *d* Antwerp, 16 July 1741) also became a printer, obtaining his patent in 1686. By clever scheming he managed to establish a virtual monopoly of music publishing for the Flemish region; however, his publications, mostly reprints and mainly of Italian music, were criticized by contemporaries, including Sir John Hawkins, for their poor typography.

HawkinsH; E. vander Straeten: *La musique aux Pays-Bas avant le XIXe siècle* (Brussels, 1867–88/ *R*1969), v (1880), vii (1885); Goovaerts (1880); P. Genard: 'De drukker Hendrik Aertssens de Jongere en de veiling zijner boeken in 1662', *Bulletin Maatschappij Antwerpsche Bibliophilen*, ii (1882–6), 87; D. F. Scheurleer: *Nederlandsche liedboeken* (The Hague, 1912–23); F. T. Arnold: 'A Corelli Forgery?', *PMA*, xlvii (1922–3), 93; R. Vannes: *Dictionnaire des musiciens (compositeurs)* (Brussels, 1947), 261; B. Huys: *Catalogue des imprimés musicaux des XVe, XVIe et XVIIe siècles* (Brussels, 1965); *Musical Documents from Two Centuries (1500 to 1700) in the Library of the Utrecht Institute of Musicology* (Buren, 1980) [title-pages]

G.S.

Åhlström, Olof (1756–1835). Swedish publisher, active in Stockholm. The first major Swedish music publisher, he began publishing in 1783, and in 1788 applied for and was given, in a Royal 'Privilegium Exclusivum', the sole right to engrave music in Sweden for the next 20 years. The privilege was eventually extended by 15 years, to 1823, though for the last five years it was undermined by the sanctioning of lithography. From 1788 the firm was given the name Kongliga priviligierade nottryckeriet. Åhlström published works of contemporary composers (including his own compositions), the first piano tutors in Sweden and two music periodicals, *Musikaliskt tidsfördrif* (1789–1834) and *Skaldeslychen satte i musik* (1794–1823). He printed at least 11 catalogues (1794–1835).

A. Wiberg: 'Olof Åhlströms musiktryckeri', *STMf*, xxxi (1949), 83–136; idem: 'Striden om Olof Åhlströms musiktryckeriprivilegium', *STMf*, xxxiv (1952), 84; idem: *Den svenska musikhandelns historia* (Stockholm, 1955)

V.H.

Aibl. German firm of publishers. The lithographer Joseph Aibl (*b* Munich, 1802; *d* Munich, 1834), a pupil of Theobald Boehm, worked from 1819 to 1825 in Berne as a musician and later as a lithographer with a music dealer. In 1825 he founded a business that published music and dealt in instruments in Munich; after his death it was continued by his widow and from 1837 by the merchant Eduard Spitzweg (*b* Munich, 1811; *d* Munich, 1884), a brother of the painter Carl Spitzweg. Under the directorship of Eduard's son Eugen Spitzweg (*b* Munich, 1840; *d* Munich 1914) the publishing house was sold in 1904 to Universal Edition. Composers represented by the firm included Peter Cornelius, Rheinberger, Alexander Ritter, Theobald Boehm, Bülow, Reger and Richard Strauss.

A. Ott: 'Richard Strauss und sein Verlegerfreund Eugen Spitzweg', *Musik und Verlag: Karl Vötterle zum 65. Geburtstag* (Kassel, 1968), 466; K. Ventzke: 'Zur Frühgeschichte des Musikverlages Joseph Aibl in München', *Mf*, xxv (1972), 316

K.V.

Aich, Arnt von (*b* ?Aachen; *d* Cologne, *c*1528–30). German printer. He came into possession of the Lupus Press in Cologne through marriage to its owner, Ida Grutter, and began publishing in 1512 or 1513. He brought out some 35 works on a variety of subjects before his death. The business was continued by his widow and son-in-law, Laurenz von der Mülen, until his son

135

Johann von Aich was old enough to take it over. Under the latter's direction some 35 more books were issued from the Lupus Press, the last of them dated 1557.

Arnt von Aich's main output consists of religious writings, a few of which exhibit Protestant sympathies and may have been printed illegally. In music his fame rests on a single collection, *LXXV hubscher Lieder*, printed by means of woodblocks. Although like many of Arnt von Aich's publications it is not dated, the repertory indicates an early date (probably between 1512 and 1520). No composers are named in the collection; some of the songs have been identified as the work of Hofhaimer, Isaac, Rener and Grefinger – all of whom were active in southern Germany and Austria. Since they had no connection with Cologne, Moser suggested that the collection may represent a reprint of an earlier Augsburg edition now lost. The repertory itself can most readily be linked to the court of the Augsburg Bishop, Friedrich II of Zollern (*d* 1505), whose setting of *Fried gib mir Herr* concludes the collection. Many of the composers and even some of these works are also found in the song collections published by Oeglin and Schoeffer.

H. J. Moser: *Paul Hofhaimer* (Stuttgart, 1929, rev. 2/1966); E. Bernoulli and H. J. Moser, eds.: *Das Liederbuch des Arnt von Aich* (Kassel, 1930); G. Domel and G. Könitzer: 'Arnd von Aich und Nachkommen. . .', *Gutenberg-Jb 1936*, 119; K. Gudewill: 'Aich, Arnt von', *MGG*; J. Benzing: 'Die Drucke der Lupuspresse zu Köln (Arnd und Johann von Aich)', *Archiv für Geschichte des Buchwesens*, i (1958), 365 [with list of publications]

M.L.G.

Aird, James (*d* Glasgow, 1795). Scottish music seller and publisher. He was in business in Glasgow from 1778 at various addresses including Candleriggs (title-page of Joshua Campbell's *Reels*, 1778), 'near McNair's Land, New Street' (trade card, *c*1780), King Street (Tait's Directory, 1783) and New Wynd (many undated half-sheet songs), and was probably the first commercial music publisher in Glasgow to run a full-time business, though music publishing had been flourishing in Edinburgh for 50 years. He aimed at a wide popular market, issuing many single songs and books of dance music. Most impressive is his *Selection of Scotch, English, Irish and Foreign Airs* (4 vols. *c*1778, 1782, 1788, 1794), the first volume of which contains the earliest known printing of the tune *Yankee Doodle*. After his death his engraved plates were purchased by the Glasgow publishers Archibald McGoun and Joseph McFadyen.

McFadyen brought out posthumous fifth and sixth volumes of Aird's *Selection*.

Kidson (1900); F. Kidson: 'Aird, James', *Grove5*

D.J.

Aitken, John (*b* Dalkeith, ?1745; *d* Philadelphia, 8 Sept 1831). American metalsmith, engraver, publisher and dealer of Scottish birth. He had arrived in Philadelphia by 1785 and began his career as a music publisher in 1787, when he brought out three large works: Reinagle's *A Selection of the most Favorite Scots Tunes*, William Brown's *Three Rondos for the Piano Forte* and his own *A Compilation of the Litanies and Vespers, Hymns and Anthems* (2/1791), the only 18th-century American collection of music for the Roman Catholic Church. In 1788 he issued another anthology by Reinagle and also probably 'Hopkinson's *Seven Songs*; a few pieces of sheet music and more of Reinagle's song collections followed in 1789. By 1793 he had brought out at least 20 titles, but between then and 1806 he published only the compendious *Scots Musical Museum* (1797) and one of his own songs, *The Goldsmith's Rant* (1802). He continued to work as a silversmith, but by 1806 he had reestablished himself in the music business. As one of Philadelphia's busiest music publishers during the years 1806–11, he brought out many secular songs and several secular collections as well as more sacred music – a total of perhaps 200 titles. Aitken's musical activity seems to have ceased after 1811, though he continued in the metalworking and printing trades in Philadelphia until at least 1825.

Aitken has been identified by Wolfe as the first professional publisher of secular music in the USA. His publications of the 1780s mark the earliest sustained commitment to the printing and sale of music of this type, and were also the first known American publications to have been produced using the intaglio method of engraving metal plates with steel punches rather than by hand.

F. J. Metcalf: *American Writers and Compilers of Sacred Music* (New York, 1925/R1967); D. W. Krummel: *Philadelphia Music Engraving and Publishing 1800–1820: a Study in Bibliography and Cultural History* (diss., U. of Michigan, 1958); Wolfe (1964); idem (1980)

R.C. (ii)

Albert. Australian firm of publishers. It was started about 1890 in Sydney when Jacques Albert (*b* Fribourg, 1850; *d* at sea, 1914) began importing violins. In 1894 he was joined by his son Michel François [Frank]

(1874–1962), who became sole proprietor in 1896. He continued to trade as J. Albert & Son and in the early 1900s negotiated Australian publishing rights with overseas music houses for the *American Annuals* and *Sixpenny Pops* series. The firm extended its merchandise to orchestral and brass band instruments but sold this stock in 1932 to Allan's in Melbourne. Shortly afterwards, J. Albert & Son Pty Ltd was formed to control the remaining music publishing interests of the family. About 1970 the firm began the Albert Edition catalogue of predominantly Australian classical compositions, which now exceeds 500 titles.

'Albert, Michel F.', *Australian Dictionary of Biography*, vii (Melbourne, 1979)

K.R.S.

Alessandri & Scattaglia. Italian firm of music and general engravers and publishers, music and print sellers. The firm was active in Venice at the sign of the Beata Vergine della Pace on the Rialto from about 1770 to at least 1803. It was founded by the engravers Innocente Alessandri (*b* Venice, *c*1740), a pupil of Bartolozzi, and Pietro Scattaglia. From about 1770, during the years of publication of their joint magnum opus, *Animali quadrupedi* (Venice: Carlo Palese, 1771–5, illustrated with 200 plates designed, engraved and hand-coloured by themselves), they also worked as engravers and selling agents for the music publisher Luigi Marescalchi; on at least one title-page they are also described as his printers, which may have been another of their regular responsibilities. Together with Marescalchi they were associated in the revival of music publishing in Italy after 70 years of almost total inactivity. The fact that their names appear on almost all title-pages of Marescalchi's Venice editions has often led cataloguers and bibliographers to ascribe to them publications that should properly be regarded as Marescalchi's, resulting in numerous errors in *RISM*, the *British Union Catalogue* and other reference works. It is probable that Alessandri & Scattaglia did not publish an edition of their own until after Marescalchi had closed his Venice business about 1775; even after that date their status is often described merely as selling agent on title-pages of editions whose publishers are not specified (it must, however, be recognized that modern definitions of the respective titles and functions of publisher and distributor may not be rigidly applicable to the music publishing trade in late 18th-century Venice).

Of the handful of editions that bear Ales-

sandri & Scattaglia's unquestioned imprint, the outstanding one is the full score of Bertoni's *Orfeo* (*c*1776); it was only the second complete opera to be published in full score in Italy since 1658. A reissue from the same plates, but without an imprint, was published for the opera's revival at the Venice Carnival (1782–3). After about 1785 the firm gradually did less music engraving, but the premises on the Rialto were retained at least until late 1803. Music of every type was sold there, including manuscript copies of numbers from the latest operas, dressed up within decoratively engraved paper wrappers. The majority of publications with which the firm was associated are in oblong format and have ornamental title-pages of uncommon elegance.

Sartori (1958), [inaccurate]

R.M.

Allan. Australian firm of publishers, active in Melbourne. It was founded by Joseph Wilkie in 1850 as a music and pianoforte saloon. In 1862 he was joined by John Campbell Webster, and a year later by the eminent singing teacher George Leavis Allan (*b* London, 1826; *d* Melbourne, 1 April 1897). Both Wilkie and Webster died in 1875 and Allan continued as sole proprietor until joined in 1881 by his son George Clark Allan (1860–1934). The Allan family, trading as Allan & Co., remained owners until the early 1900s, when the Tait brothers purchased a half-share in control and management of the business. About 1892 the firm accelerated its publishing activities. Its catalogues consistently promoted the works of Australian composers and songwriters, as did the monthly journal *Australian Musical News*, published by Allan from 1911 to 1959. In 1976 the firm was taken over by Brash Holdings Ltd.

K. Hince: 'Allan, G.L.', *Australian Dictionary of Biography*, iii (Melbourne, 1969); P. Game: *The Music Sellers* (Melbourne, 1976)

K.R.S.

Allde [Alday], **Edward** (*d* 1634). English printer. He printed a few musical works between 1610 and 1615, only his initials 'E.A.' appearing on certain imprints. He printed Thomas Ravenscroft's *A Briefe Discourse* (1614) and John Amner's *Sacred Hymnes of 3, 4, 5 and 6 parts for Voyces and Vyols* (1615). His address was 'neere Christ-Church' in London. His name appears among a list of printers granted printing monopolies by James I and his successors as

'Edw. Alday, to print sett songs et al' but he apparently made little use of any such privilege.

E. Arber: *A Transcript of the Register of the Company of Stationers of London* (London, 1875–94); R. B. McKerrow: 'Edward Allde as a Typical Trade Printer', *The Library*, 4th ser., x (1929–30), 121–62; Humphries and Smith (1954, 2/1970)

M.M.

Alsbach. Dutch firm of publishers. Carl Georg Alsbach (*b* Koblenz, 20 Jan 1830; *d* Rotterdam, 3 Jan 1906) founded the firm in Rotterdam on 15 March 1866 and it became one of the most important music publishing firms in the Low Countries in the first half of the 20th century. In 1898 the business moved to Amsterdam where the founder's son Johann Adam Alsbach (*b* Rotterdam, 12 April 1873; *d* Amsterdam, 20 May 1961) directed it from 1903 until his death, when the firm was taken over by Editions Basart. By purchasing the stock of several publishing houses, including Brix von Wahlberg (1898), Stumpf & Koning (1898), J. W. L. Seyffardt and A. A. Noske, Alsbach became the publishers for the majority of Dutch composers (e.g. J. Röntgen, Diepenbrock, Sigtenhorst Meyer and Badings). From 1910 to 1960 the firm produced the publications of the Vereniging voor Nederlandse Muziekgeschiedenis. It also issued a large number of works concerned with music teaching and practical music-making, both vocal and instrumental. J. A. Alsbach was in addition the joint proprietor of a retail firm in Amsterdam (Alsbach & Doyer).

M. van Hase: 'Johann Alsbach, Musikverleger in Amsterdam†', *Börsenblatt für den Deutscher Buchhandel*, xvii (Frankfurt, 1961), 1049; A. J. Heuwekemeijer: 'Amsterdamse muziekuitgeverijen vanaf de 18 eew tot heden', *Mededelingenblad van de Vereniging voor nederlandse muziekgeschiedenis* (1967), no.24, p. 39

H.V.

Amadino, Ricciardo (*fl* Venice, 1572–1621). Italian printer. In February 1572 he witnessed a codicil to the will of Girolamo Scotto. The fact that the will states he was a printer, rather than a bookseller, suggests that he may have worked in Scotto's shop in Venice at the time. In 1583–6 in Venice he printed jointly with Giacomo Vincenti more than 76 music books. A few were reprints of popular volumes by Arcadelt, Lassus, Marenzio, Palestrina, and Bernardino Lupacchino and Gioan Maria Tasso, but most were first editions of the works of some 33 composers, of whom the best known are Asola, Bassano, Caimo, Giuseppe Guami, Marenzio, Stivori and Virchi, as well as anthologies. For their printer's mark Vincenti & Amadino used a woodcut of a pine cone, with the motto 'Aeque bonum atque tutum'. When they began to print separately (from 1586) Vincenti kept the pine-cone symbol, while Amadino adopted a woodcut of an organ (see illustration), with the motto 'Magis corde quam organo'. The dissolution of the partnership must have been amicable, for afterwards they seem to have shared type and ornamental pieces, and some of their editions have mistakes in common. Moreover, they jointly signed several theological and philosophical books between 1600 and 1609.

Working alone from 1586, Amadino printed vocal and instrumental music in such quantity as to assure him a position among Venice's four leading music printers. His preferred composers were Gastoldi, Banchieri, Monteverdi, Agazzari and Asola; the last, who is mentioned in one of the few dedications signed by Amadino, was doubtless a personal friend. Amadino also printed several theoretical volumes, including the first edition of Bottrigari's *Il desiderio* (1594). Non-musical publications by him are rare; they include two tragedies, *La Eutheria* (1588) and *Cratasiclea* (1591), by Paolo Bozzi, who was also one of Amadino's composers.

Amadino printed several folio editions and a few octavos, but otherwise virtually his whole production was in upright quarto format (gathered apparently in half-sheets). This reflected the current trend, and indeed his whole musical production mirrors the shifting musical tastes of the time; he printed canzonettas and works for *cori spezzati* as they grew in popularity, along with *falsibordoni*, accompanied solos and duets (including those by Gastoldi, d'India and Rubini), dramatic music (e.g. Monteverdi's *Orfeo* and Domenico Belli's *Orfeo dolente*) and all types of concertato music. Many of his publications were commissioned, either by the composers or by other printer-booksellers, such as Tozzi in Padua, Bozzola in Brescia or Pietro Tini in Milan. But Amadino's own preferences must account for his persistent loyalty to certain composers, such as Asola. After 1617 he printed only one surviving work, appropriately a reprint of Asola's *Officium psalmi et missa defunctorum* (1621). Amadino deserves a place in the front rank of Italian music printers of his time for the sheer volume of his output and for his many first editions and reprints of leading composers' works.

Title-page of Banchieri's 'Il metamorfosi musicale'; published by Ricciardo Amadino (Venice, 1601)

EitnerQ; Sartori (1958); idem: 'La famiglia degli editori Scotto', *AcM*, xxxvi (1964), 19; L. G. Clubb: *Italian Plays (1500–1700) in the Folger Library* (Florence, 1968), nos. 186f; O. Mischiati: 'Adriano Banchieri (1568–†1634): profilo biografico e bibliografia dell'opere', *Annuario 1965–70 del Conservatorio G. B. Martini di Bologna*, i (1971), 38–201; T. W. Bridges: *The Publishing of Arcadelt's First Book of Madrigals* (diss., Harvard U., 1982)

T.W.B.

American Composers Alliance [ACA]. Organization owned and operated by composers, founded in 1938 by Copland, Thomson, Riegger and others to publish music and promote the interests of American composers. Because of the delay between the composition of a work and the time it is published, a special service, the Composers Facsimile Edition (known as the American Composers Edition from 1972) was established in 1952 by Roger Goeb to make copies of members' works more accessible in the interim; in 1967 the service was extended to non-members. Reproductions are made from fair masters or transparencies and offered at cost. Based in New York, the ACA also sponsors concerts, broadcasts and recordings. In 1972 it became affiliated with BMI. A bulletin was published in 1938 and in 1952–65. There were over 250 members in the mid-1980s.

F. Thorne: 'The ACA Story', *BMI: The Many Worlds of Music*, no. 1 (1984), 32

R.H.M., F.B.

American Institute of Musicology. Organization founded in Cambridge, Massachusetts, by Armen Carapetyan in 1945 as the Institute of Renaissance and Baroque Music. The primary purpose of the institute is to publish scholarly editions of compositions and theoretical works, chiefly those of the Middle Ages and the Renaissance, and thus to promote the study of these sources in the humanistic disciplines in institutions of higher education. In 1946 the new name was adopted, and headquarters were moved to Rome (though offices were maintained in Cambridge and in Dallas, the latter's circulation office moving to the firm of Hänssler-Verlag in Stuttgart in 1974). A group of eminent scholars served as an advisory board until 1949, when Carapetyan became the sole director. A choir was established in 1947, and summer sessions featuring advanced studies in medieval and Renaissance music history were held in 1947 and 1948; both were soon discontinued.

The institute's publications aim at high standards of scholarship and book production. It issues several series: *Corpus Mensurabilis Musicae*, covering the principal musical sources of the Middle Ages and Renaissance, including collected works and transcriptions of manuscript sources; *Corpus Scriptorum de Musica*, editions of theoretical treatises published in the original languages; *Musicological Studies and Documents*, consisting of monographs on various topics of medieval and Renaissance music history as well as source materials not covered by the above series; *Corpus of Early Keyboard Music*, consisting of keyboard works in modern notation; *Renaissance Manuscript Studies*; and *Miscellanea*, covering other studies and sources. The institute's yearbook, *Musica disciplina* (founded in 1946 as the *Journal of Renaissance and Baroque Music* and renamed the following year), is devoted to research studies and inventories of primary sources.

Ten Years of the American Institute of Musicology, 1945–1955 (Nijmegen, Netherlands, 1955)

P.M.(ii)

André. German firm of publishers, of French extraction. It was founded by the dilettante composer Johann [Jean] André (*b* Offenbach, 28 March 1741; *d* Offenbach, 18 June 1799). His peasant grandfather, a Huguenot, fled persecution in Languedoc and settled in 1688 in Frankfurt am Main, where he became a manufacturer of silks. When only ten years old Johann succeeded to the family business, which was directed during his minority by his mother and an uncle. His early education in music, described by Gerber as 'notes, metre and some playing of chorales', came through a friend who took lessons in nearby Frankfurt; from 1756, while he learnt business management in the family firm, he had lessons in thoroughbass for several months from a transient musician – apparently the only regular instruction he ever received. Around 1758 he went to Mannheim to further his business training, and there he enthusiastically attended concerts, plays and operas, acquainting himself with the current repertory of serious and comic Italian opera as well as the modern instrumental style specific to Mannheim.

The decisive stimulus to André's artistic career occurred when he was a volunteer clerk in Frankfurt (1760–61), where during the French occupation a French troupe presented the *opéras comiques* of Philidor for the first time to a German public. He began to make translations in 1765, including more than a dozen of French plays and operettas in 1771–2, and by 1773 had composed his first Singspiel, *Der Töpfer*, dedicated to Theobald Marchand and praised by Goethe. First performed on 22 January 1773 at the Prince's Theatre in Hanau, *Der Töpfer* was a success; and, as was characteristic of André's enterprise and practicality, he tried to turn this into a material success too. In that summer the score was published, 'at the author's expense'. The artistic and apparent financial success of *Der Töpfer* determined André's subsequent career and encouraged him to further undertakings both as a dilettante composer and as a music publisher. In 1774 he issued two collections of his songs; in the next year his setting of G. A. Bürger's *Lenore* brought him widespread acclaim.

André withdrew from the family silk concern in 1774 (1773, according to Matthäus) to found his own 'Noten-fabrique' and music publishing house in Offenbach. In 1776, perhaps through Marchand's intercession, he was appointed conductor at Theophil Doebbelin's theatre in Berlin, directing a troupe of 51. There André disclosed his full talent as a composer, producing 16 Singspiels, most of them performed in Berlin. He also continued to write songs. André's mother died in 1784, and his publishing firm had fared poorly under the administration of his uncle J. B. Pfaltz. As the removal of the firm from Offenbach to Berlin was made impossible by J. J. Hummel's exclusive privilege in that city, André, by then bearing the honorary title of Kapellmeister to the Margrave Schwedt, accordingly chose to return to Offenbach, where he immediately took over the direction of his firm. Through good fortune and acumen he was able to establish relations with Pleyel, then (through Paul Wranitzky) with Joseph Haydn and later with Adalbert Gyrowetz; by 1787 he had also taken over the music publishing business of Wolfgang Nicolaus Haueisen in Frankfurt am Main. By virtue of its circumspect treatment of authors and many technical improvements in printing and production the André firm flourished considerably, reaching its 1000th item in 1797.

Meanwhile Johann's son, Johann Anton André (*b* Offenbach, 6 Oct 1775; *d* Offenbach, 6 April 1842), had become active in the firm. He showed an early gift for music, received instruction in the piano, the violin and later in singing, and began composing small pieces at the age of six. In 1787 he took violin lessons from his brother-in-law Ferdinand Fränzl, writing his first violin sonata at this time; two years later he went to Mannheim to pursue his studies under

Ignaz Fränzl. After staying briefly in Offenbach, where he had to deputize for his father in the publishing firm, he studied composition in Mannheim with G. J. Vollweiler (1792–3). Thereupon he took a position in his father's firm, studying composition independently in his spare time. In 1796 he enrolled at Jena University as a student of fine arts, but soon had to abandon his studies when his father became ill. After his father's death he undertook an extended business journey in autumn 1799 through Germany to Vienna, accompanied by his friend, the pianist P. C. Hoffmann. It was to this journey that André owed (in his own words) 'the acquaintance of the foremost musicians of Germany' and the later, if only temporary, international importance of his firm. In Munich he acquired the rights to Senefelder's and Gleissner's lithographic process from its inventors, and engaged both of them for his Offenbach firm (in a contract of 28 September 1799). In Vienna he bought the so-called Mozart-Nachlass from the composer's widow Constanze for 3150 gulden (by a contract of 8 November 1799), and immediately had Gleissner prepare a provisional manuscript catalogue, the so-called Gleissner-Verzeichnis of 1800. The first work by the André firm to use Senefelder's lithographic method was a vocal score of André's own opera *Die Weiber von Weinsberg* (1800). The André brothers set up more or less short-lived lithographic plants in Paris (the 'Imprimerie lithographique' in Charenton from 1802) and in London (1801); a cousin in Offenbach, François Johannot, attempted at the same time to apply the process to works of art (1804).

André spent most of the rest of his life sorting and ordering the Mozart manuscripts, producing editions and laying the groundwork for later Mozart research. Of his 15 children several sons were musicians or publishers; one, Carl August André (1806–87), was a music dealer and piano maker who directed the Frankfurt music shop founded by his father in 1828. A daughter Auguste (Elisabeth) André (1802–47) married Johann Baptist Streicher, a son of the noted Viennese maker of pianos, in 1823. The direction of the family's Offenbach concern passed in 1840 from Johann Anton to his son (Johann) August André (1817–87), who successfully staved off several financial crises by issuing cheap editions of the classics and attracting such composers as Franz Abt and Heinrich Marschner. Under his direction the Frankfurt and Offenbach branches merged; they later came under the joint direction of his sons Karl (1853–1914) and Adolf André (1855–1910) and, from 1910 to 1923, of their respective widows Elisabeth and Aurelie. Their successor Karl August Johann (Hans) André (1889–1951), Adolf's son, turned the firm's emphasis towards choral and teaching material, and rebuilt the house (without a music printing shop) after its almost complete destruction in 1944. The firm continues as Johann André Musikverlag, Offenbach, and though not of importance for its new publications remains noteworthy for its archive, with rich holdings of composers' autographs, correspondence and the firm's own editions.

GerberL; *GerberNL*; H. Henkel: 'Die Familie André', *Didaskalia* [suppl. of the *Frankfurter Journal*] (1 Sept 1887); *Offenbacher Zeitung* (1 Sept 1887); H. Haupt, ed.: 'Johann Anton André', *Hessische Biographien*, i (Darmstadt, 1918); O. E. Deutsch: 'Mozarts Verleger', *MJb 1955*, 49; E. Lebeau: 'Une succursale officieuse de Johann André à Paris, de 1802 à 1806', *Kongressbericht: Wien Mozartjahr 1956*, 324; A. H. André: *Zur Geschichte der Familie André – Offenbach am Main* (Offenbach, 1962); idem: *Zur Geschichte der Familie André* (Garmisch, 1963); W. A. Bauer, O. E. Deutsch and J. Eibl, eds.: *Mozart: Briefe und Aufzeichnungen*, iv, vi (Kassel, 1963, 1971); W. Matthäus: 'Der Werk Joseph Haydns im Spiegel der Geschichte des Verlages Jean André', *Haydn Yearbook*, iii (1965), 54–110; J. Eibl: 'Aus den Briefen Constance Mozarts an die Verleger Breitkopf & Härtel und Johann Anton André', *Musik und Verlag: Karl Vötterle zum 65. Geburtstag* (Kassel, 1968), 238; W. Matthäus: 'Der Musikverlag von Wolfgang Nicolaus Haueisen zu Frankfurt am Main 1771–1789: Geschichte und Bibliographie', *Mf*, xxii (1969), 421; H. Unverricht: 'Vier Briefkopierbücher des Offenbacher Musikverlags André aus dem ersten Fünftel des 19. Jahrhunderts', *Quellenstudien zur Musik: Festschrift Wolfgang Schmieder* (Frankfurt, 1972), 161; W. Matthäus: *Johann André Musikverlag zu Offenbach am Main: Verlagsgeschichte und Bibliographie 1772–1800* (Tutzing, 1973); K. Hortschansky, H. Unverricht and others: *Johann André Musikverlag* (Offenbach, 1974); W. Plath: 'Requiem-Briefe: aus der Korrespondenz Joh. Anton Andrés 1825–31', *MJb 1976–7*, 174–203; H. Unverricht: 'Die Korrespondenz des Offenbacher Musikverlegers André mit Musikern und Musiksortimentern der östlichen Mitteleuropa am Anfang des 19. Jahrhunderts', *Musik des Ostens*, viii (1982), 107; R. Federhofer-Königs: 'Die Beziehungen von Robert Schumann zur Familie André; mit unveröffentlichten Briefen', *Gutenberg-Jb 1988*, 190

W.P.

Andrez, Benoit (*b* Liège, 1714; *d* Liège, 12 Jan 1804). South Netherlands engraver and publisher. His publications, only rarely dated, bear the address 'At Liège, behind St Thomas'. Some editions were engraved by Mlle J. Andrez, possibly his daughter, who

continued the business until after 1820. He dealt primarily with instrumental music of the 'Belgian' composers of the period, publishing works by Renotte, J.-J. Robson, J.-N. Hamal, Delange, G. G. Kennis, F.-J. de Trazegnies, Regnier, Delhaise, Coppenneur and others. He also published music by Camerloher and Schwindl, as well as Boccherini's op.4 and Beethoven's op.46. For vocal music he produced the periodical *Echo ou journal de musique françoise, italienne* (1758–73), followed by the *Journal vocal composé d'airs, duos, trios* (or *Journal de musique vocale*). Besides these, Andrez published a comedy 'interspersed with songs', *La chercheuse d'esprit* by Du Boulay, and a choral work by d'Herbois, *Hymne au printemps*. He also ventured into music theory with his publication of *Ludus melothedicus* and Morel de Lescer's *Science de la musique vocale*. With the Liège musician Jean Joiris he obtained in 1752 a licence for the publication of a *Méthode pour dresser les nouvelles contredanses françoises et angloises* and he was responsible for producing six volumes of the *Recueil de contredanses angloises*.

E. vander Straeten: *La musique aux Pays-Bas avant le XIXe siècle* (Brussels, 1867–88/R1969), i (1867), 109, v (1880), 276; Goovaerts (1880); A. Auda: *La musique et les musiciens de l'ancien pays de Liège* (Brussels, 1930); P. Deses: 'Opzoekingen naar de uitgaven van de XVIIIe eeuwse muziekdrukker Benoit Andrez', *Miscellanea musicologica Floris van der Mueren* (Ghent, 1950), 93

H.V.

Anglo-Canadian Music Publishers' Association. British-owned publishing company, based in Toronto. It was founded in 1885 to counteract the importation of cheap pirated editions or reprints of English copyrights from the USA into Canada. According to the Canadian copyright law then in force, the act of printing and publishing a work in Canada gave the copyright owner the power to stop such importation, and, even more important, prevent introduction of the cheaper editions into England via Canada. Shares in the company were offered only to owners of English music copyrights who were legitimate members of the Music Publishers' Association. These publishers then had to sell their copyrights for Canada to the company at 20 shillings per song or piano piece, plus one penny royalty per copy printed by the company. A further penny was to be paid to the publisher for transfer to any composer who had retained copyright. The first manager of the company was Frank Howe; he was succeeded by Sydney Ashdown in 1890, followed by John Hanna until 1920.

If the plate number on Leslie Stuart's 'Tell me, pretty maiden' from *Floradora* is an indication, the Anglo-Canadian Music Co. (as it became known about 1895) had issued over 1200 pieces of sheet music by 1901, including several by Canadian composers. But changes to the copyright law made publishing in Canada no longer mandatory and the firm's output decreased sharply during its last 20 years. It went into liquidation in 1920.

Americus: 'The New Anglo-Canadian Music Publishers' Association – Terms upon which it will do Business', *American Art Journal*, xlii (1888), 777; 'The Ashdown Removal', *Musical Canada*, iv/ 1 (1909), 20; Chappell & Co. Ltd.: 'Canadian Copyright', *The Times* (14 May 1927); H. Kallmann: 'The Anglo-Canadian Music Company', *Encyclopedia of Music in Canada*, (Toronto, 1981)
M.C.

Antico [Anticho, Antigo, Antiquo, Antiquis], **Andrea** (*b* Montona, Istria, *c*1480; *d* after 1539). Italian cutter of woodblocks. The known activities of his many business partners, together with surviving contracts and typographical evidence, suggest that Antico was not himself a printer or publisher. Although he appears as the first major competitor of Octaviano dei Petrucci (who had initiated the printing of polyphony at Venice in 1502), his role was different, as artisan, editor and composer. Petrucci was primarily a printer and publisher, employing and overseeing the work of compositors, pressmen and editors; Antico may well have worked alone or with one assistant. Most of what is known about Antico's life emerges from documents directly related to his publications or from the books themselves. His first book, *Canzoni nove*, was published on 9 October 1510 at Rome in collaboration with the printer Marcello Silber and the woodblock cutter Gianbattista Columba. Columba also served as witness to the contract between Antico and Ottaviano Scotto (ii) for publication of the *Liber quindecim missarum* in 1516, but he seems not to have cut anything for Antico.

Although Antico's activities before 1510 are unknown, his papal privilege of 1516 names his place of birth and calls him a 'cleric of the diocese of Parenzo now living in Rome'. On 3 October 1513 he secured a privilege from Leo X to print in the papal states with a ten-year copyright on all the music he printed. Petrucci received a similar privilege on 22 October which included the exclusive right to print organ tablature. Antico's ten-year copyright on

the music itself explains the sudden shift in repertory between his *Canzoni nove* and his *Canzoni . . . libro secondo* of 1513. The first made extensive use of Petrucci's frottola books, which had not been protected by privilege outside Venetian territory. The two privileges granted in October 1513 put Petrucci and Antico on equal footing in the papal states, while Venice remained exclusively Petrucci's.

The first edition of *Canzoni . . . libro secondo* was presumably printed in 1513, just before *Libro tertio*, which contains two compositions by Antico. Antico's next book, the sumptuous *Liber quindecim missarum*, the first large folio book of polyphony, containing masses by Josquin, Brumel, Févin, Mouton and others (for illustration *see* fig.1*b*, p.9, appeared on 9 May 1516 after a lapse of three years. Antico had obtained a privilege to print 'in magno volumine' on 15 January of that year (a right specifically withheld from Petrucci), and in the dedication to Pope Leo X he explained the three-year lapse as resulting from the labour involved in the volume, claiming to be the first to print music from woodblocks. He shared publication expenses with Ottaviano Scotto; Antonio Giunta executed the printing. The title-page depicts the pope receiving from Antico a music book which contains a canon on the text, 'Vivat Leo Decimus, Pontifex Maximus', presumably by Antico himself (see illustration). This canon reappears on the title-page of the *Canzoni . . . libro quarto* of 1517. In December 1516, Leo X transferred to Antico Petrucci's privilege for organ tablature. Petrucci had failed to issue any books of tablature but Antico issued his *Frottole intabulate da sonare organi* in January 1517, the first book of Italian keyboard music to be printed. As with the *Liber quindecim missarum*, Antico seems to have approached the pope with a complete (or nearly complete) work, confident of a new privilege as reward for his labours. He seems not to have issued a second book either of keyboard tablature or 'in magno volumine'.

Canzoni . . . libro quarto appeared in 1517 in collaboration with Nicolò de Judici, a Roman printer. Sometime before October 1517, Antico left Rome for Venice. Petrucci's privilege from the Venetian signory was due to expire in 1520. Antico apparently planned to prepare new books for publication by the time Petrucci's privilege expired. In October and November 1520, Antico issued eight separate titles including six new books. In the interim, books using Antico's blocks continued to appear in Rome. Of the four

Title-page of 'Liber quindecim missarum', engraved by Antico, and published by Scotto & Giunta (Rome, 1516)

presumably issued after 1517, two are lost and known only through entries in Columbus's catalogue. As an artisan, Antico could establish himself in trade in Venice while leaving his blocks in Rome for the printer to use. This explains the appearance of Antico's papal privilege in Mazzocchi and Giunta's edition of *Canzoni . . . libro tertio* in 1518 (a reprint of the 1513 edition).

In 1520–21 Antico worked with two partners in Venice. The 1520 volumes were published in collaboration with Luc' Antonio Giunta, uncle to Jacomo Giunta of Rome. Of special interest among these are the arrangements for voice and lute in *Frottole de Misser Bortolomio Tromboncino & de Misser Marcheto Carra*. Petrucci's 1509 and 1511 volumes of Bossinensis's intabulations may well have been Antico's model; he included a revised version of Petrucci's 'Regula' for reading the tablature at the beginning of the volume. Curiously, one year after the appearance of Antico's intabulations, Tromboncino applied to the signory for a composer's patent preventing any further dissemination of his music. Given that the intabulations of his frottolas (unlike polyphonic settings) were clearly intended for performance and were circulated among a large amateur market, any errors in transmission were more likely to become permanent features of the repertory. Tromboncino must have been reacting, therefore, to the threat of losing control over his music. In 1521 Antico entered into business with Andrea Torresani. They published sacred music, including two volumes of masses and two of motets. The inclusion of Antico's papal privilege in two volumes of 1520, the otherwise anomalous *Chansons a troys* and the tablature volume, and in all the 1521 volumes suggests that Antico used his Roman connections to sell the Venetian books in the papal states as well.

Antico's activities from 1522 until 1533 are unknown. Chapman has suggested that he may have been associated with Jacques Moderne at Lyons some time before 1530 but this hypothesis remains unproven. It is likely that Antico's absence from publishing relates to the death in 1521 of Leo X, his chief patron. His next known volume is a book of Verdelot madrigals published in 1533 on co mission from Ottaviano Scotto and printed by the Da Sabio brothers in Venice. Throughout the 1530s Antico seems to have been an artisan in Scotto's employ. His press-mark does not appear in the 1530s books though he is mentioned as 'intagliatore'. He now concentrated on the craft of cutting woodblocks and was no longer closely linked to editorial or entrepreneurial activities, although he did apparently initiate his last volume, the Willaert motet book of 1539, which displays the elegant style and craftsmanship of all his work. Both the Willaert volume and the second book of Arcadelt's four-voice madrigals (formerly dated 1537) which appeared in 1539 were probably reprints, as Scotto had changed from woodblock to single-impression type in 1538.

Antico's method of combining woodblock and type differs fundamentally from that of Petrucci, who used movable type for both text and music. The use of two different techniques not only raises questions about the printing processes used for Antico's books, but also, because his volumes display a variety of type founts, calls for consideration of his partnerships and collaborations. Despite references in the scholarly literature to Antico's 'plates', it is not at all clear or likely that he normally worked with folio-sized blocks. More likely than a large-scale, page-sized format is a series of smaller blocks locked together with the type in the forme. Antico seems to have used both single- and double-line blocks in combination with the square initial capital blocks. In general, fully texted parts, appear to be cut in single-line blocks. The lute tablature of 1520 employs single line blocks, each one containing either lute or vocal notation.

The frottola volumes, in choirbook format, present an interesting case. While it is clear from the overlapping of note stems between two adjacent staves in a given voice part that both lines had to be cut on a single block, text placement confounds the issue. Where text occupies an area on the page which should be part of the block, and assuming that the entire page was printed at one pass through the press, the type sorts cannot be explained other than as having been laid into a channel or slit in the block itself. Although this use of 'text windows' is unlikely in fully texted pieces, it appears to have been the chosen procedure where only text incipits are used. These windows place obvious constraints on the printer and compositor: the type must be of a uniform size in different editions and the length of the incipit is necessarily limited by the size of the window.

The question of method has direct bearing on that of commercial operation. Whereas Petrucci owned his press and type founts, Antico seems to have owned only his woodblocks and the tools necessary to produce them. Owing to the nature of his method, Antico could leave one set of blocks with a printer while he worked on another, as he certainly did in 1518 and 1519. These differences are significant for the editing process. A book printed from movable type will show greater variation since the type is dispersed after each printing. In Petrucci's volumes, for example, there is abundant evidence of stop-press corrections and cancels. No parallel exists in Antico's output: a woodblock, once cut, is a permanent artefact. Hence subsequent editions of the same work will be unchanged in musical text. Detectable corrections or replacement blocks are rare in Antico's work.

Two frottolas in the *Canzoni . . . libro tertio* bear the signature 'Andrea Anticho D. M.' ('de Montona' in the 1520 edition) and are presumably by Antico. The 17 pieces attributed to 'A. de Antiquis (Venetus)' in Petrucci's collections of 1505–9 and in Antico's *Canzoni nove* of 1510 are probably not his work. Antico never signed his name in this manner and was not associated with Venice so early in his career.

EDITIONS

(printer's name where known
follows date of publication)

ROME, 1510–19

Canzoni nove con alcune scelte de varii libri di canto (1510; M. Silber), 1 piece ed. IMi, iii, new ser. (1964); Canzoni, sonetti, strambotti et frottole, libro tertio (1513[1], repr. 1518; J. Mazochio & J. Giunta), ed. SCMA, iv (1941); Canzoni libro secondo con cose nuove (1516, lost [probably a revised enlarged edn. of a book first pubd in 1513 before 1513[1]], repr. 1518; J. Mazochio & J. Giunta, not in *RISM*), ed. F. Luisi (Rome, 1976); Liber quindecim missarum (1516[1]; O. Scotto & A. Giunta), 4 masses ed. MMRF, viii–ix (1894); Canzoni, sonetti, strambotti et frottole, libro quarto (1517[2]; N. de Judici); Frottole intabulate da sonare organi, libro primo (1517[3]/R1970), 7 pieces ed. IMi, iii, new ser. (1964); Frottole, libro quinto (1518, lost, mentioned in the catalogue of Columbus's library, repr. Venice, 1520 [see below]; Motetti libro primo (1518, lost, mentioned in the catalogue of Columbus's library, repr. Venice, 1521), 4 motets ed. MRM, viii (1987)

VENICE, 1520–21

B. Tromboncino and M. Cara: Frottole . . . per cantar et sonar col lauto (c1520[7]; L. A. Giunta); Chansons, 3vv (1520[6]; L. A. Giunta); Frottole libro secondo (1520, in *RISM* c1516[2] attrib. G. A. de Caneto; ?L. A. Giunta), a reissue of the 1518 Roman volume; Frottole libro tertio (1520, in *RISM* c1517[1]; ?L. A. Giunta), a reissue of the 1518 Roman volume; Frottole libro quarto (1520[5]; L. A. Giunta), a reissue of the 1518 Roman volume; Motetti novi et chanzoni franciose a quatro sopra doi (1520[3]/R1982; L. A. Giunta); Motetti novi, libro secondo [-III] (1520[1-2]; L. A. Giunta), 24 motets ed. MRM, viii; Missarum diversorum authorum liber primus

[-II] (1521[1-2]; A. Torresano); Motetti libro primo (1521[3]; A. Torresano), ?repr. of the lost 1518 Roman volume, 4 motets ed. MRM, viii; Motetti liber quartus (1521[5]; A. Torresano), 13 motets ed. MRM, viii

VENICE, 1533–9

P. Verdelot: Il primo libro de madrigali (1533[2]; G. A. Nicolini da Sabio), reissues in 1536 (not in *RISM*) and 1537 (1537[9]=V1219) by O. Scotto; P. Verdelot: Il secondo libro de madrigali (1534[16]; O. Scotto), reissues in 1536 (1536[7] = V1221) and 1537 (1537[10]=V1222) by O. Scotto; P. Verdelot: Madrigali, 5vv, libro primo (c1535=V1223; O. Scotto); Canzoni francese di messer Adriano & de altri, libro primo (1535[8]; O. Scotto), reissue in 1536 (not in *RISM*); Libro secondo delle canzoni francese (1535[9]; O. Scotto), reissue in 1536 (not in *RISM*); P. Verdelot, arr. A. Willaert: Intavolatura de li madrigali . . . da cantare et sonare nel lauto (c1536/R1980=V1224 and W1104; ?O. Scotto), ed. London Pro Musica, Renaissance Music Prints, iii (1980); La couronne et fleur des chansons, 3vv (1536[1]; A. dell'Abbate), ed. L. F. Bernstein, Masters and Monuments of the Renaissance, iii (1984); P. Verdelot: Il terzo libro de madrigali (1537[11]; O. Scotto); Madrigali, 3vv (1537[7]; O. Scotto); Dei madrigali di Verdelotto et di altri eccellentissime autori, 5vv, libro secondo (1538[21]; O. Scotto); A. Willaert: Motetti . . . libro secondo, 4vv (1539; B. & O. Scotto), ed. CMM, iii/1–2 (1950); J. Arcadelt: Il secondo libro de madrigali (c1537[6]; O. Scotto) [dated 1539, probably a reissue of an earlier volume], ed. CMM, xxxi/3 (1967)

(NOT BY ANTICO)

Motetti e canzone, libro primo (1521[6]; probably printed in 1520); Motetti et carmina gallica (c1521[7]; probably printed in 1524); Motetti, libro secondo, 4vv (1521[4])

D. P. Tomasin and G. Piber: *Andrea Antico chierico di Montona nell'Istria, primo calcografo musicale* (Trieste, 1880); A. Zenatti: 'Andrea Antico da Montona', *Archivio storico per Trieste, l'Istria e il Trentino*, i (1881–2), 167–99, but rev. iii (1884–6), 249–61; A. Gravisi: 'Andrea Antico istriano da Montona', *Atti e memorie della Società istriana di archeologia e storia patria*, i (Parenzo, 1885), 141; K. Jeppesen: *Die italienische Orgelmusik am Anfang des Cinquecento* (Copenhagen, 1943, 2/1960); A. Einstein: 'Andrea Antico's *Canzoni nove* of 1510', *MQ*, xxxvii (1951), 330; A.-M. Bautier-Regnier: 'L'édition musicale italienne et les musiciens d'outremonts au XVIe siècle (1501–1563)', *La Renaissance dans les provinces du nord: CNRS Entretiens d'Arras 1954*, 27; D. Plamenac: 'Excerpta Colombiniana: Items of Musical Interest in Fernando Colón's *Regestrum*', *Miscelánea en homenaje a Monseñor Higinio Anglés* (Barcelona, 1958–61), ii, 663; C. W. Chapman: 'Andrea Antico' (diss., Harvard U., 1964); D. Plamenac: 'The Recently Discovered Complete Copy of A. Antico's *Frottole Intabulate* (1517)', *Aspects of Medieval and Renaissance Music: a Birthday Offering to Gustave Reese* (New York, 1966), 683; C. W. Chapman: 'Printed Collections of Polyphonic Music Owned by Ferdinand Columbus', *JAMS*, xxi (1968), 34–84; K. Jeppesen: *La frottola:*

Bemerkungen zur Bibliographie der ältesten weltlichen Notendrucke in Italien (Copenhagen, 1968); E. E. Lowinsky: Introduction, *The Medici Code of 1518*, MRM, iii (1968); L. F. Bernstein: '*La Couronne et fleur des chansons a trois*: a Mirror of the French Chanson in the Years between Ottaviano Petrucci and Antonio Gardano', *JAMS*, xxvi (1973), 1–68; F. Luisi: 'Il secondo libro di frottole di Andrea Antico', *NRMI*, viii (1974), 491–535; idem: 'La nascita dell'editoria musicale romana: Andrea Antico e il *Liber quindecim Missarum*', Conservatorio de musica S. Cecilia, *Annuario dell'anno accademico 1973–4* (Rome, 1974); idem: *Il secondo libro di frottole di Andrea Antico* (Rome, 1976); idem: 'Le frottole per canto e liuto di B. Tromboncino e M. Cara nella edizione adespota di Andrea Antico', *NRMI*, x (1976), 211–58; M. Picker: 'The Motet Anthologies of Andrea Antico', *A Musical Offering: Essays in Honor of Martin Bernstein* (New York, 1977), 211; idem: 'The Motet Anthologies of Petrucci and Antico published between 1514 and 1521: a Comparative Study', *Formen und Probleme der Überlieferung mehrstimmiger Musik im Zeitalter Josquins Desprez*, ed. L. Finscher (Munich, 1981), 181; S. Boorman: 'Liber quindecim missarum', *Raffaello in Vaticano*, ed. G. Muratore (Milan, 1984), 82; idem: 'Early Music Printing: an Indirect Connection with the Raphael Circle', *Renaissance Studies in Honor of Craig Hugh Smyth* (Florence, 1985), 533; M. Picker: Introduction, *The Motet Books of Andrea Antico*, MRM, viii (1987)

B.L.M.

Apiarius [Biener], **Mathias** (*b* Berching, nr. Eichstätt, Bavaria, *c*1500; *d* Berne, autumn 1554). German printer and publisher. He settled in Basle, where he worked as a bookbinder and was given citizenship on 3 April 1527, having been admitted to the Saffran Guild on 10 December 1525. He seems to have been associated with the Reformation at an early stage; he attended the religious debates held in Berne in 1528, and it was possibly at this time that he met the Berne precentor Cosmas Alder. In 1536 he published three four-part songs by Alder, in a book of songs produced jointly with Peter Schoeffer in Strasbourg; in 1553 he also published hymns by Alder. From the middle of 1533 to 1537 he printed numerous Reformation writings (e.g. by W. F. Capito and M. Bucer) in Strasbourg, and he and Schoeffer jointly published works on music theory and practice; their association probably stemmed from Apiarius's thorough knowledge of music and his contact with composers. In 1539 he opened the first printing press in Berne, and on 19 January became a citizen. Besides music he published historical, religious and literary works, and also many songsheets (usually without the melodies). Because of their political and religious content these song publications often led to disputes within the Swiss regions. For

financial reasons Apiarius worked for many years as bookbinder to the Berne government. The works published jointly with Schoeffer were printed from two impressions, but those produced in Berne were single-impression; all were of good quality (see Bloesch for a complete bibliography of Apiarius's output). His son Samuel (*c*1530–90) took over the printing press after his father's death, but apart from a considerable number of songsheets he did not publish any new music. Mathias's second son, Sigfried, also worked as a bookbinder in Berne, where he became a Stadtpfeifer in 1553. Wannenmacher's *Bicinia* (RISM 1553[31]) were dedicated to Sigfried and two other Stadtpfeifer (Michel Copp and Wendlin Schärer). This publication also contained two bicinia by Mathias (*Ach hulff mich leid* and *Es taget vor dem walde*).

A. Thürlings: 'Der Musikdruck mit beweglichen Metalltypen im 16. Jahrhundert und die Musikdrucke des Mathias Apiarius in Strassburg und Bern', *VMw*, viii (1892), 389; A. Fluri: 'Mathias Apiarius, der erste Buchdrucker Berns (1537–1554)', *Neues Berner Taschenbuch* (1897), 196–253; idem: 'Die Brüder Samuel und Sigfrid Apiarius, Buchdrucker in Bern (1554 bis 1565)', *Neues Berner Taschenbuch* (1898), 168–233; idem: 'Mathias Apiarius, Berns erster Buchdrucker', *Schweizerisches Gutenbergmuseum*, xiv (1928), 105, xvi (1930), 6, 47, 120; W. Schuh: 'Anmerkungen zu den Berner Musikdrucken des Mathias Apiarius', *SMz*, lxix (1929), 282; A. Geering: *Die Vokalmusik in der Schweiz zur Zeit der Reformation* (Aarau, 1933); H. Bloesch, ed.: *Dreissig Volkslieder aus den ersten Pressen der Apiarius, im Faksimiledruck herausgegeben mit einer Einleitung und Bibliographie* (Berne, 1937); K. J. Lüthi: 'Die Einführung der Buchdruckerkunst in Bern 1537', *Schweizerisches Gutenbergmuseum*, xxiii (1937), 5–58 [with 16 facs.]; F. Ritter: *Histoire de l'imprimerie alsacienne au XVe et XVIe siècles* (Strasbourg, 1955); J. Benzing: 'Peter Schöffer der jüngere, Musikdrucker zu Mainz, Worms, Strassburg und Venedig (tätig 1512–1542)', *Jb für Liturgik und Hymnologie*, iv (1958–9), 133

J. S.

Arct, Michał (*b* Lublin, 31 Dec 1840; *d* Warsaw, 15 Feb 1916). Polish bookseller and publisher. He served his apprenticeship in the bookshop of his uncle Stanisław Arct in Warsaw, then at Behr & Bock in Berlin. In 1862 he took over the management of Stanisław Arct's bookshop, becoming its proprietor in 1881. In 1900 he founded his own printing house, and devoted himself almost completely to publishing, especially dictionaries, encyclopedias, school and children's literature, and music. As a distinguished authority on music publishing he developed considerably the retailing of scores, as well as introducing a system of lending music for the students of the Warsaw Conservatory. He increased his number of publications to 100 titles yearly, mainly for teaching purposes. The publishing firm M. Arct existed until 1939 and, as the firm S. Arct, from 1946 to 1949.

Music series published by M. Arct include *Etudes et exercises, Sonates et sonatines, Musique moderne, Młody muzyk* ('Young musician'), *Przyjaciółki* ('The friends'; for four hands) and *Podręcznik dla miłośników oper* ('A manual for opera lovers'). Catalogues published include *Katalog książek i nut* (Warsaw, 1892), *Wydawnictwa muzyczne Księgarni i składu nut* (1895), *Wydawnictwa pedagogiczno-muzyczne M. Arcta* (1916), *Katalog utworów muzycznych* (1929) and *Książki i nuty wydane od 1946 roku* (1949).

J. Muszkowski: *Polski słownik biograficzny,* i (Kraków, 1936), 155; *Słownik pracowników książki polskiej* [Dictionary of Polish printers] (Warsaw and Łódź, 1972), 14

K.M.(i)

A-R Editions. American firm of publishers. It was founded in New Haven in 1962 by Gary J. N. Aamodt and Clyde Rykken to provide modern critical editions of music of historical interest and artistic integrity for scholars, students and performers. The 'Recent Researches' series were launched in 1964 with volumes of music from the Renaissance and Baroque periods and expanded to include music of the Middle Ages and early Renaissance, the Classical era and the 19th century. In 1968 the firm moved to Madison, Wisconsin, and the same year took over the production and distribution of the Yale University Collegium Musicum series of historical editions. Rykken left the firm in 1971 and was replaced the following year by Lila Aamodt. The series *Recent Researches in American Music* was initiated in 1977 in collaboration with the Institute for Studies in American Music, and a series devoted to the oral traditions of music has been announced as has *Music in the United States*, co-published with the American Musicological Society. A-R executes its own music origination and pioneered the computer-driven photocomposition of music. Lewis Lockwood's edition of the masses of Vincenzo Ruffo (1979) was the first music publication to have been produced entirely in this manner. Since then, the process has proven its commercial viability not only in the Recent Researches series but also in the computerized setting that A-R undertakes for other publishers.

G. J. N. Aamodt: 'Music Publishing Today: a Symposium', *Notes*, xxxii (1975–6), 235; W. B.

Hewlett and E. Selfridge-Field: *Directory of Computer Assisted Research in Musicology, 1986* (Menlo Park, CA, 1986), 10

J.M.B.(i), S.M.W.

Arndes [Arns, Arnes, Arendes de Hamborch], **Steffen** [Stephano Aquila de Magonza di Sassonia] (*fl* 1470–1516). German printer and typecaster, active in Italy and Germany. Apparently trained in Mainz, he first appeared as a printer with Johann Neumeister in Foligno (1470), then worked with Johann Vydenast in Perugia where he opened a shop of his own (1473–81). He moved to Schleswig in 1485/6 and finally to Lübeck, printing for 30 years. His *Graduale suecicum* (Lübeck, 1493), one of the few graduals printed in the 15th century, exists in a unique incomplete copy (Kungliga Biblioteket, Stockholm). For it Arndes designed a sophisticated roman plainchant type for the complex neumes of the melismatic chant. The long-stemmed neumes are printed in black on red staves, ten to a page. He also published missals; the early *Missale slesvicense* of 1486 contains no printed music.

A. Rosso: *L'arte tipografica in Perugia* (Perugia, 1868); M. Faloci Puligrari: 'L'arte tipografica in Foligno nel secolo XV', *La bibliofilia*, i (1899–1900), 283; T. Schmid, ed.: *Graduale Arosiense impressum* (Malmö, 1959); P. Amelung: 'Steffen Arndes', *Lexikon des gesamten Buchwesens*, i/2 (Stuttgart, 1986)

M.K.D.

Arrow Music Press. American firm of publishers. It was founded in New York in 1938 by Marc Blitzstein, Aaron Copland, Lehman Engel and Virgil Thomson to encourage the composition, publication and distribution of contemporary American music. In addition to leasing the catalogue of the Cos Cob Press, it published works by Carter, Cowell, Diamond, Ray Green, Harris, Ives, Piston, Schuman and Sessions as well as its founders. Its catalogue was acquired by Boosey & Hawkes in 1956, but with the provision that composers could withdraw their works for placement elsewhere.

V. Thomson: *Virgil Thomson* (New York, 1966), 278; L. Engel: *This Bright Day: an Autobiography* (New York, 1974), 88

R.A.L.

Ars Viva. German firm of publishers. It was founded in 1950 in Zurich by Hermann Scherchen (1891–1966) to publish music by postwar avant-garde composers. The future of the Ars Viva catalogue was assured when in 1953 it was incorporated into the catalogue of B.

Artaria

Schott's Söhne, Mainz. Since then the Ars Viva list has gradually increased, the majority of its scores being by contemporary German or Swiss composers including Heinz Holliger, Klaus Huber, Giselher Klebe, Rolf Liebermann and Aribert Reimann, as well as important compositions by Luigi Dallapiccola and Niccolò Castiglioni and most of the early works of Luigi Nono. In addition, the firm published a few relatively unknown works by earlier composers, including Beethoven, Cavalieri and Pergolesi, some in editions by Hermann Scherchen himself.

A. Melichar: *Musik in der Zwangsjacke: die deutschen Musik zwischen Orff und Schönberg* (Vienna and Stuttgart, 2/1959)

A.P.(ii)

Artaria (i). Austrian firm of publishers. It was founded in Mainz in 1765 and in 1766 moved to Vienna, where it became the first important music publishing firm in the city.

1. HISTORY. The Artaria family originated in Blevio on Lake Como, Italy. On 15 January 1759 the brothers Cesare Timoteo (1706–85), Domenico (i) (1715–84) and Giovanni Casimiro Artaria (1725–97) obtained passes to visit the fairs in Frankfurt am Main, Leipzig and Würzberg; Carlo (1747–1808), son of Cesare, and Francesco (1744–1808), son of Domenico (i), accompanied them as *giovini* (commercial assistants). Cesare and Domenico (i) returned to their own country; Carlo and Francesco founded with their uncle Giovanni Casimiro the firm Giovanni Artaria & Co. in Mainz in 1765. In 1766 the brothers left Mainz and travelled to Vienna, where they at first carried on business without their own premises. According to the *Wiener Diarium* of 25 July 1770, Carlo owned a shop in the Kleine Dorotheergasse until that date, but there is no further evidence to support this. On 31 October 1770 the shop known as 'Zum König von Dänemark' was opened. The firm was called Cugini Artaria, becoming Artaria & Comp. in 1771; the licence granted to Carlo Artaria on 23 February covered only dealings in copper engravings. In 1774 connections with the firm in Mainz were re-established. The businesses developed so favourably that on 28 January 1775 the Vienna firm was able to open a shop in the Kohlmarkt, which also bore the name 'Zum König von Dänemark'.

Giovanni Casimiro's son Pasquale (1755–85) entered the business as his father's successor and from 19 October 1776 (*Wiener Diarium*, no.84) trade in printed music began with the import of

works from London, Amsterdam and particularly Paris (no first stock catalogue is extant). With the new dealing in printed music, plans for a music publishing business were also developed; the rise of the Viennese Classical period provided an encouraging context. The Paris music publisher Anton Huberty offered a stimulus to the business side of the undertaking. He had been selling his publications on the Viennese market since 1770 through various booksellers; at the beginning of 1777 he moved to Vienna with his family and established himself very successfully with a music engraving and printing shop, but his undertaking was short-lived owing to his advanced age. The Artarias seized the opportunity to issue their first publication, six trios by Bonaga, on 12 August 1778 (the plate numbers 1 and 2 of these insignificant works were later reassigned to Pleyel's quartets op.1). Huberty was an engraver for Artaria until his death on 13 January 1791.

In 1780 Ignazio Artaria (1757–1820), brother of Francesco, entered the business. He was granted a ten-year printing licence on 28 January 1782 by Emperor Joseph II: published pieces from this time bear the mark C.P.S.C.M. ('cum privilegio Suae Caesareae Majestatis'). After the death of Pasquale Artaria in 1785, his brother Domenico (ii) (1765–1823) joined the business, and in the same year the firm set up its own music engraving workshop, using at first pewter plates. Another publisher, Christoph Torricella, a competitor in the Viennese market since 31 January 1781, and now 71 years old, was soon outstripped: on 12 August 1786 Artaria bought 980 of his engraving plates at a public auction, together with all his publishing rights.

In 1789 the flourishing business was transferred to the house 'Zum englischen Gruss', in the Kohlmarkt. Domenico (ii), who with his brother Giovanni Maria (1771–1835) had carried on the Mainz branch of the firm, resigned in 1793, bringing about the final division of the firm, until then known as 'Artaria & Comp., Wien und Mainz'. The Mainz branch moved to Mannheim and combined with the firm of Fontaine to form an art bookshop and publishing business which existed until 1867.

Giovanni Cappi (whose sister, Maria, Carlo Artaria subsequently married) became an apprentice in the firm in 1773, then an employee, and finally a partner in 1792. Another employee, Tranquillo Mollo (1767–1837), from Bellinzona, also became a partner, in 1793. Finally Pietro

Cappi, a nephew of Giovanni, was employed in the firm. During these years an increasing number of music publications were transferred from the publisher Franz Anton Hoffmeister to Artaria. Between 1793 and 1798 the Artaria firm had five partners: Carlo, Francesco and Ignazio Artaria, as well as Cappi and Mollo. The war years and disagreements within the firm brought about a crisis which lasted until 1804 and had an extremely detrimental effect on the business. The contracts with Ignazio and Mollo expired in 1798; the former returned to Italy while Mollo established his own arts shop (his assets were paid over to him in publications). A further division was agreed on 16 May 1801: Francesco obtained a new licence and transferred it to his son Domenico (iii) (1775–1842), who was in partnership with Mollo, but operating from the Artaria premises; Carlo, who had continued as sole owner of the original firm, sold it to Mollo in October 1802. After the parting with Mollo in 1804 Domenico (iii) took over the sole direction of the firm at the Kohlmarkt. From 1805 to 1816 Pietro Cappi was a partner in the firm, and from 1807 until 1824 Carlo Boldrini was a third partner. In 1818 a share in the music publishing house was bought by Johann Traeg and in 1832 another by Thaddäus Weigl. In about 1830 the firm opened an auction room. After the death of Domenico (iii) on 5 June 1842, his son August (1807–93), who had entered the firm in 1833, became sole owner. The music publications of the house became fewer; new publishers were appearing and capturing the market, in particular Haslinger, Diabelli and Mechetti. In February 1858 the *Wiener Zeitung* carried the last announcement of an Artaria music publication (although the *Denkmäler der Tonkunst in Österreich* bears the Artaria imprint between 1894 and 1918). August's sons Karl August (1855–1919) and Dominik (1858–1936) entered the firm in 1881 and 1890 respectively, and after their father's death in 1893 became sole owners.

Mathias Artaria (1793–1835), son of Domenico (ii), was involved in music publishing independently of the family firm. He took over Daniel Sprenger's arts shop in 1818; his firm (which issued some Schubert first editions) was continued after his death (in 1835) by his widow (*see* MAISCH, LUDWIG).

2. PUBLICATIONS. The Artaria firm's activities began in the art trade and expanded into geography and iconography. In these areas it achieved world-wide importance, and the art and map publishing business was carried on as an integral branch of the firm into the 20th century. The arts shop offered paintings, foreign art journals, engravings, lithographs, contemporary portraits of famous men (from its own press) and numerous pictorial views; the house of Artaria gained international recognition and established itself as a cultural focus of the Viennese upper middle classes.

It was in music publishing however that the firm revealed a particularly felicitous touch (although its first owners apparently had no musical education). As early as 1779 they established contact with Joseph Haydn and on 12 April 1780 they published a set of his piano sonatas (HXVI: 20, 35–9) with plate no.7; this inaugurated a series of over 300 editions of Haydn's compositions (see illustration). Composer and publisher enjoyed a warm relationship, reflected in their lively correspondence. On 8 December 1781, a set of piano and violin sonatas by Mozart appeared; Artaria subsequently published 83 first editions and 36 early editions of Mozart in addition to publications taken over from Hoffmeister, thus becoming Mozart's chief publisher during his lifetime. The young Beethoven, on arriving in Vienna, was also quickly drawn to Artaria; his first published work, a set of piano variations, appeared on 31 July 1793, followed by first editions of his works up to op.8. Despite subsequent disagreements, the firm continued to receive new works from Beethoven, and by 1858 editions of his works – including arrangements and reprints – numbered over 100. The numerous surviving catalogues from this early period reveal many other well-known names, including Boccherini, Clementi, Gluck, Kozeluch, Pleyel, Salieri and Vanhal.

A unique business relationship developed between Artaria and the composer and music publisher F. A. Hoffmeister, who until the turn of the century several times simply surrendered portions of his publishing business to Artaria. In 1802 production had reached publication no.906, almost entirely works of fine quality. Then came the interregnum of co-production with T. Mollo & Co., which embraces publication nos.907–1000 as well as 1501–1692 and which ended by 25 August 1804. Nos.1001–1500 are found in the firm's main ledger reserved for a series with the title *Raccolta d'arie*, but in fact were used for the publication of piano reductions from current operas and of individual arias (the pieces appeared between 1787 and 1804 with the special 'Raccolta' number, as distinguished from the plate

Title-page of the first edition of Haydn's Six Quartets op.33, published by Artaria in 1782

number, on the bottom left margin). While at first using several independent music engravers, Artaria later employed its own engravers and also established its own press. Ferdinand Kauer is known to have been employed as a publisher's reader, and according to his own records carried out his duties for 17 years. Beyond its encouragement of Classical composers, the firm was committed to a demanding publishing programme; an impressive list of other composers, represented by numerous works, included Cramer, Hummel, Moscheles, Rossini, Sarti and Sterkel (Schubert, however, published only three works with Artaria).

Towards the middle of the 19th century publishing activities waned and works of poor quality began to be accepted; in 1858, under August Artaria, the music publishing house closed down. It has not been established whether he was unable to keep up with the times, or simply lost interest and gave way to younger men. Towards the end of the century the remaining assets went to the Viennese music publisher Josef Weinberger. The important collection of autographs which the family had accumulated over the years, partly through publishing activities and partly through subsequent independent purchases by Domenico Artaria (iii), was later transferred to the Preussische Staatsbibliothek.

L. von Köchel: *Chronologisch-thematisches Verzeichnis sämtlicher Tonwerke Wolfgang Amade Mozarts* (Leipzig, 1862, rev. 6/1964); G. Adler: *Verzeichnis der musikalischen Autographen von Ludwig van Beethoven . . . im Besitze von Artaria in Wien* (Vienna, 1890); F. Artaria and H. Botstiber: *Joseph Haydn und das Verlagshaus Artaria* (Vienna, 1909); K. E. Blümml and G. Gugitz: *Von Leuten und Zeiten im alten Wien* (Vienna and Leipzig, 1922); J. P. Larsen: *Die Haydn-Überlieferung* (Copenhagen, 1939); A. Weinmann: *Vollständiges Verlagsverzeichnis Artaria & Comp.* (Vienna, 1952/R1978); G. Kinsky and H. Halm: *Thematisch-bibliographisches Verzeichnis aller vollendeten Kompositionen Ludwig van Beethovens* (Munich and Duisberg, 1955); A. van Hoboken: *Joseph Haydn: thematischbibliographisches Werkverzeichnis* (Mainz, 1957–71); A. Weinmann: *Verlagsverzeichnis Tranquillo Mollo* (Vienna, 1964); idem: *Verlagsverzeichnis Giovanni Cappi bis A. O. Witzendorf* (Vienna, 1967); *Geschichte der Firmen Artaria & Compagnie und Freytag-Berndt und Artaria* (Vienna, 1970); R. Hilmar: *Der Musikverlag Artaria & Comp.: Geschichte und Probleme der Druckproduktion* (Tutzing, 1977); G. Feder and F. H. Franken: 'Ein wiedergefundener Brief Haydns an Artaria & Co.', *Haydn-Studien*, v (1982), 55; O. Hafner: 'Mozart im Steirischen Musikalienhandel vor 1800', *Mitteilungen der Internationalen Stiftung Mozarteum Salzburg*, xxix (1982), 29; G. Haberkamp: *Die Erstdrucke der Werke von Wolfgang Amadeus Mozart* (Tutzing, 1986)

A.W.

Artaria (ii). Italian family of printers and publishers, active in Milan, Novara and Genoa. Ferdinando Artaria (*b* Blevio di Como, 1781; *d* Milan, 1843), a cousin of Carlo and Francesco Artaria of Vienna, opened a music publishing and copying business at Milan in 1805 under the Coperto de' Figini. He moved to the Piazzale del Regio Teatro alla Scala in 1816, and a year later to the Contrada S Margherita. He was the first Milanese music publisher to adopt lithography, having obtained its use, by payment, from the Trentino publisher Giuseppe de Werz da Sprengenstein (who had introduced the process to Milan in 1808). Ferdinando used lithography chiefly for the city views he issued from 1814, however; most of his music editions were engraved. By 1828 he had produced about 200, mainly symphonic and chamber works in piano arrangements (e.g. *Repertorio, o sia raccolta di scelte sinfonie per pianoforte*, begun in 1821), and music treatises, including those of Adam, Boccherini, Asioli and Campagnoli. In 1829 he transferred his patent for music selling and printing to his sons Epimaco Francesco and Pasquale, retaining the copying side of the business.

Epimaco (*d* 1857), a musician, painter and man of letters, developed the publishing side and succeeded in obtaining such important works as Bellini's *I Capuleti e i Montecchi*, meanwhile continuing to issue piano arrangements. In 1837 the business was liquidated, Giovanni Ricordi acquiring all the surviving plates, but the firm was reconstituted as 'Ferdinando Artaria e Figlio' and the series of plate numbers continued. Epimaco then opened a business at Novara for typographical, lithographical and engraved music printing, which produced among other things music of Czerny and Spohr. In 1848 he moved to Genoa, where he worked on the commercial side until his death. His brother Pasquale had assumed control of the Milanese shop in 1843, but it was taken over in 1852 by Ferdinando Sacchi, under whom the production of music ceased. In all, the family's music editions number about 500.

A.Z.L.

Ascherberg, Hopwood & Crew. English firm of publishers. It was formed on the amalgamation in 1906 of Eugene Ascherberg & Co. (founded 1878) and Hopwood & Crew (founded 1860), together with their subsidiaries, the music publishers Duncan Davison & Co., John Blockley, Orsborn & Co. and Howard & Co. Its substantial catalogue covered music of every description, but was based mainly on light music including the waltzes of Waldteufel, Archibald Joyce and Charles Ancliffe. Among its successful stage works were the operettas *The Geisha* and *The Belle of New York*, and later musical comedies such as *The Maid of the Mountains* and *The Last Waltz*. The firm also held the British copyrights for Mascagni's *Cavalleria rusticana* and Leoncavallo's *Pagliacci*. Its many instrumental and choral series included works by Elgar, Reger and Coleridge-Taylor. In 1970 the firm was taken over by Chappell.

'The Music Publisher of Tradition: Ascherberg and his Amalgamations', *MO*, lxiv (1940–41), 508; Coover (1988)

J.A.F.M./P.W.J.

Ashdown, Edwin. English firm of publishers. Edwin Ashdown (1826–1912) and Henry John Parry were employed by Wessel & Co. and took over the business on the retirement of Christian Rudolph Wessel in 1860; the firm then became known as Ashdown & Parry. Parry retired in 1882 and the firm's name changed to Edwin Ashdown, becoming a limited company in 1891. The firm's publications included much new English music and the short-lived periodical *Hanover Square* (1867–9), edited by the pianist Lindsay Sloper, which consisted largely of new music. Composers in the catalogue included G. A. Macfarren, Sullivan, Elgar and Vaughan Williams, and for many years the firm was also the English agent for Bote & Bock of Berlin. Piano and choral music and solo songs came to form the core of its output. Ashdown also took over the music publishing firms of Hatzfeld & Co. (1903), Enoch & Co. (1927) and J. H. Larway (1929).

'Mr. Edwin Ashdown', *Musical Herald* (1903), 99; 'The House of Ashdown', *The Windmill*, i/13 (1958), 9; Coover (1988)

P.W.J.

Associated Board of the Royal Schools of Music. An institution set up in 1889 to organize local examinations for the Royal Academy of Music and the Royal College of Music, both in London; in 1947 it also became associated with the Royal Scottish Academy of Music, Glasgow, and the Royal Manchester College of Music (now part of the Royal Northern College of Music). It opened a publishing department in 1920, to provide the required music for its examinations without depending on outside firms; besides examination music it issued practice books for theory, sight-reading and aural tests. It soon extended its publishing to include not only educational

selections but also authoritative editions of standard repertory; notable among these are the editions of Bach's '48' (by Donald Tovey and Harold Samuel, 1924) and Beethoven's piano sonatas (by Donald Tovey and Harold Craxton, 1931), as well as many editions, notably of Schubert, by Howard Ferguson.

Associated Music Publishers [AMP]. American firm of publishers, active in New York. It was founded in 1927 by Paul Heinicke, originally as the sole American agency for leading European music publishing houses, including Bote & Bock, Breitkopf & Härtel, Doblinger, Eschig, Schott, Simrock, Union Musical Español and Universal Edition. The firm began publishing in its own right and has built up an important catalogue of American composers including John Adams, Carter, Cowell, Dello Joio, Harbison, Harris, Husa, Ives, Kirchner, Peter Lieberson, Piston, Riegger, Schuller, Surinach, Tower and Wilder. Leonard Feist (*b* 1910) served as president, 1956–64. In 1964 it was acquired by G. Schirmer, which in turn was acquired by Music Sales in 1986; as a BMI affiliate it has retained an interdependent publishing programme complementing Schirmer's affiliation with ASCAP.

A.P.(i)

Attaingnant, Pierre (*b* probably in or nr. Douai, *c*1494; *d* Paris, late 1551 or 1552). French music printer, publisher, bookseller, punchcutter and typecaster.

1. LIFE. He is probably the 'Pierotin Attaingnant', a minor, named as residuary legatee in the 1503 will of Canon Simon Attaingnant of Douai. By a document notarized 13 January 1513/14 Attaingnant, described as a 'bookseller, living in Paris', leased a press to Jean de la Roche, reserving the right to print ecclesiastical pardons and the like, should he receive commissions. He may have gone to Paris originally with a chorister's scholarship for the Collège de Dainville, which was subject to the cathedral chapters of Arras and Noyon. This institution leased the part of its buildings on the rue de la Harpe to Philippe Pigouchet (*fl* 1490–1514), the printer-engraver famous for his Hours and the master to whom Attaingnant was probably apprenticed. Marriage to one of Pigouchet's daughters, Claude, made Attaingnant his heir. Another of Pigouchet's daughters, Germaine, was married to Poncet le Preux (1481–1559), one of the

four 'grands libraires jurés' of the university, Master of the Printers' Guild and a prolific publisher of scholarly texts.

The earliest surviving book to bear Attaingnant's name is a Noyon breviary of 1525, the only book that he is known to have published in conjunction with Le Preux. Attaingnant continued to publish liturgical books for Noyon throughout his life as well as syllabuses for schoolboys. After experimenting with music types for several years he brought out the *Chansons nouvelles*, dated 4 April 1527/8. Within a year they were followed by at least seven other books in the same format. At this time he sought and obtained royal protection in the form of a privilege preventing others from copying the contents of his books for three years after printing. It specifically mentioned books 'tant en musique, jeux de Lutz, Orgues, et semblables instruments' which he had printed or at least planned. (These intentions were realized with the lute tablatures of 1529 and 1530 and the keyboard scores of 1531.)

When the protection covering his earliest music books began to run out in spring 1531, he sought a wider, six-year privilege covering 'messes, motetz, hymnes, chansons que desditz jeux de Lutz, Flustes et Orgues, en grans et petitz volumes'. The royal decree of 18 June 1531 granting this is printed in the first volume of folio masses (1532). Also in this volume is Attaingnant's dedicatory address to the Cardinal of Tournon, who was praised in a Latin poem, written by Nicolas Bourbon for the occasion. Each of the seven mass volumes was illustrated with a woodcut of the court hearing Mass by Oronce Fine, royal mathematician and cosmographer (see illustration). Further royal preferment was natural after the achievement represented by the folio masses – Tournon was a powerful statesman as well as titular head of the royal chapel. Hopes mentioned in the second privilege were also realized by the imposing 13-volume set of motets in quarto brought out in 1534 and 1535. A 14th volume devoted to Manchicourt appeared in 1539.

In 1537, in addition to a renewal of his privilege, Attaingnant received the unprecedented distinction of 'imprimeur et libraire du Roy en musique'. The other royal printers were men of learning such as Robert Estienne. About the time of Attaingnant's nomination, he began to abandon the older text types for the italics and romans more in keeping with humanist tastes. In 1538 he took a partner, Herbert Jullet, husband of his daughter Germaine, with whom he jointly signed a portion of

The French court at Mass: woodcut by Oronce Fine from 'Primus liber tres missas' printed by Attaingnant (1532)

the firm's output from then until Jullet's death in 1545. After his wife's death in 1543, an inventory of the firm's extensive stock and equipment was made. Two years later Attaingnant married Marie Lescallopier. He witnessed a contract as late as 3 October 1551 but died before the end of 1552. His widow printed a few music books between 1553 and 1557, then restricted her publications almost exclusively to the scholarly commentaries of Léger du Chesne, the last of which appeared in 1567. In the general tax of 1571 she was levied 6 livres on the considerable fortune of 300,000 livres.

2. PUBLICATIONS: In Attaingnant's method of printing music the staff-segments and notes were combined, so that both could be printed in a single impression (for illustration *see* fig.6a, p.24). This process superseded the double- or triple-impression techniques required to produce Petrucci's expensive quartos and became the first international method of music printing. The reason was primarily economic, for it allowed the time and cost of production to be reduced by half, or more. The role formerly ascribed to Pierre Haultin in this invention has been traced to the flawed account of Pierre Fournier *le jeune*, writing in 1765. A similar but more primitive method produced the music types used by John Rastell in his *Interlude*, which likely antedates the *Chansons nouvelles*. But Rastell's workmen were probably French and may have had some knowledge of experimental stages in the Attaingnant shop before the perfection of the new technique. An altogether different method that it gradually displaced was the printing of music from engraved woodblocks, of which Andrea Antico was the foremost craftsman. Attaingnant at first followed the small octavo format made popular by Antico in the 1520s, but from the mid-1530s oblong quarto became the norm for all his music publications.

The commercial success of the new method coincided with the flowering of the Parisian chanson. The leading chanson composers, Claudin de Sermisy, Clément Janequin and Pierre Certon, all in royal service of one kind or another, are very well represented in Attaingnant's collections, which diffused their works widely. The tastes and liberality of Francis I were decisive: his patronage effectively made Attaingnant the official printer of the king's music. With this development a major step was taken towards the highly centralized establishment that has characterized French musical life ever since. In compiling his extensive catalogue of sacred and secular publications Attaingnant opened the way, showing others not only how to print, but also what to print; for example, his 1546 publication of settings by Certon and Mornable of the psalms in Marot's translations, the first books of their kind, were harbingers of a wave of similar settings.

Attaingnant was the first music publisher to achieve a true mass production. The numbered series of chansons from his later years, for instance, ran to 36 volumes and many of these went through two or three editions. With press runs conservatively estimated at 1000 copies, the total number of chansons put on the market by Attaingnant alone reached a staggering figure. To sell in such quantity required outlets on an international level. These were facilitated through the publishing business of Le Preux, who had dealings with some of the large German syndicates and maintained depots in various centres. He is known to have held stocks of Attaingnant's music books and may have been responsible for their foreign distribution.

As far as is known, Attaingnant was not a composer; yet he must have been skilled enough to do his own editing. At least, no house editor was named until the very last years, when Claude Gervaise (*fl* 1540–60) was given credit for revising and correcting some books of ensemble dances (Gervaise continued to give editiorial assistance to Marie Lescallopier Attaingnant until 1558). The lutenist Pierre Blondeau may have had a hand in editing the two early lute tablatures (1529/30), in which some pieces bear his initials. The accuracy of editing was generally high, with the exception of the earliest works and some from 1550. Verbal corrigenda were sometimes used to point out errors, but more frequently cancel slips were pasted over the original to correct passages or even single notes. Concern for utility and practical convenience are evident in the listing of voice combinations in the index for the six- and eight-voice motets, and in the instrumentation indications for flutes or recorders or both in two chanson books of 1533.

For the most part, Attaingnant offered the public new and original works of French composers. The music of the generation before Francis I found scant place in his books; the same is true for composers outside France, with the exception of certain Franco-Netherlands masters working in the Low Countries (such as Gombert, Lupi and Richafort) or in Italy (Arcadelt, Verdelot and Willaert). Although he pirated Antico's canonic duets of 1520 and borrowed occasionally from Moderne, later from Susato and even from Du Chemin, he was by contemporary standards quite scrupulous. Certainly he was more imitated by other printers than imitative of them. He was chiefly responsible for starting the vogue for printing two- and three-voice arrangements of four-voice chansons – one of the clearest examples of a vast repertory created at the behest of the publishing business.

With the accession of Henri II in 1547, Attaingnant's special position soon vanished. Several other printers also received royal privileges, a fact which may explain Attaingnant's frenetic burst of activity at the end, with its concomitant lowering of standards in printing and proofreading. After Attaingnant's death, the title of 'King's Music Printers' was acquired by Le Roy & Ballard, who gradually re-established the near monopoly first held by Attaingnant.

P. Renouard: *Imprimeurs et libraires parisiens du XVIe siècle*, i (Paris, 1898/R1964) [incl. chronological list of all publications, including the non-musical ones of Attaingnant's widow]; F. Lesure: 'Pierre Attaingnant: notes et documents', *MD*, iii (1949), 34; D. Heartz: 'La chronologie des recueils imprimés par Pierre Attaingnant: la période gothique', *RdM*, xliv (1959), 176; idem: 'A New Attaingnant Book and the Beginnings of French Music Printing', *JAMS*, xiv (1961), 9; D. Heartz: *Pierre Attaingnant, Royal Printer of Music: a Historical Study and Bibliographical Catalogue* (Berkeley and Los Angeles, 1969) [lists contents of all music books, with citation of modern edns.]; idem: 'Au pres de vous – Claudin's Chanson and the Commerce of Publishers' Arrangements', *JAMS*, xxiv (1971), 193–225; A. H. King: 'The Significance of John Rastell in Early Music Printing', *The Library*, 5th ser., xxvi/3 (1971), 197; G. G. Allaire: 'L'apport de la typographie et de la musique à la poésie française du début du seizième siècle', *Renaissance et Réforme*, vii (1978), 127; L. F. Bernstein: 'The "Parisian chanson": Problems of Style and Terminology', *JAMS*, xxxi (1978), 193–240; L. Guillo: 'Les motets de Layolle et les psaumes de Piéton: deux nouvelles éditions lyonnaises du seizième siècle', *FAM*, xxxii (1985), 186

D.H.(i)

Atwill, Joseph F(airfield) (*b* Boston, 1811; *d* Oakland, CA, 1891). American publisher. From 1833 to 1849 he ran a music shop and publishing business in New York, where he also used plates of the Thomas Birch company. In 1849 Samuel C. Jollie took over the business. Atwill went to California and established the first music shop in San Francisco, at 158 Washington Street. He began publishing in 1852 with the song *The California Pioneers*, the cover of which bears the legend 'N. B. The First Piece of Music Pubd. in Cala'. A branch of Atwill & Co. was established in Sacramento the following year, but by 1854 it was being run by Dan H. Dougliss. Atwill remained in business until 1860, when he sold his interests to Matthias Gray.

Dichter and Shapiro (1941, 2/1977); M. K. Duggan: 'Music Publishing and Printing in San Francisco before the Earthquake & Fire of 1906', *Kemble Occasional*, no.24 (1980); idem: 'Music Publishing and Printing in San Francisco before the Earthquake & Fire of 1906: Directory', *Kemble Occasional*, no.30 (1983); R. Stevenson: 'California Pioneer Sheet Music Publishers and Publications', *Inter-American Music Review*, viii/1 (1986), 1

B.T.

Augener. English firm of publishers. It originated in 1853, when Charles Louis Graue set up as a foreign music importer in London with the assistance of George Augener (*b* Fechenheim, Hesse, 1830; *d* London, 25 Aug 1915), who had come to England in 1852 from employment in the firm of André in Offenbach. Graue was succeeded by Gustav Scheuermann in 1854, and in the following year Augener left the business to set up on his own as Augener & Co. In 1858 he bought the Scheuermann business at public auction and took over its premises. In November 1898 the firm acquired the trade name and goodwill of Robert Cocks, and the two businesses were fully amalgamated as Augener Ltd in 1904. With George Augener's retirement in 1910, Willy Strecker purchased full control of the concern; through him they reverted to B. Schotts Söhne of Mainz in 1913, though with the outset of the war Schott forfeited its ownership. About 1960 Augener acquired the firm of Joseph Weekes, and in 1961 that of Joseph Williams. In May 1962 the firm, together with its various concert and wholesale concerns, was purchased by Galaxy Music Corporation (New York) and made part of Galliard Ltd; this firm was subsequently absorbed by Stainer & Bell, in whose catalogue the Augener titles now appear.

The firm began mainly as importers of foreign music, and from 1873 to 1937 held the sole agency for Peters Edition. As publishers they were notable for the early adoption of lithographic methods, and were active from 1867 in producing cheap editions of the classics as well as modern works in their extensive Augener Edition. In 1878, under the direction of William Augener (*b* ?1854–5; *d* Tunbridge Wells, 19 June 1904), George's eldest son, they began printing their own publications, achieving a high standard of production; from 1871 to 1960 they published the *Monthly Musical Record*, with Ebenezer Prout (whose theoretical works they also published) as its first editor, followed by J. S. Shedlock, Richard Capell, J. A. Westrup and Gerald Abraham. The firm was particularly identified with educational music, especially piano works, and published many volumes of music for examining bodies.

'Mr. George Augener', *Musical Herald* (1900), no.631, p. 291; 'The Music Publisher of Tradition: George Augener and the Augener Edition', *MO*, lxiv (1940–41), 428

P.W.J.

Augsburg. American firm of publishers, active in Minneapolis, Minnesota. Tracing its origins to the 1841 printing of an English edition of Luther's Catechism by a lay preacher, Elling Eielsen, Augsburg was for many years the publishing arm of the American Lutheran Church. Its output includes choral and organ music, instrumental music, Sunday school materials, books, records, videotapes and denominational hymnals, notably the *Lutheran Book of Worship* (1978). In 1988 the firm merged with Fortress Press of Philadelphia, publisher for the Lutheran Church in America, to form a company serving the new Evangelical Lutheran Church in America.

G.H.S.

B

Bach-Gesellschaft. A society founded on the centenary of Bach's death (1850) to publish a complete critical edition of his works. By that time all the important keyboard and organ works had been printed, but it was obvious that a non-commercial scheme was needed for the vocal works. Schumann had raised the question in 1837, and again in 1843, when the English Handel Society was founded; the final stimulus probably came from his friend Sterndale Bennett, who organized an English Bach Society on 27 October 1849. Besides Schumann, Otto Jahn, C. F. Becker and Moritz Hauptmann were influential in founding the society. With Breitkopf & Härtel of Leipzig, they issued a preliminary announcement on 3 July 1850, and by 28 July had gained the support of Liszt, Spohr and others; they founded the society on 15 December. Their first volume (the first ten cantatas) appeared in December 1851.

Handsome and expensive, the edition long enjoyed an exaggerated reputation for scholarship. In fact its quality varied from editor to editor, but was never outstanding. For instance, the differences between Bach's writing and his wife's were not discovered (this was left to Philipp Spitta in 1873). Sources were inadequately described, and no serious attempt was made to determine their relationship on Lachmannian principles. Further, in their desire to publish the final versions of works that Bach was known to have revised, some of the editors neglected the early versions.

It is only fair to add that the society was always short of money, and that its plans were disorganized from the outset by Hermann Nägeli, who for several years refused the editors access to his autograph score of the B minor Mass, on the extraordinary grounds that the English Handel Society was doing German music quite enough honour. For its period the edition was a considerable achievement: it was essentially free from editorial additions, it was very nearly complete and it provided some form of critical apparatus. It made a tolerable foundation for aesthetic studies and served as a model for all subsequent editions of its kind.

The 46th volume of the edition was presented to the committee on 27 January 1900, and with it the society was thought to have finished its work. It was dissolved, but immediately reconstituted as the Neue Bach Gesellschaft, whose object was to popularize the music and promote discussion. The NBG has held Bach festivals, annually as far as possible, from 1901. It acquired the house in which Bach was supposed to have been born, and opened a museum there in 1907. Its popular albums of selected arias are now of no importance, but some of its publications have been of permanent value, including the newly discovered Cantata no.199 (1913) and the facsimile and transcription of the Bach Genealogy (1917). Its journal, the *Bach-Jahrbuch*, has appeared almost every year since 1904.

J. N. Forkel: *Über Johann Sebastian Bachs Leben, Kunst und Kunstwerke* (Leipzig, 1802, rev. 3/1932); H. Kretzschmar: 'Die Bach-Gesellschaft: Bericht über ihre Thätigkeit', *BJb*, xlvi (1900), p.xv; A. Schweitzer: *Johann Sebastian Bach* (Leipzig, 1908/*R*1960; Eng. trans., 1911/*R*1958); F. Blume: *Johann Sebastian Bach im Wandel der Geschichte* (Kassel, 1947; Eng. trans., 1950)

W.E.

Baethen [Batius, Bathenius], **Jacob** (*b* ?Louvain, *c*1525; *d* ?Düsseldorf, after 1557). Flemish printer whose publications are important in the history of music printing in the Low Countries. From 1545 to 1551 he worked at Louvain, probably as a university printer. Besides music, he printed mainly official documents and religious commentaries, of which a number were published by M. Rotaire and Phalèse. During this period he printed the first, third, fourth (and perhaps fifth) of *Deschansons reduictz en tablature de lut*, which were Phalèse's first music publications and the first books of lute tablature printed from type in the Low Countries.

By 1554 Baethen was in Maastricht, where his publications included a book of Flemish songs, *Dat ierste boeck vanden nievve Duytsche liedekens*, one of five such anthologies published in the Low Countries during the 16th century. In 1555 he moved to Düsseldorf, where he published three books of motets, 1555–6 (for the heirs of Arnold Byrckmann), and a theory book, *Practicae musicae* (1557). The music type used by Baethen in Maastricht and Düsseldorf is identical with that used by Phalèse at that time so it may be assumed that he took a fount with him when he left Louvain. He is sometimes confused with Johan Baethen (perhaps his brother), who was a printer in Louvain and Cologne from 1552 to 1562, but who printed no music.

E. vander Straeten: *La musique aux Pays-Bas avant le XIXe siècle* (Brussels, 1867–88/*R*1969), iii *(1875), 204; Goovaerts (1880); R. B. Lenaerts: *Het Nederlands polifonies lied in de 16de eeuw* (Mechelen, 1933); Brown (1965); S. Bain: *Music Printing in the Low Countries in the Sixteenth Century* (diss., U. of Cambridge, 1974)

S.B. (i)

Bailleux, Antoine (*b* *c*1720; *d* Paris, *c*1798). French publisher. Catalogues and title-pages of scores suggest that he founded his publishing business in Paris during the 1760s. He became one of the most important publishers of the day. During some 30 years he issued many works by both French and foreign composers, the latter including not only early masters like Corelli and Vivaldi, but also some of those who were influential in the development of the emerging Classical school: C. Stamitz, Haydn, Piccinni, Paisiello, Cimarosa, Boccherini and Clementi. French composers included Gossec, Davaux, Monsigny and Brassac, and some of the earlier generation, Lully, Lalande and Campra. One of his major publications was the *Journal d'ariettes des plus célèbres compositeurs*, comprising 240 works issued in 63 volumes (scores and parts) from 1779 to 1788. After his death (around 1798, not 1791 as has been given) Bailleux's publishing business was taken over by Erard. He was also active as a composer and teacher.

FétisB; Hopkinson (1954); Johansson (1955); J. P. Larsen: 'Der musikalische Stilwandel um 1750 im Spiegel der zeitgenössischen Pariser Verlags-katalogen', *Musik und Verlag: Karl Vötterle zum 65. Geburtstag* (Kassel, 1968), 410

D.T. (ii)

Baldini, Vittorio (*b* Venice; *d* Ferrara, 21 Feb 1618). Italian printer and engraver. He began to publish literary texts in 1578, setting up his printing works opposite the Castello Estense at Ferrara. He seems to have started music publishing in 1582 with a collection of madrigals for five voices by various • authors entitled *Il lauro secco*, in which a representative group of madrigalists from Ferrara and other Italian cities paid homage to the beauty and virtuosity of Laura Peverara, a singer from Mantua and lady-in-waiting to the Duchess of Ferrara. Baldini probably acquired the edition from the heirs of Francesco Rossi and Paolo Tortorino. He later printed many collections of madrigals, canzonettas, psalms and motets by such leading composers as Agostini, Belli, Bonfilio and Gesualdo. Between 1594 and 1597 he published several of the most significant works of the *seconda prattica* madrigalists (Luzzaschi, Venosa, Fontanelli and Macque).

Baldini also published a number of books on the theory and art of music and the theatre, including F. Patrizi's *La deca istoriale* (1586) and *La deca disputata* (1586); G. B. Aleotti's *I curiosi moti spiritali di erone alessandrino* (1589; the Italian translation, with illustrations, of a basic handbook for stage machinists); M. A. Ingegneri's *Della poesia rappresentativa* (1598); and Ercole Bottrigari's *Il melone* (1602/*R*1969, Monteverdi's reply in his own defence to the attacks of Artusi). Among the most important poetic and theatrical texts that he printed are the descriptive scenarios for intermezzos, tournaments and mock battles staged in melodramatic style at Ferrara from 1600 onwards, for example B.

Bonarelli's *Filli di Sciro* (1607, with scenery and costumes by G. B. Aleotti, engraved by F. Vallegio) and Battista Guarini's *Intermezzi* (various editions, with alterations, 1610, 1612 and 1614).

In contrast to contemporary Venetian publications, Baldini's works show a deeply cultivated and élitist tendency through the beauty of their graphic lettering, engraved decorations and superb title-pages. He used both wood and metal on fine, azure-coloured paper; his musical publications are among the most interesting of the late 16th century as they include both text and music. Baldini used several different imprints: Ducal Printer until 1597, when the Este family lost the Duchy of Ferrara, thereafter Episcopal or State Printer and Printer to the Academy of the Intrepidì. He used a large number of typographical signs including a bell, a flying Daedalus (for illustration *see* DEVICE) and the sun. After his death, his daughter Vittoria carried on the printing works until 1622, under the imprint of 'the heirs of Vittorio Baldini'.

G. Donato Cucchetti: *La pazzia favola pastorale* (Ferrara, 1581, 2/1623); Sartori (1958)

A.C. (i)

Ballard. French family of printers and composers important for over 200 years.

(1) Robert Ballard (i) (*b* Montreuil-sur-Mer, ?1525–30; *d* Paris, bur. 8 July 1588). The son of Michel Ballard and Colasse Le Roy, he was the founder, along with his cousin Adrian Le Roy, of the printing firm of Le Roy & Ballard. The first document showing their association, by which Le Roy and Ballard received a privilege for printing music from Henri II, is dated 14 August 1551. On 16 February 1553 the partners received the title of music printers to the king (the title held by Attaingnant until his death in late 1551 or 1552). It was reaffirmed in 1568 under Charles IX and in 1594 under Henri IV and was to continue for other members of the family until the mid-18th century.

On 30 October 1559 Ballard married Lucrèce Dugué, who brought him and the firm valuable connections with the musical and political life of the court. Her father Jean Dugué was organist to the king, and Dugué's nephew Pierre was attached to the retinue of the king's brother. Through her mother Perrette Edinthon she was related to Charles Edinthon, lutenist in the king's chamber from 1542 to 1572, and to Jacques Edinthon, lutenist and *valet de chambre* to the king from 1575 to 1590. Since Le Roy also had important connections with court circles and even with Charles IX himself,

the influence of the firm at court was assured.

Le Roy, a composer and lutenist of note, was unquestionably the artistic director of the firm. There is no proof that Ballard was not a musician himself, but he seems to have assumed the role of business manager. The two partners worked well together; most transactions, such as the buying of considerable properties outside Paris or contracting for shop repairs, were undertaken jointly. There was nevertheless some independence; for example, one of the rare non-musical works, *Le siège et prinse de Thionville* (1558), bears the name of Ballard alone.

After a three-year break in the firm's production on Ballard's death, Le Roy took up printing again in association with Ballard's widow Lucrèce until his own death in 1598. Le Roy, whose wife had died some time before 1570, was childless, and he left all his share of the property to the widow and heirs of Ballard. Lucrèce carried on the business after Le Roy's death with her son Pierre until 1607, when Pierre began publishing in his own name. Lucrèce was still living in 1611, when a document shows her to have been engaged in settling Le Roy's legacy for her six children.

Its important connections at court, the knowledgeable choice of repertory, the skill in printing and the beauty of its editions gave Le Roy & Ballard a virtual monopoly on music printing in France during the second half of the 16th century. Other printers in Lyons and Paris (including Fezandat, Gorlier and Granjon) issued only occasional musical editions. The firm's most important rival was Nicolas Du Chemin of Paris, who had begun to print music in 1549. Du Chemin was not a musician himself and depended on others to choose and edit the music that he printed. After his editor Claude Goudimel resigned in 1555, he was not able to maintain the brilliant pace established earlier. By about 1560 he was no longer a serious rival.

Between 1551 and 1598 Le Roy & Ballard published more than 3000 works in 350 editions. 25 books of French chansons, printed and reprinted between 1552 and 1585, and several books of older and new chansons known variously as 'Recueils' and 'Meslanges' account for almost two-thirds of the works printed – 1963 chansons in all. The next most numerous category contains 645 motets. The 491 psalms and *chansons spirituelles* reflect the strong French interest in this genre. 229 Italian (and Spanish) pieces show the role of the firm in spreading Italian influence in France; the last publication, in 1598, was a book of

TRIO.

Esté chault bouilloit, Et l'œil de ce môde Encores ne mouilloit Sa perruque blonde Dans la

mer profonde: Mais au hault seiour De sa face ronde Faisoit le my iour.

Au lict me posay
Pour freschement estre,
Et me reposay
Pour mon aise croistre:
Tant fut la fenestre
Propre à mon desir,
Qu'on n'eust sceu congnoistre
S'il fut iour ou nuict.

Voicy arriuer
Celye tant blanche,
Qu'on voit en yuer
Neige dessus branche:
Sa vesture franche
Sa ceinture ouuroit
Vne ferme hanche,
Qui rien ne couuroit.

D'elle m'aprochay
Sous amoureus signe,
Et luy arrachay
Sa chemise fine:
Elle d'une mine
Honteuse à l'ouurir,
Sa beauté diuine
S'efforçoit couurir.

Fermée à demy,
A demy ouuerte,
Melloit nuict parmy
Clarté descouuerte:
La forest couuerte
De fueillage frais
Monstroit l'herbe verte
En tel ombre espais.

Son poil long doré
Iusqu'à la racine
Pendoit esgaré
Dessus sa poictrine:
Luy faisant crespine
D'or, au blanc tetin,
Plus poignant qu'espine,
Plus lis que satin.

Mais en debatant
Comme ia batue
Fut du combatant
Bien tost abatue,
Qui la serra nue
Dans douce prison,
Aisement vaincue
Par ma trahison.

ADR. LE ROY.

3

Esté chault bouilloit.

Mon dieu quelle lors
Espaule touchay-ie,
Quels bras beaus & forts
Vey-ie & empongnay-ie:
Quel tetin cachay-ie
Tout dedans ma main.
Quelle blanche neige
Vey-ie sur son sein.

Mais qu'est il besoing
Que pour vn ie compte,
Ie vey son tout loing
De blasme & de honte:
Et pour fin du compte
La pressoye si fort,
Qu'elle me surmonte
D'un semblable effort.

Quel ventre arondi
Que ride ne plisse,
Quel bas rebondi,
Quelle ronde cuisse,
Quelle hanche propice,
Quel ferme costé,
Pour courir en lice
Du dieu de beauté.

Que diray-ie plus,
Chacun peult entendre
Quel fut le surplus
De ce debat tendre:
Contraint fus de me rendre
Lassé du combat,
Or dieu me doint prendre
Souuent tel esbat.

Two facing pages from Le Roy & Ballard's 'Cinquiesme livre de guiterre' (1554), showing the voice and guitar parts of 'L'esté chault bouilloit' by Le Roy

Marenzio madrigals. The 52 masses cover the whole period, but most are concentrated in the years 1557–9. There were 17 books of instrumental music for lute, cistre, mandora and guitar, including four instruction books for these instruments by Le Roy; they contain music by Le Roy himself (see illustration), Pierre Brunet, Gregor Brayssing of Augsburg, Alberto da Ripa and Bálint Bakfark. Two treatises on music theory were published, one in 1582 written by Jean Yssandon and one in 1583 by Le Roy.

The most frequently published composer was Lassus, who was a personal friend of Le Roy. Le Roy & Ballard played an important part in disseminating his newest works in France and in Europe generally; many of his compositions had their first publication there. Others frequently represented were Arcadelt, Certon, Costeley, Goudimel, Janequin, Le Jeune, Maillard and Claudin de Sermisy.

The typographical material was particularly fine. The elaborate woodcut borders on the title-pages, the printer's marks and the 'lettres grises' or historiated woodcut initials in several sizes in the style of Jean Cousin are superb examples of French Renaissance graphic art. At least three sets of punches of music were made by the famous typecutter Guillaume Le Bé (i). Autograph notes of Le Bé cite in 1554–5 a 'musique grosse', in 1559 a 'petite tablature d'épinette sur la moyenne musique' and at an unspecified date in the 1550s a 'grosse tablature d'épinette pour imprimer à deux foys' sold to Le Roy & Ballard (for illustration *see* GANDO). One of the sets of punches for spinet tablature was a sample, according to the notes. No book of spinet music by Le Roy & Ballard is extant, nor is there any mention of any in contemporary sources. (4) Christophe Ballard used the small set in 1678 to print a book of *Airs à 2 et 3 parties de feu monsieur le Camus*, so Le Bé's punches did not go to waste. Robert Granjon cut a set of type for lute tablature for some books he published himself in 1551 and 1552, and then it became the property of Le Roy & Ballard. Both the music types and the 'lettres grises' continued in use unchanged past the mid-18th century.

(2) Pierre Ballard (*b* Paris, ?1575–80; *d* Paris, 4 Oct 1639). Printer, son of (1) Robert Ballard (i). In partnership with his mother he carried on the business after the death of Le Roy. On 25 March 1607 Letters-patent from Henri IV officially made him music printer to the king, and henceforth the editions appeared under his name alone. The privilege was renewed by Louis XIII in 1611 and 1633. Pierre's brother, Robert Ballard (ii) (*c*1575 – in or after 1650), was a lutenist and composer of some distinction, who apparently never took part in the family business.

An example of one of the many challenges to the power of the house of Ballard over the years occurred after the musician Nicolas Métru had received a privilege to print music in 1633. Pierre Ballard brought a suit to stop him, and in 1635 the court removed Métru's privilege, forbidding him to trouble Ballard in the exercise of his office. On 29 April 1637 Louis XIII issued a decree in which he praised the beauty of the notes and characters of Ballard, which 'far surpass those made in foreign kingdoms and provinces', confirmed the title of royal music printer and stated that he would not give any privileges to print music without Ballard's consent. According to Fournier, Ballard must have granted his consent at times, because there is a record of his having sold matrices of music type called Cicero to Guillaume Le Bé (ii).

Pierre Ballard printed many collections of *airs de cour*, psalms, lute music by Claude Le Jeune, Du Caurroy, P. Guédron, A. Boësset and L. de Rigaud, organ music by Titelouze and the music examples for Mersenne's *Harmonie universelle* in 1635–6.

He had eight or ten children; on 8 January 1639 he officially named his son Robert as his heir. An inventory dated 30 November 1639, mentioned by Gando in 1766, has not been found.

(3) Robert Ballard (iii) (*b* Paris, *c*1610; *d* Paris, before May 1673). Printer, son of (2) Pierre Ballard. He received a privilege from Louis XIII dated 24 October 1639 naming him sole printer to the king for music, the first of the Ballards to have exclusivity specified in the title. Independently of his father he had started in business as a bookseller but apparently was not successful, since a judgment of 16 April 1638 allowed him to postpone paying his creditors for three years. The inheritance from his father immediately relieved him of his financial troubles, and the printing business continued to thrive under his direction.

Early in 1639 the two Jacques de Senlecque, father and son, had received a privilege for a new method of printing plainsong. On 11 February 1640 Robert Ballard brought a suit to prevent them from printing, but contrary to the earlier judgment of the king in Pierre's case the Parlement ruled that each could print what he wanted. Robert took the matter up with the king's council, since he did not consider himself, as a member of the king's household, bound by the decisions of the Parlement. A clear decision was never reached, possibly because Louis XIII died in 1643, leaving France to be governed by a regency for the five-year-old Louis XIV. When the younger Sanlecque died in 1660 Ballard offered to buy his punches and matrices from his widow, but the price she set was too high.

Nevertheless, the firm of Ballard maintained its virtual monopoly throughout Robert's tenure, printing masses, motets and collections of airs, by composers including Henri Du Mont, Bénigne de Bacilly, Mace, Parisot and Lully, as well as music treatises. Robert Ballard (iii) undertook orchestral scores for the first time, beginning with stage works by Cambert, and in 1658 with *Livre d'airs de differents autheurs à deux parties* he started a series of song collections that continued for 30 years.

In 1664 the business maintained three presses and engaged three helpers. In 1666 Robert brought in his eldest son (4) Christophe Ballard as helper. On his death the composer Estienne Droüaux wrote a five-voice *De profundis* and a six-voice *Miserere* in his memory.

(4) Christophe Ballard (*b* Paris, 12 April 1641; *d* Paris, before 28 May 1715). Printer, eldest son of (3) Robert Ballard (iii). On 11 May 1673 he was named sole music printer to the king. In anticipation of his own death his father had obtained letters-patent from the king dated 25 October 1672 to assure Christophe's succeeding him in the title. Like his father, he had started independently in business as a bookseller, besides working as a helper in the family firm. His only brother Pierre (ii) (*d* 1703) also printed music for some time, but a court edict of 8 August 1696 ordered him to turn over his supply of music type to Christophe and denied Pierre or his widow the right to print any more music.

A highpoint in the firm's success, equal to that of the 16th century, was reached in about 1700, when the house maintained four presses and employed nine helpers and two apprentices. Almost all the music of the time was printed by Ballard, including the works of Lully (for illustration *see* fig.34, p.96), Brossard, Campra, Charpentier, Collasse, the Couperins, Dandrieu, Hotteterre, Lalande, Lebègue, Marais and Montéclair. The *Airs* appeared in a new form as *Airs sérieux et à boire* with basso continuo and were issued monthly.

The firm had to undergo many expensive suits in this period, among them one against Lully's son, who had tried to reprint his father's music without Ballard's permission. But a more serious threat was the new method of printing music from engraved plates which had come increasingly into use since the second half of the 17th century. The Ballards continued to use the old movable type method invented in the 16th century and the lozenge-shaped notes that had been cast for Le Roy & Ballard in the 1550s, rarely investing in any new typographical material. In 1713 Leclair and several other musicians obtained privileges to print music from engraved plates. Ballard entered a suit against them but lost; he was considered to have the exclusive right only to print music in the old method.

(5) Jean-Baptiste-Christophe Ballard (*b* Paris, *c*1663; *d* Paris, May 1750). Printer, son of (4) Christophe Ballard and Marie Lamielle. He was established as a master printer and bookseller in the rue Frementelle on 6 June 1694. On his father's death he moved to the Ballard shop in the rue St-Jean-de-Beauvais and received his title as royal printer for music. He continued the monthly *Airs sérieux et à boire* and flooded the market with various 'Tendresses', 'Parodies', 'Amusements' and 'Menuets chantants', in an attempt to capture a wider audience. He produced monumental editions of the works of Lully, Destouches and Campra and was the publisher of Rameau's *Traité* (1722) and *Nouveau système* (1726). During his later years, as more and more engraved music was issued by others, the prestige and influence of the house of Ballard began to decline.

(6) Christophe-Jean-François Ballard (*b* Paris, *c*1701; *d* Paris, 5 Sept 1765). Printer, son of (5) Jean-Baptiste Ballard. He received the royal privilege on the death of his father. He had been active as a bookseller since 1741 and as a printer since 1742. With him the fame and success of the firm ended. A police report described him as 'lazy and untalented'. In the 18th century printing privileges had become less a matter of royal approval than a means to add to the royal treasury. In 1762 a royal decree restricted their period to 15 years and in 1790 they were abolished. The Ballards, equipped with increasingly meaningless privileges, still using lozenge-shaped notes and old-fashioned initial letters from the 16th century, were unwilling or unable to change with the times. A report from a Parlement commission in

1764 said 'the public has been disgusted for a long time with the music of Sieur Ballard'.

After his death, his widow and then his son Pierre-Robert-Christophe (*d* 23 Nov 1812) carried on after a fashion, frequently moving to new locations. In 1800 Ballard was 'printer to the theatres of the Republic and of the arts'. The last of the Ballards was Christophe-Jean-François' grandson, Christophe-Jean-François Ballard (ii) (*d* 16 Oct 1825).

Over the years the Ballard family received many of the royal favours of the *ancien régime*, · its members serving as syndics of the booksellers' guild, royal councillors, commercial judges, administrators of charity hospitals and commissioners of artillery. As a special perquisite the Ballard servants were allowed to wear royal livery. Until the declining years of the firm the care in music printing and the beauty of the results were universally praised. The music books of the house of Ballard constitute in themselves a history of French musical taste over 200 years.

P.-S. Fournier: *Traité historique et critique sur l'origine et les progrès des caractères de fonte pour l'impression de la musique* (Berne, 1765); N. and F. Gando: *Observations sur le Traité historique et critique de Monsieur Fournier le jeune sur l'origine et les progrès des caractères de fonte pour l'impresssion de la musique* (Berne, 1766); M. Brenet: 'La librairie musicale en France de 1653 à 1790 d'après les registres de privilèges', *SIMG*, viii (1906–7), 401–66; V. Fédorov: 'Ballard', *MGG*; F. Lesure and G. Thibault: *Bibliographie des éditions d'Adrian Le Roy et Robert Ballard (1551–1598)* (Paris, 1955), suppl. *RdM*, xl, (1957), 166; D. Heartz: 'Parisian Music Publishing under Henry II', *MQ*, xlvi (1960), 448; Brown (1965); M. Jurgens: *Documents du minutier central concernant l'histoire de la musique 1600–1650* (Paris, 1968), 853; J. Cain and P. Marot, eds.: *Imprimeurs et libraires parisiens du XVIe siècle, d'après les manuscrits de Ph. Renouard*, ii (Paris, 1969); D. Heartz: *Pierre Attaingnant, Royal Printer of Music* (Berkeley and Los Angeles, 1969); A. Devriès: *Edition et commerce de la musique gravée à Paris dans la première moitié du XVIIIe siècle* (Geneva, 1976)

S.F.P.

Balmer & Weber. American firm of publishers. Charles Balmer (*b* Mühlhausen, 21 Sept 1817; *d* St Louis, MO, 15 Dec 1892) and Carl Heinrich Weber (*b* Koblenz, 3 March 1819; *d* Denver, CO, 6 Sept 1892) left Germany for the USA in the 1830s; Balmer became an organist and conductor, Weber a cellist, and their early compositions were published in the eastern USA. In 1848 they entered into partnership and opened a shop in St Louis. Charles Balmer was so prolific that he adopted a number of pseudonyms, including Charles Remlab, T. van Berg, Alphonse Leduc, Charles Lange, Henry Werner, August Schumann, T. Mayer and F. B. Rider. Gradually the firm absorbed most of its competitors including Nathaniel Phillips, James & J. R. Phillips, H. A. Sherburne, H. Pilcher & Sons, W. M. Harlow, Cardella & Co. and Compton & Doan; by the end of the century it had an exceptionally large and flourishing business.

After the death of the partners, the business was managed by a company in which the Balmer family predominated. Lack of efficient direction and the rise of Kunkel Brothers, Shattinger and Thiebes-Stierlin caused the business to deteriorate, and in 1907 the catalogue was sold to Leo Feist of New York. He attempted to ship the sheet music to New York down the Mississippi, but the vessel foundered off the coast of New Jersey and its cargo sank.

E. C. Krohn: *Missouri Music* (New York, 1971); idem: *Music Publishing in the Middle Western States before the Civil War* (Detroit, 1972), 27; idem: *Music Publishing in St. Louis* (Warren, MI, 1988), 43

E.C.K.

Bärenreiter. German firm of publishers. It was founded in 1923 in Augsburg by Karl Vötterle, a bookshop assistant, then only 21 years old. Vötterle named the firm after the star Alkor ('Bärenreiter' or 'Reiterlein') in the constellation of the Great Bear. The firm's beginnings are closely associated with the musical youth movement then current in Germany. Vötterle's interest in folksong and his collaboration with the folksong researcher and singer Walther Hensel (Dr Julius Janiczek, 1887–1956), whose *Finkensteiner Blätter* was the firm's first publication, formed the basis of much of Bärenreiter's early work. The first years were characterized by the rapid growth of the *Singbewegung*, organized into the Finkensteiner Bund and developed by Vötterle; the movement was intended to revive musical interest and provide musical education for amateurs. The publication of folksong editions, beginning with the *Finkensteiner Blätter*, and later larger anthologies such as the *Bruder Singer*, characterized the early policy of the young firm. There also appeared song settings by composers such as Dowland, Hassler and Lechner. The firm's first music periodical was *Singgemeinde*, edited by Konrad Ameln. Already at that time Bärenreiter sought an involvement in the revival movement in German musicology, which during the 1920s was closely linked to the youth movement. An annotated edition of J. N.

Forkel's 1802 biography, *Über Johann Sebastian Bachs Leben, Kunst und Kunstwerke* (1924), was one of the firm's first musicological publications.

An important step forward was made when Gurlitt entrusted the firm with the publication of the report on the first Freiburg organ conference in 1926. As a result of this publication and of the association of Christhard Mahrenholz with the firm, Bärenreiter quickly grew to become the leading publisher of the *Orgelbewegung* and a specialist publisher of organ music and research material in the form of books by Klotz, Mahrenholz and others. In 1926, as its first purely musicological enterprises, Bärenreiter took over the publication of the series of the Königsberg and Tübingen musical institutes, followed later by those of Erlangen, Greifswald, Heidelberg, Jena and Münster. In 1927 the firm moved to Kassel; at that time its output comprised about 200 publications covering many aspects of music and music literature. The following five years brought further rapid growth and extension of publishing activity; in 1929 Vötterle founded the periodical *Musik und Kirche*. The rediscovery by the choirs of the musical youth movement of the works of Heinrich Schütz, with the corresponding new editions published by Bärenreiter, the discussions in *Musik und Kirche*, and the subsequent founding of the active Neue Schütz-Gesellschaft in 1930 by Vötterle, Ludwig Mahrenholz and Moser, gave a decisive impetus to the revival of Protestant church music.

In the Nazi period Bärenreiter's development was interrupted as Vötterle and his colleagues were not allowed to follow their original ideals. The Finkensteiner Bund was dissolved in 1933, and in its place Vötterle, together with Richard Baum, founded the Arbeitskreis für Hausmusik. In 1935 the firm was threatened with complete closure when Vötterle was excluded from the Reichspressekammer. As a result all religious printing had to be suspended: it was continued by the Johannes Stauda-Verlag under the direction of Paul Gümbel. The Stauda firm became the publishers of the Evangelische Michaelsbruderschaft, which aimed at a church revival; to the Reichspressekammer church music did not count as religious printing and was therefore able to make relatively undisturbed progress in spite of the anti-Christian tendencies of the time. In 1932 Bärenreiter began to publish works by Hugo Distler, beginning with his op.5. Distler's church music opened up for Bärenreiter the new category of modern church music, which in the following years it particularly cultivated. From that time on the almost exclusive cultivation of early music was challenged by the growth of that type of contemporary music which, consciously or unconsciously, was indebted to the inheritance of early music.

In the spheres of secular choral music, songbooks, domestic music and chamber music, the firm's output also increased with many publications in the period 1933–44. The practical revival of early music led to the reintroduction of early instruments, and Bärenreiter encouraged such developments with literature on the instruments and their technique, sometimes actually making instruments (notably recorders). It also began publishing orchestral and wind music, and an opera section was initiated with some works by early composers, predominantly Handel. Facsimile reprints and works of original research of all kinds appeared. Bärenreiter participated in Reichsdenkmäle, with the series *Einstimmige Werke* and *Mittelalter*, and in Landschaftsdenkmäle, devoted to various constituent states of Germany. Complete editions of the works of Gluck, Monteverdi, Pergolesi, Schein, Spohr and Walter, and selected editions of Telemann and Handel were prepared and begun, mostly in collaboration with the Staatliche Institut für Musikforschung.

In March 1945 the firm's buildings, all of its departments and nearly all of its stock were destroyed by fire. Vötterle and most of his closer colleagues survived the war, and gradually the firm was reorganized. In 1946 the Arbeitskreis für Hausmusik organized its first postwar Werkwoche. This organization was renamed Arbeitskreis für Haus- und Jugendmusik in 1952 and in 1969 became the Internationale Arbeitskreis für Musik, which is now responsible for over 70 annual courses of musical instruction and the Kasseler Musiktage (to 1974). Also in 1946 Vötterle opened the Bärenreiter second-hand bookshop which specialized in music and musicology. In 1947 he took part in the founding of the Gesellschaft für Musikforschung, whose works were published by the firm in the periodical *Die Musikforschung*, and in the book series *Musikwissenschaftliche Arbeiten*. In the same year the periodical *Musik und Kirche* restarted (with volume xviii), together with the independent *Der Kirchenchor* and the new *Musica*, covering all aspects of music. In 1948 appeared *Die neue Schau*, a cultural family periodical, and *Hausmusik*. In June 1949 the first fascicle of the encyclopedia *Die Musik in Geschichte und Gegenwart* (*MGG*) appeared, edited by Friedrich Blume, having been in preparation since 1942. In 1968 the alphabetical sequence was completed, in 14 volumes, and supplementary fascicles (in two volumes) subsequently appeared up to 1979, followed by an index (1986).

During the early 1950s the firm began to publish a number of important complete or collected editions, music series and a considerable amount of important musicological literature, notably *Acta musicologica* and *Fontes artis musicae*, both from 1954 on. Their postwar publications have included volumes of *RISM* (series A and C), the series *Documenta musicologica* and *Catalogus musicus*, complete and collected editions of numerous composers (often in conjunction with various music institutions) including Walter, Telemann, Gluck, Bach, Lechner, Handel, Mozart, Rhau, Berlioz, Berwald, Lassus, Schein, Schubert, Schütz and Janáček. Important series of musical editions include volumes of *Das Erbe deutscher Musik* (1936–), *Schweizerische Musikdenkmäler* (1955) and *Monumenta monodica medii aevi* (1956). The firm has also published collections of letters, iconography, yearbooks, congress reports, treatises on instrumental technique and manufacture, as well as works by contemporary composers, including Heinrich Kaminski, Ernst Krenek, Karl Marx, Siegfried Reda, Ernst Pepping and Johannes Driessler. To these may be added members of the younger generation of composers who have been influenced by the Second Viennese School and the avant garde, such as Günter Bialas, Klaus and N. A. Huber, Erhard Karkoschka, Rudolf Kelterborn, Giselher Klebe, Ulrich Streuz, Dimitri Terzakis, Manfred Trojahn, Gerhard Wimberger, Heinz Winbeck and many others. In 1950 the new Protestant hymnbook appeared, after years in preparation, and a new series of early domestic and chamber music, *Hortus musicus* was started. The *Nagels Musik-Archiv* series was taken over from the Nagel firm and continued in 1952, followed by *Chor-Archiv* (1953), *Flötenmusik* (1956), miniature scores (1959), *Violoncello* (1960), *Musica sacra nova* (1964), *Das 19. Jahrhundert* (1969), *Concerto vocale* (1971), 'Urtext' editions, study scores and a new series of *Hausmusik* (1986). More recently, pedagogical works have also become an important part of the firm's output.

Today Bärenreiter, following large-scale postwar expansion, is international in organization and repute. It now owns not only the Stauda and Nagel undertakings but also, since 1950, the Hinnenthal-Verlag. The Alkor-Edition was founded in Kassel in 1955, as an offshoot of the Bruckner-Verlag, Wiesbaden; it is now mainly concerned with theatre music publishing, especially opera. Bärenreiter was also the first great German publishing house to produce its own gramophone records (Musicaphon, 1959). Independent affiliates have been set up in Basle (1944), London (1957, independent since 1963; removed to Hitchin, 1977) and New York (1957).

K. Vötterle: *Haus unterm Stern* (Kassel, 1949, 4/1969); *Bärenreiter im Bild* (Kassel, 2/1968); R. Baum and W. Rehm, eds.: *Musik und Verlag: Karl Vötterle zum 65. Geburtstag* (Kassel, 1968); Plesske (1968); A. M. Gottschick, ed.: *Bärenreiter-Chronik: die ersten 50 Jahre 1923 bis 1973* (Kassel, 1973); H. Bennwitz, G. Feder, L. Finscher, W. Rehm, eds.: *Musikalisches Erbe und Gegenwart: Musiker-Gesamtausgaben in der Bundesrepublik Deutschland* (Kassel, 1975)

R.B. (i), W.R. (i)

Barley, William (*b* ?1565; *d* 1614). English publisher. His position in the history of music printing in Elizabethan London is a contentious one. In 1596 he produced *The Pathway to Musicke* and *A New Booke of Tabliture*, the latter thought to be the book that John Dowland complained of in his *The First Booke of Songes or Ayres* (1597), declaring that the versions of his lute pieces were 'falce and unperfect'. Barley was acquainted with Thomas Morley, and, when Morley acquired a music printing monopoly in 1599, six volumes appeared bearing the imprint 'imprinted at London, in Little St. Helen's by William Barley, the assigne of Thomas Morley'. An examination of these six works, however, makes it clear that they cannot all have been printed by the same man or on the same press. The most significant of this group are Anthony Holborne's *Pavans, Galliards, Almains*, the first appearance in print in England of music for instruments rather than voices, and Thomas Morley's *The First Booke of Consort Lessons*, the first appearance in print in England of music for a prescribed instrumentation. Morley's *The First Booke of Ayres* was published with Barley's imprint in 1600 but after that Barley evidently abandoned music publishing for some years. In 1606, however, he laid claim to the same music printing monopoly, which had a further 13 years to run. On Morley's death in 1602 the monopoly had fallen into disuse, but Barley managed to convince the Company of Stationers that, as Morley's business associate, he still possessed certain rights under its terms. Accordingly, Barley was made free of the company on 25 June 1606, and on the following day the company's court settled an action which Barley had brought against Thomas East for infringement of the monopoly during the years 1603 to 1606. The settlement included the stipulation that East should pay to Barley 20 shillings for each impression of music books he printed, together with six free copies of the finished volume. In addition, East and other music printers often styled themselves 'the assigne of William Barley' until Barley's death in 1614. A similar dispute with Thomas Adams was settled later.

William Barley's interest in music printing was clearly a pecuniary one. There is no evidence that he was actually a printer who had served the necessary apprenticeship. He owed his membership of the Stationers' Company to a special set of circumstances, and the six volumes published in 1599 show every sign of having been farmed out to different presses. Further, in his *A New Booke of Tabliture*, he declared 'I am myself a publisher and seller of books', and it was in this capacity that he kept his shop in Gracechurch Street, London. The exact circumstances of the disposal of his business are not clear, but there is some evidence that his music copyrights were acquired by Thomas Snodham and his partners.

E. Arber: *A Transcript of the Register of the Company of Stationers of London* (London: 1875–94); H. G. Aldis: *A Dictionary of Printers and Booksellers in England, Scotland and Ireland . . . 1557–1640* (London, 1910); C. Judge: *Elizabethan Book-Pirates* (Cambridge, MA, 1934); 160; Humphries and Smith (1954, 2/1970); J. Lievsay: 'William Barley, Elizabethan Printer and Bookseller', *Studies in Bibliography*, viii (1956), 218; W. A. Jackson, ed.: *Records of the Court of the Stationers' Company, 1602–1640* (London, 1957); R. Illing: 'Barley's Pocket Edition of East's "Metrical Psalter" ', *ML*, xlix (1968), 219; J.A. Lavin: 'William Barley, Draper and Stationer', *Studies in Bibliography*, xxii (1969), 214; J.M. Ward: 'Barley's Songs Without Words', *Lute Soviety Journal*, xii (1970), 5; Krummel (1975); I. Fenlon and J. Milsom: ' "Ruled Paper Imprinted": Music Paper and Patents in Sixteenth-century England', *JAMS*, xxvii (1984), 139; G.D. Johnson: 'The Stationers versus the Drapers: Control of the Press in the Late Sixteenth Century', *The Library*, 6th ser., v (1988), 1; idem: 'William Barley, "Publisher and Seller of Bookes", 1591–1614', *The Library*, 6th ser., xi (1989), 10–46

M.M.

Barnhouse, Charles Lloyd (*b* Grafton, WV, 20 March 1865; *d* Oskaloosa, IA, 29 Nov 1929). American publisher, bandmaster and composer. In 1886 he moved to Mount Pleasant, Iowa, where he directed the local band and set up a music publishing business. He moved his family and business first to Burlington, Iowa, in 1891, and then to Oskaloosa in 1895. For many years he directed the Iowa Brigade Band, for which he built a permanent rehearsal hall. He published more than 100 of his own band compositions, including cornet solos, marches, galops, waltzes and dirges; some works appeared under the pseudonyms Jim Fisk and A. M. Laurens. His publishing business flourished, becoming the second largest family-owned music publishing firm in the USA. In addition to his own compositions, he published the works of such important band composers as Fred Jewell, Hale A. VanderCook, Karl King, Russell Alexander and Walter English. The company bearing his name continues to publish band music of high quality under the direction of his grandsons Robert and Charles.

D. P. Walker: 'From "Hawk-Eye March and Quick Step" to "Caprice Hongrois": Music Publishing in Iowa', *American Music*, i/4 (1983), 42

R.C. (i)

Barré, Antonio (*b* Langres; *fl* Rome, 1551–79). French printer. He was a singer in the Cappella Giulia from March 1552 until at least the end of 1554, and was also active as a composer: in 1552 his *Madrigali a quattro voci* were printed in Rome by Valerio and Luigi Dorico.

In 1555 he began to print music, publishing a series of collections entitled 'delle muse', Vicentino's *L'antica musica ridotta alla moderna pratica* (1555; in 1551 Barré had witnessed the famous debate between Vicentino and Lusitano in Rome) and a few volumes devoted to single composers. His first publication, *Il primo libro delle muse a cinque* (1555), set a high standard, with canzone settings by Barré himself, Berchem, Vincenzo Ruffo and Arcadelt, including Arcadelt's superb setting of Petrarch's *Chiare, fresch'e dolci acque*. Barré's *Primo libro delle muse a quattro voci* (1555) includes his own setting of four stanzas from Ariosto's *Orlando furioso*, in a suitably declamatory and homophonic style. He coined the term 'madrigali ariosi' to describe the pieces in this collection as well as in the second and third books for four voices. It is believed to refer to madrigals in which the upper-voice melody is based on a pattern used by popular singers of stanzas from *Orlando furioso*. The collection was reprinted several times (by Gardano, Rampazetto and Vincenti & Amadino), contributing to the popularity of 'delle muse' collections among Venetian printers. The *Secondo libro delle muse a tre voci: canzoni moresche di diversi* (1555) contains the first known examples of *moresche* as partsongs. The *Primo libro. . .a tre voci* has not survived except as Scotto's *Primo libro delle muse a tre* of 1562, which contains five pieces by Barré and other works by composers better known in Rome than in Venice.

In the 1560s Barré began printing, or at least publishing, with Blado's music type (e.g. madrigals by Menta, 1560, and by Lasso, 1563), or with Dorico's, as in Brassart's *Primo libro delli soi madrigali a quattro* (1564). A contract of 1564 shows Barré and Valerio Dorico to have been partners in the publication of Eliseo Ghibel's (or Gibellino's) *De festis introitus missarum* (1565), of which they promised to deliver 30 copies to Ghibel's agent (see Masetti Zannini, 226). This suggests that similar partnerships with Dorico or Blado, or, in Venice, with Scotto or Rampazetto, were behind Barré's other editions of the 1560s. In 1563 Rampazetto printed *Liber primus musarum cum quattuor vocibus sacrarum cantionum que vulgo mottetta vocantur*, naming Barré as editor and compiler. Perhaps Barré had lost his shop and had commissioned other publishers to print his books. Temporary partnerships for one or more books were common in Rome, but most are documented too sketchily to allow confirmation of the exact role of each partner. Barré also printed a few non-musical books, including a collection of poems, *Rime . . . in vita e in morte dell'Ill. Sig. Livia Columna* (1555). No publications by him are known from later than 1565, but documents place him in Rome as late as April 1579.

Barré's music books, some 20 in number (including six or seven presumably commissioned from others), are mostly in oblong quarto format, although a few are in folio. One of these, the Vincentino treatise, is also one of the earliest books in which the natural sign is printed from type. These well-executed publications, including first editions of important music by Arcadelt, Palestrina and, notably, Lassus, demonstrate Barré's taste and initiative as well as his skill. His printer's mark was, appropriately, Apollo surrounded by a chorus of the muses; he also used a device with Orpheus playing a *lira da braccio*.

F. X. Haberl: 'Die römische "schola cantorum" und die päpstlichen Kapellsänger bis zur Mitte des 16. Jahrhunderts', *VMw*, iii (1887), 278; A. Einstein: *The Italian Madrigal* (Princeton, 1949/ *R*1971); J. Schmidt-Görg: 'Barré, Antonio', *MGG*; W. Boetticher: *Orlando di Lasso und seine Zeit 1532–1594* (Kassel and Basle, 1958); Sartori (1958); A. Ducrot: 'Histoire de la Cappella Giulia au XVIe siècle depuis sa fondation par Jules II (1513) jusqu'à sa restauration par Grégoire XIII (1578)', *Meslanges d'archéologie et d'histoire*, lxxv (1963), 179–240, 467–559; S. Simonetti: 'Barré, Antoine', *DBI*; G. Haydon: 'The First Edition of Kerle's Hymns: 1558 or 1560?', *AcM*, xxxvii

(1966), 179; H. W. Kaufmann: *The Life and Works of Nicola Vicentino (1511–c.1576)*, MSD, xi (1966), 22, 33; S. G. Cusick: *Valerio Dorico: Music Printer in Sixteenth-century Rome* (Ann Arbor, 1981); G.L. Masetti Zannini: *editori e librai a Roma nella seconda metà del cinquecento: documenti inediti* (Rome, 1981), 15, 186, 195, 226; J. Haar: 'The "Madrigale Arioso": a Mid-century Development in the Cinquecento Madrigal', *Studi musicali*, xii (1983), 203

T.W.B.

Barth, Nicolaas [Nikolaus] (*b* in the Rheingau, 3 Aug 1744; *d* Limburg, 15 March 1820). Netherlands printer of German birth. In 1778 he moved to Rotterdam, where he opened his shop and performed as a clarinettist. His editions are devoted to instrumental chamber music by recognized composers, notably Pleyel. The several dozen extant copies reflect and often announce Barth's heavy editorial activity, including transpositions, renumberings of works and free appropriations from other works. In 1803 a misleading advertisement caused a disagreement with W. van Berger in Breda, and by 1805 Barth had transferred his music publishing work to Lodewijk Plattner, who reissued several Barth editions. According to Mazure, Barth was not a good businessman but enjoyed the artistic side of his work and paid more attention to the title-pages than Plattner.

J. Mazure: 'Nicolaas Barth (1744–1820): a Contribution to the History of Music in Rotterdam', *TVNM*, xxvii (1978), 19 [incl. list of extant editions]

D.W.K.

Baumann, Georg (*b* Erfurt, 1554; *d* Breslau, 9 March 1607). German printer. He is first mentioned as a printer in 1573 at Erfurt where he remained in business until 1590. In 1589 he married the widow of Johann Scharffenburg, the Breslau printer, and was granted a privilege to print there in 1590. He certainly worked at Breslau during 1592 and 1593, but he apparently returned to Erfurt in 1594 and remained there until the following year. By 1602 he was again in Breslau and he continued to publish there until his death. His widow maintained the press until 1618, when she was succeeded by their son; the family continued printing until at least 1708. Other members of the family worked as printers elsewhere, but none of them appears to have published music. Baumann's press concentrated on the local German repertory; even his two anthologies of madrigals (*RISM* 1576^2 and 1580^7) have German contrafacta of the original Italian texts.

J. Scheibel: *Geschichte der seit 300 Jahren im Breslau befindlichen Stadtbuchdruckerey* (Breslau, 1804), 31; J. Braun: 'Geschichte der Buchdrücker und Buchhändler Erfurts im 15.–17. Jahrhundert', *Archiv für Geschichte des deutschen Buchhandels*, v (1886), 59–116; Benzing (1963, 2/1982)

S.B. (iii)

Baussen, Henri de (*fl* Paris, *c*1690–1718). French engraver. His name first appears on publications of organ music by Nicholas Lebègue and Jacques Boyvin (1690), which give his address as rue Simon le Franc. He falsely obtained a privilege on 28 April 1690 as 'musician and composer to the late Mademoiselle de Guise', allowing him to engrave his own and others' music. When he tried to issue Moreau's *La musique d'Athalie*, Christophe Ballard immediately brought suit and received a judgment against him and his partner Henry Foucault (28 June 1690). His name next appears on Boyvin's first and second books of organ music, published by Ballard (1700). Baussen often worked on editions of operas and *opéra-ballets* for the publishers Henry Foucault and Pierre Ribou, including the celebrated 'second edition' of Lully's operas (1708–11), which was the subject of a lawsuit between M. Guyenet, Lully's eldest son and Ballard.

G. Lepreux: *Gallia typographica, série parisienne* (Paris, 1911); Devriès and Lesure (1979–88)

G.H.B.

Baxter, J(esse) R(andall, jr (*b* Lebanon, AL, 8 Dec 1887; *d* Dallas, TX, 21 Jan 1960). American publisher and composer of gospel songs. He studied with some of the foremost gospel-hymn writers, including James Rowe and Charles Gabriel, and became proficient in writing both words and music; he probably wrote more conventional songs than any other gospel-music composer of his time (a compilation of his songs, *Precious Abiding Peace*, was published in 1960). He was also an outstanding singing-school teacher and conducted his own schools until 1922, when the publisher A. J. Showalter asked him to manage one of his offices, in Texarkana, Texas. In 1926 Baxter joined V. O. Stamps in the foundation of the Stamps-Baxter Music Company at Jacksonville, Texas. When the company moved to Dallas in 1929, Baxter opened a branch office in Chattanooga, Tennessee. The business was extremely successful, becoming one of the foremost publishers of gospel music in seven-shape notation. After Stamps's death in 1940, Baxter moved to Dallas and became president of the firm. In 1949 an article in *Time* likened the company to a gospel Tin Pan Alley: at that time the firm employed 50 people; its journal, *Gospel Music News*, had a circulation of 20,000.

C. Baxter and V. Polk: *Biographies of Gospel Song Writers* (Dallas, 1971); S. Beary: *The Stamps-Baxter Music and Printing Company: a Continuing Tradition, 1926–1976* (diss., Southwestern Baptist Theological Seminary, 1977)

S.B. (ii)

Beesly, Michael (*b* Sunningwell, Berks., 1700; *d* ?1760). English country psalmodist, printer and publisher. One of the first country psalmodists to engrave, print and publish, he played an important role in disseminating the fuging-tune. He was the son of a farmer and learnt music informally, possibly from the first self-proclaimed singing-master to have works published, Daniel Warner, of Ewelme. Hearne reports that Beesly learnt engraving during the mid-1720s by watching the Oxford engraver Michael Burghers, and that he 'composed and ingraved a book, about singing psalms and anthems . . . of which there are two editions'. Beesly published at least four books, all undated, some combining letterpress (printed by the Lichfields of Oxford) and his own engraved plates. He sold them to the choirs he instructed and through dealers in London, Oxford, Reading, Newbury, Winchester, Salisbury and Gloucester. Fewer than 20 copies survive.

T. Hearne: *Remarks and Collections*, ed. H.E. Salter, ix (Oxford, 1914); N. Temperley: 'The Origins of the Fuging Tune,' *RMARC*, xvii (1981), 1–32; N. Temperley and C. G. Manns: *Fuging Tunes in the Eighteenth Century* (Detroit, 1983)

D.H. (iii)

Bellère, Jean (*b* Liège, 1526; *d* Antwerp, 15 Oct 1595). Flemish publisher important for his association with the firm Phalèse. He became a citizen of Antwerp in 1553 and a member of the Guild of St Luke in 1559. His first book was published there in 1555. From 1570 he collaborated with Pierre Phalèse (i) of Louvain and, after the latter's death, with Phalèse's son. Together they issued some 50 books of music, both vocal and instrumental. During this period, Phalèse also issued some music alone, although Bellère is not known to have done so, nor to have owned music type. He was, however, one of the most prolific of Antwerp printers, issuing, independent of Phalèse, publications of the classics, literature, Spanish texts, history, mathematics and science.

Goovaerts (1880); idem: *De muziekdrukkers Phalesius en Bellerus te Leuven* (Antwerp, 1882);

Brown (1965); S. Bain: *Music Printing in the Low Countries in the Sixteenth Century* (diss., U. of Cambridge, 1974)

S.B.(i)

Belmont. American firm of music distributors and publishers. It was founded in Los Angeles in the early 1960s by Gertrud and Lawrence Schoenberg, wife and son of the composer, to make Schoenberg's music more readily available in the USA. In addition to issuing his music, Belmont Music Publishers distributes European editions of Schoenberg's works (among them those of Universal Edition, Schott and Faber & Faber) and hires out parts. The firm also deals in editions of his theoretical writings and offers slides of his works of art.

F.B.

Belwin-Mills. American firm of publishers. Belwin, Inc., was founded in 1918 by Max Winkler, and Mills Music Publishers started a year later under the aegis of Jack and Irving Mills; the two organizations merged as the Belwin-Mills Publishing Corporation in 1969, with Martin Winkler as director. The company, located in Melville, New York, has become one of the most important publishers of educational music, producing many widely used piano series, a number of class band methods and material for teaching string instruments. The firm represents such composers as Arlen, Chávez, Creston, Crumb, Davidovsky, Dello Joio, Ellington, Gould, Penderecki, Sessions, Toch and John Vincent, and also issues popular music. Divisions of the company include J. Fischer, H. W. Gray, McAfee Music, Musicord Publications and Pro Art Publications. In 1973 it became sole distributor for Edward B. Marks Music and formed a joint venture between MCA Music and the Mills Music division of the company. Subsequently it became part of the Columbia Pictures Music Group.

M. Winkler: *A Penny from Heaven* (New York, 1951); idem: *From A to X: Reminiscences* (New York, 1957)

W.T.M., M.J./R.A.L., L.A.T.

Belyayev, Mitrofan Petrovich (*b* St Petersburg, 22 Feb 1836; *d* St Petersburg, 4 Jan 1904). Russian publisher. As a boy he learnt the violin and piano, and was a member of a number of chamber music societies. Soon after leaving school he joined the business of his father, a wealthy timber merchant with large forests in Olonets. In 1882, after hearing a performance of Glazunov's Symphony no.1, he offered to finance the publication of Glazunov's works. In 1885

he decided to publish Russian music, and established a publishing house in Leipzig (under the name Belaieff) to secure international copyright which at that time did not extend to music published in Russia. He eventually brought out over 2000 compositions by Russian composers, including Balakirev, Rimsky-Korsakov, Taneyev, Borodin, Glazunov, Musorgsky, Lyadov and many others. In 1885 he instituted the Russian Symphony Concerts, which offered three to six performances (with all-Russian programmes) each season in St Petersburg. Belyayev organized similar concerts at the Paris Exhibition in 1889 and initiated 'Quartet Evenings' in St Petersburg in 1891. He also financed the Glinka Awards, offered as an incentive to young Russian composers. In honour of their patron, Borodin, Rimsky-Korsakov, Glazunov and Lyadov composed a string quartet on the notes *B–LA–F*. After the Revolution the firm continued to operate from Leipzig until World War II when it moved to Bonn; it later moved to Frankfurt am Main, where in 1971 its management passed into the hands of C. F. Peters.

V. V. Stasov: *M. P. Belyayev* (St Petersburg, 1895); M. Montagu-Nathan: 'Belaiev: Maecenas of Russian Music', *MQ*, iv (1918), 450; B. L. Vol'man: *Russkiye notnïye izdaniya XIX-nachala XX veka* [Russian music publishing in the 19th and early 20th centuries] (Leningrad, 1970); D. F. Reed: *Victor Ewald and the Russian Chamber Brass School* (diss., U. of Rochester, 1979)

R.N./G.N.

Bencard, Johann Kaspar (bap. Würzburg, 30 Oct 1649; *d* Augsburg, 24 Dec 1720). German publisher. He started publishing in Frankfurt am Main, and in 1670 took over the Jesuits' academic press in Dillingen an der Donau. In 1694 he moved to Augsburg. He produced mainly theological literature, and also occasionally printed music, including masses and *Tafelmusik* by Samuel Friedrich Capricornus (1670–71), the *Mirantische Mayen-Pfeiff* by the Capuchin monk Laurentius von Schnüffis (1692, 1707) and religious works by the Benedictine monk Cajetan Kolberer (1709–10). Bencard's widow and heirs in Augsberg and Dillingen produced a composition tutor by Justinus à Desponsatione BVM (1723).

I. Heitjan: 'Die Buchhändler, Verleger und Drucker Bencard 1636–1762', *Börsenblatt für den deutschen Buchhandel, Frankfurter Ausgabe*, xvi (1960), 1569

A.L.

Benjamin, Anton J. German firm of publishers. Its origin can be traced to 1818, when Joseph Benjamin founded a book and music shop in Altona, which his son Anton later re-established in Hamburg. John Benjamin (1868–1931), a grandson of the founder who had taken charge of the firm in 1888, bought the Böhme music shop and concert agency in Hamburg in 1907. In 1917 he acquired the music publishing house originally founded in Petersburg by A. Büttner but which had been taken over by Daniel Rahter in 1879. As Verlag Benjamin, the firm moved to Leipzig in 1920, and Richard Schauer, a nephew of John Benjamin, took over the direction. In 1925 they acquired the A. E. Fischer publishing house of Bremen, and in 1929 the Simrock music publishing firm. By taking over the Rahter and Simrock concerns, which continued to exist under their original names, the group publishing business of Benjamin acquired original publication rights on works by Tchaikovsky, Richard Strauss, Respighi, Rheinberger, Wolf-Ferrari, Beethoven, Brahms, Dvořák and others. After the Jewish pogrom of 1938 Schauer was forced to sell the publishing complex and emigrate to England. In 1951 the firm was returned to its rightful owner and Anton J. Benjamin Musikverlag GmbH was founded in Hamburg (the Leipzig house was completely destroyed during an air attack in 1943). The principal areas of publication of the Benjamin Verlag are *Hausmusik* and other light music. The firm is now run from London (at the premises of Schauer and May Ltd) by Schauer's daughter, Irene Retford.

Musikverlage in der Bundesrepublik Deutschland und in West-Berlin (Bonn, 1965), 58; C. Vinz and G. Olzog, eds.: *Dokumentation deutschsprachiger Verlage* (Munich and Vienna, 1971), 108

T.W.

Benteen, Frederick D. American publisher and piano dealer, active in Baltimore. His name first appears in the partnership of Miller and Benteen in 1838. In May 1839 Benteen acquired the business of John Cole and Son and established the firm of F. D. Benteen at 137 Baltimore Street. In 1851 he formed Benteen and Co. with William C. Miller (apparently not the same Miller of the 1838 partnership) and J. R. Beacham; in 1853 the firm became Miller and Beacham. The company moved to 104 Charles Street in 1860, and in 1865 Beacham left the partnership. The firm of William C. Miller was acquired by Oliver Ditson of Boston in 1873. The plates of Miller and Benteen were also used by George P. Reed and those of F. D. Benteen by George Willig jr. Benteen and his

successors used the plates of James G. Osbourn before 1864. Among Benteen's notable publications are a reprint of the Osbourn plates for David T. Shaw's *Columbia, Gem of the Ocean* and the first printing of the popular college song, *Vive la compagnie,* or *Vive l'amour,* both in 1844; an 1846 printing of the popular minstrel tune, *Jim Crack Corn,* also known as *The Bluetail Fly;* and the first printing of Stephen Foster's *Massa's in de cold ground,* with Firth, Pond & Co. of New York and Henry Kleber of Pittsburgh in 1852. The Maryland Historical Society holds a collection of 1500 items produced by Benteen.

Fisher (1933); Dichter and Shapiro (1941, 2/1977); D. W. Krummel and others: *Resources in American Music History* (Urbana, 1981)

C.E.

Berandol. Canadian firm of publishers, active in Toronto. It was established by Andrew Twa in 1969 with the acquisition of the music publishing division of BMI Canada Ltd. Formed in 1940, that company had published music since 1947; by 1969 it held the largest number of Canadian copyrights in the country. Berandol was acquired in 1972 by its vice-president, Ralph Cruickshank. The catalogue covers a wide spectrum, with emphasis on concert music and educational materials. The large rental library of orchestral scores includes works by François Morel, R. Murray Schafer, Harry Somers and Healey Willan. The popular music catalogue was sold to Broadland Music in 1972. In the 1970s Berandol developed MUSIcache, a microfiche edition of the standard repertory marketed by Bell & Howell; since 1975 it has been active in record production.

' "Canada First" is Berandol Policy', *Music Scene,* no.251 (1970), 10; R. Cruickshank: 'The Berandol Story', *Music Journal,* xxx/1 (1972), 26; J. J. Linden: 'Berandol Music: Ten Years of Publishing and Recording High Quality Canadian Music', *RPM Weekly,* xxxi/4 (1979), 15; M. Wehrle: 'Berandol Music Limited', *Encyclopedia of Music in Canada* (Toronto, 1981)

M.W.

Berg, Adam (*d* Munich, 1610). German printer. He took over the Schobser publishing house in Munich in 1564 and by 1568 had expanded it sufficiently to necessitate the purchase of a larger building. Under the patronage of the Bavarian Dukes Albrecht V and his son Wilhelm V, it soon became the most important business of its kind in Bavaria. Apparently not a native of Munich, Berg was Protestant, but, after having been jailed for his religious beliefs in 1569, he became a Roman Catholic and served the Counter-Reformation which his patrons enthusiastically supported. After his death his widow, Anna, ably managed the business until 1629, when she turned it over to their son Adam (*d* 1634). However, the lead in music publishing had been taken over by Berg's son-in-law and main competitor in Munich, Nikolaus Henricus.

An expert craftsman, Berg became the leading Bavarian printer of the Counter-Reformation and one of the most important German printers of his time. In addition to the official notices and reports required of him as court printer, he published a variety of books on religious and scientific topics and in the fields of literature and particularly music (which accounts for over 80 of his some 300 publications). His great interest in music reflects the brilliance of the musical establishment at the Bavarian court under the direction of Orlande de Lassus. Berg is best known for his publication of Lassus's *Patrocinium musices* in the large choirbook format generally reserved for MSS, using single-impression type and decorating the pages with handsome woodcut initials.

A. Schmid: *Ottaviano dei Petrucci da Fossombrone und seine Nachfolger im sechzehnten Jahrhunderte* (Vienna, 1845/*R*1968); P. Dirr: 'Ein Drucker und Verleger der Gegenreformation', *Buchwesen und Schrifttum im alten München 1450–1800* (Munich, 1929), 39; O. Kaul: 'Berg, Adam', *MGG*; W. Boetticher: *Orlando di Lasso und seine Zeit 1532–1594* (Kassel, 1958); Benzing (1963, 2/1982)

M.L.G.

Berg [van den Berg, vom Berg, vom Perg, Montanus], **Johann** (*b* Ghent; *d* Nuremberg, 7 Aug 1563). German printer. Berg signed many of his publications Montanus, the Latinized version of his name. After three years' study in Paris, he moved to Nuremberg, apparently because he was a Protestant. In 1541 he married Catharina Schmid and became a citizen of Nuremberg, where both he and his partner, Ulrich Neuber, were officially registered as printers in 1542. After Berg's death, his widow represented the family's interests in the firm until her marriage in 1565 to Dietrich Gerlach and the latter's entrance into the business a year later. Although Neuber left shortly thereafter, the firm continued to flourish under Gerlach's and later Catharina's direction and was ultimately taken over by Berg's grandson, Paul Kauffmann. As far as can be determined, he was not related to the Munich printer Adam Berg.

The firm of Berg & Neuber is notable more for its unusually large output than for the quality of its craftsmanship, which does not measure up to that of the older Nuremberg printers, Petreius and Formschneider. By the middle of the century it had already attained the leading position in music publication which it held until the end of the century. Interested primarily in the printing of theological literature, Berg began his efforts in the field of music by publishing liturgical books. He is best known, however, for the large multi-volume collections of sacred music by the leading Netherlands and German composers, which he apparently edited himself. He also published instruction books on music and in 1549 took over the printing of Forster's German song collections from Petreius.

Having left the firm to found his own business after Berg's death, Neuber contented himself mainly with reprints of earlier Berg & Neuber publications; his only original contributions were the collections of sacred music edited by Clemens Stephani. His output of musical publications almost entirely ceased after 1569 and the firm appears to have been on the decline even before Neuber's death in 1571. From this and the fact that he was obliged to hire an editor, it is clear that his role in the partnership with Berg was mainly that of technician, whereas Berg did the actual selection and editing of works for publication.

P. Cohen: *Musikdruck und -drucker zu Nürnberg im sechzehnten Jahrhundert* (Nuremberg, 1927); R. Wagner: 'Ergänzungen zur Geschichte der Nürnberger Musikdrucker des 16. Jahrhunderts', *ZMw*, xii (1929–30), 506; M. van Crevel: 'Coclicos Beziehungen zum Musikverleger Montanus', *Adrianus Petit Coclico* (The Hague, 1940), 230; T. Wohnhaas: 'Montanus, Johann', *MGG* [incl. list of publications]; idem: 'Neuber, Ulrich', *MGG* [incl. list of publications]; Benzing (1963, 2/1982); T. Wohnhaas: 'Zum Nürnberger Musikdruck und Musikverlag im 16. und 17. Jahrhundert', *Gutenberg-Jb 1973*, 337

M.L.G.

Bergen, Gimel [Berg, Joachim; Montanus] (*b* Lübeck, *c*1540; *d* Dresden, 1597). German printer. After apprenticeship with Jakob Lucius in Rostock and Johann Eichorn in Frankfurt an der Oder, he moved to Dresden, working at first with Matthäus Stökel. His music printing began in 1570 with vocal collections by Matthaeus Le Maistre and Antonio Scandello, followed by several Lutheran hymnals. After his death the press was continued by his widow and heirs, including his son Gimel II (*fl* 1610–37, made Hofbruckdrucker in 1616), then Gimel III (*fl* 1640–43), Christian and Melchior (*fl* 1643–88), Melchior's son Immanuel (*fl* 1688–93) and eventually Melchior's son-in-law, Johannes Riedel (*fl* 1688–1716). Their most ambitious and best-executed printing coincides with their finest music. Editions of Heinrich Schütz began to appear in 1618, including the *Psalmen Davids* (1619) and the second and third parts of the *Symphoniae sacrae* (1647, 1650, the first having been issued earlier in Venice). Other major works are the dance music (1527–8) of Carlo Farina and the dialogues (1645–71) of Andreas Hammerschmidt, the latter often with the printer Georg Beuther in nearby Freiburg. Wolfgang Seiffert (*fl* 1624–55), who married Hedwig Bergen, Gimel II's daughter, and his son Gottfried (*fl* 1655–*c*1662) are named in joint imprints and alone on works of Farina, Hammerschmidt and Schütz, notably Schütz's *Psalmen Davids* of 1661.

Benzing (1963, 2/1982)

D.W.K.

Beringen. French firm of printers. It was founded by Godefroy Beringen (*b* Germany, *fl* 1538–59; *d* ?Lyons), who was active in Lyons as a humanist; several Lyons intellectuals, including Etienne Dolet in 1538, addressed some Latin verses to him. He began to print books in 1544. In 1545 he formed an association with his brother Marcellin Beringen (*d* 1556) which lasted until the latter's death. The Beringen brothers did not publish many titles but frequently reprinted those that were apparently successful. Law, medicine, alchemy and the Roman classics dominated their production. They were in contact with Geneva through the poet Guillaume Guéroult and probably began printing music under his influence. Between 1547 and 1554 they printed a number of important music books, thus becoming the first music printers in Lyons after Jacques Moderne. The *Premier livre des chansons spirituelles* (1548) contained the first printing of Didier Lupi's *Susanne un jour*, a song that was to be the source for 38 different settings in the late 16th century. In September 1556, after Marcellin's death, Godefroy was forced to sell everything, including his six presses, to pay his debts. Nevertheless two later books appeared under his name, in 1558 and 1559. The inventory for the sale in 1556 lists three sets of music type: 'noctes grandes d'Allemaigne', 'noctes petites gloses d'Allemaigne' and 'nocte de Louain à longue queue'.

Unlike Moderne and the large Parisian music printers, the Beringens printed no anthologies. They confined themselves to separate publications of the works of only three composers – Loys Bourgeois, Dominique Phinot and Didier Lupi. The repertory has a distinct Protestant bias, and it may have been the Beringens' Protestant sympathies that caused Bourgeois to apply to them instead of to Moderne to print his psalms in 1547. There are 12 known music books and two psalters by Beringen.

H. and J. Baudrier: *Bibliographie lyonnaise* (Paris, 1895–1921/*R*1964), iii, 31; K. J. Levy: ' "Susanne un jour": the History of a 16th Century Chanson', *AnnM*, i (1953), 375; V. L. Saulnier: 'Dominique Phinot et Didier Lupi, musiciens de Clément Marot et des marotiques', *RdM*, xliii (1959), 61; L. Guillo: *Recherches sur les éditions musicales lyonnaises de la Renaissance* (diss., Ecole Pratique des Hautes Etudes, Paris, 1986)

S.F.P./L.G.

Berra, Marco (*b* Campagna, 24 Oct 1784; *d* Prague, 18 May 1853). Italian publisher, active in Prague. He was first a publisher's workman for the Artaria firm in Vienna. From 1811 to 1853 he owned his own publishing works and adjacent shop in Prague, where, in addition to music, maps and engravings, he sold instruments, strings, lithographs and oil paintings. From 1835 he also ran a large music-hire business, and maintained profitable commercial contacts with Italy, France, England, Germany and Russia. He probably issued about 1380 numbered items, of which some of the first 100 contain two separate compositions; nos. 1330 to 1380 were published jointly with his son-in-law, Jan Hoffmann. Berra's main publications were songs and pieces for guitar or piano; besides some church music and works for flute and organ, he also published works by Bach, Beethoven, Weber and other widely known composers as well as many local ones (e.g. Tomášek, Vitásek, Kníže, Mašek, Martinovský and Führer). He produced much contemporary dance music in the collections *Prager Lieblings-Galloppen* and *Prager Lieblings-Polkas*; his edition of organ compositions in the collection *Museum für Orgelspieler* is also well known. Animosity towards the competition from Hoffmann, who opened his music publishing firm in Prague in 1841, prompted Berra to decide that after his death his publishing house should be sold. It was bought by the firm Christoph & Kuhé, who continued Berra's numbering. During the 1880s it foundered and the publishing was taken over by Hoffmann's son and Berra's daughter, Emilie Hoffmannová.

ČSHS; Z. Nejedlý: *Bedřich Smetana*, ii (Prague, 1925), 372, 374, 376; J. Dostál: 'Marco Berra, první velkorysý nakladatel hudební v Praze' [Marco Berra, the first large-scale music publisher in Prague], *Slovanská knihověda*, vi (1947), 92; I. Janáčková: 'Pražští vydavatelé Václava Jana Tomáška' [Tomášek's Prague publishers], *HV*, xviii (1981), 171

Z.C.

Bertuzzi, Luigi (*b* Piacenza, *c*1787; *d* after 1847). Italian publisher. He moved to Milan in 1805 to work for Ricordi, then from 1820 set up on his own as a music seller and copyist in the Contrada di S Margherita. In 1821 he began registering his publications, but without plate numbers; the first was *XVIII Esercizi per flauto del Signor T. Berbiguier onde rendersi pratici nell'uso delle chiavi*, dedicated to Carlo Alary, the flute professor at the Milan Conservatory. Until 1830 Bertuzzi printed about 30 editions a year, mainly didactic works such as Asioli's *I transunti*, and arrangements for flute and piano of opera excerpts. Between 1828 and 1830 he printed Bellini's *Bianca e Fernando*, reprinted by Ricordi in 1837; Bertuzzi often printed arias from works by Mercadante and Morlacchi before Ricordi or Lucca did. Production increased, and by 1847 his catalogue contained more than 1500 editions. Bertuzzi published Cesare Pugni's Quartet op.3, first with G. A. Carulli in 1825, then with Lucca in 1847, the year in which he retired. He was succeeded by Domenico Vismara, who retained his plate numbers.

A.Z.L.

Bessel, Vasily Vasil'yevich (*b* St Petersburg, 25 April 1843; *d* Zurich, 1 March 1907). Russian publisher. He received his music education at the St Petersburg Conservatory, where he studied the violin with Wieniawski and music theory with Nikolay Zaremba, and graduated in 1865 from I. A. Veykman's viola class. From 1866 to 1874 he played the viola in the ballet orchestra of the imperial theatres. In August 1869 he and his brother Ivan opened a music shop on the Nevsky Prospekt and this swiftly expanded into a thriving publishing house. An important centre of Russian musical life, Bessel's firm published works by all the prominent Russian composers, notably Tchaikovsky, Dargomïzhsky, Anton Rubinstein and the members of The Five. Bessel was known also as a writer, and several of his articles appeared in the weekly journal *Muzïkal'nïy listok* ('The musical leaflet'), which he edited and published from September 1872 to May 1877. He also contributed to the *Neue allgemeine Musik-Zeitung*, and from 1878 until 1887 was the St Petersburg correspondent of the *Neue Musik-Zeitung* pub-

lished in Leipzig. From September 1885 to December 1888 he published the weekly *Muzïkal'noye obozreniye* ('Music review'), and in 1901 his book on music publishing, *Notnoye delo*, appeared in St Petersburg.

N. F. Findeyzen: *Vasily Vasil'yevich Bessel* (St Petersburg, 1909); B. L. Vol'man: *Russkiye notnïye izdaniya XIX – nachala XX veka* [Russian music publishing in the 19th and early 20th centuries] (Leningrad, 1970); G. B. Bernandt and I. M. Yampol'sky: *Kto pisal o muzïke* [Writers on music], i (Moscow, 1971) [incl. full list of writings]; R. W. Oldani: 'Editions of *Boris Godunov*', *Musorgsky in Memoriam, 1881–1981*, ed. M. H. Brown (Ann Arbor, 1982), 179–213

G.N.

Bevilacqua. Brazilian publishing firm, active in Rio de Janeiro. Isidoro Bevilacqua (*b* Genoa, 1813; *d* Rio de Janeiro, 26 Jan 1897) settled in Rio de Janeiro in 1835, and from 1857 to 1865 worked in partnership with Narcizo José Pinto Braga. In 1879 Isidoro's son Eugénio (*d* 1905) became manager, opening a branch in São Paulo in 1890. By 1900 the catalogue listed 4446 items, and by 1913, 7000. Although the company's fortunes declined in the 1920s and its catalogue was sold in 1930 (to A. Tisi Neto), Adela Bevilacqua, Eugénio's daughter, bought it back in 1941, designating Mángione & Filhos as sole selling agents. Among the more than 70 Brazilian composers published by the firm at that time were Francisco Braga, Carlos Gomes, Chiquinha Gonzaga, Leopoldo Miguez, Abdon Milanez, Ernesto Nazareth, Alberto Nepomuceno and Henrique Oswald.

R. Stevenson: *Renaissance and Baroque Musical Sources in the Americas* (Washington, DC, 1970), 267; *Enciclopédia de música brasileira: erudita, folclórica e popular*, i (São Paulo, 1977), 93, 355; *Música no Rio de Janeiro Imperial 1822–1870: Exposição comemorativa do primeiro decênio da Seção de Música e Arquivo Sonoro* (Rio de Janeiro, 1982), 69

R.S.(ii)

Bickham, George, jr (*b* ?London, ?1710–15; *d* London, 1758). English engraver. He worked in London, often for music publishers, and was probably the son of George Bickham (*d* 1769), an engraver during Queen Anne's reign. He was principally famous for his two illustrated folio volumes *The Musical Entertainer*, which was first issued in fortnightly parts, each containing four plates, from January 1737 to December 1739. The 200 plates are songs, headed and surrounded with pictorial embellishments illustrative of the song, and engraved after the style of Gravelot and Watteau (see illustration). This work was the first of its kind to be published in

'Rural Beauty; or Vaux-hal Garden' by Boyce from 'The Musical Entertainer', i (1737), printed from plates engraved by Bickham

England and quickly produced imitators such as Lampe's *British Melody*, engraved by Benjamin Cole.

A second edition, corrected by Lampe, was also issued in parts (1740–41), and a third, printed from the original plates, appeared in 1765, issued by John Ryall. Other works engraved by Bickham include *Songs in the Opera of Flora* (1737) and the frontispiece for Simpson's *The Delightful Pocket Companion for the German Flute* (c1745).

F. Kidson: 'Some Illustrated Music-books of the Seventeenth and Eighteenth Centuries: English', *MA*, iii (1911–12), 195; Humphries and Smith (1954, 2/1970)

F.K., H.G.F./P.W.J.

Biglow & Main. American firm of publishers, active in New York. A partnership was formed in 1867 between Lucius Horatio Biglow (1833–c1910) and Sylvester Main (1819–73) in order to continue the publishing activities of William B. Bradbury, who served the firm as music editor until his death in January 1868. Main had formerly been Bradbury's assistant, but it was his son Hubert Platt Main (1839–1925) who was responsible for shaping the editorial policy of the company and who built it into one of the foremost gospel-song publishers. Among the composers whose works he issued were Philip P. Bliss, William H. Doane, William J. Kirkpatrick, Robert Lowry, G. F. Root, Sankey, Sherwin, Stebbins, Sweney and Whittle. Lowry succeeded Bradbury as music editor in 1868, and a number of other composers also had editorial relationships with the firm. The poet Fanny Crosby worked closely with many of Biglow & Main's composers, contributing a total of almost 6000 texts; she formed a particularly successful collaboration with Doane.

Ira Sankey became president of the firm on the retirement of Biglow in 1895. On his death in 1908 he was succeeded by his son I. Allan Sankey (1874–1915), and for the next few years the firm was run by the Sankey family. Biglow & Main was purchased in 1922 by the Hope Publishing Co., and merged in 1933 with the E. O. Excell Co., but the company's publications continue to be issued under its own name.

C.R.

Big 3. American firm of publishers. It was formed in 1939 by Metro-Goldwyn-Mayer, which acquired three major publishers of popular music, Robbins Music Corporation, Leo Feist, Inc. and Miller Music, in order to gain control of copyrights for music used in films. The resulting company, the Big 3 Music Corporation, based in New York, has specialized in popular music, film scores and television theme music; its catalogue includes *You don't have to say you love me, Batman's Theme, The shadow of your smile* and *Somewhere my love*. In 1973 MGM sold Big 3 to United Artists.

F.B.

Billaudot. French firm of publishers. It was founded in Paris in 1895 by Louis Billaudot (1877–1936) and initially specialized in choral and theatrical music as well as works on the study of harmony. The business was expanded with the publication of new music and the acquisition of other firms: Cordier (1903), Tilliard (1914), Pinatel (1926), Thomas (1930), Librairie Théâtrale (1930) and, since World War II, Béthune (1945), Costallat (1958), Andrieu (1962), Pierre Noël (1966), Jacquot (1973) and Editions Françaises de Musique (the former publications section of Radio France; 1988).

In the 1920s Robert Billaudot (1901–81) and Gérard Billaudot (1911–86) joined the firm; from 1958 it was run by the latter as Gérard Billaudot Editeur, and from 1979 with his son-in-law François Dervaux (*b* 1940). The firm has specialized since the 1950s in educational publications, including instrumental methods and study notebooks, edited by such musicians as Maurice André, Pierre Pierlot and Daniel-Lesur; it has also established a substantial instrumental and orchestral catalogue including early French music and the works of many contemporary composers, including Arrieu, Auric, Barraud, Dutilleux, Françaix, Ibert, Jolivet, Koechlin, Ohana, Philippot and Schmitt as well as representatives of the younger generation. Theatrical publishing and bookselling continues with the Librairie Théâtrale in the Place de l'Opéra Comique.

Birchall, Robert (*b* ?London, *c*1760; *d* London, 19 Dec 1819). English music seller, instrument dealer and publisher. From his early imprints it appears that he had been apprenticed to Walsh's successors, William Randall and his wife Elizabeth. In 1783 he was in business with T. Beardmore as Beardmore & Birchall (or Birchall & Beardmore). From 1783 to May 1789 he was in partnership with Hugh Andrews as Birchall & Andrews; he also issued publications under the name Birchall & Co., and established a circulating music library. He then continued alone in the firm until 1819.

Birchall managed the series of Antient

Concerts and most of the benefit concerts of the time. In 1783 he proposed a complete reissue of Handel's works in 80 folio volumes, but the project never materialized, though Birchall subsequently published many Handel items. In addition to glees, country dance books and much Italian vocal music, his publications included the first English edition of J. S. Bach's *Das wohltemperirte Clavier*, edited by Samuel Wesley and K. F. Horn in 1810. He also published many of Beethoven's works, including the original English editions of the 'Battle' Symphony, the Violin Sonata op.96, the Piano Trio op.97, and a piano adaptation of the Seventh Symphony, the English copyrights of which he purchased from the composer.

Birchall was succeeded at his death by the firm of Birchall, Lonsdale & Mills (also known as Birchall & Co., or Mills & Co.). The firm was known as Lonsdale & Mills from about 1829 until the dissolution of the partnership in 1834. Richard Mills (*b* ?1798; *d* London, 28 Nov 1870), a nephew of Birchall, remained active until about 1868, when he was succeeded by Richard Mills & Sons, a firm which continued until 1903. The firm of Christopher Lonsdale (?1795–1877), which had a large circulating music library, continued until 1880 when it was succeeded by Alfred Hays. At an early date the firms' catalogues included vocal scores of Mozart operas.

C. Burney: *An Account of the Musical Performances . . . in Commemoration of Handel* (London, 1785); Kidson (1900); Humphries and Smith (1954, 2/1970); Neighbour and Tyson (1965)

F.K., W.C.S./P.W.J.

Birnbach. German firm of publishers. It was founded in 1911 in Berlin by Richard Birnbach (1883–1953), who quickly developed a successful catalogue, publishing a wide variety of works, including educational music, music for salon orchestra, and contemporary instrumental and vocal music. In 1919 he expanded his publishing enterprise by acquiring the catalogue of C. A. Challier & Co. Birnbach's catalogue was further extended with the purchase in 1934 of Verlag Dreililien, through which he acquired some of Schoenberg's early works (opp.1–4, 6–7). Other composers published by the firm include Rezniček, Richard Strauss, Weingartner, Leon Jessell, Oscar Straus and Gerhard Winkler. Important editions of piano music by lesser-known composers were also published. After Birnbach's death the company passed to his widow Hanna and son Richard.

Musikverlage in der Bundesrepublik Deutschland und in West-Berlin (Bonn, 1965)

A.P. (ii)

Blackmar, A(rmand) E(dward) (*b* Bennington, VT, 1826; *d* New Orleans, 28 Oct 1888). American publisher. He worked as a music teacher in Huntsville, Alabama (1845–52), and Jackson, Louisiana (1852–5). In 1858 he joined E. D. Patton's music shop in Vicksburg, Mississippi, which he bought out the following year with his younger brother Henry (1831–1909). They moved to New Orleans in 1860, where they operated publishing firms and music shops jointly, separately and often with others. From 1861 to 1866 Henry also ran a shop in Augusta, Georgia. Armand was imprisoned briefly in 1862 by the Union Army for his espousal of the Southern cause; he issued more Confederate music than any other publisher in New Orleans, including one of the earliest editions of *Dixie* (1861), and *The Bonnie Blue Flag* (1861) and *Maryland! My Maryland!* (1862). He frequently arranged or composed music under the pseudonym A. Noir. Blackmar was in San Francisco between 1877 and 1880, but was publishing again in New Orleans from 1881 to 1888.

R. B. Harwell: *Confederate Music* (Chapel Hill, 1950); P. C. Boudreaux: *Music Publishing in New Orleans in the 19th Century* (MA thesis, Louisiana State U., 1977); R. Powell: *A Study of A. E. Blackmar and Bro., Music Publishers of New Orleans, Louisiana, and Augusta, Georgia, with a Checklist of Imprints in Louisiana Collections* (MA thesis, Louisiana State U., 1978); F. W. Hoogerwerf: *Confederate Sheet-music Imprints*, ISAMm, xxi (Brooklyn, NY, 1984)

J.H.B.

Blado, Antonio (*b* Asola, nr. Mantua, 1490; *d* Rome, 1567). Italian printer. He began to print at Rome in 1516. His numerous guide-books to Rome, prognostications, reports of current events and some devotional volumes were primarily aimed at the popular market, whereas his editions of the classics, his books in Greek and Hebrew, and such works as his *Modus baptizandi* (1599) for the Ethiopian Church, using Ethiopic type, could hardly be described as commercial at all. His books show a variety of typefaces, borders, ornaments and decorated initials, and a few are lavishly illustrated with woodcuts. In 1535 he obtained the exclusive right to print Vatican documents and thereafter styled himself 'impressor camerale' or 'stampatore apostolico'. Blado was a dominant figure in Roman printing, and had one of the largest printing shops, staffed by six or seven

Bland, John

printers in 1550. He also worked in other cities: Viterbo (1546), Rieti (1549) and Foligno (1562). His usual printer's mark was a single-headed eagle resembling the imperial eagle.

Although it was Dorico who first printed music in Rome from movable type in a single impression, Blado was certainly the next. He may have printed the 1538 *Madrigale de M. Constantio Festa libro primo* (for four voices), although the surviving altus and incomplete superius do not name a printer or place of publication. The *Exercitium seraficum, madrigali di M. Hubert Naich*, signed by Blado but undated, was probably printed in 1542. This book does not use the same music type as the 1538 Festa book, and neither music type is used in any later books, at least not in Rome. When Blado printed polyphonic music again it was with other type. His later editions include Animuccia's *Secondo libro de i madrigali a cinque voci* (1551), Guerrero's *Psalmorum quatuor vocum liber primus* (1559), Zoilo's *Libro secondo de madrigali a 4 et a 5 voci* (1563) and Martelli's *La nuova et armonica compositione a quattro voci* (1564). With, or for, Antonio Barré he printed madrigal books by Francesco Menta (1560) and Lasso (1563). Blado also published the first edition of Vincenzo Lusitano's *Introduttione facilissima* (1553). He printed plainchant in a number of his liturgical books, beginning with the *Officium gloriosissimi nominis Jesu* (1539), but did not try to compete with the Venetian Giunti in this type of publishing.

After his death Blado was succeeded by his widow Paola (*d* 1588 or 1589) and son Paolo (*d* 1594). Another son, Stefano, was an important collaborator in the firm, and also conducted business on his own; his marriage to Livia Dorico, daughter of Luigi Dorico, linked the Blado firm with one of its most important competitors. The heirs continued to print both ephemera and serious editions, of which the most monumental was an 18-volume folio edition of the works of Thomas Aquinas (1570). They were among the first printers of the *laudi spirituali* edited for the Congregazione dell'Oratorio by Giovanni Animuccia and Francisco Soto. By 1594 the firm had come to rely on loans from Rodolfo Silvestri, who apparently acquired a share. Paolo's widow and then her daughter ran the business until 1626.

D. Bernoni: *Dei Torresano, Blado e Ragazzoni* (Milan, 1890); G. Fumagalli and G. Belli: *Catalogo delle edizioni romane di Antonio Blado Asolano ed eredi, possedute dalla Biblioteca nazionale centrale Vittorio Emanuele di Roma* (Rome, 1891–1942), fasc. i–iii; G. Fumagalli: *Antonio Blado tipografo romano* (Milan, 1893); F. Ascarelli: *La tipografia cinquecentina italiana* (Florence, 1953), 65; Sartori (1958); E. Vaccaro Sofia: *Catalogo delle edizioni romane di Antonio Blado Asolano ed eredi (1516–1593) possedute dalle Biblioteche Alessandrina Angelica, Casanatense, Corsiniana e Vallicelliana di Roma, dalla Biblioteca Vaticana, dall'Archivio di stato di Roma e dall' Archivio segreto Vaticano* (Rome, 1961), fasc.iv [continuation of Fumagalli and Belli, with full bibliography]; F. Barberi: 'Blado, Antonio', *DBI*; H. W. Hitchcock: 'Depriving Caccini of a Musical Pastime', *JAMS*, xxv (1972), 76; G. L. Massetti Zannini: 'Una dinastia di stampatori: i Blado', *Stampatori a librai a Roma nella seconda metà del cinquecento: documenti inediti* (Rome, 1980), 61; S. G. Cusick: *Valerio Dorico: Music Printer in Sixteenth-century Rome* (Ann Arbor, 1981)

T.W.B.

Blake, George E. (*b* England, ?1775; *d* Philadelphia, 20 Feb 1871). American engraver and publisher. He emigrated to the USA before 1793 and in 1794 began teaching the flute and clarinet. In 1802 he acquired the piano manufactory of John I. Hawkins in Philadelphia, and soon after began to publish and to operate a circulating music library. His production included many American compositions (*c*1808) and political songs (*c*1813); an early piracy of Thomas Moore's *Irish Melodies* (1808–*c*1825); a serial, *Musical Miscellany* (from 1815); and the first American edition of *Messiah* (*c*1830), along with other major vocal works by Handel. Most numerous among his output, however, were songs of the Philadelphia theatre, based on London publications. Blake also issued typeset opera librettos and engraved tunebooks. He remained active throughout the 1830s, in later years issuing minstrel music and excerpts from Italian opera. At the height of his career (*c*1810–30) he was America's most prolific music publisher.

Obituary, *Philadelphia Evening Transcript* (21 Feb 1871); J. C. White: *Music Printing and Publishing in Philadelphia, 1729–1840* (MA thesis, Columbia U., 1949); D. W. Krummel: *Philadelphia Music Engraving and Publishing, 1800–1820: a Study in Bibliography and Cultural History* (diss., U. of Michigan, 1958); Wolfe (1964); Wolfe (1980)

D.W.K.

Bland, John (*b* ?London, *c*1750; *d* ?London, *c*1840). English music seller, instrument dealer and publisher. By 1776 he was established in London, where he remained active until his comparatively early retirement in 1795. In 1789 he went to Vienna to induce Haydn to visit England and to seek compositions from him and other composers, including Hoffmeister and Kozeluch. Bland is said to have been the hero of the 'Razor' Quartet story, in which he supposedly received the manuscript of the quartet op.55 no.2 as a reward for presenting Haydn with his English-style razor; however, the op.55 quartets were published in England not by Bland, but by Longman & Broderip in 1790. Haydn did eventually send Bland three piano trios (HXV:15–17), which he subsequently published. When Haydn arrived in London in January 1791 he spent his first night as a guest of Bland at his house in Holborn. Bland published other works by Haydn, though his business relationship with him was by no means an exclusive one. He also appears to have commissioned the 1792 portrait of Haydn by Thomas Hardy (now in the Royal College of Music, London), and issued engravings from it.

Bland published many collections of catches and glees, operas and sheet music, in addition to republishing many of Handel's works, often in unusually inexpensive editions. In 1795 the business, including Bland's stock of 12,000 engraved plates, was taken over by Lewis, Houston & Hyde, who in 1797 were followed by Francis Linley (1771–1800); he in turn gave place in 1798 to William Hodsoll who kept on the business until 1831.

Letter to the editor, *Musical World*, ii (1836), 95; Kidson (1900); Humphries and Smith (1954, 2/1970); H. C. Robbins Landon, ed.: *The Collected Correspondence and London Notebooks of Joseph Haydn* (London, 1959); idem: *Haydn: Chronicle and Works*, ii, iii (London, 1976–8)

F.K., W.C.S./P.W.J.

Bland & Weller. English firm of music publishers and instrument makers, active in London. The business, not to be confused with that of John Bland, was founded in 1784 by Anne Bland, who went into partnership with E. Weller in 1792; their publishing activities included country-dance collections and the first English edition of three Mozart piano sonatas (κ280, 282, 283). In 1805 the firm purchased from Dibdin the copyrights of 360 of his songs together with his musical stock, which it then reissued. Anne Bland retired in about 1818, and a sale of plates and copyrights took place, though Weller carried on the business as Weller & Co. until 1820.

Kidson (1900); Humphries and Smith (1954, 2/1970)

F.K., W.C.S./P.W.J.

Bloom, Sol (*b* Pekin, IL, 9 March 1870; *d* Washington, DC, 7 March 1949). American publisher. He worked in newspaper publishing, the construction industry and the mail-order business before establishing his own music publishing firm in Chicago, at Wabash and Jackson streets, in 1896. His catalogue included the songs *Cinderella White* by Evelyn Henchheimer, *Don't send me away, Daddy* by Nellie Revell and *The way to a woman's heart* by Jessie Bartlett Davis (all c1896–9), *The heroes who sank with the Maine* by James O'Dea and Paul Cohn (1898), *I wish I was in Dixieland tonight* by Raymond A. Browne (1900; the first US copyright of the 20th century), *Coon, Coon, Coon* by Gene Jefferson and Leo Friedman (1901), *Sammy* by O'Dea and Edward Hutchison (1903) and *I think it must be love* by Browne and Friedman (1906). Bloom also sold, by mail, *The World's Music Library*, attracting the attention of the Hearst newspapers, which instituted a Sunday music supplement using Bloom's publications. In 1900 he moved to larger premises with a theatre, at Dearborn and Randolph streets; here he used multi-link telephone connections to 'broadcast' Sunday afternoon concerts. He acquired exclusive national distribution rights for the Victor Talking Machine and opened a gramophone shop on Fifth Avenue in New York, as well as mail-order branches there and in 12 other cities. In 1903 he moved to New York, eventually establishing 80 mail-order outlets in the USA. In 1910 he sold his publishing interests to the New York publisher Witmark, and his gramophone distribution rights back to Victor. Thereafter Bloom operated a property and construction company. In 1922 he was elected to the US House of Representatives, rising to prominence as chairman of the House Committee on Foreign Affairs. He promoted the historical music publications issued for the George Washington Bicentennial in 1932.

S. Bloom: *The Autobiography of Sol Bloom* (New York, 1948); S. Spaeth: *History of Popular Music in America* (New York, 1948); Fuld (1966, 3/1985); D. Ewen: *All the Years of American Popular Music* (Englewood Cliffs, NJ, 1977)

C.E.

Boelke-Bomart. American firm of publishers. It was founded by Margot and Walter R. Boelke in New York in 1948 and moved to Hillsdale, New York, in 1951. Affiliated to ASCAP, the firm specializes in the publication of contemporary music, and under the general editorship (1952–82) of Jacques-Louis Monod, who succeeded Kurt List, built up a small but important catalogue. Among its composers are Berger, Casanova, Lansky, Lerdahl, Perle, Schoenberg, Spies and Winkler. In 1975 a sister company, Mobart Music Publications (an affiliate of BMI), was founded; its composers include Babbitt, Gideon, Ives, Monod, Pollock, Shifrin, Weber and Webern. The distributor for both companies in the USA and Canada is Jerona Music Corporation.

G. Sturm: 'Encounters: Walter R. Boelke', *MadAminA!: a Chronicle of Musical Catalogues*, iv/1 (1983), 9

A.P.(ii)/R.A.L.

Bogard, Jan (*b* ?Louvain, ?*c*1540, *d* Douai, 1634). Flemish printer. He worked at Louvain from 1564 to 1574, when he moved to the university town of Douai and established a press at the sign of the Bible d'Or in the rue des Ecoles. From 1575 he included a number of music books among his publications, mostly volumes of motets by composers such as Gallet, Castro, Lassus and the brothers Regnard. He also reprinted popular collections, including Phalèse's *Livre 7 des chansons vulgaires* and Gastoldi's *Balletti a 5 voci*. Bogard may have acquired printing materials from Phalèse: his publication in 1578 of Pevernage's *Cantiones sacrae* show a typical Phalèse border on the title-page and is described as being printed 'typis Phalesii'. He was succeeded by his son Peter for a few years, but evidently business did not prosper; in 1655, in the accounts of the Phalèse house, Bogard is listed as owing 119 florins 12 stuivers, a debt written off as irrecoverable.

Goovaerts (1880); J. A. Stellfeld: *Andries Pevernage* (Louvain, 1943) [with list of Bogard's music publications, p. 144]; S. Bain: *Music Printing in the Low Countries in the Sixteenth Century* (diss., U. of Cambridge, 1974)

S.B. (i)

Böhm. German firm of publishers. It was established in Augsburg in 1803 by Andreas Böhm (1765–1834), and under his direction soon achieved prominence. In 1831 the ownership passed to Andreas's son Anton Böhm (1807–84) and in 1874 to his son Moritz Anselm Böhm (1846–96), when the firm became known as Anton Böhm & Sohn, a name it has retained. In 1893 M. A. Böhm established a branch in Vienna. The firm was completely destroyed in World War II but was restored under the directorship of Friedrich Ballinger (*b* 1906) and has since regained its previous importance. Anton Böhm & Sohn has specialized in the publication of Catholic church and organ music, for which it has established a lasting reputation. The firm has also pub-

lished standard editions of Haydn, Mozart and Schubert masses, many in its series *Denkmäler liturgischer Tonkunst*, and has begun to publish works by 20th-century composers including Otto Jochum, Otto Siegl, Franz Philipp, Arthur Piechler and Heinrich Lemacher.

A.P. (ii)

Boileau Bernasconi, Allessio (*b* Verona, 14 March 1875; *d* Barcelona, 27 Sept 1948). Italian publisher of French origin. He began as a music printing apprentice with Ricordi, Milan, then went as a printer to Marcello Capra of Turin. In 1904 he became a printer for Vidal Llimona y Boceta of Barcelona, whose printing works he took over in 1906. He went straight into the publishing business, founding, in partnership with others, the firm Iberia Musical in Barcelona; in 1928 he absorbed its publishing assets with those of other publishing firms to form the Editorial Boileau. He was active for several decades, publishing the standard repertory and much other music; later the firm devoted itself almost exclusively to printing music for other firms.

J.L.-C.

Boivin, François (*b c*1693; *d* Paris, 25 Nov 1733). French music seller and publisher. He was the nephew of the double bass player and composer Montéclair and brother of the string instrument maker Claude Boivin. On 15 July 1721 Boivin bought the music shop 'A la règle d'or' on the rue St Honoré, Paris, after the death of Henry Foucault who had owned it; he and his uncle went into partnership to trade there. In addition to selling scores he soon published music, including some by Montéclair. In 1724 he married Elizabeth Catherine Ballard, second daughter of Jean-Baptiste-Christophe Ballard, who assisted him. As a result of their efforts, and the family connection with Montéclair and Ballard, 'La règle d'or' became one of the foremost music shops in Paris. Works by Vivaldi, Corelli, P. A. Locatelli, Telemann and Quantz could be found there, but the mainstay of the stock was French, including cantatas by Nicolas Bernier and Clérambault, harpsichord works by François Couperin, Louis Marchand and Dandrieu, violin sonatas by J.-M. Leclair and J. B. Senaillé, sonatas for flute by Louis Hotteterre, suites for viola da gamba by Marais and Caix d'Hervelois, motets by Lalande, operas by Lully, Campra and Rameau, as well as brunettes and *airs* for amateurs. Boivin also associated with the Princess of Enghien, the Bishop of Reims, the Amsterdam publisher Le Cène and such composers as Daquin, Mouret, Boismortier, François Francoeur and P. D. Philidor.

After Boivin died his widow continued the business for 20 years, under the name 'la Veuve Boivin', assisted by her brother-in-law Claude Boivin and her father. The measure of her intelligent management is revealed by the value of the stock which increased unceasingly; worth 4500 livres in 1721 and 29,500 in 1724, its value had increased to 36,400 livres when trading ceased in 1753. She sold her shop to Marc Bayard on 2 March 1753 and died in Chartres on 13 February 1776.

S. Milliot: 'Un couple de marchands de musique au XVIIIe siècle: les Boivin', *RdM*, liv (1968), 105; A. Devriès: *Edition et commerce de la musique gravée à Paris dans la première moitié du XVIIIe siècle* (Geneva, 1976); Devriès and Lesure, (1979–88)
S.M.

Bonneüil, Hiérosme [Jérôme] [*fl* Paris, 1671–1700). French engraver and music seller. He was the engraver of Francesco Corbetta's *La guitarre royalle*, dedicated to the king of England in 1671, as well as its sole seller since Corbetta's privilege is ceded to him. He resided in the Les Halles quarter of Paris. The address on his publications is rue au Lard 'near the leather market'. His first publication adds 'near the butcher Beauvais'; all subsequent ones specify 'near SS Innocents'. Presumably he died before 1701, as the last dated publication entirely engraved by him was Pierre Gillier's *Livre d'airs* (1697). He began engraving Marais's *Pièces de violes* (livre 2, 1701), which was completed by Henri de Baussen.

Devriès and Lesure (1979–88)
G.H.B.

Boosey & Hawkes. English firm of publishers and instrument manufacturers. The Boosey family was of French origin, and though the early family history is somewhat confused, it appears that the firm's founder was the Thomas Boosey (i) who opened a bookshop in London in about 1795. This business continued until 1832, being known from 1819 as Boosey & Sons, or T. & T. Boosey. A separate music side of the business was started in 1816 under the control of the founder's son, Thomas (ii). They began as importers of foreign music, but soon became the English publishers of such composers as Hummel, Mercadante, Romberg and Rossini, and later of important operas by Bellini, Dònizetti and Verdi, until a House of Lords decision in 1854 deprived English publishers of their foreign copyrights. Among the earliest publications of T. Boosey & Co. was an English translation of Forkel's life of Bach (1820).

From about 1850 the firm also manufactured wind instruments, and from 1868 (when it purchased the business of Henry Distin) brass instruments; it pioneered the widely acclaimed design for compensating valves developed by D. J. Blaikley in 1874.

In the latter part of the 19th century Boosey & Co., as the firm had become known, centred its publishing activities on the increasingly popular ballad; to promote sales the London Ballad Concerts were established in 1867 by John Boosey, son of Thomas (ii), at St James's Hall, and later at the new Queen's Hall; Clara Butt was among the artists. From around the end of the century the firm began to emphasize educational music. In 1930 the firm of Boosey & Hawkes came into being on the amalgamation with Hawkes & Son, a firm of instrument makers and publishers founded in 1865 as Hawkes & Co. (later Rivière & Hawkes) and particularly known for handling brass and military band music, a speciality which has been continued. Boosey & Hawkes developed greater artistic ambitions, and notable musical figures such as Erwin Stein and Ernst Roth helped it to secure the copyrights or agencies for an impressive array of composers, including Richard Strauss, Stravinsky, Prokofiev, Bartók, Kodály, Copland, Mahler and Rakhmaninov, in addition to all of Benjamin Britten's output from 1938 to 1963. Maxwell Davies is the most prominent name among living English composers in the catalogue, and the firm's continuing interest in contemporary music is also reflected in the magazine *Tempo*, which it started in 1939. Boosey & Hawkes's scale of operation is now worldwide, with branches in six countries on four continents.

The New York branch of the firm, established in 1892, has developed its own catalogue, which emphasizes the works of American composers including Elliott Carter, David Del Tredici, Walter Piston and Ned Rorem. Since 1965 it has issued a newsletter, *Quarter Notes*.

W. Boosey: *Fifty Years of Music* (London, 1931); C. G. Mortimer: 'Leading Music Publishers, 3: Boosey & Hawkes Ltd.', *MO*, lxii (1938–9), 181; 'The Music Publisher of Tradition: the Booseys: Thomas and John; the Hawkes: William Henry and Oliver', *MO*, lxv (1941–2), 68; Humphries and Smith (1954, 2/1970); J. N. Moore: *Elgar and his Publishers* (London, 1987)
D.J.B.,W.C.S./P.W.J.

Borboni [Borbone], **Nicolò** (*b* ?Rome; *fl* 1615–41). Italian publisher and engraver. He probably spent his whole life in Rome and may have been related to the Roman painters Jacopo, Domenico and Matteo Borboni (the last of whom was also an engraver). Following Simone Verovio, whose pupil he may have been, he espoused the method of printing from engraved copper plates for a series of music books published between 1615 and 1637. The bulk of these comprised the various editions, seven in all, of Frescobaldi's two volumes of toccatas (and other pieces), in which the engraving was done by Cristoforo Bianchi. Like all Borboni's productions, they are accurate and elegant, with attractive decoration, and no less fine than the work of Verovio himself. Another of Borboni's productions, which he engraved himself, was his own *Musicali concenti . . . libro primo* (Rome, 1618 or perhaps 1619) for one and two voices and continuo, his only known collection of music (there are also a song and duet by him in *RISM* 1622 [11]). He may have studied music with Ottavio Catalani. He was organist of St John Lateran, Rome, from 1638 until at least 1641, and he looked after the organs at S Apollinare at least from 1 June 1633 until September 1641. Doni called him an 'excellent organist' and praised a regal he had made.

G. B. Doni: *Compendio del trattato de' generi e de' modi della musica* (Rome, 1635), 57; C. Sartori: 'Le 7 edizioni delle *Toccate* di Girolamo Frescobaldi', *La bibliofilia*, 1 (1948), 198; idem (1958); F. Hammond: *Girolamo Frescobaldi* (Cambridge, MA, and London, 1983); A. Morelli: 'Nuovi documenti Frescobaldiani: i contratti per l'edizione del primo libro di *Toccate*', *Studi musicali*, xvii (1988), 255

N.F.

Bortoli. Venetian family of printers. Giacomo reprinted in 1652 Pietro Milioni's *Modo di imparere a sonare la chitarra spagnola*, and Camillo issued Monferrato's solo motets op.6 in 1666. A more extensive music printer was Antonio Bortoli, who soon after 1700 issued concerted vocal and instrumental music by Lotti, Carlo Antonio Marini, Giulio and Luigi Taglietti and Vivaldi, besides liturgical works. His theoretical treatises include Zaccaria Tevo's *Il musico testore* (1706), the Illuminato da Torino's *Canto ecclesiastico* (1742) and Gasparini's venerable *L'armonico pratico* (1708; four later editions by his heirs up to 1764). Antonio was one of the few typographic music printers in 18th-century Italy. Several dozen published catalogues, mostly from before 1710, testify to his uncommon interest in promotion, while later ones record his slowly expanding output under cautious circumstances.

Sartori (1958); Mischiati (1984)

D.W.K.

Bosse. German firm of publishers. It was founded in 1912 by Gustav Bosse (*b* Vienenburg, 6 Feb 1884; *d* Regensburg, 27 Aug 1943) and continued after his death by his brother Walter and from 1948 by his grandson Bernhard Bosse. In 1957 Bosse Verlag merged with the Bärenreiter complex, though retaining its name and independence in the formation of its programme. The firm, based in Regensburg, has always been concerned exclusively with publishing books on music, of which the *Deutsche Musikbücherei* series is particularly notable. Besides handbooks for the study of theory in music education institutions, important current series include the *Kölner Beiträge zur Musikforschung* (from 1955), *Forschungsbeiträge zur Musikwissenschaft* (from 1955), *Studien zur Musikgeschichte des 19. Jahrhunderts* (from 1965) and *Regensburger Beiträge zur musikalischen Volks and Vöolkerkunde* (from 1969). In 1960 Edition Bosse was integrated into the book publishing side of Bärenreiter, and their projects include the publication of folk music, modern church music and school music.

E. Valentin: 'Gustav Bosse', *Musik im Kriege*, i (1943–4), 113; E. Valentin, ed.: *50 Jahre Gustav Bosse Verlag* (Regensburg, 1963); *Musikverlage in der Bundesrepublik Deutschland und in West-Berlin* (Bonn, 1965), 129

T.W.

Bossler, Heinrich Philipp Carl (*b* Darmstadt, 22 June 1744; *d* Gohlis, nr. Leipzig, 9 Dec 1812). German printer and publisher. Around 1769 he worked as a copper engraver and in 1779 invented a machine which simplified music engraving. He founded his publishing firm in Speyer in 1781; in 1785 another branch (Krämer & Bossler) was established in Darmstadt, where the company moved in 1792. By 1796 almost 300 titles had been published. After a long journey Bossler settled in Gohlis, near Leipzig, in 1799. The publishing house, later directed by his son Friedrich Bossler, closed in 1828. Bossler's publications included works by south German composers and Beethoven's three *Kurfürstensonaten* WoO47 (1783), as well as the periodical *Musicalische Realzeitung* (1788–90).

H. Schneider: *Der Musikverleger Heinrich Philipp Bossler (1744–1812)* (Tutzing, 1985)

H.-M.P.

Boston Music Company. American firm of publishers. It was founded in 1885 by Gustave Schirmer (*b* New York, 18 Feb 1864; *d* Boston, 15 July 1907) and operated from premises at 2 Beacon Street, Boston; its first publication, Arthur Whiting's *Concert Etude* for piano, was issued the following year. The firm's large catalogue, which includes many works by Ethelbert Nevin and Carrie Jacobs-Bond, is predominantly educational. Among its popular instructional series are the piano methods by John M. Williams (the 'Blue Books'), C. Paul Herfurth's series *A Tune-a-Day* (for various instruments) and *Junior Hymn Books* for piano by Rachael Beatty Kahl. Connections with the Schirmer family and firm remained close. Ernest Charles Schirmer, cousin of Gustave and founder of the E. C. Schirmer Music Company of Boston in 1921, was business manager and then partner, but left in 1917. On Gustave's death ownership passed to his son, also named Gustave (*b* Boston, 29 Dec 1890; *d* Palm Beach, FL, 28 May 1965), who engaged Carl Engel as editor and music adviser (1909–21), acquired catalogues of other publishers and joined ASCAP (1924). In 1922 publication headquarters were moved to New York. The firm has long acted as agent for both domestic and foreign publishers. From 1965 to 1976 it was owned by the Frank Music Corp., then passed into the hands of CBS for a year, during which time it ceased to publish. Williamson Music took over from 1977 to 1979, when it was sold to William Hammerstein to become a division of the Hammerstein Music & Theater Company, Inc.

Fisher (1933); C. M. Ayars: *Contributions to the Art of Music in America by the Music Industries of Boston, 1640 to 1936* (New York, 1937/R1969)

G.O.

Bosworth. Firm of publishers. The company was founded in 1889 in Leipzig by an Englishman, Arthur Edward Bosworth (1858–1923), assisted initially by Thomas Chappell and Karl Kratochwill. The aim was to protect the copyrights of the Gilbert and Sullivan operas in Austria, since at that time there was no copyright agreement between Britain and Austria. Bosworth opened a London branch in 1892, but his most far-reaching achievement was founding a publishing house in Vienna (1902) and acquiring the Austrian music publishers Kratochwill and Chmél. By doing so he obtained important copyrights, including Zeller's *Der Obersteiger* and *Der Vogelhändler* and· Heuberger's *Der Opernball*. Bosworth's sons, Laurence Owen Bosworth

(1886–1952) and Arthur Ferdinand Bosworth (1893–1959), succeeded him when he died. By World War II several more German and Austrian catalogues had been acquired. Meanwhile, in England, Bosworth's publications of Beringer's piano tutor, Ševčík's violin method and many of Moszkowski's works were having great success, and the British Empire rights to the Steingräber catalogue and the Catholic church music catalogue of Laudy were acquired. International success was achieved with the publication of Albert Ketèlbey's works. After the Leipzig premises were destroyed in the war, a new German firm was established in Cologne. Since then the firm has published more choral and educational music. Curt Gräfe took over after the Bosworth brothers died and was followed by Fritz Hartmann between 1961 and 1968. Reimar Segebrecht became director in 1969.

'The House of Bosworth', *London Musical Courier*, xxxvi/18 (1913), 236

A.P. (ii)

Bote & Bock. German firm of publishers. It was founded in Berlin on 1 February 1838 when Eduard Bote and Gustav Bock (*b* Berlin, 2 March 1813; *d* Berlin, 27 April 1863) purchased C. W. Froehlich & Co. The Berlin firms of Moritz Westphal and Thomas Brandenburg were acquired in 1840 and 1845 respectively. In 1847 Eduard Bote withdrew from the business. From 1863 to 1871 Bock's brother Emil Bock (*b* Berlin, 17 March 1816; *d* Berlin, 1 April 1871) directed the firm, followed by Gustav's son Hugo Bock (*b* Berlin, 25 July 1848; *d* Berlin, 12 March 1932), who acquired the publishing firm of Lauterbach & Kuhn in Leipzig in 1908. He was supported by his sons Gustav Bock (*b* Berlin, 17 July 1882; *d* Wiesbaden, 6 July 1953) from 1908 and Anton Bock (*b* Berlin, 7 Nov 1884; *d* Hildesheim, 28 Jan 1945) from 1911. The publishing house was completely destroyed in 1943, then under the direction of one of Hugo Bock's grandsons Kurt Radecke (*b* Freiburg, 7 July 1901; *d* Berlin 16 June 1966). The firm is a family limited partnership, and from 1966 has been under the management of Dieter Langheld (*b* Darmstadt, 2 May 1911); in 1948 a subsidiary in Wiesbaden was established.

Under Gustav Bock the publishing firm began by issuing light music and salon music of Berlin (e.g. Gustav Lange and August Conradi), as well as inexpensive new editions of works by classical composers. In the second half of the 19th century it became the leading firm in northern Germany for opera publication (e.g. Gounod's *Faust*, entitled *Margarethe*, Otto Nicolai's *Die lustigen Weiber*, Meyerbeer's *L'africaine* and operas by Flotow, Brüll, Mascagni, Kienzl and Smetana). It also acquired the rights to all Offenbach's operettas and Johann Strauss's *Waldmeister*. Through the purchase of Lauterbach & Kuhn much of Reger's work became the property of Bote & Bock. Besides further operas (e.g. d'Albert's *Die toten Augen* and *Tiefland* and Respighi's *La campana sommersa*) the firm also published important instrumental works by Liszt, Tchaikovsky, A. Rubinstein, Dvořák, Paderewski, Mahler and Richard Strauss (*Symphonia domestica*).

After 1945 the firm continued to publish editions of early music (C. P. E. Bach, Caldara and A. Scarlatti), but much of Boris Blacher's work was acquired and the firm now concentrates mainly on new music (Rudolf Wagner-Régeny, Giselher Klebe, Gottfried von Einem, Paul Dessau, Rudolf Kelterborn, Isang Yun, Nicolas Nabokov, Martin Redel and Frank Michael Beyer).

Musikverlag Bote & Bock Berlin 1838–1938 (Berlin, 1938); Deutsch (1946); H. Kunz: *125 Jahre Bote & Bock* (Berlin and Wiesbaden, 1963); *Musikverlage in der Bundesrepublik Deutschland und in West-Berlin* (Bonn, 1965); Plesske (1968)

R.E.

Brainard, Silas (*b* Lempster, NH, 14 Feb 1814; *d* Cleveland, OH, 8 April 1871). American publisher. He moved to Cleveland in 1834 and with Henry J. Mould opened a music shop, Brainard and Mould, two years later. By 1845 the company was known as S. Brainard and in that year began to publish music; this business (known as S. Brainard & Sons from 1866) became one of the most important in the country. Brainard published popular music, mostly pieces for piano and songs for solo voice with piano accompaniment, but also a few sacred hymns and quartets. Also in 1845 Brainard bought Watson Hall (built 1840, known as Melodeon Hall, 1845–60, and then Brainard's Hall until 1872), where many musical events took place. Brainard was a flautist who participated in and arranged works for musical organizations in Cleveland. The company opened branches in New York, Louisville and Chicago (where it was eventually based), and in 1864 established an influential journal, *Western Musical World*, which became *Brainard's Musical World* in 1869. Brainard married Emily Mould in 1840. Two of their seven children, Charles Silas Brainard and Henry Mould Brainard, assumed responsibility for the firm on their father's death, changing its name to S. Brainard's Sons. The firm ceased in 1931.

K. Merz: 'Silas Brainard', *Brainard's Musical World*, viii/May (1871); L. A. Brainard: *The Genealogy of the Brainard-Brainard Family in America 1649–1908*, i (Hartford, 1908), 326; S. P. Orth: *A History of Cleveland, Ohio* (Chicago and Cleveland, 1910), 111, 200; Dichter and Shapiro (1941, 2/1977); E. C. Krohn: *Music Publishing in the Middle Western States before the Civil War* (Detroit, 1972); J. H. Alexander: *It must be Heard: a Survey of the Musical Life of Cleveland, 1836–1918* (Cleveland, 1981)

J.H.A.

Brandus. French firm of publishers, active in Paris. It was established in January 1846 when Gemmy Brandus (*b* Berlin, 3 Jan 1823; *d* Paris, 12 Feb 1873) purchased the firm of Maurice Schlesinger. In partnership with his elder brother Louis (*b* Kremmen, 28 March 1816; *d* Paris, 30 Sept 1887), Brandus took over Schlesinger's premises at 97 rue Richelieu; in December 1848 a move was made (or the house was renumbered) to 87 and later, in January 1851, to 103 rue Richelieu. In October 1850 the firm of Troupenas (with which Brandus had for more than a year occasionally published) was acquired, and for a time Troupenas' premises at 40 rue Vivienne were retained. In February 1854 Sélim-François Dufour (*b* Cherbourg, 18 March 1779; *d* Paris, 25 July 1872), who had previously been manager of Brandus' branch in St Petersburg, was taken into partnership, the firm becoming known as G. Brandus, Dufour & Cie or G. Brandus & S. Dufour. When Dufour died in July 1872 the firm reverted to the name Brandus & Cie, and on Gemmy's death the next year the direction was assumed by Louis Brandus. In October 1887, after the latter's death, Philippe Maquet acquired the firm, giving it his own name; in 1899 Maquet's business was taken over by C. Joubert & Cie, which remained in existence until 1971.

Brandus took care to maintain Schlesinger's contacts with Berlioz, Chopin, Halévy and Meyerbeer. The firm published the first editions in score of Berlioz's *Harold en Italie*, *Roméo et Juliette* and the *Te Deum*, and the piano-vocal score of *Béatrice et Bénédict*. It published Chopin's opp.59–65, the last of his works to appear in his lifetime, Meyerbeer's last four operas, from *Le prophète* (1849) to *L'africaine* (1865), and, before Halévy transferred his allegiance elsewhere, seven of his operas. It also printed (though probably not always for general sale) full scores and orchestral parts of operas and operettas by Auber, Flotow, Lecocq, Maillart and Offenbach; together with its stock of earlier Schlesinger and Troupenas publications it was able in 1867 to offer performing materials of no fewer than 65 works for the stage; by 1887, excluding reissues, it had put out piano-vocal scores of a total of about 80 new stage works, including 15 by Offenbach and 25 by Lecocq. In the field of instrumental music it concentrated particularly on the piano music of Blumenthal, Victor Duvernoy, Heller and Liszt, the dance music of Musard and Labitzky, and violin works by Vieuxtemps. It published Schlesinger's *Revue et gazette musicale* until 31 December 1880, when the final number appeared. Brandus continued Schlesinger's chronological series of plate numbers, starting at about 4500 in 1846 and continuing to about 13,100 in 1887. A gap of about 3500 numbers (*c*1850) may be explained partly by the acquisition of Troupenas' stock (to which Brandus probably allocated new numbers).

Catalogue général (Paris, *c*1846), suppl. (1849), suppl. (1850); *Catalogue de Brandus et Dufour* (Paris, 1867–9); C. Hopkinson: *A Bibliography of the Musical and Literary Works of Hector Berlioz* (Edinburgh, 1951, rev. 2/1980), 195; idem (1954); Devriès and Lesure (1979–88)

R.M.

Breitkopf & Härtel. German firm of publishers and printers. It was probably established on 24 January 1719 by the printer Bernhard Christoph Breitkopf (*b* Clausthal, 2 March 1695; *d* Leipzig, 23 March 1777), who was associated with a Leipzig firm of printers and typefounders. In 1725 Breitkopf published a Hebrew Bible, the firm's first important publishing venture. His friendship with the poet Johann Christoph Gottsched led to the expansion of the firm's literary publications, with musical editions initially playing a secondary role. Well-known works produced during this period include the *Schemellische Gesangbuch* (1736) and second editions of parts of Sperontes's *Singende Muse an der Pleisse* (1740–41).

Under Bernhard's son Johann Gottlob Immanuel Breitkopf (*b* Leipzig, 23 Nov 1719; *d* Leipzig, 28 Jan 1794), one of the most versatile figures in the history of German publishing and printing, the firm achieved greater importance. In 1745 he took over his father's printing works and soon derived considerable financial benefits from his typographical inventions. His divisible and movable types, introduced in 1754–5, improved the system of printing notation so decisively that music could henceforth be published in much larger editions. His printing office had a staff of over 100. Besides pieces by Telemann, Mattheson, Leopold Mozart, Haydn, Carl

Stamitz and Reichardt, Breitkopf published works by C. P. E. Bach and J. A. Hiller, both friends of his. Virtually all notable composers of the second half of the 18th century attempted to have at least a few works printed or published by the Breitkopf firm. Marketing difficulties caused by the Seven Years War (1756–63) resulted in surplus stocks, whereupon Breitkopf published catalogues of all available works, including a thematic index (see illustration). These catalogues, brought out between 1760 and 1787, are invaluable to music bibliography. The firm also sold musical instruments and, for a time, made playing cards, fancy papers and wallpaper. Breitkopf included among his friends notable scholars and musicians of the time, a fact attested by his letters addressed to Lessing and Winckelmann, among others; the young Goethe, during his student days in Leipzig, was also drawn to the Breitkopfs' hospitable home. After 1770 Breitkopf began to devote himself to scholarly research and to publishing articles. On his death he was praised as a 'sage and philanthropist'.

Breitkopf's two sons, Bernhard Theodor (1749–*c*1820) and Christoph Gottlob (1750–1800), did not consider themselves capable of developing their father's achievements, so Gottfried Christoph Härtel (*b* Schneeberg, 27 Jan 1763; *d* Cotta, nr. Leipzig, 25 July 1827), who had studied law and had planned a diplomatic career, joined the firm as an associate in 1795. The next year he bought the firm and took over the running of the publishing house, now known as Breitkopf & Härtel; he was also appointed Breitkopf's sole heir. Härtel, who was equally gifted as an artist, scientist and economist, was commercially far-sighted. In 1806 he applied Alois Senefelder's invention of lithography to the printing of music, and published the 'Oeuvres complètes' of Mozart, Haydn, Clementi, Dussek and Cramer, forerunners of the later complete critical editions. In 1803 Härtel published the full score of Handel's *Messiah* and in 1827 produced the first of Bach's church cantatas to be printed after his death (*Ein' feste Burg*). He corresponded with Haydn and negotiated with Mozart's widow, Constanze, in connection with her husband's works. He eagerly courted Beethoven's friendship with the result that the firm was able to publish the first editions of 25 of his works (opp.29, 34, 35, all works between Symphony no.5, op.67, and the Mass in C, op.86, and the posthumously published opp.136 and 137). Härtel founded the *Allgemeine musikalische Zeitung* (1798–1848), which became the

Pages 16 and 17 from the Breitkopf Thematic Catalogue, Part iii (1763)

leading voice in music criticism in the first half of the 19th century. It was also through Härtel that the *Leipziger Literaturzeitung* (1812) was initiated. In 1807 he began manufacturing pianos; these were used by Mendelssohn, Liszt, Clara Schumann and Wagner, among others.

After Härtel's death, his nephew Florens Härtel took over the firm until his sons Raymund (*b* Leipzig, 9 June 1810; *d* Leipzig, 9 Nov 1888) and Hermann (*b* Leipzig, 27 April 1803; *d* Leipzig, 4 Aug 1875) entered the business in 1832 and 1835 respectively. It was these two members of the Härtel family who subsequently greatly expanded the firm and determined its development for the next 40 years. Hermann Härtel was keenly interested in the Italian visual arts and in 1828 had taken a doctorate of law. He was one of the co-founders of the Leipziger Kunstverein and served in numerous honorary positions connected with music. Raymund Härtel, a Leipzig city councillor, was more practically inclined and fostered the firm's technological development. Hermann Härtel was

friendly with Mendelssohn and Schumann, and it was at Schumann's instigation that he published Schubert's hitherto unknown C major Symphony ten years after the composer's death. He also acquired the rights in Brahms's early works, and in music by Chopin and Berlioz, besides giving Liszt extensive support. The firm particularly encouraged stage works; it was the first to publish operas by Meyerbeer, Cherubini, Donizetti, Bellini, Méhul, Auber, Adam, Thomas, Marschner and Lortzing, but collaboration with Wagner did not produce the expected gains. The Bach revival which began early in the 19th century found the climax in Breitkopf & Härtel's publication of the complete edition. The Beethoven edition, which required more than 13,400 plates, came out within only four years (1862–5). The adjoining book publishing division produced some of the most important standard 19th-century musicological works. With its publication of cheap, popular editions, the 'Rote Bände', the firm competed with other German publishing houses. On Hermann Härtel's death the firm's catalogue comprised 15,000 items. The Härtel brothers were largely responsible for its leading position in music publishing.

Raymund and Hermann Härtel left no male heir and the firm accordingly passed to their nephews, Wilhelm Volkmann (*b* Leipzig, 12 June 1837; *d* Leipzig, 24 Dec 1896) and Oskar von Hase (*b* Jena, 15 Sept 1846; *d* Leipzig, 26 Jan 1921), who considerably expanded the firm's programme in meeting the demands of contemporary political and economic conditions. Ludwig Volkmann (*b* Leipzig, 9 Jan 1870; *d* Leipzig, 10 Feb 1947) took over his father's responsibilities when the latter died. The Volkmann family dealt primarily with the technical processes of typesetting and printing. Oskar von Hase initiated the *Denkmäler Deutscher Tonkunst* and *Denkmäler der Tonkunst in Bayern*. In the years between 1850 and 1912 more than 20 complete critical editions were begun, including those of Mendelssohn, Mozart, Schumann, Schubert, Schütz, Berlioz, Schein, Liszt, Haydn and Wagner, as well as Bach and Beethoven.

Oskar von Hase systematically expanded the collection of concert material, and established libraries to house full scores, as well as orchestral, choral and chamber music. This fundamental reorganization of the firm's stock lasted for decades. D'Albert, Busoni and above all Sibelius were the contemporary composers whom the firm promoted. Its books on music, including collections of individual composers' correspondence, were unsurpassed in their range. The firm collaborated with leading contemporary music scholars, including Eitner, Riemann, Kretzschmar, Friedrich Ludwig, Johannes Wolf, Abert and Schering. The book division also published works on theology, medicine and aesthetics. From 1883 the firm maintained branches abroad and concluded sales agreements with almost 50 foreign publishing houses.

World War I and the ensuing economic crises were a turning-point in Breitkopf & Härtel's history. Not only Ludwig Volkmann, but also Hellmuth von Hase (*b* Leipzig, 30 Jan 1891; *d* Wiesbaden, 18 Oct 1979), who entered the business in 1919, together with Martin von Hase (1901–71) and Wilhelm Volkmann (1898–1939), all recognized that only by means of farsighted changes in publishing could they reconcile their traditional duties with modern needs in music and musical scholarship. Between 1926 and 1928 the works of Brahms were published in 26 volumes. Numerous composers, all of them in the mainstream of

international musical life, were published by the firm, including Othmar Schoeck, Kurt Atterberg, Yrjö Kilpinen, Hermann Zilcher, Kurt Thomas, Johann Nepomuk David, Günter Raphael, Hugo Distler and Helmut Bräutigam. The music textbook division produced standard reference works, and Breitkopf & Härtel also devoted themselves to the publication of music journals.

The publishing works were destroyed in a bombing raid during December 1943, and valuable autographs and archive material were lost. Part of what was saved from the archives, including copybooks and correspondence dating from about 1895, is now in the Leipzig State Archives, with the remainder in Darmstadt and West Berlin. Reconstruction work began slowly in 1945, and the firm was in effect divided into two, with one independent section in East Germany and one in West. The technical side of the business in Leipzig was separated from the publishing house, which became nationally owned in 1952. The firm of VEB Breitkopf & Härtel Leipzig has an extensive and systematically developed publishing programme. Besides publishing the well-known classics, the firm promotes the works of such contemporary East German composers as Hanns Eisler, Ernst Hermann Meyer, Paul Dessau, Wilhelm Weismann, Georg Trexler, Fidelio Friedrich Finke, Fritz Geissler, Johannes Paul Thilman, Otto Reinhold, Siegfried Kurz and Ruth Zechlin. Gunter Hempel (*b* Annaberg, 7 June 1932) was appointed head of the publishing division in 1974, when he took over from the music scholar and publisher Helmut Zeraschi (*b* 1911). The firm also publishes music books. The West German part of the firm was refounded in Wiesbaden in 1945 by Hellmuth and Martin von Hase and was later run by Lieselotte Sievers (*b* Leipzig, 18 April 1928) and Joachim Volkmann (*b* Leipzig, 30 Nov 1926). Apart from the collected edition of Max Reger's works, begun in 1954, the firm is responsible for the series *Collegium Musicae Novae*, and also publishes such contemporary composers as Driessler, Eimert, Knab, Lahusen, Karl Marx and Jens Rohwer.

For further illustration *see* fig.36, p.108.

R. Elvers: *Breitkopf & Härtel 1719–1969: ein historischer Überblick zum Jubiläum* (Wiesbaden, 1968); O. and H. von Hase: *Breitkopf & Härtel: Gedenkschrift und Arbeitsbericht* (Wiesbaden, 1968); *Pasticcio auf das 250jährige Bestehen des Verlages Breitkopf & Härtel: Beiträge zur Geschichte des Hauses* (Leipzig, 1968); Plesske (1968); R. Elvers: 'Breitkopf & Härtels Verlagsarchiv', *FAM*, xvii (1970), 24; J. Kallberg: 'Chopin in the Marketplace: Aspects of the International Music Publishing Industry in the First Half of the Nineteenth Century', *Notes*, xxxix (1982–3), 535, 795

H.-M.P./R

Bremner, Robert (*b* ?Edinburgh, *c*1713; *d* London, 12 May 1789). Scottish publisher. He established his business in Edinburgh in mid-1754, and had considerable early success: his first issues included Niccolo Pasquali's excellent *Thorough-bass Made Easy* (1757); his own *The Rudiments of Music* (1756, 3/1763), an instruction book commissioned by the Edinburgh town council for newly formed church choirs; and reprints of the fiddle variations on Scottish tunes by the locally celebrated William McGibbon. Bremner also profited from a fashionable boom in guitar playing, publishing a guitar arrangement of *Twelve Scots Tunes* (*c*1760) and *Instructions for the Guitar* (1758, 2/1765), which was probably written by his son Robert, who had been sent to London to study the guitar with Geminiani. From 1755 Bremner supplied sheet music regularly to the influential Edinburgh Musical Society, and travelled to London and Dublin to act as its agent. In 1761 he issued the Six Overtures op.1 of Lord Kelly, the first orchestral pieces in the Mannheim style ever composed in Britain.

These successes enabled Bremner to move his business to London in 1762 (the Edinburgh shop was maintained under a manager). His business continued to flourish; a notable venture was the *Periodical Overtures in Eight Parts*, a monthly series of new works for amateur orchestral societies. In 1764 he bought plates from John Simpson, in 1777 most of the stock and plates of John Johnson, and in 1779 some plates from the firm of Welcker. His own music was neatly engraved and printed on high-quality paper. After Bremner's death his London stock, plates and copyrights were bought by Preston & Son, who described their purchase as 'not only the most extensive, but also the most valuable list of works ever exhibited in this kingdom'.

An Additional Catalogue of Instrumental and Vocal Music, Printed and Sold by Preston & Son . . . Late the Property of that Eminent Dealer, Mr. Robert Bremner (London, 1790); J. Glen: *The Glen Collection of Scottish Dance Music* (Edinburgh, 1891–5), i, p. vii; Kidson (1900); H. G. Farmer: *A History of Music in Scotland* (London, 1947), 293; D. Wyn Jones: 'Robert Bremner and *The Periodical Overture*', *Soundings*, vii (1978), 63 [incl. incipit catalogue]

D.J.

Breyer. Argentine publisher, active in Buenos Aires. The firm was founded in 1882 as Casa Neumann y Breyer. G.

Neumann separated from Breyer in 1888, continuing in business to about 1960, later working with the lithographer and printer Ortelli. Alberto Breyer, with his brother Adolfo (1862–1940), had become the leading Argentine music publisher by 1910. He acquired electrically run presses in 1899, shops selling pianos and other musical articles, and branches in provincial centres. Breyer also acquired other firms, among them in 1888 Manuel de Costa Amaro (established in 1855 as an affiliate of a Brazilian firm), and in 1902 F. Stefani (founded 1887). With the acquisition in 1899 of Antonio (later Arturo) Demarchi (active in publishing since 1868, publisher of the Argentine composer Arturo Berutti), Breyer also inherited several catalogues acquired by Demarchi including Restano (1884), Lazaro Cavalleri (1885) and P. J. Hardoy (1892). The last was founded in 1886 as successor to several firms operated by Gabino Monguillot, who had been active since 1855 and incorporated Guión and Felipe P. Rodriguez. In 1899 Breyer also acquired the classical catalogue of Andrés Carrano, active as a publisher from 1891 and heir in 1896 to the firms of J. Rodriguez and Federico Guillermo Hartmann – the latter, particularly important, had been publishing since 1872, with 53,400 works in its catalogue in 1884.

The Milan firm of Ricordi, represented by Neumann y Breyer as early as 1885, acquired Breyer Hermanos in 1924, which however continued to issue works under the imprint of Ricordi-Americana, mostly popular and salon music in handsome editions.

V. Gesualdo: *Historia de la música en la Argentina* (Buenos Aires, 1961); J. M. Veniard: 'Editores de música de tango', *Antológia del Tango rioplatense*, i (Buenos Aires, 1980)

J.M.V.

Broadman Press. American publishing firm. It was formed in 1934 in Nashville, Tennessee, to produce non-curriculum materials for the Sunday School Board of the Southern Baptist Convention. Its name derives from the first secretary of the Board, John Albert Broadus (1827–95), and the first president, Basil Manly jr (1825–92). Under B. B. McKinney the music division, Broadman Music, issued its first publications in 1937; these now include hymnals, vocal and instrumental music, records and books, marketed since 1986 by the Genevox Music Group. Southern Baptist curriculum materials (choir periodicals, hymnals, records, books, handbell music) are produced separately by the Sunday School Board's Church Music Department.

Encyclopedia of Southern Baptists (Nashville, 1958), i, 194, ii, 817; R. J. Hastings: *Glorious is Thy Name!: B. B. McKinney: the Man and his Music* (Nashville, 1986)

G.H.S.

Brockhaus, Max (*b* Leipzig, 13 April 1867; *d* Lörrach, 9 May 1957). German publisher. He purchased several companies which formed the basis for his music publishing firm founded in 1893 in Leipzig. From 1906 he belonged to the Gewandhaus-Direktorium and was its chairman from 1920 to 1936. He provided 30 years of valuable stimulus for the development of Leipzig's concert life. The publishing firm was especially concerned with the promotion of contemporary opera (Humperdinck, Leoncavallo, d'Albert), and by 1918 had published 30 music dramas. From 1898 Brockhaus promoted Hans Pfitzner's work, publishing his operas and some orchestral, choral and chamber works, as well as 53 lieder and songs; he also published numerous compositions by Siegfried Wagner (Brockhaus considered himself a friend of both composers). The firm's publications have consistently achieved a high artistic standard. In 1940 Brockhaus's daughter Elisabeth Gruner took over the business, which suffered considerable war damage in 1943; reconstruction began in Lörrach in 1949.

A. Hübscher: *Hundertfünfzig Jahre F. A. Brockhaus 1805 bis 1955* (Wiesbaden, 1955)

H.-M.P.

Broome [Broom], **Michael** (*b* 1699/1700; *d* Birmingham, 21 Sept 1775). English country psalmodist, printer and publisher, active in the Midlands. Like other country psalmodists who also printed their own books, he began as a singing-master; but he renounced that career in favour of printing and publishing. His home parish was Abingdon (his earliest psalm book opens with the tune *Abingdon*) and he spent some time at Isleworth before settling in Birmingham in the early 1730s, becoming the town's first music printer. Besides engraving, printing and publishing over a dozen psalm books of his own, he issued the works of Midlands composers including John Barker and Barnabas Gunn; these comprise sacred music, secular songs and instrumental works and appear in upright format, more lavish than the oblong format used by the other printers of country psalmody.

J. Hill: *The Book Makers of Old Birmingham* (Birmingham, 1907)

D.H. (iii)

Broude, Alexander. American firm of publishers, distributors, importers and exporters. Alexander Broude (*b* New York, 1 Jan 1909) was originally associated with his brother, Irving, in Broude Brothers, and began publishing music in the 1930s in New York. In 1954 Alexander severed the association and founded his own company, Alexander Broude, Inc. (ABI Music), which from 1962 published music for all media, including educational materials and music textbooks. 20th-century American composers in the Alexander Broude catalogue include Bales, Ruth Crawford, Dahl, Etler, Frost, Daniel Kessner, Alan Schulman, Elliott Schwartz, Riegger and Westergaard. European composers of all periods, including Rakhmaninov, Casals and Dallapiccola, are also published by the firm. Alexander Broude retired in 1970. In 1982 the company was bought by Michael Lefferts (president) and Dean Streit (vice-president).

W.T.M., M.J./R

Broude Brothers. American firm of publishers, active in New York. Founded in the 1930s by Irving and Alexander Broude, it publishes scholarly editions and reference books as well as performing editions of works by modern and older composers. Its projects have included new editions of the collected works of Buxtehude, Lully, Marais, Marenzio and Rameau. It publishes the series *Monuments of Music and Music Literature in Facsimile*, as well as historical sets such as *Tudor Church Music*, *Masters and Monuments of the Renaissance* and *Music at the Court of Ferrara*. Among 20th-century composers published by the firm are Babbitt, Bacon, Berger, Bloch, Duke, Herrmann, Hovhaness, Krenek, La Montaine, Lockwood, Messiaen, Nin-Culmell and Rozsa. Alexander Broude left the organization in 1954 and established his own firm. Irving Broude's widow, Anne, took over the firm after her husband's death in 1973; when she retired in 1979, her son Ronald became president. The Broude Trust for the Publication of Musicological Editions was formed in 1981 to provide financial support for the preparation of the collected editions and historical sets.

W.T.M., M.J./R

Brzezina, Antoni (*d* Lwów, June 1831). Polish bookseller, publisher, printer and lithographer. He founded in Warsaw in

1822 a bookshop which until 1825 dealt mainly in music. He was in contact with many booksellers in Poland and abroad, and imported much music from other countries, including Schott's edition of Beethoven's collected works. One of Brzezina's regular customers was the young Chopin. After 1823 Brzezina published 309 lithographed musical works, including *Śpiewy historyczne* ('Historical songs') to words by J. U. Niemcewicz, Chopin's Rondo op.1 (1825) and *Rondo à la mazur* op.5 (1828), works by J. Damse, J. Stefani, and K. Kurpiński (keyboard method, 1829), as well as Auber, Boieldieu, Rossini, Weber and others. In 1831 Gustaw Sennewald, Brzezina's partner from 1828, purchased the firm, which then traded under his name until 1905. Brzezina also published his own trade and publishing catalogues, of which four survive (1827–30).

T. Fraczyk: *Warszawa młodości Chopina* [Chopin's early years in Warsaw] (Kraków, 1961), 278; *Słownik pracowników książki polskiej* [Dictionary of Polish printers] (Warsaw and Łódź, 1972); I. Tessaro-Kosimowa: *Historia litografii warszawskiej* (Warsaw, 1973)

K.M. (i)

Buglhat [Boglhat, Bulhat], **Johannes de** (*fl* 1528–55). Music printer. He joined the chapel of Renée of France, Duchess of Ferrara, as a clerk between 1525 and 1528, and probably travelled with her household from Paris to Ferrara in September 1528. A Ferrarese document of 1549 describes him as a priest of the diocese of Clermont and almoner to Renée, and he also served there as clerk of the chapel and surgeon to Renée until 1555 or later. Together with his associates Henrico de Campis and Antonio Hucher, he was one of the first to use the single-impression method of music printing in Italy, a technique introduced to Paris early in 1528 by Attaingnant, which Buglhat may have learnt before leaving France. Campis, possibly related to the Lyonnaise music printer Jannot de Campis (*fl* 1504–10), is listed on the rolls of the Ferrarese court chapel as a singer from 1534 until 1549. Hucher was a wood engraver, to whom the illustrations in Messi Sbugo's *Banchetti* (Ferrara, 1549) have been attributed.

Their earliest publication, *Liber cantus* (1538), was printed by Francesco Rossi (Rubeus), with Buglhat, Campis and Hucher providing 'expensis & labore'. In 1540 Campis published Alfonso della Viola's second book of madrigals and then seems to have withdrawn from publishing. Buglhat and Hucher continued as partners,

printing non-musical works and two more books of madrigals (1548 and 1550). A 1558 reprint of one of the madrigal books was described by Vogel, but no copy is known to survive.

In the dedication to Antonio Gardane's *Mottetti del frutto a sei voci* (1539), Buglhat, Campis and Hucher were attacked for impinging on Gardane's rights, but the exact nature of the rivalry is unknown, as there seems to have been no direct piracy. The two publishing houses may have been competing for the right to use the new printing process, which was just becoming established in Italy. Buglhat's first publication, the *Liber cantus*, had appeared in March 1538, one month before Gardane's earliest surviving publication, but the lack of a precise date for Gardane's lost first edition of Arcadelt's madrigals prevents definite priority being assigned to Buglhat.

A. Schmid: *Ottavio dei Petrucci da Fossombrone . . . und seine Nachfolger im sechzehnten Jahrhundert* (Vienna, 1845/R1968); I. Cittadella: *Documenti ed illustrazioni risguardanti la storia artistica Ferrarese* (Ferrara, 1868); W. Weyler: 'Documenten betreffende de muziekkapel aan het hof van Ferrara', *Vlaamsch Jb voor muziekgeschiedenis*, i (1939), 81–113; Sartori (1958); C. W. Chapman: *Andrea Antico* (diss., Harvard U., 1964); M. S. Lewis: *Antonio Gardane and his Publications of Sacred Music, 1538–55* (diss., Brandeis U., 1979); idem: 'Antonio Gardane's Early Connections with the Willaert Circle', *Music in Medieval and Early Modern Europe: Patronage, Sources and Texts*, ed. I. Fenlon (Cambridge, 1981), 209

M.S.L.

Bunting, Anthony (*b* 1765; *d* after 1843). Anglo-Irish publisher. He is listed in the Dublin directory of 1811 as a professor (piano teacher) and pianoforte seller, and was involved in the establishment of the publishers and music sellers Bunting, Walsh, Pigott & Sherwin, who traded under the name of the Dublin Harmonic Institution at 13 Westmorland Street, Dublin, from about 1825 to 1827. His better-known brother Edward (1773–1843), the Irish folksong collector, was briefly a partner in this firm after moving to Dublin in 1819. The business continued at the same address as Pigott and Sherwin in 1827, under Samuel Pigott alone from 1829 to 1836, then at a new address as the Harmonic Institution from about 1836, and finally as Pigott and Co. from about 1866.

Humphries and Smith (1954, 2/1970)

B.B.

Bureau d'Abonnement Musical. French firm of publishers. It was founded in Paris on 22 July 1765 by Antoine de Peters, a

Flemish artist, with the violinist and composer Jean-Baptiste Miroglio. De Peters was granted a privilege for the publication of music in September 1765, but a group of influential publishers, including Chevardière, Bailleux, Le Clerc and Venier, tried to stop his venture in a court battle which lasted two years; their efforts were unsuccessful and De Peters continued to issue new works. From 1778 to 1782 there is no evidence of any new activity by the firm, but in 1783 it advertised G. J. Vogler's *La kermesse ou La fête flamande*. The firm continued to appear in trade directories until 1789, though De Peters died about 1779 and Miroglio about 1785. Early catalogues of the firm include instrumental works by Wagenseil, J. P. E. Martini and Jommelli. Its most important publications were the first editions of Gluck's *Alceste* (second version, 1776) and *La Cythère assiégée* (second version, 1775) and the second edition of *Iphigénie en Aulide*, all in full scores.

Hopkinson (1954); Johansson (1955); C. Hopkinson: *A Bibliography of the Printed Works of C. W. von Gluck 1714–1787* (London, 1959, 2/1967); Devriès and Lesure, (1979–88)

N.S.

Button & Whitaker. English firm of publishers, active in London in the 19th century. S. J. Button, a bookseller, was a junior partner with Purday in the firm of Thompson in London. They directly succeeded Henry Thompson in about 1805 as Purday & Button (from 1806, Button & Purday), and in 1808 the firm was joined by John Whitaker (the organist and composer) to become Button & Whitaker. Besides republishing works originally issued by the Thompson family, such as *Apollonian Harmony*, the firm produced great quantities of popular songs, small volumes of flute music, collections of glees and country dances, and books of sacred music such as the two volumes entitled *The Seraph* (1818), edited by Whitaker. From about 1814 to 1819 the firm was variously known as Button, Whitaker & Beadnell; Button, Whitaker & Co., or Button & Co.; and from 1819 as Whitaker & Co. The business ceased in 1824 and the stock and premises were sold by auction.

Kidson (1900); Humphries and Smith (1954, 2/1970)

F.K./P.W.J.

C

Caifabri, Giovanni Battista (*fl* 1657–95). Italian publisher. He maintained a shop in the Roman suburb of Parione 'at the sign of the emperor and the Genoese cross', his own trade-mark. He owned no printing press, but made use of several Roman printers during his period of activity. The first was Carlo Ricari, who supplied for him Michelangelo Rossi's *Toccate e correnti*. The first, undated edition does not indicate the name of the printer; this appears in the 1657 reprint, with the typographer's name engraved on the border of the title-page. From this period also date publications of music by Francesco Foggia, Bonifazio Graziani and others, and several anthologies of motets and psalms drawn from composers of the Roman school (e.g. *RISM* 1663[1]), including Benevoli, Ercole, Bernabei, Berardi, Carissimi, Giuseppe Corsi, Savioni and Stamegna. Giacomo Fei, better known as Giacomo di Andrea, also worked for Caifabri; he printed Pompeo Natali's *Madrigali e canzoni spirituali e morali* (1662),

a series of masses and *sacrae cantiones* by Foggia (from 1663), and in 1665 an important group of compositions, including the first part of *Scelta di mottetti a due e tre voci* (*RISM* 1665[1]) and a new edition of Metallo's ricercares. In 1667 Amedeo Belmonti printed the second part of Caifabri's *Scelta di mottetti* (*RISM* 1667[1]), and in 1669 Caifabri entrusted Paolo Moneta with the reprinting of Galeazzo Sabbatini's *Regola facile e breve per sonare*. He also financed the reprinting by G. A. Muti of the *Primo libro a due voci* by Bernardino Lupacchino and G. M. Tasso, and G. A. Muti's printing of Foggia's *Letanie* op.16 (1672), a volume to which was appended an index of sacred and secular music published by Caifabri; this lists five works by Foggia, three by Savioni and one each by Diruta, Bernabei and Tonnani, as well as five anthologies of motets, psalms and *sacre canzoni* for one or more voices. After 1673 Caifabri entered into partnership with Vitale Mascardi, a member of a noted family of printers then active in Rome; they published together new editions of music by Foggia, Metallo, Graziani and others in *Salmi vespertini* (*RISM* 1683[1]), as well as masses by Palestrina and G. F. Anerio (*RISM* .1689[1]) and the *Sonate a tre* op.3 by Corelli (1695).

'Indice dell'opere di musica, che sono all'insegna dell'Imperatore e Croce di Genova', in F. Foggia *Letanie* op.16 (Rome, 1672); Sartori (1958); G.S. Fraenkel: *Decorative Music Title Pages: 201 Examples from 1500 to 1800* (New York, 1968)

S.A.

Camagno. Italian firm of printers and publishers, active in Milan during the second half of the 17th century and early 18th. Carlo Camagno (*d* Milan, before 1656) began as a printer, working for the bookseller and printer Bidelli, but in 1648 set up as his own publisher. He produced about a dozen titles by local composers, one in collaboration with Rolla and one with Rolla's heir. Camagno's shop was near the Chiesa della Rosa, and his heirs, his son Giovanni Francesco Camagno and his brothers, called themselves 'stampatori alla Rosa'. They continued to print music until at least 1682 and probably until 1686, rarely producing more than one book a year. The output of the firm was concentrated almost exclusively on the sacred music of local composers, of whom the most important were apparently thought to be Grancini and Bagatti.

Sartori (1958); M. Donà: *La stampa musicale a Milano fino all'anno 1700* (Florence, 1961) [incl. a nearly complete list of the firm's music publications]

S.B. (iii)

Canti, Giovanni. Italian firm of publishers and copyists. The founder, Giovanni Canti, had previously worked as an engraver for Ricordi. The firm opened in Milan, at 1042 Contrada S Margherita, in about 1835; a Turin branch was opened later 'sotto i portici di S Lorenzo'. After the founder's death the firm was run first by his widow and then by his son Carlo, who himself died in 1876. On 1 April 1878 it was taken over by Lucca. Ten years later Ricordi absorbed the firm of Lucca and the Canti plates; Canti publications are included in Ricordi's three-volume catalogue (*c*1893–7).

In 1858 Canti issued in association with Lorenzi (the Florentine publisher, who had been its agent for some 20 years) a 151-page catalogue (with ten supplements, 1858–65). By 1865 their series of plate numbers (presumed to be chronological) had passed 6800. The firm is chiefly remembered as Verdi's first publisher (the

first editions of *Sei romanze*, *c*1838, and three other vocal pieces, *c*1839); in 1865 it published his *Romanza senza parole*.

Sartori (1958); C. Hopkinson: *A Bibliography of the Works of Giuseppe Verdi*, i (New York, 1973), 88

R.M.

Cappi. Austrian firm of publishers. Founded by Giovanni Cappi (*b* Blevio, 30 Nov 1765; *d* Vienna, 5 Jan 1815) in the early 19th century, it remained active through most of the century under a succession of proprietors and changes of name. Cappi had been an employee of the Artaria firm before becoming a partner in 1792 (and later, through his sister's marriage, brother-in-law of Carlo Artaria). The dissension within Artaria & Co. around the turn of the century led to Cappi's resignation, after which he opened his own firm. In 1801 he took on his nephew Pietro Cappi as partner, but the latter returned to Artaria in 1805 as joint proprietor.

Giovanni Cappi began his plate number series at 873, the point which Artaria's own numbering had reached by that time; he kept Artaria's original numbers for all the works that had fallen to him after the division of the firm, adding only his own imprint (which enables these to be identified as earlier editions with new title-pages). A catalogue of September 1807 contains both the works taken over from Artaria and newly published ones. Cappi published numerous contemporary composers, the most noteworthy being Beethoven (opp.25–7 and 29; *recte* 31). The firm's activities coincided with the years of the war with France and the War of Liberation, and Cappi did not succeed in making any further contracts with Beethoven; during this time no advertisements appeared in the *Wiener Zeitung* so that precise dating of the firm's publications is difficult. Publication of the *Musikalisches Wochenblatt* was begun on 3 October 1806 and continued for four years.

Although legally empowered to do so from 11 November 1816, Cappi's widow Magdalena never acted publicly as proprietor of the firm; her son Carlo Cappi took over between 20 January and 25 May 1821, and on 24 April 1822 received the requisite licence. The decline in publishing in the years after 1815 and the conspicuous gaps in the series of numbers between 1683 and 2241 are probably due to the death of Giovanni Cappi and to difficulties within the firm.

On 27 September 1824 a large advertisement in the *Wiener Zeitung* announced a decisive reorganization: the founding of

191

Cappi & Comp. by Carlo Cappi and his cousin Pietro. A new series of plate numbers was begun (with no.1). The firm became Schubert's most important publisher; this connection was probably instigated by Pietro Cappi and further developed after Joseph Czerný (*b* Bohemia, 14 June 1785; *d* 22 Sept 1831) succeeded him as partner, when the firm became Cappi & Czerný (registered on 1 April 1826). From 11 April 1828 to 7 May 1831 Czerný carried on alone under his own name, while Carlo Cappi found a new career as a civil servant. The new series of publication numbers was closed at approximately 900 and the old series resumed at 2575.

The lithographer Joseph Trentsensky (*b* Vienna, *c*1793; *d* 24 Jan 1839) was proprietor from 11 July to 1 October 1831; his brother Mathias Trentsensky (*b* 1790; *d* Vienna, 19 March 1868) succeeded him in 1832. As Trentsensky & Vieweg (from 2 May 1833) the firm published the stage works of Konradin Kreutzer; its negligent business management continually brought it into difficulties with the authorities. By 29 December 1837 Eduard Mollo had become proprietor: Mathias Trentsensky continued to work as engraver and lithographer. From 13 April 1842 the name of the firm was Eduard Mollo & A. O. Witzendorf; after Mollo's death it was run by Witzendorf alone, as announced in the *Wiener Zeitung* of 2 April 1844. Struggles with the authorities continued and the firm's importance declined considerably. Its licence was returned on 2 September 1868 and the rights taken over by the firm Eduard Sieger. The business was subsequently sold to Constantin Sander (1 July 1875) and combined with his firm, F. E. C. Leuckart.

L. von Köchel: *Chronologisch-thematisches Verzeichnis sämtlicher Tonwerke Wolfgang Amade Mozarts* (Leipzig, 1862, rev. 6/1964); V. A. Heck: *Schubert-Drucke* (Vienna, 1928); *Lengfeldsche Buchhandlung*, xxxvii (Cologne, 1928); A. Weinmann: *Vollständiges Verlagsverzeichnis Artaria & Comp.* (Vienna, 1952); G. Kinsky and H. Halm: *Das Werk Beethovens: thematisch-bibliographisches Verzeichnis seiner sämtlichen vollendeten Kompositionen* (Munich and Duisburg, 1955); A. Weinmann: *Verlagsverzeichnis Giovanni Cappi bis A. O. Witzendorf* (Vienna, 1967)
A.W.

Cappi, Pietro (*fl c*1790–1830). Austrian music publisher, nephew of Giovanni Cappi. Through his uncle's influence he was engaged by the Artaria firm in Vienna in 1793. He was subsequently a partner of the new firm Giovanni Cappi (1801–5), and then of Artaria. On 30 July 1816 he was granted a licence for his own fine art business. His firm's publications appeared with the plate sign 'P: C:'; part of the catalogue later passed to the Mechetti firm. On 8 August 1818 he made over his premises to Daniel Sprenger and, on 10 December 1818 he combined with Anton Diabelli to form the firm Cappi & Diabelli. On 27 September 1824 Pietro Cappi ended this partnership and, with his cousin Carlo Cappi, established the firm Cappi & Comp. but this existed only until 1 April 1826, when Pietro Cappi made over his deed of partnership to Joseph Czerný, and ceased his activity as a publisher.

Deutsch (1946)

A.W.

Carisch. Italian firm of publishers and dealers of music and instruments. It was founded in Milan in 1887 by Giovanni Andrea Carisch (*b* Poschiavo, Switzerland, 14 March 1834; *d* Milan, 1 May 1901) and Arturo Jänichen (*b* Leipzig, 24 May 1861; *d* Leipzig, 21 Dec 1920). Music publishing began in earnest when Otto Carisch (*d* 1895) and Adolfo Carisch (*b* Tirano, 18 Nov 1867; *d* Poschiavo, 2 Oct 1936), sons and successors of Giovanni Andrea, took over the firm. In 1905 it absorbed the music publications of Genesio Venturini's publishing firm in Florence and in July 1915 altered its title to A. G. Carish & C., headed by Adolfo and Otto's son Guido (*b* Milan, 8 Feb 1892; *d* Milan, 9 July 1935). The new Carisch joint-stock company came under the management of a different group in 1936, with the musician Igino Robbiani (*b* Soresina, 18 April 1884; *d* Milan, 24 June 1966) as managing director.

The firm publishes didactic works, operas, and symphonic and chamber works as well as light music; there is also a series of instrumental music from the 18th century and the 20th (e.g. Bettinelli, Bloch, Bossi, Bucchi, Casella, Castelnuovo-Tedesco, Chailly, Dallapiccola, Ghedini, Malipiero, Mortari, Petrassi, Pick-Mangiagalli, Pizzetti, Rota and Vlad). The firm began to produce gramophone records in 1928; it issues its own recordings under the Carisch label, including the collection of ten records edited by R. Allorto, *Antologia sonora della musica italiana*, an anthology of Italian music from medieval plainchant to Baroque keyboard music. In 1963 the business administration passed to the managing director Sandro Galli, with Gino Mazzocchi as artistic director.

Sartori (1958)

S.A.

Carli. French firm of publishers. It was founded in Paris about 1805 by Nicolas-Raphaël Carli (*b* Naples, 1764; *d* Paris, 15 April 1827). The earliest publications do not bear his name, the imprint reading 'A la Typographie de la Sirène' or sometimes 'Tipografia della Sirena' (the former retained for his signboard). By January 1807 the firm was at the Péristyle du Théâtre Favart (or sometimes Théâtre-Italien), Place des Italiens; an address at 1 rue Favart, used in 1809, was perhaps Carli's residence. In about December 1817 the main premises removed to 14 boulevard Montmartre, opposite the Jardin Frascati, but for a while the Péristyle des Italiens address was also maintained. In 1827 and 1828 an alternative address, 14 boulevard St Martin, was used. Launer acquired the firm in 1828 (the year after Carli's death), probably in July, and operated at the boulevard Montmartre premises; Launer's widow was succeeded on her death in 1853 by Girod, whose firm eventually came to an end about 1919.

Among Carli's earliest publications were full scores of two operas by A. F. G. Pacini (himself soon to become a well-known publisher) and of Valentino Fioravanti's *I virtuosi ambulanti*. About 1810 two catalogues were issued, one listing the firm's publications of printed music, the other its large stock of manuscript music for sale and hire; the latter included 83 operas in full score and a series of 1037 single operatic numbers. Subsequently the firm concentrated more on piano-vocal scores of Italian operas given in Paris; of these they published more than 40, including five by Paer and, in the 1820s, no fewer than 19 by Rossini. In 1823 a prospectus was issued for an edition of several Rossini operas in full score, but nothing came of this. Among Carli's instrumental publications (again mainly by Italian composers) were numerous works for guitar by Carulli. The firm used a series of plate numbers (apparently chronological) that suggest that about 2500 publications were issued (all from engraved plates). There was evidently a close link with Richault, for each occasionally issued the other's publications with the substitution of his own title-page.

Catalogue de musique de fonds de Carli (Paris, *c*1810); *Catalogue de musique manuscrite qui se trouve chez Carli* (Paris, *c*1810); Hopkinson (1954); idem: *A Bibliographical Thematic Catalogue of the Works of John Field* (London, 1961), 164; P. Gossett: *The Operas of Rossini* (diss., Princeton U., 1970), 588; Devriès and Lesure, (1979–88)
R.M.

Carlino, Giovanni Giacomo [Giangiacomo] (*fl* 1597–1616). Italian printer. He appears to have begun printing at Naples in 1597 under contract to the bookseller Orazio Salviani; he later printed for other Neapolitan booksellers such as P. P. Riccio and G. B. Cimmino, and produced two collections of secular music edited by Marcello Magnetta (1613 and 1615). By 1598 he was collaborating in Naples with Antonio Pace, who also published on his own, and together they published madrigals by Dentice (1598) and Macque (1599); they also worked together at Vico Equense, but printed no music there. In 1600, publishing alone, Carlino was appointed *stampatore della corte arcivescovale*, a title given him on a collection of madrigals by Camillo Lambardi that he printed the same year. From 1608 for two or three years he was in partnership with Costantino Vitale. Their publications include madrigals by Meo and Dattilo Roccia (1608), Rodio's *Regole di musica* (1609), two collections of secular music by Donato Basile and Scialla (1610) and hymns by Stella (1610). In 1612–13 Carlino worked at Tricarico (but printed no music there) and then returned to Naples, where he printed madrigals and sacred works in 1616.

Most of Carlino's relatively large output of music, as with most Neapolitan music printers, is secular: he printed the earliest extant editions of Gesualdo's fifth and sixth books. His output also included secular music by Macedonio di Mutio, Puente, Trabaci, Genuino, Montella, Giaccio and Salzilli, and a few sacred collections.

Sartori (1958); P. Manzi: *La tipografia napoletana nel '500: annali de Giovanni Giacomo Carlino e di Tarquinio Longo (1593–1620)* (Florence, 1975)
S.B. (iii)

Carr. English family of publishers and musicians active in the USA.

(1) Joseph Carr (*b* England, 1739; *d* Baltimore, MD, 27 Oct 1819). Publisher. He was active in London until 1794, when on the urging of his son (2) Benjamin Carr he left for the USA and established his publishing house in Baltimore. He issued contemporary European music as well as American dances, popular ballads and patriotic songs, including the first edition of *The Star-spangled Banner* (1814). He also published the *Musical Journal for the Piano Forte*, edited by Benjamin, and *Carr's Musical Miscellany*, and sold keyboard instruments and guitars. On Carr's death the publishing firm was taken over by his son (3) Thomas Carr.

(2) Benjamin Carr (*b* London, 12 Sept 1768; *d* Philadelphia, 24 May 1831).

Publisher, composer and organist, son of (1) Joseph Carr. He learnt the music trade in his father's shop in London, studied with the leading church musicians of the day (including Samuel Arnold and Charles and Samuel Wesley), and is said to have performed in programmes given by the Concert of Ancient Music and at Sadler's Wells Theatre. He emigrated to the USA and settled in Philadelphia in 1793, and was followed the next year by the rest of his family, who went to Baltimore, where his father set up a music publishing firm. Carr established thriving music businesses in New York (sold to James Hewitt in 1797) and in Philadelphia, then the nation's capital. There he was organist of St Augustine's Catholic Church (1801–31) and of St Peter's Episcopal Church. His versatility as a publisher, editor, promoter, singer, pianist, organist, composer (he wrote songs, operas and sacred music), teacher and conductor, and his active leadership in civil musical affairs, including the founding of the Musical Fund Society of Philadelphia (1820), led him to be called the 'Father of Philadelphia Music'.

Carr's firm in Philadelphia was one of the first notable American music publishing establishments, and he and his family were leaders in supplying the young nation with patriotic music. He had an unusually fine business sense and is credited with a surprisingly large number of first American publications, including *Yankee Doodle*, *Pleyel's Hymn* and *Adeste fideles*. His *Musical Journal for the Piano Forte* (issued weekly for 24 weeks during winter and spring in the years 1800–04) was the first American music publication in magazine form of consequence; alternate issues were devoted to vocal and instrumental music. A companion publication, *Musical Journal for the Flute or Violin*, appeared concurrently on the same plan. Later *Carr's Musical Miscellany in Occasional Numbers* (1812–25) contributed significantly to the availability of good music.

(3) Thomas Carr (*b* England, 1780; *d* Philadelphia, 15 April 1849). Publisher, composer and organist, son of (1) Joseph Carr. In 1794 he went with his parents to Baltimore, where he was associated with his father's publishing firm and was organist of Christ Church (1798–1811). He was important as a composer and arranger of patriotic songs. In 1814, at the request of Francis Scott Key, he adapted the words of *The Star-Spangled Banner* to the tune *To Anacreon in Heav'n*, and in 1840 he wrote songs in support of the Whig cause and General Harrison, including *Old Tippe-*

canoe's 'Raisin'. After his father's death in 1819 he continued the publishing firm for three years, but then sold the catalogue to George Willig and John Cole and moved to Philadelphia, where he continued intermittently to publish and compose, and was also active as a teacher.

O. G. T. Sonneck: *A Bibliography of Early Secular American Music* (Washington, DC, 1905; rev. and enlarged by W. T. Upton, 2/1945/R1964); idem: *Report on 'The Star-Spangled Banner', 'Hail Columbia', 'America', 'Yankee Doodle'* (Washington, DC, 1909/R1972, rev. and enlarged 2/1914/R 1969); A. Elson: 'Carr, Benjamin', *DAB*; V. L. Redway: 'The Carrs, American Music Publishers', *MQ*, xviii (1932), 150; Fisher (1933); R. A. Gerson: *Music in Philadelphia* (Philadelphia, 1940/R1970); Dichter and Shapiro (1941, 2/1977); H. Dichter: 'Benjamin Carr's "Music [*sic*] Journal"', *Music Journal*, xv/1 (1957), 17; D. W. Krummel: *Philadelphia Music Engraving and Publishing, 1800–1820: a Study in Bibliography and Cultural History* (diss., U. of Michigan, 1958); C. E. Wunderlich: *A History and Bibliography of Early American Periodicals, 1782–1852* (diss., U. of Michigan, 1962); I. Lowens: *Music and Musicians in Early America* (New York, 1964); Wolfe (1964); H. E. Davis: 'The Carrs: a Musical Family', *Pennsylvania Genealogical Magazine*, xxiv (1965), 56; C. A. Sprenkle: *The Life and Works of Benjamin Carr* (diss., Peabody Conservatory, 1970); E. R. Meyer: 'Benjamin Carr's *Musical Miscellany*', *Notes*, xxxiii (1976–7), 253; Wolfe (1980)

W.T.M., M.J. (1), R.L.S. (2), R.A.L. (3)

Carr, John (*fl* 1672–95). English bookseller, music publisher and instrument seller. His shop at the Middle Temple Gate, London, was very near that of John Playford the elder, and they published several volumes in partnership between 1681 and 1684. One of these was Henry Purcell's *Sonnata's of III Parts* (1683), printed from plates engraved by Thomas Cross the younger (for illustration *see* CROSS, THOMAS). In spite of clear evidence of friendship as well as partnership between the Carr and Playford families, Carr began to publish independently in 1687. One volume, *Vinculum societatis*, printed that year, represents a typographical revolution, being printed from an entirely new fount of type. This fount had round note heads, and was designed to allow the printing of quavers, semiquavers etc in groups as well as separately (for illustration *see* HEPTINSTALL, JOHN). It was not possible to achieve this effect with the older diamond-headed founts used by the Playford printers, and it is noticeable that although Carr continued to publish music for the next seven years, he never did so with Henry Playford, even though Carr had many business partners. One of these partners, Sam Scott, took over the Carr business in 1695. His son Robert

Carr (*fl* 1684–7) was a member of the King's Musick in the reign of Charles II. His initials appear in the imprints of several works published by his father; in John Playford's preface to his *Choice Ayres and Songs* (1684) Playford bequeathed his great music publishing business to 'my own Son and Mr. Carr's son', but there is no evidence that Robert Carr ever took an active part in it.

Humphries and Smith (1954, 2/1970)

M.M.

Carstens, Heinrich (*fl* 1609–25). German printer, active in Hamburg. He printed a variety of religious works (Bibles, commentaries, orations) as well as scientific and educational books. Among his 15 music titles are important sacred vocal works by Hieronymus Praetorius including the *Liber missarum* (1616) and *Cantiones variae* (1618).

Benzing (1963, 2/1982)

T.D.W.

Carulli. Italian firm of publishers, active in Milan. On 22 November 1822 Giuseppe Antonio Carulli (1762–1830), a music copyist at the Milan conservatory, applied on behalf of his son Luigi for a licence to print music. He described himself as a native of Assago (Milan), 60 years old and with four children, among them Luigi, who had already been working as a music engraver and printer, and Benedetto, professor of clarinet at the conservatory. The licence was granted on 4 January 1823 and for several years, as 'Editore dell' Imperiale Regio Conservatorio', G. A. Carulli issued works by conservatory teachers or former pupils and didactic material, especially vocal and keyboard tutors. In 1827 he began the *Repertorio (nuovo) musicale: Produzioni dei più accreditati maestri ridotte per organo e pianoforte*; 24 fascicles had appeared by 1830. In 1828, with plate number 167, his address was given as S Radegonda 984. Plate number 173 marked the beginning of the *Collezione completa di Muzio Clementi*, an edition based on Breitkopf & Härtel's.

Carulli worked with Secondo Colombo in 1829, and the next year began a new series, the *Biblioteca musicale economica per flauto, organo e pianoforte*. On his death, his son Benedetto requested transfer of the patent; this was granted on 11 June 1830, though Benedetto's activity lasted less than a year. In 1832 the Carulli list of about 300 publications was acquired by Ricordi, who entered them in his catalogue with the numbers 6113–61 and 6225–6339. Four

years later another publisher, Giovanni Canti, set up in business by reprinting several Carulli editions, notably the Muzio Clementi collection.

A.Z.L.

Castagneri, Marie-Anne (*b* 1722; *d* Paris, 6 Oct 1787). French music dealer. She was descended from a Piedmont family of instrument makers; her father, André Castagneri, was born in Piedmont, but conducted his instrument making business from the Hôtel de Soissons in Paris. After her father's death she bought a licence as a stationer in 1748, and after 1762 a patent as a music seller. On 4 January 1748 she married the sculptor Pierre Hutin (*d* 1762). Her business continued to operate until 1787, handling the works of French composers of the period, including Clérambault, Daquin, Duphly, Guignon, Leclair, Balbastre and Grétry, as well as ballads, popular songs and musical journals.

G. Cucuel: 'Notes sur quelques musiciens, luthiers, éditeurs et graveurs de musique de XVIIIe siècle', *SIMG*, xiv (1912–13), 243; Hopkinson (1954); S. Milliot: 'Marie-Anne Castagneri, marchande de musique au XVIIIe siècle (1722–1787)', *RdM*, lii (1966), 185

S.M.

Cecconcelli, Pietro (*fl* 1618–30). Florentine printer. He appears in Florentine records by 1618 and apparently made his début as a music printer in 1623 with two volumes by Filippo Vitali (including Vitali's *Il secondo libro de madrigali a cinque voci*). In 1625 he printed Francesca Caccini's court opera *La liberazione di Ruggiero dall'isola d'Alcina*. His music fount and general presentation are more elegant than that of Zanobi Pignoni, his competitor in Florence. By 1630 Cecconcelli's press seems to have been taken over by Giovanni Battista Landini, who used his music type in four editions between 1630 and 1635, including Frescobaldi's two books of *Arie musicali a una, a due, e a tre voci* (1630) and music by Antonio Gardano and Domenico Anglesi.

T.C.(i)

Černý [Cžerny], **Jiří** [Nigrin, Nygryn, Georg] (*fl* Prague, 1572–1606). Czech printer. He served his apprenticeship under Kozel, probably before 1566. Between 1572 and 1606 he published many religious, philosophical, legal, medical and astronomical books, as well as sermons, felicitations and poems; he had begun printing music by 1578. He printed a series of works by the Slovenian composer Jacob Handl, as well as music by members of the Prague royal chapel (e.g. Carl Luython and

Franz Sales), Johannes Nucius and such local composers as Lomnický, Mitis z Limuz, Jevíčský, Barion, Knöfel and Benedikt-Nudožerský. In both volume and quality of production Černý was one of the foremost printers of the time.

ČSHS; J. Vanický: 'Nigrinovy hudební tisky' [Nigrin's musical prints], *HRo*, xii (1959), 608; K. Chyba: *Slovník knihtiskařů v Československu od nejstarších dob do roku 1860* [Dictionary of printers in Czechoslovakia from early times to 1860] (Prague, 1966–), 71

Z.C.

Challier. German family of publishers and booksellers. Carl August Challier (*d* Berlin, 17 July 1871) founded the music publishing house of C. A. Challier & Co. with Karl Gaillard in Berlin in 1835. He published works by Gluck, Haydn and Mozart as well as composers from Berlin; from 1844 he edited, with Gaillard, the *Berliner musikalische Zeitung*, which in 1847 merged with the *Neue Berliner Musikzeitung* (founded by Gustav Bock). His son Willibald Challier (*b* Berlin, 29 July 1849; *d* Berlin, 25 Jan 1926) took over the firm in 1865, and it was carried on from 1919 under its original name by Richard Birnbach. Ernest Challier (*b* Berlin, 9 July 1843; *d* Giessen, 19 Sept 1914), another son of Carl August, had a music shop in Giessen. Through his wide range of bibliographical publications he drew attention to much music, particularly vocal; his writings, some of which covered previously little-known subjects, provided a much needed supplement to Hofmeister's *Jahresverzeichnis*.

R. Elvers: 'Berliner Musikverleger', *Studien zur Musikgeschichte Berlins im frühen 19. Jahrhundert*, ed. C. Dahlhaus (Regensburg, 1980), 285

W.K.

Channey, Jean de (*b* Piedmont, *c*1480; *d* Avignon, *c*1539–40). French printer. He began his printing career in Lyons as an apprentice to Jacques Arnoullet. On the latter's death in 1504 or 1505, his widow Michelette du Cayre, incapable of directing the establishment herself, entrusted it to Channey, who published a book under his own name in about 1505, using Arnoullet's type. Assuming that he would have had to be in his mid-20s for such a responsibility, he was probably born in about 1480. Another book with his name as printer was published in 1510, using his printer's mark, a copy of the Aldine anchor and dolphin, for the first time.

Because Arnoullet's sons were coming of age and were ready to take over their father's business, Channey petitioned the Avignon town council in late 1512 for permission to establish a printing firm there.

In August 1513 the first of many books with the Avignon address appeared in print. Michelette du Cayre followed him to Avignon, where she married him.

His involvement with music came about through a contract with the composer Elzéar Genet, known as Carpentras, to print four books of his music. Channey was perhaps the best of the few printers in Avignon, but apart from the undated book, *Regles communes de plain chant avecques la fin des tons tant reguliers que irreguliers nottee*, he had no experience with music. (He was a publisher of books on grammar, law, theology, Marot's poetry and popular tales in French and Latin.) An agreement dated 2 January 1531, which reveals many important details about contemporary printing problems, states that Carpentras was to provide a corrector at his own expense and otherwise to supervise the project. There was great difficulty in making the note types fit the lines and spaces of the staves and instead of the six months specified in the contract it was 16 months before the first of the four books appeared (on 15 May 1532). Following this first book (of masses), a second book (of Lamentations) was published on 14 August 1532. An undated book of hymns was issued before 1534 (it is dedicated to the Cardinal Ippolito de' Medici, who died in August 1534). A fourth book, also undated and containing *Magnificat* sections, appeared later, probably not after 1536.

Although Attaingnant and Moderne had already begun printing music in the new single-impression method, Channey's books were printed in the earlier Italian method of two or more impressions. The most distinctive feature of the books is the music type, which has round instead of diamond-shaped note heads, the first ever to be used in printed music books. This was the work of the type designer Etienne Briard of Bar-le-Duc (for illustration *see* fig.5, p.22) who imitated an MS hand, perhaps that of Carpentras himself.

Channey printed no more music. His last publication, a set of ordinances of François I, is dated 1536 in the colophon and 1540 on the title-page. His four music books are an isolated example in the history of music printing, unless they served as a model for Robert Granjon in Lyons when he designed another round-note music type in 1558.

H. and J. Baudrier: *Bibliographie lyonnaise* (Paris, 1895–1921/R1964), x, 291; P. Pansier: *Histoire du livre et de l'imprimerie à Avignon du XIVe au XVIe siècle* (Avignon, 1922); D. Heartz: *Pierre Attaingnant, Royal Printer of Music* (Berkeley and Los Angeles, 1969), 110

S.F.P.

Chappell. English firm of publishers, concert agents and piano manufacturers active in London. The firm was started on 3 December 1810 by the pianist and composer Johann Baptist Cramer, Francis Tatton Latour and Samuel Chappell (*b* ?London, *c*1782; *d* London, Dec 1834), who formed a partnership. Chappell was formerly employed by the music publisher Birchall. In addition to substantial publishing activities, including educational music, the firm sold pianos, undertook concert promotion, and played a leading part in the creation of the Philharmonic Society (1813). In 1819 Cramer retired from the business; in about 1826 Latour withdrew and carried on a separate business until about 1830, when he sold it to Chappell, who was also in partnership with the instrument makers G. Longman and T. C. Bates from 1829.

After Samuel Chappell's death the business was continued by his widow Emily Chappell and her sons. The eldest, William (*b* London, 20 Nov 1809; *d* London, 20 Aug 1888), was noted for his interest in early music. In 1840, with Rimbault, Macfarren and others, he founded the Musical Antiquarian Society, which met at his firm's premises; he edited Dowland's songs for the society (1844). He had earlier published his *A Collection of National English Airs* (1838–40), copiously annotated with historical details, and this was subsequently expanded into his major work, *Popular Music of the Olden Time* (2 vols., 1855–9). William Chappell left the family firm in 1844 and went into partnership with Cramer and Beale, as Cramer, Beale & Chappell, remaining until his retirement in 1861. He also assisted in founding the Musical Association in 1874, and in the same year the first volume of his projected general history of music appeared. Meanwhile the Chappell firm prospered and greatly expanded under his brother Thomas Patey Chappell (*b* London, 1819; *d* London, 1 June 1902). The manufacture of pianos was started in the 1840s, and the firm's interests turned towards popular dance music and light opera, beginning with Balfe's *The Bohemian Girl* (1843). Under Thomas Chappell's management the Monday and Saturday Popular Concerts were begun in 1858 at St James's Hall (also a project of the Chappells). Thomas's younger brother, Samuel Arthur Chappell (*b* London, 1834; *d* London, 21 Dec 1904), directed these concerts, and many famous artists appeared there, including Charles Santley, Piatti and Clara Schumann. Thomas Chappell also organized the later seasons of Dickens's public readings from 1866 to 1870. In the 1870s the firm's association with Gilbert and Sullivan began. In addition to publishing nearly all their operas, Thomas Chappell financed the Comedy Company, which performed the works before D'Oyly Carte took over the operas in 1877. Thomas Chappell was also one of the original directors of the RCM, and a governor of the Royal Albert Hall.

The firm's fortunes declined temporarily at the end of the 19th century, and in 1894 William Boosey was engaged, initially to run a series of ballad concerts in competition with the highly successful series of Boosey & Co. These concerts also included performances by great instrumentalists such as Pachmann and Kreisler. The firm soon recovered and Boosey became managing director in 1902. Chappell also played a leading part in the campaign against musical piracy, which resulted in the effective Copyright Act of 1906. The new Queen's Hall was leased by the firm, which ran the Promenade Concerts there from 1915 until 1926 when the BBC took over their management.

In the 20th century the firm's predominance in the field of light music increased enormously. After Louis Dreyfus (*b* Kuppenheim, 11 Nov 1877; *d* London, 2 May 1967) bought the firm in 1929 his brother, Max Dreyfus (1874–1964), who had earlier been associated with Harms, created an affiliate company in New York. Chappell became the leading publisher of show music, producing scores by such composers as George Gershwin (for illustration *see* fig.39, p.121), Jerome Kern, Frederick Loewe, Cole Porter, Richard Rodgers and Sigmund Romberg, as well as works by Noël Coward and Ivor Novello. Philips (North America) bought the American company in 1968, and while the extensive show and standard catalogue has been maintained under the name of Chappell, the emphasis has shifted to rock and popular music, including works by Pink Floyd, the Police, Marvin Hamlisch and Carole Bayer Sager. The British firm continued the publication of more serious works with most of Bax's music, and from 1938 to 1973 was British agent for the Schirmer firm.

About 1904 Chappell's opened a branch in Melbourne, moving to Sydney in 1920. It prospered on the strength of successful English and American musicals (first published by Chappell UK but soon printed and distributed in Australia), and the catalogue expanded to include the works of Australian songwriters and composers. In 1973 Chappell & Co. (Australia) Pty Ltd became a wholly owned subsidiary of Chappell UK, continuing its role as agents for the increasing number of independent Australian publishers.

In 1970 Chappell acquired the music publishers Ascherberg, Hopwood & Crew. The firm, which has many subsidiary and associated companies, was taken over by the US entertainment group Warner Communications in 1988; as Warner Chappell it is now one of the largest music publishers in the world.

W. Boosey: *Fifty Years of Music* (London, 1931); C. G. Mortimer: 'Leading Music Publishers no.1: Chappell & Co., Ltd.', *MO*, lxi (1937–8), 1097; 'The Music Publisher of Tradition: Samuel Chappell and his Sons', *MO*, lxiv (1940–41), 468; Humphries and Smith (1954, 2/1970); C. Mair: *The Chappell Story, 1811–1961* (London, 1961); Neighbour and Tyson (1965)

W.H.H./P.W.J., K.R.S.

Chester, J. & W. English firm of publishers. It was founded in Brighton by John Chester and his son William in 1874 (John Chester had opened a branch office of Augener there in 1860), and established a reputation for service, maintaining both a large stock and a comprehensive lending library. In 1915 the firm was bought by Otto Marius Kling, and headquarters were set up in London, the Brighton house becoming a branch that was eventually sold. In addition to acting as agents, particularly for French and Russian publishers, the firm began its own publishing activities at this time, and soon entered into contracts not only with English composers such as Bantock, Bax, Lord Berners, Goossens and Ireland, but also with foreign composers such as Casella, Falla, Malipiero, Poulenc and Stravinsky. A small periodical, *The Chesterian*, was started in November 1915, mainly as a publishing bulletin; in 1919, when G. Jean-Aubry was appointed editor, the magazine began to publish articles by an international team of contributors. Although interrupted by World War II, it was revived in 1947 and continued until 1961. Among present-day composers in the firm's catalogue Peter Maxwell Davies, John Tavener, Robert Saxton, Anthony Payne and Geoffrey Burgon are prominent; it publishes the series *Latin Church Music of the Polyphonic Schools* and *Just Brass*, and educational music. From 1957 the firm was linked with Hansen and other Scandinavian publishers, in addition to having links with the Polish state publishing house through issuing works by Lutosławski. In 1989 it was taken over by Music Sales. The hire library has continued to expand and is among the largest in Britain.

C. G. Mortimer: 'Leading Music Publishers: J. & W. Chester Ltd.', *MO*, lxii (1938–9), 758; 'The Music Publisher of Tradition: J. & W. Chester Ltd', *MO*, lxv (1941–2), 292

E.B./P.W.J.

Choron, Alexandre(-Etienne) (*b* Caen, 21 Oct 1771; *d* Paris, 29 June 1834). French writer on music and publisher. While still a boy, he taught himself Hebrew and German and acquired a permanent interest in scientific experiment and a fascination for music theory and the techniques of composition. Although he reached the age of 16 before taking music lessons, he had already attained elementary skill on keyboard and other instruments. He greatly valued a friendship with Grétry which began in his 20th year and which suggests that he moved to Paris after his father's death.

In 1805 he set up as a publisher, first of works by Josquin, Goudimel, Palestrina and Carissimi, then of Italian and German music up to the time of Bach. There followed the two-volume *Dictionnaire des musiciens* (1810–11) in which Fayolle was his collaborator. Choron was too idealistic to be financially successful, and his attention to business was limited by his scholarly and scientific pursuits. What might have been his magnum opus, *Introduction à l'étude générale et raisonnée de la musique*, remained unfinished. He was forced to teach music and accept public appointments.

Choron had a widespread influence on teachers, organists, choralists and those who were awakening to the importance of music history. His inexpensive editions of polyphonic and choral music were invaluable, despite the later issue of most of the works in better format by Proske and the Regensburg scholars and by English and German publishers. His interest in the Baroque masters was more a revival than a novelty, and contributed indirectly to the demand for scholarly editions.

FétisB; P. Scudo: *Critique et littérature musicales* (Paris, 1852); M. and L. Escudier: *Dictionnaire de musique* (Paris, 5/1872); H. Réty: *Notice historique sur Choron et son école* (Paris, 1873); J. Carlez: *Choron, sa vie et ses travaux* (Caen, 1882) [with complete list of works]; W. Kahl: 'Zur musikalischen Renaissancebewegung in Frankreich während der ersten Hälfte des 19. Jahrhunderts', *Festschrift Joseph Schmidt-Görg zum 60. Geburtstag* (Bonn, 1957), 156; B. R. Simms: *Alexandre Choron (1771–1834) as a Historian and Theorist of Music* (diss., Yale U., 1971) [with descriptive catalogue of Choron's publications and MSS]; idem: 'The Historical Editions of Alexandre-Etienne Choron', *FAM*, xxvii (1980), 71

A.H. (ii)

Clementi

Choudens. French firm of publishers, active in Paris. It was founded by Antoine Choudens (1825–88) and is first mentioned in an advertisement in September 1844. From 1888 to 1890 the firm was run by Choudens' two sons, the second of whom, Paul, continued alone from 1890 until his death on 6 October 1925, after which the leadership was shared by Paul's sons-in-law, Gaston Chevrier (until 1952) and André Leroy (until 1958), and grandson, André Chevrier. Choudens was the original publisher of three of the most important French 19th-century operas: Berlioz's *Les Troyens* (piano-vocal scores of Parts I and II by the composer, 1863), Bizet's *Carmen* (piano-vocal score by the composer, 1875; full score, 1877) and Gounod's *Faust* (piano-vocal score by Delibes, 1859; full score, 1860); the firm also issued works by Reyer, Saint-Saëns and others. In 1891 Choudens published five of Debussy's early piano works: *Valse romantique*, *Reverie*, *Ballade*, *Marche écossaise* and *Tarantelle styrienne*. Later it published music by Marcel Landowski and others.

C. Hopkinson: *A Bibliography of the Musical and Literary Works of Hector Berlioz* (Edinburgh, 1951, rev. 2/1980); idem (1954); Devriès and Lesure (1979–88)

N.S.

Church. American firm of publishers, active in Cincinnati. On 21 April 1859 Oliver Ditson of Boston bought the catalogue of Baldwin & Truax (established in 1851 by David Truax in Cincinnati, named Curtis & Truax in 1855 and Baldwin & Truax in 1857), and in association with John Church jr (*d* Boston, 19 April 1890) founded the firm of John Church, Jr. On 1 March 1869 Church bought the half-interest of Ditson and in partnership with his bookkeeper John B. Trevor established the firm of John Church & Co., which became incorporated in 1885 as John Church Co. Church bought the catalogue of George Root & Sons of Chicago in 1872, and at about this time William Sherwin joined the firm. In 1881 James R. Murray became chief director of publications and editor of the firm's periodical, *Music Visitor* (1871–97).

Church became notable for publishing the operas and, particularly, the celebrated marches of John Philip Sousa (see illustration); the firm's other publications include operas and operettas by Julian Edwards and Reginald de Koven as well as a set of piano pieces by Theodore Presser and works by contemporary American composers. At Church's death his son-in-law R. B. Burchard became president;

W. L. Coghill became manager of publications in 1919, and in 1930 the entire catalogue was sold to Theodore Presser Co.

W. S. B. Mathews, ed.: *A Hundred Years of Music in America* (Chicago, 1889), 394; O. Thompson: *International Cyclopedia of Music and Musicians* (New York, 1939, 10/1975), 337; Dichter and Shapiro (1941, 2/1977); E. C. Krohn: *Music Publishing in the Middle Western States before the Civil War* (Detroit, 1972), 20

E.C.K.

Clausetti. Italian firm of publishers, active in Naples. It was established around 1846 by the Milanese brothers Pietro and Lorenzo Clausetti. Their father Carlo Clausetti was a dealer in pewter and other metals and supplier of plates to Giovanni Ricordi; both boys had been apprenticed to Ricordi for about ten years before leaving Milan to set up their own business in Naples, first in the via Toledo, later in the via S Carlo opposite the opera house. They took new typographical material with them and soon became known for their beautiful frontispieces. Besides issuing arrangements of well-known opera arias in the series *Miroir du Théâtre-Italien*, and obtaining the copyrights of works by Mercadante, Petrella and De Giosa, they also produced didactic works and tried (unsuccessfully) to promote German chamber music. Their last catalogue appeared in 1860.

With the annexing of the Kingdom of the Two Sicilies by Piedmont, Neapolitan music publishing diminished and many houses were absorbed by Tito Ricordi, who acquired the Clausetti business, including some 4000 plates, in 1864. Ricordi then inserted these works in his own catalogue with non-continuous numbers between 36,301 and 41,431. Until 1912, Ricordi entrusted the running of his Neapolitan interests to Pietro Clausetti's son Carlo, a lawyer and musician who founded the Società dei Concerti in Naples. On the death of Giulio Ricordi in 1912, Carlo Clausetti was called to Milan as artistic director of the Ricordi firm.

A.Z.L.

Clementi. English firm of instrument makers and publishers. The composer Muzio Clementi had invested in the London firm of Longman & Broderip probably from the early 1790s and, following its bankruptcy in 1798, he and John Longman entered immediately into a new partnership with Frederick Augustus Hyde, Frederick William Collard, Josiah Banger and David Davis. The new firm of Longman, Clementi & Co. continued in business at Longman & Broderip's former

Sheet-music cover of John Philip Sousa's march 'The Stars and Stripes Forever', first published by the John Church Co. (Cincinnati, 1897)

premises in Cheapside from October 1798 to June 1800 when Longman left to set up on his own. The firm then became known as Clementi, Banger, Hyde, Collard & Davis, or often simply Clementi & Co. In March 1807 a fire reputedly caused £40,000 worth of damage at the firm's new Tottenham Court Road premises, added in 1806. The firm was subsequently known as Clementi, Banger, Collard, Davis & Collard (from August 1810), Clementi, Collard, Davis & Collard (1819), and Clementi, Collard & Collard (1822). Clementi died in 1832 and the firm then continued as Collard & Collard; the music publishing side was taken over by Thomas E. Purday about 1834. The Clementi firm also did a great trade in the manufacture of pianos.

The firm published much new piano music by Clementi, Kalkbrenner, Steibelt and other virtuosos of the day and reprinted many items from Longman & Broderip's plates. Other notable publications included Morley's *Canzonets and Madrigals for Three and Four Voices* (1801), Haydn's *The Seasons* (1813) and a number of works by Beethoven. Clementi himself made agreements with Beethoven for the English rights of works which included the string quartets opp.59 and 74, the Violin Concerto, the Fifth Piano Concerto and the Choral Fantasia, as well as songs and piano works; the single surviving contract between Clementi and Beethoven does not mention opp.73, 74 or 80, though Clementi's firm published first editions of these compositions.

[W. F. Collard]: 'Mr Clementi', *Quarterly Musical Magazine and Review*, ii (1820), 308; M. Unger 'Muzio Clementi and his Relations with G. Chr. Härtel', *MMR*, xxxvii (1908), 246, 270; Humphries and Smith (1954, 2/1970); A. Tyson: *The Authentic English Editions of Beethoven* (London, 1963); J. C. Graue: 'The Clementi–Cramer Dispute Revisited', *ML*, lvi (1975), 47; L. Plantinga: *Muzio Clementi: his Life and his Music* (London, 1976)

P.W.J.

Clowes. English firm of printers. It was established in London in 1803 by William Clowes the elder (*b* Chichester, 1 Jan 1779; *d* London, 26 Jan 1847). The firm achieved success by making accuracy, speed and quantity its chief goals; periodicals and official reports as well as books and catalogues (from 1820 produced by steam machinery) were an important part of its output. By 1843 the firm, now called William Clowes and Sons, operated the largest printing works in the world, with 24 presses, its own type and stereotype foundries, and 2500 tons of stereo plates

and 80,000 woodcuts in store. It executed major works for the Royal Academy of Arts, the Society for the Diffusion of Useful Knowledge, the Great Exhibition and the British Museum (*General Catalogue of Printed Books*, 1881–1900).

William Clowes's achievement in music printing rests on his advocacy of musical typography at a time when engraved-plate methods predominated. Aiming specifically for the increased efficiency and lower unit costs of type-printed music in large edition sizes, he effected considerable improvements (better clarity, a more precise junction of staff lines) in this method, issuing as his pilot projects, for a variety of publishers, *The Harmonicon* (1823–33), the *Musical Library* (1834–7) and *Sacred Minstrelsy* (1834–5). These serial ventures broke new ground in the commercial marketing of serious music and musical literature in England. The firm's most successful music publication has been *Hymns Ancient and Modern*, first brought out by Novello in 1861; taken over by Clowes in 1868, it reached a sale of more than 100 million copies by 1935 and is still printed by the firm. William Clowes and Sons Limited (from 1880) became part of the McCorquodale Group in 1946. In 1983 the firm's name was changed to William Clowes Ltd.

[W. Ayrton]: 'On the Various Processes Applied to Printing Music', Monthly Supplement, *Musical Library*, i (1834), 4; S. Smiles: *Men of Invention and Industry* (London, 1884), 208; W. B. Clowes: *Family Business 1803–1953* (London, 1953); Humphries and Smith (1954, 2/1970); L. Langley: 'The Life and Death of *The Harmonicon*: an Analysis', *RMARC*, xxii (1989), 137

L.L.

Cluer, John (*b* ?London, late 17th century; *d* London, Oct 1728). English printer and publisher. As early as 1715 he was active in London as a general printer whose production included ballads, chapbooks, labels and shopkeepers' signs. He soon turned to music printing and issued some of the best engraved music of his period. A considerable innovator, he experimented, though unsuccessfully, with new methods of printing both from engraved plates and from music types. Though Walsh was Handel's chief publisher, Cluer also had business relations with the composer, starting with the printing of the *Suites de pièces pour le clavecin* in 1720. Nine of Handel's operas were published in score by Cluer, the first being *Giulio Cesare* in 1724, which was issued in the unusual format of a large pocket-size volume. Both this and the later operas are remarkable for their finely engraved title-pages and frontispieces (see

Title-page of Handel's opera 'Admeto' published by John Cluer (London, 1727)

illustration). Other notable publications include the two volumes of *A Pocket Companion for Gentlemen and Ladies* (1724–5). These small engraved songbooks were published by subscription, an innovation for a musical publication but a highly successful one, since about 1000 copies of each volume were subscribed. Imitators soon followed Cluer's lead in this and other ideas such as issuing packs of playing-cards with a song printed on each card.

Cluer was associated with the bookseller Bezaleel Creake whose name appears in some of the imprints. Thomas Cobb was employed by Cluer as an engraver and, on his marriage to Cluer's widow Elizabeth in about 1730, succeeded him in business. In 1736 the concern was purchased by Cobb's brother-in-law and associate, William Dicey of Northampton, for himself and for his son Cluer Dicey, who managed it until 1764.

Kidson (1900); Humphries and Smith (1954, 2/1870)

F.K., W.C.S./P.W.J.

Cock, Symon (*b* Antwerp, 1489; *d* Antwerp, 17 Aug 1562). Flemish printer. He was first mentioned as a printer in the Antwerp archives in 1522. He published a wide variety of books, including Bibles and religious, philosophical, legal and official publications. In 1539 Cock applied for a new privilege for a book of songs based on the psalms: in September he published the first Flemish metrical psalter, *Een devoot ende profitelijck boecxken, inhoudende veel gheestelijcke Liedekens ende Leysenen* (modern edition by D. F. Scheuleer, The Hague, 1889). It was printed by double impression, using a roman neume typeface with black notes on a red four-line staff. Christophe van Remunde had earlier used the same typeface.

The following year he published another edition, entitled *Souterliedekens*, with texts in Latin and Dutch, which also employed the double-impression method, but with a five-line staff, and diamond-shaped notes – the first dated book printed in the Low Countries to do so. This collection was so popular that it went through more than 30 editions from 1540 to 1613. The translator of the texts was Willem van Zuylen van Nyevelt; the melodies were based on popular Flemish folktunes. It differs from the Geneva Psalter in that it was primarily intended for use in the home rather than the church.

Goovaerts (1880); H. D. L. Vervliet: *Sixteenth Century Printing Types of the Low Countries* (Amsterdam, 1968); S. Bain: *Music Printing in the Low*

Countries in the Sixteenth Century (diss., U. of Cambridge, 1974); G. Hyybens: 'Een onbehende 16de-eeuwse uitgave van Dit is een suuerlijke boecxken', *Quaerendo*, xii (1982), 281

S.B. (i)

Cocks, Robert (*b* 1798; *d* London, 7 April 1887). English publisher. He established his own firm in London in 1823. In 1868 he took his two sons Arthur and Stroud into partnership, but at his death his grandson Robert M. Cocks became the proprietor and continued until his retirement in 1898 when a sale of stock took place; Augener purchased the goodwill and lease, and retained the name of the firm until 1904.

Cocks was much involved in concert management at the outset of his career and had a long association with the Hanover Square Rooms. He employed resident foreign musicians to compile and edit music. Some 16,000 works were published by the firm, including Bach's keyboard works edited by Czerny, Beethoven's quartets, and works by Czerny himself, Rode and Spohr, in addition to contemporary English music and a number of methods and books on music. A short-lived periodical, *Cocks's Musical Miscellany* (1850–53), contained original notices of Beethoven by Czerny. The firm also managed a large circulating music library and was among the first to exploit the Victorian ballad, though it soon lost this business by a reluctance to adopt the new royalty system.

Kidson (1900); 'The Music Publisher of Tradition', *MO*, lxiv (1940–41), 379; Humphries and Smith (1954, 2/1970); Neighbour and Tyson (1965); Coover (1988)

W.H.H., F.K./P.W.J.

Cole, Benjamin (*fl* London, 1740–60). English engraver. Several engravers of this name flourished in England during the 18th century, though probably only one worked at music. His first work appears in Walsh's publication of J. F. Lampe's *Songs and Duetto's in . . . The Dragon of Wantley* (1738) and music from the same composer's *Margery* (1740). His most important work was for the *British Melody, or The Musical Magazine*, published in 15 (probably fortnightly) instalments from February 1738. It reappeared as a set, published by Cole, in 1739. This was the first of the many rivals and successors to Bickham's *The Musical Entertainer*. Cole's work is of a very high standard, though less flexible and imaginative than Bickham's; the latter twice referred disparagingly to Cole in his second volume. As was customary, Cole continued to reissue separate plates for several years.

He also engraved the music plates for *The New Universal Magazine* (1751–9), a number of which he published separately as *Orpheus Britannicus* (1760).

A few of the large number of non-musical engravings signed 'B. Cole' are certainly by him, including a series in *The Gentleman's Magazine* (1755–61, and possibly as late as 1772): he may have been the engraver of a frontispiece to Tans'ur's *Works* (1748). He is probably not the engraver of a view of Leeds (1724; cited in *Grove 5* and Kidson) which can be assigned to Cole of Oxford. The Benjamin Cole who was the author of *The Ancient Hunting Notes of England* (*c*1725) is probably not the engraver.

J. Dart: *Westmonasterium* (London, 1742); R. Gough: *British Topography* (London, 1783); J. Strutt: *A Biographical Dictionary* (London, 1785–6); Kidson (1900); W. C. Smith and C. Humphries: *A Bibliography of the Musical Works Published by John Walsh, 1721–1766* (London, 1968)

S.B. (iii)

Cole, John (*b* Tewkesbury, 1774; *d* Baltimore, 17 Aug 1855). American tunebook compiler and publisher of English birth. He emigrated to the USA with his family in 1785 and settled in Baltimore. Probably self-taught, he seems at one time to have held the post of organist and choirmaster of St Paul's Episcopal Church in Baltimore. His career as a compiler of sacred tunebooks spanned almost half a century; he produced nearly 30 different issues, from *Sacred Harmony* (1799), adapted to the Methodist hymn-book, to *Laudate Dominum* (1846), for the Protestant Episcopal Church. He became involved in the printing trade as early as 1802 and published and printed several of these works himself, as well as composing some of the pieces that appeared in them. He taught at least one singing-school in Baltimore in 1819. In 1822 he opened a music shop, and from then until 1839 worked as a publisher, specializing in secular sheet music, of which, by the late 1820s, he was Baltimore's leading purveyor. The Maryland Historical Society owns a nearly complete run of Cole's musical publications, a total of some 900 items.

J. H. Hewitt: *Shadows on the Wall, or Glimpses of the Past* (Baltimore, 1877); S. P. Cheney: *The American Singing Book* (Boston, 1879/*R*1980), 186; F. J. Metcalf: *American Writers and Compilers of Sacred Music* (New York, 1925/*R*1967); L. H. Dielman: 'Old Baltimore Music and its Makers', *Peabody Bulletin* (May 1934), 26; Wolfe (1964); idem (1980)

R.C. (ii)

Colonna, Giovanni Ambrosio (*b* ?Milan; *fl* ?1616–27). Italian printer and guitarist. He belonged to the second generation of a family of Milanese printers, and according to Picinelli he was nicknamed 'lo Stampadorino'. In 1620 he was in the service of Count G. C. Borromeo and Duke Francesco Gallio of Alvito; by 1623 he was employed by Prince Theodoro Trivultio of Misocco. He compiled several books for five-course Baroque guitar containing his own *battute* (strummed) accompaniments to popular songs and dances, including passacaglias, passamezzos, galliards and folias. The music is notated in the alphabet tablature first used by Girolamo Montesardo in 1606. In the first book of 1620 Colonna included instructions on reading the tablature, on the execution of strums and on the proper tempos for certain types of piece. A book of lute works by Colonna, supposedly published by him in 1616, is lost. Colonna's own press published his first guitar anthology; he may have given up printing in about 1620, as the first anthology was reprinted, and his later works were published, by the family press under the title 'heirs of Giovanni Battista Colonna'. They also published *Scielta de canzonette*, an anonymously compiled, undated collection of canzonettas by Roman composers for solo voice, harpsichord or chitarrone, and guitar, which has sometimes, though without evidence, been attributed to Giovanni Ambrosio. It is not known in what way Giovanni Battista Colonna was related to Giovanni Ambrosio, and none of his publications survives.

F. Picinelli: *Atenco dei letterati milanesi* (Milan, 1670), 257; G. Gaspari: *Catalogo della Biblioteca del Liceo musicale di Bologna*, iv (Bologna, 1905/*R* 1961), 167; Sartori (1958); M. Donà: *La stampa musicale a Milano fino all'anno 1700* (Florence, 1961); R. Hudson: *The Development of Italian Keyboard Variations on the Passacaglia and Ciaccona from Guitar Music in the 17th Century* (diss., U. of California, Los Angeles, 1967); W. Kirkendale: *L'Aria di Fiorenza id est Il Ballo del Gran Duca* (Florence, 1972); E. Pohlmann, *Laute, Theorbe, Chitarrone* (Lilienthal and Bremen, 1972, enlarged 4/1976)

R.S. (iii)

Concordia. American firm of publishers. Concordia Publishing House was founded in St Louis in 1869 by immigrant German Lutherans for the purpose of printing their hymns and other church literature, and takes its name from the Lutheran Book of Concord (1580). Its catalogue, which has included music since 1880, consists of choral works, solo pieces and music for organ and for handbells, as well as books on the liturgy and church music. In the 1950s and 1960s, on the counsel of Walter E.

Buszin, it acted as an agent for German music publishers, notably Bärenreiter. From 1966 to 1980 the firm issued the periodical *Church Music*. Concordia is a non-profit organization and the official publishing firm of the Lutheran Church-Missouri Synod.

F.B.

Cooke, Benjamin (*b* ?London, ?between 1695 and 1705; *d* ?London, 1743 or later). English music seller and publisher. He was active in London from 1726 to 1743, and published a considerable number of vocal and instrumental works, some of them obviously pirated from other publishers, others under licence as authoritative first editions. His publications were mostly in a heavy bold style, but some were engraved in a lighter style by Thomas Cross. After Cooke's death or retirement some of his plates were acquired by John Johnson, who reissued copies from them. Cooke's publications include Roseingrave's *XII Solos for a German Flute* (1727), Handel's Sonatas op.2 (*c*1733) and 42 'suites' by D. Scarlatti in two volumes (1740). His most interesting publication, however, was that of the five books of sonatas and the 12 concertos of Corelli issued in 1732. Not only do these constitute a collected edition of the composer's works, but all, including the concertos, were published in score expressly for study purposes, an extraordinary form of publication for instrumental music at that time. Cooke's plates were used well into the 19th century for reissues of these works.

Kidson (1900); Humphries and Smith (1954, 2/1970)

W.C.S./P.W.J.

Corri. Italian family of publishers, active in Britain. The composer Domenico Corri (*b* Rome, 4 Oct 1746; *d* Hampstead, 22 May 1825) arrived in Edinburgh in August 1771 and established a music publishing business in the name of his son John (or Giovanni) about 1779. James Sutherland became a partner about 1780, and the firm of Corri & Sutherland existed until Sutherland's death in 1790.

Domenico Corri moved to London about 1790 and established himself as a music publisher in Soho. The firm specialized in publication of single numbers from operas and solo songs, sometimes as full scores. Many of them were published serially under general titles, and were decorated with the Prince of Wales's feathers, which Corri seems to have used as a mark. His daughter Sophia Giustina Corri married Jan Ladislav Dussek (*b* Čáslav, 12 Feb 1760; *d* St Germain-en-Laye or Paris, 20 March

1812) in 1792, and the latter went into partnership with his father-in-law in January 1794 as Corri, Dussek & Co. Later Lorenzo da Ponte was also associated with the firm, but about 1800 the business ran into financial trouble and Dussek fled to the Continent to avoid his creditors. Domenico Corri continued the business alone until his son Montague (*b* Edinburgh, *c*1784; *d* London, 19 Sept 1849) took it over in 1804, trading as Montague P. Corri & Co. About 1805 it briefly became Montague P. Corri, M. Hall & Co., then Corri, Pearce & Co., until about 1806 when Corri's name disappeared and the firm continued as Pearce & Co. A new firm of Corri & Co., however, existed for a short time about 1807 in Little Newport Street.

Domenico's brother, Natale (*b* Rome, 1765; *d* Wiesbaden, 24 July 1822) took over the Corri publishing firm in Edinburgh when Domenico moved to London about 1790. The Scottish business, known as Corri & Co., maintained close connections with the London firm, and many publications bear their joint imprints. Natale also undertook concert promotion, establishing concert rooms in the city, which proved financially disastrous and led to his bankruptcy at about the same time as his brother's London firm was in difficulties. Natale, however, soon re-established his activities and continued in Edinburgh until 1821, when he left for the Continent.

L. da Ponte: *Memoirs*, ed. A. Livingston (Philadelphia, 1929/*R*1988); A. Obertello: 'Una famiglia di musicisti italiani in Inghilterra', *Nuova antologia* (1930), July, 244; Humphries and Smith (1954, 2/1970)

P.W.J.

Cos Cob Press. American publishing firm, based in New York. It was founded in 1929 by Alma M. Wertheim as a non-profit-making organization for aiding and disseminating the music of American composers. Its catalogue included works by Citkowitz, Copland, Gruenberg (including his opera *The Emperor Jones*), Harris, Piston, Sessions, Thomson, Wagenaar and Whithorne. In 1938 the catalogue was leased to the newly founded Arrow Music Press, which in turn was acquired by Boosey & Hawkes in 1956.

'Cos Cob Press is Launched', *MusAm*, xlix/7 (1929), 53; C. J. Oja: 'Cos Cob Press and the American Composer', *Notes*, xlv (1988–9), 227

W.T.M., M.J./R

Cosmerovius [Cosmerov, Kosmerovius], **(Stanislaus) Matthäus** (*b* Wawrzeńczyce, 1606; *d* Vienna, 21 May 1674). Viennese printer of Polish birth. He studied in

Kraków, where he also learnt printing and managed a small press. In 1640 he married the widow of the printer Matthäus Formica (*fl* 1615–39) and assumed management of his shop on the Kölnerhof; later he became a printer for the university and court book printer. In 1649 he bought the remainder of the Formica shop, including music type from Leonard Formica (*fl* 1590–1615), and in 1655 he moved to a larger building on Unteren Bächerstrasse; known as the Cosmeroviushaus, it had five presses, more than 150 sets of type and a foundry. At his death his printing properties were transferred to his son Johann Christoph (1656–85) and thence, as the 'Cosmerovische Erben', to Johann's widow Theresia (until 1686), Matthäus's widow Susanna Christina (until 1698) and their heirs (until 1715).

Matthäus's publications include the polyphonic collection *Cultus harmonicus* (1649, 1650, 1659) by Alberik Mazák and several song collections, such as P. Sebastian a S Vincentio's *Himmels Schlüssel* (1636) and *Melodeyen des Weynächtlichen Seeln Jubel* (1657). The family also printed over 300 oratorio and opera librettos, some multilingual; several, for important court occasions, were lavish souvenir objects, with large engravings of scenes (often by Ludovico Burnacini). Cosmerovius issued the only known edition of printed Viennese ballet music of the period, J. H. Schmelzer's *Arie per il balletto a cavallo*. The most famous of the firm's librettos is for Cesti's *Il pomo d'oro* (printed 1667, performed 1668), in folio format with 25 large engravings of Burnacini's staging and settings.

A. Mayer: *Wiens Buchdrucker-Geschichte 1482–1882* (Vienna, 1887); E. Castle: *Geschichte einer Wiener Buchdruckerei 1548–1948* (Vienna, 1948); P. Riethus: 'Der Wiener Musikdruck im 16. und 17. Jahrhundert', *Das Antiquariat*, xiv (1958), 5; Benzing (1963, 2/1982); H. Lang: *Die Buchdrucker des 15. bis 17. Jahrhunderts in Österreich* (Baden-Baden, 1972), 60

T.D.W.

Costallat. French firm of publishers. It began in Paris in 1880 when Costallat (*d* 1901) went into partnership with William Enoch. Enoch Frères & Costallat were the sole agents in France for the German music publishers Litolff. In 1895 Costallat set up on his own in the rue de la Chaussée-d'Antin, and in 1898 he acquired the publishing house of Richault. When Costallat died his son-in-law Lucien de Lacour (*d* 1950) took over the business. It published many of the works of Berlioz and Alkan, and became the sole agent in France for Breitkopf & Härtel. Music is still published under the Costallat imprint, including the

series *Collection Archives de la Musique Instrumentale* and some important wind music, but the main catalogue has been taken over by the firm of Gérard Billaudot. The Costallat firm founded the Erato record company, which later became independent.

A.P. (ii)

Cottrau, Teodoro (*b* Naples, 7 Dec 1827; *d* Naples, 30 March 1879). Italian publisher. He studied the piano with F. Festa, composition with S. Pappalardo and also learnt some music from his father, Guglielmo Cottrau (*b* Paris, 9 Aug 1797; *d* Naples, 31 Oct 1847), a gifted amateur double bass player and director of the Girard firm. In 1846 Teodoro succeeded his father at Girard's and in 1848 became joint owner, later carrying on independently. He republished with greater success his father's edition of Neapolitan songs, *Passatempi musicali*. Besides the anthology Cottrau's much-admired publications include *L'ape musicale pianistica*, treatises, vocal and instrumental compositions and vocal scores of operas including Verdi's *Simon Boccanegra* and Hérold's *Le pré aux clercs*, for which he provided a translation and promoted the Italian première at the Teatro Filarmonico, Naples (1872). He was a close friend of Bellini (whom he tried unsuccessfully to persuade to set Victor Húgo's *Ernani*), Donizetti, Pacini (whose opera *Bondelmonte* he suggested to the London publisher Chappell) and the brothers F. and L. Ricci. He had the option for their operas *Chiarà di Montalbano* and *Il colonnello* from 1835.

Cottrau's name is linked with the traditional Piedigrotta Festival, for which he wrote, arranged and published the official song for many years. He was not always honest in his treatment of other Italian publishers; in April 1873 lawyers representing Ricordi and the Municipality of Rome brought a successful action against him in connection with the copyright of *La vestale* and *Lucia*. After Cottrau's death the firm, renamed the Società Musicale Napoletana, continued under different management and confined its activities to local editions. Associated with the publisher C. F. Leede of Leipzig, it used the Röder lithographical printing facilities. In 1884 it was taken over by Ricordi.

Alla memoria de T. Cottrau (Naples, 1879) [obituaries]; G. Cottrau: *Lettres d'un mélomane pour servir de documents l'histoire musicale de Naples, du 1829 à 1847* (Naples, 1885); idem: 'Le portefeuille d'un mélomane', *Revue britannique*, iv (1887), 5–58

S.A.

Couse, Adam (*b* Bethlehem, NY; *d* Detroit, MI, 6 Sept 1885). American dancing teacher, music dealer and publisher. In Detroit in June 1844 he opened Couse's Music Saloon, selling music and musical instruments. Within two years he had expanded his inventory to include fancy goods, changing the shop's name to Couse's Music and Variety Store and then to Couse's Bazaar; in time he returned to music exclusively. As Detroit's first important music publisher, he issued *The Bloomer Polka* (1851) by Wallerstein, *Walch's Detroit Grand March*, *The Detroit Polka* (1852), *The Detroit Schottisch* (1854; his own composition and most famous publication) and several other works in the 1850s, usually in association with Firth, Pond & Co. of New York. Dwight S. Amsden and Henry Hawley Cargill, Couse's shop assistants, bought the business in October 1855 and began publishing, often in conjunction with eastern firms. Their output included *Illinois Schottisch* (1855) by Charles Swinscoe, the *Young Men's Hall Polka* (1858) by J. P. Weiss, an anonymous *Pen, Ink, and Paper Polka* and several works by the Italian refugee Pietro Centemeri, including *Soon my harp shall silent be* and *When life's sad dream is o'er*. The partnership was dissolved in 1859.

M. Teal: 'Couse's Bazaar: Detroit's First Successful Music Store', *Among Friends* (Detroit Public Library), xliv (1966), 2

M.D.T.

Cousineau, Georges (*b* Merchant, Vendée, 1733; *d* Paris, 3 Jan 1800). French music seller and instrument maker, active in Paris. On 18 February 1759 he married Madeleine-Victoire Regnault and later set up shop in the rue des Poulies, opposite the Louvre, making and selling instruments. He soon specialized in harps (becoming instrument maker to Marie-Antoinette) and began issuing music engraved by his wife; she signed the plates 'Madame Cousineau de Ouvrard'. Among their publications in the early 1770s were collections of harp music and tunes from comic operas. Their son Jacques-Georges (1760–1836), a harpist at the Opéra, also helped in the business, known from 1784 as Cousineau père et fils. The firm published harp pieces by Pleyel, Krumpholz and J.-G. Cousineau, and other fashionable salon music, notably the weekly series *Les feuilles de Terpsichore* (1787–99). After his father's death Jacques-Georges abandoned instrument making but continued the publishing and retailing side of the business, which moved to the rue Dauphine in 1794; he sold it on 9 November 1822 to Lemoine.

S. Milliot: *Documents inédits sur les luthiers parisiens du XVIIIe siècle* (Paris, 1970); Devriès and Lesure (1979–88)

S.M.

Coventry & Hollier. English firm of music sellers and publishers, active in London from about 1833 to 1849. It published a number of important works, many from plates taken over when the firm succeeded Preston & Son, including many of Handel's works originally issued by Walsh, Randall and others. Some of these plates were acquired by J. Alfred Novello in 1849, after John Hollier had left the partnership. Among the original publications were four books of Bach's chorale preludes, edited by Mendelssohn, and Mendelssohn's own six organ sonatas op.65. From 1849 to 1851 Charles Coventry continued alone; at the sale of his trade stock in 1851 Novello purchased another 4780 plates of sacred works and subsequently reissued from some of them.

Humphries and Smith (1954, 2/1970); Coover (1988)

W.C.S./P.W.J.

Cowper, Edward (*b* 1790; *d* Kensington, 17 Oct 1852). English engineer and inventor. In collaboration with his brother-in-law Augustus Applegath from 1815, he made improvements to the steam printing machine (better ink distribution, use of four cylinders, conveyance of sheets from one cylinder to another) that superseded those of almost every other manufacturer. Afterwards he built and sold printing machinery with his brother Ebenezer, as E. and E. Cowper of London and Manchester (from 1838), and was Professor of Manufacturing Art and Machinery at King's College, London (1846). Cowper's contribution to music printing is connected to the firm of William Clowes. In 1826 Clowes purchased and expanded the former Applegath and Cowper premises in Stamford Street, Blackfriars, Cowper remaining in the office as engineer. By April 1827 he had patented a double-impression method for printing music (patent no. 5484), using two fixed woodblocks fitted with copper-wire characters and staff lines respectively, and a revolving tympan, so that two sheets of paper easily changed places for the separate impressions. The results were beautifully clear and accurate but expensive. Cowper lectured on his new invention at the Royal Institution in 1828 and assigned its use exclusively to Clowes, who immediately adopted it for *The Harmonicon* and other publications issued by the *Harmonicon*'s co-proprietors, notably Samuel

Chappell, Goulding, D'Almaine & Co. and Isaac Willis.

[W. Ayrton]: 'Royal Institution: Improvements in Music Printing', *Harmonicon*, vi (1828), 60; E. Cowper: Abstract of lecture to the Royal Institution, *Quarterly Journal of Science, Literature, and Art* (1828), 183; W. T. Berry and H. E. Poole: *Annals of Printing: a Chronological Encyclopaedia from the Earliest Times to 1950* (London, 1966), 218 [incl. illustration]; W. B. Todd, ed.: *A Directory of Printers and Others in Allied Trades, London and Vicinity, 1800–1840* (London, 1972), 48; J. C. Kassler: *The Science of Music in Britain, 1714–1830: a Catalogue of Writings, Lectures, and Inventions* (New York and London, 1979), 221

L.L.

Cramer, J. B. English firm of publishers, active in London. The firm was founded as Cramer, Addison & Beale in 1824 when the pianist and composer Johann Baptist Cramer (*b* Mannheim, 24 Feb 1771; *d* London, 16 April 1858) joined the partnership of Robert Addison and Thomas Frederick Beale (*b* ?1804 or 1805; *d* Chislehurst, 26 June 1863). With the addition of Cramer's name the publication of piano music became the firm's chief interest, and in 1830 it bought many of the plates of the Royal Harmonic Institution, which gave it works by Beethoven, Clementi, Dussek, Haydn, Hummel, Mozart, Steibelt and others. Italian songs and duets and English operas by composers such as Balfe and Benedict were soon added to the catalogue.

In 1844 Addison retired and was succeeded by William Chappell, and the firm then became known as Cramer, Beale & Chappell, or Cramer, Beale & Co. In 1847 Beale also became the manager and director of the Royal Italian Opera at the rebuilt Covent Garden Theatre. After the death of Cramer in 1858 and Chappell's retirement in 1861 George Wood (*b* ?1812 or 1813; *d* Hove, 22 Feb 1893), who was related to the Scottish music publishers, became Beale's partner; the firm then traded as Cramer, Beale & Wood, and also began the manufacture of pianos. After Beale's death Wood continued the business as Cramer & Co. (later Cramer, Wood & Co., and J. B. Cramer & Co.), and the piano-making side of the firm became predominant. His nephews, John Wood and George Muir Wood, succeeded to the business on his death. The firm was turned into a limited company in 1897. Many successful ballads appeared under the firm's imprint at the end of the century, and a series of ballad concerts was run by L. J. Saville from 1912 until World War II. The publishing firm of Metzler was acquired in 1931. In the 20th century publishing became the firm's main activity once again; the piano business

passed to Kemble & Co. in 1964. Choral, piano and organ music are the firm's specialities, with an emphasis on educational music.

Kidson (1900); 'The Music Publisher of Tradition: J. B. Cramer and his Successors', *MO*, lxv (1941–2), 220; Humphries and Smith (1954, 2/1970); Neighbour and Tyson (1965); Coover (1988)

C.H.P., W.C.S./P.W.J.

Cranz, August. German firm of publishers. It was founded by August Heinrich Cranz (*b* Berlin, 1789; *d* Hamburg, 1870) in 1814 in Hamburg. His son Alwin Cranz (*b* Hamburg, 1834; *d* Vevey, 10 April 1923) took over the music publishing house in 1857 and acquired the Viennese publishing firm C. A. Spina in 1876. August Cranz was the original publisher of many works by Josef, Eduard and Johann Strauss (father and son), including *Die Fledermaus, Der Zigeunerbaron* and *Eine Nacht in Venedig*. Viennese operettas and light music (e.g. Lanner, Suppé, Millöcker) have always played a large part in the publishing programme. Oskar Cranz, a partner from 1896, moved the firm to Leipzig in 1897. The August Cranz publishing house lost most of its stock in 1943; the rebuilding of the firm was carried out at first in Munich and from 1949 in Wiesbaden. Theo Nietzel was appointed director in 1972. In 1965 the firm began producing tapes and records. The firm August Cranz of Wiesbaden has branches in Brussels, London, Paris, and Vienna and is represented by agents in several countries.

H.-M.P.

Cross, Thomas (*b* ?London, ?1660–65; *d* ?London, ?1732–5). English engraver, printer, publisher and music seller. He was probably the son of the 17th-century engraver Thomas Cross, who engraved some frontispieces and portraits for John Playford's publications, including the portrait of the composer John Gamble (*Ayres and Dialogues*, 1656), and who may have engraved some music. From 1683 to about 1710 the younger Cross often signed himself 'Tho. Cross junior sculpt.', as on his first known work, Purcell's *Sonnata's of III. Parts* (1683), printed for the composer (see illustration). From about 1692 to about 1720 he kept a music shop in London. He was the first to issue songs in single sheet format rather than in collections, and from the 1690s a considerable number of these appeared under his imprint. At first they were engraved on copper plates, which was an expensive method considering the ephemeral nature of the sheet songs, but he

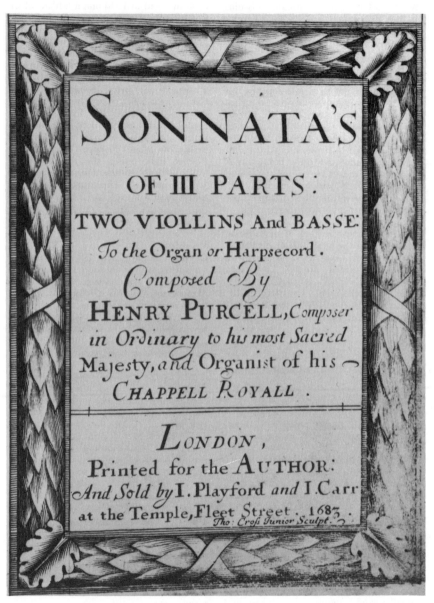

Title-page of Purcell's 'Sonnata's of III Parts' (London: Author and John Playford, 1683)

later used a cheaper material, probably pewter. He had a virtual monopoly of the music engraving trade at the end of the 17th century and worked for composers and other publishers, including Cullen, Meares and Wright, in addition to issuing his own publications. Walsh soon became Cross's great rival, despite their occasional business association. However, Cross scorned Walsh's frequent use of punches rather than pure engraving and warned on one of his sheet songs, 'beware of the nonsensical puncht ones'. It is doubtful that Cross ever did any work with punches, despite Hawkins's assertion that he did stamp the plates of a work by Geminiani. References in Purcell's *Orpheus Britannicus* (1698) and Blow's *Amphion Anglicus* (1700) attest to his fame and to the popularity of the new sheet music. He engraved in a bold style and his early work is particularly fine. It is clear, however, that he employed assistants, which probably accounts for some of the differences in engraving style which occur on plates bearing Cross's name, particularly in the later part of his career. Important works engraved in the Cross workshop included Purcell's and John Eccles's *A Collection of Songs* (*c*1696), Daniel Purcell's *Six Cantatas* (1713), Handel's *Radamisto* (1720) and Benjamin Cooke's edition of Corelli's sonatas and concertos (1732), one of Cross's last known works.

For further illustration *see* fig.13, p.44.

HawkinsH; Humphries and Smith (1954, 2/1970); Krummel (1975)

F.K., W.C.S./P.W.J.

Curci. Firm of Italian publishers. It was founded in Naples in 1912 by the brothers Giuseppe (1884–1953), Alberto (1886–1973) and Alfredo (1891–1952) Curci. Their grandfather Francesco (1824–1912) had opened a business at Naples in 1860 for the sale of musical instruments, and for music copying, an activity which was then continued by his three children, Pasquale, Achille and Concetta. Pasquale's sons, named above, started the publishing side of the 'Casa Musicale Fratelli Curci'. This part of the business was at first known as Casa Editrice di Operette e Vaudevilles (C.E.D.O.V.), and published musical comedies and operettas by Italian and foreign composers (I. Kálmán, Oscar Straus, J. Gilbert, C. Lombardo and Alberto Curci himself). The firm's address changed in 1919 from via dei Tre Re to via Roma 304/5; in this year too, the brothers founded the society 'Amici della Musica' of Naples, organizing concerts by the greatest chamber musicians. With the development of the cinema as an art form, the Casa Curci began publishing film music by well-known composers including G. Mulè, R. Rossellini and A. Veretti. In 1932 it opened a branch in Rome, and in 1936 one in Milan, which was to become a great venture under the direction of Alfredo Curci. From its premises in the Galleria del Corso in Milan, the Edizioni Curci began publishing important didactic works and collections of instrumental music of all periods, edited by such musicians as Cortot, Schnabel, Fischer, Casella, Piccioli, Agosti and Magaloff. Alfredo was active also in the field of authors' rights. At his death the management of the Milanese house was taken over by his son-in-law Giuseppe Gramitto Ricci. Besides light music, the firm publishes musicological studies and the quarterly *Rassegna musicale*. The catalogue now lists about 10,300 items.

Sartori (1958); *I cento anni della Casa Curci 1860–1960* (Milan, 1960)

M.D.

Curwen. English firm of publishers. It started from the educational work of John Curwen (*b* Heckmondwyke, 14 Nov 1816; *d* Manchester, 26 May 1880), a Congregational minister and proponent of tonic sol-fa. Having refined Sarah Glover's system, he wrote and edited a series of publications promoting his method including the *Tonic Sol-fa Reporter and Magazine of Vocal Music for the People* (1851, n.s. 1853–89; continued as *The Musical Herald and Tonic Sol-Fa Reporter* until 1891, then *The Musical Herald* until 1920). His early works were mostly issued by Ward & Co. at his own risk, but in 1863 he established the firm of J. Curwen & Son to print and publish his material. The distributing side, known as the Tonic Sol-fa Agency, continued to appear in imprints until about 1881. Works for popular singing classes were soon joined by music for schools, chiefly in tonic sol-fa notation. Then with the creation in 1885 of a grant for sight-singing in schools and official recognition of the tonic sol-fa method, Curwen's output of educational music expanded rapidly. The firm also issued music for congregational and Sunday-school use and catered to the demand for American organ and harmonium music.

John Curwen was succeeded as head of the publishing side by his eldest son John Spencer (1847–1916), while his younger son, Joseph Spedding, looked after the printing side. During Spencer's directorship the catalogue expanded to include choral music, school operettas, amateur light opera and collections for the use of such organizations as the Women's Institute, the British Legion and the Boy Scouts. His wife Annie wrote a famous piano method, first published as *The Child Pianist* (1886) and subsequently known as *Mrs Curwen's Pianoforte Method*, which became a valuable addition to the catalogue. From the end of the century the firm also took on general as well as music printing. The printing side gradually developed into the Curwen Press, noted for its fine design and quality of production; it separated from the parent company in 1933. John Kenneth Curwen (1881–1935) became head of J. Curwen & Sons in 1919 on the death of his father, Spedding, who had briefly run the whole business since Spencer's death in 1916. Although the tradition of publishing music for schools and amateur organizations continued, J. K. Curwen added orchestral music to the catalogue. Notable publications were Holst's *The Planets* and Vaughan Williams's *Hugh the Drover*, Mass in G minor and Third Symphony, as well as works by Varèse, Bantock, Boughton and Ethel Smyth. Cecil Sharp, Percy Dearmer and Martin Shaw were associated with the firm as editors, while the periodical *The Sackbut* (1920–34) also bore the Curwen imprint. J. K.'s son John Christopher (b 1911) succeeded to the firm's directorship in 1935. The American publishing group Crowell, Collier & Macmillan (now Macmillan Inc.) purchased the firm in 1969 and, while retaining ownership, closed the London office in 1971, dividing the rights for distributing the firm's catalogue between Faber Music and Roberton Publications.

J. S. Curwen: *Memorials of John Curwen* (London, 1882); C. G. Mortimer: 'Leading Music Publishers: J. Curwen & Sons, Ltd.', *MO*, lxiii (1939), 139; 'The Music Publisher of Tradition: the Curwens – John, John Spencer and John Kenneth', *MO*, lxv (1941–2), 28; H. Simon: *Songs and Words: a History of the Curwen Press* (London, 1973)

P.W.J.

D

Dale. English family of publishers, music sellers and instrument dealers, established in London. Joseph Dale (*b* 1750; *d* London, 1821) founded a business in 1783 at his private house, and from there issued his first publications, including a number of operas such as Shield's *Rosina* and *The Flitch of Bacon*. A music catalogue of 1785 announced that the copyrights and plates of these and other works had recently been purchased from William Napier; at about the same time he also purchased plates and copyrights from Charles Bennett, once the property of John Welcker. In January 1786 he moved to premises previously occupied by Samuel Babb, whose trade stock and large circulating music library Dale purchased. In 1805 he took his son William (*b* London, ?1780–85; *d* ?1827) into partnership and the firm became known as Joseph Dale & Son (or Joseph & William Dale). The partnership was dissolved in 1809, when William set up his own business as publisher, music seller and instrument dealer, issuing mainly sheet music. Joseph continued alone until his death; his firm, particularly in its early years, issued music of every description, including the operas of Storace and others, piano music by Clementi, Dussek, Krumpholtz and Steibelt, collections of English and Scottish songs, country-dance music and vast quantities of sheet music.

William's business was continued by Elspeth Dale, presumably his widow, from 1827 until about 1832; it was then succeeded by Dale, Cockerill & Co., and in 1837 by G. Gange & Co., piano manufacturers and music sellers.

Kidson (1900); Humphries and Smith (1954, 2/1970)

W.C.S./P.W.J.

Dalmas. Russian publishing firm. The founder, H. J. Dalmas, was a member of the French opera troupe in St Petersburg. In 1802, with the help of Boieldieu, he opened a music shop which swiftly developed into one of the most stable Russian publishing houses of the early 19th century. Dalmas was particularly noted for his various journals of French and Italian opera excerpts, including *Le troubadour du nord* (1804–11) and *La muse cosmopolite* (1827–8). He also published collections of songs (among them *Nouveau choix d'airs russes, ukrainiens, kosaques, etc.*, 1816) and keyboard pieces, as well as a number of important individual works by Bortnyansky (the full score and parts of *Pevets vo stane russkikh voinov*, 1813), Cavos (a piano score of the opera *Kazak-stikhotvorets*, c1812), Kozłowski (the score of the incidental music to Ozerov's *Fingal*, 1808) and others. In November 1812 the French troupe left St Petersburg, but Dalmas remained and took Russian citizenship. After his death the firm was put up for auction and bought (1829) by the publisher M. I. Bernard.

B. P. Jürgenson: *Ocherk istorii notopechataniya* [An outline of the history of music printing] (Moscow, 1928); R. A. Mooser: *Annales de la musique et des musiciens en Russie au XVIIIe siècle*, iii (Geneva, 1951); M. S. Druskin and Yu. V. Keldïsh, eds.: *Ocherki po istorii russkoy muzïki 1790–1825* [Essays on the history of Russian music 1790–1825] (Leningrad, 1956); B. L. Vol'man: *Russkiye notnïye izdaniya XIX – nachala XX veka* [Russian music publishing in the 19th and early 20th centuries] (Leningrad, 1970)

G.N.

Davidson, George Henry (*b* ?1800 or 1801; *d* London, 4 July 1875). English printer and publisher, active in London. He is first known as a general printer from about 1833. He began to publish both literary and musical works about 1844 and in 1847–8 he issued the two volumes of *Davidson's Universal Melodist*, a collection of popular and standard songs of the period. At the same time he republished a collection of Dibdin's songs, edited by George Howarth, which had originally been printed by a different George Davidson and issued by How & Parsons in 1842. From 1850 Davidson had an enormous trade in the issue of cheap editions of popular music. He published much sheet music in the *Musical Treasury* series, and from 1854 he issued *Davidson's Musical Opera Books*, a series of librettos with music of the principal airs. Some of his publications were subsequently transferred and issued with the imprint 'The Musical Bouquet Office'. From 1860 to 1881 the business continued as the Music Publishing Co.

Humphries and Smith (1954, 2/1970)

F.K., W.C.S./P.W.J.

Day, John (*b* Dunwich, Suffolk, 1522; *d* Walden, Essex, 23 July 1584). English printer, father of Richard Day. He was one of the most successful general printers of his generation, but his music printing was almost entirely limited to *The Whole Booke of Psalmes, Collected into English Metre by T. Sternhold, I. Hopkins & Others . . . with Apt Notes to Synge them withal*, known as the Sternhold-Hopkins psalter. Day first published it in 1562, under the terms of a monopoly granted to him by the crown in 1559 that gave him sole right to print the work, which became extremely popular. He had the patent of monopoly renewed in 1567 and 1577, the latter renewal extending the terms to include his son, Richard Day, who had joined him that year. Day acquired several other printing monopolies on which he built a virtual printing empire, becoming master of the Stationers' Company in 1580. In 1583 he is reported as owning four presses, from which he produced 36 separate editions of the Sternhold-Hopkins psalter. Whether or not he played any part in the choice of the psalm tunes is difficult to determine, but there is ample evidence that he regarded the book as a business asset. His only secular music printing was Thomas Whythorne's *Songes for Three, Fouer and Five Voyces* (1571), which was a commercial failure. It is difficult to accept Whythorne's claim that the book failed because it had been 'very ill printed' as all the products of the Day press are of a high standard and he must have employed journeymen of great skill. His music books show a clean, crisp impression with spacious layout and accurate registration. He had two shops in London, one in Aldersgate and another in St Paul's Churchyard; his son succeeded him when he died.

For an illustration *see* fig.32, p.90.

E. Arber: *A Transcript of the Register of the Company of Stationers of London* (London, 1875–7, 1894); R. R. Steele: *The Earliest English Music Printing* (London, 1903/R1965); E. G. Duff: *A Century of the British Book Trade* (London, 1905); Humphries and Smith (1954, 2/1970); J. M. Osborn, ed.: *The Autobiography of Thomas Whythorne* (Oxford, 1962); Krummel (1975); C. L. Oastler: *John Day, the Elizabethan Printer* (1975); J. Alpin: 'The Origins of John Day's "Certaine notes . . ." ', *ML*, lxii (1981), 295

M.M.

Day, Richard (*b* London, 21 Dec 1552; *d* before 1607). English publisher, son of John Day. He was trained as a scholar, becoming a Fellow of King's College, Cambridge, in 1574. Family pressures obliged him to return to his father's business in London, and he was admitted to the Stationers' Company in 1577. With his father he held several printing monopolies, including one that gave them sole right to print the Sternhold-Hopkins psalter, in which the metrical psalms were set to music. After his father's death in 1584 Day never printed this work himself, but assigned his rights to other printers; he authorized 46 separate printings, bringing the total printed under the monopoly to 82.

The work was continually pirated and Day was involved in several legal actions. When Thomas Morley acquired a general music-printing monopoly from the queen in 1598, the terms conflicted with Day's. Morley published Richard Alison's *Psalmes of David in Metre* (1599), in which Alison had reset the old church tunes and added an instrumental accompaniment. Day regarded this as an infringement of his long-standing monopoly, and a dispute ensued between them which the Bishop of London attempted to settle. He did not succeed, and whether any settlement was reached is not known. In 1604 James I sold all the printing monopolies to the Stationers' Company, the psalter monopoly among them. Day's fate is obscure: he had taken holy orders in 1583, becoming vicar of Reigate, but left the following year.

E. Arber: *A Transcript of the Register of the Company of Stationers of London* (London, 1875–7, 1894); *Calendar of the Manuscripts of the Marquis of Salisbury, Preserved at Hatfield House, Hertfordshire* (London, 1883–1940); H. G. Aldis: *A Dictionary of Printers and Booksellers in England, Scotland and Ireland . . . 1557–1640* (London, 1910)

M.M.

Della [Dalla] **Volpe, Lelio** (*fl* Bologna, 1720–49). Italian publisher and bookseller. His firm was active in Bologna for most of the 18th century and was famous in the art of typography and for the accuracy and elegance of its editions. In 1720, as head of a society of Bolognese printers, he acquired the printing establishment of the widow of Giulio Borsaghi. His first musical publication was Angelo Bertalotti's *Regole per il canto fermo*, first published in 1720 and reprinted in 1744, 1756, 1764 and 1778. He ordered musical type characters from the Netherlands and in 1734 began his music printing activities in earnest, starting with Giovanni Battista Martini's op.1, *Litanie e antifone a 4 voci con violini*. He was also active as a bookseller, handling the musical publications of the Bolognese printers Monti and Silvani. In 1735 he published two indexes of the musical editions of these two publishers which were sold by his firm; such a list also exists from 1747. In 1748 and 1749 he published lists of works printed by his own firm. His publications include instrumental and sacred music by G. A. Perti (1737), G. B. Martini (1747, 1763), G. M. Rutini (1765), P. Pericoli (1769, 1796), A. Caroli (1766) and P. A. Pavona (1770). He also published treatises by A. G. Minelli (*Ristretto delle regole più essenziali della musica*, 1748) and G. B. Martini (*Esemplare ossia Saggio fondamentale pratico di contrappunto sopra il canto fermo*,

1774–5), as well as Martini's *Storia della musica* (1757–81). After 1744 Della Volpe's editions were no longer printed but engraved. He died on 6 October 1749, and the firm was taken over by his son Petronio, who continued to publish under the name Lelio della Volpe. The firm's usual typographical mark is the figure of a wolf ('volpe' in Italian).

F. Vatielli: 'Editori musicali dei secoli XVII e XVIII', *Arte e vita musicale a Bologna* (Bologna, 1927/*R*1969), 239; A. Sorbelli: *Storia della stampa a Bologna* (Bologna, 1929); Sartori (1958); Mischiati (1984)

A.S. (ii)

De Santis. Italian firm of publishers, active in Rome. Pietro Giovanni De Santis (*b* Isola Liri, 1822; *d* Rome, 1914) founded the firm on returning from exile in 1852, and began by alternating publishing (harp music) with the manufacture and sale of string instruments and pianos, activities in which he had specialized with the renowned Alessandroni at the S Michele institute. His son Alberto (*b* Rome, 1876; *d* Rome, 1968), associated with the firm from 1902, enlarged the publishing programme with works by contemporary composers, including Setaccioli, Tirindelli, Bustini and Tebaldini.

Renato De Santis (*b* Rome, 1901; *d* Rome, 1974) began to take part in the business in 1916 and directed the firm until his death. Under him the firm expanded the educational and musicological sections with specialized and collected editions as well as numerous instrumental, orchestral and vocal compositions. His friendship with musicians such as Malipiero, Casella, Poulenc, Respighi, Rieti, Toscanini, Mascagni, Puccini, Cilea, Giordano, Pizzetti and Alfano led him to an interest in the new avant garde; his catalogue, besides works by some of those composers, also includes works by Porrino, Allegra, Mannino, Liviabella, Lupi, Pizzini, Turchi and Savagnone. However, the firm's most important activity has been in publishing new editions of works by earlier and often unjustly neglected composers. Under the artistic direction first of Bonaventura Somma and then of Lino Bianchi, De Santis published *Capolavori polifonici del secolo XVI* and *Polifonia vocale sacra e profana del secolo XVI*. The firm also published the 40-volume *Musiche vocali e strumentali sacre e profane dal XVII al XIX secolo*, the complete keyboard works of Pasquini, Galuppi and Rutini, and a number of important series of early music, including *Gli oratorii di Alessandro Scarlatti, Musiche rinascimentali siciliane, Polifonia napoletana del rinascimento, Musiche per sonare con ogni sorte di stromenti* and *Composizioni vocali e strumentali dal XIV al XVI secolo*; De Santis also publishes *Contributi di musicologia*.

S.A.

Desclée. Belgian firm of publishers, active in Tournai (not to be confused with Desclée de Brouwer & Cie of Bruges). It was established in 1876 by Jules Desclée (1828–1911), and four years later became Desclée, Lefebvre & Cie (Lefebvre died *c*1907) under the corporate name Société Saint-Jean-l'Evangéliste with branches in Paris and Rome. Now a division of S. A. Gedit, the firm specializes in scholarly and pastoral religious publications. In the period 1880 to 1960 Desclée contributed significantly to the publication of modern Gregorian chant books under the auspices of the Congregation of Sacred Rites at the Vatican and the Benedictine Congregation of Solesmes. According to imprint data issued during the 1950s, it published over 6100 numbered editions. With the decision of the Second Vatican Council (1962–5) to replace the ancient Latin liturgical texts and melodies with vernacular substitutes, Desclée, like other publishers, abandoned the publication of notated chant books.

Desclée's importance goes beyond the printing and marketing of modern chant books, for the company's special type fount for Gregorian melodies became the accepted standard for 20th-century publications. Its origins go back to 1877 when Dom Joseph Pothier (1835–1923), the distinguished Solesmes scholar, negotiated with Desclée, Lefebvre & Cie to publish his treatise *Les mélodies grégoriennes* (1880, 2/1890) and the *Liber gradualis* (1883, 2/1895). By the norms of Gregorian chant performance in France during the period 1830–70, these Pothier publications were revolutionary for two reasons: the mass melodies were transcribed directly from original manuscripts and bore little resemblance to the post-Tridentine melodies then in vogue, and they were printed in an entirely new, graceful notation designed by Pothier and Desclée, capable of representing the intricacies of liquescent neumes. When Pothier's books appeared, the complexity of the melodies and the novelty of the printing were much criticized; yet the authenticity of the Pothier-Desclée editions presented a major challenge to established publishers.

Desclée's more important publications include the *Breviarium romanum* (4 vols., 1877, 4/1912), *Missale romanum* (1879), *Rituale romanum* (1886), *Rassegna gregoriana*

(13 vols., 1902–14); *Ephemerides liturgicae* (xvi–xxv, 1902–11), *Revue grégorienne* (i–xxxi, 1911–52), *Paléographie musicale* (vii–xv, 1901–37), *Graduale sacrosanctae* (1908), *Antiphonale sacrosanctae* (1912) and G. M. Suñol's *Introduction à la paléographie musicale grégorienne*, (Paris and Tournai, 1935). (For other titles, see 'Plainchant', *Grove6*, xiv, 832.)

Schmidt: 'La typographie et le plain-chant', *Revue du chant grégorien*, iv (1895–6), 36, 59; A. Vermeersch: 'Desclée', *Catholic Encyclopedia*, xvi (New York, 1914), 32; L. H. Cottineau: 'Maredsous', *Répertoire topo-bibliographie des abbayes et prieurés*, ii (1937), 1744; P. Combe: *Histoire de la restauration du chant grégorien d'après des documents inédits* (Solesmes, 1969), 104; R. F. Hayburn: *Papal Legislation on Sacred Music, 95 a.d. to 1977 a.d.* (Collegeville, MN, 1979); H. Garceau: 'Notes sur la presse musicale religieuse en France de 1827 à 1861', *Periodica musica*, ii (1984), 6; K. Bergeron: *Representation, Reproduction, and the Revival of Gregorian Chant at Solesmes* (diss., Cornell U., 1989)

J.A.E.

Deutscher Verlag für Musik. German firm of publishers. It was founded as a nationally owned firm in Leipzig on 1 January 1954. Gunter Hempel became director in 1974, succeeding the music scholar Helmut Zeraschi. By the mid-1980s it had published about 300 book titles and 1400 music titles, including complete critical editions, practical editions and publications of single works and music literature (specialized musicological works, Festschriften, yearbooks, biographies, facsimile editions, reprints and children's books with music). An orchestral and theatrical agency is attached to the firm. The Deutscher Verlag für Musik has brought out numerous works by contemporary composers from the German Democratic Republic including Paul Dessau, Hanns Eisler, Friedrich Goldmann, Peter Herrmann, Georg Katzer, Günter Kochan, Wilfried Krätzschmar, Siegfried Matthus, Günter Neubert, Erhard Ragwitz, Kurt Schwaen, Siegfried Thiele, Karl Ottomar Treibmann and Udo Zimmermann, as well as works by Shostakovich, Prokofiev, Mikis Theodorakis and Takehito Shimazu. Studies, didactic works and instrumental tutors are a prominent part of its publishing programme. The firm is also responsible for the publication of the collected editions of Mendelssohn, Samuel Scheidt, Gesualdo and Eisler; with other firms (notably Bärenreiter) it is producing the collected editions of Bach, Handel and Mozart. Experts from several countries are contributing to the firm's series *Musikgeschichte in Bildern* (founded by Heinrich

Besseler and Max Schneider, now edited by Werner Bachmann), a standard work of musical iconography.

VEB Deutscher Verlag für Musik 1954–1974 (Leipzig, 1974); *VEB Deutscher Verlag für Musik Leipzig 1954–1979* (Leipzig, 1978)

H.-M.P./G.H.

Diabelli, Anton (*b* Mattsee, nr. Salzburg, 6 Sept 1781; *d* Vienna, 7 April 1858). Austrian publisher and composer. He studied music in Michaelbeuren and Salzburg and in 1800 entered the Raitenhaslach Monastery. After the dissolution of the Bavarian monasteries (1803) he went to Vienna, where he taught the piano and guitar, and soon became known for his arrangements and compositions (six masses by him had been published in Augsburg in 1799); many of his works were published in Vienna. His job as a proofreader for S. A. Steiner & Co. (as detailed in Beethoven's letters) gave him an increasing interest in music publishing, and in the *Wiener Zeitung* (15 September 1817) he advertised a subscription for some of his sacred compositions, which were to appear from his newly established publishing house in the Schultergasse. On 29 September he moved to no. 351 Am Hof. The first notice of publications (*Wiener Zeitung*, 11 February 1818) announced the appearance of further works, which were soon being distributed by most music retailers; the works in the subscription series were available on 27 April 1818.

Wishing to acquire business premises of his own, Diabelli made contact with Pietro Cappi, who had been practising as a licensed art dealer in the Spiegelgasse since 30 July 1816. After Cappi's shop passed to Daniel Sprenger on 8 August 1818, the firm Cappi & Diabelli was established in the Kohlmarkt, and advertised in the *Wiener Zeitung* (10 December 1818). From its beginning the new firm was remarkably active in publishing current operatic and dance music; anthologies such as *Philomele für die Guitarre* and *Philomele für das Pianoforte* and *Euterpe* for piano (solo and duet) were popular for decades. Similar series appeared for other types of music; the popular *Neueste Sammlung komischer Theatergesänge* reached 429 volumes. A series of light, pleasant melodies for guitar was given the title *Apollo am Damentoilette*.

As an experienced musician, Diabelli knew how to respond to the musical fashions of the time; and the connection he formed with Schubert established the company's widespread fame. Financed on commission, he published Schubert's first printed works; on 2 April 1821 *Erlkönig* appeared as op.1 and on 30 April *Gretchen am Spinnrade* as op.2. Opp.1–7 and 12–14 later became the property of Cappi & Diabelli. Diabelli's long-established acquaintance with Beethoven, however, led to only a few publications: the reissues Beethoven wanted of the sonatas opp.109–11, and a few first editions of the smaller works. The firm also published the *Vaterländischer Künstlerverein*, including Beethoven's Diabelli Variations, op.120.

Diabelli's intention in 1819 in sending his waltz theme to every composer he considered important in Austria was ostensibly to form a 'patriotic anthology'; but this altruism was mixed with sound practical sense, as in an age of domestic musicmaking he could be sure that a collection of short pieces by the best composers would catch public attention and purse. Not every composer responded, but by 1824 the inclusion of the German composer Kalkbrenner, visiting Vienna on a concert tour, brought the total to about 50, and a coda by Czerny concluded the set (see illustration). Many of the variations are similar in method, since the composers were working in ignorance of one another and since piano virtuosity and variation techniques were widely taught according to familiar principles.

In June 1824, following Cappi's retirement, the firm (renamed Anton Diabelli & Cie) entered its most productive period. Cappi's place was filled by Anton Spina (*b* Brno, 1790; *d* Vienna, 8 Sept 1857), who handled the business side while Diabelli was responsible for its artistic direction. This favourable division of responsibility led to considerable success and the firm could claim to compete successfully even with Tobias Haslinger. Lesser firms were taken over: Thadé Weigl on 19 November 1832, Mathias Artaria on 26 June 1833 and M. J. Leidesdorf (Anton Berka) on 4 September 1835.

Diabelli's programme shows that he recognized the need to finance the publication of serious or advanced music by producing popular pieces: the firm's output included a rich variety of fashionable music for entertainment and dancing. But his reputation rests on his championship of Schubert, whose principal publisher he became until 1823 when (probably through a fault of Cappi's) Schubert broke off relations with the firm and turned to other publishers. After Schubert's death Diabelli was able to obtain a large part of the estate from his brother Ferdinand; this became the property of his firm. Works owned by

Title-page of '50 Varänderungen über einen Walzer', published by Diabelli (1824)

Leidesdorf, Pennauer, Artaria and Weigl automatically became Diabelli's property as he purchased these firms. The publication of this unexpectedly rich body of compositions extended beyond Diabelli's death to his successors, so that 'new' works by Schubert were still appearing in Paris in the 1850s.

On 3 November 1851 Spina's son Carl Anton (*b* 23 Jan 1827; *d* 5 July 1906) became a partner of the firm; on 23 January 1851 Diabelli retired, dissolving the company contract. Anton Spina continued to direct the firm until the end of the year, when he retired, passing the directorship to his son. An advertisement in the *Wiener Zeitung* (11 January 1852) announced the change of the firm's name to 'C. A. Spina, vormals Diabelli'. The firm purchased the former Mechetti publishing house in 1856. Carl Anton Spina continued the tradition of Diabelli; from May 1864 the firm published works by Johann Strauss the younger and his brother Josef.

The firm's enormous productivity is most clearly reflected in the plate numbers of the published works. At the end of the period of Cappi & Diabelli (1824) the number 1558 had been reached; A. Diabelli & Cie closed at about number 9100. Spina afterwards extended the series to 10,900, then continued from about 16,000. The intermediate numbers may have been omitted to accommodate the works purchased with the Mechetti firm; these, however, never entered the enumeration. By the time the firm ceased activity the series of plate numbers had reached 24,670.

In 1872 Spina bought the catalogue of Adolf Bösendorfer, but later in the year the firm passed to Friedrich Schreiber. It remained in his possession only a few years, for in 1876 Schreiber merged with August Cranz in Hamburg, and in 1879 the name of the company became August Cranz by purchase.

A. Weiss: *Franz von Schober* (Vienna, 1907); O. E. Deutsch: 'Schuberts Verleger', *Jb von Breitkopf & Härtel* (1928), 13; L. Kantner: 'Anton Diabelli: ein Salzburger Komponist der Biedermeierzeit', *Mitteilungen der Gesellschaft für Salzburger Landeskunde*, xcviii (1958), 51; E. Anderson, ed. and trans.: *The Letters of Beethoven* (London, 1961/ R1985); A. Weinmann: *Verlagsverzeichnis Anton Diabelli & Co., 1824 bis 1840* (Vienna, 1985).

A.W.

Ditson, Oliver. American firm of publishers, pre-eminent in the USA in the second half of the 19th century. In its day, it could lay circuitous claim to being the oldest continuous American music publisher, tracing its beginning to the firm of Ebenezer Battelle, who opened the Boston Book Store in 1783 and shortly afterwards began selling music as well. Two years later Benjamin Guild purchased the shop and managed the firm until his death in 1792, when it was taken over by William Pinson Blake; William Pelham succeeded Blake in 1796, and Pelham, in turn, was succeeded by William Blagrove in 1804. Seven years later, the business became the property of Samuel H. Parker, who was the first of these owners to publish music. Oliver Ditson (*b* Boston, 20 Oct 1811; *d* Boston, 21 Dec 1888) served as an apprentice to Parker from 1823 to 1826 and then worked for two other Boston publishers, Isaac R. Butts and Alfred Mudge.

In 1835 Ditson began his own music publishing firm in the same building as Parker, and in 1836 the two became partners in the firm of Parker & Ditson. When the partnership was dissolved in 1842, Ditson acquired the remaining interest in the publishing company. Three years later John C. Haynes joined Ditson, becoming a partner when Oliver Ditson & Co. was formed in 1857. Ditson's pre-eminence among the nation's music publishers is reflected in his service as the first president (1856) of the Board of Music Trade, established in June 1855 to address problems of piracy and underpricing. Other publishers claimed more memorable editions in the 1850s and 1860s, notably those of Stephen Foster and of the music of the Civil War. But Ditson, who had quietly assembled a solid catalogue of relatively nondescript sentimental parlor songs during these years, was well off at the war's end.

A period of vast expansion followed, during which the company bought up other publishers, at first minor firms, then in 1867 Firth, Son & Co. of New York. By the time of the Board of Music Trade's massive *Complete Catalogue* (1871), just under half of its 100,000 titles identified Ditson as publisher. In 1873 Ditson acquired Miller & Beacham of Baltimore; in 1875 Wm. Hall & Son of New York and Lee & Walker of Philadelphia; in 1877 G. D. Russell & Co. of Boston and J. L. Peters of New York; in 1879 G. André of Philadelphia; and in 1890 F. A. North & Co. of Philadelphia. Through these firms Ditson inherited the catalogues of earlier firms, along with the settings for branches to be operated by his sons, Charles H. Ditson in

New York in 1867 and James Edward Ditson in Philadelphia in 1875. Other important firms were begun with Ditson's financial investment, among them John Church in Cincinnati in 1860 and Lyon & Healy in Chicago in 1864. On his death Ditson was eulogized as one who 'did send sweet song into many a humble home, and helped make "music" part of the daily life of the American citizen'. He had also been a bank president, supporter of local musical institutions and publisher of *Dwight's Journal of Music* for much of its life (1858–78). By 1900 the firm was clearly the country's largest music publisher, with a catalogue of 45,000 vocal works, 4000 octavos, 48,000 instrumental editions and 3000 books – over 100,000 titles in all. Working through the Music Publishers' Association (distinct from the Board of Music Trade), Ditson led the battle against international coverage in the US copyright law. Following the negative judgment on 6 February 1894, other firms slowly withdrew from the Board of Music Trade, often in deference to the burgeoning musical instrument market as well. Meanwhile, Ditson moved to larger quarters in 1891, 1904 and 1917.

About 1900 Ditson was criticized for neglecting ambitious music. The copyright confrontations of 1891 and the movement for musical nationalism called attention to European publishers and such American firms as Arthur P. Schmidt, who had been issuing the serious music of native composers. Under the guidance of William Arms Fisher (1861–1948), who in 1897 became editor and director of publications, Ditson's programme came to favour an increasingly eclectic repertory of art music packaged not as sheet music but in anthologies. The success of *Ditson and Co.'s Musical Record* (begun in 1878, renamed *Musical Record* in 1879 and *Musical Record and Review* in 1900 led in 1903 to acquisition of and merger into *The Musician*, founded in Philadelphia in 1896 and devoted to 'educational interests'. A cultivation of music teachers is reflected in subsequent Ditson series: *The Music Students Library* (begun in 1897): Albert G. Mitchell's instrumental class methods (1912–23); the *Music Students Piano Course* (including *The School Credit Piano Course*, 1918–22); and *A Study Course in Music Understanding* (4 vols., 1924–6) for amateur listeners. Theory and pedagogy monographs were prepared by Clarence G. Hamilton, Percy A. Goetschius and Will Earhart. The *Half-Dollar Music Series* (1905–10) contained graded teaching music for a popular market, in contrast to Ditson's most impressive series, *The*

Musicians Library (1903–28), consisting of 68 anthologies of songs and piano solos, edited by various authorities and printed by Daniel Berkeley Updike at the Merrymount Press. Fisher himself edited several Americana sets; foreign editors included Granville Bantock for folk and national songs (1911–14), Cecil Sharp for English folksongs (1916), Ernest Newman for modern Russian songs (1921) and Vincent d'Indy for Franck's piano music (1922). Other collections of classics were edited by such critics and writers as William Foster Apthorp, Henry T. Finck, Philip Hale, W. J. Henderson, Rupert Hughes, James Gibbons Huneker and H. E. Krehbiel. In 1931 the firm was absorbed by the Theodore Presser Co.

W. A. Fisher: *Notes on Music in Old Boston* (Boston, 1918/R1976); idem (1933); C. M. Ayars: *Contributions to the Art of Music in America by the Music Industries of Boston, 1640 to 1936* (New York, 1937/R1969); D. J. Epstein: 'Introduction', *Board of Music Trade: Complete Catalogue of Sheet Music and Musical Works, 1870* (New York, 1973); idem: 'Music Publishing in the Age of Piracy', *Notes*, xxxi (1974–5), 7

W.T.M., M.J./D.W.K.

Doblinger. Austrian firm of publishers. Friedrich Mainzer opened a music lending library in Vienna on 1 August 1817 which from 1825 also sold antiquarian music. Ludwig Doblinger acquired this business on 12 July 1857. On 1 August 1876 it passed to Bernhard Herzmansky (1852–1921) whose son, also Bernhard Herzmansky (1888–1954), managed it until his death, when his nephew Christian Wolf assumed ownership and took over as business manager.

Doblinger expanded the business to include music publishing; in 1874 he obtained the publishing rights of J. P. Gotthard. Under Herzmansky the undertaking had considerable success, particularly with the publication of music by Bruckner (including first editions of his symphonies nos. 1, 2, 5, 6 and 9) and other leading composers of the period, among them Dohnányi and Mahler (Fourth Symphony). At the turn of the century the publishing output was reorganized: many publications were transferred to the newly founded Universal Edition (of which Herzmansky was a co-founder) and the emphasis placed on contemporary operetta. In 1906 Herzmansky published an operetta rejected by Josef Weinberger and Karczag & Wallner, Lehár's *Die lustige Witwe*, which was to bring the firm its most spectacular and enduring success. Doblinger subsequently published Lehár's

Das Fürstenkind, *Eva* and *Die Ideale Gattin* as well as operettas by Straus, Fall, Nedbal, Eysler, Benatzky and many others. Between the wars light music and Viennese songs were prominent in the firm's output; after 1945 it began to foster the interests of music research and to encourage contemporary composers. Its popular house concerts and the series *Diletto musicale* (1958–), which includes Viennese music from the pre-Classical period to Brahms, give Doblinger a prominent place in Austrian musical life.

[B. Herzmansky]: *Verzeichnis sämtlicher im Druck erschienenen Werke von Anton Bruckner* (Vienna 1903); *1876–1926: Ludwig Doblinger (Bernhard Herzmansky), Musikalienhandlung, Verlag, Antiquariat und Leihanstalt, Wien-Leipzig* (Vienna, 1926); Weinmann (1956); Plesske (1968); H. Vogg: *1876–1976: 100 Jahre Musikverlag Doblinger* (Vienna, 1976); *Das Doblinger-Katalog von 1951: Faksimile und Preminiszenz* (Vienna, 1981)

A.W./N.S.

Doina. Romanian firm of publishers, active in Bucharest. Founded in 1914 by Braşcu and the bookseller Ştefan Theodorescu (1888–1978), it operated under Theodorescu's management from 1916 to 1947. It printed Romanian and foreign classical music, instrumental methods and vocal and instrumental chamber music, some for German publishers (P. J. Tonger). When the firm ceased, Theodorescu worked at the shop of the Composers' Union in Bucharest (1963–76).

V.C.

Dorico, Valerio (*b* Ghedi, nr. Brescia, *c*1500; *d* Rome, 1565). Italian printer. His entire professional career was spent in Rome. From March 1526 to April 1527 he collaborated with the printer Giovanni Giacomo Pasoti of Parma on six of the eight music books Pasoti printed for the Roman publisher Jacomo Giunta. By 1531 Dorico was established as an independent printer and bookseller, producing at least five collections of music and one musical treatise during the next six years. In all the music books with which his name is associated from the 1520s and 1530s, Dorico used the double-impression method of printing; after Pasoti's disappearance from Rome during the sack of 1527, Dorico retained possession of his types and decorative materials, using them in his own editions in the 1530s. After a musical hiatus of seven years, he adopted the single-impression method, devised by Attaingnant, for his edition of Morales's masses in 1544. Until his death he and his brother

Luigi printed 26 music books and two musical treatises. His heirs continued to print music until 1572, contributing seven additional publications.

The musical activity of the Dorico firm comprised about a sixth of its total production, and slightly more than half of all the music printed in Rome during the middle third of the 16th century, including masses, motets, madrigals, *laudi*, lute tablatures and instrumental ricercares. Some historical importance attaches to Dorico's otherwise limited musical activity: he is credited with the first collection to use the word 'madrigal' to describe it contents (*Libro primo de la serena*, 1530), and he was the first to print the sacred music of Palestrina and Animuccia. Dorico claimed credit for choosing the music he printed only twice in his career. Apparently he preferred to receive commissions, often from local composers, a practice that guaranteed him both financial support and free editorial assistance from the musicians he served. Dorico's surviving music books are well organized, thoughtfully illustrated and reasonably well edited. His folio editions of masses by Morales, Palestrina, Rodio and Animuccia are modelled visually on Antico's *Liber quindecim missarum*, but the belief that he inherited typographical material from Antico seems to be apocryphal.

C. W. Chapman: *Andrea Antico* (diss., Harvard U., 1964); F. Barberi: 'I Dorici, tipografi a Roma nel '500', *La bibliofilia*, lxvii (1965), 221–61; D. Kämper: 'Studien zur instrumentalen Ensemblemusik des 16. Jahrhunderts', *AnMc*, no.10 (1970) [whole vol.]; S. G. Cusick: *Valerio Dorico: Music Printer in Sixteenth-century Rome* (Ann Arbor, 1981); D. G. Cardamone: 'Madrigali a Tre et Arie Napolitane: a Typographical and Repertorial Study', *JAMS*, xxxv (1982), 436

S.G.C.

Dover. American firm of publishers. In 1941 Hayward Cirker established in New York a business as a dealer in academic remainders. He issued his first reprint in 1943 and Dover has since become known for its reissues of scholarly texts. Although it specialized initially in scientific literature, the firm soon extended its interests to other areas, including music. Notable among its reprints of music texts are the works on Bach by Albert Schweitzer and Philipp Spitta and Rimsky-Korsakov's *Principles of Orchestration*. Dover began to publish musical scores in 1963, when it brought out a reprint of the Fitzwilliam Virginal Book. Since then the firm has issued classics of the vocal, piano, chamber and orchestral repertory, as well as popular music of the past.

Its publications, mostly in paperback, are distinguished by their sturdy and attractive design and low prices.

J. Rockwell: 'A Different Kind of Music Publishing', *New York Times* (6 Jan 1980), §11, 13; J. F. Baker: 'What's Doing at Dover', *Publishers Weekly*, ccxx (14 Aug 1981), 21

F.B.

Dozza, Evangelista (*fl* Bologna, 2nd half of the 17th century). Italian printer. He was active in Rome before transferring his business to Bologna in 1638. He apparently published no music himself, but the 'Eredi di Evangelista Dozza', namely Carlo Manolesi and Pietro Dozza, probably Dozza's son, issued music during 1663 and 1664, concentrating on Cazzati's work. They also published Cazzati's reply to a critical attack on his music made by Arresti. The firm's usual mark was a pine cone in an elaborate frame.

F. Vatielli: 'Editori musicali dei secoli XVII e XVIII', *Arte e vita musicale a Bologna* (Bologna, 1927/R1969), 239; L. Gottardi: *La stampa musicale in Bologna dagli inizi fino al 1700* (diss., U. of Bologna, 1951); Sartori (1958)

A.S. (ii)

Dreher [Dreherr], **Rudolph** (*b* c1611; *d* Kempten, 28 Oct 1681). German printer and publisher. He was in charge of the press built in 1660 at the princely abbey of Kempten, but also printed on his own account works including A. Kircher's *Phonurgia nova* (1673). His music editions contain sacred music by local composers and others. In the early years the court trumpeter David Hautt worked at his firm as a typefounder; Hautt later printed song collections by Laurentius von Schnüffis in Konstanz.

A. Layer: *Musikgeschichte der Fürstabtei Kempten* (Kempten, 1975), 26

H.S.

Drei Masken Verlag. German firm of publishers. It was founded on 24 November 1910 in Munich by the composer Ludwig Friedman. In 1912 it moved to Berlin, and was taken over in 1930 by Victor Alberti and A. L. Robinson, except for the literature department, which had returned to Munich in 1920. Among the musicological works published by the Munich branch were *Musikalische Stundenbücher*, H. W. von Waltershausen's *Musikalische Stillehre in Einzeldarstellungen*, Guido Adler's *Richard Wagner*, the *Sammelbände für vergleichende Musikwissenschaft* (ed. Stumpf and Hornbostel), the first two volumes of the *Mozart-Jahrbuch* (ed. H. Abert), A. Sandberger's *Ausgewählte Aufsätze zur Musikgeschichte* and *Faksimiledrücke berühmter Musiker-Handschriften*.

The Berlin branch published mainly operas, operettas and ballets as well as dance, popular and film music. Opera and ballet composers published by the firm included Eugen d'Albert, Walter Courvoisier, Friedrich Klose, Franz Schmidt and H. W. von Waltershausen; light music was represented by works of Leo Blech, Leo Fall, Jean Gilbert, Emerich Kálmán, Walter Kollo, Eduard Künnecke, Robert Stolz and Oscar Straus. After the firm's liquidation in 1934 on racial grounds, the Dreiklang-Verlag took over the Drei Masken Verlag and its affiliated firms. During World War II the name Dreiklang- Dreimasken Bühnen- und Musikverlag was introduced. After the loss of the Berlin premises in 1943 due to war damage, the firm re-established itself in Wiesbaden on 1 January 1949; on 1 July 1957 it moved to Munich. The business is now part of an important publishing group which includes the UFA Music Press, the Wiener Bohème Press and the Ufaton Press (all based in Munich). There is still a separate firm in Munich under the name Drei Masken Verlag which publishes plays.

W. Altmann: *Kurzgefasstes Tonkünstler-Lexikon* (Regensburg, 14/1936); J. Petschull: *Musikverlage in der Bundesrepublik Deutschland und in West-Berlin* (Bonn, 1965)

E.K.

Dubois, William (*d* ?1854). American publisher. His name appears in New York City directories as piano manufacturer and music dealer from 1813. He purchased the plates of John Paff in 1817 and began to issue several of Paff's publications under his own name. In 1821 Dubois went into partnership with William Stodart, who had previously operated in Richmond; George Bacon replaced Stodart in 1835. Dubois ceased to publish in about 1841, but continued to sell music and pianos until 1854. His catalogue was devoted mostly to music from the New York theatre.

B.T.

Du Bosc, (Guillaume) Simon (*b* Rouen; *d* Geneva, 1556–7). French printer. A Simon Du Bosc, possibly identifiable with the music printer, though called a Parisian, first printed at Alençon between 1529 and 1534. He seems to have been in Paris before that time and was also there in 1534; at the end of that year he was listed as a heretic. Guillaume Simon Du Bosc appears in Geneva, where a heretic would reasonably have gone, in 1553; in that year or the next

he was joined by Guillaume Guéroult, a relative, in partnership. Between that year and 1556, when Guéroult appears to have left for Lyons, they printed at least 12 volumes of music, some of which are lost; they include collections of motets by Clemens non Papa, Crecquillon, Gombert, Goudimel, Sermisy and others, and a book of psalm settings. Du Bosc also printed on his own account, though not music. It has been suggested that he was the printer, while Guéroult acted as the financial partner and, probably, music editor.

G. Lepreux: *Gallia typographica*, iii (Paris, 1912); P. Chaix: *Recherches sur l'imprimerie à Genève de 1550 à 1564* (Geneva, 1954); P. Chaix, A. Dufour and G. Moechli: 'Les livres imprimés à Genève de 1550 à 1600', *Genava*, new ser., vii (1959), 235–394 [inc. list]; P. Pidoux: *Le psautier huguenot du XVIe siècle* (Basle, 1962–9)

S.B.(iii)

Du Boys, Michel (*fl* 1537-61). French type designer, printer and bookseller. He was active in Geneva, 1537–41, in Lyons, *c*1542–57, and again in Geneva, 1558–61. A Protestant and friend of Calvin from his first period in Geneva, he later became printer to the two great Protestant booksellers in Lyons, Jean Frellon and Antoine Vincent. During this time he printed eight works under his own name of which three contained pieces by the Lyons composer Philibert Jambe de Fer. On his return to Geneva, he printed the Huguenot psalter including the sol-fa method of Pierre Davantes, and two books of Latin motets.

R. Peter: 'Un imprimeur de Calvin: Michel Du Boys', *Bulletin de la Société d'histoire et d'archéologie de Genève*, xvi (1978), 285–335; L. Guillo: *Recherches sur les éditions musicales lyonnaises de la Renaissance* (diss., Ecole Pratique des Hautes Etudes, Paris, 1986)

L.G.

Du Chemin [Chemyn], **Nicolas** (*b* Sens, *c*1515; *d* Paris, 1576). Parisian printer. His active music printing career lasted from 1549 to 1568. He later printed one music book in 1570, two books of theory in 1571 and a single music book in 1576. He thus occupied an important position between Attaingnant, whose last music book under his own name was issued in 1550, and Le Roy & Ballard, who began a long career as royal printers of music in 1551.

Du Chemin was an engraver by trade (some music types in an inventory of Guillaume Le Bé are attributed to him) and was also described as a bookseller in a document dated November 1540. He issued his first printed book in 1541. In 1543 he moved to the rue St-Jacques-de-

Latran under the 'enseigne du Gryphon d'argent', the address from which he issued music as well as many non-musical books (on medicine, grammar, arithmetic, law and Latin literature) to the end of his career. In November 1545 he married Catherine Delahaye, ward of the printer Poncet le Preux, who was Attaingnant's brother-in-law – a circumstance that undoubtedly helped turn his attention towards music printing. He purchased punches and matrices for music from Pierre Haultin on 19 February 1547 and on 7 November 1548 received a royal privilege 'to print all new music that has not been printed before' for a period of six years from the date of his first publication. The first collection, *Premier livre contenant xxviii pseaulmes de David*, came out in 1549. The royal privilege was renewed in 1555 for ten years and again in 1566 for another six.

Du Chemin engaged musicians to supply the expertise he lacked for editing music. In a contract dated 1 October 1548 he asked Nicole Regnes to sell him four collections of his compositions, which he would print 'in the manner and of the size of those which Pierre Attaingnant has printed'; to teach him 'the art of music and . . . to sing and hold his part'; and to 'review and correct well and devotedly . . . the other books of music which said du Chemyn wants to print or have printed for him'. For this Regnes was to receive a monthly salary and his room and board. The compositions were never printed, but Regnes stayed on in his capacity as editor until 1551. Between 1551 and 1555 Du Chemin had similar assistance from Claude Goudimel, who at first was still a student at the university. From the title-pages we know that Loys Bisson acted in the same capacity between 1561 and 1567, and Henry Chandor is named as editor of the single book published in 1576.

If Regnes helped launch the music printing activity, it was under Goudimel's editorship that the house achieved its greatest success. Du Chemin was the first to print the music of Goudimel and Costeley. New and older works by Clereau, Colin, Manchicourt, Cadéac, Guyon and Janequin are also well represented in the output of this period. After the backlog of work prepared by Goudimel was exhausted, and at a time when the firm of Le Roy & Ballard was beginning to dominate the music publishing trade in Paris, Du Chemin turned more towards new and unknown composers such as Cartier, Morel, Bersoy, Besancourt and A. de Villars. One innovative event of his later career was the publication of the beautifully printed *Liber*

primus missarum Francisco Guerrero in 1566.

The approximately 100 music books contain 693 secular songs, 178 psalms and *chansons spirituelles*, 73 motets and 41 masses. The instrumental music published includes one book for lute by J. Belin (1556) and four *livres de danseries* (1559–64). Du Chemin printed two books of music theory in 1571.

P.-S. Fournier: *Traité historique et critique sur l'origine et les progrès des caractères de fonte pour l'impression de la musique* (Berne, 1765); P. Renouard: *Imprimeurs parisiens . . . jusqu'à la fin du XVIê siècle* (Paris, 1898); F. Lesure and G. Thibault: 'Bibliographie des éditions musicales publiées par Nicolas du Chemin (1549–1576)', *AnnM*, i (1953), 269–373, iv (1956), 251, vi (1958–63), 403; F. Lesure: 'Du Chemin, Nicolas', *MGG*; D. Heartz: *Pierre Attaingnant, Royal Printer of Music* (Berkeley and Los Angeles, 1969), 164

S.F.P.

Du Pré [de Pratis, a Prato], **Jean (Larcher)** (*fl* 1481–1504). Printer, active in Paris. First associated with Didier Huyn in 1481, he became a *libraire juré* for the University of Paris in 1497. He is credited with printing the earliest illustrated books in Paris, but is best known for his small books of hours with elaborate borders, made for Antoine Verard. Du Pré printed at least 20 missals with elaborate figures and borders: four with notes and staves, eight with staves, six with space for manuscript music and one without space for music. He also worked at Abbeville and Chartres.

A. Claudin: *Histoire de l'imprimerie en France* (Paris, 1900–05); K. Meyer-Baer: *Liturgical Music Incunabula: a Descriptive Catalogue* (London, 1962)

M.K.D.

Durand. French firm of publishers.

1. HISTORY. The firm was founded as Durand Schoenewerk & Cie on 30 December 1869 and that same day bought the catalogue of Gustave-Alexandre Flaxland as well as his premises at 4 place de la Madeleine, Paris. Schoenewerk withdrew from the business on 19 November 1891, and his co-founder Marie Auguste Durand (*b* Paris, 18 July 1830; *d* Paris, 31 May 1909) reorganized the firm the next day as A. Durand & Fils, in partnership with his son Jacques Massacrie Durand (*b* Paris, 22 Feb 1865; *d* Bel-Ebat, nr. Fontainebleau, 22 Aug 1928). Jacques Durand succeeded his father, and taking as partner his cousin Gaston Choisnel (*d* 9 June 1921), renamed the firm Durand & Cie on 23 December 1909. Another cousin, René Dommange, joined the firm in July 1920 and became a partner on 28 April 1921. At Jacques

Durand's death, his widow (*d* 1958) became a partner; subsequent partners have been Maquaire (1937–44), Adrien Raveau (from 1944) , Mme René Dommange and Marcel and Jean Dommange (from 1959). The company became a 'société à responsabilité limitée' from 19 June 1947. Guy Kaufmann (*b* Neuchâtel, 12 May 1923) was appointed general director in 1972. The firm continued to operate from its original premises until 1980, when it moved to 21 rue Vernet; early in 1987 the firm moved to 215 rue du Faubourg St-Honoré.

Auguste Durand, who was a classmate of Franck and Saint-Saëns at the Paris Conservatoire, studied the organ under Benoît and was organist at St Ambroise, Ste Geneviève, St Roch and St Vincent de Paul. He was also a music critic and a successful composer. His compositions include sacred and secular vocal music and many works for the piano and organ; he also had a particular liking for the harmonium, for which he composed, arranged and published extensively.

Jacques Durand also studied at the Conservatoire, where he developed lasting friendships with Dukas and Debussy. He studied harmony with Dubois and composition with Guiraud. Besides being a prolific composer, he edited and transcribed quantities of works by others. His writings include *Eléments d'harmonie* (1919); *Cours professionel á l'usage des employés de commerce de la musique* (i: *Edition musicale, historique et technique*, ii: *Abrégé de l'histoire de la musique*, both 1923); *Quelques souvenirs d'un éditeur de musique* (1924–5); and *Lettres de Claude Debussy à son éditeur* (1927).

2. PUBLICATIONS. Durand's plate numbers are, in general, reliably chronological. By 1875, after six years of publishing activity, the series of plate numbers had exceeded 2100; by 1890 the catalogue had grown to more than 4000 items, passing 6100 in 1902, 7000 in 1908, 9000 in 1915, 10,600 in 1924, 12,100 in 1932 and 15,000 in 1985.

The first major composer to be published regularly by Durand Schoenewerk & Cie was Saint-Saëns: the firm issued *Samson et Dalila* (1877), *Danse macabre* (1875) and the Third Symphony (1886), along with almost all the remainder of his mature output. *Le carnaval des animaux* was published in its complete form by Durand in 1922, after the ban imposed by the composer on performance or publication was revoked on his death in 1921. Durand Schoenewerk & Cie first published a work by Debussy in October 1884 (the piano-vocal score of *L'enfant prodigue*). In 1894 the firm issued the String Quartet and in 1903 composer and pub-

lisher began a close relationship which was to last until Debussy's death. A succession of masterpieces emerged: *La mer* (1905; see illustration), the *Préludes* (book 1, 1910; book 2, 1913), *Jeux* (piano reduction, 1912; full score, 1914), *En blanc et noir* (1915), the *Etudes* (1916) and the three sonatas (1915–17) among many others, including some works (notably *Pelléas et Mélisande*) acquired from other publishers. Ravel's *Sonatine* was published by Durand in 1905; thereafter almost all the composer's major works were issued by the firm, including *Daphnis et Chloé* (piano score, *c*1912; full score, 1913). *L'heure espagnole* (piano-vocal score, 1908; full score, 1911), *L'enfant et les sortilèges* (1925), and *Boléro* (1929), along with new editions of works acquired from other publishers, including the String Quartet and *Shéhérazade*.

Durand's pre-eminent position in French music publishing is emphasized by the other composers whose music was issued by the firm, among them Dukas, Roussel, Fauré, Schmitt, Falla, Aubert, Widor, Büsser, Milhaud, Poulenc, d'Indy (including his famous *Cours de composition musicale*), Ibert, Auric, Jolivet, Koechlin and Duruflé. In June 1931 Durand published Messiaen's Preludes for piano and subsequently issued a number of his important early works, including *Poèmes pour Mi* (1937), *Chants de terre et de ciel* (1939), *Quatuor pour la fin du temps* (1942), *Visions de l'amen* (1946), *Vingt regards sur l'enfant Jésus* (1947), *Trois petites liturgies de la Présence Divine* (1952) and the *Turangalîla-symphonie* (composed 1948, published 1953).

In 1894 Durand began to publish the collected works of Rameau, with Saint-Saëns as general editor. This monumental undertaking comprised 18 volumes by 1924 but has never been completed. In 1914 the firm embarked on the enormous series known as *Edition classique Durand & Fils*, an edition of the standard classics which was intended to have a strong French identity and be a commercially viable rival to similar editions of Peters and Breitkopf & Härtel. Principal editors were Saint-Saëns (piano works of Mozart), Fauré (piano works of Schumann), d'Indy, Debussy (complete works of Chopin), Ravel (piano works of Mendelssohn), Roussel (chamber works of Mendelssohn), Dukas, Schmitt, Ropartz, Diémer (*Les clavecinistes français*), Philipp (*Les clavecinistes allemands* and *L'école moderne du piano*), Guilmant (*Archives des maîtres de l'orgue*), Samazeuilh and Rhené-Baton. Support of French contemporary music was demonstrated by the series of Concerts Durand for new chamber music, produced by Jacques Durand from

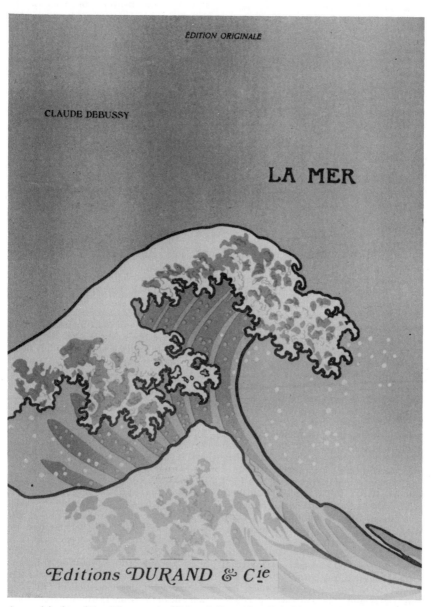

Cover of the first edition (piano score) of Debussy's 'La mer', published by Durand & Cie in 1905

1910 to 1913, and the biennial cash prize for the best French symphonic composition, which the firm instituted in 1927.

J. Durand: 'L'édition musicale', *Encyclopédie de la musique et dictionnaire du Conservatoire*, pt. 2/6 (Paris, 1931), 3334; *1869/1969: Livre du centenaire des Editions Durand & Cie* (Paris, 1969); A. Orenstein: 'Scorography: the Music of Ravel', *Musical Newsletter*, v (1975), 10; Devriès and Lesure (1979–88)

R.S.N./N.S.

Du Ry, Antoine (*fl* Lyons, 1515–34). French printer. He worked almost exclusively for the large booksellers (notably Simon Vincent and Jacques Giunta). He was probably the printer of the first musical works to be produced in Lyons, a series of motet books by Francesco de Layolle, a Florentine musician in exile in Lyons. Of these books only a fragment survives; preserved in the British Library, it can be dated to 1525. The series was engraved in wood according to the techniques of Andrea Antico, and was probably printed for Jacques Giunta. It preceded Attaingnant's Parisian publications and those of Jacques Moderne in Lyons.

L. Guillo: *Recherches sur les éditions musicales lyonnaises de la Renaissance* (diss., Ecole Pratique des Hautes Etudes, Paris, 1986)

L.G.

E

East [Easte, Este], **Thomas** (*d* London, 1608). English printer and publisher, active in London. There is no evidence to support the theory that one of the variant spellings of his name, 'Este', might indicate Italian origin. He was made free of the Company of Stationers in 1565, but during the early part of his career he was not particularly prosperous. He was one of those who signed 'The complaynt of the poor printers', a list of grievances sent to Lord Burghley in about 1577, protesting against the number of printing monopolies. He acquired a fount of music·on the death of Vautrollier and printed a work under the music printing monopoly that had been granted by Queen Elizabeth I to Tallis and Byrd in 1575. The monopoly had fallen into disuse through the commercial failure of *Cantiones sacrae* (1575), but East's 1588 volume, Byrd's *Psalmes, Sonets and Songs* apparently had an immediate success (see illustration). Byrd thought highly of East's work; the volume was reprinted the following year, and from then until his death East flourished as a music printer (he also continued to print non-musical material) and printed most of the music of Byrd and Morley, as well as *Musica transalpina* (1588 and 1597) and *The Triumphes of Oriana* (1601). In 1600 he printed John Dowland's *The Second Booke of Songs or Ayres*, and later Francis Pilkington's *The First Booke of Songs or Ayres* (1605) and John Danyel's *Songs for the Lute Viol and Voice* (1606). In 1598 he printed Lassus's *Novae cantiones*, the first Italian music by one composer printed in England, and he appears to have had plans to export English music to Italy, for in 1595 he printed two editions of Morley's five-part balletts, one in English, *The First Booke of Balletts to Five Voyces*, and the other in Italian, *Il primo libro delle ballette a cinque voci*. No evidence survives to indicate whether the venture was successful, but there is no comparable instance in East's or any other contemporary music printer's output. In 1592 East produced a version of the English metrical Psalter, entitled *The Whole Booke of Psalmes, with their Wonted Tunes, as they are Sung in Churches*, which includes settings by Giles Farnaby, Richard Alison, Michael Cavendish and John Dowland; East wrote the preface and dedication himself. It ran into two further editions during his lifetime and four after his death; after Thomas Ravenscroft's edition of it in 1611, 'newly corrected and enlarged', it became known as Ravenscroft's Psalter.

East's success was hard-won: he was continually bedevilled with lawsuits and for most of his career was obliged to work as someone else's 'assigne', a system which must certainly have cut into his profits and not offset his losses. When Morley renewed the music printing monopoly in 1598, East was one of the printers who suffered, and it was over a year before he could print music again. The monopoly was resurrected by William Barley in 1606, on the grounds that he had been Morley's business partner, and the terms under which the resulting lawsuit was settled were hardly favourable to East. In 1606 he was in dispute with

CONTRA TENOR.

Pſalmes,Sonets,& ſongs of ſadnes and pietie, made into Muſicke of fiue parts : whereof, ſome of them going abroade among diuers, in vntrue coppies, are heere truely corrected,and th'other being Songs very rare and newly compoſed,are heere publiſhed,for the recreation of all ſuch as delight in Muſicke : By *William Byrd,* one of the Gent.of the Queenes Maieſties honorable Chappell.

Printed by Thomas Eaſt, the aſſigne of VV. Byrd, and are to be ſold at the dwelling houſe of the ſaid T.Eaſt, by Paules wharfe. 1588. *Cum priuilegio Regiæ Maieſtatis.*

Title-page of Byrd's 'Psalmes, Sonets and Songs' (1588), printed and published by Thomas East

George Eastland, the publisher of John Dowland's *The Second Booke of Songs*, and the resulting lawsuit lasted for two years before the case against him was dismissed.

East was the leading music printer of his day, and may be considered the father of English music printing. He took a serious risk in printing music when the market was very uncertain, and he clearly was not easily discouraged by the vicissitudes of a music printer's life. He possessed two founts of music type and one of tablature type, together with a group of distinctive ornaments; one of these, a black horse with a crescent on the shoulder, is a pun on his address, 'Aldersgate street at the sign of the Blacke Horse', where all his music was printed. At his death his business passed to Thomas Snodham, his adopted son. He was generally supposed to have been related to Michael East, but his will (in the Gresham College Collection, Guildhall Library, London) makes no mention of him.

For another illustration *see* p.488.

E. Arber: *A Transcript of the Register of the Company of Stationers of London* (London, 1875–7, 1894); H. G. Aldis: *A Dictionary of Printers and Booksellers in England, Scotland and Ireland . . . 1557–1640* (London, 1910); M. Dowling: 'The Printing of John Dowland's Second Booke of Ayres', *The Library*, 4th ser., xii (1932), 365; Humphries and Smith (1954, 2/1970); W. A. Jackson: *Records of the Court of the Stationers' Company 1602–1640* (London, 1957); Krummel (1975); I. Fenlon and J. Milsom: ' "Ruled Paper Imprinted": Music Paper and Patents in Sixteenth-century England', *JAMS*, xxvii (1984), 139; R. Illing: 'Barley's Pocket Edition of East's Metrical Psalter', *ML*, xlix (1968), 219

M.M.

Edelmann. Cuban publishers. Jean-Frédéric Edelmann (*b* Strasbourg, 17 Feb 1795; *d* 1848) – named after his father, the composer and teacher of Méhul, who was guillotined in 1794 – settled in Havana in 1832. As Juan Federico Edelmann, he became a prominent piano teacher and director of the Sociedad Filharmónica de Santa Cecilia. From his music shop, at Calle de la Obra-pia 23, he also published operatic arrangements and Creole works. His sons Federico and Carlos operated the firm after 1848, also working as impresarios, becoming Louis Moreau Gottschalk's managers in 1854.

R. Benton: 'Jean-Frédéric Edelmann [père], a Musical Victim of the French Revolution', *MQ*, 1 (1964), 165; A. Carpentier: *La música en Cuba* (Mexico City, 1972)

M.D.M.

Eder, Joseph. Austrian firm of publishers. It was founded by Joseph Eder (*b* Vienna, 26 July 1760; *d* Vienna, 17 Feb 1835), who originally sold fancy goods and cheap engravings by the Prague publisher Balzer in the provinces. He later became a partner in the Vienna branch of Balzer's firm, and in 1789 its proprietor. On 16 September he opened a fine art and copper-engraving shop in the Trattnerhof, Vienna, which moved from there to the house 'Zum Goldenen Krone' in the Graben on 20 June 1792. With his first music prospectus on 19 April 1794, Eder began a series of isolated attempts at publishing, which gained considerable impetus when Ignaz Sauer became a partner (of Joseph Eder & Comp.) on 2 November 1796; the partnership ended in January 1798, when Sauer founded his own music publishing firm, Zu den Sieben Schwestern. Eder's brisk publishing activity is demonstrated by the fact that 511 works had appeared by 1808; the disturbances of war in 1809 and 1814, however, caused a standstill.

Eder's daughter married Jeremias Bermann (*b* 1770; *d* 2 Jan 1855), and Eder took his son-in-law into the firm in 1811 (from 25 April 1812 the firm was once again known as Joseph Eder & Comp.). At the time of the Vienna Congress (1815) numerous works appeared in joint publication with the Vienna firms Steiner, G. Cappi, Mollo, Mechetti, Maisch, Weigl and Traeg. When Eder retired in 1817 Bermann took over the business, adopting the name Besitzer der Joseph Ederschen Kunst- und Musikalienhandlung. The firm had been stagnating since 1816; despite a revival of activity that can probably be attributed to Joseph Czerný's collaboration, from 1828 it issued printed music only sporadically. In that year Jeremias Bermann took on his son Joseph Bermann as an investing partner, which legal position was recorded when the firm was renamed Bermann & Son. The firm had become unimportant as a music publisher, and on 19 October 1847 Jeremias Bermann returned his licence (Joseph Bermann had obtained a licence for a music business on 11 August 1847).

The firm's output consisted mainly of compositions by minor masters resident in Vienna as well as occasional arrangements of works by Haydn and Mozart; the only original edition is Beethoven's op.10. Beethoven's 'Pathétique' Sonata and the variations on *Tandeln und Scherzen* were taken over from F. A. Hoffmeister, and *Das Gluck der Freundschaft* op.88 from H. Löschenkohl.) J. B. Vanhal is represented by 60 works from his late period.

C. von Wurzbach: *Biographisches Lexikon des Kaiserthums Oesterreich* (Vienna, 1856–91); Deutsch

(1946); A. Weinmann: *Verzeichnis der Musikalien des Verlages Joseph Eder–Jeremias Bermann* (Vienna, 1968)

A.W.

Editio Musica Budapest [EMB]. Hungarian firm of publishers. It was founded on 1 July 1950 as the successor to the Hungarian music publishing companies Rózsavölgyi és Társa, Rozsnyai, Kálmán Nádor, Ferenc Bárd, Magyar Kórus and Imre Cserépfalvi. EMB is now the only music publishing firm in Hungary, in accordance with the socialist re-organization of economic life.

The first publication was Book 1 of Bartók's *Gyermekeknek* ('For children'), which represented the guiding principle of the enterprise: 'to serve Hungarian music, particularly music for the training of musicians and the education of the common man wishing to improve and advance his or her knowledge'. The first managing director, László Korvin, and the artistic director, András Rékai, had to rely on 'outworkers' for editorial and similar work; but in 1953 the firm acquired its own printing works and thus was able to make long-term plans and cooperate with music publishing companies outside Hungary. In 1955 Béla Tardos, a professional pianist and composer, was appointed director; he organized the editorial side into two separate departments, one for music and another for music literature, and encouraged the employment of professional musicians with practical ability and theoretical knowledge. From the 1960s connections were established with similar undertakings abroad, and in 1961 László Eösze was appointed deputy director and artistic manager. After the death of Béla Tardos (1967) László Sarlós was appointed director until his retirement in 1986, when the musicologist István Homolya succeeded to the post.

EMB's publications so far amount to around 13,000 items; 5000 are continually available. It publishes annually between 160 and 180 new editions, of which between 60 and 80 are works by contemporary Hungarian composers. Important series include the new collected edition of works by Liszt, a critical edition of the complete lute works of Valentine Bakfark, Urtext editions of works by Bach, Beethoven, Corelli, Handel and Scarlatti, miniature scores, series of piano music and violin music, *Orpheus* (music for plucked instruments), *Musica per la tastiera* (16th- and 17th-century keyboard music) and *Early Chamber Music*.

EMB has arrangements abroad with Boosey & Hawkes (London, New York, Bonn, Ontario and Artarmon, Australia), Edition Kunzelmann (Zurich), Universal (Vienna), Leduc (Paris), Ricordi (Milan), Broekmans and von Poppel (Amsterdam), Real Musical (Madrid) and Buffet Crampon (Tokyo).

M. Feuer: 'Mit teszünk mai zenénk hirnevéért?', *Muzsika*, xxi (1978), 1

J.S.W./P.M. (i)

Editions Russes de Musique. Russian publishing firm. It was founded in 1909 by Sergey Koussevitzky and his wife Natalya with the aim of subsidizing the propagation of new Russian music. Any losses were borne by the Koussevitzkys, and all profits accrued to the composers. The venture was highly successful, both artistically and financially. To ensure copyright protection the firm was first legally established in Berlin as the Russischer Musikverlag, with offices in Moscow and St Petersburg, and later in Paris, London, New York and Leipzig. The main office was moved to Paris in 1920. Originally, to ensure artistic integrity, selection of works was determined by majority vote of a jury composed of Skryabin, Rakhmaninov, Metner, Ossovsky, Struve and Koussevitzky. However, their rejection of Stravinsky's *Petrushka* was reversed when Koussevitzky threatened to withdraw from the jury. Such conflicts were obviated when, in 1914, Koussevitzky purchased the firm of A. Gutheil, which became an autonomous branch of Editions Russes under his control. Gutheil's catalogue, begun in Moscow in 1859, already contained important works by Prokofiev and Rakhmaninov, and, at a purchase price of 300,000 rubles, it also included valuable unpublished manuscripts by Glinka, Dargomïzhsky and others. From its beginning, Editions Russes offered substantial advanced and profit sharing both to promising young Russian composers and established Russian masters. These circumstances, combined with artistic foresight, accrued significant benefits to the composers, the firm and the art. Among the most noteworthy publications are Skryabin's *Prometheus* (1911, with a striking pictorial title-page by Jean Delville), Stravinsky's *Petrushka* (1912), *The Rite of Spring* (piano duet, 1913; full score, 1921), *Oedipus Rex* (1927) and *Symphony of Psalms* (piano-vocal score, 1930; full score, 1932), as well as works by Metner, Prokofiev, Rakhmaninov and Taneyev. Other composers well represented include Arensky, Balakirev, Berezovsky, Catoire, Konyus, Vernon Duke, Grechaninov, Lopatnikov, Nabokov and Ziloti. The firm also published Rimsky-Korsakov's *Principles of*

Orchestration (1913; French trans., 1914, German and English trans., 1922) and Ravel's orchestration of *Pictures at an Exhibition* (1929), which was commissioned by Koussevitzky. On 1 March 1947 the catalogue of Editions Russes de Musique was purchased by Boosey & Hawkes.

R.S.N./N.S.

Egenolff, Christian (*b* Hadamar, 26 July 1502; *d* Frankfurt am Main, 9 Feb 1555). German printer. He enrolled as a student at the University of Mainz in 1516, probably remaining there until 1519. In 1528 he established a printing business in Strasbourg. In 1530 he moved to Frankfurt am Main, where he was accepted as a citizen in the same year and began printing in 1530 or 1531. During the years 1538–43 he also maintained a subsidiary firm in Marburg where he was official university printer. He soon left this branch in the hands of his assistant, Andreas Kolbe, and returned to Frankfurt. After his death the firm was continued by his widow Margarethe until 1572, when she divided it among his heirs, who continued publishing under the name Egenolff until 1605.

Egenolff was the first printer of any importance in the city of Frankfurt, which was to become one of the main centres of the trade in the later 16th century. His production of about 500 works was large for this time; it included works in a great variety of fields such as medicine, science, history and the classics. His music publications, though a very small part of the total output, reflect his close ties to the humanistic movement and to the leaders of the Reformation. The earlier edition of Horatian odes (1532) was dedicated to Gerardus Noviomagus and the second (1551[17]) was compiled by Petrus Nigidius, both prominent teachers in Marburg. Egenolff's most valuable contribution to music lies in the various collections of secular songs. Many of the circumstances surrounding their origin and publication remain obscure. Unlike earlier song collections such as those printed by Oeglin, Schoeffer and Arnt von Aich, they are not connected with the repertory of a particular court. Egenolff apparently compiled and edited them himself, contrary to the practice of the contemporary Nuremberg publishers Forster and Ott. In spite of or perhaps because of their great popularity, virtually none of Egenolff's collections has been preserved intact. Generally entire partbooks are missing, and in some cases only a single partbook remains. Since the title, printer's mark, date of publication and complete text

were generally included only in the tenor partbook, its frequent loss has been particularly unfortunate. Although these publications can be traced to Egenolff by a comparison of the type-forms and woodcuts used, their titles can no longer be determined, and dates remain a subject of speculation often leading to controversy. On the basis of watermarks Bridgman considered that the three Paris discant books (*c*1535[14]) were published between 1532 and 1535, whereas Müller and Berz placed them after 1536. A possible criterion for chronology may be found in Egenolff's use of two very different arrangements of the song texts. In the two collections dated 1535, *Gassenhawerlin* (1535[10]) and *Reutterliedlin* (1535[11]), a text incipit is included with the music in each partbook and the complete text is written below the melody only in the tenor voice. The Paris books, which have text incipits, may also fall within this category. In the remaining collections each voice is underlaid with the first strophe. Since this group includes second editions of works first published in 1535 and 1536, it must be later.

Egenolff was the first German printer to employ the single-impression technique developed by Attaingnant and is noted also for his frequent use of woodcuts for illustrations and initials, particularly in the song collections. Although modern scholars have tended to compare the quality of his work unfavourably with that of his Nuremberg contemporaries, Formschneider and Petreius, there can be no doubt as to the success and influence of his musical publications.

H. Grotefend: *Christian Egenolff, der erste ständige Buchdrucker zu Frankfurt am Main und seine Vorläufer* (Frankfurt am Main, 1881); R. von Liliencron: 'Die horazischen Metren in deutschen Kompositionen des 16. Jahrhunderts', *VMw*, iii (1887), 26–91; D. C. McMurtrie: 'Types and Typefounding in Germany: the Work of Christian Egenolff and his Successors in the Development of the Luther Foundry', *Inland Printer* (July 1924/*R*1932 as a pamphlet); H. J. Moser: Introduction to facs. repr. of *Gassenhawer* (Augsburg and Cologne, 1927/*R*1970); K. Gudewill: 'Egenolff, Christian', *MGG*; J. Benzing: 'Christian Egenolff zu Strassburg und seine Drucke (1528 bis 1530)', *Das Antiquariat*, x (1954), 88, 92; idem: 'Die Drucke Christian Egenolffs zu Frankfurt am Main vom Ende 1530 bis 1555', *Das Antiquariat*, xi (1955), 139, 162, 201, 232 [this together with Benzing's 1954 article contains a complete list of his works]; N. Bridgman: 'Christian Egenolff, imprimeur de musique', *AnnM*, iii (1955), 77–177; Benzing (1963, 2/1982); H. C. Müller: *Die Liederdrucke Christian Egenolffs* (diss., U. of Kiel, 1964); M. Staehelin: 'Zum Egenolff–Diskantband der Bibliothèque Nationale in Paris', *AMw*, xxiii (1966), 93; E. L. Berz: *Die Notendrucker und ihre Verleger in Frankfurt am Main von den Anfängen* *bis etwa 1630*, CaM, v (1970); M.L. Göllner: 'Egenolff, Christian', *Grove6* [incl. selective list of publications]

M.L.G.

Eichorn, Johann (*b* Nuremberg, 1524; *d* Frankfurt an der Oder, 21 Aug 1583). German printer and book dealer. He probably learnt the printing trade in his native city, and he entered the University of Frankfurt an der Oder in 1547. Two years later he took over Nicolaus Wolrab's printing press and within a few years it became one of the main publishing houses in eastern Germany. He soon became official printer for the university and was made a member of the city council in 1570. On 31 October 1577 he requested and was granted the protection of Maximilian II's imperial patent. A subsidiary firm, founded by Eichorn in Stettin in 1568–9, was given to his son-in-law, Andreas Kellner (*d* 1591) in 1572. The main business was taken over in 1581 by Eichorn's son Andreas (*b* Frankfurt an der Oder, 17 Sept 1553; *d* Frankfurt, 21 Nov 1615), who had served his apprenticeship under Sigismund Feyerabend in Frankfurt am Main, and in 1615 by Andreas's son, Johann (*b* Frankfurt an der Oder, *c*1585; *d* Frankfurt, 1642), who had begun signing publications as early as 1606. Andreas compiled a publisher's list in 1606 containing 119 different items including music.

As university printer Johann Eichorn received the active support of the influential humanist Jodocus Willich, and was largely responsible for the growing importance of Frankfurt an der Oder in the international book market. By the late 16th century the city, with its three annual book fairs which attracted printers and book dealers from all over Germany, had become the main trading centre for eastern Europe. Although he printed books on a wide variety of subjects including local history, classical literature and theology, many of them decorated with woodcuts by the prominent artist Frantz Friderich, Eichorn's main contribution was in the publication of music. By 1617 the firm had brought out more than 90 works in this field, including such divergent collections as the widely used Protestant hymnbook of 1552, *Geistliche Lieder D. Martini Lutheri*, with its many subsequent editions, and lute tablatures of Waissel, Kargel and Drusina. Since he concentrated mainly on the works of local composers, Eichorn also published a great many compositions written for local special occasions (weddings, funerals, university ceremonies, etc) as well as a variety of school plays, some of which included

music. Both his son and grandson continued the business along much the same lines, relinquishing the lead, particularly in music, to the newly founded firm of Hartmann in about 1600.

P. Wackernagel: *Bibliographie zur Geschichte des deutschen Kirchenliedes im XVI. Jahrhundert* (Frankfurt am Main, 1855/*R*1961); E. Bohn: *Bibliographie der Musik-Druckwerke bis 1700 . . . zu Breslau* (Berlin, 1883/*R*1969); E. Consentius: 'Von Druckkosten, Taxen und Privilegien im Kurstaat Brandenburg während des 16. und 17. Jahrhunderts', *Forschungen zur Brandenburgischen und Preussischen Geschichte*, xxxiv (1922), 175–215 [incl. A. Eichorn's publisher's list]; W. Bake: *Die Frühzeit des pommerschen Buchdrucks* (Pyritz, 1934), 170 [incl. list of Kellner's publications]; H. P. Kosack: *Geschichte der Laute und Lautenmusik in Preussen*, Königsberger Studien zur Musikwissenschaft, xvii (Kassel, 1935); W. Maushake: *Frankfurt an der Oder als Druckerstadt* (Frankfurt an der Oder, 1936); J. Benzing: 'Der Buchdruck in Frankfurt (Oder) von 1530–1550 (Johann Hanau und Nikolaus Wolrab)', *Gutenberg-Jb 1937*, 131; H. Grimm: *Von den Drucker-Zeichen des 1549 bis 1581 in Frankfurt a.d.O. tätigen Universitätsbuchdruckers Johann Eichorn* (Frankfurt an der Oder, 1939); idem: *Meister der Renaissancemusik an der Viadrina* (Frankfurt an der Oder, 1942); A. Adrio: 'Dulichius, Philipp', *MGG*; W. Boetticher: 'Eichorn, Johann', *MGG*; H. Grimm: 'Der Medailleur, Holzschneider und Kupferstecher Frantz Friderich', *Gutenberg-Jb 1956, 205 1959*, 177; Benzing (1963, 2/1982); Brown (1965); M. L. Göllner: 'Eichorn, Johann', *Grove6* [incl. selective list of publications]

M.L.G.

Elkan, Henri (*b* Antwerp, 23 Nov 1897; *d* Philadelphia, 12 June 1980). American publisher and conductor of Belgian birth. He was trained at the Antwerp and Amsterdam conservatories, and played the violin in the Concertgebouw Orchestra before moving to the USA in 1920. He joined the Philadelphia Orchestra as a viola player, and was appointed chorus master and assistant conductor of the Philadelphia Grand Opera Company in 1927. In 1926 he opened a music shop in Philadelphia; two years later he was joined by Adolph Vogel (a cellist in the Philadelphia Orchestra) in the establishment of the Elkan-Vogel Music Co. He left the firm in 1952 but opened his own publishing house, Henri Elkan Music Publisher, Inc., in 1960. Its catalogue consists largely of teaching material, and Elkan also acts as sole agent in the USA and Canada for a number of publishers in Belgium and the Netherlands. Since Henri Elkan's death, the firm has been run by his nephew, S. Van Gobes.

Obituary, *Philadelphia Inquirer* (13 June 1980)

F.B.

Elkan-Vogel. American firm of publishers. In 1928 Henri Elkan and Adolph Vogel (*b* West Orange, NJ, 12 Feb 1893; *d* Merion, PA, 28 July 1981) founded the music retailing firm of Elkan-Vogel, and were joined in 1929 by a third partner, Bernard Kohn. First based in Philadelphia, the company soon expanded and began publishing music; in 1952 Elkan severed his relationship with the firm, and Vincent Persichetti became chief editor for the company. Elkan-Vogel credits much of its success to its early acquisition of important French agencies and assignment of copyright in the USA; these included Durand & Cie and Jean Jobert, whose catalogues contained most of the works of Debussy and Ravel. Elkan-Vogel added to its own catalogue compositions of such major composers as Jean Langlais, Harl McDonald, Milhaud, Persichetti and Yardumian; it also acquired the American agencies of Henry Lemoine, Editions Rideau Rouge, Editions Philippo, Hamelle & Cie, Consortium Musical, La Schola Cantorum & Procure Général and Dolmetsch Recorders. In January 1970 Elkan-Vogel became a subsidiary of the music publishers Theodore Presser Company and moved to Bryn Mawr, Pennsylvania.

W.T.M., M.J./R

Emerich, Johann [Emericus, Johannes] (*fl* 1487–1506). German printer, active in Venice. He came from Udenheim in the diocese of Speyer. In 1487 he printed two books with Johann Hamman, in 1492 he began printing on his own, and in 1494 for Luc'Antonio Giunta and other Venetian publishers. His speciality was liturgical books with music. Of the 71 books he issued, 67 were liturgical and at least 24 contain printed music or space for manuscript music (20 missals, one gradual, one antiphonal, two processionals and two *Libri catechumeni*). To print music he used woodcut blocks (a 1493 *Missale romanum*), metal roman plainchant types in four sizes and the first mensural music type, for the mensural Credos of the 1499 *Graduale*. The *Graduale* has been called the largest book printed in the 15th century; it uses a very large chant type with a variety of designs for different-sized neumes as well as ornamentation or liquescence. The mensural type, a black notation, preceded that of Petrucci by two years.

G. Massera: *La 'Mano musicale perfetta' di Francesco de Brugis dalle prefazione ai corali di L. A. Giunta (Venezia, 1499–1504)* (Florence, 1963); Duggan (1981)

M.K.D.

EMI Music-SBK. Anglo-American publishing firm. It was formed in 1989 with the takeover by Thorn EMI, the British entertainment and electronics group, of the publishing interests of the American company SBK Entertainment World. The SBK catalogue, begun in New York in 1986 by Stephen Swid, Martin Bandier and Charles Koppelman through the acquisition of CBS Songs, contains more than 250,000 titles, including songs from such films as *The Wizard of Oz*, *Singin' in the Rain* and *A Hard Day's Night*, and by such artists as James Taylor, Luther Vandross and Tracy Chapman. Through its constituent companies Keith, Prowse (*c*1829), Francis Day & Hunter (1877), B. Feldman & Co. (1896), Peter Maurice (1933) and Robbins Music (1952), consolidated under one umbrella company in 1974, EMI Music Publishing traces its roots back nearly 150 years. Its vast holdings include standard and contemporary songs from *Star Dust* to *Absolute Beginners*. The new company now rivals Warner Chappell for supremacy in music publishing revenues.

P. Coggan and C. Harris: 'It's Raining Money Over the Rainbow', *Financial Times* (6 Jan 1989); I. Lichtman: 'Thorn-EMI Buying SBK Pub Units', *Billboard* (14 Jan 1989), 1

L.A.T., L.L.

Enders, Karel Vilém (*b* ?1778; *d* Prague, 23 June 1841). Czech bookseller and publisher. He had a bookshop first in Leipzig and then from 1809 (or 1810) until 1835 (or 1836) in Prague, where until 1832 he also ran a publishing house. He published (up to 1812 under the name Enders & Co. and then under his own name) mostly contemporary dance music, vocal and piano pieces by Prague composers, including J. T. Held, F. M. Kníže, Jan Vitásek, B. D. Weber and V. J. Tomášek. In 1817 he produced Jakub Jan Ryba's book *Počáteční a všeobecní základové ku všemu umění hudebnímu* ('First and universal principles for all musical art'), which was of fundamental importance in the development of Czech literature on music. He also attempted to publish the first Austrian bibliography, but failed for lack of support.

K. Nosovský; *Knihopisná nauka a vývoj knihkupectví československého* [The science of book printing and the development of Czechoslovak bookselling] (Prague, 1927), 212; K. Chyba: *Slovník knihtiskařů v Československu od nejstarších dob do roku 1860* [Dictionary of printers in Czechoslovakia from early times to 1860] (Prague, 1966–), 85; I. Janáčková: 'Pražští vydavatelé Václava Jana Tomáška' [Tomášek's Prague publishers], *HV*, xviii (1981), 171

Z.C.

Endter. German family of printers and publishers. Wolfgang Endter the elder (1593–1659) began his career as a journeyman printer in Altdorf and Herborn before training as a bookseller in the shop of his father, Georg Endter the elder (1562–1630), in Nuremberg. He owed his leading position among German book printers and publishers during the Thirty Years War to his editions of the Bible and Protestant devotional works, whereas his brother Georg Endter the younger (1585–1629) and his descendants specialized in the printing and distribution of Catholic devotional literature. On being ennobled by Emperor Ferdinand III in 1651 Wolfgang the elder retired from his business in favour of his sons Wolfgang Endter the younger (1622–55) and Johann Andreas Endter (1625–70). After the death of Wolfgang the younger Johann Andreas continued to manage the firm on behalf of his brother's heirs; after his death the heirs separated. Wolfgang Moritz Endter (1653–1723), son of Wolfgang Endter the younger, has been credited with improvements in the technique of music printing, but he seems to have specialized entirely in bookselling and sold his share in the press and publishing business. The Endters' musicological importance rests on their numerous editions of hymnbooks and works of the Nuremberg school.

F. Oldenbourg: *Die Endter, eine Nürnberger Buchhändlerfamilie (1590–1740)* (diss., U. of Leipzig, 1911); C. Petzsch: 'Endter', *NDB*; L. Sporhan-Krempel: 'Zur Genealogie der Familie Endter in Nürnberg', *Börsenblatt für den deutschen Buchhandel, Frankfurter Ausgabe*, xxii/35 (1966), 1037; T. Wohnhaas: 'Die Endter in Nürnberg als Musikdrucker und Musikverleger', *Quellenstudien zur Musik: Wolfgang Schmieder zum 70. Geburtstag* (Frankfurt am Main, 1972), 197; L. Sporhan-Krempel and T. Wohnhaas: 'Zum Nürnberger Buchhandel und graphischen Gewerbe im 17. Jahrhundert', *Archiv für Geschichte des Buchwesens*, xiii (1973), 1034

T.W.

Erard. French firm of instrument makers and publishers. It began in Paris in 1780, when Sébastien Erard (*b* Strasbourg, 5 April 1752; *d* La Muette, nr. Passy, 4 Aug 1831) took his brother Jean-Baptiste (*d* 1826) into partnership to exploit the market for small, five-octave pianos. Erard frères expanded vigorously, opening a London workshop soon after the outbreak of the Revolution, and gained in the first half of the 19th century an international reputation for its grand pianos and double-action harps (the latter were manufactured mainly in London). The firm's publishing activities were in the hands of Marie-

Françoise-Catherine (1777–1851) and Catherine-Barbe (1779–*c*1815) Marcoux, nieces of Sébastien and Jean-Baptiste. In about 1798 they began trading at 37 rue du Mail, Paris (the same address as Erard frères). From November 1806 their main address is given as no.21, from 1811 to 1818 indiscriminately as no.21 and no.13 rue du Mail (respectively the *atelier* and shop of Erard frères), and from February 1818 as no.13. In September 1833 Julius Delahante announced that he had taken over the business; until 1840 both he and the Mlles Erard are listed in directories, still at 13 rue du Mail, but not thereafter.

In 1802 the Erards took over the remaining stock of 393 numbers of Bailleux's *Journal d'ariettes italiennes*, originally published by subscription from 1779 to 1795; to this they added three further volumes of their own, probably between 1802 and 1805. It is possible that they also acquired other items from, or even the whole of, the remainder of Bailleux's stock. Their earliest publications included violin concertos by Andreas Romberg and Rodolphe Kreutzer; cello concertos by Bernhard Romberg; piano concertos by Dussek, Cramer and Steibelt; several sets of piano sonatas by Clementi, Cramer, Ferrari and Steibelt; the first printing of John Field in France (op.1 sonatas); and the first French full score of Haydn's *The Creation* (1800). Between 1800 and 1805 the firm published full scores of eight operas, including Spontini's *Milton* and *Julie*, and others by Boieldieu, Dalayrac and Plantade. These were followed in 1807 and 1809 by Spontini's *La vestale* and *Fernand Cortez*, the firm's most important publications; thereafter their output seems to have diminished greatly. They concentrated on instrumental music, making only occasional operatic excursions, for example Spontini's *Olimpie*, a revised edition of *Fernand Cortez* and Hérold's *L'illusion*. All the firm's publications were engraved.

Hopkinson (1954); Devriès and Lesure, (1979–88)

R.M.

Eschig, Max(imilian) (*b* Troppau [now Opava], 27 May 1872; *d* Paris, 3 Sept 1927). French publisher of Czech birth. After an association with Schott in Mainz, he founded a music publishing house in 1907 in Paris and provided a large outlet for foreign works in France. Formerly the representative of Breitkopf & Härtel, Universal Edition, Simrock and Fürstner, the firm is still the Paris agent for Associated Music Publishers, Ricordi of Milan and Schott of Mainz and London. Eschig's production was many-faceted, but he was particularly devoted to 20th-century music. The catalogue contains works of Falla, Koechlin, Martelli, Martinu, Milhaud, Poulenc, Ravel, Satie, Szymanowski, Tansman and Villa-Lobos. Other composers represented include Auric, Charpentier, Delannoy, Halffter, Harsanyi, Honegger, Inghelbrecht, Mihalovici, Nin and Stravinsky. Eschig's noted publications for guitar include Emilio Pujol's *Bibliothèque de musique ancienne et moderne* and numerous transcriptions, classics and original 20th-century works. By 1973 the firm had published 8000 titles and had acquired an additional 5000 by purchasing the catalogues of Demets, Broussan & Cie, Jeanne Vieu, La Sirène Musicale, George Sporck and Paul Dupont.

After Eschig's death, the firm became a 'société anonyme', directed by Eugène Cools (*d* 1936), and then a 'société à responsabilité' (Editions Max Eschig). From 1936 it was directed by Jean Marietti (*b* Bastia, Corsica, 10 Nov 1900) and his brother, Philippe Marietti (*b* Bastia, 21 Aug 1905).

R.S.N.

Escudier. French firm of publishers, active in Paris. Marie-Pierre-Pascal Escudier (*b* Castelnaudary, 29 June 1809; *d* Paris, 7 April 1880) and his brother Léon (*b* Castelnaudary, 15 Sept 1815; *d* Paris, 22 June 1881) founded the firm in 1840; it developed out of the weekly journal *La France musicale* which they had founded in 1837, and which was the only serious rival in France to Schlesinger's *Revue et gazette musicale* until 1860. Whereas Schlesinger's journal concentrated primarily on French and German music, *La France musicale* redressed the balance by paying particular attention to Italian opera. For its content, its journalistic probing and for the liveliness of its style, *La France musicale* is essential for the study of contemporary music and musical events in Paris and the activity of French musicians abroad. The first number appeared on 31 December 1837, and among the journal's early collaborators were Adolphe Adam, Castil-Blaze, Schumann, Balzac and Théophile Gautier. From 38 rue Laffitte, the publishing address changed on 4 March 1838 to 14 rue de Provence, on 20 November of the same year to 20 rue de la Victoire, and on 15 July 1839 to 6 rue Neuve St Marc. From the first it had been the journal's practice to give its subscribers, about twice a month, editions of other publishers (including Richault and, particularly, Troupenas, who in

1837–42 had been distributors for the musical works published by the Escudiers). From May 1842 the firm began to publish music on its own account, under the imprint 'Au bureau de La France musicale'. By October 1842 their series of plate numbers had exceeded no.100, and their earliest really important publication, the original piano-vocal score of Donizetti's *Don Pasquale* (March 1843), bears the plate number F.M.260. The firm's name was changed first to Magasin de Musique in May 1843 and then to Bureau Central de Musique on 5 October that year, when a move was made to 29 place de la Bourse; the firm's plate numbers bear the prefix 'B.C.' from this date. In March 1848 a further move was made, to 8 rue Favart, and again, on 27 November 1853, 21 rue Choiseul. From this date the firm took the name Léon Escudier and its plate numbers were prefixed 'L.E.' In February and March 1882, some months after Léon Escudier's death, the assets were auctioned and divided among several publishers, with many lots unsold; on 26 March 1889 Ricordi acquired some or all of what remained.

In 1849 Marie Escudier had become sole director of *La France musicale*, with Léon as his co-editor; and by November 1853 at the latest Léon had taken sole responsibility for the music publishing activities of the firm. Apart from a break from April to December 1848 (and a change of title, to *La musique*, in 1849–50), *La France musicale* continued to appear as the house journal until 1860, when Marie split away from the firm. He took *La France musicale* with him, and from 21 October 1860 until its demise (on account of the Franco-Prussian War) on 31 July 1870 it was his sole concern. Meanwhile, Léon had started a new weekly journal, *L'art musical*, similar in scope to *La France musicale*. It first appeared on 6 December 1860, being edited, successively, by Oscar Comettant and P. Scudo. It managed to survive the war and was eventually sold to Girod, under whose imprint it appeared from 9 June 1881. From 6 December 1883 it was published by Alphonse Leduc, and its final number was issued on 27 September 1894; it was then merged with *Le guide musical*, edited by Maurice Kufferath.

Among the firm's earliest independent publications in 1842 were full scores of operas by Clapisson and N. Girard. In 1843 followed piano-vocal scores of *Don Pasquale* and *Marie di Rohan* and the full score of Thomas' *Mina*; and in 1844 the performing materials of Donizetti's *Dom Sébastien* and Adam's *Cagliostro*, Kastner's *Traité d'instrumentation*, piano works by Alkan, Liszt and Franck, and the vocal score of *I lombardi*. It was the first Verdi opera published by Escudier, and from this moment both the influence and the activity of the firm greatly increased, predominantly in opera. In all, some 20 operas in full score were actually published, while others (including all Verdi's works) were announced as being available, though not priced for sale; at least 65 operas were put out in piano-vocal score, almost all of them French or Italian works and many published in two editions, one with French and one with Italian text. Non-operatic publications included many piano works by Gottschalk, Krüger, Prudent and Rosellen. In all, more than 3600 works were published by the firm, judging by the chronological series of plate numbers.

The Escudier firm is chiefly important for its journals and as Verdi's French publishers. By 1845, mainly through their journal, they had become influential in Parisian musical circles; through this influence they quickly established Verdi as the Italian successor to Rossini, Bellini and Donizetti, and in so doing they were in a large way responsible for the wide dissemination of his works throughout the opera houses of the world. *Nabucco* (1845), *Ernani* and *I due Foscari* (both 1846) were the first of Verdi's works to be heard in Paris, at the Théâtre-Italien, and in 1847 *Jérusalem* (a revision, in French, of *I lombardi*) was his first to be given at the Opéra; all these productions resulted from the Escudiers' initiative, and later, in 1865, it was at Léon's suggestion that Verdi reworked *Macbeth* for Paris. Although it appears that Blanchet were Ricordi's Paris agents until about 1850, the Escudiers were in constant touch with Verdi from the mid-1840s (many of Verdi's letters to Léon have been published) and from *I lombardi* to the string quartet (1876) they published all his works and put out the first editions of *Jérusalem*, *Les vêpres siciliennes* (1855), the revised version of *Macbeth* (1865) and *Don Carlos* (1867). Escudier had close business ties with Ricordi and there seems to have been an arrangement between the two firms for simultaneous publication of Verdi's works in Italy and France.

In 1876 Léon assumed the directorship of the Théâtre-Italien at the Salle Ventadour, and on 22 April of that year launched, at a cost of 120,000 francs, the first Paris production of *Aida*, with a lavish décor, first-rate cast and Verdi on hand to supervise the rehearsals. During the run of *Aida*, Léon put on the first Paris performances of Verdi's Requiem and string quartet. His further theatrical enterprises, however, were much less successful, and the Théâtre-Italien was forced to close in June 1878. Finally, after the failure of his attempt to produce operas in French (including *Aida*) at the Salle Ventadour, Léon abandoned in August 1878 his brief career as impresario, a diversion that certainly contributed to a severe decline in the activity of his publishing business from 1876 onwards.

The Escudier brothers were also active as journalists and writers on music. In their youth they founded in Toulouse two periodicals, one of which was *La patrie*. Later, in Paris, they founded a journal, *Le réveil*, and either edited or contributed to several others; in the 1850s they contributed musical articles to *Le pays*. Between 1840 and 1856 the brothers jointly wrote five books on music, thereby extending their influence still further, and translated Verdi's *Ernani* and *I due Foscari*. After the demise in 1870 of *La France musicale* Marie Escudier returned to political journalism, contributing to *Le Figaro* under a pseudonym.

FétisB; *Oeuvres musicales dramatiques, propriétée du Bureau Central de Musique* (Paris, *c*1853); *Catalogue de musique* (Paris, *c*1863, suppl. *c*1869); G. Cesari and A. Luzio, eds.: *I copialettere di Giuseppe Verdi* (Milan, 1913/*R*1968); J. G. Prod'-homme: 'Verdi's Letters to Léon Escudier', *ML*, iv (1923), 62, 184, 375; idem: 'Lettres inédites de G. Verdi à Léon Escudier', *RMI*, xxxv (1928), 1, 171, 519; C. Gatti: *Verdi* (Milan, 1931, 2/1951); Hopkinson (1954); F. Abbiati: *Giuseppe Verdi* (Milan, 1959); G. Martin: *Verdi: his Music, Life and Times* (London, 1965); C. Hopkinson: *A Bibliography of the Works of Giuseppe Verdi* (New York, 1973–8); Devriès and Lesure (1979–88)

R.M.

Eulenburg, Ernst (Emil Alexander) (*b* Berlin, 30 Nov 1847; *d* Leipzig, 11 Sept 1926). German publisher. He studied at the Leipzig Conservatory and founded his publishing firm in Leipzig in 1874. He published chiefly educational and choral material (*Deutsche Eiche*). In 1891 he obtained the miniature score series, published by Payne in Leipzig, and in 1894 took over the London firm Donajowski's edition of scores, combining the two series. More than 1000 works have appeared in the *Eulenburgs kleine Partitur-Ausgabe* (Eulenburg Miniature Scores). The firm also publishes symphonic orchestral music, including works by Atterberg, Graener, S. W. Müller and Trapp. In 1911 Kurt Eulenburg (*b* Leipzig, 22 Feb 1879; *d* London, 10 April 1982), son of the founder, became partner and in 1926 sole proprietor; he moved the firm to London in 1939. After World War

II branches were established in Zurich (1947) and Stuttgart (1950); the original Leipzig firm ceased to exist. Kurt Eulenburg resigned in 1968, and the firm (Ernst Eulenburg und Co. GmbH, Mainz, and Ernst Eulenburg Ltd, London and Ashford, Kent) is controlled by Schott in London, though the Zurich firm remains independent.

H.-H. Schönzeler: 'Kurt Eulenburg at 100', *MT*, cxx (1979), 127

H.-M.P.

European American. American firm of publishers and distributors. It was established in New Jersey in 1977 under the joint ownership of Schott and Universal Edition. Since 1984 it has been located in Valley Forge, Pennsylvania. As a comprehensive serious music publisher, the firm distributes sheet music to dealers, hires works to orchestras, licenses opera productions and assumes administrative and artistic functions on behalf of the parent companies and their composers. The firm also operates two American publishing companies whose composers include Joseph Schwantner, Christopher Rouse and Stephen Paulus: European American Music Corporation (for ASCAP members) and Helicon Music Corporation (for BMI affiliates). In addition to representing Schott and Universal Edition, the firm is the sole US agent for Eulenburg Miniature Scores, Philharmonia Pocket Scores, Franz Lehár's Glocken Verlag, Vienna Urtext Edition, Haydn-Mozart Presse, Moeck Verlag (contemporary works only), Zen-On (contemporary works only) and Schott Frères of Brussels. The firm publishes a monthly newsletter and performance calendar, *Monthly Events*.

C.F.

Ewer. English firm of music importers, sellers and publishers, active in London. The firm was established about 1823 by John Jeremiah Ewer. A year or so later the bookkeeper Julius Johanning (*b* ?1795–6; *d* Manchester, 26 Dec 1859) joined Ewer in partnership as Ewer & Johanning; this continued until about 1829 when Johanning withdrew from the firm. It then continued as J. J. Ewer & Co., until 1867, when it merged with Novello & Co. to become Novello, Ewer & Co. The name of Ewer was finally withdrawn in 1898.

Ewer & Co. had an extensive business, and were the principal English publishers of Mendelssohn's works from about 1840, the copyrights of which passed to Novello, Ewer & Co. In 1839 they acquired the stock of Gustavus Andre, a London publisher and importer of foreign music. They also had a large circulating library, a catalogue of which was published in 1860.

Kidson (1900); Humphries and Smith (1954, 2/1970)

W.C.S./P.W.J.

F

Faber Music. English firm of publishers, active in London. It is a subsidiary company of Faber & Faber (which itself has an extensive list of books on music) and was established under the direction of Donald Mitchell in 1966 to coordinate the music publishing activities of Faber, begun in 1964 when Benjamin Britten withdrew from Boosey & Hawkes. Apart from making a small but important contribution to educational music publishing, Faber Music is active in three areas. It has a strong catalogue of works by 20th-century composers, including Britten, Holst, Searle, Malcolm Arnold, Knussen, George Benjamin, David and Colin Matthews and Nicholas Maw; it also issued several hitherto unpublished works by Mahler, Schoenberg and Stravinsky. It is developing a collection of scholarly editions which includes John Dowland's lute music, John Jenkins's consort music in five and six parts, and the complete facsimile edition of Holst's works (from 1975). The firm has also published important performing editions of opera and choral works by Monteverdi, Cavalli and other previously neglected Italian Baroque composers.

A.P. (ii)

Faber, Nicolaus [Schmidt, Nickel] (*b c*1490; *d* Leipzig, 1554). German printer. Records show that he became a citizen of Leipzig on 5 October 1510. His printing and publishing business, begun in 1521, included a book bindery and a retail bookshop. Since no publications bearing his name are dated later than 1545, he probably devoted the last years of his life to the sale rather than to the printing of books. After his death the firm was taken over by his son, Lorenz, but apparently with little success.

One of the first Protestants in Leipzig, Faber maintained close business ties with Georg Rhau in Wittenberg. His book production was largely confined to school texts and grammars and theological writings, beginning with the works by Reformation authors and later turning to those of the Catholic Church. In music he is known for a single publication, *Melodiae Prudentianae et in Virgilium magna ex parte nuper natae* (1533), which contains four-voice metric settings by Lucas Hordisch and Sebastian Forster of hymns by the 4th-century Latin poet Aurelius Clemens Prudentius. Simple note-against-note settings of antique metres, often of Horatian odes, were fairly frequent in Germany in the early 16th century and showed the influence of the contemporary humanistic movement. The quantitative rhythms of the hymns in this collection are notated in semibreves and minims with no general time signature; one note is allotted to each syllable of the text. The metric scheme is indicated at the beginning of each setting. The music is printed in choirbook format, using the old-fashioned system of block printing. Faber published the complete texts in a separate volume, *Aurelii Prudentii ... liber kathemerinon* (1533), since only the first strophe was given with the melodies.

A. Kirchhoff: *Die Entwickelung des Buchhandels in Leipzig bis in das zweite Jahrzehnt nach Einführung der Reformation* (Leipzig, 1885); H. Riemann: 'Notenschrift und Notendruck', *Festschrift zur 50-jährigen Jubelfeier des Bestehens der Firma C. G. Röder* (Leipzig, 1896); H. Springer: 'Die musikalischen Blockdrucke des 15. und 16. Jahrhunderts', *IMusSCR, ii Basel 1906*, 37; O. Clemen: 'Melodiae Prudentianae, Leipzig 1533', *ZMw*, x (1927–8), 106; H. Jentsch: *Nickel Schmidt (Nicolaus Faber) und Michael Blum, zwei Leipziger Drucker der Reformationszeit* (Wolfenbüttel, 1928); H. C. Wolff: 'Faber, Nicolaus', *MGG*; Benzing (1963, 2/1082)

M.L.G.

Falter & Sohn. German firm of music publishers. It was founded by Macarius (Franz de Paula) Falter (*b* Taiskirchen, 2 Jan 1762; *d* Munich, 24 Sept 1843), who first worked in Munich as a piano teacher. From 1788 he held a concession for the sale of manuscript music paper and printed music; the first piece of music under his imprint appeared in 1796. About 1813 Falter's son Joseph (1782–1846) was taken into the firm; he had in the meantime been involved in instrument dealing and music lending.

On 4 April 1827 the firm was sold to Sebastian Pacher and after his death on 13 March 1834 it was carried on by his widow Thekla Pacher (1805–79). From 1861 to 1874 the business was owned by Otto Halbreiter (1827–1910), who opened another music selling business which continued until 1933. Among later owners of Falter & Sohn were Ferdinand Neustätter, his wife Helene and Friedrich Schellhass (1885). On 22 June 1888 the name of Falter & Sohn was deleted from the register of firms; all the rights were transferred to the Munich publisher Joseph Aibl.

Besides works by Haydn, Pleyel and other well-known masters, the firm published principally (later almost exclusively) Munich composers, including Cannabich, von Winter, Theobald Boehm, Ett, Stuntz, Kuntz and Perfall. The plate numbers reached 200 in about 1806, 500 in 1840–41 and 700 in 1848; numerous editions appeared without numbers, many of these on commission. A series of editions bore the stamp of Falter & Sohn in conjunction with B. Schott (Mainz and Paris) and A. Schott (Antwerp).

H. Schmid: 'Falter & Sohn', *Mitteilungsblatt der Gesellschaft für bayerische Musikgeschichte*, vi (1973), 108; idem: 'Berichtigung', *Musik in Bayern*, xiv (1977), 97

H.S.

Famous. American firm of publishers. It was founded in New York in 1928 as a partnership between Famous Players-Lasky Corporation (which later became Paramount Pictures) and Warner Bros., whose interest was purchased by Paramount in 1933. Famous Music Corporation has published songs and theme music associated with Paramount films, including *Beyond the blue horizon* (1930), *Out of nowhere* (1931), *Lover* (1933), *Cocktails for Two* (1934), *Blue Hawaii* (1937), *That old black magic* (1942), *Mona Lisa* (1949), *Silver Bells* (1950), *Moon River* (1961), *Alfie* (1966), *Theme from Romeo and Juliet* (1968) and *Theme from Love Story* (1971). The company has enlarged its holdings through the acquisition of various catalogues, among them the Glaser catalogue (including *Gentle on my mind*) and the Kaiser-Phil Gernhart catalogue of songs. In 1966 Famous was acquired by Gulf & Western.

F.B.

Farrenc, (Jacques Hippolyte) Aristide (*b* Marseilles, 9 April 1794; *d* Paris, 31 Jan 1865). French publisher and scholar. Determined on a career in music despite his family's tradition in commerce, he arrived in Paris in 1815; soon an appointment as second flautist the the Théâtre-Italien propelled him directly into Parisian musical life. By the early 1820s he had established himself as a teacher and begun to compose flute music, some of which – a book of sonatas and a concerto, among other works – he issued from his own newly formed publishing concern. In 1821 he married the composer Louise Dumont (1804–75). He remained active as a publisher during the 1830s, specializing in editions of Hummel and Beethoven. His firm also brought out his wife's first piano works.

Stimulated by the revelations of Fétis's *Concerts historiques* (1832–5), Farrenc became an ardent advocate of and researcher into early music. He dissolved his business enterprise about 1840 and devoted his last 25 years to scholarship. He is particularly remembered for *Le trésor des pianistes* (20 vols., 1861–72/*R*1978; completed by his wife after his death), a comprehensive anthology of harpsichord and piano music from a repertory encompassing 300 years.

FétisB; Catalogue de la bibliothèque musicale théorique et pratique de feu M. A. Farrenc (Paris, 1866/*R*); E. Haraszti: 'Farrenc, Jacques Hyppolite Aristide', *MGG*; Z. Lissa: 'Chopin im Lichte des Briefwechsels von Verlegern seiner Zeit gesehen', *FAM*, vii (1960), 46; J. Kallberg: 'Chopin in the Marketplace: Aspects of the International Music Publishing Industry in the First Half of the Nineteenth Century', *Notes*, xxxix (1982–3), 535, 795

B.F.

Faulds, David P. (*b* Dundee, 1827; *d* Louisville, KY, 23 Jan 1903). American publisher. He went to the USA as a child, and settled in Louisville in 1841. He became the manager of the Galt House hotel there, leaving to open a music shop on Main Street in 1853. He first published music as Faulds, Stone & Morse (successors to Peters, Webb & Co.) in 1854. The next year he continued independently as D. P. Faulds, but he took James H. Huber as his business associate from 1858 to 1860, and Buck and J. P. Simmons as his associates in 1894–5. His firm became the leading music publishing house and agency for the sale of pianos in the area. At the height of his career, Faulds had a stock of over 4000 pieces and 60 books at his shops on Main and Fourth streets.

M.K.

Fazer. Finnish music company. It was founded in 1897 by K. G. Fazer in Helsinki and was at first mainly concerned with importing instruments and sheet music, but from its inception it also had a considerable publishing interest. In 1918 K. G. Fazer was succeeded by his son Georg Fazer, who substantially increased its scope, particularly in radios, gramophones and records. The company moved to their spacious premises in Aleksanterinkatu, later further extended to become one of the largest premises in Europe. In 1925 they opened a concert agency with several branches. After World War II the company developed under Roger Lindberg, grandson of the founder, who was appointed general manager in 1940; it became the agent for leading record companies and instrument makers. The firm was making its own pianos as early as 1935. Oy Finnlevy Ab, which rapidly developed into the leading record company in Finland, was founded in 1966 (general manager John Eric Westö). The music publishing division has expanded through the incorporation of several art and popular music publishing firms (R. E. Westerlund in 1967, and later Nordiska Musikförlaget) and by publishing school music. In 1971 Westö became general manager of Musik Fazer.

E. Marvia: *Oy Fazerin Musiikkikauppa 1897–1947* (Helsinki, 1947); O. Lampinen: *Musik Fazer 1897–1972* (Helsinki, 1972) [in Eng.]

E.M.

Fei. Italian family of printers, active in the 17th century. In 1615 the first work of Andrea Fei (*d* before 1658) appeared at Rome; much of his work was financed by others, in particular the Roman bookseller G. D. Franzini, who promoted musical volumes. In 1621 Fei opened a second house in Bracciano, apparently as publisher to the duke: both branches continued during the rest of his life. In 1657 Fei's son Giacomo Fei inherited the firm and retained the Bracciano branch at least into the 1660s. He seems to have printed mostly music until 1670, after which the output declined rapidly. The cost of publishing many of his titles was met by booksellers in Rome, including G. B. Caifabri, F. Franzini and Antonio Poggiolo. The firm's output, as might be expected at Rome, concentrated on editions of the late 16th-century sacred repertory.

It is not certain if Michel'angelo Fei is related to the above. He printed at Orvieto, in partnership with Rinaldo Ruuli in 1621–3. Ruuli continued to print various titles including music until 1639.

S.B.(iii)

Feist, Leo (*b* Mount Vernon, NY, 3 Jan 1869; *d* Mount Vernon, 21 June 1930). American publisher. He began a career as a corset salesman and composed songs as an avocation. When he failed to find a publisher for his work he set up his own firm to deal in popular songs, and achieved his first success with *Smokey Mokes* (1895). Feist was an astute businessman, and his self-promoting slogan 'You can't go wrong with a Feist song' was printed on every copy of the firm's sheet music. Based in New York, his company had branches in England, France, Germany and Australia through which he helped to popularize American songs abroad. He took over Balmer & Weber in 1907 and the Morse Music Co. in 1915, and in 1929 formed the Radio Music Co. with Carl Fischer and NBC, in order to enable music publishing to take advantage of the popularity of music on radio. Feist became part of the Big 3 Music Corporation in 1939. Among the most successful works in the Feist catalogue were compositions by the tenor Enrico Caruso, including *Dreams of Long Ago* (1912), and the songs *Anona* (1903), *Over there* (1917) and *The Rose of No Man's Land* (1918). Feist also published the opera *Paoletta* by Pietro Floridia (1910) and musical comedies such as *Irene* (1920) and *Rio Rita* (1926).

His son Leonard (*b* 1910) has been active in music publishing, at first in the family firm but later as president of Associated Music Publishers (1956–64) and with the National Music Publishers Association.

F.B.

Feyerabend, Sigmund (*b* Heidelberg, 1527 or 1528; *d* Frankfurt am Main, 22 April 1590). German publisher. Much of Frankfurt am Main's status as the leading city for printing in 16th-century Germany was due to his activities. His father Ägidius was a painter and engraver, and a cousin, Johann, was a printer and bookseller active in Frankfurt from 1559. Feyerabend appears to have started printing in Augsburg, before visiting Venice. He was in Frankfurt before 25 May 1559, when he was made a citizen. He set up there as a woodcutter, doing commissions for the printers Zöpfel and Rasch, and a portrait of the Doge of Venice in Keller's *Chronik*. Almost immediately he began publishing, employing most of the printers of a lively centre in the following 30 years. In 1563 he entered into an agreement with Georg Rab and the widow of the printer Weigand Han, as a result of which he printed over 60 titles in the next seven years. He employed distinguished craftsmen and artists: his engravers included Jobst Amman and Virgil Solis. He exhibited regularly at the annual Frankfurt fairs, and the extant lists show not only the range of his stock, but

also the numbers of copies of individual titles that were taken to exhibition. In 1568 these included seven music titles in 247 copies intended for sale to the trade. He also used agents at the fairs: in 1574 he sold 285 copies of an *Evangelia* to two agents who took them to the spring fair. Meiland's two pieces composed in honour of Feyerabend and his son praise them for their support of music.

H. Pallmann: 'Sigmund Feyerabend, sein Leben und seine geschäftlichen Verbindungen', *Archiv für Frankfurts Geschichte und Kunst*, new ser., vii (1881); P. Heitz: *Frankfurter und Mainzer Drucker- und Verlegerzeichen bis in das 17. Jahrhundert* (Strasbourg, 1896); C. Valentinoff: *Geschichte der Musik in Frankfurt am Main vom Anfange des 14. bis zum Anfange des 18. Jahrhunderts* (Frankfurt am Main, 1906), 51; W. von zur Westen: *Musiktitel aus vier Jahrhunderten* (Leipzig, 1921); E. Klöss: 'Der Frankfurter Drucker-Verleger Weigand Han und seine Erben: ein Beitrag zur Geschichte des Frankfurter Buchgewerbes im 16. Jahrhundert', *Archiv für Geschichte des Buchwesens*, ii (1960), 309–75; C. Becker: *Joost Amman, Zeichner und Formschneider, Kupferätzer und Stecher* (Nieuwkoop, 1961); Benzing (1963, 2/1982); E.-L. Berz: *Die Notendrucker und ihre Verleger in Frankfurt am Main von den Anfängen bis etwa 1630*, v (Kassel, 1970)

S.B.(iii)

Fezandat [Faisandat], **Michel** (*fl* Paris, 1538–66). French printer and bookseller. Also known as Dauphin (or Dauphiné), he was active in Paris as a publisher from 1538 to 1566, dealing specifically with music between 1551 and 1558. From the Hostel d'Albert on Mont St Hilaire he published works by Philandrier (1545), Habert (1549, 1551, 1557, 1560), A.-M. and J. Seymour (1551), Beuther (1551), Cockburn (1551), Rabelais (1552), Emile (1556) and Buttet (1561). He used four different marks: a pheasant and dolphin, a winged Mercury, a snake with the motto 'Ne la mort ne le venin' and a heron holding a dolphin in its claws. He collaborated variously with Buffet (1543), H. de Marnef (*c*1550), Sertenas (1551), J. Vincent (1554), Granjon (1550–51) and Morlaye (1551–8). His activity in music began on 23 December 1550 when he signed a ten-year contract with Robert Granjon, who ten months earlier had procured a privilege from Henri II to publish music of all kinds, including tablatures for lute, guitar and other instruments. The association realized at least 14 books between 1550 and 1551, including one guitar tablature by Simon Gorlier (*RISM* 1551²²), and a new agreement for 18 months was signed on 19 November 1551. But the partnership was dissolved 28 days later; its only musical product, a guitar tablature by Guillaume

Morlaye (1552[32]), appeared the following year. Granjon retained the punches, matrices, moulds and type for a small music type he himself had cut, and formed a new association with Gorlier, concentrating on the Lyons market, while Fezandat continued business at Paris in collaboration with Morlaye. On 19 April 1551 Fezandat contracted to print lute music supplied and corrected by Morlaye in sets of 1200 copies (amounting to ten folios or more as agreed) and not to reprint without permission; in return for bearing the whole cost of publication Fezandat was to sell half for his profit. This partnership produced some 15 tablatures between 1551 and 1558. These include two more books for guitar or cittern by Morlaye (1552[33], 1553[34]), three for lute by Morlaye (1552[34], 1558[18], 1558[19]) and a series of lute books by the late Albert de Rippe, edited by his pupil Morlaye (1552[36], 1554[34], 1554[35], 1554[36], 1555[36]). Others, whose present whereabouts are unknown, are listed in the Du Verdier and Fétis catalogues. Fezandat secured his own ten-year royal privilege to print music on 8 January 1552 and in 1556 used it to publish two books of four-voice psalms (1552[3], 1553[18]) and two books of four-voice chansons (1556[20], 1556[21]): the latter include one by 'G. Pelletier' who may be Guillaume le Pelletier, apprenticed to Fezandat in 1543.

La bibliothèque d'Antoine du Verdier (Lyons, 1585); *Catalogue de la bibliothèque de F.-J. Fétis acquise par l'Etat belge* (Brussels, 1877/R1969); P. Renouard: *Imprimeurs parisiens . . . jusqu'à la fin du XVIe siècle* (Paris, 1898); E. Coyecque: *Recueil d'actes notariés relatifs a l'histoire de Paris* (Paris, 1905); J. Prod'homme: 'Guillaume Morlaye éditeur d'Albert de Rippe luthiste et bourgeois de Paris', *RdM*, vi (1925), 157; D. Heartz: 'Parisian Music Publishing under Henry II', *MQ*, xlvi (1960), 448; Brown (1965)

F.D. (ii)

Filippone. Brazilian publishing firm. It was established in Rio de Janeiro in 1846, soon becoming the Imperial Imprensa de Música de Filippone e Cia and the first music publisher in South America to compete with European firms, with outlets in Bahia, Pernambuco and Buenos Aires. In 1847 it started the fortnightly *O Brasil musical* (dedicated to the Brazilian empress), which between 1848 and 1875 issued more than 500 salon pieces. Filippone was a Brazilian pioneer in using plate numbers (*O Brasil musical*, no.1 = plate no. 33) and in providing handsome engravings and publications lists on the front and back covers of its works, largely arrangements of opera airs. The firm became Filippone & Tor-

naghi in 1855 with the addition of Antonio Tornaghi, a composer and teacher, but Domenico Filippone regained complete control in 1873. In 1875 he was succeeded by his widow (to 1884) and daughter (Viuva Filippone & Filha), who published several of Ernesto Nazareth's popular polcas. Filippone issued further popular music until about 1911.

Enciclopédia de música brasileira: erudita, folclórica e popular, i (São Paulo, 1977), 353; *Música no Rio de Janeiro Imperial 1822–1870: Exposição comemorativa do primeiro decênio da Seção de Música e Arquivo Sonoro* (Rio de Janeiro, 1982), 71

R.S. (ii)

Fillmore. American family of publishers and musicians active in Ohio. Augustus D. Fillmore (1823–69) was a frontier preacher in Illinois before settling with his family in Cincinnati during the 1840s. He composed hymn tunes and revival songs and compiled a number of tunebooks using both shapenotes and a numerical notation system of his own invention; the most widely circulated were *The Christian Psalmist* (Cincinnati, 1847), edited with Silas W. Leonard, and the *Harp of Zion* (Cincinnati, 1865). Three of Fillmore's seven children took up music as a profession, jointly founding in the 1870s the publishing house of Fillmore Brothers, which specialized in educational, band and church music (the firm became Fillmore Music House about the turn of the century and was acquired by Carl Fischer in 1951). The eldest and most prominent of the three was James Henry Fillmore (1849–1936), who headed the publishing house and was well known as a gospel song composer; his works include *Songs of Gratitude* (Cincinnati, 1877). Fred(erick) A. Fillmore (*b* 1856), an organist and music teacher, also composed many gospel and Sunday school songs. Charles M. Fillmore (*b* 1860) became an ordained minister in the Christian Church and edited the monthly periodicals issued by Fillmore Brothers, the *Musical Messenger* (1891–7) and its successor, *Choir: a Monthly Journal of Church Music* (1899–1922).

Baker7; J. H. Hall: *Biography of Gospel Song and Hymn Writers* (New York, 1914/R1971), 271

P.C.E.

Filmtrax-Columbia. Anglo-American publishing firm. It was formed in 1988 when Filmtrax, the British entertainment company (founded London, 1948) which produced music for such films as *A Room with a View* and *Mona Lisa*, and, more recently, bought the British company Novello, acquired the American firms

Columbia Pictures Publications (the music publishing division of Columbia Pictures Entertainment, renamed CPP-Belwin) and Ivan Mogull Music. CPP-Belwin, based in Miami, owns the Belwin-Mills and Al Gallico Music catalogues; it arranges, prints and markets popular sheet music and songbooks. The Columbia catalogue contains some 64,000 titles, ranging from the *Ghostbusters* soundtrack to such standards as *Stand by your man*. Mogull also owns many standards, as well as songs by the pop group Abba.

N. Hunter: 'Columbia, Mogull Pub Companies', *Billboard* (16 April 1988), 1; 'Columbia Pictures Entertainment', *Wall Street Journal* (3 June 1988)
L.A.T., L.L.

Fiot & Meignen. American firm of publishers, active in Philadelphia. It was founded around 1835 by Augustus Fiot and the conductor Leopold Meignen (*b* France, 1793; *d* Philadelphia, 4 June 1873). The partnership was dissolved in 1839 but Fiot continued in business to 1855, when John E. Gould closed his New York shop and moved to Philadelphia to take over; Gould, in turn, passed the business to Beck & Lawton (1857–62). Its output consisted mostly of operatic arrangements and pieces for guitar and keyboard.

Fisher (1933); Dichter and Shapiro (1941, 2/1977); O. E. Albrecht: 'Meignen, Leopold', *GroveAM*

Firth, Hall & Pond. American firm of publishers and music dealers. It made woodwind and brass instruments, pianos and guitars, and imported a wide variety of musical goods. Based in New York, it was among the most important of American music publishers and produced material for church, home, concert hall, school and military bands; it was also one of the few firms in the USA to publish European classical music. It published some of the better-known American composers such as Gottschalk and H. C. Work, songs by Stephen Foster and tunes made popular by Christy's Minstrels.

The firm's principal partners were John Firth (*b* 1 Oct 1789; *d* Newtown, Long Island, 10 Sept 1864), William Hall (*b* Sparta, NY, 13 May 1796; *d* New York, 3 May 1874) and Sylvanus Billings Pond (*b* Milford, MA, 5 April 1792; *d* Brooklyn, NY, 12 March 1871). Firth, who was born in England, emigrated to the USA about 1810 and learnt to make flutes and fifes in the shop of Edward Riley. Hall was apprenticed to a musical instrument maker in Albany and went to work for Riley in New York about 1812. Pond also went to Albany in his youth, engaging in the commercial music business first independently and then in partnership with John Meacham.

Firth set up a business at 8 Warren Street, New York, in 1815, and Hall did so on Wooster Street in 1820; in 1820 they formed a partnership at 362 Pearl Street. In 1832 they were joined by Sylvanus Pond and moved to 1 Franklin Square. Pond wrote many Sunday school songs and some secular music. His *Union Melodies* for Sunday school singing and *The United States Psalmody* (1841) for choirs and singing societies were very successful. The firm continued until 1833 when Pond left the business for a few years, returning in 1837; his name appeared again in the title from 1842 onwards.

In 1845 additional space was acquired at 239 Broadway. When the firm was dissolved in 1847, William Hall & Son occupied 239 Broadway, and Firth, Pond & Co., who published most of Stephen Foster's songs (see illustration), continued at 1 Franklin Square. A further split in 1863 resulted in the firms of Firth, Son & Co. and William A. Pond & Co. (son of Sylvanus B. Pond). In 1867 Firth, Son & Co., and in 1875 William Hall & Son, were acquired by Oliver Ditson. William A. Pond & Co. continued into the 20th century.

F. O. Jones, ed.: *A Handbook of American Music and Musicians* (Canaseraga, NY, 1886/R1971); D. Spillane: *History of the American Pianoforte* (New York, 1890/R1969); Fisher (1933); J. T. Howard: *Stephen Foster, America's Troubadour* (New York, 1934, rev. 3/1962); S. Saunders: 'A Publication History of Stephen Foster's "Massa's in de Cold Ground" ', *Notes*, xliii (1986–7), 499
R.E.E.

Fischer, Carl. American firm of publishers. Carl Fischer was born in Buttstädt in 1849. Trained in music, he went to New York in 1872 and opened a musical instrument shop at 79 East 4th Street. He recognized the need for musical arrangements for the diversely constituted orchestras that prevailed at the time, and began to reproduce music (with permission) in longhand, eventually adopting lithography. As demand increased, he employed an engraver and an arranger, and by 1880 he had to move to larger quarters, at 6 Fourth Avenue, facing Cooper Union and its art school, and close to the principal concert halls of the city.

Fischer pursued a dual objective, both publishing music and selling instruments, music and methods (most of which were imported from Europe). Endeavouring to provide music suited to the tastes and styles of the period, he responded to the growing

Sheet-music cover of Stephen Foster's 'Jeanie with the light brown hair', published in New York in 1854

interest in band music and became the principal publisher of such figures as Arthur Pryor, John Philip Sousa and Henry Fillmore. Publication of *The Metronome*, a journal for bandleaders, was begun in 1885 and the firm still prides itself on its extensive band catalogue.

The field of school music received particular impetus under the leadership of Walter S. Fischer, who succeeded his father as president in 1923 (at which time the firm moved to its present 12-storey structure at 56–62 Cooper Square). The firm had always published the standard repertory of choral and orchestral music, and in 1907 began an invaluable monthly journal for professional musicians and music teachers, the *Musical Observer* (incorporated into the *Musical Courier* in 1931); it was to make important contributions with its accessible arrangements and easy methods (to replace the standard manuals). Leading instrumental performers provided arrangements of classical and contemporary works that have become standard material for concerts, recitals and master classes; Gustave Reese was director of publications, 1945–55.

In 1946 Frank H. Connor succeeded his father-in-law as president. He has continued the founder's policies by publishing an increasing number of new works and giving encouragement to contemporary music, especially to young composers. In the 1960s the firm participated in the Contemporary Music Project, sponsored by the Ford Foundation, and other similar undertakings, as well as the Ford Foundation's subsequent Recording-Publication Project, which encouraged collaboration between publishers and recording companies in the cause of contemporary music.

Composers represented by Carl Fischer, Inc. include Norman Dello Joio, Lukas Foss, Karl Kohn, John La Montaine, Peter Mennin, Douglas Moore, Randall Thompson and Virgil Thomson. Among the most important items in the Fischer catalogue are the Coopersmith edition of *Messiah* and the more recent addition of several early works by Webern.

While continually expanding its horizons, the Fischer firm continues to be a family-owned business; its present management is fourth-generation, with Hayden Connor jr general manager of the New York office, and Walter Fischer Connor in charge of the Boston, Chicago and San Francisco branches. The firm acquired Boosey & Hawkes in 1986.

S. F. Herz: 'The Carl Fischer Centennial', *MEJ*, lix/1 (1972), 80

W.T.M., M.J.

Fischer, J(oseph). American firm of publishers. Joseph Fischer (*b* Silberhausen, 9 April 1841; *d* Springfield, OH, 24 Nov 1901) emigrated with his brother Ignaz to the USA in their youth, and established the business of J. Fischer & Brother at Dayton, Ohio, in 1864. When the firm moved to New York (1875), Joseph became sole proprietor, being succeeded at his death by his sons George and Carl T. Fischer. In 1906 the firm was incorporated, with George as president and Carl as treasurer; in 1920 George's sons joined the business, Joseph as secretary and Eugene as assistant secretary. At first the firm specialized in music for the Roman Catholic church; later it published piano music by Abram Chasins, Hans Barth and Guy Maier, as well as many songs by Charles Wakefield Cadman, Lily Strickland, Eastwood Lane, James P. Dunn, Samuel Gaines and Howard McKinney. It had a particularly large output of octavo choral music, including compositions by Franz C. Bornschein, Harvey Gaul, William Lester, A. Walter Kramer, Joseph W. Clokey, Cecil Forsyth and Cyr de Brant; the catalogue also included two operas by Deems Taylor (*The King's Henchman* and *Peter Ibbetson*). In its last years the firm published some organ and orchestral music. It was acquired in 1970 by Belwin-Mills.

O. Thompson: *International Cyclopedia of Music and Musicians* (New York, 1939, 10/1975), 549; Dichter and Shapiro (1941, 2/1977)

E.C.K.

Flaxland, Gustave-Alexandre (*b* Strasbourg, 26 Jan 1821; *d* Paris, 11 Nov 1895). French publisher. Sent at the age of 15 by his father to Paris to make a living, he worked at various commercial jobs and then left a banking position to enter the Paris Conservatoire. He was already a fine pianist, and gave lessons to pay for his studies. Flaxland was never considered an outstanding pupil of the Conservatoire, although he composed several small piano pieces and songs and developed musical skills which helped him as a music publisher and editor. In 1847 he and his wife pooled their savings and bought a small shop at 4 place de la Madeleine, where they sold sheet music. The enterprise flourished immediately, and as their resources grew the shop became a musical and social centre in Paris. Particularly in the 1860s, Flaxland's was known for the distinguished circle of writers, musicians and wealthy patrons who convened there daily.

Flaxland's business prospered largely because he acquired the copyrights to the French editions of compositions by

Schumann (piano pieces) and Wagner, but the rights to some of Wagner's operas were controversial. During the winter of 1859–60 Franz Schott (of the Mainz firm of B. Schott's Söhne) contacted Wagner and bought the German, French and English publishing rights of the full score of *Das Rheingold*; Wagner hoped to repay his debts to Otto Wesendonk, who had advanced him money for each completed score of the *Ring*, but as the 10,000 francs he received from Schott were devoted to three Paris concerts, he sought additional funds early in 1860 by selling the French rights of three earlier operas to Flaxland. *Der fliegende Holländer* and *Tannhäuser* had been published in Germany by Meser, and his Dresden successor, Müller, claimed that Wagner was not entitled to sell the copyrights; Müller also threatened legal action against Flaxland, who avoided it by paying Müller 6000 francs. Wagner eventually (1863) conceded the foreign rights to Müller (not to Flaxland, as suggested by Dubuisson). The third opera, *Lohengrin*, had been published by Breitkopf & Härtel, who did not object to an independent French edition, but insisted that they also had a right to sell in France. Although Wagner has been accused of cheating Flaxland and failing in *Mein Leben* to give him due credit for his efforts, it seems that Wagner assumed that a contract with a German publisher applied only to Germany, leaving him free to arrange for publication elsewhere. The correspondence and documents of this period show little basis for the insinuation that he knowingly misled Flaxland; indeed the two appeared to be on the friendliest of terms and Flaxland championed Wagner's music in Paris even when feeling against Wagner was strong in France.

On 30 December 1869 Flaxland sold his enterprise to Durand Schoenewerk & Cie. He devoted his last years to composition and the manufacture of pianos, and remained an affluent and respected member of musical and literary society until his death.

FétisB; A. Dubuisson: 'Wagner et son éditeur parisien: lettres inédites de Wagner et de Minna Wagner', *ReM*, iv/11 (1923), 149 [53]; E. Newman: *The Life of Richard Wagner*, iii (New York, 1941); Hopkinson (1954); M. Gregor-Dellin, ed.: *Richard Wagner: Mein Leben* (Munich, 1963); C. Hopkinson: *Tannhäuser: an Examination of 36 Editions* (Tutzing, 1973)

T.L.

Flurschütz, Caspar [Kaspar] (*b* before 1590; *d* Augsburg, 27 Aug 1633). German music seller. In 1606 he married Regina Kreuzer, of an old Augsburg family, and from 1611 was active there as a music seller. Among his customers was the Munich court chapel. After his death the business was carried on by his widow. Together with the Augsburg family of Georg Willer, Flurschütz was among the most eminent members of the early German music trade. He sold Italian works published in Venice, Milan, Florence, Genoa, Bologna and Rome, and communicated with many German publishers. His stock catalogues are highly informative for the output of all composers active in the first third of the 17th century. As a publisher Flurschütz is notable for the collection *Flores musici* (1626).

R. Schaal, ed.: *Die Kataloge des Augsburger Musikalien-Händlers Kaspar Flurschütz, 1613–1628* (Wilhelmshaven, 1974)

R.S.

Foetisch, Charles (*b* Ballenstedt, 24 Nov 1838; *d* Pully-Lausanne, 13 Oct 1918). Swiss publisher of German birth. He lived in St Gall, before moving to Lausanne, where in 1865 he started a small music business. He bought the firm of Delavaux in 1877, and later the music firm of Hoffmann. He subsequently sold his business and his house to the four sons of his first marriage, who then founded the firm of Foetisch Frères and in 1905 made it into a joint-stock company. Two grandsons left the company in 1947 to start the business which in 1949 became the publishing house of M. P. Foetisch (to be distinguished from Foetisch Frères S.A., which no longer contains any representative of the Foetisch family).

Foetisch Frères S.A. has published numerous Swiss choral works, a small amount of instrumental music, and works by Honegger (*Le Roi David, Nicolas de Flue*). The house of M. P. Foetisch publishes Swiss choral works and Swiss contemporary music; its catalogue also includes works on musicological subjects and music appreciation.

G.-A. Bridel: 'Une famille de musiciens lausannois: les Hoffmann', *Revue historique vaudoise*, xlviii (1940), 203; J. Burdet: *Les origines du chant choral dans le canton de Vaud* (Lausanne, 1946); idem: *La musique dans le canton de Vaud au XIVe siècle* (Lausanne, 1971)

E.D.

Fog, Dan (*b* Hellerup, Copenhagen, 11 Aug 1919). Danish publisher and writer on music. He founded the publishing firm known by his name in 1953 when he purchased the Knud Larsen Musikforlag (founded 1906), and added to this an antiquarian business. He studied at the University of Copenhagen (1944–6) and the Royal Danish Conservatory (1948). From 1957 to 1977 he was in charge of the distribution of the publications of Samfundet til Udgivelse af Dansk Musik, active since 1871.

Dan Fog is regarded as the most important Scandinavian music antiquarian firm. Through the distribution of the Samfundet editions it further represents much 19th- and 20th-century Danish music, including works by J. A. P. Schulz, Niels Gade, Carl Nielsen, Knudåge Riisager and Ib Nørholm. Fog is co-editor of the *Edvard Grieg-Gesamtausgabe* and is also involved in the planning of the complete edition of works by Gade. His own writings have been concerned mainly with the bibliographical aspects of Danish music.

L.R.

Forberg, August Robert (*b* Lützen, nr. Leipzig, 18 May 1833; *d* Leipzig, 10 Oct 1880). German publisher. He opened a book and music shop in Leipzig in 1862. The company achieved international fame principally through the commission work undertaken by C. F. W. Siegel; Forberg's major activity was as a commissioning agent for well-known foreign music publishers. The founder's son Robert Max Forberg (1860–1920) became a partner in 1885 and the sole proprietor after 1888. In 1908 the company's catalogue carried over 6000 titles, which covered a wide range of musical taste. Both Forbergs contributed to the spread of Tchaikovsky's works in Germany; as the assign of the Jürgenson publishing firm, Robert Forberg's company helped the dissemination of many works by well-known Russian composers. Other composers promoted by the firm include Kienzl, Smetana, Richard Strauss, d'Albert, Hausegger and Reger. After suffering severe war damage in 1943, the firm moved to Bonn (1949) and to Bad Godesberg in 1951.

H.-M.P.

Forbes, John (*d* Aberdeen, Nov 1675). Scottish publisher. He was a stationer at Aberdeen, where he began publishing in 1656. In 1662 he and his son John (*b* Aberdeen; *d* Aberdeen, late 1704 or Jan 1705) were appointed official printers to the town and university by Aberdeen town council. They immediately ventured into music printing, presumably with town council backing; their first musical publication was *Songs and Fancies: to Thre, Foure, or Five Parts, both Apt for Voices and Viols* (1662, rev. 2/1666, rev. 3/1682), which was Scot-

land's first secular printed music book. Its presentation and contents now appear old-fashioned, resembling London madrigal partbooks of around 1600; it is prefaced by an 'Exposition of the Gamme', lifted almost word for word from Morley's *Plaine and Easie Introduction* of 1597. The three editions vary slightly in content; altogether they contain 77 different songs, of which eight are unknown elsewhere and 19 are identified from earlier manuscripts as partsongs current at the old Scottish court, which had moved to London in 1603. Curiously, only the cantus partbook was ever issued; it seems likely that Forbes was printing with sales to burgh music schools in mind (the Aberdeen music school is mentioned on the title-page). As music-school pupils mostly had unbroken voices, a preponderance of cantus copies would be required; other voice parts were perhaps supplied by Forbes in manuscript to individual order. The 1666 and 1682 editions also exist in impressions marked 'on sale in Edinburgh'. Only one copy of the 1662 edition is extant (now in the Huntington Library, San Marino, California).

In 1666 Forbes issued the first edition of the so-called Aberdeen Psalter, *Psalm Tunes to Four Voices*; it contains 14 metrical psalm tunes and one polyphonic psalm setting, 'Bon accord in reports'. This collection, too, seems to have been aimed at the educational market. It was reprinted as *The Twelve Tunes, for the Church of Scotland* in 1671 and 1706. In 1681 the firm issued *Festival Songs, or Certain Hymns Adopted to the Principall Christian Solemnities*.

After the death of the younger John Forbes the business passed, in January 1705, to his widow Margaret, then in December 1710 to his son-in-law James Nicoll. Nicoll issued the fourth and fifth editions of the Aberdeen Psalter in 1714 and 1720.

W. Kennedy: *Annals of Aberdeen* (London, 1818), i, 263, ii, 193; Kidson (1900); C. S. Terry: 'John Forbes's "Songs and Fancies" ', *MQ*, xxii (1936), 402; K. Elliott and H. Shire: Introduction to *Music in Scotland 1500–1700*, MB, xv (1957, rev. 2/1964); H. Shire: *Song, Dance and Poetry of the Court of Scotland* (Cambridge, 1969), 255; D. Johnson: *Music and Society in Lowland Scotland in the 18th Century* (London, 1972), 166

D.J.

Forckel, Andreas (*b* Mertzbach, nr. Coburg; *d* Coburg, *c*19 March 1624). German printer, active in Coburg. He was a journeyman with Jakob Winter in Lauingen, 1613–15, then by 8 November 1617 at the 'Matrikel' in Tübingen. He established himself in Coburg in 1619 and, after 1620, worked through the Fürstliche Druckerei. Besides many funeral orations and other non-musical works, he printed sacred and secular vocal music, mostly by Johann Dilliger and Melchior Franck, and a small amount of instrumental dance music. Johann Forckel (*d* Coburg, 1635), presumably his son, directed the Fürstliche Druckerei from 1624 to 1635 and continued printing music, including further works of Dilliger and Franck. On his death, the Fürstliche Druckerei was taken over by Johann Eyrich (*fl* 1635–56) and later Johann Konrad Mönch (*fl* 1655–90), both of whom continued to print music but on a smaller scale.

T. Welzenbach: 'Geschichte der Buchdruckerkunst im ehemaligen Herzogthume Franken und in benachbarten Städten', *Archiv des historischen Vereins von Unterfranken und Aschaffenburg*, xiv/2 (1857), 117–258; Benzing (1963, 2/1982)

T.D.W.

Formschneider [Andreae, Grapheus], **Hieronymus** [Jeronimus] (*b* Mergentheim, Franconia; *d* Nuremberg, 7 May 1556). German printer. There has been considerable confusion over the name 'Formschneider'. His gravestone is inscribed 'Jeronimus Andre Formschneider', which suggests that 'Andre' may actually be his family name, whereas 'Formschneider' (German for 'typecutter') is simply a designation of his trade. The Latin form 'Grapheus', found in some of his publications, is a translation of 'Formschneider'. In any case Formschneider achieved fame as a typecutter. First mentioned in the records of Nuremberg in 1515, he became a citizen in 1523 and is officially listed as a typecutter in 1526 and as a printer in the following year. Formschneider appears to have possessed a fiery temper, as frequent mention of him in later city records shows. Having been employed by the city in 1535 as a die sinker, he worked steadily for some years but became involved in a violent argument with the mayor in 1542, for which he was sentenced to 14 days in jail and fired. The years from 1544 to 1549 were spent as a typesetter in the employ of Georg Wachter and only after this could he resume his printing business.

That he succeeded after so grave a scandal is apparently due to his unquestioned excellence. One of the most prominent printers of the Reformation period, Formschneider is famous for his collaboration with Albrecht Dürer, for whom he executed numerous woodcuts, and for his editions of Luther's German Psalter and Prayer Book. Using single-impression type for his music publications, he exhibited unusual craftmanship, particularly in fitting together the individual forms. He was well known as the first printer of lute tablatures in Nuremberg and as the publisher of Hans Ott's collections and Isaac's *Choralis constantinus*.

For an illustration *see* LIGATURE.

A. Schmid: *Ottaviano dei Petrucci da Fossombrone und seine Nachfolger im sechzehnten Jahrhunderte* (Vienna, 1845/R1968); W. Tappert: 'Die Lautenbücher des Hans Gerle', *MMg*, xviii (1886), 101; P. Cohen: *Musikdruck und -drucker zu Nürnberg im sechzehnten Jahrhundert* (Nuremberg, 1927); H. Albrecht: 'Formschneider, Hieronymus', *MGG*; K. Holzmann: *Hieronymus Formschneyders Sammeldruck Trium vocum carmina, Nürnberg, 1538* (diss., U. of Freiburg, 1957); Benzing (1963, 2/1982); Brown (1965)

M.L.G.

Forster. English family of violin makers and publishers, active in London from about 1760 to 1841. William Forster (i) (*b* Brampton, Cumberland, 1739; *d* London, 14 Dec 1808), known as 'Old Forster', went to London in 1759 and within a short time had established himself in St Martin's Lane. By the early 1770s his violins were in demand, and, benefiting from royal patronage, he moved to the Strand about 1785. He issued instrumental music by J. C. Bach, G. M. Cambini and Haydn (over 100 works: in 1781 Forster made an agreement with Haydn for the publication rights in England of his music).

His son William Forster (ii) (*b* ?London, 7 Jan 1764; *d* ?London, 24 July 1824), also a violin maker, took over the selling and publishing side of his father's business in July 1786, and as well as reissuing some of his father's editions published annual country-dance books. Simon Andrew Forster (*b* 13 May 1801; *d* 2 Feb 1870), a son of William Forster (ii), carried on the business after his father's death.

Humphries and Smith (1954, 2/1970); H. C. Robbins Landon: *The Symphonies of Joseph Haydn* (London, 1955); idem, ed.: *The Collected Correspondence and London Notebooks of Joseph Haydn* (London, 1959); Neighbour and Tyson (1965); H. E. Poole: 'Music Engraving Practice in Eighteenth-century London: a Study of some Forster Editions of Haydn and their Manuscript Sources', *Music and Bibliography: Essays in Honour of Alec Hyatt King* (London, 1980), 98–131

P.W.J.

Fortier, B. (*fl c*1736–40). French engraver and printer, resident in London. Though his musical activities were apparently short-lived (according to Hawkins he was also a watchmaker), he is renowned for the excellence of his engraving, particularly in his

Opening of Sonata XXIV from Domenico Scarlatti's 'Essercizi per gravicembalo', engraved by Fortier (1738 or 1739)

superb edition of Domenico Scarlatti's *Essercizi per gravicembalo* (1739), with notes and staves of a larger size than usual (see illustration). Other fine engravings by Fortier include Porpora's *Sinfonie da camera ... opra II* (1736), De Fesch's *XII sonate, VI per il violino e basso per l'organo ... e VI a duoi violoncelli ... opera ottava* (1736), a song by Farinelli, *Ossequioso ringraziamento* (c1737), Giuseppe Sammartini's *VI concerti grossi ... opra II* (1738) and Guerini's *Sonate a violino con viola da gamba ó cembalo* (c1740).

HawkinsH; R. Kirkpatrick: *Domenico Scarlatti* (Princeton, 1953); Humphries and Smith (1954, 2/1970)

W.C.S./P.W.J.

Foucault, Henry (*fl* Paris, 1690–1720). French music dealer and publisher. It is not known whether he was related to earlier publishers with the same family name, none of whom was apparently involved in music printing. Like other 18th-century music dealers, Henry Foucault was associated with the corporation of haberdashers and jewellers rather than that of the booksellers. He was originally a paper seller, with a shop 'A la règle d'or', rue St Honoré, but seems to have branched out from this trade by 28 June 1690, when a condemnation issued by the Conseil d'Etat accused him – in association with the engraver Henri de Baussen – of contravening Christophe Ballard's royal privilege by publishing 'divers airs de musique'. Two years later Foucault's name appears on the title-page of Marais' *Pièces en trio pour les flûtes, violon & dessus de viole*, in association with Murel, Bonneüil and the composer, but he is still designated simply as 'marchand papetier'. However by 1697, in Christophe Ballard's edition of J. Campra's *L'Europe galante*, he is advertised as a music dealer offering for sale manuscript copies of extracts from Lully's operas and early ballets in six folio volumes, as well as *symphonies* for violin, books of harpsichord and organ music, Latin motets, *leçons de ténèbres* and various novelties. He also offered to buy old operas and to copy music. Foucault thus functioned as a link between the composer and printer (using the services of various engravers, notably Henri de Baussen, Claude Roussel and F. du Plessy); he occasionally risked publication at his own expense, but more often shared the expense with the composer.

Foucault was the first music publisher seriously to threaten the Ballard monopoly. The Ballards, who had long dominated movable-type printing in France, had already encountered increasing competition from engraving. Christophe Ballard's fifth *Recueil d'airs sérieux et à boire de differents auteurs* (1706) includes a catalogue of printed music sold 'A la règle d'or', and this, together with the aforementioned advertisement of 1697, suggests that the rivals had reconciled their differences and were collaborating. In 1702 Foucault had collaborated with Baussen and Claude Roussel in publishing a collection of *airs* by J.-B. Bousset, Christophe Ballard's son-in-law; in 1709 he republished this collection along with a second volume in association with Christophe Ballard's sister-in-law (P. Ballard's widow). A catalogue published by Christophe's son J.-B. C. Ballard in 1719 still advertises Foucault's shop. The links between the two families were reinforced on 2 July 1724 when Henry Foucault's successor François Boivin married Christophe Ballard's granddaughter. Foucault must have died some time between 17 October 1719 and 1720, when his widow's name appears on the title-page of a collection of motets by Campra. On 15 July 1721 his widow sold the shop and music business in the rue St Honoré to François Boivin and his uncle, the composer Michel Pignolet de Montéclair.

The catalogue of 1706 advertises sonatas by Corelli, Dandrieu, Duval and Michely, trios by La Barre, harpsichord books by D'Anglebert, Chambonnières, Lebègue, Leroux and Luc Marchand, organ books by Boyvin, Corrette, Foucquet and Lebègue, motets by Bernier, Brossard, Campra, J.-F. Lochon, Morin and Suffret, vocal anthologies (*Parodies bachiques* and *Brunettes*) and theoretical treatises (L'Affilard's *Méthode* and Masson's *Traité de composition*). Foucault also published violin sonatas by Mascitti (1704, 1706–7, 1711 and 1714) and Henry Eccles (1720; a second set was issued by Boivin in 1723), two books of motets and six books of *Cantates profanes à 1 & 2 voix* by Bernier (1703–18; two further ones by Boivin in 1723), a collection of motets by G. A. Guido (1707), a *Livre de musique d'église* by Alexandre de Villeneuve (1719), and two sets of cantatas by T.-L. Bourgeois (1709 in collaboration with Leclerc, and 1715 with Leclerc & Ribou).

G. Lepreux: *Gallia typographica, série parisienne* (Paris, 1911); A. Devriès: *Édition et commerce de la musique gravée à Paris dans la première moitié du XVIIIe siècle* (Geneva, 1976); Devriès and Lesure, (1979–88)

F.D. (ii)

Fougt, Henric [Henry] (*b* Lövånger, Swedish Lapland, 1720; *d* ?Stockholm, 1782). Swedish printer and publisher, active in London. After studies at Uppsala University and some years of clerical work he became a general book printer. About 1760 he developed his own version of Breitkopf's improvements in printing music from movable type, using a system of 166 characters. He applied for a patent in 1763, and in the following year was granted a privilege for music printing in Sweden for 25 years. Lacking economic support, however, he left Sweden in 1767 and in November of that year arrived in London, where he began to issue music in his new type. After submitting his first work, an edition of Uttini's Six Sonatas op.1, to the Society for the Encouragement of Arts, Manufactures and Commerce, he obtained a resolution from that body that his method of printing was superior and much cheaper than any that had been in use in Great Britain; he later printed this resolution as a preface to his edition of Sarti's Three Sonatas.

Fougt may be considered a pioneer of cheap music, for he sold his music at 'one penny per page, or 18 for a shilling', far less than the sixpence a page which was the average price of music at that time. He apparently aroused ill-feeling among the rest of the trade, though Hawkins was probably wrong in saying that they drove him out of the country by undercutting his publications. During his three years in London he published about 80 sheet songs and instrumental pieces, and eight more substantial items, including the sonatas mentioned above, others by Croce, Leoni, Menesini, Nardini and Sabatini, and *Twelve of the most Favourite French Songs collected from the Comic Operas*. The typography is of excellent clarity, though the results are not as elegant as the best engraved music of the period.

In 1770 Fougt sold his plant and type to Robert Falkener and returned to Stockholm, where in 1773 he was granted a new privilege by Gustavus III and enjoyed patronage as royal printer. Falkener, who was also a harpsichord maker, continued to issue sheet songs in Fougt's style until 1780, and was the author and printer of *Instructions for Playing the Harpsichord* (1770).

HawkinsH; A. Wiberg: 'Ur det svenska musiktryckets historia: Henrik Fougts musiktryckeri', *Nordisk boktryckarekonst*, 1 (1949), 211, li (1950), 78, 119, 215; Humphries and Smith (1954, 2/1970); S. G. Lindberg: 'John Baskerville och Henric Fougt', *Biblis 1958*, 67–134; A. Vretblad: 'Henric Fougts engelska musiktryck', *Biblis 1958*, 135; H.E. Poole: 'New Music Types: Invention in the Eighteenth Century', *Journal of the Printing Historical Society*, i (1965), 21, ii (1966), 23; J. A.

Parkinson: 'Henric Fougt, Typographer Extraordinary', *Music and Bibliography: Essays in Honour of Alec Hyatt King* (London, 1980), 89

P.W.J.

Fournier, Pierre-Simon (*le jeune*) (*b* Paris, 15 Sept 1712; *d* Paris, 8 Oct 1768). French typographer. The son of a typefounder, he was cutting punches and casting type by 1736, and in 1739 was registered in this craft with the printing section of the Chambre Syndicale of Paris. He issued his first specimen book, *Modéles des caractères de l'imprimerie*, in 1742. It was a tremendous achievement, showing (among other material) 4600 letters that he had cut in a wide range of styles with their sizes correlated in a logical and mathematical way. This system, quite new in typefounding, he had evolved in 1737 and he showed it in his *Modéles* as 'Table des proportions des differens caractères de l'imprimerie'.

Fournier's power of analysis and prodigious technical skill were clearly demonstrated in the six types that he devised for the printing of music. Two were for plainchant, one was for 'Hugenot music'. Three were for songs and instrumental music. The first of this group was designed for double impression, with the stave lines printed first and the notes and other signs overprinted in a second pass through the press (1756). The other two (1760) were based on a variation of a technique originated by Breitkopf which required only one pull at the press to deliver a complete copy.

In the foreword to his *Essai d'un nouveau caractère de fonte*, in which he demonstrated his 1756 type, Fournier drew attention to the stagnation that had settled over French music printing, claiming that French publishers could produce music characters in the form of squares or diamonds only. He had devised a method of rendering music from type as if it had been printed by copperplate engraving, but had laid it aside as only one person in France was allowed to undertake this sort of printing (Christophe-Jean-François Ballard, music printer to the king, 1750–65). Breitkopf had revived his interest in the subject, however, and the types he showed in the specimen were the outcome; he offered six short pieces of music set in round-headed notes as if engraved, with the words of the songs in his elegant italic, and the decorative title-page framed by some of his typographical border units: all very much in the taste of the day. Fournier had been 'obliged', as he wrote, 'to be the inventor, the cutter, the founder, the compositor and the printer'. This quotation defines his notion of the complete typographer: the master of a complex of related skills, a craftsman equipped and free to practise them all.

Unfortunately the regulations of the printing trade denied Fournier, as a cutter and founder of types, the right to print: the Ballard monopoly denied him the right to exploit his music. So in 1756 he applied to the Chambre Syndicale to be admitted as a printer, but was refused. He presented a petition, and after considerable controversy, on 27 July 1764, Parlement confirmed Ballard as sole printer of music to the king but decreed also that any other printer was authorized to print music should he so wish. Ballard, in the eyes of the establishment of the day 'a lazy man without much talent', took a serious view of this threat to his interest. On 23 October 1764, to demonstrate his still privileged status he made a gesture towards having some of Fournier's music type seized at the office of a printer who was using it to produce a book that was to be published by subscription. It was a gesture without substance: the Ballard monopoly had been broken.

During the time Fournier's petition was under consideration the reporter of the Grand Conseil had asked for a memorial on 'the affair of the music characters'. Fournier wrote one and having extended the historical part 'to make it more interesting' he published it as a general account of typographical music printing (*Traité historique et critique*, 1765). Though it is polemical, the work contains much source material collected from the archives of letter cutters and founders, from notarial records, court registers and elsewhere, which gives it permanent value. The *Traité* is rounded off with an 'Ariette, mise en musique par M. l'Abbé Dugué à Paris, des nouveaux caractères de Fournier le jeune', in which his 'petite musique' and 'grosse musique' are used in two settings of words: the 'petite musique' shown as a vocal line only, the 'grosse musique' as a vocal line with an accompaniment for the harp.

In 1765 Fournier had the satisfaction of seeing his 'petite musique' used to splendid effect in Jean Monnet's *Anthologie françoise* (see illustration). Ideally suited to the scale of the pocket book, the type was adopted by printers to set favourite airs in comedies with music and for similar purposes. The type survived well, and as late as 1819 was in case at the Imprimerie Royale in Paris.

N. and F. Gando: *Observations sur le Traité historique et critique de Monsieur Fournier le jeune sur l'origine et les progrès des caractères de fonte pour l'impression de la musique* (Berne, 1766); G. Lepreux: *Gallia typographica, série parisienne*, i (Paris,

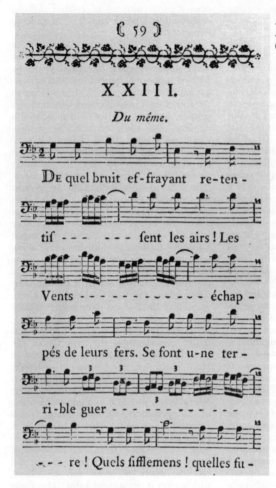

Fournier's 'petite musique' from Jean Monnet's 'Anthologie françoise', ii (1765), printed by Barbou

1911); P. Beaujon: *Pierre Simon Fournier 1712–1768, and XVIIIth Century French Typography* (London, 1926); H. Carter, ed.: *Fournier on Typefounding* (London, 1930) [trans. of P.-S. Fournier: *Manuel typographique* (Paris, 1764–8)]; A. Hutt: *Fournier the Compleat Typographer* (London, 1972)

H.E.P.

Fox, Sam. American publishing firm. It was founded in 1906 in Cleveland, Ohio, and pioneered the publication of music composed for films; it was the first to publish original scores for major film companies, including Paramount and Warner Bros., and supplied scores for short subjects, 'March of Time' newsreels, film travelogues and documentaries. The company was also one of the first to publish instructional music and has continued to produce didactic works for jazz piano, guitar and accordion. In 1917 the firm became the exclusive publisher of John

Philip Sousa and represented him until his death in 1934. About 1935 the company moved from Cleveland to New York, and subsequently offices were opened in Santa Barbara and Fort Lauderdale.

W.T.M., M.J.

Franceschi [de' Franceschi]. Italian family of printers. The best known is Francesco Franceschi (*d* in or before 1599). He signed his volumes 'Francesco dei Franceschi Senese', which implies that he came from Siena. Between 1562 and 1599 he printed a great many volumes at Venice, including the works of Zarlino. His only other musical prints were also theoretical – the writings of Maurolyco and of Paolini. His music printing is as elegant as any of the period, and he used his own fount of type. Giovanni Antonio de' Franceschi was probably his relative (there were several other contemporary printers with this name, but they did not print music); he worked at Palermo from 1592 to 1599, and produced a reprint of Arcadelt's works and the first volume of Antonio Il Verso. He printed another edition of Zarlino's works in Venice in 1602.

S.B. (iii)

Francis, Day & Hunter. English firm of publishers. It was founded by William and James Francis and David Day in 1877 (as W. & J. Francis and Day, then Francis Brothers & Day); Day had experience in music publishing, and the Francis brothers needed a publisher for the songs they wrote and performed (from 1873) with the Mohawk Minstrels. They were joined by Harry Hunter, songwriter and leader of the Manhattan Minstrels, who sold his interest in 1900. Their first offices were in Oxford Street; in 1897 they moved to Charing Cross Road, becoming the first popular music publishers in the area that became London's 'Tin Pan Alley'. They issued music-hall songs, and in 1882 published their first *Comic Annual and Dance Album*. About 1900 Day formed the Musical Copyright Association to protect the interests of songwriters and their publishers against pirate firms. Members brought the issue of music piracy to national attention; a new Copyright Act resulted (1911), and in 1914 Day helped found the Performing Rights Society.

Francis, Day & Hunter were among the first to publish inexpensive mass-produced editions of songs in sheet form, with at least 25,000 first-print copies at a much lower price than had been possible hitherto. The firm opened an office in New York in 1905 (it soon joined with T. B. Harms & Co. and in 1920 with Leo Feist Co.); a Paris office was opened in about 1920, a Berlin office in 1928. After World War I Francis, Day & Hunter became one of the most important publishers of educational, classical and popular music in Great Britain; it had exclusive publishing arrangements with various artists, including Harry Lauder and Leslie Stuart, and sold music, records and instruments. In 1945 the firm bought out the catalogue of B. Feldman & Co., and in 1972 became a subsidiary of EMI Music Publishing Ltd.

J. Abbott: *The Story of Francis, Day & Hunter* (London, 1952); E. Rogers: *Tin Pan Alley* (London, 1964)

D.L.R.

Franck, Theodor (*fl* 1480–95). German printer, active in Venice. He was known as Theodor of Würzburg. His name appears

as printer in only one book, the first edition of the *Grammatica* (Venice, 21 March 1480) by the Dominican, Franciscus Niger. Its publisher, Johann Santritter, a mathematician and astronomer from Heilbronn, was befriended by Niger upon his arrival in Venice and showed his appreciation by publishing the grammar. Book 8 contains sections on metre, rhythm and harmony, the last illustrated with six pages of the first printed mensural music. The *Grammatica* is a rare example of music type carefully printed on space left for hand-drawn staves; the reverse technique, printed staves for handwritten music, was common in the 15th century. Theodor's fount of white mensural type has nine designs, four of which are long with stems of varying lengths. The designs and measurements resemble closely the next mensural fount, used by Petrucci in Venice in 1501.

F. Geldner: *Die deutschen Inkunabeldrucker: ein Handbuch der deutschen Buchdrucker des XV. Jahrhunderts nach Druckorten*, ii (Stuttgart, 1970), 84; Duggan (1981)

M.K.D.

Frank. American firm of publishers. It was founded in New York in 1949 by the composer and lyricist Frank Loesser and specializes in the publication of musical plays and popular songs. It also publishes choral, band, orchestral, solo, ensemble and piano music, as well as textbooks and methods. Catalogues acquired by the firm include those of Carmichael Music Publications and the Walter Reade Music Corp. A former division of Frank Music Corp., Music Theatre International (also founded by Loesser), is one of the most active leasing agents for musical plays; works they represent which are published by Frank include Loesser's own *Where's Charley?*, *Guys and Dolls*, *How to Succeed in Business* and *The Most Happy Fella* (as well as his score for the film musical *Hans Christian Andersen*), and Meredith Willson's *The Music Man* and *The Unsinkable Molly Brown*.

W.T.M., M.J./R

Frey, Jacques-Joseph (*b* 1782; *d* 9 June 1838). French publisher, active in Paris. He studied the violin at the Paris Conservatoire and from 1816 to 1838 played the viola in the Opéra orchestra. In August 1811 he purchased the engraved plates, manuscripts and business of Magasin de Musique (ii), establishing himself in their premises at 76 rue de Richelieu. Shortly afterwards (by November 1812) he moved to 8 place des Victoires, and in April 1838 to 22 boulevard Montmartre. On 17 November 1839

Richault announced that he had purchased 'all the engraved plates constituting the music business of the late M. Frey'.

Frey's prime achievement was to publish orchestral scores of Mozart's seven major operas. Only two had previously appeared in France: *Die Zauberflöte*, published by Sieber *père* in a strange adaptation entitled *Les mystères d'Isis*, and *Figaro*, published by Magasin de Musique (ii); Frey engraved a correct edition of the former and reissued the latter as part of his series, which attracted more than 250 subscribers. He also reprinted 32 of Grétry's operas from the original plates, but this series had a mere 19 subscribers. He published full scores of operas by Rodolphe Kreutzer, J.-F. Le Sueur and E. N. Méhul as well as instrumental and vocal music and a number of instrumental methods; the latter included two of his own authorship, for violin and for tambour de basque. All his publications were engraved.

C. Pierre: *Le Magasin de musique à l'usage des Fêtes nationales et du Conservatoire* (Paris, 1895/R1974), 112; Hopkinson (1954); Devriès and Lesure (1979–88)

R.M.

Friedlein, Rudolf Fryderyk (*b* Kraków, 7 Aug 1811; *d* Warsaw, 20 July 1873). Polish bookseller and publisher. He worked in the bookshop run by his father, Jan Jerzy Fryderyk Friedlein, in Kraków, then from 1834 with E. Günther in Leszno. In 1839 he entered into partnership with Spiess's Warsaw firm, which he bought in 1848 and managed from 1851 under his own name. Friedlein's became one of the leading bookshops in Warsaw, being well stocked and providing a lending service. Soon after 1840 he also began to publish music, maintaining a high musical standard in the compositions he issued. His printing works were technically advanced: he was the first Warsaw publisher to number his plates and he was also the first to print Moniuszko's works. In about 1860 Friedlein was in financial difficulties and sold some of his editions to the firm newly established by Gebethner and Wolff, both of whom had been his pupils. After the January Insurrection (1865) he was arrested by tsarist authorities and sent into exile in Tver. He was released in 1870, but his firm had been liquidated in 1865.

K. Mazur: *Pierwodruki Stanisława Moniuszki* [The first editions of Moniuszko] (Warsaw, 1970), 37; F. Pieczątkowski: 'Friedlein, Rudolf', *Słownik pracowników książki polskiej* [Dictionary of Polish printers] (Warsaw and Łódź, 1972)

K.M. (i)

Fromont. French firm of publishers. It was founded in Paris about 1885 by Eugène Fromont. In 1891 the publisher Georges Hartmann sold his catalogue to Heugel and began publishing in partnership with Fromont. Under Hartmann's energetic and generous leadership the firm published a number of important works by Debussy, including the *Prélude à l'après-midi d'un faune* (1895), *Chansons de Bilitis* (1899) and *Nocturnes* (1900). The firm continued to publish Debussy's music after Hartmann's death on 22 April 1900, most importantly *Pelléas et Mélisande* (vocal score, 1902), which is dedicated to Hartmann's memory, and *Pour le piano* (1901). The firm continued in business until 1922, after which Fromont's publications were taken over and reissued by Jean Jobert of Paris.

Devriès and Lesure (1979–88)

N.S.

Fürstliche Druckerei. German printing firm, active in Wolfenbüttel from 1598 to 1614. Although no music is known to have been printed by the Fürstliche Druckerei (also called the 'Officina typographica Principalis Brunsvicensis') in its first nine years, it was responsible for printing at least 18 musical works between 1607 and 1614, including exceptionally beautiful editions of Michael Praetorius's *Musae Sioniae* (parts v–ix, 1607–10), *Terpsichore* (1612), *Urania* (1613) and several other works.

Benzing (1963, 2/1982); D. W. Krummel: 'Early German Partbook Type Faces', *Gutenberg-Jb 1985*, 80

T.D.W.

Fürstner. German firm of publishers. Adolph Fürstner (*b* Berlin, 3 April 1833; *d* Bad Nauheim, 6 June 1908) probably received part of his training as a publisher in France. Later he worked as head clerk with Bote & Bock, and in 1868 he founded his own music publishing house in Berlin, publishing mainly works by French composers. Within four years he was in a position to buy the Dresden publishing firm of C. F. Meser, thus acquiring publication rights of Wagner's *Rienzi*, *Der fliegende Holländer* and *Tannhäuser*. Apart from some of Liszt's compositions he published works by Cornelius, Massenet, Glinka and in 1889 Richard Strauss, with whom he later signed a publishing contract for some years. Both *Salome* and *Elektra* were published by Fürstner, but the latter was handled after Adolph Fürstner's death by his son and successor Otto Fürstner (*b* Berlin, 17 Oct 1886; *d* London, 18 June 1958), to whom Strauss entrusted his later operas (*Rosenkavalier*,

Ariadne auf Naxos, Frau ohne Schatten and others). The firm also published Pfitzner's *Palestrina*, a wide repertory of piano music, as well as light music for salon orchestra, which was particularly successful. In 1933 Otto left Germany and emigrated to England, where the firm of Fürstner Ltd was formed. He then leased the German publishing rights to the employees of the Johannes Oertel firm; during World War II, the Fürstner publishing house was erased from the German trade register. In 1943 a number of rights were sold to Boosey & Hawkes; those retained were administered in England by Ursula Fürstner as Fürstner Ltd. Ursula returned to Germany in the mid-1970s and died in 1986, whereupon the remaining rights were sold to Schott of Mainz.

H. Becker: 'Fürstner, Adolph', *MGG*; F. Krautwurst: 'Fürstner, Adolph & Otto', *NDB*; Plesske (1968); R. Elvers: 'Hugo Wolfs Briefe an den Verleger Adolph Fürstner in Berlin', *Musik, Edition, Interpretation: Gedenkschrift Günther Henle* (Munich, 1980), 153

T.W.

G

Galaxy. American publishing firm. It was founded in New York in 1931 by George Maxwell, who had been head of the American branch of Ricordi from 1899. Under the leadership of A. Walter Kramer, Galaxy quickly became established as a publisher of serious music, specializing in choral works. Later, under the editorship of Robert Ward, it began publishing symphonic, band and chamber music as well as opera and music for school use. American composers published by Galaxy Music Corporation include William Bergsma, Charles Wakefield Cadman, Castelnuovo-Tedesco, Richard Hageman, Hunter Johnson, Otto Luening, George Mead, Halsey Stevens and William Grant Still. From its earliest years Galaxy's name has been linked in particular with English music; the firm is the sole agent for Stainer & Bell, Delrieux, Editions Ouvrières and London Pro Musica Editions.

W. C. Rorick: 'Galaxy Music Corporation: the First Fifty Years', *FAM*, xxix (1982), 125

W.T.M., M.J./R

Galliard. English firm of publishers. It was formed in May 1962 as a wholly owned subsidiary of Galaxy Music Corporation (New York), which had purchased the firm of Augener and thereby its subsidiaries Joseph Williams and Joseph Weekes. Galliard continued to distribute the works of these firms and represented Galaxy in Great Britain, in addition to publishing numerous popular works on its own. In February 1971 the firm entered a trading partnership with Stainer & Bell, forming an independent body known as Publishing Services Partnership to distribute the works of both firms. This was dissolved in November 1972, when Galliard was bought by Stainer & Bell.

Gando. French family of typefounders. Nicolas Gando (*b* Geneva, early 18th century; *d* Paris, 1767) having first established himself in Geneva, moved in 1736 to Paris where he took over the foundry of his uncle Jean Louis Gando. Nicolas issued a specimen of his types in 1745, and another in 1758 to show the resources of Claude Lamesle's foundry, which he bought that year. His son Pierre François (*b* Geneva, 1733; *d* Paris, 1800) was a partner in the foundry and succeeded him.

The Gandos owe their place in history less to the qualities of their type than to their polemical exchanges with Pierre-Simon Fournier on the question of typographical music printing. In the course of his *Traité historique*, a general account of developments in music printing (and a bitter attack on the exclusive privilege enjoyed by the Ballard family), Fournier accused the Gandos, in terms very damaging to their reputation, of passing off as their own in 1764, music characters which he had published in 1756. The Gandos, supporting Ballard and the printing establishment, replied at length pointing out errors in Fournier's historical account and accusing him of plagiarizing the methods devised for typographical music printing by Breitkopf (1754–5). They also described their own system. They cast clefs, bar-lines, minims, crotchets, detached quavers (and sub-divisions of the quaver) in one piece as complete characters, without fragments of staff attached. Beams to join the stems of

251

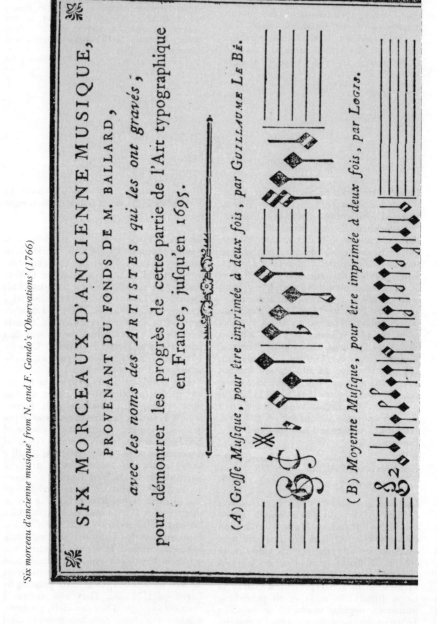

'Six morceau d'ancienne musique' from N. and F. Gando's 'Observations' (1766)

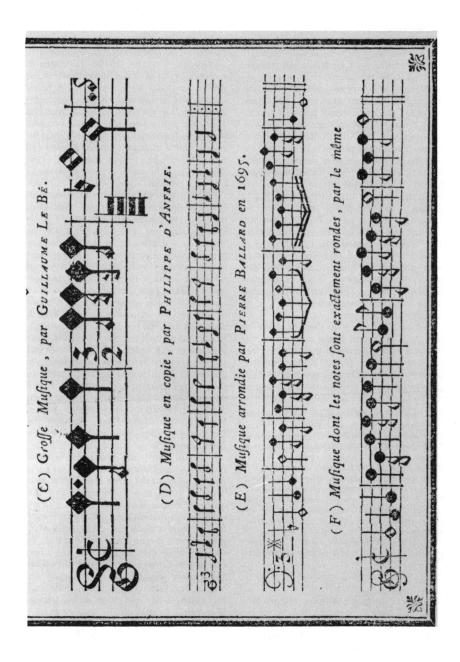

(C) *Groſſe Muſique, par* GUILLAUME LE BÉ.

(D) *Muſique en copie, par* PHILIPPE D'ANFRIE.

(E) *Muſique arrondie par* PIERRE BALLARD *en* 1695.

(F) *Muſique dont les notes ſont exactement rondes, par le même*

tied quavers and the like were also cast as single pieces in various lengths so that the only junction required was between the stem of the note (a crotchet with its stem reduced if necessary) and the small connecting strokes cast on the beam at standard intervals. The staves were made up of continuous pieces of metal.

It was necessary to pass the sheet through the press twice for a complete impression: once to print the notes, clefs, key signatures, rests, bar-lines etc, and once to print the staves, words and other ancillary material. Under normal printing conditions it was difficult to align the notes and staves exactly, because of the fine adjustments that had to be made in the relative position of type material in the two separate formes. After damping, inking and being passed through the press to take an impression of the first forme there was a danger that the paper might lose its integrity while it was waiting to be put through the press with the second forme. The Gandos claimed the invention of a press which avoided this: the two formes were worked in rapid succession and the paper was not moved from its original printing position between impressions. These two factors ensured that the size of the sheet did not vary.

In their *Observations* the Gandos offered a four-page setting of Psalm cl by the Abbé Roussier as a specimen of their types printed on their special press. Of much greater interest, they also showed specimens of six early music types from the stock-in-trade of the Ballard concern (see illustration).

P.-S. Fournier: *Essai d'un nouveau caractère de fonte pour l'impression de la musique* (Paris, 1756); idem: *Traité historique et critique sur l'origine et les progrès des caractères de fonte pour l'impression de la musique, avec des épreuves de nouveaux caractères de musique* (Berne, 1765); N. and F. Gando: *Observations sur le Traité historique et critique de Monsieur Fournier le jeune sur l'origine et les progrès des caractères de fonte pour l'impression de la musique* (Berne, 1766); P.-S. Fournier: 'Réponse à un mémoire publiée en 1766 par MM. Gando, au sujet des caractères de fonte pour la musique', *Manuel typographique*, ii (Paris, 1768), 289; M. Audin: *Les livrets typographiques des fonderies françaises créées avant 1800* (Paris, 1933, rev. 2/1964)

H.E.P.

Gardano [Gardane]. Family of printers active in Venice.

(1) **Antonio** [Antoine] **Gardano** (*b* southern France, 1509; *d* Venice, 28 Oct 1569). Venetian printer and publisher. Called 'musico francese' in Venetian documents, he was probably from the region around Gardanne in southern France, an

area that included the diocese of Fréjus, episcopal see of Gardano's first patron, Bishop Leone Orsino. Gardano's printer's mark, a lion and a bear facing each other, was inspired by the *leone* and *orso* of his patron's name. Until 1555 he used the French spelling 'Gardane' in his imprints; afterwards he and his sons adopted the Italian form. Gardano probably moved to Venice in the late 1530s, becoming a member of the city's intellectual and artistic circles, and may have conducted a music school before opening his printing house and bookshop on the calle de la Scimia in 1538. He was a friend of Pietro Aretino's secretary, Nicolò Franco, and published his letters and a dialogue before Franco fell into Aretino's bad graces and left the city. These were the only non-musical works Gardano printed.

Of his nearly 450 music books, more than half are devoted to madrigals. But since many of these were new editions of previous publications, the actual size of the repertory is much smaller than it might at first appear. Motets make up the next largest category, with about 70 editions and far fewer reprints than in the secular output. Gardano published about 40 books of *canzone villanesche* and villottas, 28 editions of lute and keyboard music, 26 of French chansons and still fewer of masses, magnificats, psalms and other sacred genres. Four composers – Arcadelt, Willaert, Rore and Lassus – figure especially prominently in Gardano's list; editions devoted chiefly to their works make up a quarter of his total output. Others whose works appear often in his publications are Ruffo, Nasco, Morales, Verdelot, Festa, Jacquet of Mantua, Janequin, Wert and Gombert, in descending order of frequency.

Many of Gardano's music books were specially commissioned by composers for a patron who underwrote the publication costs, or who had previously given the composer financial support. In other cases, composers apparently hoped to gain future favour from a dedicatee. Most such composers were minor ones or at the early stages of their careers, but there are a few exceptions. Corteccia's madrigal collections all contain dedications to Cosimo de' Medici, and Jacquet de Berchem dedicated his madrigal book of 1546 to his patron Hieronimo Bragadino. In both cases, the composers expressed in their prefaces the need to present correctly edited and attributed versions of their music.

Gardano sometimes signed dedications himself. These suggest that either the dedicatee had made a financial contribution towards the publication, or Gardano was indebted to him in some way; most of these books were devoted to the music of a single composer. At the outset of his career, Gardano wrote dedications even in Arcadelt's madrigal books and in motet books containing music of known popularity. But once his financial position was more secure, such prefaces were used mainly for editions of music by lesser-known composers, those whose commercial appeal Gardano might have doubted. By contrast, editions without obvious signs of private patronage are those that were deemed commercially viable on the basis of their composers' fame or contents' popularity. Examples include most of the publications devoted to the music of Verdelot, Willaert and Rore, and the *note nere* madrigal books of the mid-1540s.

Competition for repertory, especially in the early years of Gardano's career, is suggested by his celebrated quarrel with the Ferrarese publisher Buglhat. The dispute is reflected in Buglhat's use of satirical title-page woodcuts for his *Mottetti della scimia*, of a monkey (representing Gardano's address on the calle della Scimia) eating fruit (Gardano's *Mottetti del frutto*), and in a later *frutto* volume, of Gardano's lion and bear attacking Buglhat's monkey. Gardano's relationship with Scotto was much more complex. Comparisons of readings indicate that the two sometimes cooperated in publication or copied from each other directly (apparently with no culpability), but that at other times they had separate sources of supply for the same groups of pieces and thus competed for the same new repertory and market.

While Gardano clearly received some of the music he printed directly from composers themselves, many of his repertory sources remain obscure. His primary suppliers were undoubtedly his friends in Willaert's circle. A series of poems by Hieronimo Fenaruolo, published in 1546, depicts Gardano receiving the homage of such musicians as Rore, Cambio, Parabosco and Festa, and of the poets Gaspara Stampa and Domenico Venier. But many musicians, including Rore, were unconvinced of the benefits of publication, and Gardano was often hard-pressed to obtain works from the most famous and commercially attractive composers in Italy.

Together Gardano and Scotto created a virtual monopoly in music printing in Italy. Through their connections with leading composers and popular repertories, their use of the sophisticated Venetian distribution networks and their introduction on a large scale of the cheaper, more efficient single-impression printing method, they extended the processes of musical commerce begun in France a few years earlier by Attaingnant and Moderne. Their production of large editions at low cost made polyphonic music available to a far wider public than ever before, and introduced the element of financial gain for publishers and composers alert enough to seize the opportunity. Gardano's estate inventories and tax documents show that he became comfortably wealthy from his business, owning land, houses and many valuables.

Gardano took out a patent for a new printing method, probably a kind of forme that allowed more efficient, and hence cheaper, setting of material common to the several partbooks of an edition. Most of his editions were skilfully printed in oblong quarto, with simple but elegant decorative initials. He experimented for almost a decade before settling on a music fount that satisfied him. Later in his career he adopted a smaller, oblong octavo format for editions of villottas, introduced a large upright quarto for deluxe editions such as Willaert's *Musica nova* (1559; see illustration), and even printed a few folio choirbooks, starting with an edition of Morales's *Magnificat Omnitonum* in 1562.

Various writers have accused Gardano of fraud, particularly in some of his early editions which wrongly attribute numerous works to Arcadelt and Janequin, or freely use famous composers' names on the title-pages of collections containing only a handful of their works. Gardano, for his part, made a similar accusation against Ottaviano Scotto, and on several occasions suggested his competitor had made false claims by publishing '*Il vero libro . . .*' of one composer or another. We may never know how many of Gardano's mistaken attributions were honest errors and how many were attempts to sell more books. Most of the composers who were misrepresented – Arcadelt, Corteccia, Janequin, Naich – resided outside Venice. Gardano or his supplier could have been confused, and lack of proximity to the composer made confirmation of authorship difficult. On the other hand, that same lack of proximity would have made it easier to escape the composer's wrath while selling extra copies. At the very least, concern of composers and publishers alike over attribution is clear evidence of the growing commercialism of 16th-century musical life.

(2) Alessandro Gardano (*b* Venice, before 1540; *d* ?Rome, in or after 1591). Italian printer, son of (1) Antonio Gardano. After his father's death in 1569, he published over 100 musical editions in Venice

Title-page of Willaert's 'Musica nova' (Venice: Antonio Gardano, 1559), showing Gardano's printer's mark of a lion and a bear facing each other

together with his brother Angelo. He withdrew his assets from the family business in 1575 but still issued both musical and non-musical editions, often employing a printer's mark of two lions in place of the lion and bear associated with his father and brother. Between 1581 and 1583 he moved to Rome, where he continued his printing activity until 1591, frequently in collaboration with other printers and booksellers including Domenico Basa, Ascanio, Bernardino and Girolamo Donangeli and Jacomo Tornieri. In Rome he printed primarily sacred music, including works by some of the most important composers of the late Renaissance, among them Anerio, Guerrero, Marenzio, Palestrina and Victoria. He also published a series of *laude spirituali* edited by Francisco Soto for the Congregazione dell'Oratorio. Alessandro's output is clearly dwarfed by that of his brother Angelo. After the division of family assets in 1575, Alessandro published only about 50 musical editions and a handful of non-musical books, while Angelo issued approximately 850 musical publications. Before 1581 Alessandro used the spelling 'Gardane'; his name disappears entirely from publications and documents after 1591.

(3) **Angelo Gardano** (*b* Venice, 1540; *d* Venice, 6 or 7 Aug 1611). Italian printer, son of (1) Antonio Gardano. He and his brother Alessandro ran their deceased father's business as 'Li figliuoli di Antonio Gardano'. In 1575 Alessandro claimed his inheritance and withdrew from the firm. Angelo, with his young siblings Mattio and Lucieta, kept the remainder of the family assets together but continued the firm under his own name, retaining the lion and bear printer's mark inherited from his father. Lucieta took her dowry in 1582, but Mattio evidently stayed on as a silent partner, since his widow began legal action that forced Angelo to publish under the rubric 'Angelo Gardano et fratelli' after 1605. In all Angelo published almost 1000 editions, over twice the number produced by his prolific father. He printed music in a variety of formats, including chant books in folio and, in 1577, the first surviving score publications with more than two staves, *Tutti i madrigali di Cipriano di Rore a quattro voci, spartiti et accommodati per sonar d'ogni sorte d'instrumento perfetto* and *Musica de diversi autori ... alcune canzoni francese, partite in caselle*. In this year he seems to have issued only three editions, perhaps as a result of the problems posed by printing in score or even of the economic distress of the plague years in Venice. He and his

successors published music by most of the well-known composers of the period, including Arcadelt, Asola, d'India, A. and G. Gabrieli, V. Galilei, Gastoldi, Gesualdo, Lassus, Luzzaschi, Marenzio, Merula, Merulo, Monte, Monteverdi, Morales, Palestrina, Rore, Schütz, Striggio, Vecchi (for illustration *see* SIGNATURE LINE), Victoria, Wert and Willaert, as well as many composers with only local reputations. After Angelo's death in 1611, the firm passed to his daughter Diamante and her husband, Bartolomeo Magni, who continued the business under his own name beginning late in 1612, though he, and later his son Francesco, often referred in their imprints to the illustrious name of Gardano.

N. Franco: *Le pistole vulgari* (Venice, 1539); H. Brown: *The Venetian Printing Press* (London, 1891/R1969), 108; R. Giazotto: *Harmonici concenti in aere veneto* (Rome, 1954); C. Sartori: 'Gardane', *MGG*; idem: 'Una dinastia di editori musicali', *La bibliofilia*, lviii (1956), 176–208; idem (1958); F. Lesure: 'Les chansons à trois voix de Clément Janequin', *RdM*, xliv (1959), 193; S. F. Pogue: *Jacques Moderne: Lyons Music Printer of the Sixteenth Century* (Geneva, 1969); M. S. Lewis: *Antonio Gardane and his Publications of Sacred Music, 1538–55* (diss., Brandeis U., 1979); T. W. Bridges: 'Gardane', *Grove 6*; A. Johnson: 'The 1548 Editions of Cipriano de Rore's Third Book of Madrigals', *Studies in Musicology in Honor of Otto E. Albrecht* (Kassel, 1980), 110; M. S. Lewis: 'Antonio Gardane's Early Connections with the Willaert Circle', *Music in Medieval and Early Modern Europe: Patronage, Sources and Texts*, ed. I. Fenlon (Cambridge, 1981), 209; R. J. Agee: *The Privilege and Venetian Music Printing in the Sixteenth Century* (diss., Princeton U., 1982); T. W. Bridges: *The Publishing of Arcadelt's First Book of Madrigals* (diss., Harvard U., 1982); D. G. Cardamone: 'Madrigali a tre et arie napolitane: a Typographical and Repertorial Study', *JAMS*, xxxv (1982), 436–81; S. F. Pogue: 'A Sixteenth-century Editor at Work: Gardane and Moderne', *Journal of Musicology*, i (1982), 217; Mischiati (1984); M. S. Lewis: 'Rore's Setting of Petrarch's "Vergine Bella": a History of its Composition and Early Transmission', *Journal of Musicology*, iv (1985–6), 365; S. Boorman: 'Some Non-conflicting Attributions, and Some Newly Anonymous Compositions, from the Early Sixteenth Century', *Early Music History*, vi (1986), 109–57; M. S. Lewis: *Antonio Gardano, Venetian Music Printer 1538–1569: a Descriptive Bibliography and Historical Study* (New York, 1988–9) [incl. list of all his music editions]

M.S.L.(1), R.J.A. (2,3)

Gargano, Giovanni Battista (*fl* early 17th century). Italian printer. In partnership with Lucrezio Nucci, he was active in Naples when it was a centre for music printing: the firms of Carlino & Pace and Sottile were also flourishing at this time. A number of Gargano and Nucci's early publications were financed by the bookseller

P. P. Riccio, including *Teatro de madrigali* (*RISM* 1609[16]) edited by Scipione Riccio, Matteo Nucci replaced Lucrezio Nucci in 1617. Gargano appears to have been the technician while the two Nuccis supplied the musical expertise. Most of the music was by local composers, or reprints of popular titles. The most important publication was Cerone's treatise *El melopeo y maestro* (1613). Both Lucrezio and Matteo Nucci published music on their own account.

S.B. (iii)

Garland. American firm of publishers, active in New York. It was established by Gavin Borden in 1969 as a book reprinting concern. The firm expanded its list by 1975 to include original titles, especially reference works on a range of topics including music. Shortly thereafter Garland issued its first scores, the series *Italian Opera 1640–1770* (97 vols., begun 1977), *Early Romantic Opera* (72 vols., begun 1978) and *The Symphony 1720–1840* (60 vols., begun 1979). Since 1983 Garland has produced more than two dozen multi-volume anthologies of scores and source materials in facsimile (notably of J. S. and J. C. Bach, Brahms, Handel, the Italian cantata and oratorio, Renaissance music and 19th-century English piano music), as well as new editions devoted to the 16th-century chanson and motet, the Italian madrigal and Italian instrumental music.

C.E.

Gebauer. Romanian firm of publishers. It was founded as a music shop and publishing firm in Bucharest in 1859 by Alexis Gebauer (1815–89), a pupil of Liszt and Sechter, who published mostly Romanian folklore collections, transcriptions and opera librettos. After 1880 the firm was run by his son Constantin Gebauer (*b* Bucharest, 18 Oct 1846; *d* Bucharest, 9 March 1920) and subsequently by N. I. Eliad, Jean Feder and Georg Degen. Under Constantin Gebauer, an enthusiastic supporter of Romanian musical life, it developed considerably, publishing exquisite editions of the standard repertory as well as the central repertory of Romanian music; Gebauer was awarded the Silver Medal at the 1900 Paris World Exhibition. After 1886 he became chief editor of the musical magazine *Doina*. In 1899 he transferred the shop, which dealt in instruments and scores, to Jean Feder, licensing him to print new Romanian music in 1905. For almost half a century Feder (1869–1941), himself

an editor, supported Romanian art and folk music by his publishing activity, also issuing Romanian teaching manuals and international music literature. He published the *Revista muzicală şi teatrală* (1904–8) and the *Revista instrumentelor muzicale şi a maşinilor vorbitoare* ('Musical instruments and loudspeakers review', 1905–8). Feder paid particular attention to classical and contemporary Romanian chamber music, publishing works by Constantin Dimitrescu, Emil Monţia, G. A. Dinicu and others. The firm ceased activity in 1945.

Amadeus: 'Correspondenz (A. Gebauer)', *Siebenbürger Wochenblatt* (1839), no.27, p.221; Per: 'Un bucureştean pe zi' [A Bucharester by day], *Adevărul* (1898), no.3340, p.2; L. Predescu: 'Gebauer, Alexis', *Enciclopedia Cugetarea* (Bucharest, 1940), 346

V.C.

Gebethner & Wolff. Polish firm of booksellers and publishers. Gustaw Adolf Gebethner (*b* Warsaw, 3 Jan 1831; *d* Vladikavkaz [now Ordzhonikidze], 18 Sept 1901) served his apprenticeship at Spiess & Friedlein in Warsaw. There he met Robert Wolff (*b* Zgierz, nr. Łódź, 10 Jan 1832; *d* Sopot, 20 Aug 1910), with whom he founded in 1857 a bookshop and publishing house. Initially called Gebethner & Spółka and renamed Gebethner & Wolff in 1860, it became one of the leading bookselling and publishing enterprises in Warsaw. Its first music publication, the piano score of Moniuszko's *Halka*, appeared in 1857; this was followed by other works by Moniuszko and editions of music by many other Polish composers, including the first Polish edition of Chopin's collected works, edited by Jan Kleczyński (1864). Gebethner & Wolff also published many educational books, songbooks and manuals and numerous books on music history. They published over 7000 items of music, besides 7010 other titles, in almost 45 million copies. In 1893 they were awarded a gold medal at the Chicago Exposition. The firm was in the hands of Gebethner's successors until 1939, with numerous branches in Poland and abroad; it was nationalized in 1960.

J. Muszkowski: *Z dziejów firmy Gebethner i Wolff 1857–1937* [The history of the firm of Gebethner & Wolff] (Warsaw, 1938); K. Konarska: 'Gebethner, Gustaw Adolf', *Słownik pracowników książki polskiej* [Dictionary of Polish printers] (Warsaw and Łódź, 1972), 249

K.M. (i)

Geertsom, Jan van (*fl* Rotterdam, mid-17th century). Flemish musician and publisher. He may be related to Géry Ghersem, *maître* *de chapelle* to Philip II in Spain at the beginning of the 17th century. Archives at Rotterdam show that Geertsom rented a house there from 1665 to 1669; his publications of 1656–7 give his address as 'Rotterdam, in de Meulesteegh'. Four music collections, published between 1656 and 1661, are known. The composers represented are all Italian, including many active in Rome: Abbatini, Carissimi, Fabri, Graziani, Marcorelli (=Marco Aurelli) and Tarditi. The volume *Scelta di motetti* (1656), for example, contains (with one exception) motets by composers who held positions at various churches in Rome. Geertsom appears to have had business connections with the firm of Phalèse in Antwerp. Not only does his music type bear a distinct resemblance to that of Phalèse, but also 'Mr Jan Gersem' is listed in a 1655 inventory of the Phalèse firm as owing 27 guilders.

EitnerQ; E. vander Straeten: *La musique aux Pays-Bas avant le XIXe siècle* (Brussels, 1867–88/*R*1969), ii (1872); Goovaerts (1880); A. Smijers: 'Geertsom, Jan van', *MGG*; S. Bain: 'Geertson, Jan van', *Grover6* [incl. list of publications]

S.B. (i)

Gehrman. Swedish firm of publishers, active in Stockholm. Carl Gehrman founded the firm in 1893; in 1930 it was sold to Einar Rosenborg, who made it a joint-stock company with himself as main owner and managing director, and in 1950 Inge and Einar Rosenborg's Foundation for Swedish Music took over ownership. Lennart Bagger-Sjöbäck was managing director from 1953 to 1975, when he was succeeded by Kettil Skarby. At first the firm concentrated on popular music, although the standard repertory and Swedish art music were also published. Under Rosenborg's leadership the firm's activities expanded and a comprehensive catalogue of orchestral music was initiated. With the acquisition of Hirsch's Förlag (founded in 1837) in 1943 the art music catalogue was enlarged; it now includes four series of choral music for various voice combinations, chamber and instrumental music. The firm continues to publish popular music, and since the 1950s educational music (e.g. tutors for the recorder, piano, violin, trumpet, clarinet, flute and various ensembles, as well as booklets for compulsory school music education) has been stressed.

K.S.

Geib. German family of piano makers, organ builders and publishers who worked first in England and later in the USA. John [Johann] Geib (*b* Staudernheim, 27 Feb

1744; *d* Newark, NJ, 30 Oct 1818) emigrated to London, where he manufactured church and chamber organs and ran a successful piano factory. On 24 July 1797 he sailed with his wife and seven children to New York. In the *Argus: Greenleaf's New Daily Advertiser* for 27 December 1798 he advertised his building of an organ for the German Lutheran Church in New York. In this work he had been joined by two of his sons, the twins John (1780–1821) and Adam (1780–1849). By 1800 the firm was known as John Geib & Co. and Geib became the leading figure in American organ building of his time.

From *c*1804 until *c*1814 the firm was known as John Geib & Son (this probably refers to John Geib jr) and from 1814 their activities included music publishing – mainly patriotic and religious music. Geib seems to have retired by 1816, but Adam Geib joined his twin in the business: they had a piano warehouse at 23 Maiden Lane, New York, where Adam also taught. In 1818, the year of their father's death, a third brother, William (1763–1860), joined the firm, which then became J. A. & W. Geib. Square pianos with this inscription survive, as do instruments marked A. & W. Geib, presumably dating from 1821, when John died. In 1821 William left the business, and Adam managed it alone until 1829, when he formed a partnership with Daniel Walker. By this time it seems that the firm's activities were devoted to publishing, in which they shared engraved plates with the Ditson firm in Boston. In 1843 Walker left the company, and in 1844 Adam's son William joined it. Adam retired in 1847. Between 1849 and 1858 the firm's affairs were increasingly supervised by S. T. Gordon, of Hartford, but William Geib remained with the firm.

Dichter and Shapiro (1941, 2/1977); A. C. Gildersleeve: *John Geib and his Seven Children* (Far Rockaway, NY, 1945); Wolfe (1964)

W.T.M., M.J.

Gerig. German firm of publishers. Its founder Hans Gerig (*b* Freiburg, 16 July 1910; *d* Cologne, 15 March 1978) took the doctorate in 1935 and represented the German authors' association at the Bureau International de l'Edition Mécanique in Paris, where he was also manager of Editions Continental. In 1946 he founded the Bühnen- und Musikverlag Hans Gerig in Cologne. The Gerig group gradually expanded to 36 separate publishing houses, including Sidemton, Mondial, Rialto, Excelsior and Volk, covering a wide range of music publishing activities. Increasing internationalization led to an emphasis on dance and entertainment music, of which the Gerig group is one of the leading German publishers; chamber music and stage works are also published. An educational branch was started in 1955 with the publication of the *Neue Reihe*, a series of over 100 titles comprising works for choir and orchestra and chamber music. In 1956 *Die Garbe*, a school music publication in several volumes, was taken over from the Tonger publishing house. Tutors and orchestral studies have been published for a variety of instruments. From 1964 the side of the business dealing with serious music was reorganized and a new emphasis given to contemporary music; anthologies of contemporary piano music from various countries (including Brazil, Greece, Israel and several in eastern Europe) have been published, as well as the series *Pro Musica Nova* (studies for playing avant-garde music). Gerig also publishes the series *Instrumentalmusik des 16.–18. Jahrhunderts* (Urtext editions) and series of books on music. The Gerig group represents the Essex Group (London and New York), MCA Music and affiliated companies (New York and London), Curci (Milan), Edicije Društva Slovenskih Skladateljev (Ljubljana), from 1975 Jŭs-Aŭtor (Sofia) and from 1977 Donemus (Amsterdam).

R.L.

Gerlach [Gerlatz], **Dietrich** [Theodor] (*b* Aerdingen [=?Erding, nr. Munich]; *d* Nuremberg, 17 Aug 1575). German printer. Nothing is known of Gerlach's life before his marriage to Catharina, widow of the printer Johann Berg, in August 1565. In December of that year he became a citizen of Nuremberg and apparently entered the printing firm shortly thereafter, retaining the partnership established by Berg with Ulrich Neuber. (Publications from the year 1566 are signed either 'Neuber und Berg Erben' or 'Neuber und Gerlach'.) The association was short-lived, however, and Neuber left to found his own business in 1567 or 1568. An insight into the firm's history may be gained by comparing the imprints of the various editions of J. Meiland's *Cantiones sacrae*, in which the publisher is listed successively as U. Neuber and heirs of J. Montanus (1564), U. Neuber (2/1569), Widow and heirs of U. Neuber (3/1572) and T. Gerlach (4/1573). During the years immediately following Neuber's departure, Gerlach appears to have fallen back on the reputation of his predecessor, adding the phrase 'in officina Joani Montani' to his own name on the imprints of his publications; not until 1571

was the name Gerlach used consistently by itself. After his death in 1575 Catharina once again took over the firm, which she expanded and developed until her own death on 12 August 1591. The only heirs to the firm appear to have been those from Catharina's first marriage. 'Johann von Berg's Erben' are regularly included with her own name and the firm was eventually taken over by Berg's grandson, Paul Kauffmann.

In the field of music Dietrich and Catharina Gerlach attained a virtual monopoly, publishing over 150 books by the single-impression technique which had by then become standard. They strove to supply a large clientèle with the most popular works available. Whereas Dietrich Gerlach concentrated primarily on sacred Latin works, Catharina included many books of secular Italian and German songs in her production. Other categories, such as instrumental tablatures, instruction books and liturgical books, while also represented, form only a small part of the total. The firm has the distinction of having made the works of many contemporary composers from other countries available in Germany for the first time and of having been one of Orlande de Lassus's main publishers. In contrast to Berg, virtually all of their publications are devoted to the works of single composers. Significantly, Catharina engaged the services of the Nuremberg Kantor and composer Friedrich Lindner to assemble and edit the collections by predominantly Italian composers of sacred and secular works that she printed in the years 1585–1591.

P. Cohen: *Musikdruck und -drucker zu Nürnberg im sechzehnten Jahrhundert* (Nuremberg, 1927); R. Schaal: 'Gerlach, Dietrich', *MGG* [incl. list of publications]; Benzing (1963, 2/1982); K. Ameln: 'Ein Nürnberger Verlegerplakat aus dem 16. Jahrhundert', *Musik und Verlag: Karl Vötterle zum 65. Geburtstag* (Kassel, 1968), 136

M.L.G.

Gerstenberg, Johann Daniel (*b* Frankenhausen, 26 March 1758; *d* Hildesheim, 7 Dec 1841). German publisher. From 1778 to 1786 he attended the Gymnasium Andreanum in Hildesheim as a singer, and then studied law in Leipzig until 1788. On 26 March 1792 he opened a music and book shop in St Petersburg after spending a short period as a private tutor in Kiev; in 1793 he made his schoolfriend Friedrich August Dittmar a partner in the business, which had come to the fore with many musical and literary publications. He opened his own music engraving works in 1795, and in 1796 went to Gotha, where he founded a branch of the St Petersburg firm, but moved to Hildesheim in the same year. Connections with the parent firm in St Petersburg steadily weakened, and Dittmar carried on the business alone under many different trade names until 1808. Between 1792 and 1799 the firm published more than 200 musical works. Known as both a composer and an author, Gerstenberg wrote six piano sonatas and two collections of lieder as well as many contributions for various journals and yearbooks that he published in St Petersburg.

D. Lehmann: 'J. D. Gerstenberg und die Anfänge des musikalischen Verlagswesens in Russland am Ende des 18. Jahrhunderts', *Quellen und Studien zur Geschichte Osteuropas*, i (Berlin, 1958), 176; C. Hopkinson: *Notes on Russian Publishers* (Cambridge, 1959); R.-A. Mooser: 'L'apparition des oeuvres de Mozart en Russie', *MJb 1967*, 266; W. Gerstenberg: 'Aus Petersburger Anfängen des Verlegers J. D. Gerstenberg', *Musik und Verlag: Karl Vötterle zum 65. Geburtstag* (Kassel, 1968), 293; B. Steinpress: 'Haydns Oratorien in Russland zu Lebzeiten des Komponisten', *Haydn-Studien*, ii (1960–70), 77–112

W.G.

Gilfert, George (*d* ?December 1814). American publisher and piano dealer, active in New York. First mentioned in the 1789 city directory as an organist, he headed the city's Musical Society in 1789–91 and appeared frequently as a viola player. In 1794 he established the publishing firm of G. Gilfert & Co. at 191 Broadway, with Frederick Rausch as partner. Rausch left the firm in 1796; in 1804 Gilfert moved to 13 Maiden Lane, where he supplemented his publishing by selling pianos. The firm remained active until 1814. Gilfert was among the first to use decorative title-pages, and his output during 1794–1803 was the largest of the New York publishers. In addition to his own publishing activities he cooperated with other publishers, engraving plates for P. A. von Hagen (father and son), selling von Hagen publications and working with George Willig of Baltimore (who sold Gilfert's publications in that city). Joseph Wilson acquired Gilfert's plates in 1815 and reissued much of the Gilfert catalogue. Among Gilfert's notable publications are *Angels ever bright and fair* (said to have been sung at Washington's funeral), *Adams and Liberty*, Joseph Hopkinson's *Hail Columbia*, Victor Pelissier's *Washington and Independence* and a reprint of the extremely popular *Crazy Jane* by John Davy and M.G. Lewis, all issued during the years 1798–1801.

His son Charles (1787–1829), active in the theatre in Charleston, South Carolina,

published about a dozen works there between 1813 and 1817, mostly his own compositions, as well as several titles in New York.

Dichter and Shapiro (1941, 2/1977); Wolfe (1980)

C.E.

Girard. Italian firm of publishers. It was founded in Naples by Giuseppe Girard in 1815 and later managed by Bernardo Girard, who changed the name of the firm first to Calcografia de' Reali Teatri, then to Stabilimento Musicale B. Girard & C. From 1818 to 1847 it published much chamber music by Rossini for voice and piano and solo piano. Guglielmo Cottrau (1797–1847) was director from 1828 to 1846. Under him the firm published *Passatempi musicali* (1835–47), a collection of 129 Neapolitan songs that he edited; the first edition had been published privately in 1826 and reprinted in 1830. Bernard Latte published the collection in a translation by A. de Lauzières, and in 1833 it was sold to the Paris publisher Pacini. The firm competed with Ricordi and Lucca for the operas of Bellini, Pacini, Donizetti, Mercadante and Verdi. By paying an annual fee to the S Carlo, del Fondo and Nuovo theatres, Girard secured the copyright of the operas and ballets expressly written for and performed in those theatres; on 26 July 1834 the exclusive rights to these works were transferred to Ricordi.

Bernardo Girard died in 1835 but Cottrau's experience and reputation kept the business flourishing, thanks to the cordial rapport he enjoyed with the leading musicians of the time; his French origins possibly account for the good relations the firm enjoyed with the French publishers Troupenas, Latte and Launer, to whom rights were given for some of Bellini's operas and Donizetti's *Lucia*, *Roberto Devereux* and *Betly*. On Cottrau's retirement in 1846 he left the management of the firm to his son Teodoro Cottrau. The firm's 1847 catalogue contains 210 pages of titles. Michele Pasinati supervised the music engraving and sometimes enhanced it with rich plates and lithographic frontispieces by Richter.

Besides operas, the catalogue contains many editions of Beethoven's works, including the Third Fifth and Seventh symphonies in piano arrangements by Kalkbrenner, the sonatas for violin and piano opp.24 and 30 and the Piano Trio op.1 no.3. Other music was published in the series *Euterpe drammatica estera: scelta di pezzi vocali delle migliori opere moderne francesi e tedesche con versione italiana*. The Girard firm became known as Successori della ditta Girard or Successeurs de Girard & Cie about 1870, when Teodoro Cottrau's interest in publishing declined; it operated with difficulty for a few years longer, possibly controlled by a certain Federico Girard, a Neapolitan publisher who died in Naples in 1877. In 1884 the firm was taken over by Ricordi.

G. Cottrau: *Lettres d'un mélomane pour servir de documents à l'histoire musicale de Naples du 1829 à 1847* (Naples, 1885); idem: 'Le portefeuille d'un mélomane', *Revue britannique*, iv (1887), 5–58; Sartori (1958)

S.A.

Giudici & Strada. Italian firm of publishers. It was founded in Turin in 1859 by Augusto Giudici (*b* Milan, 1820; *d* Luino, 28 Aug 1886) and Achille Strada (*b* Milan, 10 July 1823; *d* Turin, 2 Nov 1880); both had previously been engravers for Ricordi. They inherited their firm from A. Racca, for whom they were both working. During the next three decades they increased production, enlarged the printing department and opened a new hall for exhibition and sales; between 1887 and 1894 they also developed a lithographic department. The firm is specially known for didactic works for the voice and for the piano (various works by Czerny and the Italian edition of Henri Herz's *1000 esercizi applicati all'uso del dactylion*), transcriptions for the piano and various instrumental combinations, and operas by Cagnoni, Petrella, Flotow and others.

In 1897 A. De Marchi acquired the firm from Strada's son and moved it to Milan. Under his ownership it published music by Granozio, Lanzi and Ferroni. Subsequently it was sold to P. Mariani, who published vocal scores of works by Antonio Smareglia (including *Oceàna*, 1903). From 1920 to 1930 the firm was owned by L. Stoppa.

C. Nasi: 'Augusto Giudici', *Gazzetta musicale di Milano*, xli (1886), 287; Sartori (1958); A. Basso: *Il Conservatorio di musica G. Verdi di Torino* (Turin, 1971), 58, 84, 229

S.A.

Giunta [Giunti; Zonta; Junta; Juncta; de' Giunti Modesti]. Italian family of booksellers and printers. They originated in Florence and were active from the late 15th century until well into the 17th, and had branches in Venice, Rome, Lyons and Spain.

The founder of the Venetian branch of the firm was Luc'Antonio Giunta (1457–1538), who was active in bookselling and publishing there soon after 1477. Incuna-

bula were printed for him by various printers, notably Johann Emerich of Speyer (*fl* 1487–1506), who excelled in liturgical books. The Giunta firm prospered so greatly that it was able to pay off, from 1553 to about 1561, a debt of some 100,000 ducats, notwithstanding a disastrous fire of 1557 which destroyed the company's plant and much of its stock. By then, Luc'Antonio's sons Giovan Maria (*d* 1569) and, principally, Tommaso (1494–1566) were in charge. After Tommaso's death the direction passed to Giovan Maria's son, also called Luc'Antonio (*d* 1602), and thereafter to the latter's sons, Tommaso (*d* 1618) and Giovan Maria (*d c*1632), but they left the management of the firm to a distant cousin, Bernardo di Filippo di Benedetto Giunta (*d* 1648). When Bernardo returned to Florence in 1644 the heirs of the younger Giovan Maria continued the firm until 1657, when it passed to Niccolò Pezzana whose heirs continued to print with the Giunta device until 1801.

Throughout the life of the firm liturgical books made up a large proportion of its production; no competitor produced them in such quantity, or with greater taste and skill. Those intended for choir use were so carefully edited, at first by the Franciscan monk Francesco de Brugis, that their musical texts have scarcely been superseded. Luc'Antonio's editions of the *Graduale romanum* (1499–1501) and *Antiphonarium romanum* (1503–4), printed by Emerich with new music and text types and large woodcut initials, were unrivalled in quality and size. His *Cantorinus* (1506), a compendium of chants 'for beginners', was equally reliable in its readings. These volumes were reprinted by Giunta many times, and sometimes by rival printers, as were the numerous liturgical books intended for the clergy and new types of books for choirs. About half the liturgical books contain at least some music, normally with black notes printed on a red staff in separate impressions. Virtually all are examples of fine printing, adorned with handsome woodcuts and decorative initials (see illustration).

The elder Luc'Antonio was the only member of the Venetian branch who was concerned with polyphonic music. In 1520 he cooperated with Andrea Antico in the production of eight books of frottolas, chansons and motets, using Antico's woodcuts for the notes and staves (including *RISM c*1516[2], *RISM c*1517[1]), frottolas by Tromboncino and Cara, and anthologies of chansons and motets. Giunta's collaboration in some of these is signalled only by his

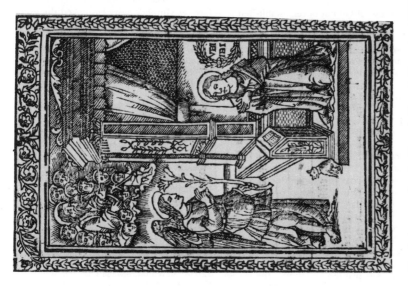

Two facing pages from Luc'Antonio Giunta's 'Cantorinus' (1513 edition), with black notes printed on red staves

printer's mark, a Florentine lily with the initials L. A. Z. (Luc'Antonio Zonta).

Luc'Antonio was not the first Giunta to collaborate with Antico, whose *Liber quindecim missarum* (Rome, 1516) was printed by, and probably on the press of, Antonio Giunta, son of Jacomo (for illustration *see* ANTICO, ANDREA). Jacomo di Biagio Giunta (1478–*c*1528), a nephew of Luc'Antonio, financed several volumes in Rome, including two of 1518 made with Antico's woodcuts and cooperation – the second and third books of *Canzoni sonetti strambotti & frottole*, both printed by Giacomo Mazzocchi. In 1522 Giunta financed the *Missarum decem clarissimis musicis compositarum . . . liber primus* printed by Giovanni Giacomo Pasoti. This was printed in two impressions, like the eight or more books that Giunta sponsored in 1526, most of them reprints of Petrucci volumes: *Canzoni frottole & capitoli . . . libro primo de la Croce*, three volumes of masses by Josquin, and the four volumes of *Motetti de la corona*. These all have colophons that identify the printers as Pasoti and Valerio Dorico. The second edition of the *Motetti de la corona, libro tertio*, also printed for Giunta by Pasoti and Dorico, was dated April 1527, shortly before the sack of Rome. This was the last music edition sponsored by Giunta, who survived the invasion but lived only about another year.

The house of Giunta never established a musical press in Florence – in 1563 Filippo Giunta (1533–1600) was obliged to send to Rampazetto in Venice the manuscript of Serafino Razzi's *Laudi spirituali*, and in 1571 and 1573 petitions by Filippo's brothers Jacopo and Bernardo, for exclusive rights to print music and to sell certain music editions in Tuscany, were denied by the Grand Duke. In 1602 Filippo's son Modesto (*c*1577–1644) reprinted Galilei's *Dialogo della musica antica e moderna*, signing the book 'Per Filippo Giunti'. This edition was not, as was for a long time supposed, composed merely of remainders of the Marescotti edition of 1581 provided with new first and last pages, but was a completely new edition. It did not lead to any other musical editions, but in early 1605 Filippo's heirs printed a catalogue of works for sale, which included a long list of musical editions. Although none of those musical works was printed by Giunta, the list is of great bibliographical interest because of its scope and size.

The activities of the Giunta family in Spain were extensive, and resulted in a number of musical editions. Juan de Junta (otherwise Giovanni di Filippo, *c*1485–1561) printed in Burgos a *Baptisterium*

(1527) and issued reprints of Martínez de Bizcargui's *Arte de canto llano* (1528 and 1535); in Salamanca he printed a *Manuale secundum consuetudinem ecclesie Salmanticensis* (1532). His son Felipe printed a *Missale romanum* (Burgos, 1580). Felipe's brothers Giulio (*fl* 1583–1618) and Tommaso (*d* 1624) worked in Madrid, from 1594 using the imprint 'Typographia Regia' or 'Imprenta Real'. They published numerous liturgical books of various kinds, including a sacramentary for use among the Indians of the New World (1617) and a few volumes of polyphony, including Philippe Rogier's *Missae sex* (1598), Victoria's *Missae, Magnificat, motecta* (1600) and *Officium defunctorum* (1605), Alonso Lobo's *Liber primus missarum* (1602) and Stefano Limido's *Armonia espiritual* (1624). After Tommaso's death his widow Teresa continued to manage the Typographia Regia, which in 1628 printed López de Velasco's *Libro de missas, motetes, salmos, Magníficas, y otras cosas*.

The Lyons branch of the firm was founded by Jacques (Jacopo di Francesco) Giunta (1487–1564), sent there around 1520 for that purpose by his uncle, Luc'Antonio. He printed no music but may have sponsored some – a series of six motet books by Francesco de Layolle, shown by Guillo to have been printed in Lyons by Antoine Du Ry not later than 1535. Jacques Giunta's heirs employed the excellent printer Corneille de Septgranges for several volumes, including three with music: *Missale ad usum romanum* (1550), *Missale sacri ordinis S. Ioannis Hierpsolymita* (1553) and *Missale iuxta ritum sancte ecclesie Lugdunensis* (1556).

A. M. Bandini: *De florentina Iuntarum typographia* (Lucca, 1791), esp. facing p.2; J. Riaño: *Critical & Bibliographical Notes on Early Spanish Music* (London, 1887/*R*1971); C. Pérez Pastor: *Bibliografía madrileña* (Madrid, 1891–1907); V. Masséna: *Etudes sur l'art de la gravure sur bois à Venise: les missels imprimés à Venise de 1484 à 1600* (Paris, 1896); H. L. and J. Baudrier: 'Giunta ou De Giunta, Jacques', *Bibliographie lyonnaise*, 6th ser. (Paris and Lyons, 1904), 77–488; A. Palau y Dulcet: *Manual del librero hispanoamericano* (Barcelona, 1923–7/*R*1948–72); H. Thomas: *Spanish Sixteenth-century Printing* (London, 1926), 32, pl.23; C. Sartori: 'Giunta, Luca Antonio', *MGG*; Sartori (1958); F. Ascarelli: *Annali tipograpfici di Giacomo Mazzocchi* (Florence, 1961), 119, 121; R. Stevenson: *Spanish Cathedral Music in the Golden Age* (Berkeley and Los Angeles, 1961); P. Camerini: *Annali dei Giunti: I, Venezia* (Florence, 1962–3); Å. Davidsson: *Bibliographie der musiktheoretischen Drucke des 16. Jahrhunderts* (Baden-Baden, 1962), 20, 22; K. Meyer-Baer: *Liturgical Music Incunabula: a Descriptive Catalogue* (London, 1962); G. Massera: *La 'Mano musicale perfetta' di Francesco de Brugis* (Florence, 1963); C. W.

Chapman: *Andrea Antico* (diss., Harvard U., 1964); P. Kast: 'Die Musikdrucke des Kataloges Giunta von 1604', *AnMc*, no.2 (1965), 41; K. Jeppesen: 'An Unknown Pre-madrigalian Music Print in Relation to Other Contemporary Italian Sources (1520–1530)', *Studies in Musicology: Essays . . . in Memory of Glen Haydon* (Chapel Hill, 1969), 3; J. Haar: 'The *Libraria* of Antonfrancesco Doni', *MD*, xxiv (1970), 119; D. Decia, R. Delfiol and L. S. Camerini: *I Giunti tipografi editori di Firenze, 1497–1570: annali* (Florence, 1978); L. S. Camerini: *I Giunti tipografi editori di Firenze, 1571–1620: annali* (Florence, 1979); W. A. Pettas: *The Giunti of Florence: Merchant Publishers of the Sixteenth Century* (San Francisco, 1980); Duggan (1981); Mischiati (1984); L. Guillo: 'Les motets de Layolle et les psaumes de Piéton: deux nouvelles éditions lyonnaises du seizième siècle', *FAM*, xxxii (1985), 186

T.W.B.

Giusti, Pedro [Pierre]. Puerto Rican publisher. In 1880 he left his native Corsica for Puerto Rico, where in San Juan he opened a shop for the sale of musical instruments, accessories and general merchandise, mainly French. First at no. 35 San Justo Street, by 1894 the Giusti shop had moved to 27 Fortaleza Street. In addition to selling music from Europe and the USA, Giusti published new music by Puerto Rican composers. Chiefly stylized Puerto Rican *danzas* for piano, these publications bore such imprints as París Bazar, París Bazar de Pedro Giusti or P. Giusti & Co., Inc., and included works by Braulio Dueño Colón, Luis R. Miranda and Juan Ríos Ovalle. Pedro Giusti died in Barcelona while on a business trip in 1926. Successor companies have remained in the Giusti family. Although no longer dealing in musical merchandise, the present company, Giusti Commercial, Inc., occasionally reprints in album form piano pieces first published by Pedro Giusti.

E. Cifre de Loubriel: *Catálogo de extranjeros residentes en Puerto Rico en el siglo XIX* (Río Piedras, 1962); A. F. Thompson: *Puerto Rican Newspapers and Journals of the Spanish Colonial Period as Source Materials for Musicological Research* (diss., Florida State U., 1980); *Album de danzas puertorriqueñas: las 10 danzas más bellas de Juan Morell Campos, Simón Madera, Angel Mislán, Luis N. Miranda, Rafael Alers, J. M. Escobar* (Santurce, n.d.); *Nuevo álbum de danzas puertorriqueñas: diez de las más bellas danzas de Luis R. Miranda, Simón Madera, Juan Morell Campos, F. Astol, Juan F. Acosta* (Santurce, n.d.); E. Díaz: 'Música para anunciar en la sociedad sanjuanera del siglo XIX', *Revista musical puertorriqueña*, i (1987), 6

D.T. (i)

Gleissner, Franz (*b* Neustadt, 1759; *d* Munich, 18 Sept 1818). German lithographer. After early training in the

seminary at Amberg he moved to Munich where he continued studies in music and philosophy. There, about 1795, he first made the acquaintance of Alois Senefelder, the inventor of lithography, and they formed a partnership that lasted throughout their careers. Gleissner first realized the potential offered by lithography to music printing. He and Senefelder founded the firm A. Senefelder, Fr. Gleissner & Co. in 1796. In 1799 they were granted a 15-year privilege by Maximilian Joseph of Bavaria. For a short time they were technical advisers to the publishing house of Johann Anton André Offenbach, but this was interrupted by a move to Vienna, where in 1803 Senefelder founded the Chemische Druckerey (*see* HASLINGER). This enterprise failed in 1806 and they returned to Munich to establish a new press under the patronage of Johann Christoph Freiherr von Aretin. Gleissner was a composer of some merit, and wrote instrumental and vocal works, many of which are among the incunables of lithography. However, his work as a composer has not survived; what remains significant today is his role as co-inventor and developer of the lithographic process. For illustration *see* fig.18, p.56.

FétisB; A. Senefelder: *Vollständiges Lehrbuch der Steindruckerey* (Munich, 1818); C. Wagner: *Aloys Senefelder: sein Leben und Wirken* (Leipzig, 1914, 2/1943); L. Dussler: *Die Incunabeln der deutschen Lithographie, 1796–1821* (Berlin, 1925); P. Gaskell: *A New Introduction to Bibliography* (London and Oxford, 1972), 267

V.D.

Godbid, William (*d* 1679). English printer. He succeeded Thomas Harper in 1656 and took over the printing of all of John Playford the elder's musical publications until his death in 1679. Godbid was a reliable and conscientious printer, if not an inspired one. In spite of the fact that the printing materials he inherited from Thomas Harper dated back over a generation, and were out of date by the middle of the 17th century, for 23 years Godbid's press produced the music volumes on which the elder Playford's remarkable business was built. He also printed Tomkins's *Musica Deo sacra* in 1668, for which he devised nested type (an ingenious invention but not significant historically). On his death in 1679, Godbid's business in Aldersgate, London, was taken over by his widow Anne and John Playford the younger.

Humphries and Smith (1954, 2/1970); Krummel (1975)

M.M.

Gombart. German firm of publishers. It was founded in Augsburg in 1795 and in its first few years produced early editions of important works by Haydn and Mozart. These include a very early edition of Haydn's symphony no.100 (1799), his symphonies nos.99 and 101 and one of the earliest editions of his *Gott erhalte den Kaiser*; and for Mozart, first editions of the Quintet for piano and wind k452 (1800) and the divertimentos k247 and k287 (1799). In 1825 Gombart produced its only Beethoven first edition, the song *An die Geliebte* WoO 140. Most of the firm's output consisted of songs by such composers as Gyrowetz and Rieff, and piano music, especially operatic arrangements. It ceased trading about 1844.

G. Haberkamp: *Die Erstdrucke der Werke von Wolfgang Amadeus Mozart* (Tutzing, 1986)

N.S.

Gordon, Stephen T. (*d* ?New York, 1890). American publisher. He published music under his own name in Hartford from 1846 to 1853 and also dealt in music and pianos. In 1850 he bought into the company of John E. Gould and the following year took over Frederick Riley's catalogue. In 1853 Berry & Gordon was established in New York, the shareholders being Gordon, Gould, Thomas S. Berry and Oliver Ditson. Gordon bought out his partners in 1855 and renamed the company S. T. Gordon; he gradually expanded his business by acquiring the catalogues of a number of other publishers in New York, including Russell & Tolman (1861) and Charles M. Tremaine, and of several in Philadelphia and Baltimore. Among his publications are early editions of *America* (1861) and *Glory hallelujah* (1862). After Gordon's death, the company was taken over by his son Hamilton S. Gordon (*b* Hartford, 1846; *d* New Jersey, 19 June 1914); it continued in the family until 1941.

Fisher (1933); Dichter and Shapiro (1941, 2/1977)

B.T.

Gorlier, Simon (*fl* Lyons, 1550–84). French printer, bookseller, composer and instrumentalist. In 1551 he prepared the third in a series of four books of music for guitar printed in Paris by Robert Granjon and Michel Fezandat (*RISM* 1551²²). In the dedication Gorlier spoke defensively of the guitar and his reasons for writing for what was evidently considered an inferior instrument, saying that he wanted to show that it was as capable as larger instruments of reproducing music in two or three voices.

Besides being an 'excellent joueur' on the guitar, as cited on the title-page, he evidently played the spinet; in an exchange of insults over Loys Bourgeois' *Droict chemin de musique* (1550) Bourgeois called him 'trougnon d'espinette' ('garbage of the spinet').

Gorlier appears as a merchant bookseller in the Lyons archives until 7 June 1584, and was granted a privilege for printing music on 17 February 1558. He published several books of music by himself and others in Lyons between 1558 and 1562. Only two of these have survived: *La lyre chrestienne*, with music by Antoine de Hauville, and *Premier livre de tablature de luth* by Jean Paladin, both dated 1560. According to the colophon of the latter, it is a reissue of a printing by Jean Pullon de Trin (Lyons, 1553). A few other titles are cited by the 16th-century bibliographer Antoine du Verdier: music for flute in tablature, 1558; for spinet in tablature, 1560; guitar tablature (possibly the Paris book), undated; and an undated book of 'music for four or five parts, in five volumes, printed in Lyons', all of which was by Gorlier. Du Verdier also cited a 1561 edition of 'chansons et vaudevilles' by Alamanne de Layolle (son of the composer Francesco de Layolle) and two books of tablature for lute by 'Antoine-François Paladin, Milanois', 1562.

R. de Juvigny, ed.: *Les bibliothèques françoises de La Croix du Maine et de Du Verdier* (Paris, 1772), iii, 42, 123, 132, v, 473; H. and J. Baudrier: *Bibliographie lyonnaise* (Paris, 1895–1921/R1964), ii, 46; F. Lesure: 'Gorlier', *MGG*; D. Heartz: 'Parisian Music Publishing under Henry II', *MQ*, xlvi (1960), 448

S.F.P.

Götz, Johann Michael (*b* c1735; *d* Worms, 15 Feb 1810). German publisher. By his own account he founded a firm of music engravers in Mannheim in 1768, but documentary evidence of his publications exists only from 1780. He soon incorporated a music shop into his publishing enterprise, buying new publications for it on his travels, especially in Paris; the publisher's catalogue he printed for the Frankfurt book fair includes works by Gossec, Rigel, Hüllmandel and Boccherini. On 23 August 1776 the Elector Carl Theodor granted his application for an exclusive patent for 20 years within the Palatinate, which was extended to include Bavaria in 1782. In view of the rapid rise of Götz's publishing business, Mozart's comment (28 February 1778), that he could not get his piano and violin sonatas printed in Mannheim, is surprising. Eschstruth praised Götz's prospectus (*Musicalische Bibliothek*, 1784, pt. i), and he was soon able to open branches in Worms and Düsseldorf. His business began to suffer from the violence and sieges of the war which began in 1794, and the firm moved entirely to Worms in 1799. The extended patent in the Palatinate was transferred in 1802 to his partner Joseph Abelshauser, who directed the firm without success until 1819.

The main publications of the firm's finest years (1776–94) were Holzbauer's *Günther von Schwarzburg* (score, 1777), Benda's melodramas *Medea* and *Ariadne* and symphonies by Cannabich and Fränzl. The catalogue consisted predominantly of piano music, and included works by the Mannheim composers Dalberg, L. A. Lebrun, Sterkel, Johann Toeschi, G. J. Vogler, J. B. Wendling and Peter Winter. The firm also published the first edition of Beethoven's Variations for piano on a march by Dressler (1782).

F. Walter: 'Der Musikverlag des Michael Götz in Mannheim', *Mannheimer Geschichtsblätter*, xvi (1915), 36; Deutsch (1946); B. S. Brook: *La symphonie française dans la seconde moitié du XVIIIe siècle*, ii (Paris, 1962), 507, 544

R.W.

Gough, John (*d* 1543). English printer and publisher. He printed Myles Coverdale's *Goostly Psalmes and Spirituall Songes*. Long conjectured on textual grounds to date from just before Gough's death, this work has been located in John Rastell's will, suggesting a publication date of before 20 April 1536. It employs the same type originally used by Rastell, with whom Gough had business connections; no other piece of music printing by Gough has survived. He worked at the 'Sign of the Mermaid', Lombard Street, London.

Humphries and Smith (1954, 2/1970); A. H. King: 'The Significance of John Rastell in Early Music Printing', *The Library*, 5th ser., xxvi/3 (1971), 197; R. J. Roberts: 'John Rastell's Inventory of 1538', *The Library*, 6th ser., i (1979), 34

M.M.

Goulart, Simon (*b* Senlis, 20 Oct 1543; *d* Geneva, 3 Feb 1628). French publisher. He studied law in Paris but then devoted his energies to the Reformation movement. He left Paris for Geneva at the beginning of 1566 and was ordained there on 20 October. He carried out his ministry first at Chancy and Cartigny, and then, after serving for a time in several French parishes, was appointed in 1571 to St Gervais, Geneva. He succeeded De Bèze as head of the Church in Geneva on the latter's death in 1605. As a historian and

publisher he brought out works by Lassus, Arcadelt, Crecquillon, Gérard de Turnhout, Jean de Castro, Noé Faignient, Goudimel, Séverin Cornet, Guillaume Boni, Antoine de Bertrand and others, with modified, and in some cases new, texts. The only composer whose works he published in their original form was Jean Servin. The prefaces he wrote to his publications throw light on relations between theologians and musicians.

O. Douen: *Clément Marot et le Psautier huguenot*, ii (Paris, 1879), 55; L.-C. Jones: *Simon Goulart* (Geneva, 1917); E. Choisy: 'Simon Goulart', *Die Religion in Geschichte und Gegenwart*, ii (1928), 1411; E. Droz: 'Simon Goulart, éditeur de musique', *Biblothèque d'humanisme et Renaissance*, xiv (1952), 265; C. S. Adams: 'Simon Goulart (1543–1628), Editor of Music, Scholar and Moralist', *Studies in Musicology in Honor of Otto E. Albrecht* (Kassel, 1977); P. Broisat-Richard: *La musique à Genève au XVIe siècle* (diss., St Etienne, 1981)

P.-A.G.

Goulding. English firm of music sellers, publishers and instrument makers, established in London. The business was founded by George Goulding in about 1786. Early in 1798 he entered into partnership with Thomas D'Almaine (*c*1784–1866) and a certain Phipps (who in 1810 left to form his own company); they obtained royal patronage, becoming 'music-sellers to the Prince and Princess of Wales', and from 1803 to 1816 operated an agency in Dublin which was first known as Goulding, Knevett & Co. Until 1823, when it was known as Goulding & D'Almaine, or Goulding, D'Almaine & Co., the firm existed under various names, and accepted a Potter and Wood into the partnership. Goulding's name was dropped by about 1834, the firm becoming D'Almaine & Co. Soon after 1840 Thomas Mackinlay joined the business and for a time some works were issued with the imprint D'Almaine & Mackinlay. With D'Almaine's death the firm was discontinued and the plates and stock sold by auction in May 1867.

George Goulding's early publications were of a minor character, but from 1800 the firm expanded its publishing interests to encompass much of the vocal music of the day, including the operas of Mazzinghi and Reeve. After moving to Soho Square in 1811 it entered its most active period, during which it published most of Henry Bishop's music. John Parry was its chief musical arranger for some time, being responsible for collections such as *The Vocal Companion* (1829), *The British Minstrel* (1830) and *Flowers of Song* (1837). Vast quantities of popular dance and vocal music continued to be issued by the firm up to the 1860s.

Kidson (1900); Humphries and Smith (1954, 2/1970)

F.K., W.C.S./P.W.J.

Grafton, Richard (*fl* 1540–50). English printer. He is noted for having printed some of the earliest books of the English church service. In 1544 he printed 'an exhortacium unto prayer, thought mete by the Kynges maiestie . . . also a Letanie with suffrage to be saide or songe in the tyme of the said processions'. He also printed John Merbecke's *The Booke of Common Praier Noted* in 1550. Grafton had his premises in what had been the house of the Grey Friars in Newgate Street, London, before the dissolution of the monasteries in the reign of Henry VIII.

Humphries and Smith (1954, 2/1970)

M.M.

Granjon, Robert (*b* Paris, 1513; *d* Rome, after 16 Nov 1589). French typefounder and printer. His chief skill was as a type designer and founder, although he was also active as a printer, both in his own name and with various associates. He is best known for the' design and execution of a typeface which imitated the cursive French gothic MS hand, known as *caractères de civilité*; he also designed roman and italic types, characters for several Near Eastern alphabets and some important music founts. He printed several books of music in two periods of his life: in Paris about 1551 and in Lyons about 1559.

A leaf of type samples dated 1583 lists the printer as 'Rob. Granjon Parisiensis' with the indication underneath 'aetatis suae LXX', thus providing the place and date of Granjon's birth. He seems to have become active as a type designer in Paris about 1543. His first known publication is a Greek and Latin New Testament printed in Paris in 1549. In February 1550 he received a royal privilege to print 'songs, masses, motets in music, tablature for lutes, guitars and other instruments', and on 23 December 1550 joined in an association with the Parisian printer of Rabelais, Michel Fezandat. The agreement was renewed for a year and a half on 19 November 1551, but by a contract dated 27 December 1551, the association was abruptly terminated and the common property divided. Fezandat agreed to take care of the firm's interests in Paris, while Granjon was to do the same in Lyons.

The fruits of the association were some books of poetry and history in Latin and French and at least two books of music for guitar in tablature: *Le premier livre de chansons* (1552) and *Le troysieme livre* (1551). A *Second livre* (1553, erroneously listed in *RISM* as having both Granjon's and Fezandat's names as printers) and a *Quatrieme livre* (1552) survive in copies which list Fezandat alone as printer. The four books form a series: they have an identical cover illustration and use the same layout and type. The tablature face, designed by Granjon, is identical with that used in the lutebooks published about that time and later by Le Roy & Ballard.

As early as 1546 Granjon had made periodic visits to Lyons to sell his types at the fairs. The record of a transaction in 1547 shows a sale to Jean de Tournes and Sebastian Gryphius of Lyons. He perhaps settled there in 1552 after the termination of the arrangement with Fezandat. In 1557 his first Lyons book, and the first in which he used *caractères de civilité*, appeared.

In December 1557 he formed a partnership with Guillaume Guéroult and Jehan Hiesse to print books of music in editions of 1500 copies, with 500 copies going to each partner for sale, but by April 1558 the partnership was dissolved. Despite a later six-year royal privilege for music, dated 12 February 1559, Granjon printed only four music books in Lyons, all in the year 1559: Beaulaigue's *Chansons nouvelles* (the tenor partbook is dated 1558) and his *Mottetz nouvellement mis en musique*, *Le premier trophée de musique* and *Le second trophée de musique*. The text of these was printed in *caractères de civilité*, and the music in a new type designed by Granjon with round note heads, inspired perhaps by the shapes designed by Etienne Briard for Jean de Channey; for illustration *see* fig.7, p.25.

Some time after 1562 Granjon settled in Antwerp. There he cut types and sold them to printers. The inventories of the famous Antwerp printer Christopher Plantin contained more than 40 types, including *caractères de civilité* and music designed by Granjon. By 1571 he was back in Paris, although he made frequent visits to Lyons up to 1575. In 1577 he is again listed as a citizen of Lyons. A year later he was in Rome, where he was to remain for the rest of his life. There he designed Armenian, Arabic, Syriac and Cyrillic type in the service of Cardinal Giulio Antonio Santoro, who supported a printing house for the propagation of the faith to Near Eastern countries. Granjon printed some books in Rome under his own name, and numerous books printed by others used his type founts. In 1582 a *Directorium chori ad usum sacrosanctae Basilice Vaticanae* appeared under his name as printer and used a plainsong music type evidently of his own design.

Granjon is important in the history of music not only for the music books he printed, but particularly for the music types he designed; some of the punches are still extant in the Plantin-Moretus Museum in Antwerp. One of the founts (probably his third) was particularly important, since it was perhaps the most widely used of all music typefaces. It was first used in Antwerp and Ghent in 1565, possibly in south Germany in 1567, definitely in Norwich, England, in 1567, and extensively by John Day in London beginning in 1571. The punches for this fount passed from Granjon to Henrik van den Keere in Ghent and then to Christopher Plantin. The type was then distributed from Antwerp, later also from Frankfurt, to printers all over northern and western Europe and was still being used in the middle of the 18th century.

H. and J. Baudrier: *Bibliographie lyonnaise* (Paris, 1895–1921/R1964), ii, 49, 429; C. Dalbanne: 'Robert Granjon, imprimeur de musique', *Gutenberg-Jb 1939*, 226; F. Lesure: 'Granjon, Robert', *MGG*; D. Heartz: 'Parisian Music Publishing under Henry II', *MQ*, xlvi (1960), 448; H. Carter and H. D. L. Vervliet: *Civilité Types*, Oxford Bibliographical Society Publications, new ser., xiv (Oxford, 1966); H. Carter: *Sixteenth-century French Typefounders: the Le Bé Memorandum* (Paris, 1967); H. D. L. Vervliet: *Robert Granjon à Rome 1578–1589* (Amsterdam, 1967); idem: *Sixteenth-century Printing Types of the Low Countries* (Amsterdam, 1968); Krummel (1975)

S.F.P.

Graupner [Graubner], **(Johann Christian) Gottlieb** (*b* Verden, nr. Hanover, 6 Oct 1767; *d* Boston, 16 April 1836). German-American publisher and musician. He was a son of the oboist Johann Georg Graupner, but no evidence has been found to link him with the earlier Christoph Graupner of Darmstadt. He followed his father's profession and joined a military regiment in Hanover as an oboist, but he also developed performing skills on many other instruments, playing in London and later Charleston, South Carolina (1795); by 1797 he had settled in Boston. In 1801, with Francis Mallet and Filippo Trajetta, Graupner established the American Conservatorio, which soon became involved in the selling, hiring and printing of music. He continued the venture alone from 1802 and during the early decades of the 19th century became Boston's leading music publisher and dealer, selling music and instruments on consignment from other dealers, and engraving and printing much music and instruction material himself. Many of Graupner's plates were later acquired by Oliver Ditson. Graupner was much in demand as a teacher on many instruments. He was leader of the Philo-Harmonic Society (founded to promote the performance of the German orchestral repertory), a charter member of the Handel and Haydn Society and a song composer. His account books are in the Brown University Libraries, Providence, and the Newberry Library in Chicago holds the J. F. Driscoll collection of Graupner's music imprints.

O. G. T. Sonneck: *A Bibliography of Early Secular American Music* (Washington, DC, 1905; rev. and enlarged by W. T. Upton, 2/1945/R1964); K. G. Stone: *History and Genealogy of the Graupner Family* (MS, 1906, Boston Public Library); F. J. Metcalf: *American Writers and Compilers of Sacred Music* (New York, 1925/R1967); F. L. G. Cole: 'Graupner, Johann Christian Gottlieb', *DAB*; H. E. Johnson: 'Mr. and Mrs. Graupner', *Musical Interludes in Boston, 1795–1830* (New York, 1943/R1967), 166–200, 305–337; Wolfe (1964); idem (1980)

D.A.L.

Gray, H. W. American firm of publishers. H. Willard Gray (*b* Brighton, 1868; *d* Old Lyme, CT, 22 Oct 1950) went to the USA in 1894 to be head of the New York branch of Novello, Ewer & Co. He bought the office and established his own company, H. W. Gray Company, Inc., in 1906. Gray specializes in choral and organ music and fosters the publication of works by American composers. It also published (*c*1908) Frederick S. Converse's *The Pipe of Desire*, which was the first American opera to be produced at the Metropolitan Opera (18 March 1910). Gray was acquired by Belwin-Mills in 1971.

F.B.

Gray, Matthias (*b* Manchester, 19 April 1829; *d* San Francisco, 23 March 1887). American publisher of English birth. He was appointed a clerk at San Francisco's first music shop, Atwill & Co., in 1851, and opened his own business in 1858. The Matthias Gray Co. became the leading music publisher in San Francisco and, with the help of the agency for Steinway, one of the largest in northern California. Gray was the first California publisher to identify his original works systematically with plate numbers. His catalogue of 1872 included works by local pianists, singers and minstrel artists, as well as excerpts from current operas and church music, and piano works by Chopin, Henri Herz and Gottschalk.

The business was dissolved in 1892, the Steinway agency sold to Sherman, Clay & Co. and the immense stock of music purchased by the Oliver Ditson Co.

M. K. Duggan: 'Music Publishing and Printing in San Francisco before the Earthquake & Fire of 1906', *Kemble Occasional*, no.24 (1980); idem: 'Music Publishing and Printing in San Francisco before the Earthquake & Fire of 1906: Directory', *Kemble Occasional*, no.30 (1983); R. Stevenson: 'California Pioneer Sheet Music Publishers and Publications', *Inter-American Music Review*, viii/1 (1986), 36

M.K.D.

Grignani, Lodovico (*fl* Rome, 1630–50). Italian printer and publisher. His few secular titles include one volume of madrigals each by Capponi and Cenci; particularly attractive is *Musiche sacre e morale*, engraved by Andrea Podestà in 1640. He concentrated mainly, however, on sacred music and treatises, and his repertory is made up mainly of motet collections by minor Roman composers, although he reprinted music by Palestrina and Anerio in 1646 and 1649, and published several volumes by Diruta. The list of theorists is more distinguished and includes Kircher, Micheli and Sabbatini.

S.B. (iii)

Grimm & Wirsung. German firm of printers and publishers. In 1517 Sigmund Grimm, who had been an Augsburg town doctor since 1507, set up a printing press and took Marx Wirsung as his partner (1518–22), but after Wirsung left the firm it began to decline and was eventually sold in 1527 or 1528. Otmar Luscinius worked with the press for some time as a proofreader. Of items printed by Grimm (nearly 300) the most important to the musicologist is the *Liber selectarum cantionum quas vulgo mutetas appellant* (1520), printed from woodcuts. A collection of 24 Latin hymns by such leading composers as Josquin, Senfl, Pierre de la Rue, Mouton and Obrecht, it includes the imperial motets *Virgo prudentissima* by Isaac and *Sancte Pater, divumque decus* by Senfl, and has woodcuts by Hans Weiditz; it is the earliest printed choirbook with the separate parts set out on two facing pages. This collection was produced at the instigation of the Augsburg humanist Konrad Peutinger, edited by Ludwig Senfl and dedicated to the Archbishop of Salzburg, Matthäus Lang von Wellenburg, a patron and lover of music who had formerly been private secretary and ambassador to the Emperor Maximilian.

Benzing (1963, 2/1982); A. Layer: 'Augsburger Musikdrucker der frühen Renaissancezeit', *Gutenberg-Jb 1965*, 124; E. T. Nauck: 'Doktor Sigmund Grimm, Arzt und Buchdrucker', *Zeitschrift des Historischen Vereins für Schwaben*, lix-lx (1969), 311; W. Senn: 'Maximilian und die Musik', *Ausstellung Maximilian I* (Innsbruck, 1969), 84; R. Steiner, Arzt und J. Bellot: 'Zur Herkunft von Dr. Sigmund Grimm, Arzt und Buchdrucker zu Augsburg', *Zeitschrift des Historischen Vereins für Schwaben*, lxxvi (1982), 183

T.W.

Grunewald, Louis (*b* Hohenhofen, 1827; *d* New Orleans, 1 March 1915). American publisher, instrument maker and impresario. He emigrated from Germany in 1852 and settled in New Orleans, where he became organist at three churches. In 1858 he opened a music shop and sold instruments and sheet music. From 1874 he also managed the Grunewald Opera House, a major concert hall. His firm manufactured musical instruments in the late 19th century and published a large quantity of music from 1870 to 1920, when G. Schirmer purchased the publishing concern. The music shop remained open until 1972, though the family sold it in 1969.

P. C. Boudreaux: *Music Publishing in New Orleans in the 19th Century* (MA thesis, Louisiana State U., 1977)

J.H.B.

Guéra. French publishing firm, active at Lyons. It was founded about 1776 by Chrétien [Johann] Gottlieb Ghera (?1745–1778), a German pianist, harpist and composer who had settled in Lyons in 1772. After his death, the business was taken over by one Graf, who apparently operated it until 1788. Some of the Guéra plates or prints were subsequently acquired by Castaud of Lyons, who was superseded by Garnier. Guéra distributed throughout Europe, using its contacts with Artaria, Breitkopf, the Bureau du Journal de Musique and Le Menu et Boyer. Its composers included Aspelmayer, Boccherini, Giordani, Giornovichi, Haydn, Hoffmeister, Ordonez, Pichl, Sterkel and Vanhal.

L. Vallas: *Un siècle de musique et de théâtre à Lyon, 1688–1789* (Lyons, 1932/R1971); A. P. Brown and R. Griscom: *The French Music Publisher Guéra of Lyon: a Dated List* (Detroit, 1987)

A.P.B., R.G.

Guéroult, Guillaume (*b* Rouen, early 16th century; *d* after 1564). French Protestant writer and publisher. He was important for his activities in the Calvinist movement, providing translations and dedicatory letters for a number of printers. He seems to have been a contentious writer, often in

270

trouble, belying his use of the motto 'patience victorieuse'. In Geneva by 1546, he translated Psalm cxxiv and the *Te Deum* for Calvin's *Deux sermones*. Although several of his subsequent publications – a dedication to Bourgeois' *Cinquante Psaulmes* (1547), translations of some of Marot's *Pseaumes de David* (1548), texts, including *Susanne un jour*, to Didier Lupi's *Premier livre de chansons spirituelles* (1548) – appeared from Lyonese printers, there is no evidence that he left Geneva before 1551, when he was expelled for infraction of religious ordinances. He went to Vienne where he worked at a branch of the Lyons firm run by his brother-in-law, Balthasar Arnoullet, and translated volumes for him. At Vienne Guéroult secretly printed religious texts: as a result, Arnoullet was imprisoned in 1553 and Guéroult fled back to Geneva.

In 1554–6 he and his relative Simon Du Bosc published in Geneva 12 volumes of music, psalm settings, *chansons spirituelles* and motets. Perhaps because of disputes with de Bèze, Guéroult had left Geneva by August 1555, probably for Lyons. In 1557 he and Jehan Hiesse entered into a contract with Granjon to publish music in editions of 1500 copies, but the contract collapsed within a few months. Guéroult's publications at this time include some psalm translations and dedicatory letters, most in Lyons. He may have been in Paris in 1559: his *L'Epistre du Segnieur de Brusquet* of that year, an attack on the Geneva Council, elicited an edict that he was to be imprisoned if he ever came from Paris to Geneva. He issued a set of texts, *La lyre chrestienne* (Lyons, 1560) and continued to publish translations, odes and epistles until 1564.

G. Becker: *Guillaume Guéroult et ses chansons spirituelles* (Paris, 1880); H. and J. Baudrier: *Bibliographie lyonnaise* (Paris, 1895–1921/*R*1964), x, 92; C. Dalbanne: 'Robert Granjon, imprimeur de musique', *Gutenberg-Jb 1939*, 226; K. J. Levy: '"Susanne un jour": the History of a 16th Century Chanson', *AnnM*, i (1953), 375; P. Chaix: *Recherches sur l'imprimerie à Genève de 1550 à 1564* (Geneva, 1954); P. Chaix, A. Dufour and G. Moechli: 'Les livres imprimés à Genève de 1550 à 1600', *Genava*, new ser., vii (1959), 235–394; P. Pidoux: *Le psautier huguenot du XVIe siècle*, (Basle, 1962–9)

S.B. (iii)

Guidi, Giovanni Gualberto (*b* Florence, 1817; *d* Florence, 18 Jan 1883). Italian publisher and double bass player. He played the double bass at the Teatro della Pergola, Florence (1849–53), and in 1844 opened his publishing firm under the name G. G. Guidi, Stabilimento Calcografico Musicale. As the publisher of the winning compositions at the Duca di S Clemente and the Società del Quartetto competitions, he printed much of the music performed at the society's concerts. His catalogue included a number of chamber works and overtures by Beethoven, Mozart and Mendelssohn, and compositions by contemporary musicians, including Bottesini and Anichini. He also published many full scores of operas, including *Guillaume Tell*, *Les Huguenots, Robert le diable* and *Il barbiere di Siviglia* by Rossini, and Peri's *L'Euridice* (1863), transcribed directly from the 17th-century manuscript. The catalogue also contained operas by Morlacchi and Mancinelli, polyphonic music, including madrigals by Tromboncino and Arcadelt (1875), E. Bertini's *Cento studi per pianoforte* and other piano music for two and four hands. Many pieces appeared in Guidi's *Biblioteca del Sinfonista* series and occasionally in his periodicals *Il piovano arlotto* and *Gazzetta musicale di Firenze* (1853–5), where chamber compositions by Rossini also appeared. The *Gazzetta* continued as *Harmonia* (1856–9) and he also issued *Boccherini* (1862–83), the journal of the Società del Quartetto.

The firm was one of the earliest to publish pocket scores (from 1858), for which it was awarded a prize at the Italian Exhibition in Florence in 1861; but the format did not achieve the desired success and was only later developed by other concerns in Germany and France. Guidi's editions were particularly admired for their clear engraving, using plates made by specially small dye-stamps. The engraving was the exclusive responsibility of Guidi's daughters Marianna and Amalia; after their father's death they continued the business until 1887 when Ricordi bought it.

A. C. P.: 'Delle nuove edizioni musicali di G. G. Guidi di Firenze', *La Esposizione italiana del 1861* (Florence, 1862), 155; *Atti dell'Accademia del R. istituto musicale di Firenze*, xxii (1884), 10; Sartori (1958); C. Hopkinson: 'The Earliest Miniature Scores', *MR*, xxxiii (1972), 138

S.A.

Gutheil [Gutkheyl']. Russian publishing firm, active in Moscow. Founded in 1859 by Alexander Bogdanovich Gutheil (1818–83), it was a strong rival to Jürgenson, Belyayev and Bessel, particularly after its amalgamation with Stellovsky in 1886. This transaction secured for Gutheil the rights to many works by Glinka, Dargomïzhsky, Serov and Balakirev, though Gutheil rejected the opportunity to become Balakirev's sole publisher after Balakirev's quarrel with Jürgenson in 1886–7. Perhaps his greatest coup was the acquisition of the publishing rights to Rakhmaninov's works. Shortly after Rakhmaninov's graduation from the Moscow Conservatory in 1892 Gutheil bought his opera *Aleko*, two cello pieces and six songs, and in October the same year he bought the First Piano Concerto. He published the cello pieces as op.2, and later included some of the songs in op.4, but, possibly unwilling to risk financial loss on a relatively unknown composer, he only issued a vocal score of *Aleko* and a two-piano arrangement of the concerto. Nevertheless from then until 1914 nearly all Rakhmaninov's major compositions appeared under the Gutheil imprint (a few were published by Jürgenson, and one by Editions Russes).

Gutheil formed an important link in the chain of ownership that characterized Russian music publishing: in 1810 Johann Petz had taken over the firm of Gerstenberg and Dittmar (then in the hands of Dittmar alone); he in turn was bought out by Klever in 1845, and Stellovsky took over the entire concern about 1850. By the time of the amalgamation with Gutheil, that firm was being run by Alexander Gutheil's son Karl, who had assumed control after his father's death. In 1914 the business was bought by Koussevitzky for 300,000 rubles and absorbed into his Editions Russes de Musique.

B. P. Jürgenson: *Ocherk istorii notopechataniya* [An outline of the history of music printing] (Moscow, 1928); A. S. Lyapunova: 'Kratkiy obzor istorii izdaniya proizvedeniy M. I. Glinki' [A short account of the history of the publication of Glinka's works], *M. A. Balakirev: perepiska s·notoizdatel'stvom P. Yurgensona*, (Moscow, 1958), 369; E. Garden: *Balakirev: a Critical Study of his Life and Music* (London, 1967); B. L. Vol'man: *Russkiye notnÿye izdaniya XIX – nachala XX veka* [Russian music publishing in the 19th and early 20th centuries] (Leningrad, 1970)

G.N.

H

Haffner, Johann Ulrich (*b* 1711; *d* Nuremberg, 22 Oct 1767). German publisher. He founded a music publishing house in Nuremberg about 1742 with the copper-engraver Johann Wilhelm Winter (1717–60), and managed the business on his own from 1745; he was the leading Nuremberg music publisher of the mid-18th century. The firm specialized in the piano and chamber music of German (central and southern) and Italian composers, including C. P. E. Bach and D. Scarlatti. During his 25 years as a publisher Haffner issued about 150 works, all first editions; almost all were engraved by the outstanding Nuremberg engraver Johann Wilhelm Stör (1705–65). The Nuremberg art dealer Adam Wolfgang Winterschmidt took charge of the publishing house in 1770, and was succeeded by his son in 1786.

L. Hoffman-Erbrecht: 'Der Nürnberger Musikverleger Johann Ulrich Haffner', *AcM*, xxvi (1954), 114, xxvii (1955), 141; idem: 'Haffner, Johann Ulrich', *NDB*; H. Heussner: 'Nürnberger Musikverlag und Musikalienhandel im 18. Jahrhundert', *Musik und Verlag: Karl Vötterle zum 65. Geburtstag* (Kassel, 1968), 319; L. Hoffmann-Erbrecht: 'Johann Sebastian und Carl Philipp Emanuel Bachs Nürnberger Musikverleger', *Nürnberger Musikverleger und die Familie Bach: Materialien zu einer Ausstellung des 48. Bach-Fests der Neuen Bach-Gesellschaft*, ed. W. Worthmüller (Zirndorf, 1973), 8

T.W.

Hagen, P. A. von [van]. American firm of publishers. Albrecht von Hagen sr (*b* Netherlands, 1755; *d* Boston, 20 Aug 1803) and his family emigrated to the USA in 1774, and by 1789 were settled in New York, where they were active as performers, teachers and concert managers. In 1796 they moved to Boston (where they changed their name from van to von) and from 1798 von Hagen became one of the most important music dealers and publishers, issuing patriotic songs, selections from ballad operas, and his own compositions. Peter Albrecht von Hagen jr (*b* ?Charleston, SC, 1779–81; *d* Boston, 12 Sept 1837) was active with his father in the family publishing firm, but owing either to his lack of interest or his incompetence, the firm's fortunes deteriorated and its stock was sold in 1804 to Gottlieb Graupner.

'A Unique Letter', *Dwight's Journal of Music*, xviii (1860), 232; O. G. T. Sonneck: *A Bibliography of Early Secular American Music* (Washington, DC, 1905; rev. and enlarged by W. T. Upton, 2/1945/R1964); H. E. Johnson: *Musical Interludes in Boston, 1795–1830* (New York, 1943/R1967); Wolfe (1964); idem (1980)

B.C., H.E.J.

Haller, Jan (*b* Rothenburg, ?*c*1467; *d* Kraków, 7 or 8 Oct 1525). Polish publisher and bookseller of German birth, active in Kraków. Granted the first royal privilege issued in Poland, he began its earliest publishing business in 1494. In 1503 he issued the *Missale Wratislaviense* in which the music in Gothic notation was printed from movable type in two colours. Possibly on his initiative, the German printer Kasper Hochfeder went to Kraków in 1503 and from 1505 to 1509 served as the firm's technical manager. Haller's output of about 250 publications included scientific books, university textbooks, state documents and liturgical books. In the field of music he is principally known for the printing of *Bogurodzica* (the knights' hymn), and two treatises by Sebastian z Felsztyna, *Modus regulariter accentuandi* (1518) and *Opusculum musicae compilatum* (1517) in addition to the missal.

Przywecka-Samecka (1969); *Słownik pracowników książki polskiej* [Dictionary of Polish printers] (Warsaw and Łódź, 1972)

T.C. (ii)

Hals, Brødrene. Norwegian firm of piano makers and publishers. It was founded by the brothers Karl (1822–98) and Petter (1823–71) Hals in Christiania in 1847. After his brother's death Karl continued to run the firm with his sons Olav (1857–83) and Thor (1852–1924). It operated solely as a piano factory and shop until 1880, when the firm built a concert hall (closed in 1919). In 1885 Brødrene Hals became co-owners of Petter Håkonsen's music shop, publishing firm and music lending library (also in Christiania). Two years later it acquired the business, founding its own shop and publishing house. Håkonsen had issued about 350 titles, and Hals brought publications to a total of 1231. Like its competitor Warmuth, Hals chiefly published Norwegian composers; among those whose names appeared most frequently were Ole Olsen, Agathe Backer-Grøndahl, Sinding, Grieg and Halvorsen. In 1908, in association with Wilhelm Hansen of Copenhagen, Brødrene Hals bought Carl Warmuth. With the merger of Hals and Warmuth, Norsk Musikforlag came into being on 1 January 1909.

Skilling-Magazin, xxix (1866); *Nordisk musiktidende*, xi (1880); T. Voss: *Warumuths Musikhandel, Brødrene Hals, Norsk Musikforlag 1843–1943* (Oslo, 1943); K. Michelsen: *Musikkhandel i Norge inntil 1929: a Historical Survey* (Oslo, 1980); idem: 'Music Trade in Norway to 1929', *FAM*, xxix (1982), 43; P. A. Kjeldsberg: *Piano i Norge 'et uunværligt Instrument'* (Oslo, 1985); K. Michelsen:

'Musikkleiebibliotekene i Norge', *SMN*, xi (1985), 81

K.M. (ii)

Hamelle. French firm of publishers. It was founded by Julien Hamelle (*d* 1917) in 1877 when he took over the business of J. Maho (founded 1851) in the boulevard Malesherbes, Paris. The firm specializes in the 19th-century French repertory, particularly piano, vocal and instrumental music. It published some of the early works of Saint-Saëns, Franck, d'Indy and Debussy as well as many works by Widor and, more especially, Fauré (virtually everything up to op.85). It also ran a successful lending library.

A.P. (ii)

Hamman, Johann [Hertzog] (*b* Landau; *d* ?Speyer, after October 1509). German printer. Between 1482 and 1509 he printed 85 books, all in Venice except the last, printed in his native Speyer diocese. Most were liturgical books for dioceses from England to Hungary; 16 contain printed notes and staves, or staves. Large, medium and small roman plainchant types appear in missals of corresponding formats – five folio, one quarto and five octavo. In addition he introduced a medium gothic plainchant type for an agenda for Passau. Together with his former partner Johann Emerich of Speyer, Hamman issued one-third of the music books printed in 15th-century Italy.

D. Rogers: 'Johann Hamman at Venice: a Survey of his Career', *Essays in Honour of V. Scholderer* (Mainz, 1970), 348; Duggan (1981)

M.K.D.

Han [Hahn], **Ulrich** [Gallus, Udalricus] (*b* Ingolstadt; *d* Rome, *c*1478). German printer, active in Rome. He claimed in colophons to have been a citizen of Vienna and may have produced the first printing there in 1462 (see Borsa). Colophons also tell us that Han was a priest (*venerabile vir*), attended a university (*magister*) and was a man of some social standing (*dominus*). He is probably the Ulrich Han from Ingolstadt who matriculated at the University of Leipzig in the winter of 1443–4 and the Udalricus of Ingolstadt registered for the winter term of 1438. He has been proposed (see Donati; reviewed by Wehmer) as the possible printer of the first book in Italy, an undated *Passio Christi* in Italian; but the engraved illustrations are more indicative of the work of Johann Numeister.

Between 1467 and 1478 Han published about 80 books in Rome. Early production focused on classical works, many edited by Giovanni Andrea Campano. Between 1471 and 1474 Han was in partnership with Simone Cardella of Lucca, a Roman publisher of legal works. He was succeeded by Stephan Planck, probably a printer in his shop, who inherited his printing equipment and re-used his music type for eight more books (Duggan, 1984). Of great importance to music is Han's *Missale romanum* (1476; Hain no.11366), the first dated use of music printed from movable type and the first appearance of roman plainchant in type. Missals without music had already appeared (*c*1472, see Tocci; 1474, Milan, Antonio Zarotto, Reichling no.997; 1475, Han, Hain no.11364). Music printed from movable type had already appeared in the *Graduale* (*c*1473), using a gothic or *Hufnagelschrift* plainchant type. Han's music type, printed in black in a second impression over red staff lines, surpasses many later examples in clarity and careful alignment of red and black printing.

L. Hain: *Repertorium bibliographicum* (Stuttgart, 1826–38); G. Erler, ed.: *Die Matrikel der Universität Leipzig*, i (Leipzig, 1895), 125, 146; D. Reichling: *Appendices ad Hainii-Copingeri Repertorium bibliographicum* (Munich, 1905–11); L. Donati: 'Passio Domini Nostri Iesu Christi', *La bibliofilia*, lvi (1954), 207; L. M. Tocci 'Incunaboli sconosciuti e incunaboli mal conosciuti della Biblioteca Vaticana', *Studi di biliografia e di storia in onore di Tammaro de Marinis* (Stamperia Valdonega, 1964), 189; F. Geldner: *Die deutschen Inkunabeldrucker: ein Handbuch der deutschen Buchdrucker des XV. Jahrhunderts nach Druckorten*, i (Stuttgart, 1968), 50, 252, 293; C. Wehmer: 'Udalricus Gallus de Bienna', *Contributi alla storia del libro italiano: Miscellanea in onore di Lamberto Donati* (Florence, 1969), 325–57; F. Geldner: 'Zum frühesten deutschen und italienischen Buchdruck (Mainz – Baiern – Foligno: Johannes Neumeister und Ulrich Han?)', *Gutenberg-Jb 1979*, 18; Duggan (1981); G. Borsa: 'Wann wurde in Österreich zum ersten Mal gedruckt?', *Biblos*, xxxii (1983), 132; M.K. Duggan: 'A System for Describing Fifteenth-century Music Type', *Gutenberg-Jb 1984*, 73 [to the seven listed titles add the 1494 *Manuale baptisterium*]

M.K.D

Handel societies. Several societies have been founded with the object of publishing Handel's works. The first was the Handel Society, founded in London 'for the production of a superior and standard edition of the works of Handel' (according to its prospectus, issued on 16 June 1843); its council for the first year included G. A. Macfarren (secretary), William Sterndale Bennett, Sir Henry Bishop, William Crotch, Ignaz Moscheles, E. F. Rimbault and Sir George Smart. By January 1848 the society had dissolved for lack of subscribers, but its publishers, Cramer, Beale & Co., sustained the production of editions until 1858, by which time 12 major works (mostly oratorios) and two collections had appeared. Mendelssohn was among the editors (*Israel in Egypt*, 1846).

The next Handel society devoted to publication was the Deutsche Händel-Gesellschaft, founded in Leipzig in 1856 for the publication of a critical and uniform edition of the whole of Handel's works. The prime movers were Friedrich Chrysander and the literary historian Gottfried Gervinus. Chrysander himself was the sole active editor, and when the society collapsed in 1860 he took over the production of the editions himself, though retaining the society's name; from 1866 he also took over the printing and distribution of the edition, working from his home in Bergedorf bei Hamburg. A Neue Händel-Gesellschaft was founded on Arnold Schering's initiative in Leipzig in 1925; it published a *Händel-Jahrbuch* (1928–33, ed. R. Steglich) and performing editions of Handel's works, and organized a number of festivals.

The Georg-Friedrich-Händel Gesellschaft was founded in Halle in 1955 for the publication of a new collected edition, known as the Hallische Händel-Ausgabe (Halle Handel Edition), and it also resumed publication of the *Händel-Jahrbuch*. The edition was begun largely as a practical edition based on Chrysander, but after criticism of the first volumes, in 1958 it was announced that the edition would continue as a full critical edition. No effective mechanism was instituted to ensure that editors consulted all sources and correctly established the relationships between them, however; as a result, some volumes, especially of the major vocal works, appeared with defective texts or inadequate critical commentaries. In 1985 new practices were established, whereby all editorial work is examined by both the office at Halle and a supervisory board of scholars from Britain, the USA and both German states, to ensure that the highest scholarly standards are consistently met. The publishers of the Halle edition, Deutscher Verlag and Bärenreiter, issued the first volumes under the new arrangement in 1988.

G. Feder: 'Händelgesellschaften', *MGG* [with full bibliography]

A.H. (ii)

Hansen. Danish firm of publishers. It was founded in Copenhagen in 1853 by Jens Wilhelm Hansen, and until 1988 was continuously owned and managed by his descendants. In 1847 he established himself as an engraver, printer and lithographer, and in 1853 began printing and publishing music from his home; in 1857 he opened a music shop that included a music hire library, and in 1874 he took into partnership his two sons, Jonas Wilhelm Hansen (1850–1919) and Alfred Wilhelm Hansen (1854–1923). The following year the publishing firm of C. E. Horneman (founded in 1861) was acquired and amalgamated with the Hansen firm. At first Hansen had published mainly educational and salon music, but it then began to issue new works by Danish composers, including Niels Gade and J. P. E. Hartmann, thus establishing a practice that is still continued. In 1879 the firm acquired a leading position in Danish music by taking over, on 25 June, the two dominating music publishers and dealers, Lose (founded in 1802) and Horneman & Èrslev (founded in 1846). Their numerous and valuable publications and their very extensive retail departments gave Hansen a virtual monopoly of the music trade in Denmark. In the following year the firm took over Lose's premises at Gothersgade 11, where it has remained.

Expansion continued with the incorporation of more Danish music publishing firms, and in 1887 a branch office was opened in Leipzig; this was very active until it was closed during World War II. In 1908 Hansen and the firm of Brødrene Hals in Oslo took over the house of Carl Warmuth (founded in 1843), and jointly established Norsk Musikforlag in Oslo (1 January 1909). When Hansen took control (1910) of the only competing Danish firm, Nordisk Musikforlag (begun 'in 1880 as Kgl. Hof-Musikhandel), the firm again acquired an exclusive status in Denmark. In 1915 a Swedish house, Nordiska Musikförlaget, was founded in Stockholm. After Alfred Wilhelm Hansen's death business was carried on by his sons Asger Wilhelm Hansen (1889–1976) and Svend Wilhelm Hansen (1890–1960), whose two daughters, Hanne Wilhelm Hansen (*b* 1927) and Lone Wilhelm Hansen (*b* 1930), subsequently took over the management. In 1951 a new German branch was established, Wilhelmiana Musikverlag in Frankfurt am Main, and in 1957 the house of J. & W. Chester, London, became associated with the Copenhagen mother firm. A Finnish branch office was opened in 1986 in Helsinki.

Since 1879 Hansen has been the leading Scandinavian music publisher, promoting the music of most northern European composers. Through the Leipzig branch many Scandinavian works were brought to the attention of a receptive international public. Denmark was represented by P. A. Heise and Emil Hartmann, and later by Carl Nielsen and the following generation, including Riisager, Tarp and Holmboe; Norway by Sinding, Backer-Grøndahl, Johan Svendsen and Halvorsen; Sweden by Alfvén, Stenhammar, Sjögren, and later Hilding Rosenberg and Sven Erik Bäck; and Finland by Sibelius (the later symphonies), Kilpinen and Palmgren. The firm has also published progressive international works, including (in the 1920s) compositions by Schoenberg, Stravinsky, Honegger and Poulenc, and (more recently) works by Lutosławski and Bibalo. It reflects educational and national trends, and its programme includes critical editions by Knud Jeppesen and others.

In November 1988 the Hansen family sold the entire business, with the exception of Norsk Musikforlag in Oslo, to Music Sales Corporation, also disposing of its retail business and concert agency. Publishing continues in Copenhagen under the name of Wilhelm Hansen.

Katalog over Wilhelm Hansen's Musik-Forlag (Copenhagen and Leipzig, 1902); *Katalog over samtlige Forlagsværker udkomne paa Wilhelm Hansen, Musik-Forlag ... Priserne ugyldige* (1923); A. Kjerulf: *Hundrede År mellem Noder: Wilhelm Hansen, Musik-Forlag 1857–1957* (Copenhagen, 1957); D. Fog: *Musikhandel og Nodetryk i Danmark efter 1750* (Copenhagen, 1984) [incl. dated plate nos.]

D.F.

Hansen, Charles. American firm of publishers. It was established in 1945 in New York by Charles Hansen (*b* Jersey City, NJ, 19 Jan 1913), who compiled songbooks by purchasing rights from the music copyright owners. The firm built its success on such songbooks representing multiple publishers, and in 1955 it moved to Miami. During the 1960s Hansen's music sheets and songbooks comprised arrangements of successful pop and rock recordings, illustrated with record-jacket artwork and celebrity photographs. For a time Hansen was the sole distributor of music copyrighted by Walt Disney, Paramount, Metromedia and other houses. In 1968 it issued about 350 song sheets and 350 songbooks; in the 1970s it was a pioneer in television marketing. The firm now operates as Hansen House, with editorial and printing offices in Miami Beach, and a catalogue of about 25,000 licensed titles and 2500 original titles.

'Hansen Presses Whirl Out Music', *Billboard* (28 June 1969); T. Ross: *The Art of Music Engraving and Processing* (Miami Beach, 1970); I. Lacher: 'His Top Tune: the Sound of Money', *Miami Herald* (4 September 1986)

J.E.H.

Hänssler. German firm of publishers. Founded in 1919 by Friedrich Hänssler in Stuttgart, it quickly built up a reputation for scholarly yet practical editions of Lutheran church music including cantatas, motets and instrumental settings. In particular, Hänssler has issued collections of the motets of Calvisius, Crüger, Gumpelzhaimer, Hammerschmidt, Raselius, Selle and Vulpius in its series *Das Chorwerk Alter Meister*. The series *Die Motette* contains many individual motets by such composers as Melchior Franck, Giovanni Gabrieli, Praetorius, Rosenmüller and Scheidt. Apart from building up a catalogue of modern German composers, the firm has started publishing the collected Stuttgarter Schütz-Ausgabe under the general editorship of Günter Graulich, as well as practical performing editions to accompany the series. In addition the *Stuttgarter Ausgabe* series contains editions of J. S. Bach, Bach's sons, Buxtehude, Eccard and Telemann. The company has become the sole German agent for publications of the American Instiute of Musicology and the scholarly publications of Friedrich Gennrich as well as agent for numerous other foreign publishers.

A.P. (ii)

Hantzsch, Andreas (*d* after 1611). German printer, son of Georg Hantzsch. He took over his father's press in 1583 and printed in Mühlhausen until 1599, when he was invited to become city printer at Hildesheim. He started there in 1600 with an ambitious list, but production fell away and he was back in Mühlhausen in 1609. His last recorded print is dated 1611; all the music that survives from his press was printed before 1600, with the exception of a treatise by Scheffer, printed in 1603. The rest comprises music by Burck and anthologies of local music, several of which are editions of music first printed by his father.

J. H. Gebauer: 'Das Buchgewerbe in der Stadt Hildesheim', *Niedersächsisches Jb*, xviii (1941), 223–58; W. Hartmann: 'Hildesheimer Drucke der Zeit vor 1650', *Alt-Hildesheim*, xxxi (1960), 1–36 [catalogue with illustrations]; Benzing (1963, 2/1982)

S.B. (iii)

Hantzsch, Georg (*b* ?c1520; *d* Mühlhausen, 1583). German printer, father of Andreas Hantzsch. When he was accorded citizenship of Leipzig in 1545 he was already called a printer. In 1550 he married the widow of Michael Blum, a local printer, and acquired his press. At Leipzig he printed some theoretical writings, editions of Zanger, and of Faber, Figulus and Listenius that had appeared elsewhere. In 1560 he went to Weissenfels and by 1567 to Mühlhausen, where he printed several volumes of music, including most of the work of Burck, and some music by Eccard and others. He also reprinted some of Faber's works and other titles. When he died his press passed to his son.

J. Rodenberg: 'Alte Leipziger Druckereien', *Graphische Nachrichten*, xiii (1934), 420; E. Sägenschnitte: 'Buchdruck und Buchhandels in Weissenfels', *25 Jahre Städtisches Museum Weissenfels* (Weissenfels, 1935), 79; H. Koch: 'Regesten zur Leipziger Buchdruckergeschichte im 16. Jhdt', *Gutenberg-Jb 1955*, 174; Benzing (1963, 2/1982)

S.B. (iii)

Hare. English family of publishers, printers and violin makers. By July 1695 John Hare (*d* London, bur. 9 Sept 1725) was established in London as a printer and publisher. In August that year he acquired additional premises in London which he probably took over from John Clarke (the 11th edition of *Youth's Delight on the Flageolet*, earlier editions of which had been issued by Clarke, was one of Hare's first publications). He gave up these two premises for new ones in April 1706 and remained in business alone until December 1721. His son Joseph Hare (*d* London, bur. 17 July 1733) joined him in January 1722, and they published jointly until John's death. Joseph then carried on the business in his name, probably on behalf of his mother Elizabeth Hare ('the elder') (*d* Islington, London, bur. 8 July 1741), until June 1728 when he formed his own business. Elizabeth apparently continued her late husband's business with John Simpson until July 1734, when it was sold and she retired to Islington; Simpson then took over her sign and set up on his own account. Joseph Hare's concern was continued after his death by his widow Elizabeth Hare ('the younger'), who was active as a publisher at least until July 1752.

The number of independent publications by the Hare family is comparatively small. From 1695 until about November 1730, however, John, and later Joseph, Hare had close ties, perhaps family ones, with John Walsh, and a great number of Walsh's publications bear their names in conjunction with his own. John Hare was also associated with Henry Playford for a time.

Kidson (1900); W. C. Smith: *A Bibliography of the Musical Works published by John Walsh during the Years 1695–1720* (London, 1948); Humphries and Smith (1954, 2/1970)

W.C.S./P.W.J.

Hargail. American firm of publishers and dealers in musical instruments. It was founded in New York in 1941 by Harold Newman, an amateur recorder player. The firm's first publication was Gail Kubik's Suite for three recorders, and Newman used his own and Kubik's forenames to form that of the company. Hargail specializes in recorder music, and though its early output was for the adult amateur, much of its music is now intended for schools; it also publishes music for Orff instruments and contemporary American music. In addition to its publishing activities, the firm deals in recorders (it manufactures the plastic Harvard model) and sells guitar kits.

K. Wollitz: 'An Interview with Harold Newman, Music Publisher', *American Recorder*, xiii (1972), 3
F.B.

Harms. American firm of publishers. It was founded in New York in 1881 by the brothers Alexander T. Harms (*b* New York, 20 Feb 1856; *d* New York, 23 Oct 1901) and Thomas B. Harms (*b* New York, 5 Jan 1860; *d* New York, 28 March 1906). T. B. Harms & Co. issued contemporary popular music, and the success of such early publications as *When the robins nest again* (1883) and *The letter that never came* (1886) led other Tin Pan Alley publishers to emulate the firm's promotional activities. In 1901 Max Dreyfus (*b* Kuppenheim, Germany, 1 April 1874; *d* Brewster, NY, 12 May 1964), who had been working for Harms as an arranger, bought a 25% interest in the firm, and over the next few years achieved complete managerial and financial control. In 1904 he employed Jerome Kern as a song plugger and Harms subsequently published all Kern's compositions. The firm also issued the works of George Gershwin, who was engaged in 1917 as a rehearsal pianist, and in the 1920s it began to publish the music of Richard Rodgers. Dreyfus sold the company to Warner Bros. in 1929 when it became part of the Music Publishers Holding Corporation, and soon after set up a company affiliated with Chappell of London, owned by his brother Louis Dreyfus (1877–1967). In 1969 that part of Harms connected with the estates of Louis Dreyfus (who had been a director of Harms) and Kern was bought by Lawrence Welk and became part of the Welk Music Group.

F.B.

Harper, Thomas (*d* ?London, March 1656). English printer. He worked in London from 1614 and acquired part of the business of Thomas Snodham. From 1650 until his death he printed all the elder John Playford's music publications, including the first edition of *The English Dancing Master* (dated 1651 but issued in 1650; for illustration *see* fig.33, p.93). His business at Paternoster Row, London, was inherited by William Godbid.

H. R. Plomer: *A Dictionary of Booksellers and Printers . . . from 1641 to 1660* (London, 1907); Humphries and Smith (1954, 2/1970)
M.M.

Harris, Frederick. Canadian publishing firm, active in Toronto and Oakville, Ontario. It was founded in London by Frederick Harris about 1904, with the support of C. J. Röder of Leipzig. Harris acquired British Empire rights to many popular songs and instrumental pieces and published new editions of works on which copyright had expired. He opened a Toronto office in 1910; an agreement with Oliver Hawkes produced the firm of Hawkes & Harris as the Canadian representative of the two British companies. Hawkes died in 1920; Harris acquired his shares three years later. After frequent trips to North America, Harris settled in Oakville, Ontario, in 1924, and formed the Frederick Harris Music Company. The London office became a branch of the Canadian operation, then in 1964 it was placed under the control of Lengnick & Co.; this association continued to 1981, after which the London office was closed. From 1916 Harris published educational material for the Toronto Conservatory, becoming its exclusive publisher in 1944. On his death a year later his shares were left in trust to the conservatory to support scholarship funds. Conservatory books and other educational materials still constitute a large segment of the company's output, which also includes piano, instrumental, vocal and choral music by such composers as Healey Willan, Sir Ernest MacMillan and Michael C. Baker.

R. Stephens: 'Frederick Harris Lists Largest Inventory', *Canadian Composer*, (1966), no.6, 16; M. Wehrle: 'Frederick Harris Music Co. Ltd.', *Encyclopedia of Music in Canada* (Toronto, 1981); W. Gilpin: *Sunset on the St. Lawrence: a History of the Frederick Harris Music Co., Limited, 1904 – 1984* (Oakville, 1984)
M.W.

Harrison. English firm of publishers, established in London. James Harrison was originally a bookseller who may have been associated with Joseph Wenman in 1778 or earlier. In 1779, from his own premises, he began to issue musical works, which included many useful reprints of works such as Arne's *Comus, Lyric Harmony* and *Thomas and Sally,* Greene's *Spenser's Amoretti,* Boyce's *The Chaplet* and *Solomon,* oratorios by Handel and early ballad operas. These were issued from 1783 in the form of a periodical publication in oblong folio format, entitled *The New Musical Magazine* and almost certainly edited by Samuel Arnold. Selling at 1s. 6d. a part (16 pages) it enabled a complete vocal score of *Messiah* to be bought for only 7s. 6d. In addition, each early number had a sheet of letterpress which comprised part of *An Universal Dictionary of Music . . . and a General History of Music,* probably compiled by Thomas Busby but unfortunately never completed. An unusual sales promotion was also given to *The Pianoforte Magazine,* a popularly priced octavo publication of operas, songs and piano pieces, started in 1797 and issued in weekly parts until 1802; each part contained a voucher, and purchasers of the entire set were apparently entitled to a free piano. Other periodical publications, which were a speciality of the firm, included *Harrison's New German Flute Magazine* (1787, also edited by Arnold), *The Lady's Musical Magazine* (1788) and *The Gentleman's Musical Magazine* (1788).

From 1783 the firm was known as Harrison & Co., and in 1788 it had an additional warehouse named 'Dr Arne's Head'. In 1798 the firm became Harrison, Cluse & Co. It ceased business about 1803.

Humphries and Smith (1954, 2/1970)

F.K., W.C.S./P.W.J.

Hart, Andro (*d* Edinburgh, Dec 1621). Scottish bookseller and printer. By 1589 he was an importer of foreign books; in 1601 his name appeared in a psalm book printed in Dordrecht, the Netherlands, to be sold in Scotland. In 1610 he became a publisher in Edinburgh, issuing a famous folio Bible in that year and many psalters (with the melodies), as well as books of Scottish court poetry, mathematics and theology.

After Hart's death, his widow (*d* Edinburgh, 3 May 1642) published more psalm books with the imprint 'the Heires of Andro Hart'. Among these is the most important 17th-century Scottish church music publication, dated 1635, which contains over 200 psalm settings, some with the metrical tunes set polyphonically.

W. Cowan: 'Andro Hart and his Press: with Handlist of Books', *Papers of the Edinburgh Bibliographical Society 1892–3* (1896), 1; K. Elliott:

'Scottish Music of the Early Reformed Church', *Transactions of the Scottish Ecclesiological Society,* xv/2 (1961), 18

D.J.

Hartknoch, Johann Friedrich (*b* Goldap, 18 Sept 1740; *d* Riga, 1 April 1789). German publisher. His father trained him as a pianist, and he became the nine-year-old J. F. Reichardt's teacher in 1761. He founded a book publishing firm in Mitau in 1763; a branch office, later established in Riga, soon became the main office, where he also published music, including Reichardt's *Vermischte Musikalien,* vocal scores of Singspiels and concertos. A catalogue of the firm (*c*1785) shows a predominance of works by the Mannheim school; the firm also published important writings by Herder (a close friend of Hartknoch's) and Kant. Hartknoch's son Johann Friedrich (1768–1819) gave up the Riga business in 1803 and moved to Leipzig. His grandson Karl Eduard Hartknoch (1796–1834) was a composer and pianist.

H. Becker: 'Hartknoch', *MGG*

G.H.

Hartmann, Georges [Romain-Jean-François] (*b* Paris, 14 May 1843; *d* Paris, 22 April 1900). French publisher. He started business in 1866, at 19 boulevard de la Madeleine, Paris. About 1878 he moved to 60 rue Neuve St-Augustin; by the end of 1881 the street name had been officially changed to rue Daunou and the number to 20. In May 1891, after he went bankrupt, his business was acquired by Heugel, but he continued publishing in association with, and under the imprint of, Eugène Fromont.

Hartmann was in a sense the ideal publisher: a philanthropist of exceptional discernment and energy. Among his first publications was Massenet's youthful song, *Poème d'avril* (1866). This led not only personally, commercially and artistically to one of the most rewarding of publisher-composer relationships, but to greatly needed new standards of presentation of music publications (which may be seen in the piano-vocal scores of *Esclarmonde* and *Le mage* as well as the de luxe editions of *Manon* and *Le Cid*). Among other composers whom Hartmann encouraged were Bizet (songs and piano works, 1868), Saint-Saëns (*La princesse jaune,* his first published opera, 1871), Franck, Lalo and Debussy (to whom he paid an annual salary of 6000 francs from about 1894). Through Fromont, Hartmann published several of Debussy's early works, and the score of

Pelléas (1902) is dedicated to his memory. In all he published just over 2000 works, his plate numbers running chronologically.

In 1873, with Edouard Colonne, Hartmann founded the Concert National (later the Concerts Colonne). He also collaborated with Alfred Ernst in a French translation of the *Ring* and was the French representative of the Wagner family and of the publisher Schott.

L. Vallas: *Claude Debussy et son temps* (Paris, 1932), 99; Hopkinson (1954): J. Harding: *Massenet* (London, 1970), 35; Devriès and Lesure (1979–88)

R.M.

Haslinger. Austrian firm of publishers.

1. HISTORY. The firm was founded as the Chemische Druckerey in Josefstadt, Vienna, on 27 July 1803, by Alois Senefelder (1771–1834), who chose the bookshop of Peter Rehm's widow as his sales outlet. As early as 7 December 1803 he transferred his outlet to the firm of Franz Grund 'beim rothen Apfel'. The very early publications bore the imprint 'A. Senefelder' and later 'Singerstr. Nr.932 à la pome rouge', which was retained after Senefelder transferred his privilege to Sigmund Anton Steiner (*b* Lower Austria, 26 April 1773; *d* Vienna, 28 March 1838). On 23 October 1805 the firm moved into premises at Graben, Paternostergässchen 612, where it remained until 1835. Between 1809 and 1812 Rochus Krasnitzky was a joint proprietor; until 1815 Steiner was again sole proprietor, trading from 6 April 1815 as K.k. priv. Kunst- und Musikalienhandlung des S. A. Steiner, and then going into partnership (14 August 1815) with his employee Tobias Haslinger (*b* Zell, 1 March 1787; *d* Vienna, 18 June 1842), as S. A. Steiner & Co. Haslinger took over the firm in his own name on 2 May 1826 and in 1832 acquired the Mollo publishing business; on 16 September 1835 the firm moved into premises in the Trattnerhof. After his death in 1842 the firm was known as Tobias Haslingers Witwe und Sohn until 19 April 1848, when it became Carl Haslinger quondam Tobias (Caroline Haslinger had died on 24 March 1848). Carl Haslinger (*b* 11 June 1816) died in 1868; his widow Josephine carried on the still considerable publishing and retail business until 1875 when she sold the publishing business to Robert Lienau (A. M. Schlesinger) in Berlin. Subsequently the music shop moved to the Tuchlauben, where it has remained until recently.

2. PUBLICATIONS. Steiner, who took over

the Chemische Druckerey shortly after Senefelder founded it, was licensed as a music dealer by the municipal authorities in 1806. The publications of the firm of Franz Anton Hoffmeister were transferred to the Chemische Druckerey in 1807. After being made a freeman of the city in 1810, Steiner was elected president of the art, book and music dealers' corporation in 1812 and licensed as an art dealer in 1813. During the partnership with Haslinger, Anton Diabelli was employed as a proofreader. Probably at Haslinger's instigation, Steiner gave up his lithographic printing licences on 7 July 1821 and part of the lithographic production was transferred to the Lithographisches Institut. The publishing rights of the K.k. Hoftheater-Musik-Verlag were acquired in 1822 and those of Josef Riedl as the successor to the Bureau des Arts et d'Industrie in May 1823.

The firm's dealings with the composers it published in this period included a paternalistic relationship with Beethoven, reflected in the entertaining correspondence with him between 1 February 1815 and 11 November 1826. The Chemische Druckerey catalogue covered a wide variety of works by all the composers then living and working in Vienna; of the great masters, however, only Mozart was represented, and then merely by a pirated edition of the Breitkopf *Oeuvres complettes*, the first edition of the parts of the Requiem, and (still in Senefelder's time) an early vocal score of *La clemenza di Tito*. Standards rose with the acquisition of the publishing house of F. A. Hoffmeister and especially after Tobias Haslinger joined the firm; he contributed greatly to its later rise in fortune by replacing the rather poor finish of lithographic printing with clear music engraving and by his dual talent for music and business.

Haslinger's partnership with S. A. Steiner (1815–26) brought the firm a worldwide reputation; he was responsible for the handsome edition of Beethoven's collected works (62 volumes), which the copyist Mathias Schwarz prepared on English vellum paper between 1817 and 1823; it was finally bought by Archduke Rudolph of Austria and bequeathed with his library to the Vienna Gesellschaft der Musikfreunde.

A notice in the *Wiener Zeitung* of 11 May 1805 lists the firm's publications to date and gives plate numbers from 1 to 134. A catalogue of publications to plate no.1881, published on 1 April 1812 (now in the Stadtbibliothek, Vienna), provides a complete record of production to that date; another notice dated 8 August 1812 contains a supplement up to plate no.1967. This is followed by six inventories printed as supplements, again with details of plate numbers, the first under 'Chemische Druckerey und S. A. Steiner' and the rest under 'S. A. Steiner & Co.'. This tradition was carried on by means of supplements or by listing publications on the last page of works. In 1817–24 the firm published its own periodical, the *Allgemeine musikalische Zeitung mit besonderer Rücksicht auf den österreichischen Kaiserstaat*. The printing process improved from 1819 and achieved an outstanding quality about 1826.

The firm's most important publications were the first editions of Beethoven's opp. 90–101, 112–18 and 121*a* (brought out by S. A. Steiner & Co.) and important editions of his works taken over from the Bureau des Arts et d'Industrie and the K.k. Hoftheater-Musik-Verlag. Mozart is represented by an edition of *Sämmtliche Werke für das Clavier mit und ohne Begleitung* in 38 volumes, and numerous works were published by other leading composers of the time including Czerny, Anton Diabelli, Eybler, Hummel, Isouard, Krommer, Mayseder, Moscheles, Onslow, Payer, J. P. Pixis, Riotte, Rossini, Spohr, Maximilian Stadler and Weber; many of these were also published later by Haslinger. The firm ran several popular series: *Kirchenmusik fürs Land*, *Musée musical des clavecinistes*, *Musica sacra*, *Sammlung komischer Theatergesänge*, *Thalia für das Pianoforte* and *Theater-Journal für Gesang und Pianoforte* (with opera music). Even in Steiner's day the large-scale production of light music was necessarily the firm's source of financial security; opportunity was provided by the demand for dance, music at Carnival time.

On 2 May 1826 Steiner handed over the publishing firm to his partner Tobias Haslinger but remained president of the dealers' corporation until 1837. At the time of the change-over, production stood at plate no.4747. Haslinger was a cathedral chorister at Linz under the Kapellmeister F. Glöggl and also worked in his music shop. Subsequently he directed the music department in F. Eurich's book and art dealer's shop. In 1810 he went to Vienna and initially worked in Katharina Gräffer's bookshop; he became known by publishing his own compositions. Under Haslinger's direction the business assumed larger dimensions. His initiative led to music printing of an exceptionally high standard, particularly evident in the many surviving de luxe editions. The business had up to 50 employees, its own music engraving establishment and a copperplate printing office with 14 presses. Haslinger's success was due to his amiable disposition, enormous industry and a marked business acumen which was, however, totally scrupulous. In 1830 he was made imperial and royal court art and music dealer, and later an honorary freeman of the city of Vienna and an honorary member of the Swedish Royal Academy of Music. The firm published his portrait in 1842.

The plan for a complete Beethoven edition, which Steiner drew up with other firms in 1810, could not be implemented for some time; this was one reason for the rift between the firm and Beethoven. In 1828 Haslinger embarked on a complete edition which reached 73 volumes in 1845. The firm published the first editions of Schubert's opp.77–83 and 89–91 (starting with the *Valses nobles* on 22 January 1827), the *Grätzer Galopp*, the quartets *Grab und Mond*, *Wein und Liebe* and, posthumously, *Schwanengesang*. Numerous composers were added to those already listed in S. A. Steiner & Co.'s catalogue, including Chopin, Gänsbacher, Handel (*Jephtha*), Carl Haslinger, Franz Lachner, the elder Adolf Müller, Bernhard Romberg, Schumann, Seyfried and Sigismund Thalberg. Attempts at complete editions of J. S. Bach and D. Scarlatti both foundered at an early stage. The popular series included *Musikalische Blumengalerie*, *Flore theatrale* for two and four hands, *Sammlung der Galoppen*, Moser's *Weiner Local-Gesänge*, *Neuigkeiten für das Pianoforte* and *Musikalische Theaterbibliothek für die Jugend*. Again dance music maintained the firm's stability; Haslinger greatly encouraged its leading exponents, publishing almost all the works of the elder Johann Strauss in up to ten different arrangements as well as a complete edition in two series, and Josef Lanner's works (previously published by Pietro Mechetti) from op.170. The firm's outstanding copperplate engravers lavished all their skill on the graphic design of the title-pages (see illustration).

Between 1842 and 1848, the six years after Haslinger's death, the firm's publication numbers ran from 9000 to 11,007. Carl Haslinger, a pupil of Czerny and Seyfried, became known as the composer of over 100 works, though of minor importance. Under his direction the firm's publishing and production standards fell considerably; arrangements and fashionable items predominated. Only the dance publications remained successful: the firm published opp.95–278 of the younger Johann Strauss but his works from op.279 were lost to C. A. Spina. At the same time Haslinger also lost Josef Strauss, whose works he had published up to op.150; he

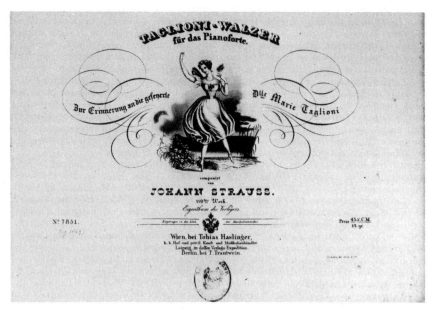

Title-page of Strauss's 'Taglioni-Walzer' op.110 (Vienna: Haslinger, 1839)

acquired C. M. Ziehrer as a replacement, publishing his works up to op.209, and then J. Kaulich. Nevertheless, through its management of midday and evening concerts, the firm remained a focal point of society. When it was sold to Lienau (1875) the final publication number was 15,170.

R. Hirsch: *Gallerie lebender Tondichter* (Vienna, 1836), 45; B. F. Voigt: *Neuer Nekrolog der Deutschen* (Weimar, 1838–44), xvi, 350, xx, 465; F. Gräffer: *Kleine Wiener Memoiren* (Vienna, 1845), i, 131, ii, 75; C. von Wurzbach: *Biographisches Lexikon des Kaiserthums Oesterreich*, viii (Vienna, 1862); A. Orel: 'Beethoven und seine Verleger', *Ein Wiener Beethoven-Buch* (Vienna, 1921), 168; M. Unger: *Ludwig van Beethoven und seine Verleger* (Berlin and Vienna, 1921); O. E. Deutsch: 'Beethovens gesammelte Werke', *ZMw*, xiii (1930–31), 60; Weinmann (1956); idem: *Vollständiges Verlagsverzeichnis Senefelder-Steiner-Haslinger* (Vienna, 1979–83)

A.W.

Hauck, Justus (*d* Coburg, 1618). German printer. He was in charge of the ducal printing house in Coburg from 1596 until his death, and from 1599 he was also a city official. He printed almost nothing but the works of Benedikt Faber, Melchior Franck and Heinrich Hartmann. Particularly interesting among his extant publications is a series of anthologies (*RISM* 1609[30a], 1610[19a], 1611[7], 1611[8], 1614[18], 1614[19], 1616[22], 1617[22]) which probably represent a larger original output. They comprise occasional music, written principally by the three composers mentioned above, in celebration of the weddings, birthdays, funerals or the assumption of civic office of noted Coburg inhabitants.

T. Welzenbach: 'Geschichte der Buchdruckerkunst im ehemaligen Herzogthume Franken und in benachbarten Städten', *Archiv des Historischen Vereins von Unterfranken und Aschaffenburg*, xiv/2 (1857), 117–258; Benzing (1963, 2/1982)

S.B. (iii)

Haultin, Pierre (*d* ?La Rochelle, ?1589). French Huguenot typographer and printer. In 1572 he began issuing music books at La Rochelle, including eight sets of Lassus partbooks (four *Mellange* collections, 1575–7, and four collections of *Moduli*, all 1576) and two books of Jean Pasquier's *Cantiques et chansons spirituelles* (1578), as well as at least five editions with music of the psalm paraphrases of Marot and de Bèze (1572–86). Haultin's nephew, Jérôme, active as a typefounder in London from 1574 to 1586, managed the firm in La Rochelle between 1590 and 1600, where he issued at least nine more psalm books as well as the 1598 edition of Le Jeune's *Dodecachorde*. Jérôme Haultin's heir was his son-in-law, Corneille Hertman, who issued Le Jeune's *Les pseaumes . . . à 4 et 5 parties* (1608) and more psalm books (the latest known one dated 1616). One more psalm book (1623) bears the imprint of Hertman's successor, Pierre Pié de Dieu.

Early in his career, Haultin was highly respected as a type designer. In 1547 he cut music punches and struck the matrices for the Parisian printer Nicolas du Chemin. Probably he also cut the two other music faces which were used in his own editions and those of his heirs. The larger of these, with several substitutions of the sorts (e.g. some note heads and the treble clefs), is the same face which appears in the partbooks printed in London by Thomas Vautrollier (Lassus: *Recueil du mellange*, 1570, also Byrd and Tallis: *Cantiones sacrae*, 1575), as well as in the madrigal partbooks printed by Thomas East, Thomas Snodham and their successors. The smaller Haultin face was probably also used in various French Haultin and Dutch music books, although it is difficult to identify conclusively.

There seems to be no likely basis in fact for two assertions made about him. In his *Traité historique et critique*, Pierre Fournier maintained that Haultin cut the first punches for music type in about 1525, but this statement conflicts with what is known about Pierre Attaingnant and the origins of French music typography. The typographer Guillaume Le Bé (ii), in his 'memorandum' of 1643, reported that Haultin was active as early as 1500; however, if there was an older Pierre Haultin, nothing is known of him. Most scholars now believe that both Fournier and Le Bé were simply in error.

P.-S. Fournier: *Traité historique et critique sur l'origine et les progrès des caractères de fonte pour l'impression de la musique* (Berne, 1765), 5; L. Desgraves: *Les Haultin* (Geneva, 1960) [incl. bibliography of Haultin publications]; D. Heartz: 'A New Attaingnant Book and the Beginnings of French Music Printing', *JAMS*, xiv (1961), 9 [esp. pp.19–20, 22–3, which presents the revised view on the Le Bé and Fournier evidence first proposed by F. Lesure in *MGG* (1956)]

D.W.K.

Heckel. German firm of publishers. It was founded in Mannheim around 1822 by Karl Ferdinand Heckel (*b* Vienna, 12 Jan 1800; *d* Mannheim, 9 April 1870), son of the court composer Johann Jakob Heckel (*c*1763–1811). After study with J. N. Hummel in Weimar, Karl Ferdinand set up an instrument shop in Mannheim in 1821 not to be confused with the more famous bassoon firm of Johann Adam Heckel in Biebrich). An art and music shop soon followed, and in 1828 Heckel bought the firm of G. Kreitner in Worms. Between 1827 and 1830 Heckel published a series of

Mozart's operas in piano-vocal scores, *Wohlfeile Ausgabe von W. A. Mozart's sämmtlichen Opern*, which included as its sixth volume the first complete edition of *La finta giardiniera*; several volumes in the series have attractive lithographed title-page vignettes and the music is lithographed throughout. Beginning in the 1840s Heckel published an unusual edition of the complete string quartets of Beethoven, Haydn and Mozart, in very small miniature scores; similar editions of Mozart's string quintets and other chamber music followed.

In 1857 the firm was managed by Karl Ferdinand's son Emil Heckel (*b* Mannheim, 22 May 1831; *d* Mannheim, 28 March 1908), sponsor of local concerts, an early admirer and later close personal friend of Richard Wagner and founder of the earliest German Richard Wagner society (1871), who was active in establishing the Bayreuth Festivals. In 1888 the firm issued the first edition of Wagner's *Die Feen*. In 1896 two Hugo Wolf first editions, the vocal score of *Der Corregidor* and Book 2 of the *Italienisches Liederbuch*, marked the start of a series of important Wolf publications. Including reissues of works previously published by Schott, Wetzler and Lacom, this series amounted to a complete edition of Wolf's songs published during his lifetime. In 1902–3 the firm published six of Wolf's songs with orchestral accompaniment. Heckel sold its rights in Wolf's music to C. F. Peters in 1908 but continues in operation to the present day.

K. Heckel, ed.: *Briefe Richard Wagners an Emil Heckel: zur Entstehungsgeschichte der Bühnenfestspiele in Bayreuth* (Berlin, 1899, 3/1911; Eng. trans., 1899); J. A. Beringer: 'Emil Heckel: ein Gedenkblatt', *Richard Wagner-Jb*, iii (1908), 387; H. Holle: 'Zum 100jährigen Bestehen der Firma K. Ferd. Heckel in Mannheim (20. Okt. 1821–1921)', *Neue Musik-Zeitung*, lxiii (1922), 24; O. Wessely: 'Heckel, Johann Jakob', *MGG*; C. Hopkinson: 'The Earliest Miniature Scores', *MR*, xxxiii (1972), 138; B. Höft: 'Ein Mannheimer Musikverleger als Wegbereiter des klassischen Erbes: Karl Ferdinand Heckel und seine "Wohlfeile Ausgabe sämtlicher Opern W. A. Mozarts" ', *Das Mannheimer Mozart-Buch*, ed. R. Würtz (Wilhelmshaven, 1977), 187

N.S.

Heckenast, Gusztáv (1811–78). Hungarian printer and publisher. He worked in Pest from 1834, in partnership with Landerer, 1840–63; from 1863 he was exclusively a publisher. His music activity was restricted to issuing 50 works of his friend Robert Volkmann from 1856.

A. Szennovitz: *G. Heckenast* (Budapest, 1890); D.P. Szemző: *H.G. a zenei kiadó* [H.G. the music publisher] (Budapest, 1961); I. Mona: *Hungarian*

Music Publication (Budapest, 1973); S. Varga: *A Magyar Könyvkereskedők Egyletének alapítása* [The foundation of the Association of Hungarian Booksellers] (Budapest, 1980)

I.M.

Heina, François-Joseph (*b* Mieschitz [now Měšic], nr. Prague, 20 Nov 1729; *d* Paris, Feb 1790). Czech musician and publisher. He was in Paris from 1764, as *cor de chasse* to the Prince de Conti and later *trompette de chevau-léger de la garde du roy*, but received his discharge in 1775. From that date he was a teacher of the trumpet and hunting horn; from 1785 until his death he was a member of the orchestra of the Comédie Française.

In January 1773 he petitioned for a six-year privilege for the publication of Stamitz's instrumental music. For at least ten years (1775–85), he published instrumental works, especially chamber music, by fellow Czechs (Vanhal, Fiala and Stamitz) and composers of the Mannheim school (Eichner and Schwindl). Heina was a good friend to Mozart in Paris, particularly at the time of his mother's illness and death. He also published the first editions of seven of Mozart's works, including three piano sonatas.

F. Lesure: 'Mozartiana gallica', *RdM*, xxxviii (1956), 121; W. A. Bauer and O. E. Deutsch, eds.: *Mozart: Briefe und Aufzeichnungen*, v (Kassel and Basle, 1971), 515; G. Haberkamp: *Die Erstdrucke der Werke von Wolfgang Amadeus Mozart* (Tutzing, 1986)

F.L.

Heinrichshofen. German firm of publishers. Wilhelm von Heinrichshofen (1780–1881) took over Theodor Keil's publishing concern in 1797; in 1806 he founded a firm under his own name and published mostly historical and theological works. His son Theodor (1805–1901) and grandson Adalbert (1859–1932) built it into a music publishing business, issuing keyboard works by J. S. Bach, Haydn, Mozart, Beethoven, Schubert, Schumann and Chopin, as well as folksongs and lieder. Otto Heinrich Noetzel, grandson of Adalbert, became director in 1932, and a subsidiary office was established in Leipzig; the head office was established at Wilhelmshaven in 1948. Heinrichshofen has issued about 30,000 titles since its foundation and represents several 20th-century composers, including Nico Dostal, Mark Lothar, G. F. Malipiero, Schoenberg and Richard Strauss. It also published school music and music for recorder.

Musikverlage in der Bundesrepublik Deutschland und in West-Berlin (Bonn, 1965), 13; C. Vinz and G. Olzog, eds.: *Dokumentation deutschsprachiger Verlage* (Munich and Vienna, 1983), 176

T.W.

Hempsted, Henry N. (*b* Albany, NY, 29 Dec 1830; *d* Kasson, MN, 22 Dec 1898). American publisher and composer. In 1849 he moved to Milwaukee, where he established himself as a music teacher; he opened a music shop two years later, which eventually became one of the largest in the upper Mid-west. He published editions of 19th-century composers (Schumann, Liszt, Strauss) as well as his own works, the most popular of which were *Iron Brigade Quickstep*, *Garibaldi's March* and *The Light Guards Quickstep*. From 1873 to 1875 he edited and published the *Musical Echo*.

J. S. Buck: *Milwaukee under the Charter from 1847 to 1853*, iii (Milwaukee, 1884)

F.S.M.

Henle. German firm of publishers. It was founded in Munich in 1948 by the Rhenish industrialist, politician, amateur musician and collector Günter Henle (*b* Würzburg, 3 Feb 1899; *d* Duisburg, 13 April 1979). His firm, later also in Duisburg, aimed to publish 'for practical use the musical works of the Classical and Romantic eras in reliable editions based solely on the sources and free from all deliberate editorial additions'. Many volumes of 'Urtext' editions of the standard piano and chamber music repertory of the 18th and 19th centuries have been published, notable for their clear engraving and printing. The firm, directed by Martin Bente since 1979, collaborates with the Beethovenhaus in Bonn and the Haydn Institute in Cologne, publishing the new complete editions of both composers and associated material, including the Kinsky-Halm Beethoven catalogue, the *Veröffentlichungen des Beethovenhauses in Bonn* and the *Haydn-Studien*. Henle is also involved in the publication of other academic volumes, notably *Das Erbe Deutscher Musik*, catalogues, congress reports and series B of *RISM*.

Musikverlage in der Bundesrepublik Deutschland und in West-Berlin (Bonn, 1965); G. Henle: *Weggenosse des Jahrhunderts* (Stuttgart, 1968; Eng. trans., 1971 as *Three Spheres: a Life in Politics, Business and Music*); idem: *25 Jahre G. Henle Musikverlag* (Munich, 1973; repr. 1983 as *Verlegerischer Dienst an der Musik*); M. Bente, ed.: *Musik, Edition, Interpretation: Gedenkschrift Günter Henle* (Munich, 1980); M. Menzel: 'Die Farbe Blau', *Börsenblatt des deutschen Buchhandels* (12 Feb 1988), 600

T.W.

Henricus [Heinrich], **Nikolaus** (*b* Oberursell, *c*1575; *d* Munich, 1654). German printer. The son of a printer, he served his apprenticeship under Adam Berg in Munich. In 1597 he married his employer's daughter, Susanna, apparently against the wishes of both families, and became a citizen of Munich. He became a Catholic and was granted permission to found his own printing house by Duke Maximilian I on 3 November 1597. Thanks to the patronage of the powerful Jesuit congregation, Henricus was soon appointed court printer and had by the turn of the century usurped the lead in publishing from Adam Berg. After his death his daughter, Jakobe, continued the business for a short time, selling it to Jakob Jäcklin in 1656.

All publishing in Bavaria was subjected to strict censorship and the dukes reserved to themselves the privilege normally exercised by city governments of granting permission to prospective publishers. Thus Henricus was the only printer, besides Berg and his descendants, who was allowed to practise his trade in Munich, until well into the 17th century. Although Henricus printed much music, his chief contribution was the publication of the important posthumous collections of Orlande de Lassus's works edited by his sons Rudolph and Ferdinand. These include otherwise unpublished masses and *Magnificat* settings and particularly the 1604 edition of motets, *Magnum opus musicum*, which was used in modern times as the basis of the edition of his complete works.

K. Fuchs: *Geschichte des Münchener Buchgewerbes* (Munich, 1912); P. Dirr: *Buchwesen und Schrifttum im alten München 1450–1800* (Munich, 1929); W. Bòetticher: *Orlando di Lasso und seine Zeit 1532–1594* (Kassel, 1958); H. W. Bieber: 'Die Befugnisse und Konzessionierungen der Münchner Druckereien und Buchhandlungen von 1485 bis 1871', *Archiv für Geschichte des Buchwesens*, ii (1960), 404; Benzing (1963, 2/1982)

M.L.G.

Heptinstall, John (*b* ?London, *c*1657; *d* ?London, 1732). English printer and manufacturer of printing ink. He set up as a Master in about 1683, and was active until about 1715. With Thomas Moore and Francis Clark he printed *Vinculum societatis* (1687; see illustration), the first musical work with the 'new tied note' (i.e. quavers and semiquavers united in groups). Before then, except in engraved music, such notes were printed separately because of the difficulty of connecting, in movable types, notes of varying intervals. The 'new tied note' was improved by William Pearson, who was in business from 1699 to 1735, and who was the best known of Heptinstall's 12

apprentices. Heptinstall and his associates also introduced the printing of round-headed notes instead of the former lozenge shape (for illustration *see* fig.8, p.29). He issued a number of works by Purcell, including *Amphitryon* (1690), *The Prophetess, or The History of Dioclesian* (1691) and *The Double Dealer* (1694), as well as a number of psalm books and publications by Henry Playford, including the 1703 edition of his *The Dancing Master*.

Krummel (1975); M. Treadwell: 'London Printers and Printing Houses in 1705', *Publishing History*, vii (1980), 23

F.K., W.C.S./D.R.H.

Hergot [Herrgott], **Hans** (*b* ?Nuremberg; *d* Leipzig, 20 May 1527). German printer. He was officially registered as a printer in Nuremberg from 1524 to 1526. Most of the actual business, however, was apparently conducted by his wife Kunegunde (*d* 7 Feb 1547), while he travelled about the country, distributing pamphlets, often of a heretical or politically radical nature. He was caught circulating one of these, *Von der newen Wandlung eynes Christlichen Lebens*, in Leipzig, then ruled by Duke Georg of Saxony, a fierce opponent of both the Reformation and peasant reform. In proceedings supervised by the duke himself he was tried and condemned to death, and after a futile attempt on his wife's part to persuade the Nuremberg city council to intercede was publicly executed. His widow continued the printing business in her own name until 1538, although she had married another Nuremberg printer, Georg Wachter, shortly after Hergot's death.

As a printer Hergot was known mainly for his piracy of Luther's writings, which he reprinted with such brazenness that the author himself was moved to complain. However, he was the first printer to include melodies for the Lutheran Mass, adding the notes by means of block printing. His widow published numerous sacred songs, generally in the form of small leaflets of four to eight folios each, making them readily saleable. Wachter also preferred this format which was continued into the 1560s by such Nuremberg printers as Valentin Neuber and Christoff and Friderich Gutknecht.

A. Kirchhoff: 'Johann Herrgott, Buchführer von Nürnberg und sein tragisches Ende 1527', *Archiv für Geschichte des deutschen Buchhandels*, i (1878), 15; idem: 'Weitere Notizen über Johann Herrgott in Nürnberg', *Archiv für Geschichte des deutschen Buchhandels*, vi (1881), 252; P. Wackernagel: *Bibliographie zur Geschichte des deutschen Kirchenliedes im XVI. Jahrhundert* (Frankfurt am Main, 1885/R1961); M. Herold: 'Die erste evangelische

A page from John Carr's 'Vinculum societatis' printed by Heptinstall (London, 1687)

deutsche Messe mit Musiknoten', *Zeitschrift Siona*
(1894); P. Cohen: *Musikdruck und -drucker zu
Nürnberg im sechzehnten Jahrhundert* (Nuremberg,
1927); R. Wagner: 'Hergot, Hans', *MGG*; Benzing
(1963, 2/1982); C. P. Clasen: *Anabaptism: a Social
History, 1525–1618* (Ithaca, NY, 1972)

M.L.G.

Heugel. French firm of publishers. The
Heugel family became associated with publishing on 1 January 1839, when Jacques
Léopold Heugel (*b* La Rochelle, 1 March
1815; *d* Paris, 12 Nov 1883) became a
partner of Jean Antoine Meissonnier (*b*
Marseilles, 8 Dec 1783; *d* Saint German-en-
Laye, 1857). Before association with
Heugel, Meissonnier, established in Paris
from 1812, published a *Journal de guitare*
(1822), *Le troubadour des salons* (1825) and
other light music. He had bought the business of Savaresse (1835); on 10 August
1838 he moved to 2 bis rue Vivienne. When
Meissonnier retired on 20 April 1842
Heugel became sole owner. In 1974 the
firm moved to Galerie de Montpensier in
the Palais Royal, and in 1980 was merged
into Leduc.

The firm had acquired the popular weekly journal *Le ménestrel* (18 June 1839) from
Jules Levy, who had founded it in 1833,
and continued publication until 1940
except during World War I. Built at first on
Le ménestrel and illustrated albums of
popular songs, the catalogue expanded
rapidly. Jacques Léopold published several
pedagogical works (including Cherubini's)
and a significant collection of harpsichord
works edited by A. Méreaux (1855–60). In
1857 Heugel founded *La maîtrise*, a journal
dedicated to renewal of religious music and
directed by D'Ortigue and Niedermeyer.
In the mid-19th century Heugel's mainstay
was theatre music. Among countless successful publications were works by David
(*Le désert*, 1844; *La perle du Brésil*, 1851);
Offenbach (*Croquefer*, 1857, then *Orphée aux
enfers, Barbe-bleue, La belle Hélène* and
many others); Thomas (*Mignon*, 1866;
Hamlet, 1868); Delibes (*Coppélia, Sylvia,
Lakmé*); and French versions of works by
Johann Strauss the younger.

In 1883 Jacques Léopold was succeeded
by his son Henri Georges Heugel (*b* Paris, 3
May 1844; *d* Paris, 11 May 1916), who had
become a partner in 1876. By 1885 Heugel
was publishing at least one work daily, and
catalogue purchases provided further
expansion: the remainder of E. Gérard
(1886, Jacques Léopold having bought part
in 1874), Hartmann (1891, numerous
works by Franck, Lalo, Reyer and
Massenet), Tellier (1898) and part of
Pérégally (1904). Henri's nephew Paul

Emile Chevalier (1861–1931) supplied the
capital to buy Hartmann's catalogue and
thereupon became Heugel's partner.
Chevalier directed the firm from May 1916
until 1919, the succession of Henri's son
Jacques Paul Heugel (1890–1979) being
delayed by the war. Chevalier retired on 22
July 1919 and Jacques led the firm alone
until 22 March 1944, when it became a
'société anonyme'. He was then appointed
president and general director. His sons
François Henri Heugel (*b* Paris, 22 Aug
1922) and Philippe Gérard André Heugel
(*b* Paris, 8 July 1924) were named artistic
director and commercial director respectively in 1947.

Under Jacques Heugel and his sons
publication of contemporary music has
been balanced with concern for earlier
music. 20th-century composers prominent
in Heugel's catalogue include Auric,
Delannoy, Fauré, Hahn, Harsányi, Ibert,
d'Indy, Jolivet, Milhaud, Poulenc, Schmitt,
Tailleferre, Tcherepnin and Widor, as well
as the later Amy, Arrigo, Boulez, Jolas,
Martinet and Mihalovici. An extensive
collection of practical editions of early
music, *Le pupitre*, began in 1967 under the
direction of François Lesure. Heugel's catalogue contains the publications of the
Société Française de Musicologie. From
1954 Heugel's current activities have been
detailed in a semi-annual *Carnet de notes*.

R.S.N.

Hewitt, James (*b* ?Dartmoor, 4 June 1770;
d Boston, 2 Aug 1827). American publisher
of English birth. He arrived in New York
on 5 September 1792. Although he advertised himself there as having had concert
experience in London under 'Haydn,
Pleyel, etc.', no evidence of this has been
found. He lived in New York until 1811, his
longest period of residence at one address
being from 1801 to 1810 at 59 Maiden
Lane. From 1792 until the end of March
1808, he was conductor of the orchestra at
the Park Street Theatre, where his duties
included arranging and composing music
for many ballad operas and other musical
productions. He also operated his own
'musical repository', where he gave lessons
and sold musical instruments and music
composed by himself and others.

Although his musical activities in Boston
began as early as 1805, the family did not
move there until 1811. The Boston city
directory for 1812 lists Hewitt at 58½ Newbury Street. He pursued the same musical
interests there as in New York, conducting the orchestra at the Federal Street
Theatre, giving lessons, and composing

and publishing music; he was also the organist at Trinity Church. In 1816 he returned to New York, taking his two eldest sons with him. Between 1820 and 1825 he travelled often between Boston, New York and several southern cities, particularly Charleston, and Augusta, Georgia.

Hewitt published at least 639 compositions, mostly by British composers such as William Shield, Michael Kelly and James Hook, though he also issued works by Handel, Haydn and Mozart, and approximately 160 of his own compositions. These include instrumental and vocal compositions and stage works (largely ballad operas). He also arranged instrumental and vocal works by others and was the author of three pedagogical treatises. In Boston his activities included business dealings with Gottlieb Graupner.

O. G. T. Sonneck: *A Bibliography of Early Secular American Music* (Washington, DC, 1905; rev. and enlarged by W. T. Upton, 2/1945/*R*1964); J. T. Howard: 'The Hewitt Family in American Music', *MQ*, xvii (1931), 25; Wolfe (1964); J. W. Wagner: *James Hewitt: his Life and Works* (diss., Indiana U., 1969); idem: 'The Music of James Hewitt: a Supplement to the Sonneck-Upton and Wolfe Bibliographies', *Notes*, xxix (1972–3), 224; Wolfe (1980); V. B. Lawrence: 'Mr. Hewitt Lays it on the Line', *19th Century Music*, v/sum. (1981), 3

J.W.W.

Hewitt, James Lang (*b* New York, 28 Sept 1803; *d* New York, 24 March 1853). American publisher, son of James Hewitt. He established a music publishing firm (unconnected with that of his father) in Boston in 1825 in partnership with James A. Dickson. In 1829 he moved to New York and maintained a publishing company there until his death. He issued works by Haydn, Rossini, Weber and Lowell Mason, in addition to compositions by his father and elder brother John Hill Hewitt. Horatio Nelson Hewitt (*b* New York, 7 Oct 1807; *d* New York, 12 Oct 1856), another son of James Hewitt, was listed as a music publisher in the Boston city directory from 1830 to 1832. No publications by his firm are extant, but he may have been the Boston representative for his brother's firm. After James Lang Hewitt's death his plates were used by many other publishing companies, including Firth, Hall & Pond.

J.W.W.

Higgins, H(iram) M(urray) (*b* Sherburne, NY, 13 Oct 1820; *d* San Diego, CA, 13 July 1897). American publisher and music dealer. He taught music until 1855, when he established a publishing partnership with his brother Adoniram Judson Higgins at 54 Randolph Street, Chicago (see illustration).

Sheet-music cover of 'Randolph Street March' (1866) showing the music store of the publisher H. M. Higgins on Randolph Street, Chicago

Higgins Brothers catered to the local market; in 1856 they issued J. P. Webster's *Lorena*, which was widely popular in the Confederacy during the Civil War. The partnership was dissolved on 1 February 1859, but the brothers continued to run independent businesses. A. J. Higgins ceased operations in November 1861, while H. M. Higgins continued to publish until he sold his plates to J. L. Peters of St Louis in May 1867. H. M. Higgins was also a composer; his best-known songs are *The Old Musician and his Harp* and *Hang up the Baby's Stocking*.

Obituary, *San Diego Union* (14 July 1897); D. J. Epstein: *Music Publishing in Chicago before 1871: the Firm of Root & Cady, 1858–1871* (Detroit, 1969)

D.J.E.

Higman, Jean (*fl* 1484–99). Printer, active in Paris. He worked from 1484 in the shop of the first printer at Paris, Ulrich Gering (*fl* 1470–1510), then established his own shop in 1489. Between that time and 1497 he printed with Wolfgang Hopyl from The Hague; at some date he printed with Guillaume Prévost. Higman printed at least 20 books with music, all liturgical and mostly missals, using both roman and gothic plainchant types. The missals include a 1497 *Missale sarisburiense* for Wynkyn de Worde and Michael Morin and a 1500 *Missale sarisburiense* for Jean Barbier and Guillaume Houtmart.

A. Claudin: *Histoire de l'imprimerie en France* (Paris, 1900–05); K. Meyer-Baer: *Liturgical Music Incunabula: a Descriptive Catalogue* (London, 1962)

M.K.D.

Hime. English and Irish firm of publishers and music 'sellers. It was started before 1790 in Liverpool by the brothers Humphrey and Morris (or Maurice) Hime. In 1790 Morris Hime (*d* Jan 1828) moved to Dublin and established an extensive business in music and instruments which was active until about 1820, when the firm was discontinued. Humphrey Hime remained in business in Liverpool; in 1805 he took his son into partnership, and as Hime & Son the firm continued until 1879, when it was purchased by the music seller Henry Lee.

The Himes did the largest provincial trade in Britain at the end of the 18th century. As English copyright protection did not extend to Ireland, Morris Hime, in common with other Irish publishers, reprinted great numbers of English works, especially vocal items from operas; many of these were sent to England for sale at cheaper rates, an arrangement which was doubtless advantageous to his brother.

Morris Hime's original publications were of a minor character and included country dances and instrumental arrangements of Irish airs; he also ran a circulating music library. Hime & Son issued a great number of single-sheet editions, most of them songs.

M. Kelly: *Reminiscences* (London, 1826, 2/1826/R1968), ii, 310; W. Gardiner: *Music and Friends* (London, 1838), i, 210; Kidson (1900); Humphries and Smith (1954, 2/1970)

F.K., W.C.S./P.W.J.

Hirsch, Abraham (1815–1900). Swedish publisher, music dealer and printer, active in Stockholm. He began his career as an apprentice in Östergrens bok-och musikhandel in 1829. The history of the Östergren shop went back as far as 1802 when Pär Aron Borg started selling music from his home in Stockholm, thus founding the firm that was to become one of Sweden's largest and most long-lived music publishing houses. By 1804 Borg, in partnership with Ulrik Emanuel Mannerhjerta, had opened a music shop (eventually taken over by Mannerhjerta). In 1816 Gustaf Adolf Östergren (1791–1825), who had been helping in the shop, took over; he not only sold music and instruments but also was a publisher. When Östergren died, his widow continued the business, during 1827 in partnership with the lithographer Carl Müller; in 1829 she sold out to Abraham Salomonsson. Abraham Hirsch, who was Salomonsson's brother-in-law, began working in the shop in 1829, and when Salomonsson died in 1831, Hirsch, at the age of 17, took over the daily leadership, but not the ownership, from his sister. This arrangement lasted until 1837 when Hirsch bought the business from his sister. A year later he acquired a lithographic printing press and continued to expand. In 1842 he bought the stock of Albert Wilhelm Möller, an earlier employee of Östergren's who had left in 1831 to set up his own business. It was not until this year that Hirsch finally changed the name of the firm from Östergrens to Hirsch musikhandel. In 1847 he sold his shop to Julius Bagge and from 1884 the publishing firm was run by Hirsch's son Otto. Both shop and stock were eventually taken over by Gehrmans.

Hirsch published works mainly by Swedish contemporary composers, including light music for piano, sonatas and chamber music, songs and male-voice quartets, but also arrangements of symphonies and operas. The growth of his stock is recorded in more than a dozen printed catalogues and in his plate numbers, which proceed in orderly succession to 2659 (1915). He also published two important music periodicals: *Stockholms musiktidning* and *Ny tidning för musik*. Hirsch was one of the initiators of the Swedish publishers' association (1843) and in 1853 he established a pension fund for Swedish music and book dealers.

A. Wiberg: *Den svenska musikhandelns historia* (Stockholm, 1955); O. Franzen: 'Hirsch, Abraham', *Svenskt biografiskt lexikon* (Stockholm, (1918–), xix (1971–3), 86; A. Helmer: 'Litet förläggarlexikon', *Svenskt musikhistoriskt arkiv: Bulletin*, iv (1970), 9

V.H.

Hitchcock, Benjamin (*b* New York, 1827 or 1836; *d* Jersey City, NJ, 14 April 1916). American publisher. He established a music shop in New York in 1869 and gradually expanded his business to include publishing. He issued popular instrumental and vocal music, such as *The culprit Fay* (1869), *In the evening by the moonlight* (1880) and *With all her faults I love her still* (1888). Although Hitchcock sold his interest in 1893, the firm continued until 1941.

B.T.

Hoffgreff [Hofgreff], **György** (*fl* 1550–59). Hungarian printer, active in Kolozsvár (now Cluj-Napoca), Romania. He probably went to Transylvania from Germany. The first book from his press, *Ritus explorendae veritatis*, was published in 1550. Thereafter he worked with Gáspár Heltai, but the partnership lasted only until 1552 and Hoffgreff continued on his own until 1559; it is not known why the business ceased. In 1553 he published a songbook with music, of which only a single, incomplete copy exists (now in the library of the Hungarian Academy of Sciences in Budapest); with its title-page missing, it is known only as the Hoffgreff Songbook. It contains 19 songs, all on biblical themes, set in mensural notation using the Haultin process. In 1554 Hoffgreff published Sebestyén Tinódi's *Cronica*, the rhymed chronicle of Hungary under the Turks in the 16th century; surprisingly, it uses the older method of double-impression printing.

G. Mátray: *Történeti, bibliai és gunyoros magyar énekek dallamai* [The melodies of historical, biblical and satirical Hungarian songs] (Pest, 1859); P. Gulyás: *A könyvnyomtatás Magyarországon a XV. és XVI. században* [Hungarian printing in the 15th and 16th centuries] (Budapest, 1929–31); B. Szabolcsi: *A 16. század históriás zenéje*. *A Hoffgreff énekeskönyv dallamainak kritikai kiadása* [The music of rhymed chronicles of the 16th century: the critical edition of the melodies of the Hoffgreff Songbook] (Budapest, 1931); K. Csomasz Tóth: *A XVI. század magyar dallamai* [Hungarian melodies of the 16th century] (Budapest, 1958)

I.M.

Hoffmann. Czech family of publishers.

(1) Jan Hoffmann (*b* Prague, 14 Feb 1814; *d* Prague, 1 Oct 1849). From 1828 to 1833 he was apprenticed to Marco Berra, under whom he worked until 1838 and whose daughter he married. In 1838 he set up a shop for *objets d'art*, engravings, maps and music; he expanded it to include a piano store, also selling strings and lending music. Probably from 1841 he had his own music printing works and publishing firm. Jointly with Berra he published 50 compositions; on his own he is reputed to have published 2300 music scores including numerous solo vocal, choral and piano works by Czech composers of the revivalist period (e.g. Tomášek, František, Škroup and his brother Jan Nepomuk Škroup, Jelen and Martinovský). In the collection *Sammlung der National-Polka* he published numerous Czech dances by F. M. Hilmar, Labický, Liehmann and others. Apart from the Prague firm he had a branch in Leipzig. After financial difficulties he sold his business, on 7 May 1844, transferring all his existing publishing contracts to his main creditor, the publisher Hofmeister in Leipzig. It has not been reliably ascertained when he took up publishing again. After his death his wife Emilie, née Berra, took over the firm.

(2) Emilie Hoffmannová (*b* Prague, 28 Aug 1816; *d* Prague, 6 July 1882). Wife of (1) Jan Hoffmann and daughter of the publisher Marco Berra. After her husband's death she carried on his business under vidual law from October 1849 to October 1879 under the name Hoffmannová Vdova. She continued publishing works by Czech composers (e.g. Karel Bendl, Václav Horák, J. T. Krov and especially the prolific J. L. Zvonař) and expanded the firm to include a concert agency; she passed the business to her son Jaromír in October 1879.

(3) Jaromír Hoffmann (*b* Prague, 7 June 1847; *d* Prague, 5 Feb 1918). Son of (1) Jan Hoffmann and (2) Emilie Hoffmannová. From 1864 until his death he was manager of Hoffmannová Vdova, which he took over from his mother in October 1879. Under him the firm took on nationalist overtones. Among the works he published were Smetana's Andante and the Concert Fantasia on Czech national songs (both in 1886) and the second edition of Smetana's marches from the year 1848 (1884), Foerster's collection *The Catholic Organist* (1858), some works by J. R. Roskošný and a series of contemporary salon music pieces.

He expanded his trade by buying the older Prague music publishing firms Christoph & Kuhé, Fleischer, Schindler and Veit (whose published scores he transferred to his own catalogue without indicating their original publishers), thus increasing his output to 4800 numbers. He continued to use the name Hoffmannová Vdova with his own name added to it.

ČSHS; J. A. Bergmann and E. Meliš: *Průvodce v oboru českých tištěných písní 1800/1862* [Guidebook to the field of printed Czech songs 1800/1862] (Prague, 1863); Z. Nejedlý: *Bedřich Smetana*, ii–iii (Prague, 1925–9); *Pazdírkův hudební slovník naučný II*. [Pazdírek's musical dictionary], i (Brno, 1937), 403; J. Dostál: 'Marco Berra, první velkorysý nakladatel hudební v Praze' [Marco Berra, the first large-scale music publisher in Prague], *Slovanská knihověda*, vi (1947), 92; R. Málek and M. Petrtýl: *Knihy a Pražané* [Books and people of Prague] (Prague, 1964), 67; I. Janáčková: 'Pražští vydavatelé Václava Jana Tomáška' [Tomášek's Prague publishers], *HV*, xviii (1981), 171; J. Černý and others: *Hudba v českých dějinách* [Music in Czech history] (Prague, 1983), 292, 340

Z.C.

Hoffmeister, Franz Anton (*b* Rothenburg am Neckar, 12 May 1754; *d* Vienna, 9 Feb 1812). Austrian publisher and composer. He went to Vienna in 1768 to study law, but after qualifying, devoted his time to music, especially publishing and composing. As early as 1783, when Viennese music publishing was still in its infancy, he began to have published two series of symphonies in Lyons (printed by Guéra), and some quartets and duets for flute. On 24 January 1784 he announced in the *Wiener Zeitung* that he planned to publish all his musical works at his own expense and under his own supervision from Rudolf Gräffer's bookshop. But in a large advertisement on 6 August 1785 he no longer mentioned Gräffer, having established a firm in his own name at his own home. This advertisement gives a list of works which had already appeared as well as a new publishing programme of three different series, including orchestral and chamber music by Haydn, Mozart, Vanhal, Albrechtsberger, Pleyel, Miča, Ordonez and other foreign composers, besides Hoffmeister's own works. Although he did not maintain his announced schedules, the business evidently flourished. Hoffmeister had connections with the Speyer publisher Bossler, whose firm acted as a kind of agent for Hoffmeister. Hence a series of announcements and some detailed reviews of works published by the Hoffmeister firm appeared in Bossler's *Musikalische Real-*

zeitung (later *Musikalische Korrespondenz*), particularly in 1789–91.

On 16 March 1791 Hoffmeister announced a branch in Linz, but this was publicly auctioned on 14 August 1793 and early in 1794 passed to the Vienna bookseller Johann Georg Binz (1748–1824). For a short time Hoffmeister had a connection with the firm J. Amon in Heilbronn, and they published various pieces jointly (1791–3). From January 1791, when the firm's most productive period was over, detailed advertisements began to appear in the *Wiener Zeitung* again. Hoffmeister's expenditure of energy as a composer seems to have forced the affairs of the firm into the background, and as a businessman he was something of a dilettante. For example, when the firm began to decline he sold many of its publications to the rival firm of Artaria, while continuing to publish other items under his own name. These transfers of individual works and large groups of works continued briskly from 1788. There was sometimes a further complication of the procedure, in that within individual works some parts were engraved by Hoffmeister and the rest by Artaria, Hoffmeister having transferred the publishing rights in the middle of production.

Hoffmeister apparently established a loose business connection with the bookseller J. G. Binz, who frequently advertised works published by Hoffmeister in the *Wiener Zeitung*. The management of the firm was also complicated by an association with the Leipzig printer Christian Gottlob Täubel, who moved his business to Vienna, reputedly at Hoffmeister's instigation, and set up his music printing press (typeprinting) in the suburb of Josefstadt by imperial decree on 5 September 1791. Despite his declared bankruptcy in 1792 Täubel evidently continued to work as a music printer, commissioned by the Musikalisch-typographische Verlagsgesellschaft until 1802. Whether he was Hoffmeister's investing partner or administrator until 1806 remains unclear; Hoffmeister's previous administrator, J. M. Auerhamer, died on 5 October 1793. After 1810 Täubel apparently ceased all business in Vienna. His publications of the 1790s include several theoretical works (by Petri, Türk, Wolf and others), a six-volume *Allgemeine Bibliothek für das Klavier und die Singekunst*, keyboard pieces by C. P. E. Bach and songs by Michael Haydn.

In the *Nachricht an die Musikliebhaber* of 23 February 1791 Hoffmeister announced a new subscription for symphonies, along with a large expansion of his business through the employment of new staff and the use of new presses and freshly cut type. But the first instalment, promised for 1 July 1791, was not ready until 1793, and the advertised clearer print on the best quality Venetian paper apparently failed to halt the general decline in business. By April 1793 the firm had reached the publication number 293, but in the next ten years it added only 30 items and lacked a coherent programme; for example, in · 1798 and 1799 three almanacs appeared, the bookseller Johann Baptist Schulmeister advertised works formerly published by the firm at reduced prices in 1797 and 1798, and at this time Hoffmeister began a new series of plate numbers at no.1. However, this period also marks the beginning of the firm's negotiations with Beethoven, whose Sonata op.13 and Six Variations on 'Tändeln und Scherzen' appeared in a first edition on 18 December 1799, but were soon transferred to Joseph Eder. An advertisement in the *Wiener Zeitung* (11 January 1800) mentions six minuets for two violins and bass by Beethoven (WoO 9) and dances by Carl van Beethoven, all evidently lost. This unsettled policy was accompanied by frequent changes of address.

About the turn of the century Hoffmeister planned a concert tour, but this led instead to the founding with Ambrosius Kühnel of the Bureau de Musique in Leipzig, which eventually became the basis of the publishing firm C. F. Peters. From 1801 to 1805 the firm led a kind of double life: the business in Vienna continued uninterrupted and published under its own initiative, albeit in a limited capacity; concurrently many Viennese publications started appearing in Leipzig, with altered plate numbers, and several new publications appeared in both towns simultaneously. It is not certain who looked after Hoffmeister's office during his absences from Vienna; his wife, who may initially have worked in the business, later followed him to Leipzig. In March 1805 he resumed business in Vienna and from 6 March left Kühnel in sole charge of the Leipzig firm. Hoffmeister's last publication appeared in 1806, after which he withdrew from business and devoted himself to composition. He arranged a life annuity with Kühnel and made over his rights of publication for his remaining works to the Chemische Druckerey (founded by Senefelder in Vienna); in many cases Hoffmeister's publication numbers were retained as both firms had reached about the same number at this time.

Hoffmeister's firm in Vienna, although unresponsive to commercial opportunities, was conscientious in its choice of com-posers; the catalogue includes Albrechtsberger, Clementi, E. A. Förster, Mederitsch, Pleyel, Süssmayr, Vanhal and Paul Wranitzky. Beethoven, Haydn and particularly Mozart (Hoffmeister's personal friend) are all represented (Mozart by several first editions between κ478 and 577, including the 'Hoffmeister' Quartet κ499). Hoffmeister's connection with Kühnel, who had more flair for business, renewed his interest in publishing and prompted serious attempts to produce complete editions of the works of Bach, Haydn and Mozart.

EitnerQ; L. R. von Köchel: *Chronologisch-thematisches Verzeichnis sämtlicher Tonwerke Wolfgang Amadé Mozarts* (Leipzig, 1862, rev. 6/1964); R. Eitner: *Buch- und Musikalienhändler* (Leipzig, 1904); E. F. Schmid: 'F. A. Hoffmeister und die "Göttweiger Sonaten" ', *Zfm*, civ (1937), 760; R. S. Hill: 'The Plate Numbers of C. F. Peters' Predecessors, *PAMS 1938*, 113; Weinmann (1956); A. van Hoboken: *Joseph Haydn: thematisch-bibliographisches Werkverzeichnis* (Mainz, 1957–71); A. Weinmann: *Die Wiener Verlagswerke von F. A. Hoffmeister* (Vienna, 1964); E. Radant: 'Ignaz Pleyel's Correspondence with Hoffmeister & Co.', *Haydn Yearbook*, xii (1981), 122–74; G. Haberkamp: *Die Erstdrucke der Werke von Wolfgang Amadeus Mozart* (Tutzing, 1986)

A.W.

Hofmeister, Friedrich (*b* Strehla, 24 Jan 1782; *d* Reudnitz, nr. Leipzig, 30 Sept 1864). German publisher and bibliographer. After learning the trade for some years as an assistant at Breitkopf & Härtel's and in Hoffmeister & Kühnel's Bureau de Musique, Hofmeister opened a retail music business in Leipzig in 1807. He soon extended this to a music publishing firm, to which he added a musical hire service and later a commission business. In his publication of vocal and instrumental pieces he served contemporary public taste. He was a close friend and the principal publisher of Heinrich Marschner, and for a time he promoted Schumann and Mendelssohn, published works by Berlioz, Chopin, Czerny, Clara Schumann and Friedrich Wieck, and issued songs and ballads by Loewe. Studies, didactic works and tutors for the popular instruments of the day were a prominent part of his publishing programme.

In 1817 Whistling published his *Handbuch der musikalischen Literatur* and Hofmeister was quick to see its importance; he published its successive supplements from the second (1819) and went on to produce further catalogues dealing with musical practice and music literature in German-speaking countries (from 1829 issued as the *Musikalisch-literarischer Monatsbericht neuer*

Musikalien, collected into an annual catalogue from 1852). This made his firm the centre of German studies in music bibliography. On Hofmeister's initiative some music publishers formed an association in Leipzig in 1829 in order to prevent the abuse of music reprints, and when he founded the Verein der Deutschen Musikalienhändler he became a spokesman for the welfare of his profession.

In 1852 Hofmeister's sons Adolph Moritz (1802–70) and Wilhelm (1824–77) took over the business, and from 1877 to 1905 it was directed by a partner, Albert Röthing. He was succeeded by Carl Wilhelm Günther (1878–1956), a great-grandson of the founder, who added to the firm's reputation. In 1897 Mahler's Second Symphony was published, and after 1909 Breuer's *Zupfgeigenhansl* proved a lasting success. The present-day Leipzig publishing house (nationalized in 1952) combines the old traditions with new editorial principles. Music for young people and for music lovers is the focus of its work; in addition to works of pedagogical interest, such as tutors and studies, its main publications include vocal and choral music, brass band music and works for folk instruments. Since 1943 the Leipzig publishing house has compiled the *Deutsche Musikbibliographie, Jahresverzeichnis der Musikalien und Musikschriften*. The branch established in Frankfurt in 1952 is now based in Hofheim am Taunus.

'Friedrich Hofmeister zum 100jährigen Geschäftsjubiläum', *Musikhandel und Musikpflege*, ix (1907), 43; M. Schumann: *Zur Geschichte des deutschen Musikalienhandels seit der Gründung des Vereins der Deutschen Musikalienhändler 1829–1929* (Leipzig, 1929); 'Der Firma Friedrich Hofmeister in Leipzig zum 125. Jahrestage ihres Bestehens am 19. März 1932', *Musikalienhandel*, xxxiv (1932), 81; *Tradition und Gegenwart: Festschrift Friedrich Hofmeister* (Leipzig, 1957); H.-M. Plesske: 'Zur Geschichte der deutschen Musikbibliographie', *BMw*, v (1963), 97; idem (1968); R. Elvers and C. Hopkinson: 'A Survey of the Music Catalogues of Whistling and Hofmeister', *FAM*, xix (1972), 1; N. Ratliff: *Handbuch der musikalischen Litteratur: a Reprint of the 1817 Edition and the ten Supplements, 1817–1827* (New York, 1975); D. W. Krummel: 'The Beginnings of Current National Bibliography for German Music', *Richard S. Hill: Tributes from Friends* (Detroit, 1987), 307

H.-M.P./G.H.

Hoftheater-Musik-Verlag. Austrian firm of publishers. It was founded in Vienna in 1796 to publish the music of operas (scores and arrangements of excerpts for piano), incidental music and ballets for the Viennese court theatre (the K.k. Hoftheater); much of this material had traditionally

been distributed in MS copies. It was first in the Burgtheater itself (at its original location on Michaelerplatz, 1796–1819) and later in what is now Bräunerstrasse 10. Officially under the direction of the current general manager of the court theatre, the operation was sporadically overseen up to 1806 by Thaddäus Weigl (1776–1844), who since 1790 had been apprenticed as a copyist of keyboard and quartet excerpts from operas and ballets performed at the theatre. Weigl opened his own art and music shop and publishing firm nearby in 1803, running it and the Hoftheater-Musik-Verlag simultaneously but with mixed success. After 1806, according to Anton Wranitzky, the newly appointed Kapellmeister of the Hoftheater, the Hoftheater-Musik-Verlag was little active because of Weigl's conflict of interest or even embezzlement. It resumed full production in 1812 under Wranitzky's supervision, but was plagued by financial difficulties and dissolved in September 1821, after which Steiner handled the publications up to March 1822. Among its composers were Boieldieu, Diabelli, Cherubini, Hummel, Molitor, Mozart, Rossini, Spontini and Süssmayr.

A. Bauer: *Opern und Operetten in Wien* (Graz, 1955); Weinmann (1956); idem: *Verzeichnis der Musikalien aus dem k.k. Hoftheater-Musik-Verlag* (Vienna, 1961); idem: *Der Alt-Wiener Musikverlag im Spiegel der 'Wiener Zeitung'* (Tutzing, 1976)

T.D.W.

Holden, Smollet (*d* Dublin, 1813). Irish publisher, instrument maker and composer of military music. In 1805, described as a 'military music master and instrument maker', he had premises in Arran Quay, Dublin. In 1806 he moved to Parliament Street, where he opened a music shop about 1807. On his death the business was continued by his widow until about 1818. Holden's publications included *A Collection of Old Established Irish Slow and Quick Tunes* (*c*1807); many of the airs may have been collected by his son Francis Holden. The elder Holden published two more collections of Irish music (issued periodically), collections of Welsh tunes, masonic songs and country dances, and many individual songs and instrumental pieces.

L.D.

Hole, William (*fl* London, 1612–18). English engraver. He engraved the plates for *Parthenia or the Maydenhead of the First Musicke that ever was Printed for the Virginalls* (*c*1612; see illustration), and Angelo Notari's *Prime musiche* (*c*1613), the earliest engraved music to be published in England. A Robert

Title-page of 'Parthenia' (c1612–13)

Hole has been thought to have been the engraver of *Parthenia In-violata* (1614), but that is now seen to be the work of several hands. The title-page states that the music was 'selected out of the Compositions of the most famous . . . by Robert Hole.'

Humphries and Smith (1954, 2/1970); R. T. Dart: 'The History of Mayden-musicke', *Bulletin of the New York Public Library*, lxv (1961), 209; R. J. Wolfe: 'Parthenia In-violata', *Bulletin of the New York Public Library*, lxv (1961), 347

M.M.

Honterus, Johannes (*b* Braşov, 1498; *d* Braşov, 23 Jan 1549). Romanian humanist, teacher and printer. He was educated at the Dominican School at Braşov and at the University of Vienna (1515–25), and after working as a teacher, Protestant preacher and professor in Regensburg, Kraków, Wittenberg and Basle (1529–33) and establishing friendships with the greatest European humanists of his time (including Erasmus), he settled in Braşov. Having brought a printing press from Switzerland (1533) he printed scientific, religious and art books. Some of his textbooks were used at the Braşov Gymnasium (Schola Coronensis, founded 1544), the first humanist school of south-east Europe. In 1548 he printed a selection for teaching music to young people, *Odae cum harmoniis ex diversis poëtis in usum ludi literarij Coronensis decerptae*. The 21 four-part polyphonic songs to texts by classical Latin and medieval writers is the oldest publication of secular music in Transylvania; the music was by Braşov composers (Lucillus, Ostermayer etc). Honterus's printing press became known throughout eastern Europe; in the 17th century Braşov was considered the main centre of Saxon printing (Valentin Wagner, Martin Wolffgang and Michael Herrmann continued the traditions of Honterus's press to 1689) and of Romanian printing (Gheorghe Coressi, his successor, continued and perfected his printing technique).

O. Netoliczka: *Beiträge zur Geschichte des Johannes Honterus und seine Schriften* (Braşov, 1930); K.K. Klein: *Der Humanist und Reformator Johannes Honterus* (Sibiu and Munich, 1938); R. Ghircoiaşiu: 'O colecţie de piese corale din secolul XVI: Odae cum harmoniis de Johannes Honterus', *Muzica*, x/10 (1960), 22; K. Göllner: *Johann Honterus* (Bucharest, 1960); H. Stǎnescu: 'Johannes Honterus, 1498–1549', *Volk und Kultur*, i (1969), 36; M. Philippi: 'Un mare umanist: J. Honterus', *Astra*, vii (1970), 5; G. Nussbächer: *Johannes Honterus: sein Leben und Werk in Bild* (Bucharest, 1973, 3/1978; Rom. trans., 1977); E. Antoni: 'Johannes Honterus "Odae cum harmoniis" ', *Forschungen zur Volks- und Landeskunde* (1982), 53

V.C.

Hope. American firm of publishers, based in Carol Stream, Illinois. It specializes in hymnals, choral music and copyright proprietorship. It was established in 1892 in Chicago by Henry Date and his cousins, George Henry Shorney and Frank Kingsbury, but through its acquisition (1922) of the New York firm of Biglow & Main, traces its roots to 1861. Hope Publishing Company remains a leading independent publisher of sacred and educational music for church and school.

D. P. Hustad: *Dictionary-Handbook to Hymns for the Living Church* (Carol Stream, IL, 1978)

G.H.S.

Horneman, Christian Frederik Emil (*b* Copenhagen, 17 Dec 1840; *d* Copenhagen, 8 June 1906). Danish publisher and composer, son of Johan Ole Emil Horneman, co-founder of Horneman & Erslev. He studied in Leipzig (1858–60) with Moscheles, Ernst Richter, Moritz Hauptmann and others; there he met Grieg, who became a firm friend.

On returning to Copenhagen in 1861 he founded the publishing firm of Chr. E. Horneman and issued, partly under pseudonyms, his own arrangements and potpourris of popular music, as well as first editions of works by Grieg. The firm also published a number of important music periodicals, including *Musikalske Nyheder* (1861–75; in collaboration with H. C. Lumbye) and *Nordiske Musikblade* (1872–5; in collaboration with Grieg and J. A. Söderman). In 1875 Horneman sold his firm to Wilhelm Hansen.

Catalog over Chr. E. Hornemans Forlagsartikler (Copenhagen, 1871); S. Berg: 'Horneman, Christian Frederik Emil', *Grove6*; D. Fog: *Notendruck und Musikhandel im 19. Jahrhundert in Dänemark* (Copenhagen, 1986)

D.F.

Horneman & Erslev. Danish firm of publishers and music dealers. It was established in Copenhagen in January 1846 by the composers J. O. Emil Horneman (1809–70) and Emil Erslev (1817–82), succeeding the firm of Horneman & de Meza (founded 1844). In 1859 Horneman left the company, which continued under Erslev. In the 1860s some editions show the firm as Horneman & Erslev (Emil Erslev), others as Emil Erslev (Horneman & Erslev). On 20 April 1869 it was taken over by the composer and musicologist S. A. E. Hagen (1842–1927), who continued publishing under the name of Horneman & Erslev.

The firm of Wilhelm Hansen took it over in June 1879.

The company held a central position in Copenhagen's music life. Horneman was a fertile and popular composer who after leaving Erslev managed the music publishing house of C. F. E. Horneman, owned by his son, the composer C. F. E. Horneman (1840–1906), a friend and publisher of Grieg. Erslev was not only an esteemed composer, but also a respected performer; he co-founded the Students' Choral Society (which his son-in-law Niels Gade conducted). S. A. E. Hagen was a composer, but is better known for his comprehensive and valuable collections of notes on Danish music history (MS in the Royal Library, Copenhagen).

The number of works published exceeds 1150. Plate numbers were used from 1850. Important music periodicals, edited in sequence by Horneman, Erslev and Hagen, include *Musikalsk museum* (31 vols., 1847–79; songs and piano music), with numerous first printings of noted compositions, and *Album for sang* (9 vols., 1867–77; songs), also including original editions of Scandinavian music. A large and important music hire library with excellent printed catalogues (1847, 1850–54, 1856, 1860) survives in the State Library at Århus.

D. Fog: *Musikhandel og Nodetryk i Danmark efter 1750* (Copenhagen, 1984), i, 332, ii, 182 [with dated plate nos.]; idem: *Notendruck und Musikhandel im 19. Jahrhundert in Dänemark* (Copenhagen, 1986), 117, 294 [with dated plate nos.]

D.F.

Howe, Elias (*b* Framingham, MA, 1820; *d* Watertown, MA, 6 July 1895). American publisher and dealer. According to several accounts he was a farmhand and fiddler. He compiled a large collection of fiddle tunes popular at local dances and persuaded the Boston publishers Wright & Kidder to publish it as *The Musician's Companion*. As a result of his success in selling this collection from door to door, he opened a music shop in Providence, Rhode Island, in 1842, and set up a similar business in Boston in 1843. His books of arrangements and instrument instruction were popular: the *Complete Preceptor for the Accordeon* (1843) sold over 100,000 copies, and his violin self-mastery volumes sold over 500,000 copies. In 1850 he sold his catalogue to the Boston publisher Oliver Ditson and agreed not to publish music for ten years. During that period he lived on his newly acquired estate in South Framingham, managed the South Reading Ice Company and compiled editions of dance music and dance instruction books.

In 1860 Howe re-entered the publishing business in Boston at 33 Court Street, where he also sold drums, fifes and other instruments needed for Civil War bands. His expanded catalogue included numerous arrangements for band, orchestra, solo instruments and voice. By 1871 he was collecting rare string instruments, and by the late 1880s was one of the largest dealers in rare violins, violas, cellos, violas da gamba, violas d'amore, guitars and banjos. After his death his sons William Hills Howe and Edward Frank Howe carried on the business, specializing in the sale and repair of violins, plucked string instruments and their fittings. When the company was sold in 1931, the music catalogue plates were destroyed and the rare instrument collection was dispersed.

R. Herndon: *Boston of Today* (Boston, 1892), 265; C. M. Ayars: *Contributions to the Art of Music in America by the Music Industries of Boston, 1640 to 1936* (New York, 1937/R1969)

C.A.H.

Huberty, Anton [Huberti, Antoine] (*b c*1722; *d* 13 Jan 1791). Engraver and publisher of Flemish descent. He worked in Paris from 1756 as a musician at the Opéra and performer on the viola d'amore, but became most prominent for his activities as an engraver and music publisher. From February 1770 he made his publications available in Vienna as well, and is credited with introducing engraving to Viennese music publishing. It was probably the bookseller Hermann Josef Krüchten who persuaded him to move to Vienna, where at that time copper engraving had been little practised; Huberty and his family moved there at the beginning of 1777 and opened a music engraving and printing business in the Alstergasse, 'Zum goldenen Hirschen'. A detailed advertisement in the *Wiener Diarium* (11 April 1778) names the Gastl art shop on the Kohlmarkt as an agency for Huberty; later Trattner and Christoph Torricella also sold his publications.

Unable to compete with the younger rival firms of Torricella and Artaria, Huberty never succeeded in having his own shop. From 1781 he engraved for Torricella; later he worked increasingly for Artaria as well as other publishers. Much engraved music of the time is recognizable as his work even without the frequent mark 'Huberty sculps:'; Geminiani's violin tutor and the *Fundamente von der Singstimmen* became particularly well known, the former a product of his own publishing firm, and the latter made for the fine-art dealer Hohenleitter.

In the last years of his life Huberty was reduced to total poverty and worked only on the technique of etching plates; his death certificate gives his occupation as 'chemist'. The benefits of his work went to the publishers Artaria, Hoffmeister and Kozeluch.

Hopkinson (1954); Johansson (1955); A. Weinmann: *Kataloge Anton Huberty (Wien) und Christoph Torricella* (Vienna, 1962)

A.W.

Hudební Matice. Czech firm of publishers, active in Prague. It was founded in 1871 at Ludevít Procházka's instigation; its aim was to publish works of Czech composers, especially piano arrangements of opera excerpts. Its first publication was Smetana's *The Bartered Bride* (1872), followed by *Libuše*, Fibich's *Bride of Messina*, and Bendl's operas *Lejla* and *The Old Bridegroom*. In 1889 the firm disbanded and its assets were taken over by the Umělecká Beseda, which continued to publish operas and piano pieces by Smetana. In 1907 it created a special foundation for its publishing activity under the name of Hudební Matice Umělecké Besedy. Its editorial work expanded to include piano excerpts from Dvořák's operas, operas by Foerster, Kovařovic, Ostrčil and Janáček, and piano excerpts of the orchestral works of Suk and Novák. It also published non-operatic works by other composers as well as opera librettos and books on music. After World War I Hudební Matice began publishing new works by those Czech composers who until then had had to rely on publishers abroad, particularly encouraging composers of the younger generation such as Ježek. It brought out most genres of art music, as well as popular music and jazz. Music literature produced by the firm includes Nejedlý's monograph on Smetana and Šourek's biography of Dvořák. The firm published several periodicals including the *Hudební revue* (1908–20), *Listy Hudebni matice* (later renamed *Tempo*; 1922–38, 1946–8) and the promotional *Hudebni noviny* (1930–38). From 1942 to 1947 it published the *Kalendář českých (československých* after World War II) *hudebníků*. Hudební Matice systematically publicized Czech music abroad by having foreign representatives, exchanging publications with foreign firms and advertising in foreign journals in exchange for space in *Tempo*; the firm also participated in festivals and exhibitions abroad (Florence, Geneva, Frankfurt am Main) and opened a bookshop in Leipzig. It finished its printing and publishing activity on 31 December 1949 but published in 1950 as the publishing house of the Czechoslovak Composers' Union. In 1951 it was merged with the Národní Hudební Vydavatelství Orbis (*see* SUPRAPHON).

ČSHS; V. Mikota: 'Hudební matice Umělecké besedy, její vznik, Vývoj a vyhlídky' [Hudební matice of the Umělecká beseda; its origin, development and prospects], *Sedmdesát let Umělecké besedy 1863–1933*, ed. F. Skácelík (Prague, 1933), 99; *Žeň Hudební matice: soupis vydaných publikací k 31. prosinc 1949* [Publications of Hudebni Matice 31 December 1949] (Prague, 1949); *Dějiny české hudební kultury 1890–1945* [The history of Czech musical culture 1890–1945], ii (Prague, 1981), 28

Z.C.

Hudgebut, John (*fl* 1679–99). English publisher and bookseller. He was one of the London music publishers to employ the printer John Heptinstall, who printed the five books of his *Thesaurus musicus*, a series of song anthologies (1693–6), and *A Collection of New Ayres: Composed for Two Flutes . . . in 1695*. He is generally taken to be the author of a work printed for him by Nathaniel Thompson in 1679, *A Vade mecum for the Lovers of Musick Shewing the Excellency of the Rechorder*, and he also published John Banister's *The Most Pleasant Companion or Choice New Lessons for the Recorder or Flute* (1681) and some of the songs from Henry Purcell's *The Indian Queen* (1695; neither Hudgebut nor his publishing partner, John May, appears to have asked the composer's permission in this venture). Hudgebut had several addresses during his career: he was first at the Golden Harp and Hoboy in Chancery Lane, then at St Paul's Churchyard and lastly in the Strand, near Charing Cross or St Martin's Lane.

Humphries and Smith (1954, 2/1970)

M.M.

Hug. Swiss firm of publishers. Jakob Christoph Hug (1776–1855), a pastor at Thalwil, was financially associated with Hans Georg Nägeli's music publishing firm in Zurich from 1802, making possible Nägeli's important series, the *Répertoire des Clavecinistes*. Owing to the Napoleonic wars Nägeli was obliged, on economic grounds, to surrender the undertaking in 1807 to Hug and his brother Kaspar. Nägeli remained closely allied with the firm as adviser and proofreader until 1818; the firm Hans Georg Nägeli & Co. was renamed Gebrüder Hug in 1817. The firm had to contend with great financial difficulties, especially as by 1819 Nägeli had already opened a rival business; J. C. Hug resumed his office of pastor in order to earn a living. In 1831 his son J. C. Hug (1801–52) took over the firm's direction and managed to profit from, and to provide impetus to, a revival of Swiss musical life. By 1842 his own publishing house and the associated music and instrument trade had regained their importance, and in 1849 his firm absorbed part of Nägeli's business. After the younger J. C. Hug's death his wife Susanna, née Wild (1814–62), in partnership with the business manager Heinrich Müller, ran the firm until 1862 when it was taken over by Emil Hug (1842–1909). Besides publishing, notably Swiss vocal music (Abt, Wilhelm Baumgartner, Attenhofer), he dealt in instruments, principally German, French and American pianos, also incorporating a workshop for restoring instruments. Branches were opened in Basle (1865), St Gall (1865), Lucerne (1871), Strasbourg (1871–1920), Konstanz (1880–1920), Leipzig (1885–1956), Winterthur (1892), Lugano (1887), Neuchâtel (1907), Lörrach (1907–1930) and Solothurn (1909), among which the Leipzig branch was particularly important. In 1879 Emil Hug began publishing the *Schweizerisches Sängerblatt* (now *Schweizerische Musikzeitung*). His sons Arnold (1866–1905) and Adolf (1867–1943) became partners in the firm in 1893. Arnold managed the St Gall branch (1894–7) and the Leipzig branch (1902–5).

The firm published works by such leading Swiss composers as Hans Huber, Schoeck, Volkmar Andreae, Fritz Brun, Willy Burkhard and Moeschinger as well as Carl Reinecke and Reger, focussing attention on vocal music (especially songbooks), educational material and musicological works. During the 1930s teaching manuals for singing and the recorder were strongly promoted. Instruments from the Hug workshop also had a good reputation. Adolf Hug directed the establishment from 1909, and was one of the pioneers of Swiss copyright and performing rights in his capacity as co-founder of the Society of Swiss Authors and Publishers (SUISA). In 1909 he founded a collection of 220 instruments, presented to the Zurich Museum of Applied Art in 1963. His son Adolf (*b* 1904) took over the management in association with H. Wolfensberger (*b* 1903) in 1943, after which there was an increase in publishing new editions of early music, including a collected edition of Ludwig Senfl's works and the series *Das*

Kammerorchester. In 1973 the undertaking was converted into a joint-stock company with Adolf Hug as director; the name of Hug & Co. has been retained. In 1966 the firm was honoured with the Hans Georg Nägeli Medal of the city of Zurich. The firm now holds a leading position in Switzerland for selling music, instruments and gramophone records.

100 Jahre Gebrüder Hug & Co. (Zurich, 1907); *125 Jahre Gebrüder Hug & Co.* (Zurich, 1932); S. F. Müller: *150 Jahre Hug & Co.* (Zurich, 1957); idem: 'Jakob Christoph Hug', *SMz*, xcvii (1957), 422; Plesske (1968)

J.S.

Hummel. Netherlands-German family of publishers. Johann Julius Hummel (*b* Waltershausen, bap. 17 Dec 1728; *d* Berlin, 27 Feb 1798) and his brother Burchard (Burghard) (*b* Waltershausen, 16 April 1731; *d* The Hague, 27 Sept 1797) were both french horn players. In the 1740s they arrived at The Hague, where Johann Julius became a citizen in 1751. By 1753 he had apparently moved to Amsterdam and established himself as a music publisher and music dealer. His first address there was in Nes, and in May 1764 he moved to Vygendam. In 1770 he opened a branch in Berlin, where he himself moved in 1774. From 1774 the imprint of his firm reads 'Chez J. J. Hummel à Berlin, à Amsterdam au Grand Magazin de Musique', often with the addition 'et aux adresses ordinaires'. He evidently delegated the management of the business in Amsterdam to his daughter Elisabeth Christina (*b* The Hague, bap. 27 Feb 1751; *d* Amsterdam, 16 April 1818), who from 1791 was helped by her second husband, Carl Wilhelm von Mettingh. In 1776 the Amsterdam branch moved to Warmoestraat and at the end of 1780 to Rokkin. After Johann Julius's death his son Johann Bernhard (1760–*c*1805) took over the firm, although it was managed by a certain Annisius; in 1800 Johann Bernhard was excluded from the firm according to a statement in the *Berlinische Nachrichten von Staats- und gelehrten Sachen* (4 September 1800). The firm continued its activities and in 1808 took over S. Markordt's music business in Amsterdam. In August and September 1822 clearance sales of the firm's stock and equipment took place in Berlin and Amsterdam, and much of it passed to C. Bachmann in Hanover and Lischke & Trautwein in Berlin. At the beginning of his activities in Amsterdam Johann Julius Hummel collaborated with the Netherlands music publisher A. Olofsen. In 1754 they published *Sei nuove* *sinfonie* by Santo Lapis, but by 1757 a sharp conflict had developed between them. Hummel's cooperation with his brother, however, continued until the early 1780s.

J. J. Hummel was enterprising, capable and energetic, and developed his business into one of the leading music publishing firms of its kind. He imported music and had agents abroad for the sale of his own publications. It is true that he had no scruples about publishing pirated prints, but this practice was relatively common at the time. He and his brother published thematic catalogues of the works they issued; only the main catalogue (1768) and six supplements (1769–74) are known, although a seventh supplement and a thematic catalogue from 1780 apparently also appeared. The firm's many publishing catalogues contain mostly instrumental music by contemporary Austrian, Bohemian, Netherlands, German and Italian composers as well as arias and ensembles from French and German operas and lieder; composers represented include Abel, J. C. and C. P. E. Bach, Boccherini, Dittersdorf, Haydn, Kozeluch, Mozart, Pleyel, Stamitz and Vanhal (for illustration *see* fig.35, p.99). Hummel's nomination to membership of the Royal Board of Commerce also testifies to contemporary recognition of his work.

Besides his short time in his father's firm, Johann Bernhard Hummel was a pianist and composer; he wrote *Modulationen durch alle Dur und Moll Töne* (Berlin, 1800) as well as some lieder and piano pieces.

Burchard Hummel settled in Agterom in The Hague, where in 1755 he received civic rights as a music dealer. In 1765 he moved his business from Agterom to Spuystraat and in 1771 he bought a house on the same street and was active there until his death. His son Leonard Hummel (*b* The Hague, bap. 8 Feb 1757) became active in the firm at an early age. From the beginning of the 1780s it was called B. Hummel et fils or B. Hummel en Zoon; its activities were carried on in Warmoestraat in Amsterdam and in Spuystraat in The Hague. In January 1801 Leonard Hummel sold a large collection of musical items, from which it can be assumed that B. Hummel's business ceased at this time. Besides orchestral and chamber music by contemporary composers Burchard Hummel published many collections of airs. His activities as a publisher were, however, not as extensive as his brother's.

Goovaerts (1880); J. W. Enschedé: 'Een magazijn-catalogus van J. J. Hummel te Amsterdam en B. Hummel te 's Gravenhage, 1778', *TVNM*, viii/4

(1908), 262; D. F. Scheurleer: *Het muziekleven in Nederland in de tweede helft der 18e eeuw in verband met Mozart's verblijf aldaar* (The Hague, 1909); E. F. Kossmann: 'De boekhandel te 's-Gravenhage tot het eind van de 18e eeuw', *Bijdragen tot de geschiedenis van den Nederlandschen boekhandel*, xiii (1937), 198; Deutsch (1946); K. Hortschansky: 'Zwei datierte Hummel-Kataloge; ein Beitrag zur Geschichte des Musikalienhandels in Frankfurt am Main', *Quellenstudien zur Musik: Wolfgang Schmieder zum 70. Geburtstag* (Frankfurt am Main, 1972), 79; Johansson (1972); J. Sachs: *Kapellmeister Hummel in England and France* (Detroit, 1977)

C.J.

Hünefeld, Andreas (*b* Halberstadt, 1581; *d* Danzig [now Gdańsk], 1666). German publisher and bookseller. He began printing in Danzig in 1609, and soon became the principal Reformation printer in Poland, with the support of King Władysław IV. He was a specialist in historical and linguistic books, although he also published a good deal of music. Much of this comprised monophonic songbooks, printed in a single impression using a Gothic notation typeface. In 1652 he transferred his printing house to Andreas and Ernest Müllers. Hünefeld's output includes Lutheran songbooks by Rybiński, Lobwasser, Schnitzkius, Optiz and Artomius, polyphonic songs by Hakenberger (1610) and Schnitzkius (1618) and treatises by Schnitzkius (1619) and Peter Johann Titz (1642).

Przywecka-Samecka (1969); *Słownik pracowników książki polskiej* [Dictionary of Polish printers] (Warsaw and Łódź, 1972)

T.C. (ii)

Hutchings & Romer. English firm of publishers, active in London. It was established in Conduit Street, Regent Street, about 1866 by Charles L. Hutchings and the composer Frank Romer (*b* London, 5 Aug 1810; *d* Malvern, 1 July 1889), brother of the soprano Emma Romer. Throughout its existence the firm did a brisk business, not only in popular music but also in plates and copyrights. Among its most lucrative properties on offer at a sale in May 1884 (according to the press one of the most important music sales in years), were Barnett's *Ancient Mariner*, Wallace's *Maritana* and *Lurline* and Crouch's *Kathleen Mavourneen* (none of them originally published by the firm). After this sale – like six successive ones to 1908 conducted by the auctioneers Puttick & Simpson – the firm seems to have branched in two, as Hutchings & Romer at Conduit Street and Hutchings & Co. at Blenheim Street. The branches reunited in 1892 at Great Marlborough Street and continued to issue popular choral and instrumental series to 1916. (For a revealing account of a publisher's 'traveller' at an auction of Hutchings & Romer material, see Coover, 1987, pp.228–9.)

J. B. Coover: 'The Dispersal of Engraved Music Plates and Copyrights in British Auctions, 1831–1931', *Richard S. Hill: Tributes from Friends* (Detroit, 1987), 223–306; Coover (1988)

L.L.

I

Imbault, Jean-Jérôme (*b* Paris, 9 March 1753; *d* Paris, 15 April 1832). French publisher and violinist, active in Paris. He made his début as a solo violinist at the age of 17 and showed great promise, according to the *Mercure de France* of 1 April 1770, but his later musical activity was for the most part confined to teaching and to participation in the orchestras of various societies (including the Concert Spirituel).

The music publishing house that Imbault founded operated during its first year in connection with the already established firm of Jean-Georges Sieber (their first joint announcement, in the *Journal de la librairie* of 2 August 1783, was for Devienne's Second Flute Concerto). Advertisements for Imbault alone appeared in various journals, beginning in November 1784 with one for J. B. Cartier's variations op.3 on *airs* from *Richard Coeur de Lion*. Until January 1811 Imbault continued to describe himself on title-pages and advertisements as both 'professor et éditeur de musique'.

The firm's considerable output is well documented by a series of catalogues issued between 1786 and about 1803 (see illustration) and by a 284-page thematic catalogue of publications (1791 or 1792). In addition to the opera arrangements and excerpts common to the period Imbault published many works by Haydn, Clementi, Viotti, Pleyel, Mozart, Boccherini, Gyrowetz, Wranitzky and other respected composers. In 1798 or 1799 he bought the shop of a publisher named Leblanc and from that time the additional location in the 'péristyle du Théâtre de l'Opéra comique' (also called the Théâtre Italien or Théâtre Favart) at 461 rue Favart appeared in his address along with the original one, 125 rue St Honoré. Imbault was still listed in the *Almanach du commerce de Paris* for 1812, with the designation of music seller to 'their imperial and royal majesties'. On 14 July 1812 Imbault sold the firm to P.-H. Janet and Alexandre Cotelle (Janet had earlier served Imbault as agent). Although the successors occupied part of the house for their commerce, Imbault continued to live at 125 rue St Honoré until his death. His bequest to his wife (there were no children) included four houses and valuable shares in the Bank of France.

Catalogue thématique des ouvrages de musique mis au jour par Imbault (Paris, 1791 or 1792/*R*1972); Hopkinson (1954); Johansson (1955); P. Guiomar: 'J. J. Imbault', *FAM*, xiii (1966), 43; R. Benton: 'J.-J. Imbault (1753–1832), violiniste et éditeur de musique à Paris', *RdM*, lxii/2 (1976), 86

R.B. (ii)

Instituto de Cultura Puertorriqueña. Puerto Rican publishing and research institute. It was established in San Juan by the legislature in 1955 to foster research, preservation and publication in the fields of Puerto Rican folklore, crafts, architecture and history. Among its initiatives has been the publication of songs, piano music and sets of performance parts for band and orchestra by native composers, individually or as inserts (*separatas*) in the agency's *Revista del Instituto de Cultura Puertorriqueña*. Published works include Juan Morel Campos's *danzas* and music by Julián Andino and other 19th-century figures, but especially the music of more recent composers, among them Héctor Campos-Parsi, Jack Délano, Narciso Figueroa, José Enrique Pedreira and Amaury Veray.

R. E. Alegría: *El Instituto de Cultura Puertorriqueña, 1955–1973: dieciocho años contribuyendo a fortalecer nuestra consciencia nacional* (San Juan, 1978); D. Thompson: 'El Archivo General de Puerto Rico: un caudal de música puertorriqueña', *Estudios en honor de Domingo Santa Cruz* (Santiago de Chile, 1986, 227; idem: 'The Music Collection of the Puerto Rico General Archive', *FAM*, xxxiii (1986), 288

D.T. (i)

Imbault catalogue, taken from a copy of Sacchini's 'Oedipe à Colone' (Paris, 1787)

Instituto Español de Musicología. Spanish publishing and research institute active in Madrid and Barcelona. It was founded by ministerial decree of the Spanish government (27 September 1943) as a branch of the Higher Council for Scientific Research. In accordance with the founding decree and other constitutive rules the institute aims to make an inventory and publish catalogues of Spanish music; to publish its source material and monographs on the history of music in Spain; to collect, edit and study popular songs of the different Spanish regions; to make a photographic archive of the most important Spanish manuscripts; and to organize musicological courses and conferences. Some of these objectives have scarcely been attempted, but much important material has been published, notably the *Monumentos de la Música Española*, the periodical *Anuario muscial* (from 1946), and a series of monographs and songbooks. The series of music catalogues began brilliantly in 1946 with the three-volume catalogue of the Madrid National Library, but then ceased. The series *Música Hispana* contains single works.

J.L.-C.

International. American firm of publishers. It was founded in New York in 1941 by A. W. Haendler (*c*1894–1979). International Music Company publishes solo instrumental music, chamber and vocal music and miniature scores of works in the standard repertory. After Haendler's death Frank Marx, executor of his estate, became head of the company, which is a subsidiary of Bourne Company.

F.B.

Israeli Music Publications. Israeli firm of publishers. It was founded in Tel-Aviv in 1949 by Peter Gradenwitz in association with the Israeli Association of Composers. From 1952 Gradenwitz managed the firm independently as a limited company. It was the first Israeli music publishing house of an international standard, and publishes works by Israeli composers of all schools and styles, as well as works by composers of any nationality that are based on biblical subjects or texts or that have a particular association with Israel or the Near East. The firm has published works written specially for Israel by Schoenberg, Milhaud, Villa-Lobos, Martinů, Martinon, Staempfli, Hovhaness, Castelnuovo-Tedesco, Rathaus and many others. The series *Early Hebrew Art Music* comprises practical scholarly editions of synagogue music from the 12th to the 19th centuries; other first publications include an *Allegro barbaro* for piano by Alkan, *Beatus vir* for soprano and alto soloists, chorus and orchestra by Galuppi, the completion of Schubert's fragmentary setting of Psalm xiii D663, and music by Joseph Achron. By 1982, when the firm was taken over by a British company and transferred to Jerusalem, the catalogue contained about 600 titles in printed editions and an orchestral lending library. Books published by the firm include biographies of composers under its aegis and theoretical works. It has outlets in most countries in Europe and elsewhere, and played a vital role in establishing the Israeli Music Publishers' Union, a member of the International Union of Publishers. Under the imprint of Illan Melody Press, the firm issued light music from 1949 to 1982.

P. Gradenwitz: 'Israeli Music Publications', *MGG*; idem: *Music and Musicians in Israel* (Tel Aviv, 1959, 3/1978)

P.G.

Israel Music Institute [IMI]. Israeli publishing institute. It was founded in Tel Aviv in November 1961 by the National Council for Culture and Art, the America–Israel Cultural Foundation and the League of Composers in Israel, as a public body to promote works by Israeli composers. The founder and first chairman was Eliezer Peri; William Y. Elias was the managing director and editor-in-chief, 1961–89; Paul Landau took over as director in 1989. The catalogue includes vocal, orchestral, chamber and educational works. Among notable composers represented are Tzvi Avni, A. U. Boskovich, Yehezkiel Braun, Arthur Gelbrun, Ami Maayani, Sergiu Natra, Ben-Zion Orgad, Odön Partos, León Schidlowsky, M. Seter, Noam Sheriff and J. Tal. The IMI also issues musicological monographs and produces recordings of Israeli music. It is the representative in Israel for Bärenreiter, Universal Edition and Ricordi.

W.Y.E., P.L.

J

Jacomo Ungaro (*fl c*1473–1513). Type-cutter, active in Venice. On 26 September 1513 he submitted a petition to the Venetian senate requesting a 15-year privilege to print mensural music. In the petition he expressed concern that others would 'harvest the fruits of his labour' after he had 'discovered the way to print mensural music [canto figurato]' in the city where he had been a cutter of letters for 40 years. The previous privilege holder, Petrucci, was by then living in Fossombrone in the papal states. The senate awarded Jacomo an exclusive privilege, but he is not known to have exercised it. Apparently he had cut Petrucci's music type; he probably was Magistro Jacomo Todesco, a typefounder for Aldus Manutius.

A. Vernarecci: *Ottaviano de' Petrucci da Fossombrone, inventore dei tipi mobili metallici fusi della musica nel secolo XV* (Bologna, 1882); S. Boorman: *Petrucci at Fossombrone: a Study of Early Music Printing, with Special Reference to the Motetti de la Corona (1514–1519)* (diss., U. of London, 1976); M. Lowry: *The World of Aldus Manutius: Business and Scholarship in Renaissance Venice* (Ithaca, 1979); Duggan (1981)

M.K.D.

Janet & Cotelle. French firm of publishers. It was founded by Pierre-Honoré Janet (*d* Orsay, Seine-et-Oise, 5 Sept 1832) and Alexandre Cotelle (*b* Montargis, 1786; *d* Paris, 5 Dec 1858). In April 1810 they started business at 17 rue Neuve des Petits-Champs, Paris, 'au Mont d'Or', their retail shop until about 1824. By July 1812 they had acquired publishing premises at 123 and 125 rue St Honoré, where, after Janet's death in 1832, the firm remained until bankrupted in 1836. On 14 July 1812 they absorbed the firm of Imbault, in 1821 that of Décombe, in March 1824 that of Boieldieu Jeune (whose premises at 92 rue de Richelieu were additionally retained), and at the end of 1825 that of Ozi et Cie (successors to Magasin de Musique (i)). After the death of Janet and dissolution of the partnership Cotelle carried on the business as A. Cotelle. In 1838 he had moved his main premises to 140 rue St Honoré (with various subsidiary addresses in the boulevard Montmartre); in 1844 he moved to 137 rue St Honoré and about 1855 to 3 rue Jean-Jacques Rousseau. After Cotelle's death the firm continued, first at the same address, then at 51 rue Jean-Jacques Rousseau (from about 1868), at 17 rue Orléans St-Honoré (from about 1883) and finally at 22 rue des Bons-Enfants (from about 1887); in about 1891 the major part of the assets were taken over by Enoch Frères & Costallat.

Mainly on account of their acquisition of four other firms, Janet & Cotelle were, in 1830, among the largest French music publishers. Their importance was transitory, however, for they made no serious attempt to encourage worthwhile contemporary composers, preferring to play safe by issuing new editions of established works. The opera full scores they published were, with a few exceptions, reissued from the plates of Imbault or the Magasin de Musique (i); and their piano-vocal scores of 17 Rossini and 13 Boieldieu operas were new editions or reissues of previously published works. The only opera of lasting fame first published by the firm was Boieldieu's *La dame blanche*.

Janet & Cotelle are best remembered for their handsome editions of 93 quintets and 52 trios by Boccherini (see illustration), 12 of the quintets being previously unpublished. They also published collections of trios, quartets and quintets by Beethoven, a collection of quartets by Haydn, a large quantity of miscellaneous instrumental and vocal music, and literary and didactic works by Fétis. But after Janet's death the firm achieved almost nothing of consequence. Up to that time the aesthetic quality of production had been high, and all their publications had been printed from engraved plates. About 2500 items had been published by 1835, with reliably chronological plate numbers.

Hopkinson (1954); P. Gossett: *The Operas of Rossini* (diss., Princeton U., 1970), 595; Devriès and Lesure (1979–88)

R.M.

Jean II de Laon (*fl* Geneva, 1582–3). French printer. In 1582–3 he printed the works of Paschal de L'Estocart using material which came from Jean Le Royer: the *150 Psalms*, two books of *Octonaires* by La Roche Chandieu, the *Quatrains* by Pybrac, the *Sacrae cantiones* and a *Meslange de chansons* (now lost). Some of these were produced for Barthélémy Vincent in Lyons, others for descendants of Eustache Vignon in Geneva. All contain extensive prefatory material and their typography is of a high quality.

L. Guillo: *Recherches sur les éditions musicales lyonnaises de la Renaissance* (diss., Ecole Pratique des Hautes Etudes, Paris, 1986)

L.G.

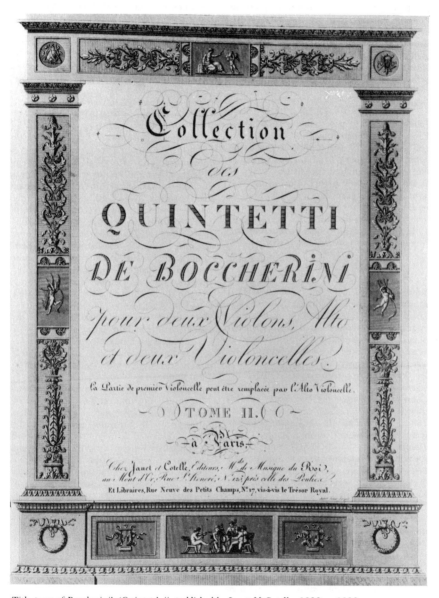

Title-page of Boccherini's 'Quintets', ii, published by Janet & Cotelle, 1822 or 1823

Jerona. American firm of publishers and distributors. It was founded in 1978 in Hackensack, New Jersey, by Joseph M. Boonin. An earlier firm, Joseph Boonin Inc., founded in 1969, became European American Music Distributors in 1977. The Jerona imprint appears on music by Edwin London, Vaclav Nelhybel and Peter Westergaard. Jerona also distributes Boelke-Bomart editions and the Rutgers *Documents of Music* series, as well as music published in Newton Centre, Massachusetts, by Gunther Schuller under the imprints Margun and GunMar.

Jobert. French firm of publishers, active in Paris. In 1922 Jean Jobert (*b* Lyons, 11 Oct 1883; *d* Paris, 27 Nov 1957) acquired the company of Eugène Fromont, for which he had worked; it had published most of Debussy's important works, including *Nocturnes*, *Suite bergamasque*, *Musiques pour le roi Lear*, *Prélude à l'après-midi d'un faune* and several song collections. In addition to 19th- and early 20th-century French music, Jobert publishes contemporary scores.

A.P. (ii)

Johnson, James (*b* Ettrick Valley, *c*1750; *d* Edinburgh, 26 Feb 1811). Scottish engraver. He was a leading Edinburgh engraver, who from 1772 to 1790 prepared plates for well over half the music issued in Scotland. The son of Charles Johnson, he was probably apprenticed with James Reed, an early Edinburgh music engraver. Johnson's first known work is Domenico Corri's *Six Canzones for Two Voices* (1772); then followed *A Collection of Favourite Scots Tunes . . . by the Late Mr Chs McLean and other Eminent Masters* (*c*1772) and Daniel Dow's *Twenty Minuets* (1773). These were cut in copper, but this later work is all stamped on pewter, a practice which his *Scots Magazine* obituary notice erroneously credits him with having invented.

Johnson worked mostly for other Scottish publishers, but he is remembered for the songbook *The Scots Musical Museum*, which he published himself in six volumes (1787–1803). The first volume is not particularly noteworthy, but in 1787 Johnson met Robert Burns and persuaded him to help with the editing. The subsequent volumes contain the bulk of Burns's work on Scottish folksong, including collecting, editing, rewriting and restoring; the collection, which contains 600 songs, has become a classic of its kind. Stephen and William Clarke supplied bass lines with figures and William Stenhouse wrote a series of scholarly notes on each song between 1817 and 1820.

About 1790 Johnson opened a music shop in the Lawnmarket, where his firm remained as Johnson & Co. until his death. He took his apprentice John Anderson into partnership about 1811; Anderson continued with Johnson's widow as Johnson & Anderson at 475 High Street (1811–12) and at North Gray's Close (1812–15). The firm appears to have ceased business in 1815.

Obituary, *Scots Magazine*, lxxiii (1811), 318; D. Laing: Preface to *The Scots Musical Museum* (Edinburgh, 1839), p.xii; D. Johnson: *Music and Society in Lowland Scotland in the 18th Century* (London, 1972), 147

F.K., W.C.S./D.J.

Johnson, John (*fl* 1740–62). English publisher, printer, music seller and violin maker, established in London. He began his business by 1740, and probably acquired part of those of Daniel Wright and Benjamin Cooke, some of whose publications he reissued from original plates. Around the mid-18th century the predominance of the Walsh engraving and publishing business began to wane, and Johnson was responsible for publishing some of the best music of the day, including works by Arne, Felton, Geminiani, Nares, Domenico Scarlatti and Stanley, as well as annual volumes and large collections of country dances. Unusually, many of Johnson's editions bore dates; their technical quality was high, some being engraved by John Phillips.

Johnson appears to have died about 1762, and from that time to 1777 most of the imprints bear the name of 'Mrs. Johnson' or 'R. Johnson', presumably his widow. The old imprint 'John Johnson' occasionally appears in these years, and may refer to her late husband or to another relative. Johnson's sign from 1748, 'The Harp and Crown', is absent from these imprints, having been adopted by J. Longman & Co. when it started business about 1767. Mrs Johnson died in 1777, and in November of that year Robert Bremner announced the purchase of most of her stock and plates.

Humphries and Smith (1954, 2/1970)

F.K., W.C.S./P.W.J.

Jones, Edward (*fl* 1687–1706). English printer. Between 1688 and 1697 he did much of the printing for Henry Playford. His press produced six editions of *The Banquet of Music*, the first two books of *Harmonia sacra*, and one or two of the

Playford family's bestsellers, like *The Dancing Master* (1690 and 1695) and *An Introduction to the Skill of Music* (1694 and 1697). He also worked for other publishers and ultimately became King's Printer. He had his premises at the Savoy in London.

Humphries and Smith (1954, 2/1970)

M.M.

Joubert, (Martin-)Célestin (*b* Saint-Savin de Blaye, Gironde, 23 July 1861; *d* Warsaw, 11 June 1934). French publisher. He worked as a lawyer in Bordeaux and then in Paris, where he became the partner (1891) of his client L. Bathlot, a music publisher (from 1868) and successor to Isidore Royol. In 1897 Joubert bought out Bathlot and moved to 25 rue d'Hauteville. He published many successful operettas and light works, including compositions by Rossini, Franck, Berlioz, Offenbach and Saint-Saëns.

The scope of his catalogue was greatly increased when he married Bathlot's daughter, the widow of Philippe Maquet. Maquet had acquired most of the Brandus brothers' catalogue (1887) which, in turn, included the catalogues of Maurice Schlesinger (acquired 1846) and E. Troupenas (1850). Joubert was president of the Société des Auteurs, Compositeurs et Editeurs de Musique for most of the years between 1903 and 1932. The business was inherited by his son, Robert André (*d* Paris, 1 April 1969), whose widow retained an interest in the firm when Editions et Productions Théâtrales Chappell bought it in 1970.

R.S.N.

Jung, P.L. American publishing firm. The name was a pseudonym created by Kurt Moebius (*b* Stollberg, 1861; *d* New York, 5 April 1932). After working in the Leipzig office of Breitkopf & Härtel, Moebius emigrated to the USA in 1885 with a boyhood friend, Reinhard Volkmann (grandson of Hermann Härtel); together they established the New York branch of Breitkopf in 1891. From 1894 to 1898 Moebius published his own copyrights, initially under the Breitkopf imprint and later under the P. L. Jung name. He issued at least two catalogues, the first in autumn 1896, the second in October 1898. Both featured music by American composers, including 45 original works and arrangements by Edward MacDowell. For a brief time around 1894 he acted as agent for MacDowell's concert appearances; in 1897 he

left the music business. He sold the Jung catalogue to A. P. Schmidt in May 1899, but retained partial ownership of the MacDowell copyrights until 1926. The Schmidt Collection at the Library of Congress contains business records and correspondence documenting Moebius's publishing activities.

'Breitkopf & Härtel: the Leipzig House Represented in New York', *Musical Courier*, xxiii (8 July 1891), 44; O. G. Sonneck: *Catalogue of First Editions of Edward MacDowell* (Washington, DC, 1917/ R1971); Obituary, *New York Times* (5 April 1932); O. and H. von Hase: *Breitkopf & Härtel: Gedenkschrift und Arbeitsbericht* (Wiesbaden, 1968); M. M. Lowens: *The New York Years of Edward MacDowell* (diss., U. of Michigan, 1971)

W.R.C.

Jürgenson [Yurgenson], **Pyotr Ivanovich** (*b* Reval [now Tallinn], 17 July 1836; *d* Moscow, 2 Jan 1904). Russian publisher. He was educated in Reval, and in 1850 was sent to St Petersburg, where from 1855 to 1859 he was an engraver at F. T. Stellovsky's publishing house. In 1859 he was appointed manager at the publishing house of C. F. Schildbach in Moscow, but in 1861, with the help of Nikolay Rubinstein, he established a music publishing business of his own, expanding this in 1867 to include a printing works. From 1870 he bought out many smaller firms, including Bernard in 1885, Meykov in 1889 and Sokolov in 1896, and the business rapidly became the largest in Russia, with a branch in Leipzig Jürgenson was the principal publisher of Tchaikovsky's works, and he also produced the complete sacred works of Bortnyansky under Tchaikovsky's editorship. His catalogue included works by many other Russian composers as well as the piano music of Mendelssohn, Beethoven, Chopin and Schumann, and the operas of Wagner. From 1862 Jürgenson was closely associated with the Moscow branch of the Russian Music Society, and in 1875 was appointed a director. After his death the publishing firm was taken over by his sons, Boris and Grigory. In 1918 it was nationalized and became the music section of the Soviet State Publishing House, which produced, among other things, Boris Jürgenson's invaluable book *Ocherk istorii notopechataniya* ('An outline of the history of music printing', Moscow, 1928).

Fuld (1966, 3/1985); B. L. Vol'man: *Russkiye notnïye izdaniya XIX – nachala XX veka* [Russian music publishing in the 19th and early 20th centuries] (Leningrad, 1970)

G.N.

305

K

Kahnt, Christian Friedrich (*b* Leipzig, 10 May 1823; *d* Leipzig, 5 June 1897). German publisher. He founded a firm in Leipzig in 1851 that brought out good contemporary music (e.g. by Liszt, Draeseke, Grabner, Ambrosius and Mahler) and a great deal of salon music. It also published careful editions of major works and various works by unfamiliar composers of the 16th and 17th centuries such as Frescobaldi, Muffat and Praetorius. Kahnt also sponsored the *Neue Zeitschrift für Musik*, and published Peter Cornelius's *Der Barbier von Bagdad* in 1886. The firm passed in that year to Oskar Schwalm, in 1888 to Paul Simon and subsequently to the banker Alfred Hoffman (1903), who enhanced its reputation by publishing musicological works (by Sandberger, Schering and Grabner) and reprinting earlier music. As C. F. Kahnt Musikalien- und Verlagsbuchhandlung the firm remained in the family's possession after Hoffmann's death (1926), moving to Bonn in 1950 and then to Wasserburg on Lake Constance.

J. Deaville: 'The C. F. Kahnt Archive in Leipzig: a Preliminary Report', *Notes*, xlii (1985–6), 502

H.-M.P.

Kallmeyer. German firm of publishers. In 1821 C. P. H. Hartmann founded a book and music shop in Wolfenbüttel, and this was extended by Ludwig Holle from 1837 to 1874. Julius Zwisler, who had founded a publishing firm in Brunswick in 1872, took over Holle's firm and moved to Wolfenbüttel, but sold Holle's business in 1894 to C. F. Siegel of Leipzig. In 1913 Georg Kallmeyer became a partner and in 1916 sole owner of the Zwisler publishing house, which he renamed Georg Kallmeyer Verlag in 1925. After Kallmeyer's death, Karl Heinrich Möseler (*b* Hildesheim, 11 Jan 1912) bought the firm in 1947 and gave it his own name. In 1951 Georg Kallmeyer (*b* Brunswick, 29 June 1924), a son of the previous owner, retrieved the rights of his father's book and art publishing house from Möseler.

Although the Holle music publishing business had made a name for itself for its numerous editions of the classics, within Zwisler's publishing programme music retired into the background. It was only through Kallmeyer's initiative that music publishing was re-established after World War I. Scholars such as Friedrich Blume (Praetorius complete edition, *Das Chorwerk, Kieler Beiträge zur Musikwissenschaft*), Fritz Jöde (*Der Musikant, Das Chorbuch, Der Kanon*) and Adolf Hoffmann (*Deutsche Instrumentalmusik*) have determined the publishing programme, which Möseler extended after World War II and which now encompasses all areas of secular music making, contemporary choral music, musicological editions and music journals.

Musikverlage in der Bundesrepublik Deutschland und in West-Berlin (Bonn, 1965), 132; C. Vinz and G. Olzog, eds.: *Dokumentation deutschsprachiger Verlage* (Munich and Vienna, 1983), 208

T.W.

Kalmus, Edwin F. (*b* Vienna, 15 Dec 1893). American publisher. He founded his firm in New York in 1926. With his son-in-law, Lawrence Galison, who became the vice-president and manager in 1961 and later chairman of the board, the firm began printing its own music, established an art and camera department, and later added a complete bindery; it is one of the largest self-contained publishing houses in the USA. Kalmus publishes orchestral music, as well as music for piano, organ and solo instruments, and reprints of standard classics. With the exception of its orchestral department, Kalmus was purchased by Belwin-Mills in 1976. The company's headquarters in Opa-Locka, Florida, continues to handle orchestral music and offers a rental service.

W.T.M., M.J./R

Kauffmann [Kaufmann]**, Paul** (bap. Nuremberg, 29 Oct 1568; bur. Nuremberg, 9 Oct 1632). German printer. His father married into one of the most important German printing families (he married Johann Berg's daughter, Gerlach's granddaughter), but was apparently not associated with printing himself. In 1589 Paul Kauffmann joined the Gerlach printing house, which then specialized in music and was run by Catharina Gerlach. On Catharina's death in 1591 the firm passed to the Kauffmann family, and Paul Kauffmann directed it from 1594 until 1617. Early titles still carried the impress 'der Gerlachschen Truckerey' although Kauffmann made new contacts. Particularly

306

important was his association with Hassler, as a result of which he published much of his music and works by the Italians who had influenced Hassler's style. Thus following the German practice of printing large-scale miscellaneous anthologies, Kauffmann introduced much fine Italian music into Germany. Individual volumes were accorded to Croce, Gastoldi and Marenzio, as well as Vecchi, while the large anthologies edited by Kaspar Hassler concentrated on the Venetian repertory. Demantius and Haussmann were among the more distinguished of his German composers. Kauffmann also printed legal and scientific books. A catalogue of his publications was prepared in 1609 by the Frankfurt bookseller Stein.

P. Cohen: *Musikdruck und -drucker zu Nürnberg im sechzehnten Jahrhundert* (Nuremberg, 1927) [incl. list of titles]; R. Wagner: 'Nachträge zur Geschichte der Nürnberger Musikdrucker im 16. Jahrhundert', *Mitteilungen des Verein für Geschichte der Stadt Nürnberg*, xxx (1931), 107–152; T. Wohnhaas: 'Kauffmann, Paul', *MGG*

S.B. (iii)

Keith, Prowse. English firm of publishers, active in London. It was established in 1815 at 91 Aldersgate Street by the instrument maker and retailer Robert William Keith, and after 1822 at 131 Cheapside as successor to Longman and Herron. In 1829 Thomas Prowse entered the business, which in 1832 moved to 48 Cheapside; it was managed by William Prowse after the death of Keith in 1846, later with W. Bryan Jones. The firm's *Complete Catalogue* from the 1930s cites more than 2000 titles, chiefly popular songs and instructional music (the most prominent composer is Richard Addinsell), along with about 300 titles from the catalogue of Sam Fox in New York. The company began its activity as a concert and theatre ticket agency in the 1880s, eventually to the exclusion of music publishing.

Humphries and Smith (1954, 2/1970); J. N. Moore: *Elgar and his Publishers* (London, 1987)

D.W.K.

Kgl. Hof-Musikhandel. Danish firm of publishers and music dealers. It was founded in Copenhagen in 1880 by the composer Henrik Hennings, whose wife was the leading actress of the Royal Theatre, and specialized in stage music and concert management. Its catalogue was wide-ranging and included music by such

Danish composers as August Enna, Peter Erasmus Lange-Müller and Ludvig Schytte, and by such Swedish composers as Hugo Alfvén, Jacob Adolf Hägg, Emil Sjögren and Wilhelm Stenhammar; at times it published in collaboration with foreign firms.

In 1895 the firm became part of Det Nordiske Forlag; in 1902 it was taken over by Nordisk Musikforlag, which in turn became part of Hansen (1929).

Kgl. Hof-Musikhandels Forlagskatalog (1889; suppl. 1892); *Fortegnelse over Det nordiske Forlags Musik-Forlag* (1896); *Tillæg til Nordisk Musikforlags Katalog* (1903); *Nordisk Musik-Forlags Katalog* (1910, 1922); D. Fog: *Notendruck und Musikhandel im 19. Jahrhundert in Dänemark* (Copenhagen, 1986), 296 [with dated plate nos.]

D.F.

Kistner & Siegel. German firm of publishers. It was formed in 1923 by a merger between two firms with long-standing traditions. In 1823 Heinrich Albert Probst (1791–1846) founded a music publishing firm in Leipzig which dealt primarily with French music and which was acquired in 1831 by the musical amateur Carl Friedrich Kistner (1797–1844), after whom it was named from 1836. Under his management it prospered and issued works by Schumann (for illustration *see* fig.37, p.109), Mendelssohn, Moscheles, David, Joachim, Hauptmann, Gade and Ferdinand Hiller. After his death it was managed by his brother Julius (1805–68) assisted by (among others) Carl Friedrich Ludwig Gurckhaus (1821–84), who became the sole proprietor in 1866. The firm had arrangements with Liszt, Smetana, Reinecke, Franz, Bruch and Goetz, and greatly stimulated the work of contemporary composers. In 1919 it was bought by the brothers Carl and Richard Linnemann, the proprietors of the music business of C. F. W. Siegel, which their family had owned since Siegel's death in 1869. This business had been founded by Carl Friedrich Wilhelm Siegel and Edmund Stoll in 1846, and was almost as important as the Kistner firm: it published works by Schumann, Spohr and Rubinstein and good light music, also issuing the popular collection *Der Opernfreund*. Under the direction of the elder Richard Linnemann (from 1870) it developed alongside the flourishing choral society movement in Germany. In 1903 Linnemann's sons bought E. W. Fritzsch's book and music publishing firm and subsequently brought out a substantial amount of Wagner literature. Distinguished musicologists collaborated closely with the firm, which had issued about 30,000 items by 1943. Severe war damage led to the decline of the Leipzig firm. In 1948 the firm of Fr. Kistner & C. F. W. Siegel & Co. was founded in Lippstadt, later moving to Porz; its publications include musicological literature and choral and organ music.

Verzeichnis des Musikalien-Verlags Fr. Kistner in Leipzig (Leipzig, 1894–1905; suppls. 1907, 1909, 1911, 1913); R. Linnemann, ed.: *Verlags-Verzeichnis von C. F. W. Siegels Musikalienhandlung* (Leipzig, 1903); idem: *Fr. Kistner 1823/1923: ein Beitrag zur Geschichte des deutschen Musik-Verlages* (Leipzig, 1923); W. Lott, ed.: *Musik aus vier Jahrhunderten, 1400–1800* (Leipzig, 1932); Z. Lissa: 'Chopin im Lichte des Briefwechsels von Verlegern seiner Zeit gesehen', *FAM*, vii (1960), 46; Plesske (1968); J. Kallberg: 'Chopin in the Marketplace: Aspects of the International Music Publishing Industry in the First Half of the Nineteenth Century', *Notes*, xxxix (1982–3), 535, 795

H.-M.P.

Kjos, Neil A. American firm of publishers. It was founded in 1936 in Chicago, moving to Park Ridge, Illinois, in 1957 and partially to San Diego in 1974, where it has been exclusively based since 1985. Its publications include piano methods, class band materials and choral and orchestral editions.

D.W.K.

Klemm [Klemme, Klemmio, Klemmius], **Johann** (*b* Oederan, nr. Zwickau, *c*1595; *d* ?Dresden, after 1651). German composer, organist and publisher. In 1605 he became a choirboy in the chapel of the electoral court at Dresden and in 1612 was appointed an instrumentalist there. The following year he went to Augsburg to study at the elector's expense with the renowned organist Christian Erbach, with whom he remained until at least 1615. When he returned to Dresden, he started working at composition under Schütz; this led to a long-lasting association between the two men typical of the close ties that Schütz formed with many of his pupils. In 1625 he was appointed court organist. He also became active as a music publisher, first in partnership with Daniel Weixer, later with Alexander Hering. His publications included some of his own music as well as collections by Schütz (the second set of *Symphoniae sacrae*, 1647, and the *Geistliche Chormusik*, 1648). In 1631 he brought out at his own expense the *Partitura seu Tabulatura italica*, a collection of 36 fugues for two,

three and four voices in the traditional 12 modes, suitable for organ or any other instruments. The fugues were printed in open score, a comparative novelty in Germany, where keyboard players were accustomed to reading from German organ tablature. Klemm followed here the example of many Italian publications (hence the 'Italian Tabulature' of the alternative title), which, while perhaps more cumbersome for the performer, allowed clearer presentation of the contrapuntal structure. The open-score layout, the strict modal part-writing 'abstaining from chromatic writing and diminutions' (to quote the postscript), indeed the entire nature of the work, all point to a deliberate attempt to provide a pedagogical model of instrumental *prima prattica* in line with the teachings of Schütz, stressing traditional strict counterpoint as the foundation of all compositional technique: in fact Klemm credited Schütz with instigating this work.

L. Schierning: *Die Überlieferung der deutschen Orgel- und Klaviermusik* (Kassel, 1961), 15; W. Apel: *Geschichte der Orgel- und Klaviermusik bis 1700* (Kassel, 1967; Eng. trans., rev. 1972), 386

A.S. (iii)

Klukowski, Franciszek (*b* Zduny, Poznań, 1770; *d* Warsaw, 6 Feb 1830). Polish bookseller and publisher. From about 1816 he managed a music bookshop in Warsaw, which sold Polish and foreign music and also engravings of composers and virtuosos. Later he established a publishing house, at first adopting the old engraving techniques but turning gradually towards lithographic processes. He published works by many Polish composers, including Elsner, Kurpiński, Stefani and Damse, and piano miniatures, arias and opera excerpts from abroad; he also produced several educational books. After his death the firm was taken over by his nephew Ignacy Klukowski (1803–65), who directed it until 1858.

M. Prokopowicz: 'Klukowski, Franciszek', *PSB*; K. Bielska: 'Klukowski Franciszek', *Słownik pracowników książki polskiej* [Dictionary of Polish printers] (Warsaw and Łódź, 1972) M. Prokopowicz: 'Wydawnictwo muzyczne Klukowskich', *Rocznik Warszawski*, xiii (1975), 135

K.M. (i)

Knight, Charles (*b* Windsor, 15 March 1791; *d* Addlestone, Surrey, 9 March 1873). English publisher. In London from 1823, he was a pioneer of popular literature; his journalistic skill, social commitment and shrewd commercial sense made him one of the most powerful forces in 19th-century English publishing. From 1827 he supervised the educational publications of the Society for the Diffusion of Useful Knowledge, many in serial form. His best-known work, the *Penny Magazine* (1832–45), reached an unprecedented sale of nearly 200,000 copies a week in 1832. In music his importance is linked with that of William Clowes, whose music printing methods and marketing strategy in *The Harmonicon* (monthly, 1823–33) Knight adopted and improved in its direct (cheaper) successor, the *Musical Library* (weekly, 1834–7). Aiming the finest musical works (including Elizabethan song) at an amateur, domestic market, Knight succeeded in his plan to reach a wider audience: the *Musical Library* found roughly 12 times as many buyers as *The Harmonicon*, and it was popular enough to be reissued from stereotyped plates in the 1840s and 1850s.

C. Knight: *Passages of a Working Life During Half a Century* (London, 1864–5); H. Curwen: *A History of Booksellers, the Old and the New* (London, 1873), 251; S. Bennett: 'Revolutions in Thought: Serial Publication and the Mass Market for Reading', *The Victorian Periodical Press: Samplings and Soundings*, ed. J. Shattock and M. Wolff (Leicester, 1982), 225; L. Langley: *The English Musical Journal in the Early Nineteenth Century* (diss., U. of North Carolina, 1983)

L.L.

Kriesstein [Kriegstein]**, Melchior** (*b* Basle, *c*1500; *d* Augsburg, 1572 or 1573). German printer. He was probably the son of the Georg Kriechstein cited as a printer in the Basle records of 1502. By 1525 Kriesstein had moved to Augsburg, where tax records from 1527 to 1573 list his name. After his death his son-in-law, Valentin Schönig, continued the business. Kriesstein's output was relatively small, and he is known mainly for his publication of Paul Hektor Mair's genealogy of Augsburg families, *Augsburger Geschlechterbuch* (1550), and of the collections of sacred music, mainly motets, but also a few masses and sacred lieder, edited by Sigmund Salminger and Johann Kugelmann, which contain numerous first editions and *unica* by German and Netherlands composers. He also printed single works by Johannes Frosch, Ulrich Brätel and Mouton. Since Salminger edited even these items, Kriesstein himself was probably not musically trained. In addition he printed various pamphlets, including reports of military actions against the Turks.

A. Schmid: *Ottaviano dei Petrucci da Fossombrone und seine Nachfolger im sechzehnten Jahrhunderte* (Vienna, 1845/R1968), 162; B. A. Wallner: *Musikalische Denkmäler der Steinätzkunst des 16. und 17. Jahrhunderts* (Munich, 1912); A. Dresler: *Augsburg und die Frühgeschichte der Presse* (Munich, 1952), 24; F. Krautwurst: 'Kriesstein, Melchior', *MGG* [incl. list of publications]

M.L.G.

Krzyżanowski, Stanisław Andrzej (*b* Laszki Wielkie, nr. Lwów, 15 Feb 1836; *d* Kraków, 11 Oct 1922). Polish bookseller and publisher. From 1855 he worked in various bookshops in Lwów, Chernovtsy, Leipzig and Kraków, where in 1870 he founded his own bookshop and swiftly developed it into one of the leading Polish music firms. He specialized in publishing the music of contemporary Polish composers, including Gall, Noskowski, Szopski, Żeleński, Friedman, Niewiadomski, Swierzyński and Wroński. His bookshop also imported the lastest editions from abroad, and provided a music lending library, amounting to 16,000 items in 1885. From 1879 Krzyżanowski also managed a concert bureau, organizing performances in Kraków by many prominent virtuosos, notably Anton Rubinstein (1879), Joachim and Brahms (1880), Paderewski (1883 and later), Sarasate, Hofmann, Friedman, Ysaÿe and others. The versatility of Krzyżanowski's firm was of great importance to musical life in Kraków, and his bookshop soon became an artistic centre. In 1908 the firm was taken over by his son Marian Krzyżanowski (1880–1964), who directed it to 1964, from 1950 solely as a second-hand bookshop.

J. Reiss: *Almanach muzyczny Krakowa*, i (Kraków, 1939), 154; B. Łopuszański and F. Pieczątkowski: 'Krzyżanowski, Stanisław, *Słownik pracowników książki polskiej* [Dictionary of Polish printers] (Warsaw and Łódź, 1972), 479

K.M. (i)

Kunkel, Charles (*b* Sipperfeld, 22 July 1840; *d* St Louis, MO, 3 Dec 1923). American pianist and publisher of German birth. He went to the USA with his father and brother, Jacob (1846–82), in 1848, and settled in Cincinnati. He studied with Thalberg and Gottschalk, and played duets with Gottschalk in the latter's recitals. In 1868 the Kunkel brothers moved to St Louis, where they established a music shop, publishing business and the periodical *Kunkel's Music Review* (1878–1906), which included articles and sheet music. Kunkel founded the St Louis Conservatory of

Music in 1872 and Kunkel's Popular Concerts (1884–1900). He was also a composer.

E. C. Krohn: 'Charles Kunkel and Louis Moreau Gottschalk', *Bulletin of the Missouri Historical Society*, xxi/4 (1965), 284, repr. in *Missouri Music* (New York, 1971), 280; P. G. Tipton: *The Contributions of Charles Kunkel to Musical Life in St. Louis* (diss., Washington U., 1978); E. C. Krohn: *Music Publishing in St. Louis* (Warren, MI, 1988)

J.M.B. (ii)

Kunst- und Industrie-Comptoir [Bureau des Arts et d'Industrie]. Austrian firm of publishers. It was founded in Vienna in 1801 by Josef Anton Kappeller, a Tyrolean painter, and Jakob Holer, who dealt mainly in fine art, maps and music. Because of illness, Kappeller had to leave the firm on 12 March 1802; the artistic direction was transferred with the deed of partnership to the writer Joseph Schreyvogel (later secretary of the Hofburg Theatre). Joseph Sonnleithner and Johann Sigmund Rizy invested in the enterprise as sleeping partners. The firm was known by its German title, as Bureau des Arts et d'Industrie, and as Contojo d'Arti e d'Industria. From 1807 Schreyvogel directed it alone, and on 16 May that year he took over J. Legrer's bookshop in Pesth, Vacznergasse, which took the name of Schreyvogel & Co. in 1808; it was managed by Josef Riedl, 1808–12 and 1815–22, and by Sigmund Rabus, 1812–15. In 1811 Jakob Holer again became a partner in the Kunst- und Industrie-Comptoir, with Riedl.

Schreyvogel was not as effective in business as he was in artistic pursuits, and the enterprise became bankrupt (probably also partly because of Holer's unreliability) and was continued by Riedl, who was granted the concession on 18 March 1814. The firm had closed by May 1823, and the music publishing rights passed to S. A. Steiner & Co., who from 1826 brought out editions from the old plates but with new title-pages and the mark 'S.u.C.H.'.

Schreyvogel published works by many well-known composers of the time, including Beethoven (among them opp.53, 58–62), Albrechtsberger, L. von Call, Eberl, Prince Louis Ferdinand of Prussia, Förster, Mauro Giuliani, Gyrowetz, Hummel, Krommer, Krufft, Méhul, Mozart, Pixis, Domenico Scarlatti, Steibelt and Vanhal.

C. von Wurzbach: *Biographisches Lexikon des Kaiserthums Oesterreich* (Vienna, 1856–91); R. Eitner: *Buch- und Musikalienhändler* (Leipzig, 1904); C. Junker: *Festschrift zur Feier des hundertjährigen Bestehens der Korporation . . . 1807–1907* (Vienna, 1907); C. Pichler: *Denkwürdigkeiten aus meinem Leben*, i (Munich, 1914), 564; F. Gräffer: *Kleine Wiener Memoiren und Wiener Dosenstücke*, i (Munich, 1917), 294; J. Stáva: 'Jos. Ant. Kappeller als Gründer des "Kunst- und Industrie-Comptoir zu Wien" ', *Tiroler Almanach* (1926), 93; Deutsch (1946); G. Kinsky and H. Halm: *Das Werk Beethovens: thematisch-bibliographisches Verzeichnis seiner sämtlichen vollendeten Kompositionen* (Munich and Duisburg, 1955); A. Weinmann: 'Vollständiges Verlagsverzeichnis der Musikalien des Kunstund Industrie Comptoirs in Wien', *SMw*, xxii (1955), 217–52; idem: *Magyar zene a bécsi zeneműpiacon 1770–1850* (Budapest, 1969); I. Mona: *Hungarian Music Publication 1774–1867* (Budapest, 1973); idem: *Magyar zeneműkiadók és tevékenységük 1774–1867* [Hungarian music publishers and their activity] (Budapest, forthcoming)

A.W., I.M.

L

Labaun [Laboun]. Family of printers. Jiří Labaun had a printing works in Prague, probably from 1686 to 1708 (some authors extend the time from 1687 or 1688 to 1710 or 1713); besides prayers, sermons, disputations, calendars, legal and other documents he also printed music by such composers as Holan Rovenský and Wentzely. After his death his son Jiří Ondřej took over the business and continued to publish music, including a new edition of Holan Rovenský's *Kaple královská zpěvní a muzikální* and works by Brenntner and Gunther Jakob. After Jiří Ondřej's death his widow continued the business; she printed Černohorský's *Laudetur Jesus Christus* and Vaňura's *Litaniae lauretanae*. The printing works, which remained in the Labaun family until probably 1769, also produced a series of occasional songs.

ČSHS; J. Volf: *Dějiny českého knihtiskařství do roku 1848* [History of Czech book printing to 1848] (Prague, 1926); K. Chyba: *Slovník knihtiskařů v Československu od nejstarších dob do roku 1860* [Dictionary of printers in Czechoslovakia from early times to 1860] (Prague, 1966–); J. Černý and others: *Hudba v českých dějinách* [Music in Czech history] (Prague, 1983), 204

Z.C.

La Chevardière, Louis Balthazard de (*b* Volx, Feb 1730; *d* Verrières-le-Buisson, 8 April 1812). French publisher. Advertisements for musical works in various periodicals in October 1758 mark the start of his activities as a music publisher. He took over the business which Jean-Pantaléon Le Clerc had passed on to his daughter Mme Vernadé. By December 1758 La Chevardière referred to himself as the 'successeur de M. Le Clerc'. Huberti seems to have been briefly associated with him in 1759 for both their names appear on the title-page of Philidor's *Blaise de Savetier* ('Paris, de La Chevardière et Huberti, successeurs de M. Leclerc'). Thereafter La Chevardière worked alone until 1780. On 5 February he handed over the management of the shop to his daughter Elisabeth-Eléonore and his son-in-law Jean-Pierre Deroullède for three years; he finally sold the business to Pierre Leduc on 1 December 1784. He then retired to Verrières, where he became mayor of the municipality.

La Chevardière showed great eclecticism in the works he published: both fashionable music (quadrilles, minuets, vaudevilles, rondos, ariettas, songs, and airs from *opéras comiques*) and more serious (chamber music, symphonies, sacred music and treatises). Haydn, J. C. Bach, Stamitz, Toeschi, Cannabich, Locatelli, Boccherini (for illustration *see* p.312), Jommelli, Pergolesi, Gossec, Grétry, Philidor, Duni, Monsigny and La Borde are among the composers represented in his catalogues. La Chevardière was one of the first French publishers to bring out weekly music magazines and most of the symphonies he published were presented in the form of periodical publications.

M. Brenet: 'Les débuts de l'abonnement musical', *BSIM*, ii (1906), 19; Hopkinson (1954); Johansson (1955); V. Fédorov: 'Louis-Balthasar de La Chevardière', *MGG*; Devriès and Lesure (1979–88)

A.D. (i)

Laet, Jean [Jan] **de** [Latius, Joannes; Latio, Giovanni] (*b* Stabroeck, *c*1525; *d* Antwerp, *c*1567). Flemish printer. He became a citizen of Antwerp in 1545 and began to print in the same year. In 1553 he registered in the Guild of St Luke under the name Jan van Stabroeck. He printed Bibles, histories, Spanish books, classical texts and, from 1554, a number of music books, either in conjunction with the Antwerp teacher and composer Hubert Waelrant, who acted as the music editor, or on his own. Together, in the years 1554–6, Waelrant and Laet published eight books of motets and four books of chansons by various composers. Alone, Laet brought out a number of music publications including Lassus's motets in 1556, the year of the composer's visit to Antwerp; thus he was one of Lassus's first publishers. Laet was on good terms with the Antwerp printer and typecutter Ameet Tavernier. He sold books printed by Tavernier and in 1566 bought some type from him. It is likely that the elegant music type used by Laet was designed by Tavernier, for it also occurs in a book published by Tavernier's widow. After Laet's death, his widow published several music books, including a reprint of Bakfark's first book for lute.

For illustration *see* WAELRANT, HUBERT.

Goovaerts (1880); A. Davidsson: *Musikbibliographische Beiträge* (Uppsala, 1954), 15; W. Boetticher: *Orlando di Lasso und seine Zeit* (Kassel and Basle, 1958); E. Roobaert and A. Moerman: 'Jean de Laet', *De gulden passer*, xxxiv (1961), 188; H.D.L. Vervliet: *Sixteenth Century Printing Types of the Low Countries* (Amsterdam, 1968); S. Bain: *Music Printing in the Low Countries in the Sixteenth Century* (diss., U. of Cambridge, 1974)

S.B.(i)

Laforge, Pierre (*fl* 1834–51). Brazilian publisher of French origin. From 1834 he worked in Rio de Janeiro as an engraver for J. B. Klier, a German clarinettist formerly of the imperial chapel in Bremen who published the first Brazilian music periodicals. In 1836 Laforge established his own *estamparia de musica*; he published modinhas, lundus and arias for the chief composers in Brazil and became the country's most prolific music publisher. In 1851 he sold his firm to Salmon & Cia, which issued piano, flute and vocal music before in turn being acquired by Narcizo José Pinto Braga in 1869.

Enciclopédia de música brasileira: erudita, folclórica e popular, i (São Paulo, 1977), 54; *Música no Rio de Janeiro Imperial 1822–1870: Exposição comemorativa do primeiro decênio da Seção de Música e Arquivo Sonoro* (Rio de Janeiro, 1982), 74

R.S. (ii)

Langinger, Herman (*b* Spas, 1908; *d* Hollywood, Dec 1979). American music engraver of Austrian birth. He studied the violin as a child before his family emigrated to

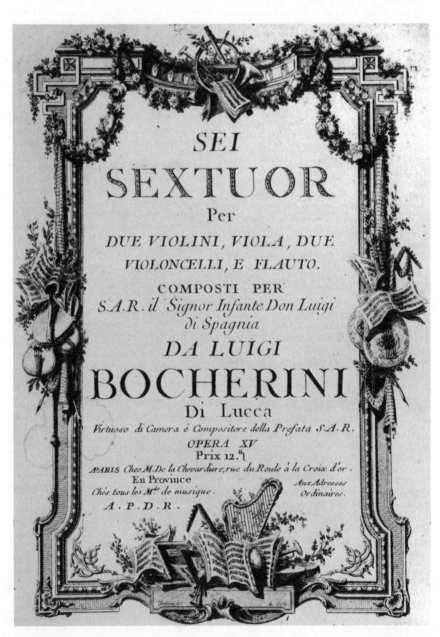

Title-page of the 'Sei Sextuor' by Boccherini, published by La Chevardière in 1775 as op.15 (Boccherini's op.16)

America, settling in Chicago. As a teenager, he was apprenticed to a music engraving firm and continued to play and teach the violin and harmony. He organized and played in the Langinger String Quartet and conducted the Langinger Symphony Orchestra in 1924, moving to New York in 1927 to continue his studies and to work in Carl Fischer's publishing house. After meeting Charles Ives there in 1928, Langinger assisted the composer in the publication of some of his most adventurous music. He moved to San Francisco in the 1930s and established the Golden West Music Press, which sustained itself by printing music for the film industry while also engraving for Henry Cowell's New Music publications (notably works by Ives, Varèse, Ruggles, Harris and Schoenberg), satisfying Langinger's interest in innovatory music. When Cowell was sent to prison in 1936, he left New Music to be run by the composer Gerald Strang and Langinger. After the film studios moved to Los Angeles Langinger moved his business to Hollywood, in 1938. There he and Strang continued New Music projects until Cowell was released and left for New York in 1940. In the early 1970s Langinger changed the name of his business to Highland Music Press, which he managed until his sudden death from a heart attack.

V. Perlis: *Two Men for Modern Music* (New York, 1978)

V.P.

La Sirène. French firm of publishers. It was founded as Editions de la Sirène in Paris in 1918, establishing a reputation from the outset for publishing new music, and in 1918 published Jean Cocteau's book *Le Coq et l'Arlequin*, with illustrations by Picasso. The firm's most celebrated publication is Stravinsky's piano transcription of his *Ragtime*, with its outstanding cover lithograph by Picasso (see illustration); it was published in 1919 in an edition of 1000 numbered copies. The following year La Sirène published Milhaud's *Le boeuf sur le toit*, with a cover lithograph by Dufy. Other important early publications include Satie's *Socrate* and Poulenc's *Bestiaire*. In about 1918 La Sirène purchased the stock of Paul Dupont, whose firm, established in 1891, was later known as the Société Nouvelle d'Editions Musicales. Dupont's publications included Debussy's Nocturne for piano (1892) and Claude Terasse's operetta *Panthéon-Courcelles* (1899; with a pictorial cover by Terasse's brother-in-law Pierre Bonnard). In 1927 Michel Dillard became director; under his leadership the firm published music by

Conrad Beck, Jean Françaix, Martinů, Nabokov, Tansman and others. In about 1927 the firm became known as La Sirène Musicale; it was acquired by Editions Max Eschig of Paris in 1936.

Hopkinson (1954); J. J. Fuld and F. Barulich: 'Harmonizing the Arts: Original Graphic Designs for Printed Music by World-famous Artists', *Notes*, xliii (1986–7), 259

N.S.

Lausch, Laurenz (*fl* late 18th century). Austrian music copyist and publisher. He began his career in Vienna on 27 March 1782 as a music copyist and subsequently developed a prominent copying business; by 13 August 1783, when he moved his premises to the Kärntnerstrasse, he was calling himself a music publisher (though the business at that time handled only the retail sale of printed and manuscript music). A few publications appeared between 1797 and 1801. The first printed edition of Haydn's *Gott erhalte den Kaiser* was probably published by Lausch, although it does not bear his imprint. He advertised in the *Wiener Zeitung* only the many works of which he had made manuscript copies; among these were a complete set of parts of Mozart's *Le nozze di Figaro* (announced 1 July 1786) and a similar set for *Don Giovanni* (24 May 1788). The German war-song κ539, written on 5 March 1788, was offered for sale by Lausch as early as 19 March in parts and vocal score.

Weinmann (1956); idem: *Wiener Musikverlag 'am Rande'* (Vienna, 1970); Fuld (1966, 3/1985)

A.W.

Lauterbach & Kuhn. German firm of publishers. It was founded in Leipzig in 1902 by Karl Lauterbach and Max Kuhn. In the same year, the firm began its relationship with Max Reger, publishing most of his works from op.66 to op.103, including three of the composer's greatest variation sets, on themes by Bach (op.81), Beethoven (op.86) and Hiller (op.100). Reger's Sinfonietta for orchestra op.90 (1905), dedicated to 'meinem lieben Freunden Karl Lauterbach und Dr. Max Kuhn', was published by the firm. In 1903 it began an important series of posthumous Hugo Wolf publications, including *Penthesilea* (in a truncated edition by Josef Hellmesberger) and the *Italian Serenade*, both issued in full scores and in arrangements for piano duet by Reger. These were followed by the String Quartet, the incidental music for *Das Fest auf Solhaug*, *Christnacht* and the *Lieder aus der Jugendzeit* (edited by Ferdinand Foll). The firm's publications usually have highly distinctive *Jugendstil* title-pages and outer wrappers.

Front cover by Picasso for the first edition (1919) of Stravinsky's piano arrangement of his 'Rag-time'

A distinguished but short-lived company, Lauterbach & Kuhn was bought by Bote & Bock at the end of 1908.

M. Reger: 'Hugo Wolf's künstlerischer Nachlass', *Süddeutsche Monatshefte*, i/2 (1904); F. Stein: *Thematisches Verzeichnis der im Druck erschienenen Werke von Max Reger einschliesslich seiner Bearbeitungen und Ausgaben* (Leipzig, 1953)

N.S.

Lavenu. English family of publishers and musicians, active in London. Lewis Lavenu (*d* London, 17 Aug 1818), a flautist, was in business as a music publisher in London from early 1796. From 1802 to 1808 he was in partnership with Charles Mitchell, the firm being known as Lavenu & Mitchell. At Lavenu's death his widow Elizabeth Lavenu succeeded to the business. She married the violinist Nicolas Mori as her second husband in 1819, and he continued the firm as Mori & Lavenu from about 1827.

Mori was succeeded at his death in June 1839 by his stepson Louis Henry Lavenu (*b* London, 1818; *d* Sydney, 1 Aug 1859), who had played the cello professionally before becoming a partner in the family firm. He maintained the firm until 1844 when it was taken over by Addison & Hodson. Lavenu also composed and published a few of his songs and short piano pieces; but, dissatisfied with his position, he emigrated to Australia and became music director at the theatre in Sydney.

The house of Lavenu was among the most prolific music publishing firms of the early 19th century, with a wide range of new vocal and instrumental music in its catalogue. It also ran a circulating music library, and by 1808 had obtained royal patronage as music sellers to the Prince of Wales.

Humphries and Smith (1954, 2/1970)

P.W.J.

Leader & Cock. English firm of publishers, active in London. Frederick Christopher Leader, trading in 1842 at 63 Old Bond Street, became in 1843 a partner of James Lamborn Cock, a close friend of Sterndale Bennett. The firm published many Bennett works, including *The May Queen* (1858), the Piano Sonata op. 46 (1862) and his edition of Bach's *St Matthew Passion*, as well as works by Benedict (*Undine*, 1860), Hatton and Smart. Art songs were a particular speciality of the firm. After the partnership ceased in 1862 Cock was briefly a partner with Charles L. Hutchings, later with Robert Addison, and then traded

alone from about 1870 to 1883. Some 35,000 engraved plates from the company's stock were auctioned on 14 November 1864; five later auctions followed, between 1872 and 1887.

J. R. S. Bennett: *The Life of William Sterndale Bennett* (Cambridge, 1907); Humphries and Smith (1954, 2/1970); J. B. Coover: 'The Dispersal of Engraved Music Plates and Copyrights in British Auctions, 1831–1931', *Richard S. Hill: Tributes from Friends* (Detroit, 1987), 223–306; Coover (1988)

D.W.K.

Le Bé, Guillaume (*b* Troyes, 1525; *d* Paris, 1598). French typecutter. He became an apprentice at the age of 15 in the household of Robert Estienne, where he learnt from Claude Garamond the art of cutting punches. After a five-year stay in Italy he returned to Paris at the end of 1550. There he worked for Garamond and then in 1552 set up in business as one of the first independent typefounders; his last type was cut in 1592.

Le Bé was well known for his Hebrew types, but his Roman and Greek types were almost as popular. Between 1554 and 1559 he engraved three music types on commission from the firm of Le Roy & Ballard (illustrated on f.26 of his type specimen book, annotated in his own hand, Paris, Bibliothèque Nationale nouv.acq.fr.4528). A fourth music type attributed to Le Bé is listed in an 18th-century inventory of the successor firm of Ballard. A plainsong music type was cut by him but evidently not sold to Le Roy & Ballard, since it is listed as still a part of Le Bé's stock in an inventory drawn up at the time of his death. This inventory also lists music punches and matrices of all kinds designed by other makers; many of these are unidentified, but several are attributed to Attaingnant, Danfrie, Granjon, Villiers and Du Chemin.

After Le Bé's death his son Guillaume (*c*1563–1645) and subsequently his grandson, also Guillaume (*d* 1685), inherited the business. They were also typecutters but probably did not make any new music types; nevertheless they continued to sell from the stock of punches and matrices they inherited. The foundry was sold by the Le Bé heirs in 1730. A document in the hand of the second Guillaume Le Bé, with additions in a later hand, known as the Le Bé Memorandum, traces the history of type making, particularly in France. It contains references (not always accurate) to music types cut by Granjon, Sanlecque, Jean Jannon and Du Chemin. For specimens of Le Bé's types *see* GANDO.

H. Omont: 'Spécimens de caractères hébreux, grecs, latins et de musique gravés à Venise et à Paris par Guillaume Le Bé (1546–1574)', *Mémoires de la Société de l'historie de Paris et de l'Ile de France*, xv (1888), 273; E. Howe: 'The Le Bé Family', *Signature*, viii (1938), l; F. Lesure and G. Thibault: *Bibliographie des éditions d'Adrian Le Roy et Robert Ballard (1551–1598)* (Paris, 1955), suppl. *RdM*, xl (1957), 166; S. Morison: *L'inventaire de la fonderie Le Bé* (Paris, 1957); H. Carter: *Sixteenth-century French Typefounders: the Le Bé Memorandum* (Paris, 1967); D. Heartz: *Pierre Attaingnant, Royal Printer of Music* (Berkeley and Los Angeles, 1969), 48

S.F.P.

Le Chevalier, Amédée (*b* Savoy, *c*1650; *d* Amsterdam, bur. 5 Dec 1720). French musician, publisher and printer. He set himself up in Amsterdam as 'muziek-meester' and on 1 December 1689 obtained a 15-year licence for music publication. On 24 July 1690 he made an agreement with D. Robethon, by which the latter promised to finance the production of 1000 copies of his first publication, *Les trios des opéra de Monsieur de Lully*. This was printed in Amsterdam by Blaeu, who worked for Le Chevalier until Le Chevalier himself became established as a printer in 1692. His publications are known from the catalogue at the end of J. de Gouy's *Airs à quatre parties sur la paraphrase des pseaumes* (1691) and from two advertisements in the *Amsterdamsche courant* (27 December 1691 and 1 July 1692). The second of these states that Le Chevalier sold not only his own publications but also music printed by A. Pointel. Le Chevalier's catalogue regularly included editions of *airs* and other compositions by C. Rosier, J. Schenck and others. In 1698 the magistrate in Ghent allowed him to establish himself in the city as a music printer without going through the prescribed period of apprenticeship. According to vander Straeten, he had returned to the Netherlands by 1702.

E. vander Straeten: *La musique aux Pays-Bas avant le XIXe siècle* (Brussels, 1867–88/R1969), v (1880), 243, 410; Goovaerts (1880); D. F. Scheurleer: 'Eene Amsterdamsche uitgave van Lully en Colasse 1690', *TVNM*, ix/4 (1914), 250; I.H. Van Eeghen: *De Amsterdamse boekhandel 1680–1725*, iii (Amsterdam, 1965), 202

H.V.

Le Clerc, Charles-Nicolas (*b* Sézanne en Brie, 20 Oct 1697; *d* Paris, 20 Oct 1774). French publisher and violinist, brother of Jean-Pantaléon Le Clerc. The brothers have often been confused owing to the similarity of their activities and the infrequent use of Jean-Pantaléon's first name. Charles-Nicolas Le Clerc's name appears for the first time in the list of violinists of the Académie Royale de Musique in 1729 and in that of the 24 Violons du Roi in

1732. He held the former post until 22 May 1750 and the latter until 1761. His talents as a violinist were frequently mentioned during that period in accounts of concerts published in the *Mercure de France*.

Le Clerc began publishing music in 1736 and remained in the business until his death; the first privileges registered in his name date from 9 March 1736 and 17 November 1738; his first catalogue (1738) shows an impressive list of works. His shop was in the rue St-Honoré and bore the signs 'A la Ville de Constantinople' (1737–8), 'A l'Image Ste Geneviève' (1759–60) and 'A Ste Cecile' (1760–74). The fact that he specialized in music publishing indicates that he was something of a pioneer, and also distinguishes his career from that of his brother and the Boivin dealers (primarily commission agents). The only works he sold to the public were those he had commissioned and had engraved. After 1760 he became a commission agent. He was the first in France to have the idea of establishing a repertory of engraved works on which he had sole rights, following the principle which Ballard had been applying for generations with printed music. He published largely foreign music by well-known Italian, German and Flemish composers; some French composers (e.g. J.-M. Leclair and Guillemain) were also listed. Up to 1760 he published mainly instrumental music, later including *opéras comiques*, ariettas and *cantatilles*. His music stock was sold in lots by his widow a few months after his death. One lot was bought in December 1774 by Mathon de la Cour on behalf of the Bureau du Journal de Musique and another in February 1775 by the composer Taillart the elder.

M. Brenet: 'Quelques musiciens français du XVIIIème siècle; les Le Clerc', *RHCM*, vi (1906), 291; G. Cucuel: 'Notes sur quelques musiciens, luthiers, éditeurs et graveurs de musique au XVIIIe siècle', *SIMG*, xiv (1912–13), 243; Hopkinson (1954); M. Ruhnke: 'Die Pariser Telemann-Drucke und die Brüder LeClerc', *Quellengeschichte der Musik: Wolfgang Schmieder zum 70. Geburtstag* (Frankfurt, 1972), 149; A. Devriès: *Edition et commerce de la musique gravée à Paris dans la première moitié du XVIIIe siècle* (Geneva, 1976); Devriès and Lesure (1979–88)

A.D. (i)

Le Clerc, Jean-Pantaléon (*b* ?Sézanne en Brie, before 1697; *d* after 1760). French publisher and violinist. He lived at the 'Croix d'Or', rue du Roule, Paris, from 1728 to 1758. Having entered the 24 Violons du Roi on 17 July 1720, he remained a member until 1760. A periodical advertisement dated October 1728 announced the start of his career as a music commission agent. Up to 1753 his name was often associated with that of Boivin, both on the title-pages of works and in music advertisements. There seems to have been a tacit agreement between the two dealers; they shared the Parisian music market and the same works are listed in their respective catalogues. Their trade was supplied by the composers themselves, mainly by those having had their works engraved at their own expense. They also represented French and foreign publishers such as Ballard, Charles-Nicolas Le Clerc and Michel-Charles Le Cène.

Three catalogues dated 1734, 1737 and 1742 provide an inventory of the music on sale at the 'Croix d'Or'; the list is supplemented by a further undated catalogue published in 1751. Some of the works listed were commissioned by Le Clerc himself; they are recorded in the 'Registres des Privilèges' and in an engraved catalogue (the French national archives contain the only surviving copy attached to a deed dated 13 April 1752). Composers listed in this catalogue include Quantz, Telemann, Bourgouin, Croes, Lavaux, Wiseman, Deltour, Noblet and Bourgeois; chamber music, dances (minuets, quadrilles, airs) and songs represent the works published by Le Clerc. The rights on these works were acquired by his younger brother Charles-Nicolas on 13 April 1752.

On 7 June 1751 Le Clerc retired and handed over the commission agency to his daughter Anne-Cécile on her marriage to the organist Claude Vernadé. He authorized her to run the business under the name of Le Clerc and this explains the alternation of the names of Le Clerc, Le Clerc-Vernadé and Vernadé on the title-pages of works sold between 1751 and 1758. In 1758 La Chevardière took over from Mme Vernadé and described himself as the successor of M. Le Clerc.

It is possible that Le Clerc was also a composer. Some dances signed Le Clerc are contained in contemporary anthologies entitled *Nouveaux menuets français et italiens . . . mis en ordre par M. Leclerc* (Paris, 1730), but this is not sufficient evidence that he was the author. The last known reference to Le Clerc is a deed drawn up by a notary in 1760 which mentions that at that time he kept a haberdashery in Paris.

For bibliography *see* LE CLERC, CHARLES-NICOLAS.

A.D. (i)

Leduc. French firm of publishers, active in Paris. It was founded by the violinist Pierre Leduc (*b* Paris, 17 Oct 1755; *d* Bordeaux, 18 Oct 1826), who first advertised as a publisher in March 1775. His brother Simon (*b* Paris, 15 Jan 1742; *d* Paris, 22 Jan 1777) also published works under the Leduc name, but these were exclusively his own compositions, and the two businesses were not related. In 1782 Pierre enlarged his firm by acquiring the stock of Preudhomme and in 1784 took over La Chevardière. Many sources say that he also absorbed Venier in 1781 or 1782, but this is not correct; Venier was active until late 1782 at least, and his stock was acquired by Boyer in 1784. Leduc published a great variety of music, particularly orchestral and serious chamber music at first, then a quantity of less weighty material for amateurs during the 1790s.

His son Auguste (*b* Paris, 1779; *d* Paris, 25 May 1823) probably assumed the directorship of the publishing house at some time between April 1803 and January 1804 (Pierre Leduc disappeared from public life shortly thereafter). He established his business in Paris at 267 rue de la Loi, but in 1805–6 the house was renumbered 78, and in 1807 the street reverted to its pre-Revolutionary name of rue de Richelieu. After his death the firm was run by his second wife, Augustine-Julie Bernier, as Mme Veuve Leduc. In August 1830 one Pierrot advertised as her successor, and in 1831 she was bankrupted; but from 1835 to 1837 she was again in business, at 47 rue Neuve-Vivienne, before selling out to Janet Frères. Finally, in 1846, she was listed at 19 rue Vivienne.

Whereas Pierre Leduc had been active both in soliciting interesting new works and in reprinting from the plates acquired from other publishers, Auguste was comparatively unenterprising and not very prolific. He, and later his widow, published full scores of a handful of operas, including three by Carafa in the 1820s; each week he continued to issue (at least until 1821) the *Journal hebdomadaire*, a periodical collection of vocal music which had been started by La Chevardière in 1764. But the contents of the *Journal*, like most of Leduc's output, tended to be second-rate. Among his more significant publications were Choron's *Principes de composition des écoles d'Italie* (1808) and a reprint of the full scores, edited by Choron, of the 26 Haydn symphonies which his father had published in 1802–3. He must also be credited with a rare flash of enlightenment for putting out the song *Le dépit de la bergère* (*c*1820), probably Berlioz's first appearance in print. Almost all Leduc's publications were printed from engraved plates, but in about 1807 he flirted briefly with lithography – one of the earliest publishers to do so.

Hopkinson (1954); Johansson (1955); R. Cotte: 'Le Duc', *MGG*; B. S. Brook: *La symphonie française dans la seconde moitié du XVIIIe siècle* (Paris, 1962); A. Devriès: 'Deux dynasties d'éditeurs et de musiciens: les Leduc', *RBM*, xxviii–xxx (1974–6), 195; Devriès and Lesure (1979–88)

J.H., R.M.

Leduc, Alphonse. French firm of publishers. It was founded in Paris about 1842 by Alphonse Leduc (*b* Nantes, 11 March 1804; *d* Paris, 17 June 1868), who was not a blood relation of Pierre and Auguste Leduc. He studied at the Paris Conservatoire and became an excellent player of the bassoon, flute and guitar as well as a prolific composer. On his death he was succeeded by his son, Alphonse-Charles (*b* Paris, 29 May 1844; *d* Paris, 4 June 1892), whose widow, Emma, daughter of the pianist Henri Ravina, directed the firm from his death until 1902, when their son, Alphonse-Henri, called Emile (*b* Paris, 17 Nov 1878; *d* Paris, 24 May 1951), and Paul Bertrand took over. Emile's two sons, Claude-Alphonse and Gilbert-Alphonse, became his partners in 1938 and succeeded to the business in 1951. Trade has been carried on under the name Alphonse Leduc except for a brief period (1902–*c*1915) when the firm was styled 'Alphonse Leduc, Paul Bertand & Cie'; about 1915 Bertrand (*d* 1953) left to join Heugel.

The firm's first premises were at 14 rue Chabanais; by November 1842 they had moved to 8 rue Vivienne and by August 1844 to 78 passage Choiseul. In 1846 or 1847 the business of Auguste Leduc was acquired, and by May 1847 the firm had moved to 18 rue Vivienne. In 1852 it moved to 2 rue de la Bourse, in 1862 to 4 rue Ménars, in about 1866 to 35 rue Le Peletier, and in November 1874 to 3 rue de Grammont; in February 1929 it moved to 175 rue St-Honoré. Although its output has probably amounted to some 50,000 publications over a period of 135 years, few significant works from notable composers have been acquired. The chief importance and pride of the firm lies rather in its contribution to music teaching in France by the publication of numerous elementary and advanced instrumental and vocal methods and studies as well as a vast quantity of instrumental music. In December 1883 Leduc took over the weekly journal *Art musical* from Girod (who had acquired it from its founder Léon Escudier); its final appearance was in September 1894, after which it was absorbed by Maurice Kufferath's *Guide musical*.

Hopkinson (1954); Devriès and Lesure (1979–88)

R.M.

Lee, Samuel (*b* ?Dublin; *d* Dublin, 21 Feb 1776). Irish publisher and music seller, active in Dublin. He was the founder of the music shop and publishing firm which carried on business at Little Green, off Bolton Street (1752–63), the Harp and Hautboy, Fownes Street (1764–8), and 2 Dame Street (1769–1821); he also appeared regularly as a violinist, 1745–56. After his death in 1776 his widow Anne had charge of the firm, with their son Edmond as assistant; Edmond himself carried on the business thereafter until John Aldridge took it over in 1821. The business operated under the name Walker & Lee in 1781 and John Lee in 1789. John, another son of Samuel, traded as a publisher, music seller and instrument maker at 64 Dame Street (1775–8) and 70 Dame Street (1778–1803).

B.B.

Lee & Walker. American firm of publishers. It was established in Philadelphia in 1848 by George W. Lee (*d* 1875) and Julius Walker (*d* 1857) and in 1856 absorbed the business of George Willig (both men had worked as clerks in Willig's music shop). The firm published early editions of such patriotic songs as *Dixie* (1860) and *Columbia, the Gem of the Ocean* (1861), as well as popular songs and dance tunes, including the *Lincoln Quick Step* (1860), the *Home Run Quick Step* (1861) and several songs by Septimus Winner. After the death of Lee the firm's catalogue was purchased by Ditson; its name was continued by Lee's son Julius Lee jr, in partnership with J. F. Morrison.

B.T.

Leeds. American publisher. It was founded in New York about 1940 by Louis Levy. The firm acquired its identity several years later through affiliation with the Am-Rus Music Corp., also founded in 1940 and soon after managed by Eugene Weintraub (*b* 1904), which arranged for publication and performance of music by Prokofiev, Shostakovich, Kabalevsky and other Soviet composers. In 1949 Leeds was involved in a celebrated lawsuit involving Igor Stravinsky's revisions, most famously to the *Firebird* suite. In 1952 it began distributing recordings from the USSR, and in 1964, following its best year, Leeds was acquired by MCA for $4.5 million. Levy remains active in negotiations involving music publishers.

E. Weintraub: 'Battle of the Conductors', *Music Journal*, xxxiv/3 (1976), 16

D.W.K.

Le Menu. French firm of publishers. Christoph Le Menu de St Philbert (*c*1720–1780) began publishing in Paris in the 1740s by issuing his own compositions, including some *cantatilles*, motets and a *Méthode de musique*. In 1774 or 1775 he was succeeded by Mme Le Menu, who joined forces with Mme Boyer about 1776. In 1783 Mme Boyer was succeeded by her husband, who published works both with Mme Le Menu and alone and who acquired Venier's plates about 1784. In 1790 Mme Le Menu ceased her activities and the music publisher Lobry possibly took over her business; Boyer himself continued publishing until 1796, when he was succeeded by Naderman. At the beginning Le Menu had published mainly *cantatilles*, motets and *ariettes*. Later the number of instrumental works grew and included symphonies and concertos, but the firm's particular interest was in chamber music by contemporary French, Italian, German, Austrian and Bohemian composers.

Hopkinson (1954); Johansson (1955)

C.J.

Lemoine. French family of publishers. Antoine Marcel Lemoine (*b* Paris, 3 Nov 1753; *d* Paris, April 1817), a guitarist, author of a guitar method, violist, theatre orchestra director and composer, founded a firm in Paris in 1772; his publications included Méhul's *Messe solennelle*, composed for Napoleon's coronation (1804). His eldest son, François (*d* 1840), published independently under the name Lemoine *aîné* (1809–40, succeeded by his widow, 1841–51). Another son, Antoine Henry Lemoine (*b* Paris, 21 October 1786; *d* Paris, 18 May 1854), succeeded him in 1816. A successful piano teacher and a harmony student of Reicha, he published most of Chopin's music and firmly established the company's production of instructional materials with Berlioz's *Traité d'instrumentation* (1844) and his own methods for piano, harmony and solfège.

Achille-Philibert Lemoine (*b* Paris, 15 April 1813; *d* Sèvres, 13 Aug 1895), son of Antoine Henry Lemoine, became a partner in 1850 and was director from 1852 to 1895. In 1858 he added engraving and printing to the business and began publication of *Panthéon des pianistes* (about 600 compositions). He acquired Schönenberger's catalogue (1862) and in 1885 inaugurated a branch in Brussels with *Le chant classique*, edited by Gevaert. His four sons became partners in 1871. They were Henry-Félicien Lemoine (*b* Paris, 8 April 1848; *d* Paris, 24 April 1924), director from 1895 to 1924;

Gaston Lemoine (1852–1930); Léon Lemoine (*b* Paris, 1855; *d* Paris, 1916), who left the firm in 1900; and Achille Lemoine (1857–1948).

Henry Jean Lemoine (*b* Paris, 10 April 1890; *d* Paris, 20 Nov 1970), son of Gaston and successor to Henry-Félicien, entered the firm in 1907. He became a partner (1920) and director (1924–70). He acquired the extensive theatrical and symphonic catalogue of Lucien Grus in 1932. André Lemoine (*b* Paris, 5 April 1907), son of Henry-Félicien, became a partner (1946) and later co-director. Max Lemoine (*b* Paris, 27 June 1922), son of Henry Jean, became a partner (1955) and later also a co-director. Publications by Editions Henry Lemoine have continued to emphasize instruction, ballet and opera.

R.S.N.

Lengnick. English firm of publishers. It was founded in 1893 by Alfred Lengnick (*d* 1904) in London. Lengnick had been appointed the British agent for the N. Simrock catalogue, and the company expanded quickly. After his death the company was acquired by Schott and was incorporated as a limited company in 1924. Although it was sole British agent for several European publishers, its main success lay with the promotion of the Simrock catalogue, especially the works of Brahms and Dvořák. But it did maintain its own publishing programme, first specializing in educational music and later expanding to include symphonic and chamber works by contemporary British composers, including Alwyn, Arnold, Maconchy, Reizenstein, Rubbra, Simpson and Wordsworth. Alfred Lengnick & Co. eventually bought the complete Simrock catalogue up to and including 1954; the firm acts as British Commonwealth agent for CeBeDeM and Donemus. In 1964 it moved to South Croydon.

'Alfred Lengnick & Co.', *MO*, xxxv (1911–12), 805

A.P.(ii)

Leonard, Hal. American firm of publishers, based in Milwaukee, Wisconsin. It was founded in 1949 by Harold 'Hal' Edstrom, Everett 'Leonard' Edstrom and Roger Busdicker, all of Winona, Minnesota. The firm issues about 1200 publications a year and has a catalogue of more than 50,000, including choral works, simplified arrangements of pop music for electronic keyboard instruments and 'fake books'. Through vertical business integration it now specializes in printing and distributing music owned by other publishers, among them Music Sales (including G. Schirmer and Associated Music Publishers), Chappell Intersong and Rubank (originally of Chicago, now in Miami). 'The company maintains large printing facilities in Winona.

J.E.H.

Le Roy, Adrian (*b* Montreuil-sur-Mer, *c*1520; *d* Paris, 1598). French printer, lutenist and composer. He was born into a wealthy merchant family from northern France. As a young man he entered successively the service of two members of the aristocracy close to the French throne. He became acquainted with the editor Jean de Brouilly in Paris, bought some properties from him in St Denis and married his daughter Denise (*d* before 1570). He moved to Brouilly's house at the sign of Ste Geneviève (later the sign of Mount Parnassus) in the rue St Jean-de-Beauvais – an address which was to become famous as the home of one of the greatest of the French music printing establishments.

On 14 August 1551 Le Roy and his cousin Robert Ballard obtained a privilege from Henri II to print and sell all kinds of music books. Their first publication appeared at the end of the same month. On 16 February 1553, the king gave Le Roy & Ballard the title of royal music printer, which had been vacant since Attaingnant's death in 1552. The title was renewed in 1568 and 1594. The history of the firm was brilliant and its successor firms continued to dominate French music printing until the middle of the 18th century. Le Roy was the artistic director, while Ballard, who was nevertheless knowledgeable in music, apparently handled the business side. Le Roy survived Ballard by ten years.

Some of the printing firm's success can be attributed to the entrée both Le Roy and Ballard had to court circles, including the king himself. Le Roy was a regular member of the salon of the Countess of Retz. There he met artists, musicians and the poets Ronsard, Baïf and Melissus, who wrote dedicatory verses for some items.

Le Roy's friendship with musicians helped assure the firm's pre-eminence. Certon, Arcadelt, Le Jeune, Costeley and Goudimel were personal acquaintances. The most valuable friendship of all was that of Orlande de Lassus, who stayed in Le Roy's house during a visit to Paris and whom Le Roy introduced at court. A letter dated 14 January 1574, from Le Roy to Lassus, describes the delight that Charles IX took in Lassus's music and tells Lassus that the king

wanted to make him composer of the royal chamber and that he had urged Le Roy to print his music as soon as possible for fear that it otherwise might be lost. Le Roy & Ballard were chiefly responsible for making Lassus's music well known in France and for disseminating his newest works to the rest of the musical world; much of his music appeared in print there for the first time.

After Ballard's death in July 1588 the firm did not publish anything until 1591, when three books of songs appeared under Le Roy's name alone. After another pause publishing began again in 1593 and continued until Le Roy's death. During this period 15 more books were published, this time under the name of Adrian Le Roy and the widow of Ballard. Le Roy died childless, turning over his interest to Ballard's heirs.

Although Le Roy was respected as a composer and pedagogue, perhaps his most lasting contribution to music history is the influence he exercised as a publisher on musical taste. His firm had very little competition in France; the favour of four kings, Henri II, Charles IX, Henri III and Henri IV, assured the dominance of Le Roy & Ballard. These conditions, together with Le Roy's discrimination and experience as a musician and artistic director of the firm, gave him a dominating role in moulding French musical taste.

For illustration *see* BALLARD.

R. de Juvigny, ed.: *Les bibliothèques françoises de La Croix du Maine et de Du Verdier* (Paris, 1772), i, 8, iii, 25; A. Sandberger: 'Roland Lassus' Beziehungen zu Frankreich', *SIMG*, viii (1906–7), 355–401; L. de La Laurencie, A. Mairy and G. Thibault, eds.: *Chansons au luth et airs de cour français du XVIe siècle* (Paris, 1934), p.xxi; F. Lesure and G. Thibault: *Bibliographie des éditions d'Adrian Le Roy et Robert Ballard (1551–1598)* (Paris, 1955), suppl. *RdM*, xl (1957), 166; F. Lesure: 'Le Roy, Adrian', *MGG*; D. Heartz: 'Parisian Music Publishing under Henry II', *MQ*, xlvi (1960), 448; J. Cain and P. Marot, eds.: *Imprimeurs et libraires parisiens du XVIe siècle, d'après les manuscrits de Ph. Renouard*, ii (Paris, 1969); D. Heartz: *Pierre Attaingnant, Royal Printer of Music* (Berkeley and Los Angeles, 1969)

S.F.P.

Le Royer, Jean (*b* 1528; *d* before 1586). French bookseller, printer and woodengraver. He was active from 1554, becoming printer in mathematics to the king. Among a number of works unconnected with music, he printed two Huguenot psalters in 1560 and 1562. A Protestant, he fled to Geneva around 1576 and printed there between 1576 and 1582 a series of works by Lassus, Goudimel, Guillaume Boni, Jean Servin and Anthoine de

Bertrand – about 15 volumes in all. These publications never bore his name, and only sometimes his trade-mark. Some of them were produced for the Lyons bookseller Charles Pesnot. It seems that he was also an associate of the printer Pierre de St-André. Le Royer used music type and letter forms partly copied from the plant of the Parisian printer Le Roy & Ballard, and these were in turn reproduced in the plant of Jean de Laon. Most of Le Royer's printing work consists of spiritual contrafacta by the Protestant minister Simon Goulart. His music editions were the first in Geneva showing the same range and scope as those being produced in Paris and Lyons at the same period.

H. J. Bremme: *Buchdrucker und Buchhändler zur Zeit der Glaubenkämpfe: Studien zur Genfer Druckgeschichte 1565–1580* (Geneva, 1969); L. Guillo: *Recherches sur les éditions musicales lyonnaises de la Renaissance* (diss., Ecole Pratique des Hautes Etudes, Paris, 1986)

L.G.

Leuckart. German firm of publishers. It was founded in 1782 in Breslau by Franz Ernst Christoph Leuckart (1748–1817) and Johann Daniel Korn (the younger) as a fine-art and music shop. As F. E. C. Leuckart, the firm was notably successful in the third generation, when Constantin Sander (1826–1905) took over its management (1849). He made agreements with talented young composers (Robert Franz, Bruch), worked with Liszt, Ferdinand Hiller, Bülow and Thuille, and encouraged the music historian A. W. Ambros to write his *Geschichte der Musik*. The firm published organ works, instructional literature and dramatic works (including Bruch's *Loreley*, 1862), and encouraged the work of Eduard Kremser (*Altniederländisches Dankgebet*) and Thomas Koschat, the Carinthian folksong collector. In 1870 the firm moved to Leipzig where it was active in promoting individual compositions by Richard Strauss, including *Ein Heldenleben* op.40 (1899) and *Eine Alpensymphonie* op.64 (1915), along with works by Pfitzner and Reger. After the death of Constantin Sander, his son Martin (1859–1930) expanded the catalogue to include Catholic liturgical music, contemporary orchestral and chamber music, the collection *Leuckarts Hausmusik* and choral music (e.g. by Richard Trunk, Armin Knab and Hugo Kaun). For several decades the hospitable Sander home was a meeting-place for distinguished musicians visiting Leipzig for world and local premières. In 1930 Martin Sander's son Horst (1904–45) inherited the firm and increased its output to almost 10,000 items. It suffered war damage and moved from Leipzig in 1945, remaining in the family's possession and resuming its activities on the same lines in Munich in 1948.

175 *Jahre Musikverlag F. E. C. Leuckart: Verlagsgeschichte und Gesamtkatalog* (Munich, 1957); J. La Rue: 'Mozart Listings in some Rediscovered Sale-Catalogues', *MJb*, xv (1967), 16; idem: 'Ten Rediscovered Sale-Catalogues: Leuckart's Supplements, Breslau 1787–1792', *Musik und Verlag: Karl Vötterle zum 65. Geburtstag* (Kassel, 1968), 424; idem: 'Haydn Listings in the Rediscovered Leuckart Supplements', *Studies in Eighteenth-century Music: a Tribute to Karl Geiringer* (London, 1970), 310

H.-M.P.

Lienau. German firm of publishers. Emil Robert Lienau (*b* Neustadt, Holstein, 28 Dec 1838; *d* Neustadt, 22 July 1920) studied philosophy and music under Moscheles and Rietz in Kiel and Leipzig. In 1863 he joined the publishing business of Schlesinger in Berlin, bought it in 1864 and continued it under the old firm name, adding 'Robert Lienau'; in 1875 he bought the Viennese firm of Haslinger. He retired from the business in 1898 and handed the management of the firms to his sons, first to Robert Heinrich Lienau (*b* Neustadt, 27 July 1866; *d* Berlin, 8 Nov 1949), and from 1907 to Friedrich Wilhelm Lienau (*b* Berlin, 6 Jan 1876; *d* Vienna, 15 Nov 1973) as well. In 1910, when the firm owned more than 25,000 titles, the brothers acquired the Viennese publishing firm of Rättig, and later also the Berlin firms of Krentzlin (1919), Wernthal (1925) and Köster (1928). Friedrich Wilhelm Lienau withdrew from the Berlin business in 1938 and directed sections of Haslinger in Vienna as an independent firm. The business in Berlin is managed by Robert Heinrich Lienau's children, Rosemarie (from 1949) and Robert Lienau (from 1958).

The elder Robert Lienau carefully continued the classical tendency of the firm of Schlesinger (Beethoven, Weber, Chopin) with Bruckner's Eighth Symphony, and expanded the catalogue considerably (from the purchase of Haslinger) with works by Schubert, Johann Strauss (father and son), Lanner and Ziehrer. His sons followed with Sibelius (opp.46–57), Paul Juon and Philipp Jarnach, also including modern composers such as Hauer and Berg (opp. 1–2). The firm specializes in neglected operas (Cimarosa, Donizetti), music for recorder and guitar, musicological literature and school music.

Verzeichnis des Musik-Verlags der Schlesingerschen Buch- und Musikhandlung (Rob. Lienau) Berlin und des Carl Haslinger qdm. Tobias (Rob. Lienau) Wien

(Berlin and Vienna, 1890); W. Altmann, ed.: *J. Brahms: Briefwechsel*, xiv (Berlin, 1920); R. Lienau: *Erinnerungen an Johannes Brahms* (Berlin, 1934); Deutsch (1946); R. Elvers: *A. M. Schlesinger – Robert Lienau: 150 Jahre Musik-Verlag* (Berlin, 1960); *Musikverlage in der Bundesrepublik Deutschland und in West-Berlin* (Bonn, 1965); Plesske (1968)

R.E.

Lillenas. American publishing firm, and music trade name of the Church of the Nazarene. It was founded at Indianapolis in 1925 by the Norwegian Nazarene pastor Haldor Lillenas; in 1930 it moved to Kansas City, Missouri, as the music department of the Nazarene Publishing House. Its output includes vocal, instrumental and teaching materials (including the catalogue of Mosie Lister Publications, acquired in 1969), and official hymnals for the church (1931, 1952, 1972).

H. Lillenas: *Down Melody Lane: an Autobiography* (Kansas City, 1953)

G.H.S.

Lithographisches Institut. Austrian firm of publishers. It was established in Vienna and owned by Adolph Count von Pötting and Ferdinand Count Palffy von Erdöd, though managed during its relatively brief existence by Schubert's friend Franz von Schober (*b* 17 May 1798; *d* 13 Aug 1882), often wrongly named as an owner. The firm's first advertisement for printed music appeared in the *Wiener Zeitung* of 26 February 1821; there were two further announcements in the same year and three more in 1822. In 1823 the publishing activity increased: on 18 November the first issue of the series *Der neue Amphion* appeared, reaching 23 issues the following year. The editor was Friedrich Kanne (1778–1833), who from 1821 also edited the *Allgemeine musikalische Zeitung mit besonderer Rücksicht auf den österreichischen Kaiserstaat* (founded 1817), which he brought into the Lithographisches Institut in 1824.

The publishing programme, apart from single works by Payer, Sechter and Voříšek, reveals only Singspiels and works by insignificant composers, including several by Kanne himself. Schubert is represented by the *Lied an den Tod* (D518), which appeared as a supplement to the *Allgemeine musikalische Zeitung* on 26 June 1824 (separate edition on 2 July), and by four songs published in 1828 (D939, 909, 768, 881: later called op.96).

When the Chemische Druckerey and S. A. Steiner & Co. (*see* HASLINGER) changed to music engraving in 1821, the Lithograph-

isches Institut took over part of their lithographic production. In 1826 the firm seems to have ceased music publishing, though a retail shop continued until at least 1833.

A. Weiss: *Franz Schober* (Vienna, 1907); Weinmann (1956)

A.W.

Litolff. German firm of publishers. Gottfried Martin Meyer founded the firm on 1 June 1828 at Brunswick as a combined music press and shop; it soon grew into a flourishing business. After Meyer's death in 1849, his widow carried on the busines successfully and in 1851 she married the French composer and pianist Henry Litolff (1818–91), who became active in the firm. Later the name was changed to Henry Litolff's Verlag. An added impetus to the publishing was given by Litolff's extensive international connections and friendships with Berlioz, Fétis, Moscheles, Liszt, Bülow, the Wieniawski brothers, Heller, Joachim, Ernst and others. Meyer's son Theodor Litolff (1839–1912), who had been adopted by Henry Litolff, took over the business when his stepfather returned to concert-giving. It was Theodor's untiring work as a farsighted administrator and ingenious inventor, improving the fast-running printing press, the printing from zinc engravings and the combined printing of music and words, that gained an international reputation for the firm. In 1862 he began to publish Beethoven's works in regular editions, and this led in 1864 to the series *Litolffs Bibliothek classischer Compositionen*, a collection of carefully edited classical compositions which achieved worldwide distribution. Soon the format was successfully adopted by other German and by foreign publishers. Litolff also quickly became a leading publisher of teaching material, most of which was carefully prepared by his brother-in-law Adolph Bente (1840–1913), who worked with him for nearly 50 years; these included new piano and violin tutors, the *Instruktives Liederalbum* and *Buch der Lieder*. Litolff also attracted leading writers such as Louis Köhler (whose *Praktischer Lehrgang des Klavierspiels* had sold over a million copies by 1914), Gurlitt, Riemann, Germer, Wohlfahrt and Götze. The series of monthly issues entitled *Die musikalische Welt: Monatshefte ausgewählter Compositionen unserer Zeit*, edited by Franz Abt and Clemens Schultze (19 vols., 1872–90), was aimed at the domestic music market, and Litolff's light music publications were immensely popular.

In 1912 the firm passed to Theodor's son Richard Litolff (1876–1937), who from

1899 had received energetic support from his brother-in-law Clemens Schultze-Biesantz, a notable editor and publisher. In 1937 the management was taken over by Richard's widow (*d* 1957). Under her careful management, in which she was advised by Franz Rühlmann, particular attention was paid to educational and domestic music (with the series *Scholasticum* and *Hausmusik der Zeit*) and to music of contemporary composers including Trapp, Graener, Kaminski, Knab, Hasse and Höffer. Musicological works were published for the first time, including Sandberger's *Neues Beethoven-Jahrbuch* (from 1935), writings of Max Seiffert, Moser, Blume and Franz Rühlmann, several volumes of the series *Das Erbe deutsher Musik*, a collected edition of the works of Weber and the series *Das weltliche Konzert im 18. Jahrhundert* (from 1932).

On 9 August 1940 Litolff was taken over by the music publishers Peters of Leipzig. It continues to publish under its own name from the Peters firm at Frankfurt am Main; its catalogue specializes in works by contemporary composers.

FétisB; R. Procházka: 'Henry Litolff', *NZM*, lxxxvii (1891), 149; *Collection Litolff (50 Jahre): Haus-Chronik von Henry Litolff's Verlag* (Brunswick, 1914); A.H. King: 'A Subscription List to Mozart's *Così fan tutte*', *The Library*, 5th ser., vii (1952) 132; F. Stein: 'Litolff', *MGG*; R. Hagemann: *Henry Litolff* (Berne, 1981)

F.S.

Lomazzo, Filippo (*fl* 1600–30). Italian printer, bookseller and publisher, who came from a family of scholars, artists and publishers in Milan. He entered into partnership with the Tini family in 1603 and until 1612 they produced much music, primarily the work of local composers. From 1612 to 1630 Lomazzo worked on his own; a number of his publications appeared from the presses of other printers. He appears to have been musically literate, for he selected the contents of some of his numerous anthologies himself: they include sacred and secular music by many composers, including Ghizzolo, Negri, Orfeo Vecchi, Gastoldi and Ricciardo Rognoni. He also published treatises by Scaletta and Rognoni.

S.B. (iii)

Longman & Broderip. English firm of publishers and instrument dealers, established in London. The business was founded in or before 1767 by James Longman and others, and was first known as J. Longman & Co. Its Harp & Crown sign, though not its premises, was apparently acquired from the widow of John Johnson.

From 1769 to 1775 the firm was known as Longman, Lukey & Co., becoming Longman, Lukey & Broderip when Francis Broderip entered the business in September 1775. Lukey withdrew from the business in 1776 and the firm remained as Longman & Broderip until its bankruptcy in 1798. From December 1782 it had a circulating music library and in 1789 it advertised that it was opening branches at Margate and Brighthelmstone (now Brighton) 'during the watering season'.

Especially in its period as Longman & Broderip the firm ranked among the most enterprising of the time. In addition to its own wide range of publications, it claimed to be able to supply any foreign publication through its contacts with continental publishers. Its own publications included English music by Arne, Avison, Shield, Storace and others, and much by foreign composers, among them J. C. Bach, Haydn (including the symphonies commissioned by Salomon), Pleyel, Schobert, and Johann and Carl Stamitz, as well as the usual country dance books and sheet songs. Its keyboard music, some of it written two or more generations earlier, had a great influence on what English harpsichordists and organists played towards the end of the century. A number of works were published in conjunction with John Johnston, and the firm acquired some of his stock and plates as well as his trading sign 'The Apollo' when he ceased business in 1778. The firm was noted for the generous sums it paid composers for their works; perhaps this was a factor in its financial downfall.

After Longman & Broderip's bankruptcy, John Longman, who had succeeded James, went into partnership with Muzio Clementi until about 1801, and then set up for himself; Giles Longman, John's successor, was in partnership with James Herron as Longman & Herron until 1822. The other partner, Francis Broderip, entered into partnership with C. Wilkinson; as Broderip & Wilkinson they reissued many of the old firm's publications in addition to publishing new ones of their own, including *Broderip and Wilkinson's New and Complete Instructions for the Lute* (*c*1800). Broderip died in 1807, and the firm became Wilkinson & Co. until 1810, when it ceased business, the stock and plates being purchased by Thomas Preston.

T. Busby: *Concert Room and Orchestra Anecdotes* (London, 1825), i, 126; Kidson (1900); Humphries and Smith (1954, 2/1970)

P.W.J.

Lorenz. American publishing firm. It was founded in 1890 by Edmund S. Lorenz in Dayton, Ohio. Serving the church choir market, it specializes in periodicals and service music, and continues in Dayton as a family-run business, with its own engraving, typesetting and printing works. Since 1967 the Lorenz Corp. has established subsidiaries including Heritage Music, Sacred Music Press and Roger Dean Publishing Co.

E. J. Lorenz: *A Critical Bibliography of the E.S. Lorenz Collection of Nineteenth-century American Songbooks* (Springfield, OH, 1977)

G.H.S.

Lorenzi, Giuseppe. Italian printer and publisher. Granted permission to open an engraving works for music in Florence on 13 May 1812, he was the first Florentine music publisher of the 19th century. In 1816 he moved from a private repository in the via della Rosina to new premises in the Piazza S Lorenzo, 'all'Insegna dell'Orfeo', where he had a printing works, warehouse and pianoforte showroom, and employed 12 families of engravers and printers. In 1817 the firm issued Campagnoli's violin method, and B. Marcello's *Salmi* with a piano reduction by Mirecki (plate no. 900). Other noteworthy works around this time were Rossini's *quartettino* 'Ridiamo cantiamo che tutto sen va' (plate no. 1024), published jointly with F. Artaria of Milan, and the series *Opere vocali serie e buffe di Gioacchino Rossini* and *Opere teatrali ridotte per il pianoforte a quattro mani da Diabelli*.

In 1819 Giovanni Ricordi acquired almost all the Lorenzi plates, generally retaining the plate number and changing only the frontispiece. Possibly Lorenzi had experienced financial difficulties, even bankruptcy, with the arrival from Bologna of Gasparo Cipriani, who for several years dominated music publishing in Florence. Lorenzi issued a catalogue in 1821, registered on 16 June, but no copies are known to survive. The firm's name appears as Giuseppe Lorenzi e Figlio in Franz Krommer's *Messa in C* (plate nos. 3189–93). Subsequently Giuseppe's son Ferdinando, who edited several numbers of the *Rivista musicale di Firenze* between 1840 and 1842, issued a few editions on his own.

A.Z.L.

Löschenkohl, Hieronymus (*b* Elberfeld, *c*1753; *d* Vienna, 11 Jan 1807). Austrian engraver and publisher. He opened an art shop in Vienna in about 1770 and became known for his topical cheap copperplate engravings: Gräffer aptly named him the 'iconographic journalist'. Through publishing calendars and almanacs he came into contact with literary and musical circles and

acquired a modest position in the Guild of Viennese Music Publishers. In the *Wiener Zeitung* of 29 September 1787 he announced a cheap music engraving process, which he evidently also used for the musical supplements to almanacs. On 15 March 1788 he published Giuseppe Sarti's three piano sonatas op.4, but until 1799 dealt chiefly in songs and dances from Singspiels and ballets. He was unfortunate in that 12 lieder and odes by Gellert in settings supposedly by Mozart (1800 and 1801) all proved to be forgeries. However he became Beethoven's publisher in 1803 with the first edition of *Das Glück der Freundschaft* op.88, which he printed on green paper in the shape of a sunflower leaf. Thereafter until 1806, apart from some works by G. J. Vogler and J. B. Vanhal and several pieces by Anton Fischer, Löschenkohl published only Austrian, French and Russian military marches. In 1806 he issued his *Musikalisches Kartenspiel*, a beautifully engraved musical card game including compositions by Mozart. At his death his shop was taken over by the music publisher and art dealer H.F. Müller.

E. K. Blümml and G. Gugitz: *Von Leuten und Zeiten im alten Wien* (Vienna, 1922); Weinmann (1956); idem: *Wiener Musikverlag 'Am Rande'* (Vienna, 1970); R. Witzmann and V. Schwarz: *Musikalisches Kartenspiel des Johann Hieronymous Löschenkohl* (Vienna, 1981) [incl. a facs. of the playing cards]

A.W./N.S.

Lose. Danish firm of publishers and music dealers. It was established in Copenhagen in 1802 when the Lose family took over the firm of E. F. J. Haly (founded 1793) in the name of C. C. Lose (1787–1835). Early publications bear the imprint C. Lose & Comp., though from 1814 they are marked C. C. Lose. On Lose's death P. W. Olsen became manager, and the firm was styled C. C. Lose & Olsen until 1846, when the younger C. C. Lose (1821–92) attained majority and entered into partnership with O. H. Delbanco. The firm was then named C. C. Lose & Delbanco, but from January 1865 Lose continued alone in his own name. On 8 November 1871 he sold the firm to F. Borchorst, and until June 1879 publications bore the imprint C. C. Lose (F. Borchorst). On 25 June 1879 the firm was incorporated into the house of Wilhelm Hansen.

In 1815 the elder Lose founded the first Danish lithographic printing works; it did not meet his expectations and he sold it in 1820, subsequently establishing his own engraving and printing shop. During the first half of the 19th century Lose was the dominating music firm in Copenhagen, with about 2000 publications in its catalogue. These include works by Weyse, Kuhlau, Gade, Hartmann and Lumbye. Dramatic music is amply represented, particularly by opera, Singspiel and ballet. Important periodical publications include the *Nye Apollo* (12 vols., 1814–27; piano music and songs), continued as *Odeon* (7 vols., 1827–34; piano music), and *Musikalsk Theaterjournal* (ed. Ludwig Zinck, 14 vols., 1817–41). Lose ran an extensive music hire library, and its printed catalogues (1818–66) provide important information on musical taste and activities in the Danish capital at that time. The collection is now in the State Library at Århus.

Fortegnelse over Musik-Forlaget af C. Lose & Comp (1813; suppls. 1815, 1817); *Fortegnelse over Musik-Forlaget af C. Lose & Comp* (1818; suppls. 1819–21); *Fortegnelse over Forlags-Musikalier . . .* (1839; suppls. 1840–42); *C. C. Lose & Delbanco's Forlags-Catalog over Musikalier . . .* (1846; suppls. 1847, 1851, 1856); *Fortegnelse over C. C. Loses Bog- og Musikhandel's (F. Borchorst) Forlag . . .* (1874; suppl. 1878); D. Fog: *Musikhandel og Nodetryk i Danmark efter 1750* (Copenhagen, 1984), i, 214–307, ii, 191 [with dated plate nos.]; idem: *Notendruck und Musikhandel im 19. Jahrhundert in Dänemark* (Copenhagen, 1986), 101, 298 [with dated plate nos.]

D.F.

Lotter. German firm of publishers and printers. Johann Jakob Lotter (i) (*b* Augsburg, *c*1683; *d* Augsburg, 1738) founded the firm in Augsburg and for over a century (before 1720 until after 1830) it held a leading position in south German music publishing. Although he himself was Protestant, he published primarily the works of Catholic composers, and his increasing prosperity was based in particular on church music. After his early death his son Johann Jakob Lotter (ii) (*b* Augsburg, 1726; *d* Augsburg, 1804) extended the publishing and printing business and published copious music catalogues in which south German masters predominate, although composers from central and north Germany, Italy, France and elsewhere are also represented. In its heyday the firm sold its publications beyond the south German area, evidence of which survives in Austrian and Swiss music inventories of the 18th century and early 19th.

Above all the firm of Johann Jakob Lotter & Sohn, as it subsequently became known, supplied many court orchestras, music colleges, monasteries, vicarages and schools with contemporary music literature of the most varied kind. In addition the firm offered young people in abbeys, at courts and in municipal music posts the opportunity to publish their works, thereby contributing to the extraordinary wealth of south German music during the 18th century. It has been estimated that more than 100 composers had their works published by Lotter. Leopold Mozart, a close friend of Johann Jakob Lotter (ii), had his violin tutor published by the firm, and carried out some business transactions for Lotter in Salzburg; their friendship is further confirmed by their correspondence (in the Stadtarchiv, Augsburg), and the fact that the publisher was the first to be informed of Wolfgang Amadeus's birth. In the third generation of the family firm Esaias Daniel Lotter (*b* Augsburg, 1759; *d* Augsburg, 1820) had to overcome the economic setbacks which had resulted from the Napoleonic wars and subsequent secularization. Two other Lotters contributed to the technical improvements of musical type printing. The last surviving music catalogue is dated 1829; the firm probably ceased to exist in the second quarter of the 19th century.

A. Layer: 'Die Augsburger Musikaliendrucker Lotter', *Gutenberg-Jb 1964*, 258; idem: *Katalog des Augsburger Verlegers Lotter von 1753* (Kassel, 1964); idem: 'Lotter und Mozart: die Geschichte einer Freundschaft', *Sieben Schwaben*, xiv (Kempten, 1964), 152, 156; idem: 'Johann Jakob Lotter der Jüngere, Leopold Mozarts Augsburger Verleger', *Leopold Mozart 1719–1787: Bild einer Persönlichkeit*, ed. L. Wegele (Augsburg, 1969), 117; H. Rheinfurth: *Der Musikverlag Lotter in Augsburg (ca. 1719–1845);* (Tutzing, 1977)

A.L.

Lowe & Brydone. English firm of printers and engravers. It was founded in London in September 1892 by G. W. Lowe and James E. Brydone. They began trading at 34 Windmill Street with a staff of six, using lithographic stone; in 1895 they introduced machine-printing from zinc plates, installing the first rotary lithographic press (invented by T. Ruddiman Johnson of Edinburgh). By 1900 Lowe had retired. In 1907 the engraver James N. Green joined the business, which expanded to premises in Park Street, Camden Town, and soon became known as the largest music printers in Britain. Offering a complete service – pewter plates made, music engraved, title drawn or engraved, paper supplied, work printed (and bound if necessary) – the company prided itself on its efficiency: in two and a half days it could deliver proofs of 87 plates of a vocal score.

In 1913 Lowe & Brydone installed its first offset machine, built by George Mann & Co. In 1916 it acquired the C. G. Röder factory in Victoria Road, North Acton, and in 1918 the music printers George Udloff & Co.

325

During the 1920s experiments with photo-lithography were carried out, and the firm installed its first offset perfecting machines. In 1937 all the branches were united under one roof at the North Acton factory. Book production, including fine lithographic colour work, made up an increasingly large proportion of its activity. In 1973 it moved to Thetford and Haverhill in East Anglia, and a few years later was bought out.

E. Austin: *The Story of the Art of Music-Printing* (London, 1913) [an account of Lowe & Brydone]; 'The Story of Lowe & Brydone (Printers) Ltd', *Printing World*, clxviii (1961), 658; 'Move to East Anglia', *Lithoprinter* 1973), Jan, 11

L.L.

Lownes, Humfrey (*fl* 1587–1629). English printer. He married the widow of Peter Short in 1604, and most of his few musical works were reprintings of Short's copyrights (e.g. Thomas Morley's *A Plaine and Easie Introduction to Practicall Musicke*) published between 1604 and 1613. It is not known if he was related to Matthew Lownes, but he seems to have ceased printing music when the latter acquired the privilege of Barley in 1614. He was succeeded by Robert Young, who printed Elway Bevin's treatise of 1631, *A Briefe and Short Instruction in the Art of Musicke*.

Humphries and Smith (1954, 2/1970); Krummel (1975)

M.M.

Lownes, Matthew (*fl* 1591–1625). English bookseller and general printer. Between 1612 and 1624 he collaborated with John Brown and Thomas Snodham in the production of several music volumes, acquiring the rights to titles previously owned by William Barley and Thomas East in 1611 and 1614. There is no evidence that he was himself a music printer.

Humphries and Smith (1954, 2/1970)

M.M.

Lucas, Stanley. English firm of publishers, active in London. It had its roots in the firm of Addison, Hollier & Lucas, in which the cellist and conductor Charles Lucas (1808–69) worked from 1857 (trading as Addison & Lucas, 1863–5). After 1873 Charles's son Stanley (1834–1903) published under the imprint of Stanley Lucas, Weber & Co., at 84 New Bond Street and 308A (after 1881 at 325) Oxford Street. The firm issued art songs, chamber music and larger works, including Benedict's Symphony in G minor op.101 (1873), Prout's Evening Service (1875), Parry's *The Birds* (1885) and *Four Shakespeare Sonnets* (1887), Balfe's Piano Trio and Cello Sonata, Charles Santley's

Mass in G (1887), choral works by Mac-farren, Parry and Stanford, and Charles Ainslie Berry's edition of the Berlioz *Te Deum*. It also served as London agents for the Russian firm of Jürgenson. In 1893 the firm of Pitt & Hatzfeld – Emile Hatzfeld was an immigrant French publisher, editor of the *Strand Musical Magazine* and Tchaikovsky's host at Cambridge – merged with Lucas to become Stanley Lucas, Weber, Pitt & Hatzfeld. In 1899 the partnership was dissolved, and Lucas sold to Weber, Pitt & Hatzfeld Ltd a total of 12,564 plates and copyrights. Other properties were sold at auction in 1899 and 1901. Stanley Lucas & Son continued to 1907.

W. H. Husk: 'Lucas', *Grove3*; G. Norris: *Stanford, the Cambridge Jubilee and Tchaikovsky* (Newton Abbot, 1980); J. B. Coover: 'The Dispersal of Engraved Music Plates and Copyrights in British Auctions, 1831–1931', *Richard S. Hill: Tributes from Friends* (Detroit, 1987), 223–306; Coover (1988)

D.W.K.

Lucca, Francesco (*b* Cremona, 1802; *d* Milan, 20 Feb 1872). Italian publisher. He worked as an apprentice music engraver with Giovanni Ricordi (1816–22) and was concurrently second clarinettist in the La Scala orchestra. Having learnt the trade he travelled abroad (1822–5) to perfect his craftsmanship and learn the new litho-graphic technique which was slow to become as popular in Italy as engraving, a more established method. On his return he opened an engraving workshop with copy-ing facilities in Contrada S Margherita, Milan, and the first samples were immed-iately admired for their clear printing and accurate copying. He later published, with Reycend of Turin, one of these, the *Metodo per violino* (*c*1835) by Baillot, Rode and Kreutzer. In Turin, where he stayed in August and December 1835, he also had an arrangement with the publisher Magrini. Probably towards the end of 1841 he went back to Ricordi to work in the copying department opposite La Scala. He announced in the press that from January 1841 he owned the rights of reproduction and transfer for Donizetti's *Adelia* (1839) and *La favorita* (1841) and was preparing vocal scores and arrangements of them; he subsequently took over a share with Ricordi of the agency for *Nabucco*. Lucca's relations with Verdi became closer when, through the friendship of his wife Giovannina Strazza (1814–94) with Giuseppina Strepponi, later Verdi's wife, he persuaded the composer to give him an album of vocal music. He brought out Verdi's *Il corsaro* in 1845, and *Attila* and *I masnadieri* in 1847, but Verdi severed the connection when Lucca, having refused to give him extra time to deliver the manuscript of *Il corsaro*, deprived him of the possibility of a lucrative contract with the London impresario Lumley, and Verdi moved to Ricordi.

Rivalry and competition increased between the two firms. The periodical *L'Italia musicale*, founded in co-ownership with and directed by G.A. Biaggi (first issue 7 July 1847), was renamed *L'Italia libera* in 1848 and became the exclusive responsibility of Francesco Lucca. (Only three issues appeared between 1847 and 1849, two under the latter title.) During this period the Lucca home was a meeting place for Mazzinian conspirators (Lucca thus gained the friendship of Garibaldi and Cavour) and also came to be known as the stronghold of musical futurism. In 1840 Lucca had already acquired *Der Freischütz* and had it translated under the bizarre title of *Il magico bersagliere* with an obvious patriotic allusion, and though it was not staged until 16 years later, his interest showed his support of the avant garde. He had major successes with operas by Mercadante, Pacini, Ricci, Petrella (*Jone*), Gomes (*Il Guarany*), Marchetti (*Ruy Blas*) and Catalani (*Edmea*) and also works by Coronaro. These operas and a large amount of chamber music, including numerous arrangements for various instruments of opera excerpts, were printed using only treble and bass clefs, for the first time.

Towards the middle of the century Lucca's wife joined the business and made an extremely valuable contribution. She bought rights for Italy of Gounod's *Faust* (La Scala, 1862), Halévy's *La juive*, Flotow's *Martha* and Meyerbeer's *L'africaine*; her greatest achievement was the acquisition (1868) of exclusive rights in Italy of all Wagner's works, for which she paid 10,000 Swiss francs. She was the sole owner of the firm after her husband's death and added to it through contracts with Berletti of Florence and Udine (1871), Ducci of Florence (1875), Canti of Milan (1878) and Vismara of Milan (1886); Bertuzzi of Milan had been purchased in 1847. This expansion threatened Ricordi, and from 1886 Verdi advised Tito Ricordi (i) to acquire Lucca; the negotiations (partly conducted by Depanis, a Turin lawyer and fervent supporter of Wagner) were protracted by Signora Lucca's determination to keep the exclusive Wagner rights. By a contract of 30 May 1888 Ricordi finally absorbed the Lucca concern at the price of a million lire plus compensation to Lucca employees, who with a few exceptions were made redundant. Ricordi acquired about 40,000 titles, and the most important compositions were reprinted with the designation 'Tito di Gio. Ricordi e F. Lucca di G. Ricordi'.

Catalogo generale delle opere pubblicate dallo stabilimento musicale 'Ditta F. Lucca' (Milan, 1884); G. Lisio: 'Su l'epistolario di casa Lucca', *Reale Istituto Lombardo di scienze e lettere*, xli (1908), 308; G. Depanis: *I concerti popolari ed il Teatro Regio di Torino*, i (Turin, 1915), 173; C. Sartori: *Casa Ricordi 1808–1958, profilo storico* (Milan, 1958); idem (1958); M. Morini: 'Francesco Lucca', *ES*; P. Rattalino: 'Editori di musica nell'Italia dell' '800', *Terzo programma*, ii (Turin, 1965), 245; A. Pasquinelli: 'Contributo per la storia di casa Lucca', *NRMI*, xvi (1982), 568

S.A.

Lundquist, Abraham (Reinold) (1817–92). Swedish music dealer and publisher. He began working in 1830 at the Östergren bok- och musikhandel in Stockholm. In 1837, when the firm was taken over by Hirsch, Lundquist decided to leave and set up his own shop and publishing business together with Ninian (Frans P.) Caron (1814–66). In 1844 the partners split up; Lundquist kept the publishing firm. He had plans for a new music shop, which were realized in 1849 when he went into partnership with the music dealer Lars Gustaf Rylander (1816–83). In 1855 Lundquist took over the new firm, changed its name from Rylander och Comp. to Lundquists musikhandel and acquired the stock of J.C. Hedbom och Comp. (1827–52). For some years, from 1863 to 1871, Lundquist owned a lithographic printing press. He continued as a music dealer and publisher until his death, when the firm was taken over by his son Georg.

Lundquist had excellent connections with music publishers on the Continent and he was the Swedish representative for Peters Verlag. His own firm was equalled only by that of Hirsch. He published mainly light piano music, including dances and salon pieces, as well as song collections of Swedish and foreign composers and tutors and songbooks for school use. The firm issued many catalogues, the largest running to 227 pages in 1876, and its chronology of plate numbers reached 4747 by 1915.

A. Wiberg: *Den svenska musikhandelns historia* (Stockholm, 1955); A. Helmer: 'Litet förläggarlexikon', *Svenskt musikhistoriskt arkiv: Bulletin*, iv (1970), 9; V. Heintz: 'Lundquist, Abraham Reinold', *Svenskt biografiskt lexikon* (Stockholm, 1918–), xxiv (1982–4), 340

V.H.

Lyon & Healy. American firm of publishers, music dealers and instrument manufacturers. It was established in Chicago on 14 October 1864, by James Washburn Lyon and Patrick J. Healy, and underwritten by Oliver Ditson of Boston as a mid-western distributor for Ditson publications; the shop, located at Clark and Washington streets, soon added music of other publishers. After the great fire of 1870 the firm moved to 150 South Clark Street and by 1871 was selling Steinway pianos and other instruments. During the 1880s it began manufacturing the Washburn line of fretted instruments and the (later famous) Lyon & Healy harp. In October 1889 Lyon retired, but allowed the firm's name to continue unchanged. It was Healy's astuteness and flair for advertising that made the company the most complete music dealer in the Midwest; he added ‹ antique violins,

gramophones, recordings, reproducing pianos, radios and teachers' guidebooks to the catalogue. In 1979 all retail activities ceased and the company changed its name to Lyon & Healy Harps. Most Lyon & Healy imprints date from 1864 to 1870, including *President Johnson's Grand Union March*, by G.R. Herbert (1865), and *The Sweet By and By* by S. Fillmore Bennett and J. P. Webster (1868).

Patrick Joseph Healy: an Appreciation (Chicago, 1907); Fisher (1933); E. M. Klock: 'Music Merchandising Moves into a House of Many Mansions', *Notes*, 2nd ser., i/2 (1944), 16

C.E.

M

McGinnis & Marx. American publishing firm. It was founded in New York in 1946 by the oboist and musicologist Josef Marx (*b* Berlin, 9 Sept 1913; *d* New York, 21 Dec 1978) in partnership with his wife, Beulah McGinnis. The catalogue features Baroque music, mostly for wind, as well as works by such composers as John Harbison, Donald Martino, Harvey Sollberger, Charles Wuorinen and notably, Stefan Wolpe. The firm is now managed by Angelina Buonamassa Marx (Marx's second wife) and Paul Sadowski.

R.B. (iii)

Magasin de Musique (i). French publishing firm, whose full name was Magasin de Musique à l'usage des Fêtes Nationales et du Conservatoire. The firm was founded by Bernard Sarrette as a result of a governmental decree of 15 February 1794; it opened at 16 rue Joseph, Paris, and in October 1794 moved to 4 rue des Fossés-Montmartre. Two months after the founding of the Paris Conservatoire in August 1795, the firm added to its name 'ou Imprimerie du Conservatoire'. In August 1797 it moved to premises within the Conservatoire, at 152 rue du Faubourg Poissonnière at the corner of the rue Bergère, at the same time changing its name to Magasin de Musique (occasionally Imprimerie) du Conservatoire. In 1806 the street number was changed from 152 to 11 and subsequently an alternative address, 3 rue Bergère, was sometimes used. From 6 March 1797 Etienne Ozi was manager,

and from the early 1800s the imprint normally read 'Le magasin de Musique du Conservatoire, tenu par M.M. Ozi et Compagnie'. After Ozi's death on 15 October 1813 his successors substituted 'MMrs. Charles, Michel, Ozi et Compagnie' and used only the 3 rue Bergère address. Janet & Cotelle took over the firm, probably late in 1825.

Sarrette directed the music corps of the National Guard, which was responsible for performing the patriotic music composed for the fêtes held in Paris from 1790. The firm primarily published music for the Parisian fêtes and patriotic music in general 'whereby to excite the courage of the defenders of la Patrie'. The profits were to be used to support widows and children of the National Guard's musicians. Two monthly periodical publications were started; the first, dating from April 1794, was a volume of some 50 pages containing an overture, a patriotic hymn or song, a military march and a rondo or quickstep; the second, launched about three months later, was a single folded leaf containing three or four patriotic songs or hymns. The government subscribed to 550 copies of the first, one for each district of the Republic, and to 12,000 copies of the second, for distribution among the land and sea forces. During the first year production costs rose by about 500% and the government, although making good the firm's deficiency, did not renew its subscription to the first periodical; the firm nevertheless continued to issue the second irregularly until 1799 and also published patriotic and military music required for fêtes and by the municipalities and armies.

As the revolutionary fever gradually subsided the needs of the newly founded Conservatoire gave the firm a new focus. It began publishing didactic works and music for the use of students, most of which was the work of Conservatoire professors themselves. Between 1800 and 1814 the *Principes élémentaires de la musique* and other treatises on harmony, singing and plainchant, two books of solfège and nine instrumental methods were published. Other publications included 17 overtures and 36 duets for wind instruments, 30 concertos, 14 symphonies concertantes for various instrumental combinations and full scores of Cherubini's *Eliza* and of six operas by Catel. After Ozi's death in 1813 production was almost entirely limited to reprinting earlier publications. All the publications of the firm were engraved.

C. Pierre: *Le Magasin de musique à l'usage des Fêtes nationales et du Conservatoire* (Paris, 1895/R1974); Hopkinson (1954); Devriès and Lesure (1979–88)

R.M.

Magasin de Musique (ii). French publishing firm, whose full name was Magasin de Musique dirigé par MMrs. Chérubini, Méhul, Kreutzer, Rode, N. Isouard et Boieldieu (each of these composers being a partner). The firm was officially founded for a period of nine years on 5 August 1802, and on 1 December announced the opening of premises at 268 rue de la Loi, Paris. In 1805–6 the street number and name were altered to 76 rue de Richelieu. Isouard left the firm, probably late in 1808, and at its dissolution (12 August 1811) the business, manuscripts and 9679 engraved plates were sold to J.-J. Frey.

In the late 18th century composers had frequently published their works from their homes, selling them personally and through music shops; this forced them to waste time in business matters, while receiving insufficient publicity and paying disproportionate fees to the music seller who took little or none of the risk. It was to overcome these disadvantages that the six composers joined forces. Each contracted to furnish at least one opera or 50 pages of their music each year; each was entitled to the proceeds from the sale of his own works, less 5%, and to a share in the profits of the firm's publications of works by non-associated composers.

Isouard was the only one of the six who regularly provided operas for publication; the firm printed nine in full score. Other operas published included Cherubini's *Anacréon*, Méhul's *Joseph* and Boieldieu's *Ma*

tante Aurore. In publishing the music of other composers precedence was given to instrumental works by contemporary musicians prominent in Paris: numerous works by Viotti (including five violin concertos), flute concertos by Devienne, piano sonatas by Steibelt and chamber music by Dussek. The most notable operatic publication was the first edition in full score of *Le nozze di Figaro* (c1807–8), which considerably preceded the Simrock edition of 1819. All together more than 650 editions were published, all from engraved plates.

C. Pierre: *Le Magasin de musique à l'usage des Fêtes nationales et du Conservatoire* (Paris, 1895/R1974), 105; Hopkinson (1954); Devriès and Lesure (1979–88)

R.M.

Magni. Italian family of printers and musicians, active in the 17th century. Bartolomeo Magni came from a family of musicians from Ravenna. Of his brothers, Benedetto Magni was a composer and organist, and Giovanni was organist at S Maria in Porto, Rome. Bartolomeo was apprenticed to Angelo Gardano and married his daughter. On Gardano's death in 1611 the estate passed to his daughter, and Magni printed as the 'heir of Angelo Gardano'. For much of his output he retained the Gardano title, presumably for commercial reasons, though he added his own in one of several formulae, such as 'Stampa del Gardano appresso Bartolomeo Magni'. He was a prolific printer, and although there were others in north Italy, he did not have to face the competition of Scotto, whose heirs had stopped printing a few years before. As a result he printed music by most of the important composers of the period to 1645, including the first editions of Monteverdi's later works, and music by Agazzari, Banchieri, Cazzati, Cifra, Gagliano, d'India, Merula, Nenna, Priuli and Vitali.

Bartolomeo Magni had two sons who were mentioned in Banchieri's *Lettere armoniche* (Bologna, 1628). One of these may have been the Paolo Magni who had a motet published in *RISM* 1679[1]; Francesco (*d* 1673) is first named in 1651. It is possible, however, that Bartolomeo had died in 1644, for the works of the intervening six years are merely signed 'Stampa del Gardano'. Francesco continued printing until his death, though his output declined in later years. He concentrated on sacred and instrumental music, including works by Cazzati, Legrenzi, Vitali and G. M. Bononcini. The firm continued in business after his death. During the second half of the century it inclined away from music towards books, but it printed some music until 1681; it ceased production in 1685. Catalogues of music published by the firm in 1619 and 1649 are extant.

E. Pastorello: *Tipografi, editori, librai a Venezia* (Florence, 1924); C. Sartori: 'Una dinastia di editori musicali', *La bibliofilia*, lviii (1956), 176–208; Mischiati (1984)

S.B. (iii)

Magyar Kórus. Hungarian firm of publishers, active in Budapest. Its full name was Magyar Kórus Zenemű- és Lapkiadó Kft. ('Hungarian Choir Music and Periodicals Publishers Ltd').It was founded in 1931 by Lajos Bárdos (1896–1986), György Kerényi (1902–86) and Gyula Kertész (1900–67), pupils of Kodály, composers and choirmasters, to supply classical and modern choral music, especially to schools. The firm's publications quickly became popular and played an important role in rejuvenating the country's musical life. All types of choral music were included: Gregorian chant, solfège (Bertalotti, Kodály's pedagogical works), sacred and secular works, classics and contemporary Hungarian compositions. Magyar Kórus first published the choral works of Bartók and Kodály. From 1934 the firm organized the 'Singing Youth' concerts. Its series titles included *From Advent to Advent* (Protestant church song), *Bicinia Hungarica* (i–iv), *From Transylvania to Upper Hungary, Singing Hungary, Western Choirs, Fallalla, Choir Music of a Thousand Years, Folk Songs for Choir*, and the Roman Catholic collections *Hungarian cantuale, Harmonia sacra* and *Sacred art Thou Lord*. The firm also published the periodicals *Magyar kórus* (ed. Bárdos and Kertész, 1931–50), *Énekszó* ('The sound of song', ed. Kerényi and Kertész, 1933/4–49), *Zenei szemle* ('Music review', ed. D. Bartha and B. Szabolcsi, 1947–9) and *Zenepedagógia* ('Music teaching', ed. E. Czövek, 1947–8). It employed translators to help in the publication of Western and classical choral works and issued instrumental tutors and books. The firm was nationalized in 1950; its legal successor is Editio Musica Budapest.

I.M.

Maisch, Ludwig (*b* Nuremberg, *c*1776; *d* Vienna, 18 April 1816). Viennese publisher. His firm began publishing in 1810, reissuing saleable works from Kozeluch's Musikalisches Magazin publishing house and the music of such composers as Gelinek, Gyrowetz, Hummel and Vanhal. While the production was for the most part of fashionable pieces and dance music, it also included some minor works by Beethoven. After Maisch's death the firm continued to trade under his name until January 1818, then for several months under that of his widow. The firm's accountant Daniel Sprenger (*b* Sülfeld, nr. Hanover, *c*1794; *d* 21 Sept 1819) took control for a further year; after his death Mathias Artaria (1793–1835), son of the Mannheim publisher Domenico Artaria (ii), assisted Sprenger's widow in carrying on the business. He married her on 4 November 1821 and the firm bore his name alone from 10 June 1822.

Under Artaria the firm's output improved markedly in quality, as shown by the publication of Beethoven's opp. 130, 133 and 134, as well as Schubert's opp. 52–4. Other composers represented included Assmayer, Jansa, Mayseder and Peháček. On 26 June 1833 the firm passed to Anton Diabelli. Artaria's widow attempted to start a publishing firm in 1838 in partnership with Gustav Albrecht and Asperl, but its importance was small and in 1850 she ceased publishing.

A. Weinmann: *Verzeichnis der Musikalien des Verlages Maisch-Sprenger–Mathias Artaria* (Vienna, 1970)

A.W.

Mangeant, Jacques (*d* ?1633). French printer. His father was probably Simon Mangeant (*d* between 1583 and 1593), who printed only two volumes with music: one of the many editions of Marot and de Bèze's psalms published in 1562, and *Cantiques spirituels*, printed for Estienne Martin in 1565. Jacques Mangeant printed from 1593 to 1633 in Caen. In 1593 he printed the *airs* of Guillaume de Chastillon who had obtained a privilege in 1590. The only other music to come from Mangeant's press was a small group of anthologies (*RISM* 1608[7], 1608[8], 1608[9], 1615[8], 1615[9], 1615[10]). His son Eleazar Mangeant does not appear to have printed any music.

G. Lepreux: *Gallia typographia*, Série départementale, iii (Paris, 1912), 484; P. Pidoux: *Le psautier huguenot du XVIe siècle*, ii: *Documents et bibliographie* (Basle, 1962)

S.B. (iii)

Manilius, Gislain (*b* ?Ghent; *d* Ghent, 1573). Flemish printer, who worked in Ghent from 1559 to 1573. Among his publications, which included proclamations, official chronicles and statutes for Ghent diocese, are two Flemish psalters (1565, 1566), the first books with music printed in Ghent. On 5 October 1564 he obtained the privilege for the first, *Psalmen Davids*, whose texts were translated by Lucas d'Heere from Clément Marot's version; however, the book was later placed on the Index. The second volume, *Alle de Psalmen Davids*, using

P. Dathenus's translation, was printed anonymously. One other book with music came from this press: Matthieu Casteleyn's *Diversche liedekens*, published by Manilius's widow in 1574.

Goovaerts (1880); P. Bergmans: *La typographie musicale en Belgique au XVIe siècle*, v (Brussels, 1929); S. Bain: *Music Printing in the Low Countries in the Sixteenth Century* (diss., U. of Cambridge, 1974)

S.B. (i)

Manwaring, William (*b* ?Dublin; *d* Dublin, 1763). Irish publisher, music seller and instrument dealer. He ran a business from about 1738 at Corelli's Head, opposite Anglesea Street in College Green, Dublin. In April 1740 he advertised a proposal for printing Geminiani's *Harmonical Guide* by subscription. Notable publications by him include collections of songs from Arne's *Comus*, Dubourg's variations on the Irish melody 'Ellen-a-Roon' and in December 1752 'six Trios for 2 Fiddles and Thorough Bass composed by Sieur Van Maldere'. From 1741 a number of publications were issued in conjunction with William Neale, including the *Monthly Musical Masque*, consisting of a collection of contemporary popular songs; the first issue was advertised in January 1744. Manwaring also imported Peter Walmsley's best violins, Roman fiddle strings and 'all the newest music published in London'. After his death his wife carried on the business until 1788.

N. Carolan, ed.: *A Collection of the Most Celebrated Irish Tunes* (Dublin, 1986) [facs., incl. list of publications by Neale and Manwaring]

B.B.

Marescalchi, Luigi (*b* Bologna, 1 Feb 1745; *d* Marseilles, 1812). Italian publisher and composer. About 1770 he began publishing in Venice and, probably in mid-1773, took the violinist and composer Carlo Canobbio (1741–1822) into partnership. Although the enterprise was temporarily abandoned about 1775, the brief period of its duration marked the revival of music publishing in Italy after 70 years of almost total inactivity. In Venice Marescalchi issued some 60 engraved publications, most in oblong format, evenly distributed between vocal pieces (mainly full scores and orchestral parts of single numbers from operas performed in Venice) and instrumental works (ballet, dance, chamber music and opera overtures). Anfossi, Boccherini, Naumann, Paisiello and Marescalchi himself were the composers of more than half of this output. In his Venice publications Marescalchi worked closely with Alessandri & Scattaglia, who were probably responsible for all his music engraving as well as being named on

most of the title-pages as his selling agents, at their premises on the Rialto; one title-page also describes them as his printers, and this may have been another of their regular responsibilities. This connection between the two firms has often led cataloguers and bibliographers to ascribe to Alessandri & Scattaglia publications which should properly be regarded as Marescalchi's, with the result that numerous entries in *RISM*, the *British Union Catalogue* and other works of reference are incorrect.

In 1775 Marescalchi probably visited Lisbon for the revival of his opera *Il tutore ingannato*; during the next ten years he was not engaged in publishing and became more active as a composer. On 15 November 1785 he obtained an exclusive royal licence for the printing of music in Naples, and, in partnership with his brother Francesco, he began to publish there in 1786. He established himself first in the new Palazzo in the strada di Chiaia beside the church of S Orsola; he was still there late in 1789 but between then and the closing of his business in 1799 he moved to 32 Vicola della Campana, Largo di Castello. For about his first year in Naples he used as retailers the booksellers Antonio Hermil and Giuseppe Maria Porcelli; thereafter he opened his own shop, where he sold music and instruments as well as running a hire library and a flourishing copisteria. His engraved publications of instrumental music included several works by Haydn and Pleyel and an early edition of Mozart's violin and viola duet κ423, probably the first work by Mozart to be published in Italy. He published many operatic excerpts in full score, particularly of Bianchi, Cimarosa, P. A. Guglielmi and Paisiello; he also reprinted (as separate numbers) most of Sarti's *Giulio Sabino* from the plates of the Vienna first edition of about 1782 and issued a second edition of Millico's *La pietà d'amore*, his largest publication.

From about 1793 Marescalchi's output of printed editions appears to have diminished, but his exclusive licence was evidently renewed and up to January 1799 the librettos of operas given at the S Carlo and del Fondo theatres still announced that the music could be obtained from him. In June 1799 political rioters destroyed his house and printing works, and he was arrested on a trumped-up charge, imprisoned and shortly afterwards exiled; he went to live in Marseilles. It is possible that the destruction of his business was incited by Neapolitan music copyists, whose livelihood had been badly affected by the licence given him and who had long since petitioned unsuccessfully against it.

Marescalchi has a reputation for unscrupulousness. In common with many contemporary publishers he was frequently guilty of piracy (e.g. his unauthorized publication in 1786 of music from Paisiello's *L'Olimpiade*) but his reputation for forgery is probably unfounded. It is based on the accusation, repeated in several reference books, that he published works of his own composition under Boccherini's name (six trios for two violins and cello op.7, Gérard 125–30). Not only are these now thought likely to be authentic works of Boccherini, but Marescalchi never himself published them: they came out in Paris and London only.

FétisB; J. F. Reichardt: '3 Fortsetzung der Berichtigungen und Zusätze sum Gerberschen Lexikon der Tonkünstler etc.', *Musikalische Monathsschrift*, iv (1792), Oct, 99 [facs. in repr. of *Gerber L, NL* (Ergänzungen)]; C. Gervasoni: *Nuova teoria di musica* (Parma, 1812/R1972), 175; A. Mazarella, ed.: *Biografia degli uomini illustri del Regno di Napoli . . . compilato da diversi letterati nazionali* (Naples, 1819), 47; F. Barberio: 'Giovanni Paisiello tra le ire di un copista e di un innovatore', *RMI*, xxii (1915), 301; U. Prota-Giurleo: *La prima calcografia musicale a Napoli* (Naples, 1923); B. Croce: 'Tra gli esuli napoletani del novantanove ancora in Francia nel 1806', *Varietà di storia letteraria e civile*, i (Bari, 1935), 221; Sartori (1958); G. de Rothschild: *Luigi Boccherini: sa vie, son oeuvre* (Paris, 1962; Eng. trans., 1965); S. Cisilino: *Stampe e manoscritti preziosi e rari della Biblioteca del Palazzo Giustinian Lolin a San Vidal (Fondazione Ugo e Olga Levi)* (Venice, 1966), 44; Y. Gérard: *Thematic, Bibliographical and Critical Catalogue of the Works of Luigi Boccherini* (London, 1969), 140

R.M.

Marescotti [Mariscotti], **Giorgio** [Georges Marescot, Mareschot] (*d* Florence, April 1602). French bookseller and printer, resident in Florence from the mid-1550s. On 7 April 1558 he matriculated in the *Arte dei medici e speziali* and became associated with Lorenzo Torrentino, the 'stampatore ducale'. By 1563 he was commissioning the Torrentino firm to print books on his behalf, and some time later he acquired the firm's equipment and stock. His production contains nothing of musical interest until Francesco Bocchi's *Discorso sopra la musica, non secondo l'arte di quella, ma secondo la ragione alla politica pertinente* (1580–81). Later in 1581 he completed Vincenzo Galilei's epochal *Dialogo della musica antica, et della moderna* (*R*1967), with numerous illustrations, including musical notation using copperplate engraving. In 1582 he published an anthology of three-part madrigals (*RISM* 1582[8]), in 1584 a volume of two-part pieces by Vincenzo Galilei, in 1585 a reprint of Arcadelt's *Il primo libro de madrigali a quattro voci*, and in 1596/7 Stefano

Venturi del Nibbio's *Il terzo libro de madrigali a cinque*.

Marescotti was the first, and during his lifetime the only, music printer in Florence. His entry into the field was perhaps spurred by the vigorous experimentation in music going on there, and he became the first printer of opera and the new monody. In 1600–01 he printed the first opera scores, Caccini's *L'Euridice* (see illustration) and Peri's *Le musiche sopra l'Euridice*. In late 1601 or early 1602 the printing of Caccini's *Le nuove musiche* was begun 'appresso i Marescotti' and, according to its colophon, was completed in late June 1602 by 'the heirs of Giorgio Marescotti'. The heirs also issued Giovanni del Turco's *Il primo libro de madrigali a cinque* in July, and Marescotti's music fount later appears in Antonio Brunelli's *Regole utilissime* printed in 1606 by a German printer working in Florence, Volcmar Timan. Giorgio Marescotti printed music only sporadically (of a total output of almost 300 titles, fewer than a dozen are devoted to music or music theory, though others are no doubt lost), in part because of the severe economic difficulties facing the printing industry in Tuscany. But his fine editions are not without distinction and interest; he used types of a handsome pattern, and the importance of his music output shows him to have been a printer of great boldness and initiative. His usual printer's mark is a ship amid the waves, with the motto 'et vult et potest'.

His eldest son and principal heir, Cristofano Marescotti (*b c*1580; *d* Sept 1611), took over the firm only after a lengthy and damaging lawsuit between members of the family on Giorgio Marescotti's death. He began to sign his own name to publications in 1604 and continued to issue Florentine monody and other music to 1610 (eight music editions bearing his imprint survive, including important volumes by Severo Bonini, Marco da Gagliano, Jacopo Peri and Francesco Rasi). His music fount differs from that of his father. In December 1611 the last Marescotti music publication, Pietro Benedetti's *Musiche* for solo voice, was published by 'the heirs of Cristofano Marescotti'. Cristofano's widow, Margherita Pugliani, then joined with a new partner, Zanobi Pignoni, who later (apparently by mid-1614) bought out the firm.

D. Moreni: *Annali dei Marescotti, I-Fr* MS Moreni 213; A. Einstein: 'Vincenzo Galilei and the Instructive Duo', *ML*, xviii (1937), 360; F. Ascarelli: *La tipografia cinquecentina italiana* (Florence, 1953), 139, figs.59–60; Sartori (1958); King (1964); F. A. D'Accone: 'The Intavolatura di M. Alamanno Aiolli', *MD*, xx (1966), 158; T. De Marinis: 'Nota sul tipografo Giorgio Marescotti',

Title-page of Caccini's 'Euridice' (1600), published in Florence by Giorgio Marescotti

La bibliofilia, lxxi (1969), 179; R. Delfiol: 'I Marescotti, librai, stampatori ed editori a Firenze tra cinque e seicento', *Studi secenteschi*, xviii (1977), 146; T. W. Bridges: *The Publishing of Arcadelt's First Book of Madrigals* (diss., Harvard U., 1982); T. Carter: 'Music-Printing in Late Sixteenth- and Early Seventeenth-century Florence: Giorgio Marescotti, Cristofano Marescotti and Zanobi Pignoni', *Early Music History*, ix (1990)

T.W.B./T.C. (i)

Margun. American firm of publishers. It was founded in 1975 in Newton Centre, Massachusetts. It has two imprints, Margun and GunMar, and issues music by nearly a hundred composers, most of them American. The president of the firm is Gunther Schuller, many of whose works and arrangements are published by Margun. Other notable composers in the list are Alec Wilder and Nikos Skalkottas, and the firm also issues music in the catalogue of Aldo Bruzzichelli, Florence, including works by contemporary Italian composers and Jean Barraqué.

Marks, Edward B(ennett) (*b* Troy, NY, 28 Nov 1865; *d* Mineola, NY, 17 Dec 1945). American publisher. In 1894 he and Joseph Stern established in New York the music publishing firm of Joseph W. Stern & Company. In 1920 Marks purchased Stern's interest and renamed the firm the Edward B. Marks Music Company; in 1932 it became the Edward B. Marks Music Corporation. The firm was a leading publisher of American and Latin American popular music. One of its earliest successes was *The Little Lost Child* (1894), written by Marks and Stern, which sold more than a million copies and was the first song to be introduced to singing audiences through illustrated slides. The firm also issued *Sweet Rosie O'Grady* (1896), *Take back your gold* (1897), *Under the bamboo tree* (1902), *Malagueña* (1928), *The Peanut Vendor* (1931) and *Paper Doll* (1942). During the 1930s Marks began to publish much serious music; its composers include Beglarian, Bolcom, Chatman, Davidovsky, Dello Joio, Robert Jager, Moevs, Alfred Reed, Sessions, Hale Smith, Thorne, Gilbert Trythall and Ward-Steinman. In 1967 Marks purchased the catalogue of the George M. Cohan Music Publishing Co. and began publishing all Cohan's songs. Marks is also the agent in the USA and Canada for parts of the catalogues of Polskie Wydawnictwo Muzyczne of Poland and Josef Weinberger of England. After Marks's death his son Herbert Edward Marks served as president of the firm until 1971; in 1973 Belwin-Mills took over the distribution of its publications.

E. B. Marks: *They All Sang: from Tony Pastor to Rudy Vallée* (New York, 1934); H. I. Brock: 'Tin Pan Alley is Always in Tune', *New York Times Magazine* (13 Feb 1944), 14, 23; ' "Little Lost Child" to "Paper Doll": 50 Years of Hits for House of Hits', *Newsweek* (21 Feb 1944), 70; 'Marks, Edward Bennett', *National Cyclopedia of American Biography*, xxxiv (New York, 1948/*R*1967), 176

R.A.L.

Mascardi. Italian family of printers. They were active at Rome from about 1620 to at least 1719. The biography of the family is difficult to unravel, partly because many works carry the impress 'Il Mascardi' or merely 'Mascardi'. At least three members were involved: Giacomo Mascardi, who ceased printing in 1640; Vitale Mascardi, who succeeded him and printed until 1667; and Giovanni Mascardi, who appears to have printed between 1667 and 1675, after which most works carry the inscription 'successor to the Mascardi', or 'Il Mascardi'. At this time the firm had a successful collaboration with the promoter G.B. Caifabri: he had employed a number of printers but from 1673 published all his musical ventures (including some anthologies edited by himself) from the Mascardi printing shop. This represented one of the more flourishing periods of the firm. There were several periods when little appears to have been published, though there were particularly lively spells during the 1650s and the early 18th century. As would be expected of a Roman printer, the bulk of the repertory is sacred music, supported by volumes of instrumental music. A volume of Palestrina and Anerio was published in 1689; several volumes of Corelli, the *Sacri concerti musicali* of Carissimi (1675) and sonatas by Leoni (1652) are among the most distinguished titles.

Sartori (1958); G. S. Fraenkel: *Decorative Music Title Pages: 201 Examples from 1500 to 1800* (New York, 1968)

S.B. (iii)

Mason Bros. American firm of publishers. It was founded in 1853 in New York by Daniel Gregory Mason (1820–69) and Lowell Mason (1823–85), sons of the celebrated music educationist, composer, anthologist and conductor Lowell Mason (1792–1872). They were joined by their brother Timothy, previously a partner in the publishing firm of Mason and Lane. The company opened a branch in Boston around 1866 and moved the entire operation there some time after 1869; it remained active until 1885, when the catalogue was acquired by Oliver Ditson. Among the firm's publications are many of the elder Lowell Mason's anthologies, including *The Glee Hive*

(1853), *The Hallelujah* (1854), *The New Odeon* (with George James Webb, 1855), *Mason's Normal Singer* (*c*1856), *Song-Book of the School-Room* (1856), *The Psaltery* (1860), *The People's Tune Book* (1860), *The Vocalist* (1860), *Asaph* (1861), *The Song-Garden* (1864), *The New Sabbath Hymn and Tune Book* (1866) and *Temple Choir* (with Theodore Frelinghuysen Seward, 1867). The firm also published anthologies by Thomas Hastings including *Sabbath School Songs* (1853), *The Shawm* (with G. F. Root, William B. Bradbury and Timothy Mason, 1853) and *Hastings' Church Music* (1860), as well as *The Dulcimer* (*c*1853) by Isaac Baker Woodbury. In addition to music, Mason Bros. published monographs, notably Lowell Mason's *Musical Letters from Abroad* (1854) and Hastings's *Dissertation on Musical Taste* (1853) and *History of Forty Choirs* (1854).

Fisher (1933); W. T. Marrocco and M. Jacobs: 'Mason', *Grove6*

C.E.

Matthysz, Paulus (*b* Harderwijk, 1613 or 1614; *d* Amsterdam, bur. 5 Dec 1684). Netherlands bookseller, printer and publisher. His shop 'in't Musyckboeck' was in the Stoof-Steegh, Amsterdam, and his business (not exclusively musical) began in 1640; his heirs, Alida and Maria Matthysz, continued it from 1681 to about 1720. He printed several editions for booksellers in Amsterdam (E. Cloppenburch, J. Jansz, L. Elzevier etc) and brought out others on his own account, including reissues. He sometimes accompanied the text with a Dutch translation or replaced it with an original Dutch text, as in Gastoldi's *Balletten . . . met drie stemmen: ende nu verrijckt met de vierde partije . . . ende op gheestelijcke gesangen gheset* (1641). Matthysz also published compositions and treatises by local composers, including Ban, J. Haffner, J. Butler, Van Eyck, Q. van Blankenburg and Hacquardt. Among his most important publications are collections of instrumental pieces, 20 *Koninklijke fantasien* (1648), *Der gooden fluyt hemel* (1644) and *'t Uitnemend kabinet* (1646–9); in this last collection he published his own 'brief dissertation on the hand-flute', and he probably composed pieces for that instrument.

E. vander Straeten: *La musique aux Pays-Bas avant le XIXe siècle* (Brussels, 1867–88/*R*1969), i (1867), 111, v (1880), 281; Goovaerts (1880); M. M. Kleerkooper and W. P. van Stockum: *De boekhandel te Amsterdam voornamelijk in de 17e eeuw* (The Hague, 1914–16); B. van den Sigtenhorst Meyer: 'Een volledig exemplaar van het "Livre septieme"', *TVNM*, xv/4 (1939), 252; B. Huys: *Catalogue des imprimés musicaux des XVe, XVIe et XVIIe siècles* (Brussels, 1965); D. van den Hul: *Jonheer Jacob van*

Eyck, *musicijn en directeur van de klockwercken tot Utrecht* (diss., U. of Utrecht, 1968); R. A. Rasch: 'Seventeenth Century Dutch Editions of English Instrumental Music: a Summary', *ML*, liii (1972), 270; idem: 'Some Mid-seventeenth Century Dutch Collections of Instrumental Ensemble Music', *TVNM*, xxii/3 (1972), 160; idem: 'Musica dîs curae est: the Life and Work of the Amsterdam Music Printer Paulus Matthysz (1613/4–1684)', *Quaerendo*, iv (1974), 86

H.V.

Mayer [Mayr]. Austrian firm of publishers. Johann Baptist Mayer founded a bookshop in Salzburg in 1655 which also published typeset music, including works by Andreas Hofer (1677). In 1704 and 1707 J. B. Samber's *Manuductio ad organum* and the *Continuatio* appeared; the firm was then J. B. Mayrs Witwe & Sohn, and in 1710 Samber's *Elucidatio musicae choralis* was published by Mayer's son Johann Joseph Mayr. The firm, subsequently called J. B. Mayrsche Buchhandlung, later issued sacred works by Michael Haydn (1797) and a *Te Deum* by J. J. Emmert. The firm continued into the 19th century.

A.W.

MCA Music. American firm of publishers. Founded in 1965 as a division of MCA Inc. (originally Merchandising Corporation of America), it is based in New York and represents Leeds Music Corp. (acquired by MCA Inc. in 1964), Duchess Music Corp. and Northern Music Co. The MCA catalogue contains over 80,000 compositions, and numerous popular songs, issued from its office in Universal City, California, are added weekly. The firm handles a wide range of music by modern Russian symphonists, and publishes works by contemporary American composers including Warren Benson, Henry Brant, Ulysses Kay, William Kraft, Elie Seigmeister, Robert Starer and Morton Subotnick. MCA also publishes educational music for band, orchestra, chorus and instrumental groups. In 1973 MCA Music formed a joint venture with the Mills Music division of Belwin-Mills.

W.T.M., M.J./L.A.T.

Meares [Mears, Meers]. English firm of instrument makers, music printers and publishers active in London in the late 17th century and early 18th. Richard Meares the elder is traceable in London by his instrument labels as early as 1669; he was a skilled maker of viols, lutes and other instruments. By 1713 he had engaged in printing and publishing music. His son Richard Meares the younger, who made a few instruments but later turned his attention entirely to publishing, appears to have been involved in the printing side of the business from 1717 or earlier, though the evidence is confused. In 1722 both the father's and the son's names are found on imprints, but Meares the elder seems to have died or retired about this time, and thereafter only the son's name appears. According to Hawkins, Meares the younger continued the business until his death about 1743. The Meares firm became one of Walsh's chief rivals, and each frequently pirated the other's publications. The firm's best publications and printed work rank among the finest of the period, and include Croft's *Musicus apparatus academicus* (1720), Handel's *Radamisto* (1720) and *Suite de pièces* (1720), John Church's *An Introduction to Psalmody* (1723), and sonatas by Castrucci, Corelli, Geminiani and others. Thomas Cross often engraved the plates of the firm's publications.

The two Richard Meares should not be confused with a typographical music printer named H. Meere, who printed one or two works for Walsh in 1716–19, or with W. Mears, a bookseller active about 1713 to 1734, who published the text and music of several ballad operas and some editions of the psalms with music.

HawkinsH; Kidson (1900); Humphries and Smith (1954, 2/1970)

P.W.J.

Mechetti. Austrian firm of publishers, active in Vienna. Carlo Mechetti (*b* Lucca, 1748; *d* Vienna, 30 Jan 1811) was for many years a steward in the service of Count Karl Colloredo. His associations with members of the higher aristocracy benefited his business transactions to such an extent that he soon acquired a considerable fortune, and on 3 November 1798 he took out an art dealer's licence. He appointed as his assistant his nephew Pietro Mechetti (*b* Lucca, 20 April 1777; *d* Vienna, 25 July 1850), whom he subsequently adopted. The deed of partnership (28 February 1807) made Pietro a public partner in the firm of Carlo Mechetti e Nipote, which was by then publishing music. Pietro Mechetti was granted a new art dealer's licence on 10 July 1810. His uncle made him sole inheritor and, after Carlo's death, Pietro showed his gratitude by always signing the name of the firm (registered on 18 February 1811) as Pietro Mechetti qdm. Carlo. The publishing of music gained impetus only after the Napoleonic wars. Through reliable business management the firm of Mechetti was always able to hold its own against its larger competitors, Haslinger and Diabelli. Pietro's son Karl (1811–47) became a manager of the firm but died at the age of 37; Pietro

survived him by three years, his widow Therese continuing the firm under the name Pietro Mechetti sel. Witwe until her death (28 June 1855). The publishing rights then passed to C.A. Spina.

The publication programme was generally above average and included the first edition of Beethoven's *Polonaise* op.89, new editions of opp.10 and 13 and some of his arrangements; the firm also issued first editions of Mendelssohn, Moscheles, Nicolai, Schubert (D356), Schumann and Spohr, and numerous works by Czerny, Donizetti, Fahrbach, Fesca, von Krufft, Leidesdorf, Payer, Pixis, Pohl, Rossini, Vanhal and Voříšek. Like Haslinger and Diabelli, Mechetti was obliged to publish light music in order to finance the less commercial publications, and thus became the principal publisher of Josef Lanner and the younger Johann Strauss. The firm ran several important series, including the *Aurora d'Italia e di Germania* (352 numbers), containing separate pieces from the most popular Italian and German operas, the *Anthologie musicale* (over 100 numbers), *Der musikalische Sammler* (95 numbers) and three series of *Terpsichore*, which included dance and ballet music. Among the firm's catalogues are the *Verlags-Katalog* (1846, 1st suppl. 1847) and two publishers' reports issued by Therese (1853–4), all in the Gesellschaft der Musikfreunde, Vienna.

Deutsch (1946); C. Junker: *Festschrift zur Feier des hundertjährigen Bestehens der Korporation . . . 1807–1907* (Vienna, 1907); M. Kratochwil: *Monographie über Carlo Mechetti* (Vienna, 1958); A. Weinmann: *Verlags-Verzeichnis Pietro Mechetti qdm. Carlo* (Vienna, 1966)

A.W.

Meltzer, Adam (*b* Neustadt an der Heide, nr. Coburg; *d* Dillingen an der Donau, 1609). German printer. In 1587 he was a journeyman at Frankfurt an der Oder; subsequently he moved to Dillingen an der Donau (1591) to work for Johann Meyer, and in 1603 he established his own business. After his death his widow ran the press until 1610, when she sold it to the printer Gregor Haenlin. Meltzer's publications consist mainly of music, and he was responsible for disseminating the works of such Swabian composers as Erbach, Aichinger, Klingenstein and Jacob Reiner.

O. Bucher: 'Adam Meltzer (1603–1610) und Gregor Haenlin (1610–1617) als Musikdrucker in Dillingen/Donau', *Gutenberg-Jb 1956*, 216

T.W.

Mense, Pascha [Mensenius, Paschen] (*fl* 1642–74). German printer, active in Königsberg. Probably the son of the court bookbinder Joachim Mense of Güstrow, he was trained in bookbinding. On 24 February 1642 he married Elisabeth, the widow of Lorenz Segebade, and with Segebade's son Josua continued the Segebade shop in Königsberg under his own name. Mostly between 1642 and 1651, Mense printed some 25 sacred and secular works, vocal and instrumental, including music by Heinrich Albert, Conrad Matthaei, Valentin Haussmann, Christoph Kaldenbach and Christoph Werner. Several were reprints of vocal music by Albert originally issued by Segebade. During most of his career he was involved in litigation with Johann Reusner, who also reprinted Segebade editions. Because of debts, he sold his shop to a Professor Reich from the university in 1671 but continued to work there until 1674.

Benzing (1963, 2/1982)

T.D.W.

Merseburger. German firm of publishers. It was founded in Leipzig on 21 September 1849 when Carl Merseburger (1816–85) purchased the C. F. Meusel publishing house in Weissenfels. From 1885 to 1898 Carl's brother Otto Merseburger (1822–98) directed the business, followed until 1918 by Otto's son Max Merseburger (1853–1935) with Georg Merseburger (1871–1958); by 1904 Georg had founded his own book publishing concern in Leipzig. In 1944 the firm in Leipzig was destroyed, but it was re-established in Berlin in 1951 by Georg's son Karl Merseburger (1905–78), with temporary subsidiaries in Heidelberg and Darmstadt. In 1956 Adolf Strube acquired the firm, which became a limited company in 1964. Wolfgang Mattei (b 1925) became principal shareholder in 1972.

Carl Merseburger was also a writer on music (*Taschenbüchlein des Musikers*, 1858, 31 editions; *Kleines Tonkünstlerlexikon*, 1860, 14/1936). He established his firm as publishers of educational music, founding an educational periodical *Euterpe* (1851–94, ed. E. J. Hentschel and Ludwig Erk); Strube, an author for the firm from 1924, followed the same policy. The firm is one of the principal Protestant church music publishers in Germany; it also issues musicological literature, new editions of old masters, and the periodicals *Der Kirchenmusiker* (1950) and *Ars organi* (1952).

Katalog der Bücher und Musikalien . . . welche in den 50 Jahren 1849–1899 erschienen sind (Leipzig, 1899); *Festgabe des Pädagogischen Verlages C. Merseburger zum 75. Gründungsgedenktage* (Leipzig, 1924); *100 Jahre im Dienste der Musik: aus der Arbeit des Verlages C. Merseburger* (Leipzig, 1949); K. Merseburger and R. Elvers, eds.: *Adolf Strube*

zum 60. Geburtstag (Berlin and Darmstadt, 1954); *Musikverlage in der Bundesrepublik Deutschland und in West-Berlin* (Bonn, 1965)

R.E.

Merulo [Merlotti], Claudio (*b* Correggio, 8 April 1533; *d* Parma, 5 May 1604). Italian composer, organist, publisher and editor. His career as a music printer, from 1566 to 1570, was brief but productive, and his editorial activities continued at least until 1575. Throughout this period he was organist at St Mark's, Venice. In 1566 he and his business partner, Fausto Bethanio, printed, with music type probably acquired from Plinio Pietrasanta, several first editions, including music by Primavera, Wert, Merulo himself and Porta, whom Merulo called 'carissimo amico mio'. The partnership was apparently very short-lived; a reprint of Verdelot for 1566 is signed by Merulo alone, and in an arbitrator's ruling of the following year, he, although assigned complete control of the firm, was required to compensate Bethanio with both equipment and a part of the stock.

Merulo continued to bring out reprints and new volumes, 32 works in all, including his own *Ricercari d'intavolatura d'organo . . . libro primo* (1567) and *Messe d'intavolatura d'organo . . . libro quarto* (1568). The numbering of these volumes conforms to a programme laid out in the 1567 *Ricercari*. Merulo planned editions of organ music by himself and others, including Andrea Gabrieli, in 12 volumes; although these two are the only ones extant from his press, book 7 (*Toccate*) survives in an edition by Verovio (1598 and 1604) and books 8 (*Canzoni*) and 12 (Gabrieli's *Ricercari*) in editions by Gardano.

Merulo's printer's mark was a woodcut representing Proserpina's golden bough with the motto 'Simili frondescat virga metallo' ('Let a bough put forth leaves in the same metal'), a variation of the phrase from the *Aeneid* (vi, 144). In 1571 this device, along with Merulo's music type, began to be used in editions signed by Giorgio Angelieri, who may previously have been Merulo's foreman. Merulo seems to have continued working with Angelieri, as an editor: Angelieri's 1571 printing of *Madrigali* by Aurelio Roccia was 'per Claudio Merulo . . . corretti', as were Angelieri's reprints of Arcadelt's first book of four-voice madrigals (1572) and Palestrina's first book (1574), and possibly books by Lasso and Rore (both 1573) as well. In some volumes, notably the 1566 edition of Verdelot's first and second books of madrigals, Merulo edited with a heavy pencil, making systematic changes of underlay and a variety of musical alterations.

He tried to remove tritones and consecutive octaves. He completed chords by adding thirds, altered chords to different inversions and changed the modal pattern by altering accidentals. In this edition, however, he left or created as many flaws as he removed, and later books showing his editorial hand are much more conservatively – and accurately – edited.

A. Catelani: 'Memorie della vita e delle opere di Claudio Merulo', *Gazzetta musicale di Milano*, xviii (1860); Q. Bigi: *Di Claudio Merulo da Correggio* (Parma, 1861); A. Einstein: 'Claudio Merulo's Ausgabe der Madrigale des Verdelot', *SIMG*, viii (1906–7), 220–54; Sartori (1958); T. W. Bridges: *The Publishing of Arcadelt's First Book of Madrigals* (diss., Harvard U., 1982)

T.W.B.

Meser, Carl Friedrich (*d* 1856). German publisher. In addition to works issued in his role as dealer for the Dresden court, he arranged to publish Richard Wagner's *Rienzi* and *Der fliegende Holländer* (1844). The music was issued in piano-vocal scores, also in orchestral scores of 25 copies, on commission and at the expense of Wagner, who, typically, called on friends for loans but still ended up considerably indebted to Meser. *Tannhäuser* was similarly issued in late 1845. Its orchestral score was copied by Wagner himself, on special paper for lithographic printing of 100 copies by an 'autographic transfer process'. In 1848 Wagner failed to persuade Breitkopf & Härtel to buy out Meser's properties in conjunction with their publication of *Lohengrin*; but on Meser's death his firm was acquired by three of Wagner's friends, including the doctor Anton Pusinelli. The business management was assigned to Hermann Müller, who in 1859 purchased the firm for 3000 Thalers, selling it in turn to Adolf Fürstner in 1872.

W. Altmann: *Richard Wagners Briefe nach Zeitfolge und Inhalt* (Leipzig, 1905/*R*1971); R. Wagner: *Mein Leben* (Munich, 1911, rev. 1963); E. Newman: *The Life of Richard Wagner* (London, 1933–47/*R*1976), i, 411, 504, ii, 33; Fuld (1966, 3/1985); C. Hopkinson: *Tannhäuser: an Examination of 36 Editions* (Tutzing, 1973); R. Strohm, ed.: *Dokumente und Texte zu 'Rienzi, der Letzte der Tribuneu'*, R. Wagner: *Sämtliche Werke*, xxiii (Mainz, 1976); H. F. G. Klein: *Erstdrucke der musikallischen Werke von Richard Wagner* (Tutzing, 1983)

D.W.K.

Métru, Nicolas (*b* Bar-sur-Aube, ?*c*1610; *d* after 1663). French composer, teacher and publisher. He was living in Paris by 1631, when he was referred to as a 'maître compositeur de musique'. On 21 June 1633 he obtained official permission 'to print, sell and distribute, through any printer or bookseller he may choose, every kind of music he has produced or may produce in the future'. To this end he took on a printer from Pierre Ballard, who at the time had a monopoly of music publishing and now used his influence in high places to suppress his rival. On 7 April 1635 he managed to get Métru's privilege withdrawn; however, a judgment of 3 July 1635 obliged him to print all of Métru's works from then on and 'to provide him with 100 copies' of each. Métru was highly thought of as a teacher: in 1643 Gantez spoke of 'Vincent, Métru and Massé, the three most celebrated teachers in Paris', and also stated that Métru was *maître de musique* to the Jesuits. A document of 1692 (*Mémoire des compositeurs*), corroborated by La Borde, states that, together with Roberday and Gigault, he was one of Lully's teachers.

A. Gantez: *L'entretien des musiciens* (Auxerre, 1643), ed. with commentary by E. Thoinan (Paris, 1878/*R*1971); *Mémoire des compositeurs, clavecinistes et luthiers, lors du procès contre les ménestriers et joueurs d'instruments* (Paris, 1692); J.-B. de La Borde: *Essai sur la musique ancienne et moderne* (Paris, 1780/*R*1972)

D.L.

Metzler. English firm of instrument dealers and publishers, established in London. The founder was Valentin Metzler, a native of Bingen am Rhein who opened a shop in London for the sale of instruments in 1788. The name Metzler first appears in the London directories in 1812, and about four years later, when the publishing side of the business was apparently started, Metzler was joined by his son George Richard Metzler (1797–1867) to form the firm Metzler & Son. In 1833, presumably the year of the elder Metzler's death, the firm became G. Metzler & Co.; by 1838 they were dealing in early forms of harmonium. George Richard Metzler retired in 1866 in favour of his son George Thomas (1835–79), a well-known writer of song lyrics. In 1867 a partnership was established with Frank Chappell, who remained with the company until his death in 1886. Their publishing activities covered all fields; many of the songs of Sullivan and Goring Thomas were published by the firm, and keyboard music was especially prominent in its catalogue. Among its operatic successes were Sullivan's *The Sorcerer* and *HMS Pinafore*, and it held the British rights for Bizet's *Carmen* and French songs and piano music by Gounod, Bizet, Godard and others. The firm became a limited company in 1893, and was taken over by J. B. Cramer in 1931.

Humphries and Smith (1954, 2/1970); Coover (1988)

P.W.J.

Michel de Toulouse [Toulouze] (*fl* 1496–1505). French printer. He was presumably from Toulouse, and may have been the first to print mensural music using movable type; his *L'art et instruction de bien dancer* uses type and is earlier than Petrucci, though in many respects rather crude. He was not the earliest music printer in Paris, though his predecessors had printed only liturgical volumes. He was living there in 1496, close to Guerson, who also printed and sold music. They seem to have collaborated, for Michel printed a volume of Guerson's and also used some of his type. He is mentioned in Guerson's will of 1503, and was last referred to in 1505.

None of Michel's four musical books is dated, although 1488 has been added by hand to *L'art*. This is certainly too early; it was probably printed about 1496. All Michel's other known publications (nearly 20) date from after this. *L'art et instruction de bien dancer* is an important collection of melodies for the basse danse, with instructions; it is closely related to a Brussels manuscript of dance tenors (Bibliothèque Royale 9085).

V. Scholderer: Introduction to facs. edn. of *L'art et instruction de bien dancer* (London, 1936); M. Dean-Smith: 'A Fifteenth Century Dancing Book', *JEFDSS*, iii (1936–9), 100; K. Meyer: 'Michel de Toulouze', *MR*, vii (1946), 178; F. Crane: *Materials for the Study of the Fifteenth Century Basse Danse* (New York, 1968); R. Rastall, ed.: *L'art et instruction de bien dancer* (Wakefield, 1971) [facs. and edn.]

S.B. (iii)

Micheletti, Gioseffo [Giuseppe] (*fl* 1683–92). Italian publisher. He was active in Bologna, keeping his printing establishment on the Pavaglione. He published sacred music by Cazzati (op.19, 1687), Cavanni (op.1, 1689) and Albergati (op.7, 1691), chamber cantatas by G. F. Tosi (op.2, 1688) and instrumental music by G. B. Degli Antoni (opp.1 and 3–6, 1687–90), G. Torelli (opp.1–3 and 5, 1686–92), Gaspardini (op.1, 1683), Clemente Monari (op.1, 1686), Mazzolini (op.1, 1687), Berri (op.1, 1688), Elia Vannini (op.1, 1691) and Belisi (op.1, 1691). Micheletti's publications are characterized by neatness and elegance; his typographical mark is an angel with a cornucopia filled with flowers, a crown or a noble coat-of-arms.

F. Vatielli: 'Editori musicali dei secoli XVII e XVIII', *Arte e vita musicale a Bologna* (Bologna, 1927/*R*1969), 239; L. Gottardi: *La stampa musicale in Bologna dagli inizi fino al 1700* (diss., U. of Bologna, 1951); Sartori (1958); Mischiati (1984)

A.S. (ii)

Miller & Beacham. American firm of publishers. It was established in Baltimore in 1853 by William C. Miller (*b* Baltimore, MD, 1826; *d* Baltimore, 30 March 1894) and Joseph R. Beacham, who took over the business of Frederick D. Benteen, a piano dealer who had also published music since 1839. From 1865 to 1872 the company operated under the name of W.C. Miller; in 1873 it was taken over by Ditson. Among the pieces published by the firm was the earliest edition (1861) of *Maryland! My Maryland*.

B.T.

Miller Music. American firm of publishers. It was founded in New York in about 1930 by William H. Woodin (1868–1934), a financier and later Secretary of the Treasury whose chief hobby was music, and the composer Charles Miller. The two men had been introduced by Jerome Kern who, with Miller, worked for the publisher Harms. The Miller catalogue consists of popular songs such as *Whispering*, *More than you know*, *The Whiffenpoof Song*, *Be my love*, *If I give my heart to you* and *Love is a many splendored thing*, as well as Hawaiian popular songs. In 1939 Miller became part of the Big 3 Music Corporation, which came under the ownership of United Artists in 1973.

F.B.

Mills, Irving (*b* New York, 16 Jan 1894; *d* Palm Springs, CA, 21 April 1985). American publisher. With his brother Jack (?1892–1979) he established Jack Mills, Inc. (later Mills Music) in New York in 1919. The firm built its reputation on developing the work of unknown songwriters; among those whose early careers it assisted are Zez Confrey, Hoagy Carmichael, Sammy Fain, Jimmy McHugh, Dorothy Fields, Harold Arlen, Fats Waller and Duke Ellington. The leading publisher of piano novelties, it became one of the most important dance-band publishers before World War II; its pioneering dance-combo orchestrations were called 'orchettes'. Mills himself managed Duke Ellington and Cab Calloway, produced records for several dozen jazz bands and in 1937 founded the short-lived Master and Variety record labels; he collaborated as lyricist on hundreds of popular songs. By 1949 Mills Music and its subsidiary American Academy of Music owned nearly 20,000 copyrights in popular, educational and 'standard' (classical, light classical and film) music, including works by Roy Harris, Leroy Anderson, Antal Dorati and Morton Gould. The firm was sold in 1965, became part of Belwin-Mills Publishing Corp. in 1969 and was later purchased by Simon & Schuster; in 1985 it was sold to Columbia Pictures Industries, Inc.

S. Kemp: 'New Talent his Specialty: Irving Mills Discovers and Develops Unknown Personalities', *The Metronome*, xlv/4 (1930), 31, 60; 'The House That Jack Built', *International Musician*, xlvii/ March (1949), 12, 33; Obituary of Jack Mills, *New York Times* (26 March 1979); Obituary of Irving Mills, *New York Times* (23 April 1985)

J.E.H.

Moderne, Jacques (*b* Pinguente, *c*1495–1500; *d* Lyons, in or after 1562). French printer of Italian birth. He was the second printer to publish music on a large scale in France. The first was Pierre Attaingnant of Paris, who began issuing his music books in 1528, using a practical and relatively inexpensive single-impression method which he had just developed. Moderne was one of the first (along with Christian Egenolff independently in Frankfurt) to adapt this new method for his own use. He began printing polyphonic music in 1532 (a book of plainsong masses is dated 1530) and continued to be Attaingnant's only rival in France for 15 years.

From the identification on his early books as 'Jacobus Modernus de Pinguento' we know that Moderne was born in the village of Pinguente (now Buzet, Yugoslavia) on the Istrian peninsula. Whether he spent some apprentice years in Venice cannot be determined. He appeared on the tax rolls of Lyons for the first time in 1523 as a bookseller and regularly thereafter in the Lyons archives until the early 1560s. According to a contract dated 28 May 1562 he rented out a room in his house, but in 1568 his widow is listed in the tax records.

He is identified in the archives and frequently on his title-pages as 'grand Jacques', no doubt because of his girth or his height, or both. His social stature must have been substantial as well, since the Lyons records show him to have been a modest landowner and an official in various Lyons activities, as well as a neighbour to some of that city's most prominent citizens.

Moderne's publishing activity was by no means restricted to music. He was an active printer of several types of popular books – on religion, home remedies, emblems and palmistry among others – in Latin and in French. Though some undated ones were undoubtedly printed before, the earliest dated one appeared in 1526. He continued printing these books throughout his career.

Music is the part of his production that brought him the greatest renown. Masses, motets, chansons and instrumental music are well represented in his books. He published a series of eight motet anthologies from 1532 to 1542, four called *Motteti del fiore* because of the woodcut of a thistle (see illustration). A similar series of 11 (or perhaps more) chanson collections, named *Le parangon des chansons*, was issued between 1538 and 1543. Later several books were devoted to the music of single composers. There were also three books of plainsong masses, some monophonic noëls and two treatises on music theory reprinted from earlier sources. There is no evidence that Moderne was a musician himself. He is never so described in the contemporary records, nor has any music written by him turned up in MSS or printed editions.

Moderne was probably persuaded to try his hand at music printing by Francesco de Layolle, a Florentine composer and the organist at Notre Dame de Confort in Lyons. He acted as editor for Moderne's first musical publication, *Liber decem missarum* of 1532, as Moderne acknowledged in the dedication. He probably continued as Moderne's editor, especially since the greater part of the musical output was published or prepared for publication before Layolle's death around 1540. After that the originality of the repertory declined.

Moderne printed about 50 music books, which contain over 800 pieces. More than half are unique to Moderne's books. Many of the rest were frequently reprinted later by others but made their first printed appearance here. These books are a particularly important source for the music of Layolle and of Pierre de Villiers, who seems to have lived in Lyons and perhaps also offered musical assistance to Moderne. Besides Layolle and Villiers, Henry Fresneau and G. Coste are other probable Lyonese composers in these collections. Pierre Colin of Autun seems to have had a special connection to Moderne, since two publications are devoted exclusively to Colin's masses, Magnificats and motets, and other motets and chansons appear frequently elsewhere. Most of the composers best represented in the collections are international figures like Gombert, Willaert, Arcadelt, Lhéritier and Jacquet of Mantua, or members of the Parisian school like Claudin de Sermisy, Maillard, Sandrin, Certon and the ubiquitous Janequin. In contrast to Attaingnant, who confined himself for the most part to French and Netherlands composers, Moderne included works by composers from Italy, Spain and

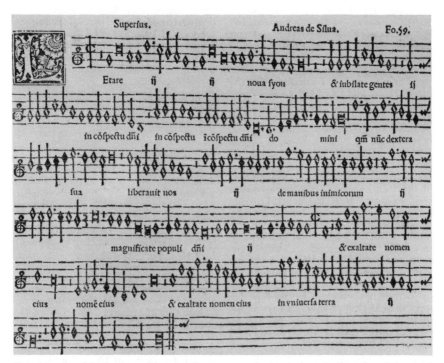

Superius voice of the first part of the motet 'Laetare nova Sion' by Andreas de Silva, from 'Motteti del fiore', printed by Jacques Moderne (Lyons, 1532)

Title-page of the superius partbook of 'Motteti del fiore', printed by Moderne (Lyons, 1532)

Germany. He devoted entire books to Italian canzonas by Layolle and Matteo Rampollini and to lute music by Francescho Bianchini and Giovanni Paolo Paladino. The first part of *Musique de joye*, reprinted from a Venetian source, contains ricercares by a number of other Italians. Morales, Mateo Flecha and Luys de Narváez represented Spain, and Leonhard Paminger and Mathias Eckel were from Germany. Moderne was the first to print the lute music of the Hungarian Balínt Bakfark.

Some explanation for the variety in Moderne's repertory lies in the character of the place where he worked. In the first half of the 16th century Lyons was a cosmopolitan city with large Italian and German colonies, an important centre for the new printing trade and a meeting ground for intellectuals. Its position on the border between France and Savoy and at the confluence of the Saône and Rhône rivers made it a crossroads. Fairs four times a year brought traders from as far away as Lebanon in the east and Portugal to the west. Thus Moderne had access to music of varied origins and a ready market to disseminate his music books throughout Europe.

F. Lesure: 'Moderne, Jacques', *MGG*; J. Vial: 'Un imprimeur lyonnais méconnu, Jacques Moderne', *Gutenberg-Jb 1962*, 256; D. Heartz: *Pierre Attaingnant, Royal Printer of Music* (Berkeley and Los Angeles, 1969), 144; S. F. Pogue: *Jacques Moderne: Lyons Music Printer of the Sixteenth Century* (Geneva, 1969); idem: 'Further Notes on Jacques Moderne', *Bibliothèque d'Humanisme et Renaissance*, xxxvii (1975), 245; idem: 'A Sixteenth-century Editor at Work: Gardane and Moderne', *Journal of Musicology*, i (1982), 217; L. Guillo: 'Les motets de Layolle et les psaumes de Piéton: deux nouvelles éditions lyonnaises du seizième siècle', *FAM*, xxxii (1985), 186; S. F. Pogue: 'The Earliest Music Printing in France', *Huntington Library Quarterly*, l/1 (1987), 35

S.F.P.

Moilli, Damiano (*b* Parma, *c*1439; *d* Parma, *c*1500). Italian printer, active at Parma. He was called a book printer and illuminator in documents of 1474 but later listed variously as a paper dealer, bookseller, ceramicist and bookbinder. He worked in the manuscript book trade before and after his publication of four printed books between 1477 and 1482, supplying the local Benedictine convent with liturgical books. His first printed book, an abbreviated *Graduale* of 1477 (issued with his brother Bernardo), was a milestone of early music printing, the third known printed music book after the *c*1473 *Graduale* and Han's 1476 *Missale*. Its giant roman plainchant type, printed in black on pages with four red staves (each 55mm high), is the largest known, nearly double that used in the *Graduale* printed by Emerich at Venice in 1499, with seven staves a page. Many of the 33 type designs were cast on abutting and kerned sorts so that they could be joined together to create complex neumes.

M. K. Duggan: 'The Music Type of the Second Dated Printed Music Book, the 1477 *Graduale Romanum*', *La bibliofilia*, lxxxix (1987), 285

M.K.D.

Moller & Capron. American firm of publishers, among the earliest in the USA devoted exclusively to music. It was founded in Philadelphia by John Christopher Moller [Möller] (*b* Germany, 1755; *d* New York, 21 Sept 1803), a composer, organist and with Alexander Reinagle co-manager of the City Concerts (1790–93), and Henri Capron (*fl* 1785–95), a cellist and singer also connected with Reinagle. In 1793 the partners opened a music shop. *Moller and Capron's Monthly Numbers* were advertised on 13 March 1793 as available on subscription, each to contain six pages. The four extant numbers include original works by both Moller and Capron as well as other music performed at the concert series and at the recently founded New Theatre in Chestnut Street. The partners soon separated, Capron to head a French boarding school in 1794, Moller to continue publishing in Philadelphia and later in New York, where he was organist at Trinity Episcopal Church and manager of the summer pleasure gardens. In November 1794 George Willig began publishing music 'in the house formerly occupied by Mr. Moller', thus continuing a business which through the subsequent succession of Ditson and Presser is still active.

O. G. T. Sonneck: *A Bibliography of Early Secular American Music* (Washington, DC, 1905; rev. and enlarged by W. T. Upton, 2/1945/*R*1964), 265; R. D. Stetzel: *John Christopher Moller (1755–1803) and his Role in Early American Music* (diss., U. of Iowa, 1965); E. C. Wolf: 'Music in Old Zion, Philadelphia, 1750–1850', *MQ*, lviii (1972), 622–52; Wolfe (1980); H. W. Hitchcock: 'Capron, Henri', *GroveAM*; R. D. Stetzel: 'Moller, John Christopher', ibid

D.W.K.

Mollo, Tranquillo (*b* Bellinzona, 10 Aug 1767; *d* Bellinzona, after 1837). Italian music publisher active in Vienna. He was first employed by the firm of Artaria in Vienna and in 1793 was made a partner. After leaving Artaria, he and Domenico Artaria (iii) founded the firm of T. Mollo & Co. in July 1798. In October 1802 Mollo purchased Carlo Artaria's firm which

Domenico Artaria then directed while Mollo remained at the parent firm. In 1804 Domenico Artaria broke with Mollo and reactivated the family firm in the Kohlmarkt; Mollo continued to run his business under his own name as a map, art and music publishing firm. The firm's basic stock consisted of the material taken over from Artaria in the years 1798 and 1804; thus the works published up until that time bear the imprint of Artaria or Mollo, but often with the plate numbers altered. Production begun after 1804 brought a confusing array of altered plate and edition numbers which have still not been clarified; current works from the old stock were also reprinted when necessary.

Music publishing, somewhat neglected during the troubled years of war in favour of map production, began to flourish again after 1815. Under Mollo's direction his sons Eduard (1799–1842) and Florian (*b* 1802) worked in the firm. On 1 January 1832 Tranquillo announced his official retirement in a printed advertisement, and on 17 February of that year the publishing house was renamed Kunsthandlung der Tranquillo Mollo's Söhne. A division soon followed: Eduard retained his father's shop, while Florian founded his own firm on 4 July 1834, which existed until June 1839. Eduard joined G. Cappi's firm in 1837 and worked there until his death. The final fortunes of the firm are reported in a contract between Mollo's sons and Tobias Haslinger, by which 630 publications on 11,348 plates were transferred to the latter. Haslinger wrote the document on 24 May 1832; it lists each work with the sum of the plates and plate numbers, providing valuable material for research into both Mollo's and Haslinger's publishing firms. Written five months after Mollo's retirement, the contract gives a detailed account of his sons' plans as well as information on Haslinger.

The output of the publishing house T. Mollo & Co. and later T. Mollo alone (after 1804) shows a wide variety of composers (most of them represented by a few works only) including Cherubini, Clementi, Fiorillo, Gyrowetz, Kreutzer, J. B. Cramer, Eberl, G. G. Ferrari, Krommer, G. J. Vogler and Vanhal. Works by Haydn and Mozart are chiefly from the Artaria period while Beethoven's (including 19 original pieces) come from both periods. After 1804 music by new and less important composers was published, including Bevilacqua, L. von Call (*c*100 works), Carulli, Diabelli, J. L. Dussek, Josef Gelinek, Mauro Giuliani, E. von Lannoy, Adolf Müller, Paer, Payer, Pleyel, Ries, Rossini, Steibel and Zumsteeg. On 30 December 1828 the first edition of Franz Schubert's choral work *Glaube, Hoffnung und Liebe* (D954) was published.

F. Gräffer: *Kleine Wiener Memoiren und Wiener Dosenstücke*, i (Munich, 1917), 292, 549; G. Gugitz: *Von Leuten und Zeiten im alten Wien* (Vienna and Leipzig, 1922), 139; A. Weinmann: *Vollständiges Verlagsverzeichnis Artaria & Comp.* (Vienna, 1952); idem: *Verlagsverzeichnis Tranquillo Mollo* (Vienna, 1964); idem: *Ergänzungen zum Verlagsverzeichnis Tranquillo Mollo* (Vienna, 1972)

A.W.

Monguillot. Argentine publisher, active in Buenos Aires. The firm was established by Gabino Monguillot, who set up shop in 1850 and published under the imprint of Monguillot & Nelson, 1855–67. In 1867 the firm of Eugenio Guión, founded in 1848, was acquired. In 1878 the firm discontinued under its own name, publishing mainly as Felipe P. Rodriguez, though some of the titles passed to De Costa Amaro. The catalogue included sheet music of a local character and some posthumous Gottschalk editions.

J.M.V.

Monti, Giacomo (*fl* Bologna, 1639–89). Italian publisher, father of Pier Maria Monti. He began his publishing activities in Bologna in 1632, establishing a printing press near the church of S Matteo delle Pescherie. Two years later he entered into partnership with Carlo Zenero, and the press was moved to the street of S Mamolo in 1638. Its first musical publication was Corbetta's *Scherzi armonici: suonate sopra la chitarra spagnola* (1639), followed in the same year by Piccinini's *Il secondo libro di intavolature di liuto*. Shortly thereafter the partnership was dissolved, and Monti continued the business alone, publishing mostly historical and sacred works. In 1662 he resumed his musical activities, having moved to a shop under the vault of the Pollaroli, and until 1689 his musical production was intense, consisting chiefly of works by Bolognese composers. He seems to have worked completely independently at first. During this period his typographical mark was a figure of S Petronio, the patron saint of Bologna.

In about 1668 the Bolognese bookseller Marino Silvani associated himself with Monti, at first using his presses for several of the anthologies he himself edited (*Sacri concerti*, 1668; *Nuova raccolta di motetti sacri*, 1670; *Canzonette per camera a voce sola*, 1670; *Scielta di suonate a 2 violini e bc. per organo*, 1680), as well as for music by Filippini (op.10), G. B. Bassani (opp.1 and 5), Albergati (op.2), Domenico Gabrielli (op.1) and Corelli (reprint of op.1), all within the period 1683–4. Apparently Silvani and Monti then made an agreement that gave Silvani the exclusive rights to sell Monti's publications. From 1685 all the publications of Giacomo Monti carried the indication 'sold by M. Silvani at the sign of the violin', and the typographical mark was nearly always a violin with the motto 'UTRElevet, MIserum FAtum SOLitosque LAbores'. The secular production of the firm during this period was somewhat limited but included madrigals by G. B. Bassani, Mazzaferrata, G. B. Bianchi and G. M. Bononcini and canzoñettas and chamber cantatas by G. M. Bononcini, Cazzati, Cherici, Cossoni, Legrenzi, Mazzaferrata and Penna. For sacred and instrumental music, however, production was far more extensive, preferred authors being G. P. Colonna, Cossoni, Filippini, G. B. Vitali, G. Bononcini, G. B. Degli Antonii, G.B. Bassani, Mazzaferrata, Cazzati, Albergati, Corelli, Berardi and Penna. Monti published an index, probably in 1682, of works printed by the firm (*Indice dell'opere di musica sin'hora stampate da Giacomo Monti in Bologna*). In 1689 the business passed to Pier Maria Monti.

F. Vatielli: 'Editori musicali dei secoli XVII e XVIII', *Arte e vita musicale a Bologna* (Bologna, 1927/*R*1969), 239; A. Sorbelli: *Storia della stampa a Bologna* (Bologna, 1929); L. Gottardi: *La stampa musicale in Bologna dagli inizi fino al 1700* (diss., U. of Bologna, 1951); Sartori (1958); Mischiati (1984)

A.S. (ii)

Monti, Pier Maria (*fl* Bologna, 1689–1709). Italian publisher, son of Giacomo Monti. He succeeded his father in 1689, taking over a well-established printing house that had been active in Bolognese music publishing since 1639. Like his father's, his publications were sold by Marino Silvani, and later also by Lelio della Volpe. The composers whose works were published by the Monti firm during these 20 years (mostly between 1690 and 1695) included G. Bononcini, Domenico Gabrielli, Corelli, G. P. Colonna, Elia Vannini, Jacchini, G. B. Bassani and Francesco Passarini. Monti's last musical edition seems to have been a reprint of Paradossi's *Il modo di suonare il sistro* (1702). After his death his heirs continued the non-musical part of the firm's publishing activities, becoming the official printers for the Holy Office; the music publishing was taken over by the Silvani firm. In general the typography of the Monti press (both father and son) lacks care and elegance and has a commercial character.

For bibliography *see* MONTI, GIACOMO.

A.S. (ii)

Monzani, Tebaldo [Theobald] (*b* Duchy of Modena, 1762; *d* London, 14 June 1839). Italian instrument maker and publisher. He moved to England, where he became well known as a solo and orchestral flautist, and in 1787 established premises in London where from various addresses he published his own compositions (mainly for flute) and other works. From 1789 he sometimes employed the piano maker and music publisher James Ball to print and sell his publications. In 1800 Monzani entered a partnership with Giambattista Cimador (*b* Venice, 1761; *d* Bath, 27 Feb 1805) as Monzani & Cimador, from about 1803 occupying a building known as The Opera Music Warehouse. They issued periodical collections of Italian and English vocal music, and published Mozart operas, advertising that 'any of the songs, Duetts, Trios, Overtures … may be had Single & the whole of Mozart's Pianoforte Compositions, published in Numbers'. Many of these were arranged or provided with piano accompaniments by Cimador. His arrangement of several Mozart symphonies for flute and strings was allegedly provoked by the refusal of the King's Theatre orchestra to play the works in their original form because of their difficulty; six of these were published by Monzani after Cimador's death. From 1805 Monzani continued alone as Monzani & Co. until about 1807, when he established a partnership with Henry Hill and the firm became Monzani & Hill; about 1815 it obtained royal patronage as 'music seller to the Prince Regent'. The partnership was dissolved in 1829 and Henry Hill and his sons continued the business until 1845, when the firm was sold by auction.

Monzani and his successors issued much sheet music, especially Italian vocal pieces, but their publications also included the piano works of Mozart and Beethoven. Monzani made many flutes and clarinets and had a high reputation as a craftsman. He also wrote a tutor, *Instructions for the German Flute* (1801, 3/*c*1820).

Humphries and Smith (1954, 2/1970); Neighbour and Tyson (1965)

W.C.S./P.W.J.

Moore, Thomas. English printer, active in the 17th century. He worked in London and was the first, with John Heptinstall and Francis Clark, to introduce the 'new tied note', wherein the tails of quavers and semiquavers are joined instead of being printed separately (*Vinculum societatis*, Book 1, 1687; for illustration *see* HEPTIN-STALL, JOHN). Moore was associated with Heptinstall in four other publications: the second and third books of both *Vinculum societatis* (1688, 1689) and *Comes amoris* (1688, 1691).

Day and Murrie (1940)

D.R.H.

Morawetz Brothers. Romanian firm of publishers, active in Timişoara. It was established in 1920 by the Morawetz brothers, then taken over in 1933 by a joint stock company, the Mentor Publishing House of Timişoara (1933–44). It published classical works for music schools and Romanian and foreign instrumental methods, and encouraged modern Romanian composers, especially those from Banat (S. Drăgoi, Z. Vancea, V. Sumski, F. Barbu). Besides the magazine *Muzica* (1921–5), it also issued monographs, folklore collections, musicological works and translations.

V.C.

Moücke, Francesco (*b* Hamburg, 1700; *d* Florence, 1758). Italian publisher, active in Florence. Besides several handsome engraved art books, which reflect his relationship with the Florentine academy, he published many opera and oratorio librettos and plainchant instruction books. His edition of Giuseppe Rigacci's *Raccolta di varie canzoni* (1739), issued in partnership with Michele Nesterus and dedicated to Lady Walpole, was one of the few vocal anthologies produced in 18th-century Italy; it provides interesting evidence of a distinctively Florentine repertory printed from music type reminiscent of the 16th and 17th centuries.

Sartori (1958); M. E. Cosenza: *Dictionary of Italian Printers* (Boston, 1968); E. Cochrane: *Florence in the Forgotten Centuries, 1527–1800* (Chicago, 1973), 319; A. Tosi: 'Stampatori e cultura scientifica a Firenze durante la reggenza lorenese (1737–1765): Francesco Moücke e Andrea Bonducci', *La bibliofilia*, lxxxvi (1984), 245

D.W.K.

Murdoch, Murdoch & Co. English firm of publishers, active in London. It was founded by J. G. Murdoch (*b* Huntingtower, Perths., 1831; *d* Margate, 22 July 1902) in Castle Street, Holborn, some time before about 1880. In 1883 it became a limited company and by 1902 occupied large premises in the Farringdon Road, moving to the West End (Princes Street, later Oxford Street) in 1916. The firm specialized in choral and orchestral music for schools, but was also the principal publisher of Arnold Bax: from 1920 to 1941 it issued some 88 of his works. At least two of the founder's six sons, G. and J. Murdoch, were in the

business; J. G. Murdoch jr, in Australia at the time of his father's death, may also have taken an active part. The company ceased about 1946.

Obituary, *MO*, xxv (1902), 860

L.L.

Musical Antiquarian Society. An organization founded in London for the 'publication of scarce and valuable works by early English composers'. Its first publications appeared from the firm of William Chappell in 1840. In a year it gathered nearly 1000 subscribing members who received the publications at cost price. By its dissolution in 1847 the society had issued 19 large folio scores, including Byrd's five-part Mass and the first book of *Cantiones sacrae*, Wilbye's *First Set of English Madrigals*, masques and madrigals by Gibbons, Purcell's *Dido and Aeneas*, *King Arthur*, *Bonduca* and the Ode for St Cecilia's Day, works by Morley, Weelkes, Dowland and East, and several anthologies of Elizabethan and Jacobean vocal music.

Music Sales. American–British publishing firm. Founded in 1935 by the Wise family, it initially produced classical and teaching material; later it moved into popular music, publishing the Beatles, Paul Simon and others. In 1970 a UK branch was established. The company expanded significantly in 1986 with the acquisition of G. Schirmer and its subsidiaries, notably Associated Music Publishers. With offices in London, New York, Copenhagen and Sydney, and vast interests in copyrights, printed music, distribution and retailing, the Music Sales Group now also includes among its constituent firms Edwin Ashdown, J. & W. Chester, Edition Wilhelm Hansen, J. Curwen & Sons, Campbell Connelly, Rae Macintosh and Yorktown Music Press.

Musikalisches Magazin. Austrian firm of publishers. It was founded by the composer Leopold Kozeluch (*b* Velvary, 26 June 1747; *d* Vienna, 7 May 1818), whose first works written in Vienna were published by Artaria and by Torricella; the desire for more profit led him to publish his works himself. On 14 April 1784 the *Wiener Zeitung* carried his first advance announcement of his two piano concertos op.12, which appeared on 1 September; on 12 November 1785 it advertised the opening of his music and art shop, the beginning of his publishing business.

Because of Kozeluch's activities as a composer, especially from 1792 when he became court composer, he was obliged to engage his brother Anton (*b* 9 Dec 1752, bap. Antonin Tomáš; *d* Vienna, 4 July 1805), who had come to Vienna in 1788, as business manager; it was at this time that the firm began to trade under the name Musikalisches Magazin, later changed to Kozeluchsche Musikhandlung. Anton did not apply to the Vienna city council for the licence left by his brother until 29 May 1802. The firm's activity however ceased completely in 1803 and the licence left to Anton Kozeluch's widow passed to Ludwig Maisch. Compared with Artaria, the Musikalisches Magazin was insignificant and lacked a definite policy. Nevertheless the publishing programme included Haydn's 'Tost' quartets, a piano reduction of Mozart's *Die Zauberflöte* and reprints of several of his works, and 13 pieces by Ignaz Pleyel. Kozeluch's own compositions make up the bulk of the output. Other composers published included Kauer, J. G. Lickl, Lipavský, Wenzel Müller, Paradis, Pasterwitz, Rieder, Vanhal, Anton Wranitzky and their lesser contemporaries.

A. Weinmann: *Verzeichnis der Verlagswerke des Musikalischen Magazins* (Vienna, 1950); C. Hopkinson and C. B. Oldman: 'Thomson's Collection of National Song', *Edinburgh Bibliographical Society Transactions*, ii (1940), 1–64; Deutsch (1946); M. Poštolka: *Leopold Koželuh; život a dílo* (Prague, 1964); A. Weinmann: 'Supplement zum Verlagverzeichnis des Musikalischen Magazins in Wien', *Beiträge zur Geschichte des Alt-Wiener Musikverlages*, 2nd ser., xiv (1970); idem: *Verzeichnis der Musikalien des Verlages Maisch-Sprenger–Mathias Artaria* (Vienna, 1970)

A.W.

Mutii. Italian family of printers and publishers, working in Rome. The first member appears to have been Nicolo, whose earliest publication is dated 1595. He printed a little music between 1596 and his presumed death in 1600, beginning with sacred works by Macque and Matelart. He also published music by Dragoni, Giovannelli, Palestrina and Soriano, as well as Cavalieri's *Rappresentatione di Anima, et di Corpo* (1600). His heirs published music by Conforti, Quagliati and Soriano between 1600 and 1602.

Giovanni Angelo Mutij published music between 1670 and 1689, sometimes at the expense of G. B. Caifabri or F. Franzini. He appears to have published mostly sacred music by, among others, Berardi, Cima, Foggia, Graziani and Steffani; he also published instrumental music by Corelli and Fontana. The few editions signed Angelo Mutij are probably his work.

Sartori (1958); Mischiati (1984)

S.B. (iii)

Muzïka. The Soviet state-controlled publisher of music and music literature. After the October Revolution the music publishing house of Jürgenson was taken over by the state, and from 1918 until 1930 formed the music department of Gosizdat (Gosudarstvennoye izdatel'stvo, 'The state publishing house'). In 1930 this became a separate entity under the name Muzgiz (Gosudarstvennoye muzïkal'noye izdatel'stvo, 'The state music publishing house'). In 1956, because of the pressure of work at Muzgiz, another establishment was founded to concentrate entirely on publishing the works of Soviet composers. Called Sovetskïy Kompozitor, this existed until 1964, when it was amalgamated with Muzgiz to form the present all-embracing publishing house. The firm has a monopoly on all music and music literature published in the Soviet Union.

The 600 to 900 items announced in the annual catalogue include orchestral and instrumental works by Soviet and foreign composers, chamber music, albums of songs and arias, folksongs and instrumental music for folk ensembles, educational material and other music for children, and books on diverse subjects. The State Publishing House has been responsible for many scholarly works; especially noteworthy are its editions of the complete works of Russian composers, including Glinka, Rimsky-Korsakov, Tchaikovsky, Balakirev, Prokofiev and others. Produced with painstaking attention to detail, these have informative introductions by distinguished Soviet musicologists, and a wealth of material, including sketches and previously unpublished works.

G.N.

N

Naderman, Jean-Henri (*b* Fribourg, 1735; *d* Paris, 4 Feb 1799). French publisher and instrument maker. He became 'maître juré de la corporation' in 1774, later styling himself 'Editeur, Luthier, Facteur des Harpes et autres instruments de musique'. With J. B. Krumpholtz, the harpist and composer, he built many single-action pedal harps, the most famous of which was the harp of Marie Antoinette (1780). As a publisher he made available all kinds of harp music. The earliest publishing licence granted to him is dated 7 November 1777, but it was not in fact until the late 1780s that he became fully active. One of his earliest catalogues (*c*1790) lists 43 publications, mainly harp or piano solos (including Krumpholtz's final six sets of harp sonatas) and *ariettes* with harp or piano accompaniment. The fullest and the latest of his catalogues that has come to light (*c*1795) lists about 320 publications, of which more than 200 are for harp or piano in various combinations; most of the remainder are for violin, wind instruments or wind band. Between 1791 and 1799 Naderman published orchestral scores of at least eight operas, including Cherubini's *Lodoïska*, Le Sueur's *La caverne* (see illustration) and Steibelt's *Roméo et Juliette*. These were, however, to remain his most substantial publications, and it was chamber music, especially for harp, that continued to predominate in his output, numerous works being either composed or arranged by his elder son François-Joseph (*b* Paris, 1781; *d* Paris, 3 April 1835). Late in 1796 Naderman took over the business and plates of Boyer, many of whose publications were subsequently reissued under Naderman's imprint. Most of Naderman's publications are elegant (with some notably handsome ornamental title-pages in the 1790s); all were printed from engraved plates. After his death his family carried on his business; eventually (*c*1835) the publishing house either went out of business or was taken over by G.-J. Sieber.

FétisB; *GerberNL*; Hopkinson (1954); Johansson (1955); Devriès and Lesure (1979–88)

R.M.

Nagel. German firm of publishers. In 1835 Adolph Nagel (1800–73) took over the music shop, music publishing firm and lending library of Georg Christian Bachmann in Hanover and ran them under his own name. In 1913 the business was acquired from his heirs by Alfred Grensser (1884–1950), who appreciated the stimulus given to music publishing after World War I by the youth music movement. He specialized in editions of early music, and produced performing editions of Baroque and early Classical works in the series *Nagels Musik-Archiv*, which numbered over 200 issues in the mid-1970s. When the Hanover premises were completely destroyed in World War II the firm moved to Celle and in 1952 was taken over by the Vötterle publishing group; it still trades from Kassel under its own name.

Musikverlage in der Bundesrepublik Deutschland und in West-Berlin (Bonn, 1965), 77; C. Vinz and G. Olzog, eds.: *Dokumentation deutschsprachiger Verlage* (Munich and Vienna, 1980), 298

T.W.

Nägeli, Hans Georg (*b* Wetzikon, nr. Zurich, 26 May 1773; *d* Zurich, 26 Dec 1836). Swiss publisher. He received his first musical instruction from his father, a parson, who had a thorough grounding in music. In 1790 he went to Zurich to study with Johann David Brünings, who gave him special instruction in Bach's music. About this time Nägeli founded a music shop and lending library, and shortly afterwards a publishing business. His lending library, the first of its kind in Switzerland, flourished in the early years of the 19th century and became known beyond the Swiss borders; it was particularly successful during the years 1801–6. Nägeli also succeeded in making contact with other European music publishing houses, and from 1803 his first editions of works by Beethoven (the op.31 piano sonatas), the Abbé Stadler, Clementi, Cramer and eight other contemporary composers appeared in the series *Répertoire des Clavecinistes*. He gradually acquired a valuable collection of autographs and copies of works by the old masters and began a subscription edition of keyboard works by Bach and Handel. With his *Musikalische Kunstwerke im strengen Stile* (1802) he revived some of Bach's neglected compositions. In 1807 the clergyman J. C. Hug (Nägeli's creditor) and his brother Kaspar took over the direction of the publishing house; Nägeli left the firm in 1818 to found one of his own. From this time he was noted especially as a choral singing teacher and lecturer on musical aesthetics.

R. Hunziker: *H. G. Nägeli: Gedächtnisrede* (Winterthur, 1924); idem: *H. G. Nägeli* (Zurich, 1938); J. J. Hassan: *Die Welt- und Kunstanshauung H. G.*

Title-page of the full score of Le Sueur's 'La caverne', published by Jean-Henri Naderman in 1793

Nägelis mit besonderer Berücksichtigung der Musik (diss., U. of Zurich, 1947); H. J. Schattner: *Volksbildung durch Musikerziehung: Leben und Wirken H. G. Nägelis* (diss., U. of Saarbrücken, 1960); M. Staehelin: *Hans Georg Nägeli und Ludwig van Beethoven: der Zürcher Musiker, Musikverleger, und Musikschriftsteller in seinen Beziehungen zu dem grossen Komponisten* (Zurich, 1982)

L.M.-S.

Napier, William (*b* ?1740–41; *d* Somerston [?Somers Town, London], 1812). Scottish publisher and musician. He is first recorded in 1758 as a violinist in Edinburgh; by 1765 he had moved to London, where he played in the private band of George III and in the Professional Concerts until prevented by gout in the hands (though he led the violas at the 1784 Handel Commemoration). He set up as a publisher in 1772, and in 1784 established a circulating music library. The publisher George Smart was employed in Napier's shop for a time, as was the caricaturist James Gillray. Napier apparently had good relationships with composers, including J. C. Bach and J. S. Schroeter, and published instrumental music, dance collections and sheet songs in addition to the popular ballad operas of the day such as Shield's *The Flitch of Bacon, The Maid of the Mill* and *Rosina*. Some of these copyrights he sold to Joseph Dale about 1785, a sign perhaps of his mounting financial difficulties. A benefit concert for his 11 surviving children was given under Cramer's direction on 11 June 1788, but this did not prevent his bankruptcy in 1791. Haydn, on his first London visit in the same year, helped Napier to re-establish himself by contributing the accompaniments to a second volume of Napier's best-known publication, *A Selection of the Most Favourite Scots Songs*. This second volume appeared in 1792 as *A Selection of Original Scots songs . . . the Harmony by Haydn*, and like the first it bore a frontispiece engraved by Bartolozzi. Its success allowed Napier to pay Haydn for his contribution and to commission from him a third volume, which he published in 1795; the three volumes eventually went through three issues. Napier continued in business until 1809.

Kidson (1900); Humphries and Smith (1954, 2/ 1970); C. Hopkinson and C. B. Oldman: 'Haydn's Settings of Scottish Songs in the Collections of Napier and Whyte', *Edinburgh Bibliographical Society Transactions*, iii (1954), 87–120; Neighbour and Tyson (1965)

F.K., H.G.F./P.W.J.

Napoleão. Brazilian firm of publishers. The pianist Arthur Napoleão (1843–1925) began publishing music in Rio de Janeiro around 1869, in partnership with Narciso José Pinto Braga (Gottschalk's publisher from 1867). The partners acquired the stock of several minor firms and in 1871 issued a 55-page catalogue. Seven years later Napoleão set up an independent firm, active in both printing music and managing concerts. He published the weekly critical journal *Revista musical e de bellas artes* (1879–80), introduced many editions of French anthologies and pioneered in publishing Debussy's piano music in Brazil; meanwhile, he issued more than 30 fantasies based on themes from Gomes's *Il Guarany*. The firm published Villa-Lobos's works as early as the 1920s.

Changes in the firm's associates resulted in name changes – in March 1880 to Narciso, A. Napoleão & Miguez; in 1882 to Narciso & A. Napoleão; in 1889 (after Narcizo's death) to Cia de Música e Pianos, Sucessora de A. Napoleão; and in 1893 to A. Napoleão & Cia. In 1913 Sampaio Araujo Cia became agents for Napoleão publications, in 1915 issuing a 209-page *Catálogo geral* (6th suppl., 1936). In 1968 Editora Fermata do Brasil bought the Napoleão catalogue.

O. Mayer-Serra: *Música y músicos de Latinoamérica*, ii (Mexico City, 1947), 675; R. Stevenson: *Renaissance and Baroque Musical Sources in the Americas* (Washington, DC, 1970), 289; *Enciclopédia de música brasileira: erudita, folclórica e popular*, i (São Paulo, 1977), 356; *Música no Rio de Janeiro Imperial 1822–1870: Exposição comemorativa do primeiro decênio da Seção de Musica e Arquivo Sonoro* (Rio de Janeiro, 1982), 34

R.S.(ii)

Neale. Irish firm of publishers and instrument makers, active in Dublin. John Neale (or Neal; *d* 1736) apparently began to print music about 1721, and seems to have taken his son William (*d* 1769) into partnership shortly afterwards. In 1723 he was elected president of the Bull's Head Society which about then became the Charitable and Musical Society; at this time he was advertising subscription concerts in his Musick Room in Christ Church Yard. William Neale was also active in the Charitable and Musical Society which, in October 1741, while he was treasurer, opened the New Musick Hall in Fishamble Street, near Christ Church, where in 1741–2 Handel gave concerts including the first performance of *Messiah* (13 April 1742). Neale appears to have given up music publishing about 1741; his last publications were issued jointly with William Manwaring of College Green.

Copies of only 13 of the Neales' publications survive; 15 more are named in advertisements or in the three surviving catalogues. One of the most important volumes was *A Collection of the Most Celebrated Irish Tunes proper for the Violin German Flute or Hautboy . . . set . . . by Senior Loranzo Bocchi*; the collection was dated *c*1721 by Bunting (*A Collection of the Ancient Music of Ireland*, 1840), though in fact it was published in 1724. It is the earliest collection known to contain works of Turlough Carolan (variously spelt in the volume as Carrollini, Carrollan and Carrallan). Another collection (defective) of Carolan tunes in the National Library of Ireland has been confused with this; it dates from 1742 or later and is not connected with the Neales.

W: H. Flood: 'John and William Neale', *Bibliographical Society of Ireland Publications*, iii (1928), 85; L. Duignan: 'A Checklist of the Publications of John and William Neale', *Irish Booklore*, ii (1972), 230; N. Carolan, ed.: *A Collection of the Most Celebrated Irish Tunes* (Dublin, 1986) [facs.]

L.D.

Nenninger. German firm of printers, active from at least 1602. It was founded by Matthäus Nenninger in Passau (not Pavia, as stated by *RISM* 1606[6]), and issued editions of music by local composers including Salomon Walthofer (1602), Michael Herrer (1606) and Urban Loth (1616, 1619). The firm's earliest printing was well executed from an important new fount of type. As early as 1616 Matthäus's son Tobias amalgamated his shop with that of Conrad Frosch. In the 1640s the business passed to the Höller family, who continued occasionally to issue music. Georg Höller printed works by Georg Kopp (1642, 1659); Georg Adam Höller and Maria Margaretha Höller issued works by Muffat (1698, 1701); and Maria Margaretha also issued music by Benedikt Aufschnaiter (1719). Her successor, from about 1728, was Gabriel Mangold.

Benzing (1963, 2/1982); D. W. Krummel: 'Early German Partbook Type Faces', *Guttenberg-Jb 1985*, 80

H.S.

Neuber, Valentin (*d* Nuremberg, 6 Feb 1590). German publisher. In 1548 he married Kunegunde Wachter, the widow of Georg Wachter, and thereby became heir to Wachter's printing firm; in the following year he received Nuremberg citizenship and from 1583 he was a member of the Greater City Council. He published over 100 songs (listed by Braungart) and some works on music theory, such as Listenius's *Musica* and several editions of Faber's *Compendiolum*.

P. Cohen: *Musikdruck und -drucker zu Nürnberg im sechzehnten Jahrhundert* (Nuremberg, 1927), 28; S. Braungart: *Die Verbreitung des reformatorischen*

Liedes in Nürnberg in der Zeit von 1525 bis 1570 (diss., U. of Erlangen, 1939), 30

T.W.

New Music. American publishing and recording venture, founded in California by Henry Cowell. The quarterly *New Music*, which first appeared in 1927, was the only journal of its day dedicated solely to the publication of new scores. These pieces, described by Cowell as 'non-commercial works of artistic value', embraced advanced and innovatory compositional techniques for which publishing houses had little sympathy. The first issue was devoted to Ruggles's *Men and Mountains*; subsequent issues included Ives's Fourth Symphony (the second movement), Ruth Crawford's String Quartet, Chávez's Sonatina, Schoenberg's *Klavierstück* op.33b, Gerald Strang's *Mirrororrim* and Slonimsky's *Studies in Black and White*. The New Music *Orchestra Series* was inaugurated in 1932 and the *Special Editions* in 1936. Although Cowell published music by European composers from time to time, works by Americans predominated. Many of these pieces were also heard in San Francisco at concerts of the New Music Society (1925–36; founded by Cowell).

In 1934 Cowell established New Music Quarterly Recordings. The discs, all first recordings, were more widely distributed than the scores, which were available only by subscription. Cowell served as head of all New Music projects until 1936. The recordings continued to be issued until 1942 under the direction of Otto Luening, while the New Music publications (*New Music Edition* from 1947) were edited by Strang, again by Cowell from 1941 to 1945, and later by Harrison, Wigglesworth and Ussachevsky. In 1954 *New Music Edition* experienced financial difficulties after the death of Charles Ives, who had for many years been its patron, and in 1958 it was transferred to Theodore Presser.

R. H. Mead: 'Cowell, Ives, and *New Music*', *MQ*, lxvi (1980), 538; idem: *Henry Cowell's New Music, 1925–1936: the Society, the Music Editions, and the Recordings* (Ann Arbor, 1981); idem: 'Henry Cowell's New Music Society', *Journal of Musicology*, i (1982), 449; idem: 'Latin American Accents in *New Music*', *Latin American Music Review*, iii (1982), 207; idem: 'The Amazing Mr. Cowell', *American Music*, i/4 (1983), 63

E.G.

Niemeyer. Chilean publisher. It was established around 1850 in Valparaiso by Carlos F. Niemeyer as a branch of the Hamburg book and music firm of G. W. Niemeyer. The firm later used the imprint of E. Niemeyer & Inghirani and was also active in Santiago, often working through Eustaquio Guzmán, a lithographer, professor, and member of Chile's foremost musical family. It issued chiefly salon music. Along with its successors, Niemeyer declined after 1914 with the opening of the Panama Canal.

E. Pereira Salas: *Biobibliografía Musical de Chile, desde los orígenes a 1886* (Santiago, 1978); S. Claro-Valdés: *Oyendo a Chile* (Santiago, 1979)

S.C.-V.

Nordheimer. Canadian firm of publishers and music dealers. It was established by Abraham and Samuel Nordheimer, who, having emigrated from Germany to New York in 1839, opened a music shop in Toronto in June 1844. By 1845 they had issued Joseph Labitzky's *The Dublin Waltzes*, the earliest engraved sheet music in Canada. Despite provision for copyright protection under Canadian law, many of the firm's early publications were engraved in New York and registered there by agents; Nordheimer did not choose to begin registering works in Canada until 1859. That year the firm became the only Canadian member of the Board of Music Trade of the USA, and nearly 300 of its publications were included in the Board's catalogue (1870).

A. & S. Nordheimer, as the company was first known, issued the usual reprints of popular European songs and piano pieces, as well as new works by such Canadian residents as J. P. Clarke, Crozier, Hecht, Lazare, Schallein and Strathy. Publications registered between 1846 and 1851 include plate numbers, but there is evidence that they were added to the plates after the first issue. Numbering resumed in the 1880s and continued after the firm changed its name, to Nordheimer Piano & Music Co., in 1898. But the highest numbers of both sequences do not even approach the number of publications issued between 1845 and 1927, of which about a thousand have been located. Nordheimer was by far the largest music publishing firm in 19th-century Canada.

After Abraham's death in 1862, Samuel was president of the firm until 1912, succeeded by his nephew Albert who retired in 1927. Branches were established at various times in Hamilton, London, Ottawa, St Catharines, Montreal, Quebec and Winnipeg. The Nordheimers were active also as impresarios, opening concert halls in Montreal and Toronto. By the quality and variety of its publications and breadth of its enterprise, the firm set a standard which later Canadian publishers were hard-pressed to emulate.

The House of Nordheimer Celebrates its 63rd Anniversary (Toronto, 1903); Nordheimer Piano & Music Co. Ltd: *Piano Teacher's Thematic Guide* (Toronto, 1914–18); M. Calderisi: *Music Publishing in the Canadas 1800–1867* (Ottawa, 1981); H. Kallmann: 'A&S Nordheimer Co.', *Encyclopedia of Music in Canada* (Toronto, 1981)

M.C.

Nordiska Musikförlaget. Swedish publishing and retailing firm. It was founded in Stockholm in 1915 as a subsidiary of the Danish publishing house Hansen; the co-owner and director of the firm was Sven Scholander. From its inception the enterprise had both publishing and retailing interests and it is now a major company in both respects. As a publishing house Nordiska Musikförlaget has constantly worked in association with large European publishers such as Peters, Hans Sikorski and, of course, its sister companies Wilhelm Hansen (Copenhagen), Norsk Musikforlag (Oslo), Chester (London) and Wilhelmiana (Frankfurt am Main); it is a representative for the orchestral music of Universal Edition, Ricordi, Schirmer and other firms.

In its publishing and promotion of Swedish and Scandinavian composers Nordiska Musikförlaget has had a considerable influence on Swedish musical life. The catalogue includes works by Stenhammar, Rangström, Nystroem and Hilding Rosenberg; during the 1960s and 1970s the firm began to publish the works of Pettersson, Bäck, Hemberg, Werle, Edlund, Bo Nilsson, Morthenson, Sven-David Sandström and many others. It also issues a substantial amount of educational and popular music. In 1988 the firm was taken over by Music Sales, then sold to Fazer of Helsinki.

I.G.

Norsk Musikforlag. Norwegian firm of publishers, active in Oslo. It was established on 1 January 1909 through the merger of two existing firms, Carl Warmuth (founded c1843) and Brødrene Hals (1847), with Hals and the Danish publishers Wilhelm Hansen as owners. Hals sold its shares to S. Kielland and A. Backer-Grøndahl in 1929, and the latter took over Kielland's share in 1938. The present managing director is Leif Dramstad.

The merger of Warmuth and Hals led to the incorporation of several established Norwegian music publishers into Norsk Musikforlag, including Edvard Winther, Hermann Neupert, Lindorff & Co., A. M. Hanche, Johan D. Behrens and Petter

Håkonsen. In 1925 the publisher Oluf By was acquired, and in 1975 Norsk Notestikk with their predecessors J. A. Røsholm and Haakon Zapffe. Thus the greater part of the practical production of Norwegian music found itself under one roof. A similar situation obtained in Denmark with Wilhelm Hansen.

In recent years Norsk Musikforlag has concentrated on educational and contemporary Norwegian music. Among composers whose work has been published by the firm are Pauline Hall, David Monrad Johansen, Sverre Jordan, Valen, Hovland, Mortensen, Nystedt and Saverud. Since its establishment Norsk Musikforlag has maintained its position as the largest music publisher in Norway. The firm also operates a large department for musical instruments.

T. Voss: *Warumuths Musikhandel, Brødrene Hals, Norsk Musikforlag 1843–1943* (Oslo, 1943); D. Fog and K. Michelsen: *Norwegian Music Publication since 1800: a Preliminary Guide to Music Publishers, Printers, and Dealers* (Copenhagen, 1976); K. Michelsen: 'Om musikkfirmaet Carl Warmuth i Christiania', *SMN*, iii (1977), 33; idem: *Musikkhandel i Norge inntil 1929: a Historical Survey* (Oslo, 1980); idem: 'Music Trade in Norway to 1929', *FAM*, xxix (1982), 43

K.M. (ii)

Novello. English firm of publishers, active in London. The origins of the firm can be traced back to Vincent Novello (*b* London, 6 Sept 1781; *d* Nice, 9 Aug 1861), who undertook the publishing expenses of the various anthologies he compiled and edited, starting with *A Collection of Sacred Music as performed at the Royal Portuguese Chapel* (1811). His eldest son, J. Alfred Novello (*b* London, 12 Aug 1810; *d* Genoa, 16 July 1896), established the business as a full commercial enterprise by opening premises in Soho in 1829. One of the first publications of Novello & Co. was the completion of the edition of Purcell's sacred music which the elder Novello had started in 1828. Alfred Novello soon discovered the artistic and commercial possibilities of cheap editions of standard works. The firm both fostered and catered for the growth of interest in choral music, through the massed singing classes of John Hullah and others, with publications such as *Novello's Choral Handbook* and Mainzer's *Singing for the Million* and by Alfred Novello's own commercial tours. Together with the issue, from 1846, of cheap vocal scores of Handel's oratorios and Mendelssohn's new choral works (*St Paul* and *Hymn of Praise*), these gave tremendous impetus to the amateur choral movement in Britain.

The founding of *The Musical Times and* *Singing Class Circular* in 1844 was a further important step in the firm's history. Each number contained one or more choral pieces in the octavo size of the journal, thus starting the 'Octavo Editions' which soon became almost universal practice for choral music. In order to reduce costs further Alfred Novello established his own printing office in 1847, and broke many of the restrictive practices of the printing trade. From then on most of the editions were produced from a fine new music type, which proved very economical for large editions, though in about 1900 the firm began to revert to engraving for many of their publications. A further contribution to the cause of cheap music was the repeal of the various taxes on paper and advertisements between 1853 and 1861, for which Alfred Novello had long campaigned. The volume of the firm's business increased steadily, and in 1849 and 1851 various plates and copyrights were bought from Coventry & Hollier. Books on music were also produced, and included a new edition of Hawkins's *History*, issued in parts in 1852–3.

On Alfred Novello's retirement in 1857 Henry Littleton (*b* London, 2 Jan 1823; *d* London, 11 May 1888), who had been employed by the firm since 1841, took over as manager, becoming a partner in 1861 and sole proprietor in 1866. Under his direction the firm expanded even more rapidly. In 1857 it began the regular publication of modern anthems by composers such as Goss, Hopkins and Monk, and in 1861 it published the first edition of *Hymns Ancient and Modern*. In 1867 the business of Ewer was acquired, along with many Mendelssohn copyrights (including *Elijah*), and the firm became Novello, Ewer & Co. Littleton soon directed more attention to the publication of secular music, with ventures such as octavo vocal scores of operas, beginning with *Fidelio* in 1870, and the catalogue came to include orchestral music as well. The firm also undertook concert promotion on a large scale, including the Oratorio Concerts and the management of the 200 free concerts given at the International Exhibition of 1873–4. It engaged Verdi to conduct four performances of his Requiem in May 1875, and from 1881 began an association with Dvořák. The firm came almost to monopolize the oratorio, and besides publishing many new works it often printed works and selections for particular festival performances. Prices were further reduced during the 1860s, and the firm pioneered pocket and tonic sol-fa editions. It issued the first volume of the Purcell Society editions in 1878, and has remained the society's publisher.

Henry Littleton retired in 1887, and was succeeded by his sons Alfred (*b* London, 15 Feb 1845; *d* London, 8 Nov 1914) and Augustus (*b* London, 8 Nov 1854; *d* London, 22 April 1942), who in turn became chairmen. In 1898 the firm became a limited company. At the end of the 19th century it began an interest in school music, with the founding of *The School Music Review* in 1892, and later with *Music in Schools* (from 1937) and its successor *Music in Education* (from 1944). From the turn of the century many important English composers, most notably Elgar, were associated with the firm. Elgar's music was championed in particular by the Novello editor A. J. Jaeger (*b* Düsseldorf, 18 March 1860; *d* London, 18 May 1909), who joined the firm in 1890 and, besides writing analytical notes for Elgar's works, helped promote the music of Horatio Parker and Coleridge-Taylor. During the late 1920s and 1930s Bantock, Holst, Bliss, and later Moeran, published with Novello. After World War II younger composers such as Joubert, Leighton and McCabe were taken on; in the early 1970s the firm's list was considerably expanded, with Richard Rodney Bennett, Thea Musgrave, David Blake and Jonathan Harvey among those exclusively associated. The firm's interests now cover every kind of music; the traditional association with oratorio was strengthened with the publication in 1959 of

Watkins Shaw's critical performing edition of *Messiah* (intended to replace the old one by Ebenezer Prout, which has, however, remained in demand). The business of Elkin & Co. was acquired in 1960, and those of Goodwin & Tabb and Paxton in 1971. The firm has acted as agent for several overseas publishers, including Hänssler, Henle, Leuckart, Molenaar, Möseler, Müller, Ricordi, Rubank and Zimmermann. In 1970 Novello became part of the Granada group of companies and in 1988 was taken over by Filmtrax.

[J. Bennett:] *A Short History of Cheap Music as exemplified in the Records of Novello, Ewer & Co.* (London, 1887); 'Soho and the House of Novello', *MT*, lvii (1906), 797; 'The Novello Centenary, 1811–1911', *MT*, lxii (1911), June suppl.; P. A. Scholes, ed.: *The Mirror of Music: 1844–1944* (London, 1947); Humphries and Smith (1954, 2/1970); *A Century and a Half in Soho* (London, 1961); Neighbour and Tyson (1965); N. Temperley: 'MT and Musical Journalism, 1844', *MT*, cx (1969), 583; M. Miller: 'The Early Novello Octavo Editions', *Music and Bibliography: Essays in Honour of Alec Hyatt King* (London, 1980), 160; M. Hurd: *Vincent Novello – and Company* (London, 1981); idem: 'The Novello Archives', *MT*, cxxvi (1986), 687; V. Cooper-Deathridge: ' "The Novello Stockbook" of 1858–1869: a Chronicle of Publishing Activity', *Notes*, xliv (1987–8), 240; J. N. Moore: *Elgar and his Publishers* (London, 1987)

H.G./P.W.J.

O

Oak. American firm of publishers. It was founded in New York in the late 1950s by Irwin Silber, who was associated with Folkways Records and was editor of the folk music journal *Sing Out!*, to publish songbooks that would be of interest to his readers. Oak's catalogue includes instruction manuals for guitar, dulcimer, banjo, pedal steel guitar, fiddle and blues harp and songbooks chiefly of blues, ragtime, bluegrass, folk and country music. Its list includes such names as Alan Lomax, Woody Guthrie, Pete Seeger, Tom Paxton, Samuel Charters and Jean Ritchie. The firm also publishes collections of folk music from other countries. In 1967 Oak Publications was purchased by Music Sales Corporation.

H. Traum: 'The Story of Oak', *Sing Out!*, xxv/6 (1977), 26

F.B.

Oeglin, Erhard (*b* Reutlingen; *d* ?Augsburg, *c*1520). German printer. In 1491 he became a citizen of Basle, where he served his printer's apprenticeship. He was registered at the University of Tübingen in 1498 and joined the printer Johann Otmar, also a native of Reutlingen, with whom he moved to Augsburg in 1502. Here he printed works on a variety of subjects, some in collaboration with Otmar, some with Georg Nadler and some alone. They include several publications commissioned by Emperor Maximilian I.

In music Oeglin is known mainly for two collections: the four-part settings of 22 Latin odes by Petrus Tritonius (1507) and a group of 42 German songs and six Latin texts, also set for four voices (1512[1]). Of a further collection of 68 German songs only the discant partbook survives (*c*1513[3]). The books of German songs include the works of such composers as Isaac, Hofhaimer and Senfl, all associated with Maximilian's court, and thus reflect its musical repertory. An excellent craftsman, Oeglin was the first German printer to use Petrucci's technique of multiple impression, although he reduced it to double impression by printing the lines and notes together. The songbooks are decorated with woodcuts by Hans Burgkmair.

A. Schmid: *Ottaviano dei Petrucci da Fossombrone und seine Nachfolger im sechzehnten Jahrhunderte* (Vienna, 1845/R1968); R. von Liliencron: 'Die horazischen Metren in deutschen Kompositionen des 16. Jahrhunderts', *VMw*, iii (1887), 26–91; R. Eitner: 'Ein Liederbuch von Oeglin', *MMg*, xxii (1890), 214 [incl. description and contents]; R. Proctor: *An Index to the Early Printed Books in the British Museum, Part 2, 1501–1520: Section I, Germany* (London, 1903/R1954), 77; H. J. Moser: *Paul Hofhaimer* (Stuttgart, 1929, rev. 2/1966); B. Meier: 'Öglin, Erhard', *MGG*; Benzing (1963, 2/1982)

M.L.G.

Oiseau-Lyre, L'. Publishing company, named after the rare Australian lyrebird. It was founded as Les Editions de L'Oiseau-Lyre ('The Lyrebird Press') in Paris in 1932 by Louise B. M. Dyer (1884–1962), an Australian patron of music; her aims were to make available early music that had never been printed in a good modern edition, and to support young contemporary composers by commissioning and publishing new works. Her first project was the publication (1932–3) of the complete works of François Couperin for the 200th anniversary of the composer's death – a 12-volume limited edition that is acknowledged to be a monument of fine scholarship, superb engraving and artistic book design. After the death of her first husband in 1938, Louise Dyer married the literary scholar Joseph ('Jeff') B. Hanson (1910–71). Over nearly 25 years they built up a remarkable catalogue of fine editions, often luxuriously produced. With music ranging from the 13th century to the 20th, L'Oiseau-Lyre's catalogue has always placed special emphasis on French music, especially the 17th- and 18th-century harpsichord repertory. The firm's most significant publishing venture has been the numbered, limited edition, *Polyphonic Music of the Fourteenth Century* (24 vols., 1956–89). Publications have always been divided between scholarly series and more straightforward performing editions of early music and of contemporary pieces. Among the many composers whom Louise Hanson-Dyer and J. B. Hanson helped in various ways were Auric, Canteloube, Ibert, d'Indy, Milhaud, Roussel, Sauguet, Britten, Holst and the Australian composers Peggy Glanville Hicks and Margaret Sutherland.

In 1947 the firm's headquarters moved to Les Remparts, Monaco, and during the 1950s the firm built up its pioneering catalogue of LP records. After his wife's death Hanson ran the firm, commissioning a new edition of the complete chansons of Janequin and taking particular interest in recordings of rare and otherwise unrecorded works; he sold the record side of the business to Decca, London, in 1970.

L'Oiseau-Lyre has been run since 1971 by Hanson's second wife, Margarita M. Hanson, who has undertaken a series of reprints and revisions of existing editions, notably the Couperin complete works (1980–); a new edition of the *Magnus liber organi* is in preparation. Louise Hanson-Dyer and J. B. Hanson bequeathed legacies to the University of Melbourne and since 1979 L'Oiseau-Lyre's publications have been produced with the university's financial assistance.

D.M.

Ortelli. Argentine publisher and lithographer, active in Buenos Aires. The firm was founded soon after the middle of the 19th century as Ortelli Hnos. G. Neumann, who had formerly worked with Breyer, joined Ortelli after separating from Breyer in 1888. The firm had extensive printing resources and issued its own music periodicals, including *Musica Reclame* (1912), and later as Imprenta Musical Ortelli Hnos. continued into the 1930s.

J.M.V.

Osterberger, Georg (*d* 1602). German printer. He began his career as a scribe and notary in the consistory of Samland (later East Prussia). In 1575 he bought Daubmann's printing press in Königsberg and subsequently received a warrant to print (1585). After his death his widow carried on the business until 1609, between 1604 and 1606 with the assistance of her son-in-law Georg Neycke. The Osterberger press published many occasional works by Königsberg musicians.

G. Küsel: *Beiträge zur Musikgeschichte der Stadt Königsberg in Preussen* (Königsberg, 1923); Benzing (1963, 2/1982); H. Heckmann: 'Johann Eccards Gelegenheitskompositionen', *Festschrift Bruno Stäblein* (Kassel, 1967), 92; Przywecka-Samecka (1969); L. Weinhold: 'Die Gelegenheitskompositionen des 17. Jahrhunderts in Deutschland', *Quellenstudien zur Musik: Wolfgang Schmieder zum 70. Geburtstag* (Frankfurt am Main, 1972), 172

T.W.

Österreichischer Bundesverlag. Austrian publishing house. It was set up in 1771 by Empress Maria Theresia to publish school books, and from its inception it published music, particularly songbooks. After the reopening of the firm in Vienna in 1945, a music department was set up under Wilhelm Rohm in 1946 which produced new music in a modern idiom required by Austrian music education, and concentrated on following modern educational principles. The resultant output has included music for all types of schools, books on music theory and history, music for amateur performance, contemporary Austrian chamber music, instrumental tutors, a series on elocution (with records), and folksongs, folkdances and wind music from all parts of Austria. In addition the series *Denkmäler der Tonkunst in Österreich* was published by the firm from volume 85 onwards. In 1961 Alois Rottensteiner was appointed head of the music department. The firm also publishes the periodical *Musikerziehung*, established by Joseph Lechthaler in 1947, which under Rohm, its chief editor until 1961, and since then under Eberhard Würzl, has published articles by Austrian and foreign authorities on every aspect of modern musical education. *Musikerziehung* was until 1961 the official journal of the Arbeitsgemeinschaft der Musikerzieher Österreichs and the mouthpiece of the Vienna Mozartgemeinde, the Österreichischer Musikrat (UNESCO) and the Franz Schmidt Gemeinde.

W. Rohm: 'Österreichischer Bundesverlag, Musikabteilung, Wien', *MGG*

W.R. (ii)

Oswald, James (*b* Scotland, 1711; *d* Knebworth, Herts., 1769). Scottish publisher. He taught dancing in Dunfermline before 1736, when he moved to Edinburgh, where he was active until 1741 as a singer, composer and concert promoter. He published *A Collection of Minuets* in Edinburgh in 1736, and *A Curious Collection of Scots Tunes* in about 1739.

In 1741 he moved to London, where he at first seems to have worked as a hack composer for the publisher John Simpson. In 1747 Simpson died and Oswald set up his own publishing firm, in St Martin's Lane. He specialized in printing popular music. *The Caledonian Pocket Companion* (15 vols., many editions), a collection of Scots folk-tunes, some with Oswald's own variations, was his outstanding publication. Oswald also fabricated a 'secret' composers' society in London, 'The Temple of Apollo', whose only other real member besides himself was Charles Burney, his editorial assistant. Oswald wrote, or contributed to, music for the theatre and was appointed chamber composer to George III in 1761.

Kidson (1900); idem: 'James Oswald and "The Temple of Apollo" ', *MA*, ii (1911), 34; H. G. Farmer: *History of Music in Scotland* (London, 1947); R. Lonsdale: *Dr. Charles Burney: a Literary Biography* (Oxford, 1965/*R*1986); D. Johnson: *Music and Society in Lowland Scotland in the 18th Century* (London, 1972), 61, 118, 127; idem: *Scottish Fiddle Music in the 18th Century* (Edinburgh, 1984), 36, 67, 107, 126, 197

D.J./R

Ott [Ottel, Otto], **Hans** (*d* Nuremberg, 1546). German publisher. He lived in Regensburg for some time before coming to Nuremberg, where he was granted citizenship in 1531. He must have been a man of some learning and at one time possessed the famous Lochamer Liederbuch. As far as can be determined, he did not own a printing press, for he is listed in the city records consistently as a bookseller rather than as a printer. With the exception of his last publication in 1544, all of Ott's collections were printed by Hieronymus Formschneider. He apparently died suddenly, since he had been granted publishing privileges for further projects just before his death, including a book on medicine, another collection of masses and Isaac's famed *Choralis constantinus*, none of which he was able to complete. The last was subsequently printed by Formschneider, who in the foreword to the first volume lamented Ott's untimely death and referred to him as 'typographus noster', a term which has given rise to speculation that Ott may have acquired a printing press in his last years.

The five collections of music published by Ott in the decade from 1534 to 1544 are notable both for their individuality and for their high quality, which indicate considerable musical knowledge on the part of their compiler. The first and last volumes (*RISM* 1534[17], selections ed. in DTÖ, lxxii, Jg.xxxvii/2, 1930/*R*, and EDM, 1st ser., xv, 1940; 1544[20], ed. in PGfM, iii, 1873–5) are devoted mainly to German secular songs, but they also include a few sacred vocal works and some songs to Latin, French and Italian texts. More than half of the pieces are by Ludwig Senfl, and indeed these two collections are the primary sources for his German songs. The three collections of sacred music (1537[1], 1538[3] and 1539[2]) contain chiefly works by prominent Netherlands composers, including Josquin, Obrecht, Gombert and Willaert.

R. Eitner, L. Erk and O. Kade: *Einleitung, Bio-graphieen, Melodieen und Gedichte zu Johann Ott's Liedersammlung von 1544*, PGfM, iv (1876); R. Wagner: 'Ergänzungen zur Geschichte der Nürnberger Musikdrucker des 16. Jahrhunderts', *ZMw*, xii (1929–30), 506; H. J. Moser: 'Hans Ott's erstes Liederbuch', *AcM*, vii (1935), 1; A. Geering and W. Altwegg: Foreword to *Lieder aus Hans Otts Liederbuch von 1534*, EDM, xv (1940; repr. in Senfl: Sämtliche Werke, iv, Wolfenbüttel, 1962); T. Wohnhaas: 'Ott, Hans', *MGG*

M.L.G.

Oxford University Press (OUP). English publishing concern, a division of Oxford University and hence a non-profit organization without shareholders. Its principal editorial centres until the 1970s were in London (from 1880) and the Clarendon Press in Oxford. From 1977 publishing was again centralized in Oxford, though the music department remained in London until 1982. Its publications are distributed by a network of affiliates and agents throughout the world. The firm celebrated its quincentenary in 1978.

The musical activities of OUP have been almost entirely a 20th-century development, though in the 19th century it had occasionally brought out works with music, such as Tallis's *Preces and Litany* (1847) and the *Yattendon Hymnal* (1899), which used original 17th-century music type cut by Peter Walpergen for John Fell. An interest in books on music began with the *Oxford History of Music* (1901–5, enlarged 2/1929–38), edited by W. H. Hadow and issued from the Clarendon Press at Oxford, but the real development dates from the employment of the 22-year-old Hubert J. Foss at the London office in 1921. Probably with the encouragement of the Bach specialist W. G. Whittaker, OUP started printing sheet music, and in June 1923 the first publications appeared in the two series *Oxford Choral Songs* and *Oxford Church Music*. Within two years a separate music department had been established in London under Foss's management, and a rapid publication programme was started, averaging over 200 works a year during the first decade. There was from the first a strong emphasis on contemporary English music; some works by Britten were published and many by Warlock, all the later works of Vaughan Williams and Gerhard (a naturalized Briton), and virtually the entire output of Lambert, Rawsthorne and Walton. In addition, anthologies such as *The Oxford Book of Carols*, *The Oxford Song Books* and *The Church Anthem Book* were issued and were soon regarded as standard collections. After the completion of the ten volumes of *Tudor Church Music* (1922–9), OUP also began to issue new editions of old English music, especially of the 16th century to the 18th, including an octavo series of 100 items taken from the Carnegie edition of *Tudor Church Music* (about 70 were later revised); the *Musica da Camera* series of 17th- and 18th-century instrumental music was initiated in 1973. With a few exceptions such as a complete Chopin edition (1932), edited by Edouard Ganche, OUP has generally avoided the publication of the standard repertory.

Apart from the continuing commitment to music by 20th-century British composers (prominent among whom are Crosse, Hoddinott and Mathias), choral, organ and educational music forms the core of its activities. In addition, the New York branch (Oxford University Press Inc.) began the separate publication in the 1960s of contemporary American music, including works by Jack Beeson and Ezra Laderman and various editions, notably Noah Greenberg's edition of *The Play of Daniel*. The Toronto branch also had its own music division until 1973.

Parallel with its printed music programme, the music department has published a large number of books on music, including such important works as Cobbett's *Cyclopedic Survey of Chamber Music*, Tovey's *Essays in Musical Analysis*, the many editions of *The Oxford Companion to Music*, *The New Oxford History of Music* and concise Oxford dictionaries of music, opera and ballet. Since 1955 it has published the scholarly quarterly *Music & Letters*, since 1973 the periodical *Early Music*, and since 1987 the *Journal of the Royal Musical Association*.

C. G. Mortimer: 'Leading Music Publishers: Oxford University Press, Music Department', *MO*, lxiii (1939–40), 187; [P.A. Mulgan]: *Oxford Music: the First Fifty Years '23–'73* (London, 1973)

P.W.J.

P

Pablos, Juan [Paoli, Giovanni] (*b* Brescia; *d* Mexico, *c*1560). Italian printer active in Mexico, the first documented printer in the New World. Sponsored by the Bishop of Mexico, Juan de Zumárraga, he went to Mexico in 1539 under a ten-year contract to the Seville printer Juan Cromberger to establish a printing monopoly in the colony. He issued 62 items in his own name from 1548. Early titles included catechisms and Castilian–Mexican dictionaries. Later the publishing programme expanded to law, science, medicine, philosophy and music, notably the first printed music in the Americas, the roman plainchant in red and black in the *Ordinarium Sacri Ordinis Heremitarum Sancti Augustini* (1556; for illustration see García Icazbalceta). The quality and quantity of Pablos's types improved after he hired a typefounder from Spain, Antonio de Espinosa, who arrived in 1551. Espinosa broke Pablos's monopoly, setting up a shop in Mexico City in 1559 and printing music in a missal (1568), antiphonal (*c*1575) and gradual (1576).

L. M. Spell: 'The First Music-Books Printed in America', *MQ*, xv (1929), 50; A. Millares Carlo and J. Calvo: *Juan Pablos, primero impresor que a esta tierra vino* (Mexico City, 1953); J. García Icazbalceta: *Bibliografía mexicana del siglo XVI* (Mexico City, 1954); H. C. Woodbridge and L. S. Thompson: *Printing in Colonial Spanish America* (Troy, NY, 1976); C. Griffin: *The Crombergers of Seville: the History of a Printing and Merchant Dynasty* (Oxford, 1988)

M.K.D.

Pachel, Leonard (*b* Ingolstadt, *c*1451; *d* Milan, 7 March 1511). German printer, active in Milan. His name first appears in 1473 as witness to a contract of the first music printer in Milan, Christoph Valdarfer. There, in 1477, his own first book was issued in association with Ulrich Scinzenzeller, with whom he printed until 1490. They issued about 400 works, only 60 with their imprint, however. Pachel printed about 11 editions with either printed music or space for it, four with music printed from three Ambrosian and roman plainchant types (three missals, one psalter) and two theory books, one with space for manuscript music, one with music printed from woodblocks. He was responsible for printing the first edition of the Ambrosian psalter (1486) and probably the first Ambrosian ritual (*c*1487).

Duggan (1981); E. Sandal: *Editori e tipografi a Milano nel Cinquecento* (Baden-Baden, 1981)

M.K.D.

Pacini, Antonio Francesco Gaetano Saverio (*b* Naples, 7 July 1778; *d* Paris, 10 March 1866). Publisher and composer of Italian birth. He studied in Naples before moving to Nîmes, where his first *opéra comique*, *Isabelle et Gertrude*, was given in 1801. In 1804 he moved to Paris, where, at least until 1822, he was active as a singing teacher. Between 1805 and 1808 *Isabelle* and three further *opéras comiques* were produced; these and a large number of songs make up the bulk of his creative output.

Pacini's career as a publisher began in 1808 when, in partnership with Momigny, he began to issue the *Journal des troubadours* (*c*1808–15); this was put out from Momigny's address, 20 boulevard Poissonnière. After a brief publishing association with Jean-Baptiste Lélu and Charles Bochsa, Pacini set up on his own at 12 rue Favart, in 1810–11. By 1819 he had moved to 11 boulevard des Italiens (he is known also to have advertised from 12 rue Favart, his residence, at least until 1829). In January 1846 Bonoldi Frères purchased the business, but by 1852 Pacini had made a new start, at 59 rue Neuve St Augustin. In April 1853 he was established at 21 rue Louis-le-Grand, where he remained until his death.

Particularly in the period 1820 to 1835, Pacini was one of Paris's most active music publishers. He was known mainly for his editions of Italian operas, of which he published at least 46 piano-vocal scores in folio format, including several operas by Mercadante, Bellini and Donizetti, and, between 1821 and 1827, 18 by Rossini. Among the Rossini works was *Ivanhoé*, a pasticcio arranged by Pacini himself (on Rossini's authority) from earlier operas, and first performed at the Odéon on 15 September 1826. Pacini also published collections of vocal exercises by Aprile, Bordogni and Rossini, and some hundreds of single numbers drawn mainly from contemporary Italian operas. None of the half-dozen operas of which he published orchestral scores between 1815 and 1834 had lasting success. In addition to the *Journal des troubadours*, a monthly collection of songs with, and solo pieces for, guitar and lyre, he published two other monthly periodical collections of vocal music: *Le troubadour ambulant* (early 1817 to at least 1828), of which each number contained four unpublished *romances* and a guitar piece; and *L'écho lyrique* (March 1827 to summer 1830), each number containing two French *romances* and an Italian aria or duet.

His output of instrumental music was relatively slight; but he issued the earliest Paris editions of Field's first six piano concertos by about 1824 and by 1828 he had published 24 caprices and 12 sonatas by Paganini. In 1823 he turned down Beethoven's offer of the Diabelli variations and four other works.

In mid-January 1838 Pacini suffered near ruin when the fire that destroyed the Théâtre Italien also wrecked his shop; much of what was not burnt was pillaged, and several valuable manuscripts are said to have been stolen. Pacini was well liked, however, and eminent Parisian composers came to his rescue, offering him manuscripts for a series of piano works to be entitled *Livre musical des cent-et-un*. He published the first number in February 1838 and, although it did not run its full course, the series was still in progress when Chopin's Waltz op.42 made its first appearance in print, as no.68, in June 1840. Pacini was a friend to all Italian musicians and had especially close links with Rossini and Paganini. For the latter he sometimes acted as concert agent, and he accompanied him on his first journey to England in April 1831. All Pacini's publications were engraved; his series of plate numbers are generally unreliable for dating purposes.

FétisBS; Hopkinson (1954); idem: *A Bibliographical Thematic Catalogue of the Works of John Field* (London, 1961), 167; B. Bardet: 'Pacini, Antonio Francesco Gaetano Saverio', *MGG*; P. Gossett: *The Operas of Rossini* (diss., Princeton U., 1970), 601; Devriès and Lesure (1979–88)

R.M.

Paff. American firm of publishers, active in New York. John Paff established a publishing firm at 112 Broadway in 1798. In 1799 he was joined by his brother Michael. Frederick Rausch may have worked for the brothers from 1800 to 1803, when the firm was located in Maiden Lane. In 1806 a branch was opened at 2 City Hotel. In 1810 Michael left the firm and John moved several times, finally, in 1817, to 15 Wall Street, where the firm was dissolved later that year. Paff was the most prolific New York music publisher in the first decade of the 19th century. Its plate stock was purchased by William Dubois in 1817, who reissued Paff plates from 1836 to 1840. Though the Paff brothers carried out their own engraving, they occasionally printed from plates engraved by William Pirsson, and later by Edward Riley. Among Paff publications are Frederick Rausch's *Liberty's Throne* (*c*1803), a collection entitled *The Gentlemen's Amusement* (probably after 1808) and *President Madison's March* (1809).

C.E.

Paling. Australian firm of publishers. It was started by the violinist and pianist William Henry Paling (*b* Rotterdam, 1 Sept 1825; *d* Sydney, 27 Aug 1895), who arrived in Sydney in 1853 and established a music shop and piano warehouse. By 1855 he had opened an Academy of Music and was publishing his own and other local compositions. Paling was prominent in music circles as an entrepreneur and performer. His congeniality and enterprise attracted custom and by 1881 he had 43 employees. The firm became W. H. Paling & Co. Ltd in 1883. Publishing activity greatly increased, benefiting local composers and music teachers especially. Operations then extended throughout New South Wales and Queensland. Importation, distribution and sales of music and musical instruments achieved record postwar levels; however, by 1975 publishing had virtually ceased. The firm is now owned by the Billy Guyatt group and trades from music shops in Sydney and Brisbane.

E. Keane: *Music for a Hundred Years: the Story of the House of Paling* (Sydney, 1954); A. D. McCredie: 'Paling, William H.', *Australian Dictionary of Biography*, v (Melbourne, 1974)

K.R.S.

Pann, Anton (*b* Sliven, 1796; *d* Bucharest, 2 Nov 1854). Romanian printer and publisher. He studied music in Bucharest (1812–18) with Dionisie Fotino and Petru Efesiu. As psalm reader and teacher of psalmody, he founded in 1843 the first printing shop in Bucharest to publish the traditional church service music in the Romanian language in place of Greek; he also published folklore collections, calendars, almanacs and folk writings. His first printed book, *Bazul teoretic și practic al muzicii bisericești* ('The theoretical and practical basis of church music', 1846), was followed by a number of church service books. He also published a book of carols (1830–54) and collected folk music, which he transcribed into church modes and published in six booklets: *Spitalul amorului sau Cîntătorul dorului* ('Love hospice or the singer of longing', 1850, 2/1852). After his death his printing shop (equipped with music printing presses) became the property of the Bucharest Metropolitan Church.

G. Dem Teodorescu: *Viața și activitatea lui Anton Pann* [Life and activity of Anton Pann] (Bucharest, 1893); I. Manole: *Anton Pann* (Bucharest, 1954); G. Ciobanu: *Anton Pann: Cîntece de lume* [Songs of the world] (Bucharest, 1955); V. Cosma: *Muzicieni români: compozitori și muzicologi* (Bucharest, 1970), 344ff

V.C.

Panton. Czech firm of publishers. It was established in Prague in 1958 as the publishing house of the Union of Czechoslovak Composers with the aim of issuing contemporary Czech (from 1964 to 1971 also Slovak) composers' music and books on music. In 1967 it expanded its activities to include the production of gramophone records. In 1971 the Czech Music Fund (1953), an umbrella organization engaged in promoting new works, took Panton under its wing. The performing materials of orchestral works published by Panton are available in the Czech Music Fund's hire library of music materials. The firm's annual production of gramophone records, including light music, reached some 70 items by the end of the 1980s. The most important record series are *Hudba přítomnosti* (symphonic and chamber works by contemporary Czech composers), *Début* (model performances by young Czech concert artists), *Panorama of Czech Music* (recordings of outstanding contemporary works) and *Impuls* (light music). Roughly 85 compositions and eight books are published annually. The editorial programmes show a permanent concern for the heritage of Janáček and Martinů, whose estates are in the hands of the Czech Music Fund.

J.L.

Paterson. Scottish firm of publishers, music dealers and instrument makers. It was started in Edinburgh about 1819 by Robert Paterson (*d* 1859) and others as Robert Paterson, Mortimer & Co. In 1826 Peter Walker Roy (*d* Edinburgh, 7 Dec 1851) joined the firm, which became Paterson & Roy and later opened a London branch. After Roy's death the business traded as Paterson & Sons. Paterson was succeeded at his death by his son Robert Roy Paterson (*b* Edinburgh, 16 July 1830; *d* Edinburgh 3 Dec 1903), who played an active part in Edinburgh's musical life and under whose direction the firm expanded to become one of the most important of its kind in Scotland, with branches in Glasgow (1857, directed by Paterson's elder brother John Walker Paterson), Perth (1864), Ayr (1868), Dundee (1882), Dumfries (1886), Paisley (1887), Kilmarnock (1892), and later Aberdeen and Oban. Its 19th-century publications included Scottish music of all kinds, with many reprints of standard editions of Scottish songs. During the 20th century its publishing activities were gradually taken over by the London branch, which, as Paterson's Publications Ltd, has concentrated largely on choral and piano music for school and amateur use. The Scottish branch of the business ceased in 1964; the

London branch was bought by Novello & Co. in 1989.

Humphries and Smith (1954, 2/1970)

P.W.J.

Pazdírek. Czech family of publishers and musicians.

(1) Bohumil Pazdírek [Johann Peter Gotthard] (*b* Drahanovice, Moravia, 19 Jan 1839; *d* Vöslau, nr. Vienna, 17 May 1919). Publisher and composer. He was the son of Josef Pazdírek (1813–96), a village teacher and musician. He settled in Vienna in 1855 and worked for various publishers (Spina, Lewy, Doblinger) until 1868 when he founded his own firm, which published many of Schubert's posthumous works. When his firm was taken over by Doblinger in 1880, he began teaching at the Theresian Academy (1882–1906), having augmented his musical training as a choirboy in Olomouc by private lessons in Vienna. He composed five operas, six string quartets, songs, chamber music and sacred music. With his brother (2) František, he published the 34-volume catalogue *Universal-Handbuch der Musikliteratur* (Vienna, 1904–10/ *R*1967), which cited all musical editions known by them to be in print and is still a valuable work of reference.

(2) František Pazdírek (*b* Citov, nr. Přerov, Moravia, 18 Dec 1848; *d* Vienna, 14 Feb 1915). Publisher, brother of (1) Bohumil. After his schooling in Olomouc, he entered his brother's firm in Vienna and gained further experience in Berlin and in Moscow (with Jürgenson). On his return he worked with his brother (3) Ludevít Raimund. He initiated the ambitious but incomplete *Prager Conservatorium Ausgabe*, published the *Musikliterarische Blätter* and worked with his brother Bohumil on the *Universal-Handbuch*.

(3) Ludevít Raimund Pazdírek (*b* Citov, nr. Přerov, Moravia, 23 Aug 1850; *d* Brno, 30 April 1914). Publisher, brother of (1) Bohumil and (2) František. After training as a teacher in Olomouc, he taught in Citov and other small Moravian towns. In 1879 he founded a publishing business in Horní Moštěnice in which he worked full time from 1889, moving to Bučovice (1891), Olomouc (1897) and finally to Brno (1911). His first publication was the frequently reprinted *Malý koledníček* ('Little carol book'). He specialized in church music and teaching manuals (e.g. Kocián's violin tutor, 1888), and himself composed some church and organ music.

(4) Oldřich Pazdírek (*b* Horní Moštěnice, nr. Přerov, Moravia, 18 Dec 1887; *d* Brno, 3 Aug 1944). Publisher, son of (3) Ludevít. He took over the family firm in Brno in 1919 and raised it to its leading position in Czech music publishing. He concentrated on the works of Moravian composers, teaching and educational literature (e.g. Ševčík's violin tutor, Černušák's music history). Notable publications included *Pazdírkův hudební slovník* ('Pazdírek's music dictionary'), which began appearing from 1929 but was stopped by German censorship in 1941, Helfert's *Leoš Janáček*, i (1939) and the historical series *Musica Antiqua Bohemica*. From 1937 he began collaborating with the Prague firm of Melantrich under the name of Melpa. After his death the family business was continued by his son Dušan until nationalized in 1948.

ČSHS; L. K. Žižka: 'Rod Pazdírkův' [The Pazdírek family], *Hudba a národ*, ed. V. Mikota (Prague, 1940), 132

J.T.

Pearson, William (*b* ?London, *c*1671; *d* ?London, 1735). English printer, active in London. A former apprentice of John Heptinstall, he set himself up in 1698 and in 1699 published *Twelve New Songs* in which he used for the first time a fount of type which he called the 'new London character'. It was a marked improvement on the older founts in use, and Pearson established a business partnership with Henry Playford. Pearson printed several notable publications for Playford, including *Mercurius musicus*, John Blow's *Amphion Anglicus*, some editions of *An Introduction to the Skill of Musick*, some parts of *Wit and Mirth*, the second volume of Henry Purcell's *Orpheus Britannicus* and parts of *Harmonia sacra*. The partnership broke up in 1703 as the result of a lawsuit and Pearson continued to print independently until 1735. After his death his business was carried on by his widow, Alice Pearson, who continued to use the 'new London character' for a few musical publications, among them John Wesley's 'Foundry' hymnbook, *A Collection of Tunes, Set to Music as they are Commonly Sung at the Foundery* (1742).

Pearson used his 'new London character' with great skill. It was one of the first used in London that could print round note heads, and quavers, semiquavers etc in groups as well as separately, and Pearson drew attention to these advantages in his preface to the *Twelve New Songs*. His work is notable for its clear impression, and the attractive layout of the pages gives it a strikingly modern appearance. Pearson was responsible for most of the typeset music produced in London, 1699–1735; his was the only fount of the time which could seriously compete with the work of engravers, who were steadily taking over music printing at the turn of the century.

For illustration *see* fig.8, p.29.

C. D. Day and E. Murrie: 'Playford v. Pearson', *The Library*, 4th ser., xvi (1935–6), 356–401; Humphries and Smith (1954, 2/1970); M. Tilmouth: 'A Note on the Cost of Printing Music in London in 1702', *Brio*, viii (1971), 1; Krummel (1975); M. Treadwell: 'London Printers and Printing Houses in 1705', *Publishing History*, vii (1980), 33; D. R. Harvey: *Henry Playford: a Bibliographical Study* (diss., Victoria U. of Wellington, 1985)

M.M./D.R.H.

Peer-Southern. American firm of publishers. It was founded in New York in 1928 by Ralph Peer as the Southern Music Publishing Co. in cooperation with the Victor Talking Machine Company. Peer had spent several years in the southern USA collecting ethnic music and jazz, and the company became a major publisher and distributor of this music. In 1932 when Victor withdrew, Peer, who was president of Southern, became its sole owner (he remained at the head of the firm until his death in 1960). In 1940 he established the Peer International Corporation. This, together with Southern, became known as the Peer-Southern Organization, which from 1940 included the American Performing Rights Society, from 1941 Melody Lane Publications and La Salle Music Publishing Company, and from 1943 the Charles K. Harris Music Publishing Company.

Peer-Southern is the principal publisher of Ives and the sole publisher of David Diamond, Anis Fuleihan, Rudolf Maros, Juan Orrego-Salas, Manuel M. Ponce, Silvestre Revueltas, Ahmet Adnan Saygun, José Serebrier and Harold Shapero. Peer also represents the catalogues of Ediciones Mexicanas de Música, Pan American Union of Washington and Wagner & Levien of Mexico City; Southern Music Publishing Co. is the exclusive representative of A. Cranz of Brussels, Editorial Argentina de Música of Buenos Aires, Editorial Cooperative Interamericana de Compositores of Montevideo, Enoch & Cie of Paris (partial catalogue), C. Gehrman of Stockholm (partial catalogue), Israeli Music Publications Ltd, Liber-Southern Ltd of London and R. E. Westerlund AB of Helsinki.

W.T.M., M.J.

Pennauer, Anton (*b c*1784; *d* Vienna, 20 Oct 1837). Viennese publisher. His father Kaspar, a musician, advertised his services as a copyist in the *Wiener Zeitung* between

360

1786 and 1799. In 1821 Anton Pennauer made an application ('as a music teacher') to open a music shop which was at first refused several times; on 20 February he was granted permission to open 'a music shop in a suburban community', and began his activities as a music publisher in Leopoldstadt on 20 May 1822. A long struggle with the authorities resulted finally on 1 March 1825 in permission for an art and music shop, which Pennauer opened in the city on 5 July 1825. The publishing house was already in difficulty at the end of 1830; in 1834 it was declared bankrupt and its stock was transferred to Anton Diabelli. Pennauer died completely impoverished. As a publisher he was extremely ambitious: he brought out works by Georg Hellmesberger, Henri Herz, Franz and Ignaz Lachner, Mayseder, Randhartinger and Voříšek, as well as 17 compositions by Schubert, including important piano works and lieder. His publications were notable for their excellent graphical production.

Deutsch (1946); A. Weinmann: *Verzeichnis der Musikalien des Verlags Anton Pennauer* (Vienna, 1981)

A.W.

Penson & Robertson. Scottish firm of publishers. It was founded in Edinburgh about 1807 by William Penson and Alexander Robertson. Penson (*b* c1776; *d* Edinburgh, ?1829) was a music teacher in Edinburgh in 1809, and from 1810 to 1816 leader of the orchestra at the Theatre Royal; in 1819 he became the first secretary of the Edinburgh Professional Society of Musicians. Robertson (*d* Edinburgh, 22 Sept 1819) was a music engraver at the Luckenbooths, Edinburgh, in 1800 and a music teacher in Libberton's Wynd in 1808.

By 1811 Penson, Robertson & Co., having started in business as music sellers, had a publishing house in Princes Street. From 1818 they also ran a music academy at Robertson's house. After Robertson's death the firm was reorganized. Penson left it to concentrate on private teaching, which he continued until his death or retirement in 1829. In 1822 Robertson's two sons, Alexander and John, took over the business, which became Alexander Robertson & Co. In 1837 John Steuart Grubb (1811–67) acquired the firm.

Among quantities of ephemeral sheet music (much of which they themselves arranged), the firm published William Marshall's outstanding *Scottish Airs* in 1822; jointly with Robert Purdie, they reissued the publications of Nathaniel Gow after the latter's bankruptcy in 1827.

Kidson (1900)

H.G.F./D.J.

Pepper, J(ames) W(elsh) (*b* Philadephia, 1853; *d* Philadelmia, 28 July 1919). American publisher and instrument maker. He worked as an engraver in his father's printing business, gave music lessons and in 1876 founded a publishing house at 9th and Filbert streets in Philadelphia. From copper plates and a manually operated press he issued instrumental tutors, quicksteps and from 1877 to 1912 a monthly periodical entitled *J. W. Pepper's Musical Times and Band Journal* (later the *Musical Times*). Around 1887 he acquired a structure at 8th and Locust streets which came to be known as the J. W. Pepper Building, accommodating a large salesroom, an instrument factory and a printing plant, equipped with steam-powered presses to produce sheet music on a large scale. During the next four decades the firm published nearly 200 new titles a year; except for a small group of sacred songs issued by Pepper Publishing Co. in 1901–4, these were all orchestral and band works intended for civic, commercial and school ensembles. Many compositions and arrangements appeared in journals – *Quickstep, Brass and Reed Band, Ballroom, Theatre and Dance* and *Opera House*. The *J. W. Pepper Piano Music Magazine* was begun in 1900, and a separate 20th-century series was also established. Among the composers whose works were published by Pepper were Sousa, Pryor, Grafulla, William Southwell, William Paris Chambers, Nick Brown, Thomas H. Rollinson, William Henry Dana and Fred Luscomb. Publication of new works ceased in 1924.

Pepper sold more than 70,000 brass instruments and a similar number of drums, woodwinds and string instruments. His instruments were moderately priced and, like his sheet music, intended for a mass audience. The manufacture of Pepper instruments continued until J. W. Pepper & Son was formed in 1910, after which most instruments sold by the firm were imported. On Pepper's death the direction of J. W. Pepper & Son was assumed by Howard E. Pepper (1882–1930), in turn succeeded by his widow, Maude E. Pepper. The firm was sold in 1942 and moved to Valley Forge, Pennsylvania, in 1973. Guided by Harold K. Burtch and his son Dean C. Burtch, who became president on his father's death in 1963, the firm grew by the mid-1980s to be the largest retailer of sheet music for instrumental ensembles in the USA.

J. W. Pepper's Musical Times and Band Journal (Philadelphia and Chicago, 1877–1912); W. H. Dana: *J. W. Pepper's Guide . . . Arranging Band Music* (Philadelphia, 1878); idem: *J .W. Pepper's Guide . . . Orchestra Music* (Philadelphia, 1879)

L.P.F.

Peters (i). German firm of publishers. On 1 December 1800 the Viennese composer and Kapellmeister Franz Anton Hoffmeister (1754–1812) and the Leipzig organist Ambrosius Kühnel (1770–1813) opened a 'Bureau de Musique' in Leipzig. Attached to this publishing house were an engraving works, a printing works and a shop selling printed music and instruments. The first publications included chamber music by Haydn and Mozart, as well as almost forgotten keyboard works by J. S. Bach, of which the firm published a complete edition in 14 volumes. J. N. Forkel entrusted his monograph on Bach to the publishers in 1802, and they also acquired several compositions by Beethoven (opp.19–22, 39–42). It has not been reliably ascertained why Hoffmeister moved back to Vienna in 1805, but he must have been a disagreeable business partner, for his sordid business methods were repeatedly the subject of complaint. Kühnel, continuing alone, increased the collaboration with Forkel, and promoted the publication of Ernst Ludwig Gerber's *Neues historischbiographisches Lexikon der Tonkünstler* (1812–14). By 1813 the firm had published works by J. F. Reichardt, Dotzauer, Streicher, Türk, Lauska, Tomášek and Vincenc Mašek; the first works by Louis Spohr were published, and Spohr continued to deal with Kühnel's successors for decades.

In 1814 the publishing business was bought by Carl Friedrich Peters (*b* Leipzig, 30 March 1779; *d* Sonnenstein, Bavaria, 20 Nov 1827), a bookseller of Leipzig, and it became known as 'Bureau de Musique C. F. Peters'. The Battle of Leipzig (1813) had a deleterious effect on the sale of printed music, and Peters's business difficulties were aggravated by the fact that he suffered from bouts of severe depression; he was subsequently committed to an asylum. Besides Spohr and Weber, Peters published works by Hummel, Grosheim, Klengel, Ries and other lesser-known composers.

The manufacturer Carl Gotthelf Siegmund Böhme (1785–1855) took over the firm in 1828. In collaboration with Czerny, Siegfried Dehn, F. C. Griepenkerl and Moritz Hauptmann he brought out many works by J. S. Bach. After Böhme's death the firm became a charity foundation under the supervision of the town council of Leipzig. On 21 April 1860 it was bought by Julius Friedländer, a book- and music-seller of Berlin, who introduced improvements in the process of printing music. In 1863 Max Abraham (1831–1900), a doctor at law, became a partner in the business and in 1880 sole owner. Under Abraham's purposeful direction C. F. Peters won a world-wide reputation. Together with Carl Gottlieb Röder, Abraham recognized the importance of the mechanical press for printing music, and used it to advantage with the *Edition Peters* series, begun in 1867. It was produced well and cheaply, with light green jackets (for earlier composers' works not affected by copyright restrictions), or pink (for original works acquired by the publisher). Abraham acquired the complete works of Grieg and from the business relationship grew a lasting friendship. First editions of Wagner, Brahms, Bruch, Köhler, Moszkowski and Sinding appeared, edited by noted musicologists and interpreters. In 1894 the Musikbibliothek Peters, founded by Abraham, was made available free of charge to the general public. Since 1953 this comprehensive collection has been in the City of Leipzig Music Library, which has made it accessible by producing bibliographies. In 1895 appeared the *Jahrbuch der Musikbibliothek Peters*, which in 1956 became the *Deutsches Jahrbuch der Musikwissenschaft*.

After Abraham's death the business was run by his nephew Henri Hinrichsen (*b* Hamburg, 5 Feb 1868; *d* Theresienstadt, 1942), who had been head clerk from 1891 and a partner from 1894. Hinrichsen developed into a far-sighted and circumspect businessman, who was also a patron of the arts. He acquired songs by Wolf, as well as works by Mahler, Reger, Pfitzner and Schoenberg, and seven symphonic poems by Richard Strauss (acquired from Aibl, 1932). In 1904 the *Volksliederbuch für Männerchor* first appeared. In 1917–18 Hinrichsen bought the Swiss firm of Rieter Biedermann and in 1927 he made possible the purchase of the Heyer collection of musical instruments in Cologne, which formed the basis for the museum of musical instruments in what is now the Karl Marx University of Leipzig. The honorary degree of doctor of philosophy was conferred on Hinrichsen by Leipzig University in 1929. In 1931, the year of the death of his assistant Paul Ollendorff, Henri Hinrichsen's eldest son Max (1901–65) joined the firm as a partner. His second son, Walter (*b* Leipzig, 23 Sept 1907; *d* New York, 21 July 1969), also joined the firm that year, followed in 1933 by the third son, Hans-Joachim (1909–40). The composer Wilhelm Weismann (*b* 1900), who had worked for the firm from 1929, had considerable influence upon its development and output until his retirement in 1966.

Walter Hinrichsen left Germany in 1936, and in 1948 founded the C. F. Peters Corporation in New York. Max Hinrichsen left the parent firm in 1937, and in 1938 created Hinrichsen Edition in London. In

1939 Henri and Hans-Joachim Hinrichsen were forced to yield to sanctions of the Nazi regime and Johannes Petschull (*b* 1901) took over the firm as managing partner. In 1940 he acquired the firm of Litolff, founded in Brunswick in 1828, and in 1950 established, in partnership with the Hinrichsen heirs, a firm at Frankfurt am Main.

After World War II the original Leipzig firm received a licence to continue publishing in March 1947. After it was transferred to public ownership in 1949–50 it was subject to new cultural, political and editorial development. In addition to its attention to the humanist musical heritage and the support of important national and international traditions it was now concerned with the promotion of the work of contemporary composers in eastern Europe (Eisler, E. H. Meyer, Butting, Dessau, Ottmar Gerster, Geissler, Khachaturian, Shostakovich). The firm produces revised editions based on the latest research into sources as well as comprehensive editions (Skryabin, Chopin, Debussy, Mahler and Vivaldi). From 1949 to 1969 the firm was under the direction of the book- and music seller Georg Hillner. In 1969 the musicologist Bernd Pachnicke (*b* 1938) took over its direction; he was succeeded by Norbert Molkenbur in 1983. Each of the three Western companies has published a substantial share of the original Peters catalogue as well as developing its own independent publishing programme. In addition the three companies maintain an entente with the state-owned Leipzig firm which is complementary rather than competing. The Hinrichsen Edition in London (renamed Peters Edition in 1975) publishes primarily early English music (e.g. Arne, Blow, Boyce, Dunstable, Pepusch, Stanley, Tallis) and 20th-century English music (Butterworth, Pitfield and Ferneyhough). The firm also publishes the *Music Book* (formerly *Hinrichsen's Musical Year Book*) series. Following Max Hinrichsen's death, his widow Carla took over the direction of the firm.

One of the first priorities of the New York branch of the firm was to reissue the *Edition Peters* publications. It also publishes the *Collection Litolff*, the *American Music Awards* sponsored by Sigma Alpha Iota, the *American Wind Symphony Editions* and the *New York Public Library Music Publications*. Another major commitment is to the publication of contemporary music; since 1948 more than 1700 works (of which 98% are contemporary) have been introduced. The Peters catalogue lists among its composers Babbitt, Cage, Cowell, Crumb, Morton Feldman, Ives, Penderecki, Schoenberg, Christian

Wolff and Wuorinen. The firm has also become the American agent for a number of European publishers. After Walter Hinrichsen's death, his widow Evelyn continued to maintain the high standards of the firm as well as expanding the catalogue. His son Henry Hans Hinrichsen became president of the firm in 1978, and was succeeded by Stephen Fisher (a staff member since 1964) in 1983. On 19 December 1983 Evelyn Hinrichsen and C. F. Peters were awarded the American Music Center's Letter of Distinction for their continued commitment to the advancement of new music.

The business transferred to Frankfurt am Main by Johannes Petschull in 1950 traded under the name C. F. Peters; Evelyn and Carla E. Hinrichsen became partners with Petschull. In 1971 the music publishers M. P. Belaieff were acquired and in 1974 Edition Schwann. In addition to the original Peters, Belaieff and Schwann catalogues the Frankfurt firm publishes much contemporary music.

H. Lindlar: *C. F. Peters Musikverlag: Zeittafeln zur Verlagsgeschichte 1800–1867–1967* (Frankfurt am Main, 1967); Plesske (1968); W. Lichtenwanger: 'Walter Hinrichsen', *Notes*, xxvi (1969–70), 491; H.-M. Plesske: *Der Bestand Musikverlag C. F. Peters im Staatsarchiv Leipzig: Geschäftsbriefe aus den Jahren 1800 bis 1926* (Leipzig, 1970); H. Lindlar: 'Zur Geschichte der Musikbibliothek Peters', *Quellengeschichte der Musik: Wolfgang Schmeider zum 70. Geburtstag* (Frankfurt, 1972), 115; 'The C. F. Peters Company', *Music Journal Annual* (1973), 56, 96; P. Gülke: 'Edition Peters: 175 Jahre Musikverlag in Leipzig', *Musik und Gesellschaft*, xxv (1975), 749; B. Pachnicke: *Edition Peters, 1800/1975: Daten zur Geschichte des Musikverlages Peters* (Leipzig, 1975); H. W. Hitchcock: 'C. F. Peters Corporation and Twentieth-century American Music', *An Introduction to Music Publishing*, ed. C. Sachs (New York, 1981), 15

H.-M.P., F.B.

Peters (ii). American family of publishers. The Peters family emigrated to the USA from England around 1820. William Cumming Peters (*b* Woodbury, Devon, 10 March 1805; *d* Cincinnati, OH, 20 April 1866) was in Pittsburgh in the early 1820s, where he opened one of the city's first music shops. In 1830 his Musical Repository was located at 19 Market Street, and in 1831 he entered into partnership with W. C. Smith and John H. Mellor at 9 Fifth Avenue. Between 1827 and 1831 he also arranged and composed music, including a Symphony in D in two movements, for the Harmony Society at Economy, near Pittsburgh. He became known as a songwriter in the 1830s, and by 1845 his work had been issued by the leading publishers in New York, Philadelphia and Baltimore, often under the pseudonym William Cumming; early titles include

There's not a word thy lip hath breath'd (1831) and *Wound not the heart that loves thee* (1835). In 1832 Peters sold his Pittsburgh business interests to his partners Smith and Mellor and moved to Louisville.

The Peters' publishing ventures may have begun as early as 1838, when *The Blooming-ton Waltz* was issued in Louisville, although early publications were probably borrowed from other publishers. There followed a succession of partnerships, the principals of which are not always identifiable: Peters & Co. (W. C. Peters and his brother Henry J. Peters, 1842); Peters & Webster (W. C. Peters and F. J. Webster, 1845); Henry J. Peters & Co. (partners, if any, not known, *c*1846); Peters & Webb (Henry Peters and Benedict Webb, *c*1848); W. C. Peters & Co. (W. C. Peters and his son Alfred C. Peters, *c*1848); Peters, Webb & Co. (Henry Peters, Webb, F. M. Burkett and R. S. Millar, *c*1849); and Peters, Cragg & Co. (Henry Peters, Timothy Cragg and Webb, *c*1851–2 and *c*1858–60). While these companies were in operation (not totally independent of one another, for some of their plate numbers interlock), W. C. Peters also issued music in Baltimore, and moved there in 1849. In 1850 he issued his *Baltimore Olio and Musical Gazette* (12 numbers), a magazine containing music, excerpts from pedagog-ical works and topics of current musical interest. Several songs by Stephen Foster helped to establish the Peters name includ-ing *There's a good time coming* (1846), *Lou'si-ana Belle* (1847), *What must a fairy's dream be?* (1847) and *Summer Longings* (1849).

W. C. Peters moved to Cincinnati in 1851 or 1852, and with his sons William and Alfred formed W. C. Peters & Sons there in 1851. This was a very successful company and a charter member of the Board of Music Trade organized in New York in 1855. In 1857 William was replaced by his brother John L. Peters, and the company continued until 1862. It issued numerous pedagogical works, music for the Roman Catholic Church, and popular sheet music, for which the plate numbers exceeded 3000 by 1862. By 1860, however, Alfred and John had registered copyrights under the names A. C. Peters & Brother, A. C. & J. L. Peters and J. L. Peters & Brother, suggesting the gradual retirement of their father, who appears to have devoted more time to composition and the compilation of sacred music, such as *Peters' Catholic Harp* (1863). On 22 March 1866 the company's entire stock was destroyed by fire; W. C. Peters died the following month, and A. C. Peters & Brother went out of business about a year later.

John Peters had also established a busi-ness with Alfred in St Louis in 1851; John L. Peters & Brother issued largely the same music as the Cincinnati firm until 1866, when John opened a music shop in New York. In 1869 the firm became J. L. Peters & Co. (John Peters and T. August Boyle). John sold his New York business to Oliver Ditson in 1877 and returned to St Louis. He was the last of the Peters family to remain active in the music trade, and continued publish-ing until 1885; he appears to have gone out of business in 1892. Henry Peters dissolved his partnership with Benedict Webb in 1877 and moved to Texas, where he died the following year.

S. V. Connor: *The Peters Colony of Texas* (Austin, TX, 1959); E. C. Krohn: *Music Publishing in the Middle Western States before the Civil War* (Detroit, 1972); R. D. Wetzel: *Frontier Musicians on the Connoquenessing, Wabash, and Ohio* (Athens, OH, 1976); idem: 'The Search for William Cumming Peters', *American Music*, i/4 (1983), 27; E. C. Krohn: *Music Publishing in St. Louis* (Warren, MI, 1988), 51
R.D.W., E.C.K.

Petreius [Petrejus, Petri, Peterlein], **Johann** (*b* Langendorf, nr. Würzburg, 1497; *d* Nuremberg, 18 March 1550). German printer. He began his studies at the Univer-sity of Basle in 1512, receiving the bacca-laureate there in 1515 and the MA two years later. In 1519 he was employed as proof-reader by his relative, Adam Petri, in Basle. He became a citizen of Nuremberg in 1523. Although Petreius was not officially entered as printer in the city records until 1526, publications survive from as early as 1524 and he appears to have established his own type foundry by 1525. After his death the business was taken over by his son-in-law, Gabriel Hayn, who continued printing until 1561.

An extremely prolific printer (about 800 publications are known) and a well-educated man, Petreius devoted his pro-fessional efforts to a variety of subjects, notably theology, science, law and the classics. Although music forms but a small part of his output, he was known for the superior quality of his work in this field, using the single-impression technique developed by Attaingnant. In addition to printing the first of Forster's collections, Petreius apparently functioned as his own editor in selecting the works for other collections. Unfortunately this tradition was not continued by Hayn, whose music publi-cations are limited to a handful of religious books.

A. Schmid: *Ottaviano dei Petrucci da Fossombrone und seine Nachfolger im sechzehnten Jahrhunderte* (Vienna, 1845/*R*1968); P. Cohen: *Musikdruck und -drucker zu Nürnberg im sechzehnten Jahrhundert* (Nuremberg,

1927); T. Wohnhaas: 'Petrejus, Johannes', *MGG* [incl. list of publications]; Benzing (1963, 2/1982); J. C. Shipman: 'Johannes Petreius, Nuremberg Publisher of Scientific Works, 1524–1550, with a Short-title List of his Imprints', *Hommage to a Bookman: Essays on Manuscripts, Books and Printing. Written for Hans P. Kraus on his 60th Birthday* (Berlin, 1967), 154; E. Soltesz: 'Bisher unbestimmte Petreius-Druckschriften', *Gutenberg-Jb 1980*, 105; M. Terramoto: *Die Psalmmotettendrucke des Johannes Petrejus in Nürnberg (gedruckt 1538–1542)* (Tutzing, 1983)

M.L.G.

Petrucci, Ottaviano (dei) (*b* Fossombrone, 18 June 1466; *d* ?Venice, 7 May 1539). Italian printer, the first significant printer of polyphonic music.

1. LIFE. Apart from the evidence of his birth and his family's residence in Fossombrone for some generations, nothing certain is known of Petrucci's life before 1498. He is thought to have been among the young men whom Guidobaldo I, Duke of Urbino, allowed to be educated at court. He may have arrived in Venice and married a citizen by 1490, for he would then have been eligible to undertake his craft by 1498 without payment of additional taxes.

On 25 May 1498 Petrucci was granted a Venetian privilege for 20 years. His petition stated that he had discovered what many had sought, a way to publish 'canto figurado'. He added that it would make the printing of chant much easier also; but this was probably no more than self-advertisement, given that he did not seek to include chant in his privilege, nor, probably, did he print any. His request was for the exclusive right to print both 'canto figurado' and 'intaboladure dorgano et de liuto'. The privilege also included a ban on the importation or sale of these repertories in the Venetian states by anyone else.

Petrucci must have spent the next three years in preparation. He would have needed to acquire a press, have special type designed and cast, recruit a staff and build up contacts for the repertory to be printed as well as sales outlets. It is not surprising that his first publication (and probably many more) was backed by Amadio Scotto and Niccolo di Raffaele, both experienced in the publishing trade.

Petrucci's first book, the *Harmonice musices odhecaton A*, does not survive intact and lacks a publication date. The dedication to Girolamo Donato, a leading Venetian nobleman, diplomat and humanist, is dated 15 May 1501. The music of this volume, a collection of 96 (not the 100 promised in the title) chansons and other secular pieces, was edited by the Dominican friar Petrus Castellanus. The success of Petrucci's first

venture must have been quickly evident: several reprintings of parts of it were needed within two years, and two new editions appeared, in 1503 and 1504. He soon broadened out into sacred music, keeping at first to a reliable repertory. The next years were devoted to books of masses by the most highly regarded composers, starting with Josquin and Brumel, as well as two motet volumes and the two books, *Canti B* and *Canti C*, which continued the *Odhecaton* series.

In 1504, with his first volume of frottolas, Petrucci launched into a new and popular repertory. This was intended from the beginning to be part of a series, and both it and many subsequent volumes went through more than one edition. In common with the chanson series, these books were in choirbook format, portable and widely usable, whereas all Petrucci's volumes of sacred music were printed in the partbooks that were to become customary for performance. From 1504 until 1509 Petrucci seems to have been consistently successful: he published at least 27 new titles, reissuing a number of these and earlier volumes, often without changing the date in the colophon.

Meanwhile, another application for a privilege to print music had been made to the signory, this time by the noted lutenist Marco dall'Aquila, who claimed in his submission of 2 March 1504 [1505, *n.s.*], to have discovered a way to print tablature and to put any piece into tablature notation. He was granted his privilege but seems not to have used it. Marco's petition may have stimulated Petrucci finally to print lute music, in 1507, and, later, frottola settings for voice and lute.

Petrucci's last publication at Venice appeared on 27 March 1509. His next volume was published in his home town on 10 May 1511. Petrucci had not lost contact with Fossombrone during his Venetian years: in 1504 he had been a councillor representing Fossombrone in Urbino, and in 1505 and 1507 a city official. In 1508 he had revisited Fossombrone, and must have resettled there sometime in 1509 or 1510. The reasons for his departure from Venice are not known, though they must have been forceful for him to have abandoned the principal centre of printing and publishing in the whole of Italy. They probably reflect his (and others') growing concern about the effect of the League of Cambrai war on Venetian business and the spread of the plague.

Petrucci's output at Fossombrone began slowly. He retained contacts with Venice through Scotto and Raffaele, and seems to have acquired the patronage of the distinguished theologian and Bishop of Fossombrone, Paulus de Middelburgh, for whom he printed two non-musical works. One of these, Paulus's *Paulina de recta Paschae* of 1513 (a plea for reform of the liturgical calendar), was Petrucci's largest and most sumptuous volume. It was probably for the text fount, and perhaps the decorative woodblock borders, that Petrucci contacted the well-known punchcutter Francesco Griffo da Bologna, who visited Fossombrone in 1511 and 1512. Petrucci's production during these years was restricted. Two volumes of music, one each in 1511 and 1512, continued series begun earlier in Venice; indeed the first appears to have been partly prepared before Petrucci left that city. Paulus's volume and a very brief book by Castiglione occupied him during 1513, and in 1514 he printed a third volume of Josquin masses.

This last was Petrucci's first volume printed under a new privilege, obtained from the pope in October 1513, protecting his books of polyphony and organ tablature in the papal states for 15 years. It was paralleled by a privilege granted to Andrea Antico, an ambitious woodcutter who appears deliberately to have set out to compete with Petrucci. In the same year, on 26 September, Jacomo Ungaro received a Venetian privilege, issued without prejudice to any earlier grant. Scotto and Raffaele petitioned on Petrucci's behalf in June 1514, pointing out that he was the inventor of music printing and that his partners had not yet recouped their investment. The second claim seems unlikely, given the continuous production for more than ten years; but the further point that Raffaele was too infirm to support his family without the benefit of Petrucci's privilege may well have been true. Their petition was no doubt a defence against not only Ungaro (who appears not to have printed any music), but also Luc' Antonio Giunta (who had recently printed *Cantorinus*, a popular musical treatise) and perhaps also Antico. However, the renewal of Petrucci's privilege, coupled with the Roman one for the papal states, encouraged him to print a volume of motets in 1514 and two of masses, besides new editions of Josquin's first two books. He also continued to be a leading member of Fossombrone's ruling councils.

The suspension of his activities between 1516 and 1519 is more apparent than real. Pope Leo X had ousted the ducal family of della Rovere from Urbino and placed Lorenzo de' Medici on the throne, and Petrucci played a significant role in the tension between the new duke and his cities.

His printing output included a few concealed editions of earlier volumes and a small text by his bishop. He was also expected to publish M. Fabio Calvo's translation of Hippocrates. An extant manuscript (in the Biblioteca Apostolica Vaticana, Rome) suggests that it appeared on 1 January 1519, but the volume itself, which caused Petrucci some contractual problems and another visit to Rome, does not appear to have been printed.

After Lorenzo de' Medici's death in 1519, Petrucci began to print again. He produced not only three motet volumes in 1519, Pisano's *Musica* and a volume of which only fragments survive (*Musica XII*), both in 1520, but also a number of reprintings of these and earlier volumes. In 1520 he opened a paper mill at Acqua Santa near Fossombrone, which seems to have been his principal source of income, for he ceased printing. (There is no evidence that Petrucci ever printed the *Prognosticon* of Paulus de Middelburgh dated 1523.) Some of his typographical material appears to surface in the volume of Eustachio Romano's duos printed by Dorico in Rome in 1523. Petrucci continued to be active in local politics for another decade. According to Schmid, he was recalled to Venice in 1536 to help print Latin and Italian classical texts. Neither his place of death nor site of burial is known.

2. PUBLICATIONS. Throughout his career Petrucci used multiple-impression type methods. The secret he averred he had discovered was that of printing both staves and music by setting and printing the two layers separately. In fact this was not new, for it had already been used by printers of liturgical music; but Petrucci did make the technique feasible for polyphony by developing much finer music sorts. His method involved twice the labour, but it produced a quality hardly to be equalled by single-impression processes, and was on a par with the best of engraved work.

At first, Petrucci seems to have sent the sheet of paper through the press three times – once for the notes and other musical signs, once for the staves and once for the text. This permitted great freedom in arranging the material of each layer, while also requiring precise accuracy of register. In this, as in other matters of technique, Petrucci's craftsmen seem to have been the equal, both in skill and in methods, of any in Venice at the time. Quite early on they adopted such efficient procedures as keeping the staves set up in the forme from one sheet, and even one book, to another; their careful handling of signatures, the particular problems of music in choirbook format, and the musical equivalents of catchwords all indicate the high level of competence Petrucci was able to call on. He seems to have employed more than one typesetter. The individual characteristics of each man's work can be distinguished, as well as the style of Petrucci's editor, known from the *Odhecaton's* introductory matter to have been the friar Petrus Castellanus. He, with Petrucci, seems to have been concerned to produce an international repertory, appealing and accessible to professional musicians.

The first frottola volumes in 1504 mark a shift in Petrucci's intended market. These books (and the volumes of lute tablature and lute songs which began to appear in 1507) offer a simpler repertory in an easier form – the choirbook layout abandoned after *Canti C* in favour of partbooks – and seem to be addressed as much to dilettantes as to professionals. At the same time, Petrucci must have acquired new suppliers of music: there is evidence suggesting contacts with the Ferrarese court.

The faster production of volumes (reaching a peak of 12 titles between March 1507 and March 1508) was possible because of a change in printing technique. This, reducing the number of impressions from three to two, appears to have occurred in May or June of 1503. From then onwards, his manner of working and the appearance of his books remained unchanged until the last two titles, although the quality of work and the state of his materials gradually deteriorated. The size of his editions probably remained small, as many titles had at least one reprinting.

When Petrucci moved back to Fossombrone, he seems to have intended continuing with a similar repertory. The hiatus caused by the political situation, or by his loss of contact with his purchasers, was partly filled by the three non-musical books, of which the *de recta Paschae* is outstanding. This book is proof that Petrucci had not yet, in 1513, abandoned his artistic standards and had maintained links with his professional colleagues: the special typefaces, two-colour printing and decorative woodblocks are all up to the highest standard.

How far he meant to continue printing in 1515–19 and how far he was responding to pressures from his patrons to compete with Antico, we cannot tell. However, his work consisted mostly of reprintings of earlier titles, and he allowed his material to deteriorate. Even the three new books of

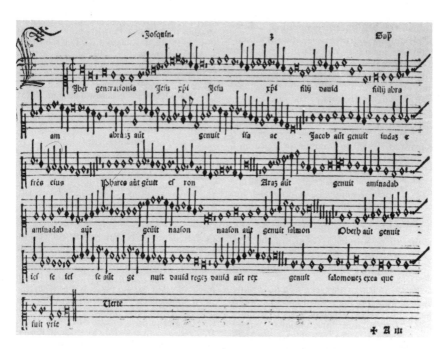

Opening of Josquin's motet 'Liber generationis Jesu Christis' from the superius partbook of 'Motetti C' (Venice: Petrucci, 1504)

1519 appear to be a political response rather than a continuation of earlier work, as they might at first seem.

By 1520 Petrucci's Venetian privilege had lapsed and he had had to replace some of his typographical material. The new sorts and blocks are of a much lower quality, perhaps the work of local craftsmen. At the same time as this (and other) evidence suggests that he was losing interest in printing, he undertook two volumes of a new Roman or Florentine repertory. Neither of these survives complete, though both show significant changes in his printing-house practice. Petrucci was by now an old man, and it is possible that his new house style reflects the presence of younger men in control. Apart from these two volumes, the year 1520 (and perhaps 1521) was devoted to the last reissues of earlier volumes.

Petrucci's production, taken as a whole, represents a major portion of the surviving music in each of the genres he covered. His three volumes devoted primarily to chansons appeared at the beginning of his career, and are representative of taste of around 1500. The many books of frottolas, on the other hand, survey the field very thoroughly, and show the various forms in their different guises and changing popularity. Petrucci's books of masses, mass sections and motets, perhaps inherently more conservative, cover the transition from works of Josquin's generation to those of his immediate successors, and even their followers, including Willaert and Festa, who formed the Italian style of the next decades. Finally, the last two books are of particular interest for their early evidence of the transition from frottola to the new madrigalian forms. Petrucci, or his editor, seems always to have been sensitive to prevailing taste: among the few volumes that were not reprinted are those for lute, or voice and lute, perhaps prompted by the position of Marco dall' Aquila.

The readings preserved in Petrucci's editions have recently been criticized for being inaccurate and arbitrary. While there is no evidence that he regarded his editorial role differently from that of a manuscript scribe, there is much evidence of the care with which he transmitted the readings, including stop-press and manuscript corrections, as well as cancel leaves.

Petrucci's legacy was seen as a major one by his contemporaries: the music he printed was widely disseminated and frequently copied into manuscripts. Various volumes were reprinted by Pasoti and Dorico in 1526 (notably Josquin's masses and the *Motetti de la corona*), by Schoeffer and probably also by Giunta. To these men, scribes as well as

printers, Petrucci's editions represented reliable usable copies of much of the most important music of the time, as trustworthy as any manuscript copy. They also presented music with an elegance which encouraged Antico or Dorico or Schoeffer (and through them many others) to continue to print music.

For another illustration *see* fig.3, p.22.

PUBLICATIONS

VENICE

Harmonice musices Odhecaton A (after 15 May 1501, 14 Jan 1503, 25 May 1504/*R*1932 and 1973); Canti B (5 Feb 1502/*R*1974 and 1975, 4 Aug 1503); Motetti A (9 May 1502, 13 Feb 1505); Josquin Desprez: Misse [I] (27 Sept 1502, [*c*1505]); J. Obrecht: Misse (24 March 1503); Motetti de passione ... B (10 May 1503, Sept 1504); A. Brumel: Misse (17 June 1503); J. Ghiselin: Misse (15 July 1503/*R*1973); P. de LaRue: Misse (31 Oct 1503/*R*1973); Canti C (10 Feb 1504/ *R*1978); A. Agricole: Misse (23 March 1504/ *R*1973); Motetti C (15 Sept 1504); Frottole I (28 Nov 1504); Frottole II (5 Jan 1505, 29 Jan 1508); Frottole III (6 Feb 1505, 26 Nov 1507); M. de Orto: Misse (22 March 1505); Motetti IV (4 June 1505); Josquin Desprez: Misse II (30 June 1505/ *R*); Fragmenta missarum (31 Oct 1505); Motetti a cinque I (28 Nov 1505; 1508, lost); Frottole IV ([1505], 31 Aug 1507); Frottole V (23 Dec 1505, 21 May 1507); Frottole VI (5 Feb 1506); Lamentationum Jeremie I (8 April 1506); Lamentationum Jeremie II (29 May 1506); H. Issac: Misse (20 Oct 1506); G. van Weerbecke: Misse (7 Jan 1507); F. Spinacino: Intabolatura de lauto I (before 27 March 1507/*R*1978); F. Spinacino: Intabolatura de lauto II (31 March 1507/*R*1978); Frottole VII (6 June 1507); Magnificats I (14 Oct 1507; lost); J. Martini: Hymnorum I (1507; lost); Laude II (11 Jan 1508); Missarum diversorum autorum I (29 Jan 1508); G. M. Alemanni: Intabolatura de lauto III (20 June 1508; lost); Dammonis: Laude I (7 July 1508); J. Dalza: Intabolatura de lauto IV (31 Dec 1508/*R*1980); Frottole IX (22 Jan 1509); F. Bossinensis: Tenori e contrabassi I (27 March 1509/*R*1978);

FOSSOMBRONE

F. Bossinensis: Tenori e contrabassi II (10 May 1511/*R*1983); Frottole X (1512; lost); Paulus de Middelburgh: de recta Paschae (8 July 1513); B. Castiglione: Epistola de vita (29 July 1513); Messa corale [1513], unlikely to be Petrucci; Josquin Desprez: Misse III (1 March 1514/*R*1973, [1516]); Motetti de la corona [I] (17 Aug 1514, [1516], [1519]); Frottole XI (24 Oct 1514); Josquin Desprez: Misse II (11 Apr 1515/*R*1973, [1517]); J. Mouton: Misse I (11 Aug 1515, [1520]); A. de Févin: Misse (22 Nov 1515, [1520]); Missarum decem libri duo (1515; lost); Josquin Desprez: Misse I (29 May 1516/*R*1973, [1517–18], [1520]); Paulus de Middelburgh: Parabola Christi (20 Nov 1516); Hippocrates, trans. Calvo (1 Jan 1519). ?not printed; Motetti de la corona II (17 June 1519, [1520]); Motetti de la corona III (7 Sept 1519); Motetti de la corona IV (31 Oct 1519); B. Pisano: Musica (23 May 1520); [Musica XII] [1520]

A. Schmid: *Ottaviano dei Petrucci da Fossombrone und seine Nachfolger im sechzehnten Jahrhunderte* (Vienna,

1845/*R*1968); F. X. Haberl: 'Drucke von Ottaviano Petrucci auf der Bibliothek des Liceo filarmonico in Bologna', *MMg*, v (1873), 49, 92; D. A. Vernarecci: *Ottaviano de' Petrucci da Fossombrone* (Fossombrone, 1881, 2/1882); E. Vogel: 'Der erste mit beweglichen Metalltypen hergestellte Notendrucke für Figuralmusik,' *JbMP 1895*, 47; M. Cauchie: 'L'Odhecaton, recueil de musique instrumentale', *RdM*, vi (1925), 148; A. Einstein: 'Das elfte Buch der Frottole', *ZMw*, x (1927–8), 613; M. Cauchie: 'A propos des trois recueils instrumentaux de la série de l'Odhecaton', *RdM*, ix (1928), 64; K. Jeppesen: 'Die neuentdeckten Bücher der Lauden des Ottaviano dei Petrucci', *ZMw*, xii (1929–30), 73; G. Reese: 'The First Printed Collection of Part-music (the Odhecaton)', *MQ*, xx (1934), 39–76; J. Marix: 'Harmonice musices odhecaton A: quelques précisions chronologiques', *RdM*, xvi (1935), 236; C. L. W. Boer: *Chansonvormen op het einde van de XVde eeuw: een studie naar aanleiding van Petrucci's 'Harmonice musices odheacaton'* (Amsterdam, 1938); E. T. Ferand: 'Two Unknown Frottole', *MQ*, xxvii (1941), 319; W. H. Rubsamen: *Literary Sources of Secular Music in Italy (ca. 1500)* (Berkeley, 1943/*R*1972); C. Sartori: *Bibliografia delle opere musicali stampate da Ottaviano Petrucci* (Florence, 1948); idem: 'A Little-known Petrucci Publication: the Second Book of Lute Tablatures by Francesco Bossinensis', *MQ*, xxxiv (1948), 234; A. Einstein: *The Italian Madrigal* (Princeton, 1949/*R*1971); C. Sartori: 'Nuove conclusive aggiunte alla "Bibliografia del Petrucci" ', *CHM*, i (1953), 175–210; A.-M. Bautier-Regnier: 'L'édition musicale italienne et les musiciens d'outremonts au XVIe siècle (1501–1563)', *La Renaissance dans les provinces du nord: CNRS Entretiens d'Arras 1954*, 27; F. J. Norton: *Italian Printers 1501–1520* (London, 1958); D. Plamenac: 'Excerpta Colombiniana: Items of Musical Interest in Fernando Colón's *Regestrum*', *Miscelánea en homenaje a Monseñor Higinio Anglés* (Barcelona, 1958–61), ii, 663; C. W. Chapman: 'Printed Collections of Polyphonic Music Owned by Ferdinand Columbus', *JAMS*, xxi (1968), 34–84; K. Jeppesen: *La frottola: Bemerkungen zur Bibliographie der ältesten weltlichen Notendrucke in Italien* (Copenhagen, 1968); S. Boorman: 'Petrucci at Fossombrone: the *Motetti de la Corona*', *IMSCR*, xi *Copenhagen 1972*, 295; idem: *Petrucci at Fossombrone: a Study of Early Music Printing, with Special Reference to the Motetti de la Corona (1514–1519)* (diss., U. of London, 1976); G. Ceccarelli and M. Spaccazocchi: *Tre carte musicali a stampa inedite di Ottaviano Petrucci* (Fossombrone, 1976); S. Boorman: 'The "First" Edition of the *Odhecaton A*', *JAMS*, xxx (1977), 183; J. Noble: 'Ottaviano Petrucci: his Josquin Editions and Some Others', *Essays presented to Myron P. Gilmore*, ii (Florence, 1978), 433; S. Boorman: 'Petrucci at Fossombrone: some New Editions and Cancels', *Source Materials and the Interpretation of Music: a Memorial Volume to Thurston Dart* (London, 1981), 129; idem: 'Petrucci's Type-setters and the Process of Stemmatics', *Formen und Probleme der Überlieferung mehrstimmiger Musik im Zeitalter Josquins Desprez*, ed. L. Finscher (Munich, 1981), 245–80; T. Noblitt: 'Textual Criticism of Selected Works published by Petrucci', ibid, 201–44; M. Picker: 'The Motet Anthologies of Petrucci and Antico published between 1514 and 1521: a

Comparative Study', ibid, 181; C. Gallico: 'Dal laboratorio di Ottaviano Petrucci: immagine, trasmissione e cultura della musica', *RIM*, xvii (1982), 187; R. A. Murányi: 'Zwei unbekannte Druckschriften aus dem 16. Jahrhundert', *SM*, xxvii (1985), 291; S. Boorman: 'A Case of Halfsheet Imposition in the Early 16th Century', *The Library*, 6th ser., viii (1986), 301

S.B.(iii)

Petrucci, Pietroiacomo (*fl* 1554–1603). Italian printer. Of a family of printers in Perugia, he was probably not related to Ottaviano dei Petrucci. He was a member of the Perugia stationers' guild after 1559, printing official documents for the city, along with literary and other texts, in partnership with Michele Porto, 1570–75. His imprint also appears on three music books: a Malvezzi book of ricercares (1577), a Vicomanni madrigal collection (1582) and a 1603 reprint of one of the many pedagogic versions of Arcadelt's *Primo libro di madrigali à 4*.

A. Vernarecci: *Ottaviano de' Petrucci da Fossombrone* (Bologna, 2/1882/*R*1971), 282; F. Ascarelli: *La Tipografia cinquecentina in Italia* (Florence, 1953), 151; Sartori (1958); T. W. Bridges: *The Publishing of Arcadelt's First Book of Madrigals* (diss., Harvard U., 1982), 238, 407

D.W.K.

Pfeyl, Johann (*fl* 1491–1519). German printer, active in Bamberg. After Johann Sensenschmidt's death (before 13 June 1491), his son Lorenz took over the shop and printed with his uncle Johann Pfeyl. Three books issued by them, one agenda and two missals for Regensburg, contain music printed from Sensenschmidt's music type. Lorenz departed and Pfeyl issued books on his own from 1495 until 1519 with newly cut types, including one gothic plainchant fount. At least four of his missals include printed music, two each for Regensburg (1497, 1500) and Bamberg (1499, 1500).

K. Meyer-Baer: *Liturgical Music Incunabula: a Descriptive Catalogue* (London, 1962); F. Geldner: *Die deutschen Inkunabeldrucker: ein Handbuch der deutschen Buchdrucker des XV. Jahrhunderts nach Druckorten*, i (Stuttgart, 1968), 52, 178, 261

M.K.D.

Phalèse. Family of music publishers, active in Louvain and Antwerp from 1545 to 1674.

(1) **Pierre Phalèse (i)** (*b* Louvain, *c*1510; *d* ?Louvain, 1573–6). He was the son of Augustin vander Phaliesen, a brewer, and Marguerite van Poddeghem. He may have been related to Arnold vander Phaliesen, a painter in Louvain from 1499, and the organist Antoine vander Phalisen (*d* 17 March 1487). Pierre Phalèse received a good

education and in 1542 became a bookseller to the University of Louvain, where from 1545 to 1550 he published a number of scientific and scholarly books, some of them jointly with another Louvain publisher and printer, Martin de Raymaker (Rotarius). During these years Phalèse also published five books of chansons arranged for lute; they were printed for him by Jacob Baethen, S. Sassen and R. Velpen, as Phalèse was at that time only a bookseller, not a printer.

Perhaps encouraged by their success or inspired by the example of Susato, who in 1543 had established the first important music printing press in Antwerp, Phalèse applied for and on 29 January 1551 received a privilege to print music from movable type. After his early lute publications Phalèse published a number of chanson and motet books featuring composers of the Low Countries, especially Clemens non Papa. Beginning in 1560, however, he showed a bolder and more international approach. In 1561 he published *Cantuale . . . usum . . . ecclesiae Amstelredamensis*, for use by the combined choirs of the Amsterdam churches, printed by single-impression type in Gothic neume notation, the only instance in which this type was used in the Low Countries during the 16th century. In 1563 Phalèse again began to issue books in French lute tablature, many of them by Sebastian Vreedman. The same year he published Francisco Guerrero's eight-part settings of the *Magnificat* using a large type (see illustration) similar to that used by Attaingnant and Du Chemin in Paris for their folio publications. Phalèse also published a number of books by Lassus and Rore, often reprints of volumes issued by Le Roy & Ballard.

In 1570 Phalèse began the association with the Antwerp printer Jean Bellère, a partnership continued by (2) Pierre Phalèse (ii) until Bellère's death in 1595. Susato's death (c1561) and that of his son (1564) had left Antwerp without a music printer, although Plantin, who had acquired Susato's printing materials, may have appeared to Phalèse a possible rival. At any rate, the partnership with Bellère ensured that Phalèse's music publications reached a wide public. Bellère came from Liège, where his brother Luc was a bookseller, and it may have been through this connection that the Liège musician Jean à Castro, whose music had already been published in Lyons and Venice, assumed an important position with the firm. Perhaps he acted as musical adviser, supplying Phalèse with the latest French and Italian compositions for publication.

Apart from the Gothic and large choir-book types, Phalèse also owned a smaller, ordinary music type, used for chanson and motet publications, and lute tablature types. The smaller music type was later used by Jan Bogard in Douai. All the types are clear and well defined, although perhaps the tablature is not as elegant as those used by French publishers. Nevertheless, Phalèse's printing is of a high standard, with texts carefully underlaid, and he was the first printer in the Low Countries to print music books in a format with the parts so arranged that players seated around a table could perform from one copy. He used this technique for songs accompanied by the lute and for music for two or more lutes. When Plantin visited Antwerp in 1570 to be examined by King Philip's proto-typographer, he declared that Phalèse was 'expert in the art of printing music, which he did exclusively, and well versed in Latin, French and Flemish.'

The date of Phalèse's death is unrecorded:

Opening of the superius voice of the 'Gloria Patri' from 'Canticum beatae Mariae quod Magnificat' by Guerrero, printed in large type by Phalèse in 1563

various books were published 'chez Pierre Phalèse' from 1574 to 1576. However, in 1574 his son Corneille also published a volume of Lassus, the first part of *Patrocinium musices* (a reprint of the Munich edition of the same year). Corneille Phalèse did not continue as a printer, but moved to Antwerp, where he became a schoolmaster. His son, Pierre Phalèse (ii), published three further parts of the *Patrocinium musices* in 1577 and 1578, signing himself on the title-page 'apud Petrum Phalesium juniorem.' As the title-pages of the volumes published by the firm between 1574 and 1576 do not carry the signature 'chez Pierre Phalèse fils', it is most likely that these were published by Pierre Phalèse the elder. He probably died, therefore, in about 1576, and not 1573–4, as is often assumed.

(2) **Pierre Phalèse (ii)** [the younger] (*b* Louvain, *c*1550; *d* Antwerp, 13 March 1629). Publisher, son of Pierre Phalèse (i). He took over the firm after his father's death and three parts of *Patrocinium musices* (1577–8) were his first publications. He moved to Antwerp and registered in the Guild of St Luke in 1581, married Elisabeth Wisschavens in 1582 and in the same year set up his press in the rue des Peignes, at the sign of 'le Lion Rouge'. He stayed there until 1608 when he moved to 'Den Coperen Pot' and shortly afterwards changed the name of the house to 'Le Roi David.' Phalèse continued the association with Jean Bellère until the latter's death in 1595. He used the same typographical material as his father, and continued to print chansons, motets and other religious music, as well as music for lute. Phalèse also published many volumes of Italian madrigals, including four celebrated collections: *Harmonia celeste* (1583, edited by Pevernage, reprinted five times between 1589 and 1628); *Musica divina* (1583, edited by Phalèse himself, reprinted seven times between 1588 and 1634); *Symphonia angelica* (1585, edited by Waelrant, reprinted four times between 1590 and 1629); and *Melodia olympica* (1591, edited by Philips, reprinted three times between 1594 and 1630). These and other collections reflect the popularity of Italian music in the Low Countries at this time. He also published a large number of madrigal books devoted to single Italian composers, including Agazzari, Anerio, Croce, Frescobaldi, Marenzio, Monteverdi, Mosto, Pallavicino, Rossi and Vecchi. Gastoldi's *Balletti a quinque voci* (1596), was reprinted seven times between 1601 and 1631, and sacred and secular music by the English composers living in Antwerp, Dering and Philips, was also published. Among

Phalèse's lute publications, *Pratum musicum* by the Antwerp lutenist Emanuel Adriaenssen (1584), containing arrangements of madrigals and chansons as well as a few Flemish songs, holds an important place.

(3) **Madeleine Phalèse** (*b* Antwerp, bap. 25 July 1586; *d* Antwerp, 30 May 1652). Publisher, daughter of Pierre Phalèse (ii). She and her sister, Marie (*b* Antwerp, bap. 10 Dec 1589; *d* Antwerp, *c*1674), enrolled in the Guild of St Luke as 'Filles Phalèse' in 1629 after their father's death, and for the next 45 years continued to run the family business, publishing some 90 volumes of madrigals, masses and motets. The proportion of madrigals to sacred music is not as high as in their father's time, but the composers are mostly Italians, and many volumes are reprints of collections originally issued by the Venetian firms of Gardano, Vincenti and Magni. After Madeleine Phalèse's death in 1652, a detailed list of the assets of the business was drawn up which gives some indication of its importance. The firm owned over 375 kilogrammes of music type and had a stock of music valued at over 3000 florins. Wages to journeymen printers and other expenses from June 1652 to July 1653 were more than 1000 florins. The document also lists the firm's outstanding debts, some of which were declared irrecoverable, and mentions its commercial ties with Italian music publishers. Although Marie Phalèse continued to manage the firm for another 20 years after her sister's death, the house of Phalèse did not recover its former stature. With the decline of Antwerp at the end of the 16th century, and the rise of Amsterdam during the 17th, music printing, like other aspects of trade and culture, became important in the northern Netherlands as it declined in the southern provinces.

Goovaerts (1880); idem: *De muziekdrukkers Phalesius en Bellerus te Leuven* (Antwerp, 1882); E. van Even: 'Phalèse, Pierre', *BNB*; S. Clercx-Lejeune: 'Les éditions musicales anversoises du XVIe siècle', *Gedenkboek der Plantin-Dagen, 1555–1955* (Antwerp, 1956), 264–375; Brown (1965); H. D. L. Vervliet: *Sixteenth Century Printing Types of the Low Countries* (Amsterdam, 1968); S. Bain: *Music Printing in the Low Countries in the Sixteenth Century* (diss., U. of Cambridge, 1974); idem: 'Phalèse', *Grove6* [incl. selective list of publications]

S.B. (i)

Phillips, John (*d* London, *c*1765). Welsh engraver, active in London. He and his wife Sarah kept a music shop from about 1740 to about 1765, and engraved many works for composers who published their own compositions. Among these were Geminiani

(*The Art of Playing on the Violin*, 1751), Arne (*Thomas and Sally*, 1761) and E. T. Warren (*A Collection of Catches, Canons and Glees*, 1763). They also worked for other publishers, including John Johnson and James Oswald. The quality of their engraving was excellent; Hawkins stated that John Phillips adopted and improved upon the ideas of Fortier, and devised his own set of punches after many experiments. On Phillips's death about 1765, his widow continued the business until 1775.

HawkinsH; Kidson (1900); Humphries and Smith (1954, 2/1970)

F.K./P.W.J.

Pignoni, Zanobi di Francesco (*fl* 1607–41). Italian bookseller and printer, active in Florence. He matriculated in the *Arte dei medici e speziali* on 15 November 1607 and by 1614 had become head of the printing firm founded by Giorgio Marescotti and continued by his son Cristofano. Significantly, he was also a musician (in 1615 he is recorded as a 'musico di cappella' of the Grand Duke of Tuscany). Pignoni made an auspicious entry into music printing in 1614–15 with no fewer than six editions, including masses and motets by Marco da Gagliano, madrigals by Giovanni del Turco, and Giulio Caccini's *Nuove musiche e nuova maniera di scriverle*. This initiative was no doubt prompted by a generous, if short-lived, financial investment in the firm (in June 1614) by three prominent Florentine musicians and patrons, Giovanni del Turco, Lodovico Arrighetti and (for Cosimo del Sera) Giovanni Battista da Gagliano: hence the imprint 'Zanobi Pignoni, e Compagni'.

Thereafter Pignoni diversified his interests, printing poetry, occasional items and *descrizioni* of court festivities, while publishing music less frequently (three titles survive from 1617, one from 1618 and two from 1619). All these music editions are closely related in format, typography and content to the earlier ones of Cristofano Marescotti, and indeed the Marescotti mark appears in several of Pignoni's books. They present the best work of Florentine composers of chamber songs of the 1610s, including Francesca Caccini, Jacopo Peri and Filippo Vitali.

By the 1620s Pignoni may have been facing competition from Pietro Cecconcelli, another Florentine printer, and for this or other reasons he produced very few new music editions. The printing quality in Marco da Gagliano's opera *La Flora* (1628) is not of the best, and Pignoni's later editions of music by Antonio Guelfi (1631), Gregorio Veneri (1631) and Bartolomeo Spighi (1641) are markedly provincial in content,

while a reprint (1637) of Giovanni Abatessa's *Cespuglio di varii fiori* (Orvieto, 1635), a set of guitar intabulations, suggests an attempt to reach a popular market. No music editions bearing the Pignoni imprint survive from after 1641, although the C. Marescotti/Pignoni music fount appears in Vitali's *Musiche a tre voci … libro quinto* (Florence, 1647), printed by Lando Landi and Giovanni Antonio Bonardi.

Sartri (1958); T. Carter: 'Music-Printing in Late Sixteenth- and Early Seventeenth-century Florence: Giorgio Marescotti, Cristofano Marescotti and Zanobi Pignoni', *Early Music History*, ix (1990)

T.C. (i)

Pisarri, Alessandro (*fl* Bologna, 1660–62). Italian publisher. He was the son of Antonio Pisarri (*d* 1650), who founded the family publishing firm in the early 1600s. Alessandro was the first to publish music, issuing ten volumes of compositions by Maurizio Cazzati between 1660 and 1662 (opp.21–30). After his death, the firm continued under the direction of the Pisarri heirs, publishing in 1689 a set of rules for members of the Accademia Filarmonica (*Ricordi per li signori compositori e per i cantori e sonatori dell' Accademia dei Filarmonici*) and in 1691 Benedetto Bacchini's treatise *De sistrorum figuris ac diferentis*.

F. Vatielle: 'Editori musicali dei secoli XVII e XVIII', *Arte e vita musicale a Bologna* (Bologna, 1927/R1969), 239; Sartori (1958)

A.S. (ii)

Plainsong & Mediaeval Music Society. English musical society. Its foundation in November 1888 (reported in the *Musical Times*, March 1889) marked an important stage in the revival in England of plainsong as music for use in the Anglican Church. Its declared aims were to form a centre for the dissemination of information, to publish facsimiles and translations of foreign works, and to form a catalogue of all plainsong and measured music in England dating from before the Reformation. H. B. Briggs was honorary secretary until 1901; Anselm Hughes became secretary in 1926, and was until his death in 1974 a leading figure in the society. Its present chairman is John Stevens, who succeeded Frank Llewelyn Harrison.

The society maintained a choir for several decades, but has laid chief stress on the scientific study of plainsong and medieval music. Its numerous publications have been its chief claim to importance. By 1959, when a list was published in Anselm Hughes's book of reminiscences, *Septuagesima*, nearly 70 had appeared. About half were either didactic essays on plainsong, including a translation of the first part of Peter Wagner's *Einführung in die gregorianischen Melodien*, or editions of plainsong with English text for modern use. Facsimiles were notably represented in W. H. Frere's *Graduale Sarisburiense* (1892–4), *Antiphonale Sarisburiense* (1901–24; with an important introduction) and the catalogue *Bibliotheca Musico-Liturgica* (1894–1901). Other early and important publications were *Early English Harmony* by H. Wooldridge and Anselm Hughes, an edition of the Old Hall Manuscript, Hughes's *Worcester Mediaeval Harmony* and Van den Borren's *Polyphonia Sacra*. A scholarly journal has been published annually since 1978.

D.H. (ii)

Planck, Stephan (*b* Passau, *c*1457; *d* Rome, 17 February 1501). German printer, active in Rome. He apparently worked with Ulrich Han; he came into possession of Han's business in 1478, issuing the first of 325 books in 1479 from 'the house of the former Udalricus'. Between 1482 and 1497 he used the earliest Roman plainchant type (that in Han's 1476 *Missale*) for eight music books – five missals (1482, 1488, 1492, 1494, 1496), two pontificals (1485, 1497) and a baptismal (1494). In addition he introduced 12 text types, some as early as 1479; he retained only the music type of his predecessor, adding a few characters of his own. Planck's ability as type designer and cutter, and his skill in setting the type for complicated melismatic chant, suggests he participated in creating the first music type in Italy.

Duggan (1981); idem: 'A System for Describing Fifteenth-century Music Type', *Gutenberg-Jb 1984*, 67

M.K.D.

Plantin, Christopher (*b* ?Tours, *c*1520; *d* Antwerp, 1 July 1589). Flemish printer of French birth. In 1551 he settled in Antwerp and became a member of the Guild of St Luke. At first he worked as a bookbinder, but after an accident he became a printer, in 1555. His combination of scholarship with business acumen made him the most prolific and important publisher of Antwerp during the 16th century. He published learned books of all kinds, including ones in specialized fields such as linguistics and science; many of the latter were illustrated with fine copperplate engraving. At one time he employed 160 men and had 22 presses in operation. He sent books all over Europe and visited the Frankfurt fairs regularly.

As official printer to King Philip of Spain, Plantin acquired a monopoly in printing missals and breviaries for Philip's domin-

ions. During the years 1570–76 he printed more than 50,000 service books, the majority of which were sent to Spain. Apart from these, he originally had no plans to print music, which he considered a risky business. However, when Philip withheld the promised subsidy for a sumptuous antiphoner (planned as a companion volume to the *Biblia royale* printed by Plantin), Plantin began to print music in order to use the 1800 reams of royal format paper ordered specially for the project. The volume that he printed, *Octo missae* by G. de la Hèle (1578; for illustration *see* fig.31, p.85), also uses the large woodcut initials designed for the antiphoner and was sold at 18 florins, a high price for the time. Plantin guarded himself against financial loss by requiring composers whose music he printed to pay for some of the copies themselves – sometimes for as many as 100 or 150 copies. During the following 11 years he printed ten other books of music by P. de Monte, J. de Brouck, A. Gaucquier, S. Cornet, J. de Kerle, C. Le Jeune and A. Pevernage. It is noteworthy that Plantin chose musicians of high standing either in Antwerp or in Philip's chapel in Spain. After Plantin's death his elder son-in-law, Jean Moretus (*b* ?Antwerp, 1543; *d* Antwerp, 1610), managed the Antwerp business, and during the first half of the 17th century four volumes by the Spanish composer Lobo and Palestrina's *Hymni sacri* (1644) were published. The firm also continued to print breviaries and missals. In Leiden, where Plantin had established a branch firm in 1583, his second son-in-law, Christofel Raphelengius (*b* Antwerp, 1566; *d* Leiden, 17 Dec 1600), issued psalm books and a volume of madrigals by the Leiden composer Schuyt in 1600; Francis Raphelengius printed three more volumes of Schuyt's music (1603–11) and Sweelinck's *Rimes françoises et italiennes* (1612).

Although Plantin's music output was small in relation to his other printing, his careful documentation of all his business affairs, including music publication, is of great historical importance. The records at his house (now the Museum Plantin-Moretus, Antwerp) include lists of books and music he took to the Frankfurt fairs, records of all books bought and sold, founts of type commissioned by him and all his business correspondence. Although his music books were expensive compared with those of his Antwerp contemporary Phalèse, the records show that his publications sold regularly into the 17th century. One reason may be the very high quality of paper, ink and presswork seen in all Plantin publications.

Throughout his life Plantin was a keen collector of typefaces, including music type. In his inventories, music type is listed from 1575 (when he had seven sorts), and on his folio type specimen from about 1579 three music types by H. van den Keere of Ghent are illustrated: 'grande, moyenne et petite musicque' (for illustration *see* TYPE SIZE). Plantin also owned three founts of music type cut by Robert Granjon, including one with round notes which, however, he is not known to have used. In 1565, he bought Susato's printing materials, including 'notte petitte & notte grosse'. He also received some type from the firm of Phalèse in settlement of debt. 28 sets of matrices for music type are in the museum. These comprise 12 double-impression plainsong types (including eight cut by Van den Keere and one by Granjon) and 16 single-impression types, of which two are plainsong, two cut by Granjon, three cut by Van den Keere and nine others.

Goovaerts (1880); J. A. Stellfeld: 'Het muziek-historisch belang der catalogi en inventarissen van het Plantinsch archief', *Vlaamsch jaarboek van muziekgeschiedenis*, ii–iii (1940–41), 5–50; idem: *Bibliographie des éditions musicales plantiniennes* (Brussels, 1949); M. Parker, K. Melis and H. D. L. Vervliet: 'Early Inventories of Punches, Matrices and Moulds in the Plantin-Moretus Archives', *De gulden passer*, xxxviii (1960), 1–139; H. Slenk: 'Christophe Plantin and the Genevan Psalter', *TVNM*, xx/4 (1967), 226; H. D. L. Vervliet: *Sixteenth Century Printing Types of the Low Countries* (Amsterdam, 1968); L. Voet: *The Golden Compasses: a History and Evaluation of the Printing and Publishing Activities of the Officina Plantiniana at Antwerp* (Amsterdam and New York, 1969–72); R. A. Rasch: 'Noord-Nederlandse Muziekuitgaven met de Plantijnse Notentypen', *De gulden passer*, li (1973); S. Bain: *Music Printing in the Low Countries in the Sixteenth Century* (diss., U. of Cambridge, 1974); idem: 'Plantin, Christopher', *Grove6* [incl. selective list of publications]; L. Voet and J. Voet-Grisolle: *The Plantin Press (1555–1589): a Bibliography* (Amsterdam, 1980–83)

S.B. (i)

Plattner, Lodewijk [Ludwig] (*b* Dettelbach am Main, 8 Aug 1767; *d* Rotterdam, 26 July 1842). Netherlands music dealer of German birth. He moved to Rotterdam and performed as a solo clarinettist as early as 5 January 1802. In January 1805 he succeeded to Nicolaas Barth's premises, where he published and sold music and musical instruments and sponsored concerts by Romberg, Spohr, Kalkbrenner and others. His output ran to about 700 titles, judging from the plate numbers, and is devoted largely to instrumental music, especially piano works. While his earliest texts are often reprints of engraved editions of Hummel and Barth, in 1809 he became the Netherlands' first music lithographer; he returned to engraving in 1817. His paste-over label may be seen on German editions of the 1820s and 1830s. The surviving stock of his shop was sold at auction beginning 19 June 1843, its catalogues listing more than a thousand instruments including Cremona violins and Broadwood pianos, as well as 3422 music lots.

Catalogue d'une collection nombreuse de musique . . . délaissée par feu Monsieur Louis Plattner [and] *Catalogue d'une collection nombreuse et très précieuse d'instruments de musique . . . laissée par feu Mr Louis Plattner* (Rotterdam, 1843); J. C. Mazure: *Lodewijk Plattner, Muziekuitgever en muziekhandelaar te Rotterdam (1767–1842)* (Utrecht, 1981) [incl. catalogue of extant imprints]

D.W.K.

Playford. English family of publishers and booksellers.

(1) **John Playford (i)** (*b* Norwich, 1623; *d* London, between 24 Dec 1686 and 7 Feb 1687). Publisher and bookseller, clerk to the Temple Church and vicar-choral of St Paul's Cathedral. During the period 1651–84 he dominated the music publishing trade (then virtually confined to London) in a business to which his son (2) Henry Playford succeeded. For the printing of his books he engaged the services of Thomas Harper (successor to Thomas Snodham, who had inherited the business of Thomas East), William Godbid (successor to Harper) and his own nephew (3) John Playford the younger, who, apprenticed to Godbid, entered business in 1679 with the latter's widow Anne. The format, style and printing of Playford's books, together with evidence from the stationers' registers, suggest with some certainty that they were printed with East's types, although for title-pages, other than those engraved, a less florid style than the earlier borders was preferred. In many instances Playford adopted East's device and its surrounding motto, 'Laetificat cor musica' (for illustration *see* DEVICE).

1. LIFE. A monument at St Michael-at-Plea, Norwich, to his father, John, a mercer, and local records show that he was one of a large family many of whom were scriveners or stationers. Since there is no record of his entry at the grammar school his brother Matthew attended, he was probably educated at the almonry or choir school attached to the cathedral, where he acquired a knowledge of music and the 'love of Divine Service' to which he later referred. Shortly after the death of his father (22 March 1639) he was apprenticed to John Benson, a London publisher of St Dunstan's Churchyard, Fleet Street (23 March 1639/40), for

seven years, achieving his freedom on 5 April 1647, when he became a member of the Yeomanry of the Stationers' Company. This entitled him to trade as a publisher.

He lost no time in securing the tenancy of the shop in the porch of the Temple Church from which all his publications were issued until his retirement. It was one of the addresses of Henry Playford until 1690, when the stock was auctioned. Royalist by family and by personal inclination, Playford began publishing political tracts culminating in *The Perfect Narrative of the Tryal of the King* and others relating to the executions of royalist nobility (reprinted in 1660 as *England's Black Tribunal*). In November 1649 a warrant was issued for the arrest of Playford and his associates. Nothing more is known of him until a year later, when on 7 November 1650 he entered in the stationers' registers 'A booke entituled The English Dancing Master'. Although registration before publishing was theoretically obligatory he entered so few of his music books that it is impossible to tell if this, subsequently published in 1651 (for illustration *see* fig.33, p.93), was his first.

In 1653 he was admitted clerk to the Temple Church, an office he held with some distinction to the end of his life, devoting himself to the repair and maintenance of the building and to promoting the seemly ordering of the services both there and, through his publications, elsewhere. At about this time he married. When his wife Hannah inherited from her father, Benjamin Allen, publisher of Cornhill, the Playfords moved (1655) from the neighbourhood of the Temple to Islington, where she established a boarding-school for girls, which she maintained until her death in 1679. Playford then moved back to London, taking a house in Arundel Street, Strand, which later passed to his son.

Temperley's examination of the court books of the Stationers' Company shows that Playford was called to the livery in 1661. In 1681 a letter from the king to the master and wardens required that he and others named be admitted to the court of assistants. He attended most of its meetings until 1684 when he declared his retirement from business in favour of his son Henry and another young man, Robert Carr. A number of books, however, retained his imprint until 1686. In his will of that year, which names Henry Purcell and John Blow as beneficiaries, he desired to be buried in the Temple Church, or in St Faith's, the stationers' chapel in the undercroft of St Paul's, but no record of the burial is known in either place. On his death Purcell wrote the *Elegy on my friend, Mr John Playford*.

2. PUBLICATIONS. Playford's publications, apart from the political tracts and miscellaneous non-musical works, fall into three categories: theory of music and lesson books for various instruments, which usually contain brief instructions followed by 'lessons' or short pieces derived from popular airs; collections of songs and instrumental pieces; and psalms, psalm paraphrases and hymns, including *The Whole Book of Psalmes* (1661) for the Stationers' Company. He began to publish music in 1651; new books succeeded one another rapidly in the early years, becoming more sparse later. Examination of the contents, however, shows that often a 'new edition' differs little from its predecessor although new 'lessons' may have been added and some others subtracted, and the later songbooks may be selections or rearrangements of earlier titles under new names. It is generally assumed that *The English Dancing Master: or, Plaine and Easie Rules for the Dancing of Country Dances, with the Tune to each Dance* addressed to the 'Gentlemen of the Innes of Court' came first, but *A Musicall Banquet* (also 1651) bears, as well as Playford's imprint, that of John Benson, his former master. *The English Dancing Master*, with many enlarged editions until 1728, is probably Playford's best-known work, because of the modern revival of the country dance and as the largest single source of ballad airs. *A Musicall Banquet* contains the genesis of later books: *Musick's Recreation* (1652), *Catch that Catch Can* (1652; entitled *The Pleasant Musical Companion* in some later editions), *A Breefe Introduction to the Skill of Musick* (1654) and *Court Ayres* (1655). All but the first continued in new and enlarged editions. *Apollo's Banquet for the Treble Violin* (1669) reflects a new fashion for this 'brisk and airy' instrument that was to last for the next 30 years, but the lessons for the cittern and the virginals, which did not last much beyond the mid-17th century, are evidence of declining sympathy with Playford's nostalgia for these instruments.

The same is true of the hymns and psalm paraphrases (as distinct from the psalter), which were an ordained part of Anglican worship, and of the songs and instrumental pieces addressed to the proficient performer. As examples of the creative genius of Henry Purcell, Matthew Locke, William and Henry Lawes, Christopher Simpson and Richard Dering, they afford interest to the scholar, but are without those qualities which enabled the vocal music of the Tudor period eventually to outlast them. These had been the property of Thomas East, and his rivals failed to find a transferee after the death of William Stansby, who had acquired them in 1625. It is possible, even probable, that they were part of the stock of East's printing house in Little Britain bought by Thomas Harper in 1634, later the workshop of John Playford the younger. In 1653 John Playford (i) offered them as part of his bookseller's stock in his *Catalogue of All the Musick Bookes printed in England*; they reappeared in the advertisements appended to many of his books. In 1690 when the stock of his shop by the Temple Church was to be sold by auction, they were again catalogued for the benefit of 'those remote from London' and offered to buyers for a few pence. The dedications and prefaces to these and his other publications reflect Playford's commercial acumen, his xenophobia, and his devotion to the restoration of the monarchy and to the divine service decently ordered.

(2) Henry Playford (*b* ?Islington, 5 May 1657; *d* London, between May and Dec 1709). Publisher, bookseller and dealer, son of (1) John Playford (i). He continued his father's business but was unable, owing to competition from the publishers of engraved music and to his conservatism and training in the old methods of bookselling, to maintain the same dominance of the music publishing trade. Nevertheless, during the late 1680s and early 1690s he was probably London's best-known music publisher.

Apprenticed to his father in 1674 and freed in 1681, he initially published in conjunction with John Playford (i), who shortly before his death handed over part of his business to his son and to Robert Carr, son of the music publisher John Carr. Henry worked from the same addresses as his father, a shop in the Temple and a house in Arundel Street. After three publications he parted company with Robert Carr, and thereafter published largely on his own account, occasionally in partnership with other publishers. His early works mainly followed the examples set by his father or were new editions of his father's titles. From 1687 he began to publish large numbers of non-musical works, which were to remain important in his output. He married Anne Baker in 1686; records of one daughter have been located. From 1690 until 1693 Playford was active in promoting sales and auctions of art works and antiquarian music books; from 1692 he was responsible for the publication of most of Purcell's music in association with that composer and later his widow Frances.

Around 1695 Playford found that competition from publishers of engraved music (notably John Walsh, John Hare and Thomas Cross) greatly affected his sales,

and so he took action to regain his share of the market. He tried issuing a series of engraved songsheets in 1697 but soon reverted to the older, more familiar methods of printing from type. In 1699 he purchased equal shares in William Pearson's improved music type fount, the 'new London character'. This partnership lasted three years and resulted in Playford's bringing suit against Pearson for alleged wrongdoing and misuse of the fount. To attract a wider audience he initiated new forms of publication, including the music periodical *Mercurius Musicus* (1699–1702) and the cheap collections of popular songs entitled *Wit and Mirth: or, Pills to Purge Melancholy*. Further, he attempted to establish a network of music clubs to promote his publications. These innovations were finally to no avail, as Playford's old-fashioned methods were quickly superseded by those of the new publishers of engraved music – themselves usually instrument sellers free from the constraints of the Stationers' Company. The last decade of his career was marked by editions or reissues of old titles, an increased interest in sacred music and religious books, and the publication of more non-musical works.

Playford never reached his father's seniority in the Stationers' Company. He was called to the livery in 1686, and awarded a half-yeomanry share in the English Stock in 1696. Records document five apprentices. His stock was sold by John Cullen from 1706, and also by John Young who probably sold them on Pearson's behalf. After his death, his saleable type-printed works were issued by John and Benjamin Sprint and William Pearson, and the engraved ones by John Walsh and John Hare. In his will he left his estate to his wife Anne.

Henry continued to reissue many of his father's titles, after updating them to suit modern tastes, until his death. Among the most successful were the collection of violin tunes *Apollo's Banquet* (four editions and a second part), *The Dancing Master* (six editions, a second part and numerous additional parts) and the catch collection entitled *The Second Book of the Pleasant Musical Companion* (three editions and several reissues). *The Division-Violin* and *The Whole Book of Psalms* (seven editions) were frequently reissued but not updated; the influential treatise *An Introduction to the Skill of Musick* (five editions) was updated in earlier editions. Among Henry's works modelled on those of his father were the song collections *The Theater of Music* (1685–7), *The Banquet of Music* (1688–92) and *Deliciae musicae* (1695–6).

Playford's non-musical publications account for approximately one-third of his total output. They include the collections of religious verse *Miscellanea sacra*, play texts and the weekly literary periodical *The Diverting Post* (1704–6). He was associated with Cavendish Weedon's 'Entertainments of Divine Musick' in 1702, and published at least four of the works issued in conjunction with these concerts. Many sale catalogues were also produced for Playford's auctions of music books and art works.

(3) John Playford (ii) (*b* Stanmore Magna, *c*1655; *d* ?20 April 1685). Printer, nephew of (1) John Playford (i). He has been confused with other members of the family also named John, and with one, believed to be a bookseller, who spelt his name Playfere, but there is now no doubt that he was the son of the Rev. Matthew Playford (brother or half-brother of John Playford (i)), vicar of Stanmore Magna, who forfeited both livelihood and property because of his royalist sympathies.

At some time, probably in the 1670s, William Godbid, a printer of scientific books and music, took young John Playford as apprentice; at Godbid's death in 1679, his widow, Anne, took John into the partnership and advertised in *The Art of Descant* (refashioned from Campion's *Art of Composing* published by 'Snodham alias Este') that 'the only Printing-house in England for Variety of Musick and Workmen that understand it, is still kept in Little Britain by A. Godbid and J. Playford Junior'. An examination of the publications suggests that much of the type and many of the ornaments and other features, including the device 'Laetificat cor musica', originally belonged to Thomas East and was used successively by Harper and Godbid.

In 1682 Playford seems to have acquired the ownership of the business and in the same year his name appears in the livery list of the Stationers' Company; in 1683 he attended the company's Court of Assistants. He died between 20 April 1685, when he signed his will, and 29 April when the will was proved, bequeathing the business to his sister Eleanor.

A year later the *London Gazette* of 3–6 May 1686 advertised 'An Ancient Printing-house in Little Britain, late in possession of Mr John Playford deceased, well-known and ready fitted . . . with good Presses and all manner of Letter for . . . Musick, Mathematicks, Navigation and all Greek and Latin Books . . . to be Sold . . . or Lett by Lease'. From subsequent events it seems that the royal printers bought some of the material; but early in 1687 Eleanor requested permission from the king to continue to print

music 'having nothing else to subsist by, yo'r Petitioner prayes that she may continue her Printing-house . . . and may have the honour to be your Majesty's servant for printing the said Musick [and] Mathematick . . . there being no other . . . that can doe the same.' She sought to further her case by referring to her father Matthew Playford, who 'suffered sequestration and was ruined', and to the continuous business carried on 'above forty years' in the same place; but James II, unlike Charles, was not well disposed to the Playford family. The royal printers were happy to assert that there were 'more Master-printers set up than there is work to be had', and to emphasize their own willingness to serve His Majesty 'in all matters of musick etc'. The petition was dismissed; the royal printers, who had 'already bought much of the Petitioner's materials', were ready to buy the rest and with that the continuity of an established business ended.

E. Arber and G. E. B. Eyre: *Archives of the Worshipful Company of Stationers . . . Transcript of the Registers 1554–1708* (London, 1875–1914); F. A. Inderwick: *Calendar of the Inner Temple 1505–1714* (London, 1895); [?F. Kidson]: 'The Petition of Mrs Eleanor Playford', *The Library*, 3rd ser., vii (1916), 346; F. Kidson: 'John Playford and 17th Century Music Publishing', *MQ*, iv (1918), 516; C. L. Day and E. B. Murrie: 'English Song-books and their Publishers 1651–1702', *The Library*, 4th ser., xvi (1936), 355; W. C. Smith: 'Some Hitherto Unnoticed Catalogues of Early Music', *MT*, lxxvii (1936), 636, 701; Day and Murrie (1940); M. J. Dean-Smith: *Playford's English Dancing Master 1651* (London, 1957) [annotated facs. edn.]; M. Tilmouth: 'Some Early London Concerts and Music Clubs 1670–1720', *PRMA*, lxxxiv (1957–8), 13; C. Blagden: 'The Stationers' Company in the Civil War Period', *The Library*, 5th ser., xiv (1959), 1; idem: *The Stationers' Company* (London, 1960); M. Tilmouth: 'A Calendar of References to Music in Newspapers 1660–1719', *RMARC*, i (1961), 1–107; L. Coral: 'A John Playford Advertisement', *RMARC*, v (1965), 1; N. Temperley: 'John Playford and the Metrical Psalms', *JAMS*, xxv (1972), 331–78; idem: 'John Playford and the Stationers' Company', *ML*, liv (1973), 203; L. Coral: *Music in English Auction Sales, 1676–1750* (diss., U. of London, 1974); Krummel (1975); M. M. Curti: *John Playford's Apollo's Banquet 1670* (diss., Rutgers U., 1977); M. Dean-Smith: 'Playford', *Grove6* [incl. selective list of publications]; P. A. Munstedt: *John Playford, Music Publisher: a Bibliographical Catalogue* (diss., U. of Kentucky, 1983); D. R. Harvey: *Henry Playford: a Bibliographical Study* (diss., Victoria U. of Wellington, 1985)

M.D.-S., D.R.H.

Pleyel, Ignace Joseph [Ignaz Josef] (*b* Ruppersthal, 18 June 1757; *d* Paris, 14 Nov 1831). Austrian composer, publisher and piano maker, active in France. In about 1772 he was Haydn's pupil and lodger in

Eisenstadt, later becoming Kapellmeister to Count Erdödy. During the early 1780s he travelled in Italy and then (probably in 1784) became assistant to F. X. Richter, Kapellmeister of Strasbourg Cathedral, whom he succeeded in 1789. Most of Pleyel's compositions date from the years 1787–95, during which period he was also active as a conductor in Strasbourg and (briefly) in London (December 1791 to May 1792).

Early in 1795 Pleyel settled in Paris, opened a music shop and founded a publishing house, which issued some 4000 works during the 39 years it existed, including many by Boccherini, Beethoven, Clementi, Cramer, J. L. Dussek, Haydn and other friends of Pleyel and his son. Some of them (e.g. Dizi, Kalkbrenner, Méhul, Rossini) were involved in the firm by financial investment. Pleyel established agents for the sale of his publications all over France, and maintained an active exchange of letters and music with some of the foremost European music publishers (e.g. Artaria of Vienna, Böhme of Hamburg, Breitkopf of Leipzig, Hoffmeister of Vienna, Hummel of Amsterdam and Simrock of Bonn), sometimes arranging for reciprocal engraving of their issues.

The most important achievement of the Maison Pleyel was probably its issue of the first miniature scores, a series entitled *Bibliothèque Musicale*. It began in 1802 with four of Haydn's symphonies, and continued with ten volumes of his string quartets, followed by chamber works by Beethoven, Hummel and Onslow (the last in 1830). In 1801 Pleyel also issued a *Collection complette des quatuors d'Haydn, dédiée au Premier Consul Bonaparte*, the title-page beautifully engraved by Aubert (see illustration), the separate parts engraved by Richomme and probably edited by the violinist Baillot. The prefatory material includes a handsome portrait of Haydn by J. Guérin and a thematic catalogue 'of all Haydn's quartets, sanctioned by the author and arranged in the order in which they appeared'. This statement and Haydn's earlier relationship with Pleyel have involved the edition in the debate concerning the authenticity and order of certain quartets generally attributed to Haydn. The edition also includes two pages of subscribers' names, many of them notable musicians (e.g. Cherubini, Dussek, Grétry, Kreutzer, Méhul, Salomon, Viotti) or aristocracy centred on Vienna (e.g. Erdödy, Esterházy, Golitsïn, Harrach, Lobkowitz, Razumovsky, Swieten, and Thurn and Taxis). The first edition contained 80 quartets, subsequent editions adding two, then one, as Haydn composed them.

In 1805 Pleyel travelled with his son Camille (1788–1855) to Vienna, mainly to establish a branch office, but this venture failed despite the support of local friends. The firm had been plagued since its inception by a series of legal contests that were not exceptional but sapped Pleyel's energy and financial resources. In 1813 he made a determined effort to sell the publishing enterprise, describing his stock in a letter to a prospective buyer as 48,000 plates of pewter (*fin étain*) or copper, printed music he had published or for which he was agent, instruments (violins, violas, double basses, trumpets, trombones, bows, strings etc), manuscripts not yet engraved and unused paper. 'In the last two years I have published more than 200 new works, of which 29% to 30% have not yet been put on sale . . . Most of my editions have been engraved by Richault, Lobry, Petit and Marquerie, the best engravers in Paris'. On 1 January 1815 Camille became a legal partner of the firm, after which it used the trade name 'Ignace Pleyel et fils aîné'. He gradually assumed more responsibility for the running of the business, especially the piano-building side of its activities.

During the 1820s Ignace Pleyel indulged his love of rural life by spending increasing amounts of time on a large farm about 50 km from Paris. During the same period the firm's output became more predominantly popular, as symphonies, sonatas and quartets were replaced by *romances, chansonnettes* and similar genres by Bayle, Bizot, Georgeon, Panseron and (especially) Pauline Duchambge, whose songs were always issued with alternative piano and guitar accompaniments. The firm also issued many fantasias, variations, rondos and potpourris of operatic *airs* by Adolphe Adam, Carulli, Duvernoy, Mayseder, Pixis and others. In 1834 the Maison Pleyel ceased its publishing activities entirely, selling its stock of plates and printed works to various Paris publishers including Lemoine, Prilipp, Delloy, Richault and Schlesinger.

C. Pierre: *Les hymnes et chansons de la Révolution* (Paris, 1904); M. Pincherle: 'L'édition musicale au dix-huitième siècle', *Musique*, i (1928), 493 [incl. letter from George Thomson to Pleyel]; H. C. R. Landon: *The Collected Correspondence and London Notebooks of Joseph Haydn* (London, 1959); J. Klingenbeck: 'Ignaz Pleyel und die Marseillaise', *SMw*, xxiv (1960), 106; A. Tyson: 'Haydn and Two Stolen Trios', *MR*, xxii (1961), 21; B. S. Brook: *La symphonie française dans la seconde moitié du XVIIIe siècle* (Paris, 1962); L. Klingenbeck: 'Pleyel, Ignaz Joseph', *MGG*; G. de Rothschild: *Luigi Boccherini: sa vie, son oeuvre* (Paris, 1962; Eng. trans., 1965); R. Benton: 'Ignace Pleyel, Disputant', *FAM*, xiii (1966), 21; idem: 'A la recherche de Pleyel perdu,

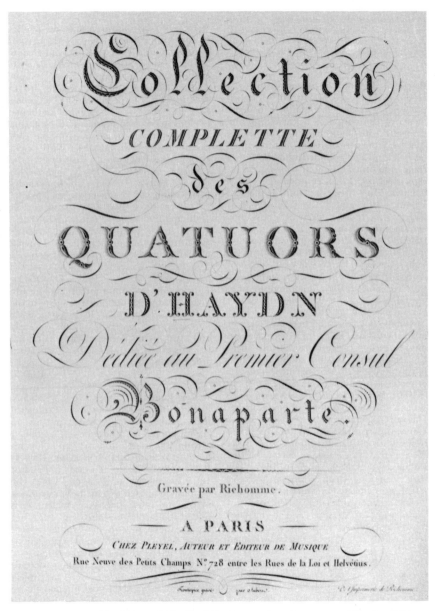

Title-page, engraved by Aubert, of Pleyel's 'Collection complette des quatuors d'Haydn, dédiée au Premier Consul Bonaparte' (1801)

or Perils, Problems and Procedures of Pleyel Research', *FAM*, xvii (1970), 9; J. Zsako: 'Bibliographical Sandtraps: the *Klavierschule*, Pleyel or Dussek?', *CMc* (1971), no.12, p.75; R. Benton: 'Pleyel's *Bibliothèque musicale'*, *MR*, xxxvi (1975), 1; idem: 'A Résumé of the Haydn–Pleyel Trio Controversy, with some Added Contributions', *Haydn-Studien*, ix (1978); idem: 'Pleyel as Music Publisher', *JAMS*, xxxii (1979), 125; E. Radant: 'Ignaz Pleyel's Correspondence with Hoffmeister & Co.', *Haydn Yearbook*, xii (1981), 122–74

R.B. (ii)

Poggioli, Antonio (*b* Samarugio, Rome, *c*1580; *d* Rome, 10 March 1673). Italian publisher and dealer. Described in documents of the period as a 'cartulario' and 'librarius', he built up his publishing concern from a bookdealer's business that he had probably founded himself. It was situated in central Rome (Parione), and his sign, which appears in his publications, was a hammer. On 4 November 1607 he married a young widow named Angela Schiavo; they had at least four children of whom one, Giovanni (*b* 17 July 1612; *d* 30 Sept 1675), followed his father's occupation. It seems that Giovanni worked independently of his father, however, for even after the death of Angela (8 June 1658) Antonio continued to work for himself. Both father and son were buried at S Maria in Vallicella (the Chiesa Nuova) in Rome.

Antonio Poggioli published most types of instrumental and sacred and secular vocal music, including reprints of Arcadelt, Lupacchino and Tasso, a complete edition of Cifra's motets and important anthologies of motets. His publications date from 1620 to 1668 and represent the work of seven Roman printers, among them Robletti, Masotti, Grignani and Mascardi. Giovanni is known only as the editor of the later of the two, slightly different, editions of the *Scelta di motetti* that appear to have been published within days of each other in 1647. The earlier edition, which is not included in *RISM*, was dedicated by Antonio Poggioli on 29 July to Ottavio Secusio, a 'senatore' and 'consiliario' of Messina, and it includes motets by composers who had connections with that city. These are replaced by Roman motets in the later edition, dedicated by Giovanni Poggioli on 31 July to Paolo Coccia, 'Signore del Poggio Sommavilla'. The *Scelta* was also published, with further slight changes, at Antwerp by Phalèse in 1652, as *Delectus sacrarum cantionum* (in Christ Church College, Oxford; not in *RISM*). It provides a representative selection of Roman *concertato* motets for two to five voices from the mid-17th century.

EitnerQ; G. Gaspari: *Catalogo della Biblioteca Musicale G. B. Martini di Bologna* (Bologna, 1890–1943/ *R*1961), ii, 356; H. Leichtentritt: *Geschichte der Motette* (Leipzig, 1908); Sartori (1958); P. Kast: 'Poggioli, Antonio', *MGG*; idem: 'Biographische Notizen zu Römischen Musikern des 17. Jahrhunderts', *AnMc* (1964), no. 1, 58

C.T.

Polskie Wydawnictwo Muzyczne [PWM; Polish Music Publications]. In 1928 a group of Polish musicologists and musicians led by Adolf Chybiński, Teodor Zalewski, Tadeusz Ochlewski and Kazimierz Sikorski organized the Towarzystwo Wydawnicze Muzyki Polskiej (TWMP; Polish Music Publishing Society), Warsaw, to publish authentic editions of Polish music. The catalogue includes music in all genres from the 15th century to the 20th. In 1934 TWMP began publishing the periodical *Muzyka polska*; the principal scholarly series is *Wydawnictwo Dawnej Muzyki Polskiej*, which includes early music by Szarzyński, Mielczewski, Pękiel, Gorczycki and Zieleński as well as 19th- and 20th-century music up to World War II. In April 1945 TWMP transferred its assets to PWM, organized by Tadeusz Ochlewski and based in Kraków; Mieczysław Tomaszewski succeeded Ochlewski on the latter's retirement in 1965. The PWM-Edition is the only music publishing house in Poland and produces a wide range of music and music literature. It is particularly important for its publications of early and avant-garde Polish music and critical editions of Chopin, Moniuszko, Wieniawski and Szymanowski.

T.C. (ii)

Power, James (*b* Galway, 1766; *d* London, 26 Aug 1836). Irish publisher and instrument maker. After starting out as an apprentice pewterer he entered the military instrument trade, and set up with his brother William in Dublin about 1802 as William Power & Co. Towards the end of 1807 he moved to London, where he established himself as a military instrument maker and music publisher. William continued the Dublin business until 1831, but the partnership with his brother ceased about 1810, although many publications were issued jointly by them up to 1820.

The brothers' major publishing venture was Moore's *Irish Melodies*. For this project they commissioned the poet Thomas Moore to provide original verses to be set to traditional melodies arranged by John Stevenson (a plan similar to the *Scottish Melodies* then being issued by the Edinburgh publisher George Thomson). The first two parts were published in London and Dublin in 1808 (not 1807 as often stated), and were an immediate success. After the sixth number (1815) a quarrel arose between the brothers, and part vii (1818) was issued by each separately. From part viii (1821) James employed Henry Bishop as arranger, though William also issued part viii, with arrangements by Stevenson. James, however, brought a successful action for breach of copyright, and the remaining two parts (1824–34) and a supplement (1834) were published by James alone.

Power also issued several other volumes of settings of Moore's poetry, including *Sacred Songs* (1816–24), *National Airs* (1818–28) and *Evenings in Greece* (1826–32). He maintained a very close relationship with the poet and paid a substantial annuity for his verses. Power's other publications included *A Selection of Scottish Melodies* (Bishop and Twiss, 1812), *Indian Melodies* (1813), *A Selection of Welsh Melodies* (John Parry, 1822) and similar works, besides many single songs, duets and glees by Stevenson, Horn, Attwood, Matthew King and others. His widow carried on the business until about 1838. The plates of the *Irish Melodies* were bought by Addison & Hodson, who reissued them in 1844, and their popularity continued well into the second half of the century.

Catalogue of the Music Plates and of the Printed Copies being the Remaining Stock in Trade of . . . J. Power (London, 1840); J. Power: *Notes from the Letters of Thomas Moore to his Music-publisher* (New York, 1854); P. H. Muir: 'Thomas Moore's Irish Melodies 1808–1834', *The Colophon* (1933), no.15; Humphries and Smith (1954, 2/1970)

P.W.J.

Prentiss, Henry. American publisher and instrument dealer, active in Boston. In 1825 he established a publishing firm and umbrella shop at 23 Court Street. The firm moved to Pemberton Hill in 1834, back to Court Street in 1838, then in 1844 to 81 Washington Street, returning to Court Street the following year. The firm's name changed to Prentiss and Clark in 1847, with shops at both Court and Washington streets. During this year, Oliver Ditson absorbed the company's publishing and Prentiss and Clark became instrument dealers exclusively. Prentiss's publications are of particular interest for their early lithographed covers and include a number of political and military songs, notably J. Friedheim's *Trip to Dedham, or Striped Pig Quickstep* (1836–7), Henry Schmidt's *Hero's Quickstep* (1836), *Tippecanoe, or Log Cabin Quickstep* and *The Whig Gathering* (both 1840), and W. C. Glynn's *Capitol Quickstep* (1844).

Fisher (1933); Dichter and Shapiro (1941, 2/1977)

C.E.

Presser. American firm of publishers. It was founded as the Theodore Presser Company in Philadelphia in 1883 by Theodore Presser (*b* Pittsburgh, PA, 3 July 1848; *d* Philadelphia, 28 Oct 1925) who earlier that year had begun publication of a monthly magazine in Lynchburg, Virginia, *The Etude*. After his death the firm was expanded by the acquisition of the John Church Company (1930), the Oliver Ditson Company (1931) and the Mercury Music Corporation (1969), which included the catalogues of Beekman Music and Merrymount Music. In 1970 Elkan-Vogel became a subsidiary and in 1981 the firm purchased the bulk of the copyrights of American Music Edition. Other subsidiaries include Merion Music, New Music Edition and Society of the Publications of American Music. Through Ditson, the company traces its history to 1783, making it the nation's oldest continuous music publisher.

Presser is the sole agent in the USA for a number of American publishers, including Columbia Music, Coronet and Peer-Southern Concert Music, as well as for foreign firms such as Durand, Editions Musicales Transatlantiques, Jobert and Novello. The company serves the needs of dealers, teachers and musicians, drawing from a huge stock of classical, educational and light music. It also maintains a large library of works for hire, including opera, ballet and orchestral music, and is the agent for the rental libraries of Belwin-Mills, Heugel, Leduc, MCA, Marks and United Artists. Among the many American composers represented by Presser are Cowell, Erb, Getty, Ives, Lazarof, Persichetti, Rochberg, Ruggles, Sapieyevski, Schickele, Schuman, Sessions, Shapey, Stucky, Weisgall, Wernick, Yardumian and Zwilich. In 1949 the company's main office was moved to Bryn Mawr, Pennyslvania; George Rochberg was director of publications, 1951–60.

A. A. Hauser: 'American Music Publishing in 1958', *Notes*, xv (1957–8), 377; C. Yoder: *Theodore Presser, Educator, Publisher, Philanthropist: Selected Contributions to the Music Teaching Profession in America* (diss., U. of Illinois, 1978); W. C. Rorick: 'Theodore Presser Company: a Bicentennial Retrospect', *FAM*, xxxi (1984), 377

W.T.M., M.J./R

Preston. English firm of publishers. It was started by John Preston (*d* Jan 1798), who by about 1774 was established as a guitar and violin maker in London. In 1789 his son Thomas entered the business, and continued it alone after his father's death until about 1834, when it was acquired by Coventry & Hollier.

The Preston firm rapidly rose to become

one of the most flourishing in the trade. Its publications covered music of every kind, and included a long annual series of country dances begun in 1786, popular operas by Arnold, Hook and Reeve, and works such as Bunting's *General Collection of the Ancient Irish Music* (1796) and J. S. Smith's collection *Musica antiqua* (1812). It was also the printer of George Thomson's collections of national songs from 1793. In addition Preston & Son bought the plates and stock of several other firms, including Robert Bremner (1789), Thomas Skillern the elder (*c*1803), H. Wright (*c*1803), and Wilkinson & Co. (*c*1810). From these it did a vast reprint business, the most notable items of which were oratorios and other works of Handel acquired from H. Wright (formerly Wright & Wilkinson), the successor of Walsh and Randall.

Kidson (1900); C. Hopkinson and C. B. Oldman: 'Thomson's Collections of National Song', *Edinburgh Bibliographical Society Transactions*, ii (1940), 1–64; Humphries and Smith (1954, 2/1970)

F.K., W.C.S./P.W.J.

Purcell Society. English publishing society. It was founded in February 1876 for the purpose, as the original prospectus states, 'of doing justice to the memory of Henry Purcell; firstly, by the publication of his works . . . and secondly, by meeting for the study and performance of his various compositions'. The idea of performances was abandoned at an early stage, and the society assumed the form simply of a body of subscribers to its publications, all of which from the start have been produced by Novello.

In 1887, by which time only two volumes had appeared, the society was reorganized with W. H. Cummings as editor and W. B. Squire as honorary secretary. Squire continued in office until 1923, by which time 20 more volumes had appeared. He was succeeded by Gerald M. Cooper and in 1923–8 four more were published. On his own account, Cooper began the publication of the Purcell Society Popular Edition in a format for practical performance, which was not part of the main scheme. There was no further activity until 1957 when, the society having been revived by Anthony Lewis, the first of the remaining volumes appeared, leading to the completion of the entire scheme in 31 volumes by 1965. Many of the pre-1928 volumes have stood up well in the light of recent scholarship, though, for example, certain continuo realizations are no longer acceptable. A programme of revision of all volumes is in progress, to be completed about 1995, employing a handier

format reduced from the splendid luxury of the original volumes.

W.S. (i)

Purday. English family of publishers, active in London. The firm of Purday & Button, established at 75 St Paul's Churchyard in about 1805, was the direct successor of the important Thompson firm (founded 1746); it was known as Button & Purday from about 1806 to 1808, when Purday retired from partnership with S. J. Button and it became Button & Whitaker. Purday was probably the father of Zenas Trivett Purday, who succeeded William Hodsoll at Bland's old shop in High Holborn in 1831, and did a large music trade, principally in humorous sheet songs. His business ceased in 1860. Thomas Edward Purday, another member of the family, also traded in sheet songs from about 1834 to 1862 at 50 St Paul's Churchyard, where he took over the music publishing part of Collard & Collard, having previously been with Clementi & Co. The business was subsequently in Oxford Street as Thomas Edward Purday & Son (*c*1862–4).

Charles Henry Purday (*b* Folkestone, 11 Jan 1799; *d* London, 23 April 1885), a composer and conductor of some repute, founded a business in 1854 in Maddox Street, publishing many of his own arrangements of sacred and secular vocal works; the firm was continued at various other addresses until 1870 when Purday apparently retired.

Humphries and Smith (1954, 2/1970); Coover (1988)

P.W.J.

Purdie, Robert (*fl* 1809–*c*1837). Scottish publisher. He was a music teacher at Jollie's Close, Canongate, Edinburgh, in 1804. In 1809 he opened a music shop and publishing house in Princes Street and by about 1820 he had become the leading music publisher in Edinburgh. Besides a great deal of sheet music, he issued the collection *The Scottish Minstrel* in six volumes (1821–4), edited by Robert Archibald Smith (1780–1829); many of the lyrics were contributed by Lady Nairne under the pseudonym 'Mrs Bogan of Bogan'. Purdie also published Smith's *Irish Minstrel* (*c*1825) and *Select Melodies with Appropriate Words* (*c*1827). He acquired and reissued (in conjunction with Alexander Robertson & Co.) several of the Gow family's works after the bankruptcy of Nathaniel Gow in 1827.

About 1837 the business passed to Purdie's son John (*d* nr. Stonehaven, 23 Aug 1891), who also published sheet music for the drawing-room market until 1887. Then Methven, Simpson & Co. continued it until 1967.

Kidson (1900)

F.K., W.C.S./D.J.

Pustet. German firm of publishers. On 30 September 1826 Friedrich Pustet (*b* Hals, nr. Passau, 25 Feb 1798; *d* Munich, 6 March 1882) founded the Pustet publishing firm and retail business in Regensburg (after 1833 the firm also produced paper). The publishing enterprise began with production of popular and academic literature on history and theology, but after 1845 it concentrated on liturgical books and thereby acquired an international reputation. Branches were founded in New York and Cincinnati in 1865 (they became independent concerns in 1912) and in Rome in 1898 (independent since 1916); Pope Pius IX appointed Pustet 'Typographus S. Sedis Apostolicae' in 1862. From 1883 until the publication of the Roman Editio Vaticana in the first decade of the 20th century, Pustet's liturgical books were regarded as the authoritative editions. The firm received a 30-year privilege for the production of all official hymnbooks (1868) and subsequently became 'Typographus Sacrorum Rituum Congregationis' (1870). Despite severe hostility the privilege was extended in 1898 for two years, but expired with the abolition of the so-called Medicaea. The company concurrently developed an equal interest in the publication of church music, serving the Regensburg movement for the restoration of church music; it issued Mettenleiter's *Enchiridion Chorale*, Proske's *Musica Divina* and *Selectus Missarum* and Haberl's continuation of *Musica Divina* and *Repertorium Musicae Sacrae*. The catalogue also contained many works by minor composers. After 1945 Pustet issued the new series *Musica Divina* (edited by Stäblein), *Regensburger Tradition* (Schrems), *Die Chorsammlung* (Haberl and Quak) and the collection of early organ pieces *Cantantibus Organis* (Eberhard Kraus). The firm acquired considerable importance by publishing periodicals and yearbooks of church music including the *Fliegende Blätter für katholische Kirchenmusik* (1866, later *Caecilienvereinsorgan*, 1911–37), *Musica sacra* (1868–1937) and the *Caecilien-Kalender* (1876, later *Kirchenmusikalisches Jahrbuch*, 1886–1932). It also published writings on church music by Haberl, Gottron, Johner, Karl Weinmann, Peter Wagner, Hugo Riemann and Kroyer. In 1978 Pustet was acquired by Feuchtinger and Gleichauf of Regensburg.

H. Bohatta: *Liturgische Drucke und Liturgische Drucker: Festschrift zum 100jährigen Jubiläum des Verlags Friedrich Pustet Regensburg* (Regensburg, 1927); T. Emmerig: *Wolfgang Joseph Emmerig und Franz Anton Niedermayr: ein Beitrag zur Geschichte des Steindrucks in Regensburg* (Regensburg, 1981)

A.S. (i)

R

Rab [Raabe, Rabe], **Christoph** [Corvinus, Christopher] (*b* Zurich, 1552; *d* Herborn, 19 Jan 1620). German printer and publisher. After studying at the universities of Heidelberg, Wittenberg and Vienna (1567–74) he worked in the press of his father Georg Rab (*d* 1580); later he worked with the Frankfurt publisher Sigismund Feyerabend and the printers Johann Wechel and Paul Rab (1581–5). In 1585 he moved to Herborn, where Count Johann VI the elder of Herborn helped him to establish and expand an efficient printing firm. Rab mainly printed works for the new University of Herborn (founded 1584), moving with it to Siegen (1595–9) and then following it back to Herborn. His publications include many Calvinist psalm books, including George Buchanan's in Latin, Ambrosius Lobwasser's in German and at least one Hungarian version, as well as several editions of hymnbooks and works by Meiland, Melchior Schramm and other composers.

Benzing (1963, 2/1982); H. Hüschen: 'Hessische Gesangbuchdrucker und -verleger des 16. und 17. Jahrhunderts', *Festschrift Hans Engel* (Kassel, 1964), 166

T.W.

Rampazetto, Francesco (*b* Lona, *c*1510; *d* Venice, ?1576). Italian printer and bookseller, active in Venice. He worked in the parish of S Giovanni Novo, with a shop on the calle delle Rasse, and in 1572 was elected Prior of the Guild of Booksellers and Printers, succeeding Girolamo Scotto. Working mainly on commission for other printers and booksellers, he produced at least 190 books in Italian, Latin, Greek or Spanish; literary works, notably reprints of Ariosto and Boccaccio, figure prominently in his output.

From 1561 until 1568 he printed music – 31 sets of partbooks, one theory book and a book of *laudi spirituali*. The last, Serafino Razzi's voluminous collection (*RISM* 1563⁶), was sent to Rampazetto by the Florentine publisher Filippo Giunta because Florence had no musical press at the time. Among his other commissions were an anthology of motets (1563³) compiled and edited by the printer Antonio Barré, and the second book⁻ of Vinci's five-part madrigals (1567²⁴), financed by Giovanni Comencino. Besides commissions for first editions, Rampazetto reissued works by Rore, Lassus and Arcadelt. In reprints he made few musical changes, but often altered spellings, contractions and text underlay.

Rampazetto's activity as a music printer falls within the years that Girolamo Scotto and Antonio Gardano monopolized the Venetian industry, and indeed he was the only other bookman until 1566 to produce more than a handful of musical editions. There is evidence of a connection between Rampazetto and Scotto. Printing materials first used by Scotto, including music type, historiated initials and a woodcut, appear in editions printed later by Rampazetto. Furthermore, several Rampazetto madrigal books, notably Primavera's third (1566¹³) and Vinci's second book of five-part settings, complete editions of the same composers' works issued by Scotto. Apparently Scotto's overflow of work prompted him to send material to Rampazetto. A correlation exists also between the time that Rampazetto stopped printing music and the years the Scotto firm increased its music production. From the late 1560s Girolamo's nephew Melchiore took a more active role in the family business; music which earlier would have been passed to Rampazetto may have remained with the Scotto press.

Printers' marks hint at another possible source of support in Rampazetto's work. He had four of his own marks. An early woodcut containing his initials, a serpent and an eel and a four-*putti* border, appears on the colophon of only one publication, Ariosto's *Orlando furioso* (1554). The other three marks, similar in design, have the motto 'Et animo et corpore' above *putti* bearing laurel wreaths. Rampazetto used these marks on a variety of books including musical ones but he also used marks belonging to other bookmen. On nine Rampazetto music books of 1565–8, the title-page has a woodcut of 'Virtue' holding a banner and palm fronds. Since the Venetian printer Plinio Pietrasanta used the same mark on four music books in the 1550s, it is possible that he was Rampazetto's silent partner for these nine editions.

Rampazetto may have died in the Venetian plague of 1575–7. His son Giovan Antonio took over the firm at his death, using the imprint 'heredi di Francesco Rampazetto' from 1578 until 1583, and his own name until around 1607. In 1610 another Francesco Rampazetto printed at least one volume. The firm is known to have continued until 1662.

H. Brown: *The Venetian Printing Press* (New York, 1891/*R*1969), 87, 253; C. Sartori: 'Rampazetto, Francesco', *MGG*; idem (1958); M. E. Cosenza: *Biographical and Bibliographical Dictionary of the Italian Printers and of Foreign Printers in Italy* (Boston, 1968); C. Marciani: 'Editori, tipografi, librai veneti nel regno di Napoli nel cinquecento', *Studi veneziani*, x (1968), 512, 514, 540; P. F. Grendler: *The Roman Inquisition and the Venetian Press, 1540–1605* (Princeton, 1977), 177, 277; T. W. Bridges: *The Publishing of Arcadelt's First Book of Madrigals* (diss., Harvard U., 1982); C. I. Nielsen: 'Francesco Rampazetto, Venetian Printer, and a Catalogue of his Music Editions' (M.A. thesis, Tufts U., 1987)

C.I.N.

Randall, William (*b* London, *c*1728; *d* London, ?Jan 1776). English music seller and publisher. He was a son or more probably a grandson of Peter Randall, a London music publisher associated with John Walsh, and was presumably the Randall found among the Children of the Chapel Royal from 1736 to 1745. At the death of his cousin John Walsh the younger in 1766 he and John Abell inherited the extensive Walsh business, where they had doubtless been employed. They published for the first time the complete full scores of a number of Handel oratorios, starting with *Messiah* (1767). After Abell's death on 29 July 1768 Randall remained in business alone. Besides reprinting Walsh publications, sometimes with the original imprint in addition to his own, he published many interesting works, including a reissue in 1771 of Morley's *A Plaine and Easie Introduction to Practicall Musicke*. Collections of country dances and pleasure-garden songs also came from his press. At his death his widow Elizabeth carried on the business until 1783, when it was taken over by Wright & Wilkinson.

Kidson (1900); W. C. Smith: *A Bibliography of the Musical Works published by John Walsh during the Years 1695–1720* (London, 1948); idem: 'John Walsh and his Successors', *The Library*, 5th ser., iii/4 (1949), 291; Humphries and Smith (1954, 2/

1970); W. C. Smith: *Handel: a Descriptive Catalogue of the Early Editions* (London, 1960, 2/1970); W. C. Smith and C. Humphries: *A Bibliography of the Musical Works published by John Walsh, 1721–1766* (London, 1968)

F.K., W.C.S./P.W.J.

Rastell, John (*b* London, *c*1475; *d* London, 1536). English Member of Parliament, dramatist, writer on law, historian, adventurer, and printer of books and music. Although the quantity of extant music printed by him is small, it is of great historical importance. It consists of a three-part song (see illustration) printed in rough score in his own play, *A New Interlude and a Mery of the Nature of the iiii Elements* (modern edition by R. Coleman, Cambridge, 1971, as *The Four Elements*), and a broadside ballad (unique copies in the British Library, London). Unfortunately both lack a date.

The three-part song 'Tyme to pas' from the play 'A New Interlude' written and printed by John Rastell (GB-Lbm)

The circumstantial and bibliographical evidence is extremely complex, but strongly suggests that neither the play nor the broadside is likely to have been printed much later than 1525 and the play possibly some years earlier. The broadside, a fragment of a much larger sheet (with little more than one line of a voice part) which contained the music of either a two-part or a three-part song, is the earliest known broadside with music printed from type in any country. The music type used by Rastell, though rather rough and produced from twice-struck matrices, enabled him nevertheless to print the staves, notes and

directs at the same impression with the text. Since no type of any kind was first cut and cast in England until some time after Rastell's death, he must have obtained the fount from some continental source, possibly in the Low Countries or northern France. The type has been found later only once, in a book of psalms printed by John Gough probably in the mid-1530s.

Rastell's two productions antedate by at least three years the first book of Attaingnant's chansons which appeared in April 1528 and have long been considered the first example of one-impression music printing. Although Attaingnant used type cast from once-struck matrices, and was a better printer, he must on present evidence yield priority to Rastell as the pioneer in the use of this far-reaching innovation in the history of music printing.

A. H. King: 'Rastell Reunited', *Essays in Honour of Victor Scholderer* (Mainz, 1970), 213, repr. in *Musical Pursuits* (London, 1987); idem: 'The Significance of John Rastell in Early Music Printing', *The Library*, 5th ser., xxvi/3 (1971), 197, repr. in *Musical Pursuits*; idem: 'An English Broadside of the 1520's', *Essays on Opera and English Music in Honour of Sir Jack Westrup* (Oxford, 1975), 19; R. J. Roberts: 'John Rastell's Inventory of 1538', *The Library*, 6th ser., i (1979), 34

A.H.K.

Ratdolt, Erhard (*b* Augsburg, 1447; *d* Augsburg, late 1527 or early 1528). German printer. According to his own diary covering the years 1462–1523 (Vienna, Österreichische Nationalbibliotek 15473) he first went to Venice in 1462, after the death of his father. Returning there in 1474, he began printing with two German partners, Peter Löslein and Bernardus Pictor (whether 'Pictor' is a latinized version of the surname, 'Maler', or whether it refers to its bearer's profession of illuminator, remains uncertain). Following the departure of both partners in 1478 or 1479 and after a one-year interim, he resumed business by himself in 1480. In 1485 the diocese of Augsburg commissioned a breviary from Ratdolt, which particularly pleased the bishop; efforts were made to persuade the printer to return to Augsburg, first by Bishop Johann von Werdenberg and, after his death in 1485, by his successor, Friedrich von Hohenzollern. He apparently did so shortly afterwards (his last Venetian publication is dated 18 March 1486) and continued printing until his retirement in 1522, although his son Georg officially took over the business in 1515.

Ratdolt was one of the major craftsmen of his time, known primarily, however, for publications outside the field of music. In Venice his efforts were devoted mainly to writings on astronomy and mathematics (about 50 works), but his Augsburg publications (over 70) are almost exclusively liturgical, principally consisting of missals, breviaries and obsequials for various dioceses in southern Germany, Austria and Switzerland (Augsburg, Brixen, Chur, Konstanz, Freising, Passau, Regensburg and Salzburg). He introduced musical notes into his liturgical books in 1487, using woodblocks at first, in 1491 changing to movable type. Ratdolt was the first printer to employ decorated title-pages and the first to print in three, and even four, different colours, using woodcuts by such prominent artists as Hans Burgkmair and Jörg Breu. A proof sheet of 14 different type models, dated 1 April 1486 (made just before his return to Augsburg and apparently in connection with that offer), is extant (in the Bayerische Staatsbibliothek, Munich).

G. R. Redgrave: *Erhard Ratdolt and his Work at Venice*, Bibliographical Society, Illustrated Monographs, i (London, 1894, 2/1899) [incl. list of publications]; R. Proctor: *An Index to the Early Printed Books in the British Museum, Part 2, 1501–1520: Section 1, Germany* (London, 1903/R1954), 74; R. Molitor: *Deutsche Choral-Wiegendrucke* (Regensburg, 1904); R. Proctor: *Catalogue of Books Printed in the XVth Century now in the British Museum*, ii (London, 1912/R1963), 379; E. H. Voullième: *Die deutschen Drucker des 15. Jahrhunderts* (Berlin, 1916, 2/1922), 13; K. Schottenloher: *Die liturgischen Druckwerke Erhard Ratdolts aus Augsburg 1485–1522* (Mainz, 1922) [incl. numerous facs. and list of publications]; I. Schwarz: 'Die Memorabilien des Augsburger Buchdruckers Erhard Ratdolt (1462–1523)', *Werden und Wirken: Festgruss K. W. Hiersemann zugesandt* (Leipzig, 1924), 399; R. Diehl: *Erhard Ratdolt: ein Meisterdrucker des XV. und XVI. Jahrhunderts* (Vienna, 1933); D. C. McMurtrie: *Erhard Ratdolt, the Father of Typographic Decoration* (Chicago, 1936); K. Meyer-Baer: *Liturgical Music Incunabula: a Descriptive Catalogue* (London, 1962); Benzing (1963, 2/1982); T. Wohnhaas: 'Ratdolt, Erhard', *MGG*; A. Layer: 'Augsburger Musikdrucker der frühen Renaissancezeit', *Gutenberg-Jb 1965*, 124; M. K. Duggan: 'A System for Describing Fifteenth-century Music Type', *Gutenberg-Jb 1984*, 67; C. W. Gerhardt: 'Wie haben Ratdolt und Callierges Ende des 15. Jahrhunderts in Venedig ihre Drucke mit Blattgold hergestellt?', *Gutenberg-Jb 1984*, 145

M.L.G.

Ratti, Cencetti & Comp. Italian firm of publishers, active in Rome. Giovanni Battista Cencetti ran a copying business at 8 via Canestrari that was established by the second decade of the 19th century, and began music publishing with Leopold Ratti, probably in 1821. The firm, originally styled Stamperio Litografica di Leopoldo Ratti e Gio: Batta Cencetti, was first at 24 via de Spagnuoli. From about 1823 to 1830 it was at 23 via della Posta Vecchia (also referred to as 23 via de' Sediari), with additional premises at 17 via della Croce (from c1828); in about 1830 the latter became its main address, with 154 via di Ripetta also in use (c1830–31). Cencetti's name was dropped from the imprint in about 1834, but as Ratti & Comp. the firm continued in business until at least late 1837.

To judge by plate numbers (which appear to be chronological) the firm issued some 600 publications, all probably in lithography, mainly of excerpts from contemporary operas. It is best remembered, however, for the enterprising series of complete full scores of eight Rossini operas: *Mosè in Egitto* (c1825), *L'inganno felice* and *Semiramide* (c1826), *Il barbiere di Siviglia* (c1827), *Ricciardo e Zoraide* (c1828), *L'assedio di Corinto* (c1830), *Matilde di Shabran* (c1832) and *Guillaume Tell* (c1835). Although Rossini probably did not supervise their preparation, they were the first full scores of his operas to appear in Italy (five of them have never been republished in full score). They are landmarks both in Italian and in lithographic music publishing; only a few operatic full scores were published in Italy in the 19th century, and it was at this time exceptional for such large-scale works to be printed by lithography anywhere.

P. Gossett: *The Operas of Rossini* (diss., Princeton U., 1970), 572

R.M.

Rättig. Austrian firm of publishers. Theodor Rättig began his publishing activities in Vienna about 1877, working as a partner in the firm of Bussjäger & Rättig in 1878–80. In 1878 he was responsible for publishing the first edition of Bruckner's Third Symphony (1877 version) after hearing the work's première on 16 December 1877: he was almost alone among the Viennese musical establishment in his enthusiasm. He issued a full score and, shortly afterwards, a version for piano duet by the 18-year-old Mahler, the latter's first publication. By the end of 1880 Rättig was operating on his own. He continued his passionate advocacy of Bruckner's music with the publication of the *Te Deum* (1885), four *Graduale* (1886) and the revised 1889 version of the Third Symphony (1890). Other composers in his catalogue are almost all minor Viennese musicians, though Rättig did publish works by Josef Schalk, and he had limited success with Josef Forster's ballet *Der Spielmann*. In the late 1890s the firm moved to Leipzig; it was taken over by Schlesinger (Lienau) in 1910.

H. Rättig: 'Ein Wegbereiter Anton Bruckners', *Gedanke und Tat*, i (1959), 1; R. Grasberger: *Werkverzeichnis Anton Bruckners* (Tutzing, 1977); N. Simeone: 'Two interesting Bruckner Editions', *Mitteilungsblatt der Internationalen Bruckner-Gesellschaft*, xxvii (1986), 11

N.S.

Raverii, Alessandro (*fl* Venice, early 16th century). Italian printer. His father Constantin Raverii was a member of a minor printing family and married one of the Bindoni family, famous as Venetian printers though little associated with music. Through them he became related to the Gardano family. Alessandro Raverii printed music only between 1606 and 1609, during which time he printed a large number of volumes of which over 50 are extant. He appears to have had close ties with Angelo Gardano, for many of Raverii's titles are clearly no more than reprints of volumes from Gardano's house after 1588. Raverii also printed three titles (by Bonini, Caccini and Peri) which he seems to have taken from Marescotti in Florence.

C. Sartori: 'Una dinastia di editori musicali', *La bibliofilia*, lvii (1956), 176–208; idem (1958); L. Bartholomew: *Alessandro Raverii's Collection of 'Canzoni per sonare' (Venice, 1608)* (Fort Hayes, KS, 1965)

S.B. (iii)

Rebenlein. German firm of printers. Georg Rebenlein (1575–1657) was one of Hamburg's four official book printers; his son Jakob Rebenlein (*d* Hamburg, 1662) inherited the printing firm, whose output included music. The business was continued by Jakob's sons, Georg Jürgen Rebenlein (1634–84) and Johann Hans Rebenlein (1637–78). Its chief musicological significance is its connection with he origins and development of the Hamburg school of song.

Benzing (1963, 2/1982); T. Wohnhaas: 'Rebenlein', *MGG*

T.W.

Regent's Harmonic Institution [Royal Harmonic Institution]. English firm of publishers, active in London. It was founded in 1818 as a joint-stock company of 23 professional musicians, including Attwood, Ayrton, Cramer, William Hawes, Ries, George Smart, Thomas Welsh and Samuel Wesley, to finance reconstruction of the Argyll Rooms, Regent Street. The plan, apparently led by the Regent Street architect, John Nash, in conjunction with the Philharmonic Society, called for the investors' money to be recouped through

profits from the sale of music, pianos and harps in a lower saloon. The company was formed by January 1819 and its first publications were registered in April; the shop and concert room were ready in January 1820. Internal dissension and financial instability soon led several investors to withdraw, notably Smart, Ries and Charles Neate, and the speculation foundered. The Philharmonic Society dissociated itself and by spring 1823 Welsh and Hawes were the principal shareholders. The imprint, altered to 'Royal Harmonic Institution' in December 1820, became 'Welsh and Hawes, at the Royal Harmonic Institution', 246 Regent Street, in September 1825. After Hawes declared bankruptcy in July 1827, Welsh continued alone until fire destroyed the building in February 1830. It was soon rebuilt and he resumed trading at the New Argyll Rooms in 1831, continuing to May 1833.

The firm's output consisted chiefly of light music – glees and songs, arrangements of opera airs, piano pieces – by its members, especially Walmisley, Griffin, Rawlings, Calkin, Beale, Attwood and Ries. Its most notable publication however was Beethoven's Piano Sonata op.106, the 'Hammerklavier' (registered at Stationers' Hall in September 1819), in an edition authorized by the composer.

The English Musical Gazette; or, Monthly Intelligencer (1819), 16, 34; W. H. Husk: 'Argyll Rooms', *Grove1*; Humphries and Smith (1954, 2/1970); A. Tyson: *The Authentic English Editions of Beethoven* (London, 1963); Neighbour and Tyson (1965)

L.L.

Rellstab, Johann Carl Friedrich (*b* Berlin, 27 Feb 1759; *d* Berlin, 19 Aug 1813). German publisher. From 1768 to 1775 he performed in student concerts at the Joachimsthal Gymnasium, playing keyboard concertos by J. S. and C. P. E. Bach. He studied with J. F. Agricola from 1773 (mainly the keyboard) and with C. F. C. Fasch in 1776–8 (mainly composition). In 1779 his father, who had acquired Berlin's oldest printing firm, had a stroke, and Rellstab was forced to step into the business and to abandon plans for study with C. P. E. Bach. Soon he enlarged the business, adding a new printing press, a publishing firm and a music shop where keyboard (both English and German), string and wind instruments, musical clocks and tuning pipes were sold, and where from 1792, harpsichords, pianos, harps and violin bows were manufactured. In 1783 he established a music lending library, and his firm issued printed music at least as early as 1785; from this time also he was active as a composer. In 1787 he acquired G. L. Winter's publishing firm, applied for a music printing monopoly in Prussia and in the same year instituted a series of weekly public subscription 'Concerts for Connoisseurs and Amateurs' at the English House, a series he was forced by financial necessity in 1788 to continue as private fortnightly concerts at members' homes. The concerts were often attended by Fasch, Reichardt, Zelter and others, and included both sacred and secular works such as Bach's *Magnificat* and Gluck's *Alceste*. Unfortunate political conditions forced the temporary cancellation of the concerts in 1806 and the sales of many instruments in 1808; in 1812 the lending library almost ceased to function and the press was permanently shut down. Rellstab continued selling some music and wind instruments, giving lessons in singing, declamation, composition and continuo realization. From 1808 to 1813 he was critic for the *Vossische Zeitung*.

Recent scholarship has again drawn attention to the dispute between Rellstab and C. P. E. Bach in 1785. Rellstab claimed to have acquired the rights to Bach's keyboard sonatas 'with altered repeats' w50 (H126, 136–40; 1760) from G. L. Winter's widow. Bach, who had invested money with G. L. Winter in a joint venture for their sales, had later at least partially settled with Winter's widow and received some of the unsold copies. He claimed that the sonatas could not be republished without his release and offered his copies to Rellstab at a low price. Rellstab declined, infuriating Bach by replying that he planned to print 300 copies by September and that Bach could become a partner if he advanced a printing fee. To punish Rellstab, Bach sent his copies to Breitkopf, urging the Leipzig publisher to issue them as soon as possible. Breitkopf's edition (?October) followed closely on the heels of Rellstab's and must have deprived the younger man of anticipated profits, although after Bach's death, Rellstab still professed great admiration for the master.

GerberNL; C. von Ledebur: *Tonkünstler-Lexicon Berlin's* (Berlin, 1861/R1965); H. F. L. Rellstab: *Aus meinem Leben* (Berlin, 1861); O. Guttmann: *Johann Karl Friedrich Rellstab: ein Beitrag zur Musikgeschichte Berlins* (Berlin, 1910); H. von Hase: 'Carl Philipp Emanuel Bach und Joh. Gottl. Im. Breitkopf', *Bjb*, viii (1911), 86; W. Hitzig: 'Ein Berliner Aktenstück zur Geschichte des Notendruckverfahrens', *Festschrift Peter Wagner* (Leipzig, 1926/R1969), 81; R. Elvers: 'Die bei J. K. F. Rellstab in Berlin bis 1800 erschienenen Mozart-Drucke', *MJb 1957*, 152; idem: *Alt-Berliner Musikverleger* (Berlin, 1961); idem:

'Datierte Verlagsnummern Berliner Musikverleger', *Festschrift Otto Erich Deutsch* (Kassel, 1963), 291; idem: 'Winter, Georg Lud(e)wig', *MGG*; H. Heussner: 'Rellstab', *MGG*; R. Wade: *The Keyboard Concertos of Carl Philipp Emanuel Bach* (Ann Arbor, 1981); H. Serwer: 'C. P. E. Bach, J. C. F. Rellstab, and the Sonatas with Varied Reprises', *C. P. E. Bach Studies*, ed. S. L. Clark (Oxford, 1988), 233

S.D.

Remick, Jerome H. (*b* Detroit, MI, 15 Nov 1868; *d* Grosse Pointe Farms, MI, 15 July 1931). American publisher. He worked initially for his family's logging firm, one of the largest in Michigan. In 1898 he purchased an interest in the Whitney-Warner Publishing Co., which moved to New York in 1904 and was reorganized as Shapiro, Remick & Co. (later Jerome H. Remick & Co.). Remick was one of the largest and most powerful firms of Tin Pan Alley, publishing such popular songs as *Hiawatha, In the shade of the old apple tree, Smiles, Pretty Baby, Sweet Georgia Brown* and *Shine on, harvest moon*. George Gershwin was employed at the age of 15 by Remick as a song plugger and had an early rag published by the firm. Remick also issued songs by Richard Whiting, Harry Akst, Gus Kahn, J. Fred Coots and Walter Donaldson. In the 1920s Remick returned to Detroit where he became active in many local businesses. The firm was acquired by Warner Bros. in 1930 as part of the Music Publishers Holding Corporation.

S.S.B.

Remunde [Ruremunde; Endoviensis], **Christophe van** (*b* Eindhoven, ?1475–1500; *d* London, 1531). Dutch printer. He worked in Antwerp from 1523 to 1531, where he published an important series of liturgical books 'ad usum ecclesie Sarum' – a series which helped to establish Antwerp as a rival to Paris in liturgical music printing. It includes: *Manuale* (1523), *Processionale* (1523), *Hymnorum cum notis opusculum* (1524), *Psalterium cum hymnis* (1524), *Breviarium* (1525), *Missale* (1527) and *Horae Beatae Mariae Virginis* (1530). Remunde had two sizes of type with Roman neumes and one with Gothic neumes (used for the Utrecht missal of 1527). All were printed by double impression, with black notes on red staves. The smaller of the two Roman faces (found in his publications from 1528 onwards) was also used by Symon Cock for his first music publication of 1539.

Besides liturgical books, Remunde published an English translation of the New Testament, an English almanac and Lyndewood's *Provinciale seu constitutiones Anglie*. Many of his books were printed for Peter Kaetz and Francis Birckmann, booksellers in London. In 1531 Remunde himself visited London where he was arrested for selling English New Testaments. He was sent to prison where he died. His widow Catharine continued to manage the business in Antwerp from 1532 to 1546. Her publications were similar to those of her husband and included some reprints of his books.

F. van Ortroy: 'Remunde, Christophe van', *BNB*; P. Bergmans: *La typographie musicale en Belgique au XVIe siècle*, v (Brussels, 1929); H. D. L. Vervliet: *Sixteenth Century Printing Types of the Low Countries* (Amsterdam, 1968); S. Bain: *Music Printing in the Low Countries in the Sixteenth Century* (diss., U. of Cambridge, 1974)

S.B. (i)

Reusner, Johann (*b* Rostock; *d* Königsberg, 30 April 1666). German printer. In October 1639 he moved to Königsberg, where he operated a printing shop and foundry under contract with the university. In 1640 he received a special privilege, and in 1660 the privilege to print a newspaper, the *Europäischer Mercurius*. After his death, his son Friedrich managed the shop until 1678, succeeded by Johann's widow Katharina and other 'Reusner Erben' until 1723. The Reusners printed nearly 100 music editions between 1639 and 1693, including many reprints, some unauthorized, such as Heinrich Albert's first seven collections of *Arien* (printed by Mense, 1638–50; repr. 1648–54). Johann was continually involved in legal battles with Lorenz Segebade's widow Elisabeth, or with her second husband Pascha Mense, perhaps because he reprinted so many of Segebade's works.

Benzing (1963, 2/1982)

T.D.W.

Reyser, Georg (*fl* 1468–*c*1504). German printer. With his brother Michael he apparently learnt the art of printing at Strasbourg, where in 1471 he became a citizen and member of the printer's guild. Anonymously printed books from 1468 to 1478 have been assigned to him. When he moved to Würzburg in 1479 he was awarded a monopoly on liturgical books by Bishop Rudolph of Scherenberg (1446–99), renewed by Bishop Lorenz von Beba (1495–1519). His printed music books for the Würzburg diocese include at least eight missals, a giant three-volume gradual and antiphonal, an agenda and a vigil, besides a missal (1482) for the Mainz diocese. Long noted for the beauty and clarity of his text types, Reyser is also to be praised for his two gothic plainchant types. Printed in large folio books, black notes on red staves, they reveal his mastery, from the first design of about 1481 to the improved and more elaborate fount of the *Graduale* of 1496–9.

After working with Georg, Michael Reyser established a branch in 1483/4 at Eichstätt, where he used a new gothic plainchant type for the elaborate chant of the 1488 *Obsequiale eystettense*. His three editions of the *Missale eystettense* contain no printed music, but he printed a separate edition of the music of the prefaces for Eichstätt (Nuremberg, Landeskirchliches Archiv, Ka 2).

R. Molitor: *Deutsche Choralwiegendrucke: ein Beitrag zur Geschichte des Chorals und der Notendrucker in Deutschland* (Regensburg, 1904); K. Ohly: 'Georg Reysers Wirken in Strassburg und Würzburg', *Gutenberg-Jb 1956*, 121; F. Geldner: *Die deutschen Inkunabeldrucker: ein Handbuch der deutschen Buchdrucker des XV. Jahrhunderts nach Druckorten*, i (Stuttgart, 1968), 63, 230, 261

M.K.D.

Rhames, Benjamin (*d* 16 Sept 1774). Irish publisher and dealer in music and haberdashery. He traded at 'The Sun', 16 Upper Blind Quay (later Exchange Street), Dublin, from about 1750. The business was carried on by his widow, Elizabeth, after his death in 1774. When she died in 1778, their son Francis carried on, using his mother's name until 1806, and then his own name until 1810. The firm was prolific in its production of sheet music, much of it pirated from London editions.

Humphries and Smith (1954, 2/1970)

B.B.

Rhau [Rhaw], **Georg** (*b* Eisfeld an der Werre, Suhl, 1488; *d* Wittenberg, 6 Aug 1548). German publisher. Working in Wittenberg, rather removed from the main centres of European music publication, he became one of the most important publishers of music, particularly for the Reformation church, and of schoolbooks and works of musical theory. On 15 April 1512 he enrolled at the University of Wittenberg, and in 1514 completed requirements for the BA degree. He then began a long association with the publishing business, working for four years in the publishing house of Johann Rhau-Grunenberg (presumably his uncle). In the summer of 1518 he left Wittenberg to become Kantor of the Thomasschule and Thomaskirche in Leipzig, a position he held until at least 1 May 1520. On 18 September 1518 he also joined the faculty of the University of Leipzig, lecturing in music theory.

Whether Rhau was associated at this early date with the circle of theologians surrounding Luther in Wittenberg is not clear. Nevertheless, as a former student at the University of Wittenberg and a resident of that city at the time of the nailing of the 95 theses, Rhau was certainly aware of Luther's position. In Leipzig, he seems to have become more directly involved. In June 1519 he wrote the *Missa de Sancto Spirito* for the service at the Thomaskirche which marked the opening of the disputations between Luther and Eck. This in itself implied no particular sympathy towards Luther's position, since such activity would have been normal to his duties as Kantor of the cathedral church. However, the growing enmity towards the Wittenbergers and Rhau's apparent sympathies put his position at the Thomaskirche in jeopardy, and it was necessary for him to leave Leipzig in 1520. He moved to Eisleben, where he accepted the post of *Ludimagister* of one of the Winkelschulen of the city. In 1521 or 1522 he became a teacher at Hildburghausen, and in 1523 he returned to publishing in Wittenberg, where he remained until his death.

Rhau's publishing activities reflected his relationship to the new church. Publications to meet the literary and musical needs of the church appeared in large quantities, including many books on theology, exegeses of the books of the Bible written by Luther, Melanchthon and Bugenhagen, editions of Luther's Catechism, his sermons, the Augsburg Confession and doctrinal treatises, both apologetic and polemic. Rhau's close association with the Wittenberg theological circle is further demonstrated by the prefaces by Luther, Melanchthon and Bugenhagen for his various musical publications; also a number of the young theologians, while studying at the university, worked in varying capacities in Rhau's shop. He was held in great esteem by his contemporaries for his contributions to theology, mathematics and music, and for his services as a citizen.

Rhau's enthusiasm for music had begun at an early age; he remarked in the preface of his *Postremum vespertini officii opus* (*RISM* 1544[4]) that he had been occupied with music 'a pueritia'. It is also likely that, since the music curriculum at the University of Wittenberg was well developed, Rhau attended lectures in music. No known compositions of Rhau are extant, but his accomplishments as composer as well as performer are suggested by his having been appointed to the position of Kantor at the Thomaskirche. Even as late as 1548 (the year of his death), he assumed direction of the electoral choir in Torgau succeeding Johann Walter – a fact which suggests his continuing ability and interest in musical performance.

In publication of musical materials, Rhau's first efforts were directed towards theory. In 1517, while still employed in the offices of Grunenberg, he published the first part of his own treatise on musical theory, *Enchiridion utriusque musicae practicae*, devoted to the subject of plain-chant (*musica choralis*). The second part, *Enchiridion musicae mensuralis*, appeared in 1520, while Rhau was in Leipzig. Although neither portion of the treatise was innovatory, the work enjoyed considerable success, appearing in successive editions – even after his death, as continued in publication by his heirs – until 1553. Beginning in 1517, he also brought out publications or new editions of theoretical works, with music examples cut in woodblock, by Martin Agricola, Nikolaus Listenius, Wenceslaus Philomathes, Johann Galliculus and Johann Spangenberg.

In 1538 Rhau's interest turned chiefly to the publication of collections of polyphonic music. In his preface to *Vesperarum precum officia* (1540[5]) he stated that it had always been his desire particularly to assist schoolboys by providing them with materials through which they might praise God and learn the truths of the Scriptures, and through which they might also love and study the honourable discipline of music. He further stated that from their early years the pupils should be exposed to the precepts of the musical art and through the singing of worthy examples learn to apply the rules to practical experience.

To fulfil these intentions Rhau published 15 major collections between 1538 and 1545, ranging from very simple works to those representative of the most highly developed Franco-Flemish polyphony, and which in keeping with his aims provided an extensive repertory of artistically significant music for both Mass and Vespers. For these works he used movable type of the same face seen earlier in editions of Formschneider in Nuremberg. The *Opus decem missarum* (1541[1]) furnished settings of the Ordinary of the Mass in general, while the *Officia paschalia, de resurrectione et ascensione Domini* (1539[11]) and the *Officiorum . . . de nativitate, circumcisione, epiphania Domini, et purificationis, etc* (1545[5]) supplied settings of both 'Ordinary and Proper, as complete services, for the Mass on the high feasts from Christmas to the Purification and from Easter to the Ascension respectively.

The *Selectae harmoniae quatuor de passione Domini* (1538²) provided similar works, as well as appropriate motets, for

Three of the collections were for Vespers. The *Vesperarum precum officia* included complete settings of the choral portions (opening responses, antiphons and psalms, responsory, hymn, versicle, *Magnificat* with antiphon and *Benedicamus Domino*) for each day of the week; the *Sacrorum hymnorum* (1542¹²) contained 134 settings of vesper hymns; and the *Postremum vespertini officii opus* 25 *Magnificat* settings. Three other collections provided settings by single composers of specific portions of Vespers: the *Novum ac insigne opus musicum* (1541) with settings by Sixt Dietrich of antiphons for each day of the week; the *Responsorum numero octoginta* (1542) with two volumes of responsories by Balthasar Resinarius; and the *Novum opus musicum* (1545) with three volumes of hymns by Sixt Dietrich.

Of the remaining volumes, four comprised materials for more general use within the school. The *Symphoniae iucundae* (1538⁸) contained 52 motets, many of which were appropriate for use in the service. The *Tricinia* and *Bicinia*, each of two volumes, however, contained secular materials only, selected for their artistic merit, to serve in the development of the pupils' musical ability and taste. The final volume, the *Wittembergisch deudsch geistlich Gesangbüchlein* (1544), constituted a new and enlarged edition of Johann Walter's *Gesangbüchlein* which had appeared in earlier editions (1524, 1525 and 1535) from other presses, but which now, because of its continuing usefulness, was issued by the press which had come to represent the very centre of publishing activities for the new church.

Rhau's musical publications as a whole present compositions which reflect procedures that had been traditionally associated with settings of liturgical texts at the beginning of and just before the Reformation, as seen in the works of the generation of Obrecht and Josquin. This generation is rather well represented in the publications. However, there is also a fairly extensive literature representative of a younger generation of German composers associated directly with the new church, and whose compositions are known through Rhau's publications. The publications are important, not only for the general quality and accuracy of the musical printing (Rhau probably made corrections himself as work on an edition progressed), but also for the preservation of a repertory useful for the study of the early Reformation worship service, its music, and the conservative attitudes towards musical style held by its composers.

J. Reusch: *Epitaphia Rhauorum* (Wittenberg, 1550); F. W. Rost: *Was hat die Leipziger Thomasschule für die Reformation getan?* (Leipzig, 1817); R. Eitner: 'Georg Rhaw: Biographie', *MMg*, x (1878), 120; O. Kade: 'Georg Rhaw', *MMg*, xi (1879), 27; G. Buchwald: 'Stadtschreiber M. Stephan Roth in Zwickau', *Archiv für Geschichte des deutschen Buchhandels*, xvi (1893), 6–246; F. Spitta: 'Die Chorsammlung des Georg Rhaw 1544', *Monatschrift für Gottesdienst und kirchliche Kunst*, xv (1910), 2; T. W. Werner: 'Die Magnificat-Kompositionen Adam Reners', *AMw*, ii (1919–20), 235; W. Wölbing: *Der Drucker und Musikverleger Georg Rhaw: ein Beitrag zur Drucker- und Verlagstätigkeit im Zeitalter der Reformation* (diss., U. of Berlin, 1922) [incl. complete list of Rhau's theological publications]; H. Zenck: *Sixt Dietrich, ein Betrag zur Musik und Musikanschauung der Reformation* (Leipzig, 1928); W. Gosslau: *Die religiöse Haltung in der Reformationsmusik, nachgewiesen an den 'Newen Deudschen Geistlichen Gesengen' des Georg Rhaw* (Kassel, 1933); H. Albrecht: 'Sacrorum hymnorum liber primus, Besprechung der Neuausgabe', *Mf*, i (1948), 203; L. Schrade: 'The Editorial Practice of Georg Rhaw', *The Musical Heritage of the Church*, iv (1954), 31; I.-M. Schröder: *Die Responsorienvertonungen des Balthasar Resinarius* (Kassel, 1954); H. Albrecht: 'Zur Rolle der Kontrafaktur in Rhaus "Bicinia"', *Festschrift Max Schneider* (Leipzig, 1955), 67; A. Boes: 'Die reformatorischen Gottesdienste in der Wittenberger Pfarrkirche von 1523 an', *Jb für Hymnologie und Liturgik*, iv (1958–9), 1–40, vi (1961), 49–61; M. Geck: 'Rhau, Georg', *MGG*; V. H. Mattfield: *Georg Rhaw's Publications for Vespers* (Brooklyn, 1966); C. Parrish: 'A Renaissance Music Manual for Choirboys', *Aspects of Medieval and Renaissance Music: a Birthday Offering for Gustave Reese* (New York, 1966), 649; C. T. Gaines: *Georg Rhau: Tricinia, 1542* (diss. Union Theological Seminary, 1970); B. A. Bellingham: *The Bicinium in the Lutheran Latin Schools during the Reformation Period* (diss., U. of Toronto, 1971); W. Steude: *Untersuchungen zur Herkunft, Verbreitung und spezifischem Inhalt mitteldeutscher Musikhandschriften des 16. Jahrhunderts* (diss., U. of Rostock, 1973); V.H. Matfield: 'Rhau, Georg', *Grove6* [incl. list of publications]

V.H.M.

Rhetus [Rhete], **Georg** [Jerzy] (*b* Stettin [now Szczecin], 16 Jan 1600; *d* Stettin, 5 June ?1645). German printer. He came from a family of printers living in Stettin; in 1619 he purchased Georg Rhode's printing house, the most eminent in Danzig (now Gdańsk), and in 1629 he was appointed 'Reipublicae et gymnasii typographus'. After his death the firm was run by his widow and then by his sons until the end of the 17th century. His music publications included volumes by Eccard and Stobaeus (*RISM* 1634³), Opitz (1639), Stobaeus (1640), Siefert (1640) and Spielenberger (1641). He used a high quality of type and

391

his publications present an attractive appearance.

Przywecka-Samecka: (1969); *Słownik pracowników książki polskiej* [Dictionary of Polish printers] (Warsaw and Łódź, 1972)

T.C. (ii)

Ribou, Pierre (*fl* Paris, 1704–20). French publisher. Probably the son of Jean Ribou and the father of Guillian Ribou, he was the only significant music publisher contemporary with the Ballards and Henry Foucault. In 1705 he began a lifelong collaboration with Foucault, publishing instrumental music. Besides several treatises, he published two important dance collections by Pecour (*c*1712). His name is first found in the imprint of a collection of *Airs de la Comédie-Française* (1704–13) by Jean Claude Gillier, where his address is given as 'near the Augustine monastery at the descent from Pont Neuf at the sign St Louis'; he remained there until his death in mid-1720. He maintained a close relationship with the Académie Royale de Musique, publishing extracts from its productions and naming himself their 'sole printer' on a score by Campra (1710) and 'sole book seller' on the score of Mouret's *Didon*.

Devriès and Lesure (1979–88)

G.B.

Richault. French firm of publishers. It was founded in Paris by Jean-Charles-Simon Richault (*b* Angerville, Essonne, 5 May 1780; *d* Paris, 20 Feb 1866). After an apprenticeship with the publisher J. J. de Momigny, Richault set up on his own in 1816 at 7 rue Grange-Batelière, occasionally also publishing jointly with Momigny for up to 20 years afterwards. His firm, normally styled 'Simon Richault', moved to 16 boulevard Poissonnière some time between September 1823 and July 1825; between 14 and 28 November 1841 it moved (or the house was renumbered) to no. 26; and on 19 October 1862 it had just moved to 4 boulevard des Italiens. Meanwhile, in November 1839, Richault purchased the business of J.-J. Frey, many of whose publications he subsequently reissued. On his death, Charles-Simon was succeeded by his son Guillaume-Simon (*b* Chartres, 2 Nov 1805; *d* Paris, 7 Feb 1877) and the firm became known as Richault & Cie. Guillaume-Simon was in turn succeeded by his widow, Marie (*b* Naples, 30 Oct 1813; *d* after 1898) in partnership with their son Léon (*b* Paris, 6 Aug 1839; *d* Paris, 10 April 1895), who traded as Richault & Cie or Richault Fils & Cie. After León's death the firm was directed by his mother until in June 1898 it was acquired by Costallat & Cie (still in existence).

Particularly under the management of Charles-Simon, Richault was one of the most important music publishers in Paris during the 19th century, issuing a total of some 20,000 publications. Its catalogue included orchestral, chamber and vocal music, especially the works of important non-Italian contemporary composers, such as Beethoven, Czerny, Fesca, Liszt, Mendelssohn, Schumann, Spohr, Weber and notably Schubert. Among the French composers it encouraged were Alkan, Massé, Reber, Thomas and Berlioz; Richault was the first to publish Berlioz's *La damnation de Faust*, *L'enfance du Christ*, *Lélio*, four of the overtures and several vocal works, as well as a collection of his *mélodies* with piano accompaniment. Rather less attention was paid to opera, but full scores or orchestral parts or both were published of works by Adam, Monpou, Onslow and Thomas, as well as the handsome critical edition of Gluck operas edited by F. Pelletan and others (issued in association with Breitkopf & Härtel, in 1873–96). Piano-vocal scores of at least 30 operas were published. According to Pougin (*FétisBS*) the firm acquired and reissued many editions previously published by Naderman, Sieber, Pleyel, Erard and others and, after Pacini's death in 1866, at least part of his stock, including his operatic publications. Richault's plate numbers were applied chronologically and are generally reliable for dating purposes.

FétisBS; C. Hopkinson: *A Bibliography of the Musical and Literary Works of Hector Berlioz* (Edinburgh, 1951, 2/1980); idem (1954); idem: *A Bibliographical Thematic Catalogue of the Works of John Field* (London, 1961), 168; Devriès and Lesure (1979–88)

R.M.

Richel, Bernhard (*fl* 1472–82). Printer active in Basle. The first known music printer north of the Alps, he is credited with an unsigned and undated *Missale basiliense* (Stuttgart, Württembergische Landesbibliothek Ink. 11332.C). The edition is usually dated 1480/81, but an annotation in the catalogue at Stuttgart suggests *c*1483. It contains 17 pages of music printed with a black gothic chant type on red four-line staves. Two earlier missals for Basle, one unsigned in about 1478 and one with Richel's printer's mark dated 22 January 1480, were printed without music but with space for manuscript music on some 50 pages. He died between 20 February and 6 August 1482.

A. Pfister: 'Vom frühsten Musikdruck in der Schweiz', *Festschrift Gustav Binz zum 70. Geburtstag am 16. Januar 1935* (Basle, 1935); F. Geldner: *Die deutschen Inkunabeldrucker: ein Handbuch der deutschen Buchdrucker des XV. Jahrhunderts nach Druckorten*, i (Stuttgart, 1968), 112, 114, 120, 191

M.K.D.

Ricordi. Italian firm of publishers.

1. HISTORY. The firm of Ricordi was founded in Milan in 1808 by Giovanni Ricordi (*b* Milan, 1785; *d* Milan, 15 March 1853); it was directed from 1853 to 1888 by his son Tito (i) (*b* Milan, 29 Oct 1811; *d* Milan 7 Sept 1888), from 1888 to 1912 by Tito's son Giulio (*b* Milan, 19 Dec 1840; *d* Milan, 6 June, 1912) and from 1912 to 1919 by Giulio's son Tito (ii) (*b* Milan, 17 May 1865; *d* Milan, 13 March 1933). The firm was managed from 1919 to 1940 jointly by Renzo Valcarenghi and Carlo Clausetti, from 1940 to 1944 by Valcarenghi and Alfredo Colombo and from 1944 to 1952 by Colombo, Eugenio Clausetti and Camillo Ricordi. In 1952 it became a limited company, under the presidency first of Colombo, then from 1961 of Guido Valcarenghi and from 1976 of Carlo Origoni.

Giovanni Ricordi, a violinist, was leader of the orchestra of a small Milanese theatre, the Fiando. Probably in 1803 he had started a *copisteria* (copying establishment) beneath the portico of the Palazzo della Ragione. From 1804 to 1807 he was under contract as official copyist and prompter to the Teatro Carcano and in 1807 to the Teatro del Lentasio. In 1807 he spent several months in Leipzig studying the techniques of Breitkopf & Härtel and, after returning to Milan, on 16 January 1808 he formed a publishing partnership with Felice Festa, an engraver and music seller. Their first, and probably only, joint publication was a duet from Farinelli's *Calliroe*, which they issued as the first in a series entitled *Giornale di Musica Vocale Italiana*; the imprint gave Ricordi's address as Contrada di S Margherita (not mentioning the house number, 1108) and Festa's as Pantano no. 4705. The partnership was terminated on 26 June 1808, and at about the same time Ricordi took a shop at 4068 Contrada di Pescaria Vecchia, from which address his plate number 1 (Antonio Nava's *Le quattro stagioni*) was issued. In 1811 he was appointed publisher to the Milan Conservatory. In the following year, probably in August, he moved to 1065 Contrada di S Margherita, and in the winter of 1815–16 to no. 1118 of the same street. About 1824 the shop, which he used as his publishing address, transferred to Ferdinando Artaria's former premises, favourably loca-

ted opposite La Scala (Dirimpetto all'I. R. Teatro alla Scala no. 1148) and in 1828 he moved his printing works from 1118 Contrada di S Margherita to 1635 via Ciovasso. From 1838 Ricordi's imprints read '1720 Contrada degli Omenoni', but after about 1860 the firm's address was normally omitted from its publications. In 1844 a new shop was opened at the side of La Scala, 'di fianco alla Scala', and soon became known as the Casino Ricordi. By 1867 the main offices, and probably the works too, were at 1 via Omenoni; from 1875 at the latest there was a shop at the Galleria Vittorio Emmanuele; in 1884 new printing works were erected at 21 viale Porta Vittoria; and in January 1889 a shop was opened at 9 via S Margherita. In 1910 the works were moved to 42 viale Campania and the offices to 2 via Berchet. Both these premises were bombed in 1943, with the loss of machinery and the stock of unsold copies, hire material and almost all the non-autograph manuscripts. The reconstructed via Berchet premises were reopened in February 1950. The most valuable of Ricordi's rich archives survived the war and are still in the possession of the firm; they include some 4000 music manuscripts (chiefly autograph), a large quantity of correspondence, and approximately 25,000 printed editions; details of much of the collection are listed at the Ufficio Ricerca Fondi Musicali (the Italian *RISM* centre) in Milan.

During his first decade in business Giovanni Ricordi issued an average of 30 publications a year; in his second the yearly average was about 300. This expansion was largely the result of a succession of contracts starting from December 1814, which he won as prompter and exclusive copyist to La Scala, giving him the right to publish the music performed there; in 1825 he purchased their entire musical archives. In 1816 he had a similar contract as copyist to the Teatro Re, and in the 1830s and 1840s concluded highly favourable agreements with the opera houses of Venice and Naples. By the end of 1837 he had not only purchased the stock and plates of Ferdinando Artaria but was able to boast more than 10,000 publications, the exclusive rights to operas written for Milan and Naples, an archive of 1800 autograph manuscripts and a branch in Florence. The latter, Ricordi Grua & Co., was opened towards the end of 1824; its name was changed to Ricordi Pozzi & Co. (1827), to G. Ricordi & Co. (1828) and to G. Ricordi & S. Jouhaud (*c*1840). In 1860 the association with Jouhaud terminated, and in 1865 Tito (i) opened an independent branch in

Florence. A London branch, Grua Ricordi & Co., had been opened (1824), but it was closed four years later. In December 1840 Ricordi purchased the small business of Gaetano Longo (of Este), and expansion within the firm continued at such a rate that by his death in 1853 Giovanni had issued 25,000 publications.

Tito (i), a good pianist, had worked in the firm since 1825. Under his management, new printing methods were introduced, branches in Naples (1860), Rome (1871), London (1875), Palermo and Paris (both 1888) were opened, and the substantial businesses of Clausetti (1864), Del Monaco and Guidi (both 1887) and finally Lucca (30 May 1888) were taken over. The acquisition of Lucca, which had been Ricordi's chief rival from the 1840s and had itself between 1847 and 1886 absorbed five firms (including Canti), brought to the Ricordi catalogue some 40,000 editions as well as the Italian rights to Wagner's operas.

Shortly before his death, Tito (i) gave over the management of the firm to his son Giulio, a highly cultured man and the best musician in the family. Usually under the pseudonym J. Burgmein (or sometimes Grubmeni), he composed many piano pieces and songs as well as some orchestral music and stage works, culminating in a comic opera *La secchia rapita*, performed at Turin in 1910. He worked for his father for a short time from 1856 and permanently from 1863. It was he who regularly dealt with Verdi on the firm's behalf (from c1875) and who played a central role in Puccini's artistic development. Under his management, branches at Leipzig (1901) and New York (1911) were opened, part of the stock of Escudier, Ricordi's former Paris agent, was acquired (1889), and the firms of Pigna and Schmidl (both 1902) and Carelli (1905) were taken over. His son Tito (ii), who succeeded him, appears to have lacked both charm and judgment. He and Puccini disliked each other, and Puccini had *La rondine* published by Ricordi's rival Sonzogno. When Tito (ii) retired in 1919, the management of the firm passed out of the hands of the Ricordi family. Business expansion continued, however, and in South America the publishers Breyer-Hermanos (1924, Buenos Aires; Breyer had been representing Ricordi since 1885), Canulli (1925), Harrods (1928), Oerthmann (1935), Balerio y Bonini (1940) and Romero y Fernandez (1947) were all taken over; the Walter Mocchi musical archives were acquired in 1929, and the Naples firm of Pasquariello absorbed in 1946. Further branches were set up in São Paolo (1927),

Basle (1949), Genoa (1953), Toronto (1954), Sydney (1956) and Mexico City (1958). Since then, branches or agencies have been opened in Bari, Florence, Turin and Munich, and the branch in Leipzig has closed. The New York branch was purchased by Alfredo Colombo's son, Franco (*b* Milan, 4 Aug 1911), who had been its managing director since 1949, and became known as Franco Colombo Inc. in 1962. By 1975 Ricordi had published more than 132,000 editions and included gramophone records and light music in its catalogue.

2. PUBLICATIONS. The firm's earliest editions were printed from engraved plates, but in 1821 or 1822 several publications were printed by lithography. About 1824 Ricordi took over Ferdinando Artaria's lithographic department, and a year or so later Tito (i) was sent to Germany to study the process. Nevertheless the firm only rarely used lithography, and printing direct from engraved plates remained the normal practice until the 1870s, when chromolithographic and offset processes were introduced. In their publications of vocal music Ricordi invariably used, until about 1844, the soprano and tenor clefs in addition to the treble and bass, and it was a further 20 years before the former were finally dropped. In 1877 the firm devised a new modification of the treble clef to indicate a line sung an octave lower, by a tenor. Ricordi's plate numbers are in general reliably chronological (but certain caveats are sounded by Gossett and Hopkinson). The sudden, curious leap in 1890 from about 55,000 to about 94,000 is explained by the application in that year of Ricordi numbers to their recently acquired Lucca stock. Another useful Ricordi practice was the blind-stamping of dates on most of their publications issued between about 1860 and 1932; in all probability these stamps related not to the date of printing but rather to that of the binding or wrappering of a particular batch of copies. In the Ricordi archives there is a further valuable source of precise chronological information – a series of manuscript notebooks giving the dates on which many works to be published by the firm were sent, apparently, for engraving or printing.

Ricordi's first catalogue (1814) lists his first 176 publications. These were mainly piano arrangements of and variations on operatic tunes, pieces for one and two guitars (including several by Antonio Nava), and the operatic numbers that formed part of his *Giornale di Musica Vocale Italiana* (which did not run beyond its fourth volume). The most notable single

Ricordi

items from these early years were Asioli's *Trattato d'armonia* and Pollini's *Metodo per forte-piano o clavicembalo*, both published for the Milan Conservatory, and Ricordi's first complete vocal score, Mayr's *Adelasia ed Aleramo*, issued in association with the firm of G. C. Martorelli. Several supplementary catalogues were printed during the next few years, and then, in 1825, appeared a major catalogue of Ricordi's total production (more then 2300 items) to the end of 1824. By this time the firm was offering a range of instrumental music by international composers, methods and theoretical works for students, a large selection of Italian operatic numbers for piano solo and piano and voice (including many pieces by Rossini), and dance and ballet music for piano solo. Especially noteworthy are the first appearances of Paganini's works in print (opp. 1–5), many pieces for violin by Rolla and for guitar by Nava and Giuliani, and vocal scores of five complete operas. The catalogue lists in full score about 60 operatic excerpts but only two complete works: Weigl's cantata *Il ritorno d'Astrea* and Beethoven's *Christus am Ölberge*. Much of the music in the catalogue first appeared in the series *Biblioteca di Musica Moderna*, a periodical collection offered by subscription in four (1820) and six (1821–30) categories, three consisting of piano music and one each of vocal, violin and flute music.

The next general catalogue appeared in 1838 and advertised the firm's 10,000 publications to the end of 1837. During this period Ricordi had, through his connections with opera houses, established both an extremely powerful position for himself in the operatic world and a highly profitable business. Rossini had effectively retired and Bellini was dead; but Ricordi had published vocal scores and was in a position to hire out performing material of 19 operas by Rossini and eight by Bellini. Donizetti was still flourishing, and Ricordi either already had published, or was about to publish, all but a handful of his works composed after 1830. Also on Ricordi's books were the best of the other Italian opera composers – Mercadante, Vaccai, Pacini and Luigi and Federico Ricci – as well as Meyerbeer, whose *Crociato in Egitto* had been published by the firm in 1824 and whose French operas were now achieving widespread success. In 1839, by publishing Verdi's first opera, *Oberto, Conte di S Bonifacio*, Ricordi took the most significant single step in the entire history of the firm. Except for *Attila*, *I masnadieri* and *Il corsaro*, published by Lucca between 1846 and 1848, Ricordi published all Verdi's remaining operas (for

illustration *see* fig.38, p.112), the Requiem and, after 1848, almost all his smaller works.

Shortly afterwards Italy's first regular musicological and critical journal, the *Gazzetta musicale di Milano*, was founded by Ricordi. From 2 January 1842 it was weekly, with monthly musical supplements that were reissued annually, until 1848, in a series entitled *Antologia Classica*. For a short time in 1848 it appeared as the *Gazzetta musicale di Milano ed Eco delle notizie politiche*, the greater part being given over to political comment, but, after a break in publication, it reverted in 1850 to exclusively musical content. Apart from occasional breaks, it survived until 25 December 1902, after which it merged with Ricordi's *Musica e musicisti*, which had been started in June 1902. This was renamed *Ars et labor – Musica e musicisti* from 1906 until December 1912, when it merged with *Il secolo XX*. From 1865 to 1883 the firm had published a second periodical, the *Rivista minima*, a fortnightly review of politics, literature, art and theatre; it was edited until 1874 by Verdi's librettist Antonio Ghislanzoni, then by Ghislanzoni and Salvatore Farina, and from 1878 by Farina alone. In 1919 *Musica d'oggi* was launched, quarterly for its first year and thereafter monthly, until 1942, when it lapsed temporarily. From 1951 to 1957 it reappeared as *Ricordiana* and in 1958 reverted to *Musica d'oggi*; it ceased publication in December 1965.

The Italian passion for operatic and vocal music coupled with the paucity of original instrumental works composed in Italy during the 19th century was not unnaturally reflected in Ricordi's catalogues, and during the second and third quarters of the century a large proportion of the immense quantity of instrumental music, especially for piano, put out by the firm consisted of operatic arrangements. Specially large contributions were made by Czerny, Liszt, Döhler, Henri Herz, the Strauss family, Golinelli, Prudent, Truzzi, Adolfo Fumigalli, Ascher, Bonamici and Martucci; the firm also published numerous methods and exercises for all instruments. The Ricordi catalogue of 1875 advertised the *Biblioteca di Musica Populare*, which came to be known as the *Edizioni Economiche*. Designed to be produced inexpensively, this at first consisted only of vocal and piano scores of opera, printed in a new smaller format (subsequently used for all Ricordi's vocal scores); later, publications in all genres were added to the series. This catalogue shows that in the second half of the century the firm was maintaining its operatic tradition. Pedrotti and Boito had already been taken on, and from the 1870s operas by Ponchielli and Catalani were published. In 1884 Ricordi published Puccini's first opera, *Le villi*, after it had been turned down by Sonzogno; and, apart from *Le rondine*, the firm went on to publish all Puccini's operas. After Verdi, Puccini has been Ricordi's most valuable asset by far. Sonzogno, however, proved to be their strongest rival since Lucca; he was the main publisher of Puccini's most successful contemporaries, Mascagni and Leoncavallo, leaving Ricordi the less profitable Alfano, Franchetti, Montemezzi and Zandonai.

After World War I the character of Ricordi's catalogue altered: much more emphasis was now given to new editions of earlier composers, both Italian and foreign. These undertakings included editions of Domenico Scarlatti, Beethoven and Chopin, and an anthology of early music; in 1947 an important collected edition of Vivaldi's instrumental works was launched. At the same time Ricordi continued to publish, though with far more competition and perhaps rather less energy and inspiration than in the 19th century, the works of contemporary Italian composers, including operas and other music by Pizzetti, Malipiero, Respighi, Wolf-Ferrari, Rocca, Tosatti, Rossellini, Bettinelli, Rota and Testi, and non-operatic works by Arrigo, Bussotti, Casella, Castelnuovo-Tedesco, Gentilucci, Ghedini, Maderna, Mannino, Nono, Petrassi, Turchi, Veretti and Zafred. A department dealing in American popular music was set up in Italy after World War II, while the New York branch, under the directorship of Franco Colombo, operated as a publishing house rather than an agency for the parent firm, and issued the music of such composers as Creston, Dello Joio, Hoiby, Kubik, Menotti, Thomson and Varèse. The Buenos Aires branch, as a continuation of the Breyer firm, similarly issued popular and serious music for the local market. Ricordi's output of literature has been small; the more substantial items include Franco Abbiati's useful biography *Giuseppe Verdi* (1959) and the *Enciclopedia della musica*, edited by Claudio Sartori (1963–4).

Between 1700 and 1770 Italian music publishing was in eclipse. Marescalchi and Zatta brought about a temporary revival, but both had retired before Giovanni Ricordi opened his business in 1808. At this time Italian music normally circulated in manuscript copies; it needed a man of Ricordi's training, taste, energy and ambition to realize, after himself spending four years as a copyist, that through publication music could be circulated much more accurately, widely, swiftly and cheaply, as well as far more profitably, to everybody's advantage. His rise to power in his first 20 years seems to have been achieved with a simplicity and orderliness that are hard to believe; it is interesting to speculate what sort of opposition, if any, he encountered in clinching that useful appointment to the conservatory and those vital contracts with La Scala and other theatres. The fact is, however, that he brushed aside, and continued to brush aside, almost all competition, just as his son and grandson were to do after him. All three had the happy knack of recognizing quality when they saw it; they also had the tact, the persistence and the influence to patronize and market it. In the entire history of music publishing there has been no other firm that through its own efforts, astuteness, initiative and flair has achieved a position of dominance such as Ricordi enjoyed in Italy in the 19th century, nor of power such as it has been able to maintain (on account of its rights on Verdi's and Puccini's operas) in the 20th.

Yet with power should go responsibility, and it must be noted that Ricordi have been criticized for allowing considerations of art to take second place to those of commerce. Verdi himself complained bitterly about the elder Tito's sanctioning, for financial gain, mutilated performances of his works. There is a clear moral obligation for the publisher owning the rights and autograph manuscripts of almost every one of Verdi's and Puccini's operas to make those works available, and in correct texts. All but three of Ricordi's Puccini operas were by 1975 available in orchestral score; the final three were in preparation in 1976. But the Ricordi catalogue of 1975 advertised the full scores of only seven Verdi operas; the others had never been put on sale and were available only for hire. Further, there is a widely held view that the existing scores of these composers' operas, whether on sale or for hire, contain inaccurate texts. From 1958 to 1963 there raged a battle at least as fierce as the Querelle de Bouffons between, on the one hand, Denis Vaughan and his supporters, who maintained that the scores were riddled with actual errors (Vaughan claimed to have counted 27,000 in *Falstaff*) and, on the other, Ricordi and their defenders, who held that the alleged divergences between autograph and printed texts were authorized modifications that had gradually evolved over successive contemporary performances and productions. This dispute could be resolved only by Ricordi's allowing unfettered access to their Verdi and Puccini archives and publishing a critical edition of the works of both composers. The critical edition of Rossini's operas, under the general editorship of Philip Gossett and Alberto Zedda, and the Verdi critical edition, published in association with the University of Chicago Press, represent promising developments.

CATALOGUES
(selective list; all published in Milan)
'Catalogo della musica stampata nella nuova calcografia di Giovanni Ricordi', in A. Rolla: *Tre divertimenti a violino e viola* (1814); *Catalogo della musica di fondo e degli spartiti di Giovanni Ricordi* (1825); *Catalogo della musica pubblicata . . . di Giovanni Ricordi* (1838); *Catalogo delle opere pubblicata . . . di Giovanni Ricordi* (1844); *Catalogo generale degli spartiti manoscritti d'opere teatrali* (1844, suppl. c1847); *Secondo catalogo delle opere pubblicate* (1848, suppls. 1–32, 1848–55); *Catalogo delle opere pubblicate* (1855–64); *Catalogo (in ordine numerico) delle opere pubblicate* (1857–c1896) [1857 catalogue repr. in *Il catalogo numerico Ricordi 1857 con date e indici*, ed. A. Z. Laterza (Rome 1984)]; *Catalogo delle pubblicazioni* (1875); *Catalogo generale delle edizione G. Ricordi e C.* (c1893–7, suppls. 1904–23); *Catalogo generale delle edizione economiche e popolare* (1919); *Catalogo di musica sinfonia, sinfonico-vocale e da camera* (1965, suppl. 1969); *Catalogo edizioni* (1985)

RicordiE; E. Rosmini: *Legislazione e giurisprudenza sui diritti d'autore* (Milan, 1890); *Internationale Musik- und Theater-Ausstellung 1892 Wien . . . G. Ricordi & C.* (Milan, 1892); N. Tabanelli: 'Giurisprudenza la causa Ricordi–Leoncavallo', *RIM*, vi (1899), 833; idem: 'Giurisprudenza teatrale: la ditta Ricordi contro il tenore Bonci', *RIM*, viii (1901), 703; 'Fascicolo dedicato al centenario della ditta Ricordi & C. di Milano', *Il risorgimento grafico*, v (1907), 169; G. Cesari and A. Luzio, eds.: *I copialettere di Giuseppe Verdi* (Milan, 1913/R1968); G. Adami, ed: *Epistolario di Puccini* (Milan, 1928; Eng. trans., 1931, rev. 2/1974); G. Adami: *Giulio Ricordi e i suoi musicisti* (Milan, 1933); A. Luzio, ed.: *Carteggi verdiani* (Rome, 1935–47); G. Adami: *Giulio Ricordi: l'amico dei musicisti italiani* (Milan, 1945); O. Vergiani: *Piccolo viaggio in un archivio* (Milan, 1953); M. Carner: *Puccini* (London, 1958); E. Gara, ed.: *Carteggi pucciani* (Milan, 1958); C. Sartori: *Casa Ricordi 1808–1958, profilo storico* (Milan, 1958); idem (1958); D. Vaughan: 'Discordanze tra gli autografi verdiani e la loro stampa', *La scala* (1958), no. 104, pp. 11, 72; G. Gavazzeni: *Problemi di tradizione dinamico-fraseologica e critica testuale, in Verdi e Puccini* (Milan, 1961) [in It., Eng. and Ger.]; C. Sartori: 'Ricordi', *ES*; F. Walker: *The Man Verdi* (London, 1962); C. Sartori: 'Ricordi', *MGG*; G. Martin: *Verdi* (New York, 1963, rev. 2/1964); H. Weinstock: *Donizetti and the World of Opera* (New York, 1963); C. Gatti: *Il teatro alla Scala*, i (Milan, 1964), 49; Fuld (1966, 3/1985); C. Hopkinson: 'Bibliographical Problems concerned with Verdi and his Publishers', *I° congresso internazionale di studi verdiani: Venezia 1966*, 431; idem: *A Bibliography of the Works of Giacomo Puccini* (New York, 1968); Plesske (1968); H. Weinstock: *Rossini* (New York and London, 1968); C. Sartori: 'The Bibliographer's Occupation', *Notes*, xxvi (1969–70), 711; P. Gossett: *The Operas of Rossini* (diss., Princeton U., 1970), 594;

T. F. Heck: 'Ricordi Plate Numbers in the Earlier 19th Century', *CMc*, (1970), no. 10, p. 117; idem: 'The Role of Italy in the Early History of the Classic Guitar: a Sidelight on the House of Ricordi', *Guitar Review* (1971), no. 34, p. 1; H. Weinstock: *Vincenzo Bellini: his Life and his Operas* (New York, 1971); J. Budden: *The Operas of Verdi* (London, 1973–81); C. Hopkinson: *A Bibliography of the Works of Giuseppe Verdi* (New York, 1973–8); M. Chusid: *A Catalog of Verdi's Operas* (Hackensack, 1974), 192; C. Sartori: 'I sospetti di Puccini', *NRMI*, xi (1977), 232; F. Degrada and others: *Musica, musicisti, editoria: 175 anni di Casa Ricordi, 1808–1983* (Milan, 1983); P. Gossett: 'The Ricordi Numerical Catalogues: a Background', *Notes*, xlii (1985–6), 22; A. Z. Laterza: 'Le edizioni Ricordi in Pazdirek Handbuch', *FAM*, xxxiii (1986), 240; L. Jensen: *Giuseppe Verdi and the Milanese Publishers of his Music from 'Oberto' to 'La Traviata'* (diss., New York U., 1987)

R.M.

Ries & Erler. German firm of publishers. It was founded in Berlin on 1 July 1881 by the violinist Franz Ries (*b* Berlin, 7 April 1846; *d* Naumburg, 20 Jan 1932) and Hermann Erler (*b* Radeberg, 3 June 1844; *d* Berlin, 13 Dec 1918). Ries, who was the nephew of Ferdinand Ries, started selling music in 1874 but in 1884 he sold his business (which also incorporated a concert management agency) and entered publishing; he had already made the first step in this direction in 1881, when he became associated with the publishing house that Erler had founded in Berlin in 1872. They acquired the rights to the compositions of Heinrich Hofmann; in 1882 they took over the publication of educational works (principally songs) from the firm of M. Schloss in Cologne and the following year took over Voigt of Kassel. They began to publish salon music, including pieces by Ries himself. After Erler's death Ries acquired the publishing rights to works by many composers, including Humperdinck, Pfitzner and Rezniček; he also published tutors by Carl Flesch, and the firm subsequently absorbed the R. Sulzer and Jatho houses.

When Ries retired in 1924 the business was taken over by his son Robert Ries (1889–1942), who extended the range of its publications, particularly of orchestral music. In 1927 he was elected to the governing body of the Musikverleger-Verein, and was its deputy chairman until 1929; also in 1927 he was elected to the governing body of the Verband Deutscher Musikverleger, of which he was president from 1930 to 1933. His particular interests were amateur and contemporary music, both of which he promoted vigorously. After his death the business was inherited by his daughter Waltraud Ries, who rebuilt the firm in 1948 after its wartime destruction; since 1968 it has been directed by her sister Ingrid Meurer-Ries. Its present publications consist mainly of symphonic and light orchestral music by Theodor Berger, Dressel, Frommel, Genzmer, Lothar and others, as well as solo instrumental, chamber and vocal music and didactic and theoretical works.

T.-M. Langner: 'Ries & Erler', *MGG*; *100 Jahre Musikverlag Ries & Erler Berlin, 1881–1981*

T.-M.L.

Rieter-Biedermann, Jakob Melchior (*b* Winterthur, 14 May 1811; *d* Winterthur, 25 Jan 1876). Swiss publisher. He was originally a part owner of his father's spinning mill and engineering firm. In 1833 he studied engineering design in Paris, where he met Berlioz and Rossini; subsequently he was librarian and timpanist of the Winterthur Musikkollegium (1835–48). His enthusiasm for music led him to found a music shop and publishing firm (1849), which had issued 900 items by 1876. The firm's publications included works by Berlioz, Kirchner, Herzogenberg, Schumann and, after 1858, 22 works by Brahms, including opp. 14, 15, 34, 39 and 45. Rieter-Biedermann's son-in-law Edmund Astor (1845–1918) directed the branch established in Leipzig (1862), which became the headquarters after the original office closed in 1884. Rieter-Biedermann also founded the *Leipziger Allgemeine musikalische Zeitung*, which the firm published from 1866 to 1882. In 1917 C. F. Peters bought the company.

Katalog des Musikalien-Verlags von J. Rieter-Biedermann (Leipzig, 1897); *Verzeichniss der Compositionen von Johannes Brahms nebst ihren Bearbeitungen aus dem Verlage von J. Rieter-Biedermann in Leipzig* (Leipzig, 1898, 3/1908); *Katalog des Musikalien-Verlages von J. Rieter-Biedermann* (Leipzig, 1909); W. Altmann, ed.: *Johannes Brahms im Briefwechsel mit Breitkopf & Härtel, Bartolf Senff, J. Rieter-Biedermann* (Berlin, 1920); M. Fehr: '18 Briefe von H. Berlioz an den Winterthurer Verleger J. Rieter-Biedermann', *Schweizerisches Jb für Musikwissenschaft*, ii (1927), 90; idem: *Das Musikkollegium Winterthur 1629–1837* (Winterthur, 1929); Plesske (1968); K. Hoffmann: *Die Erstdrucke der Werke von Johannes Brahms* (Tutzing, 1975)

H.-M.P.

Riley, Edward (*b* England, 1769; *d* Yonkers, NY, 18 Aug 1829). American engraver and publisher. He engraved and published music in England from 1795 to 1803 before emigrating to the USA and settling in New York in 1805 or 1806. He worked as a music teacher, flautist and singer for at least ten years after his arrival, and also established himself as an instrument maker and repairer, specializing in flutes and fifes. John Firth and Sylvanus Pond (who, with William Hall, formed Firth, Hall & Pond in 1832) were apprentices in Riley's instrument shop. Riley worked as an engraver for various publishers in the city, including John Paff and John Appel, then about 1811 set up his own publishing business. He published his own compositions, the best known of which are probably *La Fayette's Grand March and Quick Step* (1824), texts on flute instruction including *Riley's New Instructions for the German Flute* (1811), and four volumes of flute melodies. *Riley's Flute Melodies* (1814–16/*R*1973, 1817–20/*R*1973, 1820–25, ?1826–30) reflect the popular musical taste of the time, and include folk tunes, excerpts from operas and melodies from Haydn, Mozart and Beethoven, as well as contemporary American pieces.

Riley's firm continued first under his widow, Elizabeth Riley, then from 1832 to 1842 under the direction of his son Edward C. Riley (*b* England, *c*1800; *d* ?New York, 1871). Another son, Frederick Riley, assumed responsibility for the firm from 1842 to 1851, when its catalogue was absorbed by S. T. Gordon.

M. A. D. Howe: *Music Publishers in New York City before 1850: a Directory* (New York, 1917); Dichter and Shapiro (1941, 2/1977); Wolfe (1964); idem (1980)

B.T., R.J.

Robbins. American firm of publishers. It was founded in New York in 1927 by John Jacob (Jack) Robbins (*b* Worcester, MA, 15 Sept 1894; *d* New York, 15 Dec 1959), who had formerly worked for Harms and for Enterprise. Robbins Music Corporation was one of the earliest firms to publish popular songs associated with films; their successes included *Spring is here* and *You were meant for me* (1929), *Goodnight sweetheart* (1931), *Try a little tenderness* (1932), *All I do is dream of you* and *Blue Moon* (1934) and *A-tisket, A-tasket* (1938). Robbins also published theme songs for the bands of Jimmy Dorsey, Glenn Miller, Benny Goodman, Stan Kenton and Count Basie, Grofé's *Grand Canyon Suite* and popular Latin American music. Metro-Goldwyn-Mayer bought an interest in the firm in 1929, and in 1939 it became part of the Big 3 Music Corporation; Robbins was vice-president of the new company until 1946.

F.B.

Roberts, Henry (*fl* 1737–*c*1765). English engraver, active in London. From 1737 until about 1762 he kept a music and print shop in Holborn from which he issued several notable books of songs with pictorial embellishments heading each piece. The earliest, the two-volume *Calliope, or English Harmony*, was issued from 1737 by and for the engraver in periodical numbers of eight octavo pages each. The first volume of 25 numbers was completed in 1739; the parts of the second volume began to appear in the same year, though it was probably not finished until about 1746. A second issue of both volumes, appearing in 1746–7, was undertaken by the printer and publisher John Simpson. The plates later came into the possession of Longman & Broderip, who reprinted from them about 1780. Roberts's other famous work, *Clio and Euterpe, or British harmony*, was similar in style, and issued by him in parts (from 1756) and in two volumes (1758–9). A later edition, dated 1762, had a third volume engraved by Roberts, and a fourth volume was added when John Welcker reissued the work about 1778.

Among other examples of Roberts's fine ornamental engraving are the dedicatory leaf in Giuseppe Sammartini's *XII sonate* op. 3 (1743) and the title-page engraving of William Jackson's *Elegies* (c1762).

F. Kidson: 'Some Illustrated Music-books of the Seventeenth and Eighteenth Centuries: English', *MA*, iii (1911–12), 195; Humphries and Smith (1954, 2/1970)

F.K., W.C.S./P.W.J.

Robletti, Giovanni Battista (*fl* Rome, 1609–50). Italian printer. He usually published at his own expense at a time when printers were frequently financed either by a bookseller or the author or composer. However, he did occasionally print 'at the author's request' (e.g. Pugliaschi's *La gemma musicale*, 1618) or on behalf of booksellers, among them A. Poggioli (books 1, 4, 5 and 6 of Rontani's *Varie musiche*, 1620–23) and G. D. Franzini (Silvestri's *Florida verba* of 1648). Like other publishers of the time he brought out several anthologies of music he chose himself: two of sacred music (*Lilia campis*, RISM 1621[3], and *Litanie*, 1622[1], both for voices and organ) and three of secular music (*Giardino musicale*, 1621[15], *Vezzosetti fiori* 1622[11], *Le risonanti sfere*, 1629[9]). He also published non-musical works.

Robletti's publications are accurate and clear, if not particularly elegant. A list of those extant shows that he catered for a wide range of styles and interests. He included many famous and lesser-known names in his output: G. F. Anerio (at least 16 vols., 1609–29), Cifra (1609–20), Quagliati (1611–27) and Alessandro Capece (1615–25), as well as Frescobaldi, Landi,

Nanino, Sabbatini, Soriano, Viadana, Agazzari, Falconieri, Fiorillo and d'India. Between 1631 and 1633, at the printing house of the Hospitio dei Letterati, Rome, he printed Agostino Diruta's *Messe concertate* for five voices op. 13, Serpieri's *Missa at vespertinum officium* and Sacchi's *Missarum liber primus*. Contemporary with these are F. Vitali's *Arie* for one to three voices and the *Varie musiche* for one to five voices 'concertate con il basso continuo' by Giulio Pasquali, which were published by a press of Robletti's in Orvieto.

Most of Robletti's output was produced in Rome, but he is known to have worked also in Tivoli, where a subsidy from the town granted in 1620 enabled him to print for almost 25 years, and in Rieti in 1636. His last publication is thought to be Giamberti's *Antiphonae et motecta* (1650).

Sartori (1958)

S.A.

Rodeheaver, Homer A(lvan) (*b* Union Furnace, OH, 4 Oct 1880; *d* Winona, IN, 18 Dec 1955). American publisher. During the first half of the 20th century he greatly influenced the creation and popularization of gospel song both in the USA and elsewhere. He worked for 20 years with the evangelist Billy Sunday. In 1910, with Bentley DeForrest Ackley, he established the Rodeheaver-Ackley publishing house in Chicago, which became the Rodeheaver Co. in 1911. With the purchase of the Hall-Mack Co. of Philadelphia in 1936 Rodeheaver's company, now the Rodeheaver Hall-Mack Co., became a leader in the field of gospel music. The firm moved to Winona Lake, Indiana, in 1941 and changed its name back to the Rodeheaver Co.; in 1969 it became a division of Word, Inc. During the 1920s Rodeheaver established Rainbow Records, one of the earliest labels devoted solely to gospel song recordings. Although he composed little, Rodeheaver edited or compiled some 80 collections of gospel songs.

T. H. Porter: *Homer Alvan Rodeheaver (1880–1955): Evangelist Musician and Publisher* (diss., New Orleans Baptist Theological Seminary, 1981)

T.H.P.

Röder, Carl Gottlieb (*b* Stötteritz, nr. Leipzig, 22 June 1812; *d* Gohlis, nr. Leipzig, 29 Oct 1883). German printer active in Leipzig. After a ten-year apprenticeship as a music engraver and printer with Breitkopf & Härtel, he opened his own music engraving business in 1846. In 1863, after many attempts, he succeeded in adapting the lithographic mechanical press built by G. Sigl to the printing of music; his subsequent improvements to the mechanical music printing process were used for various musical editions (from 1867) and considerably furthered the developments of German music publishing. The Röder printing works were among the most important of their kind and collaborated with music publishers around the world. In the 1870s Röder's two sons-in-law and later their successors (e.g. Carl Johannes Reichel) ensured the constant expansion of the firm. It became a joint-stock company in 1930; having suffered severe damage in World War II, it was subsequently nationalized and as the 'Röderdruck' printing works has a considerable international reputation.

Festschrift zur 50 jährigen Jubelfeier des Bestehens der Firma C. G. Röder, Leipzig (Leipzig, 1896); W. von zur Westen: *Musiktitel aus vier Jahrhunderten: Festschrift anlässlich des 75 jährigen Bestehens der Firma C. G. Röder G.m.b.H.* (Leipzig, 1921); O. Säuberlich: 'Leipzig als Hauptsitz des Notenstichs und Musikaliendrucks', *Archiv für Buchgewerbe und Gebrauchsgraphik*, lix (1922), 19; A. H. King: 'C. G. Röder's Music-printing Business in 1885', *Brio*, ii/2 (1965), 2

H.-M.P.

Roger, Estienne (*b* Caen, 1665 or 1666; *d* Amsterdam, 7 July 1722). French printer active in Amsterdam. He and his family, as Protestants, left Normandy after the revocation of the Edict of Nantes in 1685 and moved to Amsterdam, as is attested by Estienne Roger's registration as a member of the Walloon church there in February 1686. He soon went into the printing trade, apprenticed successively between 1691 and 1695 to Antoine Pointel and Jean-Louis de Lorme. On 11 August 1691, listed in the records as 'marchand', he married Marie-Suzanne de Magneville (*c*1670–1712). On 7 November 1695 he was on the rolls of the association of booksellers, printers and binders. By 1697 he was publishing music and other books (including histories, grammars and a dictionary of antiquities) under his own name.

Roger had two daughters. He designated the elder, Jeanne (1692–1722), as his successor in the business in a will dated 11 September 1716, and from that date he used her name alone on the titles of the books he printed. The younger daughter, Françoise (1694–1723), married Michel-Charles Le Cène (1684–1743) in May 1716. Le Cène worked for his father-in-law for a few years after his marriage, but by 1720 was operating his own printing establishment.

After Roger's death Jeanne maintained her father's business with the help of a faithful employee, Gerrit Drinkman. But she soon fell ill, and died in December of the same year, after cutting Françoise out of her will (because, she said, her sister had left her ill and did not help her in her

Part of the Adagio from 'Sonata a violino o cimbalo di Arcangelo Corelli' (Amsterdam, 3/1715), printed by Estienne Roger from engraved plates, showing the written-out embellishments claimed to be Corelli's own

weakness), and leaving the business to Drinkman. Within a short time Drinkman was also dead. At this point Le Cène arranged to buy the printing firm from Drinkman's widow. In an advertisement in the *Gazette d'Amsterdam* of June 1723 he was able to announce that he was continuing 'the business of the late Mr Estienne Roger, his father-in-law, which had been interrupted since his demise'. His wife Françoise, the last of the Rogers, died two months later.

Le Cène carried on the business for 20 years more until his death in 1743. Although he was not as active as Roger, he added the works of many new composers to the house's roster. He frequently reprinted from Roger's plates, listing the firm's name then as 'Estienne Roger & Le Cène'. Music books for which Le Cène was the originator carried only his name. Since the earlier firm had used the names of 'Estienne Roger' and 'Jeanne Roger' there were then four names under which the business was identified.

After Le Cène's death his inventory was bought by the bookseller G. J. de la Coste, according to an advertisement in the *Nouvelles d'Amsterdam* of 18 October 1743. Shortly after this La Coste published a catalogue of 'the books of music, printed at Amsterdam, by Estienne Roger and Michel-Charles Le Cène'. There is no evidence that La Coste was engaged in any printing activity; apparently he bought the books to add to his stock.

In the period from 1696 to 1743, 600 titles (not including reprints) were printed by the two firms. More than 500 of them were issued by Roger between 1696 and 1722 and less than 100 during Le Cène's regime, although Le Cène continued to republish and to retain in stock much of Roger's output. Under both Roger and Le Cène the firm's music books were carefully edited and beautifully printed from copperplate engravings; they were valued for their quality.

Besides seeking new MSS through direct contacts with composers, Roger's practice from the beginning was to copy music of publishers in other countries, and since there were no copyright laws he could do so with impunity. While most other music printers had little distribution outside their own countries or even outside their own cities and printed the works of local composers only, Roger's distinction was that he could offer an international and not just a parochial repertory. Furthermore his distribution network was highly effective. At various times he had agents in Rotterdam, London, Cologne, Berlin, Liège, Leipzig, Halle, Brussels and Hamburg.

Early in the 18th century, as engraving superseded movable type, music printers discontinued the practice of dating their books. Roger was the first to use publishers' numbers, a practice soon imitated by others (such as Walsh and Balthasar Schmid) and one that continued to identify books through the 18th century and part of the 19th. In 1716 he assigned numbers to all books in stock, without regard, however, to their chronological order of printing. The numbers after that time follow directly in chronological order.

Though the plate numbers of books printed before 1716 do not help in dating them, another of Roger's practices provides an approximation. From 1698 to 1716 he printed catalogues of his music books in the back of dated non-musical books. He also printed his music catalogues in advertisements in the Amsterdam and London papers over this period of time. Thus the listing of a new work in these sources serves as a *terminus ante quem*.

Roger's repertory was particularly strong in works by Italian composers. He printed the second editions of Vivaldi's opp. 1 and 2, and beginning with op. 3, *L'estro armonico*, the first editions of all Vivaldi's printed works but two were published by Roger or his successors. Roger also published all Corelli's works and although these were copied from Italian sources, the description of them from a catalogue of 1716 shows that the printer sometimes improved on the original editions as a result of his personal relations with the composer: 'Corelli opera quinta, new edition engraved in the same format as the four first works of Corelli, with the embellishments marked for the adagios, as Mr Corelli wants them played (see illustration), and those who are curious to see the original of Mr Corelli with his letters written on this subject, can see them at Estienne Roger's'. Other Italian composers in Roger's catalogues were Albicastro, Albinoni, Bassani, Bonporti, Caldara, Gentili, Marcello, C. A. Marino, Alessandro Scarlatti, Taglietti, Torelli, Valentini and Veracini. From Ballard in Paris he reprinted works by La Barre, Lebègue, Lully, Marais and Mouton, and Ballard's annual *Airs sérieux et à boire*. During Le Cène's time Geminiani, Handel, Locatelli (whom Le Cène evidently knew as a friend), Quantz, Tartini and Telemann, among others, were added to the catalogue.

Although Roger copied the music of others, he also had to defend himself against plagiarism of his own publications. There was an altercation with John Walsh (i) of London around 1700, but the dispute was settled satisfactorily and later Walsh even became Roger's London agent. More serious was the threat from the Amsterdam printer Pierre Mortier, who copied many of Roger's books in 1708 and advertised them for sale at a lower price. This problem was only resolved with Mortier's death in 1711, when Roger bought his plates and later even issued some of Mortier's editions under his own name. The importance of the firm in the distribution of music in the first half of the 18th century cannot be overestimated.

J. W. Enschedé: 'Quelques mots sur E. Roger, marchand libraire à Amsterdam', *Bulletin de la commission de l'histoire des églises wallonnes* (1896), 209; C. Veerman: 'Estienne Roger, muziekuitgever te Amsterdam omstreaks 1700', *De muziek* (1932), May, 337; M. Pincherle: 'De la piraterie dans l'édition musicale aux environs de 1700', *RdM*, xiv (1933), 136; idem: 'Note sur E. Roger et M. C. Le Cène', *RBM*, i (1946–7), 82; F. Lesure: 'Un épisode de la guerre des contrafaçons à Amsterdam: Estienne Roger et P. Mortier', *RdM*, xxxviii (1956), 35; C. G. Kneppers and A. J. Heuwekemeijer: 'De muziekuitgever E. Roger', *Ons Amsterdam* (1959), 187; A. Koole: 'Roger', *MGG*; F. Lesure: *Bibliographie des éditions musicales publiées par Estienne Roger et Michel-Charles Le Cène (Amsterdam 1696–1743)* (Paris, 1969)

S.F.P.

Rolla, Giorgio (*d* Milan, ?1651). Italian printer and publisher, active in Milan. He was a printer for Milan Cathedral in 1619, and his press published music until 1651. He appears to have produced only one or two music publications each year, almost all of local minor composers and not running to second editions. Most of the music is sacred. In 1649 he collaborated with Carlo Camagno for one title; he composed a little music, printing it in some of his collections (*RISM* 1619³, 1619⁴, 1623³, 1649¹). He was succeeded by his son, Carlo Francesco Rolla, who had started printing in 1650, and who continued either in his own name or as his father's heir. He printed one title with Camagno in 1651, and fewer than ten on his own; he seems to have stopped printing by the end of the decade.

Sartori (1958); M. Donà: *La stampa musicale a Milano fino all'anno 1700* (Florence, 1961) [incl. a nearly complete list of Rolla's music publications]

S.B. (iii)

Rönnagel [Rennagel], **Johann Wilhelm** (*b* Nuremberg, 29 Oct 1690; *d* Ansbach, 30 March 1759). German publisher. In 1716 he settled in Ansbach as the court book dealer with the margrave's special permission. From 1716 to 1738 he also worked in Nuremberg as a book dealer and publisher and produced approximately 20 music items, including a work by Pachelbel. However, he had insufficient musical knowledge to compete with other Nuremberg music publishers. He became bankrupt, his premises were sold by auction in 1739–40 and he retired to Ansbach.

R. Eitner: *Buch- und Musikalienhändler* (Leipzig, 1904); A. Bayer: *Ansbacher Buchdruck in 350 Jahren* (Ansbach, 1952); R. Merkel: *Buchdruck und Buchhandel in Ansbach* (Erlangen, 1965), 307

W.S. (ii)

Root & Cady. American firm of publishers and music dealers. Founded by Ebenezer Towner Root and Chauncey Marvin Cady in December 1858, it soon became Chicago's leading music dealer and publisher; in 1860 George Frederick Root joined as chief of publications. It initially conducted a general music trade, publishing simple sheet music for a local market. With the outbreak of the Civil War, trade in instruments for regimental bands soared and the firm found a national market for its succession of patriotic songs by G. F. Root, Henry Clay Work and others, including *The Vacant Chair* (1861), *Kingdom Coming*, *The Battle Cry of Freedom* (both 1862), *Tramp! Tramp! Tramp!* and *Marching through Georgia* (both 1865).

Beginning with *The Silver Lute* (1862), the firm issued a succession of popular instruction books for schools, music conventions and choirs, again reaching a national market. After the Civil War, while American public taste grew more diversified, the policies of the firm remained almost unchanged. Crippling losses followed the Chicago fire of October 1871 and the firm did not recover. On 24 October 1871 G. F. Root and his sons withdrew, leaving the original partners, who (with William Lewis) retained the name Root & Cady. The new firm sold the sheet music catalogue on 17 November 1871 to S. Brainard's Sons of Cleveland and the book catalogue to John Church & Co. of Cincinnati on 23 February 1872. In October 1872 Root & Cady were bankrupt. Cady withdrew, and a new firm, Root & Lewis, was formed, continuing until 1 January 1875, when it merged with Geo. F. Root & Sons and Chandler & Curtiss to form the Root & Sons Music Co.

G. F. Root: *The Story of a Musical Life* (Cincinnati, 1891/R1970); D. J. Epstein: *Music Publishing in Chicago before 1871: the Firm of Root & Cady, 1858–1871* (Detroit, 1969)

D.J.E.

Rossi, Giovanni (*fl* Bologna, 1558–95). Italian publisher. He opened his first printing house in Venice in 1557 and transferred it to Bologna in 1558 or 1559, at first in partnership with the brothers Benacci. From 1561, however, his publications were signed with his name alone. In 1563 his printing press was on the street of S Mamolo, bearing the title 'Episcopal printer' (i.e. official printer to the church). In 1572 he was elected the official typographer of a Bolognese society of men of letters, historians etc. A senate decree (renewed in 1593) declared that Rossi was obliged to provide good type characters, in particular musical ones, to be replaced whenever necessary. He was the first to print music in Bologna using movable metal type, producing an elegant edition of Camillo Cortellini's *Il secondo libro di madrigali a cinque voci* (11 May 1584); his typographical mark was a winged Mercury with the motto 'Coelo demissus ab alto'. His only other musical work that survives is a small publication by Ascanio Trombetti, *Musica sopra le conclusioni di legge* (1587).

Giovanni died in 1595 and his son Perseo succeeded to the printing business, using the title 'Heredi di G. Rossi'. The firm published some works by Adriano Banchieri – *Conclusioni nel suono dell'organo* (1609), *Terzo libro di pensieri ecclesiastici* (1613), *Cartellina del canto fermo gregoriano* (1614), *Due ripieni in applauso musicale* (1614) and *Prima parte del primo libro al direttorio monastico di canto fermo* (1615) – as well as Ercole Porta's *Vaga ghirlanda di . . . fiori musicali* (1613) and Coma's *Sacrae cantiones* (1614). Giovanni Rossi's publications are characterized by a finesse and elegance which the firm did not retain after his death.

L. Sighinolfi: 'La prima stampa della musica in Bologna', *L'archiginnasio*, xvii (1922), 192; F. Vatielli: 'Editori musicali dei secoli XVII e XVIII', *Arte e vita musicale a Bologna* (Bologna, 1927/R1969), 239; A. Sorbelli: *Storia della stampa a Bologna* (Bologna, 1929); L. Gottardi: *La stampa musicale in Bologna dagli inizi fino al 1700* (diss., U. of Bologna, 1951); Sartori (1958); Mischiati (1984)

A.S. (ii)

Rossiter, Will [Williams, W. R.] (*b* Wells, England, 15 March 1867; *d* Oak Park, IL, 10 June 1954). American publisher and composer. After moving to the USA in 1881 he settled in Chicago and became a draughtsman. His musical career started in 1891 when, under the pseudonym W. R. Williams, he wrote and published his first song, *Sweet Nellie Bawn*. It was a success, and was followed by further popular titles during the 1890s. In 1898 he appeared at Tony Pastor's Music Hall in New York, performing and publicizing his own songs. By the turn of the century he had become the most successful and best-known popular music publisher in Chicago. In 1910 he purchased the rights to *Meet me tonight in dreamland* by Leo Friedman and Beth Slater Whitson; in the same year he issued Shelton Brooks's *Some of these days*, which became Sophie Tucker's theme song, and his own *I'd love to live in loveland with a girl like you*, which eventually sold over two million copies. Brooks's *The Darktown Strutters' Ball* (1917) also achieved lasting popularity. Other songwriters, lyricists and performers whose careers were furthered by their association with Rossiter include Charles K. Harris, Percy Wenrich, J. Will Callahan, Fred Fisher and Egbert Van Alstyne. An aggressive promoter of his publications, Rossiter initiated innovatory techniques in marketing: he sponsored live performances of songs in retail shops, issued inexpensive collections of popular song texts, distributed free music folders imprinted with the Rossiter name to orchestras and bands and made use of radio broadcasting for promotional purposes.

T. E. Gauthier: 'Will Rossiter: Popular Publisher of Popular Songs', *The Rotarian*, xxxi/1 (1927), 31; I. Goldberg: *Tin Pan Alley: a Chronicle of the American Popular Music Racket* (New York, 1930/R1961), 104; Obituary, *Chicago Daily Tribune* (11 June 1954); T. W. Thorson: *A History of Music Publishing in Chicago: 1850–1960* (diss., Northwestern U., 1961), 186, 230

J.G.

Rouart-Lerolle. French firm of publishers. It was founded in Paris in 1905 by Alexis Rouart (1869–1921) through the acquisition of the publishing companies Meuriot and Badoux. Badoux had published several works of Jacques-Dalcroze and Lefebvre, as well as Satie's *Le fils des étoiles*. Satie's cabaret works, which had been published in 1903–4 by Bellon, Ponscarme & Cie, were also acquired. In 1908 Jacques Lerolle, a nephew of Chausson, joined the company and directed it after Rouart died. With Jacques Durand, Rouart had the idea of creating a collected French classical edition, and he began issuing new editions by d'Indy, Bordes and others. The company maintained a progressive programme, publishing works by notable French and Spanish composers including Albéniz, Chausson, Duparc, d'Indy, Koechlin, Hüe, Ladmirault, Poulenc, Ropartz, Satie, Séverac and Turina. In October 1941 the company was bought by Francis Salabert, and its publications were incorporated into the Salabert catalogue.

P. Bordes: *L'éditon musicale* (Paris, 1947)

A.P. (ii)

Rózsavölgyi és Társa. Hungarian firm of publishers. It was founded in Pest in 1850 by Gyula Rózsavölgyi (1822–61, son of Márk Rózsavölgyi) and Norbert Grinzweil (1823–90), and immediately established links with music publishers in Austria, France, Germany and England. Through the founders' excellent work the firm prospered and by the end of the century had become the largest music publisher in Hungary, having taken over smaller firms including Wagner (1858) and Treichlinger (1874), and later incorporating Rozsnyai (1936). After Rózsavölgyi's death, Grinzweil went into partnership with his brother-in-law János Nepomuk Dunkl, but the firm continued operating under its former name, except in 1862–6 when the branch in Vienna was known as J. N. Dunkl. From 1908 the owners were Gusztáv Bárczi, Victor Alberti and Béla Ángyán. The company issued works by leading contemporary composers including Erkel, Liszt, Mosonyi and Volkmann, and at the turn of the century works by Bartók, Kodály, Dohnányi, Weiner, Lajtha and others. (It should be noted that the three old Hungarian dances by 'Liszt' in the collection of 1852–4, *30 eredeti magyar zenedarab*, were by János Liszt, a doctor and amateur musician.) From 1873 Rózsavölgyi also promoted concerts ('Evenings of new music', 'Concerts populaires'); its music lending library contained some 100,000 items. From 1883 the firm held a royal appointment and from 1894 it published the periodicals *Zeneirodalmi szemle* ('Review of music literature') and *Művészeti lapok* ('Arts news'). Its publishing activities expanded in the 1930s to include books on music.

The firm always gave plate numbers to its publications; until Rózsavölgyi's death the number was preceded by a combination containing his initial (R. et C., R. et Co., R. és T.Sz. etc), thereafter, to 1869, Grinzweil's initials were sporadically used (G.N., N.G., G.No.N., N.G.Sz. etc). From 1870 to 1885 there were no initials, and from 1885 R. et C. appeared again. Unfortunately the numerical sequence does not indicate the chronological order of publication; from the beginning, the firm re-used old plates without changing the numbers, so that it is not uncommon to find the same number on two completely different editions. The plate numbers of incorporated firms were retained, although on the cover the former publisher's name was replaced. At one time agency publications were separately indicated (C.1. etc). Rózsavölgyi is now the name of the biggest Hungarian music retailer; since nationalization (1949) the publishing activities of the firm have been continued by its legal successor Editio Musica Budapest.

K. Ábrányi: *A magyar zene a 19-k században* [Hungarian music in the 19th century] (Budapest, 1900); E. Major: *Három tévesen Liszt Ferencnek tulajdonitott kompozicióról* [On three compositions erroneously attributed to Ferenc Liszt] (Budapest, 1926); K. Isoz: 'Á Rózsavölgyi és Társa cég története 1850–1908', and R. Alberti: 'Á Rózsavölgyi és Társa cég története 1908–1949' [History of Rózsavölgyi & Co.], *Magyar zenetörténeti tanulmányok* (Budapest, 1973); I. Mona: *Magyar zeneműkiadás 1850–1975* [Hungarian music publication 1850–1975] (Budapest, 1975); idem: *Magyar zeneműkiadók es tevékenységük 1774–1867* [Hungarian music publishers and their activity] (Budapest, forthcoming).

I.M.

Rozsnyai. Hungarian firm of publishers. It was founded in Budapest by Károly Rozsnyai in 1889 and later run by Róbert Rozsnyai. Its publications were primarily pedagogical and are still of value, having been written by teachers at the then National Academy of Music including József Bloch (violin), Kálmán Chován and Árpád Szendy (piano) and Albert Siklós (singing and composition). Bartók's editions of *Das wohltemperirte Clavier* and the works of Mozart, Scarlatti and Couperin were also published by Rozsnyai, as well as Bartók's own works, including the 14 Bagatelles, the two Elegies for piano and the *Gyermekeknek* ('For children') cycle for violin and piano (with Tivadar Országh). In 1936 the firm was taken over by Rózsavölgyi és Társa.

I.M.

Runge. German firm of printers, active in Berlin. From 1611 Georg Runge managed the press belonging to his father Christoph Runge the elder in the Berlin Minorite monastery. After Georg's death (1639) his widow and heirs carried on the business until 1644, when Georg's son Christoph Runge the younger was able to take it over. Half of the 128 musical works from Berlin (listed by Lenz) were printed on the Runge press, which was particularly active in disseminating the works of Zangius, Johannes Crüger, Hentzschel and others.

H. U. Lenz: *Der Berliner Musikdruck von seinen Anfängen bis zur Mitte des 18. Jahrhunderts* (diss., U. of Rostock, 1932); Benzing (1963, 2/1982)

T.W.

Russell, George D. (*b* Boston, 1822; *d* Roxbury, MA, 3 Feb 1910). American publisher and music dealer. He was initially a clerk in the music shop of the instrument dealer and publisher George P.

Reed (*b* Boston, *c*1814; *d* Boston, 18 March 1890), who had established his business in Boston in 1838. In 1849 Russell became a partner in the firm, which in 1855 became a founding member of the Board of Music Trade. From 1856 to 1858 he had another partner, Nathan Richardson, and published Reed's former catalogue. He also formed a brief partnership in 1858 with Fuller (possibly Francis Fuller, a piano maker, or William Fuller, an instrument maker). Russell & Tolman was formed in 1858 from combining the catalogues of Reed & Russell and Russell & Richardson with that of Henry Tolman (*b* Boston, 15 Jan 1821; *d* Cohasset, MA, 20 Nov 1888), who had operated his own firm dealing in musical instruments and umbrellas since 1846 and publishing since 1849. Russell & Tolman became one of the most important music publishers in the USA in the 19th century, issuing a great quantity of American popular music, marches, polkas and comic songs, as well as the works of established American composers such as George F. Root; they also dealt in music and pianos. The firm maintained close business ties with the Chicago

firm of Root & Cady and printed some of their first publications. After the dissolution of Russell & Tolman in 1862, Tolman took over the catalogue and continued until 1870 as Henry Tolman & Co., though he sold his sheet music plates to Root & Cady in 1868; he became sole publisher from 1862 to 1868 of the *Boston Musical Times* and in 1865 was elected vice-president of the Board of Music Trade. Russell was joined by his brother Joseph M. Russell in 1863 to form G. D. Russell & Co., a similar publishing and dealing business, which also undertook printing work. The firm continued to operate, later with other partners, for 14 years; when the brothers separated, their catalogue was taken over by Oliver Ditson. By 1883 a company named Russell Brothers was active in the city, and G. D. Russell remained in business until his retirement in 1888.

Fisher (1933); C. M. Ayars: *Contributions to the Art of Music in America by the Music Industries of Boston, 1640 to 1936* (New York, 1937/R1969); Dichter and Shapiro (1941, 2/1977); D. J. Epstein: *Music Publishing in Chicago before 1871: the Firm of Root & Cady, 1858–1871* (Detroit, 1969)

G.O.

S

Sabbio, Vincenzo. Italian printer, active in Brescia. He opened a shop in Bergamo in February 1576 but sold it in August 1578 and returned to Brescia, where he began printing music editions for publishers including Giovanni Antonio degli Antoni of Venice (Ruffo's *Messe à 6 voci*, 1580), Pietro Bozzola of Brescia (Monteverdi's *Madrigali spirituali à 4 voci*, 1583), Francesco and Simone Tini of Milan (Casulana's *Primo libro di madrigali à 4 voci*, 1583) and Francesco e eredi di Simone Tini (Colombani's *Armonia super Davidicos vesperarum psalmos . . . 5 vocibus*, 1584). In addition to commission work, Sabbio printed independently music by Falconio, Colombani, Antegnati, Canale, Mensa and Bertani. His final publication was the celebrated anthology *L'amorosa Ero rappresentata da più celebri musici d'Italia con l'istesse parole et nel medesimo tuono* (1588).

Sartori (1958); H. B. Lincoln: *The Madrigal Collection L'Armorosa Ero* (Albany, NY, 1968); M. T. Rosa Barezzani: 'La musica nelle antiche

stamperia bresciane', *La musica a Brescia* (Brescia, 1979), 138

C.E.

Sadelar [Sadeler], **Johan** (*b* Brussels, 1550; *d* Venice, 1610). Flemish copperplate engraver. Of a family of engravers, he worked in several German cities, notably Munich, and in Italy. His works include a number of devotional music publications (1584–90; some ed. in *Organum*, 1st ser., xix-xx, Leipzig, 1930). These show angels or biblical figures singing and playing from partbooks and were probably intended as religious propaganda for the Counter-Reformation cause (see illustration). The compositions are complete and legible; although their influence on Verovio is largely conjectural, they are important in their own right as particularly beautiful and unusual examples of early music engraving.

M. Seiffert: 'Bildniszeugnisse des 16. Jahrhunderts für die instrumentale Begleitung des

Devotional print showing the Virgin and Child with St Anne, and the four-part motet 'Ave gratia plena' by Cornelis Verdonck, engraved by Johan Sadeler after Martin de Vos (Antwerp, 1584)

Gesanges und den Ursprung des Musikkupfers-tichs', *AMw*, i (1918–19), 49; P. Bergmans: *La typographie musicale en Belgique au XVIe siècle*, v (Brussels, 1929); King (1964); P. E. Ritter and F. W. Riedel: *Musik, Theater, Tanz, vom 16. Jahrhundert bis zum 19. Jahrhundert* (St Pölten, 1966); S. Bain: *Music Printing in the Low Countries in the Sixteenth Century* (diss., U. of Cambridge, 1974)

S.B. (i)

Sala, Giuseppe (*fl* 1676–1715). Italian publisher, printer and bookseller. He was active in Venice, and the most important part of his output appeared between 1685 and 1705. He conducted his business, under the sign of King David playing the harp, at S Giovanni Crisostomo in the house of the musician Natale Monferrato. Sala's first essay in printing, financed by the composer, was Monferrato's *Salmi concertati a 2 voci con violini e senza* (op.11). At some date before 1684, Sala took a share in the publishing side as a partner and, on Monferrato's death in 1685, he became its sole proprietor. In 1682 he published anonymously, *L'armonia sonora delle sonate di diversi autori*, an anthology, edited by himself, of 12 sonatas for three instruments by various composers.

An *Indice dell'opere di musica sin hora stampate da Giuseppe Sala in Venezia* (?1714) enumerates his output of psalms, motets, cantatas and sonatas, in particular those of Bassani, Monferrato, Taglietti and Corelli; he published at least 14 editions of Corelli's first five opus numbers. The index also shows that he published psalms by Sartorio, D. F. Rossi, Cazzati and Benedetti, motets by Legrenzi, Allegri, Bonporti, G. M. Bononcini and Gasparini, cantatas by Caldara, Gregori and Albinoni and sonatas by Vitali, Legrenzi, de Castro, Corelli, Torelli, Bernabei and Marcello.

Sartori (1958); idem: 'Le origini di una casa editrice veneziana', *FAM*, vii (1960), 57; idem: *Un catalogo di G. Sala del 1715* (Florence, 1966); Mischiati (1984)

S.A.

Salabert. French firm of publishers. It was founded in Paris between 1878 and 1895 by Edouard Salabert (*b* London, 1 Dec 1838; *d* Paris, 8 Sept 1903); he was paralysed in 1901, and the company was taken over by his son Francis Salabert (*b* Paris, 27 July 1884; *d* nr. Shannon, Ireland, 28 Dec 1946). Salabert was among the first to internationalize popular music; his enterprises were diversified and mostly successful, including music from and for films, recordings, music-hall and concert productions, artist management, and publication of arrangements and original versions of all varieties of light music – European,

Latin American and American. Successes in light music permitted Salabert to expand production of the classics, educational materials and modern art music. He published some compositions of Auric, Honegger, Milhaud, Poulenc and others, and by 1946 had bought the catalogues of 51 other publishers, among them Dufresne (1923), Gaudet (1927), Mathot (1930), Christiné (1937), Rouart-Lerolle (1941), Senart (1941) and Deiss (1946).

Under Mme Salabert, Francis's widow, Editions Salabert remains a leading publisher of new works. In 1968 a catalogue of the *Jeune école contemporaine* was initiated; it contains hundreds of compositions by young composers, many of them avant-garde.

Salabert informations, i (1967), ii (1968); *Jeune école contemporaine* (Paris, 1969; suppl. 1972) [Salabert catalogue]

R.S.N.

Salvadori, Angelo (*fl* 1618–28). Italian printer. He does not appear to be related to the contemporary librettist of the same name. He worked in Vicenza and is most important for Sabbatini's *Regola facile* (1628), Monte's *Vago fior* (probably printed in the mid-1620s) and for a series of five volumes of canzonettas (*RISM* 1618[17], 1620[22], 1622[20], 1623[11], *c*1625[12]) of which at least three went into second editions.

S.B. (iii)

Samfundet til Udgivelse af Dansk Musik. Danish publishing society. It was founded on 18 December 1871 by Jacob Christian Fabricius (1840–1919) as a private, non-commercial enterprise with the aim of furthering knowledge of Danish music by publishing major Danish works. The catalogue comprises over 300 works by 110 composers of all periods, and includes Mogens Pedersøn's madrigals (*c*1620), works by late 18th-century masters such as F. L. A. Kunzen and J. A. P. Schulz, works of the 19th century by Weyse, Kuhlau, Hartmann and Gade, the music of Carl Nielsen and his successors, Riisager, Høffding, Weis, Tarp and Holmboe, and later works by N.V. Bentzon, Maegaard, Mogeus Winkel Holm and Nørholm, and the succeeding generation. (The society has issued detailed lists of works by Riisager and Høffding.) Works are published in their original form, mainly in full scores (and parts); for modern compositions, where necessary, traditional notation and format have been replaced by graphic notation. From the outset historical editions included informative prefatory material; facsimile editions and critical editions by leading scholars have also been produced. In the mid-1960s the society began issuing gramophone records of works in its catalogue. Samfundet til Udgivelse af Dansk Musik is largely financed by subsidies from the state's cultural fund.

D. Fog, ed.: *Samfundet til udgivelse af dansk musik 1871–1971: Catalogue* (Copenhagen, 1972) [in Eng.]

D.F.

Sassetti. Portuguese firm of publishers and retailers. It was founded in Lisbon in 1848 as Sassetti & Co. by João Baptista Sassetti (1817–89), and published educational works, classical choral and piano music and works by Portuguese composers (e.g. João Arroio, Luis de Freitas Branco, Cláudio Carneyro, Rui Coelho, Rey Colaço, Armando José Fernandes, Frederico de Freitas, Victor Hussla, Alfredo Keil and José Vianna da Motta). In 1973 Sassetti & Co. started a new company, Sassetti-Sociedade Portuguese de Música e Som, which is involved in the manufacture of records and music, also handling its own sales; it specializes in records, and its programme includes the systematic recording of works by major Portuguese composers (e.g. Carlos Seixas, João Domingos Bomtempo, Fernando Lopes Graça, Jorge Peixinho and Emanuel Nunes). Sassetti & Co. continues as an independent retail business.

C. de P.L.

Sauer. Austrian firm of publishers, active in Vienna. Its founder Ignaz Sauer (*b* Bohemia, 1 April 1759; *d* Vienna, 2 Dec 1833) began his activities in the art and music business as a partner in Joseph Eder's firm (founded 1794); Sauer terminated this relationship at the end of 1797. On 17 January 1798 he advertised his own 'Kunstverlag zu den sieben Schwestern'; this name refers to his seven daughters by his first marriage and appears in the plate inscriptions of his publications, which always bore an 'S.S.' in front of the number. His publications were initially commissioned to Leopold Kozeluch and Johann Traeg. In March 1801 he became the Viennese agent for the firm of André in Offenbach. In a large advertisement in the *Wiener Zeitung* of 25 July 1801 (two years before Senefelder's firm was founded) he announced the first attempt at lithographic printing in Austria with an edition of 12 ländler by Pechatschek. The confusion of war in 1805 and 1809 caused a financial decline, and on 25 November 1813 Sauer was obliged to give his stock-in-trade on commission to H. F. Müller.

On 9 December 1822 Sauer was joined by Marcus (Maximilian Josef) Leidesdorf (1787–1840), the son of a Jewish merchant, and as Sauer & Leidesdorf the firm revived, producing about 750 numbers in the next five years. Sauer relinquished his art dealer's licence on 30 April 1826, possibly because of his advanced age. On 9 May 1826 the firm was renamed M. J. Leidesdorf and continued to prosper until 18 July 1832, when Leidesdorf left for Italy; the licence was kept in abeyance until 15 May 1834, when Anton Berka took over the firm. On 4 September 1835 it passed to Diabelli & Co.

Ignaz Sauer's firm, while interesting for the history of publishing, was musically less significant; apart from issuing single works by Asioli, Clementi, Eybler, Mederitsch and Pasterwitz, it published many of Vanhal's late works and some of Sauer's own compositions. But as Sauer & Leidesdorf its calibre improved greatly; Leidesdorf's compositions were superficial fashionable pieces, but under his guidance the company published music by Beethoven and Weber, 49 works by Schubert (many of them first editions, including *Die schöne Müllerin*) and piano reductions of many of Rossini's operas with notable title decorations by Moritz von Schwind.

J. Jureczek: 'Die Kaiserliche Privatbibliothek im Jahre 1809', *Die Kultur*, ix (1908), 187; 'P. Beda Planks Fluchtreise 1800 bis 1801', *63. Programm des k.k. Obergymnasiums zu Kremsmünster* (Linz, 1913), 35; F. Gräffer: *Kleine Wiener Memoiren und Wiener Dosenstücke*, ed. A. Schlosser and G. Gugitz (Munich, 1917–18); G. Gugitz: 'Alt-Wiener Kunsthändler', *Von Leuten und Zeiten im alten Wien* (Vienna and Leipzig, 1922); Deutsch (1946); A. Weinmann: *Vorlagverzeichnis Ignaz Sauer (Kunstverlag zu den Sieben Schwestern), Sauer und Leidesdorf und Anton Berka & Comp.* (Vienna, 1972)

A.W.

Schetky [Shetky], **J(ohn) George** (*b* Edinburgh, 1 June 1776; *d* Philadelphia, 11 Dec 1831). American publisher of Scottish birth. He was the son of the Edinburgh cellist and composer J. G. C. Schetky and a nephew of Alexander Reinagle. Schetky emigrated to the USA in 1787 and became active as a cellist and music teacher in Philadelphia, where he lived with the musicians Benjamin Carr and Joseph C. Taws. With Carr he was co-editor of *The Musical Journal for the Piano Forte* (vols.iii–v) and published over 350 works from about 1803 to 1809; in addition they reissued 238 titles from the *Musical Journal* in 1806–7. Between 1812 and 1818 Schetky apparently visited Britain, for he published piano compositions by his father and himself in London and Edinburgh. He was a co-founder in 1820 of the Musical Fund

Society in Philadelphia, which owns a portrait of him.

O. G. Sonneck: *A Bibliography of Early Secular American Music* (Washington, DC, 1905; 2/1945, ed. W. T. Upton; 3/1964); J. Campbell: 'Old Philadelphia Music', *Philadelphia History*, ii (1926), 181; L. O. Schetky: *The Schetky Family: a Compilation of Letters, Memoirs and Historical Data* (Portland, OR, 1942); Wolfe (1964)

A.D.S.

Schirmer, E. C. American firm of publishers. It was founded in Boston in 1921 by Ernest Charles Schirmer (*b* Mount Vernon, NY, 15 March 1865; *d* Waban, MA, 15 Feb 1958), who had previously worked in New York for his brother Gustave, also a music publisher, and had later become a partner in the Boston Music Company. When Ernest Schirmer died, E. C. Schirmer jr became president and remained the head of the firm until his death on 6 May 1966, when Robert MacWilliams became president. In addition to standard works, Schirmer publishes electronic music, the choral repertory of the Harvard University, Radcliffe, Vassar and Wellesley college glee clubs, the St Dunstan Edition of Sacred Music and books on music theory and appreciation. American composers in its catalogue include Avshalomov, Howard Boatwright, Copland, Felciano, Korte, Donald Martino, Alice Parker, Perera, Piston, Pinkham, Rorem, Conrad Susa and Randall Thompson. E. C. Schirmer maintains offices in London and Hamburg, and represents Galaxy Music Corporation and Highgate Press of New York, Nova Music of London and Foetisch Frères of Switzerland.

W.T.M., M.J.

Schirmer, G. American firm of publishers. One of the largest and most important of its kind in the USA, it began in New York as an outgrowth of the Kerksieg & Bruesing Company (founded 1848), of which Gustav Schirmer (*b* Königsee, 19 Sept 1829; *d* Eisenach, 5 Aug 1893) became manager in 1854 (he had gone to New York in 1837). With Bernard Beer, Schirmer took over the business in 1861, and in 1866 he bought out Beer's interest and established the house of G. Schirmer, Music Publishers, Importers and Dealers. As its activities increased and the firm grew in standing, it several times moved to new quarters and in 1891 founded its own engraving and printing plant – one of the few maintained into the 1980s by American music publishing houses (it ceased to operate in 1984). After Gustav's death the business was incorporated under the management of his sons:

Rudolph Edward (*b* New York, 22 July 1859; *d* Santa Barbara, CA, 19 Aug 1919) was president, and Gustave (*b* New York, 18 Feb 1864; *d* Boston, 15 July 1907) secretary. When Rudolph died, Gustave's son, also named Gustave (*b* Boston, 29 Dec 1890; *d* Palm Beach, FL, 28 May 1965), succeeded him as president; he was followed in 1921 by W. Rodman Fay. In May 1929 Carl Engel assumed the presidency and held that office until his death in 1944. Gustave Schirmer (grandson of the founder) was again made president and was succeeded in 1957 by Rudolph Tauhert. The subsequent president, Edward P. Murphy, was succeeded by John A. Santuccio on 1 March 1984. In 1964 Associated Music Publishers, with a catalogue including many internationally known composers, became a subsidiary of G. Schirmer. In 1968 the firm was acquired by the American book publisher, Macmillan. In 1986 the music publishing activities were taken over by Music Sales, and its publications distributed by Hal Leonard; the book publishing was retained by Macmillan, as Schirmer Books.

Schirmer publishes for all media; its catalogue includes works by Stephen Albert, Barber, Bloch, Corigliano, Creston, Anthony Davis, Morton Gould, Griffes, Roy Harris, Laderman, Menotti, Douglas Moore, John Jacob Niles, Schumann and Thomson. In addition, Schirmer as an ASCAP affiliate and AMP, as a BMI affiliate, are the sole American representatives for 40 publishers, including Bote & Bock, Chester and Wilhelm Hansen, Editions Max Eschig, Faber Music, Editions Salabert and Hans Sikorski. Since 1974 they have been assigned American publishing and related rights to all Soviet music through an agreement with VAAP, the Soviet copyright agency. Among the firm's publications are *Schirmer's Library of Musical Classics* (introduced in 1892), opera and orchestral study scores and instructional materials for all instruments. Schirmer maintains a vast library of rental materials of the larger 20th-century works as well as the standard repertory.

The lexicographer Theodore Baker served as Schirmer's literary editor and translator, 1892–1926, and was active in founding the *Musical Quarterly* in 1915. Its first editor, Oscar G. Sonneck, joined the firm in 1917 and was vice-president from 1921 to his death in 1928. Engel succeeded him on the *Musical Quarterly*. Among later editors at the firm were Nathan Broder (manager of publications, 1945–54), Paul Henry Lang (ed. *Musical Quarterly*, 1945–73) and Hans W. Heinsheimer (1947–74).

Baker's Biographical Dictionary of Musicians, which has been regularly updated, was first published by Schirmer in 1900. Schirmer established, and for many years maintained, the principal circulating music library in the USA (in 1906 it was transferred to the Institute of Musical Art).

For an illustration *see* fig.40, p.123.

H. W. Heinsheimer: *Menagerie in F sharp* (Garden City, NY, 1947); idem: *Fanfare for Two Pigeons* (Garden City, NY, 1952); P. H. Lang: 'Portrait of a Publishing House', *One Hundred Years of Music in America* (New York, 1961/R1985), 9; H. W. Heinsheimer: *Best Regards to Aida* (New York, 1968); S. Craft: 'G. Schirmer: the Music Publishing Experience', *AB Bookman's Weekly*, lxxii (1983), 4155

W.T.M., M.J./R

Schlesinger. German firm of publishers. Adolph Martin Schlesinger (*b* Sülz, Silesia, 4 Oct 1769; *d* Berlin, 11 Oct 1838) worked before 1795 as a book dealer in Berlin, and later incorporated printed music into his business; he founded the music publishing house in April 1810. After his eldest son Maurice Schlesinger had established himself in Paris and his second son Carl (1808–31) had died, the youngest son Heinrich (*b* Berlin, 1810; *d* Berlin, 14 Dec 1879) received full control in 1831. After his father's death he directed the business with his mother, Philippine, and alone from 1844. In 1864 he sold the firm to Robert Lienau.

From 1811 Schlesinger did its own printing, orginally producing works by local Berlin composers. It soon established contacts with Spontini, Mendelssohn, Loewe and Weber, and in August 1814 secured the rights for Weber's works, becoming his original publisher. Encouragement from the Prussian royal house resulted in the *Sammlung preussischer Armeemärsche*, which comprised over 200 numbers. In 1819 Maurice Schlesinger established contact with Beethoven in Vienna, which led to the publication of opp.108–112, 132 and 135. Through the efforts of Adolph Bernhard Marx, who edited the *Berliner allgemeine musikalische Zeitung* (formerly the *Zeitung für Theater und Musik*, 1821–3) for Schlesinger from 1824 to 1830, the company issued the first edition of Bach's *St Matthew Passion*. With more than 2000 publications issued by 1836, Schlesinger ranked among the most important Prussian music publishers. Under Heinrich Schlesinger the firm acquired works by Berlioz, Cornelius, Liszt and notably Chopin's posthumous works. It concentrated on inexpensive editions of well-known works and, for copyright reasons, revised editions of earlier publications. The periodical *Echo* (1851–65),

chiefly edited by Heinrich Schlesinger himself, was designed to revitalize the musical life of Berlin. A certain stagnation in the firm's activities was overcome when Robert Lienau took it over in 1864. A complete catalogue was never published.

A. B. Marx: *Erinnerungen aus meinem Leben* (Berlin, 1865); A. Kalischer: *Beethoven und Berlin* (Berlin, 1908); R. H. Lienau: 'Die Schlesinger'sche Buch- und Musikhandlung in Berlin', *Börsenblatt für den deutschen Buchhandel*, lxxvii (1910), 3891; M. Unger: *Ludwig van Beethoven und seine Verleger* (Berlin, 1921); R. Elvers: *A.M. Schlesinger – Robert Lienau: 150 Jahre Musik-Verlag* (Berlin, 1960); idem: 'Acht Briefe von Lea Mendelssohn an den Verleger Schlesinger in Berlin', *Das Problem Mendelssohn*, ed. C. Dahlhaus (Regensburg, 1974), 47

R.E.

Schlesinger, Maurice [Moritz Adolf] (*b* Berlin, 30 Oct 1798; *d* Baden-Baden, 25 Feb 1871). French publisher of German descent. He was the eldest son of Adolf Martin Schlesinger, the Berlin publisher. Before settling in Paris in 1816, he served in the Prussian army (1814–15) and worked in his father's firm. In Paris he worked first for the bookseller Bossange Père. In summer 1819 he visited Beethoven in Vienna and Mödling to cultivate his friendship. Not later than July 1821 he started his own business, his first advertisements bearing Bossange's address, 13 quai Malaquais. By October 1822 he had moved to 107 rue Richelieu and by February 1824 he was at no.97 of the same street, where he remained until his retirement. In 1826 his business survived a fire that destroyed many manuscripts including letters of Beethoven. On 20 November 1842 *La France musicale* announced that Schlesinger was gradually selling the stock of his firm; it was not until January 1846 that he sold the entire business to Brandus. A few years later he retired to Baden-Baden.

Schlesinger's earliest publications include a series of piano-vocal scores of Mozart's operas, with title-page vignettes by Horace Vernet, and the full score of Méhul's *Valentine de Milan* (1823). These were followed by numerous other operatic publications: piano-vocal scores of at least 50 operas and some two dozen full scores, including the first editions of Meyerbeer's *Robert le diable* and *Les Huguenots*, Halévy's *La juive* and at least 11 of his other works, Adam's *Le postillon de Longjumeau* and Donizetti's *La favorite*. Among his employees between 1840 and 1842 was Wagner, who, then quite impoverished, was engaged to make piano (and other) arrangements of *La favorite* and of Halévy's *La reine de Chypre*. Schlesinger published a great deal of instrumental music. In the 1820s he brought out substantial collections of piano music by Moscheles, Weber and Hummel, and early in 1829 he announced complete editions first of Beethoven's piano works and then of his string trios, quartets and quintets. In 1822–3 he published authentic simultaneous first editions of Beethoven's opp.110 and 111 piano sonatas and in 1827 of the opp.130, 132, 133 and 135 string quartets. In the late 1820s and the early 1830s he published early works by Mendelssohn, Liszt and Berlioz; among his Berlioz publications were the first editions of the *Huit scènes de Faust* (see illustration), Liszt's piano arrangement of the *Symphonie fantastique* and the full scores of the *Requiem*, the *Symphonie fantastique* and the *Symphonie funèbre et triomphale*. He published about 40 of Chopin's works, most of them authentic simultaneous first editions. In the 1830s and 1840s he also published a vast quantity of piano music by Heller, Thalberg, Lanner, Labitzky and the elder Johann Strauss. In all, about 4500 editions were published, judging by the chronological series of plate numbers.

Schlesinger's most enduring publication was the weekly *Gazette musicale de Paris*, first published on 5 January 1834. From November 1835 (vol.ii, no.44) it was merged with *Revue musicale* (edited by Fétis), subsequently appearing as *Revue et gazette musicale*; in 1880 it ceased publication. Among the early contributors were Berlioz, Wagner, Liszt and Schumann. It is an invaluable source of information on music and music publishing in Paris.

Schlesinger was imaginative, reckless, hard in business and a considerable rogue. He is said to be accurately portrayed by Flaubert as Jacques Arnoux in *L'éducation sentimentale*; Madame Arnoux is just as closely modelled on Schlesinger's wife, Elisa, with whom Flaubert was for many years in love. Irascible by nature, Schlesinger not infrequently became entangled with his colleagues in wrangles over publication rights or allegedly defamatory statements; his clashes with Escudier in 1839, with Troupenas in 1841 and with Rossini in 1843 provide three interesting examples documented in *La France musicale* (1839–43). The autographs from his estate were auctioned by Liepmannssohn in Berlin on 4 November 1907.

FétisB; F. C. Busset: *M. Fétis mis à la portée de tout le monde* (Paris, 1838); *Catalogue général* (Paris, *c*1846) [Brandus & Cie catalogue listing all works published by Schlesinger to 30 June 1845]; M. Unger: *Ludwig van Beethoven und seine Verleger* (Berlin, 1921); Deutsch (1946); C. Hopkinson: *A Bibliography of the Musical and Literary Works of Hector Berlioz* (Edinburgh, 1951, rev. 2/1980), 195; H. Steinhart-Leins: *Flauberts grosse Liebe: Elisa Foucault, das Urbild der Mde. Arnoux* (Baden-Baden, 1951); Hopkinson (1954); Z. Lissa: 'Chopin im Lichte des Briefwechsels von Verlegern seiner Zeit gesehen', *FAM*, vii (1960), 46; E. Anderson, ed. and trans.: *The Letters of Beethoven* (London, 1961/*R*1985), ii–iii; M. Gregor-Dellin, ed.: *Richard Wagner: Mein Leben* (Munich, 1963); A. Tyson: 'Maurice Schlesinger as a Publisher of Beethoven, 1822–27', *AcM*, xxxv (1963), 182; P. Gossett: *The Operas of Rossini* (diss., Princeton U., 1970), 607; Devriès and Lesure (1979–88); A. Devriès: 'Un editeur de musique "à la tête ardente": Maurice Schlesinger', *FAM*, xxvii (1980), 125; J. Kallberg: 'Chopin in the Marketplace: Aspects of the International Music Publishing Industry in the First Half of the Nineteenth Century', *Notes*, xxxix (1982–3), 535, 795; A. Devriès: 'La "musique à bon marché" en France dans les années 1830', *Music in Paris in the Eighteen-Thirties*, ed. P. Bloom (Stuyvesant, NY, 1987)

R.M.

Schmid [Schmidt]**, Balthasar** (*b* Nuremberg, bap. 20 April 1705; bur. 27 Nov 1749). German printer and composer. He was born into a family of artisans and craftsmen, and continued in the tradition of artistic craftsmanship to become one of the best-known music engravers in 18th-century Germany. Church records first mention him as an engraver in 1726, later as a musician and engraver (1734), and again as organist at St Margaretha in Nuremberg (1737). He was highly regarded by Mattheson, who praised him in his *Grundlage einer Ehren-Pforte* (1740) as an organist and fine engraver of musical works; and Ludwig Gerber, writing later in the century, credited Schmid's engraving of some parts of J. S. Bach's *Clavier-Übung* as an important factor in the renown and distribution of those works.

Schmid devoted his early efforts as a printer to his own compositions, but after 1738 his catalogue included the names of some of the leading musical figures in north Germany: G. P. Telemann (sacred vocal works, portrait, autobiography); G. A. Sorge (organ sonatas, preludes and suites for keyboard); C. Nichelmann (12 keyboard sonatas); J. L. Krebs (sonatas for violin and obbligato keyboard, miscellaneous keyboard works); J. Agrell (at least three keyboard sonatas, sonatas for violin and obbligato keyboard); F. W. Marpurg (six keyboard sonatas); C. F. Schale (six keyboard sonatas); C. P. E. Bach ('Prussian' sonatas, keyboard concertos, trio sonatas, a sinfonia); and J. S. Bach (*Clavier-Übung*, iv: Goldberg Variations and the canonic variations on *Vom Himmel hoch*). Schmid maintained a standard of accuracy and legibility

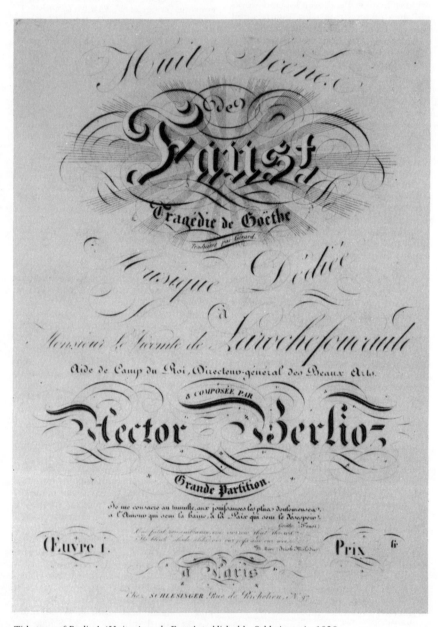

Title-page of Berlioz's 'Huit scènes de Faust', published by Schlesinger in 1829

unusual for the time, and it was probably through the high quality of his editions of the Bach keyboard works that he first came to the attention of modern scholars. He was also among the earliest publishers to ascribe numbers to his printed works, a practice which makes it possible for scholars to establish the dates and chronology of compositions. Unfortunately, Schmid's numbering is very erratic in that it includes both arabic and roman numerals, as well as a few entries designated with the letter N. An index of his printed works remains (Vienna, Gesellschaft der Musikfreunde 272/20), and has been reproduced by H. Heussner with probable dates of publication inserted. Schmid's widow, Maria Helena Volland (1710–91), continued the publishing activities after his death; from about 1751 printed works of the firm were identified with 'Balth. Schmids seel. Wittib'.

As a composer Schmid is known primarily by his keyboard works, intended for the growing society of amateurs. The *Nürnbergische alte und neue Kirchen-Lieder*, his only venture into vocal music as a composer, consists of 208 chorale melodies set in an open two-part texture with figured bass; the work is a model of the printer's art in its clarity and format. Johann Michael Schmidt (1741–93; this spelling appeared on his published works), son of Balthasar, continued the engraving trade and operated the publishing house during the last quarter of the century. He was most active in the realm of vocal music and published many important lieder collections between 1773 and 1791.

J. Mattheson: *Grundlage einer Ehren-Pforte* (Hamburg, 1740), ed. M. Schneider (Berlin, 1910/R1969); *Verzeichnis der musicalischen Wercker, welche bey Balthasar Schmid seel Wittib in Nürnberg zu haben sind* (MS, A-Wgm 272/20); C. F. Cramer: *Magazin der Musik*, i (Hamburg, 1783/R), 1135, ii (Hamburg, 1784/R), 489; W. B. Squire: 'Publishers' Numbers', *SIMG*, xv (1913–14), 420; G. Kinsky: *Die Originalausgaben der Werke Johann Sebastian Bachs* (Vienna, 1937); Deutsch (1946); H. Heussner: 'Der Musikdrucker Balthasar Schmid in Nürnberg', *Mf*, xvi (1963), 348; W. Wörthmüller, ed.: *Nürnberger Musikverleger und die Familie Bach: Materialien zu einer Ausstellung des 48. Bach-Fests der Neuen Bach-Gesellschaft* (Zirndorf, 1973)

D.A.L.

Schmidt, Arthur P(aul) (*b* Altona, Germany, 1 April 1846; *d* Boston, 5 May 1921). American publisher. He emigrated to the USA in January 1866 and worked in Boston for the G. D. Russell & Co. publishing house. In October 1876 he established his own firm as the A. P. Schmidt Co. He began as an importer of foreign music, acting as US agent for the Litolff Edition and for publications from such London firms as Edwin Ashdown Ltd., W. Morley & Co., and Patey & Willis. He entered his first copyright on 26 March 1877 and in 1880 became the first American publisher to issue a symphony by a native American composer (Paine's *Spring Symphony*). Known as the 'pioneer publisher of American music', he brought out works by many New England composers including Mrs H. H. A. Beach, George Chadwick and Horatio Parker, as well as almost the entire body of compositions by Arthur Foote. He became MacDowell's chief publisher after purchasing the P. L. Jung catalogue in 1899.

In 1889 he sold his retail business in Boston to Miles and Thompson and expanded his publishing operations into Europe. He engaged Franz Schäffer of the Leipzig firm Kistner to act as his agent on commission, enabling Schmidt to obtain manuscripts from European composers and gain international copyright protection for his American publications. This arrangement lasted until 1908, when Schmidt established his own branch in Leipzig. In 1910 B. Schott's Söhne bought the European rights to the Schmidt catalogue; the firm's Leipzig interests continued to be represented by an agent until 1938. Schmidt kept his Boston and Leipzig catalogues completely separate, although he issued some American works from Leipzig; the Boston list had over 15,000 titles, and the Leipzig list over 500. He had subpublishing contracts with the London publishers Boosey, Enoch, Elkin, Lengnick and Schott, to whom he assigned the English rights for numerous songs and some piano and choral works. From 1894 to 1937 the firm had a branch in New York.

In 1899 Schmidt helped establish the business of a Boston music dealer, Charles W. Homeyer & Co., remaining a partner until 1912. He also published a journal, the *Musical World* (1901–4). Educational music became the major focus of the firm after Schmidt's retirement in 1916, when three long-time employees, H. B. Crosby, F. J. Emery and H. R. Austin, became partners in the firm. Austin became president of the Arthur P. Schmidt Co., Inc., in 1949, and sold it to Summy-Birchard in 1959, assigning the copyrights in 1960. A vast collection of the firm's archival records, together with correspondence with composers, and autograph manuscripts used for published editions, is in the Library of Congress.

'Publisher Arthur P. Schmidt: Quarter-Centennial Anniversary', *Musical Courier*, xliii/14 (1901), 34; Obituary, *Boston Evening Transcript* (6 May

1921); [H. Levine]: 'A. P. Schmidt, Pioneer Publisher of American Music, is Dead', *Musical America*, xxxiv/3 (1921), 55; [J. Freund]: 'Arthur P. Schmidt', *Musical America*, xxxiv/5 (1921), 22; A. Foote: 'Schmidt, Arthur Paul', *DAB*; Fisher (1933); C. M. Ayars: *Contributions to the Art of Music in America by the Music Industries of Boston, 1640 to 1936* (New York, 1937/R1969); Dichter and Shapiro (1941, 2/1977)

W.R.C.

Schmitt, Joseph [Georgius Adamus Josephus] (*b* Gernsheim am Rhein, bap. 18 March 1734; *d* Amsterdam, 28 May 1791). German publisher and composer, active in the Netherlands. His musical education under Carl Friedrich Abel must have taken place in Dresden before 1758, the year Abel left the court chapel there and settled in London. On 2 October 1753 Schmitt took vows at the Cistercian monastery at Eberbach im Rheingau, where he wrote many sacred and secular works. On 9 October 1757 he was ordained priest. From 1763 at the latest the care of the music in the monastery seems to have been entrusted to him as *regens chori*. Before 1767 he established a connection with the music publisher Hummel in Amsterdam, who from this time until 1773 took six luxuriously printed collections of instrumental pieces by Schmitt into his catalogue. In 1771 payments by the monastery for music abruptly ceased, and by 1774 Schmitt had printed his op.7 in Amsterdam under his own imprint.

In Schmitt's early years in the Netherlands he earned his livelihood from his publishing firm (which at first brought out only his own compositions) and perhaps by teaching, as is indicated by his *Principes de la musique dédiés à tous les commençans* and by the violin duos op.8 (printed before 1774) which exhibit a strong didactic bias. When the Felix Meritis Society of Amsterdam opened a new building in 1788, Schmitt was appointed director of the music section. At his death he was succeeded in this post by Bartholomeus Ruloffs, and in his publishing firm by Vincent Springer (a relative of Schmitt's by marriage), a basset-horn player who continued the business until the end of the century.

Schmitt was in keen competition with Hummel – a catalogue of 1793 cited by Gerber apparently carried over 500 titles. Works published by Schmitt and Springer achieved wide international distribution, particularly in the Scandinavian countries, where they were the primary means of making known the works of the Viennese Classical composers (Schmitt's was principally a reprint firm). As a composer he was particularly esteemed for his orchestral and chamber music. He should not be confused with Karl Joseph Schmitt, a native of Eltville (Rheingau) who worked as a music director in Amsterdam and Frankfurt.

EitnerQ; GerberL; GerberNL; D. F. Scheurleer: *Het muziekleven in Nederland in de tweede helft der 18e eeuw in verband met Mozart's verblijf aldaar* (The Hague, 1909); O. Andersson: 'Musikliterarische Fäden zwischen Holland und Finnland am Ende des 18. Jahrhunderts', *Gedenboek aangeboden aan Dr. D. F. Scheurleer* (The Hague, 1925), 43; D. J. Balfoort: *Het muziekleven in Nederland in de 17de en 18de eeuw* (Amsterdam, 1938); A. Dunning: *Joseph Schmitt: Leben und Kompositionen des Eberbacher Zisterziensers und Amsterdamer Musikverlegers (1734–1791)* (Amsterdam, 1962); A. Gottron: 'Musik in sechs mittelrheinischen Männerklöstern im 18. Jahrhundert', *SMw*, xxv (1962), 214

A.D. (ii)

Schoeffer [Schöffer], **Peter**, jr (*b* Mainz, *c*1475–80; *d* Basle, 1547). German printer. He learnt the printing trade from his father, Peter Schoeffer, associate of Gutenberg and co-publisher (with Johannes Fust) of the famous Mainz *Psalterium* (1457). After the elder Schoeffer's death in 1502 or 1503 his son established his own printing business, which, as a Protestant sympathizer, he was forced to sell in the summer of 1512. For the rest of his life he moved from one city to another. As early as 1518 he began printing in Worms, although he did not move his business there until 1520. Once again he was expelled from the city, this time because of his involvement with the Anabaptist movement. In 1529 he became a citizen of Strasbourg through his marriage to Anna Pfintzer and set up his business there, associating himself first with his former typesetter in Worms, Johann Schwintzer, then in 1534 with Mathias Apiarius, with whom he published only music books. In 1539 he can be traced in Basle and in 1541–2 in Venice, where he published at least seven works before his final return to Basle. His last years appear to have been spent working as a type-founder for other printers.

Although the number of his music publications was relatively small (14 out of about 100 works), he is perhaps best known for his superb craftsmanship in this field, producing unusually elegant notation by means of multiple impression. His collections of German songs, including works by such composers as Hofhaimer, Schönfelder, Sies and Virdung, represent the repertory of the Stuttgart court chapel under Ulrich of Württemberg.

A. Schmid: *Ottaviano dei Petrucci da Fossombrone und seine Nachfolger im sechzehnten Jahrhunderte* (Vienna, 1845/R1968); J. J. Maier: 'Unbekannte Sammlungen deutscher Lieder des XVI. Jahrhunderts, I: Peter Schöffer's des Jüngeren II. Liederbuch', *MMg*, xii (1880), 6; A. Thürlings: 'Der Musikdruck mit beweglichen Metalltypen im 16. Jahrhundert und die Musikdrucke des Mathias Apiarius in Strassburg und Bern', *VMw*, viii (1892), 389; E. H. Voullième: *Die deutschen Drucker des 15. Jahrhunderts* (Berlin, 1916, 2/1922); H. J. Moser: *Paul Hofhaimer* (Stuttgart, 1929, rev.2/1966); M. E. Kronenberg: 'Het Kamperliedboek, c.1540', *Het Boek*, xxiii (1935–6), 165; A. Geering:'Apiarius, Matthias', *MGG*; H. Lehmann-Haupt: *Peter Schoeffer of Gernsheim and Mainz* (Rochester, NY, 1950); J. Benzing: 'Peter Schöffer der Jüngere, Musikdrucker zu Mainz, Worms, Strassburg und Venedig (tätig 1512–1542)', *Jb für Liturgik und Hymnologie*, iv (1958–9), 133; K. Meyer-Baer: *Liturgical Music Incunabula: a Descriptive Catalogue* (London, 1962); J. Benzing: 'Schöffer, Peter', *MGG*; H. Carter: *A View of Early Typography* (Oxford, 1969); E. Thausing: 'Bemerkungen zu einigen illuminierten Schöffer-Drucken', *Gutenberg-Jb 1973*, 185; S. Bain: *Music Printing in the Low Countries in the Sixteenth Century* (diss., U. of Cambridge, 1974); S. V. Lenkey: 'Migrations of Sixteenth Century Printers', *Gutenberg-Jb 1976*, 218

M.L.G.

Schonenberger, Georges (*b* Mitlödi, Glaris, Switzerland, 22 July 1807; *d* Pfäfers, Switzerland, July 1856). French publisher. His earliest advertisement dates from 10 April 1830, and his first address, 10 boulevard Poissonnière, Paris, was that of Dufaut & Dubois, whose business he acquired and many of whose publications he reissued. The house number was changed, or a move was made, first to no.20 in November or December 1841, and then to no.28 boulevard Poissonnière between December 1842 and January 1843. From 1837 Schonenberger's brother-in-law Jost Wild (1793–1875) was a partner in the firm. In the 1860s Wild's name was usually added to or substituted for that of Schonenberger in the imprints. In June 1875, on Wild's death, the business was advertised for sale for 250,000 francs. Schonenberger died in the St Pirminsberg asylum in the St Gallen canton of Switzerland.

Schonenberger is interesting for his enterprise in publishing full scores and orchestral parts of four Donizetti operas, including *La fille du régiment* (1840). He put out full scores of some 27 other operas, all but a handful of which were reissues from the plates of other publishers (including Pleyel, Dufaut & Dubois and Bochsa). He published about 50 operas in piano-vocal scores, including several little-known works by Rossini and Donizetti. Among his other publications should be noted Berlioz's *Grand traité d'instrumentation* (1843), piano concertos in parts by Hummel, Mendelssohn and Thalberg, numerous piano works by F. Beyer, J. Herz and Hünten, new

editions or reissues of a large proportion of Bochsa's harp music, violin music by Delphin Alard and Paganini, a highly successful piano method by H. Bertini, a certain amount of Spanish music, and translations into Spanish of didactic works published by the firm.

Catalogue de musique: Schonenberger éditeur (Paris, *c*1860); Hopkinson (1954); Devriès and Lesure (1979–88)

R.M.

Schönig [Schoneck]. German family of printers. Valentin Schönig (*b* Gnodstadt, 1544; *d* Augsburg, 1614) acquired Augsburg citizenship in 1567 through his marriage to Barbara Kriesstein, a daughter of the Augsburg printer Melchior Kriesstein, whose business Schönig probably inherited. With his purchase of Philipp Ulhard's workshop in 1581, he established an efficient printing firm and, in spite of his adherence to Reformation teaching, worked continually for the episcopal court. Gumpelzhaimer's *Compendium musicae* (1591) was one of his most successful publications. The Thirty Years War and unfavourable economic conditions prevented his descendants Hans Ulrich Schönig (1589–1655) and Johann Schönig (1616–80) from extending the firm. Only Johann Jakob Schönig (1657–94), who had married a daughter of the Augsburg music publisher Andreas Erfurt, succeeded in giving it fresh impetus. Valentin Schönig, unlike his predecessors Kriesstein and Ulhard, had restricted himself to printing works of composers active in Augsburg, but Johann Jakob printed mainly catholic church music. After his early death his widow married J. C. Wagner, who then took over the workshop. In 1710 Johann Jakob's son Johann Matthias Schönig (1685–1753) acquired his own printing business, which published individual editions of songs.

T. Wohnhaas: 'Die Schönig, eine Augsburger Druckerfamilie', *Archiv für Geschichte des Buchwesens*, v (1964), 5

T.W.

Schott. German firm of publishers. It was founded by Bernhard Schott (*b* Eltville, 10 Aug 1748; *d* Sandhof, nr. Heidesheim, 26 April 1809) in Mainz. Eitner gave 1770 as the year of foundation, and the firm celebrated its bicentenary in 1970, but the publishing house was probably not founded until 1780 when Schott was granted a *privilegium exclusivum* and the title of music engraver to the court of the elector at Mainz. Schott had studied from 1768 to 1771 at the University of Mainz

Schott

(graduating as magister artium), was clarinettist in a Strasbourg regiment from 1771 to 1773 and travelled in the Netherlands and England; in addition to his musical education, he gained a knowledge of copperplate engraving and particularly of music engraving. He was thus more thoroughly trained for the profession of music publishing than many of his contemporaries. He began his publishing venture with editions of the works of Abbé Vogler and his circle and with the composers for the Hofkapelle at Mainz, especially the works of G. A. Kreusser and F. X. Sterkel. Above all he brought out music for which there was a popular demand, such as piano scores and arrangements of popular operas; he published the first piano score of Mozart's *Die Entführung aus dem Serail* (1785) and of *Don Giovanni* (1791). He frequently reprinted the works of popular composers, especially Pleyel, and boasted that his own editions were of superior quality. The numerous flute duets and other pieces published in the 1790s are evidence of a marked leaning towards salon music.

Bernhard's sons Johann Andreas (1781–1840) and Johann Joseph (1782–1855), who gave the name 'B. Schott's Söhne' to the firm, enlarged the enterprise both by increasing the scope of the publishing programme and by taking over other publishers. By 1818 they had absorbed partly or completely the firms of Amon of Heilbronn, Falter of Munich and Kreitner of Worms (together with a part interest in Götz of Mannheim and Worms), as well as the firms of Karl Zulehner of Mainz and Georg Zulehner of Eltville. Subsequently the firm established branches in Antwerp (1824, transferred to Brussels in 1843 by Peter Schott, a son of Johann Andreas, where it has been independent from 1889 under the name of Schott Frères), Paris (1826), London (1835; managed by Bernhard's third son Adam Joseph Schott, 1794–1840) and Leipzig (*c*1840). The firm first achieved eminence through the connection it formed with Beethoven in 1824 and through its first publication of such late works as the *Missa solemnis*, the Ninth Symphony (see illustration) and the string quartets opp.127 and 131. The firm continued its tradition of publishing popular works by issuing the compositions of Italian and French opera composers, including Bellini, Donizetti, Rossini, Adam, Auber, Gounod and Halévy. In addition it brought out many works for piano by Ascher, Herz, Hünten, Sydney Smith and Thalberg, and works for violin by de Bériot, Dancla and Paganini. From 1824 to 1848 it published

the music periodical *Cäcilia*, edited by Gottfried Weber, which was continued until 1869 as the *Süddeutsche Musikzeitung*, edited by Siegfried Dehn. From 1835 it published, together with the Brussels firm of Leroux, Fétis's *Biographie universelle des musiciens et bibliographie générale de la musique*.

From 1855 until his death Franz Philipp Schott (1811–74), the son of Johann Andreas, carried on the publishing house as sole proprietor. Under him a connection with Wagner was formed in 1859, after which the firm published his music dramas *Der Ring des Nibelungen, Die Meistersinger von Nürnberg* and *Parsifal*. Other composers of Wagner's circle turned to Schott, including Liszt, with whom there had already been a slight connection since 1837, as well as Cornelius, Wolf and Humperdinck.

After the death of Franz Philipp Schott the publishing house was bequeathed to Ludwig Strecker (1853–1943) who came from an old Hessian civil service family not related to the Schotts. From 1920 he made his sons Ludwig (1883–1978) and Willy (1884–1958) partners in the publishing house. With the publication of Stravinsky's *Fireworks* (1908) it began to encourage modern music and this is still an important part of the firm's policy. 20th-century composers whose works have been published by Schott include Hindemith, Orff, Fortner, Egk, Françaix, Henze, Schoenberg, Zimmermann, Weill, Ligeti and Penderecki, as well as Goehr and Tippett in association with the English branch of the firm.

In 1907 Willy Strecker assisted Max Eschig in the foundation of his publishing house in Paris, and in 1910 he took over the London firm of Augener; both were expropriated during World War I. Heinz Schneider-Schott, Ludwig Strecker's son-in-law, became a director of the firm in 1952, and in 1974 Arno Volk (the founder of Volk), who had held a leading position in the firm since 1957, became chairman of the board of directors, the other members being Peter Hanser-Strecker and Günther Schneider-Schott; Volk was succeeded on his retirement in 1977 by Ludolf Freiherr von Canstein.

The more important works of musicology published by Schott since World War II include the 12th edition of the *Riemann Musiklexikon* and the Haydn thematic catalogue edited by Anthony van Hoboken. In addition Schott has undertaken critical editions of the complete works of Wagner, Hindemith and Schoenberg.

The firm has also been much involved in music education. It publishes a number of perodicals including *Melos, Neue Zeitschrift*

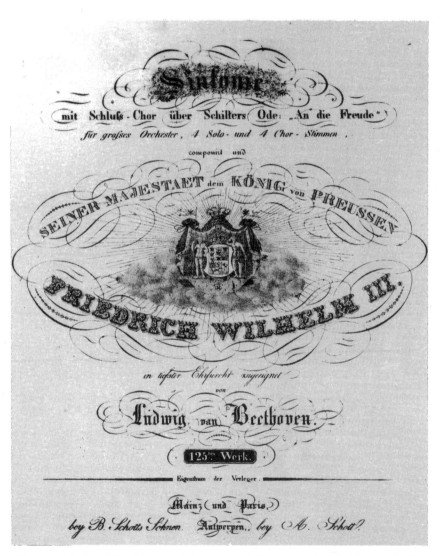

Title-page of the first edition of the score of Beethoven's Ninth Symphony, published by Schott in 1826

für Musik (these two combined in 1974), *Musik and Bildung* (formerly *Musik im Unterricht*), *Forschung in der Musikerziehung, Das Orchester, The World of Music* and *Darmstädter Beiträge zur neuen Musik*. In 1953 Schott bought the publishing house of Ars Viva and in 1971 the gramophone record company of Wergo. It cooperates with Universal Edition, Vienna, with which the joint publishing house of Wiener Urtext Edition was formed in 1973. Musifactory, a subsidiary firm which publishes light music, was founded in 1975 and a branch established in the USA in 1977. In 1986 Schott bought the firm of Fürstner (London), for whose Richard Strauss edition it had been the German agent.

The firm survived World War II almost unscathed and is still in possession of its largely complete archives. Some 600 letters of Beethoven and other 19th-century composers were donated by Franz Philipp Schott to the Mainz Stadtbibliothek.

The London branch of the firm was managed, after the death in 1840 of A. J. Schott, by Johann Baptist Wolf, to be followed by Charles G. J. Volkert (1854–1929) who had joined the staff in 1873 and who took over the management in 1887. Under his direction the firm began to develop independently. In 1914 Volkert acquired the firm and it became a limited company in 1924. After his death in 1929 his son-in-law Max R. B. Steffens took over as joint director with Willy Strecker; Strecker was succeeded on his death by Heinz Schneider-Schott. In 1957 Schott acquired the firm of Ernst Eulenburg. In 1961 Peter W. Makings was appointed managing director, and the firm entered on a period of expansion; additional premises were built at Ashford, Kent, in 1965, to house a new printing works, and the Great Marlborough Street premises, purchased in 1909, were redesigned in 1966 to include a retail shop. John S. Harper became managing director in 1980. Though autonomous from 1914 until 1980, when Schott of Mainz resumed control, Schott & Co. kept close links with the parent firm while maintaining a publishing policy of its own, which it continues to pursue. Contemporary music is strongly represented (Banks, Maxwell Davies, Fricker, Gilbert, Goehr, Hamilton, Martland, Sackman, Searle, Seiber, Tippett and Turnage), and educational and school music are an important feature, with an extensive list of recorder music. The firm has taken a special interest in the recorder and early music revival; in 1963 it established the *Recorder and Music Magazine* and in 1986 the Early Music Shop was incorporated in the retail department.

EitnerQ; M. Seiffert: 'Das Haus Schott', *AMz*, xx (1893); E. Istel, ed.: 'Elf ungedruckte Briefe Liszts an Schott', *Die Musik*, v/3 (1905–6), 43; A. Börckel: *Aus der Mainzer Vergangenheit* (Mainz, 1906); W. Altmann: *Richard Wagners Briefwechsel mit seinen Verlegern*, ii: *Briefwechsel mit B. Schott's Söhnen* (Leipzig, 1911); H. Schrohe: *Bilder aus der Mainzer Geschichte*, Hessische Volksbücher, xlviii (Friedberg, 1922); M. Unger: 'Zu Beethovens Briefwechsel mit B. Schott's Söhnen', *NBJb*, iii (1926–51); B. Ziegler: 'Zur Geschichte des Privilegium exclusivum des Mainzer Musikstechers Bernhard Schott', *Festschrift für Georg Leidinger* (Munich, 1930), 293; K. Schweickert: *Die Musikpflege am Hofe der Kurfürsten von Mainz im 17. and 18. Jahrhundert* (Mainz, 1937); L. Strecker: *Richard Wagner als Verlagsgefährte* (Mainz, 1951); A. Gottron: *Mainzer Musikgeschichte 1500–1800*, Beiträge zur Geschichte der Stadt Mainz, xviii (Mainz, 1959); Plesske (1968); *Musikverlag B. Schott's Söhne Mainz: Kurze Verlagsgeschichte* (Mainz, 1971); *Festschrift für einen Verleger: Ludwig Strecker zum 90. Geburtstag* (Mainz, 1973); H.-C. Müller: *Bernhard Schott, Hofmusikstecher in Mainz: die Frühgeschichte seines Musikverlages bis 1797, mit einen Verzeichnis der Verlagswerke 1779–1797* (Mainz, 1977); *Ludwig van Beethoven: der Briefwechsel mit dem Verlag Schott*, ed. Beethoven-Haus, Bonn (Munich, 1985)

H.-C.M., F.D. (i), C.C.

Schuberth, E(dward). American firm of publishers. Edward Schuberth began his association with the New York branch of the Leipzig publisher Julius Schuberth in 1858. When the branch closed in 1872, he established his own publishing business in Union Square. His earliest publications were by German and German-trained musicians, and included songs with English and German words, German-American pieces such as Fritz Neumüller's *Campaign March for Grover Cleveland* (1884) and a series of European piano pieces edited by William Mason. Schuberth was the first American publisher of Victor Herbert's music, issuing his first five operettas, the Second Cello Concerto and some orchestral music. In the 1890s the firm published English translations of European operettas by Ludwig Engländer and Ede Poldini, which were popular in New York, as well as those by the American composer De Koven. Schuberth became recognized as one of the major American publishers of serious music and was among the few to participate in an exhibition organized by the highly esteemed Manuscript Society in 1895.

In 1902 E. Schuberth moved to 22nd Street. The firm had published songs by American composers such as Frederick Ritter, C. W. Cadman and W. W. Gilchrist as early as 1879, and by 1917 new items had doubled the size of its catalogue. Some of these songs enjoyed immense sales, especially *For You Alone*, made famous by

Caruso. The number of new titles soon declined sharply, however, and the New York office was closed. Schuberth moved to Carlstadt, New Jersey, in February 1971.

J.B.Y.

Schuberth, Julius (Ferdinand Georg) (*b* Magdeburg, 14 July 1804; *d* Leipzig, 9 June 1875). German publisher. He was the founder of the well-known firm of J. Schuberth & Co. at Leipzig and New York. After learning the business of a music publisher at Magdeburg, he started his own firm at Hamburg in 1826. He founded branch establishments at Leipzig (1832) and New York (1850). In 1854 he gave up the original Hamburg business to his brother Friedrich (1817–after 1890), who operated it as Fritz Schuberth; Julius then devoted himself to the Leipzig and New York branches. He edited a *Musikalisches Fremd-wörterbuch* (Hamburg, 1840, 8/1870), a *Musikalisches Conversationslexicon* (Leipzig, 1850, 10/1877; Eng. trans., 1895), the *Kleine Hamburger Musik Zeitung* (1840–50), the New York *Musik Zeitung* (1867) and *Schuberths kleine Musik Zeitung* (1871–2). In 1840 he founded the Norddeutscher Musikverein and received many decorations in recognition of his services to music. In 1874 he settled at Leipzig. His business, which by 1877 had issued over 6000 publications including works by Mendelssohn, Chopin, Schumann and Liszt, was carried on after his death with increasing success by his widow and nephew until 1891, when it was bought by F. Siegel.

Zur Geschichte des Musikverlags J. Schuberth & Co., Leipzig (Leipzig, 1926); Plesske (1968)

W.B.S./R

Schwickert. German firm of publishers, active 1772–1845. Founded by Engelhard Benjamin Schwickert, it was the most important typographic printer in Leipzig in the late 18th century. It issued many important works, including keyboard sonata collections by J. W. Hässler (1776, 1778) and D. G. Türk (1787, 1789), and other works by Türk; Georg Benda's keyboard concertos (1779, 1784) and violin concertos (1783); anthologies of keyboard pieces and songs (1779, 1783–8); and numerous opera vocal scores. His theoretical and pedagogical works include reprints of Leopold Mozart's violin school (1792), Albrechtsberger's *Gründliche Anweisung zur Composition* (1790), two editions of C.P.E. Bach's *Versuch* (1780, 1787) and J. N. Forkel's *Allgemeine Litteratur der Musik* (1792) as well as many other musical and literary works. The firm had a branch in Halle, 1792–1802.

A. Kirchhoff: 'Lesefrüchte aus den Acten des städtischen Archivs zu Leipzig', *Archiv für Geschichte des deutschen Buchhandels*, xiv (1891), 262; F. G. Meyer: 'Zum Transitrecht', ibid, 275

T.D.W.

Scotti, Luigi (*fl* Milan, *c*1815–1845). Italian engraver and publisher. He applied for permission to print music on 20 October 1826, declaring himself 43 years old and 'by profession a violinist at the Imperiale Regio Teatro alla Scala, and a teacher both of violin and cembalo in various private houses'. The licence was granted in December in recognition of his already well-known activity as an engraver. He had begun engraving music around 1815, his first works appearing in the *Catalogo di musica stampata di proprio fondo d'Antonio Monzino fabbricatore d'instrumenti e corde armoniche in Milano nella Contrada della Dogana al N. 4037*. Here the 21 pieces marked with an asterisk are given as the work of 'Luigi Scotti, music teacher and engraver in Milan'; they are all from before 1817 and include two arias from Rossini's *La pietra del paragone* (a joint edition with the publisher Carlo Bordoni), guitar music by Moretti and Monzino and instrumental chamber music, mostly by Milanese composers such as Pontelibero, Santambrogio, Soliva and Savj.

Scotti often changed premises, from the Contrada del Monte to the Contrada de' Bigli, and then to the Contrada delle Orsole. He worked until 1845, producing only a few editions each year but most of them engraved and printed on the best paper. The last known plate number is 167, *Sei duetti e canone per soprano e tenore o violino e violoncello con accompagnamento di pianoforte* by Carlo Soliva (issued jointly with G. Cattaneo of Turin and dedicated to Count Cesare di Castelbarco), almost all of whose compositions Scotti had printed.

A.Z.L.

Scotto. Italian family of booksellers, printers and composers.

(1) Ottaviano Scotto (i) (*b* Monza; *d* Venice, 24 Dec 1498). Printer and bookseller. He worked in Venice and, as a member of a patrician family, styled himself 'nobilis vir'. Philosophy, medicine, law and classical literature were prominent among his publications, and he was an important publisher of liturgical incunabula containing printed notes and staves. Scotto's 1481 edition of the Roman missal has spaces for music and, in some copies, printed staves on which music has been added by hand. Three books printed by Scotto in 1482 (two Roman missals and a Dominican missal) include black musical notation and red four-line staves, printed in two impressions, essentially the same method as that used by Petrucci. At least ten other printers occasionally worked for Scotto, and on his commission Johann Hamman printed, in the smaller octavo format, a Roman missal (1493), a Dominican missal (1494 or 1495) and another Roman missal (1497), all containing music and possibly printed from his type. Scotto's missals were notable achievements: that of 1481 was perhaps the second illustrated book to be printed in Venice; those of 1482 made him the first Venetian printer and the first native Italian to print music from movable type; and his missal of 1493 was the first in the small octavo format. The delicacy of his note forms and the accuracy of his registration set standards infrequently surpassed in the next three centuries of liturgical music printing. His printer's mark was an orb-and-cross device with the initials O[ctavianus] S[cotus] M[odoetiensis].

Ottaviano Scotto's heirs were his nephews, who published under the imprint 'heirs of Ottaviano Scotto' until 1532. Amadio Scotto (*fl* 1498–1532) supported Petrucci financially and Paolo Scotto (*fl* 1507–14) was a composer as well as a bookseller (Petrucci printed several frottolas and a *lauda* by him), but neither published any music.

(2) Ottaviano Scotto (ii) (*b* *c*1495; *d* ?Venice, *c*1568). Printer and bookseller, cousin of Amadio and nephew of (1) Ottaviano (i). His connection with music publishing began in 1516 when, according to a Roman contract, he was a financial backer of Andrea Antico's *Liber quindecim missarum*. In 1533 he took over the firm's main branch, presumably after Amadio's death, and from then until 1539 dominated Venetian music printing. Works by Verdelot, Willaert, Festa and Arcadelt, mostly madrigals, motets and chansons, make up the bulk of his 14 extant editions. All were xylographically produced by Antico.

Although he remained an owner of the press until at least 1566, Ottaviano left its active management to his brother (3) Girolamo in 1539, possibly because of his interests in medicine and philosophy, or because of illness, suggested by his drawing up of a will in 1544 and again in 1547. Very few books, none containing music, were printed by him after 1539. His last surviving publication is an Aristotelian

commentary issued jointly with Girolamo in 1552. Ottaviano died some time between 1567, when he was named in a contract, and 1569, when Girolamo referred to himself as sole owner of the press. Respected as an editor and scholar, Ottaviano is mentioned in the writings of several men of letters including Pietro Aretino, Antonio Mintorno and Antonfrancesco Doni.

In 1539 Ottaviano (iii) (*fl* 1539–63) and Brandino Scotto, Amadio's sons, printed Antico's last music publication, Willaert's second book of four-voice motets. The following year they issued a music treatise, Giovanni del Lago's *Breve introduttione di musica misurata* (1540/*R*1969). From 1541 until at least 1558 Ottaviano (iii) ran his own press, issuing publications in several subjects, many duplicating those of the family's main branch. He also worked as an agent for his cousin Girolamo. Ottaviano di Amadio probably had a hand in the printing of 18 unsigned musical works of 1545–7.

(3) Girolamo [Gerolamo, Geronimo] **Scotto** (*b* *c*1505; *d* Venice, 3 Sept 1572). Printer, bookseller and composer, nephew of (1) Ottaviano Scotto (i) and brother of (2) Ottaviano Scotto (ii). He is first named in a petition for a printing privilege of 1536. He assumed directorship of the press in 1539, when he issued seven music editions and an Aristotelian commentary, and financed a liturgical book. The advent of single-impression printing enabled him to make the house of Scotto one of the foremost music publishers of the 16th century. Of the over 800 publications that emanated from his press during his 33-year tenure, some 396 music editions survive, a number rivalled only by the output of his contemporary, Antonio Gardano.

Scotto favoured music editions devoted to individual composers rather than the anthologies so popular in northern European centres. His earliest books feature works by Willaert as well as by composers outside the Venetian orbit, including Gombert, Morales and Jacquet of Mantua. In 1540 he published Veggio's *Madrigali a quattro voci . . . con la gionta di sei altri di Arcadelth della misura a breve*, the first book of *note nere* madrigals to acknowledge the new style in its title. The following year he introduced to Venice the three-voice Neapolitan *canzone villanesche* with Nola's first and second books. In 1544 Scotto experimented with the layout of his publications. He issued Doni's *Dialogo della musica*, a musico-literary work, and five other editions in upright rather than the usual oblong quarto format. Upright quarto was not used again until 1564, after which all his quarto publications were upright.

A curious gap occurred in Girolamo's production of music in 1545–7, when only one music theory book, Pietro Aaron's *Lucidario*, was signed by him. Between these same years 22 music editions, including six lute books, were issued without a printer's name. Title-pages to four of them contain a woodcut of a burning salamander, a device used by Girolamo and other printers on several non-music publications (a larger version of this woodcut had appeared in Scotto's 1543 edition of Lupacchino's *Madrigali a quattro*). Typographical and archival evidence suggests that a consortium of bookmen delegated 18 of the editions to the house of Scotto. But Girolamo, busy with at least 56 non-music items, probably sub-contracted the music to other printers, in particular his cousin Ottaviano di Amadio (iii). At least three of the remaining editions, which use the same music type fount, were printed by Giacomo Fabriano and Bernardo Bindoni in Padua: Fabriano, a close associate of Scotto's, probably borrowed the fount from him.

Scotto continued to emphasize motets and madrigals in the 1550s and 1560s, turning to the works of a new generation of composers including Rore, Donato, Ruffo, Hoste da Reggio, Contino, Lassus and Striggio. In 1549–50 he also printed a handful of chanson collections, and in 1556 he brought out *Villancicos de diversos autores*, one of the few 16th-century editions of Spanish song to be printed outside Spain and the only Scotto publication in choir-book format.

Scotto issued many anthologies of *canzone villanesche*, changing their format in 1562 from oblong quarto to upright octavo. Between 1565 and 1568 the singer Giulio Bonagiunta published several important anthologies at the Scotto press. As noted in his dedications, Bonagiunta obtained and edited the music; he might also have helped finance the publications. Of special interest is the *Corona delle morte*, a collection honouring the literary figure Annibale Caro to which 15 composers and poets contributed madrigals, many based on Caro's name. Other significant editions during this period include Maddalena Casulana's two books of four-voice madrigals (1568, 1570), the first extant publications by a woman composer; Vincenzo Galilei's *Il Fronimo* (1568–9) and Barbetta's *Primo libro dell'intavolatura de liuto* (1569), Scotto's only music works issued in folio; and *Musica de virtuosi* (1569), an anthology assembled by Massimo Troiano containing madrigals by Lassus and others at the Bavarian court.

Early in his career Girolamo issued three editions of his own music. His *Primo libro a due voci* proved the most popular, being printed at least five times from 1541 to 1572. The didactic purpose of this and of his three-voice madrigals is unmistakable, since Scotto organized and labelled the pieces according to genre and mode.

Although Scotto frequently changed the designs of his title-pages, initials and text founts, he employed the same music fount for more than 20 years. He probably owned the punches and sold or leased the matrices to several other printers (including Gardano) who used the fount briefly in the 1540s. In 1554 he introduced a larger music fount ('stampa grosetta'), which he used more frequently in the 1560s.

Girolamo owned over 20 different printer's marks. The three main designs, which incorporated symbols of Venice and appeared in sizes to match various formats, are an anchor (symbolizing stability) surrounded by a palm frond (virtue) and an olive branch (peace) with the initials, S[ignum] O[ctaviani] S[coti]; a device depicting Fame with the initials O.S.M.; and a figure representing Peace atop a globe (see illustration).

Two of Girolamo Scotto's printer's marks from reprints (1558, 1551) of his own 'Il primo libro de i madrigali a due voci' (1541)

Scotto maintained close relationships with several music printers, including Francesco Rampazetto, whose music fount and initials appear in two Scotto publications of 1555 and 1556, Ricciardo Amadino, who witnessed Girolamo's will, and possibly Antonio dell'Abbate (? dell' Rovigo), publisher of *La courone et fleur des chansons a troys* (1536). His precise connection with Antonio Gardano is more difficult to ascertain. Scotto underwrote Gardano's 1541 edition of Jhan Gero's *Madrigali italiani*, *et canzoni francese a due voci*, which was in fact a reprint of a 1540 edition printed by Scotto. Throughout their long careers Scotto and Gardano reprinted a significant number of each other's titles, occasionally in the same year. Accusations of piracy have been levelled at one or the other, but no evidence substantiates a rivalry between the two. On the contrary, reprinting was common practice among Venetian printers in all fields. Scotto and Gardano obviously prospered from this relationship, since they maintained a near monopoly on Italian music printing for over 30 years.

Music printing was only one aspect of Girolamo's business. He also marketed books throughout Europe, held interests in retail shops in several Italian cities and acted as a publisher by underwriting the editions of other printers. He continued to issue liturgical books and works in medicine, classical literature, theology, vernacular history and literature and law. The speciality that won him respect and financial success was scholasticism, notably the Latin translations, commentaries and interpretations of Aristotle. In his *Pandectarum* of 1548 the Swiss bibliographer Conrad Gesner dedicated the preface on civic philosophy to Scotto, whose importance as a printer and publisher did not go unnoticed by his peers. In 1571 he was elected the first Prior of the Venetian Guild of Printers and Booksellers.

(4) **Melchiorre** [Marchiore, Marchiò] **Scotto** (*fl* 1565–1613). Printer and bookseller, nephew and heir of (3) Girolamo Scotto. He joined the Scotto press as early as 1565, when he was an agent for Girolamo. Taking over the firm at his uncle's death in 1572, he continued to print music in great quantity, with many editions of Asola, Palestrina, Ferretti, Giovannelli, Lassus, Monte and Alessandro Striggio and numerous anthologies and lute tablatures. He issued almost no music in the new concertato genres. Among his most elaborate books are Gasparo Fiorino's *La nobiltà di Roma* (1571–3), three volumes of compositions by Fernando de las Infantas (1578–9) and a reprint of Galilei's *Il Fronimo* (1584). His output represents the more conservative side of the market, both in his editions of earlier music and in his choice of contemporary composers. He continued the family's practice of printing non-musical books, but in much smaller numbers than previously. In his will he named his natural son Baldissera as heir, but because of Baldissera's illegitimacy the authorities confiscated the property and sold it at public auction.

RicordiE; VogelB; C. Gesner: *Pandectarum sive Partitionum universalium . . . libri XXI* (Zurich, 1548), 311; G. B. di Crollalanza: *Dizionario storico-blasonico delle famiglie nobili e notabili italiane estinte e fiorenti* (Pisa, 1886–90/R1965), iii, 513; H. Brown: *The Venetian Printing Press* (London, 1891/R1965), 87, 251; H. Riemann: *Notenschrift und Notendruck: bibliographisch-typographische Studie* (Leipzig, 1896/R1969), 51; R. Molitor: *Die nach-tridentinische Choral-Reform zu Rom*, i (Leipzig, 1901), 94; G. Scotti: 'L'antica famiglia varennate degli Scotti', *Periodico della Società storica per la provincia e antica diocesi di Como*, xxii (1915), 65–97; C. Volpati: 'Gli Scotti di Monza, tipografi-editori in Venezia', *Archivio storico lombardo*, xlix (1922), 365; V. Scholderer: *Catalogue of Books Printed in the XVth Century now in the British Museum*, v: *Venice* (London, 1924), pp.xxii, xxxix, 275; L. Moe: *Dance Music in Printed Italian Tablatures from 1507 to 1611* (diss., Harvard U., 1956), 8; K. Meyer-Baer: *Liturgical Music Incunabula: a Descriptive Catalogue* (London, 1962); C. W. Chapman: *Andrea Antico* (diss., Harvard U., 1964); B. Disertori: *Le frottole per canto e liuto intabulate da Franciscus Bossinensis*, IMi, new ser., iii (1964), 56, 582; C. Sartori: 'La famiglia degli editori Scotto', *AcM*, xxxvi (1964), 19; J. Haar: 'The Note Nere Madrigal', *JAMS*, xviii (1965), 22; G. Pollard: *The Distribution of Books by Catalogue from the Invention of Printing to A.D. 1800* (Cambridge, 1965); J. Haar: 'Notes on the "Dialogo della Musica" of Antonfrancesco Doni', *ML*, xlvii (1966), 198; C. Marciani: 'Editori tipografi librai veneti nel regno di Napoli nel Cinquecento', *Studi veneziani*, x (1968), 500; P. F. Grendler: *The Roman Inquisition and the Venetian Press, 1540–1605* (Princeton, 1977), 23; M. S. Lewis: *Antonio Gardane and his Publications of Sacred Music, 1538–55* (diss., Brandeis U., 1979); D. G. Cardamone: *The canzone villanesca alla napolitana and Related Forms, 1537–1570*, i (Ann Arbor, 1981), 13; R. J. Agee: *The Privilege and Venetian Music Printing in the Sixteenth Century* (diss., Princeton U., 1982); T. W. Bridges: *The Publishing of Arcadelt's First Book of Madrigals* (diss., Harvard U., 1982); D. G. Cardamone: *Madrigali a tre et arie napoletane: a Typographical and Repertorial Study*, *JAMS*, xxxv (1982), 436–81; R. J. Agee: 'The Venetian Privilege and Music-Printing in the Sixteenth Century', *Early Music History*, iii (1983), 1–42; Mischiati (1984); J. Bernstein: 'The Burning Salamander: Assigning a Printer to some 16th-century Music Prints', *Notes*, xlii (1985–6), 483; R. J. Agee: 'A Venetian Music Printing Contract and Edition Size in the Sixteenth Century', *Studi musicali*, xv (1986), 59; S. Boorman: 'Some Non-conflicting Attributions, and Some Newly Anonymous Compositions, from the Early Sixteenth Century', *Early Music History*, vi (1986), 109–57; G. M. Ongaro: *The Chapel of St. Mark's at the Time of Adrian Willaert (1527–1562): an Archival Study* (diss., U. of North Carolina, 1986), 207

T.W.B.(1,4), J.A.B.(2,3)

Segebade, Lorenz (*b* Krummenhagen, 1584; *d* Königsberg, 22 Aug 1638). German printer. Trained as a bookbinder, he registered as a university book dealer in Königsberg on 27 March 1620. After 4 April 1623 he also became known as a printer, and, having bought Johann Schmidt's printing facilities, received a privilege on 6 July 1626. His several dozen vocal editions are mostly by the local composers Jonas Zornicht, Heinrich Albert and especially Johann Stobaeus. After his death his wife Elisabeth oversaw the shop for two years, but it was his son Josua, with Elisabeth's second husband Pascha Mense, who operated it until 1671. Works by Albert and Stobaeus were occasionally reprinted by Mense and by Johann Reusner.

Benzing (1963, 2/1982); D. W. Krummel: 'Early German Partbook Type Faces', *Gutenberg-Jb 1985*, 80

T.D.W.

Senart. French firm of publishers, active in Paris. It was founded by Maurice Senart (*b* Paris, 29 Jan 1878; *d* Paris, 23 May 1962) in 1908 in partnership with B. Roudanez. Senart directed the company alone from 1912 to 1920, when, in association with Albert Neuburger, it was reorganized as the Société Anonyme des Editions Maurice Senart.

Senart rapidly created a large catalogue (5000 works by 1925), including a number of important collections. The first was a series of popularly priced classics, edited by Vincent d'Indy and chiefly selected from the repertory of the Schola Cantorum. The firm later published *Les maîtres contemporains de l'orgue* (8 vols., 1912, ed. J. Joubert); *La musique de chambre* (extensive periodic collection of vocal and instrumental music with emphasis on modern works, ed. J. Peyrot and J. Rebuffat); *Edition nationale de musique classique* (begun in 1930, including Cortot's editions of music by Chopin, Liszt and Schumann); *Les maîtres français du violon au XVIIIe siècle* (ed. J. Debroux); *Chants de France et d'Italie* and *Les maîtres musiciens de la renaissance française* (both ed. H. Expert). The Senart catalogue includes compositions by Cras, Casella, Delannoy, Harsányi, Inghelbrecht, Jaques-Dalcroze, Koechlin, Malipiero, Migot, Milhaud and Rivier, and most of Honegger's early works. Editions Salabert bought the entire catalogue in 1941.

R.S.N.

Senefelder, Alois (*b* Prague, Nov 1771; *d* Munich, 26 Feb 1834). Bavarian actor and playwright and the inventor of lithography. He was the son of Franz Peter Senefelder, an actor who joined the court theatre of the Elector of Bavaria in 1778. Educated first at the Munich Gymnasium and the Electoral Lyceum, he then followed his father's wishes and studied law at Ingolstadt University; however, after his father's death he left the university and took up acting.

Even as a student he had written successful plays, and as he wrote more he sought a cheap method of printing them because letterpress and engraving were very expensive. He first experimented with etched Solnhofen stone (apparently in ignorance of the fact that this process had been in limited use since 1550) and in association with Franz Gleissner (a composer and player in the electoral band) printed some music in 1796 (for illustration *see* fig.18, p.56) and early 1797 which was issued by the Munich music publisher Falter. Later in 1797 Senefelder discontinued etching and perfected his 'chemical printing'. He wrote on the stone with greasy ink and coated the surface with a mixture of water, acid and gum arabic. He inked the surface and the ink was absorbed by the writing. The resulting impression could be taken directly from the surface of the stone. The first music so printed was a selection from *Die Zauberflöte* made by Franz Danzi.

Thenceforward, almost until his death, Senefelder continued to experiment and improve the process, which had vast commercial possibilities. He received a 15-year privilege in 1799 and in partnership with the influential music publisher J. A. André of Offenbach began to develop lithography all over Europe. Late in 1800 Senefelder went to London where he received letters patent on 20 June 1801; he established his Chemische Druckerey in Vienna on 27 July 1803 (*see* HASLINGER).

From its early days, lithography was used for the reproduction of works of art as well as for music. The famous *Specimens of Polyautography* (London, 1803) is an example of the delicacy of this new medium and the inspiration it could give to artists. But it was in the cheap, clear printing of music that there lay the most far-reaching benefits of lithography and its revolutionary development later in the 19th century. Senefelder himself described his work in *Vollständiges Lehrbuch der Steindruckerey* (Munich, 1818), which was translated into English by A. Schlichtegroll as *A Complete Course of Lithography* (London, 1819), and later as *The Invention of Lithography*, translated by J. W. Muller (London, 1911).

F. M. Ferchl: *Uebersicht der einzig bestehenden, vollständigen Incunabeln-Sammlung der Lithographie* (Munich, 1856); W. Graeff: *Die Einführung der Lithographie in Frankreich* (Heidelberg, 1906); C. Wagner: *Aloys Senefelder: sein Leben, und Wirken* (Leipzig, 1914, 2/1943); B. A. Wallner: 'Die Senefelder-Ausstellung in der Bayerische Staatsbibliothek zu München', *ZMw*, iv (1921); 182;

L. Dussler: *Die Incunabeln der deutschen Lithographie, 1796–1821* (Berlin, 1925); E. Metzger: *Weltruhm aus bayerischen Steinplatten: Alois Senefelder, der deutsche Erfinder der Steindruckkunst* (Leipzig, 1938); E. Lebeau: *Les débuts ignorés de l'imprimerie lithographique, Charenton, Paris, 1802–1806* (Auxerre, 1952); King (1964); F. H. Man, ed.: *Homage to Senefelder: Artists' Lithographs from the Felix H. Man Collection* (London, 1971) [Victoria and Albert Museum exhibition catalogue]; A. Weinmann: *Vollständiges Verlagsverzeichnis Senefelder-Steiner-Haslinger* (Munich, 1979–83)

A.H.K.

Senff, Bartolf Wilhelm (*b* Friedrichshall, nr. Coburg, 2 Sept 1815; *d* Badenweiler, 24 June 1900). German publisher. He served his apprenticeship with the music publisher C. F. Kistner in Leipzig, and in 1843 founded the periodical *Signale für die musikalische Welt*, which he edited up to his death. He left Kistner in 1847 to set up an independent publishing house that issued works by Schumann, Liszt, Brahms, Schubert, Bruch, Rubinstein, Bülow, Marschner, Raff, Hiller, Reinecke, Reitz and others; his catalogue of 1898 also includes 46 operas (with piano reductions by Kleinmichel). In his capacity as editor of *Signale* he was often reproached with being lukewarm towards Wagner. After his death the publishing firm was managed by his niece, and in 1907 it was sold with the *Signale* to Simrock.

Katalog des Musikalien-Verlages von Bartolf Senff (Leipzig, 1890; suppl. 1898); R. Kleinmichel: Obituary, *Signale für die musikalische Welt*, lviii (1900), 657

T.W.

Sennewald. Polish firm of publishers. It was founded by Gustav Adolf Sennewald (*b* Bielsko, 26 Jan 1804; *d* Warsaw, 16 July 1860), who worked in the firm of Antoni Brzezina during the 1820s. In 1829 he became a joint owner, taking over after Brzezina's death in 1831. Sennewald was a publisher, bookseller and owner of a lithographic works. The firm was continued by his son Karol Gustav Sennewald (*b* Warsaw, 9 April 1833; *d* Warsaw, 11 March 1896) who was also a founder of the Warsaw Music Society. His son Władysław Gustav Sennewald (*b* Warsaw, 9 Sept 1860; *d* Warsaw, 19 April 1929) took over the firm after his father's death; he sold it in 1901. It continued until 1905 under the name Gustav Sennewald – Księgarnia i Skład Nut Muzycznych.

The firm published mainly vocal and piano music, including melodies from contemporary European operas, songs and romances for voice and piano by such 19th-century Polish composers as Stefani,

Troszel, Zarzycki and Zeleński, and mazurkas, waltzes and polkas for the piano by Kraszewski, Kania, Roguski, Troszel and Lewandowski. The firm also published Moniuszko's operas *Flis* and *Verbum nobile* and his operetta *Jawnuta*, some pieces for the violin, string orchestra and military band, a few school books, and editions of early Polish music including ten psalms by Gomółka and two masses by Gorczycki.

T.C. (ii)

Sensenschmidt, Johann (*b* Eger; *d* Bamberg, before 13 June 1491). German printer. In 1496 he was in Nuremberg, working partly with Knefl and Andreas Frisner. In 1480 he moved to Bamberg at the request of Abbot Ulrich III of the Michaelsberg monastery and set up a printing press there to print the *Missale benedictinum* (1481). As an itinerant printer (the first of Freising, Regensburg and Dillingen), he accepted commissions to print the liturgical books of various south German dioceses and monasteries. In 1487 he began to use a strong, well-cut gothic chant type to print at least eight missals with music. After his death, his son Lorenz inherited the press and, with the music printer Johann Pfeyl, issued three more liturgical books with music in 1491 and 1492. Pfeyl took over the press in 1495 and continued printing music with his own types.

K. Meyer-Baer: *Liturgical Music Incunabula: a Descriptive Catalogue* (London, 1962); F. Geldner: *Die deutschen Inkunabeldrucker: ein Handbuch der deutschen Buchdrucker des XV. Jahrhunderts nach Druckorten*, i (Stuttgart, 1968), 52

M.K.D.

Seres, William (*fl* 1546–77). English printer. In 1553 he acquired a monopoly for printing psalms, through the influence of Sir William Cecil; in the same year he printed two volumes that included music, Francis Seagar's *Certayne Psalmes select out of the Psalter of David, and drawen into Englyshe Metre, with Notes to every Psalme* and Christopher Tye's *The Actes of the Apostles*. Seres continued to work as a printer, but no other example of printed music survives from his press. He is generally supposed to have been in partnership with John Day, who acquired the sole right to print the English Metrical Psalter with music in 1559. Seres had several addresses in London during his career; in 1553 he was working 'at the sygne of the Hedge-Hogg'.

H. G. Aldis: *A Dictionary of Printers and Booksellers in England, Scotland and Ireland . . . 1557–1640* (London, 1910); Humphries and Smith (1954, 2/ 1970); Krummel (1975)

M.M.

Shapiro, Bernstein & Co. American firm of publishers. It was founded in New York in 1895 by Maurice Shapiro (*b* Germany, Jan 1873; *d* New York, 1 June 1911) and Louis Bernstein (*b* New York, 13 March 1878; *d* New York, 15 Feb 1962) after they had purchased the Orphean Music Co., which had had a great success with Harry Von Tilzer's song *My old New Hampshire home.* Shapiro and Bernstein engaged Von Tilzer as a staff songwriter, and in 1897 made him a partner in the firm Shapiro, Bernstein & Von Tilzer. (Von Tilzer later left the company and in 1902 founded his own business.) After Shapiro's death Bernstein established the firm Shapiro, Bernstein & Co., with himself and his sister Fanny (Shapiro's widow) as owners. Fanny's son Elliott Shapiro (*b* New York, 1895; *d* New York, 2 Feb 1956) became a vice-president of the company and was expected to succeed his uncle, but died before him; on Bernstein's death in 1962 the firm was taken over by his son-in-law, Richard Voltter. The firm published several successful songs, including *Let me call you sweetheart* (1910), *My melancholy baby* (1912), *Sweet Sue, just you* (1928), *On the sunny side of the street* (1930), *Wagon Wheels* (1934) and *Melody of Love* (1954).

F.B.

Shaw, Joseph P. (*b* England, 1808; *d* Rochester, NY, 1899). American publisher. He opened a music shop in Rochester, New York, in 1854, though his earliest publication is believed to be John Kalbfleisch's piano nocturne *Twilight Hour* (1857). He went on to issue more than 200 titles between 1857 and 1899, becoming Rochester's principal music publisher; his works were widely distributed in the eastern USA. The bulk of his sheet music output consisted of songs, dances and short instrumental pieces by local and international composers, but he also published collections and pedagogical works, including Cecilia Cary's *Piano Class Book* in at least four editions, and the *Rochester Musical Times* (1869–77). Carefully chosen and tastefully printed, Shaw's publications reveal a cross-section of late 19th-century middle-class taste; they often celebrate memorable events and places in local history.

Dichter and Shapiro (1941, 2/1977); S. A. Kohler, ed.: *Music Publishing in Rochester, 1859–1930* (Rochester, 1975)

R.T.W.

Shawnee Press. American firm of publishers. It was founded by Fred Waring in Delaware Water Gap, Pennsylvania in 1939 as Words and Music and incorporated as the Shawnee Press in 1947; it is a division of Waring Enterprises, Inc. The firm was originally set up to provide copies for loan of the popular choral arrangements performed by Waring's Pennsylvanians. Public demand eventually was such that the press was established to publish the editions under the series title *Fred Waring Choral Arrangements.* Since then Shawnee has expanded and specializes in educational material, catering to the needs and abilities of elementary and secondary school ensembles and college performing groups, both instrumental and choral. In 1970 the firm purchased Harold Flammer, Inc., which manages the church music catalogue; other divisions are GlorySound, specializing in gospel music, and Omnisound, which issues recordings. Although Shawnee publishes works composed mainly in a serious contemporary idiom (besides music for schools, it has published Andrew Imbrie's opera *Angle of Repose* and some of the works of the pianist Alec Templeton), its repertory encompasses music from all periods, as well as folk music, spirituals and music from shows; all items are graded according to their degree of difficulty. The firm has also introduced a video cassette series, the *Choreo Collection*, to help performers learn choreography or movement while singing.

G. le Coat: 'L'édition musicale et l'enseignement du chant dans les écoles des Etats-Unis', *Revue musicale de Suisse Romande*, xxi/4 (1968), 4

F.B.

Sherman, Leander S. (*b* Boston, 28 April 1847; *d* San Francisco, 5 April 1926). American music dealer and publisher. He went to San Francisco in 1861 as a clerk and repairer of music boxes, and opened his first music shop there in 1870. In 1871 he formed a partnership with his brother-in-law F. A. Hyde (Sherman & Hyde), but Hyde sold his holdings in 1876 to Clement Comer Clay, a wholesale grocer from Memphis. Music publishing began as a minor part of the activities of Sherman, Clay & Co. in the 1870s (notably in *Sherman and Hyde's Musical Review*; monthly, 1874–9), but the firm flourished in the first decades of the 20th century, when sales of popular sheet music reached more than a million copies and publishing offices were set up in many American cities. With the acquisition of the Steinway agency from Matthias Gray in 1892 and the exclusive West Coast agency for the Victor Talking Machine Company, Sherman's business grew to a position of prominence in northern California. Sherman, Clay continues today as an instrument and music dealer.

D. W. Ryder: *The Story of Sherman, Clay & Co., 1870–1952* (San Francisco, 1952); M. K. Duggan: 'Music Publishing and Printing in San Francisco before the Earthquake & Fire of 1906', *Kemble Occasional*, no.24 (1980); idem: 'Music Publishing and Printing in San Francisco before the Earthquake & Fire of 1906: Directory', *Kemble Occasional*, no.30 (1983); R. Stevenson: 'California Pioneer Sheet Music Publishers and Publications', *Inter-American Music Review*, viii/1 (1986), 48

M.K.D.

Short, Peter (*d* 1603). English printer. He already had a flourishing general printing business when, in 1597, he first began to print music. From about 1584 he had established premises in Bread Street Hill, London, at the 'signe of the Starre'; all his printed music bears that imprint. In 1597 he issued six major musical works, John Dowland's *The First Booke of Songes or Ayres*, Antony Holborne's *The Cittharn Schoole*, William Hunnis's *Seven Sobs of a Sorrowfull Soule for Sin* and Morley's *Canzonets or Little Short Aers, Canzonets or Little Short Songes* and *A Plaine and Easie Introduction to Practicall Musicke* (see illustration).

The layout of the pages in the Dowland volume established the English 'table-book' style for printing lutesongs, a style adopted by all other London printers for music of this kind. The *Plaine and Easie Introduction to Practicall Musicke*, a remarkably complex volume, includes among its many diagrams and illustrations the only surviving example of two-colour printing from London at this period; this volume alone would have been sufficient proof of Short's skill. He worked with type and possessed one of the few tablature founts known to have been used in London at that time. He printed only seven more music volumes, two of which were reprints of Dowland's *First Booke of Songes or Ayres*. On his death in 1603, Short's widow published a few titles, and in 1604 married Humfrey Lownes, who took over the business.

S. P. Thompson: 'Peter Short, Printer, and his Marks', *Transactions of the Bibliographical Society*, iv (1898), 123; O. E. Deutsch: 'The Editions of Morley's *Introduction*', *The Library*, 4th ser., xxiii (1942–3), 127; Humphries and Smith (1954, 2/1970); Krummel (1975)

M.M.

Sidler, Joseph (Anton) (*b* Munich, 1785; *d* Munich, 24 March 1835). German lithographer and publisher. He was the son of the court violin maker Gregor Sidler (1753–1829). First active as a court viola player, he trained as a lithographer with

Senefelder's colleagues and in 1807 founded his own shop, which was granted a special privilege in 1811. Besides trading in lithography and printing copperplate pictures, he executed from 1812 a series of music editions, both on his own account and for other publishers (notably Falter & Sohn). He seems to have employed no plate numbers (the few exceptions were probably added later). In spite of his long-standing activity as a music printer, he was known chiefly as an art dealer and not officially recognized as a music publisher until 6 February 1827. He was appointed 'Hofmusikalien- und Instrumentenhändler' on 5 November 1827, but for unknown reasons gave up the music publishing side of his lithography business to Falter & Sohn as early as 1828 or 1829.

L. Weinhold: *Joseph Anton Sidler: ein Münchner Lithograph, Musikalienhändler und Musikverleger der Biedermeierzeit (1785–1835)*, Musik in Bayern, xxii (1981), 163–239

H.S.

Sieber, Georges-Julien (*b* Paris, 15 Nov 1775; *d* Passy, 22 Jan 1847). French publisher and composer, son of Jean-Georges Sieber. He studied harmony with H.-M. Berton at the Paris Conservatoire, and worked in his father's publishing business from about 1795. In August 1798 he married Anne-Marie, daughter of the publisher Pierre Leduc. On 25 January 1799 he announced that he had just opened a shop at 1245 rue de la Loi, where he traded as Sieber Fils at the sign of 'La flûte enchantée'. The house was renumbered 28 between 10 May and 28 September 1805, and the street reverted to its pre-Revolutionary name, rue de Richelieu, between July 1806 and July 1807. In 1812 Sieber moved to 21 rue des Filles St Thomas, where the firm remained. In 1824 he took over his father's business and in 1834 retired, being succeeded by his son Adrien-Georges (*b* Paris, 26 June 1802; *d* Paris, 17 Oct 1872). By 1847 Adrien was a bandmaster and in April the plates and stock were sold by auction. With that of Jean-Georges, Georges-Julien's output as a publisher was strongly biased towards instrumental music by foreign composers. In particular he published a great quantity of piano music, including numerous works by Clementi, J. B. Cramer, Dussek, Gelinek and Steibelt. He also published at least 35 of his own works, mainly piano sonatas, fantasias, variations, contredanses and quadrilles, and nocturnes for piano and horn. All the firm's publications were engraved. From his shop, as well as retailing the music of all publishers, he sold

426

Title-page of Thomas Morley's 'A Plaine and Easie Introduction to Practicall Musicke' (1597)

instruments, ran a lending library and offered music binding facilities.

For bibliography *see* SEIBER, JEAN-GEORGES

R.M.

Sieber, Jean-Georges (*b* Reiterswiesen, 2 Feb 1738; *d* Paris, 13 Jan 1822). French publisher and instrumentalist. He went to Paris in 1758 and was employed as a horn player in several orchestras there, 1762–86; he also worked occasionally as a harpist and a trombonist.

At some time between 2 July 1770 and 28 January 1771, in partnership with a Signor Fischer, he took over the stock and premises (in the rue des Deux Ecus) of the publisher Huberty; but the arrangement was short-lived, for between August and November 1771 Huberty resumed publishing, reclaiming both his former stock and premises. Sieber moved to the rue St-Honoré, where he established his business in the Hôtel d'Aligre (formerly Hôtel du Grand Conseil). By March 1782 he had moved to the building opposite, 92 rue St-Honoré, which was renumbered 85 in, or soon after, 1792. About 1802 he moved back to the Hôtel d'Aligre; at first the house number was 99, but in 1803 it was altered to 199 and in 1805 to 123. In February 1813 Sieber moved to 22 rue Coquillière, remaining there until his death. His son, Georges-Julien Sieber, worked with him from about 1795, when the firm was called Sieber Père et Fils. After Georges-Julien had left to found his own business in 1799, Sieber styled himself Sieber Père.

According to Choron and Fayolle, it was J. C. Bach who dissuaded Sieber from buying an existing business and suggested that he would do better to start afresh and make direct approaches to eminent foreign composers. Whether or not Bach had any part in it, Sieber certainly showed uncommonly good judgment in the works he chose to publish. Unlike most of his Parisian contemporaries, he did not indulge the popular taste for trivia: the greater part of his output consisted of good editions of music by first-rate international composers. Among the publications of his first two years were chamber works by J. C. Bach, Dittersdorf, Eichner, Gossec, Haydn, Schobert and Stamitz; he continued to publish the instrumental and symphonic works of the Mannheim school, of Italians like Boccherini, Cambini, Fiorillo, Giardini, Pugnani, Tessarini and Viotti, and of J. C. Bach, Gossec, Gyrowetz, Kreutzer, Pleyel, Vanhal and Wranitzky. He published the first editions of six of Mozart's piano and violin sonatas (к301–6/293*a–d*, 300*c* and 300*l*) in 1778 and of the Paris Symphony

(к297/300*a*) in *c*1778, as well as early editions of some two dozen other works; but in 1783 he turned down Mozart's offer of three piano concertos and six string quartets. He published more than 50 of Haydn's symphonies in parts and numerous chamber works. Sieber also published or reissued at least 35 operas in full score, mainly French adaptations of Italian works; these included operas by J. C. Bach (*Amadis des Gaules*), Cimarosa, Duni (12 works), Kreutzer (*Lodoïska*), Paisiello and Sarti, and *Laurette* (based on *La vera costanza*), the only Haydn opera published in contemporary full score. He also enjoyed the dubious distinction of being the first to publish the full score of *Die Zauberflöte*, but in the infamous version by Lachnith entitled *Les mistères d'Isis* (1801).

All Sieber's publications were engraved and from about 1789 bore plate numbers (earlier works were given plate numbers when reissued). The date of his death is often given as 1815, but there are references to him in directories until 1822 as a 'pensionnaire de l'Opéra'. His firm continued to advertise their publications in his name until September 1822; but the last advertisement that month was inserted by 'Veuve Sieber.'

Les Spectacles de Paris, xii–xxxvi (Paris, 1763–87); A. Choron and F. Fayolle: *Dictionnaire historique des musiciens*, ii (Paris, 1811/*R*1970), 316; G. Cucuel: 'Notes sur quelques musiciéns, luthiers, éditeurs et graveurs de musique au XVIIIe siècle', *SIMG*, xiv (1912–13), 243; G. de Saint-Foix: 'Les éditions françaises de Mozart 1765–1801', *Mélanges de musicologie offerts à M. Lionel de la Laurencie* (Paris, 1933), 247; Hopkinson (1954); Johansson (1955); H. C. R. Landoň: *The Collected Correspondence and London Notebooks of Joseph Haydn* (London, 1959), 84ff; D. W. Krummel: 'Late 18th Century French Music Publishers' Catalogues in the Library of Congress', *FAM*, vii (1960–62), 61; A. Devriès: 'Les éditions musicales Sieber', *RdM*, lv (1969), 20; Devriès and Lesure (1979–88)

R.M.

Siegling. American publisher and music dealer, active in Charleston, South Carolina. John Siegling founded a publishing firm at 69 Broad Street in 1819. In 1831 it moved to King Street at the corner of Beaufain, where it remained in operation until 1955. It was the most extensive music publisher in the early South. In 1858 the firm was headed by Henry Siegling, and in 1905 the name was changed to Siegling Music House. Among Siegling's publications is *The Palmetto State Song* (1860), commemorating South Carolina's secession from the union. The South Carolina Historical Society houses the Siegling Music

House Collection, consisting of music and business records relating to the company's operations from 1820.

Dichter and Shapiro (1941, 2/1977); Wolfe (1964); D. W. Krummel and others: *Resources in American Music History* (Urbana, 1981)

C.E.

Sikorski. German firm of publishers. In 1935 Hans Sikorski (*b* Posen [now Poznań], 30 Sept 1899; *d* Tegernsee, 22 Aug 1972) founded a drama and music publishing concern whose main publications were popular and entertainment music. In 1948 Hamburg became the headquarters of the group, which now includes more than 20 subsidiary firms. Publications cover a wide range of music including operas, symphonies, chamber music, operettas and musicals. The firm has published works by such contemporary composers as W. Abendroth, T. Berger, N. Dostal, H. Herrmann, K. Höller, Kabalevsky, Khachaturian, Künnecke, Prokofiev, Riethmüller, Shostakovich, Wellesz and H. Wirth. It is also noted for its publications of school music, methods for guitar, recorder, violin and other instruments, and music literature.

Musikverlage in der Bundesrepublik Deutschland und in West-Berlin (Bonn, 1965), 66

T.W.

Silvani, Giuseppe Antonio (*b* Bologna, 21 Jan 1672; *d* Bologna, *c*1727). Italian publisher and composer. Son of the Bolognese music publisher Marino Silvani, he and his brother Matteo took over the business after their father's death in 1711. He was the sole owner possibly from 1712, and certainly from 1716. In addition to printing works by Aldrovandini, Pistocchi, Tosi and Mazzaferrata, he also published several of his own compositions of sacred music in the Bolognese late Baroque style.

The publishing house of Silvani found itself in serious financial difficulties in 1723 and had to be mortgaged; evidently the firm was liquidated by 1727. A list of works published by the firm exists, probably from 1724. The date of Silvani's death is reported in the index of the *Defonti della celebre Accademia de' Filarmonici di Bologna* as 1728. However, an index of the firm's printed works dating from 1727 mentions the heirs of G. Silvani, so his death probably occurred shortly before that date.

P. M. Monti: *Indice dell'opere di musica sin'ora stampate in Bologna, e si vendono da G. A. Silvani* (Bolgona, 1724); *Indice dell'opere in musica sin'ora stampate in Bologna, e si fanno vendere dalli eredi di G. A. Silvani* (Bologna, 1727); *Inventario di tutte le opere di musica ritrovate nello stato del fù Sig. Giuseppe Silvani* (MS, Bologna, Civico Museo Bibliografico Musicale H/67, ff.124–8); *Defonti della celebre Accademia de' Filarmonici di Bologna* (Bologna, 1764); F. Vatielli: 'Editori musicali dei secoli XVII e XVIII', *Arte e vita musicale a Bologna* (Bologna, 1927/R1969); Sartori (1958); Mischiati (1984)

A.S. (ii)

Silvani, Marino (*d* Bologna, 1711). Italian publisher and editor. He began his career as a seller of books and music, trading 'at the sign of the violin'. He occasionally used the presses of the Bolognese printer Giacomo Monti, particularly for the anthologies of Bolognese music that he edited (*Sacri concerti*, 1668[2]; *Nuova raccolta di motetti sacri*, 1670[1]; *Canzonette per camera a voce sola*, 1670[3]; *Scielta di suonate a due violini, con il basso continuo*, 1680[7]), and for several other publications in 1683–4. From at least 1665 until his death he also did his own printing. His music publications include both sacred and instrumental music by Bassani, Cazzati, Aldrovandini, Cherici, G. P. Colonna, and his son Giuseppe Antonio Silvani, Corelli, Jacchini and Manfredini. He published at least three lists of his printed works in 1698–9, 1704 [?1701] and 1709 [?1707]. After his death his heirs continued the firm, publishing a reprint of Corelli's op.5 and G. A. Silvani's op.7 (both in 1711). Later the firm took the name of G. A. Silvani; its typographical mark was a basket of fruit and musical instruments, or a violin with the motto 'UTRElevet MIserum FAtum SOLitosque LAbores'.

F. Chrysander: 'Der italienische Musikverlag um 1700', *AMZ*, iv (1869), 137; F. Vatielli: 'Editori musicali dei secoli XVII e XVIII', *Arte e vita musicale a Bologna* (Bologna, 1927/R1969), 239; L. Gottardi: *La stampa musicale in Bologna dagli inizi fino al 1700* (diss., U. of Bologna, 1951); Sartori (1958); Mischiati (1984)

A.S. (ii)

Silver Burdett. American firm of publishers. It was founded in Boston in 1885 by Edgar O. Silver (*b* Bloomfield, VT, 1860; *d* East Orange, NJ, 18 Nov 1909), whose interest in elementary music education led him to buy the rights to *The Normal Music Course* (1883) by Hosea E. Holt and John W. Tufts from its original publisher, Appleton. Silver continued to address the needs of the school music system, planning arrangements of works to fit the vocal capabilities of children. Frank W. Burdett (*b* Boston, 29 Oct 1858; *d* Brookline, MA, 5 Nov 1919) entered the publishing business after completing his education at Harvard University, and purchased a partnership in the firm. Silver Burdett has expanded to become a major publisher of primary and secondary school textbooks, and also issues instrumental methods, choral material and recordings. *Making Music your Own*, a graded programme of music education for children, first issued in 1966, includes recorded discussions of their music by ten composers: Barber, Carlos Chávez, Copland, Cowell, Creston, Dello Joio, Luening, Richard Rodgers, William Schuman and Stravinsky. The company moved to Morristown, New Jersey, in 1955, and is part of the SFN group of publishing companies. Patrick Donaghy became president in 1981.

F.B.

Simpson, John (*d* London, *c*1749). English publisher, instrument maker and engraver, established in London. He was employed by John Hare's widow, Elizabeth, until her retirement in 1734, when he set up in business for himself, taking over the trade sign from Mrs Hare and probably also her stock and plates. He also had connections for a short time with Thomas Cobb, and when James Oswald arrived in London in 1741 he may have worked for Simpson, who published some of his compositions.

Simpson's early publications were mostly sheet songs, which were later gathered into the two volumes of *Thesaurus musicus* containing the earliest known appearance of *God Save the King*. Other notable publications were Henry Carey's *The Musical Century* (3/1744), *The Delightful Pocket Companion* (*c*1745), a reissue of *Calliope* (1746–7), Thomas Arne's *The Musick in the Masque of Comus* (*c*1749) and *Lyric Harmony* (*c*1746–8), and Gluck's *Six Sonatas for Two Violins & a Thorough Bass* (1746).

After his death Simpson was succeeded by his widow Ann, with Maurice Whitaker as manager, and the business continued in her name until she married John Cox in 1751. At Cox's retirement in 1764 many of Simpson's plates were acquired by Robert Bremner, Henry Thorowgood, the Thompson family and John Walsh the younger. The business passed into the hands of James Simpson, son of John and Ann, who about 1767 took his own son, John, into the firm, which continued until about 1795. They were mainly active as violin and flute makers, but published a small quantity of music, mostly single sheet songs. They were presumably related to James Simpson jr, who was at Sweeting's Alley from about 1796 to 1799.

Humphries and Smith (1954, 2/1970)

F.K., W.C.S./P.W.J.

Simrock. German firm of publishers. Nicolaus Simrock (*b* Mainz, 23 Aug 1751; *d* Bonn, 12 June 1832), a horn player in the electoral orchestra in Bonn who by 1780 was dealing in printed music and musical instruments, founded the firm there in 1793; Heinrich [Henri] Simrock founded a branch in Paris in 1802 and in 1812 Peter Joseph Simrock (*b* Bonn, 18 Aug 1792; *d* Cologne, 13 Dec 1868) founded a branch in Cologne, taking over the firm from his father Nicolaus Simrock in 1832. He was followed in 1868 by his son Friedrich August [Fritz] Simrock (*b* Bonn, 2 Jan 1837; *d* Ouchy, 20 Aug 1901), who moved the firm to Berlin in 1870. From 1901 to 1910 one of Fritz Simrock's nephews, Johann Baptist [Hans] Simrock (*b* Cologne, 17 April 1861; *d* Berlin, 26 July 1910) directed the firm and established a subsidiary in Leipzig (1904) as well as agencies in London, New York and Paris. In 1907 the firm acquired the Bartolf Senff publishing house of Leipzig. Richard Chrzescinski was manager from 1910 to 1920; he was succeeded by Fritz Auckenthaler (*b* 17 Nov 1893), a nephew of Fritz Simrock who took over the publisher Eos in 1925. The firm was sold to the Anton J. Benjamin-Verlag of Leipzig in 1929 but retained its original name; from 1938 to 1951 it belonged to the group of Sikorski music publishing houses, Leipzig. The firm was then returned to the Schauer family (the heirs of the former owners, Benjamin), who manage it in Hamburg and London within the Benjamin-Rahter-Simrock publishing organization.

Through his friendship with the young Beethoven, Nicolaus Simrock published the Kreutzer Sonata op.47 (1805) and the Variations for flute and piano op.107; and when Haydn visited Bonn in 1790, Simrock met him and the firm subsequently published *Sechs leichte Trios* op.21 (1796), the London symphonies nos. 7, 9 and 10 (1801) and a collection of 37 symphonies under the title *Symphonies à grand orchestre* (1810). Simrock published compositions by Carl Maria von Weber from 1808 and encouraged the reprinting of works by Bach (*Das wohltemperirte Clavier*, 1800; solo, violin sonatas, 1802; *Magnificat*, 1811; Mass in B minor, 1833, with Nägeli of Zurich) and Handel (Psalm c, 1821; *Messiah*, 1823; *Alexander's Feast*, 1825; *Israel in Egypt*, 1826); he was also interested in promoting German folksong. Under Peter Joseph Simrock works by Mendelssohn (*Lieder ohne Worte, St Paul, Elijah*), Hiller and Schumann (Symphony no.3) were acquired for the firm. The collection *Classische Kirchenwerke alter Meister für Männerchor* (1845), edited by J. J. Maier and including works by Josquin, Lassus and Palestrina, was published during this period. From 1860 Simrock published

Title-page of Brahm's Violin Sonata in D minor op.108, published by Simrock (Berlin, 1889)

most of Brahms's opp.16–122 (see illustration) and, at Brahms's suggestion, pieces by Dvořák, including *Klänge aus Mähren* op.32 (1877) and *Slavische Tänze* op.46 (1878), most works by Bruch from 1869 to 1890 and some by the younger Johann Strauss. Simrock's successors acquired music by Kirchner and Reger, Pfitzner, Graener and Dohnányi. The firm publishes compositions by Wellesz, Manicke, T. Blumer and others, as well as editions of earlier works.

Verzeichnis des Musikalien-Verlages N. Simrock (Berlin, 1898) [3 suppls., 1902–27, incl. pl. nos.]; M. Kalbeck, ed.: *Johannes 'Brahms' Briefe an P. J. Simrock und Fritz Simrock* (Berlin, 1917–19); E. H. Müller, ed.: *Simrock-Jb* (Berlin, 1928–34); Deutsch (1946); W. Ottendorf-Simrock: *Das Haus Simrock* (Ratingen, 1954); K. Stephenson: *Johannes Brahms und Fritz Simrock: Weg einer Freundschaft* (Hamburg, 1961); H. Unverricht: 'Die Simrock-Drucke von Haydns Londoner Sinfonien', *Karl Gustav Fellerer zum 60. Geburtstag* (Cologne, 1962), 235; R. Elvers, ed.: *Felix Mendelssohn Bartholdy: Briefe an deutsche Verleger* (Berlin, 1968); Plesske (1968); O. Wenig: *Buchdruck und Buchhandel in Bonn* (Bonn, 1968); H. Unverricht: 'Nicolaus Simrock als Lieferant von Opernpartituren für die Mainzer Bühne, 1786–1792', *Mitteilungen der Arbeitsgemeinschaft für Rheinischen Musikgeschichte*, xx (1970), 202; S. Brandenburg: 'Die Gründungsjahre des Verlags N. Simrock in Bonn', *Beiträge zur rheinischen Musikgeschichte*, cxvi (1978), 87

R.E.

Skillern, Thomas. English engraver and publisher, active in London. On the death of John Walsh the younger in 1766 two of his engravers, Thomas Straight and Thomas Skillern, set up in partnership on their own as engravers and publishers. The firm of Straight & Skillern lasted until about the end of 1777 and then split into two separate businesses. Straight evidently published and sold music only until about 1783, although his engraving activities continued into the 1790s and included some work on Arnold's Handel edition. Skillern remained in business until 1802, his plates being subsequently bought by Thomas Preston. Besides books of pleasure-garden songs, country dances and the like, many single sheet songs were issued by both firms, often using only the letters 'Str: & Sk:', 'Str:', 'T.Sk:' or 'Sk:' as an imprint. An apparently different Thomas Skillern, probably a son, set up as a music seller and publisher at a new address around 1802; this business, later known as Skillern & Challoner, and then as Skillern & Co., survived until about 1826.

Kidson (1900); Humphries and Smith (1954, 2/1970)

P.W.J.

Snodham, Thomas (*d* 1624). English printer. He was the apprentice and adopted son of Thomas East and inherited East's business some time between 1608 and 1611. Two of his early imprints read 'Printed by Tho. Easte, alias Snodham', which has given rise to the conjecture that either East or Snodham changed his name, but the adoption details in East's will refute this. Snodham seems to have inherited East's position as the leading London music printer. He later formed a partnership with Matthew Lownes and John Brown, which lasted until his death, and printed many musical works in conjunction with them. Most of his music output is entirely original: although he acquired the copyrights of two other printers he rarely reprinted any of their works. He printed William Corkine's *The Second Booke of Ayres* (1612), four books of madrigals by Michael East (1610–24), the *Ayres* and *Lessons for 1, 2 and 3 Viols* (both 1609) by Alfonso Ferrabosco and Martin Peerson's *Private Musick* (1620). He was a worthy successor to East; he did not maintain such uniformly high standards, but he was more ready to experiment with existing styles of layout, as seen in Peerson's *Private Musick*, where he adapted the prevailing 'table-book' style, and George Mason's and John Earsden's *Ayres that were sung and played at Brougham Castle* (1618), which demonstrates an early example of a printed score, a remarkable achievement for a printer who worked with type. His premises were at St Botolph without Aldersgate but, curiously, he never included this address in any of his music imprints. His lack of care in dating volumes makes an exact chronolgy of his output difficult to establish. He was a printer in his own right for less than 13 years and there was no one of comparable skill to succeed him. Most of his printing materials were acquired by Thomas Harper and, later, William Godbid.

Humphries and Smith (1954, 2/1970); Krummel (1975)

M.M.

Society for the Publication of American Music [SPAM]. An American non-profit-making organization founded in 1919 by Burnet C. Tuthill in New York for the publication of contemporary American chamber music. It flourished for half a century and had several hundred subscribers. A selection committee was appointed to examine manuscripts and listen to live performances, and about 85 works were published. The composers chosen include Daniel Gregory Mason, Leo Sowerby, Arthur Shepherd, Quincy Porter, Edward

Burlingame Hill, David Diamond, Ingolf Dahl, Irving Fine, Lukas Foss, William Bergsma and Mel Powell. The first president of the society was John Alden Carpenter, William B. Tuthill was secretary until his death in 1929, and Burnet C. Tuthill was treasurer until 1949. From 1920 the society sponsored the Aliénor Harpsichord Composition Awards. In 1969 it was dissolved and the rest of its music stock turned over to the Theodore Presser Company, which had been its publisher and distributor for the last few years of its existence.

B. C. Tuthill: 'Fifteen Years of Service to an American Ideal', *MusAm*, liv/13 (1934), 5; W. M. Holman: *A History of the Society for the Publication of American Music, 1919–1969* (diss., U. of Iowa, 1977)

W.T.M., M.J.

Soldi, Luca Antonio (*fl* 1619–25). Italian printer. He worked in Rome at S Spirito in Sassia. He was an undistinguished printer using an unattractive typeface, and is most important for his editions of Cifra, G. F. Anerio and Kapsberger and for Frescobaldi's first book of *Capricci*. He printed music, mostly sacred, by other Roman composers, sometimes financed by the bookseller Masotti. Further research might well show some connection between Soldi and Robletti or Zannetti, both of whose printed repertories seem to have passed to him.

Sartori (1958)

S.B. (iii)

Sønnichsen, Søren (*b* Copenhagen, 9 June 1765; *d* Copenhagen, 5 Nov 1826). Danish publisher and printer. He matriculated at the University of Copenhagen when he was 15 and soon devoted his time and effort to music. Having started business as a music dealer (1783), he embarked on a publishing career in 1784 by issuing 12 minuets for small orchestra by P. M. Lem, printed from plates engraved in London. He took an interest in the process of printing from movable type after the model of Breitkopf, and in June 1787 he finally obtained a privilege as a music printer. Thereafter he published about 300 works, all in type print, securing him a lasting position in Danish music history. He was closely connected with the Royal Theatre and worked as the prompter at the opera from 1788 to 1799, partly overlapping with J. A. P. Schulz's time as director (1787–95). Concurrently he produced several important vocal scores such as Schulz's *Høstgildet* ('The harvest home'), *Peters bryllup* ('Peter's wedding') and the oratorio *Maria og Johannes*, operas by F. L. A. Kunzen and others and

piano scores of several early ballets by C. Schall, as well as outstanding song collections, for example those by Haydn (1785), Pleyel and Mozart.

Sønnichsen also initiated the music periodical *Apollo*, which became an influential element of Danish musical life. Between 1795 and 1808 six volumes were published, containing abundant examples of Danish and foreign works of that period. As a music dealer and importer he was also remarkably active, frequently advertising new shipments of music from Amsterdam, Paris, Vienna, London and elsewhere, for which he printed small catalogues. His music hire library, begun in 1786, contained over 550 keyboard items by 1808. After 1809 Sønnichsen's activity apparently decreased, although there were occasional publications until 1816. After his death certain of his editions appeared in the catalogues of the firm of C. C. Lose.

D. Fog: *Musikhandel og Nodetryk i Danmark efter 1750*, i (Copenhagen, 1984), 167; idem: *Notendruck und Musikhandel im 19. Jahrhundert in Dänemark* (Copenhagen, 1986), 94

D.F.

Sonzogno. Italian firm of publishers. It was founded in Milan at the end of the 18th century by Giovan Battista Sonzogno and was devoted at first to the production of single editions of various kinds. The firm passed successively to Giovan Battista's sons Francesco and Lorenzo and in 1861 to Lorenzo's son Edoardo (*b* Milan, 21 April 1836; *d* Milan, 14 March 1920), who began in 1874 to specialize in music. His first music publication was an arrangement for piano of *Il barbiere di Siviglia* in the *Musica per Tutti* series, which was in the charge of the composer Amintore Galli, who wrote the arrangements and compiled the introductory history notes. Among the firm's notable achievements were obtaining the Italian rights for *Carmen* in 1897 and, later, those for Thomas' *Mignon* and *Hamlet*; the Sonzogno Competition was instituted in 1883 (also held in 1889, 1892 and 1903 – the young Mascagni won that of 1889, with his *Cavalleria rusticana*; see illustration). The firm promoted the Italian *verismo* school associated with Mascagni, Giordano, Filiasi, Leoncavallo and Cilea, as well as some foreign composers and some of the more famous operettas of Hervé, Lecocq and Offenbach. Its greatest successes were *Pagliacci*, *Andrea Chénier*, *Fedora*, *L'amico Fritz* and *La gioconda*. During the season of Carnival and Lent in 1875, Edoardo Sonzogno took over the management of the Teatro S Redegonda in Milan; the experiment was repeated with lasting success in

433

Title page of piano score of Mascagni's 'Cavalleria Rusticana' published in 1890 by Sonzogno

1894, when on 22 September he opened a theatre of his own, the Lirico Internazionale (founded on the site of the Canobbiana), with the opera *La martire*, based on a short theatre piece by Luigi Illica, with music by the Greek composer Spyridon Samaras. Sonzogno also published the periodicals *Il teatro illustrato* (1881–92) and *La musica popolare* (1882–92).

On Edoardo's retirement in 1909 the publishing house came under the direction of his son Riccardo (*d* Montecatini, 6 or 8 July 1915), who was succeeded by his cousin Renzo (*b* Milan, 21 Jan 1877; *d* Milan, 3 April 1920). Renzo had been introduced to music and publishing by his uncle Edoardo and had been established with the separate music publishing firm of Lorenzo Sonzogno, founded in 1910 to promote Italian and foreign operettas, and comic and serious operas, among which were Mascagni's *Parisina* and Pizzetti's *Fedra*.

A legal document dated 17 November 1915 records the amalgamation of the two firms with Lorenzo as president and Edoardo Banfi, Arturo Catalani and the lawyer Leopoldo Barduzzi as advisers. On Renzo's death the house passed to Banfi and later to Barduzzi. The firm assumed the name Società Anonima Sonzogno in 1923 and is now known as the Società per Azioni Sonzogno. In August 1943 the offices and archive were destroyed by bombing. When activities were resumed, the house was administered by Enzo Ostali, son of Pietro Ostali who had been director from 1923.

Catalogo delle pubblicazioni musicali dell'editore E. Sonzogno (Milan, 1911); *Catalogo generale 1916–1917 della casa musicale Sonzogno* (Milan, 1917); Sartori (1958)

S.A.

Spehr, Johann Peter (*b* *c*1770; *d* *c*1860). German publisher. He was the proprietor of the Musik- und Kunsthandlung auf der Höhe (from 1794, Musikalisches Magazin auf der Höhe), which he founded at Brunswick in 1791. Through trading contacts with London, France, the Netherlands and elsewhere, the firm expanded until by 1816 it could announce a catalogue containing 1500 works. Among its most enterprising early publications was *Collection complette de tous les oeuvres pour le fortepiano de Mozart*, which was offered for subscription 'up to Easter 1797' and appeared in six parts (five numbers in each) early in 1798; their contents are listed in the sixth edition of Köchel's catalogue. No complete copy is known (an imperfect one is in the British Library, London. This collection seems to have caused Breitkopf &

Härtel to hasten their own plans for the much larger, complete edition of Mozart which was brought out from 1798. Besides editions of these classics, Spehr published mainly popular music, fashionable dances, operatic extracts and educational works. In 1860 he sold the business to the Brunswick music publisher Carl Weinholz, whose business was taken over in 1872 by Julius Bauer and Julius Pahlmann. From 1873, under Bauer's name alone, the firm continued until the destruction of its premises in 1944.

L. von Köchel: *Chronologisch-thematisches Verzeichnis sämtlicher Tonwerke Wolfgang Amade Mozarts* (Leipzig, 1862, rev. 6/1964), 915

A.H.K.

Stainer & Bell. English firm of publishers, active in London. It was founded in 1907 by a group of composers as an outlet for British compositions (the names 'Stainer' and 'Bell' were chosen merely for euphony). The firm's reputation was quickly established, and it published the later music of Stanford, as well as works by Holst (*Hymn of Jesus*, 1919), Vaughan Williams (*A Sea Symphony*, 1918; *London Symphony*, 1920), Bantock and Boughton. In 1917 it was appointed by the Carnegie Trust to publish the Carnegie Collection of British Music. Since then the firm has undertaken the publication of several major scholarly series, notably E. H. Fellowes's editions of the *English Madrigal School* (1913–24), the *Complete Works of William Byrd* (1937–50), and the *English School of Lutenist Song Writers* (1920–31), which was taken over from the firm of Winthrop Rogers in 1924. Revised editions of all three series were published under the supervision of Thurston Dart, musical adviser to the firm from 1953 until his death in 1971. In 1951 the firm was entrusted with the publication of the *Musica Britannica* series for the Royal Musical Association, and a further important series, *Early English Church Music*, has been published for the British Academy since 1963; the facsimile series *Music for London Entertainment* was taken over in 1987. In addition the firm has published many sheet editions in its series *Choral Library*, *Church Choir Library*, *Unison Songs*, *Organ Library*, and *Modern Church Services*, all orginally devoted to new works by British composers and latterly noted for fine editions of older music. In February 1971 the firm entered a partnership with Galliard Ltd; with its purchase of that firm in November 1972 titles published by Augener, Joseph Williams and Joseph Weekes entered the catalogue. In 1968 Bernard Braley became the firm's managing director, succeeding his grandfather Ellis R. Howard (1920–48) and father Arthur E. Braley (1948–57). In 1978 Allen Percival became editorial director.

P.W.J.

Stansby, William (*d* 1638). English printer, active in London. He was apprenticed to John Windet in 1591 and made free of the Stationers' Company in 1597. He succeeded to Windet's business in 1611, and in 1628 he acquired some of the music copyrights of Thomas Snodham. In this way Stansby inherited two of the most important music printing businesses in 17th-century London, yet he made little use of them, printing only eight music volumes in his relatively long career. Stansby's press was astonishingly variable in the standard of its printing. Whereas Thomas Leighton's *Teares or Lamentacions of a Sorrowful Soule*, published over Stansby's imprint in 1614, is an elaborate, almost virtuoso piece of printing, his other publications appear slapdash and untidy. In fact, Stansby was severely taken to task by the Stationers' Company over the low standard of his work, and his relations with the company deteriorated so badly, over his unruly behaviour as much as his printing, that in 1627 his share of the English stock was sequestered and he was banned from entering Stationers' Hall. Stansby cannot be described as either a distinguished or an enthusiastic music printer, yet the importance of his output is such that it seems likely he was the only printer in London who had the requisite materials to print music at that time. In 1629, for example, he printed *French Court-aires*, a volume of songs by Pierre Guédron and Antoine Boësset, originally published in Paris by Pierre Ballard, but appearing in England *with their Ditties Englished . . . Collected, Translated, Published by Ed. Filmer*. This volume marks the first appearance of a slur in English music printing, and his publication of Martin Peerson's *Motets* of 1630 has the first figured bass to appear in a printed volume in England. The year after he died his widow assigned his business to Richard Bishop. At the beginning of his career Stansby appears to have worked at the Cross Keys, St Paul's Wharf, which was his old master John Windet's address; he later moved to his own shop in St Dunstan's Churchyard, Fleet Street.

Humphries and Smith (1954, 2/1970); C. Hill: 'William Stansby and Music Printing', *FAM*, xix (1972), 7; J. K. Bracken: 'Books from William Stansby's Printing House and Jonson's Folio of 1616', *The Library*, 6th ser., x/1 (1988), 18

M.M.

Stark, John (Stillwell) (*b* Shelby Co., KY, 11 April 1841; *d* St Louis, 20 Nov 1927). American publisher. He grew up on a farm near Gosport, Indiana, and settled in Missouri in the early 1870s. By 1882 he had moved to Sedalia, Missouri, where he opened a piano and music shop under the name of John Stark & Son. Within a few years he had entered music publishing by buying out a local competitor, J. W. Truxel, including Truxel's seven music copyrights. It is probable that Stark himself (under the pseudonyms O. B. Ligato and L. G. Wezbrew) composed some of the firm's earliest publications; others were written by his son E. J. Stark. In 1899 he issued *Maple Leaf Rag* by a local composer, Scott Joplin; a masterpiece of ragtime, it became the firm's best-selling item with half a million copies printed by 1909. In 1900 Stark moved his firm to St Louis. From 1905 to 1910 he operated editorial offices in New York while maintaining a printing plant in St Louis. From about 1908, however, after disagreements with Stark over two extended works – *The Ragtime Dance* and *Tree-monisha* – Joplin left the firm and published nearly all his works elsewhere.

Stark was best known for his ragtime publications, though he issued other types of popular, parlor and teaching pieces using the imprints 'John Stark & Son', 'Stark Music Company' and 'American Music Syndicate'. He also published briefly *The Intermezzo* (*c*1905–6), a genteel music magazine to which he contributed articles on ragtime. By 1918 his business had declined considerably, but he continued to publish a few rags until 1922. A unique and pioneering figure, Stark was the most significant of all ragtime publishers. He helped Joplin establish himself, and was the primary publisher of other important writers of piano rags, notably James Scott, Joseph F. Lamb, Artie Matthews, Arthur Marshall and Scott Hayden. He apparently coined the term 'classic ragtime' for the work of these composers, and in publishing pieces by black composers generally avoided the racial stereotyping found on the title-pages of contemporary sheet music. Stark's small firm competed against the giants of Tin Pan Alley, relying on the excellence of its composers' rags and on a long series of hyperbolic advertisements, letters and articles in the music press. It published more than 100 piano rags, ranking second only to Jerome H. Remick & Co. in output of instrumental ragtime.

A. W. Christensen: 'Chicago Syncopations: John Stark Pioneer Publisher', *Melody*, ii/10 (1918), 8; R. Blesh and H. Janis: *They All Played Ragtime* (New York, 1950, rev. 4/1971); D. Brockhoff:

'Missouri Was the Birthplace of Ragtime: Widow of Music Publisher Recalls', *Saint Louis Post-Dispatch* (18 Jan 1961); W. J. Schafer and J. Riedel: *The Art of Ragtime* (Baton Rouge, LA, 1973/R1977); D. A. Jasen and T. J. Tichenor: *Rags and Ragtime: a Musical History* (New York, 1978); J. E. Hasse: 'Ragtime: from the Top', *Ragtime: its History, Composers and Music* (New York, 1985), 22, 338

J.E.H.

Starý, Emanuel (*b* Pardubice, 27 July 1843; *d* Prague, 1 Aug 1906). Czech publisher. In 1867 he founded a lithographic works with Antonín Vítek in Prague, taking sole charge in November 1870. He was on friendly terms with the leading Czech composers and published a series of works by Smetana, Dvořák, Bendl, Fibich, Foerster and others. His collection of male choruses, *Hlahol*, was important in the development of Czech choral songs. He published *Dalibor* (1873–5) and *Hudební a divadelní věstník* ('Music and theatre bulletin', 1877–8). He was active in a number of artistic societies in Prague.

After his death his son Emanuel (*b* Prague, 18 Jan 1874; *d* Prague, 20 April 1928) took over the firm. In 1908 he reorganized it and introduced engraving and note printing on the Leipzig pattern. Apart from choral and solo vocal compositions, he published a number of instrumental works, particularly Foerster's and Ostrčil's. After his death his widow, Růžena Stará, née Meruňková, ran the firm until 1949. In addition to Foerster's Cello Concerto and Second Violin Concerto (with piano arrangement) she brought out a series of Foerster's choral works and reprints of earlier publications of choral music.

ČSHS

Z.C.

Stein, Nikolaus (*b* Steinau an der Strasse; *d* Frankfurt am Main, *c* 20 Jan 1629). German music dealer and publisher. In 1602 he and the printer Wolfgang Richter founded a printing and publishing association in Frankfurt am Main which existed until 1615 under the name of Typographia Musica; it was one of the leading German music publishing firms before the Thirty Years War, and concentrated on Catholic church music, also publishing numerous collections of dances and lieder.

E. L. Berz: *Die Notendrucker und ihre Verleger in Frankfurt am Main von den Anfängen bis etwa 1630*, (Kassel, 1970), 80

T.W.

Stein & Buchheister. American firm of publishers, active in Detroit. Charles F. Stein and William Buchheister, who were members of the Germania Society orchestra of Boston when it disbanded at the end of its second mid-western tour, settled in Detroit and opened the Boston Music Store on 27 October 1854. They immediately began publishing music, the first item being Buchheister's *Bell Polka*, composed in remembrance of the Germania Musical Society. Their output included songs, piano pieces, dance music, orchestral works and the series *Ballroom Delights* and *New and Pleasing Dances, Mazurkas, Rondos*. Despite early success, the Boston Music Store closed around 1865, when Stein returned to Germany; Buchheister was remanded to an insane asylum a year later.

H. E. Johnson: 'The Germania Musical Society', *MQ*, xxxix (1953), 75

M.D.T.

Steingräber, Theodor Leberecht (*b* Neustadt an der Orla, 25 Jan 1830; *d* Leipzig, 5 April 1904). German publisher. He acquired a reputation as a music teacher and under the pseudonym Gustav Damm published a world-famous piano tutor (1868); subsequently he founded the Steingräber publishing house in Hanover (1878), moving it to Leipzig in 1890. The central feature of the publishing programme was a series of editions of classical works (*Edition Steingräber*) prepared by Hans Bischoff, Hermann Keller, Franz Kullak, Henri Marteau and others. The arrangers and editors of school and teaching material included M. A. Frey, Julius Klengel and Richard Kleinmichel. A son-in-law of Steingräber, Walter Friedel, managed the firm from 1903 to 1916 and it has remained in the family's possession. After suffering severe damage in World War II it moved to Frankfurt in 1953, and to Offenbach am Main in 1956.

H.-M.P.

Stellovsky, Fyodor Timofeyevich (*b* 1826; *d* 1875). Russian publisher. He built up his firm on the basis of Klever's publishing house, which he acquired in about 1850. He also took over the smaller business of Gurskalin, who had been publishing music in St Petersburg from 1838 and who owned Denotkin's printing press, established in 1844. Stellovsky was particularly known as the publisher of Glinka's music; in fact it was his editions that first introduced Rimsky-Korsakov to Glinka's two operas. He also published the works of Balakirev (who, in his early, impecunious years, helped Stellovsky to prepare other composers' scores for publication), Serov and Dargomïzhsky. After Stellovsky's death the business was carried on by his widow and

437

then by his sister; in 1886 it was taken over by Gutheil.

B. P. Jürgenson: *Ocherk istorii notopechataniya* [An outline of the history of music printing] (Moscow, 1928); A. S. Lyapunova: 'Kratkiy obzor istorii izdaniya proizvedeniy M. I. Glinki' [A short account of the history of the publication of Glinka's works], *M. A. Balakirev: perepiska s notoizdatel'stvom P. Yurgensona*, ed. V. A. Kiselyov and A. S. Lyapunova (Moscow, 1958), 369; E. Garden: *Balakirev: a Critical Study of his Life and Music* (London, 1967); B. L. Vol'man: *Russkiye notnïye izdaniya XIX – nachala XX veka* [Russian music publishing in the 19th and early 20th centuries] (Leningrad, 1970)

G.N.

Stephens, Roe (*b* Coburg, North West Territories, *c*1844; *d* ?Detroit, MI, 18 Jan 1897). American music dealer and publisher. He spent some time in piano factories in Boston learning the mechanical and professional sides of the music business. He then moved to Detroit, where he worked as a piano tuner and repairer. Around 1868 he became associated with J. Henry Whittemore, whose business then became known as J. Henry Whittemore, Swan & Stephens. Three years later it became Whittemore & Stephens, and by 1875 Stephens was sole owner. Although he was bankrupt within the first two years of his ownership, Stephens's business recovered rapidly, and by 1880 he was considered the largest sheet music publisher in Michigan. The firm published dance tunes by well-known composers of the day as well as some of Stephens's own compositions, and between 1874 and 1885 also issued *The Amphion*, a popular monthly music magazine. While continuing to operate his music emporium, Stephens became involved in another business venture in 1885 when he joined William Scott in operating a brass foundry, Stephens, Scott & Co. Two years later that firm became Roe Stephens Manufacturing Co., with a new set of associates. For about nine years Stephens directed both his music establishment and the manufacturing company, but apparently the latter proved more profitable, for some time in 1893 he ceased operation of the music shop.

M.D.T.

Stern. German family of printers and publishers. The bookbinder Johann Stern (*d* 1614) set up a printing and publishing business in Lüneburg, where it is still active. His sons Johann (*d* 1656) and Heinrich (1592–1665) established a branch at Wolfenbüttel which became one of the most important publishing concerns during the Thirty Years War; they received royal privileges and were ennobled in recognition of their achievements. The founder's grandson Johann (1633–1712) published particularly interesting works of H. Rist and his circle, including works by J. W. Franck, F. Funcke, F. E. and J. Praetorius, T. Selle and J. J. Weiland.

H. Dumrese and F. C. Schilling: *Lüneburg und die Offizin der Sterne* (Lüneburg, 1956); H. Walter: *Beiträge zur Musikgeschichte der Stadt Lüneburg im 17. Jahrhundert und beginnenden 18. Jahrhundert* (diss., U. of Cologne, 1962), 32, 160, 187; Benzing (1963, 2/1982); H. Walter: *Musikgeschichte der Stadt Lüneburg: vom Ende des 16. bis zum Anfang des 18. Jahrhunderts* (Tutzing, 1967); H. Hüschen: 'Hamburger Musikdrucker und Musikverleger im 16. und 17. Jahrhundert', *Beiträge zur Musikgeschichte Nordeuropas: Kurt Gudewill zum 65. Geburtstag* (Wolfenbüttel, 1977), 255

T.W.

Stuchs [Stüchs, Stöchs], **Georg** (*b* ?Sulzbach, Upper Palatine; *d* Nuremberg, 1520). German printer. Although Stuchs himself gave Sulzbach as his place of birth in his publications, he may have been the son of the Nuremberg organ builder Friedrich Stuchs. He became a citizen of Nuremberg in 1484 and began printing in the same year. His last publication is dated 1517; after this he was active only as a bookseller, leaving the printing business in the hands of his son, Johann, under whose name publications had been issued as early as 1509.

The elder Stuchs, whose known publications number 132, was famous above all as a printer of liturgical books, particularly missals. He served a large circle of clients from all parts of Europe, including, for example, the bishoprics of Regensburg, Salzburg, Prague, Kraków, Magdeburg and Linköping. In 1491 he introduced musical notes into his liturgical books, using the double-impression technique. Stuchs was known for the superior quality of his type forms, which he frequently sold to other printers, and for the woodcuts, often by prominent artists, with which he decorated his volumes. The younger Stuchs devoted himself in later years to the cause of the Reformation, printing many of the writings of Luther and his followers. His sole contribution to music consists of a reprint of Johannes Cochlaeus's treatise *Tetrachordum musices* in 1512.

P. Molitor: *Deutsche Choral-Wiegendrucke* (Regensburg, 1904); W. Baumann: 'Die Druckerei Stuchs zu Nürnberg (1484–1537)', *Gutenberg-Jb 1954*, 122 [with list of publications]; J. Benzing: 'Die Stuchsdruckerei zu Nürnberg im Dienst der Reformation', *Archiv für Geschichte des Buchwesens*, iv (1961–3), 1585; K. Meyer-Baer: *Liturgical*

Music Incunabula: a Descriptive Catalogue (London, 1962); T. Wohnhaas: 'Stuchs, Georg', *MGG*

M.L.G.

Summy-Birchard. American firm of publishers. In 1931 John Sengstack acquired the Clayton F. Summy Company, founded in Chicago in 1888. In 1957 Summy took over C. C. Birchard & Co., a Boston firm founded in 1901, and the resulting firm took the name Summy-Birchard Company; at that time it was based in Evanston, Illinois, but it later moved to Princeton, New Jersey, and is now known as Birchtree, Ltd. Clarence Birchard had a particular interest in American music; he commissioned American composers to write for his pioneering school and community songbooks and was an early publisher of Bloch, Copland, Hanson, Ives and Varèse David Sengstack succeeded his father as president of the firm in 1958. In 1960 Summy-Birchard acquired the Arthur P. Schmidt Company of Boston (established 1876) and in 1969 McLaughlin & Reilly (founded in 1903), a Boston firm devoted primarily to music for the Catholic church. Summy-Birchard now specializes in instructional materials, notably piano series and Suzuki method books. In December 1988 Warner Chappell purchased the firm, including its most valuable possession, *Happy Birthday to you*, originally published in Summy's *Song Stories for Kindergarten* (1893). The song's copyrights are not due to expire until 2010; its royalties reportedly amount to a million dollars a year.

Fuld (1966, 3/1985)

W.T.M., M.J./L.A.T.

Supraphon. Czech firm of publishers of gramophone records, music and books on music. It arose out of the change of name, on 20 February 1967, of the Státní Hudební Vydavatelství (State Music Publishers); before the foundation of that firm on 1 January 1961 records were made by the Gramofonové Závody (Gramophone Works, nationalized 1946), while the production of music and books on music (after the nationalization of the publishing firms in 1949) was conducted first by the firms Orbis and Hudební Matice and then (1953–60) by Státní Nakladatelství Krásné Literatury, Hudby a Umění (State Publishers of Literature, Music and Art).

The production of gramophone records in the early 1970s had reached an annual total of about 2000 titles, including most genres of classical and popular music, jazz and all types of folk music. In addition Supraphon produces anthologies of music from the Czech and Moravian archives, and

early Czech organ music. It also exchanges recordings for publication with well-known foreign firms. The firm publishes annually about 275 scores and 20 books on music. A wide range of music is covered, including editions of Smetana, Dvořák, Fibich and Janáček. Early music is published in the series *Musica Antiqua Bohemica, Musica Viva Historica, Documenta Historica Musicae* and *Medailon*, and the firm also publishes works by contemporary composers. The publicity department issues the magazine *G-Gramorevue*, and is responsible for cultural societies in Prague and Ostrava as well as an exhibition hall in Prague. In 1971, when state music publishing activities were decentralized, an independent publishing firm, Opus, was founded in Bratislava, and this took over Supraphon's activities in Slovakia.

Z.C.

Susato, Tylman (*b* ?*c*1500; *d* ?Antwerp, 1561–4). Publisher and composer active in Antwerp. Because of the name Susato (= De Soest) it is generally thought that he came from Soest in Westphalia. Soest lay within the bishopric of Cologne, which perhaps explains why he occasionally styled himself Tylman Susato Agrippinensis (or Agrippinus), from the old name, Colonia Agrippina. On the other hand, he may have been born in Antwerp, into a family from Soest: for in 1377 a citizen of Antwerp, 'Tielmano de susato Coloniensis', is mentioned in the cathedral archives, and in the preface to the first *Musyck boexken* (1551), a book of Flemish songs, Susato referred to 'our Flemish mother tongue'.

In 1529 and 1530 Tylman worked as a calligrapher at Antwerp Cathedral and in 1531 also as a trumpeter there. The following year 'Tielman van Colen' appears in the Antwerp archives as a town player who owned several instruments: 9 flutes in a case, 3 trumpets and a tenor pipe. He continued as a town player until 1549, but from 1543 until 1561 worked mainly as a music publisher, establishing the first important music press in the Low Countries. In 1541 he formed a partnership with two other Antwerp printers, Henry ter Bruggen, an engraver and publisher of maps, who received a privilege to print music dated 22 December 1541, and Willem van Vissenaecken; however, this partnership did not flourish. Susato formed another on 12 September 1542 with Vissenaecken and the same year a volume of motets, *Quatuor vocum musicae modulationes numero XXVI*, was published by Vissenaecken alone; on 9 April 1543 this second contract was dissolved. Susato acquired his own privilege on 20 July 1543 and that year established his press in the Twaalfmaandenstraat. He stayed there until 1551 when he moved to a new house, called the 'Cromhorn', where he may have combined his printing activities with a musical instrument business. During his 18 years as a publisher, Susato issued 25 books of chansons (mostly in two series); 3 books of masses; 19 books of motets (in two series); and 11 *Musyck boexken*, the first two being collections of Flemish songs, the third a book of dances arranged by Susato, based on popular tunes, and the remaining eight books of *Souterliedekens* (psalter songs).

In his printing he used two founts of single-impression music type: the first (which may have been cut by Henry ter Bruggen) until 1551 and the second (from Petreius in Nuremberg) from 1551 onwards. When Susato died, he was succeeded by his son Jacques, who published Lassus's *Premier livre de chansons* in 1564. Jacques died on 19 November 1564. His widow sold all the printing materials to Christopher Plantin, and a fragmentary set of matrices for the second music type is in the Museum Plantin-Moretus, Antwerp.

Susato, who was himself a practical musician, composer and calligrapher, was well qualified for the profession of music printing – an art which, according to the dedication of his first publication, he had long sought to master. Many of his volumes are dedicated to persons of high standing, including prominent citizens of Antwerp, some of whom appear to have been his friends. In 1546 three citizens of Antwerp testified to Susato's good character, perhaps in connection with the renewal of his printing privilege. Most of his chanson and motet publications were anthologies, although he occasionally published a book devoted to one composer, for example Manchicourt and Crecquillon. He often printed music by Flemish composers, such as Crecquillon, Clemens non Papa, Canis, Gombert, Baston, Appenzeller, Guyot, Handl and Lupi. His seventh book of chansons (1545) was a retrospective publication, containing pieces by Josquin Desprez and three epitaphs on his death. Susato also published Janequin's popular chanson *La bataille* (see illustration) in a volume of programme chansons (1545). On the other hand, a forward-looking

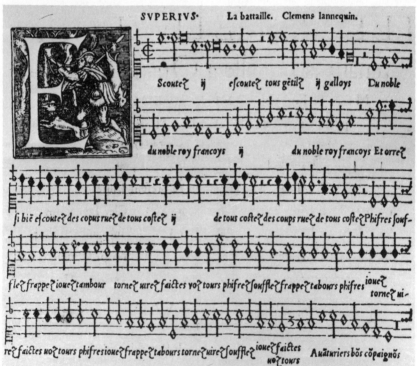

Opening of the superius voice of the chanson 'La bataille' from 'Le dixiesme livre contenant la Bataille a quatre de Clement Jannequin . . .', printed by type from single impression by Susato (Antwerp, 1545)

approach is seen in his publication of Lassus's chansons in 1555 (he was one of Lassus's first publishers); in 1560 Susato also published a volume of his motets. He showed enterprise in his *Musyck boexken* series; in the preface to the first book he asked Flemish composers to send him songs 'suitable for publication' so that he could prove that Flemish songs were as agreeable and artistic as those with French, Latin or Italian words. However, very few were published during the century: two of Susato's 1551 books, one by Baethen (1554) and one by Phalèse (1572) are the only dated volumes containing only Flemish songs. In the publication of *Souterliedekens* in polyphonic arrangements by Clemens non Papa (1556–7) and his pupil G. Mes (1561), Susato undoubtedly met public demand. These metrical Dutch psalm settings, intended for domestic rather than for church use, were very popular during the 16th century in the Netherlands.

As a composer, Susato is particularly important as the author of two books of cantus firmus chansons composed 'à 2 ou à 3 parties' (i.e. with an optional bass part); these 50 chansons are the largest number extant by any composer and may have been the model for those composed by Claude Gervaise.

FétisB; Goovaerts (1880); U. Meissner: *Der Antwerpener Notendrucker Tylman Susato* (Berlin, 1967); H. D. L. Vervliet: *Sixteenth Century Printing Types of the Low Countries* (Amsterdam, 1968); S. Bain: *Music Printing in the Low Countries in the Sixteenth Century* (diss., U. of Cambridge, 1974); K. K. Forney: *Tielman Susato, Sixteenth-century Music Printer: an Archival and Typographical Investigation* (diss., U. of Kentucky, 1978); S. Bain: 'Susato, Tylman,', *Grove6* [incl. selective list of publications]; K. K. Forney: 'New Documents on the Life of Tielman Susato, Sixteenth-century Music Printer and Musician', *RBM*, xxxvi–xxxviii (1982–4), 18–52

S.B. (i)

Suvini Zerboni. Italian firm of publishers. It was founded in Milan in 1930, and owes its development to Paolo Giordani who was its head from 1932 until his death in 1948. He aimed to build up a collection of Italian compositions and make them internationally known, but his efforts were interrupted by World War II. He was joined after the war by the Hungarian Ladislao Sugar, who became head of the firm. Sugar brought Hungarian composers into the firm's catalogue, so that it now includes many compositions by Sándor Veress, Dorati, Seiber and others. He also negotiated an agency agreement with Editio Musica of Budapest and important reciprocal agency

agreements with Schott and other firms. Suvini Zerboni publishes works by contemporary Japanese composers as well as editions of Italian classical music (including the series *Orpheus Italicus*). By far the greater part of its catalogue, (which numbered about 4000 items in 1975) is contemporary Italian music, including many of the works of Berio, Castiglioni, Aldo Clementi, Dallapiccola, Donatoni, Ghedini, Maderna, Gianfrancesco and Riccardo Malipiero, and Pizzetti.

Miscèllanea del cinquantenario: die Stellung der italienischen Avantgarde in der Entwicklung der neuen Musik (Milan, 1978)

A.P. (ii)

Szarfenberg [Szarffenberck, Scharpfenberg, Szarfenberger, Szarffemberg, Ostrowski, Ostrogórski]**, Maciej** (*b* Liebenthal, nr. Jelenia Góra; *d* Kraków, between 21 March and 15 June 1547). Polish printer active in Kraków. He established his printing house in 1530. Among his music publications are secular and religious partsongs, liturgical books, and music treatises by Jerzy Liban (*De accentuum ecclesiasticorum exquisita ratione, c*1539) and Jan Spanenberg (*Questiones musicae in usum Scholae Northusianae*, 1544) which contain numerous classical examples, including some complete compositions. He used exclusively woodblock printing.

His relative Marek Szarfenberg (*b* Liebenthal; *d* Kraków, 1545) was a Kraków bookseller who first started printing in about 1543. He mainly published liturgical books with Gothic notation, using movable type in a double-impression technique, as well as woodblock printing.

Marek's grandson Mateusz Siebeneicher [Siebeneich, Sybeneycher, Zybenaicher] (*b* Liebenthal; *d* Kraków, 1582) married the widow of Maciej's son Hieronim and thus became the owner of the Szarfenberg printing house in 1557. He was one of the most eminent Polish publishers of his time and specialized in the printing of textbooks and Catholic devotional literature. He also issued many popular partsongs and psalms of Cyprian Bazylik z Sieradza, Wacław z Szamotuł and others (mostly published singly), and Krzysztof Klabon's collection, *Pieśni Kalliopy slowienskiey* ('Songs of the Slavonic Calliope', 1588), all printed from movable mensural type. After his death the firm continued until 1627.

Przywecka-Samecka (1969); *Słownik pracowników książki polskiej* [Dictionary of Polish printers] (Warsaw and Łódź, 1972)

T.C. (ii)

T

Táborszky, Nándor [Ferdinánd] (1831–88). Hungarian publisher. He was the son of János Mihály Táborszky, for whose benefit Liszt gave a concert in Pest on 8 January 1840. He opened his shop in 1868 as a branch of the Rózsavölgyi firm, but soon became independent and, with József Parsch, set up as Táborszky & Parsch. As early as 1873 they received a letter of commendation at the Viennese Exhibition. Their publications are marked with the letters 'T & P' or 'T és P' followed by the plate number (usually accurate). Táborszky not only had business relations with Liszt, between 1871 and 1886 publishing more than 18 of his works; he enjoyed the composer's personal friendship, as Liszt's correspondence in Hungarian collections shows. The firm ceased in 1895 with the death of József Parsch, after more than 25 years of activity. The legal successor was Kálmán Nádor; since nationalization it has been Editio Musica Budapest.

M. Prahács, ed.: *Franz Liszt: Briefe aus ungarischen Sammlungen, 1835–1886* (Budapest, 1966)

I.M.

Tebaldini, Nicolò (*fl* Bologna, 1620–46). Italian publisher. Between 1627 and 1639 he printed four music publications: Costanzo Fabrizio's *Fior novello, libro primo di concerti* (1627); Bartolomeo Guerra's *Il diletto del notturno* (1634; the publication, however, is without the intended music); and two books of Ascanio Trombetti's *Intavolatura di sonate per chitarra* (1639). The last-named uses an unusual kind of tablature notation, which, as the author explained in his advice to the reader, incorporates letters of the alphabet and celestial symbols such as the sun to indicate repetitions. The same letter notation but without celestial signs is employed in the *Fior novello*; in this publication each page is printed half in the normal way and half upside-down so that it may be read by a person facing the first performer. All the pages are enclosed in an ornamental frame and every canzona finishes with an elegant frieze. Tebaldini also published Adriano Banchieri's *Lettere scritte a diversi patroni ed amici* (1636).

F. Vatielli: 'Editori musicali dei secoli XVII e XVIII', *Arte e vita musicale a Bologna* (Bologna, 1927/R1969), 239; A. Sorbelli: *Storia della stampa a Bologna* (Bologna, 1929); L. Gottardi: *La stampa musicale in Bologna dagli inizi fino al 1700* (diss., U. of Bologna, 1951); Sartori (1958)

A.S. (ii)

Thomas, Isaiah (*b* Boston, 19 Jan 1749; *d* Worcester, MA, 4 April 1831). American printer and publisher. He was apprenticed to a printer at the age of seven and worked in print shops in Halifax, Nova Scotia, Charleston, South Carolina, and elsewhere. In 1770 he was in Boston publishing the *Massachusetts Spy*, a newspaper strongly opposed to the English government. He fought briefly in the War of Independence, then in 1778 moved to Worcester, where he continued to publish the *Spy*. There he established a business that made him the leading American printer and publisher of his time, with more than 400 titles coming from his press.

Before 1786, when Thomas first expanded his enterprise to include the publication of tunebooks, American sacred collections were normally printed from engraved copper plates. Thomas imported a fount of movable music type from England and brought out *The Worcester Collection of Sacred Harmony* (Worcester, 1786), printed typographically. The work was a conspicuous success, running to eight editions by 1803. Its repertory was a carefully chosen blend of favourite pieces from English and American composers, and its typography presented a clean and legible image to the eye. Considering its ample size (parts i–iii encompassed 200 pages), its price was low, for typographical printing and a well-established network of agents allowed Thomas to print and sell in quantity. Admitting that he himself was 'unskilled in musick', Thomas recruited knowledgeable musicians to aid him in compiling his work. The emphasis in *The Worcester Collection* on familiar pieces was copied by almost every American tunebook of the next two decades that enjoyed three or more editions.

Between 1789 and his retirement in 1802, Thomas published or printed more sacred tunebooks that any other American, most of them through his partnership with Ebenezer T. Andrews in Boston. The list of compilers whose works he printed includes a few psalmodists associated with the earlier New England style (Belcher, Billings, French, Wood). Also represented were several who were schooled in a more cosmopolitan, Europeanized idiom (Samuel Babcock, Bartholomew Brown, Amos Bull, William Cooper, Holden, Holyoke and Kimball), and inveterate reformers like the European-born John Cole and, especially, Hans Gram. Thomas also published the *Massachusetts Magazine*, a literary and

442

political journal that between 1789 and 1792 occasionally carried secular songs, including some by the local composers Gram, Holyoke, Elias Mann and Selby. Thomas was the first professional printer in America to involve himself energetically in the publication of sacred music. That others followed suit suggests that profits, if not careers, could be made at the commercial end of the American sacred music trade in the late 18th and early 19th centuries.

R. W. G. Vail: 'Thomas, Isaiah', *DAB*; C. K. Shipton: *Isaiah Thomas* (Rochester, NY, 1948); I. Lowens: *Music and Musicians in Early America* (New York, 1964), 73; K. D. Kroeger: *The Worcester Collection of Sacred Harmony and Sacred Music in America 1786–1803* (diss., Brown U., 1976); idem: 'Isaiah Thomas as a Music Publisher', *Proceedings of the American Antiquarian Society*, lxxxvi (1976), 321; R. Crawford and D. W. Krummel: 'Early American Music Printing and Publishing', *Printing and Society in Early America*, ed. W. L. Joyce and others (Worcester, MA, 1983), 187, 193, 195, 215

R.C. (ii)

Thompson. English firm of publishers, printers and violin makers, established in London. The business was founded about 1746 by Peter Thompson and was continued after his death (*c*1757) by his widow Ann and son Charles, sometimes under the imprint Thompson & Son. About 1761 they were joined by a second son, Samuel Thompson (*d* Aug 1795), to become Thompson & Sons. Ann left the firm in about 1763, and thereafter it was under the direction of various family members whose names appeared on its imprints: it was under the joint management of Charles and Samuel until about 1776, after which Samuel continued alone for a year; he was then joined by another Ann (whose relationship to the preceding Ann is not known), and these two remained with the firm until Samuel's death, on their own (*c*1777–9), then with Peter (*c*1779–93), with Peter and Henry (*c*1793–4) and finally with Henry (*c*1794–5). During the several changes of membership after 1792 the imprints frequently give 'Messrs Thompson' or 'Thompsons' Warehouse'. After Samuel's death Ann and Henry managed the firm together until about 1798, after which it continued under the sole ownership of Henry Thompson. About 1805 the business was taken over by Purday & Button (later Button & Whitaker).

The early publications of the firm were mostly of a minor character and included many tutors for violin, flute, harpsichord and other instruments. From 1751 Thompson published annual collections of *Twenty Four Country Dances*, which were continued throughout the whole period of the firm's existence and also collected into five cumulative volumes of 200 dances each; later the firm initiated a similar series of minuets. In 1764 the Thompsons acquired some plates at the auction of John Cox's stock and reissued a number of works from them. From about 1765, while under the direction of Charles and Samuel, the firm gradually became one of the most important in London. Further advances took place under the direction of Samuel, Ann and Peter, who published yearly catalogues of their newly issued works (*c*1781–90). Many works by Arne, Arnold, Dibdin, Philip Hayes, James Hook, Thomas Linley the elder, F. X. Richter, Samuel Webbe the elder and others appeared with the firm's imprint.

Robert Thompson, probably brother of Peter Thompson, had a music shop in London from 1748 until 1785. He was an instrument maker and published a number of single sheet songs.

Humphries and Smith (1954, 2/1970)

F.K., W.C.S./P.W.J.

Thompson, Gordon V. Canadian firm of publishers, active in Toronto. It originated in 1909 as Gordon V. Thompson's Revival Publishing Bureau, which became the Thompson Publishing Company in 1911. Gordon V. Thompson (1888–1965) was a prolific writer of patriotic and religious songs who financed his education by door-to-door sales of his *Life Songs* and *Heart Songs*. The business grew as he acquired the rights to other popular songs, and was especially successful during the two world wars. The firm was taken over by the US company Leo Feist in 1919, becoming Radio Music Company Ltd in 1930; Thompson purchased its Canadian branch in 1932, renaming it Gordon V. Thompson Ltd. He remained its president until his death, when he was succeeded by John C. Bird; in 1984 the company was acquired by Gage Publishing Ltd (now Canada Publishing Corporation). Educational material became an important part of the business in the 1930s, and concert music in the 1950s, with orchestral works by Robert Fleming, Oskar Morawetz and Godfrey Ridout, among others. The choral catalogue is particularly wide-ranging and includes the *Elmer Iseler Choral Series* and the *Toronto Children's Chorus Series*. Thompson is the Canadian agent for Columbia Pictures Publications, Bourne Music Company and the rental library of G. Schirmer Inc.

'Gordon V. Thompson: Profile of the Man and the Firm', *Canadian Music Educators' Association Newsletter* (1983), no. 56, p. 7; 'This Man Gordon V. Thompson', *Musical Canada*, xiii/8 (1932), 12; G. V. Thompson: 'My First 50 Years of Music Publishing in Canada', *Canadian Composer* (1965), no. 1, p. 14; H. Kallmann and M. Wehrle: 'Thompson, Gordon V.' and 'Gordon V. Thompson Ltd.', *Encyclopedia of Music in Canada* (Toronto, 1981)

M.W.

Thomson, George (*b* Limekilns, Fife, 4 March 1757; *d* Leith, 18 Feb 1851). Scottish amateur folksong editor and publisher. He spent his childhood in Turriff, northern Scotland, and then at the age of 17 settled in Edinburgh. In 1780 he took a clerical post with the Board of Trustees for the Encouragement of Art and Manufactures in Scotland for whom he worked for the next 59 years. Financially secure, he devoted his spare time to music. He joined the influential Edinburgh Musical Society about 1780, playing the violin in the orchestra and singing in the choir. He also developed a taste for Scots folksongs in 'classical' arrangements by hearing foreign singers, notably the castrato Tenducci, perform them at the Edinburgh Musical Society's weekly concerts. Folksongs in their unadorned state, such as he must have heard in his childhood, do not seem to have appealed to him.

About 1791 Thomson decided to publish a prestigious collection of Scottish folksongs arranged for voice and piano trio by the greatest living European composers. This collection was to occupy him until 1841 and to cost him a great deal of his own money. Haydn and Pleyel visited London in 1791 and the publisher William Napier signed on Haydn to arrange folksongs (published in 1792 and 1795): Thomson then engaged Pleyel for the same purpose and issued the first part of his *A Select Collection of Scottish Airs* in Edinburgh (1793).

In 1797 Pleyel stopped arranging for Thomson, who then turned to Kozeluch (1797–1809), Haydn himself (1799–1804), Beethoven (1803–*c*1820), Weber (briefly in 1825), Hummel (1826–*c*1835) and Bishop (1841). Beethoven wrote 126 settings for Thomson, and Haydn 187. (A thematic catalogue of Haydn's and Beethoven's contributions is given in Hopkinson and Oldman, 1940.) Haydn also made a further 221 Scots song settings for William Napier and for William Whyte, another Edinburgh publisher. Musically the collection is unsatisfactory. Most of Thomson's arrangers had never heard genuine Scottish folksongs and tried to accommodate the melodies to Viennese harmony. Thomson, moreover, infuriated Beethoven by simplifying his piano parts for the drawing-room market. The folktunes were largely culled from earlier printed collections, only a few being personally collected by Thomson and his correspondents.

Many distinguished Scottish poets, such as Burns, Scott, James Hogg and Joanna Baillie, also worked for Thomson, rewriting the words of the songs at Thomson's insistence to remove their bawdiness and substitute a pathetic sensibility. The collection contained 300 songs in six folio volumes (1793–1841). Six octavo volumes of selections were issued in 1822. But the collection was not an artistic success; it was criticized even in its own time for its lack of national spirit and is now considered not the standard classic that Thomson intended but an historical curiosity.

Other significant publications of his included three volumes of *Welsh Airs* in 1809, 1811, and 1817, and two of *Irish Airs* in 1814 and 1816. In 1817 he commissioned a cantata from Sir Henry Bishop on Burns's poem, *The Jolly Beggars*. From 1803 he made several attempts to get Beethoven to write chamber works incorporating Scots folktunes, but negotiations were unsuccessful because Beethoven asked for too much money.

J. C. Hadden: *George Thomson, the Friend of Burns* (London, 1898); R. Aldrich: 'Beethoven and George Thomson', *ML*, vii (1927), 234; F. Lederer: *Beethovens Bearbeitungen schottischer und anderer Volkslieder* (Bonn, 1934); C. Hopkinson and C. B. Oldman: 'Thomson's Collection of National Song', *Edinburgh Bibliographical Society Transactions*, ii (1940), 1–64; K. Geiringer: 'Haydn and the Folksong of the British Isles', *MQ*, xxxv (1949), 179; C. B. Oldman: 'Beethoven's Variations on National Themes', *MR*, xii (1951), 45; C. Hopkinson and C. B. Oldman: 'Haydn's Settings of Scottish Songs in the Collections of Napier and Whyte', *Edinburgh Bibliographical Society Transactions*, iii (1954), 87–120; D. Johnson: *Music and Society in Lowland Scotland in the 18th Century* (London, 1972), 41, 142, 162; M. Bröcker: 'Die Bearbeitung schottischer und irischen Volkslieder von Ludwig van Beethoven', *Jb für Musikalische Volks- und Völkerkunde*, x (1982), 63

D.J.

Thornton, Robert (*fl* Dublin, 1682–1701). Printer and publisher. His advertisement for 'Choicest new Songs with Musical Notes, set by the best Masters . . . 2d a piece' (*Dublin News Letter*, 13–18 Feb 1686) is the earliest known evidence for music printed and published in Dublin. He carried on his

444

business at the Leather Bottle in Skinner Row between 1682 and 1701.

Humphries and Smith (1954, 2/1970)

B.B.

Tini. Italian family of printers in Milan, active from at least 1572. The brothers Francesco and Simone Tini were the first to print music, beginning in 1583 with a volume of works by Maddalena Casulana. Simone was dead before the end of 1584, as the company signed itself 'Francesco e eredi di Simone Tini' between 1584 and 1590. Francesco apparently died in 1590 or 1591, although the firm continued to publish. Donà believes that Michele Tini, who had signed books in 1590, was the heir to the firm. Between 1598 and 1603 the 'erede di Simone Tini' published with G. F. Besozzi and from 1603 to 1612 with Filippo Lomazzo, to whom the business then passed. Their output represents the extent to which popular music was in demand in Milan, including editions of Anerio (1590), Belli (1586), Dentice (1593), Andrea Gabrieli (1588, 1590), Lassus (1590), Palestrina (1587, 1593) and Orfeo Vecchi (1586, 1588, 1596). A Pietro Tini, probably a brother of Francesco and Simone, published a few works in 1584–6.

M. Donà: *La stampa musicale a Milano fino all'anno 1700* (Florence, 1961); Sartori (1958); I. Fenlon: 'Il foglio volante editoriale Tini, circa il 1596', *RIM*, xii (1977), 231; I. Horsley: 'Full and Short Scores in the Accompaniment of Italian Church Music in the Early Baroque', *JAMS*, xxx (1977), 466–99; Mischiati (1984)

S.B. (iii)

Tonger, P. J. German firm of publishers. Augustin Josef Tonger (1801–81) founded a music shop and publishing firm in Cologne in 1822. The retail business was taken over as an independent concern in 1872 by his son Peter Josef (i) (1845–1917). The latter's son, Peter Josef (ii) (1875–1960), and grandson, Peter Josef (iii) (*b* 1902), did much to develop a flourishing business. Tonger's *Taschen-Alben* series, of which 62 volumes had appeared by World War II, reached an overall circulation of more than three million copies. The firm has also published choral and school music, Hausmusik and music literature. After the Cologne premises were destroyed in World War II, it moved to Rodenkirchen. Contemporary composers whose works it publishes include Bresgen, Driessler, Kolneder, Lemacher, Mersmann, Siegl and Schroeder. Peter Tonger (*b* 1937), son of Peter Josef (iii), joined the firm in 1965.

Musikverlage in der Bundesrepublik Deutschland und in West-Berlin (Bonn, 1965), 115

T.W.

Torricella, Christoph (*b* Switzerland, *c*1715; *d* Vienna, 24 Jan 1798). Swiss publisher and art dealer. He established his business in Vienna in the early 1770s, and on 5 April 1775 advertised the arrival of new copper engravings in the *Wiener Zeitung*. His first dealings in music consisted of imports from England, the Netherlands and Paris, his source for Anton Huberty's publications. In 1781 his own first publications appeared. Initially he was a commission agent for Huberty, who had moved to Vienna and eventually became only an engraver for Torricella, gradually handing over many of his pieces; one of the most important was Geminiani's violin tutor, which Torricella published in a splendid new edition on 16 October 1782. The firm flourished in its early days, but increasing competition from Artaria & Co. culminated in a public auction (12 August 1786), at which most of Torricella's plates were obtained by Artaria. He continued to run his art shop until he died, completely impoverished.

Torricella was a pioneer of music publishing in Vienna, but because of his advanced age his enterprising programmes were never fulfilled. He published several symphonies by Haydn, Mozart's piano sonatas κ333/315*c*, 284/205*b* and 454, the variations κ398/416*e*, 265/300*e* and 455 and a piano reduction of the overture to *Die Entführung aus dem Serail*, as well as three piano concertos and six accompanied sonatas by J. C. Bach, Clementi's three sonatas op.10, several works by F. A. Hoffmeister and Leopold Kozeluch, two arias by Sarti, five arias by Salieri and three caprice-sonatas and seven variations by Vanhal. Works by Georg Druschetzky, P. Mandrup Lem, Antonio Rosetti, Maximilian Stadler and A. F. Titz were also published; these editions are now very rare.

A. Weinmann: *Verlagsverzeichnis Anton Huberty und Christoph Torricella* (Vienna, 1962)

A.W.

Torresani, Andrea (*b* Asola, 4 March 1451; *fl* 1479–1529). Italian printer active in Venice. He produced two missals with music in 1496 and 1497, using roman chant type. After Manutius's death in 1515 he took over the Aldine press. He was the partner of Andrea Antico in 1521.

Duggan (1981)

M.K.D.

Title-page of Geminiani's 'Art of Playing on the Violin' in an edition published by Artaria using Torricella's plates

Tournes, Jean de (*fl* Lyons 1564–85, then Geneva 1585–1615). French humanist printer. His musical output has long been underestimated. A Protestant associate of Claude Goudimel, he printed in Lyons from 1572 works by Orlande de Lassus, Claude Goudimel (both under the pseudonym Jean Bavent), Corneille de Blockland, Gilles Maillard and Jacques Arcadelt. After fleeing to Geneva for religious reasons, apart from reprinting works by de Blockland and Arcadelt he printed pieces by Lassus and Johann Tollius for Jerome Commelin (Heidelberg), and works by Sweelinck for Hendrik Barentsen (Amsterdam). Comprising 17 volumes, his output is meticulous and typographically varied, two-thirds of it being devoted to a Protestant repertory.

L. Guillo: *Recherches sur les éditions musicales lyonnaises de la Renaissance* (diss., Ecole Pratique des Haute Etudes, Paris, 1986)

L.G.

Tradate. Italian family of publishers, active in Milan. Agostino Tradate, who was among the first to print full scores, issued music from 1598. His publications include works of Biffi, Soderini, Cantone, Cavalieri, Comandeo, Vecchi, Cangiasi, d'India, Nantermi, Beccari and Aquilino Coppini (*Musica tolta da i madrigali di Claudio Monteverde e d'altri autori à 5 et 6 voci*, 1607). From 1608 to 1610 the firm's name appears variously as 'Gli Heredi di Agostino Tradate' or 'Alessandro ed Eredi di Agostino Tradate', mostly on music associated with Monteverdi. Editions of 1610–12 devoted to music of Cavalieri, Coppini, Beccari, Cangiasi and Biumo identify Melchiorre (Melchion) as heir to Agostino Tradate. Publication ceased after 1612.

Sartori (1958); M. Donà: *La stampa musicale a Milano a fino all'anno 1700* (Florence, 1961), 108

C.E.

Traeg, Johann (*b* Gochsheim, Lower Franconia, 20 Jan 1747; *d* Vienna, 5 Sept 1805). Austrian publisher and copyist. He was the son of Johann Veit Traeg, a musician, after whose death the family moved to Vienna (by 1779), where Johann established his business. After his death his son Johann Traeg the younger (*b* 15 Sept 1781; *d* after 1831) acquired the firm by decree of the town council on 12 February 1808.

Johann Traeg the elder began his music publishing activities as a copyist in the early 1780s. His first announcement in the *Wiener Zeitung* on 10 August 1782 advertised that all genres of music could be purchased from him. The undertaking subsequently developed into the most prominent copying workshop in Vienna. Between 21 December 1782 and 15 January 1794 frequent advertisements in the *Wiener Zeitung* announced new manuscripts, and also mentioned items for sale by other publishers. On 19 February 1794 Traeg opened a music shop. His publishing concern was launched with the three quartets op. 1 by Eybler, published on commission on 9 April 1794, though until 1800 it pursued a somewhat hesitant course. Manuscript copies continued to be sold as well as items from foreign firms; from 16 June 1798 Traeg was an agent for Breitkopf & Härtel. By 1803 the business was firmly established, and on 22 October was renamed Johann Traeg und Sohn. This period ended on 7 August 1805 when three short masses by Kajetan Freundthaler were published with the imprint 'Giovanni Traeg' (i.e. the son), though after the father's death, the official permit being still valid, publications with the imprint 'Johann Traeg und Sohn' continued to appear until the beginning of 1808. The firm subsequently prospered and by 1818 had reached the publication no. 604; growing competition from other firms led to a gradual decline in activity and to bankruptcy which enforced the sale of the majority of the publications to Artaria & Co. (July 1817). The bankruptcy was, however, unexpectedly cancelled two years later (20 August 1819). The final liquidation of the firm took place on 27 July 1820, the rest of the current publications passing to Cappi & Diabelli and Pietro Mechetti. Johann Traeg the younger was registered as an art shop bookkeeper in October 1823 and in April 1831 he was living in Leopoldstadt.

The most important years of the publishing house were mainly its earliest. Its publications included the first edition of Haydn's Piano Trio hXV:31 and some of his lesser pieces and arrangements; the first editions of Mozart's k174, 298 and 608 and early editions of the quartets k387–465; the first edition of Beethoven's opp.9 and 66 as well as WoO65, 69, 70, 72, 77, 83, 123 and 124, and several arrangements as well as pieces by C. P. E. Bach. Among the other composers represented in Traeg's catalogue are Cherubini, Cramer, Dussek, Eybler, Förster, Gyrowetz, M. Haydn, Hummel, Krommer, Mederitsch, Pleyel, A. Polzelli, A. Reicha, F. Ries, P, Rode, Starke, Steibelt, Vanhal and Woelfl. The firm also published music by Johann the elder's brother Andreas (*b* Gochsheim, 2 Dec 1748).

J. Traeg: *Verzeichnis alter und neuer sowohl geschriebener als gestochener Musikalien, welche bei Johann Traeg erschienen sind* (Vienna, 1799/*R*, suppl. 1804/*R*); L. von Köchel: *Chronologisch-thematisches Verzeichnis sämtlicher Tonwerke Wolfgang Amade Mozarts* (Leipzig, 1862, rev. 6/1964); G. Kinsky and H. Halm: *Das Werk Beethovens: thematisch-bibliographisches Verzeichnis seiner sämtlichen vollendeten Kompositionen* (Munich and Duisburg, 1955); A. Weinmann: 'Verzeichnis der Musikalien des Verlages Johann Traeg in Wien 1794–1818', *SMw*, xxiii (1956), 135; A. van Hoboken: *Joseph Haydn: thematisch-bibliographisches Werkverzeichnis* (Mainz, 1957–71); A. Weinmann: *Johann Traeg: die Musikalienverzeichnisse von 1799 und 1804 (Handschrift und Sortiment)* (Vienna, 1973); idem: *Die Anzeigen des Kopiaturbetriebes Johann Traeg in der Wiener Zeitung zwischen 1782 und 1805* (Vienna, 1981); G. Haberkamp: *Die Erstdrucke der Werke von Wolfgang Amadeus Mozart* (Tutzing, 1986)

A.W.

Trattner, Johann Thomas, Edler von (*b* Hungary, 11 Nov 1717; *d* Vienna, 31 July 1798). Austrian publisher of Hungarian birth. He was the leading music publisher and retailer in Vienna between 1770 and 1790. He arrived there in 1739, and worked as a journeyman in Van Ghelen's printing office before buying J. J. Jahns's business in 1748. Subsequently he became court bookseller (1751) and court printer (1754). The numerous privileges resulting from the Empress Maria Theresia's patronage and his own efficiency and business acumen helped his firm to flourish. The house he bought in Alt Lerchenfeld in 1759 was transformed into a 'typographical palace'; in 1773 he bought the Freisingerhof on the Graben and built the new Trattnerhof there in 1777. His standing is strikingly demonstrated by the fact that the future Emperor Joseph II learnt printing from him.

Trattner started advertising music in the *Wiener Diarium* in 1756, but only on a small scale before 1764; the firm's *Catalogus universalis liborum* (1765) and further catalogues (1776, 1777, 1780, 1784) indicate increased activity. His fame as a music publisher rested particularly on the scores of two works by Gluck, *Alceste* (1769) and *Paride ed Elena* (1770). He was also responsible for the *Missale romanum* of 1758. Mozart lived in the Trattnerhof from 23 January to 29 September 1784, and taught Trattner's second wife, Theresia, to whom he dedicated the Fantasy and Sonata κ475 and 457. He gave three concerts in Trattner's concert hall.

In 1793 Trattner made his grandson Johann Thomas Trattner the younger a partner; the latter carried on the business after Trattner's death. In 1805 the printing office was sold to the manager Georg Überreuter and the bookshop to Josef Tendler.

Überreuter's press has become part of the Viennese firm of Salzer.

A. Mayer: *Wiens Buchdrucker-Geschichte 1482–1882*, ii (Vienna, 1887); H. Cloeter: 'Johann Thomas von Trattner', *Jb des Vereines für Geschichte der Stadt Wien*, i (1939), 82; E. Castle: *Geschichte einer Wiener Buchdruckerei 1548–1948* (Vienna, 1948); H. Cloeter: *Johann Thomas Trattner: ein Grossunternehmer im Theresianischen Wien* (Graz and Cologne, 1952); Weinmann (1956); H. Gericke: *Der Wiener Musikalienhandel von 1700 bis 1778* (Graz and Cologne, 1960); O. Hafner: 'Mozart in Steirischen Musikalienhandel vor 1800', *Mitteilungen der Internationalen Stiftung Mozarteum Salzburg*, xxix (1982), 29

A.W.

Trautwein, Traugott. German publisher. After apprenticeship at Breitkopf & Härtel he moved to Berlin and in 1820 published Friedrich von Drieberg's essays on ancient Greek music. In 1821 the local patrician Ferdinand Mendheim entered the firm, further emphasizing its scholarly and historical bent. Its output was devoted to pedagogical and critical topics and to Renaissance and Baroque music, often edited by Franz Commer. Series included Johann Gottfried Hientzsch's *Eutonia* (1835–7), Ludwig Rellstab's *Iris im Gebiete der Tonkunst* (1830–41), the *Auswahl vorzügliche Musik-Werke* (1835–46) of the Preussische Akademie der Künste and the collected works of Carl Friedrich Fasch (6 vols., 1839). After 1840, imprints of the Trautwein'sche Buch- und Musikalien Handlung usually specify the subsidiary retail shop of J. Guttentag. The firm was acquired in 1858 by Martin Bahn, who issued music by Franz Gläser, Eduard Grell and Karl Reissiger, among others. The Trautwein imprint also appears on early issues of the *Monatshefte für Musikgeschichte* (1869–84). On Bahn's death in 1902 the business passed to Heinrichshofen in Magdeburg.

R. Schaal: 'Trautwein, Traugott', *MGG*; R. Elvers, 'Berliner Musikverleger', *Studien zur Musikgeschichte Berlins im frühen 19. Jahrhundert*, ed. C. Dahlhaus (Regensburg, 1980), 285

D.W.K.

Treichlinger, József (*b* Vienna, 1807; *d* after 1866). Hungarian publisher. From 1828 he made regular public appearances as a solo violinist and in a formal letter he described himself as a 'musician, honorary member of several philharmonic societies at home and abroad, conductor, committee member and archivist of the Pest-Buda Musical Association'. In 1844 he took over Vince Grimm's publishing house in the city of Pest, thus becoming the last owner of the

Kunst und Industrie Comptoir (founded in 1805). He published mostly dance music that aimed to serve average tastes, and occasionally also piano scores of operas (Ferenc Erkel's *Hunyadi László*, György Császár's *A kunok*, Ferenc Doppler's *Benyovszky* and *Vanda*). He kept plate numbering in exemplary order, with only rare instances of duplication. More than 400 of his publications are known. Surprisingly, the plate numbers 1–105 are missing; his first known plate number is J. T. 106. There are, however, some unnumbered specimens, and some with only alphabetical markings. According to present information it may be assumed that his alphabetically marked plates date from before 1850; numbered and unnumbered plates appear to be characteristic of the entire span of his activities. In 1866 he handed over the firm to his son József Treichlinger jr, who sold it to Rózsavölgyi és Társa in 1874.

K. Isoz: *Zeneműkereskedelem és kiadás a régi Pest-Budán* [Music trade and publication in old Pest-Buda] (Budapest, 1941); I. Mona: *Hungarian Music Publication 1774–1867* (Budapest, 1973); idem: *Magyar zeneműkiadók és tevékenységük 1774–1867* [Hungarian music publishers and their activity] (Budapest, forthcoming)

I.M.

Troupenas, Eugène-Théodore (*b* Paris, 17 Dec 1799; *d* Paris, 11 April 1850). French publisher, active in Paris. After training as a mathematician, he acquired the publishing firm of Isouard (who traded as Nicolo) in 1825, taking premises at 3 rue de Ménars. In September 1828 he moved to 23 rue St Marc. In 1835 he moved again, to 40 rue Neuve-Vivienne (sometimes given simply as rue Vivienne). For a short time after his death his firm continued to advertise, but in October 1850 it was taken over by Brandus (with whom Troupenas had occasionally published in partnership).

Troupenas' success in business mainly derived from his contacts with Rossini and Auber. Between 1826 and 1829 he published the first editions of Rossini's last four operas – *Le siège de Corinthe, Moïse, Le comte Ory* and *Guillaume Tell* (see illustration); later he published the *Soirées musicales,* the *Stabat mater* and the adaptation *Robert Bruce* (in 1841 he was involved in a lawsuit with Schlesinger and Aulagnier over the rights to the *Stabat mater*). It was Rossini who encouraged him to publish Auber's *La muette de Portici* in 1828, and this was followed by scores of 19 further Auber operas (including all the famous ones). In addition he published full scores of operas by Bazin, Gomis and Labarre and reissued 13 of Isouard's works. He also put out piano-vocal scores of more than 40 operas, ending with Meyerbeer's *Le prophète* (in association with Brandus). In all he issued rather over 2300 publications (judging by the plate numbers, which in general are reliably chronological), all from engraved plates. Notable among them were didactic works by Kastner and Fétis, a collection of Beethoven's symphonies edited by Fétis (for which, and for *Guillaume Tell*, he employed Berlioz as proofreader), and a large quantity of instrumental music, including string quartets and quintets by Onslow and numerous works for violin by de Bériot, for flute by Tulou, for harp by Bochsa and Labarre, for piano by Czerny, Herz, Kalkbrenner and Thalberg, and quadrilles and waltzes by Lanner, Labitzky and Musard. In 1840–41 he published the first editions of Chopin's opp.35–41 and 43. During summer 1838 and subsequently he advertised publications of the former Magasin de Musique (i) which he seems to have purchased from Janet & Cotelle at the period of the dissolution of that partnership.

Troupenas composed some church music and a few *romances,* and in 1832 contributed to the *Revue musicale* three theoretical articles which were published separately that year. According to Fétis, when he died he left unfinished a work elucidating his theories.

FétisB; E. Troupenas: *Résumé des opinions de la presse sur le Stabat de Rossini* (Paris, 1842); Hopkinson (1954); H. Weinstock: *Rossini* (New York, 1968); Devriès and Lesure (1979–88)

R.M.

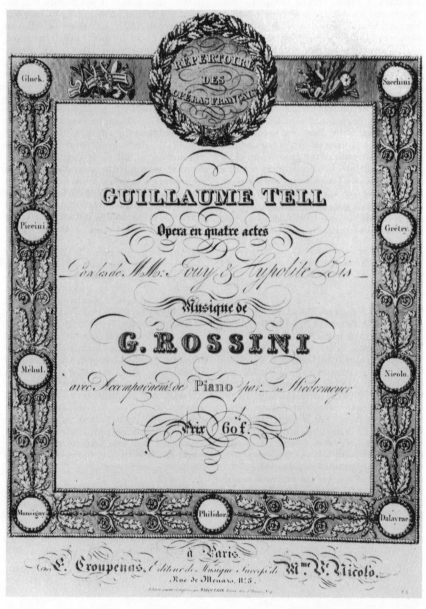

Title-page of the first edition of the vocal score of Rossini's 'Guillaume Tell' (Paris: Troupenas, 1829)

U

Ugrino. German firm of publishers. In 1921 Gottlieb Harms and Hans Henny Jahnn founded the firm in Hamburg; in 1923 it was registered as an 'association for safeguarding the interests of the Ugrino religious community, publishing section'. Hilmar Trede joined the firm in 1925 as director. The first undertaking (in 1921), was a complete edition of the works of Vincent Lübeck which was followed by complete editions of Scheidt and Buxtehude. Jahnn was forced to emigrate in 1933, and apart from works already in preparation when he left, which continued to appear until 1935, publishing did not resume until his return in 1952. In 1956 the firm was again incorporated in the commercial register. After Jahnn's death in 1959 it was taken over by his daughter Signe Trede. On 1 October 1971 the VEB Deutscher Verlag für Musik in Leipzig acquired the publishing rights of Ugrino, which still continues to produce works by Buxtehude, Gesualdo, Scheidt, Schlick and others.

Musikverlage in der Bundesrepublik Deutschland und in West-Berlin (Bonn, 1965), 69

T.W.

Ulhart [Ulhard], **Philipp** (*d* Augsburg, 1567 or 1568). German printer. In 1522 he began printing in Augsburg, using the typefaces of Sigmund Grimm, who had in turn acquired them from Erhard Oeglin. Ulhart's first efforts in publishing, as Schottenloher showed, were devoted almost exclusively to promoting the cause of various Reformed sects then active in Augsburg, particularly that of the Anabaptists, whose leaders included his friends Jacob Dachser and Sigmund Salminger. On 7 March 1523 in an attempt to curb sectarianism, the city council required Ulhart and seven other Augsburg printers to swear a formal oath that they would not publish anonymously. The order was rescinded shortly afterwards, and almost 200 anonymous pamphlets can be traced from typographical evidence to Ulhart's press from the period 1523–9. In connection with the vigorous persecution of the Anabaptists he was imprisoned for eight days in 1526 and arrested again in 1528, but released for lack of evidence. In 1548 he became a citizen of Augsburg, though his reputation as a printer had been established long before. After his death the business was continued by his son, also

called Philipp (*d* 1579 or 1580), and was bought in 1581 by Valentin Schönig, son-in-law of the Augsburg printer Melchior Kriesstein.

As well as religious publications, which included the writings of Luther and other Reformation leaders, Ulhart printed various theoretical works and school plays, many of which contain religious songs. In music, however, he is known principally for issuing collections edited by Sigmund Salminger; these contain settings of hymns and psalms. The two volumes of 1545 and 1548 contain works for the Catholic liturgy, many of them *unica*, by well-known Netherlands composers.

P. Wackernagel: *Bibliographie zur Geschichte des deutschen Kirchenliedes im XVI. Jahrhundert* (Frankfurt am Main, 1855/R1961); idem: *Das deutsche Kirchenlied*, i (Leipzig, 1864/R1964), 389, 407; K. Schottenloher: *Philipp Ulhart, ein Augsburger Winkeldrucker und Helfershelfer der 'Schwärmer' und 'Wiedertäufer' (1523–1529)* (Munich, 1921/R1967) [incl. list of publications]; A. Dresler: *Augsburg und die Frühgeschichte der Presse* (Munich, 1952), 23; Benzing (1963, 2/1982)

M.L.G.

Ungler, Florian (*b* Bavaria; *d* Kraków, 1536). Polish printer of German birth, active in Kraków. From 1510 to 1516 he worked with other printers, including Jan Haller, but later he established his own printing house. He was the first in Poland to publish music in mensural notation (printed from woodblock), in his editions of musical theorists. His output was over 240 titles. When he died his widow continued the business until her death in 1551, when Siebeneicher acquired the firm for the Szarfenberg publishing house.

Przywecka-Samecka (1969); *Słownik pracowników książki polskiej* [Dictionary of Polish printers] (Warsaw and Łódź, 1972)

T.C. (ii)

Unión Musical Española. Spanish firm of publishers. At the end of the 19th century Ernesto Dotesio Paynter established a music shop in Bilbao, and also engaged in music publishing. On 14 March 1900 he founded the music publishing firm Casa Dotesio, having in 1898 bought the Casa Romero, one of the most important publishing houses in Spain; this was founded by Antonio Romero y Andía in 1856, and was active throughout the second half of the 19th century. In the weeks following its foundation the Casa Dotesio absorbed other important houses, including Zozaya,

Fuentes y Asenjo and, most significant, Eslava (founded by Bonifacio San Martín Eslava); the Casa Romero and Eslava are notable for having published many 19th-century Spanish works, not only in large numbers but also exquisitely printed. In the following years the Casa Dotesio continued to absorb other smaller publishers. On 26 May 1914 it changed its name to Unión Musical Española, a name that better reflected the character of the firm, since it had united all the previously disparate parts of the nation's music publishing under one roof, and continued to do so in subsequent years. In 1942 it acquired the Editorial Orfeo Tracio, which in turn had absorbed such important houses as Vidal Llimona y Boceta, Luis Tena and Salvat.

The Unión Musical Española has continually fostered the development of Spanish music. It has published works by all the major 20th-century Spanish composers; for some, such as Eduardo Toldrá, Regino Sáinz de la Maza and Graciano Tarragó, it is the sole publisher. The firm's most important work is possibly represented by historic Spanish music, with such monumental collections as *La Tonadilla Escénica*, edited by José Subirá (24 volumes), the sonatas of Antonio Soler, edited by Samuel Rubio, and numerous editions of songs, as well as music for guitar, organ and other instruments.

J.L.-C.

Universal Edition. Austrian firm of publishers.

1. HISTORY. Universal Edition (UE) was founded in Vienna on 1 June 1901 by three Viennese publishers: Josef Weinberger, Adolf Robitschek and Bernhard Herzmansky sr (of Doblinger) in conjunction with the music engraving and printing firm of R. v. Waldheim, Josef Eberle & Co. The original idea probably came from Weinberger and the banker Josef Simon (Johann Strauss's brother-in-law). UE was almost certainly the earliest joint-stock publishing company in Austria. Its initial aims were described in the *Neue Wiener Tagblatt* on 9 August 1901: 'The new music publisher is a joint venture founded by leading publishers of Austria-Hungary. . . . As well as publishing the classics and significant instructive works, it will also publish compositions by important modern masters'. The main purpose of UE at the outset was to provide an Austrian edition of the standard repertory which could compete successfully with those of Peters and Breitkopf & Härtel. The firm's financial position was strengthened by the instruction from the Austrian Ministry of Education on 5 July 1901 that all Austrian music schools should buy UE publications in preference to German editions. Further stability was offered by Weinberger who undertook to purchase a substantial quantity of UE's output. Weinberger also provided the firm with its first premises, in his own building at 11 Maximilianstrasse (later Mahlerstrasse). In 1914 it moved to the Musikvereinsgebäude where it remains. In 1904 UE purchased the firm of Aibl, which had published a number of major works by Richard Strauss and Reger. The rapid expansion of the catalogue was made possible not only by such outright purchases, but also by issuing under licence, in UE wrappers, a large number of works from other publishers.

In 1907 Emil Hertzka (*b* Budapest, 3 Aug 1869; *d* Vienna, 9 May 1932) was appointed managing director of UE, with far-reaching consequences. Along with the senior editor Josef V. von Wöss (*b* Cattaro, Dalmatia, 13 June 1863; *d* Vienna, 22 Oct 1943) Hertzka changed the firm's publishing policy, concentrating almost exclusively on new music. He presided over the most exciting years in UE's history and after his death Paul Stefan wrote: 'When the history of the music of our time is written, Hertzka's name will stand above all others as the great originator'. Alfred Kalmus joined the firm in 1909; he remained until his death in 1972, apart from the years 1923–5 when he established the Wiener Philharmonischer Verlag. Hans Heinsheimer (*b* Karlsruhe, 25 Sept 1900) joined in 1923 as head of the opera department, a post he held until 1938. Alfred Schlee (*b* 1901) began working for the company in 1927.

Hertzka's successors were Hugo Winter and Kalmus, but the changing political climate drove Kalmus to leave Vienna in 1936, the year he established UE London, and in 1938 Winter was dismissed by the Nazis; Heinsheimer left Vienna on 11 March 1938, the day before the Anschluss. In 1940 all the shares in UE were acquired by Johannes Petschull (*b* Diez, 8 May 1901), who also worked as managing director of C. F. Peters during the war years. Alfred Schlee remained in Vienna throughout the war, maintaining such contact as was possible with UE composers and, in particular, helping Webern by employing him as arranger and reader. Schlee also made frequent trips to Switzerland during the war, usually to promote Webern's music. The rapid reconstruction of UE after the war owed much to the energetic initiatives of Schlee in Vienna and Kalmus in London. In 1949 the London branch became independent from Boosey & Hawkes under whose aegis it had operated during the war; on 5 June 1951 UE Vienna was re-established, with restoration of all the original shareholders' rights and three directors: Schlee, Kalmus and Ernst Hartmann. From that time UE, both in Vienna and London, once again established itself as the pre-eminent European publisher of modern music, a position which it maintains with authority to the present day. The remarkable achievement of UE was well described by Franz Schreker in 1926: 'It has not only encouraged and sponsored the modern music movement, it has founded it'.

2. PUBLICATIONS. UE's publisher's numbers are, in general, reliably chronological. The firm issued 400 titles in its first year of business (1901), passing the stated original target of 1000 titles in 1904 and reaching 3200 in the Spring 1911 supplement to the 1910 complete catalogue. The 1937 *Gesamt-Katalog* lists over 10,000 titles. The catalogue has continued to grow at a considerable rate since the war; by the time UE celebrated its 75th anniversary in 1976 the main numerical series had exceeded 15,000.

In UE's early years, from 1901 to 1907, most of its publications were of the classics. Their editing and arranging was entrusted to some of Vienna's leading musicians, including Hellmesberger, Heuberger, Kienzl, Rosé, Schenker, Schoenberg and Zemlinsky. With the appointment of Hertzka as director in 1907 the policy of publishing new music became apparent almost at once: among the 'recent publications' listed in the 1910 catalogue are new works by Korngold, Mahler, Schoenberg, Schreker, Bruno Walter and Zemlinsky. Hertzka made contracts with many of the most important composers of the time, excepting Hindemith, Stravinsky, Prokofiev and the French school. The list of composers contracted to UE before 1938 is imposing: Bartók, Berg, Bittner, Braunfels, Casella, Delius, Gál, Graener, Grosz, Hába, Hauer, Janáček, Kodály, Krenek, Mahler, Malipiero, Marx, Novák, Schmidt, Schoenberg, Schreker, Szymanowski, Webern, Weigl, Weill, Weinberger, Wellesz and Zemlinsky, among many others.

With such composers as these it is hardly surprising that UE published many of the most significant works of the time. The firm's pre-war opera catalogue is particularly notable, including Bartók's *Bluebeard's Castle* (1922), Berg's *Wozzeck* (1926) and *Lulu* (1936), Max Brand's *Maschinist Hopkins* (1929), Gál's *Die heilige Ente* (1922), Janáček's *Jenůfa* (1917), *Mr Brouček's*

Excursions (1919), *Kát'a Kabanová* (1922), *The Cunning Little Vixen* (1924), *The Makropulos Affair* (1926) and *From the House of the Dead* (1930), Kodály's *Háry János* (1929), Krenek's *Jonny spielt auf* (1926), Schoenberg's *Erwartung* and *Die glückliche Hand* (both 1916), Schreker's *Der ferne Klang* (1911, vocal score by Berg), Weill's *Dreigroschenoper* (1928) and *Aufstieg und Fall der Stadt Mahagonny* (1930), Weinberger's *Shvanda the Bagpiper* (1927) and Zemlinsky's *Der Zwerg* (1921). In other genres UE's list before 1938 is scarcely less impressive, with Bartók's *The Miraculous Mandarin* (1927) and Music for Strings, Percussion and Celesta (1937), Berg's Violin Concerto (1936), Janáček's Sinfonietta (1927) and *Glagolitic Mass* (1928), Kodály's *Psalmus hungaricus* (1924), Mahler's *Das Lied von der Erde* (1911) and Ninth Symphony (1912), Schoenberg's *Gurrelieder* (1912, vocal score by Berg), First Chamber Symphony (1912) and *Pierrot lunaire* (1914), Webern's Passacaglia op.1 (1922) and Zemlinsky's Lyric Symphony (1923).

From the time of the Anschluss on 12 March 1938 until the end of the war, UE's activities were much curtailed; nevertheless, several interesting works were issued by the firm. Only two serve as a grim reminder of the period – Franz Schmidt's posthumous work *Deutsche Auferstehung* (1940) and Josef Reiter's *Festgesang an den Führer des deutschen Volkes* (1938), a cantata in praise of Hitler. Important publications include Webern's *Das Augenlicht* (April 1938), Schmidt's *Das Buch mit sieben Siegeln* (1938), Wagner-Régeny's *Johanna Balk* (1941, vocal score by Webern), Schoeck's *Schloss Dürande* (1942, vocal score by Webern) and Frank Martin's *Le vin herbé* (1943), the first of his many works brought out by the firm. After the war UE published works by Berio, Boulez, Bussotti, Cerha, Dallapiccola, Einem, Halffter, Haubenstock-Ramati, Kagel, Kurtág, Ligeti, Pärt, Pousseur, Schnittke, Skalkottas, Stockhausen and Takemitsu. Among the most notable publications are Boulez's *Le marteau sans maître* (1955), Stockhausen's *Studie II* (1956, the first electronic music to be published), Kagel's *Ludwig van* (1970) and Berio's *Sinfonia* (1972).

The firm has an established tradition of issuing periodicals. Much the most important of these was *Musikblätter des Anbruch* (1919–38; *Anbruch* from 1929), the leading journal of new music, with an inevitable bias towards UE composers. Other journals include *Pult und Taktstock* (1924–30; ed. E. Stein, 1924–7), *Musica divina* (1913–38), *Schrifttanz* (1928–31), the *Haydn Yearbook* (1962–75) and *Die*

Title-page of Mahler's Ninth Symphony; published by Universal Edition (Vienna and Leipzig, 1912)

Reihe (1955–62). UE's book catalogue is also substantial, including Schoenberg's *Harmonielehre* (1911), Schenker's series of Beethoven analyses, Hauer's theoretical writings and Hába's *Harmonielehre* (1927). UE has also been active as a publisher of educational music: the *Rote Reihe*, started in the 1960s, is a comprehensive attempt to apply new educational methods to the teaching of avant-garde music.

UE London was founded by Alfred Kalmus on 1 July 1936. Despite close ties with the Vienna firm, it is an independent company which has pursued a vigorous policy of publishing new music by such British and American composers as Bedford, Bennett, Birtwistle, Earle Brown, Feldman, Finnissy, Holt, Hoyland, Muldowney, Osborne, Patterson, Rands and Schafer. UE London's 50th anniversary in 1986 saw the highly successful première of one of its most important recent publications, Birtwistle's *The Mask of Orpheus*.

25 Jahre neue Musik: Jb 1926 der Universal-Edition (Vienna, 1926); *Universal-Edition Gesamt-Katalog 1937* (Vienna, 1937); H. W. Heinsheimer: *Menagerie in F sharp* (Garden City, NY, 1947); *1901 bis 1951 Universal Edition Wien* (Vienna, 1951); Plesske (1968); E. Hilmar: *15 Jahre Universal Edition (1901–1976)* (Vienna, 1976) [exhibition catalogue]; R. Klein: 'Kodály és az Universal Edition', *Magyar zenetörténeti tanulmámyok Zoltan Kodály* (Budapest, 1977), 136; H. Schneider: *Katalog Nr. 205: 75 Jahre Universal Edition (1901–1976)* (Tutzing, 1977); A. H. Bartosch: 'Prozessbeendigung in Sachen *Lulu*: Einigung über Beachtung und Interessensphären', *ÖMz*, xxxv (1980), 300; T. Chylinska: *Karol Szymanowski: Briefwechsel mit der Universal Edition* (Vienna, 1981); R. Stephan: 'Ein Blicke auf die Universal Edition: aus Anlass von Alfred Schlees 80. Geburtstag', *ÖMz*, xxxvi (1981), 639; M. G. Hall: *Österreichische Verlagsgeschichte 1918–1938* (Vienna, 1985); Burnett & Simeone Ltd: *Catalogue 22: Universal Edition* (Tunbridge Wells, 1988); E. Hilmar: *Leoš Janáček: Briefe an die Universal Edition* (Tutzing, 1988)

N.S.

Urbánek, František Augustin (*b* Moravské Budějovice, 24 Nov 1842; *d* Prague, 4 Dec 1919). Czech publisher, father of Mojmír Urbánek. After his Gymnasium studies in Znojmo and Brno he was employed from 1862 by the bookseller and publisher J. L. Kober in Prague, for whom he became general manager (1866–70). In 1872 he established his own bookselling and publishing firm in Prague, as Fr. A. Urbánek, where he first produced pedagogical publications and school textbooks. During the 1870s he gradually began to publish music,

bringing out new works by Smetana, almost all of Fibich's compositions, and the early works of Foerster, Novák, Suk, Janáček, Křička, Axman and others. His series *Dalibor*, *Lumír*, *Zora*, *Vesna*, *Lýra* and *Vlasta* were important in the development of choral song; he also published tutors for the piano, violin, flute and harmonium as well as books on music and the journals *Dalibor* (1879–99) and *Kalendář českých hudebníků* (1881–1908), serving as editor of both for some years. Besides reviewing Czech books and scores for the journal *Oestrreich-ung. Buchhändler-Correspondenz* (from 1864), he published *Knihopisný slovník* ('Book dictionary', 1865) and published and edited the *Věstník bibliografický* ('Bibliographical bulletin', 1869–84). In 1913 his sons František Augustin and Vladimír became partners in the firm and its name was changed to Fr. A. Urbánek a synové. Subsequently the firm published revisions of earlier publications and a new series of popular compositions. The firm was nationalized in 1949.

ČSHS; V. Nejdl: *30 let českého hudebního nakladatele 1872–1902* [30 years of a Czech music publisher] (Prague, 1902); L. K. Žižka: *Mistři a mistříčkové: vzpomínky na české muzikanty let 1881–1891* [Masters and lesser masters: reminiscences of Czech musicians 1881–91] (Prague, 1939, enlarged 2/1947); *Vzpomínka k stoletému výročí narozenin ceského nakladatele Fr. A. Urbánka a na sedmdesát let trvání závodu: 1842–1872–1942* [Recollections on the 100th anniversary of the birth of the Czech publisher Urbánek and on the 70 years of the firm's existence] (Prague, 1942)

Z.C.

Urbánek, Mojmír (*b* Prague, 6 May 1873; *d* Prague, 29 Sept 1919). Czech publisher, son of František Augustin Urbánek. After an apprenticeship with his father and experience in Germany, France, England and the USA, he founded his own publishing house in Prague in 1900. Under the name Edition M.U. the firm published music by Foerster, Novák, Suk and Vojtěch Říhovský. Besides books on music Urbánek published the journal *Dalibor* (from 1900). He owned a keyboard instrument shop and in 1908 set up the Mozarteum concert hall; he also ran a successful concert agency, and after World War I acquired a music printing works. After his death his widow Iška Urbánková ran the firm, followed from 1925 by his son Mojmír Urbánek. The firm was nationalized in 1949.

Z.C.

V

Valdarfer, Christoph (*b* Regensburg; *fl* 1470–88). German printer, active in Venice, Milan and Basle. After an unsuccessful attempt to set up a printing shop in Milan in 1470 he moved to Venice and issued several books. He returned to Milan to print between 1474 and 1478, and then went to Basle to work with Bernhard Richel from 1479 to 1482. Valdarfer returned to Milan a second time, issuing the *Missale ambrosianum* of 15 March 1482 with the first printed Ambrosian plainchant, the first music printed in Milan. His *Missale romanum* of 1 September 1482 used a roman plainchant type of the same size. The irregularity and thinness of the long stems of Valdarfer's notes, together with their frequent lack of connection to the note head, suggests that the stems were printed from various lengths of metal rule, as were the bar-lines.

F. Geldner: *Die deutschen Inkunabeldrucker: ein Handbuch der deutschen Buchdrucker des XV. Jahrhunderts nach Druckorten*, ii (Stuttgart, 1970), 109; Duggan (1981)

M.K.D.

Valentim de Carvalho. Portuguese firm of publishers. It was founded in Lisbon in 1914 by Valentim de Carvalho (1888–1957). In 1953 it took over the firms of Newparth & Carneiro and Heliodoro de Oliveira. Its record company, established in 1945, issues Portuguese music and re-recordings from about 20 foreign firms. The firms also owns studios for recording film soundtracks. Valentim de Carvalho publishes educational works, piano music by Portuguese and foreign composers, and the 'Polyphonia' collection of scores in two series, one of popular Portuguese music, the other devoted to Portuguese music from the 16th century to the 18th (works by Manuel Cardoso, Francisco Martins, Filipe de Magalhães, King John IV, Diogo Dias Melgaz, Francisco António de Almeida and Carlos de Seixas). The company's record catalogue includes works by all the major Portuguese composers.

T. Borba and F. Lopes Graça: *Dicionário de música*, ii (Lisbon, 1958), 503, 657

C. de P.L.

Valesi, Fulgenzio (*b* Parma, ?*c*1565; *d* ?after 1614). Italian composer and printer. From the dedication of his *Primo libro di napolitane* (Venice, 1587) it appears that he was born and grew up in Parma and that this was his first work. He was a Cistercian monk at the convent of S Croce in Gerusalemme, Rome, from 1593 to 1600. At this time many references to him appeared in documents relating to the plan for the printing of the Roman Gradual, corrected in accordance with the dictates of the Council of Trent. Together with Leonardo Parasoli, Valesi obtained from Pope Clement VIII on 16 September 1593 the privilege of printing the books of chants by a presumably new process of their own invention, using notes and letters of large proportions. The musical text to be printed should have been corrected by Palestrina, who died, however, before finishing the work. Iginio, the son and heir of Palestrina, supplied a text tampered with by other hands, which led to a long lawsuit, begun in 1596. During the complicated proceedings Valesi, originally the holder, with other associates, of Palestrina's MS, left the association and was instructed by the Congregation of Rites to examine the MS with G. M. Nanino, A. Dragoni and Marenzio to see if it corresponded to correct liturgical usage; the lawsuit occasioned several informed and authoritative statements from Valesi. Soon after 1600 he left Rome and seems to have begun a life of adventure.

R. Molitor: *Die nachtridentinische Choralreform zu Rom* (Leipzig, 1902); N. Pelicelli: 'Musicisti in Parma nei secoli XV–XVI', *NA*, ix (1932), 127; A. Bernier: 'Intorno alla edizione medicea del canto gregoriano: un documento inedito', *NA*, xiii (1937), 91

M.D.

Van Ghelen. Austrian firm of publishers. Johann Peter van Ghelen (1673–1754), son of an Antwerp bookdealer, served an apprenticeship in Brussels and in his father's Viennese printing works, which he took over in 1721. In 1722 he bought the *Wiener Diarium* (renamed the *Wiener Zeitung* in 1780), which remained in the firm's ownership into the 19th century and exercised an important monopoly as the advertising organ of the book and music publishing trade until 1848. In 1725 Van Ghelen published Fux's *Gradus ad Parnassum* and reissued Georg Muffat's *Apparatus musico-organisticus* (1690). His eldest son Johann Leopold took over the business in 1754, succeeded in the 1760s by Jakob Anton van Ghelen, with whom the family's male line died out in 1782. The amount of music advertised by the firm increased greatly under his management after 1770; with Trattner and Krüchten the firm was the biggest music dealer in Vienna. After Jakob Anton's death the firm changed its name to Edle v. Ghelenschen Erben.

Weinmann (1956); H. Gericke: *Der Wiener Musikalienhandel von 1700 bis 1778* (Graz and Cologne, 1960)

A.W.

Van Ohr, Phillipp (*b* Marsberg or Obermarsberg; *d* Hamburg, 1608). German printer. Active in Hamburg after 1597, presumably as successor to Heinrich Binder (*fl* 1587–97), he printed non-musical works and at least six small collections of songs and three of dances, by Zacharias Füllsack, Christian Hildebrand and William Brade. Among other composers represented in his musical output of about 16 titles are Hieronymus Praetorius (*Cantiones sacrae*, 1599, repr. 1607; *Magnificat*, 1602) and J. P. Sweelinck (*Canticum nuptiarum*, n.d.). Van Ohr is associated with one of two distinctive music typefaces in early 17th-century north German music.

Benzing (1963, 2/1982); D. W. Krummel: 'Early German Partbook Type Faces', *Gutenberg-Jb 1985*, 80

T.D.W.

Vaughan, James D(avid) (*b* between Lawrence Co. and Giles Co., TN, 14 Dec 1864; *d* Lawrenceburg, TN, 9 Feb 1941). American publisher. He was a composer and compiler of gospel songs in shape notation. From 1890 to 1911 he produced gospel songbooks under his own name, beginning with the volume *Gospel Chimes*. In 1912 he established the Vaughan Co. in Lawrenceburg, which by 1964 had issued over 105 collections of music, most of them known as convention books because they were intended for use in singing conventions and other gatherings of gospel singers. The firm also published five instruction books for singing-school use and a trade journal, the *Musical Visitor* (later *Vaughan's Family Visitor*; ceased 1986), which publicized activities of gospel singers. Vaughan has been credited with having originated the idea of the male gospel quartet in about 1891 and beginning radio broadcasts by such groups; later his firm employed up to 16 quartets at one time. In 1921 he established the first radio station in Tennessee, to promote Vaughan songs and songbooks. His firm also sponsored singing-schools and normal music schools to train singing-school teachers. Since 1965 the Vaughan Company has been managed by Pathway Press of Cleveland, Tennessee, the trade division of the Church of God publishing house. Selected Vaughan books are kept in print, including the famous *Rudiments*, and a new one produced each year.

G. P. Jackson: 'Rural Shape-note Song Books by the Million: Publishers of Seven-shape Song Books', *White Spirituals in the Southern Uplands* (Chapel Hill, 1933/*R*1965), 366; J. L. Fleming: *James D. Vaughan, Music Publisher, Lawrenceburg, Tennessee, 1912–1964* (diss., Union Theological Seminary, 1971)

H.E.

Vautrollier, Thomas (*d* 1587). English printer, publisher and bookseller of French birth. He was a Huguenot refugee who settled in London (*c*1562) and worked in London and Edinburgh. He ran a general printing and publishing business, and in 1570 he published an English edition of Lassus's *Recueil du mellange*. He also printed in 1575 the *Cantiones sacrae* of Tallis and Byrd (see illustration and *see* fig.6, p.24), the first work published under the terms of a music printing monopoly granted to the two composers by Elizabeth I. Neither the quality of the music nor the high standard of the printing stopped the venture from being a failure and Vautrollier printed no more music under this licence, although he printed two psalm books in 1587, which were exempt from the monopoly. His type was almost certainly acquired from the Netherlands, and on his death his partbook fount passed to Thomas East. A street was named after Vautrollier in the Blackfriars district of the City of London.

Humphries and Smith (1954, 2/1970); J. Kerman: 'An Elizabethan Edition of Lassus', *AcM*, xxvii (1955), 71; Krummel (1975)

M.M.

Venier, Jean Baptiste (*fl* 1755–84). French publisher. He lived in Paris, and his first privilege for music publishing dates from 1755. At that time he apparently had no premises of his own, but in 1760 the address of his firm is given as rue St Thomas du Louvre. After September 1778 he moved to rue Traversière St Honoré, where he was active until about 1784, when Boyer acquired his stock.

Venier published mostly instrumental works – symphonies, concertos and chamber music. His catalogues give a picture of the international character of Parisian musical life at that time as well as the different influences on the development of the French symphony. At first he published Italian symphonies by Castrucci, Galuppi, Jommelli and Giuseppe Sammartini and, later, works by contemporary German, Bohemian and Austrian composers, including J. C. Bach, Bode, Hasse, Kammel, Mysliveček, Dittersdorf and

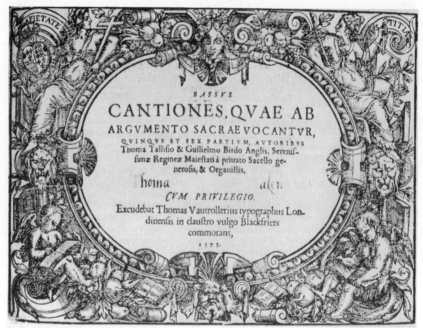

Title-page of the 'Cantiones', published by Byrd and Tallis in 1575 under their royal patent for music printing: it has the first continental-style music title-page used in England, adapted from Le Roy by the printer Vautrollier for his London edition of Lassus's chansons in 1570

Wagenseil. The Mannheim school is richly represented in his catalogues with works by Franz Beck, Christian Cannabich, Filtz, Fränzl, Holzbauer, F. X. Richter and Johann Stamitz. He also published many works by Boccherini, and he was the first to publish a symphony by Haydn, *Sinfonie a più stromenti composte da vari autori*, no.14 (1764; HI:2).

M. Brenet: 'La librairie musicale en France de 1653 à 1790, d'après les registres de privilèges', *SIMG*, viii (1906–7), 401–66; Hopkinson (1954); Johansson (1955); B. S. Brook: *La symphonie française dans la second moitié du XVIIIe siècle*, i (Paris, 1962)

C.J.

Verovio, Simone (*b* 's-Hertogenbosch; *fl* Rome, 1575–1608). Netherlands calligrapher, editor and engraver of music. He went to Rome in 1575; in 1586 he edited volumes of music, among the first to be printed entirely from engraved plates. (The *Intabolatura da leuto del divino Francesco da Milano*, imperfectly engraved in about 1535, inspired no immediate imitations of the technique.) Two of these were entitled *Diletto spirituale*, one with keyboard score and lute tablature (see illustration), and one with only the vocal parts; the third was Peetrino's *Primo libro delle melodie spirituali*. In two of the books Verovio called himself

'scrittore', but in all three books the phrase 'Martinus van Buyten incidit' appears on the title-page. Van Buyten may have engraved all of the plates for the Peetrino book and the purely vocal version of *Diletto spirituale*; however, the version with instrumental music was 'collected by Simon Verovio, engraved and printed by the same'. In some later editions Verovio clearly stated that he was the engraver, others he signed 'appresso Simone Verovio' or 'stampate da S.V.', and some he did not sign at all.

Verovio also wrote or contributed to at least five writing books between 1587 and 1598, two of them broadsides. The music books show Verovio's cursive hand; the music hand is neat, with shaded and rounded note heads. They are largely devoted to *canzonette spirituali*, often with optional instrumental parts, by composers then active in Rome. The most impressive music from his press consists of Luzzaschi's *Madrigali* (1601) and Merulo's two books of *Toccate d'intavolatura* (1598, 1604).

SartoriB; *VogelB*; R. Casimiri: 'Simone Verovio: Aggiunte', *NA*, xi (1934), 66; B. Becherini: 'Giovanni Francesco Anerio ed alcune sue gagliarde per cembalo', *La bibliofilia*, xlii (1939), 159; A. F. Johnson: 'A Catalogue of Italian Writing-books of the Sixteenth Century', *Signature*, new ser., x (1950), 22; C. Bonacini: *Bibliografia*

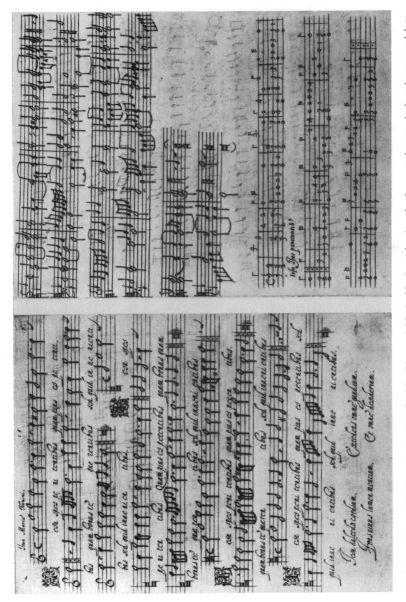

Opening of the motet 'Jesu spes penitentibus' by Giovanni Maria Nanino (showing the four vocal parts, keyboard score and lute tablature) from 'Diletto spirituale canzonette' engraved and printed by Verovio (Rome, 1586)

delle arti scrittorie e della calligrafia (Florence, 1953); Sartori (1958); King (1964); Brown (1965); C. Sartori: 'Verovio, Simone', *MGG*; A. J. Ness, ed.: *The Lute Music of Francesco Canova da Milano (1947–1543)* (Cambridge, MA, 1970), 12

T.W.B.

Vigoni [Vigone]. Italian firm of publishers. Francesco Vigoni (*b* Milan, *c*1624; *d* Milan, 1699) founded the firm in Milan in 1660. He lived first at S Sebastiano and from 1682 in Pescheria Vecchia; he printed books of various kinds (many on religious subjects) including the *Ateneo dei letterati milanesi* by Abbé Filippo Picinelli (1670), an important biographical source book for Milanese writers and artists. His music publications include sacred vocal and instrumental chamber music by such composers as C. G. San Romano, M. S. Perucona, Giacinto Pestalozza, Tomaso Motta, Bartolomeo Trabattone, G. M. Angeleri and Gerolamo Zanetti. He also published many oratorio and opera librettos. Of Francesco's five sons, Carlo Federico Vigoni (1658–*c*1693) shared the management of the firm with his father; their successors, including Carlo Federico's son Giuseppe (until 1730), published many librettos but apparently no music. The firm continued until about 1750.

Sartori (1958); M. Donà: *La stampa musicale a Milano fino all'anno 1700* (Florence, 1961)

M.D.

Vincenti [Vincenci, Vincenzi], **Giacomo** (*d* Venice, 1619). Italian bookseller and printer. He may have been of Spanish origin, since at the beginning of his career – in 1583, and for the next few years – he often signed his books 'Vincenci'; his edition of Guerrero's *Canciones y villanescas espirituales* (1589) was signed 'en la emprenta de Iago Vincentio'. He also used the spelling 'Vincenzi' in 1583, and that was the usual form until 1588; thereafter he used the form 'Vincenti', which had already appeared in some volumes of 1584.

Between 1583 and 1586 Vincenti printed, in partnership with Ricciardo Amadino, some 20 editions of music each year. Vincenti seems to have been the more assertive partner; he signed several dedications of joint works while Amadino signed none. Moreover, when they began to print separately in 1586, Vincenti kept the joint printer's mark, a pine cone. Although they probably printed no more music together, they continued to use the same typefaces, type ornaments and decorative initials, and printed jointly a number of books on philosophy and theology (1600–09). The music books issued by each printer separately do not include any of which the first edition was by the other, although a few first published by the two in partnership were reprinted by Vincenti. Perhaps they divided their copyrights when they divided their other assets in 1586. One apparent exception is Marenzio's fourth book of madrigals for six voices, which Vincenti issued in 1587 with Marenzio's dedication of 10 December 1586. Amadino's edition followed shortly, 'newly reprinted and purged of many errors', and with slightly changed contents, but with the same dedication. Evidently they had not agreed on the disposition of this book.

Vincenti's separate production from 1586 onwards was extensive and included music of most of the principal north Italian composers of the day: Croce (54 or more editions), Viadana, Marenzio, Asola, Banchieri (music and theory), Cifra, Alessandro Grandi (i), Felice Anerio, Girolamo Diruta, Ignazio Donati, Giovannelli and many other composers. He also printed numerous anthologies; theatre music (such as the *Intermedii et concerti*, 1591; composed by Malvezzi, Marenzio, Cavalieri, Bardi and Peri for the wedding in 1589 of Ferdinando de Medici and Christine of Lorraine); and a reprint of Caccini's *L'Euridice* (1615). He reprinted Caccini's *Le nuove musiche* (1615; abridged as *Nove arie*, 1608), and he printed much instrumental music as well as tutors and *passaggi*. These include works by Bassano (1591), Riccardo Rognoni (1592), Diruta (1593), Bovicelli (1594), Spadi (1609) and Bottazzi (1614). With Amadino he printed Artusi's *L'arte del contraponto ridotta in tavole* (1586), and alone he printed a *Seconda parte* (1589; repr. 1598). In 1600 he printed *L'Artusi, overo Delle imperfettioni della moderna musica*, attacking Monteverdi, with a *Seconda parte* (1603), and in 1608 Artusi's *Discorso secondo . . . di Antonio Braccino da Todi*, answering the reply in Monteverdi's *Scherzi musicali* (1607). He also printed Banchieri's *Cartella musicale* (1601) and Romano Micheli's letter *Alli molt'illustri . . . musici della cappella di N.S.* (1618), concerning the composition of canons.

Vincenti's non-musical production was small. Besides the books already mentioned there were three Tasso editions, a few plays (including one by Banchieri) and books on history, medicine and geography. His main competition was with the firms of Gardano, Scotto and Amadino. Two sons, Vincenzo and Alessandro (Allessandro), together published 12 volumes of *Villanelle, et arie napolitane* (Venice, n.d.). Vincenzo seems not to have taken any other part in the firm, and it was Alessandro Vincenti

Vitale

(*fl* 1619–67) who faced vigorous Venetian competition from Gardano's successors, Bartolomeo and Francesco Magni, while competition from Rome and other cities was also growing.

Alessandro was enthusiastic and energetic and printed copiously. His output included music by Cazzati, Donati, Grandi, Merula, Martino Pesenti and Galeazzo Sabbatini, and in lesser quantity the music of Banchieri, Gasparo and Girolamo Casati, Cozzolani, Crivelli, Ghizzolo, Salamone Rossi, Giovanni Valentini and many others. He took a solicitous interest in the blind Pesenti, whose works he usually dedicated, although Pesenti often supplied a preface to the reader and sometimes his own dedication. Pesenti's third book of *Correnti alla francese* op.12 (1641) was dedicated to 'the most illustrious and excellent Signore Domenico Vincenti' by his 'most devoted and obliged relative Allessandro Vincenti', though with no indication of how they were related.

Some Vincenti editions merit special mention: Monteverdi's eighth and ninth books of madrigals (1638, 1651) and *Messa . . . et salmi* (1650); reprints of Frescobaldi's *Capricci* (1626, 1628), and first editions of his *Canzoni* (1635), *Fiori musicali* (1635) and *Canzoni alla francese* (1645); and Cavalli's *Musiche sacre* (1656). His last known work is Rosenmüller's *Sonate da camera* (1667). He also printed music theory and criticism: Zacconi's *Prattica di musica seconda parte* (1622) and Scacchi's polemical *Cribrum musicum* (1643); and reprints of Banchieri's *L'organo suonarino* (1622, 1627, 1638) and *Cartella musicale* (as *La Banchierina*, 1623), the second part of Diruta's *Il transilvano* (1622), Scaletta's *Scala di musica* (1622, 1626, 1656, 1664) and Sabbatini's *Regola facile* (1644).

Of great historical interest are several Vincenti trade lists, beginning with *Indice di tutte l'opere di musica, che si truova alla Stampa della Pigna* (1591), which contains brief, sometimes ambiguous, indications of music for sale, not all printed by Vincenti, along with the prices. Other catalogues followed in 1621, 1635, 1649, 1658 and 1662, usually with prices (repr. in Mischiati). These generally reflect the inflation characteristic of the times, although some old copies of out-of-date music depreciated in price.

The Vincenti music editions, made from movable type, met the needs of their times but typify a period of technical stagnation and artistic decline in Italian music printing generally (except in music engraving, which Vincenti did not practise). Most are mediocre in appearance, and some are marred by ugly decoration, worn type, poor inking and errors in text and pagination. The best, however, are accurate and well executed, and a few have excellent engraved title-pages.

SartoriB; *VogelB*; A. Segarizzi: *Bibliografia delle stampe popolari italiane della R. Biblioteca nazionale di S. Marco di Venezia* (Bergamo, 1913), 223; G. Thibault: 'Deux catalogues de libraires musicaux: Vincenti et Gardane (Venise 1591)', *RdM*, xiii (1929), 177; Sartori (1958); H. W. Hitchcock: 'Depriving Caccini of a Musical Pastime', *JAMS*, xxv (1972), 58; Mischiati (1984); T. W. Bridges: *The Publishing of Arcadelt's First Book of Madrigals* (diss., Harvard U., 1982)

T.W.B.

Vissenaecken, Willem van (*fl* Antwerp, *c*1540–45). Netherlands printer. He worked with Adrien Verbrugghen in the house of Willem Vorsterman. In 1541 he formed a partnership with Henry ter Bruggen and Tylman Susato in order to print music, but quarrels led to its dissolution in 1542, and Vissenaecken and Susato formed a new, short-lived partnership. Subsequently Vissenaecken brought an unsuccessful court action against Susato. A volume of motets (*Quatuor vocum musicae modulationes numero XXVI*) was published by Vissenaecken alone in 1542, a year before Susato's first publication. It is the earliest dated music printed by a single impression in the Low Countries, and appears to have been printed independently of the partnership, the music type being quite different from any used by Susato. In 1545 Vorsterman's house and its contents, including the music type, were sold to Martin Nutius. Nutius did not print music, but after his death (1558) Vissenaecken's type reappeared in two editions of *Souterliedekens*, one published by Symon Cock (1559), the other by Claes van der Wouwere (1564).

Goovaerts (1880); H. D. L. Vervliet: *Sixteenth Century Printing Types of the Low Countries* (Amsterdam, 1968); S. Bain: *Music Printing in the Low Countries in the Sixteenth Century* (diss., U. of Cambridge, 1974)

S.B. (i)

Vitale. Brazilian publishing firm, active in São Paulo. Vicente Vitale (*b* São Paulo, 8 May 1903) set up shop in São Paulo in September 1923, publishing both Brazilian and foreign light music. Soon he incorporated with his brothers Emilio, João, Alonso and José, and the group took the name Empresa Editora Musical Irmãos Vitale. With the acquisition of the Edição Brasília de Nicolini e Pó in 1931, Vitale Irmãos began competing with foreign firms in the standard European classics. On the advice of João de Sousa Lima, its new

461

artistic director, it then began issuing a mix of commercial and serious music, including works by Villa-Lobos, Lorenzo Fernândez, Osvaldo Lacerda and Marlos Nobre; after World War II the company became Brazil's chief music publisher. It publishes catalogues of teaching materials and thematic catalogues of all music required in Brazilian conservatories. In 1973, to celebrate its 50th year, the firm issued a *Suplemento Vitale*.

Enciclopédia de música brasileira: erudita, folclórica e popular, ii (São Paulo, 1977), 356

R.S. (ii)

Vitale, Costantino (*fl* 1603–23). Italian printer. He specialized in music printing in Naples from 1603 to 1623, except for a brief period in the service of the Archbishop of Trani in 1617–18. He published secular vocal music by Macedonio di Mutio and Montella (1603), Gesualdo (1604), Albano (1616), Camillo Lambardi (1616) and others, instrumental music by Mayone and Trabaci and a number of anthologies and music treatises. From 1608 for two or three years he was in partnership with G. G. Carlino, with whom he published madrigals by Meo and Dattilo Roccia (1608), Rodio's *Regole di musica* (1609), and two collections of secular music by Donato Basile and Scialla and one of hymns by Stella (all 1610).

S.B. (iii)

Vitali, Bernardino (*fl* 1494–1529). Italian printer. He printed a number of volumes in partnership with his brother Matteo, who may have done no more than provide financial support. The most significant music printing that can certainly be assigned to them comprises the treatises of Aaron and Spataro, printed in Venice between 1523 and 1531. By then Bernardino, based in Venice, had also printed in Rome (1507–10) and in Rimini (1521). The printing of degli Silvestri's *Della origine delli volgari proverbi* (1526) is thought to have led directly to the establishment of Venetian censorship. The most important volume associated with Bernardino Vitali is Girolamo Cavazzoni's *Intavolatura* (1543), marked with a printer's device but no name. This has also been ascribed to Bernardus Vercellensis and even to Bernardinus de Vianis. It is now thought likely that it was printed by Vitali, which would make it his last printed work.

D. Zasso: *Introduzione della censura della stampa in Venezia nell'anno 1527* (Venice, 1880); C. Sartori: 'Precisazioni bibliografiche sulle opere di Girolamo Cavazzoni', *RMI*, xliv (1940), 239

S.B. (iii)

Volk. German firm of publishers. It was founded by Arno Volk (*b* Würzburg, 14 Jan 1914), who studied music at the University of Cologne, taking the doctorate there in 1943. In 1950 he founded the Arno Volk Verlag in Cologne; it was bought by the Gerig publishing group in 1957, when it became known as the Arno Volk-Verlag Hans Gerig KG; from that year Volk held a leading position with B. Schott's Söhne in Mainz, becoming chairman of the board of directors in 1974. Since its foundation the Volk-Verlag has concentrated on publishing works in musicology and music education. The firm's most ambitious project is the series *Das Musikwerk*, edited by K. G. Fellerer with the collaboration of internationally known musicologists; 47 volumes were produced in the 25 years from 1950, and from 1954 some items were issued in English as the *Anthology of Music*. A series of records associated with the anthology *Opus Musicum* (planned to run to 12 boxed sets) was begun in 1972. In 1952 the firm began the *Beiträge zur Rheinischen Musikgeschichte* and the *Veröffentlichungen des Staatlichen Instituts Preussischer Kulturbesitz*; the periodical *Analecta Musicologica* and the series *Concentus Musicus* (publications of the musicological section of the German Historical Institute in Rome, from 1973) are also noteworthy. Among the firm's performing editions are the series *Polyphonia Sacra*, choral music based on original texts (French chansons, German lieder, English madrigals, community songs) and solo cantatas of the 17th and 18th centuries.

K. G. Fellerer: 'Volk, Arno', *Rheinische Musiker*, viii (Cologne, 1974); *Festschrift für Arno Volk* (Cologne, 1974)

R.L.

Von Tilzer, Harry [Gumm, Harold] (*b* Detroit, MI, 8 July 1872; *d* New York, 10 Jan 1946). American publisher and songwriter. He added 'Von' to his mother's maiden name and used this as a professional pseudonym. He worked in a circus and medicine show as a singer and tumbler, and published his first song in 1892 (*I love you both*). In New York the same year, he performed his songs in vaudeville. The success of *My Old New Hampshire Home* (1898) was such that he was made a partner in the publishing firm Shapiro, Bernstein & Co., for whom he then wrote *A Bird in a Gilded Cage* (1900) and worked as a song plugger. In 1902 he founded the Harry Von Tilzer Music Co., which became one of the most successful American popular-music publishers in the early 20th century, earning him the nickname 'the Man who Launched a Thousand Hits'. Von Tilzer engaged Irving Berlin as a song plugger, issued George Gershwin's first song and is reputed to have published about 2000 of his own songs, including *Down where the Wurzburger flows* (1902), *I want a girl just like the girl that married dear old dad* (1911), *When my baby smiles at me* (1920) and many other sentimental ballads. He also wrote 'coon' songs for blackface minstrel and vaudeville acts. He may have been responsible for the invention of the name 'Tin Pan Alley' in about 1903, when a journalist noticed that he had stuffed paper between the strings of his office's upright piano to produce a more percussive sound. Von Tilzer was one of few publishers in the late 1920s to remain independent of the radio and cinema companies that bought up music firms and their songwriting staffs. His introduction to E. M. Wickes's manual *Writing the Popular Song* (1916) gives a brief philosophy of the profession.

Von Tilzer's brothers were also involved in music publishing and adopted his pseudonym: Julie Von Tilzer was a manager of Remick's and later president of the Harry Von Tilzer Music Co.; Will Von Tilzer was a lyricist and head of Broadway Music Co.; Jack Von Tilzer was a co-founder, in 1903, and director of the York Music Co. together with Albert Von Tilzer, who was also a successful songwriter.

I. Goldberg: *Tin Pan Alley: a Chronicle of the American Popular Music Racket* (New York, 1930/ R1961); S. Spaeth: *A History of Popular Music in America* (New York, 1948); D. Ewen: *Popular American Composers* (New York, 1962; suppl., 1972); idem: *The Life and Death of Tin Pan Alley* (New York, 1964); K. A. Kanter: *The Jews on Tin Pan Alley: the Jewish Contribution to American Popular Music, 1830–1940* (New York, 1982)

D.L.R.

W

Wachter, Georg (*b* ?Bamberg; *d* Nuremberg, 24 July 1547). German printer. By his marriage on 15 December 1527 to Kunegunde (i), widow of Hans Hergot, he became a citizen of Nuremberg and acquired the latter's printing business, which continued to issue Reformation songs under her name until 1538. After her death (Nuremberg, 7 Feb 1547), Wachter married Kunegunde (ii) Hermann, who later became wife of Valentin Neuber.

P. Cohen: *Musikdruck und -drucker zu Nürnberg im sechzehnten Jahrhundert* (Nuremberg, 1927); R. Wagner: 'Nachträge zur Geschichte der Nürnberger Musikdrucker im 16. Jahrhundert', *Mitteilungen des Vereins für Geschichte der Stadt Nürnberg*, xxx (1931),107–152; S. Braungart: *Die Verbreitung des reformatorischen Liedes in Nürnberg in der Zeit von 1525 bis 1570* (diss., U. of Erlangen, 1939); Benzing (1963, 2/1982)

T.W.

Waelrant [Waelrand], **Hubert** [Huberto] [Waelrandus, Hubertus] (*b* between 20 Nov 1516 and 19 Nov 1517; *d* Antwerp, 19 Nov 1595). Flemish composer, editor and publisher. He was associated from 1554 with the printer Jean de Laet; the dedications to their volumes indicate that he served as music editor while Laet managed

the details of typesetting. 16 products of this joint venture are extant. The last is dated 1558 (a collection of five-part Italian madrigals and *canzoni francesi* by Waelrant himself; see illustration), but some early bibliographies also include a *Symphonia angelica* of 1565; thus their association may have continued until Laet's death in about 1567. The 16 editions consits chiefly of sacred music. Waelrant and Laet also issued sacred and secular works by French composers, among them metrical psalms and madrigals and chansons. Their repertory is notable for its progressive choice of music, for the quality of type used and the care taken over text underlay and *musica ficta*.

R. L. Weaver: *The Motets of Hubert Waelrant (c1517–1595)* diss., Syracuse U., 1971); A. Rouzet: *Dictionnaire des imprimeurs, libraires et éditeurs belges des XVe et XVIe siècles* (Nieuwkoop, 1975), 115; G. Persoons: 'De genealogie van de Antwerpse Toonkundige Hubertus Waelrant (1517–1595)', *De gulden passer*, lvii (1979), 142

R.L.W.

Wagenmann, Abraham (*b* Öhringen, *c*1570; *d* Nuremberg, 19 March 1632). German printer. He was a printer at Öhringen, but became a citizen of Nuremberg

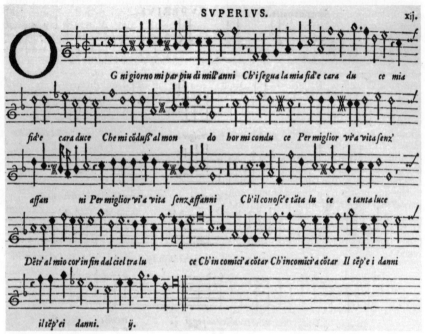

Superius of Waelrant's 'Ogni giorno' from 'Il primo libro de madrigali' (1558), published by Waelrant and Laet

on his marriage to Ursula Adelhart in 1593. He printed or published over 150 items of which almost a third are music. His publications include works by German and Italian composers, notably Vecchi; he was a particularly staunch promoter of the music of Austrian exiles.

T. Wohnhaas: 'Nürnberger Gesangbuchdrucker und -verleger im 17. Jahrhundert', *Festschrift Bruno Stäblein* (Kassel, 1967), 311

T.W.

Wagner, A. Mexican firm of publishers. It was active during the middle of the 19th century in Mexico City under the imprint of A. Wagner y Levien; it also made pianos and had retail shops throughout Mexico. Most Wagner editions bear no copyright date, leaving the firm's origins and chronology uncertain. A 16-page typescript 'Lista de Obras Archivio Wagner' cites nearly a thousand titles, most of them in popular forms (*canción*, bolero, foxtrot, *paso doble*, *ranchero*) and by local composers. The expediencies of Mexico's turbulent history are reflected in their issues of occasional music, including serious works in the 1850s by the liberal politician Miguel Lerdo de Tejada (*c*1814–1861); marches after 1876 in honour of the dictator Porfirio Diaz, written by his chief of engineers; and, later, music to promote the revolutions. A wider market is suggested by editions of national hymns of other Latin American nations and works by foreign composers, including the Cuban Ernesto Lecuona. Wagner plates were often engraved in Leipzig by Röder, Brandstetter, or Engelmann, while a few works bear joint imprints with foreign publishers, notably Schirmer, Jos. W. Stern and Southern in New York, Lyon & Healy in Chicago and Hofmeister in Leipzig. Wagner's most successful titles were Juventino Rosas's *Sobre las olas* (*c*1888) and Manuel Ponce's *Estrellita* (1914). By 1936 the bankrupt firm was taken over by a bank, but acquired by its present owners in 1938, who reissued several of its editions and today maintain the archives of the firm and of other Mexican publishers.

G. Baqueiro Foster: 'Aportación musical de Mexico para la formación de la Biblioteca Americana de Caracas, 1882–1883', *Revista musical mexicana*, ii/2 (1942), 27; Fuld (1966, 3/1985)

J.R.B.

Wagner, József (*b* Stockerau, 1791; *d* after 1861). Hungarian publisher, seller of books and printed music, and lithographer. He settled in Hungary in his youth as a cellist at the German theatre in Pest, but in 1837 ill-health obliged him to abandon his musical career, and after two years of uncertainty he opened his shop 'Musical Merchandise' in Pest. Besides working as a publisher he participated keenly in the musical life of the city, being closely connected with the Pest-Buda Musical Association; as early as 1837 he submitted to it his draft of a pension scheme for artists, which however was 'temporarily set aside'. The contemporary press criticized him for his anti-Hungarian attitude but mentioned with approval that 'at the time of the last Polish uprising he showed sympathy and helped the refugees'. His firm published works by the leading Hungarian composers (e.g. Ferenc Erkel's Hungarian national anthem and opera *Hunyadi László* and Béni Egressy's *Szózat*). Unfortunately he did not establish the sequence of his publications: some have only a number (notably works of 1840–44), some have only his initials (J.W., I.W., W.I., W.J.P.) and some are unnumbered, marked by letters of the alphabet (B, C, D, Dd, O etc, particularly in 1844–9). Surviving issues with a regular publisher's plate number (e.g. J.W.41–1846) apparently do not exceed 200, and these appeared only between 1846 and 1858. The chronology of the firm's activities is equally difficult to determine. For some time another member of the family, Ferenc Wagner, was involved in the management; some publications were issued under his name. After the music printing firm was sold to the publishers Rózsavölgyi és Társa in 1858, József Wagner dealt solely in lithography.

K. Isoz: *Zeneműkereskedelem és kiadás a régi Pest-Budán* [Music trade and publication in old Pest-Buda] (Budapest, 1941); I. Mona: *Hungarian Music Publication 1774–1867* (Budapest, 1973); idem: *Magyar zeneműkiadók és tevékenységük 1774–1867* [Hungarian music publishers and their activity] (Budapest, forthcoming)

I.M.

Wagner, Michael (*b* Deubach; *d* Innsbruck, 1669). Bavarian printer and publisher. In 1639 he married Maria, widow of the Innsbruck printer Johann Gäch, and assumed ownership of Gäch's printing shop. The same year he received official permission to print and sell books, and ten years later a weekly newspaper. After the death of Hieronymus Paur, his collaborator in several large projects, Wagner bought his shop and became court book printer in 1668. He also printed musical works on a regular basis, primarily sacred song collections and masses by such composers as the court organists Johann Stadlmayr and Ambrosius Reiner, but also works by Felician Schwab (a Franciscan Kapellmeister in Switzerland), Fidel Molitor (a Cistercian at Wettingen), Michael Kraf

(director of music at Weingarten), Georg Arnold (court organist at Bamberg), Christoph Sätzl and others. Wagner's activities resulted in the widest circulation of printed music in his area up to that time. He also issued librettos for opera performances at the Innsbruck court, including several for works by Cesti: *L'Argia* (1655), *La Dori* (1660), *La magnanimità d'Alessandro* (1662) and probably *La Cleopatra* (1654). The libretto for *L'Argia* was exceptionally extravagant, with engraved title-page, borders, vignettes and scenes. After Wagner's death, his son Jakob Christoph (*fl* 1669–1701; widow 1701–5) and grandson Michael Anton (from 1706) continued printing librettos but not music.

Verlags-Catalog der Wagner'schen Universitäts-Buchhandlung: Nebst einer Geschichte der Firma 1554–1881 (Innsbruck, 1881); E. Schumacher: 'Geschichte unserer Firma', *Verlagskatalog der Wagner'schen Univ.-Buchhandlung in Innsbruck: Oster-Messe 1904* (Innsbruck, 1904), pp. iii–xliii; A. Dörrer: '100 Innsbrucker Notendrucke aus dem Barock', *Gutenberg-Jb 1939*, 243; R. Hittmair: *300 Jahre Wagnerische Buchhandlung* (Innsbruck, 1939); A. Dörrer: '400 Jahre Wagner in Innsbruck', *Gutenberg-Jb 1955*, 154; K. M. Klier: 'Innsbrucker Lied-Flugblätter des 17. Jahrhunderts', *Jb des österreichischen Volksliedwerkes*, iv (1955), 56; Benzing (1963, 2/1982); H. Lang: *Die Buchdrucker des 15. bis 17. Jahrhunderts in Österreich* (Baden-Baden, 1972), 24

T.D.W.

Waldkirch, Henrik (*d* Copenhagen, 1629). Danish printer. He was the first Danish music printer of any importance and probably a member of a Danish printing family in Schaffhausen, where he may have been born. In 1586 he was granted a privilege to print a Danish Bible, and in 1598 he established with Mads Vingard a printing business at Copenhagen University, continuing on his own when Vingard died in 1623. Waldkirch visited the Frankfurt book fairs and took publications from Nuremberg houses to Denmark. The bulk of the 25 musical titles that can be assigned to Waldkirch (listed in Davidsson) is made up of psalm books and other liturgical volumes in Danish. He also published the Danish music by Borchgrevinck, Brachrogge and Pedersøn, who were working in Venice at that time, and Hans Kraft's treatise, *Musicae practicae rudimenta* (1607).

Å. Davidsson: *Dansk musiktryck intill 1700-talets mitt*, Studia musicologia Upsaliensia, viii (Uppsala, 1962)

S.B. (iii)

Walsh, John (*b* ?1665 or 1666; *d* London, 13 March 1736). Music seller, engraver, printer, publisher and instrument maker, probably of Irish extraction. He was established in London by about 1690. On 24 June 1692 he was appointed musical instrument-maker-in-ordinary to William III in succession to John Shaw, whose trade sign of 'The Golden Harp and Hoboy' he also adopted; in the same year he married Mary Allen, by whom he had 15 children, of whom only three survived infancy.

In 1695, when he began publishing, Walsh had no powerful rival in the trade. John Playford was dead, and his son Henry evidently lacked the initiative to maintain the family firm as a flourishing concern. Walsh was quick to take advantage of the situation, and engraved music soon appeared from his premises on a scale previously unknown in England. In addition to works by English composers he printed much popular continental music (including Corelli's sonatas) which he often copied from Dutch editions. From about 1716, however, he seems to have established a friendly relationship with Estienne Roger of Amsterdam; Walsh's labels are found pasted over Roger's imprint, and he occasionally used Roger's plates, substituting his own imprint.

· With his own publications he soon replaced the use of copper plates with less costly pewter ones, and also began using punches rather than engraving as Thomas Cross preferred to do. Hawkins dated these innovations from around 1710, they were probably implemented by 1700. There was no necessary connection between the two: punches could be used on copper plates, provided the plates were manufactured soft or were heated before engraving. Nonetheless the innovations seem to have been conceived in tandem. It is unlikely that Walsh would continue to employ both metals extensively, not only because of the differences in working them and the cost advantage of pewter, but also because different inks and alteration of the rolling press were required. Pewter plates, while generally regarded as softer than copper, could produce 2000 impressions if handled well. As initial print runs were usually in the range of 50–200 copies, plate stamina was not a concern. The uniformity of plate size evident from the plate marks found in extant copies suggests that the plates were mould-made, resembling the flatware more typical of the pewterer's output.

Although Walsh was criticized by Thomas Cross for the introduction of punches, he did not entirely dispense with the burin. Only a few musical signs, mainly clefs and note heads, were punched. Stems, rests, slurs and other linear markings were engraved (punches for a wider range of musical signs, letters and numbers were developed only later in the century). Indeed etching, rather than engraving alone, was his probable technique. It required less initial effort to work the plate, and in any event the variations in depth and tone typical of art work, which could only be produced by pure engraving, were not required.

Walsh was the first music printer and publisher to adopt regularly the passe-partout technique of printing title-pages. This involved the creation of title-page plates with a blank area within which title information could be printed from a second, small plate or written in manuscript. Some title-pages and blue wrappers exist with only the small plate's information. Passe-partout title-pages are often elaborate. Walsh obtained two of his plates for these from other publishers. The royal arms title-page (see illustration) was first used, with a different coat of arms, for Godfrey Finger's *VI Sonatas or Solo's* of 1690. Conveniently, passe-partout title plates had long lives. Walsh's plate engraved by James Collins was first used in about 1690, came to Walsh in 1698 and lasted until 1769; it graced nearly 60 editions or issues.

Most of Walsh's imprints up to 1730 also bear the name of John Hare (later John and Joseph Hare) of Cornhill, who provided him with a City outlet for his publications. It is uncertain whether the Hares were in partnership with him, but there may have been family ties. In 1706 Walsh also associated himself with Peter Randall, who probably married Walsh's sister (the William Randall who ultimately succeeded to the Walsh business was either Randall's son or grandson). About October 1708 Randall probably entered into partnership with Walsh, and remained with him until December 1710, having given up his own shop in 1709.

Walsh was an excellent businessman, advertising widely and using plates economically. He was quick to adopt new methods, including subscription issues and free copies, and to imitate the innovations of others (the periodical music collections *The Monthly Mask of Vocal Music* and *Harmonia Anglicana* were modelled on Henry Playford's publications). By 1700 his publications covered the whole range of current music, including single songs, English operas and instrumental works. About this time he began to encounter rivals, beginning with Cullen in 1702, and continuing with Pippard, Wright, Meares, Cooke and Cluer. Publishers recognized

Title-page of 'Songs in the Opera Calld Loves Triumph' by Carlo Francesco Cesarini, printed from engraved plates by John Walsh in 1709

that textual accuracy was a selling point. When John Cullen issued editions of the Italianate operas *Camilla*, *Thomyris* and *Pyrrhus and Demetrius* he proclaimed them 'more correct than the former editions' of Walsh, and emphasized that his editions were printed from copper, not pewter, plates. Walsh responded by reducing the price of his editions. Cullen ceased music publishing in 1713.

Luke Pippard set up his own business in 1709, following his apprenticeship with Walsh. Immediately Walsh began to apply the full panoply of commercial pressures to drive Pippard out of business. Pippard and Walsh had an advertising battle over William Topham's six sonatas op.3. The composer supported Pippard. Their advertisement in the *Post Man* of 26–9 November 1709 states that Walsh 'has Printed such mistakes in the Thorough-Base as only he himself, and no Masters could possibly have overlooked', which lends support to the view that Walsh's musical knowledge was indifferent. Walsh continued to use misleading advertisements, competitive editions and predatory pricing, so that Pippard left music printing and publishing in 1713. Another Walsh apprentice, William Smith, who established his business in 1720, was more successful.

Piracy was common. Before 1710 no copyright protection existed unless a composer or publisher registered his text with the Stationers' Company or had a royal licence for sole publication. After passage of the 1709/10 Copyright Act, publishers including Walsh sought to deny composers their right to protection (as Lord Mansfield was later to determine it), issuing competitive editions based either on texts from alternative sources (theatre personnel rather than composers) or on the first edition.

Walsh, however, remained pre-eminent, and it was natural for Handel, on his first visit to England in 1710, to turn to him for the publication of *Rinaldo* (1711), by which it is said Walsh made £1500, undoubtedly an exaggerated figure. Walsh apparently had no further links with the composer until 1720, when Handel, who by now was well aware of the need for copyright protection, had obtained a royal licence. Walsh then issued Handel's works as agent. The firm did not become Handel's regular publisher until about 1730, when the younger John Walsh (*b* London, 23 Dec 1709; *d* London, 15 Jan 1766) began to take over the firm.

The elder Walsh was also noted for his strong opposition to the government stamp duty and was imprisoned for non-payment

in 1726, being released in the following year. Duty was payable on single-sheet items. First levied in 1712, the duty may have led not only to the demise of music periodicals such as the *Monthly Mask of Vocal Music* but also to a decline in the number of single-sheet songs.

Walsh was buried in the vaults of the church of St Mary-le-Strand, where he had been a churchwarden. The *Gentleman's Magazine* announced that he had left £30,000, and the *London Daily Post and General Advertiser* put the figure at £20,000.

When the younger Walsh took over the firm, the relationship with the Hare family apparently ceased and the numbering of the firm's publications started. On 8 May 1731 Walsh succeeded to the appointment of instrument maker to the king. Although John Johnson and other rivals arose, the business continued to prosper and maintained its excellent engraving and paper. Walsh fully developed the firm's relationship with Handel, publishing all his later works and in 1739 being granted a monopoly of his music for 14 years; the op.4 concertos were apparently dedicated to Walsh. The firm also sold other publishers' works, and bought up the stock of smaller firms when they ceased business. Many of Walsh's apprentice engravers later set up on their own, including John Caulfield, Thomas Straight and Thomas Skillern. On Walsh's death the *Public Advertiser* placed his fortune at £40,000. The business was left, under specific conditions, to his cousin William Randall and John Abell, who had presumably both been in his employ.

F. Kidson: 'Handel's Publisher, John Walsh, his Successors and Contemporaries', *MQ*, vi (1920), 430; W. C. Smith: 'John Walsh, Music Publisher: the First Twenty Five Years', *The Library*, 5th ser., i/1 (1946), 1; idem: *A Bibliography of the Musical Works published by John Walsh during the Years 1695–1720* (London, 1948); idem: 'John Walsh and his Successors', *The Library*, 5th ser., iii/4 (1949), 291; idem: 'New Evidence concerning John Walsh and the Duties on Paper', *Harvard Library Bulletin*, vi/2 (1952), 252; J. Walsh: *A Catalogue of Music Published by John Walsh and his Successors* (London, 1953); Humphries and Smith (1954, 2/1970); W. C. Smith: *Handel: a Descriptive Catalogue of the Early Editions* (London, 1960, 2/1970); W. C. Smith and C. Humphries: *A Bibliography of the Musical Works published by John Walsh, 1721–1766* (London, 1968); D. Burrows: 'Walsh's Editions of Handel's opera 1–5: the Texts and their Sources', *Music in Eighteenth-century England: Essays in Memory of Charles Cudworth* (Cambridge, 1983); D. Hunter: 'The Publication and Dating of an Early Eighteenth-century English Song Book', *Bodleian Library Record*, xi (1984), 231; idem: 'Music Copyright in Britain to 1800', *ML*, lxvii (1986), 269; idem:

English Opera and Song Books 1703–1726: their Contents, Publishing, Printing and Bibliographical Description (diss., U. of Illinois, 1989); idem: 'The Printing of Opera and Song Books in England, 1703–1726', *Notes*, xlvi (1989–90)

F.K., W.C.S./P.W.J., D.H. (ii)

Warmuth, Carl. Norwegian firm of publishers, founded in Christiania (now Oslo). It was the leading music firm in the country in the 19th century. It started as a modest shop for strings, run in his home by the German emigré Carl Warmuth sr (1811–92). According to the firm, the business was established in 1843, but it seems that the actual date is a few years later. Wind and bowed stringed instruments and sheet music were added to the business, which moved in 1861 to larger premises. Its scope radically increased with the return of Warmuth's son Carl jr (1844–95) from his studies in Braunschweig; he joined the firm and took over the management in 1874. He was an exceptionally enterprising and efficient businessman and the firm bought up almost all its competitors: Lindorff & Co. in 1864, Edvard Winther in 1878, Hermann Neupert in 1879, A. M. Hanche in 1881 and Johan D. Behrens in 1890.

The firm's first publication appeared in 1851, followed soon by two more, but serious publishing activity did not begin before 1862. Warmuth's list eventually amounted to 2870 publications. The firm was of considerable significance to Norwegian cultural life because most of its publications were by native composers, including a large number of women. Such important composers as Kjerulf, Grieg and Svendsen had some of their well-known works published by Warmuth.

From 1880 to 1892 Warmuth edited and published the first Norwegian music periodical to gain recognition outside Norway, *Nordisk musik-tidende*. The firm also operated an important concert agency and a lending library of 65,000 volumes, probably one of the largest in northern Europe. Carl Warmuth jr was awarded many Norwegian and foreign honours. After his death in 1895 the firm began to decline. There were various changes in management until it was bought by the partnership of Brødrene Hals and Wilhelm Hansen of Copenhagen in 1908. On 1 January 1909 Hals and Warmuth were incorporated into Norsk Musikforlag.

T. Voss: *Warumuths Musikhandel, Brødrene Hals, Norsk Musikforlag 1843–1943* (Oslo, 1943); D. Fog and K. Michelsen: *Norwegian Music Publication since 1800: a Preliminary Guide to Music Publishers, Printers and Dealers* (Copenhagen, 1976) [with dated plate nos.]; K. Michelsen: 'Om musikkfirmaet Carl Warmuth i Christiania', *SMN*, iii (1977), 33; idem: *Musikkhandel i Norge inntil 1929: a Historical Survey* (Oslo, 1980); idem: 'Music Trade in Norway to 1929', *FAM*, xxix (1982), 43; P. A. Kjeldsberg: *Piano i Norge 'et uunværligt Instrument'* (Oslo, 1985); K. Michelsen: 'Musikkleiebibliotekene i Norge', *SMN*, xi (1985), 81; idem: 'Historien om Harz-Musikverein', *SMN*, xiv (1988), 147

K.M. (ii)

Warner Bros. Music. American firm of publishers. It was formed by Warner Bros. in Los Angeles in 1929 to gain control of copyrights for music used in its films. Four separate publishers of popular music, Harms, Remick, Witmark and New World Music, were purchased and amalgamated to form the Music Publishers Holding Corporation. The companies' catalogues included the works of such composers as Walter Damrosch, Rudolf Friml, George Gershwin, Victor Herbert, Jerome Kern and Sigmund Romberg. In 1937 two divisions of the firm were established, the popular and the standard (the latter dealing with educational music and texts). In 1968 the company became known as Warner Bros. Music. In 1988 its parent company Warner Communications took over the English firm Chappell, forming the Warner Chappell Music Group, one of the largest music publishing concerns in the world.

F.B.

Waterloo. Canadian firm of music dealers and publishers. It was established in Waterloo, Ontario, in 1922 by Charles F. Thiele, a local band director who imported sheet music and distributed it by mail to bands and silent film houses. He began publishing Canadian music in 1925, primarily educational materials; these have since become the main emphasis of the firm's publishing activities, although the sale of instruments and accessories forms most of its business. The company publishes music texts for schools, piano examination books and band and choral music. Among the Canadian composers in its catalogue are John Beckwith, Jean Coulthard, Barbara Pentland and Godfrey Ridout. The company has also produced recordings, and in 1979 it established its own printing shop, Action Press. Waterloo became a limited company in 1951 with Thiele as president until 1954.

D. Grayhurst: 'Waterloo Music,' *Music Scene* (1968), no. 240, p. 6; M. Wehrle: 'Waterloo Music Company Ltd.,' *Encyclopedia of Music in Canada* (Toronto, 1981); J. Mellor: *Music in the Park: C. F. Thiele, Father of Canadian Band Music* (Waterloo, Ont., 1988)

M.W.

Waters, Horace (*b* Jefferson, ME, 1812; *d* New York, 1893). American publisher. In 1845 he established a music shop in New York which was expanded in 1880 to include the manufacture and sale of pianos. The business was maintained by the family for nearly a century. As a music publisher, Waters is best known for his first editions of 47 songs by Stephen Foster, including 21 hymns which first appeared in *The Athenaeum Collection* (1863) and *Waters' Golden Harp* (1863). Waters purchased the rights to several of Foster's songs in the early 1860s, and on Foster's death in January 1864 was the first publisher to capitalize on the sales potential of the 'last songs', issuing five publications of posthumous ' pieces. Many of Waters's publications during this time bore the copyright name of E. A. Daggett, believed to have been his brother-in-law. After his retirement Waters continued to be a prominent figure in the music business through honorary membership on the US Board of Music Trade.

D. Spillane: *History of the American Pianoforte* (New York, 1890); Dichter and Shapiro (1941, 2/1977); E. F. Morneweck: *Chronicles of Stephen Foster's Family* (Pittsburgh, 1944); J. J. Fuld: *Pictorial Bibliography of the First Editions of Stephen C. Foster* (Philadelphia, 1957); C. E. Claghorn: *Biographical Dictionary of American Music* (West Nyack, NY, 1973)

A.M.R.

Watts, John (*b* 1678; *d* London, 26 Sept 1763). English bookseller and printer. He was established in Lincoln's Inn Fields, London, before 1726, and in conjunction with the publisher Jacob Tonson issued plays, librettos and miscellaneous works. The introduction of the ballad opera at Lincoln's Inn Fields Theatre gave Watts a brisk trade in the publication of the operas performed there. He issued the first and later editions of *The Beggar's Opera* (1728), and after this practically the whole of the series of ballad operas (more than 27 all together) as soon as they were performed. These editions present the airs for the songs, printed from engraved woodblocks, as an appendix, and are especially valuable for giving the old names of the tunes. Another important work is the six-volume *The Musical Miscellany* (1729–31), also printed from woodblocks and considered the finest pocket songbook of the period. The third to fifth volumes of this set were reissued by J. Wren about 1750 with different titles (*The Harp, The Spinnet* and *The Violin* respectively).

Kidson (1900); H. R. Plomer: *A Dictionary of the Printers and Booksellers . . . in England, Scotland and Ireland from 1668 to 1725* (London, 1922); Humphries and Smith (1954, 2/1970)

F.K./P.W.J.

Wa-Wan Press. American firm of publishers. It was founded in Newton Centre, Massachusetts, in 1901 by the composer Arthur Farwell (*b* St Paul, MN, 23 April 1872; *d* New York, 20 Jan 1952) to publish neglected music by contemporary American composers and music using American folk material. Named after an Omaha Indian ceremony for peace, fellowship and song, it began idealistically to further the cause of American music and a new indigenous music that Farwell believed would emerge from a study of ragtime and of black, Indian and cowboy songs. The press published the works of 37 composers (including nine women) whose main interest was in American Indian music, and Farwell, H. W. Loomis and Carlos Troyer were among those whose works used such material. Other composers whose music was published by the firm include Frederic Ayres, Rubin Goldmark, E. S. Kelley, Arthur Shepherd, Henry Gilbert, E. B. Hill and Gena Branscombe. Two collections of music were issued each quarter, one vocal and one instrumental, in volumes beautifully designed and printed, often with introductions by Farwell. Later each composition was published separately in sheet-music form; Farwell designed many of the abstract covers himself, taking pride in their distinctive appearance. In 1907, encouraged by public acceptance and demand, the firm began to publish monthly instead of quarterly. In 1908 loss of subscriptions caused the publishing house to founder, and in 1912 it was acquired by G. Schirmer of New York.

E. N. Waters: 'The Wa-Wan Press: an Adventure in Musical Idealism', *A Birthday Offering to Carl Engel* (New York, 1943), 214; G. Chase: *America's Music* (New York, 1955, rev. 2/1966); J. R. Perkins: *An Examination of the Solo Piano Music Published by the Wa-Wan Press* (diss., Boston U., 1969); V. B. Lawrence, ed.: *The Wa-Wan Press, 1901–1911* (New York, 1970) [repr. of the entire press run incl. introduction by G. Chase: 'The Wa-Wan Press: a Chapter in American Enterprise']; E. Brody: 'Vive la France: Gallic Accents in American Music from 1880 to 1914', *MQ*, lvx (1979), 200

W.T.M., M.J.

Weidner, Johann (*b* Dornburg; *d* Jena, 2 Nov 1625). German printer, active in Jena. After serving apprenticeship in Leipzig and Torgau, he moved to Jena in 1605 and bought the printing facilities of the Richtzenhan family (*fl* 1559–1605). Besides

THE

WA-WAN·PRESS

THE FAREWELL

SONG FOR BARITONE

BY

ARTHUR FARWELL

NEWTON·CENTER·
MASSACHUSETTS

'The Farewell' by Arthur Farwell, published by the Wa-Wan Press in 1910

funeral orations and other non-musical works, he printed many sacred and secular songs, individually and in collections, as well as motet, madrigal and dance collections. Composers represented include Volckmar Leisring, (Johannes) Lippius, Sethus Calvisius, Melchior Vulpius, Georg Quitschreiber, Johann Thüring and Johann Lyttich. On his death the shop was run by his widow, later with her second husband, Christoph Küche, until 1629.

Benzing (1963, 2/1982)

T.D.W.

Weigel [Waigel]. German family of engravers and publishers. Christoph Weigel (i) [*der Ältere*] (*b* Marktredwitz, bap. 30 Nov 1654; *d* Nuremberg, 5 Feb 1725) learnt the craft of copper engraving in Augsburg (1673–81) and worked in Vienna, Frankfurt am Main and Regensberg before settling in Nuremberg, where he married in 1698. He founded an art publishing firm which, through the heirs Tyroff and later Schmidt, existed into the 19th century; in it he also engraved and published music. His *Ständebuch* of 1698 follows very closely in its sections on music Michael Praetorius's *Organographia* of 1618 and Kircher's *Musurgia* of 1650. But it contains interesting details of the instrumental practice of the time, and stresses 'the predominance of the organ among the instruments and the leading role of Nuremberg in the construction of wind instruments' (Krautwurst).

Christoph's brother, Johann Christoph (*b* Marktredwitz, bap.15 July 1661; *d* Nuremberg, bur. 3 Sept 1726), also settled in Nuremberg and worked there as an engraver and art dealer. Notable among the works he published are Pachelbel's *Erster Theil etlicher Chorale* (*c*1700) and above all his own *Musicalisches Theatrum* (*c*1722). The latter is a collection of folio plates illustrating various instruments being played with a conductor, and is closely related to Mattheson's *Das neu-eröffnete Orchestre* (Hamburg, 1713). After Johann Christoph Weigel's death his wife continued the business, which was taken over by their son Christoph Weigel (ii) [*der Jüngere*] (*b* 1703; *d* Nuremberg, bur. 19 June 1777) in 1734. The most important work published by the 'jüngere Weigelsche Handlung' (which survived with A.G. Schneider's bookshop until 1807) was book 2 of Bach's *Clavier-Übung*.

J. C. Weigel: *Musicalisches Theatrum* (Nuremberg, *c*1722/*R*1961); J. G. Doppelmayr: *Historische Nachrichten von den Nürnbergischen Mathematicis und Künstlern* (Nuremberg, 1730); C. Schaper: 'Neue archivalische Forschungen zur Lebensgeschichte von Professor Erhard Weigel (1625–

1699)'. *Archiv für Geschichte von Oberfranken*, xxxix (1959), 97–140; F. Krautwurst: 'Weigel', *MGG*; W. Wörthmüller, ed.: *Nürnberger Musikverleger und die Familie Bach: Materialien zu einer Ausstellung des 48. Bach-Fests der Neuen Bach-Gesellschaft* (Zirndorf, 1973)

W.S. (ii)

Weigl, Thaddäus [Thadé] (*b* 8 April 1776; *d* Vienna, 29 Feb 1844). Austrian composer, conductor and publisher, son of Joseph Weigl (the cellist). He studied music theory with Albrechtsberger, who acquainted him with the works of Bach and Handel; his brother Joseph Weigl (ii) introduced him to the music of Haydn and Mozart. From 1795 he worked as an arranger (especially of piano scores) for the Viennese court theatre's music publishing house, and in 1796 the firm sent him on a business journey that took him all over Europe. In 1801 he was granted a licence for a publishing firm of his own, which he founded in 1803. From that time he often stood in for his brother as vice-Kapellmeister at the Kärntnertortheater, and in 1806 he was granted the title of composer to the court theatre. Between 1799 and 1805 he had five operettas and 15 ballets performed. As vice-Kapellmeister of the court theatre he took over the direction of the musical archives and thoroughly reorganized them. Later he resigned from practical music-making to devote himself entirely to his work as a publisher. Apart from works by his brother, he chiefly published works by Viennese contemporaries and operatic arrangements. Several songs by Schubert first appeared under his imprint. In 1831 the firm went bankrupt, and its publishing rights were taken over by the firms of Diabelli and Artaria.

A. Weinmann: *Verzeichnis der Musikalien aus dem k.k. Hoftheater-Musik-Verlag* (Vienna, 1962); R. Angermüller: 'Zwei Selbstbiographien von Joseph Weigl (1766–1846)', *DJbM*, xvi (1973), 46; A. Weinmann: *Verzeichnis der Musikalien des Verlages Thadé Weigl* (Vienna, 1982)

R.A.

Weinberger, Josef (*b* Lipto St Miklos, Moravia, 6 May 1855; *d* Vienna 8 Nov 1928). Austrian publisher. On 1 November 1885 he founded a music publishing firm in Vienna in partnership with Carl Hofbauer. In 1890 Weinberger started to publish on his own. His earliest significant work was the lavish *Album der Wiener Meister*, issued for the International Music and Theatre Exhibition in Vienna in 1892 and including pieces by Brahms, Bruckner, Goldmark, Johann Strauss (ii), Suppé and others. In 1897 Weinberger was a founder-member of the Gesellschaft der Autoren, Komponisten und Musikverleger (AKM), one of the earliest societies of its kind; for the rest of his life he was either its chairman or its honorary president. Also in 1897 Weinberger began to publish works by Mahler, starting with the *Lieder eines fahrenden Gesellen*; this was followed by the First Symphony (1899), *Des Knaben Wunderhorn* (1900), Third Symphony (1902) and *Das klagende Lied* (1902). Weinberger was a co-founder of Universal Edition (1901), which he allowed to use his premises until it moved into the Musikvereinsgebäude in 1914. He published operas by various composers of the Austrian Empire, such as Kienzl, Goldmark and Brüll, and later issued Franz Schmidt's *Fredigundis* and Korngold's *Die Kathrin* and *Die stumme Serenade*. He acquired the stage rights for operettas by Suppé, Millöcker, Zeller, Genée and, most importantly, J. Strauss (ii), meanwhile publishing operettas by Eysler, Fall, Straus, Kálmán, Lehár, Robert Stolz and many others. Foreign composers in the catalogue included Smareglia and Wolf-Ferrari (eight operas).

After Weinberger's death the firm was run by Otto Blau (1893–1980). In 1938 it was taken over by the Berlin firm of Sikorski and Weinberger's name was erased from the German trade register for the duration of World War II. After the war it was successfully re-established in Vienna. In the mid-1950s several of Franz Schmidt's works were acquired, including the three quintets written for Paul Wittgenstein and two organ works. The firm remains active and has branches in London (where Malcolm Williamson and Paul Patterson are among the composers represented) and Frankfurt am Main.

A. Weinmann: 'Weinberger, Josef', *MGG*; *100 Years Remembered: a History of the Theatre and Music Publishers Josef Weinberger. Vienna, Frankfurt am Main, London, 1885–1985* (London, 1985)

A.W./N.S.

Weintraub, Eugene (*b* Stalnoye, Ukraine, 10 March 1904). American publisher. An accomplished musician, he started publishing music in 1940 in New York. He was director of the Am-Rus Music Corp., in charge of Soviet music distribution in the USA, and in this capacity arranged the first American performances of works by Prokofiev, Shostakovich, Kabalevsky and Myaskovsky. He obtained the highest ever rental fee ($10,000) in 1944 for the first American performance of Shostakovich's Symphony no. 8. From 1944 to 1950 he was head of the department of Soviet music at Leeds Music Corporation. In 1950 he established the Weintraub Music Company,

which specialized in works by American composers, including George Antheil, Virgil Thomson, Robert Kurka, Howard Swanson and Benjamin Lees, issuing about ten new titles each year. Music Sales Corporation acquired the Weintraub firm in 1987, although Weintraub continues as music editor.

W.T.M., M.J.

Welcker. English family of music publishers, printers and music sellers, established in London. Peter Welcker (*d* London, 1775) founded a business in or before 1762, publishing many important works, including much of J. C. Bach's instrumental music, works of the Mannheim school (using plates from Hummel of Amsterdam) and several of the early volumes of Thomas Warren's *A Collection of Catches, Canons and Glees*. At his death the business was continued by his widow Mary Welcker (*d* London, early 1778), probably with her son-in-law James Blundell as manager. Her executors carried on the business for a few months after her death, but by July 1778 Blundell had taken over the business, and in the following year Robert Bremner purchased some of her plates and music. John Welcker (*fl* 1775–*c*1785), the son of Mary and Peter Welcker, set up his own business as a music seller and publisher in 1775, but in 1780 he became bankrupt. His premises were taken over by Blundell, and the trade stock was offered for sale in July 1780. Welcker started business again in August of that year, and continued for about five years. He issued the opera dances and ballets performed at the Haymarket Theatre and continued to publish the sort of music which his parents had issued. About 1778 he reissued the three volumes of *Clio and Euterpe* which had been engraved and first published by Henry Roberts, with an added fourth volume.

Kidson (1900); Humphries and Smith (1954, 2/1970)

F.K., W.C.S./P.W.J.

Wening, Michael (*b* Nürnberg, 11 July 1645; *d* Munich, 21 April 1718). Bavarian copperplate engraver. His chief work was the four-volume *Beschreibung des Kurfürsten- und Herzogtums Ober- und Niederbayern – Historico topographica descriptio* (1701–26), which contains hundreds of pictures of places. Though only a single music book of his survives, it is of exceptionally high quality: J. K. Kerll's *Modulatio organica super Magnificat* (Munich, 1686).

G. Stetter: *Michael Wening* (Munich, 1977)

H.S.

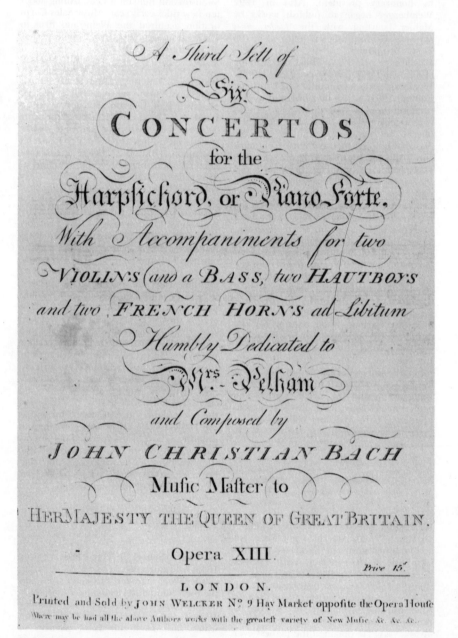

Title-page of J. C. Bach's 'A Third Sett of Six Concertos' op.13, published by John Welcker (London, 1777)

Wenssler, Michael (*b* Strasbourg; *fl* 1472–99). Alsatian printer, active at Basle. He established his printing shop in 1472, working with the first printer at Basle, Berthold Ruppel, and with Bernhard Richel. His name appears with Jacob von Kilchen's ('impensis spectatissimorum virorum MW et JK') on a spectacular series of printed music books of 1488: a gradual, two antiphonals, missals, and agendas. Another gradual of about 1486 has been attributed to him and a *Missale sarumburiense* was shipped to England in 1489 at the expense of Wenssler, Kilchen and Hans Wiler. In 1490 financial disaster forced Wenssler to sell his shop; he fled Basle and spent the next decade printing for others in Speyer and Basle and on his own in Cluny, Macon and Lyons. He was allowed to return in 1499. Several missals, vigils and psalters with printed music are attributed to him, but ownership of his types after 1490 is unclear.

Three music types were used in Wenssler's books and in books printed for Peter Drach in Speyer and others: a very large gothic chant type for the choirbooks and two missals for Worms (1486, 1488, 1489–90); a large gothic type chant for quarto vigils, agendas, psalters and folio missals (1490–1501 and later); and a roman chant type for the Sarum missal (1489). The use of black mensural type for the mensural chant of Glorias and Credos in the graduals is the second known use of mensural music type, after the 1480 Niger *Grammatica* printed at Venice by Theodor Franck of Würzburg. It is striking that the first printed music attributed to Wenssler is a reprint of that title in Basle, dated about 1485, with music printed from woodcuts.

K. Meyer: 'Der Musikdruck in den liturgischen Inkunabeln von Wenssler und Kilchen', *Gutenberg-Jb 1935*, 117; F. Geldner: *Die deutschen Inkunabeldrucker: ein Handbuch der deutschen Buchdrucker des XV. Jahrhunderts nach Druckorten*, i (Stuttgart, 1968), 79, 109, 112, 173, 192

M.K.D.

Werlein, Philip P. (*b* Rheinkreiss, 30 March 1812; *d* New Orleans, 17 April 1885). American publisher. He received his early musical training as a pianist in Germany, then emigrated to the USA in 1831, settling in Vicksburg, Mississippi, where he taught music and in 1842 opened a music shop. In the early 1850s he moved to New Orleans, opening a music shop with L. C. Ashbrand in 1853. The following year Werlein bought the publishing business of W. T. Mayo, which he then ran under his own name. In 1860 he moved to Canal Street, where the Werlein business is still located. Because of strong Southern loyalties (his was the first pirated edition of *Dixie*, 1860), he fled New Orleans in 1862, returning only in 1867. One of the most important publishers of Confederate music, he went on to issue several hundred pieces, a *Song Journal* and *Werlein's Journal of Music*. Werlein was succeeded by his son Philip (ii) (1847–99), and grandson Philip (iii) (1878–1917) and further descendants, who ran the business until about 1940; Dave Franck of New Orleans then bought the publishing concern, but the music shop has remained in the family.

F. W. Hoogerwerf: *Confederate Sheet-music Imprints*, ISAMm, xxi (Brooklyn, NY, 1984)

J.H.B.

Wessel, Christian Rudolph (*b* Bremen, 1797; *d* Eastbourne, 15 March 1885). English publisher of German origin. He emigrated to London, where, with a piano maker named William Stodart, he established the firm of Wessel & Stodart in 1823. They began as importers of foreign music, but also issued their own publications from 1824. Their main interest was piano music often issued in the form of periodical albums, and besides the usual popular arrangements of operatic airs and dance music they published the sonatas of Beethoven and Mozart, and the works of piano virtuosos such as Heller, Henselt and Thalberg. They also helped at an early date to promote the music of Schubert, Schumann, Mendelssohn, Gade, Liszt and others in England. Stodart retired in 1838 and Wessel continued the business alone until 1839, when he took in Frederic Stapleton as a partner. From 1833 they began to publish Chopin's works and in 1836 entered into a contract with the composer for the exclusive rights to his works in England. The firm's complete edition of Chopin's works, finished with op. 64 in 1848, was the first collected edition of his music to be issued. In 1845 Stapleton left the firm, and Wessel again carried on the business alone. The firm was among those particularly affected by the House of Lords decision of 1854 to ban exclusive agencies for foreign publications. In 1860 Wessel retired in favour of his managers, Edwin Ashdown and Henry John Parry, and the business eventually became the firm of Edwin Ashdown Ltd.

Humphries and Smith (1954, 2/1970); M. J. E. Brown: 'Chopin and his English Publisher', *ML*, xxxix (1958), 363; idem: *Chopin: an Index of his Works* (London, 1960, 2/1972), 188; Neighbour and Tyson (1965); J. Kallberg: 'Chopin in the Marketplace: Aspects of the International Music Publishing Industry in the First Half of the

Nineteenth Century', *Notes* xxxix (1982–3), 535, 795; Coover (1988)

A.C. (ii)/P.W.J.

Whaley, Royce & Co. Canadian publisher, instrument maker and dealer. It was founded in Toronto in 1888 by E. Whaley and G. C. Royce, with a branch in Winnipeg 1889–1922. Its earliest publications were deposited at the copyright office in 1890. Although plate numbers were used irregularly, a 1923 copyright bearing the number 1601 is consistent with the some 1500 pieces known to have been published to that date. By 1920 the firm's output surpassed that of all other Canadian music publishers. Unlike most of its competitors, Whaley, Royce & Co. owned a printing plant and functioned also as a job printer. Evidence of the firm's enterprise is contained in its *Descriptive and Select Catalogue of Sheet Music and Music Books published and for sale by Whaley, Royce & Co.* (1895). Besides the usual popular and light classical repertory, the company published serious works including a piano arrangement of Sibelius's *Finlandia* (1894) and Rhakmaninov's Prelude op.3 no.2 (1923), as well as the music of many Canadian composers, notably R. S. Ambrose, Gena Branscombe, W. O. Forsyth, C. A. E. Harriss and Clarence Lucas. Calling itself 'Canada's Greatest Music House', the firm also produced songbooks, operatic vocal scores, cantatas and oratorios, educational music and two periodicals. Its publishing activities waned considerably from 1920 and had virtually ceased, apart from reprints, by 1940.

H. Kallmann: 'Whaley, Royce & Co. Ltd.', *Encyclopedia of Music in Canada* (Toronto, 1981)

M.C.

Wheatstone. English firm of publishers and instrument makers. It was said to have been established in London about 1750. Charles Wheatstone, who was presumably not the founder, was associated with it from about 1791. From about 1815 the firm was known as C. Wheatstone & Co., and from about 1815 to 1816 it had a branch or agency at Bath. William Wheatstone (*fl* from 1813), probably the brother of Charles, was a flute teacher and manufacturer, and held patents for improvements to the instrument. In about 1826 he apparently amalgamated with Charles, and for some time around the middle of the century the firm was known as William Wheatstone & Co. William also published a number of books of airs for the flute.

The eminent physicist Sir Charles Wheatstone (*b* Gloucester, Feb 1802; *d* Paris, 19 Oct 1875), probably a nephew or cousin of William and the son of a music seller at Gloucester, invented the concertina, the patent of which, taken out in June 1829, was held by the Wheatstone firm for many years. The firm published a prodigious amount of sheet music, mostly of a popular nature but including several interesting collections of glees such as *The Naval and Convivial Vocal Harmonist* (*c*1807). It also did an extensive trade as makers of and dealers in musical instruments, especially concertinas. In 1961 it was acquired by Boosey & Hawkes, who continue to use the name.

Humphries and Smith (1954, 2/1970)

F.K., W.C.S./P.W.J.

Whistling. German family of publishers. Carl Friedrich (*b* Kelbra, Thuringia, 1788; *d* after 1849) studied in Leipzig and after 1811 worked in the Bureau de Musique of Franz Anton Hoffmeister and Ambrosius Kühnel, from 1814 C. F. Peters. Whistling's *Handbuch der musikalischen Literatur*, a serious attempt at a list of music in print, was first issued in 1817 by Anton Meysel, whose shop Whistling acquired on 13 November 1821. Friedrich Hofmeister issued Whistling's supplements to the *Handbuch* between 1819 and 1825, although Whistling's own imprint appears after 1826. On 28 May 1830 Hofmeister purchased both the shop and the *Handbuch*, which by then had evolved into a current list of new music publications, edited by Whistling and later his sons, Friedrich Wilhelm (1809–61) and August Theodor (1812–69). Carl Friedrich later had a music shop in Hamburg, eventually in Vienna, while Friedrich Wilhelm in Leipzig became a publisher in his own right in 1835, introducing important works by Schumann, songs by Robert Franz and other serious vocal and chamber music. In 1858 part of the publishing firm was sold to Gustav Heinze. August Theodor, a senior employee at C. F. Peters in 1855, in 1861 maintained the Whistling imprint, which was dissolved in 1870.

H.-M. Plesske: 'Zur Geschichte der deutschen Musikbibliographie', *BMw*, v (1963), 97; R. Elvers and C. Hopkinson: 'A Survey of the Music Catalogues of Whistling and Hofmeister', *FAM*, xix (1972), 1; N. Ratliff: *Handbuch der musikalischen Literatur: a Reprint of the 1817 Edition and the ten Supplements, 1817–1827* (New York, 1975); G. Borghetto: 'Una lettera inedita di Robert Schumann all'editore Whistling di Lipsia', *Richerche musicali*, v (1981), 46; D. W. Krummel: 'The Beginnings of Current National Bibliography of German Music', *Richard S. Hill: Tributes from Friends* (Detroit, 1987), 307

D.W.K.

Whitney, Clark J. (*b* Avon, MI, 12 July 1832; *d* New York, ?2 March 1903). American publisher and music dealer. He ran several businesses and factories at various locations in Detroit from about 1857 to 1895; one of these was for the manufacture of melodeons and organs. During the 1870s he published the *Song Journal*, a monthly publication devoted to music literature, and the *Concert Goer*. He established Whitney's Grand Opera House in Detroit in 1875, and within 15 years was also manager of opera houses in Toledo, Ohio, and London and Hamilton, Ontario. He was perhaps the most important music dealer in Detroit during the second half of the 19th century. His brother, W. W. Whitney, was a music dealer in Toledo, Ohio, and published *Whitney's Musical Guest* (1868).

Obituary, *Detroit News* (23 March 1903)

M.D.T.

Whittemore, J(oseph) Henry (1834–75). American composer, music dealer and publisher. He opened his 'New Music Establishment' in Detroit in conjunction with John E. Schonacker in March 1858; later he was in partnership with J. B. Staring, still later with Joseph A. Swan and Roe Stephens. In Whittemore's most prolific years as a music publisher, 1863–9, he issued such patriotic songs as *The Volunteer's Wife*, *What will they say in Michigan* and *The old flag will triumph yet*, all to his own music, as well as William James Robjohn's *Abraham Lincoln's Funeral March*. His later topical output included the *Flight and Capture of Jeff Davis*, *Father don't drink any now*, *The Blue Line Galop*, *Detroit Rink Waltz* and *The Velocipede Galop*. With an output of more than 500 titles he was second only to Clark J. Whitney among Detroit music publishers of the 1860s.

M.D.T.

Widmanstetter, Georg (*d* Graz, 20 May 1618). Austrian printer. One of an artisan family of Nellingen bei Ulm, he was in Bavaria by 1564. He married the daughter of the printer Daser, and between 1568 and 1584 was employed as a typesetter and proof corrector by the music printer Adam Berg of Munich. In 1585 Widmanstetter travelled to Graz, where he was appointed as 'katholischer Hofbuchdrucker' to the court, and to the Jesuit College and the university. His salary was 100 florins a year with a free house. He remained there as a printer until his death, with a total production of over 200 titles. He exhibited at the Frankfurt book fairs between 1588 and 1596 (after which date no Graz names appear in the list for 70 years), including some music in his catalogue. His music production was not very large, and surprisingly does not include the music of the Italians who were employed at Graz. (Almost all of this was first printed in Venice.) His most famous titles were Lassus's *Cantiones sacrae* (1594), Ferdinand de Lassus's *Cantiones sacrae* (1587) and Beuttner's *Catholisch Gesangbuch* (1602 and later editions).

Widmanstetter's son Ernst took over the firm's work in 1610, taking charge of it completely on his father's death. The firm continued until 1806 but did not print any music.

F. Ahn: 'Die Druckerpresse Georg Widmanstetters zu Graz', *Mitteilungen des Österreichischen Vereins für Bibliotheks-Wesen*, viii (1904), 144; F. Bischoff: 'Steiermärkischer Notendruck im 16. Jahrhundert', *Zeitschrift des Historischen Vereins für Steiermark*, xiv (1916), 107; F. Bayer: *G. Widmanstetter und seine Grazer Drucke, 1587–1618* (diss., U. of Graz, 1934); V. Thiel: 'Geschichte der Offizin Widmanstetter in Graz', *Gutenberg-Jb 1935*, 193; H. Federhofer: 'Grazer Musiknotendruck aus alter Zeit', *Neue Chronik zur Geschichte und Volkskunde der innerösterreichischen Alpenländer*, vii (1952), 3; Benzing (1963, 2/1982)

S.B. (iii)

Wiener Philharmonischer Verlag. Austrian firm of publishers. It was founded in Vienna on 5 April 1923 by Alfred Kalmus (*d* 1972). The firm is best known for its series of Philharmonia miniature scores in grey covers, each with a frontispiece portrait of the composer. Kalmus established the company after 14 years at Universal Edition. From the start there was a close relationship between the two firms, though Wiener Philharmonischer Verlag was an independent company in which UE were shareholders. In 1923 Wiener Philharmonischer Verlag published a notable group of facsimiles: Bach's Coffee Cantata, Mozart's Jupiter Symphony and Strauss's *Tod und Verklärung*. The firm also issued books, including Hans Gál's *Anleitung zum Partiturlesen*, Eckstein's *Erinnerungen an Anton Bruckner* and a new edition of Sechter's analysis of the finale of Mozart's Jupiter Symphony. In 1925 UE purchased the firm; since then, Philharmonia miniature scores have been issued by UE, with a separate series of plate numbers.

Wiener Philharmonischer Verlag: September 1924 (Vienna, 1924) [catalogue]

N.S.

Wiener Urtext Edition. Publishing company, founded in 1972 by Schott's Söhne, Mainz, and Universal Edition, Vienna. It continues the work of the Wiener Urtext Ausgabe of Universal Edition, publishing 18th- and 19th-century music for practical and scholarly use. A first series, which appeared in 1973, consisted of 39 volumes of works by Bach, Mozart, Haydn, Beethoven, Schubert, Schumann, Chopin and Brahms. More recently, works by Debussy and Hindemith have been issued by the firm.

L.R.

Wietor [Büttner, Philovalensis, Doliarius], **Hieronim** (*b* Lubomierz, Silesia, *c*1480; *d* 1546 or 1547). Polish printer, publisher and bookseller. Probably a pupil of Jan Haller he worked in Vienna from 1510 to 1517 and moved to Kraków in 1519. Around 1527 he became 'royal printer'. He was the first in Poland to use an italic type and the first to print music from movable mensural type in double- and, later, single-impression methods. Among his music publications were treatises, songbooks and numerous anonymous secular and sacred partsongs. After his death Andrysowicz Łazarz (*b* Stryków; *d* Kraków, 1577) married Wietor's widow and took over the firm. He published many works by Polish composers, mostly popular partsongs, psalms and hymns. After his death his son Jan Łazarzowicz Januszowski (*b* Kroki, 1550; *d* Kraków, 1613) continued the printing firm. Known for publications of a high standard, he too became 'royal printer'. In music he widened the firm's output to include lute tablatures, missals and other service books, as well as treatises and partsongs.

Przywecka-Samecka (1969); *Słownik pracowników książki polskiej* [Dictionary of Polish printers] (Warsaw and Łódź, 1972)

T.C. (ii)

Williams, (William Sidney) Gwynn (*b* Llangollen, 4 April 1896; *d* Llangollen, 13 Nov 1978). Welsh publisher. In the early 1920s he gave up a career in law in favour of music publishing, gaining experience as superviser of publications at Hughes & Son, Wrexham, until he established his own firm, Gwynn Publishing Company, Llangollen, in 1937. It issued over 600 items, mostly of vocal music. Many were arranged by Williams himself, all vocal works were issued with voice parts in staff and tonic sol-fa notations, and all had English and Welsh words. A number also had French, Gaelic, German, Hungarian, Italian, Latin, Norwegian or Russian words. Supplying the need for test pieces at the National Eisteddfod of Wales (with which Williams was intimately connected) and at the Llangollen International Musical Eisteddfod (of which he was the first musical director, 1946–78), these editions had a revitalizing influence on Welsh choral societies and enhanced the reputation of Welsh music abroad. Williams wrote authoritatively on folk music, edited many collections of Welsh folksongs and dances which he published himself (1927–62), and was active in several folksong and professional societies. In July 1981 the firm was absorbed in the Cwmni Cyhoeddi Gwynn, Penygroes, Caernarvon.

O.E.

Williams, Joseph. English firm of printers and publishers. It was established in London in 1808 by Lucy Williams, a music and copperplate printer who printed some works for Clementi & Co. In 1843 she took her son Joseph William Williams (1819–83) into the firm, which was known as Lucy Williams & Son until the following year, after which Joseph continued in his own name. He was succeeded in 1883 by his son, Joseph Benjamin Williams (1847–1923), who, under the pseudonym of Florian Pascal, also composed some 200 songs, piano pieces, cantatas, comic operas and operettas. He in turn was succeeded by his eldest son, Florian Williams (1879–1973), for some time helped by his brother Ralph Williams (1881–1948). A family company, Joseph Williams Ltd, was formed in 1900; from 1930 they were joined by Montagu Normington Williams (1911–42). In July 1961 Augener took over the business but continued to operate the firm separately until May 1962, when Galliard was formed; this in turn was taken over by Stainer & Bell, in whose catalogue Joseph Williams's works now appear.

The firm published almost every kind of work, with particular emphasis on light opera and ballads. The acquisition of the British rights of Robert Planquette's highly successful operetta *Les cloches de Corneville* in 1877 laid the foundations of the firm's fortunes. The serious side of the firm's catalogue included works by Elgar, Vaughan Williams, Bax, Bantock, Ireland and others, and they were concerned in the publication of G. E. P. Arkwright's *Old English Edition* (1889–1902) of Elizabethan and Jacobean music. They also had a strong interest in educational music, and published books of music for various examining bodies.

C. G. Mortimer: 'Leading Music Publishers: the House of Joseph Williams', *MO*, lxii (1938–9),

1092; F. Williams: 'After Forty Years: Recollections of a Music Publisher', *MO*, lxiii (1939–40), lxiv (1940–41) [13-pt. ser.]; Humphries and Smith (1954, 2/1970)

P.W.J.

Williamson, T(homas) G(eorge) (*b* London, 1758–9; *d* Paris, Oct 1817). English army officer, composer, author and publisher. He joined the Bengal Army at 19 and served in India from 1778 to 1798, when his career as an officer came to a sudden end. On his return to London Williamson opened a warehouse at 20 The Strand, 'where a great variety of Music, Instruments, as also Prints and Drawings, may be had'. He published from this address works by other composers and some of his own numerous compositions and writings. These show strong Indian and military connections.

Humphries and Smith (1954, 2/1970); O. Edwards: 'Captain Williamson's Compositions: Fashionable Music by an Army Officer', *MR*, xlii (1981), 116

O.E.

Willig, George (*b* Germany, 1764; *d* Philadelphia, 30 Dec 1851). American publisher. He took over John Christopher Moller's business in Philadelphia in 1794 and established one of the most active and enduring music publishing firms of the early 19th century. He built up a large and varied catalogue of instrumental and vocal music and popular songs, including Stephen Foster's first published song, *Open thy lattice, love* (1844). In 1856 the firm was taken over by Lee & Walker, which was in turn acquired by Oliver Ditson in 1875. In 1822 Willig acquired the business of Thomas Carr in Baltimore, and his son George Willig jr took control of that firm (which was renamed after him) in 1829. The Baltimore firm also published popular songs, especially minstrel music such as *Clare de Kitchen*, *Jim Crow* and *Zip Coon*. At the death of George Willig jr in 1874, his sons Joseph E. Willig and Henry Willig, who had joined him in 1868, inherited the business, which they continued until 1910 under the name Geo. Willig & Co.

Dichter and Shapiro (1941, 2/1977); D. W. Krummel: *Philadelphia Music Engraving and Publishing, 1800–1820: a Study in Bibliography and Cultural History* (diss., U. of Michigan, 1958); C. E. Claghorn: *Biographical Dictionary of American Music* (West Nyack, NY, 1973); Wolfe (1980)

R.A.L.

Windet, John (*fl* London, 1584–1611). English printer. He owned one of the most successful general printing businesses in London. He held several important offices in the Company of Stationers and ultimately became Printer to the City of London. From 1592 he printed several editions of the Sternhold and Hopkins psalm book for John Day and for his son Richard Day. His publications began with John Dowland's *Lachrimae* (dated 2 April 1604 in the Stationers' register; see illustration); it was financed by Thomas Adams and was one of the most important musical publications of the time. Windet's music output is not large, numbering only a dozen volumes, including Coprario's *Funeral Teares* (1610), Robert Jones's *The First Set of Madrigals* (1607) and *Ultimum vale* (1605) and Thomas Ford's *Musicke of Sundrie Kinds* (1607). Windet worked with type and his printing was always of a high standard, distinguished by spacious layout and a clean, sharp impression. His skill must have been stretched to its limits by the eccentric demands of Tobias Hume's *The First Part of Ayres* (1605) and *Poeticall Musicke* (1607), both of which he printed. His secular music bears the imprint of 'the Crosse Keys at Powles Wharfe' where he carried on his business from about 1594 until 1611, when he assigned most of his copyrights to William Stansby, formerly his apprentice.

E. Arber: *A Transcript of the Register of the Company of Stationers of London* (London, 1875–7, 1894); H. G. Aldis: *A Dictionary of Printers and Booksellers in England, Scotland and Ireland . . . 1557–1640* (London, 1910); Humphries and Smith (1954, 2/1970)

M.M.

Winner, Joseph E(astburn) (*b* Philadelphia, 1837; *d* Philadelphia, 1918). American composer and publisher. He was the son of Joseph Winner, a Philadelphia violin manufacturer. In 1845 he opened a music business in Philadelphia with his brother Septimus Winner (1827–1902), though each went on to establish a separate business in 1854. Under the pseudonym Eastburn, Joseph Winner composed and published several pieces of popular music, the most famous of which was *The Little Brown Jug* (1869). He was active as a publisher throughout the second half of the 19th century, particularly in the late 1860s. He was later succeeded by his son, who continued the family business until 1918. Septimus wrote and published simple instrumental pieces and arrangements, and issued a succession of concise, low-priced and highly popular instrumental methods. Under the pseudonym Alice Hawthorne he published some enormously successful popular songs, including *Listen to the mocking bird* (1855), *Whispering Hope* and *Ten Little Injuns* (both 1868).

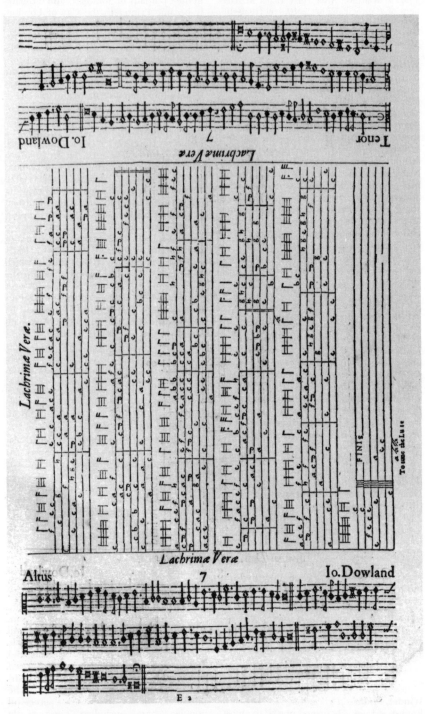

Pavan no.7, in table-book format, from John Dowland's 'Lachrimae' (London: John Windet, 1604)

Fischer (1933); C. E. Claghorn: *The Mocking Bird: the Life and Diary of its Author* (Philadelphia, 1937); Dichter and Shapiro (1941, 2/1977)

A.M.R., N.E.T.

Winter, Georg Ludwig (*d* Berlin, before 1772). German printer and publisher. He founded his firm in Berlin in 1750 and introduced there Breitkopf's improved typeface. He published primarily works by Berlin composers (Quantz, Agricola, Benda, C. P. E. Bach) and collections such as *Musicalisches Mancherley* (1762–3) and *Lieder der Deutschen mit Melodien* (1767). From June 1772 his widow continued the business; in 1787 J. K. F. Rellstab took over the printed music and Winter's firm ceased business.

R. Eitner: *Buch- und Musikalienhändler* (Leipzig, 1904); A. Potthast: *Geschichte der Buchdruckerkunst zu Berlin im Umriss* (Berlin, 1926); R. Elvers: 'Musikdrucker, Musikalienhändler und Musikverleger in Berlin 1750 bis 1850, eine Übersicht', *Festschrift Walter Gerstenberg* (Wolfenbüttel, 1964), 37

R.E.

Winther, H. T. Norwegian firm of publishers. It was opened in Christiania in 1822 by the Dane Hans Thøger Winther (1786–1851). He traded in books, sheet music and instruments and also published books on music. In 1823 he set up the first music lending library in Norway. His firm was the most important music shop and publishing house in the country for the first half of the 19th century; it issued almost 200 light musical titles, some through the periodical *Amphion*. After Winther's death in 1851 the business was sold by auction.

Winther's son Edvard ran his own publishing and printing business from 1841. He published three music periodicals, *Lyra*, *Musikalsk Løverdagsmagazin* and *Musikalsk Album*, in which many Norwegian compositions appeared for the first time. Other Norwegian music publishers made much use of his printing firm. The business was taken over by Carl Warmuth in 1878.

K. Mitchelsen: *Musikkhandel i Norge inntil 1929: a Historical Survey* (Oslo, 1980); idem: 'Music Trade in Norway to 1929', *FAM*, xxix (1982), 43; idem: 'Musikkleiebibliotekene i Norge', *SMN*, xi (1985), 81

K.M. (ii)

Wirzbięta [Wierzbięta], **Maciei** (*b* Kraków, 1523; *d* Kraków, 15–17 June 1605). Polish printer and bookseller active in Kraków. He was probably a pupil of Florian Ungler. For the high standards of his publications Wirzbięta received the title 'Sacrae Maiestatis Regiae chalcographus'. A Calvinist, he became the principal printer for the Reformation in Poland. He published much music, almost entirely consisting of songbooks in which Protestant solo songs are well represented. In Walenty z Brozowa's *Cantional* (1569), for example, Wirzbięta reproduced the music partly by type and partly by woodblock.

Przywecka-Samecka (1969); *Słownik pracowników książki polskiej* [Dictionary of Polish printers] (Warsaw and Łódź, 1972)

T.C. (ii)

Witmark. American firm of publishers. It was founded in 1885 by Isidore Witmark (*b* New York, ?1871; *d* New York, 9 April 1941) and his younger brothers Julius and Jay, when they realized that Julius, a popular vaudeville and minstrel performer, was not receiving the promised royalties from the publisher of the songs he was publicizing. The firm was originally called Witmark Brothers, but its name was soon changed to M. Witmark & Sons (after the boys' father, Marcus), because the brothers were too young to open a bank account. Witmark's first successful publication was *President Grover Cleveland's Wedding March* (1886), issued just after the announcement of the President's engagement. In addition to Isidore's own compositions, the firm later published works by Victor Herbert, George M. Cohan, Chauncey Olcott, Weber and Fields, Romberg, Charles K. Harris and Ernest M. Ball. It was an early publisher of ragtime and was among the founding members of ASCAP; it was also the first company to supply free orchestrations and vocal arrangements to those who publicized its songs. Witmark was purchased by Warner Bros. in 1929 as part of the Music Publishers Holding Corporation, but the firm's name remained in use until 1941.

I. Witmark and I. Goldberg: *The Story of the House of Witmark: from Ragtime to Swingtime* (New York, 1939/R1976)

S.S.B., F.B.

Witvogel, Gerhard Fredrik (*b* Varel, *c*1669; *d* Aachen, July 1746). Netherlands music publisher and organist of German origin. It is possible that he was given instruction in music by his father, himself an organist. In 1724 he became organist for the Lutheran Oude Kerk in Amsterdam. His request to be transferred to the Nieuwe Kerk was granted in 1726, and he held that post until his death. On 21 May 1731 he received a government privilege for printing two collections of psalms and spiritual songs which he had compiled for use in the Protestant church. In this way he began his activity as publisher, eventually bringing out at least 93 publications. At his death his firm was taken over by Jan Covens, who later also bought the publications of Roger & Le Cène.

As a composer Witgovel is of little significance, though as an organist he was evidently skilled enough to have held his own among eminent colleagues in Amsterdam at that time. His greatest importance, however, certainly lies in music publishing; during a decade or so he brought out an impressive series of works. His editions are now comparatively rare; only about 75 of his publications survive, in public and private collections. He was even more unscrupulous in acquiring originals for printing than was common at that time: one contemporary document states that he made use of a 'compositeur bien plus habile que luy', who revised pirated editions for printing. Authenticity and reliability of the musical text and authorship of his publications must be considered with the greatest caution. Nevertheless, Witgovel was important for having contributed to the rapid dissemination throughout Europe of the works of the late Italian Baroque. He published catalogues in 1733, 1742 and 1742–3.

D. F. Scheurleer: 'De nalatenschap van G. F. Witgovel', *TVNM*, ix/4 (1914), 245; E. F. Kossman: 'Het fonds van G. F. Witgovel, Amsterdam 1730–1742', *Het boek*, new ser., xxv (1938–9), 53; Deutsch (1946); A. Dunning: *De muziekuitgever Gerhard Frederik Witgovel en zijn fonds: een bijdrage tot de geschiedenis van de Nederlandse muziekuitgeverij in de 18e eeuw* (Utrecht, 1966)

A.D. (ii)

Wood, John Muir (*b* Edinburgh, 31 July 1805; *d* Armadale, Cove, 25 June 1892). Scottish publisher and writer on music. He was the son of Andrew Wood, a music publisher in Edinburgh, who named him after his partner John Muir. He received his initial musical education in Edinburgh, partly with Kalkbrenner, who visited the city in 1814. After periods of study in Paris with J. P. Pixis and in Vienna with Czerny, he returned to Edinburgh in 1828 for a while and taught music. For a number of years he was in London, where his interests were mostly literary. In 1848 he became director of the newly established Glasgow branch of the family publishing firm Wood & Co.; the branch became known as J. Muir Wood & Co., though it retained close links

with the parent firm, and survived until 1899. He provided many notes for the later editions of Graham's *The Songs of Scotland* (the Edinburgh house's most important publication), especially the one-volume edition of 1884. Wood edited later editions of J. T. Surenne's *The Dance Music of Scotland*, originally published in about 1830, contributed excellent articles on Scottish music to *Grove 1*, and edited the short-lived periodical *The Scottish Monthly Musical Times* (1876–8). He played a prominent part in Scottish musical life, promoting Chopin's concerts in Scotland in 1848 as well as initiating the visit of Sir Charles Hallé and the Hallé Orchestra to Glasgow.

'Mr. J. Muir Wood', *Musical Herald* (1892), no. 533, p. 249; H. G. Farmer: *A History of Music in Scotland* (London, 1947); Humphries and Smith (1954, 2/1970)

P.W.J.

Word. American publisher. It was founded in 1951 by Jarrell McCracken in Waco, Texas, as a sacred music and book publisher. In 1969 it acquired the Rodeheaver Company of Winona Lake, Indiana, whose copyrights included *The Old Rugged Cross* and *In the Garden*; in 1974 it was purchased by ABC, and in 1986 merged with Capital Cities Communications. Word produces a wide range of material for the broad evangelical market, including traditional anthems, keyboard, handbell and church orchestral music, hymnbooks and contemporary gospel music. Corporate headquarters are now located in Irving, Texas.

T. H. Porter: *Homer Alvan Rodeheaver (1880–1955): Evangelistic Musician and Publisher* (diss., New Orleans Baptist Theological seminary, 1981)

G.H.S.

Wright, Daniel (*fl* London, 1709–35). English publisher. He was established in London by 1709, and occasionally employed the engraver Thomas Cross. He also claimed to be a musical instrument maker, and died or retired about 1735. His son Daniel Wright had a business at different premises from 1730 to about 1735, for a while using a sign which his father had briefly used before him. He probably gave up trading about 1740, and John Johnson (*fl* 1740–62) may have founded his business on that of the Wrights, as he issued some works from their plates. From about 1730 to 1735 the names of both Wrights appear on some imprints.

Hawkins summed up the character of the elder Wright as a man 'who never printed anything he did not steal'. The Wrights were perhaps the most notorious musical pirates of their time, copying numerous publications, especially those of John Walsh. They also issued works under the same titles as those of Walsh or very similar ones, including a *British Musical Miscellany*, a *Merry Musician* and a *Monthly Mask of New Songs*. Hawkins also maintained that the elder Wright published a set of harpsichord lessons by Maurice Greene without the composer's permission, although, as with many of these pirated editions, no copy has survived. Their publications included instrumental works by Handel, Vivaldi, Corelli, George Hayden, J. S. Humphries, Loeillet and Robert Valentine, as well as sheet songs, instruction books for the flute and books of dances and airs for the flute or violin including *Aria di Camera: being a Choice Collection of Scotch, Irish & Welsh Airs* (c1730). A list of the elder Wright's publications appeared in his edition of Giulio Taglietti's *Concerti e sinfonie a tre* (c1734).

A music seller named Thomas Wright published sheet songs and a number of works around 1732 to 1734 in conjunction with the two Daniel Wrights, to whom no doubt he was related.

HawkinsH; Kidson (1900); W. Grattan Flood: ' "Aria di Camera": Oldest Printed Collection of Irish Music, 1727', *Bibliographical Society of Ireland Publications*, ii/5 (1923), 97; Humphries and Smith (1954, 2/1970)

F.K., W.C.S./P.W.J.

Wright & Wilkinson. English firm of music sellers, printers and publishers, established in London. As Wright & Wilkinson, or Wright & Co., they succeeded Elizabeth Randall and advertised themselves as 'Successors to Mr. Walsh', whose business had passed to her through her husband William Randall. From February 1785 to 1803 the firm was known by the name of H. Wright, standing for Hermond or Harman Wright. It is chiefly notable for the reissue of many of Handel's works from the Walsh plates, and for the first publication in full score of a number of his oratorios, including *Belshazzar* (c1784), *Joseph* (c1785), *The Occasional Oratorio* (1784) and *Solomon* (c1788). After Wright ceased business his entire stock of plates was purchased by Preston & Son.

Humphries and Smith (1954, 2/1970)

W.C.S./P.W.J.

Wust, Balthasar [the elder] (*b* Wittenberg, 1630; *d* Frankfurt am Main, 1704). German printer. By his marriage with Anna Margarete Rötel he acquired the printing office of Kaspar Rötel in Frankfurt am Main. Despite a succession of financial difficulties, he managed to establish himself in the second half of the 17th century as a Bible printer in competition with Endter and Stern, and published several interesting hymnbooks.

Benzing (1963, 2/1982); H. Hüschen: 'Hessische Gesangbuchdrucker und -verleger des 16. und 17. Jahrhunderts', *Festschrift Hans Engel* (Kassel, 1964), 166

T. W.

Wynkyn de Worde (*b* c1455; *d* London, 1534). English printer. He was Caxton's assistant at Westminster, London, about 1480, and in 1495 he published an edition of Ranluf Higden's *Polycronicon*, the first book published in England to include musical notes. Wynkyn's reputation as an influential music printer rested for many years on the theory that he printed the *XX Songes*, a set of partbooks published in London in 1530, but this was later found to be the work of another printer who remains unidentified.

R. Steele: *The Earliest English Music Printing* (London, 1903/R1965); H. M. Nixon: 'The Book of XX Songs', *British Museum Quarterly*, xvi (1951), 33; Humphries and Smith (1954 2/1970); J. Moran: *Wynkyn de Worde* (London, 1976); M. C. Erler: 'Wynkyn de Worde's Will', *The Library*, 6th ser., x (1988), 107

M.M.

Wyssenbach, Rudolf (*b* Zurich, ?1517–27; *d* before 1572). Swiss typecutter and printer. Son of Heinrich Wyssenbach, a shopkeeper, he was a typecutter in the employ of the Zurich printer Christoph Froschauer the elder from 1554. Around 1548 Wyssenbach set up his own press. In October 1551 he went into business with the printer Andreas Gessner the younger, but the partnership was dissolved by the end of 1553. Apparently he again worked as a typecutter and printer for Gessner from around 1557 to 1559.

Wyssenbach took the pieces in his *Tabula-turbuch uff die Lutten* (Zurich, 1550, 2/1663 as *Ein Schön Tabulaturbuch*) from Francesco Canova da Milano and Barrono's *Intabula-tura di lauto, libro secondo* (Venice, 1546). He transcribed them from Italian into German lute tablature, as he pointed out in the title and in the preface, in which he explained the ornamentation. He omitted the fantasias and included only two of Janequin's songs in arrangements by Francesco. However, he adopted exactly the same order as that of the original for Borrono's eight dance suites. Each comprises a pavan followed by three *Spryngerdänntze* (saltarellos), of which the first is a rhythmic variation of the pavan; in a few instances the second and third *Spryngerdänntze* should be taken from other suites. Most of the dances are in a chordal style, but several have virtuoso variations. One pavan and *Spryngerdanntz* are arranged for just two lutes.

W. J. von Wasielewski: *Geschichte der Instrumentalmusik im XVI. Jahrhundert* (Berlin, 1878); T. Norlind: 'Zur Geschichte der Suite', *SIMG*, vii (1905–6), 175; J. Dieckmann: *Die in deutscher Lautentabulatur überlieferten Tanze des 16. Jahrhunderts* (Kassel, 1931); P. Leeman-van Elck: *Zürcher Drucker um die Mitte des 16. Jahrhunderts* (Berne, 1937); idem: *Die Offizin Gessner zu Zürich im 16. Jahrhundert* (Berne, 1940); Brown (1965)

H.R.

Y

Young, John (*b* ?London, ?*c*1660; *d* London, 1732). English printer, publisher and instrument maker. He may have been a son of the John Young who was appointed musician-in-ordinary to the king as a viol player on 23 May 1673, and who had died by 1680 (according to the Lord Chamberlain's records). Young was established in London by 1695. His publications included *A Choice Collection of Ayres for the Harpsichord or Spinett* by Blow and others (1700), William Gorton's *A Choice Collection of New Ayres, Compos'd and Contriv'd for Two Bass-Viols* (1701), *The Flute-Master Compleat Improv'd* (1706), the fifth and sixth editions of Christopher Simpson's *Compendium* (1714) and other works. Some were issued in conjunction with other publishers, including Henry Playford, Thomas Cross, John Cullen, John Walsh and John Hare, so that such works as Clarke's *Choice Lessons*

for the Harpsichord or Spinett (1711), and editions of *The Dancing Master, Wit and Mirth: or Pills to Purge Melancholy* and Purcell's *Orpheus Britannicus* include his imprint. A number of interesting works known to have been published by Young are now lost, including John Banister's *The Compleat Tutor to the Violin* (1699), Philip Hart's *A Choice Set of Lessons for the Harpsichord or Spinet* (1702) and Alex Roathwell's *The Compleat Instructor to the Flute* (1699). Young also had a high reputation as a violin maker.

EitnerQ; *HawkinsH*; Kidson (1900); J. Pulver: *A Bibliographical Dictionary of Old English Music* (London, 1927); Day and Murrie (1940); Humphries and Smith (1954, 2/1970); M. Tilmouth: 'A Calendar of References to Music in Newspapers published in London and the Provinces 1660–1719', *RMARC*, i (1961)

P.W.J.

Z

Zanibon. Firm of Italian publishers. It was founded at Padua in 1908 by Guglielmo Zanibon (*b* Padua, 5 Oct 1878; *d* Padua, 21 April 1966). After studying music in his native city he moved to New York, where in 1903 he founded the review *The Mandolin*. He played the double bass with various touring companies until Cleofonte Campanini appointed him general secretary and librarian to the orchestra of the Manhattan Opera House. Back in Padua in 1908, he associated himself with A. Parisotto and managed a small music publishing house, of which he then took sole control, calling it 'Edizioni Zanibon'. He worked with many well-known musicians, among them Marco Enrico Bossi, Oreste Ravanello and Luigi Dallapiccola.

His large output included sacred music, instrumental and polyphonic works and Italian music of the 17th and 18th centuries. At his death the management of the house passed to his adopted son Guglielmo Travaglia Zanibon, who paid particular attention to the classical guitar repertory, early Italian music (notably for keyboard, Urtext editions), contemporary composers (Chailly, Bettinelli, Margola), didactic works and books on music; the *Opera Omnia* of Luigi Boccherini is in progress. The catalogue of Casa Zanibon contains at present about 7000 items.

Sartori (1958); E. Parenzan: *Guglielmo Zanibon a cent'anni dalla nascita* (Padua, 1978)

M.D.

Zannetti [Zanetti]. Italian family of printers. They were active in the 16th and 17th centuries and three of them printed music in Rome. An early member of the family, Bartholomeo de Zanetti da Bressa, printed Bonini's treatise *Acutissime observationes* at Florence in 1520. His name gives the only indication of the probable origin of the family. The first music printer in the family was Luigi Zannetti, who worked at Rome between 1602 and 1606 and printed mostly sacred music by Agostino Agazzari, Antonio Cifra and their contemporaries. Bartolomeo, probably his son, appears to have taken over at once, for he began to produce music in 1607. Between 1618 and 1621 he was printing at Orvieto but he later returned to Rome. His output was much larger than his father's and included music by most contemporary Roman composers and sacred music by other Italians. He published a series of anthologies of sacred works edited by Fabio Constantini (*RISM* 1614³, 1616¹, 1618³ and 1620¹) and the first edition of Frescobaldi's *Ricercari et canzoni franzese* (1615). In 1638 Francescho Zannetti published three volumes of music by Domenico Mazzocchi. He was probably related to Bartolomeo.

S.B. (iii)

Zarotto, Antonio (*b* Parma, *c*1450; *d* Milan, 1510). Italian printer. He was the first printer in Milan, from 1471. His *Missale romanum* of 1474, the first dated printed missal, and its successor, the first *Missale ambrosianum* (1475), contain no printed music; scribes filled in the notation, in the latter book with a two-line red and yellow staff. Zarotto later printed the music of Ambrosian plainchant in the missal (1488,

1490), ritual (*c*1487) and psalter (1496). He added roman plainchant characters to his fount to print the music of other missals (1488, 1492, 1504).

Duggan (1981); A. Ganda: *I primordi della tipografia milanese: Antonio Zarotto da Parma (1471–1507)* (Florence, 1984)

M.K.D.

Zatta, Antonio (*fl* late 18th century). Venetian printer and publisher. He was in business with his sons under the name 'Antonio Zatta e figli Librai e Stampatori veneti', with premises in Venice 'al traghetto di S Barnaba'; theirs was the largest engraving works in the city. The output included philosophical texts, novels, daily papers, illustrated books and 47 volumes of Carlo Goldoni's comedies (1788), besides music – instrumental works (by Corelli, Bertoni, Boccherini, Capuzzi, Andreozzi, Cirri, Cambini, Pichl, Fodor, Stabinger, Grazioli, Haydn, Mozart, Salieri) and vocal (arias by Cimarosa, Guglielmi, Paisiello, Anfossi, Naumann, Gazzaniga, Borghi, Traetta, Piccinni). From 1786 the firm began printing, on their own press from engraved plates, a weekly piece of instrumental music for sale by subscription; in the following years this initiative expanded to include trios, duos, quartets, symphonies or sonatas for various instruments, and even vocal pieces, issued on a monthly basis. In the letters circulated to 'professori e dilettanti di musica', inviting them to become subscribers, the firm explained the preponderance of instrumental music by the fact that Italy 'abounds without doubt more in professional and amateur players than in singers'. Zatta also published didactic methods (Pfeiffer, *La bambina al cembalo*) and music theory. One of Antonio's daughters, Marina, married the publisher Sebastiano Valle, who continued the work of the Zatta family until about 1806.

Sartori (1958); Mischiati (1984)

M.D.

Zondervan. American firm of publishers. It was founded as a religious book publisher by Pat Zondervan in Grand Rapids, Michigan, in 1931. Committed to evangelical activities, the firm entered the field of music in 1960 by acquiring Singspiration Music of Wheaton, Illinois, the owner of John W. Peterson's widely popular *Inspiring Hymns* (1951). In 1972 Zondervan acquired the Stamps-Baxter Music Co., founded in

1926 by V. O. Stamps and J. R. Baxter as a specialist in shape-note songbooks, and later a major producer of gospel songs. The Nashville firm of John T. Benson, specialists in record production and distribution, was also acquired in 1980, at which time the Zondervan group was relocated in Nashville.

PART THREE
Glossary

'Aprill is in my mistris face': page from the cantus partbook of Morley's 'Madrigalls to Foure Voyces'
printed by Thomas East (London, 1594)

Glossary

This glossary does not claim to present a comprehensive reference guide to the terms used by printers and publishers in various periods, or to those used by modern scholars of the printed book. To offer such a compendium would drastically alter the balance of the whole volume.

Rather, it attempts to explain current usage for those terms which a musician or musical scholar might reasonably expect to meet when reading musicological literature. Thus, while the principal implements and processes of printing are defined, no attempt has been made to describe, for example, all the implements involved in preparing an engraving of a musical score. The musical reader interested in such detail would, in any case, expect to turn to the professional literature in the field of music printing.

In the same way, there are many detailed concepts employed in the study of printed books, including musical volumes, which have not yet made their way into the musicological writings. Few of them will be found here, and those that are present are included for their value as potent tools in describing and analysing printed music; others may be pursued through references at the end of the entry 'Bibliography'. Instead, a number of key analytical concepts have been treated at greater length. These, the compiler hopes, will encourage greater precision in bibliographical writing about music, and also help to illumine the manner in which printed volumes of music represent histories of transmission as complex as those for manuscripts.

Abdruck [Abzug] (Ger.). A term, used interchangeably with *Abzug*, to denote an IMPRESSION. Both terms are also used to refer to a PROOF, as are *Probeabzug* and *Probeabdruck*.

Abzug (Ger.). *See* ABDRUCK.

Advertisement. The advertising of musical publications, as such, lies beyond the scope of this glossary. Publishers' advertisements from earlier periods, however, which even in the late 16th century may appear on the title-page or the back cover of a music book and became common during the 19th century (often comprising the whole of one or two sides of the cover; *see* BINDING), may be invaluable aids to the dating and identification of surviving music. Listed works had not necessarily been published by the time a catalogue was printed, but the great majority had been, especially those listed with prices. These may provide effective dates (*termini ante quem*) not only for the listed items but also for the work that accompanies the catalogue. Especially with engraved or lithographed music, this may be the most sure way of arriving at a date for any copy printed after the first issue.

Walsh is the most studied, though by no means the only, publisher who advertised the imminent appearance of his editions in the daily press. Later many music publishers advertised their editions (among others) in their own journals; notable examples are Breitkopf & Härtel (*Allgemeine musikalische Zeitung*) and Novello (*Musical Times*). It is reasonable to assume that publishers who continued the same methods of advertisement for a number of years were satisfied with the responses to their publicity.

Ascender. Term used for the part of a letter that extends above the height of an x, as in b, d, f etc.

Auflage (Ger.). Term used in German bibliographical work, roughly corresponding with Issue. *See also* AUSGABE.

Ausgabe (Ger.). Term used in German bibliographical work, generally to mean EDITION. Strictly, it is translated more closely as 'issue', and is so used in many non-bibliographical contexts. *Auflage*, on the other hand, seems to imply the whole of an edition, by reference to the act of printing, but is used in bibliographical work to represent a smaller distinct unit, the ISSUE.

Author. The phrase 'for the Author', often found in early English editions, refers to the practice among composers and authors of employing printers and music dealers to act on their behalf. A composer or author undertook the cost and responsibility of printing and publishing his own work, contracting with a printer merely that he should deliver printed copies, and often with a dealer that he should take, advertise and sell them. Evidence of the same practice is found in French editions of the late 18th and early 19th centuries. *See* SELBSTVERLAG.

Bed. The smooth surface of a letterpress printing PRESS on which the FORME of type rests during printing.

Bibliography. A term which, while clearly related to the description and classification of books, has acquired several different meanings.

   1. The subject.   2. Descriptive bibliography.   3. Analytical bibliography.

1. THE SUBJECT. The uses of the word 'bibliography' encompass: (*a*) a list of books, articles or other references pertaining to a specific topic; (*b*) 'reference bibliography': essentially an extension of (*a*), this means a listing of the extant material in a particular field or genre (such as a dictionary of musical themes, an itemization of settings of poems by Goethe, or a catalogue of all the music published in England in the current year). For the study of music publishing and printing, relevant examples are the volumes of *RISM* and catalogues of first or early editions of a composer's music, or of the output of individual publishers or printers. Ideally, such volumes contain detailed lists of locations as well as of contents, full details of title-pages and enough other description to allow scholars to identify new copies exactly. This area of bibliography spills over into (*c*) 'descriptive bibliography', the aim of which is to give details of a book's construction and of its components – typeface, paper, format etc. Such a description, normally a somewhat cumbersome process, is essential for an understanding not only of how the book was prepared and printed but also of where it stands in the publisher's and the composer's oeuvre. The last, so closely related to (*c*) as to be often seen as indistinguishable, is (*d*) 'analytical bibliography'. This takes the details of the description, studies the processes in the printing house (the range of decisions made by the house editor, the patterns of problems with type or paper etc) and as a result throws light on the reliability of the text and music, on possible causes for 'error' or change in the readings and on questions of taste or the possible market. It is (*c*) and (*d*) that are the concern of the remainder of the present article. (For a discussion of reference bibliography, see *Grove 6*, 'Bibliography of music', § 2.)

   Descriptive and analytical bibliography for musical volumes differs somewhat from the processes for most other books, although many of the general principles are similar. The biggest single difference lies in the nature of music as a graphic object and in the wide extent to which engraving or similar processes are used to depict it. The nature of the printing plate directly affects the layout of the material and its presentation from one issue or edition to another, the range of errors likely to occur, the manner in which a volume is printed, stored and marketed, and a number of other matters.

2. DESCRIPTIVE BIBLIOGRAPHY. The description of a copy of printed music involves a number of basic elements, common to all descriptive bibliography. (Fuller commentary on some of these will be found elsewhere in this glossary; *see also* CATCHWORD, COLLATION, COLOPHON, DEDICATION, EDITION, FORMAT, ISSUE, PLATE NUMBER, RUNNING HEAD, SIGNATURE, STATE and WATERMARK.) Ideally, it should include any of the following that are relevant:

(i) Transcription of the title-page; this serves as the first approximation for identifying a copy and for comparison with one in the reader's hand. A photograph and a printed transcription are not interchangeable, for each will reveal different information.

(ii) Collation and format, including any printed (or MS) pagination. These help to define the completeness of the copy in hand.

(iii) Colophon, or any publication data appearing on pages other than the title-page.

(iv) Description of the paper: watermark, chain-lines etc; quality and character. Often this will help to indicate whether the copy in the hand was printed at the same time as other copies.

(v) Size, both of the actual pages and of the printed area (or text-block). The latter will be related to the size of the plate or of the forme used in printing.

(vi) The process involved in printing the music. In the case of type, description and measurements should be made. In the case of engraved plates, woodblocks etc, characteristics of the artist's work need to be described. Any plate numbers should be given, with their position on the page.

(vii) Any running heads, signatures, catchwords or other details regularly printed on the pages of the book. These may indicate much about the printer's procedures and his concern to avoid errors.

(viii) A full list of contents, including scoring, tempo indications, key and any unusual features, with reference to other important editions of the piece or pieces.

(ix) A transcription of the table of contents, if extant. If this gives no information not to be found at the head of the music, it may be enough merely to mention its presence.

(x) Dedication (if not on the title-page) or subscription list.

(xi) The presence of any page or section advertising other publications, with some description of its contents, particularly the heading and the most recent items listed.

(xii) A list of examples of the edition being described, giving any major differences in content or appearances.

(xiii) For each copy examined, (*a*) condition, including description of the binding; (*b*) any MS corrections; (*c*) details of any differences from other copies – corrected plates, etc; and (*d*) anything known about the history or provenance of the volume.

(xiv) The date of the edition or issue, if deduced from evidence not present in the volume.

(xv) A note on related editions, issues and states if they are described elsewhere.

For much music, in particular sheet music from the late 18th century onwards, a number of these items will be irrelevant, but it is just such repertories, many of which were subject to frequent reprintings (by the same or a different company), that need careful bibliographical description. The many editions of a nocturne by Chopin need as careful distinction as those of a song by the Beatles, for the opportunity for variation is just as great.

If the description of a copy has been carried out thoroughly, the owner of another example of the same piece or volume should be able to tell whether his copy corresponds to any one of those described; the scholar should be able to decide which version, and therefore which exemplar, is to attract his or her attention; and finally, the information in the description may serve as a starting-point for the processes of analytical bibliography.

3. ANALYTICAL BIBLIOGRAPHY. This has several related objectives. One is to determine the extent to which the copy in hand carries a reliable text; one is to decide the particular function of the copy; and a third is to determine the place of that copy in the history of printing and publishing in general. These are necessarily related: a book printed by an obsolete technology, with an old-fashioned format or as a 'vanity' publication may well not do justice to the details of the musical text, or may not be able to display them in a manner convenient for the performer. On the other hand, a book destined exclusively for the performer, and subjected to editing by the publishing house, may equally distort the composer's intention. (Comparison of any edition of Beethoven's sonatas from the end of the 19th century with any so-called Urtext edition will quickly reveal the possible range of variation.)

While some analysis of the printed object itself is necessary in order to describe it adequately, reference to secondary literature is also important, especially since the majority of music printed between 1600 and 1900 is undated. The publisher's name and address should be compared with details in biographies or collections of data on the publisher, and plate numbers compared with published lists of numbers used by the house. The names on a list of subscribers or the name and rank of a dedicatee may be helpful, as may a comparison of the musical text with those of other editions published at about the same time.

Another essential facet of analytical bibliography comprises a study of 'printing house practice', the procedures adopted by editor, COMPOSITOR and printer in preparing the printed music, as well as by the publisher in deciding how to display and caption the work, in claiming contact with the composer, in asserting that the contents are really 'revised', or in incorporating music into a series of publications. A few examples of the impact of such research follow:

(i) detailed description of the typographical material used in several music books of the 1540s and 50s, which carry no publisher's or printer's name, but include the DEVICE of a salamander, has shown that they were connected with a major Venetian publisher of the time; this raises questions about why he chose not to acknowledge the editions.

(ii) The dates of composition of Byrd's masses have to some extent been revised as a result of a study of the undated editions, which yielded approximate printing dates for all surviving copies.

(iii) Poole's study (1980) of how London engravers divided up their work on some editions of Haydn, and his comparison of their work with the MS exemplars have enabled him to identify the characteristics of each craftsman and the range of errors each was liable to make – knowledge which can then be extended to other music engraved by the same men.

(iv) Study of the arrangements for publishing Beethoven's works in England shows that some of the English editions reflect his intentions more closely than any published elsewhere.

(v) Close examination of copies of the original editions of works by Brahms throws light on the lack of care with which engravers handled many details of the composer's score, as well as the extent to which Brahms notated corrections and improvements on the proof.

(vi) Study of the engraved full or vocal scores of certain 19th-century Italian

Bifolium

operas often reveals that some pages, while carrying the same plate numbers as their neighbours, are engraved in a different hand. While in some cases these pages are replacements for defective ones, in many they represent necessary adjustments in layout as more popular individual numbers, published earlier, were incorporated into the complete edition.

Very often, such research seems to be far removed from the actual music in the volumes studied. However, any analyses that throw light on the musical text are valuable: and it is evident that the many ways in which music has at different times been printed may have equally diverse effects on the extant versions of that music.

DESCRIPTIVE BIBLIOGRAPHY: GENERAL

R. B. McKerrow: *An Introduction to Bibliography for Literary Students* (Oxford, 1927); F. Bowers: *Principles of Bibliographical Description* (Princeton, 1949); G. A. Glaister: *Glossary of the Book* (London, 1960); P. Gaskell: *A New Introduction to Bibliography* (Oxford, 1972); G. T. Tanselle: 'The Description of Non-letterpress Material in Books', *Studies in Bibliography*, xxxv (1982), 1–42

DESCRIPTIVE AND ANALYTICAL BIBLIOGRAPHY: MUSIC

W. B. Squire: 'Publisher's Numbers', *SIMG*, xv (1913–14), 420; K. Meyer: 'Was sind musikalische Erstausgaben?', *Philobiblon*, viii (1935), 181; Deutsch (1946); W. C. Smith: 'The Meaning of the Imprint', *The Library*, 5th ser., vii (1952), 61; C. Hopkinson: 'Fundamentals of Music Bibliography', *Journal of Documentation*, xi (1955), 119; Johansson (1955); A. van Hoboken: 'Probleme der musikbibliographischen Terminologie', *FAM*, v (1958), 6; L. Weinhold: 'Musiktitel und Datierung', *FAM*, xiii (1966), 136; D. W. Krummel: 'Oblong Format in Early Music Books', *The Library*, 5th ser., xxvi (1971), 312; H. Lenneberg: 'Dating Engraved Music: the Present State of the Art', *Library Quarterly*, xli (1971), 128; D. W. Krummel: *Guide for Dating Early Published Music* (Hackensack, 1974), suppl. in *FAM*, xxiv (1977), 175; idem: 'Musical Functions and Bibliographical Forms', *The Library*, 5th ser., xxxi (1976), 327; D. Fog: 'Random Thoughts on Music Dating and Terminology', *FAM*, xxiv (1977), 141; M. Przywecka-Samecka: *Początki drukarstwa muzycznego w Europie wiek XV* (Wrocław, 1981); D. W. Krummel: 'Citing the Score: Descriptive Bibliography and Printed Music', *The Library*, 6th ser., ix (1987), 329

ANALYTICAL BIBLIOGRAPHY: CASE STUDIES

Å. Davidsson: *Studier rörande svenskt musiktryck före år 1750* (Uppsala, 1957); idem: 'Das Typenmaterial des älteren nordischen Musikdrucks', *Annales Academiae regiae scientiarum upsaliensis*, vi (1962), 76; Alan Tyson: *The Authentic English Editions of Beethoven* (London, 1963); P. Clulow: 'Publication Dates for Byrd's Latin Masses', *ML*, xlvii (1966), 1; K. Hortschansky: 'Die Datierung der früen Musikdrucke Etienne Rogers', *TVNM*, xxii/2 (1971), 152–86; K. Hofmann: *Die Erstdrucke der Werke von Johannes Brahms* (Tutzing, 1975); S. Boorman: 'The "First" Edition of the *Odhecaton A*', *JAMS*, xxx (1977), 183; H. E. Poole: 'Music Engraving Practice in Eighteenth-century London: a Study of some Forster Editions of Haydn and their Manuscript Sources', *Music and Bibliography: Essays in Honour of Alec Hyatt King* (London, 1980), 98–131; N. Del Mar: *Orchestral Variations* (London, 1981); M. K. Duggan: *Italian Music Incunabula: Printers and Typefonts* (diss., U. of California, Berkeley, 1981); D. G. Cardamone: '*Madrigale a tre et arie napoletane*: a Typographical and Repertorial Study', *JAMS*, xxxv (1982), 436–81; L. Cyr: 'Le Sacre du printemps: petite historie d'une grande partition', *Stravinsky: Etudes et temoignages*, ed. F. Lesure (Paris, 1982), 91–147; R. Pascall: 'Brahms and the Definitive Text', *Brahms*, ed. R. Pascall (Cambridge, 1983), 59; J. Bernstein: 'The Burning Salamander: Assigning a Printer to some 16th-century Music Prints', *Notes*, xlii (1985–6), 483

Bifolium. The term used for a pair of folios which are 'conjugate', joined together through the fold at the spine of a book. The two leaves of a bifolium comprise four pages of content; in most books, these are adjacent only at the centre of a GATHERING.

The concept is useful in the study of music printing, for it draws attention to the pages which must have been prepared and printed together. If the four pages are numbered 1, 2, 3 and 4, then pages 1 and 4 are on the same side of a bifolium and will have been printed together, and pages 2 and 3 are on the other. In a gathering of several folios, the conjugate pages may be further apart. With four bifolia, there are eight folios, 16 pages: then pages 1 and 16, 2 and 15, 3 and 14, etc are conjugate.

Binding. The binding of a printed volume is not always strictly part of the original book; at least until the time, in the 19th century, when publishers' bindings became common. Before then, the binding involved a separate process, whether undertaken by the publisher or his agent, for a book-dealer or for the eventual owner. Thus the binding of a book normally tells us little or nothing about its printing and publishing, though it may reveal much about its subsequent history.

This is particularly true for music. Many musical volumes as they now appear are anthologies bound up at some time after their individual pieces were purchased or copied. Clearly, the binding of such a volume can have little to do with the printing of any one item. But in many cases the binding carries a label (on the outside of the board) or an inscription or book-plate (inside the front board or on a flyleaf) indicating the name of an early owner. In addition, the binding will reveal much about its own provenance through the use of specific punches, stamps or rolls, each of which produces its own identifiable design on the leather.

Many other musical volumes have an institutional provenance (for it is often only through the careful preservation of collections from cathedrals or noble households that such books survive); this may be identifiable through the design of the binding. Examples include the collections owned by the French court in the 17th century (now in the Bibliothèque Municipale, Versailles and the Bodleian Library, Oxford), those from the Bavarian court chapel of the Renaissance (in the Bayerische Staatsbibliothek, Munich) and the volumes bound up for the British Royal Library in the 18th century (now in the British Library, London). Such bindings may also indicate the original ownership of the music they protect. (*See* KONVOLUT.)

While many early publishers and printers owned binderies – a notable example is that of Christopher Plantin – they undertook binding work under contract for purchasers, or occasionally provided simple bindings as a service. (Liturgical books are sometimes cited as available bound or not, in publishers' catalogues of the 16th century and the early 17th.) The earliest publishers' bindings as such, in which the publisher offered volumes for sale in a standard bound form, date from the very end of the 17th century. By the middle of the 18th century, publishers were issuing books bound in plain board, usually with separately printed paper labels attached. This practice appears to have spread only slowly to music: among the first to adopt it were Monzani & Cimador, in London, who were selling bound scores of Mozart's operas soon after 1800. The inconvenience and additional cost involved were more than offset, for the publisher used the paper covers of the boards to carry not only the title and publication details but also announcements of his other publications. Such announcements had appeared in published music since the early 17th century, although only sporadically at first and as space on the pages allowed. But they became more widespread during the 18th, often filling a whole page if one was available (for illustration *see* IMBAULT, JEAN-JÉRÔME). The arrival of publishers' bindings guaranteed the existence of such a page, on the back board.

These advertising pages could be left in standing TYPE and re-used in several volumes. For example, during the 1870s Breitkopf & Härtel's editions of Brahms regularly appeared with publishers' bindings, each carrying (on the front board) a list of others of the composer's works available from that house: the page could be used for any issue of any of the listed works, and the title of the one in question could be marked with red pencil. The back board also had a printed list, in this case of works by other composers. These lists were regularly updated, as were the lists on the back covers of Universal Edition's publications of Schoenberg and Webern. (These lists often carry an abbreviated date of their preparation.)

The technique of binding music, essentially the same as that of binding all printed matter, lies outside the scope of this discussion. One additional feature of interest to musicologists, however, lies in the regular use of printer's waste (discarded sheets) for padding the boards or as binding strips. In a significant number of cases, this has been found to derive from musical volumes, yielding new MSS, new editions and, in a few cases, evidence of lost titles or fragments of lost works, as in the Bagford collection in the British Library.

Blind impression. An impression made by an uninked printing surface. In most cases this is the result of an error in inking. Particularly with hand-presses, it is possible to miss part of the page when inking the forme: the content will then not show black but will often show indentations. Some printers deliberately used type which was not intended to be inked on large blank areas on the forme. These sorts, called 'bearers', will also show an indentation in surviving copies.

Blind stamping. (1) The impression of a binding punch or roll on a leather binding, without the use of colour or gold leaf. It is more common than gold-leaf stamping on many musical volumes, where the bindings were utilitarian rather than decorative. (2) The impression by Ricordi & Co. of a date on the lower left-hand corner of the title-page of their publications. This date, also sometimes found on the other preliminary pages, seems to represent the date on which the sheets were assembled ready for sale. Ricordi started the practice in the 1850s; it continued well into the present century. Hopkinson (1978) used the term blind-stamp for these marks, which provide important information for the date of otherwise undated later issues of engraved works.

C. Hopkinson: *A Bibliography of the Works of Giuseppe Verdi*, ii (New York, 1978), p. xv.

Block. A loose term for a block, usually of wood, into which any unique design has been cut. Initials are the matter most commonly printed from woodblocks; they can usually be distinguished from large type initials, both by their uniqueness (in details if not in overall design) and through study of the forms of damage to which they are subject. During the 19th century many initials on blocks were actually made from metal mounted on a wooden block; this construction produced a durable surface without adding excessively to the weight. Some printers use the term 'block' for any such design, on any surface, that can be printed on the same press as type or letterpress.

The earliest woodblock printed music appeared in the 15th century, in the form of examples in treatises; these were treated in the same way as the diagrams in architectural or medical books or the purely graphic illustrations of specula-tive music theory still being presented in new treatises. Many woodblock examples of actual music are of a low quality. The first complete piece of music printed from woodblock appeared at the end of Verardus's *Historia beatica* in 1493, and music continued to be printed in this fashion until the 19th century. Several volumes of plays printed in Germany around 1500 included one or two choruses, which were regularly printed from woodblock. However, beginning with Andrea Antico in 1510, whole musical volumes were also printed by this means. Probably the survival of the technique resulted from a reluctance among printers to buy music type when they had little prospect of working on many musical volumes. This does not explain the extensive use of woodblocks by Antico, who continued to cut them for musical volumes until the emergence of single-impression music type in 1538. For illustration *see* fig.1, pp.8–9.

Broadsheet [broadside]. A single sheet of paper, usually printed only on one side, as a self-contained unit, not to be folded or cut, and containing a complete work. While the best known use of broadsheets for nearly two centuries was as political leaflets, they were frequently used for music and for verse intended to be sung. The history of single-sheet music printing is obscure and will probably remain so, at least in detail. The survival of sheets is more haphazard than that of other printed music. Most do not show the name of their printer or publisher, or the place or date of publication. While a number contain topical references, many others lack specific information. Finally, bibliographical control of broadsheets, especially those with music, is relatively poor.

Single sheets were important vehicles of religious texts in Germany from before 1500. Some of the earliest with music also include translations from Latin texts (made by Sebastian Brant). Many of these are not strictly broadsheets, since they are too small and apparently printed on halfsheets; they typically measure between 38 × 25 mm and 23 × 15 mm, with a preponderance of the smaller sizes. Most carry a single vocal line, although one, printed in 1515 probably by Gutknecht of Nuremberg, has a four-part setting. In the early years of the Reformation, single-sheet hymns were frequently published, but small anthologies of four or eight pages were the norm by the 1540s.

Of the many broadsides carrying ballads and published in England before 1700, a few (probably less than 5%) contain musical notation. Nearly all that survive date from the last decades of the 17th century. Many are printed with a line stating 'To the tune of . . .', implying that the majority of the tunes cited were well known. Indeed, several broadsheets carry nonsense music.

The broadside ballad in England declined at the end of the 17th century, and the songsheet became popular during the ensuing years (see Krummel, 1975). The songsheet, which seems normally to have been printed on a half-sheet of paper, was a much more sophisticated creation. It contained songs (with basslines) by established composers, and was often carefully engraved.

Such sheets evidently commanded a viable market, for they continued to be published into the 19th century, in both Europe and America, although they gradually gave way to the four-page folded sheet, often printed on only one side (i.e. on the second and third pages).

In addition to these repertories, there have been other occasional broadsheet publications in music, including basic instructions in plainchant, elementary lute tutors and presentations of the rudiments of musical notation. Most of these await serious study.

W. Bäumker: *Das katholische deutsche Kirchenlied* (Freiburg im Breisgau, 1889–1911); R. Lamson: *English Broadside Ballad Tunes (1550–1700)* (diss., Harvard U., 1935); Krummel (1975)

Burin. The principal tool of the engraver (in US usage, a 'graver'). It is a steel rod, square in cross-section, mounted on a wooden handle, with the other end ground to an angle of (usually) 45°. This creates a point, which is used to cut the plate.

Burins or gravers are also produced in other shapes. 'Lozenge' gravers, which are often used for wood engraving, produce finer lines. 'Scorpers' are shaped like gouges, with either flat or rounded ends; they can be used for removing solid areas or for creating broad lines, for example, beams between notes.

Burnisher. An engraver's tool consisting of a tapered rod, oval in cross-section. Its use is the third of the principal stages of engraving a plate, after scraping (*see* SCRAPER). The burnisher smooths out scratches and unwanted surface marks on the plate, and can also be used to thin shading.

Burr. The ridge of metal forced up on either side of a line cut in a plate with a Burin. If left in place during printing, burrs attract extra ink to the line, making it thicker and ugly; they are therefore removed with a Scraper.

Camera copy [camera-ready copy]. A final version, ready to be photographed for the making of printing plates, of material to be printed, laid out page by page with all preliminary and incidental matter (such as page numbers, running heads etc), exactly as it is to appear when published.

Cancel [cancellans]. A new sheet or bifolium prepared to replace one containing a major textual error or affected by some practical mishap; the rejected sheet or bifolium is called a 'cancelland' (or 'cancellandum'). If the printer and publisher effect the change quickly and efficiently, no trace of the original need remain, and the cancel may later prove impossible to detect. Thus some volumes printed by Petrucci, for example, include individual sheets which appear to modern scholars to have been prepared later than the rest: but it cannot be proved that they are cancels, since no defective originals survive, and they may merely represent additional sheets run off to supplement the stock.

The process of cancelling seems rare when dealing with engraved plates or later techniques; it is then often simpler merely to correct the plate, producing not a cancel but a later state.

Cancelland [cancellandum]. *See* Cancel.

Cancellans. Cancel.

Caractère (Fr.). Sort.

Case. (1) The tray in which sorts of type are stored when being used for setting up text or music for printing. There are two cases for text: capital letters are kept in the 'upper case', small ones in the 'lower case'. The layout of text cases is standardized, but music founts vary so considerably that no standard layout has emerged.

(2) The hard cover of a bound book.

Casting off. A process in the printing house whereby a senior craftsman marks up the text of an exemplar (the printer's Copy or Stichvorlage) to show where line- and page-ends should fall in the printed edition. A highly demanding exercise, this involves considerations of economy as well as of facility in use, and is even more complex for music than for literary texts. The printer will wish to finish the music at the foot of a page, using a whole number of sheets, rather than waste paper (and money) by running on to the start of another sheet. At the same time, he will ensure that there are no undue problems for the reader: in performing parts, page-turns must be carefully placed (as these affect the layout of the rest of the page), and for orchestral scores, decisions as to the number of systems on a page and the retention of blank staves for silent parts are equally important. With few (and usually deliberate) exceptions, the linear spacing of notes is rarely consistent and proportional, even with type, but is arrived at with the skilled eye and judgment of the craftsman casting off and of his colleagues preparing the material to be printed. Satisfactory spacing presents the most intractable problem in computer typesetting of music, just as it is the hallmark of a good craftsman's work.

Catchword. A cue, printed at the foot of a page, indicating the first word of the next page; it usually appears at the right-hand end of the Signature line. Catchwords were normally printed only on the last page of a gathering as a check that the gatherings were in the correct order for binding. However, in a number of volumes, among them Glarean's *Dodecachordon* (1547) and some early editions of *The Beggar's Opera*, they appear at the foot of most pages. In Mersenne's *Harmonie universelle* (1636–7) they are found on most versos.

A musical equivalent of the catchword is obviously impractical, although there are two analogous devices. One is the use of a *custos*, or direct, the sign at the end of a line of music indicating the first pitch of the next line; the other is the curious practice, found in Petrucci's *Canti C* (1504), of indicating the first few notes after the page-turn for each of the voices. Both of these, however, are intended as guides to the reader or performer rather than aids to the binder. For illustration *see* p.488.

Chain-lines. Part of the impress of the mould used in making PAPER, formed by the chain-wires that keep the laid-wires in place. They run parallel to the short side of a sheet of paper and are more widely spaced than the LAID-LINES. *See also* WATERMARK.

Chase. The metal frame that holds a FORME laid-out ready for printing.

Coffin. The part of the PRESS into which a forme of type or plate is fitted, once it is ready for printing, and in which it rests when pulled under the platen. The tympan, folded over the coffin, holds the sheet of paper on which an impression is to be taken from the type. For illustration *see* PRESS, fig.1.

Collating mark. A black mark on the outside of the fold of a GATHERING, a modern equivalent of the SIGNATURE. The marks on consecutive gatherings are usually placed in adjacent positions to show the sequence of binding.

Collation. A description of the structure of a book or MS as it is prepared for binding. It is a formulaic presentation of the number of leaves in each GATHERING, and provides (with the book's FORMAT) a first step towards determining many details of the completeness of the volume and, where applicable, of how the printer worked with the music he was to print in it. Published collations are usually those of an IDEAL COPY, a notional perfect example of the book collated; since many copies will vary in their completeness, it is essential to note which copy is being collated.

For the simplest examples, in which the number of leaves in every gathering of a book is the same, collation simply indicates the sequence of signatures (*see* SIGNATURE) and, by a superscript numeral, the number of leaves in each gathering: $A–G^4$, for instance, represents a 28-folio book with four folios to each of seven gatherings, signed consecutively from A to G. A number of musical volumes are organized as simply as this, especially those published in partbooks: the first extant edition of Arcadelt's first book of madrigals (1539) has the collation [Tenor] $A–G^4$; [Cantus] $H–O^4$; [Altus] $P–X^4$; [Bassus] Y–Z, AA–EE^4. (It is more usual for the sequence of signatures to begin with the Cantus book, followed by the Tenor, as is the case in the next edition of this collection.)

In many early volumes, especially those containing short works (madrigals, chansons etc), the printer appears to have selected just enough works to fill a predetermined number of regular gatherings. Many more volumes, however, have relatively complex structures. Most texts do not fit exactly into a series of regular gatherings, and at least one gathering must be of an irregular size. Each of the partbooks of Gombert's first set of five-part motets, *Pentaphthongos* (1541), collates $a–d^4e^6$, each one having a different style of letters (a, aa, A, AA or Aa). In other cases a complex structure results from the inclusion in an individual gathering of material that is in some manner distinctive. A common example concerns the Proper of the Mass in printed missals which was frequently set in larger type than the rest of the volume and therefore prepared separately. It may then be in a gathering of a different size; so, consequently, may be the preceding material, which would not necessarily have finished at the end of a normal gathering. Even more commonly, the PRELIMINARY PAGES comprise a separate batch of material. Often, because they contain a table of contents or index, or a dedication page, they will have been printed last (even though they appear first in the volume) and may also not have filled regular complete gatherings.

Ravenscroft's collection *Pammelia* of 1601 has the collation A^2B–G^4H^2. The two folios of gathering A have the title-page and a letter to the reader; the two folios of H contain the last compositions and an index. Glarean's *Dodecachordon* of 1547 collates a^6b^4A–Z^6Aa–$Pp^6Qq^4Rr^6$; gatherings a and b contain, besides the title and dedication, a series of indexes that can have been prepared only after the rest of the volume had been printed. (The short gathering Qq illustrates a not-uncommon practice whereby, if the volume did not end with an exact number of regular gatherings, the smaller gathering was not the last one. This practice had advantages in binding and is still followed by paperback printers.)

Sometimes these preliminary gatherings have a different signature from the rest of the volume (e.g. an asterisk) or no signature at all. In the latter case, the Greek letter *chi* is used to indicate conventionally that the gathering was not signed. For instance, the first book of Mersenne's *Harmonie universelle* (1636–) has a complex collation which reads χ^2 A^6¶ ^{4}¶ ¶ ^{4}¶ ¶ ¶ ^{4}¶ ¶ ¶ ^{4}†^{6}ã^{4}A–T^6 etc. The first gathering contains two titles, with a large engraving on the second; gathering A carries the 'Preface Generale'; the next four gatherings have a 'Table des Propositions', with some errata at the end; gathering † has a list of contents; gathering ã has the dedication and a further preface; and the text proper begins with A1. Each of these layers represents a separate part of the volume and a different stage in its printing. (An alternative to the Greek *chi* for unsigned gatherings, followed by some musicologists and perhaps clearer to the layman, involves using a conventional sign, often an asterisk, but placing it within square brackets to indicate editorial intervention.)

Other similar anomalies, such as the presence of a single tipped-in frontispiece (*see* TIP IN), an engraving or similar plate elsewhere in the volume, need to be shown. The loss of pages which were originally part of a volume must also be noted, as must the (rarer) addition of pages. The most common such loss is that of blank leaves; the manner of presenting these in a collation is shown in Bowers (1949). Here the process of collation spills over from the description of an IDEAL COPY to the description of a copy as it survives, with any defects it may have. Since very few books before 1700, including musical books, were actually identical in all published copies (thereby thwarting one of the apparent aims of printing), the accurate description of a surviving copy is as important as the attempted description of an ideal copy.

F. Bowers: *Principles of Bibliographical Description* (Princeton, 1949); G. T. Tanselle; 'Title-page Transcription and Signature Collation Reconsidered', *Studies in Bibliography*, xxxviii (1985), 45–81

Collette. PASTE-OVER.

Colophon. In early printing, a verbal statement appearing at the end of the book, often in conjunction with the DEVICE and a statement of privilege. In such cases it may provide the only identification of the printer or publisher. In such example, the famous Dorico edition of Palestrina's first book of masses (1554) has no evidence of place or date of printing until the page after the last notes of music, where the colophon is printed: 'Impressum Romae apud Valerium / Doricum & Aloysium Fratres / Anno Domini / M.D. LIIII. / [Device of the Dorico brothers] / Cum Gratia & Privilegio'.

With the gradual adoption of the IMPRINT during the 16th century, the colophon fell into disuse. It was still occasionally used in the 17th century, especially in England, though rarely in musical volumes.

In some modern usage, especially in the USA, the term 'colophon' denotes a publisher's device, wherever it appears in a volume.

Compartment. A specially prepared decorative or pictorial FRAME for a title-page, into which type is inserted to give the actual title; it is to be distinguished from the more common type of frame, which comprises material from the printer's stock (either standard type ornaments or a series of decorative cuts or blocks butted together). Although intended to be used for more than one title, a compartment is conceived as a unit. It was usually constructed as a decorative or pictorial block, with a hole in the centre, into which different type could be inserted for each use. Compartments necessarily comprise large cuts, and as a result became more usual with the rising popularity of engraving for music printing. The London printer John Walsh the elder used several engraved compartments for various series; these are a special example of the PASSE-PARTOUT. For illustration *see* p.467.

W. C. Smith: *A Bibliography of the Musical Works published by John Walsh during the Years 1695–1720* (London, 1948)

Compositor [typesetter]. The craftsman in a printing shop who sets up the type, taking the individual sorts from the case and preparing the forme for printing. It is terminologically unfortunate for musicologists that this craftsman practises the art of composing, as does the creative musician.

Copper plate. The use of copper plates for ENGRAVING goes back, probably, to the early 16th century, although many early plates for etching and engraving were made of iron. Until recently, copper has been the most acceptable material: although not as durable as iron, steel, brass or aluminium, it is easier to work. It has gradually been replaced for some purposes by zinc alloy. *See also* PEWTER.

Copy (Ger. *Druckvorlage*). The version of a text from which the printer prepares type or plates; copy may be in MS or typescript, or may be an earlier printed edition. In music the German term *Stichvorlage* is often preferred.

Printer's copy normally shows annotations by a house editor or a supervising compositor or engraver which indicate the required layout. *See* CASTING OFF.

Copyright. The right to prevent another person from copying a printed (or, later, an MS) document. A direct descendant of the earlier grants of PRIVILEGE, copyright protection was at first usually accorded to printers and publishers rather than authors or composers as today; in many cases it was considered to exist in perpetuity.

According to the first copyright act, passed in England in 1709, protection for a volume was awarded to its author for a specified period, but was largely the responsibility of the printer or publisher, who had to register the text by 'entering' a printed copy at Stationers' Hall in London. In practice this system did not work perfectly, as many editions, especially of music, were published without being entered and some were entered but not published. Registered volumes were later sent to the British Museum and other deposit libraries. The length of protection granted has varied with the acts passed since that time; it is now regularly related to the lifetime of the author, composer or creator of a work, though it may be sold or assigned to a publisher without affecting its duration.

In the USA, the first federal law concerning copyright was passed in 1790 and followed laws first passed in Connecticut in 1783 in applying only to American authors and composers; music was specified as a separate category in 1831. Other countries followed suit, and the first international copyright convention was held in Berne in 1886.

Music was not often registered in the early years, perhaps because much of it was considered ephemeral. But with the increasing recognition, by both composers and printers, of the value of copyright protection for music, increasing amounts were copyrighted and deposited in the receiving libraries.

Correction. An early printer had several ways of making corrections when he discovered or was notified of errors in his publications: all seem to have been followed at one time or another by printers of music.

The most drastic method was to produce a CANCEL. In music printed from type, this involves preparing a new version of at least the bifolium (and usually the whole sheet) containing the error, printing a complete set of copies and discarding copies of the erroneous sheet. In engraving and later processes it sometimes entails preparing a new plate and going through the same procedure.

More frequently encountered is the STOP-PRESS CORRECTION, in which the press is stopped during the print run and a correction made. In such cases it is rare for the printer to discard the sheets printed before the press was stopped; more frequently they are released for sale as they stand.

Corrections of both these kinds are often difficult to distinguish from other anomalies. Apparent cancel sheets, of which either the paper or the style of type or engraving is at odds with the rest of the volume, exist in the output of a number of printers, and the scholar may be unable to determine whether they are truly revisions or merely copies made up to supplement stock. This is particularly true in the case of editions prepared from plates, when it is often impossible to tell whether a surviving copy contains a true cancel or stop-press correction or is in fact a variant ISSUE.

The easiest method was merely to provide a list of ERRATA and corrigenda, printed usually on one leaf of the book. Examples abound in musical treatises, from at least 1547, in Glarean's *Dodecachordon*, but they are almost never found with early printed music, perhaps because there was no easy way of indicating either the site of an error or the corrected version.

It may be for this reason that printers of music sometimes turned to two other ways of making corrections, of which both were even rarer outside music. One was to run off paste-overs, small slips of paper showing a corrected reading, to be glued into place (*see* PASTE-OVER); these have been found in the work of Moderne and Gardano, as well as some later printers. The other was to make individual corrections by hand; MS corrections were fairly common in the early 16th century and have been found in editions from the house of Petrucci and from some German printers. In both cases, the printer could correct only those copies still in stock; but the presence of identical corrections in several copies, especially those of very different provenances, proves that the printer was involved in making the alterations.

Cotage (Fr.). A term used to mean both PLATE NUMBER and PUBLISHER'S NUMBER.

Countermark. A secondary WATERMARK in the half-sheet of paper opposite to that containing the main mark, either in the centre or in the lower outer corner. It often includes the name or device of the papermaker, or a date.

Cropped. A term used to describe pages so heavily trimmed (usually by the binder) that some of their content is missing. A common result of cropping in music is the whole or partial loss of a composer's name.

Cut. An alternative term for an illustrative engraving; that is, one that does not include part of the content of a musical volume.

Dedication. The dedication or dedicatory letter attached to an edition of music is an important document in the biography of the composer or printer, and often in the artistic biography of the dedicatee. As such it should be transcribed and included in any description of a volume.

Dedicatory letters appear in non-musical works from before 1500, including (for example) Gaffurius's *Practica musicae*, although the earliest examples in musical volumes come from the mid-16th century. Many early dedications apparently have at least as much to do with the printer as with the composer, although their function was the same. The dedication was thought of as a way of acquiring the cachet of being associated with a noble patron or leading citizen, especially one known to be a connoisseur of the arts. A tangible reward was not necessarily expected, although many composers of the late 16th century and the 17th dedicated their volumes to their employers or patrons.

In the late 18th century and the 19th, the nature of the dedication was different. First, it regularly appeared on the title-page, and was not accompanied by a dedicatory letter. Secondly, it increasingly took the form of a personal statement from composer to friend, lover or student: the beneficiary was the recipient rather than the composer. Thirdly, and most significantly, it was attached specifically to the piece of music, not to the edition. In MSS of the earlier 18th century, such as those of Bach, it is not always clear whether a dedication applies to the work or merely to the copy of it being presented to the dedicatee. This is rarely a problem in music of after 1800. All these three conditions still prevail in 20th-century editions, although the dedication more frequently appears not on the title-page but on the following recto. For illustration *see* p.446.

Deposit. The requirement to deposit a copy of a publication in an archive or library is usually part of a Copyright law or agreement; books and music are deposited in national libraries in Great Britain, France and the USA, for example. However, in so far as the act of copyrighting a volume of music is optional rather than compulsory, such libraries will not necessarily be sent copies of books for which neither composer nor publisher has sought copyright protection. The date of receipt of a deposit copy (which may be stamped in it or recorded elsewhere) may not always correspond with the date of publication.

Dépôt légal. The French practice of depositing copies of published works in the Bibliothèque Nationale in order to register publication. It began at least as early as 1839; registration records go back nearly 30 years earlier.

Descender. Term used for the tail of a letter, in letterpress type, that extends below the depth of an x, such as g, j, p etc.

Device (Ger. *Druckvermerk*). A design, usually printed with a woodblock, which a printer or publisher adopted as his own and which he used regularly on the title-page or with the Colophon of a book. Petrucci's device, found at the end of all his books, is a typical geometrical design incorporating his initials. Gardano, Scotto and many later printers used a pictorial design (see illustration). In a number of cases the device appears without any inscription. Some of Antico's volumes from 1521 contain Torresano's device on the title-page and that of Antico himself, with his colophon, at the end. Devices seem to have gone out of use during the late 17th century and are now rarely found outside the work of specialist or private presses; one present-day example is that of the bear appearing on Bärenreiter's editions. In modern usage, especially in the USA, a publisher's device is sometimes called a colophon. For further illustration *see* Gardano and Scotto.

Device adopted by Playford's printer, Thomas Harper, from Thomas East

The motif of Daedalus, one of the typographical signs used by V. Baldini, from the 'Registro' (last page) of the second part of G. B. Aleotti's 'I curiosi moti spiritali di erone alessandrino' (Ferrara, 1589)

E. Vaccaro: *Le marche dei tipografi ed editori italiani del secolo xvi*, (Florence, 1983); J. Bernstein: 'The Burning Salamander: Assigning a Printer to some 16th-century Music Prints', *Notes*, xlii (1985–6), 483

Direction line. SIGNATURE LINE.

Druck (Ger.). A general term for printing, for printed matter (it may denote either an impression or an edition in non-specialized literature) and for type. A number of other terms derive from it: *im Druck*, in print; *Druckbogen*, a printed sheet of paper; *Druckbuchstabe*, type, or more commonly a capital or display letter; *Drucker*, printer; *Druckfehler*, printing error; *Druckplatte*, engraved plate; *Druckprobe*, proof; *Druckvermerk*, printer's mark or colophon; and *Druckvorlage*, printer's copy.

Duodecimo [twelvemo]. A FORMAT involving 12 leaves to the gathering, all produced from folding the original sheet of paper four times. In duodecimo, the leaf is always in upright format, with the chain-lines running across the page. Any watermarks will be found on the outside edge of pages.

Duodecimo is not a common format, being reserved largely for small volumes, pocket books, librettos and psalters. A number of the latter were produced in this format in the North Netherlands (for both home and English consumption) and France during the later 18th century.

Éditeur (Fr.). The French term, not for 'editor' (*rédacteur*) but for 'publisher'.

Edition (Ger. *Ausgabe*). One of four terms used by bibliographers to explain the relationships between different printed copies of the same material. The present article aims both to define the term 'edition' and to outline the complex interlocking relationships of that term and the other three, IMPRESSION, ISSUE and STATE. Although there is general agreement on the broad pattern of their relationships as applied to literary texts, and even to music printed from type, any attempt to extend this to other printed music presents problems, many of which arise from the differences in publishing (and even printing) procedures resulting from the use of engraved or lithographed plates, woodblocks or film.

1. Typeset music. 2. Music printed by other methods. 3. Conclusion.

1. TYPESET MUSIC. The definitions developed for literary texts seem to apply well to music printed from type. An 'edition' traditionally includes all the copies of a text printed from the same setting of type. Until standing type began to be allowed in the 18th century and photographic processes were adopted in the 19th, it was not usually possible to preserve a setting of type, for the sorts would be needed for use in another setting of different material. By and large, therefore, an edition consists of copies prepared and printed in a single sequence. If the type was reassembled, the content reset and more copies printed, these copies would necessarily represent a new edition, even if the detailed layout of the first edition was followed exactly.

Of course, not all the copies of such an edition would be identical: in the case of most early (pre-1700) editions, surviving copies vary with regard to such features as stop-press corrections, cancel leaves and inserted or deleted dedication leaves. These serve to distinguish different 'states' within the edition, each state being represented by copies with one variant or more. States cannot always be arranged chronologically (and they can very rarely be dated), for they are all part of the larger group comprising the whole edition, and the order of many of the changes can only be surmised.

A number of books (such as psalters or missals) that were frequently reprinted show a progression from one edition to the next through many intervening states, suggesting that the printer reset and reprinted individual sheets as stock ran low. A copy of the first edition of such a book with only one or two replacement sheets is evidently a later state of that edition; with the inclusion of more and more replacement sheets, however, eventually a whole volume may consist only of new sheets, and must accordingly be defined as belonging to a second edition. The point at which bibliographers decide that the transition to a new edition has occurred is necessarily arbitrary. It may be compared with the more common situation in which copies of a nominal second edition survive with a few sheets of the first, apparently included as a means of using up old stock. Bowers (1949) argues that the scholar should try to determine whether the printer intended merely to supplement his stock of the first edition or to produce a second while using up old stock. Krummel (1974), writing about other processes of printing, suggests that a copy should be defined as a new edition if more than 20% of the sheets are newly prepared; this would seem to be too small a proportion for letterpress work, for it implies that some four or five 'editions' must appear before a true second edition is established. In many cases, the title-page or some other feature will indicate the printer's or publisher's intention; any single copy can then be defined either as part of one edition with sheets from the other or as a reissue of the earlier edition with some new sheets. The latter represents both a new state and a new 'issue'.

An 'edition', then, may easily contain more than one issue, for the latter term refers to the arrangements under which copies were published – offered for sale – and not to how they were prepared or printed. If a publisher had occasion to change the address given on the title-page, if a new publisher took over the stock of a volume and added his name or if a year of publication was changed, a new issue is involved. This is also the case where printer and publisher agree to issue a new set of copies.

Separate issues within an edition may also be produced when a work is published in two different guises, for example as part of a composer's collected works as well as separately. The only difference between them may be that the collected edition carries a series title on a separate page, but the different conditions of sale are sufficient to indicate different issues.

The term 'impression' is traditionally used for all the copies that went through the press at the same time. Because of the need to re-use type in other contexts, the number of copies in an impression often comprises the whole of an edition, even though some individual sheets may be represented by two impressions. However, with the emergence of photographic processes, it has become possible to use the film from a single setting of type to produce later impressions of the same edition. An extreme example would be a photographic facsimile of an early volume. The modern facsimiles of the first edition of Petrucci's *Canti B* (1502), published in 1975 and 1976, are new impressions but must be seen as part of the original edition, for they were produced from photographic copies of the setting of type. (They are also new issues, since they were published under different arrangements.)

'Edition' stands at the head of the grouping of four terms, for it represents a single large-scale series of actions, the preparation of one version of the text in one form. The other terms are all subordinate. The nearest is 'impression', which often represents the same group of copies. 'Issue' and 'state' can both stand for parts of an edition; the number of copies in an issue is in many cases the same as in the whole edition (for the selling plans were not changed) but the state is more likely to change from copy to copy.

It should be noted that both 'impression' and 'state' may refer (the first often, the second normally) to an individual sheet in the first instance, and only then to the whole volume. Where a single sheet is reprinted, that sheet is in both a second impression and a new state, while the whole volume may otherwise be exactly like other copies of the first edition. In bibliographical study it is therefore wise to examine every page of a typeset volume.

2. MUSIC PRINTED BY OTHER METHODS. The situation underlying these terms is fundamentally different when applied to music printed by methods other than by typesetting. The printing surface – be it engraved plate, woodblock, lithographic stone or film – can be preserved almost indefinitely and re-used many times. The concept of an 'edition' therefore relates to a much greater period of time, that of an 'impression' is much more important and 'issue' and 'state' have very different resonances.

There is considerable uncertainty over the way in which the terms should be defined in these contexts, involving rare book librarians, bibliographers and musicologists. The only scholars who have regularly had to struggle with the problem have, until recently, been those dealing with such work as engravings, woodblock prints, printed atlases and plate-books. For them the concept of an 'edition' does not apply to individual prints, for each is a separate work of art; a new edition of an atlas or similar volume is produced when its contents are changed by the addition or substitution of plates. (It must be added that some early plate-books, apparently represent a situation in which each purchaser could make his own selection from among the available plates.) On the other hand, 'impression' and 'state' have a central importance. The state of a print, usually the more readily definable of the two, refers to the exact condition of the plate or block from which it was printed, in so far as this is evident from the copy. This definition differs from that used in letterpress printing in one important particular: a new state can be produced through accidental damage as easily as it can by deliberate change. As a corollary, the states within an edition can usually be arranged in an exact sequence, even if they cannot be dated precisely, for the changes in the printing surface that define them are irreversible.

Since such changes can be made at any time, even in the middle of a print run, states do not necessarily coincide with impressions. Nevertheless plates, blocks and film can engender a long run of impressions (of which many may be intended to present identical versions of the content), permitting the printer or publisher to maintain only a small stock of printed copies and run off new impressions as required. Further, a plate can easily be replaced (producing a new version of that page) or can be re-used in a different context. Both of these possibilities were exploited in the printing of opera scores in the 19th century: plates produced for individual numbers of an opera were re-used for printing scores of the whole work, and individual plates were replaced with others incorporating bridging material between numbers.

The definition of 'edition' in this context is essentially the same as that proposed for music printed from type: it consists of all the copies printed from 'substantially the same printing surfaces . . . at any time or times' (Krummel, 1974, p.30). This conveniently releases the word from any implications as to the passage of time. For as long as the printing surfaces for a volume survive, they can be used to print more copies within the same edition.

Copies produced in any printing after the first, however, represent part of a new impression. The identification of impressions is therefore the key to arranging copies in chronological order and to finding out what changes, if any, are of significance. Unfortunately, although identifying new impressions remains the key to determining the significance of an individual copy, individual impressions cannot always be detected. In many cases, both printer and publisher intended the new impressions to be added to the stock of a volume, so that the book could remain on sale for longer: they therefore make no particular indication that new copies represent a new process. Often a new impression can be detected only because of changes in the state of the content, or as a result of changes in the issuing details; occasionally a difference in paper or in format provides the necessary evidence. As in typeset music, an 'issue' represents all the copies of a volume put on sale as a single group and under the same arrangements. However, these publication arrangements are again not restricted in time, and may apply to several successive impressions. The first issue of an engraved edition usually contains all the copies that were prepared – in any number of impressions and over any length of time – until some change in the arrangements for publication occurred: the plates might be sold to a new publisher, the piece might be incorporated into a larger volume or a series of volumes, the publisher might change his address. It is possible to have two simultaneous issues of a musical work: a piece may be available both as a separate item and as a part of a series, or in both a de luxe issue (e.g. one printed on vellum) and a standard issue. In these cases, the two issues would be seen as parts of the same impression, although it is more likely that they represent two immediately successive printings. The most common form of reissue of engraved music, however, involves so-called TITELAUFLAGE. It has been argued (Tanselle, 1981, p.20) that the nature of the term 'issue' precludes its referring to more than one impression, 'for a group of copies forming a discrete publishing unit could not comprehend the output of several different press runs over a period of time'. However, it is evident that many music publishers did see just that possibility, and planned 'open-ended' issues, adding later impressions as demand required. Many of these later impressions would also contain later states, as advertising matter or minor details of the plates were altered.

The term 'state' also starts with the meaning it carries for music printed from type, denoting those copies of an edition that carry the same content. But because of the nature of plates, blocks etc, changes in state can occur much more freely, and in much less consistent a relationship to either impression or issue. It was as easy to make a change on an engraved plate as to make a stop-press correction with type, and such changes can be made to plates throughout their existence. In addition, accidental damage, wear and distortion continued to occur as plates were re-used. Any of these changes can happen in the process of making a single impression, although they seem to occur more frequently when a new impression is undertaken. Thus a single state may represent only part of a single impression (if some change, accidental or deliberate, is made to some of the plates), or the whole of an impression or even, if no changes are apparent, several successive impressions.

The hierarchy of the four terms is not necessarily the same for editions prepared from such surfaces as plates and blocks as it is for those printed from type. If, for 'type', 'edition' and 'impression' are normally identical in the number of copies represented, and 'issue' often covers the same copies, the same is not consistently true for volumes printed by other means. The concept of an edition remains central, but variant issues and different impressions occur within an edition much more often. A state may extend over more than one impression; indeed, the impression and state of a particular copy may well both be different from those of another copy of the same issue.

3. CONCLUSION. By and large, therefore, the definitions adopted by the bibliographers of literary texts stand up well to use in musical bibliography, so long as it is recognized that their relationships are necessarily slightly different in this context. The term 'state' (and even 'impression') can refer to an individual sheet in a volume, while 'issue' and 'edition' refer to the whole copy only: but all sheets need to be examined with respect to all four conditions before any single copy of a printed volume can be adequately placed in the history of the music it contains. It is unwise to assume that a copy in the hand is the same as the one described elsewhere, for in the work of many printers the process of change was almost continuous. Unfortunately, however, we can go no further in many cases than detecting obviously different states or issues, without being able to accord them a hierarchy or a date. Only the bibliographical study of many copies of an edition will demonstrate the true pattern of relationships and allow dates to be suggested for the various impressions, issues and states.

F. Bowers: *Principles of Bibliographical Description* (Princeton, 1949); C. Hopkinson: 'Fundamentals of Music Bibliography', *Journal of Documentation*, xi (1955), 119; idem: 'Towards a Definition of Certain Terms in Musical Bibliography', *HMYB*, xi (1961), 147; H. Lenneberg: 'Dating Engraved Music: the Present State of the Art', *Library Quarterly*, xli (1971), 128; D. W. Krummel: *Guide for Dating Early Published Music* (Hackensack, 1974), suppl. in *FAM*, xxiv (1977), 175; G. T. Tanselle: 'The Bibliographical Concepts of "Issue" and "State" ', *Papers of the Bibliographical Society of America*, lxix (1975), 17–66; idem: 'The Description of Non-letterpress Material in Books', *Studies in Bibliography*, xxxv (1982), 1–42

Editor (Fr. *rédacteur*; Ger. *Herausgeber*). A present-day publishing house uses editors, whether full-time or casual employees, in two different roles. (The role of the editor, or creator, of scholarly editions of music is not discussed here.) Editors of one kind take decisions as to which books, editions etc should be published, selecting from submissions and occasionally commissioning volumes; they are also concerned with the general balance and shaping of volumes, suggesting to authors and composers ways of avoiding what they see as defects. Editors of the other kind deal with detail, an especially important task in music publishing. They are responsible for maintaining the house style: this may concern such matters as spelling, punctuation and layout in literary texts, or the treatment of beaming, text division and transposing instruments in musical editions. They also ensure the accuracy (grammatical and factual) and stylishness of the finished product. A good music editor will use his knowledge of a composer's style to check for mistakes in copying and preparation, but will be aware of the danger of imposing excessive consistency and thereby obscuring nuances in sound and style, particularly in anthologies of works by several composers.

In earlier periods, editors of music felt free to make much greater changes than are customary today, and would (for example) rescore, alter notes and harmonies and provide their own piano reductions. Petrus Castellanus, a friar who prepared music for Petrucci, seems to have added a fourth part to certain three-part chansons, and occasionally rewrote sections of the originals. In the 19th century, George Thomson apparently overhauled the folksong arrangements prepared for him, acting as his own house editor. A remnant of such activities today is the 'edition' produced by a famous performer, which will frequently show alterations to readings as well as to dynamics, tempos, pedalling and so on; but it may not represent his considered view of how he would perform the music (and may just as well have been produced hastily or even 'ghosted'). The same can sometimes be said of modern 'scholarly' editions; in particular, these rarely take full account of the bibliographical or codicological strengths and weaknesses of the sources, factors which necessarily have great bearing on the merit of individual readings and overall versions.

Editore (It.). The Italian term, not for 'editor' (*redattore*) but for 'publisher'.

Electrotype. A process involving electrolysis to prepare a printing surface: also the printing surface itself. This technique seems first to have been applied to printing during the 1840s. A soft mould made of wax, lead or (in modern processes) plastic, covers the original type or plates; a layer of copper or nickel is deposited by electrolysis. The new metal shell is the material from which copies are printed; it is light and easy to store, while still durable, and thus has many of the advantages of engraved plates without their weight. In addition, as in offset processes, the original surface is not used for printing and so remains undamaged.

Em. A unit of length in type, originally based on the letter *m*. Strictly, it means a horizontal measurement equal to the Point size of the type being used (*see* Type size); in practice it often refers to the Pica em, approximately one sixth of an inch (4.206 mm). Gamble (1923) states that black note heads in music founts are usually reckoned as 1½ em in size. (Standard spacing sorts are necessarily built on the same scale; the most common are the em and the en.)

W. Gamble: *Music Engraving and Printing: Historical and Technical Treatise* (London, 1923/ R1971)

En. A unit of length in type, half of an Em in type sizes. Originally based on the letter *n*, it is approximately the average width of type characters in a fount.

End-paper. The extra sheets of paper used at the front and back of a volume to attach the book to its binding: each is a bifolium, with one folio pasted to the binding board itself (the Paste-down) and the other standing free. Usually the end-papers are of a different paper from the printed pages of the book; and they may therefore provide useful information on the history of a particular copy. The term is also often used to refer to a Flyleaf.

Engraving (Fr. *gravure*; Ger. *Stich*; It. *incisione, intaglio*). In an engraving, the design to be printed is cut into a plate in reverse; plates for music have traditionally been of copper or pewter. The earliest engravings were all cut freehand, but punches were later introduced for frequently recurring symbols – clefs, note heads, accidentals etc. For a detailed discussion of engraving, see pp.40–54.

Errata. Errors in a printed volume are not, of course, restricted to lapses on the part of printing staff, but not infrequently result from mistakes made by the author, either in preparing his Copy or when reading Proof. They normally necessitate small changes to the text – removing faulty spellings of names, revising inaccurate dates or correcting page references in footnotes or index, for example.

Many volumes contain a printed list of errata, and corrigenda, either on the last leaf or at the end of the PRELIMINARY PAGES (which are often printed after the rest of the book). An 'errata slip' is a separate piece of paper, usually smaller than the size of a whole page, which is tipped into the binding (*see* TIP IN); it contains a list of errors as printed and indicates the corrections to be entered by the reader. An 'errata leaf' is a page containing a list of errata, or an errata slip the size of a page. For other methods of corrrecting a printed volume, *see* CORRECTION.

État (Fr.). STATE.

Explicit (from Lat.: 'here ends'). A special form of COLOPHON, appearing at the end of a volume and beginning with the word 'Explicit'.

Facsimile. This word is often loosely used; strictly, it refers to a reproduction of an original that is true in every respect, including size. Very few so-called facsimiles, however, conform to this definition. Among the better facsimiles of musical MSS are some issued in the series 'Codices selecti' and by specialized presses. Interesting examples include the reproduction of working material for Mahler's Tenth Symphony, in which the gathering structure of the original is preserved; the 'facsimile' of Berg's *Symphonie-fragmente*; and the reproductions of performing parts for works by Bach. Some facsimiles use full colour printing, with four or even six photographic colour separations, to reproduce every nuance of an original where a composer's faint indications, and perhaps different layers of work, may be significant. Other, commercial facsimile series are monochrome, sometimes using line rather than half-tone processes, which for some originals may serve adequately; a two-colour process is also common, allowing many of the refinements of the original to be perceived.

Printed editions might seem easier to reproduce, but few 'facsimiles' of such material have the exact size of the original, much less its collation. Many are 'touched up' by removing apparent imperfections and redrawing the image where it is faint: often this generates new errors. From a bibliographical point of view, a facsimile of a printed volume should ideally represent not merely that volume but a specific copy (which should be identified), reproducing its annotations, 'errors' and variations in printing quality. Until the history of music printing is much better understood, and the house practice of individual printers are better known (especially with regard to correction), the omission or alteration of any features of the original will lessen the worth of the facsimile and indeed disqualify it from being described as such. (*See also* REPRINT.)

Fascicle. The increasingly common use of this word as synonymous with 'gathering' is to be deplored. A fascicle is a unit of content of a volume, which may (but need not) coincide with a structural unit. In the study of musical MSS, many of which clearly show evidence of various layers of content, the distinction is essential. Even printed anthologies of music may show similar evidence: volumes of polyphony may be arranged by composer or by number of voices, while other volumes show more subtle signs of being collected from diverse sources.

In certain series, among them editions of collected works and large-scale anthologies, an individual issue may be called a fascicle. For instance, the principal Italian edition of Scribe's librettos was published in series, each libretto reaching the market in a number of *fascicoli*, each of up to 12 gatherings.

Flower. A small TYPE ORNAMENT used to divide sections of text or to build up patterns for borders. Such ornaments may represent leaves or other simple objects rather than flowers, or may be simple abstract patterns. For illustration *see* p.488.

Flyleaf. A blank folio at the front or back of a book which is not part of the printed volume. Many bound books have flyleaves within the fold of the end-papers (*see* END-PAPER), which help to attach the book to its binding.

In some cases the printed book itself has a blank leaf at the front or back, part of a GATHERING of the book. Such leaves were commonly included in early printing, for the blank folios protected the text of the book until it was bound. Many early books have now lost these leaves.

Foliation. Sequential numbering which applies to the leaves of a volume rather than the pages (*see* PAGINATION). Foliation was the norm in the editions of many early printers and usually appears on the recto of each folio. Like pagination, it sometimes begins after the PRELIMINARY PAGES.

Folio. (1) A single leaf of a book, front and back (recto and verso) together, thus comprising two pages.

(2) A term used to describe one FORMAT or physical structure of a book. It implies that each original sheet of paper was folded only once, to make four pages or two leaves.

(3) Increasingly, the term is used to describe the approximate size of a volume, tending to refer to a page size larger than about 250×200 mm. Conductor's scores of all sizes are called folio. This application of the term is useless for the study of printed music and is to be discouraged outside publisher's catalogues.

(4) The term has also been used to stand for an anthology of items, such as individual piano solos or songs, which are related but were not necessarily printed or copied at the same time; this may be equivalent to a KONVOLUT. A 'song folio' is thus a printed anthology of popular songs. The term 'folio' may also refer to an individual popular songsheet.

Font. *See* FOUNT.

Format. A description of the traditional relationship between an individual leaf of a volume and the original sheet of paper, which in almost all cases consists of more than one leaf. The most widely used terms for format are 'folio' (abbreviated 2°), 'quarto' (4°, or 4to), 'octavo' (8°, or 8vo) and 'sedecimo', also called 'sextodecimo' (16mo, or 'sixteen mo'), while the less common terms include 'thirtytwo-mo' (32mo); each describes the number of leaves made by folding a single sheet. Some of these can exist in both 'upright' format (with the vertical axis longer than the horizontal) and 'oblong' format (in the opposite orientation), especially in music.

In all books, printed and MS, each leaf is normally 'conjugate' with another, that is, joined to it through the spine: such a join is necessary to allow the leaves to be sewn to the spine. (In so-called 'perfect binding', now found in many paperbacks, occasionally some other books, and even some miniature scores, this join is cut away; but it was there when the book was printed.) The practice of folding sheets to make pairs of leaves dates back to early MSS, but it was convenient to retain the same arrangement in printed books. The printer could print the whole of one side of a sheet of paper simultaneously, no matter how many leaves were eventually to be made from it.

The format of a printed volume therefore shows how many pages were printed at the same time. The folding sequences have been standardized from the earliest years of printing, and the description of the format therefore indicates how the pages were arranged on the sheet, reflecting the arrangement

Format

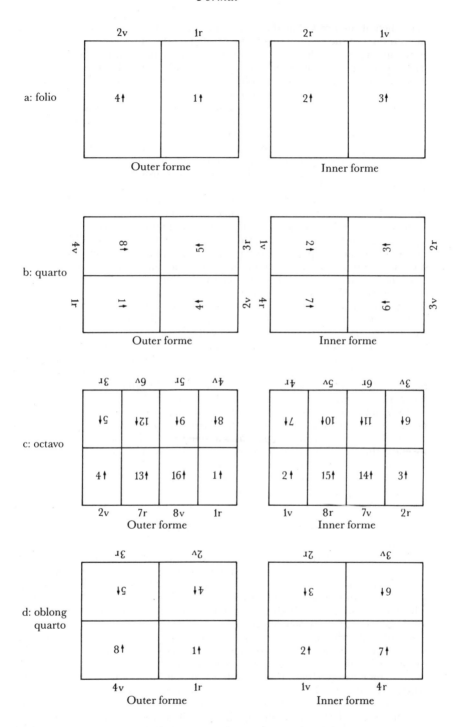

Diagram showing the layouts as they appear on both sides of the printed sheet, one printed on the outer forme and the other on the inner; the numbers indicate the order of the pages after folding and the arrows point towards the heads of the pages on the bed of the press. The diagrams on p. 511 show the layouts as they appear on both sides of the printed sheet, one printed on the outer FORME and the other on the inner; the numbers indicate the order of the pages after folding, and the arrows point towards the heads of pages. A number of bibliographical manuals show mirror images of these diagrams, presenting the layout in the press itself.

'Folio format' implies that the sheet of paper is folded once, parallel with its shorter sides, to produce two leaves (folios) joined together at the spine. These are normally taller than they are wide (i.e. in upright format) and contain four pages (laid out as in *a*). Much of the sheet music printed in upright format in the 18th and 19th centuries is in folio. Apart from the general size, evidence for this lies in the pattern of watermarks (if present) and chain-lines in the paper. There should be one watermark for each pair of leaves, usually in the centre of one leaf, and the chain-lines should run vertically. As in the other formats, these features will normally help to determine the format even where a gathering contains leaves from more than one sheet of paper or from only part of a sheet.

Quarto, the other principal upright format in early music, was used, for example, for many volumes of madrigals. It requires a second fold across the centre of the sheet of paper, at right angles to the first (shown in *b*). The vertical side of a volume in quarto is still longer than the horizontal, although in many cases the two are more nearly equal than in a folio volume. Any watermark will normally be split across two joined folios (the first and fourth or second and third), of each GATHERING. Chain-lines run horizontally across the page.

Octavo involves yet another fold, this time in the direction of the first (as in *c*). Any watermark in the standard position will be largely invisible, being hidden in the spine of the book; chain-lines run vertically. Clearly the size of the printed page will be smaller with each fold, but it does not follow that all octavo pages are smaller than all quarto pages: the size depends on that of the original sheet of paper and on how much has been cut away by the guillotine. For details of sedecimo and other rarer formats, see McKerrow (1928).

Much music has been printed in oblong format, from the earliest editions of polyphony onwards; it was popular for 17th- and 18th-century operatic music and has been used for most repertories at one time or another. In all the oblong formats, the first fold is made parallel with the longer side. Subsequent folds alternate in direction. In oblong folio the pages are very long and the chain-lines run across the page. Much more common is oblong quarto, in which a second fold produces pages of the proportions familiar in present-day organ and piano duet music (shown in *d*). Earlier pages in this format tended to be somewhat smaller, although the modern sizes began to appear during the 17th century. Oblong octavo has also frequently been used for music; it was particularly common during the 16th century.

Once machine-made paper became widely available for printing, during the early 19th century, a much greater flexibility in sizes and formats became possible. There was now theoretically no limit to the length of a sheet of paper, while the width was controlled only by the width of the paper-making machine. The more complicated foldings of 16mo and 32mo become more common, yielding pages of a reasonable size.

Since a gathering need not be made up only of the leaves resulting from one whole sheet of paper but may contain several sheets or even part of a sheet, it is often hard to determine the format of 19th- and 20th-century music. Machine-made paper rarely shows the chain-lines or watermarks that would help the scholar reconstruct the format. However, modern printed books still often use signatures and have gatherings with consistent numbers of leaves, which, together with other more subtle signs, often allows the bibliographer to analyse their structure. Many volumes of piano, chamber and vocal music, however, consist of only one gathering. It is tempting to use the terminology of formats loosely and assume that almost all 19th-century piano music, for example, is in folio format, or that the regular sewing of some Ricordi opera scores by four or eight leaves implies an oblong quarto format. While these statements are valid for many editions, the existence of new designs of press, coupled with the use of larger sheets of paper, means that we cannot make such simple generalizations. *See also* COLLATION.

R. B. McKerrow: *An Introduction to Bibliography for Literary Students* (Oxford, 1927); W. H. Bone: 'Imposition in Half-sheets', *The Library*, 4th ser., xxii (1941–2), 163; D. W. Krummel: 'Oblong Format in Early Music Books', *The Library*, 5th ser., xxvi (1971), 312

Forme. An arrangement of prepared type or blocks, locked into a CHASE and ready for printing. It contains all the pages to be printed on one side of a sheet of paper: the 'outer forme' includes the first page contained on a sheet, and the 'inner forme' the second, which lies on the other side of the paper.

The term has been transferred to later processes, as has the procedure. In engraving, some printers used plates that each covered more than one page (two pages of a volume in folio, or four of one in quarto); these would then have to be laid out in correct FORMAT.

The word 'forme' is also used in filmsetting to refer to the completely corrected film or to CAMERA COPY.

Fount. A complete set of type sorts of any one design and size. (The US equivalent is 'font'.) Thus a fount for a normal alphabet includes all the sorts of upper- and lower-case letters and of abbreviations, numerals etc of (for example) a specific roman or italic design and of a certain body size. A printer holds founts of each design in different sizes.

Music founts are much less consistent in their contents: much depends on the repertory being printed, on the technique of printing (especially if multiple impression type is involved, or if NESTED TYPE is used) and on the extent to which the printer allows aesthetic criteria to influence his choices and working habits. When examining a printed volume of music it is therefore much harder to determine both the full range of symbols in a fount – and hence the range of punches needed to make them (*see* PUNCH) – and the number of sorts (individual copies) of each symbol. However, a number of sets of punches survive, notably in the Plantin-Moretus Museum in Antwerp, and others can be reconstructed from type specimen sheets used as advertisements by founders (for illustration *see* fig.10a, p.38).

Foxing. The discolouration of paper leaves through damage by fungus or paper mildew, so called because it consists of gingery or reddish-brown patches. It may be the result of the paper's having been stored in a damp place; in books from many periods it is caused by the fungus growing in the felts used for making the paper.

Frame. A decorative border around a page. Normally built of pre-existing material, it may consist of straight lines (*see* RULE) or of ornaments arranged together to make a complete border, or it may be a COMPARTMENT. For illustration *see* p.488.

Frisket. An essential part of a hand-press, it consists of a sheet (usually of paper or card) into which holes have been cut corresponding in shape and size to the text area to be printed (for illustration *see* PRESS, fig.1). It is laid over the inked type or plates before each sheet is printed in order to prevent ink from reaching the surrounding area – furniture, spaces etc – and then transferring to the sheet of paper under the pressure of the press. The frisket acts to mask the unwanted.

Many copies of early printed music survive in which parts of the outer edge of a page's content are not printed – the composer's name or the lowest line of underlaid text, for example, may be wholly or partly lacking. Often this is a result not of a defect in the type or plate but of a poorly cut or misaligned frisket; other copies may survive with the same material properly printed.

Front matter. All the printed material of a volume that precedes the formal content (the first chapters of text or the first bars of music); it is printed on the PRELIMINARY PAGES. It normally comprises some or all of the following: HALF-TITLE, frontispiece, TITLE, COLOPHON or copyright statement, letter of DEDICATION, letter to the reader, table of contents and preface.

Furniture. Blocks of wood or metal used to help lock type into place before presswork. The completed pages of type, ready to be locked into the forme, do not normally fill it exactly. While it will correspond to the intended page size, the forme is designed to take various page-sizes and formats. In order to lock the type in place, and prevent it from moving under the pressure of the press, furniture blocks are placed around it and wedged securely into position. Early plates were nailed to wooden blocks, themselves surrounded by furniture. A similar process is necessary for all press-work, although actual furniture is no longer used.

Gathering. The prime structural element of a book, consisting of a group of bifolia which have been folded together to allow them to be sewn or stapled as a unit into the binding (*see* BIFOLIUM). Although it is clearly possible for each bifolium to be bound separately, this is usually impractical because of the ensuing bulk of the binding; in practice, several bifolia are normally collected together in each gathering. There are also practical upper limits to the size of a gathering. Some musical volumes seem to press close to this limit: Antico published several editions with 20 folios to a gathering, and Italian printers of the early 17th century produced even larger gatherings: these are exceptional, for each makes up the whole of a single partbook and will therefore not have been so difficult to bind as a book consisting of a set of such gatherings.

The number of folios in a gathering relates directly to the FORMAT of the volume, and thus to the number of pages on a sheet of the paper. If a score is in quarto format, for example, a gathering will normally contain four folios; it will contain eight if two sheets have been folded, one inside the other, to produce 'quarto-in-eights'. Many earlier printers seem to have favoured these structures. By contrast, many of the upright engraved editions from the end of the 18th century and later are in folio format and thus show a greater range of gathering sizes: a single gathering is often used for a set of three sonatas or for each part in a series of string quartets. The piano part of the first edition of Brahms's Piano Quintet op. 34 consists of 34 folios (17 bifolia) in one gathering.

The size of the gatherings in a larger volume, and the points at which they begin and end, need have nothing to do with the musical content of the book (*see* FASCICLE). It is easiest to prepare a large volume, for instance an opera score, with gatherings that are (as far as possible) regularly structured. This practice was followed by Carli in Paris in his vocal scores of several operas by Rossini, and by Ricordi in his 'complete' versions of operas by Bellini and Donizetti, regardless of the lengths of the individual arias and choruses. In each case many of the individual numbers had previously been published separately; while the collected edition is printed from the plates of these separate issues, its bibliographical structure does not reflect theirs. If it did, we might suspect that the complete edition was merely a collection of unsold copies of the separate numbers. (There are cases where the presence of irregular gatherings does reflect the content of a book: *see* COLLATION.)

Graver. *See* BURIN.

Gravure (Fr.). ENGRAVING.

Gutter. The blank area of an opening nearest to the spine, made up of the inner margins of two facing pages.

Half-title. The title of a book, usually in a concise form, printed (sometimes with the author's name) on the recto of the folio preceding the title-page. The term is also applied to the page on which the half-title appears.

Head line. RUNNING HEAD.

Ideal copy. A bibliographical figment, the term is used to refer to a notional copy of a volume representing the form in which it was intended to leave the publisher. It is a useful concept, as it acts as a yardstick against which surviving copies can be measured. If all, for example, lack a title-page or have lost one or more folios, the COLLATION describing the book will be that of an ideal copy.

G..T. Tanselle: 'The Concept of Ideal Copy', *Studies in Bibliography*, xxxiii (1980), 18–54; D. C. Hunter: 'The Publication and Dating of an Early Eighteenth-century Song Book', *Bodleian Library Record*, xi (1984), 231.

Imposition. The act of arranging a series of pages of type in a FORME so that they will appear in the correct sequence when the sheet of paper is printed and folded. *See* FORMAT.

Impression (Fr. *tirage*; Ger. *Abdruck, Abzug*). One of a set of four terms (the others being EDITION, ISSUE and STATE) used by bibliographers to define and explain the relationship between different printed copies of the same material. It denotes the group of copies of a work that were all printed at the same time. There need be no visible distinction between sequential impressions of the same work, for the term has no implications regarding the other circumstances under which the copies were printed. Thus both the plates or type and the arrangements for publication and sale (as indicated on the title-page) may be consistent, and the discernible differences may concern only other elements of the book, for instance the paper. An impression may therefore comprise the whole of an edition (as in music printed from type, for example) or may contain fewer copies than either an issue or a state of a volume (as in much music printed from plates, of which additional copies can easily be run off as needed, without any other change being made).

For further discussion of the term and its relationship with the other three, *see* EDITION, where the special problems of musical bibliography are considered.

Imprint. The material, usually appearing at the foot of the title-page – or beneath the title and above the first system of music in sheet-music editions that lack a title-page – that states where and when the book was printed or published; it also sometimes indicates for whom the book was printed or where it could be bought. This information gradually moved from the COLOPHON to the imprint during the first century of printing.

The imprint on the title-page of *Musica Transalpina* reads: 'Imprinted at London by Tho-/mas East, the assigne of William / Byrd. 1588. / *Cum Privilegio Regiae Maiestatis*'. That for Walsh's edition of Handel's *XXIV Overtures* reads: 'London. *Printed for and Sold by* John Walsh *Musick Printer and Instrument / maker to his Majesty at the Harp and Hoboy in Catherine Street in the Strand*'. Subsequently, the imprint came to be reduced to the name and town of the publisher, together with references to publishers elsewhere with whom the main publisher had an agreement; a date was not usually given for music. This kind of imprint is typical of most 19th-century musical publications from major houses, Ricordi and Breitkopf & Härtel among them. On many, more ephemeral publications the imprint details may appear in one of a number of places: immediately beneath the caption to the music (as in early 19th-century editions), at the foot of the first page of music, on a paper wrapper etc.

Details of the imprint, especially the publisher's address, are of considerable importance, for they are often the only guides to the date of publication. For illustration *see* p.379.

Incisione (It.). An ENGRAVING or an engraved PLATE.

Incunable (pl. *incunabula*). A book printed during the early years of the history of printing, before the year 1501. Incunabula have been catalogued with considerably greater thoroughness than have books from later periods and have been subjected to much closer analytical study. As a result, we know many details of the history of early printing, of the methods by which it developed new technical resources and of the means by which it became increasingly stream-lined.

Recent counts suggest that at least 200 editions of chant with printed music and staves were published before 1501; in addition, some 60 other editions survive with only printed staves (so that the music could be added by hand) and approaching 20 with neither staves nor notes but with spaces left for their addition. Over 30 treatises with printed music appeared before 1501, although some of the earliest used spacing sorts to represent notes. Virtually no poly-phony was printed during the incunable period; perhaps the first was a four-voice chorus added to the end of Verardus's *Historia Beatica* of 1493 (Rome: Silber). About half a dozen broadsheets or small books with songs were published in Basle and Strasbourg before the turn of the century, and Michel de Toulouse, working in Paris during the 1490s, published musical notation in his *L'art et instruction de bien danser*, among other books.

H. Bohatta: *Liturgische Bibliographie des XV. Jahrhunderts* (Vienna, 1911); *Gesamtkatalog der Wiegendrucke* (Stuttgart and Leipzig, 1925–); W. H. J. Weale: *Bibliographia liturgica* (London, 1928); K. Meyer-Baer: *Liturgical Music Incunabula: a Descriptive Catalogue* (London, 1962); M. K. Duggan: *Italian Music Incunabula: Printers and Typefonts* (diss., U. of California, Berkeley, 1981); M. Przywecka-Samecka: *Poczatki drukarstwa muzycznego w Europie wiek XV* (Wrocław, 1981)

Intaglio (It.). ENGRAVING. The term is often used in English-language writing.

Issue (Fr. *tirage*; Ger. *Auflage, Titelauflage*). One of a set of four terms (the others being EDITION, IMPRESSION and STATE) used by bibliographers to define and explain the relationships between different printed copies of the same material. It denotes all the copies of a work prepared for sale under the same publishing arrangements. An entire issue may often be printed at the same time. If a volume is printed for publication by two different publishers, sharing costs and profits, then the one printing ('impression') actually represents two issues, so long as the different arrangements are indicated on the different copies. On the other hand, if a publisher begins to run out of stock and orders a further impression, this is part of the same issue.

For further discussion of the term and its relationship with the other three, *see* EDITION, where the special problems of musical bibliography are considered.

Kerned type. Type in which the symbol to be printed overhangs the edge of the body of the type (for illustration *see* fig.2, p.19). In most founts of type (including music founts), there are considerable advantages in arranging for all the sorts to have bodies of exactly the same size, since they will then fit well next to each other when the type is composed. However, a few symbols of kerned type can usually be accommodated, the protruding part of each lying over the body of an adjacent piece of type.

Kerning has been found in printed music of most periods, even where the type itself or its punches no longer survive. The evidence may lie in the patterns of damage to the type as revealed in the printed copy or in the way in which some sorts seem to be butted together. Kerned type was well known to incunable printers, and has been found in Italian liturgical music books of the 15th century as well as in early printed volumes of polyphony. It was very useful in single-impression music printing, for the kerned note tails could, if necessary, project beyond the area occupied by the staves and into the space between.

Konvolut (Ger.). A miscellany of separate items kept together. First used before the invention of printing, the term originally referred to an MS collection in which the items often were related only by function or by provenance. In music bibliography it has been increasingly used to denote a collection of separate sheets and bifolia – most commonly sheet pieces ('sheet music') or performing parts – bound together (*see* FOLIO). Such collections became common in the late 18th century, when there was an expansion in both the publication of individual songs and sheet pieces (some of them taken from larger works) and the number of amateur performers who had their music bound.

Label. (1) A small rectangular strip of paper pasted on the title-page of a volume (usually over the publisher's name and address), carrying the name of a new publisher or of a bookseller.

(2) A panel on an engraved title-page or illustration, carrying a title, dedication or other inscription. It is usually rectangular but may be oval (a 'cartouche') or in the shape of a shield, a banner etc.

(3) In binding, a label is any small patch pasted onto the spine or front cover. It may be of leather or paper, and carries an inscription, usually an abbreviated form, of the title or description of the contents, or else the name of an owner.

Laid-lines. Part of the impress of the mould used in making PAPER, formed by the laid-wires. They are close together, usually fainter than CHAIN-LINES, and run parallel to the long side of a sheet of paper. *See* WATERMARK.

Landscape format. The more standard term for what music bibliographers usually refer to as OBLONG FORMAT.

Leading. The process of inserting extra white space between consecutive lines of text; also the strips inserted to procure that space. Most founts of text are so constructed that the ascenders and descenders reach to the end of each sort, if they are not actually KERNED. As a result, consecutive lines of text can seem to be very close to each other, especially when a descender (of, say, a 'g') in one line lies immediately above an ascender (perhaps an 'h') on the line below. The process of leading involves inserting a small strip of lead or wood (if the latter, strictly called a 'reglet') below each row of text.

Much the same problem and solution occurs with many founts of single-impression music type, where the note stems again run to the edge of sorts. The solution of adding leading is common in music, especially between a line of text underlaid to music and the next line of music notation.

Many type designs, made in the standard sizes, are also made on larger bodies, where in effect a row of leading is built in. The main text of the present volume is printed in 10-point type on an 11½-point body, this glossary in 9-point on 10; thus the leading is respectively 1½-point and 1-point.

The presence of leading or of type on a different-sized body can make the measurement of type size more complicated. *See* TYPE SIZE.

Leaf. A single piece of paper in a book, consisting of two pages, front and back. The term Folio is often used in the same sense; the only reason for preferring 'leaf' is that there might otherwise be confusion with other meanings of 'folio'.

Letterpress. Printing with movable type. The phrases 'letterpress printing' and 'letterpress typography' refer specifically to the use of type for printing literary texts, and by extension they have also been used in connection with the printing of music from type.

Ligature. This term has a meaning for printing similar to that in musical notation, denoting two or more separate symbols bound together as one unit. Among the most common ligatures in text printing used to be *fl, ct, sc*. During the centuries in which the long *s* was in general use, *sl, st, ss* and a few others were regularly ligated, especially in italic founts.

Opening of the discantus part of the introit 'Benedicta sit Sancta Trinitas' from 'Choralis constantinus', book 1, by Isaac, published by Formschneider in 1550

Music printers of the 16th century regularly used ligatures (see illustration). Petrucci had only two-note ligatures, as did most of his successors, and had to butt together individual sorts to make longer ones. It has been argued (Lewis, 1979) that Gardano was persuaded, by Rore, to have ligatures cast. Even into the 17th century some printers retained a few simple ligatures, almost exclusively those *cum opposite proprietate* for common small intervals, but it was often easier to use *longas* or *breves* butted closely together for most other combinations. It is not clear that the beginning of the decline of the ligature (even in MSS) during the first half of the 16th century was influenced by music printers' reluctance to have cast sorts for the many possible intervals.

Lithography. The process of drawing a design or music on a stone, which is then inked so that copies may be printed from it. Invented by Alois Senefelder and apparently first used in 1796, it was from the first closely associated with music. For details of the process, including the development of the Transfer process and of Photolithography, see pp.55–65 and figs.18–21.

Manuscript paper. Paper on which staves have been ruled or printed for writing music. It has been printed at least from the middle of the 16th century. The earliest examples appear to be German in origin. In England the distribution of MS paper was included in the restrictive privilege awarded to Byrd and Tallis in 1575.

In one respect, the printing of MS paper, while not obviously linked to the printing of music itself, provides a direct analogy with the complex range of possibilities available when preparing music for printing. MS paper has always been available in many different sizes and formats, and sometimes in special layouts, for example with braces for songs with piano accompaniment and even with irregular groupings of staves. A curious example is in a mid-17th-century Italian MS containing cantatas by Marazzoli: the paper is in oblong format, with only two printed staves on each recto and five on each verso.

Matrix. A piece of metal from which the individual sorts of TYPE are cast. The individual type designs are originally cut (in reverse) on a PUNCH, which is then used to strike the matrix. For illustration *see* fig.2*b*, p.19.

Mosaic type. A modern term for a fount of music type in which each note is made up of several smaller units – one for the head, one for the beam and one or more for the stem. Each unit carries only a small part of the staff, and they must be fitted together with small sections of blank staff. Although there are precedents in the 16th and 17th centuries (including the founts developed for lute tablature in England in about 1600), the modern use of mosaic type derives from the innovations of Breitkopf, Fleischmann and Fournier in the 1750s; well-known examples of its use are the vocal scores published by Novello, of Handel's oratorios and other works, in the 19th century. For illustration *see* figs.9 and 10, pp.32, 33 and 38.

Multiple impression. Any printing process in which paper goes through the press more than once. An obvious example is colour print, which is to be found in most volumes of liturgical music from before the 19th century: in these, the staves and rubrics were traditionally printed in red, the sung text and the notes themselves in black. Notable among other music printed in two colours is the repertory of Spanish 16th-century songs to the vihuela, in which the vocal part is printed in tablature with the vihuela part, but in red. In a few other works red notation is used for some special reason; for example, in Maxwell Davies's String Quartet it distinguishes precise notation from the notation of relative proportions, and in the movement 'Constellations-miroirs' of Boulez's Third Piano Sonata both red and green are used to distinguish different textures. In these cases the different colours represent two distinct processes, from preparing the material to printing in two colours.

In most liturgical books, however, only some of the red material, the staves, had to be set up separately. Some of the red material, the rubrics, was usually set up in type at the same time as the blocks, though the two were inked and printed separately, employing specially cut friskets (*see* FRISKET). Exactly the same arrangement – red staves and some (red) text, black notes and other (black) text – appears in *L'art et instruction de bien danser*, published by Michel de Toulouse (*c*1496) and in Cock's 1540 editions of *Souterliedekens*.

Some polyphonic music was also printed by multiple impression. Petrucci's innovation in 1501 consisted in creating beautiful music type which could be elegantly printed. The type did not include staves, which had to be printed at a second impression; he seems to have printed the text at a third impression for two or three years, amalgamating it with the staves only during 1504. Other printers, among them Oeglin, Grimm and Wirsung, Peter Schoeffer jr and Etienne Briard, used double-impression printing in the early 16th century. Before the invention of single-impression music type in the late 1520s and its widespread dissemination a decade later, the only alternative to the double-impression printing of music was the equally laborious process of cutting woodblocks.

A. B. Barksdale: *The Printed Note: 500 Years of Music Printing and Engraving* (Toledo, OH, 1957/*R*1981) [Exhibition catalogue, Toledo Museum of Art]; K. Meyer-Baer: *Liturgical Music Incunabula: a Descriptive Catalogue* (London, 1962); M. K. Duggan: *Italian Music Incunabula: Printers and Typefonts* (diss., U. of California, Berkeley, 1981); S. Boorman: 'A Case of Half-sheet Imposition in the Early 16th Century', *The Library*, 6th ser., viii (1986), 301

Nested type. A term, introduced by Greer Allen and Krummel (1975), to refer to single-impression type in which the musical symbols are accompanied by fewer than the standard five staff lines. Sorts with tails (crotchets, minims etc) were usually made with four lines, though fewer where feasible. The compositor, when setting the music, supplied the missing lines (most frequently the top or bottom ones only) by adding longer rules which extended over several symbols and thereby helped stabilize the rest of the contents of the forme.

Krummel (1975)

Oblong format [landscape format]. A FORMAT in which the first fold of the sheet is made parallel with the long side; this usually, though not always, produces pages in which the long axis is horizontal as opposed to the more normal vertical. Oblong format cannot necessarily be identified from the proportions of the page, for these will depend on the size of the original sheet and the number of foldings, not to mention any trimming resulting from binding. The distinguishing features are instead the position of the WATERMARK and the direction of the CHAIN-LINES. Thus, whereas in upright quarto format the watermark is in the gutter (at the spine of the book) and the chain-lines are horizontal, in oblong quarto the mark is split between two adjacent folios, in the centre of the top edge, and the chain-lines are vertical.

The first printers of polyphony adopted oblong format almost exclusively, although why is not known, for it was also new in MSS. It has been suggested (Krummel, 1971) that musicians preferred the longer lines of music that it allowed, although this does not explain the format's sudden adoption. It is possible that the longer staff rules (used for multiple-impression printing) and the longer blocks (in woodblock printing) were more stable, while single-impression type was more satisfactory in the shorter lines of upright format. Certainly, during the last quarter of the 16th century, an increasing amount of music was being printed in the upright format that is conventional today. However, oblong quarto, in particular, remained associated with music printing, and was described in 17th- and 18th-century printers' manuals as being used for this. It seems that most music volumes in oblong format were prepared in quarto: Krummel lists examples from the 17th century, as well as presenting format diagrams and listing surviving examples of oblong folio, sexto and octavo. Oblong octavo was the only widely used alternative to oblong quarto, and was especially popular for such small 'pocket-books' as the German lieder volumes of the early 16th century, Attaingnant's early chanson volumes and the songbooks of Le Roy and Ballard.

The popularity of oblong format for certain repertories and in certain countries subsisted well into the 19th century. Thus Ricordi's editions of Rossini and Donizetti, for instance, are in oblong format, whereas Parisian editions are upright: Schubert's lieder are in oblong format, while French or English songs of the same date are upright; and American tune books were oblong while European psalters are upright. Modern publishers continue to use oblong format extensively for organ and piano duet music, and in smaller sizes for recorder music and for performance parts for marching bands.

D. W. Krummel: 'Oblong Format in Early Music Books', *The Library*, 5th ser., xxvi (1971), 312

Octavo. A term, like 'folio' or 'quarto', used to define the format of a book. In octavo format, each sheet of paper is folded three times after printing, to produce eight folios or 16 pages. *See* FORMAT.

The term is now frequently and loosely used to indicate the approximate size of a printed volume, referring to books with a page size of about 200 × 130 mm. This usage is not to be encouraged in bibliographical work.

Offset. (1) Term for a printing process in which the paper is not printed directly from a plate or lithographic stone but from an intermediate rubber-covered cylinder which has received an impression from the plate or stone. The cylinder then offsets the impression to the sheet of paper. This may be 'photo-offset', done by a TRANSFER PROCESS. The process gives a better quality of impression on matt or rough-surfaced papers. It is accordingly supposed to be particularly advantageous for music printing, allowing the use of papers without a smooth reflective surface.

(2) Ink transferred from a printed page to another page. This may be from the facing page: although that is more common in MSS, it does occur in printed books that have been bound for hundreds of years. More commonly the offset text or music is from the back of another copy of the same sheet or from some completely different material.

Pagination. The practice of numbering each page of a volume (rather than each folio: *see* FOLIATION). It rarely appears in musical volumes before the 16th century. While foliation remains a feature of MSS, printers seem to have found it more useful to number each page. Even so, many printers either did not number the PRELIMINARY PAGES or gave them a separate pagination, so that the principal content of the volume could begin at page 1.

In some musical books the pieces rather than the pages are numbered. In cases where each page presents a new piece, the method used can be distinguished only by bibliographical analysis.

Paper. Paper has remained by far the most common surface for printing, especially for music. Very little music has ever been printed on vellum, except for liturgical volumes, and the most recent surfaces are of little interest for musical work.

Traditionally, paper historians and others who deal with early paper divide papers into two broad classes: 'hand-made' and 'machine-made'; this distinction closely approximates that between 'laid' and 'wove' papers. 'Hand-made' paper is produced by dipping a sieve-like mould into a vat of pulp, and then turning out the wet sheets of pulp so formed, separated by layers of felt, on to a pile (or 'post'). The sheets show a pattern impressed by the wires in the mould, usually as heavier CHAIN-LINES and lighter LAID-LINES (visible when the paper is held up to the light), together with any WATERMARK that may be present. The full sheet has a 'deckle edge', a thinner feathery border formed by the edges of the mould, but this is usually trimmed away when a book is bound. (Modern machine-made papers can be produced with both the patterns of chain-lines and watermarks and a deckle edge.)

Machine-made paper was first produced when a machine was invented, just before 1800, that could produce a continuous strip of paper. Because the paper pulp rests on a woven 'mould' in the form of a belt, the appearance of wove paper reflects the texture of the pulp and of the wove felt, without chain-lines or other patterns. Machine-made paper can be of any size, corresponding to the width of the machine, and can have different finishes applied to its surface more easily than can hand-made paper.

While machines have been made that duplicate the impress of the earlier hand-mould, it is also true that not all 'wove' paper was machine-made. In about 1795, John Baskerville of Birmingham introduced a hand-mould with a woven pattern of wires which made papers with a machine-made appearance. Some of this paper survives in printed music of the period and may show a date in the texture, like a watermark.

Paper for printing must have certain basic characteristics: (*a*) it must not expand too much with moisture in the atmosphere; (*b*) it must be flexible enough to fit closely to the printing surface (there are many volumes in which the paper has not taken ink consistently, resulting in slight white patches in individual notes); (*c*) the two sides of the paper should ideally have the same type of surface (this was almost impossible to achieve with hand-made papers); and (*d*) the paper must absorb ink well – though not too well – while still remaining opaque. Paper for engraved music has to be relatively soft and flexible, so that it will take the detail of the engraved lines; on the other hand, paper for lithographic work needs to be very firm and smooth and particularly stable in the presence of the moisture intrinsic to the process.

Much paper used for music printing has not been of high quality, and it has been very variable in both texture and sizing. Almost any music book of the Renaissance reveals differences in weight and finish between one sheet and another, and much music paper of the 17th century, especially that made in Italy, is lightweight and of poor quality. Particularly in the last hundred years, papers of a wide range of kinds have been used for different processes and in different areas. Papers in lithographic editions and in many Ricordi publications have remained whiter and less brittle than many French papers, owing to their different chemical composition. Even in a modern volume, however, the presence of a sheet or bifolium with a different 'feel' does not mean that it was printed at a different time from the rest: there is still a degree of variation in the material. This is even more true of earlier musical editions, where the variation in texture is often much more marked, and is therefore an even less reliable guide to bibliographical anomalies.

The size of a leaf in a printed book depends on the size of the original sheet of paper and on the number of times it is folded (the FORMAT of the book), as well as the extent to which it was trimmed during binding.

Sizes of paper have varied considerably over the centuries; details of many sizes from different periods can be found in Labarre (1952). Relatively few of these sizes have been used for music printing at any time, as far as we can now tell. By far the most common, found throughout the 19th century, is a size which is now (after trimming and binding) about 13½ × 21 inches (343 × 533 mm). This, which has a wide range of variation, gives pages of about 13½ × 10½ inches (343 × 267 mm). The actual measured sizes of individual leaves can vary considerably, from 12¼ × 9½ inches (312 × 242 mm) for music from Florence to 13¾ × 10 inches (350 × 255 mm) for books in publishers' bindings from London in the earliest years of the century. These sizes seem to correspond to what is called 'Music Demy', a paper whose average size at the paper mill is about 21 × 14½ inches (343 × 368 mm).

At this and other periods, other sizes have been used, depending much on the intended eventual format as well as on different practices at different times. Thus quarto volumes were more frequently printed on paper corresponding to the English size, 19 × 15 inches (483 × 381 mm), called Post. Early music printing seems often to be on a size of about 20 × 13½ inches (508 × 343 mm), which was called 'Mezane' (or 'Medium').

The presence of an anomalous sheet or bifolium in a printed book of music from any period is often less significant than it would be in an MS: because of the much larger quantities of paper involved, the occasions for the printer to introduce a new batch, or even a few different sheets to complete a press-run, were much more frequent. However, any unexpected paper should be the signal for a careful examination of the printed text in order to see whether it confirms the presence of some bibliographical anomaly.

E. J. Labarre: *Dictionary and Encyclopaedia of Paper and Papermaking* (Amsterdam, 1937, rev. 2/1952, suppl. 1967); D. Hunter: *Papermaking* (London, 1947)

Passe-partout (Fr.: 'passes everywhere'). A title-page designed to be used in different publications with little or no adaptation. The term is also applied to a plate from which a passe-partout is printed. The passe-partout became common

1. Example of passe-partout with a list of issue numbers

after the widespread adoption of engraving, in which plates were normally retained and could therefore be used over a long period. Its attractiveness to publishers lay in the opportunity to spread the cost of an illustrated title-page over many publications.

Two kinds of passe-partout title-page can be identified. The earlier, introduced by John Walsh about 1700, consists merely of a series title (with any other necessary publication details) and a blank area in which details of a particular issue were printed from a second plate or added by hand. Many of the operas issued by Walsh have such title-pages, as have the first year's issues of his *Monthly Mask of Vocal Music* (1703), on which the name of the month was hand-written. Perhaps the most attractive passe-partout pages of this kind are those with compartments, essentially pictorial frameworks into which the individual title was inserted in type (*see* COMPARTMENT; for illustrations *see* CLUER, JOHN and WALSH, JOHN). Other examples include the many sets of 'Three Sonatas' issued separately but with the same title-page.

A later version of the passe-partout carries a list of the compositions in a set or series and is used for editions of all the music listed, with an MS indication on the title-page of the pieces actually presented inside. This practice goes back to the early 19th century; the separate issues in Clara Schumann's edition of her

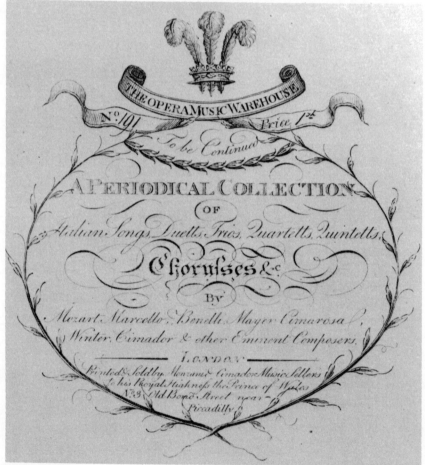

2. *An example of passe-partout giving the series title and showing the handwritten issue number and price*

husband's works are relatively early examples. Among more recent publications of the kind are the editions of piano sonatas by Mozart, Beethoven and Schubert by the Associated Board of the Royal Schools of Music.

Some long-running series started with this form of title-page and later graduated to the simpler style of passe-partout. Figs.1 and 2 show title-pages of such a series, published by Monzani & Cimador in London from about 1800. The early editions of the series, which was also called 'Vocal Italian', carried a passe-partout title intended to list every item; from issue no.43 the size of engraving was reduced, but only 84 items were listed on a full page (see fig.1). By the time the series had reached 200 issues, however, the publishers had introduced a true passe-partout title, to which the item number was added by hand (see fig.2); the title 'Vocal Italian' was still given on the signature line.

W. C. Smith: *A Bibliography of the Musical Works published by John Walsh during the Years 1695–1720* (London, 1948); D. W. Krummel: *Guide for Dating Early Published Music* (Hackensack, 1974), 90

Paste-down. The leaf of paper pasted to the inside of the binding board of a book. This leaf is half a bifolium, the other half of which is sewn with the book itself. The two folios therefore strengthen the connection between the book and its binding. They are jointly called 'end papers' (*see* END PAPER).

Paste-over [Collette]. A piece of paper carrying a corrected reading, pasted over the incorrect notes or words. Surprising as it may seem, printers did in fact adopt this method, among others, of making corrections (*see* CORRECTION). It seems to have involved printing a series of single notes or words on a sheet, then cutting it up and pasting the individual corrections into each copy.

It is difficult to know how widespread this practice was. Often the corrections must have fallen out as the paste dried; and in many cases copies must have been sold and distributed before the correction was made. Some paste-overs have been discovered in the work of Gardano and Moderne and in English music printing. In certain cases, brown patches can be seen over single notes, as if a paste-over correction has been lost. Some printers had corrections made in manuscript, which may have been quicker.

R. Steele: *The Earliest English Music Printing* (London, 1903/R1965); H. C. Slim: *Musica Nova*, MRM, i (1964); D. W. Krummel: 'Musical Functions and Bibliographical Forms', *The Library*, 5th ser., xxxi (1976), 327

Perfect. To print the second side of a sheet of paper after the first has been finished. This involves aligning both the text and music to be printed and the pile of half-printed sheets, so that the two sides will be correctly arranged. Many modern presses print both sides of a sheet simultaneously. For 'perfect binding', *see* BINDING.

Pewter. An alloy of tin, lead and antimony, in variable proportions according to cost and function, widely used to make engraving plates. It is softer and easier to work than either zinc or copper and therefore wears down the punches less readily; it was especially suitable for the small press-runs involved in producing song-sheets. Pewter plates are much more satisfactory when used in conjunction with modern transfer processes than they were with earlier printing methods, even for popular works requiring many impressions, as the plates themselves do not go through the press and are therefore not subject to excessive wear and tear.

Photolithography. A lithographic process in which, instead of writing music or other matter directly on to a lithographic stone, a photographic negative is used as part of a TRANSFER PROCESS. Any original which can be photographed – a composer's autograph, for example – can be reproduced directly by this means. It has also opened the way to the production of facsimile editions of printed and MS music of all periods.

Pica. One of the most common type sizes, now also called '12 point' (*see* POINT).

Piracy. In publishing, as in other contexts, this term refers to the cavalier theft of another person's property. It also implies an awareness of the owner's right to the property; many instances in which the same music has been issued by different publishers are therefore not strictly examples of piracy. Often in the past, neither the publisher, the composer or any other person was aware of, or sensitive to, exclusive rights on the part of any other; such seems to have been the position for almost all cases of publication in more than one centre before the late 17th century, and even in cases of publication by firms in the same state or city, such as those of Gardano and Scotto in Venice.

In other cases, the publication of a work by more than one firm was provided for by special provisions in the contract or permitted by loopholes in the conditions of international copyright conventions. Beethoven was among the first composers to negotiate contracts providing for 'simultaneous' publication by two or more publishers in different markets. Later, the special position of the USA with regard to the Berne Convention of 1948 led to the appearance there of many editions apparently pirated from European publishers. Other instances of apparent theft can be traced to the use of false imprints, perhaps in order to avoid religious persecution or to benefit from the prestige of the printer being imitated.

Nevertheless, there are many editions that seem to represent conscious attempts to gain financial advantage from printing another publisher's property. Estienne Roger of· Amsterdam was notorious in this; he seems from the beginning of his career to have pirated editions from other publishers, most of them abroad. Indeed, most of his output seems to have been copied from elsewhere. He and Walsh stole from each other; Walsh went one step further and prepared editions of new music (e.g. Handel's opp.1 and 2) and issued them with Roger's imprint. It is likely that, while Roger's contemporaries found the practice reprehensible (and he himself objected to others' copying from his editions), they had little hope of redress unless the thieving publisher worked in the same market. Even then, the 'owner' of the music or edition might·have little prospect of preventing the piracy, as is evident from Roger's inability to suppress the cheaper editions of Pierre Mortier.

With the development of photographic printing processes, it became possible to copy not merely the contents of a volume, but even the plates that carried them. Piracy became easier and quicker, as well as much cheaper.

Plate. In engraving, a sheet, usually of copper or pewter, on which the matter to be printed is incised. The edge of a plate frequently leaves a mark on a printed leaf. Plates are also used in photolithography and other photographic processes.

Plate number (Fr. *cotage*; Ger. *Plattennummer*). A number used by the printer to ensure that plates will be stored in the correct place between printings; it usually appears on the plates themselves. A number is not unique to an individual plate but rather identifies a series of plates – often those for a complete work, though for a large-scale work (e.g. an opera or a symphony) several numbers are used.

The plate number of an edition can usually be found at the foot of a printed page, often in the centre, and usually also on the title-page (for illustration *see* DIABELLI, ANTON). If a plate covered two conjugate pages, the number is often divided between their inner margins. (In some 19th-century opera scores, the title-page and list of contents have a number different from those of the music pages.)

Many editions have additional letters alongside the plate number. Often these are the initial letters of the publisher: 'D. et C.' represents the Viennese firm Diabelli et Companie; 'B. et B.', Bote & Bock of Berlin. Boosey & Hawkes still use the letters 'B. & H.', and Universal Edition's publications are identified with 'U. E.'. Many Ricordi editions show the initials of the engraver of each plate: the letters appear on either side of the plate number. Publishers have used particular formulae to distinguish special series: the various collected editions issued by Breitkopf & Härtel in the 19th century carry the composer's initials, a series number and an item number, for example 'J.S.B.I.175' for Bach's Cantata no. 175; and Hart & Co. of London published a series of vocal scores of oratorios with a series letter and number (e.g. '0-5') in the lower left-hand corner. When Monzani & Hill collected numbers from their series 'Vocal Italian' to make a vocal score of Mozart's *Così fan tutte*, in about 1810, 'A.2' was added at the foot of each page of Act 2.

Because their function is solely an organizational one, plate numbers seldom appear to follow a chronological sequence through a publisher's output; in many cases they approximate to this order, though with major anomalies and, no doubt many, barely detectable minor discrepancies. Some publishers reserved series of numbers for individual composers or repertories; Breitkopf & Härtel allocated different series according to printing method (type, engraving, lithography); many publishers' sequences of plate numbers appear to be arbitrary. In addition, the same plate number could be re-used by a publisher, presumably when the work to which it originally belonged ceased to be worth reprinting or was revised. This can produce serious anomalies in an apparently chronological ordering. More minor variations are no doubt a product of the practice of assigning numbers as work on volumes was begun, without taking into account the different lengths of time needed to complete them.

Despite the problems in their interpretation, plate numbers are of considerable value in bibliographical work, and they have been the subject of considerable study (see Krummel, 1974). Treated with due caution, and with awareness of the habits of the publisher in question, they will often suggest when an undated edition was printed. Some publishers keep in their files the plate numbers for works, alongside dates and other details (Bote & Bock, Heugel and Ricordi are important examples), and will occasionally indicate replaced plates. In a composite volume, the sequence of plate numbers may reveal the order in which the individual items were prepared; in the case of an opera, this will sometimes indicate which arias the publisher thought to be the most popular. *See also* PUBLISHER'S NUMBER.

W. B. Squire: 'Publisher's Numbers', *SIMG*, xv (1913–14), 420; Deutsch (1946); A. Weinmann: *Beiträge zur Geschichte des alt-Wiener Musikverlages*, 2nd ser. (Vienna, 1950–); Neighbour and Tyson (1965); D. W. Krummel: *Guide for Dating Early Published Music* (Hackensack, 1974)

Platen. The part of a printing press that actually exerts the pressure on paper and type or plates; for illustration, *see* PRESS, fig.1.

Point. The basic unit of measurement in printing, equivalent to 0.0138 inches, or about 0.35 mm (in British and US usage; a European Continental point is 0.0148 mm, or about 0.376 mm). 72 points are equivalent to very nearly an inch. Type is described as being of so many points in size. Pica, the most commonly used, is 12-point: thus six rows of pica type stand approximately one inch tall on the page.

Portrait format. The more standard term for what many music bibliographers call UPRIGHT FORMAT.

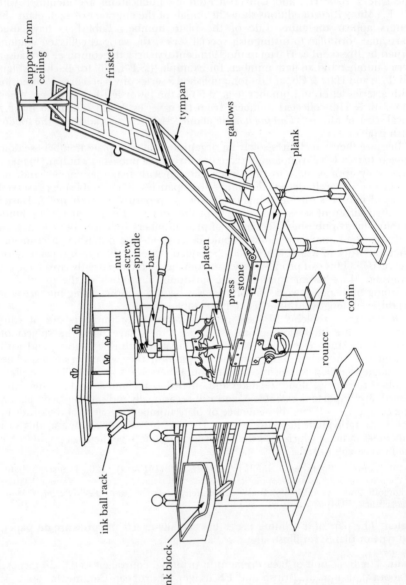

support from ceiling

frisket

tympan

gallows

plank

nut
screw
spindle
bar

platen

press
stone

coffin

rounce

ink ball rack

ink block

1. Diagram of a printing press

Preliminary pages. The pages in a book that precede the first page of its formal content; they contain the FRONT MATTER. Often the last pages to be printed, they may include a list of contents (with page numbers), a letter of dedication, a list of errata or an imprimatur, none of which can be fully prepared until the main text is finished. The preliminary pages then represent a separate bibliographical unit, comprising separate gatherings with their own sequence of signatures. This is also the case in volumes of engraved music of which the title-page and other front matter are set in type and consequently printed on a different press. For examples of such volumes *see* COLLATION.

Press. The invention of the press, as much as that of movable type, laid the foundations for the rapid dissemination of printed matter, especially music. Neither stencils nor a child's 'printing set' are appreciably faster to use or more reliable than MS copying. But the efficient press, even in its 16th-century form, allowed for mass production of each setting of type. The role of the press has been especially important for music, because so much of it has been printed from blocks or plates.

The function of a printing press is threefold. It holds the material to be printed (the type, plate or other surface) exactly in position, so that each copy will be printed evenly and correctly placed; it arranges for the printing surface to be freshly inked before each sheet of paper is in position; and it allows for (or, in more modern presses, ensures) the accurate placing of individual sheets of paper to be imprinted and then presses them against the printing surface.

These processes have been increasingly mechanized. In the early stages, the paper had to be placed and aligned by hand, the type or block was inked by hand using ink-balls, the paper was then placed against the type, and pressed closely to it using a platen and a screw turned by hand. The press and details to be described stayed largely unchanged until the start of the 19th century.

Fig.1 shows a typical press with its constituent parts labelled, and fig.2 its method of use. The type, arranged correctly in its forme, is laid in the coffin. The sheet of paper is placed in the tympan and correctly aligned by being pressed on to two points sticking up from the tympan. The frisket, to be turned down over the sheet of paper, has holes cut into it corresponding with the matter to be printed; otherwise it protects the paper from unwanted ink marks. The forme is inked in place and the tympan, covered by the frisket, is folded on to it. The whole is then drawn to the bed of the press, below the platen. The platen is pressed on to the forme by turning the bar, which winds the spindle down the screw and ensures a clear, even impression. Finally, the bar is returned to its previous position so that screw and platen are lifted and the coffin, forme and printed sheet of paper are drawn away.

The gradual mechanization of this process began in the early 19th century. Devices were invented to control the platen, ink the type, feed the paper into the press, and continuous rolls of paper were adopted: but the process remained essentially the same. Two developments had particular importance for music. One was the invention of the so-called rolling press, which seems to have been specifically designed for printing from engraved plates. In this a sheet of paper and a protective layer of felt are both laid on the inked plate, and the whole is then rolled between two cylinders. The felt allows a good even impression to be made without damaging the copper plate. The earliest such presses appear to have existed before 1650.

At least as important in the history of music printing is the rotary press. This resembles the rolling press but differs from it, in that the printing surface is itself on one of the rollers. This arrangement is ideally suited to photographic and STEREOTYPE plates, which can easily be attached to a roller; but it has also been used with type and engraved plates. By having plates attached to both rollers it was equally possible to print both sides of the paper at once. The rotary press has

2. The printing press in operation: to the left, the pressman is fitting a clean sheet of paper on to the tympan, prior to folding over the frisket. His second or 'boy' is inking the type with two ink balls. To the right, a pressman is 'pulling', forcing the platen down against the forme to make a clean inked impression, while his assistant is 'beating' the ink balls together to spread the ink over them.

several other advantages, all of them conducive to greater speed. The roller carrying the plate can be run against an ink roller immediately before it touches the paper; the press can be fed either by single sheets of paper or from a continuous roll (in both cases there are fewer problems of alignment); and much larger sheets can be printed, the only restriction (apart from the size of the paper) being the length and diameter of the roller. Rotary presses are also constructed as twin presses to print different sections of a volume simultaneously, and then feeding them together into a folding machine (this is particularly useful for newspapers); and others have consecutive pairs of rollers for colour printing. Neither of these kinds of press has seen much use in music printing, however.

A. Senefelder: *Vollständige Lehrbuch der Steindruckerey* (Munich, 1818; Eng. trans., 1819/R1968 as *A Complete Course of Lithography*); J. Moxon: *Mechanick Exercises, or the Whole Art of Printing*, ed. H. Davis and H. Carter (London, 1958–62/R1978); J. Moran: *Printing Presses: History and Development from the Fifteenth Century to Modern Times* (Berkeley, 1973)

Print. In current usage, the term refers to a copy of a work of art taken from a plate (or other surface) by printing. The former use of the word, to refer to a printed book or journal, is now obsolete; the habit among musicologists of referring to printed music as 'musical prints' should be discouraged.

Printer (Fr. *imprimeur*; Ger. *Drucker*; It. *stampatore*). The work of a printer, in preparing the printed sheets of a volume, is distinct in all respects from that of the PUBLISHER; the only possible area of overlap lies in the matter of editing the copy. This has been the case in music for some time, the printer acting as an agent contracted by the publisher. Thus he usually receives the copy already edited (and, increasingly, laid out or even camera-ready) and prints the required number of copies in the prescribed manner.

This distinction seems to have been blurred in early music printing, where many publishers were their own printers. Contracts between printers and financial backers (who seem to have acted as publishers) survive for a number of non-musical volumes from the early 16th century; but the earliest evidence of a clear distinction for musical volumes concerns the special case of the production of Calvinist psalters in 1560. By the end of the century a number of Italian booksellers were beginning to act as publishers, commissioning volumes of music from different printers.

Privilege. A document issued by local rulers to a printer (or an author or composer), assuring him of protection from rivals for a specific period. Privileges fall into several main categories:

(*i*) *For technical processes*. In 1513 Jacomo Ungaro received a Venetian privilege for his 'method of printing music'. This was probably a woodblock process, and Ungaro was protecting himself against Antico, who was then in Rome. In 1536 Francesco Marcolini received a privilege for printing music from type, allowing anyone who wanted to do so to continue printing with woodblocks. Both of these instances are analogous to the later patents for technical processes, such as those acquired by Senefelder in 1799–1801.

(*ii*) *For whole repertories*. Petrucci's privilege for mensural music, issued in 1498, followed a tradition of such privileges, including those for liturgical music and for books in Greek. Similar privileges were granted by the French court to Attaingnant in 1531, to Le Roy & Ballard in 1553 (indeed the Ballard family held a monopoly, although only for music printed from type, until 1789); by the English court to Tallis and Byrd in 1575 (while Day already held a patent for psalters); and by Maximilian I to Adam Berg.

(*iii*) *For individual works and collections*. These too were familiar outside music before they began to be sought by music printers and composers. Costanzo Festa applied for a privilege for all his music in 1538, echoing Tromboncino's request of 1521. Lassus received an imperial privilege for all his music in 1581. Most such petitions, however, came from printers, who sought to protect specific volumes planned for publication. These privileges were antecedents of the later COPYRIGHT.

The granting of privileges declined in later years as patents and copyrights came into use. Courts and the Papal See, among others, continued to retain appointed printers, with responsibility for all authorized publications, but such printers increasingly restricted their work to official documents. They may be considered the last representatives of the tradition of the granting of privileges.

Proof (Fr. *épreuve*; Ger. *Abdruck, Abzug, Druckprobe, Probleabdruck, Probeabzug*; It. *bozza, bozza di stampa*). A copy of the content of a volume, 'pulled' (i.e. printed) before the main print-run begins, for the purpose of checking it for accuracy.

Proof copies of music, where they exist, present important evidence of a composer's later thoughts. Proofs seen and marked up by the composer exist for works by (among others) Brahms, Stravinsky and Carter. In some cases, these show significant compositional changes, though in many others they show little more than corrections of minor printing errors. Very few proofs survive from earlier periods, and the fact that there are virtually none for musical sources has led scholars to question whether proof copies were pulled at all. In many instances volumes exist both in copies with stop-press or other corrections and in copies without these corrections. This may imply that printing continued while the copy was being read for errors (*see* CORRECTION, STOP-PRESS CORRECTION).

Publisher (Fr. *éditeur*; Ger. *Verleger*; It. *editore*). The person or company responsible for presenting a printed volume to the public. A music publisher need have nothing to do with the technical aspects of printing, and is principally concerned with the selection of music to be published, editorial decisions as to its content and manner of presentation (*see* EDITOR), control over the style and format (so that it will fit into the publishing house's normal style or image), and marketing and dissemination.

In the early years of music printing and publishing, the two functions were often undertaken by the same person, and the editorial decisions made by the publisher were closely informed by details of printing technique. With the emergence of engraving and then lithography, editorial decisions could be based more on purely musical criteria: these processes allowed much greater freedom over the exact representation on the printed page of the composer's or publisher's wishes. Since the adoption of modern processes of photo-reproduction the publisher is again more closely in touch with many details of the finished product.

W. C. Smith: 'The Meaning of the Imprint', *The Library*, 5th ser., vii (1952), 61

Publisher's number (Fr. *cotage*; Ger. *Verlagsnummer*). A number used to identify a whole work in a specific form and edition. Publisher's numbers have appeared on the title-pages of many editions from the time of Roger and Walsh in the early 18th century, and are still used by a number of major music publishers. Like the ISBN (International Standard Book Number), the publisher's number can be retained from one impression and issue to the next, in so far as it identifies the contents rather than the bibliographical or technical details; also, as with the ISBN, publishers regularly have used different numbers for paper-bound and hardbound copies of the same edition, that is for different issues, even when prepared from the same plates. (A similar comparison might be made with the proposed ISMN International Standard Music Number, for which plans have been mooted.) However, a publisher's number has, in theory, a different function from a PLATE NUMBER. The latter identifies the physical objects from which a volume is to be printed; the former identifies the volume. In practice the distinction is often somewhat blurred.

Among the most widely evident of publisher's numbers of present-day music publishing are those in the series of miniature scores issued by such publishers as Eulenburg. They may be seen in the catalogues published by these firms, in which items are listed either by genre (with a number attached) or in numerical sequence. The ordering of these publisher's numbers often represents an organized publishing plan. It does not, however, tell us anything about the order of work on the titles involved, or whether a copy in hand is of a first or a later edition or set of plates. More information on both these points can be drawn from the plate numbers.

For example, three volumes with consecutive publisher's numbers in Boosey & Hawkes's collection of 'Pocket Scores' have plate numbers reflecting when the work was actually undertaken: Stravinsky's Symphony of Psalms (publisher's number 637), *Rite of Spring* (638, larger format) and *Petrushka* (1947 version; 639, smaller format) have the plate numbers 16328, 16333 and 16236 respectively. In the same way, Hindemith's *Kammermusik* nos.2–5, issued by Schott with the publisher's numbers 3440 to 3443, have the plate numbers 31213, 31299, 31456 and 31927. A similar system is evident in much modern music publishing, even though (because of modern techniques of printing) fewer and fewer volumes now show plate numbers.

The value of publisher's numbers to both publisher and music seller is most evident when examining large-scale works printed during the late 18th century and the 19th. Many vocal scores of operas and first collected editions of major composers contain a diversity of plate numbers, corresponding either to the order of preparation of the different components or to different layers of printing activity. The publisher's number was added to the title-page and other preliminary pages so that the publisher and printer could identify the whole volume. Sometimes, as in Carli's editions of Rossini, this number corresponds with the first plate number of the music – that of the overture, for example.

Publisher's numbers sometimes served a similar function in the 18th century, when they were more widespread. Walsh identified most of his editions by numbers in the lower right of the title-page; in anthologies, such as those of Handel's overtures in parts, this number identified the edition as a whole rather than the location of the individual plates, which related to several other works and were drawn from several sources.

In practice, the distinction between publisher's numbers and plate numbers is often unclear, and may be non-existent. Many works, on the one hand, are short enough to have been printed with only one series of plates, and are identified only by what appears to be a single plate number. (In such cases, this number may also appear on the cover, in which case it can be identified as a plate number only by study of the printer's or publisher's house practice.) On the other hand there are editions, such as Ricordi's of Donizetti and Bellini, which carry on the title-page a list of the plate numbers for the individual items. Further, there are modern editions for which the publisher's number – or at least the number that corresponds in sequence and placing with the publisher's number in other editions from the same house – also appears at the foot of each page of the score. For example, in most of Universal Edition's scores of Boulez's works, the same number is to be found on the cover and on each page. The same firm's miniature score (1966) of Berg's *Der Wein* has the number 14286 on the cover and each page; current copies of his *Orchesterlieder* op.4 (printed with the plates of an edition of 1953, but in a new cover) have the number 14325 on the cover but 12124 as a plate number. It appears that Universal Edition may have been systematizing their publisher's and plate numbers so that the two corresponded.

In these and many other cases, it is not always easy to tell whether a number on the cover or title-page is truly a publisher's number or simply a plate number.

The only guide is a determination of the manner in which the publisher and the printer (and also the music seller) used the numbers, as a reference to an issue of specific music in a specific form, and this must sometimes rely on subjective judgment.

Punch. (1) A piece of metal, usually steel, carrying the incised design for a type symbol in mirror image (for illustration *see* fig.2*a*, p.19). There is only one punch for each design in a FOUNT, for it is not used directly to make the many individual sorts of type; it is used to strike the design on an intermediary, the MATRIX, which itself is employed for casting the type, thereby protecting the punch from damage. The punch thus remains the master from which new matrices can be made as needed to replenish the supply of type. A punch used in making type has to be cut in mirror image so that the matrix will be the 'right way', the type in mirror image and the printed impression as needed for reading.

(2) A piece of metal used for impressing a frequently recurring symbol in engraved plates; it is cut in direct, not mirror, image. Dynamic signs, certain common words, clefs, note heads and accidentals are among the symbols found on these punches, which are cut in relief, reading normally so that the impression on the plate will be in mirror image. The use of punches appears to date from the 18th century (for illustration *see* fig.15, p.48): earlier engraving seems to be completely freehand.

Quarto. Term, like 'folio' or 'octavo', used to define the format of a book. In quarto format, each sheet of paper is folded twice after printing, to produce eight pages or four folios. *See* FORMAT.

The term is now frequently and loosely used to indicate the approximate size of a printed book, tending to refer to books with a page size of about 250 × 200 mm. Miniature scores of all sizes are often described by publishers and dealers as quarto. This usage should be discouraged in bibliographical work as leading to confusion.

Rastrum (Lat.: 'rake'). A multi-nibbed pen, or scorer, used to draw all the lines of a staff at once. Used for music MSS at least since the 15th century, rastra have at various times been made with four, five and six nibs, and even with ten for drawing pairs of staves. The study of the use of rastra and of stave layout generally, which has acquired the name 'rastrology', often reveals much about scribes' working habits, about layers of work in individual MSS and about batches of paper prepared at the same time. There is evidence that some kinds of machine-operated rastra were used in the late 18th century.

Similar five-line scorers are used for engraving staves on plates. Each scorer has its own characteristics; the manner in which it is used by the engraver can also vary, although such variation is hard to detect.

Recto. The first side of a folio and the right-hand page of a book when open. It is usually paginated with an odd number; if the book is foliated, the numbers usually appear on the recto.

Register. In multiple impression printing, the alignment of elements, e.g. of two different colours, printed at separate runs through the press (impressions). In music, precise register is normally significant only in liturgical books, using red staves, or for some early printing, although there are other examples. *See* MULTIPLE IMPRESSION.

Reprint. A loosely used term, which implies no more than its literal meaning, a new IMPRESSION. It does not necessarily indicate a new STATE or EDITION, nor (technically) a new Issue, for it is often used (outside music publishing) to refer to copies produced to 'top up' an issue. In publications of the 19th century and earlier, the word or an equivalent (e.g. *ristampata*) does frequently refer to a new edition and seems to have been used as a means of attracting the potential purchaser – often with the addition of some such phrase as 'newly revised and enlarged'.

In 20th-century publications, however, the term seems never to refer to a new edition, although it may well signal a new issue, for example when the price or the publisher's address is changed. A reprint could clearly include a new state, either through the correction of minor errors or from the addition of a new catalogue or advertising page, for instance. One of the most common uses of the word 'reprint' is in connection with 'facsimiles' of much earlier editions: here the publisher, not unnaturally, is wary of calling the new issue a part of a first edition of possibly hundreds of years before (even where that is usually what it is).

The term is perhaps best avoided in bibliographical description (except, of course, when transcribing from a copy which uses it), and its vagueness replaced by the use of one of the more specific terms, 'edition', 'issue', 'state' or 'impression'. *See* EDITION.

Rule. A strip of brass or type metal used to print a straight line on the page; also a line on the page printed with this. Many 17th- and 18th-century books have rules around the text, in particular on the title-page. They may be on either side of the running head in Playford's editions, and also appear in Walsh's engraved music, where they are cut into the plate. Shorter rules commonly separate portions of text on musical title-pages, and must be included in bibliographical transcriptions for study (*see* TITLE-PAGE).

A 'French rule' is a rule divided in the middle by a diamond-shaped ornament; an 'Oxford rule' is thin at either end and swells towards the middle.

Running head [headline]. A caption that appears at the top of every page of a volume or section of a volume, usually in a distinctive type. Running heads are a normal feature of literary texts and accordingly appear in musical treatises. The great majority of partbooks have the name of the part (e.g. Bassus, Quintus, Violino primo) as a running head (for illustration *see* p.488); the practice continues to the present day in orchestral, chamber music and choral parts but has otherwise become rare in printed music. The headline often also contains the page number, sometimes also an item number or the composer's name.

Saddle-stitching. A form of binding, common in piano music and scores of the 19th century, in which a whole volume is made up of one large gathering sewn together through the fold.

Scorer. *See* RASTRUM.

Scraper. An engraver's tool consisting of a steel rod, triangular in cross-section and tapering to a point. It is used to remove the burrs (*see* BURR) resulting from the use of a BURIN.

Sedecimo [sextodecimo; sixteenmo]. A FORMAT resulting from folding the printed sheet of paper four times, to produce 16 folios or 32 pages. Sedecimo is rare in printed music, being found most often in pocket format books such as psalters or librettos.

Selbstverlag (Ger.: 'self-publisher'). A term, now found in English as well as German writing, which refers principally to the publication of a work by its author or composer. It may be applied, for instance, to the songs of Charles

Ives, keyboard works of J. S. Bach and sacred music by Maurizio Cazzati, which appeared under the name of the composer, even though in each case professional printers actually prepared the copies. Friedrich Gennrich published much of his own musicological writing in the same way. Such an arrangement was commonly indicated in early English editions by the phrase 'for the Author'.

It is difficult to justify extending use of the term much further, to include, for example, the many volumes that appeared under the name of a publisher even though they were heavily subsidized by the composer. It seems probable that this practice was widespread at certain times; in any case, it was almost certainly the publisher of record, rather than the composers, who undertook the responsibilities for such a volume.

Serif. A serif is á decorative element on a letter, comprising a short, thin horizontal stroke at the end of a vertical or slanting part of the letter. Thus serifs appear at the base and top of both verticals of a capital H, as well as at top and bottom of the vertical and diagonals of a capital K. Serifs come in different styles and are an integral part of the design of each typeface. A typeface without serifs belongs to a general family of designs called 'sans-serif'.

Serifs, of considerable importance in some manuscript writing styles, were produced by a lateral movement of the pen, which helped to square off the ends of letters. Type designers regard them as important, for they give a forward impetus to letters and help to maintain a horizontal momentum for the eye of the reader.

Serifs are virtually unknown in music founts, although they can be seen in some volumes printed by Berg in Munich in the later 16th century, and in the work of Marescotti in Florence (e.g. in Peri's *Euridice* of 1600).

Sexto. A FORMAT in which the original sheet of paper is folded so as to produce six folios. There is more than one way of producing such a structure, in each of which the page is in oblong format. Some authorities have asserted that sexto is useful for music, but it is almost never found (as it occasionally is in atlases).

Sextodecimo. *See* SEDECIMO

Sheet. The name given to the whole piece of paper, as it comes from the paper mill and as it is run through the press, before being folded for binding.

One side of a sheet was normally printed in its entirety at one run through the press and the other side was printed later; with modern presses, both sides can be printed simultaneously or in close succession, but this does not affect the patterns of evidence. Thus all the pages on one side, pages which are not normally consecutive, had to be ready for printing at one time; the pages for the other side would be treated similarly.

The sheet is a bibliographical concept of considerable importance. An awareness of the relationship of the sheet size to the format of a volume can illuminate many analytical details – the division of work among engravers or typesetters, the patterns of running heads, or the distribution of different papers in a volume, for example.

Signature. A letter appearing on the first page of each GATHERING of a book and on subsequent pages with the addition of a numeral, indicating the position of the gathering in the book and that of the page within the gathering. Signatures have traditionally been used in non-musical books (although they are now included only occasionally); in music they are usually found only in volumes printed from type or blocks. They always appear on a line below the lowest line of content (i.e. on the signature line), most frequently at its outside (right-hand) end. In modern books, however, signatures are often in the inner margin (in the gutter), while larger books (in folio) and many 17th-century volumes in general have the signature in the centre of the signature line.

Signatures act as aids to the binder, allowing him to check that he has all the gatherings, that they are in the correct order and that they are folded correctly. For this purpose they are more useful than page numbers, which are hidden in the fold at the top of a folio in quarto and smaller formats.

The first recto of a gathering is usually signed only with a letter; the second leaf contains the same letter plus some form of the numeral 2, the third has the letter and 3, etc. Normally signatures run only to the folio before or the one after the centre of a gathering (e.g. to that marked 4 or 5 in an OCTAVO); if the numbers are in sequence and the first half of the gathering is correctly folded, the second half must be too.

The usual signing alphabet contains only 23 letters – either I or J and either U or V are omitted, as is W. If necessary the sequence continues either with a second alphabet, usually of double letters, or, if only one or two gatherings remain, with other signs (e.g. an ampersand). *Der ander Theil des Lautenbuchs* of Hans Neusidler (1536) has 30 gatherings, signed from A to Z and then from Aa to Gg; his lutebook of 1549 is signed a to z and then, for the last two gatherings, uses the standard abbreviation signs for the Latin *et* and *con* (which resemble the modern 7 and 9 respectively).

In books with FRONT MATTER, gathering A usually begins after the PRELIMI-NARY PAGES, which may be unsigned or may be signed with an obelus or an asterisk. Though normal in treatises, this arrangement is rarely met with in musical volumes. One example is *Musica transalpina*, where the first page of music, signed A, is preceded by a separate bifolium of title and dedicatory letter, the second folio carrying the italic signature *Aij*.

Sets of partbooks raise interesting issues: while the individual parts of a set needed to be signed in a similar style, to show that they belonged together, they also needed to be distinguished from each other. The simplest method, adopted by Petrucci and retained by many Italian printers during the 16th and 17th centuries, was to letter the partbooks consecutively, using the signatures A–D for the Superius, E–H for the Tenor, J–M for the Altus and N–Q for the Bassus, for example (for illustration *see* p.488). In some cases, printers would also distinguish one title from another, for example by using one letter for the first volume of a series, doubling it for the second etc, or by introducing another symbol or a short title before the signature. A modification of this procedure was adopted by Attaingnant. He signed each partbook consecutively from A, with a distinguishing emblem, continuing the series of letters with the next volume in his series of publications. For instance, the volumes of *Chansons nouvelles* are all signed consecutively, but with the prefix of a different Greek letter for each partbook. All the partbooks of *Trente et troys chansons nouvelles* are signed a–d, those of *Vingt et huit chansons nouvelles* are signed e–h, etc. German publishers also started each volume with a letter A but distinguished the parts by using a different fount for each. These more complicated practices soon became obsolete, however, as the techniques of music printing became as highly developed as any other printing process.

Signatures largely went out of use with the development of engraving. The plate number, appearing in the same area of the page, served to confirm that sheets belonged to the same volume. It is probable, too, that the different nature of the business of printing from plates, as well as the growing tendency to bind soon after printing, contributed to a weakened need for signatures.

Signatures are of prime importance to the scholar. By studying the pattern of signatures in a volume and preparing a COLLATION, he can often detect the loss of folios or the subsequent insertion of other leaves. In the case of a complex volume, especially a liturgical book, the signatures may be more reliable as a guide to its condition than would be study of the contents.

D. Heartz: *Pierre Attaingnant: Royal Printer of Music* (Berkeley and Los Angeles, 1969); D. W. Krummel: 'Musical Functions and Bibliographical Forms', *The Library*, 5th ser., xxxi (1976), 334–5

Signature line [direction line]. The line immediately beneath the lowest line of content on a page. It is used to carry information for the printer and binder, in particular the SIGNATURE and CATCHWORD (for illustration *see* p.488). The term is usually restricted to volumes set from type or blocks. In some musical volumes, especially those without a RUNNING HEAD, the signature line also carries an abbreviated version of the title of the book. The edition of Vecchi's *L'Amfiparnasso* published by Gardano in 1597 has the phrase 'Comedia di Horatio Vecchi A5.' on the first recto of the second and following gatherings (see illustration).

Signatures ceased to be used once plate numbers became the norm in engraved work. However, these usually appear in the same position on a page, and are sometimes accompanied by an abbreviated title; the concept of the 'signature line' therefore remains useful.

Sixteenmo. *See* SEDECIMO

Sort (Fr. *caractère*). An individual piece of TYPE.

Spiegel. *See* TEXTBLOCK

State (Fr. *état*; Ger. *Variante*). One of a set of four terms (the others being EDITION, IMPRESSION and ISSUE) used by bibliographers to define and explain the relationships between different printed copies of the same material. Perhaps the most precise of the four, 'state' is defined by the content of a book: any two copies with identical content are deemed to belong to the same state. Any change in the content, whether a deliberate alteration to the text or music, the title-page or other ancillary matter, or even a marked deterioration in plates or blocks, is enough to produce a new state. Thus each state usually consists of fewer copies than either an issue or an impression.

The practice of bibliographers dealing with material printed from type has been to exclude accidental changes and damage from the criteria for determining a new state, arguing that this should represent some change effected by the printer or publisher. On the other hand, art historians, who deal with material similar to musical plates, have regularly included accidental damage to a plate (in so far as it shows on the printed material) as one of the ways of distinguishing states and by this means have been able to arrange different copies into a provisional chronological order and even to supply approximate dates for some. It seems that such an approach might be useful for bibliographers working with music printed from plates or blocks or even by the more recent film processes.

For further discussion of the term and its relationship with the other three, *see* EDITION, where the special problems of musical bibliography are considered.

Stencil. There is some evidence of the use of stencils to produce musical books before the 20th century. One of the best-known examples is a large and elegant liturgical volume (now in *US-Tm*), apparently prepared in France during the 18th century: the notes and text, as well as a series of ornamental flourishes and decorations, were produced with stencils using three colours throughout.

The drawback with stencilling was that each copy had to be prepared separately. Now that photographic processes are central to much printing, however, stencils have come into their own. A single master prepared from a set of stencilled symbols can be used, as frequently as one engraved or copied by hand, to produce many printed copies.

E. Judd O'Meara: 'Notes on Stencilled Choir Books', *Gutenberg-Jb 1933*, 169

Opening of Act 1 scene i of Vecchi's 'L'Amfiparnaso' (Venice: Angelo Gardano, 1597)

Stereotype. A printing process which, in conjunction with the rotary PRESS, permitted much faster press-work than was previously possible. The first stereotype process appears to have been invented by Johann Müller in 1701. More important, however, were the developments of William Ged (*c*1725) and Andrew Foulis and Alexander Tilloch (who started work in 1781), all of which used methods of making plates from type. In Ged's procedure, once the type was set up, it was covered with a pulp of plaster of Paris and water, producing a reversed image of the type, which was allowed to dry and then baked. This was then, in turn, pressed into molten type-metal, making an impression corresponding to that of the original type. Once the type-metal cooled, the plaster mould could be removed and the new 'plate' was ready for printing. The original type was thereby preserved from damage, and could be used to make replacement plates as needed.

The crucial innovation, made by Edward Cowper in 1815, was to curve the plates while they were still warm and then fit them to a roller for printing. In 1829 French printers began to use 'flong', made of papier mâché with layers of clay, instead of plaster of Paris compounds; this was more flexible and facilitated the manufacture of curved plates for the rotary press. The final stage in the establishment of stereotype plates occurred with the modifications made to the rotary press by Hoe and Co. of Philadelphia in 1861. These mean both that printing from a stereotype was now much faster than printing from letterpress, and also that newspaper publishers, among others, could print simultaneously from several stereotype plates, all made from the same original.

Stich (Ger.). An engraved PLATE (another German term is *Druckplatte*). The term is also used, especially in writing on art history, for a single sheet pulled from such a plate.

Stichvorlage (Ger.). Term for the MS COPY of material to be published, from which an engraver prepares plates. Like other printer's copy, it usually shows evidence of the engraver's decisions as to CASTING OFF, etc. The term has been widely adopted in musicological writing; there is no simple English-language counterpart.

Stop-press correction. As the term implies, a CORRECTION to printed material made during the process of printing. It may be made when errors in the text or music are discovered, presumably through a careful reading of one of the first copies to come from the press, akin to the process of reading a proof. In the same manner as when corrections are made after a proof copy, the type or plate is taken from the press and corrected before being returned for the rest of the run. However, the evidence of surviving copies of early printed music argues that the copies printed before the correction were not normally discarded: the output of every printer studied in sufficient detail includes copies of editions both with and without such corrections. In the case of Petrucci, some copies printed before the press was stopped have corrections inserted by hand, apparently by a member of the printing house.

Not all errors were amenable to stop-press correction, either because they were too numerous or because they affected the layout of a whole page; in such cases a CANCEL might be needed.

Stub. The traditional processes of binding require that each folio be attached to another, through the spine, so that the stitching may grip on the paper. A single folio, if it is to be bound (rather than a TIP-IN), must have a part of the leaf on the other side of the spine as otherwise it would slip from the binding. The slip, called a 'stub', is usually kept as narrow as possible. Occasionally it is also glued to an adjacent folio, especially if it is the conjugate of a special page such as a plate or a list of contents. A stub may also be the remains of a folio that has been torn or cut out; the stub is then all that prevents the conjugate leaf from falling out of the book.

Subsidiary edition. A term coined by Bowers (1949) to refer to an edition which stems from another in some way. It may be a revised or enlarged edition which none the less largely uses the plates or typesetting of the original; it may be published in a different country, in a limited edition or in a 'facsimile' issued under a new aegis. The concept may have some value in musical bibliography for it allows for a clear statement about the relationship both of the two 'editions' and of the readings they contain. An example would be a miniature score produced by photo-reduction from a full or 'conducting' score: this has the same contents and is prepared from the same plates, but is in a different format, with a different title-page. Although it is a different edition, it is clearly subsidiary to the original score. However, since 'subsidiary edition' is not a bibliographical term, the relationship of such a volume to other copies should also be described formally; *see* EDITION, ISSUE, IMPRESSION and STATE.

F. Bowers: *Principles of Bibliographical Description* (Princeton, 1949), 383–4

Sugar paper. A thin paper of poor quality, usually coloured blue, although some is purple or white. Made from waste paper, it received its name from its use for wrapping sugar loaves and making sugar bags. It survives from the late 18th and early 19th centuries in the form of loose paper wrappers for sheet music and librettos, often stabbed together with the content in an informal binding. There is no evidence as to whether these were applied by music retailers or by subsequent owners.

Text-block (Ger. *Spiegel*). Term for the total area occupied by the text or music on a page, including any other printed material (page number, signature, running head etc). It provides a measure of the total area available to the typesetter for laying out his material. Analogous to the measurement of the size of a plate in engraving and other processes, it has similar implications as regards the craftsman's patterns of work of the material but quite different ones as regards bibliographical analysis.

Tip-in. A separately prepared leaf inserted into a volume by gluing or pasting it to the adjacent page along a narrow strip at the spine. Material printed on different paper from the rest of a volume or by a different method (such as a letterpress title-page in an engraved edition of music) might be added in this manner and tipped in before binding. The most common tipped-in pages, however, are those inserted after a volume has been prepared, as later additions; these will often be in MS but may contain printed material, such as a list of errata.

An alternative method of inserting single leaves into a volume involves a STUB. The two have different implications for the structure of a book and need to be distinguished. A tipped-in leaf is not part of the gathering to which it is attached; this must be shown in a COLLATION.

Tirage (Fr.). Term used to mean either IMPRESSION or ISSUE.

Titelauflage (Ger.). Term used to describe a new ISSUE in which the only or principal difference from a previous one is the presence of a newly prepared title. Strictly, it is applied only if the original publisher is involved. The term has acquired general usage in English-language writing, occasionally even in cases where a different publisher initiates the new issue.

Title-page. The page of a volume that carries full details of its title, the name of the author or composer and (almost always) full details of publication; these last may include the name of the publisher, the place and date of publication, information about secondary publishers or dealers, a copyright statement and, worked into the design, the name of the engraver. The HALF-TITLE carries much less information.

For the study of music printing and for the bibliographical study of music – the works of one composer, the output of a publisher – title-pages are of central importance. Details of the statements that the publisher chooses to make there may be dishonest or erroneous: supplying an incorrect or inconsistent opus number to the works of Mozart or Beethoven; claiming revisions or corrections in a new edition of Arcadelt; suppressing evidence of the incompleteness of an edition or the presence of works by other composers in a madrigal volume attributed to Marenzio. But these details themselves are part of the image that the publisher wishes to project. Before the presence of publisher's bindings, or of catalogues of their editions, the title-page was the first evidence seen by the potential purchaser.

The title-page of a new issue or edition had equally to be effective: it needed to attract the interest of new purchasers. An immediate result is the clear statement that a new edition is 'revised' or 'corrected'. Often these changes are minimal; but they were enough to justify the attempt at reaching a new audience.

Detailed transcription of the title-page is essential in bibliographical study. Unfortunately, for many musical editions it is also almost impossible. There is no way to transcribe adequately the luxurious growth of curling lines and delicate filigree surrounding a title-page of Brahms; to describe the artistic design on a Debussy title; or even to distinguish the many different founts of display type on 19th-century editions. A title-page printed entirely from type or using only letters and numerals, presents few problems for there have long been methods of transcription (see Bowers, 1949, pp.135 ff, and Gaskell, 1972, pp.322 ff). A transcription of more complex titles should be prepared as far as possible in some form that will give many of the details: perhaps the subject of a lithographed picture or the use of type ornaments. The presence of MS annotations showing a price or number in a series or of later ownership marks is only one reason why such transcriptions cannot be adequately replaced by photographs.

R. B. McKerrow: *An Introduction to Bibliography for Literary Students* (Oxford, 1927); F. Bowers: *Principles of Bibliographical Description* (Princeton, 1949); L. Weinhold: 'Musiktitel und Datierung', *FAM*, xiii (1966), 136; G. S. Fraenkel: *Decorative Music Title Pages: 201 Examples from 1500 to 1800* (New York, 1968); P. Gaskell: *A New Introduction to Bibliography* (Oxford, 1972); R. Schaal: *Musiktitel aus fünf Jahrhunderten* (Wilhelmshaven, 1972); G. T. Tanselle: 'Title-page Transcription and Signature Collation Reconsidered', *Studies in Bibliography*, xxxviii (1985), 45–81; see also BIBLIOGRAPHY, section x

Tranchefiles. Two wires in a mould for hand-made paper, one at each side of the mould, running parallel to the chain-wires. They leave impressions in the paper similar to the chain-lines. Since each is nearer to the next chain-wire than the spacing of wires themselves, the presence of these impressions gives some guide as to how heavily a sheet has been trimmed. *See* WATERMARK.

Transfer process. A lithographic press in which, instead of being written directly on to a lithographic stone, the design or music is written on a sheet of special transfer paper which is then treated with dilute nitric acid. When the sheet is laid on the stone, the musical notation is impressed on the stone in reverse. More often, the original is engraved on to a plate. A paper copy is pulled, printed from the plate, and then transferred to the stone. This process, more than any other adaptation, ensures the continuing use of lithography for music printing. It was probably adopted in the 1840s.

Photolithography is a similar process; here a photographic process is used to produce the intermediary, rather than transfer paper.

Tympan. The part of a printing Press that held the blank sheet of paper ready to receive an impression from type or plates (for illustration *see* Press, fig.1). The tympan folded on to the coffin, holding the type or plate, and provided a flat and strong backing against which the platen could exert pressure. In modern rolling presses, there is no need for a tympan; the paper is conveyed between rollers, on one of which the plates are mounted.

Type. An individual piece, usually of metal, used in printing. It is a small rectangular block of a specified height (usually 0.9175 inches, or approximately 23.3 mm) with a raised design on its top representing a letter, a numeral or some other symbol in reverse.

The word 'type' occurs in such terms as Typeface; 'movable type', a collection of such pieces, as distinct from plates or woodblocks; 'standing type', type left in the forme ready to print more copies; 'typesetter' (*see* Compositor); and 'type-specimen', a printed sheet showing samples of the various characters in available typefaces.

Typeface. A design for a complete range of printed characters – letters (in upper and lower case), numerals and other symbols. It will be available in various point sizes and also usually in roman and italic styles (or analogous forms); in some cases a bold-face version (and in modern type usage a variety of related styles such as condensed or ultra-bold) will be included in the basic design. A Fount is usually a complete set of one typeface in one size and one style (roman, italic etc). Among the variable characteristics of text faces are the length of ascenders and descenders, the presence, extent and design of serifs, the degree of contrast between thick and thin parts of a letter and the shape of the ends of thick sections.

Music typefaces have similar distinguishing features – the length of stems, the width of the angle at the corners of notes (in early diamond-shaped founts), the point at which the tail emerges from the note head (in *Civilité* and later founts) and the treatment of the ends of stems and of flags on quavers and semiquavers. More obvious features include the styles of clefs and of dynamic marks, the designs of accidentals and the angles between beams and stems in linked short notes (in mosaic founts these angles are highly specific; *see* Mosaic type).

Multiple-impression music typefaces have relatively few sorts, since only one is needed for each note value and rest, regardless of pitch; but early single-impression designs needed a sort for each value at each level on the staff. Thus while Petrucci's fount may have had only about 50 characters, single-impression founts of his time had some 200. With the adoption of mosaic typefaces, the number of sorts incresed dramatically. Fig.10a (p.38) shows part of a typeface with 452 different sorts.

T. Tanselle: 'The Identification of Type-faces in Bibliographical Description', *Papers of the Bibliographical Society of America*, lx (1966), 185

Type ornament. Any ornamental design that is cast and punched like ordinary type. Type ornaments exist in multiple copies in a printer's stock, unlike woodblock ornaments, each of which is unique; they are often used in sets to make borders or frames for title-pages. A small type ornament is called a Flower.

Type size. Even though type is three-dimensional, the principal element of type size is the height on the page, or 'body', measured at right angles to the lines of text. This is constant for all the sorts of a single fount. The width of the type, measured along a line on the page, varies according to the symbol, letter or note value. The third measure, the 'height-to-paper', is that of the distance from the foot of a piece of type, resting on the press, to the top of the letter, on which the paper rests; this is the same throughout a fount (usually 0.9175 inches, or approximately 23.3 mm).

The body of a piece of text type is necessarily longer than the largest letters in the alphabet, for it must extend beyond the top of the ascenders (of f or h, for example) and below the descenders (of g or j) to prevent letters from rubbing against each other (the same is not true for music typefaces). For some exceptions, *see* KERNED TYPE.

Type sizes have traditionally been measured in points, each of which is 0.0138 inches or approximately 0.35 mm (in British and US usage; a European Continental point is 0.0148 inches or 0.376 mm). Pica typefaces are 12 points high (0.166 inches, or about 4.206 mm); thus six lines of a pica typeface will fit into one inch. Other traditional names for type sizes – pearl, agate, brevier etc – have been replaced by point sizes. In fact a double measurement is often given, since the length of the letters is independent of that of the actual piece of type, the body, and since larger bodies are often used to allow for extra white space between lines; thus '9/10' indicates a nine-point face on a ten-point body. The present volume is printed in a 10/11½ point face, with 9/10 for this glossary and the bibliography, and 8/9 for the dictionary (the bibliography sections within the glossary and the dictionary are respectively 8/9 and 7/8).

Earlier text types are measured in different ways: two measurements are taken, which together provide a guide to the sizes of both the typeface and its body. The 'x'-height (like all such details) measured in millimetres, is the height of any letter that has no ascenders or descenders (such as an x or an n); the '20-line' measurement is the total height of 20 lines of text, from the foot of an x (or similar letter) in one line to the foot of one 21 lines above.

Music type cannot be measured in the same ways: it is much larger, and varies too much in its height on the page. A MOSAIC TYPE has widely divergent sort sizes. Indeed, early type founders and printers seem not to have standardized their names for mosaic-type sizes as they did with text faces. Le Bé called his various music founts after their function and the format of the book in which they were used, for example 'Musique moienne des chansons 4°' or 'Musique petite pour psaume'. Plantin's founts (see illustration) were 'Grande musicque', 'Moyenne musicque' and 'Petite musicque'.

The type founders of the 19th and 20th centuries adopted the names used for text sizes when advertising their music types. Various founders listed their founts as being in Brilliant, Gem, Diamond, Ruby, Pearl, Semi-nonpareil and Nonpareil. Gamble, writing in 1923, noted that music founts had not adopted the 'new' point system, although he described Semi-nonpareil as being about three point and Ruby as about half-pica, or six point. Examples of Diamond appear in fig.10, p.38. The numerals after the fount names, as in Diamond no.3, Diamond no.5 etc, indicate different styles of note shapes, corresponding to the names of text type styles (e.g. Bembo, Times Roman).

It is difficult to find such standardization in earlier music types, or even in most from the 19th century. However, certain measurements are characteristic of each individual fount and can be used, if not to identify typefaces, at least to segregate them. One is the height of the staff, which even in mosaic types has to remain constant within any one fount: if it did not, the individual sorts would not fit well together, making the music much harder to read.

Other features of music type have been measured in different ways, depending to some extent on the character of the fount in use. Heartz (1967) used the heights of the minim and of the staff, presented as a ratio, to provide a convenient identification for single-impression typefaces. Berz (1970, pp.122–43) developed a more complex system to cope with the range of similar

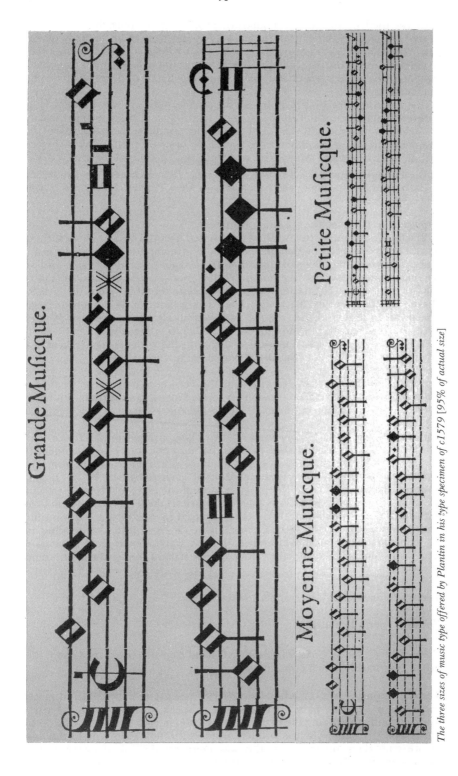

The three sizes of music type offered by Plantin in his type specimen of c1579 [95% of actual size]

typefaces used by printers in Frankfurt, measuring not only the size of the symbol printed by each sort on the paper, but also the size of the body of the type. With a NESTED TYPE or mosaic typefaces, such detailed measurements may be the only way of distinguishing different founts; the same is true for so-called 'double-struck' types, which are made using the same punches in different combinations.

The measurement of size is by no means the only way of distinguishing different typefaces, nor is it always the most useful. In a music type in particular, the style of clefs (especially the G clef), of accidentals (particularly the sharp), of time signatures or mensuration signs and of 'decorative' features such as braces is often more distinctive and specific to a typeface.

W. Gamble: *Music Engraving and Printing: Historical and Technical Treatise* (London, 1923/*R* 1971); D. Heartz: 'Typography and Format in Early Music Printing', *Notes*, 2nd ser., xxiii (1967), 702; Berz (1970)

Typography. (1) The art of printing from type.

(2) The arrangement, or layout, of the printed material on a page. As such, it reflects decisions made by the members of the printing house. These decisions concern technical problems of spacing, format, typefaces and type size, and of the relationship between content and ancillary matter; they also involve artistic matters such as the relationship of the text-block to the whole page, the density of type on the page (its 'blackness'), the balance between decoration or large capitals and the rest of the content, and particularly the appearance of title-pages, starts of chapters or movements, and other 'free' layouts.

(3) In some recent work on musical bibliography the term has been treated as a synonym for 'typeface', but this usage should not be encouraged.

Upright format. Any FORMAT in which the vertical axis is longer than the horizontal; it is the normal orientation for printed matter. In the trade, it is more often referred to as 'portrait format'. *See also* OBLONG FORMAT.

Variant, Variant issue. Term used, in describing printed music, for a copy which differs from another copy in ways that may not be precisely defined. It may mean an ISSUE that, while otherwise identical with another, differs from it in some detail of publication – date, address or even publisher. By definition, however, this represents a different issue, even if the two are otherwise part of the same impression, and is better defined as such. If the term is taken to denote slight differences in content, it is better replaced by one of the other readily understood terms – STATE (as in German usage) or IMPRESSION – depending on the extent and nature of the differences. Indeed, 'variant issue' seems to be used largely to avoid making any other more specific statement as to the relationship of copies.

Verlagsnummer (Ger.). PUBLISHER'S NUMBER.

Verleger (Ger.). PUBLISHER.

Verso. The second side of a folio or the left-hand page of a book when open. It is usually paginated with an even number.

Vertical setting. Term coined by Lewis (1988) and useful in the study of music preserved in separate parts. It refers to a printer's working on all the parts simultaneously, preparing the first piece or section in each before moving on to the second. In most volumes, printers worked through each part to the end before embarking on the next; this was more economical of material, and perhaps of time. However, evidence of vertical setting has been found in the work of 16th- and 17th-century printers; analogous procedures can be seen in some engraved editions. The range of bibliographical and musical anomalies that result from vertical setting differ from those produced by working through the parts one at a time.

M. S. Lewis: *Antonio Gardano, Venetian Music Printer 1538–1569* (New York, 1988), 68

Watermark. The trace left in paper, usually in hand-made paper, by the wires in the mould; these produce a visible thinning in the paper. A sheet of paper may have up to four elements of these marks, of which two are usually referred to as the watermark and countermark. The other two, always to be found in hand-made paper, are the traces of the basic structure of the mould. LAID-LINES, reflecting the parallel laid-wires that support the pulp in the mould while allowing the water to drip through, are close together and run parallel to the longer sides of the sheet of paper. CHAIN-LINES run at right angles to them: these are regularly thicker, for they are formed by the stronger supporting chain-wires that keep the laid-wires in place. Laid-lines and chain-lines can best be seen when the paper is held up to the light.

The watermark proper is produced in the same manner, by a wire device mounted on the chain-wires of the mould. It is usually in the middle of one half of a complete sheet; the original reason for this seems to have been that it would then be in the middle of a leaf when the paper is folded once, to make folio format. If there is a countermark, it would appear either in the middle of the other half of the sheet (especially if it consists of the name of the papermaker), or in its lower outer corner (in which case it may consist of the initials or device of the maker, a date or a small and simple design).

Since paper was made using two moulds, dipped alternately into the vat of pulp, which were intended to have the same design, watermarks come in matching pairs, called 'twins'. These will be very similar in many details as well as in general design, although the watermark (and hence the countermark) will appear in opposite halves of the mould.

Many marks are long-lived. An individual device, wires tied to the mould, may not actually last very long: it is fairly fragile and subject to stresses during use, and so tends to become increasingly distorted. There is no reliable way of estimating how long a specific mark may stay in use, for this damage, like all wear and tear, occurs haphazardly. However, there is evidence that many makers replaced devices with close copies in order to retain the same basic design. Some designs had an even wider and longer circulation. The early designs of an oxhide, a cardinal's hat or an anchor within a circle all lasted for over a century, and were used by many makers, although often within a small geographical area. Later designs such as the 'Strasbourg bend' were also long-lived and widespread (see illustration). Many of these designs were intended to be statements, not about their manufacturer, but about the quality and size of the paper; several terms still in use, such as 'foolscap', derive from this convention. Together with a countermark bearing the manufacturer's name or device, they ensured that both quality and source of paper were apparent to the stationer.

In bibliographical work today, the patterns of deterioration of individual marks, coupled with those of the use and spread of general designs, mean that a close study of the details of marks is essential before any statement can be made about the consistency or otherwise of the paper used for a book. The analysis of the marks in paper includes a study of laid- and chain-lines, which in the case of incomplete sheets may be the only evidence available. Manufacturers tended to have their own particular patterns of distances between chain-lines; these were not necessarily consistent over long periods but appear distinct enough when different papers are compared. Thus the measurement of the space between chain-lines, as well as of the number of laid-lines to the centimetre, will help to confirm whether the same or different moulds were used for different sheets of paper. The presence and spacing of marks left by the TRANCHEFILES is also particularly valuable.

Alan Tyson (1975) has devised a formula and schematic representation for analysis, which have been widely adopted for studies of musical MSS. In it, a notional whole sheet of paper is divided into four 'quadrants', each with its own characteristic pattern of marks and lines. The division ensures that the scholar is aware of which parts of each sheet of paper have been used, and which might (or could not) be conjugate with each other.

A second element in Tyson's method is that all sheets should be examined from the side on which they touched the mould, and that the 'twins' should be correctly distinguished. By means of this consistent approach, as Tyson's subsequent studies have demonstrated, it is possible to link folios, reconstructing a complete sheet. It also produces a corpus of quarter-sheets with which to compare any other folios that may subsequently come to light.

The value of watermarks for the study of sources falls into two general areas: dating the source, and examining its consistency and structure. Both depend on precise description of the individual marks. Their use as a tool for dating MSS and printed volumes is fraught with problems. It requires exact dating of the individual mark and reliable knowledge as to how long a batch of paper might take to be completely used, neither of which are currently available. With the exception of the very few marks (made principally in France from 1742 and in England between 1794 and 1811) that carry a date, we normally have no indication of when a specific sheet of paper was made; we only have information as to when it was used. Much of this comes from the study of large archives (see Briquet, 1907, and Gerardy, 1983), where each batch of paper might be used over a long period but where each document written on that paper was precisely dated. This therefore provides a *terminus ante quem* for the use of a mark as represented by a specific sheet of paper, but it does not prove that another sheet with the same mark (if its identity can even be confirmed) was used at the same time. There has been considerable controversy over how long one batch of paper might last in a scriptorium or printing house. Much of the controversy has surrounded MS copyists and printers of incunabula, and the patterns of paper use in later printing are far from clearly understood. There is considerable evidence that many printers ordered paper for specific volumes, but this does not seem to resolve the general problem (see Bühler, 1973).

Watermarks are much more useful for studying the consistency or integrity of a printed book. Tyson's method is ideal when studying MS sources. It is usually less essential, however, when examining printed books. There are two reasons for this. One is the necessarily large amount of paper involved in printing a book, even in a short run: 500 copies of a printed score take up 500 times as much paper as one MS copy, and there is thus proportionally more room for variation between sheets due to the deterioration or replacement of a mark or to the many moves involved in bringing a stack of paper from the papermill to the press. The second reason is a corollary of the first. In an MS, two adjacent sheets of paper may very well have been made consecutively: in a printed book, they will normally have been separated by, on average, as many sheets as there are copies in the print-run. Thus detailed analysis of the status of each individual sheet and watermark tells little about consistency and order of construction of the whole, both of which can often be studied as easily from an examination of typefaces or engraving styles.

On the other hand, the pattern of watermarks running through a book, folio by folio, may be very revealing. It can be significant in a number of ways:

(*i*) The presence of a different watermark on one sheet often suggests that this sheet was prepared at a different time. Other analyses will confirm the suggestion or else indicate that the sheet was merely a random one inserted into the stock at the press.

(*ii*) The shift part-way through a book from one watermark to another may confirm the order of work, possibly indicating a hiatus of some sort, or may argue that earlier layers of the book (such as the preliminary pages) were actually printed last. In sets of partbooks, such changes sometimes occur in each part at the same place, implying that they were prepared simultaneously (*see* VERTICAL SETTING).

(*iii*) The most precise and revealing evidence is that of a single leaf or bifolium bearing the 'wrong' mark, while the rest of the sheet has the same mark as surrounding sheets. This requires that the folio concerned must be a replacement of some sort, possibly a CANCEL. It is this situation that is most amenable to Tyson's approach. While most known cancels have been found as a result of gross differences in watermarks, it is probable that others would surface if similar analysis of the quadrants in several copies of each printed book were ever undertaken.

Descriptions or freehand drawings of watermarks may be sufficient for analyses of consistency within printed volumes, where the different sheets can be compared *in situ*. They are hardly satisfactory, however, for the study of MSS or for comparison between copies of printed books in different libraries. Thus the drawings in the major collections (Briquet etc in the series produced by the Paper Publications Society) are no more than a guide to families of marks and their approximate dates of use. The development of beta-radiography (see illustration) has enabled precise photographs of marks to be taken (see Gerardy).

Beta-radiograph of a blank page showing the 'Strasbourg bend' (named after the arms of that city), one of the more common 18th-century watermarks; note the horizontal laid-lines of the mould and the vertical chain-lines which kept them in place

While the value of these photographs in the study of printed music is subject to the limitations outlined above, as they become more normally available they will allow the study of the watermark itself to advance to an acceptable level of accuracy.

C. M. Briquet: *Les filigranes: dictionnaire historique des marques du papier* (Geneva, 1907/R1968 with addns); W. A. Churchill: *Watermarks in Paper in Holland, England, France etc. in the XVII and XVIII Centuries* (Amsterdam, 1935); E. J. Labarre: *Dictionary and Encyclopaedia of Paper and Papermaking* (Amsterdam, 1937, rev. 2/1952, suppl. 1967); E. Heawood: *Watermarks, Mainly of the 17th and 18th Centuries* (Hilversum, 1950/R1957, and 1969 with suppl.); A. Stevenson: 'Watermarks are Twins', *Studies in Bibliography*, iv (1951–2), 57–91, 235; G. Eineder: *The Ancient Paper-mills of the Former Austro-Hungarian Empire and their Watermarks*

(Hilversum, 1960); G. Piccard: *Veröffentlichungen der Staatlichen Archivverwaltung Baden-Württemberg: Sonderreihe die Wasserzeichenkartei Piccard im Hauptstaatsarchiv Stuttgart* (Stuttgart, 1961–83); J. LaRue: 'Watermarks and Musicology', *AcM*, xxxiii (1961), 120 [with extensive annotated bibliography]; idem: 'Classification of Watermarks for Musicological Purposes', *FAM*, xiii (1966), 59; C. Bühler: 'Last Words on Watermarks', *Papers of the Bibliographical Society of America*, lxvii (1973), 1; A. Tyson: 'The Problem of Beethoven's "First" *Leonore* Overture', *JAMS*, xxviii (1975), 292–334; S. Boorman: 'The "First" Edition of the *Odhecaton A*', *JAMS*, xxx (1977), 183; T. Gerardy: 'Datierung mit Hilfe des Papiers', *Quellenstudien zur Musik der Renaissance*, ii: *Datierung und Filiation von Musikhandschriften der Josquin-Zeit* (Wiesbaden, 1983), 217; P. Pulsiano: 'A Checklist of Books and Articles containing Reproductions of Watermarks', *Essays in Paper Analysis* (London, 1987), 115–53

Woodblock. A printing BLOCK made of wood. Because wood is resilient and strong yet lightweight, and because it can be easily carved, it was widely used for large plates and also for whole pages of music from the early years of printing until long after the earliest engraved metal plates were produced.

Wrappers. A binding made of paper leaves rather than boards.

Bibliography

Bibliography

Key to the short forms used in the
Dictionary section

Benzing (1963, 2/1982) – F.*D*
Brown (1965) – C.
Coover (1988) – F.*GB*
Day and Murrie (1940) – F.*GB*
Deutsch (1946) – D.
Devriès and Lesure, (1979–1988) –
  F.*F*
Dichter and Shapiro (1941, 2/1977) –
  F.*AM*
Duggan (1981) – D.
Fisher (1933) – F.*AM*
Fuld (1966, 3/1985) – C.
Goovaerts (1880) – F.*RE*

Hopkinson (1954) – F.*F*
Humphries and Smith (1954, 2/1970)
  – F.*GB*
Johansson (1955) – F.*F*
Johansson (1972) – G.
Kidson (1900) – F.*GB*
King (1964) – B.
Krummel (1975) – F.*GB*
Mischiati (1984) – F.*I*
Neighbour and Tyson (1965) – F.*GB*
Plesske (1968) – C.
Przywecka-Samecka (1969) – F. *RE*
Sartori (1958) – F.*I*
Weinmann (1956) – F.*D*
Wolfe (1964) – F.*AM*
Wolfe (1980) – D.

A. *Printing in General*

Joseph Moxon: *Mechanick Exercises, or the Doctrine of Handy-Works applied to the Art of Printing*, 2 vols. (London: Joseph Moxon, 1683–4); issued as *Mechanick Exercises, or the Whole Art of Printing*, ed. Herbert Davis and Harry Carter (London: Oxford U. Press, 1958–62)

Geoffrey Ashall Glaister: *Glossary of the Book* (London: Allen & Unwin, 1960, 2/1979 as *Glaister's Glossary of the Book*); also issued as *An Encyclopedia of the Book* (Cleveland: World, 1960)

Marshall Lee: *Bookmaking: the Illustrated Guide to Design/Production/Editing* (New York: Bowker, 1965, 2/1979)

W. Turner Berry and H. Edmund Poole: *Annals of Printing: a Chronological Encyclopaedia from the Earliest Times to 1950* (London: Blandford, and Toronto: U. of Toronto Press, 1966)

Adrian Wilson: *The Design of Books* (New York: Reinhold, 1967; London: Studio Vista, 1968)

Herbert Spencer: *The Visible Word* (London: Royal College of Art, and New York: Hastings House, 1968; London: Lund Humphries, rev. 2/1969)

Michael Twyman: *Lithography 1800–1850* (Oxford: Clarendon Press, 1970)

Philip Gaskell: *A New Introduction to Bibliography* (Oxford: Clarendon Press, 1972/R1974; New York: Oxford U. Press, 1972/R1975) [the second is the most authoritative; see review by James Green in *Book Arts Press*, Occasional Publication no. 4 (New York: Columbia U., School of Library Service, 1975)]

B. Histories of Music Printing and Publishing

[J. Alfred Novello]: *Some Account of the Methods of Musick Printing, with Specimens of the Various Sizes of Moveable Types; and of Other Matters* (London: Novello, 1847)

J.-B. Weckerlin: 'Histoire de l'impression de la musique, principalement en France, jusqu'au dix-neuvième siècle', *La chronique musicale*, vi (1874), 241–50; vii (1875), 55–64, 170–82

Friedrich Chrysander: 'A Sketch of the History of Music-Printing, from the 15th to the 18th Century', *MT*, xviii (1877), 265–8, 324–6, 375–8, 470–75, 524–7, 584–7; Ger. trans. as 'Abriss einer Geschichte des Musikdruckes vom 15. bis 19. Jahrhundert', *AMZ*, xiv (1879), 161–7, 177–83, 193–200, 209–14, 225–32, 241–8

Hugo Riemann: 'Notenschrift und Notendruck: bibliographisch-typographische Studie', *Festschrift zur 50jährigen Jubelfeier des Bestehens der Firma C. G. Röder, Leipzig* (Leipzig: C. G. Röder, 1896)

William Barclay Squire: 'Notes on Early Music Printing', *Bibliographica*, iii (1897), 99–122

Kathi Meyer and Eva J. O'Meara: 'The Printing of Music, 1473–1934', *The Dolphin*, ii (1935), 171–207 [of continuing value for the clarity and charm with which it presents technical matters]

Bruce Pattison: 'Notes on Early Music Printing', *The Library*, 4th ser., xix (1939), 389–421 [admirable in its special concern for the historical context of music printing]

Ernst Laaff: *Musik mit Fleiss gedruckt* (Eltville: Wiesbadener Kurier, 1956)

A. Beverly Barksdale: *The Printed Note: 500 Years of Music Printing and Engraving* (Toledo, OH: Toledo Museum of Art, 1957/R New York: Da Capo, 1981) [exhibition catalogue]

Raoul Castelain: *Histoire de l'édition musicale; ou, du droit d'éditeur au droit d'auteur, 1501–1973* (Paris: Lemoine, 1957)

A. Hyatt King: *Four Hundred Years of Music Printing* (London: British Museum, 1964) [excellent brief historical overview]

Maria Przywecka-Samecka: *Drukarstwo muzyczne w Europie do końca XVIII wieku* [Music printing in Europe up to the end of the 18th century] (Wrocław: Ossolineum, 1987)

D.W. Krummel: *The Memory of Sound: Observations on the History of Music on Paper* (Washington, DC: Library of Congress, 1988) [text of Engelhard lecture, 29 Oct 1987]

C. Reference Works and Bibliographies of Early Printed Music

Emil Vogel: *Bibliothek der gedruckten weltlichen Vocalmusik Italiens, aus den Jahren 1500 bis 1700* (Berlin: A. Haack, 1892; repr., with revisions by Alfred Einstein, Hildesheim: Georg Olms, 1962) [index of printers by city, pp. 527–43]; also issued without the index, as *Bibliografia della musica italiana vocale profana, pubblicata dal 1500 al 1700*, ed. François Lesure and Claudio Sartori, 3 vols. (Staderini:Minkoff, 1977)

Robert Eitner: *Biographisch-bibliographisches Quellen-Lexikon der Musiker und Musikgelehrten der christlichen Zeitrechnung bis zur Mitte des neunzehnten Jahrhunderts* (Leipzig: Breitkopf & Härtel, 1900–04, rev. 2/1959–60) [indexed in Eitner (1904) below]

——— : *Buch- und Musikalienhändler, Buch-und Musikaliendrucker nebst Notenstecher, nur die Musik betreffend* (Leipzig: Breitkopf & Härtel, 1904) [a complement to the *Quellen-Lexikon* above; not as meticulously edited as its agendum but the only general source for many names of minor music printers and publishers before *c*1850]

Michel Brenet: 'Bibliographie des bibliographies musicales', *L'année musicale*, iii (1913), 1–152 [section v lists nearly 200 'Catalogues d'éditeurs et de libraires']

Der Musikverlag und Musikalienhandel in der Welt (Leipzig: Bureau International d'Information et de Coopération des Editeurs de Musique, 1938) [brief reports on music publishing activity in 19 countries]

Åke Davidsson: 'Litteraturen om nottyyckets historia: en översikt jämte bibliografi', *STMf*, xxix (1947), 116–30; xxx (1948), 137–8; 2nd edn. as 'Die Literatur zur Geschichte des Notendruckes', in his *Musikbibliographische Beiträge* (Uppsala: A. B. Lundequist, 1954), 91–115; 3rd edn. as *Bibliographie zur Geschichte des Musikdrucks* (Uppsala: Almquist & Wiksell, 1965)

Répertoire international des sources musicales [RISM]. The following volumes are devoted to printed music:

François Lesure, ed.: *Recueils imprimés XVIe–XVIIe siècles: liste chronologique* (Munich and Duisburg: Henle, 1960) [*RISM* B/I/1; index, pp. 597–606]

——, ed.: *Recueils imprimés, XVIIIe siècle* (Munich and Duisburg: Henle, 1964) [*RISM* B/II; index, pp. 411–18]

——, ed.: *Ecrits imprimés concernant la musique* (Munich and Duisburg: Henle, 1971) [*RISM* B/VI/1–2; index, ii, 1039–69]

Karlheinz Schlager, ed.: *Einzeldrucke vor 1800* (Kassel: Bärenreiter, 1971–81) [*RISM* A/I; printer and publisher index to follow]

Konrad Ameln, Markus Jenny and Walther Lipphardt, eds.: *Das deutsche Kirchenlied: kritische Gesamtausgabe der Melodien* (Kassel: Bärenreiter, 1975–80) [*RISM* B/VIII/1; index, ii, 119–48]

Guy A. Marco: *The Earliest Music Printers of Continental Europe: a Checklist of Facsimiles Illustrating their Work* (Charlottesville: Bibliographical Society of the U. of Virginia, 1962) [a publisher and printer index to reproductions of their work in modern reference books]

Harald Heckmann: *Deutsche Musikgeschichtliches Archiv, Kassel – Katalog der Filmsammlung* (Kassel: Bärenreiter, 1963–) [indexes at the end of each vol.]

Howard Mayer Brown: *Instrumental Music Printed before 1600: a Bibliography* (Cambridge, MA: Harvard U. Press, 1965) [publishers included in the name index, pp. 481–95]

Bernard Huys: *Catalogue des imprimés musicaux des XVe, XVIe et XVIIe siècles* (Brussels: Bibliothèque Royale, 1965) [index, pp. 418–22]

James J. Fuld: *The Book of World-Famous Music* (New York: Crown, 1966, rev. 2/1971; New York: Dover, 3/1985) [brief essays identifying the first printed edns. of some 500 works]

Wolfgang Schmieder and Gisela Hartwieg: *Kataloge der Herzog-August-Bibliothek, Wolfenbüttel*, xii: *Musik: alte Drucke bis etwa 1750* (Frankfurt am Main: Vittorio Klostermann, 1967) [Register III: 'Namen, Titel, Sachen und Orte', pp. 219–310]

Hans-Martin Plesske: 'Bibliographie des Schrifttums zur Geschichte deutscher und österreichischer Musikverlage', *Beiträge zur Geschichte des Buchwesens*, iii (1968), 135–222 [a systematic list of nearly 800 writings]

D. W. Krummel: *Guide for Dating Early Published Music: a Manual of Bibliographical Practices* (Hackensack, NJ: Joseph Boonin, 1974) [incl. 'National Reports' on the publishing history and scholarly resources of particular regions]; suppl. in *FAM*, xxiv (1977), 175–84; see also Linda Solow, 'An Index to Publishers, Engravers and Lithographers and a Bibliography of the Literature cited in the IAML Guide', *FAM*, xxiv (1977), 81–95

D. W. Krummel: 'Musical Functions and Bibliographical Forms', *The Library*, 5th ser., xxxi (1976), 327–50

Bibliographical Inventory to the Early Music in the Newberry Library, Chicago (Boston: G. K. Hall, 1977) [incl. 'Index to Printers, Engravers, Artists, Copyists, and Publishers', pp. 565–87]

D. Analytical and Technical Studies

D'Almaine & Co.: *A Day at a Music Publisher's* (London, *c*1848); repr., with commentary by H. Edmund Poole, in *Journal of the Printing Historical Society*, xiv (1979–80), 59–81

August Marahrens: 'Der Musiknotensatz', *Vollständiges theoretisch-praktisches Handbuch der Typographie*, i (Leipzig: Verlag des Leipziger Vereinsbuchdr., 1870), 512–34

Robert Dittrich: *Anleitung zum Satz der Musiknoten-Typen* (Leipzig: Alexander Waldow, 1872)

Théophile Beaudoire: *Manuel de typographie musicale* (Paris: Author, 1891)

Henri Robert: *Traité de gravure de musique sur planches d'étain et des divers précédés de simili gravure de musique* (Paris: Author, 1902, 2/1926 as *Gravure de musique et similigravure*)

William Gamble: *Music Engraving and Printing: Historical and Technical Treatise* (London: Pitman, 1923/R New York: Da Capo, 1971)

Hubert J. Foss: 'Modern Styles in Music Printing in England', *The Fleuron*, iii (1924), 89–106

Desmond Flower: 'On Music Printing, 1473–1701', *Book-Collector's Quarterly*, iv (1931), 76–92

Hubert J. Foss: 'The Printing of Music: some Problems of Today', *Gutenberg-Jb 1931*, 293–300

Otto Kinkeldey: 'Music and Music Printing in Incunabula', *Papers of the Bibliographical Society of America*, xxvi (1932), 89–118

Georg Kinsky: *Erstlingsdrucke der deutschen Tonmeister der Klassik und Romantik* (Vienna: Reichner, 1934); also in *Philobiblon*, vii (1934), 347–64

Cecil B. Oldman: *Collecting Musical First Editions* (London: Constable, 1934); also in John Carter: *New Paths in Book Collecting* (London: Constable, 1934), 95–124

Paul Koch: 'Die Musiknoten im Buchdruck', *Klimschs Jb des graphischen Gewerbes*, xxxiii (1940), 61–6

Otto Erich Deutsch: *Music Publishers' Numbers: a Selection of 40 Dated Lists, 1710–1900* (London: Aslib, 1946; Ger. trans., rev., 1961 as *Musikverlagsnummern*)

Karl Hader: *Aus der Werkstatt eines Notenstechers* (Vienna: Waldheim-Eberle, 1948)

Leonard Feist: 'Music as a Graphic Art', *Juilliard Review*, i (1954), 26–31

'Music Printing: An Ancient Craft Successfully Adopts Modern Techniques', *British Printer*, lxx/11 (1957), 56–63

Donald W. Krummel: 'Graphic Analysis: its Application to Early American Engraved Music', *Notes*, xvi (1958–9), 213–33

Åke Davidsson: 'Das Typenmaterial des älteren nordischen Musikdrucks', *Annales Academiae regiae scientiarum upsaliensis*, vi (1962), 76–101

Kathi Meyer-Baer: *Liturgical Music Incunabula: a Descriptive Catalogue* (London: The Bibliographical Society, 1962)

Alan Tyson: *The Authentic English Editions of Beethoven* (London: Faber & Faber, 1963)

H. Edmund Poole: 'New Music Types in the Eighteenth Century', *Journal of the Printing Historical Society*, i (1965), 21–38; ii (1966), 23–44

Bibliography

Ted Ross: *The Art of Music Engraving and Processing* (Miami Beach: Hansen Books, 1970)

A. Hyatt King: 'The 500th Anniversary of Music Printing', *MT*, cxiv (1973), 1220–23

Richard J. Wolfe: *Early American Music Engraving and Printing: a History of Music Publishing in America from 1787 to 1825* (Urbana: U. of Illinois Press, 1980)

Mary Kay Duggan: *Italian Music Incunabula: Printers and Typefonts* (diss., U. of California, Berkeley, 1981)

Eckart Morat: 'Notenstecher – ein aussterbender Beruf?', *Das Orchester*, xxix (1981), 117–21

Hans Lenneberg: 'Music Publishing and Dissemination in the Early Nineteenth Century – some Vignettes', *Journal of Musicology*, ii (1983), 174–83

Mary Kay Duggan: 'A System for Describing Fifteenth-century Music Type', *Gutenberg-Jb 1984*, 67–76

Eckart Morat: 'Die Entwicklung der Herstellung von Druckvorlagen für den Druck von Musiknoten seit 1945', *Gutenberg-Jb 1984*, 77–82

D. W. Krummel: Early German Partbook Type Faces', *Gutenberg-Jb 1985*, 80–99

Stanley Boorman: 'Early Music Printing: Working for a Specialized Market', *Print and Culture in the Renaissance: Essays on the Advent of Printing in the Renaissance*, ed. Gerald P. Tyson and Sylvia S. Wagonheim (Newark: U. of Delaware Press, and London and Toronto: Associated U. Presses, 1986), 222–45

D. W. Krummel: 'Clarifying the Musical Page: the Romantic *Stichbild*', *Printing History*, xvi (1986), 26–36

E. Anthologies of Examples of Music Printing

Oscar Comettant: 'Les Publications musicales', *La Musique, les musiciens, et les instruments de musique . . . a l'Exposition internationale de 1867* (Paris: M. Levy, 1869), 466–515 [exhibition catalogue]

Gabriel Mourey: 'The Illustration of Music', *International Studio*, vi (1898), 86–98

J. Grand Carteret: *Les titres illustrés et l'image au service de la musique* (Turin: Bocca Frères, 1904)

An Illustrated Catalogue of the Music Loan Exhibition held . . . by the Worshipful Company of Musicians at Fishmongers' Hall, June and July, 1904 (London: Novello, 1909) ['Music Printing', pp. 1–123]; discussed in D. W. Krummel, 'An Edwardian Gentlemen's Musical Exhibition,' *Notes*, xxxii (1975–6), 711–18

A. H. Littleton: *A Catalogue of one hundred Works illustrating the History of Music Printing from the Fifteenth to the End of the Seventeenth Century, in the Library of Alfred Henry Littleton* (London: Novello, 1911) [derived from the 1904 exhibition, based on the library of a main exhibitor and of the Novello firm]

William E. Imeson: *Illustrated Music-Titles* (London: n.p., ?1912)

Walter von zur Westen: *Musiktitel aus vier Jahrhunderten: Festschrift anlässlich der 75-jährigen Bestehens der Firma C. G. Röder* (Leipzig, 1921)

Grolier Club, New York: Catalogue of an Exhibition of Printed Music, 17 Dec 1937 – 16 Jan 1938 (New York: Recordak, 1938) [microfilm of selected pages from some 100 items in various collections, with captions suggesting ties to the Meyer and O'Meara essay in *The Dolphin* (1935) above]

Marian Hannah Winter: *Art Scores for Music* (Brooklyn: Brooklyn Museum, 1939)

Sacheverell Sitwell: *Morning, Noon, and Night in London* (London: Macmillan,
1948) [narrative prose based on illustrations on sheet-music covers]
A. Hyatt King: 'English Pictorial Music Title-pages, 1820–1885', *The Library*, 5th
ser., iv (1949–50), 262–72
Gottfried S. Fraenkel: *Decorative Music Title Pages: 201 Examples from 1500 to 1800*
(New York: Dover, 1968)
Richard Schaal: *Musiktitel aus fünf Jahrhunderten* (Wilhelmshaven:
Heinrichshofen, 1972) [essentially a slightly abridged version of Zur
Westen (1921) above]
Mary Kay Duggan: *Early Music Printing in the Music Library* (Berkeley: U. of
California, 1977) [exhibition for the 12th Congress of the IMS]
Cinque secoli di stampa musicale in Europa (Naples: Electa, 1985) [a handsomely
illustrated catalogue of an exhibition at the Museo di Palazzo Venezia]
*Harmonizing the Arts: Original Graphic Designs for Printed Music by World-Famous
Artists* (New York: New York Public Library, 1986) [checklist of 43 titles
illustrated by French artists, 1851–1965, with an introduction by James
J. Fuld]

F. National Studies

GREAT BRITAIN (*GB*)
Frank Kidson: *British Music Publishers, Printers and Engravers* (London: W. E. Hill,
1900/R New York: Benjamin Blom, 1967)
Robert Steele: *The Earliest English Music Printing* (London: The Bibliographical
Society, 1903/R 1965)
Charles G. Mortimer: 'Leading Music Publishers', *MO*, lxi (1937–8); lxii (1938–
9); lxiii (1939–40) [17-part ser.]
Florian Williams: 'After Forty Years: Recollections of a Music Publisher', *MO*,
lxiii (1939–40); lxiv (1940–41) [13-pt. ser.]
—— : 'The Music Publisher of Tradition', *MO*, lxiv (1940–41); lxv (1941–2) [13-
pt. ser.]
Cyrus L. Day and Eleanore B. Murrie: *English Song-Books, 1651–1702: a
Bibliography* (London: The Bibliographical Society, 1940)
Charles Humphries and William C. Smith: *Music Publishing in the British Isles from
the Beginning until the Middle of the Nineteenth Century: a Dictionary of
Engravers, Printers, Publishers and Music Sellers, with a Historical
Introduction* (London: Cassell, 1954; Oxford: Basil Blackwell, rev. 2/
1970)
O. W. Neighbour and Alan Tyson: *English Music Publishers' Plate Numbers in the
First Half of the 19th Century* (London: Faber & Faber, 1965)
D. W. Krummel: *English Music Printing, 1553–1700* (London: The
Bibliographical Society, 1975)
—— : 'Music Publishing,' *Music in Britain: the Romantic Age*, ed. Nicholas Temperley
(London: Athlone, 1981), 46–59
James B. Coover: *Music Publishing, Copyright, and Piracy in Victorian England: a
Twenty-Five Year Chronicle, 1881–1906* (London: Mansell, 1985)
—— : 'The Dispersal of Engraved Music Plates and Copyrights in British Auctions,
1831–1931', *Richard S. Hill: Tributes from Friends* (Detroit: Information
Coordinators, 1987) 223–306
—— : *Music at Auction: Puttick and Simpson (of London), 1794–1971* (Warren, MI:
Harmonie Park Press, 1988)

FRANCE (*F*)
Since French music printing was at first dominated by Attaingnant and Moderne,
later by Du Chemin and Ballard, the studies of them (see section G. below) cover

most of the early output. The 17th century is poorly covered, but for the 18th, the works by Devriès, Brenet and Cucuel are of particular importance. Hopkinson's directory, which surveys the remainder of the history, is now in process of being superseded by Devriés-Lesure.

Michel Brenet: 'La librairie musicale en France de 1653 à 1790, d'après les registres de privilèges', *SIMG*, viii (1906–7), 401–66

Georges Cucuel: 'Quelques documents sur la librairie musicale au XVIIIe siècle', *SIMG*, xiii (1911–12), 385–92

—— : 'Notes sur quelques musiciens, luthiers, éditeurs et graveurs de musique au XVIIIe siècle', *SIMG*, xiv (1912–13), 243–52

Cecil Hopkinson: *A Dictionary of Parisian Music Publishers, 1700–1950* (London: Author, 1954/R New York: Da Capo, 1979)

Cari Johansson: *French Music Publishers' Catalogues of the Second Half of the Eighteenth Century*, 2 vols. (Stockholm: Almquist & Wiksell, 1955) [incl. facsimiles]

Anik Devriès and François Lesure: *Dictionnaire des éditeurs de musique français*, i: *Des origines à environ 1820*, ii: *De 1820 à 1914* (Geneva: Minkoff, 1979–88)

ITALY *(I)*

Claudio Sartori: *Dizionario degli editori musicali italiani* (Florence: Olschki, 1958)

Mariangela Donà: *La stampa musicale a Milano fino all'anno 1700* (Florence: Olschki, 1961)

Angelo Pompilio: 'Editoria musicale a Napoli e in Italia nel cinque-seicento', *Musica e cultura a Napoli dal XV al XIX secolo*, ed. Lorenzo Bianconi and Renato Bossa (Florence: Olschki, 1983), 79–102 [followed by Keith A. Larson and Angelo Pompilio: 'Cronologia delle edizioni musicali napoletane del cinque-seicento', pp. 103–39]

Oscar Mischiati: *Indici, cataloghi e avvisi degli editori e librai musicali italiani dal 1591 al 1798* (Florence: Olschki, 1984) [incl. facsimiles]

Franco Piperino: *Gli 'Eccelentissimi musici della città di Bologna', con uno studio sull'antologia madrigalistica del cinquecento* (Florence: Olschki, 1985) [incl. imprint lists, pp. 44–56]

Giancarlo Rostirolla: 'L'editoria musicale a Roma del Settecento', *Le Muse Galanti: la musica a Roma del settecento*, ed Bruno Cagli (Rome: Instituto della Enciclopedia Italiana, 1985)

Tim Carter: 'Music Publishing in Italy, *c*1580–*c*1625: some Preliminary Observations', *RMARC*, xx (1986–7), 19–37

GERMAN-SPEAKING COUNTRIES *(D)*

Göhler lists much of the early production, while Plesske's bibliography (see C. above) lists the sources for later periods. Gericke covers the pre-history of modern Viennese publishing, and Weinmann the extensive activity from the 1780s.

Albert Göhler: *Die Messkataloge im Dienste der musikalischen Geschichtsforschung* [and] *Verzeichnis der im den Frankfurter und Leipziger Messkatalogen der Jahre 1564 bis 1759 angezeigten Musikalien* (Leipzig: Kahnt, 1901–2/R Hilversum: Knuf, 1965) [a discussion and brief listing of the music in the semi-annual book fair catalogues]

Paul Cohen: *Die Nürnbeger Musikdrucker im sechzehnten Jahrhundert* (diss., U. of Erlangen, 1927); pubd as *Musikdruck und -drucker zu Nürnberg im sechzehnten Jahrhundert* (Nuremberg: Zierfuss, 1927)

Rudolf Wagner: 'Ergänzungen zur Geschichte der Nürnberger Musikdrucker des 16. Jahrhunderts', *ZMw*, xii (1929–30), 506–8

—— : 'Nachträge zur Geschichte der Nürnberger Musikdrucker im 16.
   Jahrhundert', *Mitteilungen des Verein für Geschichte der Stadt Nürnberg.*
   xxx (1931), 107–51
Alexander Weinmann: *Beiträge zur Geschichte des alt-Wiener Musikverlages*
   (Vienna: v.p., 1948–) [separate vols. on individual publishers, built
   around reconstructed plate-number lists]
—— : *Wiener Musikverleger und Musikalienhändler von Mozarts Zeit bis gegen 1860*
   (Vienna: Rohrer, 1956) [a directory that establishes the context of the
   publishers covered in more detail in the above series]
Hannelore Gericke: *Der Wiener Musikalienhandel von 1700 bis 1778* (Graz:
   Hermann Böhlaus, 1960)
Josef Benzing: *Die Buchdrucker des 16. und 17. Jahrhunderts im deutschen
   Sprachgebiet* (Wiesbaden: Harrassowitz, 1963, rev. 2/1982) [directory of
   printers, excluding publishers who were not also printers; invaluable
   for music]

REST OF EUROPE *(RE)*

Alphonse Goovaerts: *Histoire et bibliographie de la typographie musicale dans les Pays-
   Bas* (Antwerp: P. Kockx, 1880/*R* Hilversum: Knuf, 1963)
Paul Bergmans: 'La typographie musicale en Belgique au XVIe siècle', *Histoire
   du livre et de l'imprimerie en Belgique des origines à nos jours* (Brussels: Le
   Musée du livre, 1923–9), v, (1929), pt. 2, pp. 47–75
Boris L'vovich Vol'man: *Russkiye pechatnïye notï XVIII veka* [Russian 18th-century
   printed music] (Leningrad: Gosudarstvennoe muzykal'noe izdatel'stvo,
   1957)
Cecil Hopkinson: *Notes on Russian Music Publishers* (London: Author, 1959)
Åke Davidsson: 'Isländskt musiktryck i äldre tider', *STMf*, xliii (1961), 99–108
Higini Anglès: 'Der Musiknotendruck des 15.–17. Jahrhunderts in Spanien,'
   Musik und Verlag: Karl Vötterle zum 65. Geburtstag (Kassel: Bärenreiter,
   1968), 143–9
Maria Przywecka-Samecka: *Drukarstwo muzyczne w Polsce do końca XVIII wieku*
   [Music printing in Poland up to the end of the 18th century] (Kraków:
   PWM, 1969)
Georgii Ivanov: *Notoizdatelskoe delo v Rossii: istoricheskaia spravka* [Russian music
   publishing: a historical study] (Moscow: Sov'etskii kompozitor, 1970)
Boris L'vovich Vol'man: *Russkiye notnïye izdaniya XIX – nachala XX veka* [Russian
   music publishing in the 19th and early 20th centuries] (Leningrad:
   Muzïka, 1970)
Dan Fog: *Dänische Musikverlage und Notendruckereien* (Copenhagen: Fog, 1972);
   greatly expanded version covering the later period as *Musikhandel og
   Nodetryk i Danmark efter 1750*, 2 vols. (1984); slightly abridged Ger.
   version as *Notendruck und Musikhandel im 19. Jahrhundert in Dänemark*
   (1986) [complemented by an imprint list, *Dansk Musikfortegnelse*, of
   which i (1979) covers 1700–1854]
Ilona Mona: *Hungarian Music Publication, 1774–1867: First Summary*
   (Budapest: IAML, Hungarian National Committee, 1973)
Susan Bain: *Music Printing in the Low Countries in the Sixteenth Century* (diss., U. of
   Cambridge, 1974)
Dan Fog and Kari Michelsen: *Norwegian Music Publication since 1800: a
   Preliminary Guide to Music Publishers, Printers and Dealers* (Copenhagen:
   Fog, 1976)
Ilona Mona: 'Music Publishing in Hungary', *FAM*, xxix (1982), 40–43
Maria Przywecka-Samecka: 'Z dziejów węgierskiego drukarstwa muzycznego
   (XVI–XVIII w.) ', *Roczniki biblioteczne*, xxix (1985), 115–27 ['From the
   history of Hungarian music printing, 16th to 18th centuries'; Eng.
   summary, pp. 128–9]

Bibliography

Lennart Reimers: 'Music Publishing in Sweden', *FAM*, xxxiv (1987), 100–08

Bernard Huys: 'Les imprimeurs de musique à Bruxelles au XIXe siècle', *FAM*, xxxv (1988), 158–62

USA, CANADA *(AM)*

Willaim Arms Fisher: *One Hundred and Fifty Years of Music Publishing in the United States: an Historical Sketch with Special Reference to the Pioneer Publisher Oliver Ditson Company, Inc., 1783–1933* (Boston: Ditson, 1933)

Harry Dichter and Elliott Shapiro: *Early American Sheet Music: its Lure and its Lore, 1768–1889* (New Bowker, 1941); rev. as *Handbook of Early American Sheet Music* (New York: Dover, 2/1977)

Richard J. Wolfe: 'Index of Publishers, Engravers and Printers', 'Publishers' Plate and Publication Numbering Systems', *Secular Music in America, 1801–1825: a Bibliography*, iii (New York: New York Public Library, 1964), 1133–1200

Ernst C. Krohn: *Music Publishing in the Middle Western States before the Civil War* (Detroit: Information Coordinators, 1972)

Helmut Kallmann: 'Canadian Music Publishing', *Papers of the Bibliographical Society of Canada*, xiii (1974), 40–48

Christopher Pavlakis: *The American Music Handbook* (New York: Free Press, 1974) [the directory of 'Music Publishers' provides information on some 150 firms]

Barclay McMullen: 'Tune-book Imprints in Canada to 1867: a Descriptive Bibliography', *Papers of the Bibliographical Society of Canada'*, xvi (1977), 31–57

Leonard Feist: *An Introduction to Popular Music Publishing in America* (New York: National Music Publishers' Association, 1980)

Maria Calderisi: *Music Publishing in the Canadas, 1800–1967* (Ottawa: National Library of Canada, 1981)

Richard Crawford and D. W. Krummel: 'Early American Music Printing and Publishing', *Printing and Society in Early America* (Worcester, MA: American Antiquarian Society, 1983), 186–227

Russell Sanjak: *From Print to Plastic: Publishing and Promoting America's Popular Music (1900–1980)* (Brooklyn: Institute for Studies in American Music, 1983)

D. W. Krummel: *Bibliographical Handbook of American Music* (Urbana: U. of Illinois Press, 1987) [see esp. chap. 16]

Ernst C. Krohn: *Music Publishing in St. Louis* (Warren, MI: Harmonie Park Press, 1988)

Russell Sanjek: *American Popular Music and its Business* (New York: Oxford U. Press, 1988)

OTHER

Eugenio Pereira Salas: 'La creación musical en Chile, 1850–1900', *Historia de la música en Chile (1850–1900)* (Santiago: U. of Chile, 1957), 357–62

F. Z. Van der Merwe: *Suid-Afrikaanse Musiekbibliografie, 1787–1952* (Pretoria: J. L. Van Schaik, 1958; Kaapstad, rev. 2/1974)

Vicente Gesualdo: *Historia de la música en la Argentina* (Buenos Aires: Editorial Beta S. R. I., 1961) [incl. references to music publishers and a list of 1650 items pubd 1852–1900 (ii, 929–1063)]

Robert Stevenson: *Music in Aztec and Inca Territory* (Berkeley and Los Angeles: U. of California Press, 1968) [music printing in the New World, 16th – 18th centuries, discussed on pp. 172–99]

Kazuo Fukushima: *Printing and Publishing of Music in Japan from the Beginning to the Meiji Restoration, 1868* (Tokyo: Ueno Gakuen College, Research Archives for Japanese Music, 1980)

Robert Stevenson: 'Brazilian Music Publishers', *Inter-American Music Review*, ix/2 (1988), 91–103

G. Publishers

Among works on individual music printers and publishers cited in the Dictionary, the following are particularly significant.

Oskar and Hellmuth von Hase: *Breitkopf & Härtel: Gedenkschrift und Arbeitsbericht*, i–ii (Leipzig: Breitkopf & Härtel, 1917–19); iii (Wiesbaden: Breitkopf & Härtel, 1968)
Claudio Sartori: *Bibliografia delle opere musicali stampate de Ottaviano de Petrucci* (Florence: Olschki, 1948)
William C. Smith: *A Bibliography of the Musical Works published by John Walsh during the Years 1695–1720* (London: The Bibliographical Society, 1948, enlarged 2/1968)
François Lesure and Geneviève Thibault: 'Bibliographie des éditions musicales publiées par Nicolas du Chemin (1549–1576)', *AnnM*, i (1953), 269–373; iv (1956), 251–3; vi (1958–63), 403–6
—— : *Bibliographie des éditions d'Adrian Le Roy et Robert Ballard (1551–1598)* (Paris: Heugel, 1955); suppl., *RdM*, xl (1957), 166–72
Ernst Roth: *Die Musik als Kunst und Ware: Betrachtungen und Begegnungen eines Musikverlegers* (Zurich: Atlantis, 1966; Eng. trans. as *The Business of Music: Reflections of a Music Publisher*, London, 1969); pt. 2 repr. as *Erfahrungen eines Musikverlegers: Begegnungen mit . . . Komponisten unserer Zeit* (Zurich: Atlantis, 1982)
William C. Smith and Charles Humphries: *A Bibliography of the Musical Works published by the Firm of John Walsh during the Years 1721–1766* (London: The Bibliographical Society, 1968)
Daniel Heartz: *Pierre Attaingnant, Royal Printer of Music: a Historical Study and Bibliographical Catalogue* (Berkeley and Los Angeles: U. of California Press, 1969)
Cari Johansson: *J. J. & B. Hummel: Music Publishing and Thematic Catalogues* (Stockholm: Almquist & Wiksell, 1972)
Anik Devriès: *Edition et commerce de la musique gravée à Paris dans la première moitié du XVIIIe siècle: les Boivin, les Leclerc* (Geneva: Minkoff, 1976)
Stanley Boorman: 'Petrucci's Type-setters and the Process of Stemmatics', *Formen und Probleme der Überlieferung mehrstimmiger Musik im Zeitalter Josquins Desprez*, ed. Ludwig Finscher (Munich: Kraus, 1981), 245–80
Francesco Degrada and others: *Musica, musicisti, editoria: 175 anni di Casa Ricordi, 1808–1983* (Milan: Ricordi, 1983)

Computers and Music Printing

(compiled by Richard Vendome)

Barry S. Brook and Murray Gould: 'Notating Music with Ordinary Typewriter Characters', *FAM*, xi (1964), 142–59
Gardner Read: *Music Notation: a Manual of Modern Practice* (New York: Taplinger, 1964, 2/1979)
Lejaren A. Hiller and R. A. Baker: 'Automated Music Printing', *JMT*, ix (1965), 129–50

Bibliography

Leland Smith: 'Editing and Printing Music by Computer', *JMT*, xvii (1973), 292–309

Donald Byrd: 'A System for Music Printing by Computer', *Computers and the Humanities*, viii (1974), 161–72

Raymond F. Ericson: 'The DARMS Project: a Status Report', *Computers and the Humanities*, ix (1975), 291–8

Armondo Dal Molin: 'The X – Y Typewriters and their Application as Input Terminals for the Computer', *Proceedings of the Second Annual Music Computation Conference* (Urbana: U. of Illinois, Office of Continuing Education and Public Service in Music, 1975), iv, 28–53

Donal Byrd: 'An Integrated Computer Music Software System', *Computer Music Journal*, i/2 (1977), 55–60

David A. Gomberg: 'A Computer-oriented System for Music Printing', *Computers and the Humanities*, xi(1977), 63–80

W. Buxton and others: 'The Evolution of the SSSP Score Editing Tools', *Computer Music Journal*, iii/4 (1979), 14–25

Dean Walraff: 'NEDIT: a Graphical Editor for Musical Scores', *Proceedings of the 1978 International Computer Music Conference*, ii (Menlo Park, CA: Computer Music Journal, 1979), 410–49

Mario Baroni and Laura Callegari: *Musical Grammars and Computer Analysis: Atti del convegno, Modena, 4–6 octobre 1982* (Florence: Olschki, 1984)

Hélène Charnassé: 'Les bases de données en musicologie', *FAM*, xxxi (1984), 153–76 [incl. essays by Harry B. Lincoln, Warren E. Hultberg, Helmut Rösing, Joachim Schlichte and Philip J. Drummond]

G. Haus: *Elementi di informatica musicale* (Milan: Gruppo Editoriale Jackson, 1984)

J. T. Maxwell and S. M, Ornstein: 'Mockingbird: a Composer's Amanuensis,' *Byte*, ix (1984), 384–401

Carla Scaletti: 'The CERL Music Project at the University of Illinois', *Computer Music Journal*, ix/1 (1985), 45–58

Christoph Schnell: *Die Eingabe musikalischer Information als Teil eines Arbeitinstrumentes: ein Beitrag zur Computeranwendung in der Musikwissenschaft* (Berne and New York: Peter Lang, 1985)

John S. Gourlay: 'A Language for Music Printing', *Communications of the Association for Computing Machinery*, xxix (1986), 388–401

Gary E. Wittlich, John W. Schaffer and Larry R. Babb: *Microcomputers and Music* (Englewood Cliffs, NJ: Prentice-Hall, 1986)

Walter B. Hewlett and Eleanor Selfridge-Field: *Directory of Computer Assisted Research in Musicology, 1987* (Menlo Park, CA: Center for Computer Assisted Research in the Humanities, 1987) [3rd annual edn.; the 1986 discussion is here greatly expanded as 'Music Printing: an Update', pp. 26–76, with 46 illustrations of presentations from different music printing programs]

Deta S. Davis: *Computer Applications in Music: a Bibliography* (Madison, WI: A-R Editions, 1988)

Index

Names entered in bold in the Index have entries of their own in the dictionary. References are given as page numbers if they are to be found in the main text or glossary. Entries in the dictionary are indicated by the headword under which the reference is to be found. (If the headword is lengthy, it is given in a form sufficient for identification.)

Aamodt, Gary J.N.   A-R Editions
Aamodt, Lila   A-R Editions
Aaron, Pietro   Scotto, Vitali (B.)
Abatessa, Giovanni   Pignoni
Abba   Filmtrax-Columbia
Abbate, Antonio Dell'   Scotto
Abbatini, Antonio Maria   Geertsom
Abbiati, Franco   Ricordi
ABC   Word
Abel, Carl Friedrich   Hummel, Schmitt
Abell, John   Randall, Walsh
Abelshauser, Joseph   Götz
Abendroth, Walter   Sikorski
Abert, Hermann   Breitkopf & Härtel, Drei
   Masken Verlag
ABI Music   Broude (A.)
Abraham, Gerald   Augener
Abraham, Max   Peters (i)
Abt, Franz Wilhelm   André, Hug, Litolff
ACA   American Composers Alliance
Achron, Joseph   Israeli Music Publications
Ackely, Bentley DeForrest   Rodeheaver
Action Press   Waterloo
Adam, Adolphe   Artaria (ii), Breitkopf & Härtel,
   Escudier, Pleyel, Richault, Schlesinger (M.),
   Schott
Adams, John   Associated Music Publishers
Adams, Thomas   92, Barley, Windet
Addinsell, Richard   Keith, Prowse
Addison, Robert   102, Cramer, Lavenu, Leader
   & Cock, Lucas, Power
Adelhart, Ursula   Wagenmann
Adler, Guido   Drei Masken Verlag
Adriaenssen, Emanuel   Phalèse
Aertssens [Aertsen], **Hendrik**   92
Agazzari, Agostino   Amadino, Magni, Phalèse,
   Robletti, Zannetti
Agosti, Guido   Curci
Agostini, Lodovico   Baldini
Agrell, Johann Joachim   Schmid
Agricola, Johann Friedrich   Winter
Agricola, Martin   Rhau
Agrippinensis [Agrippinus], Tylman
   Susato   Susato
Åhlström, Olof   111
Aibl   Falter, Universal
Aibl, Joseph   110, Aibl
Aich, Arnt von   82, Egenolff
Aichinger, Gregor   Meltzer
Aird, James   103
Aitken, John   114
Akst, Harry   Remick
Alard, Delphin   Schonenberger

Alary, Carlo   Bertuzzi
Albano, Marcello   Vitale
Albéniz, Isaac   Rouart-Lerolle
Albergati (Capacelli), Pirro   Micheletti,
   Monti
Albert
Albert, Heinrich   87, Mense, Reusner,
   Segebade
Albert, Jacques   128, Albert
Albert, Stephen   Schirmer (G.)
Alberti, Victor   Drei Masken Verlag, Rózsavölgyi
Albicastro, Henrico del Biswang   Roger
Albinoni, Tomasso   Roger, Sala
Albrecht, Gustav   Maisch
Albrecht V, Duke   Berg (A.)
Albrechtsberger, Johann Georg   Hoffmeister,
   Kunst- und Industrie-Comptoir, Schwickert
Alder, Cosmas   Apiarius
Aldine Press   Torresani
Aldridge, John   Lee
Aldrovandini, Giuseppe   Silvani (G. A., Marino)
Aleotti, Giovanni Battista   Baldini
Alessandri & Scattaglia   111, Marescalchi
Alessandroni   De Santis
Alexander, Russell   Barnhouse
Alfano, Franco   De Santis, Ricordi
Alfvén, Hugo   Hansen (W.), Kgl. Hof-
   Musikhandel
Al Gallico Music   Filmtrax-Columbia
Alison, Richard   Day (R.), East
Alkan, (Charles-) Valentin   Costallat, Escudier,
   Israeli Music Publications, Richault
Allan   128, Albert
Allde [Alday], **Edward**   92
Allegra, Salvatore   De Santis
Allegri, Giovanni Battista   Sala
Allen, J.   10, 94
Allorto, Riccardo   Carisch
Allyn & Bacon   126
Almeida, Francisco António de   Valentim de
   Carvalho
Alsbach   120
Alvito, Duke Francesco Gallio of   Colonna
Alwyn, William   Lengnick
Amadino, Ricciardo   83, Scotto, Vincenti
Ambros, August Wilhelm   Leuckart
Ambrose, Robert Steele   Whaley, Royce & Co.
Ambrosio, Giovanni   Colonna
Ambrosius   Kahnt
Ameln, Konrad   Bärenreiter
America–Israel Cultural Foundation   Israel
   Music Institute
American Academy of Music   Mills

American Book Company 126
American Composers Alliance [ACA] 127
American Institute of Musicology 118
American Lutheran Church Augsburg
American Music Centre 127
American Music Edition Presser
American Musicological Society A-R Editions
American Music Syndicate Stark
Amman, Jobst Feyerabend
Amner, John Allde
Amon, Johann Andreas Hoffmeister, Schott
Am-Rus Music Corp. 127, Leeds, Weintraub
Amsden, Dwight S. Couse
Amy, Gilbert Heugel
Ancliffe, Charles Ascherberg, Hopwood &
    Crew
Anderson, John Johnson (James)
Anderson, Leroy Mills
Andía, Antonio Romero y Unión Musical
    Española
Andino, Julián Instituto de Cultura
    Puertorriqueña
André 106, 107, Augener, Gleissner,
    Senefelder
André, Gustavus Ditson, Ewer
André, Johann [Jean] [father] 105, André
André, Johann Anton [son] 58, André
André, Maurice Billaudot
Andreae, Hieronymus *see* Formschneider
Andreae, Volkmar Hug
Andreozzi, Gaetano Zatta
Andrews, Ebenezer T. Thomas
Andrews, Hugh Birchall
Andrez, Benoit 100
Andrieu, Jean François Billaudot
Anerio, Felice Vincenti
Anerio, Giovanni Francesco Caifabri, Gardano,
    Grignani, Mascardi, Phalèse, Robletti, Soldi,
    Tini
Anfossi, Pasquale Marescalchi, Zatta
Angeleri, Giuseppi Maria Vigoni
Anglesi, Domenico Cecconcelli
Anglo–Canadian Music Publishers' Association
Ángyán, Béla Rózsavölgyi
Anichini Guidi
Animuccia, Giovanni Blado, Dorico
Annisius Hummel
Antegnati, Constanzo Sabbio
Antheil, George Weintraub
Antico [Anticho, Antigo, Antiguo, Antiquis],
    Andrea 7, 82, 89, 496, 503, 532,
    Attaingnant, Dorico, Du Ry, Giunta, Petrucci
    (O.), Scotto, Torresani
Apiarius [Biener], **Mathias** 22, 26, 86,
    Schoeffer
Appel, John Riley
Appenzeller, Benedictus Susato
Applegarth, Augustus Cowper
Aprile, Giuseppe Pacini
Apthorp, William Foster Ditson
Aquinas, Thomas Blado
Arcadelt, Jacques 83, 499, 543, Amadino,
    Antico, Attaingnant, Ballard, Barré, Buglhat,
    Franceschi, Gardano, Goulart, Guidi,
    Le Roy, Marescotti, Merulo, Moderne,
    Petrucci (P.), Poggioli, Rampazetto, Scotto,
    Tournes
Arct, Michal 122
A-R Editions 68, 118
Arendes de Hamborch *see* Arndes
Arensky, Anton Editions Russes de Musique

Aretin, Johann Christoph Freiherr
    von Gleissner
Aretino, Pietro Gardano, Scotto
Ariosto, Ludovico Barré, Rampazetto
Aristotle Scotto
Arkwright, G.E.P. Williams (J.)
Arlen, Harold Belwin-Mills, Mills
Armbrüster, Anton 113
Arndes [Arns, Arnes], **Steffen** 81
Arne, Thomas Harrison, Johnson (John),
    Longman & Broderip, Manwaring, Peters (i),
    Phillips, Simpson, Thompson
Arnold, Georg Wagner (M.)
Arnold, Malcolm Faber, Lengnick
Arnold, Samuel 118, Carr, Harrison, Preston,
    Skillern, Thompson
Arnoullet, Balthasar Guéroult
Arnoullet, Jacques Channey
Arrieu, Claude Billaudot
Arrighetti, Lodovico Pignoni
Arrigo, Girolamo Heugel, Ricordi
Arroio, João Sassetti
Arrow Music Press 127, Cos Cob Press
Ars Viva 119, Schott
Artaria (i) 106, Berra, Cappi (G., P.),
    Hoffmeister, Huberty, Mollo, Musikalisches
    Magazin, Pleyel, Torricella, Traeg, Weigl
Artaria (ii) 111, Lorenzi, Ricordi
Artaria, Carlo 106, Artaria (i), Artaria (ii),
    Cappi
Artaria, Domenico (ii) Artaria (i), Maisch
Artaria, Domenico (iii) 106, Artaria (i), Mollo
Artaria, Ferdinando 111, Artaria (ii)
Artaria, Francesco 106, Artaria (i), Artaria (ii)
Artaria, Mathias Artaria (i), Diabelli, Maisch
Artomius, Piotr Krzesichleb Hünefeld
Artusi, Giovanni Maria Vincenti
Ascanio Gardano
Ascher, Leo Ricordi, Schott
Ascherberg, Hopwood & Crew 120, Chappell
Ashbrand, L.C. Werlein
Ashdown, Edwin 102, Wessel
Ashdown, Sydney Anglo-Canadian Music
Asioli, Bonifacio Artaria (ii), Bertuzzi,
    Ricordi, Sauer
Asola, Giovanni Matteo Amadino, Gardano,
    Scotto, Vincenti
Aspelmayer, Franz Guéra
Asperl Maisch
Asser, Eduard I. 61
Assmayer, Ignaz Maisch
**Associated Board of the Royal Schools of
    Music** 526
Associated Music Publishers [AMP] 127, Feist,
    Leonard, Schirmer (G.)
Astor, Edmund Rieter-Biedermann
Attaingnant, Marie Lescallopier [second
    wife] Attaingnant
Attaingnant, Pierre 23, 25, 39, 40, 82–3, 84,
    86, 129, 521, 532, 538, Ballard, Buglhat,
    Channey, Dorico, Du Ry, Egenolff, Gardano,
    Haultin, Le Be, Le Roy, Moderne, Petreius
Attenhofer, Karl Hug
Atterberg, Kurt Breitkopf & Härtel, Eulenburg
Attwood, Thomas Power, Regent's Harmonic
    Institution
Atwill, Joseph F(airfield) 115, Gray (M.)
Auber, Daniel–François–Esprit Brandus,
    Breitkopf & Härtel, Brzezina, Schott,
    Troupenas
Aubert 49, Durand, Pleyel

Auckenthaler, Fritz   Simrock
Auerhamer J.M.   Hoffmeister
Aufschnaiter, Benedikt   Nenninger
Augener   102, Chester, Cocks, Galliard, Schott, Stainer & Bell, Williams (J.)
Augsburg
Aulagnier   Troupenas
Auric, Georges   Billaudot, Durand, Eschig, Heugel, Oiseau-Lyre, Salabert
Austin, H.R.   Schmidt
Avison, Charles   Longman & Broderip
Avni, Tzvi   Israel Music Institute
Avshalomov, Jacob   Schirmer (E. C.)
Axman   Urbánek
Ayr   Paterson
Ayres, Frederic   Wa-Wan Press
Ayrton, Edward   Regent's Harmonic Institution

Babb, Samuel   Dale
Babbitt, Milton   Boelke-Bomart, Broude Brothers, Peters (i)
Babcock, Samuel   Thomas
Bacchini, Benedetto   Pisarri
Bach, Carl Philipp Emanuel   Bote & Bock, Breitkopf & Härtel, Haffner, Hoffmeister, Hummel, Rellstab, Schmid, Schwickert, Traeg, Winter
Bach, Johann Christian   Forster, Garland, Hummel, La Chevardière, Longman & Broderip, Napier, Sieber, Torricella, Venier, Welcker
Bach, Johann Sebastian   100, 118, 510, 528, 537, Associated Board of the Royal Schools of Music, Bach-Gesellschaft, Bärenreiter, Berra, Birchall, Boosey & Hawkes, Breitkopf & Härtel, Cocks, Coventry & Hollier, Deutscher Verlag für Musik, Dover, Editio Musica Budapest, Garland, Hänssler, Heinrichshofen, Hoffmeister, Lauterbach & Kuhn, Leader & Cock, Nägeli, Peters (i), Schlesinger, Simrock, Weigel, Wiener Philharmonischer Verlag, Wiener Urtext Edition
Bach's sons   Hänssler
Bach Gesellschaft
Bachmann, Georg Christian   Hummel, Nagel
Bachmann, Werner   Deutscher Verlag für Musik
Bacilly, Bénigne de   Ballard
Bäck, Sven Erik   Hansen (W.), Nordiska Musikförlaget ·
Backer-Grøndahl, Agathe   Hals, Hansen (W.), Norsk Musikforlag
Bacon, Ernst   Broude Brothers
Bacon, George   Dubois
Badings, Henk   Alsbach
Badoux, Emil   Rouart-Lerolle
Baethen [Batius, Bathenius], **Jacob**   86, Phalèse, Susato
Bagatti, Francesco   Camagno
Bagge, Julius   Hirsch
Bagger-Sjöbäck, Lennart   Gehrmans
Bahn, Martin   Träutwein
Baïf, Jean Antoine de   Le Roy
Bailleux, Antoine   104, Bureau d'Abonnement Musical, Erard
Baillie, Joanna   Thomson
Baillieul, F.   49
Baillot, Pierre   Lucca, Pleyel
Baker, Michael C.   Harris
Baker, R.A.   66

Baker, Theodore   124, Schirmer (G.)
Bakfark, Balínt [Valentin]   Ballard, Editio Musica Budapest, Laet, Moderne
Balakirev, Mily   Belyayev, Editions Russes de Musique, Gutheil, Muzïka, Stellovsky
Balbastre, Claude-Bénigue   Castagneri
Baldini, Vittorio   89
Baldwin, John   Church
Bales, Richard   Broude (A.)
Balfe, Michael William   Chappell, Cramer, Lucas
Ball, Ernest M.   Witmark
Ball, James   Monzani
Ballard   39, 88, 92, 95, 104, 521, 532, Foucault, Gando, Le Clerc (C.-N.), Ribou, Roger
Ballard, Christophe   Ballard, Baussen, Foucault
Ballard, Christophe-Jean-François (i)   Ballard, Fournier
Ballard, Jean-Baptiste-Christophe   Ballard, Boivin, Foucault
Ballard, Pierre (i)   25, Ballard, Metru, Stansby
Ballard, Pierre (ii)   25, Ballard
Ballard, Pierre (ii), widow of   Ballard, Foucault
Ballard, Robert (i)   25, 84, Ballard, Le Roy
Ballinger, Friedrich   Böhm
Balmer & Weber   116, Feist
Balsach, Llorenc   73
Balzac, Honoré de   Escudier
Balzer   Eder
Ban, Joan Albert   Matthysz
Banat   Morawetz
Banchieri, Adriano   Amadino, Magni, Rossi, Tebaldini, Vincenti
Bandier, Martin   EMI Music-SBK
Banfi, Edoardo   Sonzogno
Banger, Josiah   Clementi
Banister, John   Hudgebut, Young
Banks, Paul   Schott
Bantock, Granville   Chester, Curwen, Ditson, Novello, Stainer & Bell, Williams (J.)
Bapst, Valentin   7
Barber, Samuel   Schirmer (G.), Silver Burdett
Barbetta, Giulio Cesare   Scotto
Barbier, Jean   Higman
Barbu, Filaret   Morawetz
Bárczi, Gusztav   Rózsavölgyi
Bárd, Ferenc   Editio Musica Budapest
Bardi, Giovanni de   Vincenti
Bárdos, Lajos   Magyar Kórus
Barduzzi, Leopoldo   Sonzogno
Bärenreiter   62, 68, 118, 503, Bosse, Deutscher Verlag für Musik, Handel societies
Barentsen, Hendrik   Tournes
Barjona Madelka, Simon   Černý
Barley, William   91, 92, Adams, East, Lownes
Barnard, John   79
Barnett, John   Hutchings & Romer
Barnhouse, Charles Lloyd   126
Barraud, Henry   Billaudot
Barré, Antonio   89, Rampazetto
Barry   128
Barth, Hans   Fischer
Barth, Nicolaas   100, Plattner
Bartha, Denes   Magyar Kórus
Bartók, Bela   119, Boosey & Hawkes, Editio Musica Budapest, Magyar Kórus, Rózavölgyi, Rozsnyai, Universal
Bartolozzi, Bruno   Napier
Basa, Domenico   Gardano
Basie, Count [William]   Robbins
Basile, Donato   Carlino, Vitale

Baskerville, John 522
Bassani, Giovanni Battista   Monti, Roger, Sala,
    Silvani
Bassano, Giovanni   Amadino, Vincenti
Bastien, James   Kjos
Baston, Josquin   Susato
Bates, T.C.   Chappell
Bathenius, Jacob   *see* Baethen
Bathlot L.   Joubert
Batius, Jacob   *see* Baethen
Battelle, Ebenezer   Ditson
Bauer, Julius   Spehr
Bauer-Mengelberg, Stefan   66
Baum, Richard   Bärenreiter
Baumann, George 86–7
Baumgartner, Wilhelm   Hug
Baussen, Henri de   Bonneüil, Foucault
Bavent, Jean   Tournes
Bax, Arnold   Chappell, Chester, Murdoch,
    Williams (J.)
Baxter, J(esse) R(andall, Jr.)   124, Zondervan
Bayard, Marc   Boivin
Bayle, François   Pleyel
Bayreuth Festivals   Heckel
Bazin, François   Troupenas
Bazylik z Sieradza, Cyprian   Szarfenberg
Beach, Mrs. H. H. A. (Amy Cheney)   Schmidt
Beacham, Joseph R.   Benteen, Miller &
    Beacham
Beadnell   Button & Whitaker
Beale, Thomas Frederick   Chappell, Cramer,
    Handel societies
Beale, William   Regent's Harmonic Institution
Beardmore, T.   Birchall
Beaudoire, T.   35
Beaulaigue, Barthélemy   24, Granjon
Beba, Bishop Lorenz von   Reyser
Beccari, Fabio   Tradate
Beck   Fiot & Meignen
Beck, Conrad   La Sirène
Beck, Franz   Venier
Becker, Carl Ferdinand   Bach-Gesellschaft
Beckwith, John   Waterloo
Bedford, David   Universal
Beekman Music   Presser
Beer, Bernard   Schirmer (G.)
Beesley, Michael 103
Beeson, Jack   Oxford University Press
Beethoven, Carl van   Hoffmeister
Beethoven, Ludwig van   103, 106, 107, 118, 493,
    526, 527, 543, Associated Board of the Royal
    Schools of Music, Andrez, Ars Viva, Artaria
    (i), Benjamin, Berra, Birchall, Bossler,
    Breitkopf & Härtel, Brzezina, Cappi,
    Clementi, Cocks, Cramer, Diabelli, Eder,
    Editio Musica Budapest, Farrenc, Girard,
    Gombart, Götz, Guidi, Haslinger, Heckel,
    Henle, Heinrichshofen, Hoffmeister, Janet
    & Cotelle, Jürgenson, Kunst- und
    Industrie-Comptoir, Lauterbach & Kuhn,
    Lienau, Litolff, Löschenkohl, Maisch,
    Mechetti, Mollo, Monzani, Nägeli, Pacini,
    Peters (i), Pleyel, Regent's Harmonic
    Institution, Richault, Ricordi, Riley, Sauer,
    Schlesinger, Schott, Simrock, Thomson,
    Traeg, Troupenas, Wessel, Wiener Urtext
    Edition
Beglarian, Grant   Marks
Behr & Bock   Arct
Behrens, Johan D.   Norsk Musikforlag,
    Warmuth

Belaieff [Belyayev], M. P.   Belyayev, Peters (i)
Belcher   Thomas
Belisi, Filippo   Micheletti
Bell & Howell   Berando
Bellère, Jean   84, Phalèse
Belli, Domenico   Amadino
Belli, Girolamo   Baldini, Tini
Bellini, Vincenzo   515, 534, Artaria (ii), Bertuzzi,
    Boosey & Hawkes, Breitkopf & Härtel,
    Cottrau, Girard, Pacini, Ricordi, Schott
Bellon, Jean Bénédikt   Rouart-Lerolle
Belmont 27
Belmonti, Amedeo   Caifabri
Belwin-Mills 68, 125, Filmtrax-Columbia,
    Fischer, Gray, Kalmus, MCA Music, Mills,
    Presser
Belyayev, Mitrofan Petrovich 122, Gutheil
Benacci, Vittorio   91, Rossi
Benatzky, Ralph   Doblinger
Bencard, Johann Kaspar 87
Benda, Georg   Götz, Schwickert, Winter
Bendl, Karel   Hoffmann, Hudební Matice, Starý
Benedetti, Francesco Maria   Sala
Benedetti, Piero [Pietro]   Marescotti
Benedict, Julius   Cramer, Leader & Cock, Lucas
Benedictine Congregation   Desclée
Benedictus Hectoris   7
Benedikti-Nudožersky, Vavřinec   Černý
Benevoli, Orazio   Caifabri
Benjamin, Anton J. 110, 119, Simrock
Benjamin, George   Faber
Bennett, Charles   Dale
Bennett, Richard Rodney   Novello, Universal
Bennett, S. Fillmore   Lyon & Healy
Bennett, William Sterndale   102, Bach-
    Gesellschaft, Handel societies,
    Leader & Cock
Benson, John   Playford
Benson, John T.   Zondervan
Benson, Warren   MCA Music
Bente, Adolph   Litolff
Bente, Martin   Henle
Bentcen, Frederick D. 115, Miller & Beacham
Bentzon, Niels Viggo   Samfundet til Udgivelse
    af Dansk Musik
Berandol 128
Berardi, Angelo   Caifabri, Monti, Mutii
Berchem, Jacquet de   Barré, Gardano
Berezowsky, Nicolai   Editions Russes de
    Musique
Berg, Adam 87, 537, Henricus, Widmanstetter
Berg, Alban   510, 534, Lienau, Universal
Berg, Catharina (née Schmid)   Berg (J.),
    Gerlach, Kauffmann
Berg [van den Berg, vom Berg, vom Perg,
    Montanus]**, Johann** 84, Gerlach,
    Kauffmann
Berg, T. van (pseud.)   Balmer & Weber
Bergen, Gimel [Berg, Joachim; Montanus]   87
Berger, Arthur (Victor)   Boelke-Bomart,
    Broude Brothers
Berger, Theodor   Ries & Erler, Sikorski
Berger, W. van   Barth
Bergsma, William   Galaxy, Society for the
    Publication of American Music
Beringen
Beringen, Godefroy   86, 88, Beringen
Beringer, Oscar   Bosworth
Berio, Luciano   Suvini Zerboni, Universal
Bériot, Charles-Auguste de   Schott, Troupenas
Berka, Anton   *see* Leidesdorf, M. J.

Berkeley, Lennox   Chester
Berletti, Luigi   Lucca
Berlin, Irving   125, Von Tilzer
Berlioz, Hector   Bärenreiter, Brandus,
    Breitkopf & Härtel, Choudens, Costallat,
    Hofmeister, Joubert, Leduc, Lemoine,
    Litolff, Richault, Rieter-Biedermann,
    Schlesinger, Schonenberger
Bermann, Jeremias   106, Eder
Bermann, Joseph   Eder
Bernabei, Ercole   Caifabri, Sala
Bernard, Matvey Ivanovich   Dalmas, Jürgenson
Bernardino di Copertino, Desa
    Giovanni   Gardano
Bernasconi, Allessio Boileau   *see* Boileau
    Bernasconi, Allessio
Berners, Lord   Chester
Bernier, Augustine-Julie   Leduc
Bernier, Nicolas   44, Boivin, Foucault
Bernstein, Louis   Shapiro, Bernstein
Berra, Marco   111, Hoffmann
Berri   Micheletti
Berry, Thomas S.   63, Gordon
Bertalotti, Angelo Michele   Della Volpe
Bertani, Lelio   Sabbio
Berthiaud   47
Bertini, E.   Guidi
Bertini, Henri   Schonenberger
Bertoni, Ferdinando (Gasparo)   Alessandri &
    Scattaglia, Zatta
Bertrand, Anthoine de   Goulart, Le Royer
Bertrand, Paul   Leduc, Leduc (A.)
Bertuzzi, Luigi   111, Lucca
Berutti, Arturo   Breyer
Berwald, Franz   Bärenreiter
Berwinckel, Joannes   43
Besozzi, Giovanni Francesco   Tini
Bessel, Ivan   Bessel, Gutheil
Bessel, Vasily Vasil'yevich   122
Besseler, Heinrich   Deutscher Verlag für Musik
Bethanio, Fausto   Merulo
Béthune, Charles Albert   Billaudot
Bettinelli, Bruno   Carisch, Ricordi, Zanibon
Beuther, Georg   Bergen
Beuther, Michael   Fezandat
Beuttner   Widmanstetter
Bevilacqua   128, Mollo
Bevin, Elway   Lownes (H.)
Beyer, Ferdinand   Schonenberger
Beyer, Frank Michael   Bote & Bock
Bèze, Théodore de   88, Guéroult, Haultin
Biaggi, Girolamo A.   Lucca
Bialas, Günter   Bärenreiter
Bianchi, Cristoforo   43, Borboni
Bianchi, Francesco   Marescalchi
Bianchi, G.B.   Monti
Bianchi, Lino   De Santis
Bianchini, Francesco   Moderne
Bibalo   Hansen (W.)
Bickham, George, Jr.   101, Cole (B.)
Bidelli, Marteo   Camagno
Biener, Mathias   *see* Apiarius
Biffi, Gioseffo   Tradate
Biglow, Lucius Horatio   Biglow & Main
Biglow & Main   124, Hope
Big 3   125, 126, Feist, Miller, Robbins
Billaudot
Billaudot, Gérard   Billaudot, Costallat
Billings, William   113, Thomas
Binder, Heinrich   Van Ohr
Bindoni, Bernardo   Scotto

Bindoni family   Raverii
Binney & Ronaldson   113
Binz, Johann Georg   Hoffmeister
Birch, Thomas   Atwill
Birchall, Robert   102, Chappell
Birchard, Clarence   Summy-Birchard
Birchtree   Summy-Birchard
Birckmann, Francis   Remunde
Bird, John C.   Thompson (G. V.)
Birnbach   110, Challier
Birnbach, Richard   Birnbach
Birtwistle, Harrison   Universal
Bischoff, Hans   118, Steingräber
Bishop, Sir Henry R(owley)   Goulding, Handel
    societies, Power
Bishop, Richard   Stansby
Bittner, Julius   Universal
Biumo, Giacomo Filippo   Tradate
Bizcargui, Martínez de   *see* Martínez de
    Bizcargui, Gonzalo
Bizet, Georges   Choudens, Hartmann, Metzler
Bizot, Léon   Pleyel
Blackmar, A(rmand) E(dward)   116
Blado, Antonio   89
Blaeu   Le Chevalier
Blaikely, D.J.   Boosey & Hawkes
Blake, David   Novello
Blake, George E.   114
Blake, William Pinson   Ditson
Blanchet   F. Escudier
Bland, John   102, Bland & Weller, Purday
Bland & Weller
Blankenburg, Quirinius van   Matthysz
Blau, Otto   Weinberger
Blech, Leo   Drei Masken Verlag
Bliss, Arthur   Novello
Bliss, Philip P.   Biglow & Main
Blitzstein, Marc   Arrow Music Press
Bloch, Ernest   Broude Brothers, Carisch,
    Schirmer (G.), Summy-Birchard
Bloch, József   Rozsnyai
Blockland, Corneille de   Tournes
Blockley, John   Ascherberg, Hopwood & Crew
Blondeau, Pierre   Attaingnant
Bloom, Sol   125
Blow, John   Cross, Pearson, Peters (i), Playford,
    Young
Blum, Michael   Hantzsch (G.)
Blume, Friedrich   Bärenreiter, Kallmeyer,
    Litolff
Blumenthal, Christian Adolph
    Gottfried   Brandus
Blumer, Theodor   Simrock
Blundell, James   Welcker
Boatwright, Howard   Schirmer (E.C.)
Bocanegra, Juan Perez   94
Boccaccio, Giovanni   Rampazetto
Boccherini, Luigi   Artaria (i), Artaria (ii),
    Bailleux, Benoit, Götz, Guéra, Hummel,
    Imbault, Janet & Cotelle, La Chevardière,
    Marescalchi, Pleyel, Sieber, Venier, Zanibon,
    Zatta
Bocchi, Francesco   Marescotti
Bochsa, Nicholas Charles   Schönenberger,
    Troupenas
Bock, Gustav   Bote & Bock, Challier
Bodé, (Johann Joachim Christoph)   Venier
Boehm, Theobald   Aibl, Falter
Boelke-Bomart   127
Boësset, Antoine   Ballard, Stansby
'Bogan, Mrs. Bogan of'   *see* Lady Nairne

Bogard, Jan 92, Phalèse
Boglhat, Johannes de Buglhat
Bohemian Brethren 40, 87
Böhm
Böhme, Carl Gotthelf Siegmund Peters (i)
Böhme, Johann August 106,110, Benjamin, Pleyel
Boieldieu, (François-)Adrien Brzezina, Dalmas, Erard, Hoftheater-Musik-Verlag, Janet & Cotelle, Magasin de Musique (ii)
Boieldieu, (Adrien-) Louis (-Victor; "Jeune") Janet & Cotelle
Boileau Bernasconi, Alessio 122
Boitard, P. 47
Boito, Arrigo Ricordi
Boivin, Elizabeth Catherine (née Ballard) Boivin, Foucault
Boivin, François 104, Foucault, Le Clerc
Böker-Heil, Norbert 68
Bolcom, William Marks
Boldrini, Carlo Artaria (i)
Bomtempo, João Domingos Sassetti
Bonaga, Paolo Artaria (i)
Bonagiunta, Giulio Scotto
Bonamici, Ferdinando Ricordi
Bonardi, Giovanni Antonio Pignoni
Bonarelli della Rovere, Guidobaldo Baldini
Bonfilio, Paolo Antonio Baldini
Boni, Guillaume Goulart, Le Royer
Bonini, Balerio y Ricordi
Bonini, Pier-Maria Zannetti
Bonini, Severo Marescotti, Raverii
Bonneüil, Hiérosme 95, Foucault
Bonoldi Frères Pacini
Bononcini, Giovanni Maria Magni, Monti (G., P. M.), Sala
Bonporti, Francesco Antonio Roger, Sala
Boonin, Joseph M. Jerona
Boosey, Thomas (i) 102, Boosey & Hawkes
Boosey, William Chappell
Boosey & Co. Boosey & Hawkes, Chappell, Schmidt
Boosey & Hawkes 120, 528, 534, Arrow Music Press, Cos Cob Press, Editions Russes de Musique, Faber, Fischer (C.), Fürstner, Universal, Wheatstone
Borboni [Borbone], **Nicolò** 43, 94
Borchgrevinck, Melchior Waldkirch
Borchorst, Carl Ferdinand Lose
Borden, Gavin Garland
Bordes, Charles Rouart-Lerolle
Bordogni, Giulio (Marco) Pacini
Bordoni, Carlo Scotti
Borg, Pär Aron Hirsch
Borghi, Giovanni Battista Zatta
Bornschein, Franz C. Fischer (J.)
Borodin, Alexander Porfir'yevich Belyayev
Borren, Charles van den Plainsong & Mediaeval Music Society
Borromeo of Alvito, Count G.C. Colonna
Borrono, Pietro, Paolo Wyssenbach
Borsaghi, Giulio Della Volpe
Borsaghi, Giulio, widow of Della Volpe
Bortnyansky, Dmitry Stepanovich Jürgenson
Bortoli 91
Bösendorfer, Adolf Diabelli
Bossange Père Schlesinger
Bosse
Bosse, Gustav 119, Bosse
Bossi, Marco Enrico Carisch, Zanibon
Bossinensis, Franciscus Antico

Bossler, Heinrich Philipp Carl 106, Hoffmeister
Boston Book Store Ditson
Boston Music Company 124–5, Schirmer (E. C.)
Boston Music Store Stein & Buchheister
Bosworth 120
Bote & Bock 110, 528, Fürstner, Lauterbach & Kuhn, Schirmer (G.)
Bottazzi, Bernardino Vincent.
Bottesini, Giovanni Guidi
Bottrigari, Ercole Amadino, Baldini
Boughton, Rutland Curwen, Stainer & Bell
Boulez, Pierre 520, 534, Heugel, Universal
Bourbon, Nicolas Attaingnant
Bourgeois, Loys Beringen, Guéroult
Bourgeois, Thomas-Louis Foucault, Le Clerc (J. P.)
Bourgouin (Le Cadet) Le Clerc
Bourne Music Company International
Bousset, Jean Baptiste de Foucault
Bovicelli, Giovanni Battista Vincenti
Bowman, Henry 94
Boyce, William Harrison, Peters (i)
Boyer, Jean Leduc, Le Menu, Naderman, Venier
Boyer, Mme Le Menu
Boyle, T. August Peters (ii)
Boyvin, Jacques 95, Baussen, Foucault
Bozzi, Paolo Amadino
Bozzola, Pietro Amadino, Sabbio
Brachrogge, Hans Waldkirch
Bradbury, William B. Biglow & Main, Mason Bros.
Brade, William Van Ohr
Braga, Francisco Bevilacqua
Bragadino, Hieronimo Gardano
Brahms, Johannes 107, 493, 495, 515, 530, 543, Benjamin, Breitkopf & Härtel, Doblinger, Garland, Krzyżanowski, Lengnick, Peters (i), Rieter-Biedermann, Senff, Simrock, Weinberger, Wiener Urtext Edition
Brainard, Silas 116
Brainard's sons, S. Brainard, Root & Cady
Braley, Arthur E. Stainer & Bell
Braley, Bernard Stainer & Bell
Branco, Luís de Freitas Sassetti
Brand, Max Universal
Brandenburg, Thomas Bote & Bock
Brandstetter, Johann 51, Wagner
Brandus 110, Joubert, Schlesinger (M.), Troupenas
Branscombe, Gena Wa-Wan Press, Whaley, Royce
Brant, Cyr de Fischer (J.)
Brant, Henry MCA Music
Brant, Sebastian 497
Braşcu Doina
Brash Holdings Ltd. Allan
Brassac, René de Bearn Bailleux
Brassart, Johannes Barré
Brätel, Ulrich Kriesstein
Braun, Yehezkiel Israel Music Institute
Braunfels, Walter Universal
Bräutigam, Helmut Breitkopf & Härtel
Brayssing, Grégoire [Gregor] Ballard
Breitkopf, Johann Gottlob Imanuel 3, 28–30, 31, 34, 36, 98–100, 105, 107, Fougt, Fournier, Gando, Haslinger, Pleyel, Rellstab, Sønnichsen, Winter

Breitkopf & Härtel   3, 105, 106, 107, 118, 119,
   120, 127, 490, 495, 517, 520, 528, Bach-
   Gesellschaft, Carulli, Durand, Flaxland,
   Hofmeister, Jung, Meser, Richault, Ricordi,
   Roder, Spehr
Bremner, Robert   101, 103, Johnson (J.),
   Preston, Simpson, Welcker
Brentner, Joseph   Labaun
Bresgen, César   Tonger
Breu, Jörg   Ratdolt
Breuer   Hofmeister
Breyer   128, Ortelli, Ricordi
Briard, Etienne   22, 86, 520, Channey, Granjon
Briggs, H.B.   Plainsong & Mediaeval Music
   Society
Britannico, Angelo   10
Britten, Benjamin   62, 120, Boosey & Hawkes,
   Faber, Oiseau-Lyre, Oxford University
   Press
Broadland Music   Berando
Broadman Press   126
Broadus, John Albert   Broadman
Broadway Music Co.   Von Tilzer
Brockhaus, Max   119
Broder, Nathan   Schirmer (G.)
Broderip, Francis   102, Longman & Broderip
Broderip & Wilkinson   Longman & Broderip
Brook, Barry S.   66
Brooks, Shelton   Rossiter
Broome, [Broom] **Michael**   103
Brossard, Sébastien de   Ballard, Foucault
Brouck, Jacob de   Plantin
Broude, Alexander   127, Broude Brothers
Broude Brothers   127
Brouilly, Jean de   Le Roy
Broussan   Eschig
Brown, Bartholomew   Thomas
Brown, Earle   Universal
Brown, Geoff   73
Brown, John   Lownes, Snodham
Brown, Nick   Pepper
Brown, William   Aitken
Browne, Raymond A.   Bloom
Brozowa, Walenty z   Wirzbięta
Bruch, Max   Kistner & Siegel, Leuckart,
   Peters (i), Simrock
Bruckner, Anton   119, Doblinger, Lienau,
   Rättig, Weinberger
Bruckner-Verlag   Bärenreiter
Bruggen, Henry ter   Susato, Vissenaecken
Brugis, Francesco de   Giunta
Brüll, Ignaz   Bote & Bock, Weinberger
Brumel, Antoine   Antico, Petrucci (O.)
Brun, Fritz   Hug
Brunelli, Antonio   Marescotti
Brunet, Pierre   Ballard
Brünings, Johann David   Nägeli
Brzezina, Antoni   111, Sennewald
Bucchi, Valentino   Carisch
Bucer (Butzer), Martin   Apiarius
Buchanan, George   89
Buchheister, William   Stein & Buchheister
Buffet   Fezandat
Bufford, John H.   115
Bugenhagen   Rhau
Buglhat [Bulhat], **Johannes de**   89, Gardano
Bull, Amos   Thomas
Bull, John   43
Bülow, Hans von   Aibl, Leuckart, Litolff, Senff
Bunting, Anthony   103
Bunting, Edward   Bunting, Neale, Preston

Burchard, R.B.   Church
Burck, Joachim á   Hantzsch (A., G.)
Burdett, Frank W.   Silver Burdett
Bureau Central de la Musique   Escudier
Bureau d'Abonnement Musical
Bureau de Musique   Hoffmeister, Peters (i),
   Whistling
Bureau des Arts et d'Industrie   Haslinger,
   Kunst- und Industrie-Comptoir
Bureau du Journal de Musique   Le Clerc
Bürger, Gottfried August   André
Burghers, Michael   Beesly
Burgkmair, Hans   Oeglin, Ratdolt
Burgmein, J.   *see* Ricordi
Burgon, Geoffrey   Chester
Burkett, F.M.   Peters (ii)
Burkhard, Willy   Hug
Burnacini, Ludovico   Cosmerovius
Burney, Charles   Oswald
Burns, Robert   Johnson (James), Thomson
Burtch, Dean C.   Pepper
Burtch, Harold K.   Pepper
Burtius, Nicolaus   7
Busby, Thomas   Harrison
Busdicker, Roger   Leonard
Busoni, Ferrucio   Breitkopf & Härtel
Büsser, Henri   Durand
Bussjäger & Rättig   Rättig
Bussotti, Sylvano   Ricordi, Universal
Bustini, Alessandro   De Santis
Buszin, Walter E.   Concordia
Butler, Joseph   Matthysz
Butt, Clara   Boosey & Hawkes
Butterworth, Arthur   Peters (i)
Buttet   Fezandat
Butting, Max   Peters (i)
Büttner, A.   Benjamin
Büttner, Hieronim   *see* Wietor
Button, S.J.   102, Button & Whitaker, Purday
Button & Whitaker   102, Purday, Thompson
Buxtehude, Dietrich   Broude Brothers,
   Hänssler, Ugrino
Buyten, Martin van   43
By, Oluf   Norsk Musikforlag
Byrckmann, Arnold   Baethen
Byrd, Donald   68
Byrd, William   43, 80, 91, 490, 519, East, Musical
   Antiquarian Society, Stainer & Bell,
   Vautrollier

Caccini, Francesca   Cecconcelli, Pignoni
Caccini, Giulio   532, Marescotti, Pignoni,
   Raverii, Vincenti
Cadman, Charles Wakefield   Fischer (J.),
   Galaxy, Schuberth (E.)
Cady, Chauncey Marvin   Root & Cady
Cage, John   Peters (i)
Cagnoni, Antonio   Giudici & Strada
Caifabri, Giovanni Battista   91, Fei, Mascardi,
   Mutii
Caimo, Giuseppe   Amadino
Caix d'Hervelois, Louis de   Boivin
Calcografia de' Reali Teatri   Girard
Caldara, Antonio   Bote & Bock, Roger, Sala
Caligraving   62
Calkin, Joseph   Regent's Harmonic Institution
Call, Leonhard von   Kunst- und Industrie-
   Comptoir, Mollo
Callahan, J. Will   Rossiter
Calloway, Cab   Mills
Calvin, Jean   88, Guéroult

Calvisius, Sethus   Hänssler,
Calvo, M. Fabio   Petrucci (O.)
Camagno
Camagno, Carlo   89, 92, Camagno, Rolla
Cambert, Robert   Ballard
Cambini, Giuseppe Maria (Gioacchino)   Forster,
   Sieber, Zatta
Cambio, Perissone   Gardano
Camerloher, Placidus Cajetan von   Andrez
Campagnoli, Bartolemeo   Artaria (ii)
Campano, Giovanni Andrea   Han
Campbell, Joshua   Aird
Campis, Henrico (Jannot de)   89, Buglhat
Campos, Juan Morel   Instituto de Cultura
   Puertorriqueña
Campos-Parsi, Héctor   Instituto de Cultura
   Puertorriqueña
Campra, André   44, Bailleux, Ballard, Boivin,
   Foucault, Ribou
Canada Publishing Corporation   Thompson
   (G. V.)
Canale, Floriana   Sabbio
Caneto   82
Cangiasi, Giovanni Antonio   Tradate
Canis, Cornelis   Susato
Cannabich, (Johann) Christian (Innocenz
   Bonaventura)   Falter, Götz, La Chevardière,
   Venier
Canobbio, Carlo   Marescalchi
Canstein, Ludolf Freiherr von   Schott
Canteloube, Joseph   Oiseau-Lyre
Canti, Giovanni   111, Carulli, Lucca, Ricordi
Cantone, Serafino   Tradate
Canulli   Ricordi
Capece, Alessandro   Robletti
Capell, Richard   Augener
Capital Cities Communications   Word
Capito, Wolfgang Fabricius   Apiarius
Cappi   Cappi (P.), Eder, Mollo
Cappi, Carlo   Cappi (G., P.)
Cappi, Giovanni   106, Artaria (i), Cappi
   (G., P.)
Cappi, Pietro   106, Artaria (i), Cappi, Diabelli,
   Traeg
Capponi, Giovanni Angelo   Grignani
Capra, Marcello   Boileau Bernasconi
Capricornus, Samuel Friedrich   Bencard
Capron, Henri   114, Moller & Capron
Capuzzi, Giuseppe Antonio   Zatta
Cara, Marchetto   Giunta
Carafa de Colobrano, Michele   Leduc
Carapetyan, Armen   American Institute of
   Musicology
Cardella, Frank   Balmer & Weber
Cardella, Simone   Han
Cardoso, Mánuel   Valentim de Carvalho
Carelli, Beniamino   Ricordi
Carey, Henry   Simpson
Cargill, Henry Hawley   Couse
Carisch   122
Carisch, Giovanni Andrea   Carisch
Carissimi, Giacomo   Caifabri, Choron,
   Geertsom, Mascardi
Carli
Carli, Nicolas-Raphaël   110, 515, Carli
Carlino, Giovanni Giacomo   91, 534, Gargano,
   Vitale
Carl Theodor, Elector of the Palatinate   Götz
Carmichael, Hoagy   Mills
Carmichael Music Publications   Frank
Carneyro, Cláudio   Sassetti

Caro, Annibale   Scotto
Carolan, Turlough   Neale
Caroli, Angelo Antonio   Della Volpe
Caron, Ninian (Franz P.)   Lundquist
Carpenter, John Alden   Society for the
   Publication of American Music
Carpentras, Elzéar Genet de   22, 24,
   Channey
Carr
Carr, Benjamin   Carr, Schetky
Carr, John   92, Playford
Carr, Joseph   114, Carr
Carr, Richard   92
Carr, Robert   Carr (J.), Playford
Carr, Thomas   Carr, Willig
Carrano, Andrés   Breyer
Carstens, Heinrich   87
Carter, Elliott   533, Arrow Music Press,
   Associated Music Publishers, Boosey &
   Hawkes
Cartier, Jean Baptiste   Imbault
Carulli   111
Carulli, Ferdinando   Carli, Mollo, Pleyel
Carulli, Giuseppe Antonio   Bertuzzi, Carulli
Caruso, Enrico   Feist, Schuberth (E.)
Cary, Cecilia   Shaw
Casa Editrice di Operette e Vaudevilles
   [C.E.D.O.V.]   Curci
Casals, Pablo   Broude (A.)
Casanova, Franco   Boelke-Bomart
Casati, Gasparo   Vincenti
Casati, Girolamo   Vincenti
Casella, Alfredo   Carisch, Chester, Curci,
   De Santis, Ricordi, Senart, Universal
Caslon, W.   30, 31, 98, 113, 114
Castagneri, Marie-Anne   104
Castaud   104, Guéra
Castelbarco, Count Cesare di   Scotti
Casteleyn, Matthieu   Manilius
Castellanus, Petrus   Petrucci (O.)
Castelnuovo-Tedesco   Carisch, Galaxy, Israeli
   Music Publications, Ricordi
Castiglione, Baldissare   Petrucci (O.)
Castilglioni, Niccolò   Ars Viva, Suvini Zerboni
Castil-Blaze, François-Henri   Escudier
Castro, Antonio de   30
Castro, Jean de [Jean à]   Bogard, Goulart,
   Phalèse
Castro e Ascarrega, Colonello D. Bernardo   Sala
Castrucci, Pietro   Meares, Venier
Casulana, Maddalena   Sabbio, Scotto, Tini
Catalani, Alfredo   Lucca, Ricordi
Catalani, Arturo   Sonzogno
Catel, Charles-Simon   Magasin de Musique (i)
Catoire [Katuar], Georgy   Editions Russes de
   Musique
Cattaneo, G.   Scotti
Caulfield, John   Walsh
Cavalieri, Emilio de'   Ars Viva, Mutii, Tradate,
   Vincenti
Cavalleri, Lazaro   Breyer
Cavalli, Francesco   Faber, Vincenti
Cavanni, Francesco   Micheletti
Cavazzoni, Girolamo   82, Vitali
Cavendish, Michael   East
Cavos, Catterino   Dalmas
Cavour, Benso di   Lucca
Caxton, William   Wynkyn de Worde
Cazzati, Maurizio   91, 537, Dozza, Magni,
   Micheletti, Monti, Pisarri, Sala, Silvani,
   Vincenti

CBS   Boston Music Company
CBS Songs   EMI Music-SBK
Cecconcelli, Pietro   89, Pignoni
Cecil, Sir William   Seres
Cencetti, Giovanni Battista   Ratti, Cencetti & Comp.
Cenci, Lodovico   Grignani
Centemeri, Pietro   Couse
Cerha, Friedrich   Universal
Černohorský, Bohuslav Matěj   Labaun
Cernušák, Gracian   Pazdírek
Černý [Cžerny], **Jiří** [Nigrin, Nygryn, Georg]   87
Cerone, Pietro   Gargano
Certon, Pierre   Attaingnant, Ballard, Le Roy, Moderne
Cesti, Marcantonio   Cosmerovius, Wagner (A.)
Chadwick, George Whitefield   Schmidt
Chailly, Luciano   Carisch, Zanibon
Challier   107, Birnbach
Challier, Carl August   Challier
Challoner, Neville Butler   Skillern
Chambers, William Paris   Pepper
Chambonnières, Jacques Champion, Sieur de   95, Foucault
Chandieu, La Roche   Jean II de Laon
Chandler, Francis S.   Root & Cady
Chandler & Curtiss   Root & Cady
Channey, Jean de   22, 28, 82, Granjon
Chapman, Tracy   EMI Music-SBK
Chappell   102, 120, 128, Ascherberg, Hopwood & Crew, Musical Antiquarian Society, Warner Bros.
Chappell, Frank   Metzler
Chappell, Samuel   Chappell, Cowper
Chappell, Thomas Patey   Bosworth, Chappell
Chappell, William   Chappell, Cramer
Chappell Intersong   Leonard
Charles   Magasin de Musique (i)
Charles II   Bonneüil
Charles IX   Ballard, Le Roy
Charlier de Gerson, Jean   5
Charnassé, Hélène   69
Charpentier, Gustave   Eschig
Charpentier, Marc-Antoine   Ballard
Charters, Samuel   Oak
Chase, Gilbert   Wa-Wan Press
Chasins, Abram   Fischer (J.)
Chastillon, Guillaume de   Mangeant
Chatman, Stephen   Marks
Chausson, (Amedée) Ernest   Rouart-Lerolle
Chávez (y Ramirez), Carlos (Antonio de Padua)   Belwin-Mills, Silver Burdett
Chemische Druckerey   106, Gleissner, Haslinger, Hoffmeister, Lithographisches Institut, Senefelder
Chemyn, Nicolas   *see* Chemin
Cherici, Sebastiani   Monti, Silvani
Cherubini, Luigi   Breitkopf & Härtel, Heugel, Hoftheater-Musik-Verlag, Magasin de Musique (i), Magasin de Musique (ii), Mollo, Naderman, Pleyel, Traeg
Chester, J. & W.   120, Hansen, Nordiska Musikförlaget, Schirmer (G.)
Chester, John   Chester
Chevalier, Paul Emile   Heugel
Chevardière   *see* La Chevardière
Chevrier, André   Choudens
Chevrier, Julius Gaston   Choudens
Chicago University Press   62
Chmél, J.   Bosworth
Choisnel, Gaston   Durand

Chopin, Fryderyk Franciszek   102, Brandus, Breitkopf & Härtel, Brzezina, Durand, Gebethner & Wolff, Gray (M.), Haslinger, Heinrichshofen, Hofmeister, Jürgenson, Lemoine, Lienau, Maurice, Oxford University Press, Pacini, Peters (i), Polskie Wydawnictwo Muzyczne, Ricordi, Schlesinger, Schuberth (J.), Senart, Troupenas, Wessel, Wiener Urtext Edition
Choron, Alexandre(-Etienne)   Leduc
Choudens
Choudens, Antoine   110, 120, Choudens
Chován, Kálmán   Rozsnyai
Christiné, Henri   Salabert
Christoph   Berra, Hoffmann
Christy's Minstrels   Firth, Hall & Pond
Chrysander, Friedrich   118, Handel societies
Chrzesciński, Richard   Simrock
Church   124, 126, Ditson, Presser, Root & Cady
Church, John   Meares
Church of God Publishing House   Vaughan
Church of the Nazarene   Lillenas
Chybinski, Adolf   Polskie Wydawnictwo Muzyczne
Cifra, Antonio   Magni, Poggioli, Robletti, Soldi, Vincenti, Zannetti
Cilea, Francesco   De Santis, Sonzogno
Cima, Giovanni Paolo   Mutii
Cimador, Giambattista   102, Monzani
Cimarosa, Domenico   Bailleux, Lienau, Marescalchi, Sieber, Zatta
Cimmino, G. B.   Carlino
Cipriani, Gasparo   Lorenzi
Cirker, Hayward   Dover
Cirri, Giovanni Battista   Zatta
Citkowitz, Israel   Cos Cob Press
Clapisson, (Antoine-)Louis   Escudier
Clarendon Press   Oxford University Press
Clark   Prentiss
Clark, Francis   Heptinstall, Moore
Clarke, James Paton   Nordheimer
Clarke, John   Hare, Young
Clarke, Stephen   Johnson (James)
Clarke, William   Johnson (James)
Clausetti   111, Ricordi
Clausetti, Carlo   Clausetti, Ricordi
Clausetti, Eugenio   Ricordi
Clay, Clement Comer   Gray, Sherman
Clemens (non Papa), Jacobus   Du Bosc, Phalèse, Susato
Clement VIII, Pope   Valesi
Clementi   102, Artaria (i), Bailleux, Breitkopf & Härtel, Carulli, Cramer, Dale, Erard, Hoffmeister, Imbault, Longman & Broderip, Mollo, Nägeli, Pleyel, Purday, Sauer, Sieber, Torricella, Williams (J.)
Clementi, Aldo   Suvini Zerboni
Clérambault, Louis Nicolas   44, Boivin, Castagneri
Clokey, Joseph W.   Fischer (J.)
Cloppenburch, E.   Matthysz
Clowes   103, Cowper
Clowes, William, the elder   37, Clowes, Cowper, Knight
Cluer, John   101, Meares, Walsh
Cluse   Harrison
Cobb, Thomas   Cluer, Simpson
Cobbett, Walter Wilson   Oxford University Press
Coccia, Paolo   Poggioli

Index

Cochlaeus, Johannes   Stuchs
Cock, Symon   84, 520, Remunde,
  Vissenaecken
Cockburn   Fezandat
Cockerill   Dale
Cocks, Robert   102, Augener
Cocteau, Jean   La Sirène
Coelho, Rui   Sassetti
Coghill, W.L.   Church
Cohan, George M.   125, Marks, Witmark
Cohn, Paul   Bloom
Colaço, Rey   Sassetti
Colasse, Pascal   Ballard
Colburn, William S.   116
Cole, Benjamin   101, Bickham
Cole, John   115, Benteen, Carr, Thomas
Coleman, Roger   Rastell
Coleridge-Taylor, Samuel   Ascherberg,
  Hopwood & Crew, Novello
Colin, Pierre   Moderne
Collaert, Adriaen   42
Collard, Frederick William   Clementi,
  Purday
Collins, James   Walsh
Colloredo, Count Karl   Mechetti
Colombani, Orazio   Sabbio
Colombo, Alfredo   Ricordi
Colombo, Franco   Ricordi
Colón, Braulio Dueño   Giusti
Colonna, Giovanni Ambrosio   91, Monti
  (G., P. M.), Silvani
Colonne, Edouard   Hartmann
Columba, Gianbattista   Antico
Columbia Pictures
  Entertainment   Filmtrax-Columbia
  Industries Inc   Mills
  Music Group   Belwin-Mills
  Publications   Filmtrax-Columbia
Coma, Antonio   Rossi
Comanedo, Flaminio   Tradate
Comencino, Giovanni   Rampazetto
Comettant, Oscar   Escudier
Commelin, Jerome   Tournes
Commer, Franz   Trautwein
Compañeros Alemanes   5
Compton, John   Balmer & Weber
Concordia   126
Conforti, Giovanni Luca   Mutii
Confrey, Zez   Mills
Congregation of Sacred Rites   Desclée
Connor, Dennis   103
Connor, Frank H.   Fischer (C.)
Connor, Hayden jr.   Fischer (C.)
Connor, Walter Fischer   Fischer (C.)
Conradi, August   Bote & Bock
Constantini, Fabio   Zannetti
Contino, Giovanni   Scotto
Contojo d'Arti e d'Industria   Kunst- und
  Industrie-Comptoir
Converse, Frederick S.   Gray (H. W.)
Cooke, Benjamin   101, Cross, Johnson (John),
  Meares
Cools, Eugène   Eschig
Cooper, Gerald M.   Purcell Society
Cooper, William   Thomas
Coots, J. Fred   Remick
Copland, Aaron   American Composers Alliance,
  Arrow Music Press, Boosey & Hawkes, Cos
  Cob Press, Schirmer (E. C.), Silver Burdett,
  Summy-Birchard
Coppenneur, Jean-Herman   Andrez

Coppini, Aquilino   Tradate
Coprario, John   Windet
Corbetta, Francesco   95, Bonneüil, Monti (G.)
Cordier, Baude   Billaudot
Corelli, Arcangelo   Bailleux, Boivin, Caifabri,
  Cooke, Cross, Editio Musica Budapest,
  Foucault, Mascardi, Meares, Monti
  (G., P. M.), Mutii, Roger, Sala, Silvani,
  Walsh, Wright, Zatta
Coressi, Gheorghe   Honterus
Corigliano, John   Schirmer (G.)
Corkine, William   Snodham
Cornelius, Peter (i)   Aibl, Fürstner, Kahnt,
  Schlesinger, Schott
Cornet, Séverin   Goulart, Plantin
Coronaro, Gaetano   Lucca
Corrette, Michel   Foucault
Corri, Domenico   103, Corri, Johnson (J.)
Corsi, Giuseppe   Caifabri
Corteccia, (Pier) Francesco   Gardano
Cortellini, Camillo   Rossi
Cortot, Alfred   Curci, Senart
Corvinus, Christopher   see Rab
Cos Cob Press   127, Arrow Music Press
Cosmerovius [Cosmerov, Kosmerovius],
  (Stanislaus) Matthäus   88
Cossoni, Carlo Donato   Monti
Costa Amaro, Manuel de   Breyer
Costallat   110, 120, Billaudot, Janet & Cotelle,
  Richault
Coste, G.   Moderne
Costeley, Guillaume   83, Ballard, Le Roy
Coster   43
Cottrau, Guglielmo   Cottrau, Girard
Cottrau, Teodoro   111, Girard
Coutlhard, Jean   Waterloo
Couperin, François   49, Ballard, Boivin,
  Oiseau-Lyre, Rozsnyai
Couperin, Louis   Ballard
Cour, Mathon de la   Le Clerc (C. N.)
Courvoisier, Walter   Drei Masken Verlag
Couse, Adam   125
Cousin, Jean   Ballard
Cousineau, George   104
Covens, Jan   Witvogel
Coventry & Hollier   102, Novello, Preston
Coverdale, Myles   23, Gough
Coward, Noël   Chappell
Cowell, Henry   127, Arrow Music Press,
  Associated Music Publishers, Langinger,
  New Music, Peters (i), Presser, Silver
  Burdett
Cowper, Edward   35, 541
Cox, John   Simpson, Thompson
Cozzolani, Chiara Margarita   Vincenti
CPP-Belwin   Filmtrax-Columbia
Cragg, Timothy   Peters (ii)
Cramer, J. B.   102, Artaria (i), Breitkopf &
  Härtel, Chappell, Erard, Handel societies,
  Metzler, Mollo, Nägeli, Napier, Pleyel,
  Regent's Harmonic Institution, Sieber, Traeg
Cranz, August   110, Diabelli
Cras   Senart
Crawford, Ruth   Broude (A.), New Music
Craxton, Harold   Associated Board of the Royal
  Schools of Music
Creake, Bezaleel   Cluer
Crecquillon   Du Bosc, Goulart, Susato
Creston, Paul   Belwin-Mills, Ricordi, Schirmer
  (G.), Silver Burdett
Crivelli   Vincenti

Croce, Giacomo   Fougt
Croce, Giovanni   Fougt, Kauffmann, Phalèse, Vincenti
Croes, Henri-Jacques de   Le Clerc (J. P.)
Croft, William   Meares
Cromberger, Juan   Pablos
Crosby, Fanny   Biglow & Main
Crosby, Harry B.   Schmidt
Cross, Thomas   44, 49, 101, Carr (J.), Cooke, Meares, Playford, Walsh, Wright, Young
Crosse, Gordon   Oxford University Press
Crotch, William   Handel societies
Crouch. Frederick Nicholls   Hutchings & Romer
Crowell, Collier & Macmillan   Curwen
Crozier, St George B.   Nordheimer
Crüger, Johannes   87, Hänssler, Runge
Cruickshank, Ralph   Berandol.
Crumb, George   Belwin-Mills, Peters (i)
Csaszar, György   Treichlinger
Cserépfalvi, Imre   Editio Musica Budapest
Cullen, John   Cross, Playford, Walsh, Young
Cummings, W.H.   Purcell Society
Cummings, William   Peters (ii)
Curci 122
Curmer 35
Currier, Nathaniel 115
Curtis & Truax   Church
Curwen 103
Czech Music Fund   Panton
Čžerny, Carl   Artaria (ii), Cocks, Diabelli, Giudici & Strada, Haslinger, Hofmeister, Mechetti, Peters (i), Richault, Ricordi, Troupenas
Čžerny, Jiří   *see* Černý
Čžerny, Joseph   Cappi, Eder
Czövek, Erna   Magyar Kórus

Dachser, Jacob   Ulhart
Daggett, E.A.   Waters
Daguerre 61
Dahl, Ingolf   Broude (A.), Society for the Publication of American Music
Dalayrac, Niclos-Marie   Erard
Dalberg, Johann Friedrich Hugo, Freiherr von   Götz
D'Albert, Eugene   Bote & Bock, Breitkopf & Härtel, Brockhaus, Drei Masken Verlag, Forberg
Dale, Joseph   Dale, Napier
Dallapiccola, Luigi   Ars Viva, Broude (A.), Carisch, Suvini Zerboni, Universal, Zanibon
Dall'Aquila, Marco   Petrucci (O.)
Dalla Volpe, Lelio   *see* Della Volpe
D'Almaine, Thomas   59, 102, Cowper, Goulding
Dalmas
Dal Molin, Armando   64, 66, 67
Dal Molin, Cecil   64, 66, 67
Damiano da Moilli   5
Damm, Gustav   Steingräber
Damrosch, Walter   Warner
Damse, Joseph   Brzezina, Klukowski
Dana, William Henry   Pepper
Dancla, (Jean Baptiste) Charles   Schott
Dandrieu, Jean-François   Ballard, Boivin, Foucault
Danfrie, Philippe   24, 28, Le Bé
D'Anglebert, Jean-Henri   95, Foucault
Daniel-Lesur   Billaudot
Danyel, John   East
Danzi, Franz   56, Senefelder
Daquin, Louis-Claude   Castagneri

Dargomizhsky, Alexander Sergeyevich   Bessel, Editions Russes de Musique, Gutheil, Stellovsky
Dart, Thurston   Stainer & Bell
Da Sabio brothers   Antico
Daser, Ludwig   Widmanstetter
Dataland 68
Date, Henry   Hope
Dathenus, P.   89, Manilius
Daubmann   Osterberger
Dauphin [Dauphiné]   Fezandat
Davantes, Pierre   88, Du Boys
Davaux, Jean Baptiste   Bailleux
David, Félicien   Heugel, Kistner & Siegel
David, Johann Nepomuk   Breitkopf & Härtel
Davidovsky, Mario   Belwin-Mills, Marks
Davidson, George Henry 102
Davies, Peter Maxwell   Boosey & Hawkes, Schott
Davis, Anthony   Schirmer (G.)
Davis, David   Clementi
Davis, Jessie Bartlett   Bloom
Davison, Duncan   Ascherberg, Hopwood & Crew
Davy, John   Gilfert
Dawkins, Henry 113
Dawson, William 113
Day, John   39, 89, 532, Day (R.), Granjon, Seres, Windet
Day, Richard   89, 91, Day (J.), Windet
Day, Stephen 94
Dean, Roger Publishing Co.   Lorenz
Dearmer, Percy   Curwen
De Baussen, Henri 95
De Bèze, Théodore   *see* Bèze
Debroux, J.   Senart
Debussy, (Achille) Claude   122, 543, Choudens, Durand, Fromont, Elkan-Vogel, Hamelle, Georges Hartmann, Jobert, La Sirène, Napoleão, Peters (i), Wiener Urtext Edition
Décombe   Janet & Cotelle
De Costa Amaro   Monguillot
De Fesch, Willem   Fortier
De'Franceschi   *see* Franceschi
Degen, Georg   Gebauer
De Giosa, Nicola   Clausetti
De'Giunti Modesti   *see* Giunta
Degli Antoni, G.B.   Micheletti, Monti
Degli Antoni, Giovanni Antonio   Sabbio
Degli Silvestri   Vitali
Dehn, Siegfried   Peters (i), Schott
Deiss, Lucien   Salabert
De Koven, Reginald   Schuberth (E.)
De Laet, Jean 84
Delahante, Julius   Erard
Delange, Hermann François   Andrez
Delannoy, Marcel   Eschig, Heugel, Senart
Délano, Jack   Instituto de Cultura Puertorriqueña
Delavaux   Foetisch
Delbanco, O.H.   Lose
Delhaise, Nicolas-Joseph   Andrez
Delibes, Léo   Choudens, Heugel
Delius, Frederick   Universal
Del Lago, Giovanni   Scotto
Della Viola, Alfonso   Buglhat
Della [Dalla] Volpe, Lelio 98, Monti
Dello Joio, Norman   Associated Music Publishers, Belwin-Mills, Fischer (C.), Marks, Ricordi, Silver Burdett
Delloy, Henri-Louis   Pleyel
Del Monacom Giorgio   Ricordi

Index

Deltour   Le Clerc
Del Tredici, David   Boosey & Hawkes
Del Turco, Giovanni   Pignoni
Delusse, Mme   44–5, 46
Delville, Jean   Editions Russes de Musique
Demantius, (Johannes) Christoph   Kauffmann
De Marchi [Demarchi], Arturo   Breyer, Giudici
   & Ştrada
Demets, Eugène   Eschig
De Meza   Horneman & Erslev
Denotkin   Stellovsky
Dentice, Fabrizio   Tini
Dentice, Scipione   Carlino
Depanis, Giuseppe   Lucca
Dering, Richard   Phalèse, Playford
Deroullède, Jean-Pierre   La Chevardière
Derriey   35
Dervaux, François   Billaudot
De Santis   112
Desclée
Desclée de Brouwer   Desclée
Desponsatione BVM, Justinus à   Bencard
Dessau, Paul   Bote & Bock, Breitkopf & Härtel,
   Deutscher Verlag für Musik, Peters (i),
Destouches, André Cardinal   Ballard
Det Nordiske Forlag   Kgl. Hof-Musikhandel
Deutsche Händel-Gesellschaft   Handel societies
Deutscher Verlag für Musik   119, Handel
   societies
Devienne   Imbault, Magasin de Musique (ii)
D'Heere, Lucas   Manilius
D'Herbois   Andrez
Diabelli, Anton   106, 528, Artaria (i), Càppi,
   Haslinger, Hoftheater-Musik-Verlag,
   Maisch, Mechetti, Mollo, Pennauer, Sauer,
   Traeg, Weigl
Diamond, David   Arrow Music Press, Peer-
   Southern, Society for the Publication of
   American Music
Diaz, Porfirio   Wagner (A.)
Dibdin, Charles   Bland & Weller, Davidson,
   Thompson
Dicey, Cluer   Cluer
Dicey, William   Cluer
Dickens, Charles   Chappell
Dickson, James A.   Hewitt
Diémer, Louis(-Joseph)   Durand
Diepenbrock, Alphons   Alsbach
Dietrich, Sixt   Rhau
Dillard, Michel   La Sirène
Dilliger, Johann   Forckel
Dimitrescu, Constantin   Gebauer
D'India, Sigismondo   see India, Sigismondo d'
D'Indy, Vincent   see Indy, Vincent d'
Dinicu, Grigoras   Gebauer
Diruta, Agostino   Caifabri, Grignani, Robletti
Diruta, Girolamo   Vincenti
Disney, Walt   Hansen (C.)
Distin, Henry   Boosey & Hawkes, Pepper
Distin, John   102
Distler, Hugo   Bärenreiter, Breitkopf & Härtel
Ditson C.H.   Ditson
Ditson, Oliver   116, 124, Benteen, Church,
   Firth, Hall & Pond, Geib, Gordon, Graupner,
   Gray (M.), Howe, Lee & Walker, Mason
   Bros., Miller & Beacham, Moller & Capron,
   Peters (ii), Prentiss, Presser, Russell, Willig
Dittersdorf, Carl Ditters von   Hummel, Sieber,
   Venier
Dittmar, Friedrich August   Gerstenberg, Gutheil
Dizi, François Joseph   Pleyel

Doan, Thomas C.   Balmer & Weber
Doane, William H.   Biglow & Main
Doblinger   107, Pazdírek, Universal
Dobson, Thomas   114
Döhler, Theodor   Ricordi
Dohnanyi, Ernö   Doblinger, Rózsavölgyi,
   Simrock
Doina   122
Dolet, Etienne   Beringen
Doliarius, Hieronim   see Wietor
Dommange, Jean   Durand
Dommange, Marcel   Durand
Dommange, René   Durand
Donaghy, Patrick   Silver Burdett
Donajowski   118, Eulenburg
Donaldson, Walter   Remick
Donangeli, Girolamo   Gardano
Donati, Ignazio   Vincenti
Donato, Baldassare   Scotto
Donato, Girolamo   Petrucci (O.)
Donatoni, Franco   Suvini Zerboni
Doni, Antonfrancesco   Scotto
Donizetti, Gaetano   515, 521, 534, Boosey &
   Hawkes, Breitkopf & Härtel, Cottrau,
   Escudier, Girard, Lienau, Lucca, Mechetti,
   Pacini, Ricordi,.Schlesinger, Schonenberger,
   Schott
Doolittle, Amos   113, 114
Doppler, Ferenc   Treichlinger
Dorati, Antal   Mills, Suvini Zerboni
Dorico, Valerio   82, 89, 499, Barré, Blado,
   Giunta, Petrucci (O.)
Dorico, Luigi   Barré, Dorico
Dorsey, Jimmy   Robbins
D'Ortigue   see Ortigue, Joseph d'
Dostal, Nico   Heinrichshofen, Sikorski
Dotesio, Luis E.   113 Unión Musical Española
Dotesio Paynter, Ernesto   Unión Musical
   Española
Dotzauer, (Justus Johann) Friedrich   Peters (i)
Dougliss, Dan H.   Atwill
Dover   127
Dow, Daniel   Johnson (James)
Dowland, John   Adams, Bärenreiter, Barley,
   Chappell, East, Faber, Musical Antiquarian
   Society, Short, Windet
Dowland, Robert   Adams
Doyer   Alsbach
D'Oyly Carte   Chappell
Dozza, Evangelista
Dozza, Pietro   91, Dozza
Drach, Peter   Wenssler
Draeseke, Felix (August Bernhard)   Kahnt
Drăgoi, Sabin V(asile)   Morawetz
Dragoni, Giovanni Andrea   Mutii, Valesi
Dramstad, Leif   Norsk Musikforlag
Dreher, Rudolph   87, Dreher
Dreiklang-Verlag   Drei Masken Verlag
Dreililien, Verlag   Birnbach
Drei Masken Verlag   119
Dressel   Ries & Erler
Dreyfus, Louis   120, 125, Chappell, Harms
Dreyfus, Max   120, Chappell, Harms
Drieberg, Friedrich von   Trautwein
Driessler, Johannes   Bärenreiter, Breitkopf &
   Härtel, Tonger
Drinkman, Gerrit   Roger
Druschetzky, Georg   Torricella
Drusina, Benedict   Eichorn
Dubois, William   114, Paff
Du Bosc, (Guillaume) Simon   88, Guéroult

Du Boulay   Andrez
Dubourg, Matthew   Manwaring
Du Boys, Michel   88
Du Caurroy, François-Eustache   Ballard
Ducci, Carlo   Lucca
Duchambge, Pauline   Pleyel
Du Chemin [Chemyn]**, Nicolas**   84,
   Attaingnant, Ballard, Haultin, Le Bé, Phalèse
Du Chesne de Quercu, Guillaume   Attaingnant
Dufaut & Dubois   Schonenberger
Dufour, Sélim-François   Brandus
Dufresne   Salabert
Dugué, L'Abbé   Fournier
Dugué, Lucrèce   Ballard
Dukas, Paul   Durand
Duke, Vernon   Broude Brothers, Editions
   Russes de Musique
Du Mont, Henri   Ballard
Du Mont, Louise   Farrenc
Duni, Egidio   La Chevardière, Sieber
Dunkl, János Nepomuk   Rózsavölgyi
Dunn, James P.   Fischer (J.)
Dunn, John   69
Dunstable, John   Peters (i)
Duparc, Henri   Rouart-Lerolle
Duphly, Jacques   Castagneri
DuPlessis (du Plessy), F.   49, Foucault
Dupont, Paul   Eschig, La Sirène'
Du Pré [de Pratis, a Prato]**, Jean (Larcher)**   88
Durand   122
Durand, Jacques Massacrie   Durand, Rouart-
   Lerolle
Dürer, Albrecht   Formschneider
Duruflé. Maurice   Durand
Du Ry, Antoine   86
Dussek, Jan Ladislav   102, Breitkopf & Härtel,
   Corri, Cramer, Dale, Erard, Magasin de
   Musique (ii), Mollo, Pleyel, Sieber, Traeg
Dutilleux, Henri   Billaudot
Du Tour, Henri   *see* Van den Keere, Henrik
Duval, François   Foucault
Duval, Peters   115
Du Verdier, Antoine   Fezandat
Duverger, Eugène   34
Duverger, M.   37
Duvernoy, Victor   Brandus, Pleyel
Dvořák, Antonín   107, 120, Benjamin, Bote &
   Bock, Hudební Matice, Lengnick, Novello,
   Simrock, Starý, Supraphon
Dydo, Stephen   73
Dyer, Louise B.M.   *see* Hanson-Dyer, Louise

Earhart, Will   Ditson
Earsden, John   Snodham
East, Michael   East, Musical Antiquarian Society
East [Easte, Este]**, Thomas**   91, 516, Barley,
   Haultin, Lownes, Playford, Snodham,
   Vautrollier
Eastburn (pseud.)   Winner
Eastland, George   East
Eberl, Anton (Franz Josef)   Kunst- und
   Industrie-Comptoir
Eberle & Co., Josef   Universal
Eccard, Johannes   Hänssler, Hantzsch, Rhetus
Eccles, Henry   Foucault
Eccles, John   Cross
Eckel, Mathias   Moderne
Eckstein, Friedrich   Wiener Philharmonischer
   Verlag
Edelmann
Eder, Joseph   106, Hoffmeister, Sauer

Ediçaõ Brasília de Nicolini e Pó   Vitale
Edinthon family   Ballard
Editio Musica Budapest   122, Magyar Kórus,
   Rózsavölgyi, Taborszky
Edition M.U.   Urbánek
Editions Basart   Alsbach
Edition Schwann   Peters (i)
Editions Continental   Gerig
Editions et Productions Théâtrales
   Chappell   Joubert
Editions Françaises de Musique   Billaudot
Editions Russes de Musique   122, Gutheil
Editora Fermata do Brasil   Napoleão
Editorial Boileau   Boileau Bernasconi
Editorial Orfeo Tracio   Unión Musical Española
Edlund, Lars   Nordiska Musikförlaget
Edstrom, Everett 'Leonard'   Leonard
Edstrom, Harold 'Hal'   Leonard
Edwards, Julian   Church
Efesiu, Petru   Pann
Effinger, Cecil   65, 66
Egenolff, Christian   23, 86, Moderne
Egk, Werner   Schott
Egressy, Béni   Wagner (J.)
Eichorn, Andreas   86
Eichorn, Johann   86, Bergen
Eichner, Ernst   Heina, Sieber
Eielsen, Elling   Augsburg
Eimert, Herbert   Breitkopf & Härtel
Einem, Gottfried von   Bote & Bock, Universal
Eisler, Hanns   Breitkopf & Härtel, Deutscher
   Verlag für Musik, Peters (i)
Eitner, Robert   Breitkopf & Härtel
Elgar, Sir Edward   120, Ascherberg, Hopwood
   & Crew, Ashdown, Breitkopf & Härtel,
   Novello, Williams
Eliad, N.I.   Gebauer
Elias, William Y.   Israel Music Institute
Elizabeth I   East, Vautrollier
Elkan, Henri   Elkan-Vogel
Elkan-Vogel   127, Elkan, Presser
Elkin & Co.   Novello, Schmidt
Ellington, Duke   Belwin-Mills, Mills
Ellis, E. F.   126
Elsner, Jósef Antoni Franciszek   Klukowski
Elzevier, Ludwig   Matthysz
EMB   Editio Musica Budapest
Emerich, Johann [Emericus, Johannes]   6, 20,
   Moilli, Hamman
Emery, F.J.   Schmidt
Emile   Fezandat
EMI Music-SBK   Francis, Day & Hunter
Emmert, Johann Joseph   Mayer
Enders, Karl Wilem   111
Endoviensis, Christophe van   *see* Remunde
Endter   87, Wust
Engel, Carl   124, Boston Music Company,
   Schirmer (G.)
Engel, Lehman   Arrow Music Press
Engelmann (Leipzig engraver)   51, 57, 58, 128,
   Wagner (A.)
Engländer, Ludwig   58, 128, Schuberth (E.)
English, Walter   Barnhouse
English Bach Society   Bach-Gesellschaft
English Handel Society   Bach-Gesellschaft
Enna, August   Kgl. Hof-Musikhandel
Enoch, William   Costallat
Enoch & Co.   110, Ashdown, Schmidt
Enoch Frères   110, Janet & Cotelle
Enschedé, Izaac   30, 31, 98, 113
Enschedé, Johannes   28, 31, 113

Enterprise   Robbins
Eos   Simrock
Eösze, László   Editio Musica Budapest
Erard   110, Bailleux, Richault
Erato   Costallat
Erb, Donald   Presser
Erbach, Christian   Meltzer
Erdöd, Ferdinand Count Palffy
   von   Lithographisches Institut
Erdődy, Count   Pleyel
Erfurt, Andreas   87, Schönig
Erk, Ludwig   Merseburger
Erkel, Ferenc   Rózsavölgyi, Treichlinger,
   Wagner (J.)
Erler, Hermann   110, Ries & Erler
Ernst, Alfred   Hartmann
Ernst, Heinrich Wilhelm   Litolff
Erslev, Emil   Horneman & Erslev
Eschig, Max(imilian)   122, La Sirène, Schirmer
   (G.), Schott
Escudier   110, 120, Ricordi, Schlesinger
Escudier, Léon   Escudier, Leduc
Eslava, Hilarión   Unión Musical Española
Espinosa, Antonio de   Pablos
Este, Thomas   *see* East
Esterhazy, Pál   Pleyel
Estienne, Robert   Attaingant, Le Bé
Estocart, Paschal de l'   *see* L'Estocart, Paschal de
Etler, Alvin   Broude (A.)
Ett, Kaspar   Falter
Eulenburg, Ernst (Emil Alexander)   118, 534,
   Schott
Eurich, Friedrich Emanuel   Haslinger
European American Music Corporation   127,
   European American
European American   Jerona
Evangelical Lutheran Church   Augsburg
Evans, Dorothy   43
Ewer   102, Gray, Novello
Ewer, John Jeremiah   Ewer
Excell, E. O.   Biglow & Main
Excelsior   Gerig
Expert, Henri   Senart
Eybler, Joseph Leopold   Haslinger, Sauer,
   Traeg
Eyrich, Johann   Forckel
Eysler, Edmund S.   Doblinger, Weinberger

Faber, Benedikt   Hauck
Faber, Heinrich   Hantzsch, Neuber
Faber, Nicolaus
Faber & Faber   Faber
Faber Music   120, Schirmer (G.)
Fabri, Stefano   Geertsom
Fabriano, Giacomo   Scotto
Fabricius, Jacob Christian   Samfundet til
   Udgivelse af Dansk Musik
Fabrizio, Costanzo   Tebaldini
Fahrbach, Philipp   Mechetti
Faignient, Noé   Goulart
Fain, Sammy   Mills
Fairlight   72
Faisandat, Michel   *see* Fezandat
Falconi, D. Giacomo   30
Falconieri, Andrez   Robletti
Falconio, Placido   Sabbio
Falkener, Robert   31, 98, Fougt
Fall, Leo(pold)   Doblinger, Drei Masken Verlag,
   Weinberger
Falla, Manuel de   Chester, Durand, Eschig
Falter, Macarius (Franz de Paula)   106, Falter

Falter & Sohn   56, 58, Schott, Senefelder, Sidler
Famous   125
Famous Players – Lasky Corporation   Famous
Farina, Carlo   Bergen
Farina, Salvatore   Ricordi
Farinelli (Carlo Broschi)   Fortier (B.), Ricordi
Farnaby, Giles   East
Farrenc, (Jacques Hippolyte) Aristide
Farwell, Arthur   127, Wa-Wan Press
Fasch, Carl Friedrich   Trautwein
Faulds, David   116
Fauré, Gabriel   122, Durand, Hamelle, Heugel
Fay, W. Rodman   Schirmer (G.)
Fayolle, François   Choron
Fazer   120
Fazer, K. G.   Fazer
Feder, Jean   Gebauer
Fei
Fei, Andrea   91, Fei
Fei, Giacomo   91, Caifabri, Fei
Fei, Michel'angelo   Fei
Feist, Leo   125, Balmer & Weber, Big 3, Francis,
   Day & Hunter, Thompson (G. V.)
Feist, Leonard   Associated Music Publishers,
   Feist
Felciano, Richard   Schirmer (E. C.)
Feldman, B. & Co.   EMI Music-SBK, Francis,
   Day & Hunter
Feldman, Morton   Peters (i), Universal
Fell, John   Oxford University Press
Fellerer, Karl Gustav   Volk
Fellowes, Edmund H.   Stainer & Bell
Felsztyna, Sebastian z   *see* Sebastian z Felsztyna
Felton, William   Johnson (John)
Fenaruolo, Hieronimo   Gardano
Ferguson, Howard   Associated Board of the
   Royal Schools of Music
Fernandes, Armando Jose   Sassetti
Fernández, Lorenzo   Vitale
Ferneyhough, Brian   Peters (i)
Ferrabosco, Alfonso   Snodham
Ferrari, Benedetto   Erard
Ferretti, Giovanni   Scotto
Ferroni, Vincenzo   Giudici & Strada
Fesca, Friedrich   Mechetti, Richault
Festa, Costanzo   532, Gardano, Petrucci (O.),
   Scotto
Festa, Felice   Ricordi
Fétis, François-Joseph   Farrenc, Fezandat, Janet
   & Cotelle, Litolff, Schott, Troupenas
Feuchtinger   Pustet
Févin, Antoine de   Antico
Feyerabend, Sigismund   87, Eichorn, Rab
Fezandat [Faisandat], Michel   84, Ballard,
   Gorlier, Granjon
Fiala, Joseph   Heina
Fibich, Zdeněk   Hudební Matice, Starý,
   Supraphon, Urbánek
Field, John   Erard, Pacini
Fields, Dorothy   Mills
Fields, Lew   Witmark
Figgins, V.   37
Figueroa, Narciso   Instituto de Cultura
   Puertorriqueña
Figulus, Wolfgang   Hantzsch
Filiasi, Lorenzo   Sonzogno
Filippini, Stefano   Monti
Filippo, Giovanni di   Giunta
Filippone
Filippone, Domenico   128, Filippone
Fillmore

Fillmore, Henry   Fischer (C.)
Filmtrax   Filmtrax-Columbia, Novello
Filmtrax-Columbia
Filtz, Anton   Venier
Finck, Henry T.   Ditson
Fine, Irving   Society for the Publication of
  American Music
Finé, Oronce   Attaingnant
Finger, Godfrey   Walsh
Finke, Fidelio Friedrich   Breitkopf & Härtel
Finnissy   Universal
Fioravanti, Valentino   Carli
Fiorillo, Federigo   Robletti, Sieber
Fiorino, Gasparo   Scotto
Fine, Oronce   Attaingnant
Fiot, Augustus   115, Fiot & Meignen
Fiot & Meignen
Firth, Hall & Pond   116, Hewitt
Firth, John   Benteen, Couse, Ditson, Firth, Hall
  & Pond, Riley
Fischer, A.E.   Benjamin
Fischer, Anton   Löschenkohl
Fischer, Carl   124, 126, Feist, Fillmore,
  Langinger
Fischer, Edwin   Curci
Fischer, Fred   Rossiter
Fischer, J(oseph)   124, Belwin-Mills
Fischer, Signor   Sieber
Fischer, Stephen   Peters (i)
Fisher, William Arms   Ditson
Fisk, Jim (pseud.)   Barnhouse
Five, The   Bessel
Flammer, Harold Inc.   Shawnee
Flaxland, Gustave-Alexandre   110, Durand
Flecha, Mateo   Moderne
Fleetwood, Anthony   115
Fleischer, Friedrich Gottlob   Hoffmann
Fleischmann, J. M.   30, 31, 520
Fleming, John   114
Fleming, Robert   Thompson (G. V.)
Flesch, Carl   Ries & Erler
Floridia, Pietro   Feist
Flotow, Friedrich   Bote & Bock, Brandus,
  Giudici & Strada, Lucca
Flurschütz, Caspar
Flurschütz, Regina (née Kreuzer)   88, Flurschütz
Fodor, Joseph   Zatta
Foerster, Josef Bohustav   Hoffmann, Hudební
  Matice, Starý, Urbánek
Foetisch, Charles   122
Fog, Dan   120
Foggia, Francesco   Caifabri, Mutii
Foley, Charles   125
Foll, Ferdinand   Lauterbach & Kuhn
Follett   126
Fontaine   Artaria (i)
Fontana, Giovanni Battista   Mutii
Fontanelli, Alfonso   Baldini
Foote, Arthur   Schmidt
Forberg, August Robert   107
Forbes, John   92
Forckel, Andreas
Ford, Thomas   Windet
Forkel, Johann Nikolaus   Bärenreiter, Boosey &
  Hawkes, Peters (i), Schwickert
Formica, Leonard   Cosmerovius
Formica, Matthäus   Cosmerovius
Formschneider [Andreae, Grapheus],
  Hieronymus [Jeronimus]   23, 83, 86, Berg,
  Egenolff, Ott
Forster

Förster, Emanuel Aloys   Hoffmeister, Kunst-
  und Industrie-Comptoir, Traeg
Forster, Georg   Berg, Egenolff, Petreius
Forster, Josef   Rättig
Forster, Sebastian   Faber
Forster, William (i)   49, 101, Forster
Forsyth, Cecil   Fischer (J.)
Forsyth, W.O.   Whaley, Royce & Co.
Fortier, B.   101, Phillips
Fortner, Wolfgang   Schott
Fortress Press   Augsburg
Foss, Hubert J.   Oxford University Press
Foss, Lukas   Fischer, Society for the Publication
  of American Music
Foster, Stephen   116, Benteen, Ditson, Firth,
  Hall & Pond, Peters (ii), Waters, Willig
Fotino, Dionisie   Pann
Foucault, Henry   95, Baussen, Boivin, Ribou
Foucquet, Pierre-Claude   Foucault
Fougt, Henric   30, 31, 98
Foulis, Andrew   541
Fournier, Pierre-Simon (le jeune)   27, 29, 31,
  98, 520, Attaingnant, Gando, Haultin
Fox, Sam   125, Keith, Prowse
Foxley, Eric   69
Françaix, Jean   Billaudot, La Sirène, Schott
Franceschi [de' Franceschi]   89
Francesco Canova da Milano   Wyssenbach
Franchetti, Baron Alberto   Ricordi
Francis, Day & Hunter   120, EMI Music-SBK
Franck, César   Ditson, Escudier, Hamelle,
  Hartmann, Heugel, Joubert
Franck, Dave   Werlein
Franck, Johann Wolfgang   Stern
Franck, Melchior   Forckel, Hänssler, Hauck
Franck, Theodor   20, 80, Wenssler
Franco, Nicolò   Gardano
François I   Attaingnant, Channey
Frank   Boston Music Company
Frank
Frank Music Corp.   125, Frank
Franklin, J.   43, 113
Franz, Robert   Kistner & Siegel, Leuckart,
  Whistling
Franzini, F.   Fei, Mutii
Franzini, G.D.   Fei, Robletti
Fränzl, Ignaz   Götz, Venier
Freitas, Frederico de   Sassetti
Frellon, Jean   Du Boys
French, Jacob   Thomas
Frere, Walter Howard   Plainsong & Mediaeval
  Music Society
Frescobaldi, Girolamo   43, Borboni, Cecconcelli,
  Kahnt, Phalèse, Robletti, Soldi, Vincenti,
  Zannetti
Fresneau, Henry   Moderne
Freundthaler, Kajetan   Traeg
Frey, Jacques-Joseph   110, Magasin de Musique
  (ii), Richault
Frey, M.A.   Steingräber
Fricker, Peter Racine   Schott
Friderich, Frantz   Eichorn
Friedel, Walter   Steingräber
Friedheim, J.   Prentiss
Friedlein, Rudolf Fryderyk   111, Gebethner &
  Wolff
Friedman, Ignacy   Krzyżanowski
Friedman, Leo   Bloom, Rossiter
Friedman, Ludwig   Drei Masken Verlag
Friedrich II of Zollern, Bishop   Aich
Frieländer, Julius   Peters (i)

Friml, Rudolf   Warner
Frisner, Andreas   Sensenschmidt
Fritzsch, E. W.   Kistner & Siegel
Froehlich, C. W. & Co.   Bote & Bock
Frommel, Hermann   Ries & Erler
Fromont   122, Hartmann, Jobert
Frosch, Conrad   Nenninger
Frosch, Johannes   22, 26, Kriesstein
Froschauer the elder, Christoph   Wyssenbach
Frost   Broude (A.)
Fuentes y Asenjo   Unión Musical Española
Führer, Robert (Jan Nepomuk)   Berra
Fuleihan, Anis   Peer-Southern
Fuller, Francis   Russell
Fuller, William   Russell
Füllsack, Zacharias   Van Ohr
Fumigalli, Adolfo   Ricordi
Funcke, Friedrich   Stern
Fürstliche Druckerei   87, Forckel
Fürstner   119, Schott
Fürstner, Adolf   110, Fürstner, Meser
Fust   4
Fux, Johann Joseph   Van Ghelen
Fyner, Conrad   5

Gabrieli, Andrea   Gardano, Merulo, Tini
Gabrieli, Giovanni   Gardano, Hänssler
Gabrielli, Domenico   Monti
Gäch, Johann   Wagner (M.)
Gach, Maria   *see* Wagner, Maria
Gade, Neils (Wilhelm)   Fog, Hansen (W.),
   Kistner & Siegel, Lose, Samfundet til
   Udgivelse af Dansk Musik, Wessel
Gaffurius   7, 10, 503
Gage Publishing Ltd.   Thompson (G.)
Gagliano, Giovanni Battista da   Pignoni
Gagliano, Marco da   Magni, Marescotti, Pignoni
Gaines, Samuel   Fischer (J.)
Gál, Hans   Universal, Wiener Philharmonischer
   Verlag
Galaxy   120, 127, Augener, Galliard
Galilei, Vincenzo   41, 89, Gardano, Giunta,
   Marescotti, Scotto
Galison, Lawrence   Kalmus
Galitsin   *see* Golitsïn, Prince Nikolay Borisovich
Gall, Jan Tomasz   Krzÿzanowski
Galle, Philip   42
Gallet, François   Bogard
Galli, Amintore   Sonzogno
Galli, Sandro   Carisch
Galliard   120, Augener, Stainer & Bell, Williams
Galliard, Karl   Challier
Galliculus, Johann   Rhau
Gallus, Udalricus   Han
Galuppi, Baldassare   De Santis, Israeli Music
   Publications, Venier
Gamble, John   Cross
Ganche, Edouard   Oxford University Press
Gando
Gando, Nicolas   98, Gando
Gange, George & Co.   Dale
Gänsbacher, Johann Baptist   Haslinger
Gantez, Annibal   Métru
Garamond, Claude   Le Bé
Gardane   Gardano
Gardano   39, 519, 526, 527, Barré, Merulo,
   Phalèse, Raverii, Scotto, Vincenti
Gardano, Angelo   Gardano, Magni, Raverii
Gardano, Antonio   23, 83, 89, 502, 503, 539,
   Buglhat, Cecconcelli, Gardano, Rampazetto,
   Scotto

Gargano, Giovanni Battista   91
Garibaldi, Giuseppe   Lucca
Garland   73, 118
Garnier   Guéra
Gaspardini, Gasparo   Micheletti
Gasparini, Francesco   Bortoli, Sala
Gastoldi, Giovanni Giacomo   Amadino, Bogard,
   Gardano, Kauffman, Lomazzo, Matthysz,
   Phalèse
Gaucquier, Alard du   Plantin
Gaudet   Salabert
Gaul, Harvey   Fischer (J.)
Gaultier   95
Gautier, Théophile   Escudier
Gaveaux   104
Gazzaniga, Giuseppe   Zatta
Gebauer
Gebauer, Alexis   111, Gebauer
Gebethner, Gustaw Adolf   Friedlein, Gebethner
   & Wolff
Gebethner & Wolff   111
Gebrüder Hug   111, Hug
Ged, William   541
Geertsom, Jan van
Gehrman   120 Hirsch
Geib   114
Geissler, Fritz   Breitkopf & Härtel, Peters (i)
Gelbrun, Artur   Israel Music Institute
Gelinek, Josef   Maisch, Mollo, Sieber
Gellert, Christian Fürchtegott   Löschenkohl
Geminiani, Francesco   Bremner, Cross,
   Huberty, Johnson (John), Manwaring,
   Meares, Phillips, Roger, Torricella
Genée, Franz   Weinberger
Genet, Elzéar   *see* Carpentras
Gennrich, Friedrich   537, Hänssler
Gentili, Giorgio   Roger
Gentilucci, Armando   Ricordi
Genuino, Francesco   Carlino
Genzmer, Harald   Ries & Erler
Georgeon, Henriette   Pleyel
Georg-Friedrich-Handel Gesellschaft   Handel
   societies
Gérard, Edmond   Heugel
Gerber, Ernst Ludwig   Peters (i)
Gerhard, Roberto   Oxford University Press
Gerig   Volk
Gerig, Hans   119, Gerig
Gering, Ulrich   Higman
Gerlach, Catharina   *see* Berg, Catharina
Gerlach [Gerlatz]**, Dietrich** [Theodor]   28, 84,
   Berg, Kauffmann
Gerle, Hans   83
German Historical Institute   Volk
Germer, Heinrich   Litolff
Gero, Jhan   Scotto
Gerrish, Samuel   43, 113
Gershwin, George   Chappell, Harms, Remick,
   Tilzer, Warner
Gerstenberg, Johann Daniel   111, Gutheil
Gerster, Ottmar   Peters (i)
Gervaise, Claude   Attaingnant, Susato
Gervinus, Gottfried   Handel societies
Gesellschaft der Autoren, Komponisten und
   Musikverleger   Weinberger
Gesellschaft für Musikforschung   Bärenreiter
Gesner, Conrad   Scotto
Gessner the younger, Andreas   Wyssenbach
Gesualdo, Carlo, Prince of Venosa   91, Baldini,
   Carlino, Deutscher Verlag für Musik,
   Gardano, Ugrino, Vitale

Getty, Gordon   Presser
Gevaert, François-Auguste   Lemoine
Ghedini, Giorgio Federico   Carisch, Ricordi,
   Zerboni
Ghera, Chrétien [Johann] Gottlieb   Guéra
Ghersem, Géry   Geertsom
Ghislanzoni, Antonio   Ricordi
Ghizzolo, Giovanni   Lomazzo, Vincenti
Giaccio, Orazio   Carlino
Giacomo di Andrea   *see* Fei, Giacomo
Giamberti, Giuseppe   Robletti
Giardini, Felice (de)   Sieber
Gibbons, Orlando   43, 94, Adams, Musical
   Antiquarian Society
Gideon, Miriam   Boelke-Bomart
Gigault, Nicolas   Métru
Gilbert, Anthony   Schott
Gilbert, Henry   Wa-Wan Press
Gilbert, Jean   Curci, Drei Masken Verlag
Gilbert & Sullivan   120, Bosworth, Chappell
Gilchrist, William Wallace   Schuberth (E.)
Gilfert, George   114, 115
Gillier, Jean Claude   Ribou
Gillier, Pierre   Bonneüil
Gillray, James   Napier
Gilman, John Ward   113
Ginastera, Alberto   128
Ginn   126
Gionichi, Giovanni   Mane
Giordani, Paolo   Suvini Zerboni
Giordani, Tommaso   Guéra
Giordano, Umberto   De Santis, Sonzogno
Giovannelli, Ruggiero   Mutii, Scotto, Vincenti
Girard   Cottrau
Girard, Giuseppe   111, Girard
Girard, Narcisse?   Escudier
Girod, Etienne   Carli, Escudier, Leduc
Giudici & Strada   111
Giuliani, Mauro   Kunst- und Industrie-
   Comptoir, Mollo, Ricordi
Giunta [Giunti; Zonta; Junta; Juncta; de' Giunti
   Modesti]   81
Giunta, Antonio   Antico, Giunta
Giunta, Filippo   Giunta, Rampazetto
Giunta, Jacomo di Biagio   Antico, Dorico,
   Giunta
Giunta, Jacques (Jacopo di Francesco)   Du Ry,
   Giunta
Giunta, Luc'Antonio   81, Antico, Emerich,
   Giunta, Petrucci
Giusti, Pedro
Glarean   499, 500, 502
Glaser   Famous
Gläser, Franz   Trautwein
Glazunov, Alexander Konstantinovich   Belyayev
Gleichauf   Pustet
Gleissner, Franz   55, 57, 58, André, Senefelder
Glinka, Mikhail Ivanovich   Editions Russes de
   Musique, Fürstner, Gutheil, Muzïka,
   Stellovsky
Glover, Sarah   Curwen
Gluck, Christoph Willibald Ritter von   Artaria
   (i), Bärenreiter, Bureau d'Abonnement
   Musical, Challier, Richault, Simpson,
   Trattner
Gluck, Johann   87
Glynn, W.C.   Prentiss
Godard, Benjamin   Metzler
Godbid, Anne   Godbid, Playford
Godbid, William   40, Harper, Playford,
   Snodham

Godefroi   34
Goeb, Roger   American Composers Alliance
Goehr, Alexander   Schott
Goetschius, Percy A.   Ditson
Goetz, Hermann   Kistner & Siegel
Golden West Music Press   Langinger
Goldmann, Friedrich   Deutscher Verlag für
   Musik
Goldmark, Karl   Weinberger
Goldmark, Rubin   Wa-Wan Press
Goldoni, Carlo   Zatta
Golinelli, Stefano   Ricordi
Golitsïn [Galitzin], Prince Nikolay Borisovich
   Pleyel
Gombart   110
Gombart, G.   106
Gombart, H.   55
Gombert, Nicolas   499, Attaingnant, Du Bosc,
   Gardano, Moderne, Ott, Scotto, Susato
Gomes, Carlos   Bevilacqua, Lucca, Napoleão
Gomis   Troupenas
Gomółka   Sennewald
Gonzaga, Chiquinha   Bevilacqua
Goodman, Benny   Robbins
Goodwin & Tabb   Novello
Goossens, Eugene   Chester
Gorczycki, Grzegorz Gerwazy   Polskie
   Wydawnictwo Muzyczne, Sennewald
Gordon, Stephen T.   115, Geib, Riley
Gorlier, Simon   88, Ballard, Fezandat
Gorton, William   Young
Gosizdat   Muzïka
Goss, Sir John   Novello
Gossec, François-Joseph   Bailleux, Götz,
   La Chevardière, Sieber
Gossett, Philip   Ricordi
Gotthard, Johann Peter   Doblinger, Pazdírek
Gottron, Adam   Pustet
Gottschalk, Louis Moreau   Edelmann, Escudier,
   Firth, Hall & Pond, Gray (M.)
Gottsched, Johann Christoph   Breitkopf &
   Härtel
Götz, Johann Michael   105, Schott
Götze, Heinrich   Litolff
Goudimel, Claude   Ballard, Choron, Du Bosc,
   Goulart, Le Roy, Le Royer, Tournes
Gough, John   Rastell
Goulart, Simon   Le Royer
Gould, John E.   Fiot & Meignen, Gordon
Gould, Morton   Belwin-Mills, Mills, Schirmer
   (G.)
Goulding   102, Cowper
Gounod, Charles (François)   Bote & Bock,
   Choudens, Lucca, Metzler, Schott
Gouy, Jacques de   Le Chevalier
Gow, Nathaniel   Penson & Robertson, Purdie
Grabner, Hermann   Kahnt
Graça, Fernando Lopes   Sassetti
Gradenwitz, Peter   Israeli Music Publications
Graener, Paul   Eulenburg, Litolff, Simrock,
   Universal
Graf   Guéra
Grafe, Curt   Bosworth
Graffer, Katharina   Haslinger
Graffer, Rudolf   Hoffmeister
Grafische Industrie   62
Grafton, Richard
Grafulla, Claudio S.   Pepper
Graham, George Farquhar   Wood
Gram, Hans   Thomas
Granada   Novello

Grancini, Michel'Angelo   Camagno
Grandi, Alessandro (i)   Vincenti
Granjon, Robert   24, 27, 28, 88, Ballard,
   Channey, Fezandat, Gorlier, Guéroult, Le
   Bé, Plantin
Granozio   Giudici & Strada
Grapheus, Hieronymus   *see* Formschneider
Graue, Charles Louis   Augener
Graulich, Günter   Hänssler
Graupner, Christoph   Graupner
Graupner [Graubner]**, (Johann Christian)**
   Gottlieb   114, Hagen, Hewitt
Gravelot, Hubert (François) Bourgignon-
   Bickham
Gray, H.W.   126, Belwin-Mills
Gray, Matthias   115, Atwill, Sherman
Graziani, Bonifazio   Caifabri, Geertsom, Mutii
Grazioli, Giovanni Battista   Zatta
Grechaninov, Alexander   Editions Russes de
   Musique
Green, B.   10, 94
Green, James N.   Lowe & Brydone
Green, Ray   Arrow Music Press
Greenberg, Noah   Oxford University Press
Greene, Maurice   Harrison, Wright
Grefinger, Wolfgang   Aich
Gregori, Giovanni Lorenzo   Sala
Grell, Eduard   Trautwein
Grensser, Alfred   Nagel
Grétry, André   Castagneri, Frey, La
   Chevardière, Pleyel
Grieg, Edvard (Hagerup)   Hals, Horneman,
   Peters (i), Warmuth
Griepenkerl, Friedrich Conrad   Peters (i)
Griffes, Charles Tomlinson   Schirmer (G.)
Griffin   Regent's Harmonic Institution
Griffo, Francesco, da Bologna   22, Petrucci (O.)
Grignani, Lodovico   91, Poggioli
Grimm, Sigmund   520, Grimm & Wirsung,
   Ulhart
Grimm, Vince   Treichlinger
Grimm & Wirsung   82
Grinzweil, Norbert   Rózsavölgyi
Grofé, Ferde   Robbins
Grosheim, Georg Christoph   Peters (i)
Grosz, Wilhelm   Universal
Grua, Paul   Ricordi
Grubb, John Steuart   Penson & Robertson
Grubmeni (pseud.)   *see* Ricordi, Giulio
Grund, Franz   Haslinger
Grunewald, Louis   116
Gruenberg, Louis   Cos Cob Press
Gruner, Elisabeth   Brockhaus
Gruninger, J.   7
Grus, Lucien   Lemoine
Grutter, Ida   Aich
Gryphius, Sebastian   Granjon
Guami, Giuseppe   Amadino
Guarini, Battista   Baldini
Guedron, Pierre   Ballard, Stansby
Guelfi, Antonio   Pignoni
Guéra   104, Hoffmeister
Guerini, Francesco   Fortier
Guéroult, Guillaume   88, Beringen, Du Bosc,
   Granjon
Guerra, Bartolomeo   Tebaldini
Guerrero, Francisco   Gardano, Phalèse, Vincenti
Guerson, Guillaume [Guillermus]   20, Michel de
   Toulouse
Guglielmi, Pietro Alessandro   Marescalchi, Zatta
Guidi, Giovanni Gualberto   111, 118, Ricordi

Guido, Giovanni Antonio   Foucault
Guignon, Jean Pierre   Castagneri
Guillemain, Louis-Gabriel   Le Clerc
Guilmant, Alexandre   Durand
Guión, Eugenio   Breyer, Monguillot
Gulf & Western   Famous
Gümbel, Paul   Bärenreiter
Gumm, Harold   Von Tilzer
Gumpelzhaimer, Adam   Hänssler, Schönig
Gunn, Barnabus   Broome
Günther, Carl Wilhelm   Hofmeister
Günther, E.   Friedlein
Gurckhaus, Carl Friedrich Ludwig   Kistner &
   Siegel
Gurlitt, Cornelius   Litolff
Gurlitt, Willibald   Bärenreiter
Gurskalin   Stellovsky
Gustavus III   Fougt
Gutenberg, Johann   80
Gutheil [Gutkheyl']   122, Editions Russes de
   Musique, Stellovsky
Guthrie, Woody   Oak
Gutkheyl'   *see* Gutheil
Gutknecht, Christoff   Hergot
Gutknecht, Friderich   Hergot
Guttentag, J.   Trautwein
Guyatt, Billy   Paling
Guyenet   Ballard, Baussen
Guyot (de Châtelet) [Castileti], Jean   Susato
Guzmán, Eustaquio   Niemeyer
Gwynn Publishing Company   Williams (G.)
Gyrowetz, Adalbert   André, Gombart, Imbault,
   Kunst- und Industrie-Comptoir, Maisch,
   Mollo, Sieber, Traeg

Hába, Alois   Universal
Haberl, Franz Xaver   Pustet
Habert   Fezandat
Hacquardt, Carolus   Matthysz
Hadow, William Henry   Oxford University
   Press
Haendler, A.W.   International
Haenlin, Gregor   Meltzer
Haffner, Johann Ulrich   105, Matthysz
Hageman, Richard   Galaxy
Hagen, P. A. von   Gilfert
Hagen, S.A.E.   Horneman & Erslev
Hägg, Jacob Adolf   Kgl. Hof-Musikhandel
Hahn, Reynaldo   Heugel
Hahn, Ulrich   *see* Han
Haken, Lippold   69
Hakenberger, Andress   Hünefeld
Håkonsen, Petter   Hals, Norsk Musikforlag
Halbreiter, Otto   Falter
Hale, Philip   Ditson
Halévy, (Jacques-François) Fromental   Brandus,
   Lucca, Schlesinger, Schott
Halffter, Ernesto   Eschig, Universal
Hall, M.   Corri
Hall, Pauline   Norsk Musikforlag
Hall, Thomas   68
Hall, William   Ditson, Firth, Hall & Pond, Riley
Haller, Jan   81, Ungler, Wietor
Hall-Mack Co.   Rodeheaver
Hals, Brødrene   Hansen (W.), Norsk
   Musikforlag, Warmuth
Hals, Karl   120, Hals
Hals, Petter   120, Hals
Halvorsen, Johann   Hals, Hansen (W.)
Haly, E.F.J.   Lose
Hamal, Jean-Noël   Andrez

Hamel, Keith 73
Hamelle 122
Hamelle, Julien Hamelle
Hamilton, Clarence G. Ditson
Hamilton, Iain Schott
Hamlisch, Marvin Chappell
Hamman, Johann 6, 80, 81, Emerich, Scotto
Hammerschmidt, Andreas Bergen, Hänssler
Hammerstein, William Boston Music Company
Hammerstein Music & Theater
  Company Boston Music Company
Han [Hahn], Ulrich 5, 80, Planck
Han, Weigand, widow of Feyerabend
Hanche, Anton Marius Norsk Musikforlag,
  Warmuth
Handel, George Frideric 31, 101, 118, 515,
  520, 527, 534, Bärenreiter, Blake, Bland,
  Breitkopf & Härtel, Cluer, Cooke, Coventry
  & Hollier, Cross, Deutscher Verlag für
  Musik, Editio Musica Budapest, Garland,
  Handel societies, Harrison, Haslinger,
  Hewitt, Meares, Nägeli, Novello, Preston,
  Randall, Roger, Simrock, Skillern, Walsh,
  Wright, Wright & Wilkinson
Handel societies
Handl, Jacob 87, Černý, Susato
Handy, W. C. 125
Hanna, John Anglo-Canadian Music Publishers'
  Association
Hansard, Thomas Curson 14
Hansen 120, Chester, Hals, Horneman,
  Horneman & Erslev, Kgl. Hof-Musikhandel,
  Lose, Nordiska Musikförlaget, Norsk
  Musikforlag, Schirmer (G.), Warmuth
Hansen, Charles 126
Hanser-Strecker, Peter Schott
Hanson, Howard (Harold) Summy-Birchard
Hanson, Joseph ('Jeff') B. Oiseau-Lyre
Hanson, Margarita M. Oiseau-Lyre
Hanson-Dyer, Louise Oiseau-Lyre
Hänssler 119, American Institute of
  Musicology
Hantzsch, Andreas 86, Hantzsch
Hantzsch, Georg Hantzsch
Harbison, John Associated Music Publishers,
  McGinnis & Marx
Hardoy, P.J. Breyer
Hare
Hare, Elizabeth ('the elder') Hare, Simpson
Hare, John Hare, Playford, Walsh, Young
Hare, Joseph 101, Hare, Walsh
Hargail 127
Harlow, W.M. Balmer & Weber
Harms Chappell, Miller Music, Robbins,
  Warner Bros.
Harms, Gottlieb Ugrino
Harms, Thomas B(rush) 125, Francis, Day &
  Hunter, Harms
Harper, John S. Schott
Harper, Thomas Godbid, Playford, Snodham
Harrach Pleyel
Harris, Charles K. Peer-Southern, Rossiter,
  Witmark
Harris, Frederick 128
Harris, Roy Arrow Music Press, Associated
  Music Publishers, Cos Cob Press, Langinger,
  Mills, Schirmer (G.)
Harrison
Harrison, James 101, 114, Harrison
Harrison, Lou New Music
Harriss, C.A.E. Whaley, Royce & Co.

Harrods Ricordi
Harsányi, Tibor Eschig, Heugel, Senart
Hart, Andro 89, 528
Hart, Philip Young
Härtel, Gottfried Christoph Breitkopf & Härtel
Härtel, Hermann 107, Breitkopf & Härtel,
  Jung
Hartknoch, Johann Friedrich 105
Hartmann, C.P.H. Kallmeyer
Hartmann, Emil Hansen (W.)
Hartmann, Ernst Universal
Hartmann, Federico Guillermo Breyer
Hartmann, Friedrich Eichhorn
Hartmann, Fritz Bosworth
Hartmann, Georges 110, Fromont, Heugel
Hartmann, Heinrich Hauck
Hartmann, Johan Peter Emilius Hansen (W.),
  Lose, Samfundet til Udgivelse af Dansk
  Musik
Harvey, Jonathan Novello
Hase, Hellmuth von Breitkopf & Härtel
Hase, Martin von Breitkopf & Härtel
Hase, Oskar von Breitkopf & Härtel
Haslinger 107, Artaria (i), Diabelli, Lienau,
  Mechetti, Mollo
Haslinger, Tobias 107, Haslinger
Hasse, Johann Adolf Venier
Hasse, Karl Litolff
Hassler, Hans Leo Bärenreiter, Kauffman
Hassler, Kaspar Kauffman
Hässler, Johann Wilhelm Schwickert
Hastings, Thomas Mason Bros.
Hatton, John Liptrot Leader & Cock
Hatzfeld, Emile Ashdown, Lucas
Haubenstock-Ramati, Roman Universal
Hauck, Justus 87
Haueisen, Wolfgang Nicolaus André
Hauer Lienau, Universal
Haultin, Pierre 88, Attaingnant, Hoffgreff
Hauptmann, Moritz Bach-Gesellschaft, Kistner
  & Siegel, Peters (i)
Hausegger, Sigmund von Forberg
Haussmann, Valentin Kauffmann, Mense
Hautt, David Dreher
Hauville, Antoine de Gorlier
Hawes, William Regent's Harmonic Institution
Hawkes, Oliver Harris
Hawkes, Ralph 115, Boosey & Hawkes
Hawkins, A. 31, 43
Hawkins, Sir John Novello
Hawthorne, Alice Winner
Hayden, George Wright
Hayden, Scott Stark
Haydn (Franz) Joseph 49, 493, André, Artaria
  (i), Bailleux, Bland, Böhm, Breitkopf &
  Härtel, Challier, Clementi, Cramer, Eder,
  Erard, Falter, Forster, Gombart, Guéra,
  Heckel, Heinrichshofen, Henle, Hewitt,
  Hoffmeister, Hummel, Imbault, Janet &
  Cotelle, La Chevardière, Lausch, Leduc,
  Longman & Broderip, Marescalchi,
  Musikalisches Magazin, Napier, Peters (i),
  Pleyel, Riley, Schott, Sieber, Simrock,
  Sønnichsen, Thomson, Torricella, Traeg,
  Venier, Wiener Urtext Edition, Zatta
Haydn, Michael Hoffmeister, Mayer, Traeg
Hayes, Philip Thompson
Hayn, Gabriel Petreius
Haynes, John C. Ditson
Hays, Alfred Birchall
Healy, Patrick J. Lyon & Healy

Index

Hebel, Kurt   69
Hecht   Nordheimer
Heckel   117
Heckel, Johann Adam   Heckel
Heckel, Karl Ferdinand   110, Heckel
Heckenast, Gusztáv   111
Hedbom, Johan Carl   111, Lundquist
Heina, François-Joseph   104
Heinicke, Paul   Associated Music Publishers
Heinrich, Nikolaus   *see* Henricus
Heinrichshofen   110, 119, Trautwein
Heinsheimer, Hans (Walter)   119, Schirmer (G.),
   Universal
Heinze, Gustav   Whistling
Heise, Peter Arnold   Hansen (W.)
Held, Johann Theobald   Enders
Hèle, George de la   Plantin
Helfert, Vladimir   Pazdírek
Helicon Music Corporation   European
   American
Heller, Stephen   Brandus, Litolff, Schlesinger,
   Wessel
Hellmesberger, Georg (i)   Pennauer‧
Hellmesberger, Josef   Lauterbach & Kuhn,
   Universal
Heltai, Gáspár   Hoffgreff
Hemberg   Nordiska Musikförlaget
Hempel, Günter   Breitkopf & Härtel, Deutscher
   Verlag für Musik
Hempsted, Henry N.   116
Henchheimer, Evelyn   Bloom
Henderson, William James   Ditson
Henle
Hennings, Henrik   Kgl. Hof-Musikhandel
Henri II   Attaingnant, Ballard, Fezandat, Le
   Roy
Henri III   Le Roy
Henri IV   Ballard, Le Roy
Henricus [Heinrich], **Nikolaus**   87, Berg (A.)
Henricus, Susanna (née Berg)   Henricus
Hensel, Walther   Bärenreiter
Henselt, Adolf   Wessel
Hentschel E.J.   Merseburger
Hentzschel, Johann   Runge
Henze, Hans Werner   Schott
Heptinstall, John   28, 94, Hudgebut, Moore,
   Pearson
Herbert, G.R.   Lyon & Healy
Herbert, Victor   Schuberth (E.), Warner Bros.,
   Witmark
Herder, Johann Gottfried   Hartknoch
Herfurth, C. Paul   Boston Music Company
Hergot [Herrgott], **Hans**   86, Wachter
Hergot, Kunegunde   Hergot, Wachter
Hering, Alexander   Klemm
Heritage Music   Lorenz
Hermil, Antonio   Marescalchi
Hérold, (Louis Joseph) Ferdinand   Cottrau,
   Erard
Herrer, Michael   Nenninger
Herrmann, Bernard   Broude Brothers
Herrmann, Hugo   Sikorski
Hermann, Michael   Honterus
Herrmann, Peter   Deutscher Verlag für
   Musik
Herron, James   Keith, Prowse, Longman &
   Broderip
Hertman, Corneille   Haultin
Hertzka, Emil   119, Universal
Hertzog, Johann   Hamman
Hervé [Ronger, Florimond]   Sonzogno

Herz, Henri   Giudici & Strada, Gray (M.),
   Pennauer, Ricordi, Schott, Troupenas
Herz, Jacques Simon   Schonenberger
Herzmansky, Bernhard jr.   Doblinger
Herzmansky, Bernhard, sr.   Doblinger,
   Universal
Herzogenberg   Rieter-Biedermann
Heuberger, Richard   Bosworth, Universal
Heugel   110, 120, Escudier, Fromont,
   Hartmann, Leduc, Presser
Hewitt, James   114, Carr, Hewitt
Heyer   Peters (i)
Hicks, Peggy Glanville   Oiseau-Lyre
Hientzsch, Johann Gottfried   Trautwein
Hiesse, Jehan   Granjon, Guéroult
Higden, RanulF   Wynkyn de Worde
Higgins, Adoniram Judson   Higgins
Higgins, H(iram) M(urray)   116
Highland Music Press   Langinger
Higman, Jean   6, 81
Hildebrand, Christian   Van Ohr
Hill, Edward Burlingame   Society for the
   Publication of American Music, Wa-Wan
   Press
Hill, Henry   102, Monzani
Hiller, Ferdinand   Kistner & Siegel
Hiller, Johann Adam   Breitkopf & Härtel,
   Lauterbach & Kuhn, Leuckart, Senff,
   Simrock
Hiller, Lejaren   66
Hillner, Georg   Peters (i)
Hilmar, Franz   Hoffmann
Hime   103
Hindemith, Paul   534, Schott, Universal, Wiener
   Urtext Edition
Hinnenthal-Verlag   Bärenreiter
Hinrichsen, Carla   Peters (i)
Hinrichsen, Evelyn   Peters (i)
Hinrichsen, Hans-Joachim   Peters (i)
Hinrichsen, Henri   Peters (i)
Hinrichsen, Henry Hans   Peters (i)
Hinrichsen, Max   120 Peters (i)
Hinrichsen, Walter   Peters (i)
Hirsch, Abraham   111–3, Gehrman,
   Lundquist
Hitchcock, Benjamin   125
Hoboken, Anthony van   Schott
Hochfeder, Kasper   Haller
Hoddinott, Alun   Oxford University Press
Hodsoll, William   Bland, Purday
Hodson, William   102, Lavenu, Power
Hoe   541
Hofbauer, Carl   Weinberger
Hofer, Andreas   Mayer
Hoffding, (Niels) Finn   Samfundet til Udgivelse
   af Dansk Musik
Höffer, Paul [Hofgreff]   Litolff
Hoffgreff, György   86
Hoffmann   Foetisch, Charles
Hoffmann, Adolf   Kallmeyer
Hoffmann, Alfred   Kahnt
Hoffmann, Jan   111, Berra, Hoffmann
Hoffmann, Jaromir   Berra, Hoffmann
Hoffmannová, Emilie (née Berra)   Berra,
   Hoffmann
Hoffmeister, Franz Anton   106, Artaria (i),
   Bland, Eder, Guéra, Haslinger, Hoffmann,
   Hofmeister, Huberty, Peters (i), Pleyel,
   Whistling
Hofhaimer, Paul   Aich, Oeglin, Schoeffer
Hofmann, Josef   Krzyżanowski

Index

Hofmann, Heinrich   Ries & Erler
Hofmeister, Friedrich   107, Challier, Wagner
   (A.), Whistling
Hoftheater-Musik-Verlag   106, Haslinger
Hogg, James   Thomson
Höhe, Musikalisches Magazin auf der   Spehr
Hohenleitter   Huberty
Hohenzollern, Friedrich von   Ratdolt
Hoiby, Lee   Ricordi
Holborne, Antony [Anthony]   Barley, Short
Holden, Smollet   103, Thomas
Hole, William   43, 94
Holer, Jakob   Kunst- und Industrie-Comptoir
Holle, Ludwig   Kallmeyer
Höller, Georg   87, Nenninger
Höller, Georg Adam   Nenninger
Höller, Karl   Sikorski
Höller, Maria Margaretha   Nenninger
Hollier, John   Coventry & Hollier, Lucas,
   Novello, Preston
Holliger, Heinz   Ars Viva
Holm, Mogens Winkel   Samfundet til Udgivelse
   af Dansk Musik
Holmboe, Vagn   Hansen (W.), Samfundet til
   Udgivelse af Dansk Musik
Holst, Gustav   Curwen, Faber, Novello,
   Oiseau-Lyre, Stainer & Bell
Holt, Hosea E.   Silver Burdett
Holt, Simeon ten   Universal
Holyoke, Samuel   Thomas
Holzbauer, Igaaz Jakob   Götz, Venier
Homeyer & Co., Charles W.   Schmidt
Homolya, István   Editio Musical Budapest
Honegger, Arthur   Eschig, Foetisch, Hansen
   (W.), Salabert, Senart
Honterus, Johannes   86
Hook, James   Hewitt, Preston, Thompson
Hope   126, Biglow & Main
Hopkins, Edward John   89, Novello
Hopkinson, Francis   113, 114, Aitken
Hopkinson, Joseph   Gilfert
Hopyl, Wolfgang   5, Higman
Horák, Václav   Hoffmann
Hordisch, Lucas   Faber
Horn, Charles Edward   Power
Horn, Karl Friedrich   Birchall
Hornbostel, Erich M(oritz) von   Drei Masken
   Verlag
Horneman, Christian Frederik Emil   120,
   Hansen (W.), Horneman & Erslev
Horneman, Johan Ole Emil   Horneman,
   Horneman & Erslev
Horneman & Erslev   113, 120, Hansen (W.),
   Horneman
Hoste da Reggio   Scotto
Hotteterre, Louis   Ballard, Boivin
Houtmart, Guillaume   Higman
Hovhaness, Alan   Broude Brothers, Israeli
   Music Publications
Hovland, Egil   Norsk Musikforlag
How & Parsons   Davidson
Howard, Ellis R.   Stainer & Bell
Howard, John M. & Co.   Ascherberg, Hopwood
   & Crew
Howarth, George   Davidson
Howe, Elias   115
Howe, Frank   Anglo-Canadian Music
   Publishers' Association
Hoyland, Vic   Universal
Huber, Hans   Hug
Huber, James H.   Faulds

Huber, Klaus   Ars Viva, Bärenreiter
Huber, Nicolaus A.   Bärenreiter
Huberty, Anton [Huberti, Antoine]   104,
   106, Artaria (i), La Chevardière, Sieber,
   Torricella
Hucher, Antonio   89, Buglhat
Hudební Matice   122, Supraphon
Hudgebut, John
Hué, Georges (Adolphe)   49, Rouart-Lerolle
Hug
Hug, Jakob Christoph   Hug, Nägeli
Hug, Kaspar   Hug, Nägeli
Hughes   Williams (G.)
Hughes, Anselm   Plainsong & Mediaeval Music
   Society
Hughes, Hugh   37
Hughes, Rupert   Ditson
Hullah, John   Novello
Hüllmandel, Nicolas-Joseph   Götz
Hume, Tobias   Windet
Hummel   105, Plattner, Pleyel, Schmitt, Welcker
Hummel, Johann Nepomuk   100, 103, Artaria
   (i), Boosey & Hawkes, Cramer, Farrenc,
   Haslinger, Hoftheater-Musik-Verlag, Kunst-
   und Industrie-Comptoir, Maisch, Peters (i),
   Schlesinger, Schonenberger, Thomson,
   Traeg
Humperdinck, Engelbert   Brockhaus, Ries &
   Erler, Schott
Humphries, J.S.   Wright
Hünefeld, Andreas   88
Huneker, James Gibbons   Ditson
Hunnis, William   Short
Hünten, Franz   Schonenberger, Schott
Husa, Karel   Associated Music Publishers
Hussla, Victor   Sassetti
Hutchings, Charles L.   Hutchings & Romer,
   Leader & Cock
Hutchings & Romer   120
Hutchison, Edward   Bloom
Huyn, Didier   Du Pré
Hyde, Frederick A.   Sherman
Hyde, Frederick Augustus   Clementi

Iberia Musical   Boileau Bernasconi
Ibert, Jacques   Billaudot, Durand, Heugel,
   Oiseau-Lyre
Illan Melody Press   Israeli Music Publications
Illuminato da Torino   Bortoli
Il Verso, Antonio   Franceschi
Imbault, Jean-Jérôme   104, Janet & Cotelle
Imbrie, Andrew   Shawnee Press
India, Sigismondo d'   Amadino, Gardano,
   Robletti, Tradate
Indy, Vincent d'   Ditson, Durand, Hamelle,
   Heugel, Magni, Oiseau-Lyre, Rouart-
   Lerolle, Senart
Infantas, Fernando de las   Scotto
Ingegneri, Marć Antonio   Baldini
Inghelbrecht, Désiré-Emile   Eschig, Senart
Inghirani   Niemeyer
Institute for Studies in American Music   A-R
   Editions
Institute of Renaissance and Baroque
   Music   American Institute of Musicology
Instituto de Cultura Puertorriqueña
Instituto Español de Musicología
   International   122, 127
Ireland, John   Chester, Williams
Isaac, Heinrich   83 Aich, Formschneider,
   Grimm & Wirsung, Oeglin, Ott

Index

Isouard, Nicolo   Haslinger, Magasin de Musique (ii), Troupenas
Israeli Association of Composers   Israeli Music Publications
Israeli Music Publications   122
Israel Music Institute
Ives, Charles   127, 536–7, Arrow Music Press, Associated Music Publishers, Boelke-Bomart, Langinger, New Music, Peer-Southern, Peters (i), Presser, Summy-Birchard

Jacchini, Giuseppe Maria   Monti, Silvani
Jäcklin, Jakob   Henricus
Jackson, William   Roberts
Jacobs-Bond, Carrie   Boston Music Company
Jacomo Ungaro   20, 532, Petrucci (O.)
Jacquet of Mantua   Gardano, Moderne, Scotto
Jacquot, Jean   Billaudot
Jaeger, A.J.   Novello
Jager, Robert   Marks
Jahn, J.J.   Trattner
Jahn, Otto   Bach-Gesellschaft
Jahnn, Hans Henny   Ugrino
Jakob, Gunther   Labaun
Jambe de Fer, Philibert   88, Du Boys
James, Henry   61
James I   Allde, Day
Janáček   Bärenreiter, Hudební Matice, Panton, Supraphon, Universal, Urbánek
Janequin, Clément   83, Attaingnant, Ballard, Gardano, Moderne, Oiseau-Lyre, Susato, Wyssenbach
Janet, Pierre-Honoré   Janet & Cotelle
Janet & Cotelle   110, Imbault, Magasin de Musique (i), Troupenas
Janet Frères   Janet & Cotelle, Leduc
Jänichen, Arturo   Carisch
Janiczek, Julius   Bärenreiter
Jannon, Jean   Le Bé
Jansa, Leopold   Maisch
Janssen, Joannes   43
Jansz, J.   Matthysz
Januszowski, Jan Lazarzowicz   Wietor
Jaques-Dalcroze, Emile   Rouart-Lerolle, Senart
Jarnach, Philipp   Lienau
Jatho-Verlag   Ries & Erler
Jean-Aubry, Georges   Chester
Jean II de Laon   88, Le Royer
Jefferson, Gene   Bloom
Jelen, A.   Hoffmann
Jenkins, John   Faber
Jeppesen, Knud   Hansen
Jerona
Jessell, Leon   Birnbach
Jevíčský   Černý
Jewell, Fred   Barnhouse
Ježek   Hudební Matice
Joachim, Joseph   Kistner & Siegel, Krzyżanowski, Litolff
Joanne de Colonia   23
Jobert   Fromont
Jochum, Otto   Böhm
Jöde, Fritz   Kallmeyer
Johann VI the elder, Count   Rab
Johannes Petrus de Lomatio   10
Johanning, Julius   Ewer
Johannot, François   André
Johansen, David Monrad   Norsk Musikforlag
John IV   Valentim de Carvalho
Johner, Dominicus   Pustet
Johnson, Hunter   Galaxy

Johnson, James   103
Johnson, John   101, Bremner, Cooke, Phillips, Walsh, Wright
Johnson, John, widow of   Johnson (John), Longman & Broderip
Johnson, T. Ruddiman   Lowe & Brydone
Johnston, John   Longman & Broderip
Johnston, Thomas   113
Joiris, Andrez
Jolas, Betsy   Heugel
Jolivet, André   Billaudot, Durand, Heugel
Jollie, Samuel C.   Atwill
Jommelli, Nicolò   Bureau d'Abonnement Musical, La Chevardière, Venier
Jones, Edward   94
Jones, Robert   Windet
Jones, W. Bryan   Keith, Prowse
Joplin, Scott   125, Stark
Jordan, Sverre   Norsk Musikforlag
Joseph II   Artaria (i), Trattner
Josquin Desprez   82, Antico, Choron, Giunta, Grimm & Wirsung, Ott, Petrucci (O.), Simrock, Susato
Joubert, (Martin-)Celestin   122, Brandus
Joubert, J.   Senart
Joubert, John (Pierre Herman)   Novello
Joubert, Robert André   Joubert
Jouhaud, S.   Ricordi
Joyce, Archibald   Ascherberg, Hopwood & Crew
Judici, Nicolò de   Antico
Jullet, Germaine (née Attaingnant)   Attaingnant
Jullet, Herbert   Attaingnant
Jullien & Co.   59
Juncta   see Giunta
Jung, P.L   127, Schmidt
Junta   see Giunta
Juon, Paul   Lienau
Jürgenson [Yurgenson], Pyotr Ivanovich   107, 122, Forberg, Gutheil, Pazdírek

Kabalevsky, Dmitry   Leeds, Sikorski, Weintraub
Kaetz, Peter   Remunde
Kagel, Mauricio   Universal
Kahl, Rachael Beatty   Boston Music Company
Kahn, Gus   Remick
Kahnt, Christian Friedrich
Kaiser-Phil Gernhart   Famous
Kaizen   10
Kalbfleisch, John   Shaw
Kaldenbach, Christoph   Mense
Kalkbrenner, Friedrich Wilhelm   Clementi, Diabelli, Girard, Plattner, Pleyel, Troupenas
Kallmeyer
Kallmeyer, Georg   119, Kallmeyer
Kálmán, Emerich   Curci, Drei Masken Verlag, Weinberger
Kalmus, Alfred   119, 127, Universal, Wiener Philharmonischer Verlag
Kalmus, Edwin F.   119
Kaminske, Heinrich   Bärenreiter, Litolff
Kammel, Antonín   Venier
Kania, Emmanuel   Sennewald
Kanne, Friedrich   Lithographisches Institut
Kant, Immanuel   119, Hartnoch
Kappeller, Josef Anton   Kunst- und Industrie-Comptoir
Kapsberger, Johann Hieronymus   43, Soldi
Karczag & Wallner   Doblinger
Kargel, Sixt   Eichorn
Karkoschka, Erhard   Bärenreiter
Kastner, Alfred   Escudier, Troupenas

Katzer, George   Deutscher Verlag für Musik
Kauer, Ferdinand   Artaria (i), Musikalisches
　　Magazin
Kauffmann [Kaufman], **Paul**   84, Berg, Gerlach
Kaufmann, Guy   Durand
Kaulich, Josef   Haslinger
Kaun, Hugo   Leuckart
Kay, Ulysses   MCA Music
Keaton, Robert H.   27
Keere, Henrik van den   *see* Van den Keere,
　　Henrik
Keil, Alfredo   Sassetti
Keil, Theodor   Heinrichshofen
Keith, Prowse   102, EMI Music-SBK
Keller, Andress   Feyerabend
Keller, Hermann   Steingräber
Kelley, Edgar Stillman   Wa-Wan Press
Kellner, Andreas   Eichorn
Kelly, Michael   Hewitt
Kelly, Thomas Alexander Erskine (6th Earl
　　of)   Bremner
Kelterborn, Rudolf   Bärenreiter, Bote & Bock
Kemble & Co.   Cramer
Kennis, Guillaume Gommaire   Andrez
Kenton, Stan   Robbins
Kerényi, György   Magyar Kórus
Kerksieg & Bruesing Company   Schirmer (G.)
Kerle, Jacobus de   Plantin
Kerll, Johann Kaspar   Wening
Kern, Jerome   125, Chappell, Harms, Miller,
　　Warner Bros.
Kertész, Gyula   Magyar Kórus
Kessner, Daniel   Broude (A.)
Ketèlbey, Albert   Bosworth
Key, Francis Scott   Carr
Kgl. Hof-Musikhandel   120, Hansen
Khachaturian, Aram   Peters (i), Sikorski
Kidder (Wright & Kidder)   Howe
Kielland, S.   Norsk Musikforlag
Kienzl, Wilhelm   Bote & Bock, Forberg,
　　Universal, Weinberger
Kilchen, Jacob von   Wenssler
Killan, Lucas   94
Kilpinen, Yrjö   Breitkopf & Härtel, Hansen
Kimball, Jacob   Thomas
King, Karl   Barnhouse
King, Matthew Peter   Power
Kircher, Athanasius   Dreher, Grignani, Weigel
Kirchner, Leon   Associated Music Publishers,
　　Rieter-Biedermann, Simrock
Kiritescu, Stefan   122–4
Kirkpatrick, William J.   Biglow & Main
Kistner, Carl Friedrich   107, Kistner & Siegel,
　　Schmidt, Senff
Kistner & Siegel
Kjaer, Mogens   68
Kjerulf, Halfdan   Warmuth
Kjos, Neila   126
Klabon, Krzysztof   Szarfenberg
Klebe, Giselher   Ars Viva, Bärenreiter, Bote &
　　Bock
Kleber, Henry   Benteen
Kleczyński, Jan   Gebethner & Wolff
Kleinmichel, Richard   Senff, Steingräber
Klemm, Johan
Klengel, August (Stephan) Alexander   Peters (i)
Klengel, Julius   Steingräber
Klever   Gutheil, Stellovsky
Klier, J.B.   128, Laforge
Kling, Otto Marius   Chester
Klingenstein, Bernhard   Meltzer

Klose, Friedrich   Drei Masken Verlag
Klotz, Hans   Bärenreiter
Klukowski, Franciszek   111
Knab, Armin   Breitkopf & Härtel, Leuckart,
　　Litolff
Knapton, Phillip   102
Knapton, Samuel   102
Knefl   Sensenschmidt
Knevett   Goulding
Knight, Charles   103
Kníže, František Max   Berra, Enders
Knöfel, Johann   Černý
Knussen, Oliver   Faber
Kober, J.L.   Urbánek
Kochan, Gunter   Deutscher Verlag für Musik
Kocián, Jaroslav   Pazdírek
Kodály, Zoltán   Boosey & Hawkes, Magyar
　　Kórus, Rózsavölgyi, Universal
Koechlin, Charles   Billaudot, Durand, Eschig,
　　Rouart-Lerolle, Senart
Köhler, Louis   Litolff, Peters (i)
Kohn, Bernard   Elkan-Vogel
Kohn, Karl   Fischer (C.)
Kolbe, Andreas   Egenolff
Kolberer, Cajetan   Bencard
Kollo, Walter   Drei Masken Verlag
Kolneder, Walter   Tonger
Kongliga priviligierade nottryckeriet   Ahlström
Koning (Stumpf & Koning)   Alsbach
Konyus, Georgy Eduardovich   Editions Russes
　　de Musique
Kopp, Georg   Nenninger
Koppelman, Charles   EMI Music-SBK
Korn, Johann Daniel, the younger   Leuckart
Korngold, Erich Wolfgang   Universal,
　　Weinberger
Korte, Karl   Schirmer (E.C.)
Kórus, Magyar   Editio Musica Budapest
Korvin, László   Editio Musica Budapest
Koschat, Thomas   Leuckart
Kosmerovius, Matthaus   *see* Cosmerovius
Köster   Lienau
Koussevitzky, Natalya   Editions Russes de
　　Musique
Koussevitzky, Sergey   122, Editions Russes de
　　Musique, Gutheil
Kovařovic, Karel   Hudební Matice
Koven, Reginald de   Church
Kozel   Černý
Kozeluch, Johann Antonin [J.E. Antonín
　　Tomáš]   Musikalisches Magazin
Kozeluch, Leopold   106, Artaria (i), Bland,
　　Huberty, Hummel, Maisch, Musikalisches
　　Magazin, Sauer, Thomson, Torricella
Kozeluchsche Musikhandlung   Musikalisches
　　Magazin
Kozowski, Józef   Dalmas
Kraf, Michael   Wagner (M.)
Kraft, Hans   Waldkirch
Kraft, William   MCA Music
Kramer, A. Walter   Fischer (J.), Galaxy
Krämer (& Bossler)   Bossler
Krasnitzky, Rochus   Haslinger
Kraszewski, Gaétann   Sennewald
Kratochwill, Karl   Bosworth
Kratochwill, Vincenz   Bosworth
Krätzschmar, Wilfried   Deutscher Verlag für
　　Musik
Kraus, Eberhard   Pustet
Krebs, Johann Ludwig   Schmid
Krehbiel, Henry Edward   Ditson

Index

Kreitner, G. Heckel, Schott
Kremser, Eduard Leuckart
Krenek, Ernst Bärenreiter, Broude Brothers, Universal
Krentzlin, R. Lienau
Kretzschmar Breitkopf & Härtel
Kreusser, G.A. Schott
Kreutzer, Konradin Cappi
Kreutzer, Rodolphe Erard, Frey, Lucca, Magasin de Musique (ii), Mollo, Pleyel, Sieber
Křička, Jaroslav Urbánek
Kriesstein, Barbara Schönig
Kriesstein [Kriegstein], **Melchior** 86, Schönig, Ulhart
Krommer, Franz (Vinzenz) Haslinger, Kunst- und Industrie-Comptoir, Lorenzi, Mollo, Traeg
Krov, Jósef, Theodor Hoffmann
Kroyer, Theodor Pustet
Krüchten, Hermann Josef Huberty, Van Ghelen
Krufft, Nikolaus, Freiherr von Kunst- und Industrie-Comptoir, Mechetti
Krüger Escudier
Krumpholtz, J.B. Cousineau, Dale, Naderman
Kryżanowski, Stanislaw 111
Kubik, Gail Hargail, Ricordi
Küche, Christoph Weidner
Kufferath, Maurice Escudier, Leduc
Kugelmann, Johann Kriesstein
Kuhé, Wilhelm Berra, Hoffmann
Kuhlau, Friedrich Lose, Samfundet til Udgivelse af Dansk Musik
Kuhn, Max Lauterbach & Kuhn
Kühnel, Ambrosius 106, Hoffmeister, Hofmeister, Peters (i), Whistling
Kullak, Franz Steingräber
Kunkel, Jacob Kunkel
Kunkel Brothers Balmer & Weber
Künnecke, Eduard Drei Masken Verlag, Sikorski
Kunst- und Industrie-Comptoir 106, 111, Treichlinger
Kuntz Falter
Kunzen, Friedrich Ludwig Aemilius Samfundet til Udgivelse af Dansk Musik, Sønnichsen
Kurka, Robert Weintraub
Kurpiński, Karol Kazimierz Brzezina, Klukowski
Kurtág, György Universal
Kurz, Siegfried Breitkopf & Härtel
Kurzweil 72

La Barre, Michel de Foucault, Roger
Labarre, Théodore(-François-Joseph) Troupenas
Labaun
Labaun, Jiri 92, Labaun
Labický Hoffmann
Labitzky, Joseph Brandus, Nordheimer, Schlesinger, Troupenas
La Borde, Jean Benjamin de 49, La Chevardière, Métru
Lacerda, Osvaldo Vitale
La Chevardière, Louis Balthazard de 104, Bureau d'Abonnement Musicale, Le Clerc (J.P.), Leduc
Lachner, Franz Haslinger, Pennauer
Lachner, Ignaz Pennauer
Lachnith, Ludwig Venceslav Sieber
Lacom, C. Heckel

La Coste, G.J. de Roger
Lacour, Lucien de Costallat
Laderman, Ezra Oxford University Press, Schirmer (G.)
Ladmirault, Paul Rouart-Lerolle
Laet, Jean de [Latius, Joanes, Latio, Giovanni] Waelrant
L'Affilard, Michel Foucault
Laforge, Pierre 128
Lahusen, Christian Breitkopf & Härtel
Lajtha, László Rózsavölgyi
Lalande, Michel-Richard de 44, Bailleux, Ballard, Boivin
Lalo, Edouard Hartmann, Heugel
Lamb, Joseph F. Stark
Lambardi, Camillo Carlino, Vitale
Lambert, Constant Oxford University Press
Lambert, Michel 43, 95
Lamesle, Claude Gando
La Montaine, John Broude Brothers, Fischer
Lampe, John Frederick Bickham, Cole
Landerer Heckenast
Landi, Lando Pignoni
Landi, Stefano Robletti
Landini, Giovanni Battista Cecconcelli
Landowski, Marcel Choudens
Lane Mason Bros
Lane, Eastwood Fischer (J.)
Lang, Paul Henry Schirmer (G.)
Langdon, Chauncey 114
Lange, Charles Balmer & Weber
Lange, Gustav Bote & Bock
Lange-Müller, Peter Erasmus Kgl. Hof-Musikhandel
Langheld, Dieter Bote & Bock
Langinger, Herman 127
Langlais, Jean Elkan-Vogel
Lankisch, Johann 87
Lanner, Josef Cranz, Haslinger, Lienau, Mechetti, Schlesinger, Troupenas
Lannoy, Eduard Freiherr von Mollo
Lansky, Paul Boelke-Bomart
Lanzi, Maria Giudici & Strada
Lapis, Santo Hummel
Larsen, Knud Fog
La Rue, Pierre de Grimm & Wirsung
Larway, Joseph Henry Ashdown
La Salle Music Publishing Company Peer-Southern
La Sirene 122, Eschig
Lassus, Ferdinand de Widmanstetter
Lassus, Orlande de 87, 91, 533, Amadino, Ballard, Bärenreiter, Barré, Berg (A.), Bogard, East, Gardano, Gerlach, Goulart, Haultin, Henricus, Laet, Le Roy, Le Royer, Merulo, Phalèse, Rampazetto, Scotto, Simrock, Susato, Tini, Tournes, Vautrollier, Widmanstetter
Latour, Francis Tatton Chappell
Latte, Bernard Girard
Lauder, Harry Francis, Day & Hunter
Laudy, Joseph, & Co. Bosworth
Launer Carli, Girard
Launer, widow of Carli
Laurens, A.M. (pseud) Barnhouse
Lausch, Laurenz 106
Lauska, Franz Seraphinus Peters (i)
Lauterbach, Karl Lauterbach & Kuhn
Lauterbach & Kuhn 119, Bote & Bock
Lauzières, A. de Girard

Lavaux, Nicolas   Le Clerc
Lavenu
Lavenu, Lewis   102, Lavenu
Law, Andrew   114
Lawes, Henry   Playford
Lawes, William   Playford
Lawrence, Vera B.   Wa-Wan Press
Lawton, Dennis   Fiot & Meignen
Layolle, Alamanne de   Gorlier
Layolle, Francesco de   Du Ry, Gorlier, Giunta, Moderne
Làzare   Nordheimer
Lazarof   Presser
Łazarz, Andrysowicz   Wietor
Lazarz, Andrysowicz, wife of   Wietor
Leader & Cock   102
League of Composers in Israel   Israel Music Institute
Le Barbier   49
Le Bé, Guillaume (i)   25, 84, 545, Ballard
Le Bé Guillaume (ii), son of Guillaume   Ballard, Haultin, Le Bé
Lebègue, Nicolas-Antoine   Ballard, Baussen, Foucault, Roger
Lebègue   95
Leblanc   Imbault
Le Bouleux   49
Lebrun, Ludwig August   Götz
Le Cene, Francoise (née Roger)   Roger
Le Cène, Michel-Charles   100, Roger, Witvogel
Le Chevalier, Amédée   100
Lechner, Leonnhard   Bärenreiter
Lechthaler, Joseph   Österreichischer Bundesverlag
Leclair, Jean-Marie   Ballard, Boivin, Castagneri, Le Clerc
Leclair, Mme   104
Le Clerc, Charles-Nicolas   104
Le Clerc, Jean-Pantaléon   Bureau d'Abonnement Musical, Foucault, La Chevardière
Lecocq   Brandus, Sonzogno
Lecuona, Ernesto   Wagner (A.)
Leduc   104, 110, 120, Heugel, La Chevardière, Presser, Sieber
Leduc, Alphonse   Escudier
Leduc, Alphonse [pseud. of Balmer, Charles]   Balmer & Weber
Lee, George W.   Lee & Walker
Lee, Henry   Hime
Lee, Samuel   101
Lee & Walker   115, Ditson, Willig
Leede, C.F.   Cottrau
Leeds   127, Weintraub
Lees, Benjamin   Weintraub
Lefebvre, Charles Edouard   Rouart-Lerolle
Lefebvre (Desclée, & Co.)   Desclée
Lefferts, Michael   Broude (A.)
Legrenzi, Giovanni   Magni, Monti, Sala
Legrer, J.   Kunst- und Industrie-Comptoir
Lehár, Franz   Doblinger, Weinberger
Leidesdorf, Marcus (Maximilian Josef Anton Berka)   Diabelli, Mechetti, Sauer
Leighton, Kenneth   Novello
Leighton, Thomas   Stansby
Leisring, Volckmar   Weidner
Le Jeune, Claude   Ballard, Haultin, Le Roy, Plantin
Lem, P. Mandrup   Sønnichsen, Torricella
Lemacher, Heinrich   Böhm, Tonger
Le Maistre, Matthaeus   Bergen

Le Menu
Le Menu de St. Philibert, Christoph   104, Le Menu
Lemercier, R.J.   61
Lemoine   104, 120, Pleyel
Lengnick   Harris, Schmidt
Leo X   Antico
Leonard, Hal   126
Leonard, Silas W.   Fillmore
Leoncavallo, Ruggiero   Ascherberg, Hopwood & Crew, Brockhaus, Ricordi, Sonzogno
Leoni, Benedetto   Fougt, Mascardi
Le Preux, Poncet   Attaingnant
Lerdahl, Fred   Boelke-Bomart
Lerdo de Tejada, Miguel   Wagner (A.)
Lerolle, Jacques   Rouart-Lerolle
Leroux, Maurice   Schott
Leroux, Gaspard   Foucault
Le Roy, Adrian   25, 184, 521, 532, Ballard
Leroy, André   Choudens
Le Roy, Denise (née de Brouily)   Le Roy
Le Roy & Ballard   Attaingnant, Ballard, Granjon, Le Bé, Le Roy, Le Royer, Phalèse
Le Royer, Jean   88, Jean II de Laon
Lescer, Morel de   Andrez
Le Signerre, Guillemus   10
Les Six   122
Lester, William   Fischer (J.)
L'Estocart, Paschal de   Jean II de Laon
Le Sueur, Jean-François   Frey, Naderman
Lesure, François   Heugel
Leuckart
Leuckart, Franz Ernst Christoph   106, 107, Leuckart, Cappi
Levin [Levien]   Wagner (A.)
Levy, Jules   Heugel
Levy, Louis   Leeds
Lewandowski, Lazarus (Leopold)   Sennewald
Lewis, Anthony   Purcell Society
Lewis, Houston & Hyde   Bland
Lewis, Matthew Gregory   Gilfert
Lewis, William   Root & Cady
Lewy, Gustav   Pazdírek
Lhéritier, Jean   Moderne
Liban, Jerzy   Szarfenberg
Librairie Théâtrale   Billaudot
Lichfield, Leonard   Beesley
Lickl, Johann Georg   Musikalisches Magazin
Liebermann, Rolf   Ars Viva
Lieberson, Peter   Associated Music Publishers
Liehmann, Jósef   Hoffmann
Lienau   107, Haslinger
Lienau, (Emil) Robert   Lienau, Schlesinger
Lienau, Robert (A.M. Schlesinger)   Haslinger
Ligato, O.B. (pseud.)   Stark
Ligeti, György   Schott, Universal
Lillenas
Lillenas, Haldor   126, Lillenas
Lima, João de Sousa   Vitale
Limido, Stefano   Giunta
Limuz, Mitis z   Černý
Lindberg, Roger   Fazer
Lindner, Friedrich   Gerlach
Lindorff & Co.   Norsk Musikforlag, Warmuth
Linley, Francis   Bland
Linley, Thomas the elder   Thompson
Linnemann, Carl   Kistner & Siegel
Linnemann, Richard, the elder   Kistner & Siegel
Linnemann, Richard, the younger   Kistner & Siegel

Lipavsky, J.   Musikalisches Magazin
Lippius, (Johannes)   Weidner
Lischke & Trautwein   Hummel
List, Kurt   Boelke-Bomart
Listenius, Nikolaus   Hantzsch, Neuber, Rhau
Liszt, Franz   110, 111, Bach-Gesellschaft, Bote & Bock, Brandus, Breitkopf & Härtel, Editio Musica Budapest, Escudier, Fürstner, Hempsted, Kahnt, Kistner & Siegel, Leuckart, Litolff, Richault, Ricordi, Rózsavölgyi, Schlesinger, Schott, Schuberth (J.), Senart, Senff, Taborszky, Wessel
Liszt, János   Rózsavölgyi
Lithographisches Institut   107, Haslinger
Litolff   110, Costallat, Peters (i)
Littleton, Alfred   Novello
Littleton, Augustus   Novello
Littleton, Henry   Novello
Liviabella   De Santis
Llimona y Boceta, Vidal   Boileau Bernasconi, Unión Musical Española
Lobkowitz, Prince Joseph Franz Maximilian   Pleyel
Lobo, Alonso   Giunta, Plantin
Lobry, Andreas   Le Menu, Pleyel
Lobwasser, Frédéric   89, Hünefeld
Locatelli, Pietro Antonio   Boivin, La Chevardière, Roger
Locher, J.F.   22
Lochon, Jacques-François   Foucault
Locke, Matthew   Playford
Lockwood, Lewis   A-R Editions
Lockwood, Normand   Broude Brothers
Loeillet, Jean Baptiste   Wright
Loesser, Frank   Frank
Loewe, (Johann) Carl (Gottfried)   Schlesinger
Loewe, Frederick   Chappell, Hofmeister
Logier, F.   128
L'Oiseau Lyre   *see* Oiseau Lyre, L'
Lomax, Alan   Oak
Lomazzo, Filippo   89, Tini
Lombardo, (Carol *or* Constantino)   Curci
Lomnicky   Černý
London, Edwin   Jerona
Longman, Giles   Chappell, Keith, Prowse, Longman & Broderip
Longman, James   Johnson (J.), Longman & Broderip
Longman, John   101, Clementi, Longman & Broderip
Longman & Broderip   Bland, Clementi, Roberts
Longo, Gaetano   Ricordi
Lonsdale, Christopher   Birchall
Loomis, Harvey Worthington   Wa-Wan Press
Lopatnikoff, Nikolas   Editions Russes de Musique
Lorenz
Lorenz, Edmund S.   126, Lorenz
Lorenzi, Giuseppe   111, Canti
Lorme, Jean-Louis de   Roger
Lortzing, Albert   Breitkopf & Härtel
Löschenkohl, Hieronymus   106, Eder
Lose   113, 120, Hansen (W.), Sønnichsen
Löslein, Peter   Ratdolt
Loth, Urban   Nenninger
Lothar, Mark   Heinrichshofen, Ries & Erler
Lotter
Lotter, Johann Jakob (i)   31, 98, Lotter
Lotti, Antonio   Bortoli
Louis XIII   Ballard

Louis XIV   Ballard
Louis XVIII   59
Louis Ferdinand of Prussia, Prince   Kunst- und Industrie-Comptoir
Low de Vinne, Theodore   39
Lowe, G.W.   43, Lowe & Brydone
Lowe & Brydone   51, 61
Lownes, Humfrey   92, Short
Lownes, Matthew   Lownes, Snodham
Lowry, Robert   Biglow & Main
Lübeck, Vincent   Ugrino
Lucas, Clarence   Whaley, Royce & Co.
Lucas, Stanley   120
Lucca, Francesco   111, Bertuzzi, Canti, Girard, Ricordi
Lucillus   Honterus
Lucius, Jakob   Bergen
Ludwig, Friedrich   Breitkopf & Härtel
Luening, Otto   Galaxy, New Music, Silver Burdett
Lukey   Longman & Broderip
Lully, Jean-Baptiste   44, 84, 92, 95, Bailleux, Ballard, Baussen, Boivin, Broude Brothers, Foucault, Métru, Roger
Lumbye, Hans Christian   Horneman, Lose
Lumley, Benjamin   Lucca
Lundquist, Abraham (Reinold)   111–113
Lupacchino, Bernardino   Amadino, Caifabri, Poggioli, Scotto
Lupi, Didier   Beringen, Guéroult
Lupi, Johannes   Attaingnant, Susato
Lupi, Roberto   De Santis
Lupus Press   Aich
Luscinius, Otmar   Grimm & Wirsung
Luscomb, Fred   Pepper
Luther, Martin   86, 88, 119, 126, Augsburg, Formschneider, Hergot, Rhau, Stuchs, Ulhart
Lutheran Church-Missouri Synod   Concordia
Lutosławski, Witold   Chester, Hansen (W.)
Luython, Carl   Černý
Luzzaschi, Luzzasho   Baldini, Gardano, Verovio
Lyadov, Anatol   Belyayev
Lyndewood   Remunde
Lyon, James Washburn   113, Lyon & Healy
Lyon & Healy   125, Ditson, Wagner (A.)
Lyrebird Press, The   Oiseau-Lyre
Lyttich, Johann   Weidner

Maas, Kurt   68
Maayani, Ami   Israel Music Institute
McAfee Music   Belwin-Mills
McCabe, John   Novello
McCaffrey, Henry   115
McCorquodale Group   Clowes
McCracken, Jarrell   Word
McCulloch, William   113
McDonald, Harl   Elkan-Vogel
Macdowell, Edward   127, Jung
Macé, Denis   Ballard
Macedonio di Mutio, Giovanni Vincenzo   Carlino, Vitale
McFadyen, Joseph   Aird
Macfarren, George A.   Ashdown, Chappell, Handel societies, Lucas
McGibbon, William   Bremner
McGinnis & Marx
McGoun, Archibald   Aird
McHugh, Jimmy   Mills
Mackellar   38–39
Mackellar, Smiths & Jordan   13

Mackinlay, Thomas   Goulding
McKinney, B.B.   Broadman Press
McKinney, Howard   Fischer (J.)
McLaughlin & Reilly   Summy-Birchard
Macmillan, Sir Ernest   Harris
Macmillan Inc.   Schirmer (G.), *see also* Crowell, Collier & Macmillan
Maconchy, Elizabeth   Lengnick
Macque, Giovanni de   Baldini, Carlino, Mutii
MacWilliams, Robert   Schirmer (E.C.)
Maderna, Bruno   Ricordi, Suvini Zerboni
Maegaard, Jan   Samfundet til Udgivelse af Dansk Musik
Magalhães, Filipe de   Valentim de Carvalho
Magaloff, Nikita   Curci
Magasin de Musique   Escudier
Magasin de Musique (i)   104, Janet & Cotelle, Troupenas
Magasin de Musique (ii)   105, Frey
Magnetta, Marcello   Carlino
Magni   Phalèse
Magni, Bartolomeo   Gardano, Magni, Vincenti
Magni, Diamante (née Gardano)   Magni
Magni, Francesco   83, Gardano, Magni, Vincenti
Magonzo de Sassonio, Stephano Aquila de Arndes
Magrini, G.   Lucca
Magyar Kórus   122
Mahler, Gustav   119, 510, Boosey & Hawkes, Bote & Bock, Doblinger, Faber, Hofmeister, Kahnt, Peters (i), Rättig, Universal, Weinberger
Maho, J.   Hamelle
Mahrenholz, Christhard   Bärenreiter
Mahrenholz, Ludwig   Bärenreiter
Maier, Guy   Fischer (J.)
Maier, Julius Joseph   Simrock
Maillard, Jean   Ballard, Moderne, Tournes
Maillart, Aimé   Brandus
Mainwaring, William   *see* Manwaring
Mainzer, Friedrich   Doblinger
Mainzer, Joseph   Novello
Mair, Paul Hektor   Kriesstein
Maisch, Ludwig   Eder
Makings, Peter W.   Schott
Malipiero, Gian Francesco   Carisch, Chester, De Santis, Heinrichshofen, Ricordi, Senart, Suvini Zerboni, Universal
Malipiero, Riccardo   Suvini Zerboni
Mallet, Francis   Graupner
Malvezzi, Cristofano   Petrucci (P.), Vincenti
Manchicourt, Pierre de   Attaingnant, Susato
Mancinelli, Luigi   Guidi
Manfredini, Francisco   Silvani
Mangeant, Jacques
Mangold, Gabriel   Nenninger
Manicke, Dietrich   Simrock
Manilius, Gislain   89
Manly Basil, jr.   Broadman Press
Mann, Elias   Thomas
Mann, George   Lowe & Brydone
Mannerhjerta, Ulrik Emanuel   Hirsch
Mannheim school   Hartnoch, Welcker
Mannino, Franco   De Santis, Ricordi
Manolesi, Carlo   Dozza
Manutius, Aldus   22, Jacomo, Torresani
Manwaring [Mainwaring], **William**   101, Neale
Maquaire   Durand
Maquet, Philippe   Brandus, Joubert
Marais, Marin   95, Ballard, Boivin, Bonneüil, Broude Brothers, Foucault, Roger

Marazzoli   520
Marcello, Benedetto   Lorenzi, Roger, Sala
Marchand, Louis   Boivin
Marchand, Luc   Foucault
Marchetti, Tomasi   Lucca
Marco   68
Marcolini, Francesco   41, 532
Marcolini da Forli   40
Marcorelli (Marco Aurelli)   Geertsom
Marcoux, Catherine-Barbe   Erard
Marcoux, Marie-Francoise-Catherine   Erard
Marenzio, Luca   543, Amadino, Ballard, Broude Brothers, Gardano, Kauffman, Phalèse, Valesi, Vincenti
Marescalchi, Luigi   110, Alessandri & Scattaglia, Ricordi
Marescot [Mareschot], Georges   *see* Marescotti (G.)
Marescotti, Cristofano   Marescotti, Pignoni
Marescotti, Giorgio   41, 89, Giunta, Pignoni, Raverii
Margola, Franco   Zanibon
Margun
Maria Theresa, Empress   Österreichischer Bundesverlag, Trattner
Mariani, Paolo   Giudici & Strada
Marietti, Jean   Eschig
Marietti, Philippe   Eschig
Maringo, Giovanni Battista   91
Marini, Carlo Antonio   Bortoli
Marino, Carlo Antonio   Roger
Mariscotti, Giorgio   *see* Marescotti (G.)
Mark of the Unicorn   73
Markordt, S.   Hummel
Marks, Edward B(ennett)   125, Presser
Marnef, H. de   Fezandat
Maros, Rudolf   Peer-Southern
Marot, Clement   88–9, Attaingnant, Channey, Gueroult, Haultin, Mangeant, Manilius
Marpurg, Friedrich Wilhelm   Schmid
Marquerie, (Jean?)   Pleyel
Marschner, Heinrich August   André, Breitkopf & Härtel, Hofmeister, Senff
Marshall, Arthur   Stark
Marshall, William   Penson, Robertson
Marteau, Henri   Steingräber
Martelli, Henri   Eschig
Martin, Estienne   Mangeant
Martin, Frank   Universal
Martinet, Jean-Louis   Heugel
Martinez de Bizczrgui, Gonzalo   Giunta
Martini, Giovanni Battista   Della Volpe
Martini, Johann Paul Aegidius   Bureau d'Abonnement Musical
Martino, Donald   McGinnis & Marx, Schirmer (E.C.)
Martinon, Jean   Israeli Music Publications
Martinovsky   Berra, Hoffmann
Martins, Francisco   Valentim de Carvalho
Martinů, Bohuslav   Eschig, Israeli Music Publications, La Sirène, Panton
Martorelli, G.C.   Ricordi
Martucci, Giuseppe   Ricordi
Marx, Adolph Bernhard   Schlesinger, Universal
Marx, Angelina Buonamassa   McGinnis & Marx
Marx, Frank   International
Marx, Joseph   McGinnis & Marx
Marx, Karl   Bärenreiter, Breitkopf & Härtel
Mascagni, Pietro   Ascherberg, Hopwood & Crew, Bote & Bock, De Santis, Ricordi, Sonzogno

Mascardi 91, Poggioli
Mascardi, Vitale   Caifabri, Mascardi
Mascitti, Michèle   Foucault
Mašek, Vincenc   Berra, Peters (i)
Mason, Daniel Gregory   Mason Bros., Society
   for the Publication of American Music
Mason, George   Snodham
Mason, Lowell (i)   114, 124, 126, Hewitt, Mason
   Bros.
Mason, William   Schuberth (E.)
Mason Bros.   124
Masotti, Paolo   91, Poggioli, Soldi
Massé, Victor   Métru, Richault
Massenet, Jules   Fürstner, Hartmann, Heugel
Masson, Charles   Foucault
Matelart, Johannes   Mutii
Mathias, William (James)   Oxford University
   Press
Mathot, Albert Zunz   Salabert
Mattei, Wolfgang   Merseburger
Matthaei, Conrad   Mense
Mattheson, Johann   Breitkopf & Härtel
Matthews, Artie   Stark
Matthews, Colin   Faber
Matthews, David   Faber
Matthus, Siegfried   Deutscher Verlag für Musik
Matthysz, Paulus   92
Maurice, Peter   EMI Music-SBK
Maurolyco   Franceschi
Maw, Nicholas   Faber
Maximilian I   Henricus, Oeglin
Maximilian II   Eichorn
Maximilian Joseph of Bavaria   Gleissner
Maxwell, George   Galaxy
Maxwell, John   69
Maxwell Davies   520
May (Schauer & May)   Benjamin
May, John   Hudgebut
Mayer
Mayer, Johann Baptist   87, Mayer
Mayer, T. (pseud. of Charles Balmer)   Balmer &
   Weber
Mayo, William T.   116, Werlein
Mayone, Ascanio   Vitale
Mayr, Johann Joseph   Mayer
Mayr, (Johannes) Simon   Ricordi
Mayseder, Joseph   Haslinger, Maisch, Pennauer,
   Pleyel
Maza, Regino Sáinz de la   Unión Musical
   Española
Mazák, Alberik   Cosmerovius
Mazzaferrata, Giovanni Battista   Monti, Silvani
Mazzinghi, Joseph   Goulding
Mazzocchi, Domenico   Zannetti
Mazzocchi, Giacomo   Antico, Giunta
Mazzocchi, Gino   Carisch
Mazzolini, Carlo Andrea   Micheletti
MCA Music   126, Belwin-Mills, Leeds, Presser
Meacham, John   Firth, Hall & Pond
Mead, George   Galaxy
Meares [Mears, Meers]   Cross, Walsh
Meares, Richard, the elder   101, Meares
Mears, W.   Meares
Mechetti   107, Artaria (i), Cappi, Diabelli, Eder
Mechetti, Carlo   106, Mechetti
Mechetti, Pietro   106, Haslinger, Mechetti,
   Traeg
Mederitsch, Johann   Hoffmeister, Sauer, Traeg
Medici, Cardinal Ippolito de'   Channey
Medici, Cosimo de'   Gardano
Meere, H.   Meares

Méhul, Etienne-Nicolas   Breitkopf & Härtel,
   Frey, Kunst- und Industrie-Comptoir,
   Lemoine, Magasin de Musique (ii), Pleyel,
   Schlesinger
Meignen, Leopold   115, Fiot & Meignen
Meiland, Jacob   28, Feyerabend, Gerlach, Rab
Mein, John   114
Meissonnier, Jean Antoine   Heugel
Melanchthon, Philipp   Rhau
Melantrich   Pazdírek
Melgaz, Diogo Dias   Valentim de Carvalho
Melissus, Paul   Le Roy
Mellor, John H.   Peters (ii)
Melody Lane Publications   Peer-Southern
Melpa   Pazdírek
Meltzer, Adam   87
Mendelssohn(-Bartholdy), (Jakob Ludwig)
   Felix   102, Breitkopf & Härtel, Coventry &
   Hollier, Deutscher Verlag für Musik,
   Durand, Ewer, Guidi, Handel societies,
   Hofmeister, Jürgenson, Kistner & Siegel,
   Mechetti, Novello, Richault, Schlesinger,
   Schonenberger, Schuberth (J.), Simrock,
   Wessel
Mendheim, Ferdinand   Trautwein
Menesini, Bartolomeo   Fougt
Mennin, Peter   Fischer (C.)
Menotti, Gian Carlo   Ricordi, Schirmer (G.)
Mensa, Didaco   Sabbio
Mense, Elisabeth   see Segebade, Elisabeth
Mense, Pascha [Mensenius, Paschen]   87,
   Reusner, Segebade
Mentor Publishing House   Morawetz
Meo, Ascanio   Carlino, Vitale
Merbecke, John   Grafton
Mercadante, Saverio   Bertuzzi, Boosey &
   Hawkes, Clausetti, Girard, Lucca, Pacini,
   Ricordi
Merchandising Corporation of America   MCA
   Music
Mercury Music Corporation   Presser
Méreaux, Jean-Amédé Le Froid de   Heugel
Merion Music   Presser
Merlotti, Claudio   see Merulo
Merritt Ives, J.   115
Merrymount Music   Ditson, Presser
Merseburger
Merseburger, Carl   107, Merseburger
Mersenne, Marin   499, 500, Ballard
Mersmann   Tonger
Merula, Tarquinio   Gardano, Magni, Vincenti
Merulo, Claudio [Merlotti, Claudio]   83,
   Gardano, Verovio
Mes, Gheradis   Susato
Meser, Carl Friedrich   Flaxland, Fürstner
Mesler, Edwards   115
Messiaen, Olivier   Broude Brothers, Durand
Metallo, Grammatico   Caifabri
Metner, (Medtner), Nikoby   Editions Russes de
   Musique
Metro-Goldwyn-Mayer   Big 3, Robbins
Metromedia   Hansen (C.)
Métru, Nicolas   Ballard
Mettenleiter, Johann Georg   Pustet
Mettingh, Carl Wilhelm von   Hummel
Metzler   102, Cramer, Metzler
Meurer-Ries, Ingrid   Ries & Erler
Meuriot, Emile   Rouart-Lerolle
Meusel, C.F.   Merseburger
Meyer, Ernst Hermann   Breitkopf & Härtel,
   Peters (i)

591

Meyer, Gottfried Martin Litolff
Meyer, Johann Meltzer
Meyerbeer, Giacamo Bote & Bock, Brandus,
  Breitkopf & Härtel, Lucca, Ricordi,
  Troupenas
Meykov, K.I. Jürgenson
Meysel, Anton Whistling
Miča, Franntišek Adam Hoffmeister
Michel, (Alphonse?) Magasin de Musique (i)
Michel de Toulouse [Toulouze] 20, 514, 517
Micheletti, Gioseffo 91
Micheli, Romano Grignani, Vincenti
Michely Foucault
Middelburgh, Paulus de (Bishop of
  Fossombrone) Petrucci (O.)
Mielczewski, Marcin Polskie Wydawnictwo
  Muzyczne
Migot, Georges Senart
Miguez, Leopoldo Bevilacqua
Mihalovici, Marcel Eschig, Heugel
Milanez, Abdon Bevilacqua
Milano, Francesco Canova da *see* Francesco
  Canova da Milano
Miles, Jonas or Septimus (Miles &
  Thompson) Schmidt
Milhaud, Darius Durand, Elkan-Vogel, Eschig,
  Heugel, Israeli Music Publications, La Sirène,
  Oiseau Lyre, Salabert, Senart
Milioni, Pietro Bortoli
Millar, R.S. Peters (ii)
Miller, Charles Miller
Miller, Glenn Robbins
Miller, William C. Benteen, Miller & Beacham
Miller & Beacham 115, Benteen, Ditson
Miller & Richard 37
Miller & Robbins 125
Miller Music Big 3
Millico, Giuseppe Marescalchi
Millöcker, Carl Cranz, Weinberger
Mills, Irving Belwin-Mills
Mills, Jack Belwin-Mills, Mills
Mills, Richard Birchall
Mills Music 125, Belwin-Mills, MCA Music,
  Mills
Minciacchi, Diego 68
Minciacchi, Marco 68
Minelli, Angelo Gabriele Della Volpe
Mintorno, Antonio Scotto
Miranda, Luis R. Giusti
Mirecki, Franz Lorenzi
Miroglio, Jean-Baptiste Bureau d'Abonnement
  Musical
Misocco, Prince Theodoro Trivultio of Colonna
Mitchell, Albert G. Ditson
Mitchell, Charles Lavenu
Mitchell, Donald Faber
Mobart Music Publications Boelke-Bomart
Mocchi, Walter Ricordi
Moderne, Jacques 23, 39, 86, 502, 526, Antico,
  Attaingnant, Beringen, Channey, Du Ry,
  Gardano
Moebius, Kurt Jung
Moeran, E(rnest) J(ohn) Novello
Moeschinger, Albert Hug
Moevs, Robert Marks
Mogull Music, Ivan Filmtrax-Columbia
Moilli, Bernardo 80
Moilli, Damiano 5, 80
Molitar, Fidel Hoftheater-Musik-Verlag,
  Wagner (M.)
Molkenbur, Norbert Peters (i)

Möller, Albert Wilhelm Hirsch
Moller [Möller], John Christopher 114, Moller
  & Capron, Willig
Mollo, Eduard Cappi, Mollo
Mollo, Tranquillo 106, Artaria (i), Eder,
  Haslinger
Molter & Capron
Momigny, J.J. de Pacini, Richault
Monari, Clemente Micheletti
Mönch, Johann Konrad Forckel
Mondial Gerig
Moneta, Paolo Caifabri
Monferrato, Natale Bortoli, Sala
Mongeant, Jacques 88
Monguillot
Monguillot, Gabino Breyer
Moniuszko, Stamstan Friedlein, Gebethner &
  Wolff, Polskie Wydawnictwo Muzyczne,
  Sennewald
Monk, William Henry Novello
Monnet, Jean Fournier
Monod, Jacques-Louis Boelke-Bomart
Monpou, Hippolyte Richault
Monsigny, Pierre-Alexandre Bailleux, La
  Chevardière
Montanus *see* Berg (J.), Bergen
Monte, Lodovico Salvadori
Monte, Philippe de Gardano, Plantin, Scotto
Montéclair, Michel Pignolet de Ballard, Boivin,
  Foucault
Montella, Giovanni Domenico Carlino, Vitale
Montemezzi, Italo Ricordi
Montesardo, Girolamo Colonna
Monteverdi Claudio Amadino, Bärenreiter,
  Faber, Gardano, Magni, Phalèse, Sabbio,
  Tradate, Vincenti
Monti, Giacomo 91, Della Volpe, Silvani
Monti, Pier Maria
Monția, Emil Gebauer
Monzani, Tebaldo 102
Monzani & Cimador 495, 526
Monzani & Hill 528
Monzino, Antonio Scotti
Moore, Douglas S(tuart) Fischer (C.), Schirmer
  (G.)
Moore, Thomas Heptinstall
Moore, Thomas Blake, Power
Mora 49
Morales, Cristóbal de Dorico, Gardano,
  Moderne, Scotto
Morawetz, Oskar 122, Thompson
Morawetz Brothers
Moreau, Jean Baptiste 49, Baussen
Morehen, John 69
Morel, François Berando
Moretti, Nicola Scotti
Moretus, Jean Plantin
Mori, Nicolas Lavenu
Morin, Jean Baptiste Foucault
Morin, Martin 4
Morin, Michael Higman
Morlacchi, Francesco Bertuzzi, Guidi
Morlaye, Guillaume Fezandat
Morley, Thomas 80, 91, Barley, Clementi, Day,
  East, Forbes, Lownes, Musical Antiquarian
  Society, Randall, Short
Mornable, Antoine de Attaingnant
Morrison, J.F. Lee & Walker
Morse Faulds
Morse Music Co. Feist
Mortari, Virgilio Carisch

Index

Mortensen, Finn Norsk Musikforlag
Morthenson, Jan Wilhelm Nordiska
    Musikförlaget
Mortier, Pierre 527, Roger
Mortimer, Frederick Paterson
Moscheles, Ignaz Artaria (i), Handel societies,
    Haslinger, Kistner & Siegel, Litolff, Mechetti,
    Schlesinger
Möseler, Karl Heinrich Kallmeyer
Moser, Hans Joachim Bärenreiter, Litolff
Mosonyi, Mihály Rózsavölgyi
Mosto, Giovannni Battista Phalèse
Moszkowski, Moritz Bosworth, Peters (i)
Motta, José Vianna da Sassetti
Motta, Thomaso Vigoni
Moücke, Francesco 98
Mould, Henry J. Brainard
Mouret, Jean Joseph Ribou
Mouton, Charles Roger
Mouton, Jean Antico, Grimm & Wirsung,
    Kriesstein
Moxon 18
Mozart, Constanze André, Breitkopf & Härtel
Mozart, Leopold 31, Breitkopf & Härtel, Lotter,
    Schwickert
Mozart, Wolfgang Amadeus 107, 118, 495, 526,
    528, 543, André, Artaria (i), Bärenreiter,
    Birchall, Bland & Weller, Böhm, Breitkopf &
    Härtel, Challier, Cramer, Deutscher Verlag
    für Musik, Durand, Eder, Frey, Gombart,
    Guidi, Haslinger, Heckel, Heina,
    Heinrichshofen, Hewitt, Hoffmeister,
    Hoftheater-Musik-Verlag, Hummel,
    Imbault, Kunst- und Industrie-Comptoir,
    Lausch, Löschenkohl, Marescalchi, Mollo,
    Monzani, Musikalisches Magazin, Peters (i),
    Riley, Rozsnyai, Schlesinger, Schott, Sieber,
    Sønnichsen, Spehr, Torricella, Traeg,
    Wessel, Wiener Philharmonischer Verlag,
    Wiener Urtext Edition, Zatta
Muffat, Georg Kahnt, Nenninger, Van Ghelen
Muir, John 103, Wood
Muldowney, Dominic Universal
Mulè, Giuseppe Curci
Mülen, Laurenz von der Aich
Müller, Adolf, the elder Haslinger, Mollo
Müller, Carl Hirsch
Müller, H.F. Löschenkohl, Sauer
Müller, Heinrich Hug
Müller, Hermann Flaxland, Meser
Muller, J.W. Senefelder
Müller, S.W. Eulenburg
Müller, Wenzel Musikalisches Magazin
Müllers, Andreas Hünefeld
Müllers, Ernest Hünefeld
Murdoch, Murdoch & Co. 120
Murel Foucault
Murphy, Edward P. Schirmer (G.)
Murray, James R. Church
Musard, Philippe Brandus, Troupenas
Musgrave, Thea Novello
Musical Antiquarian Society 118
'Musical Bouquet Office' Davidson
Musical Copyright Association Francis, Day &
    Hunter
Musicord Publications Belwin-Mills
Music Publishers' Association Ditson
Music Publishers Holding Corporation Harms,
    Remick, Warner Bros., Witmark
Music Publishing Co. Davidson
Music Reprographics 68

Music Sales Associated Music Publishers,
    Leonard, Oak, Schirmer (G.), Weintraub
Music Theatre International Frank
Musifactory Schott
Musikalisches Magazin 106, Maisch
Musikalisches Magazin auf der Höhe Spehr
Musikalisch-typographische
    Verlagsgesellschaft Hoffmeister
Musikstaatsverlag 124
Musorgsky [Moussorgsky], Modest Petrovich
    Belyayev
Mutii
Mutii, Giovanni Angelo 91, Caifabri, Mutii
Muzgiz Muzïka
Muzïka 122
Myaskovsky, Nikolay Yakovlevich Weintraub
Mysliveček Venier

Nabokov, Nicolas Bote & Bock, Editions Russes
    de Musique, La Sirène
Naderman, Jean-Henri 104, Le Menu, Richault
Nadler, Georg Oeglin
Nádor, Kálmán Editio Musica Budapest,
    Táborsky
Nagel 110, Bärenreiter
Nägeli, Hans Georg 111, Hug
Nageli, Hermann Bach-Gesellschaft
Naich, Hubert Blado, Gardano
Nairne, Lady Purdie
Nanino, Giovanni Bernardino Robletti
Nanino, Giovanni Maria Valesi
Nantermi, Orazio Tradate
Napier, William 101, Dale, Thomson
Napoleão
Nardini, Pietro Fougt
Nares, James Johnson (John)
Národní Hudební Vydavatelství Orbis Hudební
    Matice
Narváez, Luys de Moderne
Nasco, Giovanni Gardano
Nash, John Regent's Harmonic Institution
Natali, Pompeo Caifabri
National Council for Culture and Art Israel
    Music Institute
National Eisteddfod of Wales Williams (G.)
National Music Publishers' Association Feist
Natra, Sergiu Israel Music Institute
Naumann, Johann Gottlieb Marescalchi, Zatta
Nava, Antonio Ricordi
Nazareth, Ernesto Bevilacqua, Filippone
Nazarene Publishing House Lillenas
NBC Feist
Neale
Neale, John 101, Neale
Neale, William Manwaring, Neale
Neate, Charles Regent's Harmonic Institution
Nedbal, Oskar Doblinger
Negro, (Negri), Giulio Santo Pietro del
    Lomazzo
Nejedlý, Zdeněk Hudební Matice
Nelhybel, Vaclav Jerona
Nenna, Pomponio Magni
Nenninger
Nenninger, Matthäus 87, Nenninger
Nenninger, Tobias 87
Nepomuceno, Alberto Bevilacqua
Ness, A.J. 40
Nesterus, Michele Moücke
Neto, A. Tisi Bevilacqua
Neuber, Kunegunde see Wachter (ii),
    Kundegunde

Neuber, Ulrich   84, Berg, Gerlach
Neuber, Valentin   Hergot, Wachter
Neubert, Günter   Deutscher Verlag für
　　Musik
Nèuburger, Albert   Senart
Neue Bach Gesellschaft   Bach-Gesellschaft
Neue Händel-Gesellschaft   Handel societies
Neue Schütz-Gesellschaft   Bärenreiter
Neumann y Breyer   Breyer
Neumann, Georg   Breyer, Ortelli
Neumeister, Johann   Arndes
Neumüller, Fritz   Schuberth (E.)
Neupert, Hermann   Norsk Musikforlag,
　　Warmuth
Neusidler   538
Neustätter, Ferdinand   Falter
Neustätter, Helene   Falter
Nevin, Ethelbert   Boston Music Company
Newman, Ernest   Ditson
Newman, Harold   Hargail
New Music   Langinger, Presser
New Music Society   New Music
Newparth & Carneiro   Valentim de Carvalho
New World Music   Warner Bros.
Neycke, Georg   Osterberger
Nibbio, Stefano Venturi del   *see* Venturi del
　　Nibbio, Stefano
Nichelmann, Christoph   Schmid
Nicolai, Otto   Bote & Bock, Mechetti
Nicoll, James   Forbes
Niedermeyer, (Abraham) Louis   Heugel
Nielsen, Carl   Fog, Hansen, Samfundet til
　　Udgivelse af Dansk Musik
Niemcewicz, J.U.   Brzezina
Niemeyer   128
Niemeyer, Carlos F.   Niemeyer
Niepces   61
Nietzel, Theo   Cranz
Niewiadomski, Stanisław   Krzyżanowski
Niger, Franciscus   7, 20, Franck, Wenssler
Nigidius, Petrus   Egenolff
Nigrin, Georg   Černý
Niles, John Jacob   Schirmer (G.)
Nilsson, Bo   Nordiska Musikförlaget
Nin (y Castellanos), Joaquín   Eschig
Nin-Culmell, Joaquím María   Broude Brothers
Nivers   95
Noblet, Charles   Le Clerc
Nobre, Marlos   Vitale
Noël, Pierre   Billaudot
Noetzel, Otto Heinrich   Heinrichshofen
Noir, A. (pseud.)   Blackmar
Nola, Giovannia   Scotto
Nono, Luigi   Ars Viva, Ricordi
Norddeutscher Musikverein   Schuberth (J.)
Nordeheimer   128
Nordiska Musikförlaget   Hansen (W.)
Nordisk Musikforlag   Hansen, Kgl. Hof-
　　Musikhandel
Nørholm, Ib   Dan Fog, Samfundet til Udgivelse
　　af Dansk Musik
Norman, William   113
Norman & White   31
Norsk Musikforlag   120, Hals, Hansen (W.),
　　Nordiska Musikförlaget, Warmuth
Norsk Notestikk   Norsk Musikforlag
North, F.A.   Ditson
North, Roger   43
Noske, A.A.   Alsbach
Noskowski, Zygmunt   Krzyżanowski
Notari, Angelo   94, Hole

Novák, Vitězslav (Augustin Rudolf)   Hudební
　　Matice, Universal, Urbánek
Novello   102, 120, 127, 490, 520, Clowes, Ewer,
　　Filmtrax-Columbia, Gray (H.W.), Purcell
　　Society
Novello, J. Alfred   37, Coventry & Hollier,
　　Novello
Novello, Ivor   Chappell
Novello & Ewer   102
Noviomagus, Gerardus   Egenolff
Nucci, Lucrezio   91, Gargano
Nucci, Matteo   Gargano
Nucius, Johannes   Černý
Numeister, Johann   Han
Nunes, Emanuel   Sassetti
Nutius, Martin   Vissenaecken
Nyevelt, Willem van Zuylen van   Cock
Nystedt, Knut   Norsk Musikforlag
Nystroem, Gösta   Nordiska Musikförlaget

Oak
Obrecht, Jacob   Grimm & Wirsung, Ott
Ochlewski, Tadeusz   Polskie Wydawnictwo
　　Muzyczne
O'Dea, James   Bloom
Oeglin, Erhard   22, 26, 82, 520, Aich, Egenolff,
　　Ulhart
Oertel, Johannes   Fürstner
Oerthmann   Ricordi
Offenbach, Jacques   Joubert
Ohana, Maurice   Billaudot
Oiseau-Lyre, L'   118
Olcott, Chauncey   Witmark
Oliveira, Heliodoro de   Valentim de Carvalho
Oliver, François   34
Oliver, Robert M.   66
Ollendorff, Paul   Peters (i)
Olofsen, A.   Hummel
Olsen, Ole   Hals
Olsen, P.W.   Lose
Ondřej, Jiří   Labaun
Ondřej, Jiří, widow of   Labaun
Onslow, (André) Georges (Louis)   Haslinger,
　　Pleyel, Richault, Troupenas
Opitz, Martin   Hünefeld, Rhetus
Opus   Supraphon
Orbis   Supraphon
Ordonez, Carlo d'   Guéra, Hoffmeister
Orff, Carl   Schott
Orgad, Ben-Zion   Israel Music Institute
Origoni, Carlo   Ricordi
Ornstein, Severn   69
Orphean Music Co.   Shapiro, Bernstein & Co.
Orrego-Salas, Juan   Peer-Southern
Orsborn, George Hunt   Ascherberg, Hopwood
　　& Crew
Orsini, Bishop Leone   Gardano
Országh, Tivadar   Rozsnyai
Ortelli
Ortigue, Joseph d'   Heugel
Osborne, Nigel   Universal
Osbourn, James G.   115, Benteen
Ossovsky, Alexander   Editions Russes de
　　Musique
Ostali, Enzo   Sonzogno
Ostali, Pietro   Sonzogno
Osterberger, Georg   87
Östergren, Gustaf Adolf   Hirsch
Östergren bok – och musikhandel   Hirsch,
　　Lundquist
Ostermaier   Honterus

Österreichischer Bundesverlag 119
Ostrčil, Otakar   Hudební Matice, Starý
Ostrogorski [Ostrowski]   *see* Szarfenberg
Oswald, Henrique   Bevilacqua
Oswald, James   101, Phillips, Simpson
Otmar, Johann   Oeglin
Ott [Ottel, Otto]**, Hans**   Egenolff,
   Formschneider
Ovalle, Juan Ríos   Giusti
Oxford University Press [OUP]   68, 120
Ozerov, V.A.   Dalmas
Ozi, Etienne   Magasin de Musique (i)
Ozi et Cie   Janet & Cotelle, Magasin de
   Musique (i)

Pablos [Paoli, Giovanni]**, Juan**   94
Pace, Antonio   Carlino, Gargano
Pace, Charles Henry   124
Pace & Handy   125
Pachel, Leonard   80
Pachelbel, Johann   Rönnagel, Weigel
Pacher, Sebastian   Falter
Pacher, Thekla   Falter
**Pacini, Antonio Francesco Gaetano
   Saverio**   110, Carli, Girard, Richault
Pacini, Giovanni   Cottrau, Lucca, Ricordi
Paderewski, Ignacy Jan   Bote & Bock,
   Krzyżanowski
Paer, Ferdinando   Carli, Mollo
Paff   114, Dubois, Riley
Paganini, Nicolò   Pacini, Ricordi,
   Schonenberger, Schott
Pahlmann, Julius   Spehr
Paine, John Knowles   Schmidt
Paisiello, Giovani   Bailleux, Marescalchi, Sieber,
   Zatta
Paladin, Antoine-François   Gorlier
Paladino [Paladin], Giovanni Paolo [Jean
   Paul]   Gorlier, Moderne
Palestrina, Giovanni Pierluigi da   80, 500,
   Amadino, Barré, Caifabri, Dorico, Grignani,
   Mascardi, Mutii, Plantin, Scotto, Tini, Valesi
Palestrina, Iginio   Valesi
Paling, William Henry   128, Paling
Pallavicino, Benedetto   Phalèse
Palmgren, Selim   Hansen
Paminger, Leonhard   Moderne
Pann, Anton   111
Pannetier, Mme   59
Panseron, Auguste   Pleyel
Panton
Paoli, Giovanni   *see* Pablos
Paolini, Aurelio   Franceschi
Paolucci, Giuseppe 30
Parabosco, Girolamo   Gardano
Paradies, Maria Theresia   Musikalisches
   Magazin
Paradossi   Monti
Paramount Pictures   Famous, Fox, Hansen (C.)
Parasoli, Leonardo   Valesi
París Bazar   Giusti
Parisot, Nicolas   Ballard
Parisotto, A.   Zanibon
Parker, Alice   Schirmer (E.C.)
Parker, Horatio (William)   Novello, Schmidt
Parker, John   Broome
Parker, John Rowe   114
Parker, Samuel H.   Ditson
Parry, Henry John   Ashdown, Wessel
Parry, (Charles) Hubert (Hastings)   Lucas
Parry, John   Goulding, Power

Parsch, József   Táborszky
Partos, Odön   Israel Music Institute
Pascal, Florian [Williams, Joseph
   Benjamin]   Williams
Pasinati, Michele   Girard
Pasoti, Giovanni Giacomo   Dorico, Giunta,
   Petrucci (O.)
Pasquali, Giulio   Robletti
Pasquali, Niccolo   Bremner
Pasquariello   Ricordi
Pasquier, Jean   Haultin
Pasquini, Bernardo   De Santis
Passarini, Francesco   Monti
Paterno, Anton   106
Pasterwitz   Musikalisches Magazin, Sauer
Paterson
Paterson, Robert   103, Paterson
Pathway Press   Vaughan
Patrizi (Patrici), F.   Baldini
Patterson, Paul   Universal, Weinberger
Patton E.D.   Blackmar
Paulus, Stephen   European American
Paur, Hieronymus   Wagner
Pavona, Pietro Alessandro   Della Volpe
Paxton, Stephen   Novello
Paxton, Tom   Oak
Payer, Hieronymus   Haslinger,
   Lithographisches Institut, Mechetti, Mollo
Payne, Albert   118, Eulenburg
Paynter, Ernesto Dotesio   *see* Dotesio Paynter,
   Ernesto
Pazdírek
Pazdírek, Bohumil   110, Pazdírek
Pearce   Corri
Pearson, William   28, 94, Heptinstall, Playford
Pechatschek (Pechacek)   Maisch, Sauer
Pecour, Louis Guillaume   Ribou
Pederson, Mogens   Samfundet til Udgivelse af
   Dansk Musik, Waldkirch
Pedreira, José Enrique   Instituto de Cultura
   Puertorriqueña
Pedrotti, Carlo   Ricordi
Peerson, Martin   Snodham, Stansby
Peer-Southern   127
Peetrino, Jakob   Verovio
Peháček   Ludwig Maish
Peixinho, Jorge   Sassetti
Pekiel, Bartlomiej   Polskie Wydawnictwo
   Muzyczne
Pelissier, Victor   Gilfert
Pelletan, Fanny   Richault
Pelletier, Guillaume le   Fezandat
Penderecki, Krzysztof   Belwin-Mills, Peters (i),
   Schott
Pendleton J.B.   115
Pendleton W.S.   115
Penna, Lorenzo   Monti
Pennauer, Anton   106, Diabelli
Penson & Robertson   103
Pentland, Barbara   Waterloo
Pepper, J(ames) W(elsh)   126
Pepping, Ernst   Bärenreiter
Pepusch, Johann Christoph   Peters (i)
Percival, Allen   Stainer & Bell
Pérégally   Heugel
Perera, Ronald   Schirmer (E.C.)
Perfall, Kari   Falter
Performing Rights Society   Francis, Day &
   Hunter
Pergolesi, Giovanni Battista   Ars Viva,
   Bärenreiter, La Chevardière

Peri, Jacopo   89, Guidi, Marescotti, Pignoni, Raverii, Vincenti
Peri, Eliezer   Israel Music Institute
Pericoli, Pasquale   Della Volpe
Perle, George   Boelke-Bomart
Perry, Michael   94
Persichetti, Vincent   Elkan-Vogel, Presser
Perti, Giovanni Antonio   Della Volpe
Perucona, Maria Saveria   Vigoni
Pesenti, Martino   Vincenti
Pesnot, Charles   88, Le Royer
Pestalozza, Giacinto   Vigoni
Peterde Warpurgen   28
Peterlein, Johann   *see* Petreius
Peters (i)   117, 119, 120, 127, Belyayev, Durand, Heckel, Hoffmeister, Litolff, Rieter-Biedermann, Whistling
Peters (ii)
Peters, Antoine de   Bureau d'Abonnement Musical
Peters, Henry J.   Faulds, Peters (ii)
Peters, John L.   Ditson, Higgins, Peters (ii)
Peters, William Cumming   115, Peters (ii)
Peterson, John W.   Zondervan
Petit, Philippe   Pleyel
Petrarch [Francesco Petrarca]   Barré
Petrassi, Goffredo   Carisch, Ricordi
Petreius [Petrejus, Petri, Peterlein], **Johann**   83, 84, Berg, Egenolff
Petrella, Errico   Clausetti, Giudici & Strada, Lucca
Petri, Adam   Petreius
Petri, Johann Samuel   Hoffmeister
Petrucci, Ottaviano (dei)   20, 23, 41, 82, 97, 129, 498, 499, 502, 503, 506, 519, 520, 532, 538, 541, 544, Antico, Attaingnant, Emmerich, Franck, Giunta, Jacomo, Michel de Toulouse, Oeglin, Scotto
Petrucci P.   91
Petrushka, Shabtai   Israel Music Institute
Petschull, Johannes   Peters (i), Universal
Pettersson, (Gustaf) Allan   Nordiska Musikförlaget
Petz, Johann   Gutheil
Peutinger, Konrad   Grimm & Wirsung
Pevernage, Andreas   41, 42, Bogard, Phalèse, Plantin
Peyrot, J.   Senart
Pezzana, Niccolò   Giunta
Pfaltz, J.B.   André
Pfeyl, Johann   80, Sensenschmidt
Pfitzner, Hans   Brockhaus, Fürstner, Leuckart, Peters (i), Ries & Erler, Simrock
Phalèse   Baethen, Bellère, Bogard, Geertsom, Plantin, Poggioli, Susato
Phalèse, Pierre (i)   24, 84, Phalèse
Phalèse, Pierre (ii)   84, 92, Bellère, Phalèse
Philandrier   Fezandat
Philidor, François-André Danican   La Chevardière
Philip II   Plantin
Philipp, Franz   Böhm
Philipp, Isidore   Durand
Philippot, Michel   Billaudot
Philips, Peter   Phalèse
Phillips, J.R.   Balmer & Weber
Phillips, James   Balmer & Weber
Phillips, John   102, Johnson (John)
Phillips, Nathaniel   Balmer & Weber
Phillips, Sarah   Phillips
Philomathes, Wenceslaus   Rhau

Philovalensis, Hieronim   *see* Wietor
Phinot, Dominique   Beringen
Phipps   Goulding
Piatti, Alfredo   Chappell
Pibac, Guy de Faur   Jean II de Laon
Picasso, Pablo   La Sirène
Piccinini, Alessandro   Monti, (G.)
Piccinni, Niccolò   Bailleux, Zatta
Piccioli, Giacomo Antonio   Curci
Pichl, Wenzel   Zatta
Picinelli, Abbé Filippo   Vigoni
Pick-Mangiagalli, Riccardo   Carisch
Pictor, Bernardus   Ratdolt
Piechler, Arthur   Böhm
Pié de Dieu, Pierre   Haultin
Piedigrotta Festival   Cottrau
Pierlot, Pierre   Billaudot
Pierrot   Leduc
Pietrasanta, Plinio   Rampazetto
Pietroiacomo
Pigna, Alessandro   Ricordi
Pignoni, Zanobi di Francesco   89, Cecconcelli, Marescotti
Pigott, Samuel   Bunting
Pigouchet, Claude   *see* Attaingnant, Marie
Pigouchet, Philippe   Attaingnant
Pilcher, H. & Sons   Balmer & Weber
Pilkington, Francis   East
Pinatel   Billaudot
Pink Floyd   Chappell
Pinkham, Daniel   Schirmer, (E.C.)
Pinto Braga, Narcizo José   Bevilacqua, Laforge, Napoleão
Pipphard, Luke   Walsh
Pirsson, William   Paff
Pisano, Bernardo   Petrucci (O.)
Pisarri, Alessandro
Pisarri, Antonio   91, Pisarri
Pistocchi, Francesco   Silvani
Piston, Walter   Arrow Music Press, Associated Music Publishers, Boosey & Hawkes, Cos Cob Press, Schirmer (E.C.)
Pitfield, Thomas   Peters (i)
Pitt & Hatzfeld   Lucas
Pius IX   Pustet
Pixis, Johann Peter   Haslinger, Kunst- und Industrie-Comptoir, Mechetti, Pleyel
Pizzetti, Ildebrando   Carisch, De Santis, Ricordi, Sonzogno, Suvini Zerboni
Pizzini, Carlo Alberto   De Santis
Plainsong and Medieval Music Society   118
Planck, Stephan   80, Han
Planquette, Robert   Williams
Plantade, Charles Henri   Erard
Plantin, Christopher   24, 27, 84, 92, 94, 495, 545, Granjon, Phalèse, Susato
Plattner, Lodewijk   100, Barth
Playford   533, Jones
Playford, Henry   Carr, Hare, Heptinstall, Jones, Pearson, Playford, Walsh, Young
Playford, John (i)   89, 92, 94, 100, Carr, Cross, Godbid, Harper, Playford
Playford, John (ii)   Godbid, Playford
Plessy, F. du   *see* Du Plessis, F.
Pleyel, Ignace Joseph [Ignaz Josef]   103, 104, André, Artaria (i), Barth, Cousineau, Falter, Hoffmeister, Hummel, Imbault, Longman & Broderip, Marescalchi, Mollo, Musikalisches Magazin, Richault, Schonenberger, Schott, Sieber, Sønnichsen, Thomson, Traeg
Podestà, Andrea   Grignani

Index

Poggiolo, Antonio 91, Fei, Robletti
Pohl, Carl Ferdinand Mechetti
Pointel, Antoine Le Chevalier, Roger
Poitevin, Alphonse 61
Poldini, Ede Schuberth (E.)
Police Chappell
Polish Music Publications Polskie Wydawnictwo Muzyczne
Polish Music Publishing Society Polskie Wydawnictwo Muzyczne
Pollini, Cesare Ricordi
Pollock Boelke-Bomart
Polonus, Stanislaus 26
Polskie Wydawnictwo Muzyczne 122
Polygram Chappell
Polzelli, Anton Traeg
Ponce, Manuel M. Peer-Southern, Wagner (A.)
Ponchielli, Amilcare Ricordi
Pond, Sylvanus Billings Benteen, Couse, Firth, Hall & Pond, Riley
Pond, William A. Firth, Hall & Pond
Ponscarme, & Cie Rouart-Lerolle
Ponte, Lorenzo da Corri
Pontelibero, Ferdinando Scotti
Porcelli, Giuseppe Maria Marescalchi
Porpora, Nicolo Antonio Fortier
Porrino, Ennio De Santis
Porta, Costanzo Merulo
Porta, Ercole Rossi
Porter, Cole Chappell
Porter, (William) Quincy Society for the Publication of American Music
Porto, Michele Petrucci (P.)
Pothier, Dom Joseph Desclée
Potter Goulding
Pötting, Adolph Count von Lithographisches Institut
Poulenc, Francis (Jean Marcel) Chester, De Santis, Durand, Eschig, Hansen (W.), Heugel, La Sirène, Rouart-Lerolle, Salabert
Pousseur, Henri Universal
Powell, Mel Society for the Publication of American Music
Power, James 103
Power, William 103, Power
Pozzi, Escot (Olga) Ricordi
Praetorius, Friedrich Emanuel Stern
Praetorius, Hieronymus Carstens, Van Ohr
Praetorius, Jacob (ii) Stern
Praetorius, Johannes 87
Praetorius, Michael Fürstliche Druckerei, Hänssler, Kahnt, Kallmeyer, Weigel
Pratis, Jean de see Du Pré
Prato, Jean a see Du Pré
Prentiss, Henry 115
Presser Church, Ditson, Elkan-Vogel, Moller & Capron, New Music, Presser, Society for the Publication of American Music
Presser, Theodore 124
Preston Bremner, Coventry & Hollier, Wright & Wilkinson
Preston, John 101, Preston
Preston, Thomas 101, Longman & Broderip, Preston, Skillern
Preussische Akademie der Künste Trautwein
Prevost, Guillaume Higman
Prilipp [Philippe] Pleyel
Primavera, Giovan Leonardo Merulo, Rampazetto
Priuli, Giovanni Magni
Pro Art Publications Belwin-Mills

Probst, Heinrich Albert 107, Kistner & Siegel
Procházka, Ludevít Hudební Matice
Progin, Xavier 63
Prokofiev, Sergey (Sergeyevich) Boosey & Hawkes, Deutscher Verlag für Musik, Editions Russes de Musique, Leeds, Muzïka, Sikorski, Universal, Weintraub
Proske, Karl Choron, Pustet
Prout, Ebenezer Augener, Lucas, Novello
Prowse, Thomas Keith, Prowse
Prudent, Emile Escudier, Ricordi
Prudentius, Aurelius Clemens Faber
Prudhomme Leduc
Prüss, Johann 7
Pryor, Arthur Carl Fischer, Pepper
Ptolemy, Claudius 40
Publishing Services Partnership Galliard
Puccini, Giacomo (Antonio Domenico Michele Secondo Maria) De Santis, Ricordi
Puente, Giuseppe de Carlino
Pugliani, Margherita Marescotti
Pugliaschi Robletti
Pugnani, (Guilio) Gaetano (Gerolamo) Sieber
Pugni, Cesare Bertuzzi
Pujol, Emilio Eschig
Purcell, Daniel Cross
Purcell, Frances Playford
Purcell, Henry 101, Carr, Cross, Heptinstall, Hudgebut, Musical Antiquarian Society, Novello, Pearson, Playford, Purcell Society, Young
Purcell Society Novello
Purday 102, Button & Whitaker, Thompson
Purday, Thomas Edward Clementi, Purday
Purdie, Robert 103, Penson, Robertson
Pusinelli, Anton Meser
Pustet
Pustet, F. 110
PWM Polskie Wydawnictwo Muzyczne
Pybrac, Guy de Faur Jean II de Laon
Pye 49
Pynson 5

Quagliati, Paolo Mutii, Robletti
Quak, Arend Pustet
Quantz, Johann Joachim Boivin, Le Clerc, Roger, Winter
Quitschreiber, Georg Weidner

Rab [Corvinus, Christopher], **Christoph** 89, [Raabe, Rabe]
Rab, Georg Feyerabend, Rab
Rabelais, François Fezandat, Granjon
Rabus, Sigmund Kunst- und Industrie-Comptoir
Racca, A., e Balegno Giudici & Strada
Radecke, Kurt Bote & Bock
Radio Music Company Feist, Thompson (G.V.)
Raff, Joachim Senff
Raffaele, Niccolò di Petrucci (O.)
Ragwitz, Erhard Deutscher Verlag für Musik
Rahter, Daniel Benjamin, Simrock
Rakhmaninov 122, Boosey & Hawkes, Broude (A.), Editions Russes de Musique, Gutheil, Whaley, Royce & Co.
Ralson 95
Rameau, Jean-Phillippe Ballard, Boivin, Broude Brothers, Durand
Rampazetto, Francesco 83, Barré, Giunta, Scotto
Rampollini, Matteo Moderne

Randall, Elizabeth Birchall, Randall, Wright & Wilkinson
Randall, Peter Randall, Walsh
Randall, William 101, Birchall, Coventry & Hollier, Preston, Walsh, Wright & Wilkinson
Randhartinger, Benedikt Pennauer
Rands, Bernard Universal
Rangström Nordiska Musikförlaget
Raphael, Günter Breitkopf & Härtel
Raphelengius, Christofel Plantin
Raphelengius, Francis Plantin
Rasch, Johann Feyerabend
Raselius, Andreas Hänssler
Rasi, Francesco Marescotti
Rastell, John 22–3, 27, Attaingnant, Gough
Ratdolt, Erhard 5, 26, 81
Rathaus, Karel Israeli Music Publications
Ratti, Cencetti & Comp. 111
Ratti, Leopoldo Ratti, Cencetti & Comp.
Rättig 119, Lienau
Rättig, Theodor Rättig
Rausch, Frederick 114, Gilfert, Paff
Ravanello, Oreste Zanibon
Raveau, Adrien Durand
Ravel, (Joseph) Maurice 122, Durand, Editions Russes de Musique, Elkan-Vogel, Eschig
Ravenscroft, Thomas 500, Allde, East
Raverii, Alessandro 83
Ravina, Henri Leduc
Rawlings, Thomas A. Regent's Harmonic Institution
Rawsthorne, Alan Oxford University Press
Raymaker, Martin de (Rotarius) Phalèse
Raymundi, D. 41
Razumovsky, Count Andrey Kyrillovich Pleyel
Razzi, Serafino Giunta, Rampazetto
Read, Daniel 113
Reade, Music Corp., Walter Frank
Rebenlein
Rebenlein, Georg 87, Rebenlein
Reber, (Napoléon-) Henri Richault
Rebuffat, J. Senart
Reda, Siegfried Bärenreiter
Redel, Martin Bote & Bock
Reed, Alfred Marks
Reed, George P. 115, Benteen, Russell
Reed, James Johnson
Reese, Gustave Fischer (C.)
Reeve, William Goulding, Preston
Regent's Harmonic Institution
Reger, Max Aibl, Ascherberg, Hopwood & Crew, Bote & Bock, Breitkopf & Härtel, Forberg, Hug, Lauterbach & Kuhn, Leuckart, Peters (i), Simrock, Universal
Reggio, Pietro 94
Regnard brothers Bogard
Regnault, Madeleine-Victoire *see* Madeleine-Victoire Cousineau
Regnier, Nicolas *see* Renier
Rehm, Peter Haslinger
Rehm, Peter, widow of Haslinger
Reich, Professor Mense
Reicha, Antoine(-Joseph) Lemoine, Traeg
Reichardt, Johann Friedrich Breitkopf & Härtel, Hartnoch, Peters (i)
Reichel, Carl Johannes Röder
Reimann, Aribert Ars Viva
Reinagle, Alexander 114, Aitken, Moller & Capron, Schetky
Reinecke, Carl Hug, Kistner & Siegel, Senff
Reiner, Ambrosius Wagner (M.)

Reiner, Jacob Meltzer
Reinhard of Strasbourg 33
Reinhold, Otto Breitkopf & Härtel
Reisch, Gregor 7
Reissiger, Karl Trautwein
Reiter, Josef Universal
Reizenstein, Franz Lengnick
Rékai, András Editio Musica Budapest
Rellstab, Johann Carl Friedrich 105, Winter
Rellstab, Ludwig Trautwein
Remick, Jerome H. 125, Stark, Tilzer, Warner Bros.
Remlab, Charles Balmer & Weber
Remunde [Ruremunde; Endoviensis], **Christophe van** 81, Cock
Rener, Adam Aich
Renier (Regnier), Nicolas Andrez
Rennagel, Johann Wilhelm Rönnagel
Renotte, Hubert Andrez
Resinarius, Balthasar Rhau
Respighi, Ottorino Benjamin, Bote & Bock, Ricordi
Restano, (Casar) Breyer
Retford, Irene Benjamin
Retz, Countess of Le Roy
Reusner, Friedrich 87
Reusner, Johann 87, Mense, Segebade
Revell, Nellie Bloom
Revere, Paul 113
Revueltas, Silvestre Peer-Southern
Reycend, Fratelli e C. Lucca
Reyer, Louis-Etieene-Ernest Choudens, Heugel
Reyser, Georg 5, 80
Rezniček, E(mil) N(ikolaus) von Birnbach, Ries & Erler
Rhames, Benjamin 103
Rhau [Rhaw], **Georg** 23, 86, Bärenreiter, Faber
Rhau, Johann Rhau
Rheinberger, Joseph Aibl, Benjamin
Rhené-Baton Durand
Rhetus [Rhete], **Georg** 88
Rhode, Georg Rhetus
Rialto Gerig
Ribou, Pierre 95, Baussen, Foucault
Ricari, Carlo Caifabri
Ricci, Federico Cottrau, Lucca, Ricordi
Ricci, Giuseppe Gramitto Curci
Ricci, Luigi Cottrau, Ricordi
Riccio, P.P. Carlino, Gargano
Riccio, Scipione Gargano
Rice, Henry 114
Richafort, Jean Attaingnant
Richardson, Nathan 115, Russell
Richault 110, Carli, Costallat, Escudier, Pleyel
Richault, Charles-Simon Frey, Richault
Richel, Bernhard 5, 80, Valdarfer, Wenssler
Richers 43
Richomme, Jean-Thomas Pleyel
Richter Girard
Richter, Franz Xaver Thompson, Venier
Richter, Wolfgang 87, Stein
Richtzenhan family Weidner
Ricordi 62, 63, 111, 127, 496, 514, 515, 517, 521, 522, 528, 534, Bertuzzi, Boileau Bernasconi, Breyer, Canti, Carulli, Cottrau, Escudier, Galaxy, Girard, Giudici & Strada, Guidi, Lucca
Ricordi, Giovanni Artaria (ii), Clausetti, Lorenzi, Lucca, Ricordi
Ricordi, Giulio Clausetti, Ricordi
Ricordi, Tito (i) Clausetti, Lucca, Ricordi

Index

Ricordi-Americana Breyer
Rider, F.B. Balmer & Weber
Ridout, Godfrey Thompson (G.), Waterloo
Riedel, Johannes Bergen
Rieder, Ambrosius Musikalisches Magazin
Riederer, F. 22
Riedl, Josef Haslinger, Kunst- und Industrie-
  Comptoir
Rieff, Georg Joseph Gombart
Riegger, Wallingford American Composers
  Alliance, Associated Music Publishers,
  Broude (A.)
Riemann, Hugo Breitkopf & Hartel, Litolff,
  Pustet
Ries, Ferdinand Regent's Harmonic Institution,
  Ries & Erler, Peters (i)
Ries, Franz 110, Ries & Erler, Traeg
Ries & Erler 110
Rieter-Biedermann, Jakob Melchior 111,
  Peters (i)
Riethmüller, Heinrich Sikorski
Rieti, Vittorio De Santis
Rietz, Julius Senff
Rigacci, Giuseppe Moüche
Rigaud, Louis de 49, Ballard
Rigel, Heinrich Joseph Götz
Řihovský, Vojtěch Urbánek (W.)
Riisager, Knudåge Fog, Hansen (W.),
  Samfundet ti Udgivelse af Dansk Musik
Riley, Edward 114, Firth, Hall & Pond, Paff
Riley, Frederick Gordon, Riley
Rimbault, Edward Francis Chappell, Handel
  societies
Rimsky-Korsakov, Nikolay Andreyevich
  Belyayev, Dover, Editions Russes de
  Musique, Muzïka, Stellovsky
Riotte, Philipp Jakob Haslinger
Ripa (da Mantova), Alberto da Ballard,
  Fezandat
Rippe, Albert de see Ripa (da Mantova), Alberto
  da
Rist, Johann von 92, Stern
Ritchie, Jean Oak
Ritter, Alexander Aibl
Ritter, Frédéric Louis Schuberth (E.)
Rivier, Jean Senart
Rivière, Jules Prudence Boosey & Hawkes
Rizy, Johann Sigmund Kunst- und Industrie-
  Comptoir
Roathwell, Alex Young
Robbiani, Igino Carisch
Robbins Big 3, EMI Music-SBK
Robbins, John Jacob (Jack) 125, Robbins
Robbins Music EMI Music-SBK
Roberday, François Métru
Roberts, Henry 102, Welcker
Robertson, Alexander Penson & Robertson
Robertson, Alexander, son of Alexander
  Penson & Robertson, Purdie
Robertson, John Penson & Robertson
Robethon, D. Le Chevalier
Robinson, A.L. Drei Masken Verlag
Robitschek, Adolf Universal
Robjohn, William James Whittemore
Robletti, Giovanni Battista 91, Poggioli, Soldi
Robson, Jean-Jacques Andrez
Rocca, Lodovico Ricordi
Roccia, Aurelio Merulo
Roccia, Dattilo Carlino, Vitale
Rochberg, George Presser
Roche, Jean de la Attaingnant

Rode, (Jacques) Pierre (Joseph) Cocks, Magasin
  de Musique (ii), Lucca, Traeg
Rodeheaver, Homer A(lvan) 124, 126, Word
Röder, Carl Gottlieb 51, 117, Cottrau, Lowe &
  Brydone, Peters (i), Wagner (A.)
Röder, Carl Johannes Harris
Rodgers, Richard 125, Chappell, Harms, Silver
  Burdett
Rodio, Rocco Carlino, Dorico, Vitale
Rodriguez, Felipe P. Breyer, Monguillot
Rodriguez, J. Breyer
Roger, Estienne 47, 100, 527, 533, Walsh,
  Witvogel
Rogers, Stephen 43
Rogers, Winthrop Stainer & Bell
Rogier, Philippe Giunta
Rognoni, Ricciardo Lomazzo, Vincenti
Roguski, Gustav Sennewald
Rohm, Wilhelm Österreichischer Bundesverlag
Rohwer, Jens Breitkopf & Härtel
Rolla, Alessandro Ricordi
Rolla, Carlo Francesco Camagno, Rolla
Rolla, Giorgio 89, Camagno
Rollinson, Thomas H. Pepper
Romano, Eustachio Petrucci (O.)
Romberg, Bernhard Erard, Haslinger
Romberg, Sigmund Chappell, Warner Bros.,
  Witmark
Romberg brothers Boosey & Hawkes, Erard,
  Plattner
Romero, Mateo Unión Musical Española
Romero y Fernandez Ricordi
Rönnagel, Johann Wilhelm 100
Ronsard, Pierre de Le Roy
Rontani, Rafaello Robletti
Röntgen, Julius Alsbach
Root, Ebenezer Towner Root & Cady
Root, George Frederick Biglow & Main,
  Church, Mason Bros., Root & Cady, Russell
Root & Cady 116, Russell
Ropartz, (Joseph) Guy (Marie) Durand, Rouart-
  Lerolle
Rore, Cipriano de 519, Gardano, Merulo,
  Phalèse, Rampazetto, Scotto
Rorem, Ned Boosey & Hawkes, Schirmer (E.C.)
Rosart, Jacques-François 28, 98
Rosas, Juventino Wagner (A.)
Rosé, Arnold Universal
Roseingrave, Thomas Cooke
Rosellen, Henri Escudier
Rosenborg, Einar Gehrman
Rosenberg, Hilding Hansen (W.), Nordiska
  Musikförlaget
Rosenborg, Inge and Einar's Foundation for
  Swedish Music Gehrman
Rosenmüller, Johan Hänssler, Vincenti
Rosetti, Antonio Torricella
Rosholm, J.A. Norsk Musikforlag
Rosier, Rosiers, Charles Le Chevalier
Roskošný, J.R. Hoffmann
Rossellini, Renzo Curci, Ricordi
Rossi, D.F. Sala
Rossi (Rubeus), Francesco Baldini, Buglhat
Rossi, Giovanni 89
Rossi, Michelangelo Caifabri
Rossi, Salamone Phalèse, Vincenti
Rossini, Giachino (Antonio) 110, 515, 521, 534,
  Artaria (i), Boosey & Hawkes, Brzezina,
  Carli, Girard, Guidi, Haslinger, Hewitt,
  Hoftheater-Musik-Verlag, Janet & Cotelle,
  Joubert, Lorenzi, Mechetti, Mollo, Pacini,

599

Pleyel, Ratti, Cencetti & Comp., Ricordi, Sauer, Schlesinger, Schonenberger, Schott, Scotti, Troupenas
Rossiter, Will
Rota, Nino Carisch, Ricordi
Rotaire, M. Baethen
Rötel, Anna Margarete Wust
Rötel, Kaspar Wust
Roth, Ernst 119, Boosey & Hawkes
Röthing, Albert Hofmeister
Rottensteiner, Alois Österreichischer Bundesverlag
Rouart-Lerolle 122, Salabert
Roudanez, Benjamin Senart
Rouse, Christopher European American
Roussel Durand, Foucault, Oiseau-Lyre
Roussier, Abbé Gando
Rovenský, Holan Labaun
Roy, Peter Walker Paterson
Royal Musical Association Stainer & Bell
Royol, Isidore Joubert
Rozsa, Miklos Broude Brothers
Rózsavölgyi, Gyula (Rosenthaler, Julius) Rózsavölgyi
Rózsavölgyi és Társa 122, Editio Musica Budapest, Rozsnyai, Táborszky, Treichlinger, Wagner
Rozsnyai 122, Editio Musica Budapest, Rózsavölgyi
Rubank Leonard
Rubbra, Edmund Lengnick
Rubini, Nicolò Amadino
Rubinstein, Anton (Grigor'yevich) Bessel, Bote & Bock, Kistner & Siegel, Krzyżanowski, Senff
Rubinstein, Nikolay Jürgenson
Rubio, Samuel Unión Musical Española
Ruffo, Vincenzo A-R Editions, Barré, Gardano, Sabbio, Scotto
Rugeriis, Ugo de 7
Ruggles, Carl (Sprague) Langinger, New Music, Presser
Rühlmann, Franz Litolff
Rullman, Fred J. 126
Runge
Runge, Georg 87, Runge
Ruppel, Berthold Wenssler
Ruremunde, Christophe van *see* Remunde
Russell, George D. 115, Ditson, Gordon, Schmidt
Russischer Musikverlag Editions Russes de Musique
Rutini, Giovanni Maria Della Volpe, De Santis
Ruuli, Rinaldo Fei
Ryall, John Bickham
Ryba, Jakub Jan Enders
Rybiński, Jean Hünefeld
Rykken, Clyde A-R Editions
Rylander, Lars Gustaf Lundquist

Sabbatini, Galeazzo Caifabri, Grignani, Robletti, Salvadori, Vincenti
Sabbatini, Giovanni Andreas Fougt
Sabbio, Vincenzo 89
Sacchi, Ferdinando Artaria (ii)
Sacred Music Press Lorenz
Sadelar [Sadeler], **Johan** 41, 94
Sadowski, Paul McGinnis & Marx
Saeverud, Harald Norsk Musikforlag
Sage, John 116
Sager, Carole Bayer Chappell

St-André, Pierre de Le Royer
Saint-Quentin 49
Saint-Saëns, (Charles) Camille 122, Choudens, Durand, Hamelle, Hartmann, Joubert
Sala, Giuseppe 91
Salabert 122, Schirmer (G.), Senart
Salabert, Edouard Salabert
Salabert, Francis Rouart-Lerolle, Salabert
Sales, Franz Černý
Salieri, Antonio Artaria (i), Torricella, Zatta
Salminger, Sigmund Kriesstein, Ulhart
Salmon, Lily 64
Salmon & Cia. Laforge
Salomon, Johann Peter Longman & Broderip, Pleyel
Salomonsson, Abraham Hirsch
Salvadori, Angelo 91
Salvat Unión Musical Española
Salviani, Orazio Carlino
Salzer Trattner
Salzilli, Crescenzio Carlino
Samazeuilh, Gustave Durand
Samber, Johann Baptist Mayer
Sambonetto 82
Samfundet til Udgivelse af Dansk Musik 120
Sammartini, Giuseppe Fortier, Roberts, Venier
Samuel, Harold Associated Board of the Royal Schools of Music
Sandberger, Adolf Drei Masken Verlag, Kahnt, Litolff
Sander, Constantin Cappi, Leuckart
Sander, Horst Leuckart
Sander, Martin Leuckart
Sandrin [Regnault, Pierre] Moderne
Sandström, Sven-David Nordiska Musikförlaget
Sankey, I. Allan Biglow & Main
Sankey, Ira David Biglow & Main
Sanlecque, Jacques de Ballard, Le Bé
San Romano, Carlo Giuseppe Vigoni
Santambrogio Scotti
Santley, Charles Chappell, Lucas
Santoro, Cardinal Giulio Antonio Granjon
Santritter, Johann Franck
Santuccio, John A. Schirmer (G.)
Sapieyevski, Jerzy Presser
Sarasate, Pablo Krzyżanowski
Sarlós, László Editio Musica Budapest
Sarony, Major & Knapp 115
Sarony, Napoleon 115
Sarrette, Bernard Magasin de Musique (i)
Sarti, Giuseppe Artaria (i), Fougt, Löschenkohl, Marescalchi, Sieber, Torricella
Sartori, Claudio Ricordi
Sartorio, Antonio Sala
Sassen (Sassenus), Servatius Phalèse
Sassetti
Sassetti, João Baptista 113, Sassetti
Sassetti – Sociedade Portuguese de Música e Som Sassetti
Satie, Erik (Alfred Leslie) Eschig, La Sirène, Rouart-Lerolle
Sätzl, Christoph Wagner (M.)
Sauer
Sauer, Ignaz 106, Eder, Sauer
Sauguet, Henri Oiseau-Lyre
Saur, Christopher 31, 113
Savagnone, Giuseppe De Santis
Savaresse, Philibert Heugel
Saville, L.J. Cramer
Savioni, Mario Caifabri
Savj Scotti

Saygun, Ahmet Adnan   Peer-Southern
SBK Entertainment World   EMI Music-SBK
Sbugo, Messi   Buglhat
Scacchi, Marco   Robletti, Vincenti
Scaletta, Orazio   Lomazzo, Vincenti
Scandello, Antonio   Bergen
Scarlatti, (Pietro) Alessandro (Gaspare)   Bote & Bock, Roger
Scarlatti, Domenico   101 Cooke, Editio Musica Budapest, Fortier, Haffner, Johnson (John), Kunst- und Industrie-Comptoir, Ricordi, Rozsnyai
Scattaglia, Pietro   Alessandri & Scattaglia
Schaeffer, Franz   Schmidt
Schafer, R. Murray   Berandol, Universal
Schale, Christian Friedrich   Schmid
Schalk, Joseph   Rättig
Schall, C.   Sønnichsen
Schallehn   Nordheimer
Scharffenburg, Johann   Baumann
Scharpfenberg   *see* Szarfenberg, Maciej
Schauer, Richard   Benjamin
Schauer family   Simrock
Scheffer, Martin   Hantzsch
Scheidt, Samuel   Deutscher Verlag für Musik, Hänssler, Ugrino
Schein, Johann Hermann   87, Bärenreiter, Breitkopf & Härtel
Schellhass, Friedrich   Falter
Schenck, Johannes   Le Chevalier
Schenker, Heinrich   Universal
Scherchen, Hermann   119, Ars Viva
Scherenberg, Rudolf, Bishop of   Reyser
Scherer, Sebastian Anton   95
Schering, Arnold   Breitkopf & Härtel, Handel societies, Kahnt
Schetky, J.G.   103, Schetky
Scheuermann, Gustav   36, Augener
Scheurleer,Daniel François   Cock
Schickele, Peter   Presser
Schidlowsky, León   Israel Music Institute
Schildbach, C.F.   Jürgenson
Schindler, Anton   Hoffmann
Schirmer, E.C.   Boston Music Company
Schirmer, Ernest Charles   Boston Music Company, Schirmer (E.C.)
Schirmer, G.   51, 124, 125, 126, 127, Associated Music Publishers, Chappell, Grunewald, Leonard, Wagner (A.), Wa-Wan Press
Schirmer, Gustav   Schirmer (G.)
Schirmer, Gustave [son]   Boston Music Company, Schirmer (G.)
Schirmer, Gustave [grandson]   Boston Music Company, Schirmer (G.)
Schlee, Alfred   Universal
Schlesinger   Lienau, Rättig
Schlesinger, Maurice   107, 110, Brandus, Escudier, Joubert, Pleyel, Schlesinger, Troupenas
Schlichtegroll, Friedrich von   Senefelder
Schlick, Arnold   Ugrino
Schloss, M.   Ries & Erler
Schmelzer, Johann Heinrich   Cosmerovius
Schmid [Schmidt], Balthasar   105, Roger
Schmid, Catharina   Berg (J.)
Schmidl, Carlo   Ricordi
Schmidt   Weigel
Schmidt, Arthur P(aul)   120, 124, 127, Ditson, Jung, Summy-Birchard
Schmidt, Franz   Drei Masken Verlag, Universal, Weinberger

Schmidt, Henry   Prentiss
Schmidt, Johann   Segebade
Schmidt, Nickel   Faber
Schmitt, Florent   Billaudot, Durand, Heugel
Schmitt, Joseph
Schmitt, Karl Joseph   100, Schmitt
Schnabel, Artur   Curci
Schneider, A.G.   Weigel
Schneider, Max   Deutscher Verlag für Musik
Schneider-Schott, Günther   Schott
Schneider-Schott, Heinz   Schott
Schnitke, Alfred   Universal
Schnitzkius, Gregor   Hünefeld
Schnüffis, Laurentius von   Bencard, Dreher
Schober, Franz von   Lithographisches Institut
Schobert, Johann   Longman & Broderip, Sieber
Schobser, Andreas   Berg (A.)
Schoeck, Othmar   Breitkopf & Härtel, Hug, Universal Edition
Schoeffer [Schöffer], Peter   4, 22, 26, 82, 520, Aich, Apiarius, Petrucci (O.)
Schoenberg, Arnold   119, 127, 496, Belmont, Birnbach, Boelke-Bomart, Faber Music, Hansen (W.), Heinrichshofen, Israeli Music Publications, Langinger, New Music, Peters (i), Schott, Universal
Schoenberg, Gertrud   Belmont
Schoenberg, Lawrence   Belmont
Schoenewerk   Durand, Flaxland
Scholander, Sven   Nordiska Musikförlaget
Scholes, Percy   Oxford University Press
Schonacker, John E.   Whittemore
Schönenberger, Georges   Lemoine
Schönfelder, Jörg   Schoeffer
Schönig
Schönig, Johann Jakob, widow of   *see* Wagner, Christoph, widow of
Schönig, Valentin   87, Kriesstein, Schönig, Ulhart
Schott   68, 107, 119, 120, 534, Brzezina, Eulenberg, European American, Falter, Fürstner, Heckel, Lengnick, Schmidt
Schott, A.   Falter
Schott, Bernhard   105, Schott
Schott, Franz Philipp   Flaxland, Schott
Schott, Johann   7
Schott Frères   Schott
Schott's Söhne, B.   Ars Viva, Augener, Flaxland, Schmidt, Schott, Volk, Wiener Urtext Edition
Schramm, Melchior   Rab
Schreiber, Friedrich   Diabelli
Schreker, Franz   Universal
Schrems, Joseph   Pustet
Schreyvogel, Joseph   Kunst- und Industrie-Comptoir
Schroeder, Hermann   Tonger
Schroeter, Johann Samuel   Napier
Schubert, Franz (Peter)   107, 521, 526, Artaria (i), Associated Board of the Royal Schools of Music, Bärenreiter, Böhm, Breitkopf & Härtel, Cappi, Diabelli, Haslinger, Heinrichshofen, Israeli Music Publications, Lienau, Lithographisches Institut, Maisch, Mechetti, Mollo, Pazdírek, Pennauer, Richault, Sauer, Senff, Weigl, Wessel, Wiener Urtext Edition
Schuberth, Edward
Schuberth, Julius (Ferdinand Georg)   110, Schuberth (E.)

Schuller, Gunther   Associated Music Publishers, Jerona
Schulman, Alan   Broude (A.)
Schulmeister, Johann Baptist   Hoffmeister
Schultze, Clemens   Litolff
Schultze-Biesantz, Clemens   Litolff
Schulz, Johann Abraham Peter   Fog, Samfundet til Udgivelse af Dansk Musik, Sønnichsen
Schuman, William   Arrow Music Press, Presser, Schirmer (G.), Silver Burdett
Schumann, August   Balmer & Weber
Schumann, Clara   525, Breitkopf & Härtel, Chappell, Hofmeister
Schumann, Robert (Alexander)   110, Bach-Gesellschaft, Heinrichshofen, Mechetti, Richault, Rieter-Biedermann, Schlesinger, Schuberth (J.), Senart, Senff, Simrock, Wessel, Urtext Edition Wiener
Schütz, Heinrich   Bärenreiter, Bergen, Breitkopf & Härtel, Gardano, Klemm
Schuyt, Cornelis   41, Plantin
Schwab, Felician   Wagner
Schwaen, Kurt   Deutscher Verlag für Musik
Schwalm, Oskar   Kahnt
Schwantner, Joseph   European American
Schwartz, Elliott   Broude (A.)
Schwarz, Mathias   Haslinger
Schweitzer, Albert   Dover
Schwertel, Johann   86
Schwickert
Schwickert, Engelhard Benjamin   105, Schwickert
Schwind, Moritz von   Sauer
Schwindl, Friedrich   Andrez, Heina
Schwintzer, Johann   Schoeffer
Schytte, Ludvig   Kgl. Hof-Musikhandel
Scialla, Alessandro   Carlino, Vitale
Scinzenzeller, Ulrich   Pachel
Scott, James   Stark
Scott, Sam   Carr
Scott, Sir Walter   Thomson
Scotti, Luigi   111
Scotto   23, 39, 81, 82, 83, 503, 527, Barré, Magni, Vincenti
Scotto, Amadio   Petrucci (O.), Scotto
Scotto, Girolamo   Amadino, Gardano, Rampazetto, Scotto
Scotto, Melchiore   Rampazetto, Scotto
Scotto, Ottaviano (ii)   Antico, Scotto
Scotus   5
Scribe   510
Scudo, Paul   Escudier
Seagar, Francis   Seres
Searle, Humphrey   Faber, Schott
Sebastian z Felsztyna   Haller
Sechter, Simon   Lithographisches Institut, Wiener Philharmonischer Verlag
Secusio, Ottavio   Poggioli
Seeger, Pete   Oak
Seeger, Ruth. *see* Crawford, Ruth
Segebade, Elisabeth   Mense, Reusner, Segebade
Segebade, Josua   Mense, Segebade
Segebade, Lorenz   87, Mense
Segebrecht, Reimar   Bosworth
Seiber, Mátyás   Schott, Suvini Zerboni
Seiffert, Max   Litolff
Seiffert, Wolfgang   Bergen
Seixas, Carlos de   Sassetti, Valentim de Carvalho
Selby, William   Thomas
Selle, Thomas   Hanssler, Stern
Senaillé, Jean Baptiste   Boivin

Senart   122, Salabert
Senefelder, Alois   55, 56–8, 59, 61, 106, 107, 519, 532, André, Breitkopf & Härtel, Gleissner, Haslinger, Hoffmeister, Sauer, Sidler
Senff, Bartolf Wilhelm   Simrock
Senfl, Ludwig   Grimm & Wirsung, Hug, Oeglin, Ott
Sengstack, David   Summy-Birchard
Sengstack, John   Summy-Birchard
Senlecque, Jacques de   *see* Sanlecque, Jacques de
Sennewald
Sennewald, Gustaw Adolf   111, Brzezina, Sennewald
Sensenschmidt, Johann   6, 80, Pfeyl
Sensenschmidt, Lorenz   Pfeyl, Sensenschmidt
Septgranges, Corneille de   Giunta
Sera, Cosimo del   Pignoni
Serebrier, José   Peer-Southern
Seres, William
Sermisy, Claudin de   Attaingnant, Ballard, Du Bosc, Moderne
Serov, Alexander Nikolayevich   Gutheil, Stellovsky
Serpieri   Robletti
Serres, Marcel de   58
Sertenas   Fezandat
Servin, Jean   Goulart, Le Royer
Sessions, Roger   Arrow Music Press, Belwin-Mills, Cos Cob Press, Marks, Presser
Setaccioli   De Santis
Seter, Mordicai   Israel Music Institute
Ševčík, Otakar   Bosworth, Pazdírek
Séverac, (Marie Joseph Alexandre) Deodat de   Rouart-Lerolle
Seward, Theodore Frelinghuysen   Mason Bros.
Seyffardt, J.W.L.   Alsbach
Seymour, A.-M.   Fezandat
Seymour, J.   Fezandat
Sfarzenberg   87
Shapero, Harold   Peer-Southern
Shapey, Ralph   Presser
Shapiro, Bernstein & Co.   122, Von Tilzer
Shapiro, Maurice   Remick, Shapiro, Bernstein & Co.
Sharp, Cecil   Curwen, Ditson
Shattinger, Thomas   Balmer & Weber
Shaw, David T.   Benteen
Shaw, Joseph P.
Shaw, Martin   Curwen
Shaw, Oliver   115
Shaw, Watkins   Novello
Shawnee Press   126
Shedlock, John South   Augener
Shepherd, Arthur   Society for the Publication of American Music, Wa-Wan Press
Sherburne, Henry   Balmer & Weber
Sheriff, Noam   Israel Music Institute
Sherman, Leander S.   Gray
Sherman & Hyde   115
Sherwin, John Frederick   Bunting
Sherwin, William F(isk)   Biglow & Main, Church
Shetky, J(ohn) George   Schetky
Shield, William   Dale, Hewitt, Longman & Broderip, Napier
Shifrin   Boelke-Bomart
Shimazu, Takehito   Deutscher Verlag für Musik
Short, Peter   91, Adams, Lownes
Short, Peter, widow of   Lownes, Short

Shostakovitch, Dmitry (Dmitriyevich)   Deutscher
    Verlag für Musik, Leeds, Peters (i), Sikorski,
    Weintraub
Showalter, A.J.   Baxter
Sibelius, Jean (Julius Christian)   Breitkopf &
    Härtel, Hansen (W.), Lienau, Whaley, Royce
    & Co.
Sidemton   Gerig
Sidler, Joseph (Anton)   110
Siebeneich (Siebeneicher), Mateusz
    Szarfenberg, Ungler
Sieber, Georges-Julien   Naderman, Richault,
    Sieber
Sieber, Jean-Georges   Frey, Imbault, Richault,
    Sieber
Siefert, Paul   Rhetus
Siegel, Carl Friedrich Wilhelm   Forberg,
    Kallmeyer, Kistner & Siegel
Siegel, F.   Schuberth (J.)
Sieger, Eduard   Cappi
Siegl, Otto   Böhm, Tonger
Siegling
Siegling, John   115, Siegling
Siegmeister, Elie   MCA Music
Sieradza, Cyprian z   *see* Bazylik, Cyprian
Sies [Siess], Johannes   Schoeffer
Sievers, Lieselotte   Breitkopf & Härtel
Sigl, G.   Röder
Sigma Alpha Iota   Peters (i)
Sigtenhorst Mayer, Bernhard van den   Alsbach
Siklós, Albert   Rozsnyai
Sikorski   Simrock, Weinberger
Sikorski, Hans   119, Schirmer (G.), Sikorski
Sikorski, Kazimierz   Polskie Wydawnictwo
    Musyczne
Silber, Eucharius   7, 517
Silber, Irwin   Oak
Silber, Marcello   Antico
Silvani, Giuseppe Antonio   Silvani
Silvani, Marino   Della Volpe, Monti, Silvani
Silver, Edgar O.   Silver Burdett
Silver Burdett   124
Silvestri, Florido de   Robletti
Silvestri, Rodolfo   Blado
Simmons, Buck   Faulds
Simmons, J.P.   Faulds
Simon, Josef   Universal
Simon, Paul   Kahnt
Simon & Schuster   Mills
Simpson, Christopher   15, Playford, Young
Simpson, John   101, Bickham, Bremner, Hare,
    Oswald, Roberts
Simpson, Robert   Lengnick
Simrock   107, 119, 120, Benjamin, Lengnick,
    Magasin de Musique (ii), Pleyel, Senff
Simrock, Nicolaus   106, Simrock
Sinclair, Thomas   115
Sinding, Christian   Hals, Hansen (W.), Peters (i)
Singspiration Music   Zondervan
Sjögren, Emil   Hansen (W.), Kgl. Hof-
    Musikhandel
Skalkottas, Nico(lao)s   Universal
Skarby, Kettil   Gehrmans
Skillern, Thomas   Preston, Walsh
Škroup, František   Hoffmann
Škroup, Jan Nepomuk   Hoffmann
Skryabin, Alexander (Nikolayevich)   Editions
    Russes de Musique
Slatyer, William   94
Slonimsky, Nicolas   New Music
Sloper, Lindsay   Ashdown

Smareglia, Antonio   Giudici & Strada,
    Weinberger
Smart, George   Handel societies, Leader &
    Cock, Napier, Regent's Harmonic Institution
Smetana, Bedřich   120, Bote & Bock, Forberg,
    Hoffmann, Hudební Matice, Kistner &
    Siegel, Starý, Supraphon, Urbánek
Smith, Hale   Marks
Smith, Harold   62
Smith, J.S.   114
Smith, John Stafford   Preston
Smith, Leyland   68
Smith, Robert Archibald   Purdie
Smith, Stanley   62
Smith, (Edward) Sydney   Schott
Smith, W.C.   47, Peters (ii)
Smith, William   Meares
Smyth, Ethel   Curwen
Snodham, Thomas   92, Adams, Barley, East,
    Harper, Haultin, Lownes, Playford, Stansby
Société Française de Musicologie   Heugel
Société Saint-Jean-l'Evangéliste   Desclée
Society for the Publication of American Music
    [SPAM]   127, Presser
Soderini, Agostino   Tradate
Soderman, John August   Horneman
Sokolov   Jürgenson
Soldi, Luca Antonio   91
Soler, Antonio   Unión Musical Española
Solis, Virgil   Feyerabend
Soliva, Carlo   Scotti
Sollberger, Harvey   McGinnis & Marx
Somers, Harry   Berando
Somma, Bonaventura   De Santis
Soncino   22
Sonneck, Oscar   124, Schirmer (G.)
Sønnichsen, Søren   113, 120
Sonnleithner, Joseph   106, Kunst- und
    Industrie-Comptoir
Sonzogno   111, Ricordi
Sorge, Georg Andreas   Schmid
Soriano, Francesco   Mutii, Robletti
Soto, Francisco   Blado, Gardano
Sottile, Giovanni   Gargano
Sourek, Otakar   Hudební Matice
Sousa, John Philip   Church, Fischer, Fox,
    Pepper
Southern Baptist Convention   Broadman
Southern Music Publishing Co.   Peer-Southern,
    Wagner (A.)
Southward, John   37
Southwell, William   Pepper
Sovetskïy Kompozitor   Muzïka
Soviet State Publishing House   Jürgenson
Sowerby, Leo   Society for the Publication of
    American Music
Spadi, Giovanni Battista   Vincenti
Spanenberg, Jan   Szarfenberg
Spangenberg, Johann   Rhau
Spataro, Giovanni   Vitali
Spechtshart, Hugo   7
Spehr, Johann Peter   106
Sperontes [Scholze, Johann
    Sigismund]   Breitkopf & Härtel
Spielenberger, Martin   Rhetus
Spies, Claudio   Boelke-Bomart
Spiess, Meinrad   Friedlein, Gebethner & Wolff
Spighi, Bartolomeo   Pignoni
Spina, Anton   Diabelli
Spina, Carl Anton   107, 110, Cranz, Diabelli,
    Haslinger, Mechetti, Pazdírek

Index

Spina, S.A.   107
Spitta, Philipp   Bach-Gesellschaft, Dover
Spitzweg, Carl   Aibl
Spitzweg, Eduard   Aibl
Spitzweg, Eugen   Aibl
Spohr, Louis   Artaria (ii), Bach-Gesellschaft, Bärenreiter, Cocks, Haslinger, Kistner & Siegel, Mechetti, Peters (i), Plattner, Richault
Spólka   Gebethner & Wolff
Spontini, Gasparo   Erard, Hoftheater-Musik-Verlag, Schlesinger
Sporck, George   Eschig
Sprengenstein, Giuseppe de Werz da   Artaria (ii)
Sprenger, Daniel   Artaria (i), Cappi, Diabelli, Maisch
Springer, Vincent   Schmitt
Sprint, Benjamin   Playford
Sprint, John   Playford
Squire, W.B.   Purcell Society
Staatliche Institut für Musikforschung   Bärenreiter
Stabingher   Zatta
Stäblein, Bruno   Pustet
Stabroeck, Jan van   Laet
Stadler, Abbé Maximilian   Haslinger, Nägeli, Torricella
Stadlmayr, Johann   Wagner (M.)
Staempfli, Edward   Israeli Music Publications
Stainer & Bell   120, Augener, Galliard, Williams
Stamegna, Nicolò   Caifabri
Stamitz, Carl   Bailleux, Breitkopf & Härtel, Heina, Hummel, La Chevardière, Longman & Broderip, Sieber
Stamitz, Johann   Hummel, La Chevardière, Longman & Broderip, Venier
Stampa, Gaspara   Gardano
Stamps, V.O.   Baxter, Zondervan
Stamps-Baxter Music Company   Baxter, Zondervan
Stanford, Sir Charles Villiers   Lucas, Stainer & Bell
Stanhope, Earl   18
Stanley, John   Johnson (John), Peters (i)
Stansby, William   92, Playford, Windet
Stapleton, Frederic   Wessel
Stará, Růžena, (née Meruňková)   Starý
Starer, Robert   MCA Music
Staring, J.B.   Whittemore
Stark, John Stillwell   125
Starke, Friedrich   Traeg
Starý, Emmanuel   111, 122
Státní Hudební Vydavatelství   Supraphon
Státní Nakladatelství Krâsné Literatury, Hudby a Umění   Supraphon
Stauda, Johannes   Bärenreiter
Stebbins, George Waring   Biglow & Main
Stefani, F.   Breyer
Stefani Jozef   Brzezina, Klukowski, Sennewald
Steffani, Agostino   Mutii
Steffens, Max R.B.   Schott
Steglich, Rudolf   Handel societies
Steibelt, Daniel Gottlieb   Clementi, Cramer, Dale, Erard, Kunst- und Industrie-Comptoir, Magasin de Musique (ii), Naderman, Sieber, Traeg
Stein, Charles F.   Stein & Buchheister
Stein, Erwin   Boosey & Hawkes, Universal
Stein, Nikolaus   87, Kauffmann
Stein & Buchheister   125

Steiner, Sigmund Anton   58, 107, Diabelli, Eder, Haslinger, Hoftheater-Musik-Verlag, Kunst- und Industrie-Comptoir, Lithographisches Institut
Steingräber, Theodor Leberecht   118, 119, Bosworth
Steinway   Gray (M.)
Stella, Scipione   Carlino, Vitale
Stellovsky, Fyodor Timofeyevich   Gutheil, Jürgenson
Stenhammer, Wilhelm   Hansen (W.), Kgl. Hof-Musikhandel, Nordiska Musikförlaget
Stenhouse, William   Johnson (James)
Stephani, Clemens   Berg
Stephens, Roe   125, Whittemore
Sterkel, (Johann) Franz Xaver   Artaria (i), Götz, Schott
Stern   92 Wust
Stern, Joseph W.   125, Marks, Wagner (A.)
Sterngold   89
Stevens, John   Plainsong & Mediaeval Music Society
Stevens, Halsey   Galaxy
Stevens, R.J.S.   49
Stevenson, John   Power
Stichter, Johannes   43
Stierlin, Frederick C.   Balmar & Weber
Still, William Grant   Galaxy
Stivori, Francesco   Amadino
Stobaeus, Johann   Rhetus, Segebade
Stöchs, Georg   Stuchs
Stöckel, Matthaus   Bergen
Stockhausen, Karlheinz   68, Universal
Stodart, William   102, Dubois, Wessel
Stoll, Edmund   Kistner & Siegel
Stolz, Robert   Drei Masken Verlag, Weinberger
Stone (Faulds, Stone & Morse)   Faulds
Stone, Henry   115
Stoppa, L.   Giudici & Strada
Stör, Johann Wilhelm   Haffner
Storace, Stephen (John Seymour)   Dale, Longman & Broderip
Strada, Achille   Giudici & Strada
Straet, Jaen von de   42
Straight, Thomas   49, Skillern, Walsh
Strang, Gerald   Langinger, New Music
Strathy, George William   Nordheimer
Straus, Oscar   Birnbach, Doblinger, Drei Masken Verlag, Weinberger
Strauss, Eduard   Cranz
Strauss, Johann [the elder]   Cranz, Häslinger, Lienau, Schlesinger
Strauss, Johann [the younger]   107, Bote & Bock, Cranz, Diabelli, Haslinger, Heugel, Lienau, Mechetti, Simrock, Weinberger
Strauss, Josef   Cranz, Diabelli, Haslinger
Strauss, Oscar   Curci
Strauss, Richard   110, Aibl, Benjamin, Birnbach, Boosey & Hawkes, Bote & Bock, Forberg, Fürstner, Heinrichshofen, Hempsted, Leuckart, Peters (i), Schott, Universal, Wiener Philharmonischer Verlag
Strauss family   Ricordi
Stravinsky, Igor (Fyodorovick)   122, 533, 534, Boosey & Hawkes, Chester, Editions Russes de Musique, Faber, Hansen, La Sirène, Leeds, Schott, Silver Burdett, Universal
Strazza, Giovannina   Lucca
Strecker, Ludwig   Schott
Strecker, Ludwig, son of Ludwig   Schott
Strecker, Willy   Augener, Schott

Index

Streicher, Johann Andreas   Peters (i)
Streit, Dean   Broude (A.)
Strepponi, Giuseppina   Lucca
Streuz, Ulrich   Bärenreiter
Strickland, Lily   Fischer (J.)
Striggio, Alessandro (i)   Gardano, Scotto
Strube, Adolf   Merseburger
Struve, Nikolai   Editions Russes de Musique
Stuart, Leslie   Anglo-Canadian Music
   Publishers' Association, Francis, Day &
   Hunter
Stuchs [Stüchs, Stöchs], **Georg**   80
Stucky, Steven   Presser
Stumpf, (Friedrich) Carl   Drei Masken Verlag
Stumpf & Koning   Alsbach
Stuntz, Joseph Hartmann   Falter
Subira, Jose   Unión Musical Española
Subotnick, Morton   MCA Music
Suffret   Foucault
Sugar, Ladislao   Suvini Zerboni
Suk, Josef   Hudební Matice, Urbánek
Sullivan, Arthur   Ashdown, Metzler
Sulzer, R.   Ries & Erler
Summy, Clayton F.   Summy-Birchard
Summy-Birchard   126, Schmidt
Sumski, Vadim   Morawetz
Sunday, Billy   Rodeheaver
Suppé, Franz (von)   Cranz, Weinberger
Supraphon   122
Surenne, John Thomas   Wood
Surinach, Carlos   Associated Music Publishers
Susa, Conrad   Schirmer (E.C.)
Susato, Tylman   23, 39, 84, Attaingnant,
   Phalèse, Plantin, Vissenaecken
Süssmayr, Franz Xaver   Hoffmeister,
   Hoftheater-Musik-Verlag
Sutherland, James   Corri
Sutherland, Margaret   Oiseau-Lyre
Suvini Zerboni   122
Svendsen, Johan (Severin)   Hansen (W.),
   Warmuth
Swan, Joseph A.   Stephens, Whittemore
Swanson, Howard   Weintraub
Swedish Publishers' Association   Hirsch
Sweelinck, Jan Pieterszoon   Plantin, Tournes,
   Van Ohr
Swid, Stephen   EMI Music-SBK
Świerzyński   Krzyżanowski
Swieten, Gottfried Bernhard (Baron) van   Pleyel
Swinscoe, Charles   Couse
Sybeneycher, Mateusz   Szarfenberg
Synclavier   72
Szabolcsi, Bence   Kórus Magyar
Szamotuł, Wacław z   Szarfenberg
Szarayński   Polskie Wydawnictwo Muzyczne
Szarfenberg [Szarffenberck, Scharpfenberg,
   Szarfenberger, Szarffemberg, Ostrowski,
   Ostrogórski], **Maciej**   Ungler
Szendy, Árpád   Rozsnyai
Szopski, Felicjan   Krzyżanowski
Szymanowksi, Karol   Eschig, Polskie
   Wydawnictwo Muzyczne, Universal

Tabb (Goodwin & Tabb)   Novello
Táborszky, Nándor   111
Taglietti
Taglietti, Giulio   Bortoli, Roger, Sala, Wright
Taglietti, Luigi   Bortoli
Taillart the elder   Le Clerc
Tailleferre, Germaine   Heugel
Tait brothers   Allan

Takemitsu, Tōru   Universal
Tal, Josef   Israel Music Institute
Talbot, W.H.   Fox   61
Tallis, Thomas   80, 91, 519, East, Oxford
   University Press, Peters (i), Vautrollier
Taneyev, Sergey Ivanovich   Belyayev, Editions
   Russes de Musique
Tansman, Alexandre   Eschig, La Sirène
Tans'ur, William   113, Cole
Tantestein   35
Tardos, Bela   Editio Musica Budapest
Tarp, Svend-Erik   Hansen (W.), Samfundet til
   Udgivelse af Dansk Musik
Tarragó, Graciamo   Unión Musical Española
Tartini, Giuseppe   Roger
Tasso, Gioan Maria   Amadino, Caifabri, Poggioli
Tasso, Torquato   Vincenti
Täubel, Christian Gottlob   34, 37, Hoffmeister
Tauhert, Rudolph   Schirmer (G.)
Tavener, John   Chester
Tavernier, Ameet   Laet
Taws, Joseph C.   Schetky
Taylor, Deems   Fischer (J.)
Taylor, James   EMI Music-SBK
Tchaikovsky, Pyotr Il'yich   122, Benjamin,
   Bessel, Bote & Bock, Forberg, Jürgenson,
   Muzïka
Tcherepnin, Alexander   Heugel
Tebaldini, Nicolò   91, De Santis
Telemann, Georg Philipp   Bärenreiter, Boivin,
   Breitkopf & Härtel, Hänssler, Le Clerc,
   Roger, Schmid
Tellier, Henri   Heugel
Templeton, Alec   Shawnee Press
Tena, Luis   Unión Musical Española
Tendler, Josef   Trattner
Terasse, Claude   La Sirène
Terzakis, Dimitri   Bärenreiter
Tessarini, Carlo   Sieber
Tessaro, Angelo   63
Testi, Flavio   Ricordi
Tevo, Zaccaria   Bortoli
Thalberg, Seyfried   Haslinger
Thalberg, Sigismond (Fortuné
   François)   Haslinger, Schlesinger,
   Schonenberger, Schott, Troupenas, Wessel
Thayer, B.W.   115
Theodorescu, Ştefan   Doina
Theodor of Würzburg   see Franck, Theodor
Theodorakis, Mikis   Deutscher Verlag für Musik
Thiebes-Stierlin Music Co.   Balmer & Weber
Thiele, Charles F.   Waterloo
Thiele, Siegfried   Deutscher Verlag für Musik
Thilman, Johannes Paul   Breitkopf & Härtel
Thomas   Billaudot
Thomas, (Charles Louis) Ambroise   Breitkopf &
   Härtel, Escudier, Heugel, Richault,
   Sonzogno
Thomas, Arthur Goring   Metzler
Thomas, Isaiah   31, 113
Thomas, Kurt   Breitkopf & Härtel
Thompson   101, 102, 128, Simpson
Thompson (Miles & Thompson; C.W. Thompson
   & Co.)   Schmidt
Thompson, Gordon
Thompson, Henry   Button & Whitaker, Purday,
   Thompson
Thompson, Nathaniel   Hudgebut
Thompson, Peter   Thompson
Thompson, Randall   Fischer (C.), Schirmer (E.C.)
Thomson, George   103, Power, Preston

605

Thomson, Virgil   American Composers
    Alliance, Arrow Music Press, Cos Cob Press,
    Fischer (C.), Ricordi, Schirmer (G.),
    Weintraub
Thomson, William   101
Thorne, Francis   Marks
Thornton, Henry   92
Thornton, Robert   92
Thorowgood, Henry   Simpson
Thuille, Ludwig   Leuckart
Thüring, Johann   Weidner
Thurn und Taxis, Princes of   Pleyel
Tilliard   Billaudot
Tilloch, Alexander   541
Timan, Volcmar   Marescotti
Tini   Lomazzo
Tini, Francesco   Sabbio, Tini
Tini, Pietro   Amadino, Tini
Tini, Simone   89, Sabbio, Tini
Tinödi, Sebestyén   Hoffgreff
Tin Pan Alley   Harms, Remick, Stark, Tilzer
Tippett, Sir Michael (Kemp)   120, Schott
Tirindelli, Pierre Adolfo   De Santis
Titelouze, Jehan   Ballard
Titz, August Ferdinand   Torricella
Titz, Peter Johann   Hünefeld
Toch, Ernst   Belwin-Mills
Todesco, Magistro Jacomo   Jacomo
Toeplitz, Uri   Israel Music Institute
Toeschi   Götz, La Chevardière
Toldrá, Eduardo   Unión Musical Española
Tollius, Johann   Tournes
Tolman, Henry   115, Gordon, Russell
Tomášek, Václav Jan Křtitel   Berra, Enders,
    Hoffmann, Peters (i)
Tomaszewski, Mieczyslaw   Polskie Wydawnictwo
    Muzyczne
Tomkins, Thomas   40, Godbid
Tonger, Augustin Josef   Tonger
Tonger, P.J.   Doina, Gerig
Tonnani, Alessandro   Caifabri
Tonson, Jacob   Watts
Toppan   68
Torelli, Giuseppe   Micheletti, Roger, Sala
Tornaghi, Antonio   Filippone
Tornieri, Jacomo   Gardano
Torrentino, Lorenzo   Marescotti
Torresani, Andrea   503, Antico
Torricella, Christoph   106, Artaria (i), Huberty,
    Musikalisches Magazin
Tortorino, Paolo   Baldini
Torun, Thorn   88
Tosatti, Vieri   Ricordi
Toscanini, Arturo   De Santis
Tosi, Giuseppe Felice   Micheletti
Tosi, Pier Francesco   Silvani
Tournes, Jean de   89, Granjon
Tournon, Cardinal of   Attaingnant
Tovey, Donald   Associated Board of the Royal
    Schools of Music, Oxford University Press
Towarzystwo Wydawnicze Muzyki
    Polskiej   Polskie Wydawnictwo Muzyczne
Tower   Associated Music Publishers
Tozzi   Amadino
Trabaci, Giovanni Maria   Carlino, Vitale
Trabattone, Bartolomeo   Vigoni
Tradate
Tradate, Agostino   89, Tradate
Traeg, Johann   106, Artaria (i), Eder,
    Sauer
Traetta, Tommaso   Zatta

Trajetta, Filippo   Graupner
Trapp, Max   Eulenburg, Litolff
Trattner, Johann Thomas   98, Huberty, Van
    Ghelen
Trautwein, Traugott   107
Trazegnies (Treseniers), François Joseph
    de   Andrez
Trede, Hilmar   Ugrino
Trede, Signe   Ugrino
Treibmann, Karl Ottomar   Deutscher Verlag
    für Musik
Treichlinger, József   111, Rózsavölgyi
Tremaine, Charles M.   Gordon
Trentsensky, Joseph   Cappi
Trentsensky, Mathias   Cappi
Trevor, John B.   Church
Trexler, Georg   Breitkopf & Härtel
Trin, Jean Pullon de   Gorlier
Tripp, Louis   116
Tritonius, Petrus   22, 23, Oeglin
Troiano, Massimo   Scotto
Trojahn, Manfred   Bärenreiter
Trombetti, Ascanio   Rossi, Tebaldini
Tromboncino, Bartolomeo   533, Antico, Giunta,
    Guidi
Troszel, Wilhelm   Sennewald
Troupenas, Eugène-Theódore   Brandus,
    Escudier, Girard, Joubert, Schlesinger
Troyer, Carlos   Wa-Wan Press
Truax, David   Church
Trunk, Richard   Leuckart
Truxel, J.W.   Stark
Truzzi, Luigi   Ricordi
Trythall, Gilbert   Marks
Tucker, Sophie   Rossiter
Tufts, John W.   43, 113, Silver Burdett
Tulou, Jean Louis   Troupenas
Turchi, Guidi   De Santis, Ricordi
Turco, Giovanni del   Marescotti
Turina, Joaquin   Rouart-Lerolle
Türk, Daniel Gottlob   Hoffmeister, Peters (i),
    Schwickert
Turnhout, Gérard de   Goulart
Tuscany, Grand Duke of   Giunta
Tuthill, Burnet C.   Society for the Publication of
    American Music
Tuthill, William B.   Society for the Publication of
    American Music
Twa, Andrew   Berandol
Twiss, Richard   Power
TWMP   Polskie Wydawnictwo Muzyczne
Tye, Christopher   Seres
Typographia Musica   Stein
Typographia Regia   Giunta
Tyroff   Weigel

Überreuter, Georg   Trattner
Udloff, George   Lowe & Brydone
UFA Music Press   Drei Masken Verlag
Ufaton Press   Drei Masken Verlag
Ugrino   119
Ulhart [Ulhard], Philipp   86, Schönig
Ulrich III, Abbot   Sensenschmidt
Umelěcké Beseda   Hudební Matice
Ungaro, Jacomo   *see* Jacomo Ungaro
Ungler, Florian   87, Wirzbięta
Ungut, Meinardus   26
Unión Musical Española   113
Union of Czechoslovak Composers   Hudební
    Matice, Panton
United Artists   Big 3, Miller, Presser

Universal Edition 68, 119, 496, 528, 534, Aibl,
　Doblinger, European American, Schott,
　Weinberger, Wiener Philharmonischer
　Verlag, Wiener Urtext Edition
University of Chicago Press　Ricordi
Updike, Daniel Berkeley　Ditson
Urbánek, František Augustin　Urbanek (M.)
Urbánek, Mojmir　111, 120, 122, Universal,
　Urbánek (F.A.)
Ussachevsky, Vladimir　New Music
Uttini, Francesco　Fougt

Vaccai, Nicola　Ricordi
Valcarenghi, Guido　Ricordi
Valcarenghi, Renzo　Ricordi
Valdarfer, Christoph　5, 80, Pachel
Valen, Fartein　Norsk Musikforlag
Valentin de Carvalho　122
Valentine, Robert　Wright
Valentini, Giovanni　Vincenti
Valentini, Giuseppe　Roger
Valerius, Adriaen　92
Valesi, Fulgenzio
Valle, Sebastiano　Zatta
Vallegio, F.　Baldini
Vallet, Nicolas　43, 94
Van Alstyne, Egbert　Rossiter
Van Buyten, Martin　Verovio
Vancea, Zeno　Morawetz
Van den Keere, Henrik　Granjon, Plantin
Vander Cook, Hale A.　Barnhouse
Vandersloot　126
Vandross, Luther　EMI Music-SBK
Van Eyck　Matthysz
Van Geertsom, Jan　92
Van Ghelen　98, Trattner
Van Ghelen, Johann Peter　Van Ghelen
Van Gobes, S.　Elkan
Vanhal, Johann Baptist　Artaria (i), Eder, Guéra,
　Heina, Hoffmeister, Hummel, Kunst- und
　Industrie-Comptoir, Löschenkohl, Maisch,
　Mechetti, Mollo, Musikalisches Magazin,
　Sauer, Sieber, Torricella, Traeg
Vannini, Elia　Micheletti, Monti
Van Ohr, Philipp　87
Vaňura [Waniura, Wanjura], Česlav　Labaun
Varese, Edgard (Victor Achille Charles)
　Curwen, Langinger, Ricordi, Summy-
　Birchard
Vaughan, Denis　Ricordi
Vaughan, James D(avid)　124, 126
Vaughan Williams, Ralph　120, Ashdown,
　Curwen, Oxford University Press, Stainer &
　Bell, Williams
Vautrollier, Thomas　39, 88, 91, East, Haultin
VEB Deutscher Verlag für Musik　Ugrino
Vecchi, Orfeo　539, Gardano, Kauffman,
　Lomazzo, Phalèse, Tini, Tradate,
　Wagenmann
Veggio, Claudio Maria　Scotto
Veit, Václav Jindřich　Hoffmann
Velasco, López de　Giunta
Velpen [Velpius], R.　Phalèse
Vendome, Richard　68
Veneri, Gregorio　Pignoni
Venier, Domenico　Gardano
Venier, Jean Baptiste　104, Bureau
　d'Abonnement Musical, Leduc, Le Menu
Venosa, Carlo Gesualdo, Prince of　*see* Gesualdo
Venturi del Nibbio, Stefano　Marescotti
Venturini, Genesio　Carisch

Veracini, Francesco　Roger
Veradrus, Carolus　7, 496, 517
Verard, Antoine　Du Pré
Veray, Amaury　Instituto de Cultura
　Puertorriqueña
Verbrugghen, Adrien　Vissenaecken
Vercellensis, Bernardus　Vitali
Verdelot, Philippe　Antico (A.), Attaingnant,
　Gardano, Merulo, Scotto
Verdi, Giuseppe (Fortunino Francesco)　62, 111,
　Boosey & Hawkes, Canti, Cottrau, Escudier,
　Girard, Lucca, Novello, Ricordi
Verdier, Antoine du　Gorlier
Verein der Deutschen Musikalien-
　händler　Hofmeister
Vereniging voor Nederlandse
　Musiekgeschiedenis　Alsbach
Veress, Sándor　Suvini Zerboni
Veretti, Antonio　Curci, Ricordi
Vernadé, Anne-Cécile (née Le Clerc)　La
　Chevardière, Le Clerc
Vernadé, Claude　Le Clerc
Verndonck, Cornelius　41
Vernet, Horace　Schlesinger
Verovio, Simone　42–3, 94, Borboni, Merulo,
　Sadelar
Verso, Antonio Il　*see* Il Verso
Viadana, Lodovico　Robletti, Vincenti
Vianis, Bernardinus de　Vitali
Vicentino, Nicola　Barré
Vicomanni, Democrito　Petrucci (P.)
Victoria, Tomas Luis de　Gardano, Giunta
Victor Talking Machine　Bloom, Peer-Southern
Vieu, Jeanne　Eschig
Vieuxtemps, Henri　Brandus
Vieweg　Cappi
Vignon, Eustache　Jean II de Laon
Vigoni
Vigoni, Francesco　89–91, Vigoni
Villa-Lobos, Heitor　Eschig, Israeli Music
　Publications, Napoleão, Vitale
Villeneuve, Alexandre de　Foucault
Villiers, Pierre de　Le Bé, Moderne
Vincent　Métru
Vincent, Antoine　88, Du Boys
Vincent, Barthélemy　Jean II de Laon
Vincent, J.　Fezandat
Vincent, John　Belwin-Mills
Vincent, Simon　Du Ry
Vincenti [Vincenci, Vincenzi], **Giacomo**　83,
　Amadino, Barré, Phalèse
Vinci, Pietro　Rampazetto
Vingard, Mads　Waldkirch
Viotti, Giovanni Battista　Imbault, Magasin de
　Musique (ii), Pleyel, Sieber
Virchi, Paolo　Amadino
Virdung, Sebastian　Schoeffer
Vismara, Domenico　Bertuzzi, Lucca
Vissenaecken, Willem van　23, 84, Susato
Vitale
Vitale, Costantino　91, Carlino
Vitale, Vicente　128, Vitale
Vitali, Bernardino　82
Vitali, Filippo　Cecconcelli, Magni, Pignoni,
　Robletti
Vitali, Giovanni Battista　Monti (G.), Sala
Vitásek, Jan (Matyáš Nepomuk) August　Berra,
　Enders
Vítek, Antonín　Starý
Vivaldi, Antonio Lucio　Bailleux, Boivin,
　Bortoli, Peters (i), Ricordi, Roger, Wright

Vlad, Roman   Carisch
Vogel, Adolph   Elkan, Elkan-Vogel
Vogler, [Abbé] George Joseph   Bureau
  d'Abonnement Musical, Götz, Löschenkohl,
  Mollo, Schott
Voigt   Ries & Erler
Volk   Gerig, Schott
Volk, Arno   Schott, Volk
Volkert, Charles G.J.   Schott
Volkmann, Joachim   Breitkopf & Härtel
Volkmann, Ludwig   Breitkopf & Härtel
Volkmann, Reinhard   Jung
Volkmann, (Friedrich) Robert   Heckenast,
  Rózsavölgyi
Volkmann, Wilhelm   Breitkopf & Härtel
Volland, Maria Helena   Schmid
Voltter, Richard   Shapiro, Bernstein & Co.
Von Aich, Arnt   82
Von Hagen, Peter Albrecht   114
Von Tilzer, Harry   125, Shapiro, Bernstein
  & Co.
Vořišek, Jan Václav   Lithographisches Institut,
  Mechetti, Pennauer
Vorsterman, Willem   Visssenaecken
Vos, Martin de   41
Vötterle, Karl   Bärenreiter, Nagel
Vreedman, Sebastian   Phalèse
Vulpius, Melchior   Hänssler, Weidner
Vydenast, Johann   Arndes

Wachter, Georg   Formschneider, Hergot,
  Neuber
Wachter, Kunegunde (i)   *see* Hergot Kunegunde
Wachter, Kunegunde (ii)   Neuber, Wachter
Waelrant [Waelrand], Hubert [Huberto]
  [Waelrandus, Hubertus]   84, Laet, Phalèse
Wagenaar, Bernard   Cos Cob Press
Wagenseil, Georg Christoph   Bureau
  d'Abonnement Musical, Venier
Wagner, A.   128
Wagner, Jakob Christoph   Schönig, Wagner
  (M.)
Wagner, József   111, Rózsavölgyi
Wagner, Maria   Wagner (M.)
Wagner, Michael   87
Wagner, Peter   Plainsong & Mediaeval Music
  Society, Pustet
Wagner, Richard   59, Breitkopf & Härtel,
  Flaxland, Fürstner, Heckel, Jürgenson,
  Kistner & Siegel, Lucca, Meser, Peters (i),
  Ricordi, Schlesinger, Schott, Senff
Wagner, Siegfried   Brockhaus
Wagner, Valentin   Honterus
Wagner family   Hartmann
Wagner-Régeny, Rudolf   Bote & Bock,
  Universal
Wahlberg, Brix von   Alsbach
Waissel, Matthäus   Eichorn
Waldheim, R.   Universal
Waldkirch, Henrick   88
Waldteufel   Ascherberg, Hopwood & Crew
Walker, Daniel   Geib
Walker, Julius   Lee & Walker
Walker & Lee   Lee
Wallace, William Vincent   Hutchings & Romer
Waller, Fats [Thomas Wright]   Mills
Wallerstein   Couse
Walmisley, Thomas Forbes   Regent's Harmonic
  Institution
Walmsley, Peter   Manwaring
Walpergen, Peter   Oxford University Press

Walpole, Lady   Moücke
Walpurgis, Electress Maria Antoniade   31
Walsh   47, 487, Bunting
Walsh, John   101, 500, 516, 525, 527, 533, 534,
  536, Birchall, Cluer, Cole, Coventry &
  Hollier, Cross, Hare, Johnson (John),
  Meares, Playford, Preston, Randall, Roger,
  Wright, Young
Walsh, John [the younger]   101, Randall,
  Simpson, Skillern, Walsh, Wright &
  Wilkinson
Walter, Bruno   Universal
Walter, Johann   Bärenreiter, Rhau
Walter, Thomas   43, 113
Waltershausen, Hermann Wolfgang von   Drei
  Masken Verlag
Walthofer, Salomon   Nenninger
Walton Sir William   120, Oxford University
  Press
Wannenmacher [Vannius], Johannes   Apiarius
Ward, Robert   Galaxy
Ward & Co.   Curwen
Ward-Steinman   Marks
Waring, Fred   126, Shawnee
Waring Enterprises, Inc.   Shawnee
Warlock, Peter   Oxford University Press
Warmuth, Carl   113, 120, Hals, Hansen (W.),
  Norsk Musikforlag, Winther
Warner, Daniel   Beesley
Warner Bros. Music   126, Famous, Fox, Harms,
  Remick, Witmark
Warner Chappell   Chappell, EMI Music-SBK,
  Summy-Birchard, Warner Bros.
Warner Communications   Chappell, Warner
  Bros.
Warren, Edmund Thomas   Phillips
Warren, Thomas   Welcker
Waterloo
Waters, Horace   115
Watteau, Jean Antoine   Bickham
Watts, John   101
Wa-Wan Press   127
Webb, Benedict   Faulds, Peters (ii)
Webb, George James   Mason Bros.
Webbe, Samuel [the elder]   Thompson
Weber   Lucas
Weber, Bedřich Diviš [Friedrich Dionys]   Enders
Weber, Ben   Boelke-Bomart
Weber, Carl Heinrich   Balmer & Weber
Weber, Carl Maria (Friedrich Ernst) von   103,
  Berra, Brzezina, Haslinger, Hewitt, Lieanu,
  Litolff, Peters (i), Richault, Sauer,
  Schlesinger, Simrock, Thomson
Weber, Gottfried   Schott
Weber, Joe   Witmark
Weber & Co.   120
Webern, Anton (Friedrich Wilhelm von)   496,
  Boelke-Bomart, Fischer (C.), Universal
Webster, F.J.   Peters (ii)
Webster, John Campbell   Allan
Webster, Joseph Philbrick   Higgins, Lyon &
  Healy
Wechel, Johann   Rab
Weedon, Cavendish   Playford
Weekes, Joseph   Augener, Galliard, Stainer &
  Bell
Weelkes, Thomas   Musical Antiquarian Society
Weiditz, Hans   Grimm & Wirsung
Weidner, Johann   87
Weigel [Waigel]   105
Weigl, Joseph (ii)   Ricordi

Weigl, Karl   Universal
Weigl, Thaddäus   106, Artaria (i), Diabelli,
   Eder, Hoftheater-Musik-Verlag
Weiland, Julius Johann   Stern
Weill, Kurt   Schott, Universal
Weinberger, Jaromír   Universal
Weinberger, Josef   119, Artaria (i), Doblinger,
   Universal
Weiner, Nikolaus   Rózsavölgyi
Weingartner, Felix   Birnbach
Weinholz, Carl   Spehr
Weinmann, Karl   Pustet
Weintraub, Eugene   127, Leeds
Weis, Flemming   Samfundet til Udgivelse af
   Dansk Musik
Weisgall, Hugo   Presser
Weismann, Wilhelm   Breitkopf & Härtel,
   Peters (i)
Weiss, J.P.   Couse
Weixer, Daniel   Klemm
Welack, Matthäus   86
Welcker
Welcker, John   Bremner, Dale, Roberts,
   Welcker
Welcker, Peter   101, Welcker
Welk, Lawrence   Harms
Welk Music Group   Harms
Wellenburg, Matthäus Lang von [Archbishop of
   Salzburg]   Grimm & Wirsung
Weller, E.   Bland & Weller
Wellesz, Egon   Sikorski, Simrock, Universal
Welsh, Thomas   Regent's Harmonic Institution
Wendling, Johann Baptist   Götz
Wening, Michael
Wenker, Jerome   68
Wenman, Joseph   Harrison
Wenrich, Percy   Rossiter
Wenssler, Michael   6, 80–81
Wentzely, Mikuláš František Xaver   Labaun
Werdenberg, Bishop Johann von   Ratdolt
Werle, Lars Johan   Nordiska Musikförlaget
Werlein, Philip P.   116
Werner, Christoph   Mense
Werner, Henry   Balmer & Weber
Wernick, Richard   Presser
Wernthal   Lienau
Wert, Giaches de   Gardano, Merulo
Wertheim, Alma M.   Cos Cob Press
Wesendonk, Otto   Flaxland
Wesley, Charles   Carr
Wesley, John   Pearson
Wesley, Samuel   Birchall, Carr, Regent's
   Harmonic Institution
Wessel, Christian Rudolph   102, Ashdown
Westergaard, Peter   Jerona
Westerlund, R.E.   Fazer
Westö, John Eric   Fazer
Westphal, Moritz   Bote & Bock
Westrup, Sir Jack Allan   Augener
Wetzler, Hermann   Heckel
Weyse, Christoph Ernst Friedrich   Lose,
   Samfundet til Udgivelse af Dansk
   Musik
Wezbrew, L.G. (pseud.)   Stark
Whaley, Royce & Co.   128
Wheatstone
Wheatstone, Charles   102, Wheatstone
Whistling, Carl Friedrich   107, Hofmeister
   Whistling
Whitaker, John   Button & Whitaker, Purday
Whitaker, Maurice   Simpson

White-Smith Co.   125
Whithorne, Emerson   Cos Cob Press
Whiting, Arthur   Boston Music Company
Whiting, Richard   Remick
Whitney, Clark J.   125, Whittemore
Whitney-Warner Publishing Co.   Remick
Whitson, Beth Slater   Rossiter
Whittaker, Hubert   Oxford University
   Press
Whittemore, J(oseph) Henry   125, Stephens
Whittle, Daniel Webster   Biglow & Main
Whyte, William   Thomson
Whythorne, Thomas   Day
Wickes, E.M.   Von Tilzer
Widmanstetter, Georg   87
Widor, Charles-Marie   Durand, Heugel
Wieck, Friedrich   Hofmeister
Wiener Bohème Press   Drei Masken
   Verlag
Wiener Philharmonischer Verlag   118,
   Universal
Wiener Urtext Edition   118, Schott
Wieniawski, Henryk   Polskie Wydawnictwo
   Muzyczne
Wieniawski brothers   Litolff
**Wietor, [Büttner, Philovalensis, Doliarius]
   Hieronim**   81
Wigglesworth, Frank   New Music
Wilbye, John   Musical Antiquarian Society
Wilder, Alec   Associated Music Publishers
Wiler, Hans   Wenssler
Wilhelm V   Berg (A.)
Wilkie, Joseph   128, Allan
Wilkinson, C.   Longman & Broderip, Preston,
   Wright & Wilkinson
Willaert, Adrian   Antico, Attaingnant, Gardano,
   Moderne, Ott, Petrucci (O.), Scotto
Willan, Healey   Berando, Harris
Willer, Georg   88, Flurschütz
Williams, (William Sidney) Gwynn   120
Williams, John M.   Boston Music Company
Williams, Joseph   120, Augener, Galliard,
   Stainer & Bell
Williams, Joseph Benjamin [Pascal, Florian]
   102, Williams
Williams, W.R.   Rossiter
Williamson, Malcolm   Weinberger
Williamson, T(homas) G(eorge)
Williamson Music   Boston Music Company
Willich, Jodocus   Eichorn
Willig, George   114, 115, Carr, Gilfert, Moller &
   Capron
Willig, George (jr.)   Benteen, Lee & Walker,
   Willig
Willis, Isaac   Cowper
Willson, Meredith   Frank
Wilson, Joseph   114, Gilfert
Wimberger, Gerhard   Bärenreiter
Wirtbeck, Heinz   Bärenreiter
Windet, John   91, Stansby
Winkler, Gerhard   Birnbach
Winkler, Martin   Belwin-Mills
Winkler, Max   125, Belwin-Mills
Winkler, Peter K(enton)   Boelke-Bomart
Winner, Joseph E(astburn)   115
Winner, Septimus   115, Lee & Walker, Winner
Winter, Georg Ludwig   105, Rellstab, Winter
Winter, Hugo   Universal
Winter, Jakob   Forckel
Winter, Johann Wilhelm   Haffner
Winter, Peter   Falter, Götz

Winterschmidt, Adam Wolfgang   Haffner
Winther, Edvard   Norsk Musikforlag, Warmuth, Winther
Winther, H.T.   120, Winther
Wirsung, Marx   520, Grimm & Wirsung
Wirth, Helmut   Sikorski
Wirzbięta [Wierzbięta], **Maciei**   87
Wiseman, Charles   Le Clerc
Witmark   125, Bloom, Warner Bros.
Wittgenstein, Paul   Weinberger
Witvogel, Gerhard Fredrik   100
Witzendorf, Adolf Othmar   Cappi
Władysław IV   Hünefeld
Woelfl, Joseph   Traeg
Wohlfahrt, Johann   Litolff
Wolf   Hoffmeister
Wolf, Christian   Doblinger
Wolf, Hugo   110, Heckel, Lauterbach & Kuhn, Peters (i), Schott
Wolf, Johann Baptist   Schott
Wolf, Johannes   Breitkopf & Härtel
Wolfe   113
Wolfensberger, H.   Hug
Wolff, Christian   Peters (i)
Wolff, Robert   Friedlein
Wolf-Ferrari, Ermanno   Anton J. Benjamin, Ricordi, Weinberger
Wolffgang, Martin   Honterus
Wolpe, Stefan   McGinnis & Marx
Wolrab, Nicolaus   Eichorn
Wood   Goulding
Wood, Abraham   Thomas
Wood, Andrew   103
Wood, George   Cramer
Wood, George Muir   103, Cramer
Wood, John   Cramer
Woodbury, Isaac Baker   Mason Bros.
Woodin, William H.   Miller
Wooldridge, Harry Ellis   Plainsong & Mediaeval Music Society
Word   126, Rodeheaver
Worde, Wynkyn de   *see* Wynkyn de Worde
Words and Music   Shawnee Press
Wordsworth, William   Lengnick
Work, Henry Clay   Firth, Hall & Pond, Root & Cady
Wornum, Robert   101
Wöss, Josef V. von   Universal
Wouwere, Claes van der   Vissenaecken
Wranitzky, Anton   Hoftheater-Musik-Verlag, Musikalisches Magazin
Wranitzky, Paul   André, Hoffmeister, Sieber, Imbault
Wren, J.   Watts
Wright, Daniel   101, Cross, Johnson (John), Walsh
Wright, Hermond [Harman]   Preston, Wright & Wilkinson
Wright & Kidder   Howe
Wright & Wilkinson   101, Preston, Randall
Wroński, Adam   Krzyżanowski
Wuorinen, Charles   McGinnis & Marx, Peters (i)
Würzl, Eberhard   Österreichischer Bundesverlag

Wust, Balthazar   87
Wynkyn de Worde   Higman
Wyssenbach, Rudolf   86

Yamaha   72
Yardumian, Richard   Elkan-Vogel, Presser
York Music Co.   Von Tilzer
Young, John   101, Playford
Young, Robert   Lownes
Ysaÿe, Eugène   Krzyżanowski
Yssandon, Jean   Ballard
Yun, Isang   Bote & Bock
Yurgenson, Pyotr Ivanovich   *see* Jürgenson

Zacconi, Lodovico   Vincenti
Zafred, Mano   Ricordi
Zalewski, Teodor   Polskie Wydawnictwo Muzyczne
Zandonai, Riccardo   Ricordi
Zanetti, Gerolamo   Vigoni
Zanetti da Bressa, Bartholomeo de   Zannetti
Zanger, Johann   Hantzsch
Zangius, Nikolaus   Runge
Zani, Agostino   10
Zanibon   122
Zannetti   Soldi
Zannetti, Bartolomeo   91
Zapffe, Haakon   Norsk Musikforlag
Zarlino, Gioseffo   89, Franceschi
Zarotto, Antonio   80
Zarzycki, Alexander   Sennewald
Zatta, Antonio   111, Ricordi
Zechlin, Ruth   Breitkopf & Härtel
Zedda, Alberto   Ricordi
Żeleński, Władysław   Krzyżanowski, Sennewald
Zeller, Carl   Bosworth, Weinberger
Zemlinsky, Alexander (von)   Universal
Zenero, Carlo   Monti
Zeraschi, Helmut   Breitkopf & Härtel, Deutscher Verlag für Musik
Ziehrer, C(arl) M(ichael)   Haslinger, Lienau
Zielénski, Mikotas   Polskie Wydawnictwo Muzyczne
Zilcher, Hermann   Breitkopf & Härtel
Ziloti, Alexander   Editions Russes de Musique
Zimmermann, Bernd Alois   Schott
Zimmermann, Udo   Deutscher Verlag für Musik
Zinck, Ludwig   Lose
Zondervan   126
Zonta   *see* Giunta
Zöpfel, David   Feyerabend
Zornicht, Jonas   Segebade
Zozaya y Guillen, Emilio   Unión Musical Española
Zu den Sieben Schwestern   Eder
Zulehner, Georg   Schott
Zulehner, Karl   Schott
Zumárraga, Juan de   Pablos
Zvonař, Josef Leopold   Hoffmann
Zwilich, Ellen Taafe   Presser
Zwisler, Julius   Kallmeyer
Zybenaicher, Mateusz   Szarfenberg

Index

Index of Cities

Branches, distribution centres and other secondary offices are shown in square brackets

Aberdeen Forbes, Paterson
Altona Benjamin
Amsterdam 43, 61, 100, 105, Alsbach, Le
  Chevalier, Hummel, Matthysz, Roger,
  Schmitt, Witvogel
Ansbach Rönnagel
Antwerp 23, 40, 41, 42, 84, 95, 514, Aertssens,
  Bellère, Cock, Granjon, Laet, Phalèse,
  Plantin, Remunde, Schott, Susato,
  Vissaecken
  Cathedral Susato
Ashford, Kent Eulenburg, Schott
Augsburg 86, 87, 88, 94, 126, Bärenreiter,
  Bencard, Böhm, Flurschütz, Gombart,
  Grimm & Wirsung, Kriesstein, Lotter,
  Oeglin, Ratdolt, Schönig, Ulhart
Augusta, GA Blackmar
Avignon 24, Channey

Bad Godesberg Forberg
Bahia Filippone
Baltimore, MD Benteen, Carr, Cole, Miller &
  Beacham, Peters (ii), Willig
Bamberg Pfeyl, Sensenschmidt
Barcelona Boileau Bernasconi, Instituto
  Español
Bari [Ricordi]
Bar-le-Duc 22
Basle 7, 517, [Bärenreiter], [Hug], Richel,
  Ricordi, Valdarfer, Wenssler
Bath Wheatstone
Beccles [Clowes]
Bergedorf bei Hamburg Handel societies
Berlin 68, 100, Birnbach, Bote & Bock, Challier,
  [Drei Masken], Editions Russes de Musique,
  [Francis, Day & Hunter], Fürstner, Hummel,
  Lienau, Merseburger, Rellstab, Ries & Erler,
  Runge, Schlesinger, Simrock, Trautwein,
  Winter
Berne 507, Apiarius
Bilbao Unión Musical Española
Birmingham 521, Broome
Bloomington, IN 68, Indiana University
Bologna 7, 22, 40, 91, Della Volpe, Dozza,
  Micheletti, Monti, Pisarri, Rossi, Silvani,
  Tebaldini
  Accademia Filarmonica Pisarri
Bonn Belyayev, Forberg, Kahnt, Simrock
  Beethovenhaus Henle
Boston 10, 43, 94, 113, 115, 125, Boston Music
  Company, Ditson, [Fischer (C.)], Graupner,
  Hagen, Hewitt, Howe, Mason Bros., Prentiss,
  Russell, Schirmer (E. C.), Schmidt, Silver
  Burdett
  American Conservatorio Graupner
Bracciano [Fei]
Brașov Honterus
Bratislava Supraphon
Brescia Sabbio
Breslau Baumann, Leuckart
Brighton Chester
Brisbane Paling
Brno [Pazdírek]
Brunswick Litolff, Kallmeyer, Spehr
Brussels Cranz, Lemoine, Schott
Bryn Mawr, PA Elkan-Vogel, Presser
Bucharest 124, Doina, Gebauer, Pann

Bučovice [Pazdírek]
Budapest Editio Musica Budapest, Rozsnyai
  National Academy of Music Rozsnyai
Buenos Aires Breyer, Filippone, Monguillot,
  Ortelli, Ricordi,
Burgos [Giunta]
Burlington, IA Barnhouse

Caen Mangeant
Calcutta 128
Cambridge, MA American Institute of
  Musicology
Cape Town 128
Carol Stream, IL Hope
Celle Nagel
Charleston, SC Gilfert, Siegling
Chattanooga, TN Baxter
Chicago 124, Bloom, Brainard, [Ditson],
  [Fischer, (C.)], Higgins, Hope, Kjos, Lyon &
  Healy, Pepper, Rodeheaver, Root & Cady,
  Rossiter
Christiania (now Oslo) Hals, Warmuth,
  Winther
Cincinnati, OH Church, [Ditson], Fillmore,
  Peters (ii), [Pustet]
Cleveland, OH Brainard, Fox
Cluj-Napoca see Kolozsvár
Coburg Forckel, Hauck
Cologne 87, Aich, [Bosworth], Gerig, [Peters
  (i)], [Simrock], Tonger, Volk
  Haydn Institute Henle
Copenhagen 88, Fog, Hansen (W.), Horneman,
  Horneman & Erslev, Kgl. Hof-Musikhandel,
  Lose, Samfundet til Udgivelse af Dansk
  Musik, Sønnichsen, Waldkirch
  Royal Theatre Sønnichsen
  University Waldkirch

Dallas, TX American Institute of Musicology,
  Baxter
Danzig 87, Hünefeld, Rhetus
Darmstadt Bossler, Merseburger
Dayton OH Fischer (J.), Lorenz
Delaware Water Gap, PA Shawnee
Denver, CO 65
Detroit, MI Couse, Remick, Stein
  & Buchheister, Stephens, Whitney,
  Whittemore
Dillingen an der Donau Bencard, Meltzer,
  Sensenschmidt
Douai Bogard, [Phalèse]
Dresden Bergen, Klemm, Meser
Dublin 103, Bunting, [Goulding], Hime,
  Holden, Lee, Manwaring, Neale, Power,
  Rhames, Thornton
  Harmonic Institution Bunting
Duisburg Henle
Dumfries [Paterson]
Dundee [Paterson]
Düsseldorf [Baethen], [Götz]

Edinburgh Bremner, Corri, Hart, Johnson
  (James), Oswald, Paterson, Penson &
  Robertson, Purdie, Schetky, Thomson,
  Vautrollier, Wood
  Edinburgh Musical Society Bremner
Eichstätt Reyser

Index

Erfurt Baumann
Evanston, IL Summy-Birchard

Ferrara 80, 89, Baldini, Buglhat
  Academy of the Intrepidi Baldini
Florence 40, 523, 537, Cecconcelli, Giunta,
  Guidi, Lorenzi, Marescotti, Moücke, Pignoni,
  [Ricordi]
  Duca di S. Clemente Guidi
  Società del Quartetto Guidi
Fort Lauderdale, FL Fox
Fossombrone Petrucci (O.)
Frankfurt am Main 86, 87, 113, 547, [André],
  Belyayev, Egenolff, Feyerabend, [Hansen
  (W.)], Hofmeister, Litolff, Peters (i), Stein,
  [Steingräber], [Weinberger], Wust
Frankfurt an der Oder Eichorn
  University of Eichorn
Freiburg 7
Freising Sensenschmidt

Gdańsk see Danzig
Geneva 89, Du Bosc, Du Boys, Goulart,
  Guéroult, Jean II de Laon, Tournes
Genoa [Artaria (ii)], [Ricordi]
Germantown, PA 31, 113
Ghent [Le Chevalier], Manilius
Giessen [Challier]
Glasgow Aird, Associated Board of the Royal
  Schools of Music, Paterson, Wood
  Royal Scottish Academy of Music Associated
  Board of the Royal Schools of Music
Goetha Gerstenberg
Grand Rapids, MI Zondervan
Graz Widmanstetter
Greifswald 87

Haarlem 28, 30
Hackensack, NJ Jerona
Hague, The [Hummel]
Halle Handel societies, Schwickert
Hamburg Benjamin, Carstens, Cranz, Diabelli,
  Rebenlein, Schirmer (E.C.), [Schuberth (J.)],
  Sikorski, Simrock, Ugrino, Van Ohr,
  Whistling
Hamilton, Ont. Nordheimer
Hanover Nagel, [Steingräber]
Hartford, CT Gordon
Havana 128, Edelmann
Haverhill Lowe & Brydone
Heidelberg Merseburger
Helsinki 120, Fazer
Herborn Rab
  University Rab
Hildesheim Hantzsch
Hillsdale, NY Boelke-Bomart
Hitchin [Bärenreiter]
Hofheim an der Taunus Hofmeister
Hollywood, CA 125, Langinger
Horní Moštěnice Pazdírek

Illinois University of 69
Indianapolis, IN Lillenas
Ingolstadt 55
Innsbruck Wagner

Jacksonville, TX Baxter
Jena Weidner
Jerusalem Israeli Music Publications

Kaliningrad see Königsberg

Kansas City, MO Lillenas
Kassel Bärenreiter, Nagel
Kempton Dreher
Kilmarnock Paterson
Kolozsvár 86, Hoffgreff
Königsberg Mense, Osterberger, Reusner,
  Segebade
Konstanz Hug
Kōyasan 10
Kraków Haller, Krzyżanowski, Szarfenberg,
  Ungler, Wietor, Wirzbięta

La Rochelle Haultin
Lausanne Foetisch
Lawrenceburg, TN Vaughan
Leiden [Plantin]
Leipzig 7, 34, 51, 87, 98, 106, 107, 117, Bach
  Gesellschaft, Belyayev, Benjamin, Bosworth,
  Bote & Bock, Breitkopf & Härtel, Brockhaus,
  Cranz, Deutscher Verlag für Musik,
  [Editions Russes de Musique], Faber,
  Forberg, Handel societies, [Hansen],
  Hantzsch, Heinrichshofen, Hoffmann,
  Hoffmeister, Hofmeister, [Hudební Matice],
  Hug, Jürgenson, Kahnt, Kistner & Siegel,
  Lauterbach & Kühn, Leuckart, Merseburger,
  Peters (i), Rättig, [Ricordi], Rieter-
  Biedermann, Röder, Roger, Schmidt, Schott,
  Schuberth (J.), Schwickert, Senff, Simrock,
  Steingräber, Whistling
Leningrad see St Petersburg
Les Ramparts, Monaco Oiseau-Lyre
Liège Andrez
Lima 94
Linz [Hoffmeister]
Lippstadt Kistner & Siegel
Lisbon Sassetti, Valentim de Carvalho
Liverpool Hime
Llangollen International Musical
  Eisteddfod Williams (G.)
London 26, 36, 37, 59, 79, 98, 100–101, 105,
  129, 493, 527, 528, Adams, Allde, André,
  Ascherberg, Hopwood & Crew, Ashdown,
  Associated Board of the Royal Schools of
  Music, Augener, Barley, Benjamin, Bickham,
  Birchall, Bland, Bland & Weller, Boosey
  & Hawkes, Bosworth, Bremner, Button
  & Whitaker, Carr (J.), Chappell, Chester,
  Clementi, Clowes, Cluer, Cocks, Cole (B.),
  Cooke, Corri, Coventry & Hollier, Cowper,
  Cramer, [Cranz], Cross, Curwen, Davidson,
  Day (J.), Day (R.), East, [Editions Russes
  de Musique], Eulenburg, Ewer, Faber,
  Filmtrax-Columbia, Forster, Fortier, Fougt,
  Francis, Day & Hunter, Galliard, Godbid,
  Gough, Goulding, Grafton, Handel societies,
  Hare, Harper, Harris, Harrison, Heptinstall,
  Hole, Hudgebut, Hutchings & Romer,
  Johnson (John), Jones, Keith, Prowse,
  Knight, Lavenu, Leader & Cock, Lengnick,
  Longman & Broderip, Lowe & Brydone,
  Lownes, Lucas, Meares, Metzler, Monzani,
  Moore, Murdoch, Musical Antiquarian
  Society, Napier, Novello, Oswald (J.), Oxford
  University Press, Paterson, Pearson (W.),
  Phillips (J.), Plainsong & Mediaeval Music
  Society, Playford, Power, Preston, Purcell
  Society, Purday, Randall, Rastell, Regents
  Harmonic Institution, Ricordi, Roberts,
  Schetky, Schirmer [E.C.], Schott, Seres,
  Short, Simpson, Simrock, Skillern, Snodham,

Index

Stainer & Bell, Stansby, Thompson,
[Universal Edition], Vautrollier, Walsh,
Watts, Weinberger, Welcker, Wessel,
Wheatstone, Williams (J.), Williamson,
Windet, Wright, Wright & Wilkinson,
Wynkyn de Worde, Young
British Academy   Stainer & Bell
British Museum   Clowes
Comedy Company   Chappell
Great Exhibition   Clowes
Haymarket Theatre   Welcker
King's Theatre   Monzani
Lincoln's Inn Fields Theatre   Watts
London Ballad Concerts   Boosey & Hawkes
Musical Antiquarian Society   Chappell
Musical Association   Chappell
Philharmonic Society   Regent's Harmonic
Institution
Royal Academy of Arts   Clowes
Royal Academy of Music   Associated Board of
the Royal Schools of Music
Royal College of Music   Associated Board of
the Royal Schools of Music
Royal Harmonic Institution   Cramer (J.B.),
Regent's Harmonic Institution
Royal Musical Association   Stainer & Bell
Society for the Diffusion of Useful
Knowledge   Clowes, Knight
Temple of Apollo   Oswald
London, Ont.   [Nordheimer]
Lörrach   Brockhaus, [Hug]
Los Angeles   125, Belmont, Warner Bros.
Louisville, KY   Brainard, Faulds, Peters (ii)
Louvain   Baethen, Phalèse
University   Phalèse
Lübeck   87, Arndes
Lucerne   [Hug]
Lugano   [Hug]
Lüneberg   Stern
Lyons   86, 88, Beringen, Channey, Du Boys,
Du Ry, [Giunta], Gorlier, Granjon, Guéra,
Gueroult, Hoffmeister, Moderne, Tournes,
Wenssler

[Maastricht]   Baethen
Madison, WI   A-R Editions
Madrid   [Giunta], Instituto Español
Magdeburg   110
Mainz   Artaria (i), [Augener], [Eulenburg],
Schott
Manchester   103, Associated Board of the Royal
Schools of Music, Cowper
Royal Manchester College of Music
Associated Board of the Royal
Schools of Music
Mannheim   [Artaria (i)], Götz, Heckel
Marburg   [Egenolff]
University   [Egenolff]
Marseilles   63
Mechlin   80
Melbourne   128, Allan, Chappell
Melville, NY   Belwin-Mills
Mexico City   Pablos, [Ricordi], Wagner (A.)
Miami, FL   Hansen (C.)
Miami Beach   Hansen (C.)
Milan   7, 10, 91, Artaria (ii), Bertuzzi, Camagno,
Canti, Carisch, Carulli, Colonna, Curci,
Lomazzo, Lucca, Pachel, Ricordi, Rolla,
Scotti, Sonzogno, Suvini Zerboni, Tini,
Tradate, Valdarfer, Vigoni, Zaroni
Cathedral   Rolla

Conservatory   Carulli
La Scala   Lucca, Ricordi
Teatro Carcano   Ricordi
Teatro del Lentasio   Ricordi
Teatro Re   Ricordi
Milwaukee, WI   Hempsted, Leonard
Minneapolis, MN   Augsburg
Misocco   [Colonna]
Mitau [Jeglava]   [Hartknoch]
Montreal   [Nordheimer]
Moravia   110
Morristown, NJ   Silver Burdett
Moscow   Editions Russes de Musique, Gutheil,
Jürgenson, Muzïka
Mount Pleasant,IA   Barnhouse
Mühlhausen   Hantzsch (A.), Hantzsch (G.)
Munich   58, Aibl, Berg (A.), Cranz, Drei Masken
Verlag, Falter, Gleissner, Henle, Henricus,
[Leuckart], [Ricordi], Sadelar, Senefelder,
Sidler, Wening
Court Chapel   Flurschütz

Naples   23, Carlino, [Clausetti], Cottrau, Curci,
Gargano, Girard, Marescalchi, [Ricordi],
Vitale
'Amici della Musica'   Curci
Teatro del Fondo   Girard
Teatro Nuovo   Girard
Teatro S. Carlo   Girard
Nashville, TN   26, Broadman Press,
Zondervan
Neuchâtel   [Hug]
New England   113
New Haven, CT   114, A-R Editions
New Orleans, LA   Blackmar, Grunewald,
Werlein
Newton Centre, MA   Jerona, Wa-Wan Press
New York   114, 115, American Composers
Alliance, Arrow Music Press, Associated
Music Publishers, Atwill, [Bärenreiter], Big 3,
Bloom, Boelke-Bomart, Boosey & Hawkes,
[Boston Music Company], [Brainard],
Broude (A.), [Carr], Chappell, Cos Cob
Press, [Ditson], Dover, Dubois, [Editions
Russes de Musique], EMT Music-SBK, Feist,
Firth, Hall & Pond, Fischer (C.), Fischer (J.),
Fox, [Francis, Day & Hunter], Frank, Galaxy,
Garland, Geib, Gilfert, Gordon, Gray,
Hansen (C.), Hargail, Harms, Hewitt (J.),
Hewitt (J.L.), Hitchcock, International, Jung,
Kalmus, Leeds, McGinnis & Marx, Marks,
Mason Bros., MCA Music, McGinnis & Marx,
Miller, Mills, Moller & Capron,
[Nordheimer], Oak, [Oxford University
Press], Paff, Peer-Southern, [Pepper], Peters
(i), Peters (ii), [Pustet], Remick, [Ricordi],
Riley, Robbins, Schirmer, [Schmidt],
Schuberth (E.), Schuberth (J.), Shapiro,
Bernstein & Co., Society for the Publication
of American Music, Stark, Von Tilzer,
Waters, Weintraub, Witmark
Queen's College   66
Novara   [Artaria (ii)]
Nuremberg   83–4, 86, 88, 95, 98, 497, Berg,
Endter, Formschneider, Gerlach, Haffner,
Hergot, Kauffmann, Neuber, Ott, Petreius,
Rönnagel, Schmid, Sensenschmidt, Stuchs,
Wachter, Wagenmann, Weigel

Oakville, Ont.   Harris
Oban   [Paterson]

Index

Offenbach am Main André, [Brandus], [Heugel], [Sonzogno], [Steingräber]
Olomouc Pazdírek
Opa-locka, FL Kalmus
Orvieto [Fei]
Oskaloosa, IA Barnhouse
Oslo (see also Christiania) [Hansen (W.)], Norsk Musikforlag,
Ottawa [Nordheimer]
Oxford 28, Beesley, Oxford University Press

Padua Zanibon
Paisley [Paterson]
Palermo Franceschi, [Ricordi]
Palo Alto CA 69
Paris 34–5, 37, 59, 84, 89, 95, 98, 104–5, 129, 521, [André], Attaingnant, Bailleux, Ballard, Baussen, [Bergen], Boivin, Bonneuil, Brandus, Bureau d'Abonnement Musicale, Carli, Castagneri, Choron, Choudens, Costallat, Cousineau, [Cranz], [Desclée], Du Pré, Durand, Editions Russes de Musique, Erard, Eschig, Escudier, Farrenc, Fezandat, Flaxland, Foucault, Fournier, [Francis, Day & Hunter], Frey, Fromont, Gando, Granjon, Hamelle, Hartmann (Georges), Heina, Heugel, Higman, Huberty, Imbault, Janet & Cotelle, Jobert, Joubert, La Chevardière, La Sirène, Le Bé, Le Clerc, Leduc, Le Menu, Lemoine, Le Roy, Magasin de Musique (i), Magasin de Musique (ii), Métru, Michel de Toulouse, Naderman, Oiseau-Lyre, Pacini, Pleyel, Ribou, Richault, Ricordi, Rouart-Lerolle, Salabert, Schlesinger, Schonenberger, [Schott], Senart, Sieber, [Simrock], Troupenas, Venier
Académie Royale de Musique Ribou
Centre National de la Recherche Scientifique 69
Conservatoire 110, Magasin de Musique (i)
Schola Cantorum Senart
University (Sorbonne) Du Pré
Park Ridge, IL Kjos
Parma Moilli
Passau Hamman, Nenninger
Pernambuco [Filippone]
Perth Paterson
Perugia Petrucci (P.)
Pest (see also Budapest) Heckenkast, Magyar Kórus, Rózslavölgyi, Táborsky, Treichlinger, Wagner
Philadelphia 38, 39, 113, 114, 115, 124, 541, Aitken, Blake, Carr, [Ditson], Elkan, Elkan-Vogel, Fiot & Meignen, Lee & Walker, Moller & Capron, Pepper, Presser, Schetky, Willig
Pittsburgh, PA Peters (ii)
Porz [Kistner & Siegel]
Prague Berra, Cerny, Enders, Hoffmann, Hudební Matice, Labaun, Panton, Stáry, Supraphon, Urbánek
Princeton, NJ Summy-Birchard
Providence, RI [Howe]

Québec [Nordheimer]

Regensburg Bosse, Pustet
Reutlingen 7
Riga Hartknoch
Rio de Janeiro 128, Bevilacqua, Filippone, Laforge, Napoleão

Rochester, NY Shaw
Rodenkirchen Tonger
Rome 7, 40, 41, 91, 517, American Institute of Musicology, Antico, Barré, Blado, Borboni, Caifabri, Curci, De Santis, [Desclé], Dorico, Fei, Gardano, Giunta, [Granjon], Grignani, Han, Mascardi, Mutii, Planck, Poggioli, Pustet, Ratti, Cencetti & Comp., Ricordi, Robletti, Soldi, Valesi, Verovio, Zannetti, Zarotto
Congregazione dell' Oratorio Gardano
Rostock 87
Rotterdam Alsbach, Barth, Geertsom, Plattner
Rouen 4

Sacramento Atwill
St Catherines, Ont. [Nordheimer]
St Gall [Hug]
St Louis, MO Balmer & Weber, Concordia, Kunkel, Peters (ii), Stark
St Petersburg Bessel, Dalmas, Editions Russes de Musique, Gerstenberg, Stellovsky
Salamanca [Giunta]
Salzburg 87, Mayer
San Diego, CA Kjos
San Francisco, CA Atwill, [Fischer (C.)], Gray (M.), Langinger, New Music, Sherman
San Juan Giusti, Instituto de Cultura Puertorriqueña
Santa Barbara, CA Fox
Santiago (Chile) Niemeyer
São Paolo [Bevilacqua], [Ricordi], Vitale
Sedalia, MO Stark
Seville 26
Solothurn [Hug]
Speyer Bossler, Hamman
Stanford, CA Stanford University 68
Stettin 87, [Eichorn]
Stockholm 88, Ahlstrom, Fougt, Gehrmans, [Hansen (W.)], Hirsch, Lundquist, Nordiska Musikförlaget
Stoke on Trent North Staffordshire Polytechnic 69
Strasbourg 7, 35, 128, 517, Apiarius, Egenolff, Hug, Reyser, Schoeffer
Stuttgart [Eulenburg], Hänssler
Sydney Albert, Paling, [Ricordi], [Schott]

Tel-Aviv Israel Music Institute, Israeli Music Publications
Thetford 62, Lowe & Brydone
Timisoara Morwetz
Tivoli [Robletti]
Toronto Anglo-Canadian Music Publishers' Association, Berando, Harris, Nordheimer, [Ricordi], Thompson (G.V.), Whaley, Royce & Co.
Conservatory of Music Harris
Tournai Desclée
Turin Canti, Giudici & Strada, [Lucca], [Ricordi]

Universal City, CA MCA Music
Urbana-Champaign, IL University of Illinois 66, 69

Valley Forge, PA European American, Pepper
Valparaiso (Chile) Niemeyer
Venice 10, 23, 30, 83, 91, 95, 289, Alessandri & Scattaglia, Amadino, Antico, Bortoli, Emerich, Franceschi, Franck, Gardano,

Index

Giunta, Hamman, Jacomo, Magni, Marescalchi, Merulo, Petrucci (O.), Rampazetto, Ratdolt, Raverii, Sala, Scotto, Torresani, Valdarfer, Vincenti, Vitali, Zatta
Vicenza   Salvadori
Vicksburg, MS   Blackmar
Vienna   58, 98, 104, 106, Artaria (i), [Böhm], [Bosworth], Cappi, Cosmerovius, [Cranz], Diabelli, Doblinger, Eder, [Gleissner], Guérroult, Haslinger, Hoffmeister, Hoftheater-Musik-Verlag, Huberty, Kunst- und Industrie- Comptoir, Lausch, Lienau, Lithographisches Institut, Loschenkohl, Maisch, [Marescalchi], Mechetti, Mollo, Musikalisches Magazin, Osterreichischer Bundesverlag, Pazdírek, Pennauer, [Pleyel], Rättig, [Rózsavölgyi], Sauer, Senefelder, Torricella, Traeg, Trattner, Universal, Van Ghelen, Weigl, Weinberger, [Whistling], Wiener Philharmonischer, Wiener Urtext Edition
  Court Theatre   Hoftheater-Musik-Verlag
  University   Cosmerovius

Waco, TX   Word

Warsaw   Arct, Brzezina, Friedlein, Gebethner & Wolff, Klukowski, Sennewald
Wasserburg   [Kahnt]
Waterloo, Ont.   Waterloo
Weissenfels   [Hantzsch]
Wiesbaden   Bote & Bock, Breitkopf & Härtel, Cranz, [Drei Masken Verlag]
Wilhelmiana   [Hansen], Nordiska Musikförlaget
Wilhelmshaven   Heinrichshofen
Winnipeg   [Nordheimer], [Whaley, Royce & Co.]
Winona, MN   Leonard
Winona Lake, IN   Rodeheaver
Winterthur   Heinrichhofsen, [Hug], Rieter-Biedermann
Wittenberg   Rhau
Wolfenbüttel   Fürstliche Druckerei, Kallmeyer, [Stern]
Worcester, MA   Thomas
Worms   [Götz], Schoeffer
Wrocław   see Breslau
Würzburg   Reyser

Zurich   Ars Viva, Eulenburg, Hug, Nägeli, Wyssenbach